THE RETIREMENT ACCOUNT CALCULATOR

Complete Savings and Withdrawal Tables for IRA and Keogh Plans

Michael Sherman, Ph.D.

CONTEMPORARY
BOOKS, INC.
CHICAGO ▪ NEW YORK

Acknowledgments

Computer Analyst: Thomas Locke

Great care has been taken to ensure exact figures in the production of these tables, but there is no guarantee of accuracy assumed by the author or publisher of this book.

Copyright © 1986 by Delphi Information Sciences Corporation
All rights reserved
Published by Contemporary Books, Inc.
180 North Michigan Avenue, Chicago, Illinois 60601
Manufactured in the United States of America
International Standard Book Number: 0-8092-5002-0

Published simultaneously in Canada by Beaverbooks, Ltd.
195 Allstate Parkway, Valleywood Business Park
Markham, Ontario L3R 4T8 Canada

CONTENTS

INTRODUCTION

The popularity of Individual Retirement Accounts (IRAs) has grown enormously in the past few years. Most consumers prefer to place their IRAs in fixed-rate savings investments. This book is directed toward this class of consumer investor. It is designed as a tool to help investors compare investments with differing interest rates and to solve a variety of mathematical problems associated with such investments.

The scope of rates and terms chosen encompasses almost every conceivable problem encountered in the calculation of fixed-rate investments. The book is organized in an easy-to-use format. You need no advanced mathematical skills to understand the tables. First read these introductory instructions. Then follow the directions as described in the examples at the beginning of each tabular section.

All fixed-rate investments have one common attribute. They have a stated interest rate, the so-called nominal annual rate. Two investments with the same nominal rate may produce significantly different earnings due to the magic of compound interest. To avoid confusing the consumer, the federal government through the Federal Reserve Board (FRB) has suggested a new national standard against which to measure the return on fixed-rate investments. In January 1986, the FRB proposed a revision to Regulation Q to simplify advertising of interest rates. All fixed-rate investments would be required to state the effective annual yield (EAY) on such investments. The proposed name for this new standard is the annual percentage yield, and it is synonymous with the EAY used throughout this book.

If the proposed revisions to Regulation Q are adopted, the EAY will undoubtedly become to savers what the annual percentage rate (APR) of Regulation Z has become to borrowers. All of the tables in this book are based on this universal measure for fixed-rate investments.

This book is organized into three basic sections: Deposit Tables, Withdrawal Tables, and the Effective Annual Yield Table. Before you attempt to follow the examples shown in the deposit or withdrawal tables, please turn to the Instructions for the Effective Annual Yield Table starting on page 263. It is in this section that the concept of interest compounding is reviewed. Certain interest rate nomenclature is

1

discussed including the concepts of nominal interest rates, ordinary interest, exact day interest, and bank interest rates.

Interpolation. The deposit tables and the withdrawal tables have been designed to cover a wide range of EAYs. Each EAY is a column index for either set of tables. When you convert a nominal annual rate to an EAY, you may not get an EAY that exactly matches a column index in a table. Interpolation is the method used to find a value in the tables when the desired EAY is not shown as a column index.

Interpolation problems are like simple algebra problems. For example, if 6 pounds of apples cost 18 cents and 9 pounds cost 27 cents, then 7 pounds should cost 21 cents. You found the answer by using interpolation. Here's how to apply the technique to the tables.

Let's say that you made an initial investment in an account with a nominal rate of 7.2% compounded semiannually. You wish to know how much the account will be worth after 120 months. From the Effective Annual Yield Tables on page 267, you find that 7.2% compounded semiannually is equivalent to an EAY of 7.33%. First find the two nearest EAY indices that bracket the desired EAY. Then use simple proportion to find the desired table entry.

Turn to the Single Deposit Table on page 13 to find the desired EAY of 7.33%. There is no EAY column index for 7.33%. The bracketing EAY indices on either side of the desired EAY are 7.30% and 7.35%. The two associated table entries on the 120-month row are 2.02301 and 2.03245. For illustrative purposes, construct a table of these values as follows:

EAY	120-Month Entry
7.30	2.02301
7.35	2.03245

The proportional relationship below then gives the desired entry.

$$\text{entry} = 2.02301 + \left[\frac{(7.33 - 7.30)}{(7.35 - 7.30)} \times (2.03245 - 2.02301) \right]$$

$$\text{entry} = 2.02301 + \left(\frac{0.03}{0.05} \times 0.00944 \right)$$

$$\text{entry} = 2.02867$$

An account of $100,000 will be worth $202,867 after 120 months when invested at 7.2% compounded semiannually. Whenever you complete an interpolation, always check to see if the interpolated value falls between the two table entries.

DEPOSIT TABLES INSTRUCTIONS

These sections of the book are designed to solve problems concerning the growth of money in fixed interest rate investments. All calculations are based on deposits made at the beginning of each period. The table entries are figures for the end of each period, and are based on one dollar deposits. Be sure to read the Effective Annual Yield (EAY) Table Instructions starting on page 263 before you attempt to solve any problems. And remember that most problems start with finding the EAY on the investment.

The Deposit Tables consist of four tables: Single Deposit, Monthly Deposits, Quarterly Deposits, and Annual Deposits. Six basic problems can be solved with these tables.

1. How much a single deposit will be worth after a certain period of time.
2. How big an initial single deposit is required to accrue to a specified amount after a certain period of time.
3. How much a series of periodic deposits will be worth after a certain period of time.
4. How big a series of periodic deposits are required to accrue to a specified amount after a certain period of time.
5. How many periodic deposits are required to accrue to a specified amount, if the periodic deposit amount is known.
6. What EAY must be earned to achieve a specific financial result.

EXAMPLE: How much will $2,000 invested in a 7.5% compounded daily 365/360 certificate of deposit (CD) be worth after 36 months? First turn to page 268 of the EAY Table to find the EAY on the CD. Move down the nominal annual rate (NAR) column at the left-hand side of the page to the 7.5% row. Read across this row to find 7.9% EAY under the daily 365/360 compounding column.

Turn to page 15 of the Single Deposit Table and move down the number of months column to 36 months. Then move across this row until you find the table entry 1.25622 under the 7.9% EAY column.

Multiply $2,000 by the table entry to get $2,512.44 as the future value of the initial investment.

EXAMPLE: How much should be paid for a zero-coupon bond to earn a nominal rate of 10% if the bond will be worth $10,000 in 10 years? The answer is called the Compound Accreted Value by bond investors. One must remember that most bonds pay interest semiannually. Hence in order to compare a zero-coupon bond to those with interest payments, you must first convert the nominal rate (yield) to the universal standard EAY. Turn to page 271 of the EAY Table to find the EAY. Move down the NAR column at the left-hand side of the page to the 10% row. Read across this row to find 10.25% EAY under the semiannual compounding column.

Turn to page 21 of the Single Deposit Table and move down the number of months column to 120 months. Then move across this row until you find the table entry 2.65330 under the 10.25% EAY column. Divide $10,000 by the table entry to get $3,768.89 as the Compound Accreted Value for this zero-coupon bond.

EXAMPLE: How much will have accrued in an IRA after one year if $150 is invested every month in an account paying 7% interest, compounded daily 365/365? Turn to page 267 of the EAY Tables to find the EAY. Move down the NAR column at the left-hand side of the page to the 7% row. Move across this row to find the EAY of 7.25% under the daily 365/365 compounding column.

Turn to page 49 of the Monthly Deposits Table and move down the number of monthly deposits column to find 12 months. Move across this row to the 7.25% EAY column and find the table entry 12.46621. Multiply this table entry times $150 to get $1,869.93 as the future value of the 12 monthly deposits made to the account.

EXAMPLE: How big a monthly deposit must be placed into a credit union account that pays 8% interest compounded monthly, so that $200,000 is saved at the end of 20 years? Turn to page 268 of the EAY Table to find the EAY. Read down the NAR column at the left-hand side of the page to the 8% row. Then read across this row to find the EAY of 8.3% under the monthly compounding column.

Turn to page 52 of the Monthly Deposits Table and move down the number of monthly deposits column to find 240 months (20 years). Read across this row to the 8.3% EAY column and find the table entry 592.95062. Divide $200,000 by 592.95062 to get $337.30 as the monthly deposit required.

EXAMPLE: How long will it take to save $50,000 in an account paying 11.6% interest compounded continuously if $2,500 is deposited every month? First turn to page 273 of the EAY Table to find the EAY. Read down the NAR column at the left-hand side of the page to the 11.6% row. Then read across this row to find the EAY of 12.3% under the continuous compounding column.

4

Next, find the required growth factor. If a $2,500 monthly deposit must grow to $50,000, then the required growth factor, found by dividing $50,000 by $2,500, is 20. Turn to page 62 of the Monthly Deposits Table and find the 12.3% EAY column. Move down this column until you find the first table entry that exceeds 20. It is 20.95778. Move across to the left-hand column and read 19 as the number of monthly deposits required to reach the goal. The last monthly deposit will be somewhat less than $2,500 to achieve the goal.

EXAMPLE: What EAY must an investment earn if you wish to double your money in ten years? The Single Deposit Table is used to solve this problem. If money is to double in 10 years, then the single deposit growth factor we must find is two (2). Begin scanning the Single Deposit Tables by reading across the 120 months row on each page.

Continue to do so until you find the first table entry that exceeds 2, on page 13. The factor is 2.00423. Read up to the top of the column and find the EAY of 7.20%. It takes an EAY of 7.20% to double your money in ten years.

This example demonstrates the "Rule of 72." To find out how long it takes to double your money, simply divide 72 by the EAY of the investment. The answer is the number of years it takes to double your money. In the above example 72 divided by 7.2 equals 10 years. This rule of thumb works very well for most interest rates.

EXAMPLE: What EAY must be earned on a $175 monthly deposit to build a $28,000 nest egg after 8 years (96 months)? First calculate the monthly deposit growth factor by dividing $28,000 by $175 to get 160. Start from the first page of the Monthly Deposits Table (page 44) on the 96 months row and begin to move across each column until you find the first column where the table entry exceeds 160. On page 62 of the Monthly Deposits Table find the table entry 160.30981. Read up the column to the EAY of 12.5%. In order to build the required nest egg, the account must earn 12.5% EAY.

The previous seven examples are typical of the problems that can be solved using the Deposit Tables in conjunction with the EAY Table starting on page 265 of this book. One additional problem requires using a combination of both these Deposit Tables and the Withdrawal Tables in the next section.

In certain retirement plans, your retirement goal may be to withdraw a predetermined amount (the Defined Benefit) from your nest egg for a period of time equal to your life expectancy at retirement. How much must be deposited periodically (the Defined Contribution) until retirement so that you will have the Defined Benefit for the rest of your expected life? An example of this problem is found in the Withdrawal Tables Instructions starting on page 151.

The Simple Interest Approximation to Deposit Table Problems. This book does not contain simple interest tables. However, some problems

5

require using simple interest rates to find the answer. These are problems where periodic deposits to an account are made more frequently than interest is compounded.

In order to solve such problems you must convert the stated problem to one in which the deposits are refigured as equivalent deposits for the compounding period. Then you use the tables to solve the equivalent problem. For example, let's say that you deposited $100 each month in an account paying interest at 6.30% compounded quarterly. How much would accrue to the account after 36 months?

First turn to page 266 of the Effective Annual Yield Table and find the EAY of 6.45%. Next, figure out what $100 per month accumulates to at 6.30% *simple interest* at the *end* of one quarter. The first month's deposit earns three months interest, the second month's deposit earns two months interest and the third month's deposit earns one month interest. Thus the total interest earned in one quarter for the three deposits is 6 months simple interest, or 3.15% on a $100 deposit. This equals $3.15 which when combined with three $100 monthly deposits gives a total accumulated value of $303.15 per $100 of initial monthly deposit.

Next turn to page 83 of the Quarterly Deposits Table and move down the 6.45% EAY column. For one quarterly deposit the table entry is 1.01575. Since $303.15 is the value of three $100 deposits at the *end* of one quarter, if you divide this amount by 1.01575, you get the equivalent quarterly deposit at the beginning of the first quarter. The resultant equivalent quarterly deposit is $298.44942. Move down the same 6.45% EAY column to 12 quarterly deposits (36 months) and find the table entry 13.30224. If you multiply this table entry times $298.44942, you get $3,970.05 as the balance in the account after three years.

The same simple interest approximation can be applied to any other type of Deposit Tables problem. Simply remember to convert the more frequent deposits to the equivalent deposit by figuring simple interest for the duration of the specified compounding period. Then use the table entries for the applicable EAY to solve the remainder of the problem.

TABLE 1. SINGLE DEPOSIT

NUMBER OF MONTHS	EFFECTIVE ANNUAL YIELD							
	5.00%	5.05%	5.10%	5.15%	5.20%	5.25%	5.30%	5.35%
1	1.00407	1.00411	1.00415	1.00419	1.00423	1.00427	1.00431	1.00435
2	1.00816	1.00824	1.00832	1.00840	1.00848	1.00856	1.00864	1.00872
3	1.01227	1.01239	1.01251	1.01263	1.01275	1.01287	1.01299	1.01311
4	1.01640	1.01656	1.01672	1.01688	1.01704	1.01720	1.01736	1.01752
5	1.02054	1.02074	1.02094	1.02114	1.02135	1.02155	1.02175	1.02195
6	1.02470	1.02494	1.02518	1.02543	1.02567	1.02591	1.02616	1.02640
7	1.02887	1.02916	1.02944	1.02973	1.03001	1.03030	1.03058	1.03087
8	1.03306	1.03339	1.03372	1.03405	1.03437	1.03470	1.03503	1.03536
9	1.03727	1.03764	1.03801	1.03838	1.03875	1.03912	1.03949	1.03986
10	1.04150	1.04191	1.04232	1.04274	1.04315	1.04356	1.04398	1.04439
11	1.04574	1.04620	1.04665	1.04711	1.04757	1.04802	1.04848	1.04893
12	1.05000	1.05050	1.05100	1.05150	1.05200	1.05250	1.05300	1.05350
13	1.05428	1.05482	1.05537	1.05591	1.05645	1.05700	1.05754	1.05809
14	1.05857	1.05916	1.05975	1.06034	1.06093	1.06151	1.06210	1.06269
15	1.06289	1.06352	1.06415	1.06478	1.06542	1.06605	1.06668	1.06732
16	1.06722	1.06789	1.06857	1.06925	1.06993	1.07061	1.07128	1.07196
17	1.07156	1.07229	1.07301	1.07373	1.07446	1.07518	1.07590	1.07663
18	1.07593	1.07670	1.07747	1.07824	1.07901	1.07977	1.08054	1.08131
19	1.08031	1.08113	1.08194	1.08276	1.08357	1.08439	1.08520	1.08602
20	1.08471	1.08558	1.08644	1.08730	1.08816	1.08902	1.08988	1.09075
21	1.08913	1.09004	1.09095	1.09186	1.09277	1.09368	1.09459	1.09550
22	1.09357	1.09453	1.09548	1.09644	1.09739	1.09835	1.09931	1.10026
23	1.09803	1.09903	1.10003	1.10103	1.10204	1.10304	1.10405	1.10505
24	1.10250	1.10355	1.10460	1.10565	1.10670	1.10776	1.10881	1.10986
25	1.10699	1.10809	1.10919	1.11029	1.11139	1.11249	1.11359	1.11469
26	1.11150	1.11265	1.11380	1.11494	1.11609	1.11724	1.11839	1.11954
27	1.11603	1.11723	1.11842	1.11962	1.12082	1.12202	1.12322	1.12442
28	1.12058	1.12182	1.12307	1.12432	1.12556	1.12681	1.12806	1.12931
29	1.12514	1.12644	1.12773	1.12903	1.13033	1.13163	1.13293	1.13423
30	1.12973	1.13107	1.13242	1.13377	1.13511	1.13646	1.13781	1.13916
31	1.13433	1.13572	1.13712	1.13852	1.13992	1.14132	1.14272	1.14412
32	1.13895	1.14040	1.14185	1.14329	1.14474	1.14620	1.14765	1.14910
33	1.14359	1.14509	1.14659	1.14809	1.14959	1.15109	1.15260	1.15410
34	1.14825	1.14980	1.15135	1.15290	1.15446	1.15601	1.15757	1.15913
35	1.15293	1.15453	1.15613	1.15774	1.15934	1.16095	1.16256	1.16417
36	1.15763	1.15928	1.16094	1.16259	1.16425	1.16591	1.16758	1.16924
37	1.16234	1.16405	1.16576	1.16747	1.16918	1.17090	1.17261	1.17433
38	1.16708	1.16884	1.17060	1.17236	1.17413	1.17590	1.17767	1.17944
39	1.17183	1.17365	1.17546	1.17728	1.17910	1.18092	1.18275	1.18457
40	1.17661	1.17847	1.18035	1.18222	1.18409	1.18597	1.18785	1.18973
41	1.18140	1.18332	1.18525	1.18718	1.18911	1.19104	1.19297	1.19491
42	1.18621	1.18819	1.19017	1.19215	1.19414	1.19613	1.19812	1.20011
43	1.19105	1.19308	1.19512	1.19715	1.19919	1.20124	1.20328	1.20533
44	1.19590	1.19799	1.20008	1.20217	1.20427	1.20637	1.20847	1.21058
45	1.20077	1.20292	1.20506	1.20722	1.20937	1.21153	1.21369	1.21585
46	1.20566	1.20786	1.21007	1.21228	1.21449	1.21670	1.21892	1.22114
47	1.21057	1.21283	1.21510	1.21736	1.21963	1.22190	1.22418	1.22646
48	1.21551	1.21782	1.22014	1.22247	1.22479	1.22712	1.22946	1.23179
60	1.27628	1.27932	1.28237	1.28542	1.28848	1.29155	1.29462	1.29770
72	1.34010	1.34393	1.34777	1.35162	1.35548	1.35935	1.36323	1.36712
84	1.40710	1.41180	1.41651	1.42123	1.42597	1.43072	1.43548	1.44026
96	1.47746	1.48309	1.48875	1.49443	1.50012	1.50583	1.51157	1.51732
108	1.55133	1.55799	1.56468	1.57139	1.57813	1.58489	1.59168	1.59849
120	1.62889	1.63667	1.64447	1.65231	1.66019	1.66810	1.67604	1.68401
132	1.71034	1.71932	1.72834	1.73741	1.74652	1.75567	1.76487	1.77411
144	1.79586	1.80615	1.81649	1.82689	1.83734	1.84784	1.85841	1.86902
156	1.88565	1.89736	1.90913	1.92097	1.93288	1.94486	1.95690	1.96901
168	1.97993	1.99317	2.00649	2.01990	2.03339	2.04696	2.06062	2.07436
180	2.07893	2.09383	2.10883	2.12392	2.13912	2.15443	2.16983	2.18534
192	2.18287	2.19957	2.21638	2.23331	2.25036	2.26753	2.28483	2.30225
204	2.29202	2.31064	2.32941	2.34832	2.36738	2.38658	2.40593	2.42542
216	2.40662	2.42733	2.44821	2.46926	2.49048	2.51187	2.53344	2.55518
228	2.52695	2.54991	2.57307	2.59643	2.61999	2.64375	2.66771	2.69188
240	2.65330	2.67868	2.70430	2.73014	2.75623	2.78254	2.80910	2.83590
252	2.78596	2.81396	2.84222	2.87075	2.89955	2.92863	2.95798	2.98762
264	2.92526	2.95606	2.98717	3.01859	3.05033	3.08238	3.11476	3.14746
276	3.07152	3.10534	3.13951	3.17405	3.20894	3.24421	3.27984	3.31585
288	3.22510	3.26216	3.29963	3.33751	3.37581	3.41453	3.45367	3.49324
300	3.38635	3.42690	3.46791	3.50939	3.55135	3.59379	3.63672	3.68013
312	3.55567	3.59996	3.64477	3.69013	3.73602	3.78246	3.82946	3.87702
324	3.73346	3.78176	3.83066	3.88017	3.93029	3.98104	4.03242	4.08444
336	3.92013	3.97273	4.02602	4.08000	4.13467	4.19005	4.24614	4.30296
348	4.11614	4.17336	4.23135	4.29012	4.34967	4.41002	4.47119	4.53317
360	4.32194	4.38411	4.44715	4.51106	4.57585	4.64155	4.70816	4.77569
420	5.51602	5.60870	5.70289	5.79862	5.89591	5.99479	6.09527	6.19739
480	7.03999	7.17534	7.31322	7.45369	7.59678	7.74255	7.89105	8.04232

SINGLE DEPOSIT

NUMBER OF MONTHS	EFFECTIVE ANNUAL YIELD							
	5.40%	5.45%	5.50%	5.55%	5.60%	5.65%	5.70%	5.75%
1	1.00439	1.00443	1.00447	1.00451	1.00455	1.00459	1.00463	1.00467
2	1.00880	1.00888	1.00896	1.00904	1.00912	1.00920	1.00928	1.00936
3	1.01323	1.01336	1.01348	1.01360	1.01372	1.01384	1.01396	1.01408
4	1.01769	1.01785	1.01801	1.01817	1.01833	1.01849	1.01865	1.01881
5	1.02216	1.02236	1.02256	1.02276	1.02296	1.02316	1.02337	1.02357
6	1.02665	1.02689	1.02713	1.02738	1.02762	1.02786	1.02811	1.02835
7	1.03115	1.03144	1.03172	1.03201	1.03230	1.03258	1.03287	1.03315
8	1.03568	1.03601	1.03634	1.03667	1.03699	1.03732	1.03765	1.03798
9	1.04023	1.04060	1.04097	1.04134	1.04171	1.04208	1.04245	1.04282
10	1.04480	1.04521	1.04563	1.04604	1.04645	1.04687	1.04728	1.04769
11	1.04939	1.04985	1.05030	1.05076	1.05122	1.05167	1.05213	1.05258
12	1.05400	1.05450	1.05500	1.05550	1.05600	1.05650	1.05700	1.05750
13	1.05863	1.05917	1.05972	1.06026	1.06081	1.06135	1.06189	1.06244
14	1.06328	1.06387	1.06446	1.06504	1.06563	1.06622	1.06681	1.06740
15	1.06795	1.06858	1.06922	1.06985	1.07048	1.07112	1.07175	1.07238
16	1.07264	1.07332	1.07400	1.07468	1.07536	1.07603	1.07671	1.07739
17	1.07735	1.07808	1.07880	1.07952	1.08025	1.08097	1.08170	1.08242
18	1.08208	1.08285	1.08362	1.08439	1.08517	1.08594	1.08671	1.08748
19	1.08684	1.08765	1.08847	1.08929	1.09010	1.09092	1.09174	1.09256
20	1.09161	1.09247	1.09334	1.09420	1.09506	1.09593	1.09679	1.09766
21	1.09641	1.09732	1.09823	1.09914	1.10005	1.10096	1.10187	1.10278
22	1.10122	1.10218	1.10314	1.10410	1.10505	1.10601	1.10697	1.10793
23	1.10606	1.10706	1.10807	1.10908	1.11008	1.11109	1.11210	1.11311
24	1.11092	1.11197	1.11303	1.11408	1.11514	1.11619	1.11725	1.11831
25	1.11580	1.11690	1.11800	1.11911	1.12021	1.12132	1.12242	1.12353
26	1.12070	1.12185	1.12300	1.12415	1.12531	1.12646	1.12762	1.12878
27	1.12562	1.12682	1.12802	1.12923	1.13043	1.13164	1.13284	1.13405
28	1.13056	1.13181	1.13307	1.13432	1.13557	1.13683	1.13809	1.13934
29	1.13553	1.13683	1.13813	1.13944	1.14074	1.14205	1.14336	1.14466
30	1.14052	1.14187	1.14322	1.14458	1.14593	1.14729	1.14865	1.15001
31	1.14553	1.14693	1.14834	1.14974	1.15115	1.15256	1.15397	1.15538
32	1.15056	1.15201	1.15347	1.15493	1.15639	1.15785	1.15931	1.16077
33	1.15561	1.15712	1.15863	1.16014	1.16165	1.16316	1.16468	1.16619
34	1.16069	1.16225	1.16381	1.16537	1.16694	1.16850	1.17007	1.17164
35	1.16578	1.16740	1.16901	1.17063	1.17225	1.17387	1.17549	1.17711
36	1.17091	1.17257	1.17424	1.17591	1.17758	1.17926	1.18093	1.18261
37	1.17605	1.17777	1.17949	1.18122	1.18294	1.18467	1.18640	1.18813
38	1.18121	1.18299	1.18477	1.18655	1.18833	1.19011	1.19189	1.19368
39	1.18640	1.18823	1.19006	1.19190	1.19373	1.19557	1.19741	1.19925
40	1.19161	1.19350	1.19539	1.19728	1.19917	1.20106	1.20296	1.20485
41	1.19685	1.19879	1.20073	1.20268	1.20462	1.20657	1.20853	1.21048
42	1.20210	1.20410	1.20610	1.20810	1.21011	1.21211	1.21412	1.21613
43	1.20738	1.20944	1.21149	1.21355	1.21561	1.21768	1.21974	1.22181
44	1.21269	1.21480	1.21691	1.21903	1.22115	1.22327	1.22539	1.22752
45	1.21801	1.22018	1.22235	1.22453	1.22670	1.22888	1.23107	1.23325
46	1.22336	1.22559	1.22782	1.23005	1.23229	1.23452	1.23677	1.23901
47	1.22874	1.23102	1.23331	1.23560	1.23789	1.24019	1.24249	1.24480
48	1.23413	1.23648	1.23882	1.24117	1.24353	1.24589	1.24825	1.25061
60	1.30078	1.30387	1.30696	1.31006	1.31317	1.31628	1.31940	1.32252
72	1.37102	1.37493	1.37884	1.38277	1.38670	1.39065	1.39460	1.39856
84	1.44505	1.44986	1.45468	1.45951	1.46436	1.46922	1.47409	1.47898
96	1.52309	1.52888	1.53469	1.54051	1.54636	1.55223	1.55812	1.56402
108	1.60533	1.61220	1.61909	1.62601	1.63296	1.63993	1.64693	1.65395
120	1.69202	1.70007	1.70814	1.71626	1.72440	1.73259	1.74080	1.74906
132	1.78339	1.79272	1.80209	1.81151	1.82097	1.83048	1.84003	1.84963
144	1.87969	1.89042	1.90121	1.91205	1.92295	1.93390	1.94491	1.95598
156	1.98120	1.99345	2.00577	2.01817	2.03063	2.04317	2.05577	2.06845
168	2.08818	2.10209	2.11609	2.13018	2.14435	2.15860	2.17295	2.18739
180	2.20094	2.21666	2.23248	2.24840	2.26443	2.28057	2.29681	2.31316
192	2.31980	2.33747	2.35526	2.37319	2.39124	2.40942	2.42773	2.44617
204	2.44506	2.46486	2.48480	2.50490	2.52515	2.54555	2.56611	2.58682
216	2.57710	2.59919	2.62147	2.64392	2.66655	2.68937	2.71238	2.73556
228	2.71626	2.74085	2.76565	2.79066	2.81588	2.84132	2.86698	2.89286
240	2.86294	2.89023	2.91776	2.94554	2.97357	3.00186	3.03040	3.05920
252	3.01754	3.04774	3.07823	3.10902	3.14009	3.17146	3.20313	3.23510
264	3.18049	3.21384	3.24754	3.28157	3.31594	3.35065	3.38571	3.42112
276	3.35223	3.38900	3.42615	3.46369	3.50163	3.53996	3.57870	3.61783
288	3.53325	3.57370	3.61459	3.65593	3.69772	3.73997	3.78268	3.82586
300	3.72405	3.76847	3.81339	3.85883	3.90479	3.95128	3.99829	4.04585
312	3.92515	3.97385	4.02313	4.07300	4.12346	4.17452	4.22620	4.27848
324	4.13710	4.19042	4.24440	4.29905	4.35437	4.41039	4.46709	4.52450
336	4.36051	4.41880	4.47784	4.53765	4.59822	4.65957	4.72171	4.78465
348	4.59598	4.65962	4.72412	4.78949	4.85572	4.92284	4.99085	5.05977
360	4.84416	4.91357	4.98395	5.05530	5.12764	5.20098	5.27533	5.35071
420	6.30117	6.40664	6.51383	6.62275	6.73344	6.84593	6.96025	7.07641
480	8.19642	8.35340	8.51331	8.67620	8.84213	9.01115	9.18332	9.35869

SINGLE DEPOSIT

EFFECTIVE ANNUAL YIELD

NUMBER OF MONTHS	5.80%	5.85%	5.90%	5.95%	6.00%	6.05%	6.10%	6.15%
1	1.00471	1.00475	1.00479	1.00483	1.00487	1.00491	1.00495	1.00499
2	1.00944	1.00952	1.00960	1.00968	1.00976	1.00984	1.00992	1.01000
3	1.01419	1.01431	1.01443	1.01455	1.01467	1.01479	1.01491	1.01503
4	1.01897	1.01913	1.01929	1.01945	1.01961	1.01977	1.01993	1.02009
5	1.02377	1.02397	1.02417	1.02437	1.02458	1.02478	1.02498	1.02518
6	1.02859	1.02883	1.02908	1.02932	1.02956	1.02981	1.03005	1.03029
7	1.03344	1.03372	1.03401	1.03429	1.03457	1.03486	1.03514	1.03543
8	1.03830	1.03863	1.03896	1.03928	1.03961	1.03994	1.04026	1.04059
9	1.04319	1.04356	1.04393	1.04430	1.04467	1.04504	1.04541	1.04578
10	1.04810	1.04852	1.04893	1.04934	1.04976	1.05017	1.05058	1.05099
11	1.05304	1.05350	1.05395	1.05441	1.05487	1.05532	1.05578	1.05623
12	1.05800	1.05850	1.05900	1.05950	1.06000	1.06050	1.06100	1.06150
13	1.06298	1.06353	1.06407	1.06462	1.06516	1.06570	1.06625	1.06679
14	1.06799	1.06858	1.06917	1.06976	1.07034	1.07093	1.07152	1.07211
15	1.07302	1.07365	1.07429	1.07492	1.07555	1.07619	1.07682	1.07746
16	1.07807	1.07875	1.07943	1.08011	1.08079	1.08147	1.08215	1.08283
17	1.08315	1.08387	1.08460	1.08532	1.08605	1.08678	1.08750	1.08823
18	1.08825	1.08902	1.08979	1.09056	1.09134	1.09211	1.09288	1.09365
19	1.09337	1.09419	1.09501	1.09583	1.09665	1.09747	1.09829	1.09911
20	1.09852	1.09939	1.10025	1.10112	1.10199	1.10285	1.10372	1.10459
21	1.10370	1.10461	1.10552	1.10644	1.10735	1.10827	1.10918	1.11009
22	1.10889	1.10986	1.11082	1.11178	1.11274	1.11370	1.11467	1.11563
23	1.11412	1.11513	1.11614	1.11715	1.11816	1.11917	1.12018	1.12119
24	1.11936	1.12042	1.12148	1.12254	1.12360	1.12466	1.12572	1.12678
25	1.12464	1.12574	1.12685	1.12796	1.12907	1.13018	1.13129	1.13240
26	1.12993	1.13109	1.13225	1.13341	1.13456	1.13572	1.13689	1.13805
27	1.13525	1.13646	1.13767	1.13888	1.14009	1.14130	1.14251	1.14372
28	1.14060	1.14186	1.14312	1.14438	1.14564	1.14690	1.14816	1.14942
29	1.14597	1.14728	1.14859	1.14990	1.15121	1.15253	1.15384	1.15515
30	1.15137	1.15273	1.15409	1.15545	1.15682	1.15818	1.15955	1.16091
31	1.15679	1.15820	1.15962	1.16103	1.16245	1.16386	1.16528	1.16670
32	1.16224	1.16370	1.16517	1.16664	1.16811	1.16958	1.17105	1.17252
33	1.16771	1.16923	1.17075	1.17227	1.17379	1.17532	1.17684	1.17837
34	1.17321	1.17478	1.17636	1.17793	1.17951	1.18108	1.18266	1.18424
35	1.17874	1.18036	1.18199	1.18362	1.18525	1.18688	1.18851	1.19015
36	1.18429	1.18597	1.18765	1.18933	1.19102	1.19270	1.19439	1.19608
37	1.18986	1.19160	1.19334	1.19507	1.19681	1.19855	1.20030	1.20204
38	1.19547	1.19726	1.19905	1.20084	1.20264	1.20444	1.20624	1.20804
39	1.20110	1.20294	1.20479	1.20664	1.20849	1.21035	1.21220	1.21406
40	1.20675	1.20866	1.21056	1.21247	1.21438	1.21629	1.21820	1.22011
41	1.21244	1.21440	1.21636	1.21832	1.22029	1.22225	1.22422	1.22620
42	1.21815	1.22016	1.22218	1.22420	1.22623	1.22825	1.23028	1.23231
43	1.22388	1.22596	1.22803	1.23011	1.23219	1.23428	1.23637	1.23845
44	1.22965	1.23178	1.23391	1.23605	1.23819	1.24034	1.24248	1.24463
45	1.23544	1.23763	1.23982	1.24202	1.24422	1.24642	1.24863	1.25083
46	1.24126	1.24351	1.24576	1.24802	1.25028	1.25254	1.25480	1.25707
47	1.24710	1.24941	1.25173	1.25404	1.25636	1.25868	1.26101	1.26334
48	1.25298	1.25535	1.25772	1.26010	1.26248	1.26486	1.26725	1.26964
60	1.32565	1.32878	1.33193	1.33507	1.33823	1.34138	1.34455	1.34772
72	1.40254	1.40652	1.41051	1.41451	1.41852	1.42254	1.42657	1.43061
84	1.48388	1.48880	1.49373	1.49867	1.50363	1.50860	1.51359	1.51859
96	1.56995	1.57589	1.58186	1.58784	1.59385	1.59987	1.60592	1.61198
108	1.66101	1.66808	1.67519	1.68232	1.68948	1.69666	1.70388	1.71112
120	1.75734	1.76567	1.77402	1.78242	1.79085	1.79931	1.80781	1.81635
132	1.85927	1.86896	1.87869	1.88847	1.89830	1.90817	1.91809	1.92806
144	1.96711	1.97829	1.98953	2.00084	2.01220	2.02362	2.03509	2.04663
156	2.08120	2.09402	2.10692	2.11989	2.13293	2.14604	2.15924	2.17250
168	2.20191	2.21652	2.23123	2.24602	2.26090	2.27588	2.29095	2.30611
180	2.32962	2.34619	2.36287	2.37966	2.39656	2.41357	2.43070	2.44794
192	2.46474	2.48344	2.50228	2.52125	2.54035	2.55959	2.57897	2.59848
204	2.60769	2.62872	2.64991	2.67126	2.69277	2.71445	2.73629	2.75829
216	2.75894	2.78250	2.80626	2.83020	2.85434	2.87867	2.90320	2.92793
228	2.91896	2.94528	2.97183	2.99860	3.02560	3.05283	3.08029	3.10799
240	3.08826	3.11758	3.14716	3.17701	3.20714	3.23753	3.26819	3.29913
252	3.26738	3.29996	3.33285	3.36605	3.39956	3.43340	3.46755	3.50203
264	3.45688	3.49300	3.52948	3.56633	3.60354	3.64112	3.67907	3.71741
276	3.65738	3.69734	3.73772	3.77852	3.81975	3.86141	3.90350	3.94603
288	3.86951	3.91364	3.95825	4.00335	4.04893	4.09502	4.14161	4.18871
300	4.09394	4.14259	4.19179	4.24154	4.29187	4.34277	4.39425	4.44631
312	4.33139	4.38493	4.43910	4.49392	4.54938	4.60551	4.66230	4.71976
324	4.58261	4.64145	4.70101	4.76130	4.82235	4.88414	4.94670	5.01003
336	4.84840	4.91297	4.97837	5.04460	5.11169	5.17963	5.24845	5.31814
348	5.12961	5.20038	5.27209	5.34476	5.41839	5.49300	5.56860	5.64521
360	5.42713	5.50460	5.58314	5.66277	5.74349	5.82533	5.90829	5.99239
420	7.19446	7.31442	7.43633	7.56021	7.68609	7.81400	7.94399	8.07607
480	9.53733	9.71929	9.90463	10.09342	10.28572	10.48158	10.68108	10.88429

SINGLE DEPOSIT

NUMBER OF MONTHS	EFFECTIVE ANNUAL YIELD							
	6.20%	6.25%	6.30%	6.35%	6.40%	6.45%	6.50%	6.55%
1	1.00503	1.00506	1.00510	1.00514	1.00518	1.00522	1.00526	1.00530
2	1.01008	1.01016	1.01023	1.01031	1.01039	1.01047	1.01055	1.01063
3	1.01515	1.01527	1.01539	1.01551	1.01563	1.01575	1.01587	1.01599
4	1.02025	1.02041	1.02057	1.02073	1.02089	1.02105	1.02121	1.02137
5	1.02538	1.02558	1.02578	1.02598	1.02619	1.02639	1.02659	1.02679
6	1.03053	1.03078	1.03102	1.03126	1.03150	1.03175	1.03199	1.03223
7	1.03571	1.03600	1.03628	1.03657	1.03685	1.03713	1.03742	1.03770
8	1.04092	1.04124	1.04157	1.04190	1.04222	1.04255	1.04288	1.04320
9	1.04615	1.04652	1.04689	1.04726	1.04763	1.04800	1.04836	1.04873
10	1.05141	1.05182	1.05223	1.05264	1.05306	1.05347	1.05388	1.05429
11	1.05669	1.05715	1.05760	1.05806	1.05851	1.05897	1.05943	1.05988
12	1.06200	1.06250	1.06300	1.06350	1.06400	1.06450	1.06500	1.06550
13	1.06734	1.06788	1.06843	1.06897	1.06951	1.07006	1.07060	1.07115
14	1.07270	1.07329	1.07388	1.07447	1.07506	1.07565	1.07624	1.07683
15	1.07809	1.07873	1.07936	1.08000	1.08063	1.08126	1.08190	1.08253
16	1.08351	1.08419	1.08487	1.08555	1.08623	1.08691	1.08759	1.08827
17	1.08895	1.08968	1.09041	1.09113	1.09186	1.09259	1.09331	1.09404
18	1.09443	1.09520	1.09597	1.09675	1.09752	1.09829	1.09907	1.09984
19	1.09993	1.10075	1.10157	1.10239	1.10321	1.10403	1.10485	1.10567
20	1.10545	1.10632	1.10719	1.10806	1.10893	1.10980	1.11066	1.11153
21	1.11101	1.11193	1.11284	1.11376	1.11467	1.11559	1.11651	1.11743
22	1.11659	1.11756	1.11852	1.11949	1.12045	1.12142	1.12238	1.12335
23	1.12220	1.12322	1.12423	1.12524	1.12626	1.12727	1.12829	1.12930
24	1.12784	1.12891	1.12997	1.13103	1.13210	1.13316	1.13422	1.13529
25	1.13351	1.13462	1.13574	1.13685	1.13796	1.13908	1.14019	1.14131
26	1.13921	1.14037	1.14153	1.14270	1.14386	1.14503	1.14619	1.14736
27	1.14493	1.14615	1.14736	1.14858	1.14979	1.15101	1.15222	1.15344
28	1.15069	1.15195	1.15322	1.15448	1.15575	1.15702	1.15829	1.15956
29	1.15647	1.15779	1.15910	1.16042	1.16174	1.16306	1.16438	1.16570
30	1.16228	1.16365	1.16502	1.16639	1.16776	1.16913	1.17051	1.17188
31	1.16812	1.16954	1.17097	1.17239	1.17381	1.17524	1.17667	1.17809
32	1.17399	1.17547	1.17694	1.17842	1.17990	1.18138	1.18286	1.18434
33	1.17989	1.18142	1.18295	1.18448	1.18601	1.18755	1.18908	1.19062
34	1.18582	1.18740	1.18899	1.19057	1.19216	1.19375	1.19534	1.19693
35	1.19178	1.19342	1.19506	1.19670	1.19834	1.19998	1.20163	1.20327
36	1.19777	1.19946	1.20116	1.20285	1.20455	1.20625	1.20795	1.20965
37	1.20379	1.20554	1.20729	1.20904	1.21079	1.21255	1.21431	1.21606
38	1.20984	1.21164	1.21345	1.21526	1.21707	1.21888	1.22069	1.22251
39	1.21592	1.21778	1.21964	1.22151	1.22338	1.22525	1.22712	1.22899
40	1.22203	1.22395	1.22587	1.22779	1.22972	1.23165	1.23357	1.23551
41	1.22817	1.23015	1.23213	1.23411	1.23609	1.23808	1.24007	1.24206
42	1.23434	1.23638	1.23842	1.24046	1.24250	1.24454	1.24659	1.24864
43	1.24055	1.24264	1.24474	1.24684	1.24894	1.25104	1.25315	1.25526
44	1.24678	1.24893	1.25109	1.25325	1.25541	1.25758	1.25974	1.26191
45	1.25305	1.25526	1.25748	1.25970	1.26192	1.26414	1.26637	1.26860
46	1.25934	1.26162	1.26389	1.26617	1.26846	1.27074	1.27303	1.27533
47	1.26567	1.26801	1.27035	1.27269	1.27503	1.27738	1.27973	1.28209
48	1.27203	1.27443	1.27683	1.27923	1.28164	1.28405	1.28647	1.28888
60	1.35090	1.35408	1.35727	1.36047	1.36367	1.36687	1.37009	1.37331
72	1.43465	1.43871	1.44278	1.44685	1.45094	1.45504	1.45914	1.46326
84	1.52360	1.52863	1.53367	1.53873	1.54380	1.54889	1.55399	1.55910
96	1.61807	1.62417	1.63029	1.63644	1.64260	1.64879	1.65500	1.66122
108	1.71839	1.72568	1.73300	1.74035	1.74773	1.75514	1.76257	1.77003
120	1.82493	1.83354	1.84218	1.85087	1.85959	1.86834	1.87714	1.88597
132	1.93807	1.94813	1.95824	1.96840	1.97860	1.98885	1.99915	2.00950
144	2.05823	2.06989	2.08161	2.09339	2.10523	2.11713	2.12910	2.14112
156	2.18584	2.19926	2.21275	2.22632	2.23996	2.25369	2.26749	2.28137
168	2.32136	2.33671	2.35215	2.36769	2.38332	2.39905	2.41487	2.43080
180	2.46529	2.48276	2.50034	2.51804	2.53586	2.55379	2.57184	2.59001
192	2.61814	2.63793	2.65786	2.67793	2.69815	2.71851	2.73901	2.75966
204	2.78046	2.80280	2.82531	2.84798	2.87083	2.89385	2.91705	2.94042
216	2.95285	2.97797	3.00330	3.02883	3.05456	3.08051	3.10665	3.13301
228	3.13593	3.16410	3.19251	3.22116	3.25006	3.27920	3.30859	3.33823
240	3.33035	3.36185	3.39364	3.42570	3.45806	3.49071	3.52365	3.55688
252	3.53684	3.57197	3.60744	3.64324	3.67938	3.71586	3.75268	3.78985
264	3.75612	3.79522	3.83470	3.87458	3.91486	3.95553	3.99661	4.03809
276	3.98900	4.03242	4.07629	4.12062	4.16541	4.21066	4.25639	4.30258
288	4.23632	4.28444	4.33310	4.38228	4.43199	4.48225	4.53305	4.58440
300	4.49897	4.55222	4.60608	4.66055	4.71564	4.77135	4.82770	4.88468
312	4.77790	4.83674	4.89626	4.95650	5.01744	5.07911	5.14150	5.20463
324	5.07413	5.13903	5.20473	5.27123	5.33856	5.40671	5.47570	5.54553
336	5.38873	5.46022	5.53263	5.60596	5.68023	5.75544	5.83162	5.90876
348	5.72283	5.80149	5.88118	5.96194	6.04376	6.12667	6.21067	6.29579
360	6.07765	6.16408	6.25170	6.34052	6.43056	6.52184	6.61437	6.70816
420	8.21028	8.34666	8.48524	8.62606	8.76914	8.91453	9.06225	9.21236
480	11.09125	11.30206	11.51677	11.73545	11.95818	12.18503	12.41607	12.65139

SINGLE DEPOSIT

EFFECTIVE ANNUAL YIELD

NUMBER OF MONTHS	6.60%	6.65%	6.70%	6.75%	6.80%	6.85%	6.90%	6.95%
1	1.00534	1.00538	1.00542	1.00546	1.00550	1.00554	1.00558	1.00561
2	1.01071	1.01079	1.01087	1.01095	1.01102	1.01110	1.01118	1.01126
3	1.01611	1.01623	1.01634	1.01646	1.01658	1.01670	1.01682	1.01694
4	1.02153	1.02169	1.02185	1.02201	1.02217	1.02233	1.02249	1.02265
5	1.02699	1.02719	1.02739	1.02759	1.02779	1.02799	1.02819	1.02839
6	1.03247	1.03271	1.03296	1.03320	1.03344	1.03368	1.03392	1.03417
7	1.03799	1.03827	1.03855	1.03884	1.03912	1.03941	1.03969	1.03997
8	1.04353	1.04386	1.04418	1.04451	1.04483	1.04516	1.04549	1.04581
9	1.04910	1.04947	1.04984	1.05021	1.05058	1.05095	1.05132	1.05168
10	1.05470	1.05512	1.05553	1.05594	1.05635	1.05677	1.05718	1.05759
11	1.06034	1.06079	1.06125	1.06171	1.06216	1.06262	1.06307	1.06353
12	1.06600	1.06650	1.06700	1.06750	1.06800	1.06850	1.06900	1.06950
13	1.07169	1.07224	1.07278	1.07333	1.07387	1.07442	1.07496	1.07551
14	1.07742	1.07801	1.07860	1.07918	1.07977	1.08036	1.08095	1.08154
15	1.08317	1.08380	1.08444	1.08508	1.08571	1.08635	1.08698	1.08762
16	1.08895	1.08964	1.09032	1.09100	1.09168	1.09236	1.09304	1.09372
17	1.09477	1.09550	1.09622	1.09695	1.09768	1.09841	1.09914	1.09987
18	1.10062	1.10139	1.10217	1.10294	1.10371	1.10449	1.10527	1.10604
19	1.10649	1.10732	1.10814	1.10896	1.10978	1.11061	1.11143	1.11225
20	1.11240	1.11327	1.11414	1.11501	1.11588	1.11675	1.11763	1.11850
21	1.11834	1.11926	1.12018	1.12110	1.12202	1.12294	1.12386	1.12478
22	1.12432	1.12528	1.12625	1.12722	1.12819	1.12915	1.13012	1.13109
23	1.13032	1.13134	1.13235	1.13337	1.13439	1.13541	1.13642	1.13744
24	1.13636	1.13742	1.13849	1.13956	1.14062	1.14169	1.14276	1.14383
25	1.14242	1.14354	1.14466	1.14578	1.14689	1.14801	1.14913	1.15025
26	1.14853	1.14969	1.15086	1.15203	1.15320	1.15437	1.15554	1.15671
27	1.15466	1.15588	1.15710	1.15832	1.15954	1.16076	1.16198	1.16321
28	1.16083	1.16210	1.16337	1.16464	1.16591	1.16719	1.16846	1.16974
29	1.16702	1.16835	1.16967	1.17100	1.17232	1.17365	1.17498	1.17631
30	1.17326	1.17463	1.17601	1.17739	1.17877	1.18015	1.18153	1.18291
31	1.17952	1.18095	1.18238	1.18381	1.18525	1.18668	1.18812	1.18955
32	1.18582	1.18730	1.18879	1.19028	1.19176	1.19325	1.19474	1.19623
33	1.19215	1.19369	1.19523	1.19677	1.19831	1.19986	1.20140	1.20295
34	1.19852	1.20011	1.20171	1.20330	1.20490	1.20650	1.20810	1.20970
35	1.20492	1.20657	1.20822	1.20987	1.21153	1.21318	1.21484	1.21650
36	1.21136	1.21306	1.21477	1.21648	1.21819	1.21990	1.22161	1.22333
37	1.21782	1.21959	1.22135	1.22312	1.22488	1.22665	1.22842	1.23020
38	1.22433	1.22615	1.22797	1.22979	1.23162	1.23344	1.23527	1.23710
39	1.23087	1.23274	1.23462	1.23650	1.23839	1.24027	1.24216	1.24405
40	1.23744	1.23938	1.24131	1.24325	1.24520	1.24714	1.24909	1.25103
41	1.24405	1.24604	1.24804	1.25004	1.25204	1.25404	1.25605	1.25806
42	1.25069	1.25275	1.25480	1.25686	1.25892	1.26099	1.26305	1.26512
43	1.25737	1.25949	1.26160	1.26372	1.26584	1.26797	1.27010	1.27223
44	1.26409	1.26626	1.26844	1.27062	1.27280	1.27499	1.27718	1.27937
45	1.27084	1.27307	1.27531	1.27755	1.27980	1.28205	1.28430	1.28655
46	1.27762	1.27992	1.28222	1.28453	1.28684	1.28915	1.29146	1.29378
47	1.28445	1.28681	1.28917	1.29154	1.29391	1.29628	1.29866	1.30104
48	1.29130	1.29373	1.29616	1.29859	1.30102	1.30346	1.30590	1.30835
60	1.37653	1.37976	1.38300	1.38624	1.38949	1.39275	1.39601	1.39928
72	1.46738	1.47152	1.47566	1.47981	1.48398	1.48815	1.49233	1.49653
84	1.56423	1.56937	1.57453	1.57970	1.58489	1.59009	1.59531	1.60054
96	1.66747	1.67374	1.68002	1.68633	1.69266	1.69901	1.70538	1.71177
108	1.77752	1.78504	1.79259	1.80016	1.80776	1.81539	1.82305	1.83074
120	1.89484	1.90374	1.91269	1.92167	1.93069	1.93975	1.94884	1.95798
132	2.01990	2.03034	2.04084	2.05138	2.06198	2.07262	2.08331	2.09406
144	2.15321	2.16536	2.17757	2.18985	2.20219	2.21460	2.22706	2.23959
156	2.29532	2.30936	2.32347	2.33767	2.35194	2.36629	2.38073	2.39525
168	2.44681	2.46293	2.47914	2.49546	2.51187	2.52839	2.54500	2.56172
180	2.60830	2.62671	2.64525	2.66390	2.68268	2.70158	2.72061	2.73976
192	2.78045	2.80139	2.82248	2.84372	2.86510	2.88664	2.90833	2.93017
204	2.96396	2.98768	3.01159	3.03567	3.05993	3.08437	3.10900	3.13382
216	3.15958	3.18636	3.21336	3.24057	3.26800	3.29565	3.32352	3.35162
228	3.36811	3.39826	3.42866	3.45931	3.49023	3.52141	3.55285	3.58455
240	3.59041	3.62424	3.65838	3.69282	3.72756	3.76262	3.79799	3.83368
252	3.82738	3.86525	3.90349	3.94208	3.98104	4.02036	4.06005	4.10012
264	4.07998	4.12229	4.16502	4.20817	4.25175	4.29576	4.34020	4.38508
276	4.34926	4.39643	4.44408	4.49222	4.54087	4.59002	4.63967	4.68984
288	4.63631	4.68879	4.74183	4.79545	4.84965	4.90443	4.95981	5.01579
300	4.94231	5.00059	5.05953	5.11914	5.17942	5.24038	5.30204	5.36438
312	5.26850	5.33313	5.39852	5.46468	5.53162	5.59935	5.66788	5.73721
324	5.61623	5.68779	5.76022	5.83355	5.90777	5.98291	6.05896	6.13594
336	5.98690	6.06602	6.14616	6.22731	6.30950	6.39274	6.47703	6.56239
348	6.38203	6.46941	6.55795	6.64766	6.73855	6.83064	6.92394	7.01848
360	6.80325	6.89963	6.99733	7.09637	7.19677	7.29854	7.40169	7.50626
420	9.36488	9.51985	9.67731	9.83730	9.99986	10.16502	10.33284	10.50334
480	12.89105	13.13513	13.38372	13.63689	13.89473	14.15732	14.42475	14.69710

12

SINGLE DEPOSIT

EFFECTIVE ANNUAL YIELD

NUMBER OF MONTHS	7.00%	7.05%	7.10%	7.15%	7.20%	7.25%	7.30%	7.35%
1	1.00565	1.00569	1.00573	1.00577	1.00581	1.00585	1.00589	1.00593
2	1.01134	1.01142	1.01150	1.01158	1.01166	1.01173	1.01181	1.01189
3	1.01706	1.01718	1.01730	1.01741	1.01753	1.01765	1.01777	1.01789
4	1.02281	1.02297	1.02313	1.02329	1.02345	1.02361	1.02376	1.02392
5	1.02859	1.02879	1.02899	1.02919	1.02939	1.02959	1.02979	1.02999
6	1.03441	1.03465	1.03489	1.03513	1.03537	1.03562	1.03586	1.03610
7	1.04026	1.04054	1.04082	1.04111	1.04139	1.04167	1.04196	1.04224
8	1.04614	1.04646	1.04679	1.04712	1.04744	1.04777	1.04809	1.04842
9	1.05205	1.05242	1.05279	1.05316	1.05353	1.05390	1.05427	1.05463
10	1.05800	1.05841	1.05883	1.05924	1.05965	1.06006	1.06047	1.06089
11	1.06398	1.06444	1.06490	1.06535	1.06581	1.06626	1.06672	1.06717
12	1.07000	1.07050	1.07100	1.07150	1.07200	1.07250	1.07300	1.07350
13	1.07605	1.07659	1.07714	1.07768	1.07823	1.07877	1.07932	1.07986
14	1.08213	1.08272	1.08331	1.08390	1.08449	1.08508	1.08567	1.08626
15	1.08825	1.08889	1.08952	1.09016	1.09080	1.09143	1.09207	1.09270
16	1.09441	1.09509	1.09577	1.09645	1.09713	1.09782	1.09850	1.09918
17	1.10059	1.10132	1.10205	1.10278	1.10351	1.10424	1.10497	1.10570
18	1.10682	1.10759	1.10837	1.10914	1.10992	1.11070	1.11147	1.11225
19	1.11307	1.11390	1.11472	1.11555	1.11637	1.11720	1.11802	1.11884
20	1.11937	1.12024	1.12111	1.12198	1.12286	1.12373	1.12460	1.12548
21	1.12570	1.12662	1.12754	1.12846	1.12938	1.13030	1.13123	1.13215
22	1.13206	1.13303	1.13400	1.13497	1.13594	1.13692	1.13789	1.13886
23	1.13846	1.13948	1.14050	1.14152	1.14255	1.14357	1.14459	1.14561
24	1.14490	1.14597	1.14704	1.14811	1.14918	1.15026	1.15133	1.15240
25	1.15137	1.15249	1.15362	1.15474	1.15586	1.15698	1.15811	1.15923
26	1.15788	1.15906	1.16023	1.16140	1.16258	1.16375	1.16493	1.16611
27	1.16443	1.16565	1.16688	1.16811	1.16933	1.17056	1.17179	1.17302
28	1.17101	1.17229	1.17357	1.17485	1.17613	1.17741	1.17869	1.17997
29	1.17764	1.17897	1.18030	1.18163	1.18296	1.18430	1.18563	1.18697
30	1.18429	1.18568	1.18706	1.18845	1.18984	1.19122	1.19261	1.19400
31	1.19099	1.19243	1.19387	1.19531	1.19675	1.19819	1.19964	1.20108
32	1.19772	1.19922	1.20071	1.20221	1.20370	1.20520	1.20670	1.20820
33	1.20450	1.20604	1.20759	1.20915	1.21070	1.21225	1.21381	1.21536
34	1.21131	1.21291	1.21452	1.21612	1.21773	1.21934	1.22095	1.22257
35	1.21816	1.21982	1.22148	1.22314	1.22481	1.22648	1.22814	1.22981
36	1.22504	1.22676	1.22848	1.23020	1.23193	1.23365	1.23538	1.23710
37	1.23197	1.23375	1.23552	1.23730	1.23908	1.24087	1.24265	1.24444
38	1.23894	1.24077	1.24261	1.24444	1.24628	1.24813	1.24997	1.25181
39	1.24594	1.24783	1.24973	1.25163	1.25353	1.25543	1.25733	1.25923
40	1.25299	1.25494	1.25689	1.25885	1.26081	1.26277	1.26473	1.26670
41	1.26007	1.26208	1.26410	1.26612	1.26814	1.27016	1.27218	1.27421
42	1.26719	1.26927	1.27134	1.27342	1.27550	1.27759	1.27967	1.28176
43	1.27436	1.27649	1.27863	1.28077	1.28292	1.28506	1.28721	1.28936
44	1.28156	1.28376	1.28596	1.28816	1.29037	1.29258	1.29479	1.29700
45	1.28881	1.29107	1.29333	1.29560	1.29787	1.30014	1.30241	1.30469
46	1.29610	1.29842	1.30075	1.30308	1.30541	1.30774	1.31008	1.31243
47	1.30343	1.30581	1.30820	1.31060	1.31299	1.31539	1.31780	1.32020
48	1.31080	1.31325	1.31570	1.31816	1.32062	1.32309	1.32556	1.32803
60	1.40255	1.40583	1.40912	1.41241	1.41571	1.41901	1.42232	1.42564
72	1.50073	1.50494	1.50917	1.51340	1.51764	1.52189	1.52615	1.53043
84	1.60578	1.61104	1.61632	1.62161	1.62691	1.63223	1.63756	1.64291
96	1.71819	1.72462	1.73107	1.73755	1.74405	1.75057	1.75711	1.76367
108	1.83846	1.84621	1.85398	1.86179	1.86962	1.87748	1.88537	1.89330
120	1.96715	1.97636	1.98561	1.99490	2.00423	2.01360	2.02301	2.03245
132	2.10485	2.11570	2.12659	2.13754	2.14854	2.15959	2.17069	2.18184
144	2.25219	2.26485	2.27758	2.29037	2.30323	2.31615	2.32915	2.34220
156	2.40985	2.42453	2.43929	2.45413	2.46906	2.48408	2.49917	2.51436
168	2.57853	2.59545	2.61248	2.62960	2.64684	2.66417	2.68161	2.69916
180	2.75903	2.77843	2.79796	2.81762	2.83741	2.85732	2.87737	2.89755
192	2.95216	2.97431	2.99662	3.01908	3.04170	3.06448	3.08742	3.11052
204	3.15882	3.18400	3.20938	3.23495	3.26070	3.28665	3.31280	3.33914
216	3.37993	3.40847	3.43724	3.46624	3.49547	3.52494	3.55463	3.58457
228	3.61653	3.64877	3.68129	3.71408	3.74715	3.78050	3.81412	3.84803
240	3.86968	3.90601	3.94266	3.97964	4.01694	4.05458	4.09255	4.13086
252	4.14056	4.18138	4.22259	4.26418	4.30616	4.34854	4.39131	4.43448
264	4.43040	4.47617	4.52239	4.56907	4.61621	4.66381	4.71188	4.76042
276	4.74053	4.79174	4.84348	4.89576	4.94857	5.00193	5.05584	5.11031
288	5.07237	5.12956	5.18737	5.24581	5.30487	5.36457	5.42492	5.48592
300	5.42743	5.49119	5.55567	5.62088	5.68682	5.75351	5.82094	5.88913
312	5.80735	5.87832	5.95013	6.02277	6.09627	6.17063	6.24587	6.32198
324	6.21387	6.29275	6.37259	6.45340	6.53520	6.61801	6.70182	6.78665
336	6.64884	6.73638	6.82504	6.91482	7.00574	7.09781	7.19105	7.28547
348	7.11426	7.21130	7.30962	7.40923	7.51015	7.61240	7.71599	7.82095
360	7.61226	7.71970	7.82860	7.93899	8.05088	8.16430	8.27926	8.39579
420	10.67658	10.85259	11.03142	11.21311	11.39771	11.58525	11.77580	11.96938
480	14.97446	15.25692	15.54457	15.83751	16.13583	16.43963	16.74900	17.06404

SINGLE DEPOSIT

EFFECTIVE ANNUAL YIELD

NUMBER OF MONTHS	7.40%	7.45%	7.50%	7.55%	7.60%	7.65%	7.70%	7.75%
1	1.00597	1.00601	1.00604	1.00608	1.00612	1.00616	1.00620	1.00624
2	1.01197	1.01205	1.01213	1.01220	1.01228	1.01236	1.01244	1.01252
3	1.01801	1.01813	1.01824	1.01836	1.01848	1.01860	1.01872	1.01884
4	1.02408	1.02424	1.02440	1.02456	1.02472	1.02488	1.02503	1.02519
5	1.03019	1.03039	1.03059	1.03079	1.03099	1.03119	1.03139	1.03159
6	1.03634	1.03658	1.03682	1.03706	1.03730	1.03755	1.03779	1.03803
7	1.04252	1.04281	1.04309	1.04337	1.04366	1.04394	1.04422	1.04450
8	1.04874	1.04907	1.04939	1.04972	1.05005	1.05037	1.05070	1.05102
9	1.05500	1.05537	1.05574	1.05611	1.05647	1.05684	1.05721	1.05758
10	1.06130	1.06171	1.06212	1.06253	1.06294	1.06336	1.06377	1.06418
11	1.06763	1.06809	1.06854	1.06900	1.06945	1.06991	1.07036	1.07082
12	1.07400	1.07450	1.07500	1.07550	1.07600	1.07650	1.07700	1.07750
13	1.08041	1.08095	1.08150	1.08204	1.08259	1.08313	1.08368	1.08422
14	1.08686	1.08745	1.08804	1.08863	1.08922	1.08981	1.09040	1.09099
15	1.09334	1.09398	1.09461	1.09525	1.09589	1.09652	1.09716	1.09780
16	1.09986	1.10055	1.10123	1.10191	1.10260	1.10328	1.10396	1.10465
17	1.10643	1.10716	1.10789	1.10862	1.10935	1.11008	1.11081	1.11154
18	1.11303	1.11381	1.11458	1.11536	1.11614	1.11692	1.11770	1.11847
19	1.11967	1.12050	1.12132	1.12215	1.12297	1.12380	1.12463	1.12545
20	1.12635	1.12723	1.12810	1.12897	1.12985	1.13072	1.13160	1.13248
21	1.13307	1.13400	1.13492	1.13584	1.13677	1.13769	1.13862	1.13954
22	1.13983	1.14081	1.14178	1.14275	1.14373	1.14470	1.14568	1.14665
23	1.14663	1.14766	1.14868	1.14971	1.15073	1.15176	1.15278	1.15381
24	1.15348	1.15455	1.15562	1.15670	1.15778	1.15885	1.15993	1.16101
25	1.16036	1.16148	1.16261	1.16374	1.16486	1.16599	1.16712	1.16825
26	1.16728	1.16846	1.16964	1.17082	1.17200	1.17318	1.17436	1.17554
27	1.17425	1.17548	1.17671	1.17794	1.17917	1.18041	1.18164	1.18288
28	1.18125	1.18254	1.18382	1.18511	1.18639	1.18768	1.18897	1.19026
29	1.18830	1.18964	1.19098	1.19232	1.19366	1.19500	1.19634	1.19768
30	1.19539	1.19678	1.19818	1.19957	1.20097	1.20236	1.20376	1.20516
31	1.20253	1.20397	1.20542	1.20687	1.20832	1.20977	1.21122	1.21268
32	1.20970	1.21120	1.21271	1.21421	1.21572	1.21722	1.21873	1.22024
33	1.21692	1.21848	1.22004	1.22160	1.22316	1.22473	1.22629	1.22786
34	1.22418	1.22580	1.22741	1.22903	1.23065	1.23227	1.23389	1.23552
35	1.23149	1.23316	1.23483	1.23651	1.23819	1.23986	1.24155	1.24323
36	1.23883	1.24056	1.24230	1.24403	1.24577	1.24750	1.24924	1.25098
37	1.24623	1.24801	1.24981	1.25160	1.25339	1.25519	1.25699	1.25879
38	1.25366	1.25551	1.25736	1.25921	1.26107	1.26293	1.26478	1.26664
39	1.26114	1.26305	1.26496	1.26688	1.26879	1.27071	1.27263	1.27455
40	1.26867	1.27064	1.27261	1.27458	1.27656	1.27854	1.28052	1.28250
41	1.27624	1.27827	1.28030	1.28234	1.28438	1.28642	1.28846	1.29050
42	1.28385	1.28595	1.28804	1.29014	1.29224	1.29434	1.29645	1.29856
43	1.29151	1.29367	1.29583	1.29799	1.30015	1.30232	1.30449	1.30666
44	1.29922	1.30144	1.30366	1.30588	1.30811	1.31034	1.31258	1.31481
45	1.30697	1.30925	1.31154	1.31383	1.31612	1.31842	1.32071	1.32302
46	1.31477	1.31712	1.31947	1.32182	1.32418	1.32654	1.32890	1.33127
47	1.32261	1.32503	1.32744	1.32986	1.33229	1.33471	1.33714	1.33958
48	1.33051	1.33299	1.33547	1.33796	1.34045	1.34294	1.34544	1.34794
60	1.42896	1.43229	1.43563	1.43897	1.44232	1.44567	1.44903	1.45240
72	1.53471	1.53900	1.54330	1.54761	1.55194	1.55627	1.56061	1.56496
84	1.64828	1.65366	1.65905	1.66446	1.66988	1.67532	1.68078	1.68625
96	1.77025	1.77685	1.78348	1.79012	1.79679	1.80348	1.81020	1.81693
108	1.90125	1.90923	1.91724	1.92528	1.93335	1.94145	1.94958	1.95774
120	2.04194	2.05147	2.06103	2.07064	2.08028	2.08997	2.09970	2.10947
132	2.19304	2.20430	2.21561	2.22697	2.23839	2.24985	2.26138	2.27295
144	2.35533	2.36852	2.38178	2.39511	2.40850	2.42197	2.43550	2.44910
156	2.52962	2.54497	2.56041	2.57594	2.59155	2.60725	2.62304	2.63891
168	2.71681	2.73458	2.75244	2.77042	2.78851	2.80670	2.82501	2.84343
180	2.91786	2.93830	2.95888	2.97959	3.00043	3.02142	3.04253	3.06379
192	3.13378	3.15720	3.18079	3.20455	3.22847	3.25255	3.27681	3.30124
204	3.36568	3.39242	3.41935	3.44649	3.47383	3.50137	3.52912	3.55708
216	3.61474	3.64515	3.67580	3.70670	3.73784	3.76923	3.80087	3.83275
228	3.88223	3.91672	3.95149	3.98656	4.02192	4.05758	4.09353	4.12979
240	4.16952	4.20851	4.24785	4.28754	4.32758	4.36798	4.40874	4.44985
252	4.47806	4.52204	4.56644	4.61125	4.65648	4.70213	4.74821	4.79472
264	4.80944	4.85894	4.90892	4.95940	5.01037	5.06184	5.11382	5.16631
276	5.16533	5.22093	5.27709	5.33383	5.39116	5.44908	5.50758	5.56669
288	5.54757	5.60989	5.67287	5.73654	5.80089	5.86593	5.93167	5.99811
300	5.95809	6.02782	6.09834	6.16965	6.24176	6.31467	6.38841	6.46297
312	6.39899	6.47690	6.55572	6.63546	6.71613	6.79775	6.88031	6.96385
324	6.87251	6.95942	7.04739	7.13643	7.22656	7.31777	7.41010	7.50355
336	7.38108	7.47790	7.57595	7.67523	7.77577	7.87758	7.98068	8.08507
348	7.92728	8.03501	8.14414	8.25471	8.36673	8.48022	8.59519	8.71166
360	8.51390	8.63361	8.75496	8.87794	9.00260	9.12895	9.25702	9.38682
420	12.16606	12.36587	12.56887	12.77511	12.98463	13.19749	13.41373	13.63342
480	17.38486	17.71156	18.04424	18.38301	18.72798	19.07925	19.43695	19.80118

14

SINGLE DEPOSIT

EFFECTIVE ANNUAL YIELD

NUMBER OF MONTHS	7.80%	7.85%	7.90%	7.95%	8.00%	8.05%	8.10%	8.15%
1	1.00628	1.00632	1.00636	1.00640	1.00643	1.00647	1.00651	1.00655
2	1.01260	1.01267	1.01275	1.01283	1.01291	1.01299	1.01307	1.01314
3	1.01895	1.01907	1.01919	1.01931	1.01943	1.01954	1.01966	1.01978
4	1.02535	1.02551	1.02567	1.02583	1.02599	1.02614	1.02630	1.02646
5	1.03179	1.03199	1.03219	1.03239	1.03259	1.03279	1.03299	1.03318
6	1.03827	1.03851	1.03875	1.03899	1.03923	1.03947	1.03971	1.03995
7	1.04479	1.04507	1.04535	1.04563	1.04592	1.04620	1.04648	1.04676
8	1.05135	1.05167	1.05200	1.05232	1.05265	1.05297	1.05330	1.05362
9	1.05795	1.05832	1.05868	1.05905	1.05942	1.05979	1.06015	1.06052
10	1.06459	1.06500	1.06541	1.06582	1.06624	1.06665	1.06706	1.06747
11	1.07127	1.07173	1.07218	1.07264	1.07310	1.07355	1.07401	1.07446
12	1.07800	1.07850	1.07900	1.07950	1.08000	1.08050	1.08100	1.08150
13	1.08477	1.08531	1.08586	1.08640	1.08695	1.08749	1.08804	1.08858
14	1.09158	1.09217	1.09276	1.09335	1.09394	1.09453	1.09512	1.09572
15	1.09843	1.09907	1.09971	1.10034	1.10098	1.10162	1.10226	1.10289
16	1.10533	1.10601	1.10670	1.10738	1.10806	1.10875	1.10943	1.11012
17	1.11227	1.11300	1.11373	1.11446	1.11519	1.11593	1.11666	1.11739
18	1.11925	1.12003	1.12081	1.12159	1.12237	1.12315	1.12393	1.12471
19	1.12628	1.12711	1.12793	1.12876	1.12959	1.13042	1.13125	1.13208
20	1.13335	1.13423	1.13510	1.13598	1.13686	1.13774	1.13861	1.13949
21	1.14047	1.14139	1.14232	1.14325	1.14417	1.14510	1.14603	1.14696
22	1.14763	1.14860	1.14958	1.15056	1.15153	1.15251	1.15349	1.15447
23	1.15483	1.15586	1.15689	1.15792	1.15894	1.15997	1.16100	1.16203
24	1.16208	1.16316	1.16424	1.16532	1.16640	1.16748	1.16856	1.16964
25	1.16938	1.17051	1.17164	1.17277	1.17390	1.17504	1.17617	1.17730
26	1.17672	1.17791	1.17909	1.18027	1.18146	1.18264	1.18383	1.18502
27	1.18411	1.18535	1.18658	1.18782	1.18906	1.19030	1.19154	1.19278
28	1.19154	1.19283	1.19413	1.19542	1.19671	1.19800	1.19930	1.20059
29	1.19903	1.20037	1.20172	1.20306	1.20441	1.20576	1.20711	1.20846
30	1.20655	1.20795	1.20935	1.21076	1.21216	1.21356	1.21497	1.21637
31	1.21413	1.21559	1.21704	1.21850	1.21996	1.22142	1.22288	1.22434
32	1.22175	1.22326	1.22478	1.22629	1.22781	1.22932	1.23084	1.23236
33	1.22942	1.23099	1.23256	1.23413	1.23571	1.23728	1.23886	1.24043
34	1.23714	1.23877	1.24040	1.24203	1.24366	1.24529	1.24692	1.24856
35	1.24491	1.24660	1.24828	1.24997	1.25166	1.25335	1.25504	1.25674
36	1.25273	1.25447	1.25622	1.25796	1.25971	1.26146	1.26321	1.26497
37	1.26059	1.26240	1.26420	1.26601	1.26782	1.26963	1.27144	1.27325
38	1.26851	1.27037	1.27224	1.27410	1.27597	1.27785	1.27972	1.28159
39	1.27647	1.27840	1.28032	1.28225	1.28418	1.28612	1.28805	1.28999
40	1.28449	1.28647	1.28846	1.29045	1.29245	1.29444	1.29644	1.29844
41	1.29255	1.29460	1.29665	1.29871	1.30076	1.30282	1.30488	1.30694
42	1.30067	1.30278	1.30489	1.30701	1.30913	1.31125	1.31338	1.31551
43	1.30883	1.31101	1.31319	1.31537	1.31755	1.31974	1.32193	1.32412
44	1.31705	1.31929	1.32153	1.32378	1.32603	1.32828	1.33054	1.33280
45	1.32532	1.32763	1.32994	1.33225	1.33456	1.33688	1.33920	1.34153
46	1.33364	1.33601	1.33839	1.34077	1.34315	1.34553	1.34792	1.35031
47	1.34201	1.34445	1.34690	1.34934	1.35179	1.35424	1.35670	1.35916
48	1.35044	1.35295	1.35546	1.35797	1.36049	1.36301	1.36553	1.36806
60	1.45577	1.45915	1.46254	1.46593	1.46933	1.47273	1.47614	1.47956
72	1.56932	1.57370	1.57808	1.58247	1.58687	1.59129	1.59571	1.60014
84	1.69173	1.69723	1.70275	1.70828	1.71382	1.71939	1.72496	1.73056
96	1.82369	1.83046	1.83726	1.84409	1.85093	1.85780	1.86469	1.87160
108	1.96593	1.97416	1.98241	1.99069	1.99900	2.00735	2.01572	2.02413
120	2.11928	2.12913	2.13902	2.14895	2.15892	2.16894	2.17900	2.18910
132	2.28458	2.29626	2.30800	2.31979	2.33164	2.34354	2.35550	2.36751
144	2.46278	2.47652	2.49033	2.50422	2.51817	2.53220	2.54629	2.56046
156	2.65487	2.67093	2.68707	2.70330	2.71962	2.73604	2.75254	2.76914
168	2.86195	2.88059	2.89935	2.91821	2.93719	2.95629	2.97550	2.99482
180	3.08519	3.10672	3.12840	3.15021	3.17217	3.19427	3.21651	3.23890
192	3.32583	3.35060	3.37554	3.40065	3.42594	3.45141	3.47705	3.50287
204	3.58525	3.61362	3.64221	3.67101	3.70002	3.72925	3.75869	3.78836
216	3.86489	3.89729	3.92994	3.96285	3.99602	4.02945	4.06315	4.09711
228	4.16636	4.20323	4.24041	4.27790	4.31570	4.35382	4.39226	4.43102
240	4.49133	4.53318	4.57540	4.61799	4.66096	4.70430	4.74803	4.79215
252	4.84166	4.88909	4.93685	4.98512	5.03383	5.08300	5.13263	5.18271
264	5.21931	5.27282	5.32687	5.38144	5.43654	5.49218	5.54837	5.60510
276	5.62641	5.68674	5.74769	5.80926	5.87146	5.93430	5.99779	6.06192
288	6.06527	6.13315	6.20176	6.27110	6.34118	6.41201	6.48361	6.55596
300	6.53876	6.61460	6.69169	6.76965	6.84848	6.92818	7.00878	7.09028
312	7.04836	7.13385	7.22034	7.30784	7.39635	7.48590	7.57649	7.66813
324	7.59813	7.69386	7.79075	7.88881	7.98806	8.08852	8.19019	8.29309
336	8.19078	8.29782	8.40621	8.51597	8.62711	8.73964	8.85359	8.96897
348	8.82966	8.94920	9.07031	9.19299	9.31727	9.44318	9.57073	9.69994
360	9.51838	9.65171	9.78686	9.92383	10.06266	10.20336	10.34596	10.49049
420	13.85660	14.08333	14.31366	14.54764	14.78534	15.02682	15.27212	15.52131
480	20.17207	20.54972	20.93427	21.32583	21.72452	22.13048	22.54383	22.96471

15

SINGLE DEPOSIT

EFFECTIVE ANNUAL YIELD

NUMBER OF MONTHS	8.20%	8.25%	8.30%	8.35%	8.40%	8.45%	8.50%	8.55%
1	1.00659	1.00663	1.00667	1.00671	1.00674	1.00678	1.00682	1.00686
2	1.01322	1.01330	1.01338	1.01346	1.01353	1.01361	1.01369	1.01377
3	1.01990	1.02002	1.02013	1.02025	1.02037	1.02049	1.02060	1.02072
4	1.02662	1.02678	1.02693	1.02709	1.02725	1.02741	1.02757	1.02772
5	1.03338	1.03358	1.03378	1.03398	1.03418	1.03438	1.03458	1.03477
6	1.04019	1.04043	1.04067	1.04091	1.04115	1.04139	1.04163	1.04187
7	1.04705	1.04733	1.04761	1.04789	1.04817	1.04846	1.04874	1.04902
8	1.05395	1.05427	1.05459	1.05492	1.05524	1.05557	1.05589	1.05622
9	1.06089	1.06126	1.06163	1.06199	1.06236	1.06273	1.06310	1.06346
10	1.06788	1.06829	1.06870	1.06911	1.06953	1.06994	1.07035	1.07076
11	1.07492	1.07537	1.07583	1.07628	1.07674	1.07719	1.07765	1.07810
12	1.08200	1.08250	1.08300	1.08350	1.08400	1.08450	1.08500	1.08550
13	1.08913	1.08967	1.09022	1.09077	1.09131	1.09186	1.09240	1.09295
14	1.09631	1.09690	1.09749	1.09808	1.09867	1.09926	1.09985	1.10044
15	1.10353	1.10417	1.10480	1.10544	1.10608	1.10672	1.10736	1.10799
16	1.11080	1.11149	1.11217	1.11285	1.11354	1.11422	1.11491	1.11559
17	1.11812	1.11885	1.11958	1.12032	1.12105	1.12178	1.12251	1.12325
18	1.12549	1.12627	1.12705	1.12783	1.12861	1.12939	1.13017	1.13095
19	1.13290	1.13373	1.13456	1.13539	1.13622	1.13705	1.13788	1.13871
20	1.14037	1.14125	1.14213	1.14301	1.14388	1.14476	1.14564	1.14652
21	1.14788	1.14881	1.14974	1.15067	1.15160	1.15253	1.15346	1.15439
22	1.15545	1.15643	1.15741	1.15839	1.15937	1.16035	1.16133	1.16231
23	1.16306	1.16409	1.16512	1.16615	1.16718	1.16822	1.16925	1.17028
24	1.17072	1.17181	1.17289	1.17397	1.17506	1.17614	1.17723	1.17831
25	1.17844	1.17957	1.18071	1.18184	1.18298	1.18412	1.18526	1.18639
26	1.18620	1.18739	1.18858	1.18977	1.19096	1.19215	1.19334	1.19453
27	1.19402	1.19526	1.19650	1.19775	1.19899	1.20024	1.20148	1.20273
28	1.20189	1.20318	1.20448	1.20578	1.20708	1.20838	1.20968	1.21098
29	1.20981	1.21116	1.21251	1.21386	1.21522	1.21657	1.21793	1.21929
30	1.21778	1.21919	1.22059	1.22200	1.22341	1.22482	1.22624	1.22765
31	1.22580	1.22727	1.22873	1.23020	1.23166	1.23313	1.23460	1.23607
32	1.23388	1.23540	1.23692	1.23845	1.23997	1.24150	1.24302	1.24455
33	1.24201	1.24359	1.24517	1.24675	1.24833	1.24992	1.25150	1.25309
34	1.25019	1.25183	1.25347	1.25511	1.25675	1.25840	1.26004	1.26169
35	1.25843	1.26013	1.26183	1.26353	1.26523	1.26693	1.26864	1.27034
36	1.26672	1.26848	1.27024	1.27200	1.27376	1.27552	1.27729	1.27906
37	1.27507	1.27689	1.27871	1.28053	1.28235	1.28418	1.28600	1.28783
38	1.28347	1.28535	1.28723	1.28911	1.29100	1.29289	1.29477	1.29666
39	1.29193	1.29387	1.29581	1.29776	1.29971	1.30166	1.30361	1.30556
40	1.30044	1.30245	1.30445	1.30646	1.30847	1.31048	1.31250	1.31452
41	1.30901	1.31108	1.31315	1.31522	1.31730	1.31937	1.32145	1.32353
42	1.31764	1.31977	1.32190	1.32404	1.32618	1.32832	1.33047	1.33261
43	1.32632	1.32852	1.33072	1.33292	1.33512	1.33733	1.33954	1.34176
44	1.33506	1.33732	1.33959	1.34186	1.34413	1.34640	1.34868	1.35096
45	1.34385	1.34618	1.34852	1.35085	1.35319	1.35554	1.35788	1.36023
46	1.35271	1.35511	1.35751	1.35991	1.36232	1.36473	1.36714	1.36956
47	1.36162	1.36409	1.36656	1.36903	1.37151	1.37399	1.37647	1.37896
48	1.37059	1.37313	1.37567	1.37821	1.38076	1.38331	1.38586	1.38842
60	1.48298	1.48641	1.48985	1.49329	1.49674	1.50020	1.50366	1.50712
72	1.60459	1.60904	1.61351	1.61798	1.62247	1.62696	1.63147	1.63598
84	1.73616	1.74179	1.74743	1.75308	1.75875	1.76444	1.77014	1.77586
96	1.87853	1.88549	1.89246	1.89947	1.90649	1.91354	1.92060	1.92770
108	2.03257	2.04104	2.04954	2.05807	2.06663	2.07523	2.08386	2.09251
120	2.19924	2.20942	2.21965	2.22992	2.24023	2.25059	2.26098	2.27142
132	2.37958	2.39170	2.40388	2.41612	2.42841	2.44076	2.45317	2.46563
144	2.57470	2.58902	2.60340	2.61786	2.63240	2.64700	2.66169	2.67644
156	2.78583	2.80261	2.81949	2.83646	2.85352	2.87068	2.88793	2.90528
168	3.01427	3.03383	3.05350	3.07330	3.09321	3.11325	3.13340	3.15368
180	3.26144	3.28412	3.30694	3.32992	3.35304	3.37632	3.39974	3.42332
192	3.52887	3.55506	3.58142	3.60797	3.63470	3.66162	3.68872	3.71601
204	3.81824	3.84835	3.87868	3.90923	3.94001	3.97102	4.00226	4.03373
216	4.13134	4.16584	4.20061	4.23565	4.27098	4.30657	4.34245	4.37862
228	4.47011	4.50952	4.54926	4.58933	4.62974	4.67048	4.71156	4.75299
240	4.83666	4.88155	4.92685	4.97254	5.01864	5.06514	5.11205	5.15937
252	5.23326	5.28428	5.33578	5.38775	5.44020	5.49314	5.54657	5.60049
264	5.66239	5.72024	5.77865	5.83762	5.89718	5.95731	6.01803	6.07934
276	6.12671	6.19215	6.25827	6.32507	6.39254	6.46070	6.52956	6.59912
288	6.62910	6.70301	6.77771	6.85321	6.92951	7.00663	7.08457	7.16334
300	7.17268	7.25601	7.34026	7.42545	7.51159	7.59869	7.68676	7.77581
312	7.76084	7.85463	7.94950	8.04548	8.14257	8.24078	8.34014	8.44064
324	8.39723	8.50263	8.60931	8.71727	8.82654	8.93713	9.04905	9.16232
336	9.08580	9.20410	9.32388	9.44517	9.56797	9.69232	9.81822	9.94570
348	9.83084	9.96344	10.09776	10.23384	10.37168	10.51132	10.65277	10.79605
360	10.63697	10.78542	10.93588	11.08836	11.24290	11.39952	11.55825	11.71912
420	15.77445	16.03159	16.29281	16.55816	16.82707	17.10151	17.37964	17.66217
480	23.39324	23.82957	24.27383	24.72616	25.18670	25.65560	26.13302	26.61908

SINGLE DEPOSIT

NUMBER OF MONTHS	EFFECTIVE ANNUAL YIELD							
	8.60%	8.65%	8.70%	8.75%	8.80%	8.85%	8.90%	8.95%
1	1.00690	1.00694	1.00698	1.00701	1.00705	1.00709	1.00713	1.00717
2	1.01385	1.01392	1.01400	1.01408	1.01416	1.01423	1.01431	1.01439
3	1.02084	1.02096	1.02107	1.02119	1.02131	1.02143	1.02154	1.02166
4	1.02788	1.02804	1.02820	1.02836	1.02851	1.02867	1.02883	1.02899
5	1.03497	1.03517	1.03537	1.03557	1.03577	1.03597	1.03616	1.03636
6	1.04211	1.04235	1.04259	1.04283	1.04307	1.04331	1.04355	1.04379
7	1.04930	1.04958	1.04987	1.05015	1.05043	1.05071	1.05099	1.05127
8	1.05654	1.05687	1.05719	1.05751	1.05784	1.05816	1.05849	1.05881
9	1.06383	1.06420	1.06456	1.06493	1.06530	1.06567	1.06603	1.06640
10	1.07117	1.07158	1.07199	1.07240	1.07281	1.07322	1.07363	1.07405
11	1.07856	1.07901	1.07947	1.07992	1.08038	1.08083	1.08129	1.08175
12	1.08600	1.08650	1.08700	1.08750	1.08800	1.08850	1.08900	1.08950
13	1.09349	1.09404	1.09458	1.09513	1.09567	1.09622	1.09676	1.09731
14	1.10104	1.10163	1.10222	1.10281	1.10340	1.10399	1.10459	1.10518
15	1.10863	1.10927	1.10991	1.11055	1.11118	1.11182	1.11246	1.11310
16	1.11628	1.11697	1.11765	1.11834	1.11902	1.11971	1.12039	1.12108
17	1.12398	1.12471	1.12545	1.12618	1.12691	1.12765	1.12838	1.12912
18	1.13173	1.13252	1.13330	1.13408	1.13486	1.13565	1.13643	1.13721
19	1.13954	1.14037	1.14120	1.14204	1.14287	1.14370	1.14453	1.14536
20	1.14740	1.14828	1.14917	1.15005	1.15093	1.15181	1.15269	1.15357
21	1.15532	1.15625	1.15718	1.15811	1.15905	1.15998	1.16091	1.16184
22	1.16329	1.16427	1.16525	1.16624	1.16722	1.16820	1.16919	1.17017
23	1.17132	1.17235	1.17338	1.17442	1.17545	1.17649	1.17752	1.17856
24	1.17940	1.18048	1.18157	1.18266	1.18374	1.18483	1.18592	1.18701
25	1.18753	1.18867	1.18981	1.19095	1.19209	1.19323	1.19438	1.19552
26	1.19572	1.19692	1.19811	1.19931	1.20050	1.20170	1.20289	1.20409
27	1.20397	1.20522	1.20647	1.20772	1.20897	1.21022	1.21147	1.21272
28	1.21228	1.21358	1.21489	1.21619	1.21750	1.21880	1.22011	1.22142
29	1.22064	1.22200	1.22336	1.22472	1.22608	1.22745	1.22881	1.23017
30	1.22906	1.23048	1.23190	1.23331	1.23473	1.23615	1.23757	1.23899
31	1.23754	1.23902	1.24049	1.24196	1.24344	1.24492	1.24639	1.24787
32	1.24608	1.24761	1.24914	1.25068	1.25221	1.25374	1.25528	1.25682
33	1.25468	1.25627	1.25786	1.25945	1.26104	1.26264	1.26423	1.26583
34	1.26333	1.26498	1.26663	1.26828	1.26994	1.27159	1.27325	1.27490
35	1.27205	1.27376	1.27547	1.27718	1.27889	1.28061	1.28232	1.28404
36	1.28082	1.28259	1.28437	1.28614	1.28791	1.28969	1.29147	1.29325
37	1.28966	1.29149	1.29333	1.29516	1.29700	1.29884	1.30068	1.30252
38	1.29856	1.30045	1.30235	1.30425	1.30615	1.30805	1.30995	1.31186
39	1.30752	1.30947	1.31143	1.31339	1.31536	1.31732	1.31929	1.32126
40	1.31654	1.31856	1.32058	1.32261	1.32464	1.32667	1.32870	1.33073
41	1.32562	1.32770	1.32979	1.33188	1.33398	1.33607	1.33817	1.34027
42	1.33476	1.33692	1.33907	1.34123	1.34339	1.34555	1.34771	1.34988
43	1.34397	1.34619	1.34841	1.35064	1.35286	1.35509	1.35732	1.35956
44	1.35324	1.35553	1.35782	1.36011	1.36240	1.36470	1.36700	1.36930
45	1.36258	1.36493	1.36729	1.36965	1.37201	1.37438	1.37675	1.37912
46	1.37198	1.37440	1.37683	1.37926	1.38169	1.38413	1.38656	1.38901
47	1.38144	1.38394	1.38643	1.38893	1.39144	1.39394	1.39645	1.39896
48	1.39097	1.39354	1.39611	1.39868	1.40125	1.40383	1.40641	1.40899
60	1.51060	1.51408	1.51757	1.52106	1.52456	1.52807	1.53158	1.53510
72	1.64051	1.64505	1.64959	1.65415	1.65872	1.66330	1.66789	1.67249
84	1.78159	1.78734	1.79311	1.79889	1.80469	1.81050	1.81633	1.82218
96	1.93481	1.94195	1.94911	1.95629	1.96350	1.97073	1.97799	1.98526
108	2.10121	2.10993	2.11868	2.12747	2.13629	2.14514	2.15403	2.16294
120	2.28191	2.29244	2.30301	2.31362	2.32428	2.33499	2.34573	2.35653
132	2.47815	2.49073	2.50337	2.51607	2.52882	2.54163	2.55450	2.56744
144	2.69127	2.70618	2.72116	2.73622	2.75136	2.76657	2.78186	2.79722
156	2.92272	2.94027	2.95790	2.97564	2.99348	3.01141	3.02944	3.04757
168	3.17408	3.19460	3.21524	3.23601	3.25690	3.27792	3.29906	3.32033
180	3.44705	3.47093	3.49497	3.51916	3.54351	3.56801	3.59268	3.61750
192	3.74349	3.77117	3.79903	3.82709	3.85534	3.88378	3.91243	3.94127
204	4.06544	4.09737	4.12955	4.16196	4.19461	4.22750	4.26063	4.29401
216	4.41506	4.45179	4.48882	4.52613	4.56373	4.60163	4.63983	4.67832
228	4.79476	4.83688	4.87934	4.92216	4.96534	5.00888	5.05277	5.09703
240	5.20711	5.25526	5.30385	5.35285	5.40229	5.45216	5.50247	5.55322
252	5.65492	5.70985	5.76528	5.82123	5.87769	5.93468	5.99219	6.05023
264	6.14124	6.20375	6.26686	6.33058	6.39493	6.45990	6.52549	6.59173
276	6.66939	6.74037	6.81208	6.88451	6.95768	7.03160	7.10626	7.18169
288	7.24296	7.32341	7.40473	7.48691	7.56996	7.65389	7.73872	7.82445
300	7.86585	7.95689	8.04894	8.14201	8.23611	8.33126	8.42747	8.52473
312	8.54231	8.64516	8.74920	8.85444	8.96089	9.06858	9.17751	9.28770
324	9.27695	9.39297	9.51038	9.62920	9.74945	9.87115	9.99431	10.11895
336	10.07477	10.20546	10.33778	10.47175	10.60740	10.74475	10.88380	11.02459
348	10.94120	11.08823	11.23717	11.38803	11.54085	11.69566	11.85246	12.01129
360	11.88214	12.04736	12.21480	12.38449	12.55645	12.73072	12.90733	13.08630
420	17.94915	18.24066	18.53677	18.83754	19.14306	19.45338	19.76859	20.08876
480	27.11396	27.61781	28.13078	28.65303	29.18474	29.72606	30.27716	30.83823

17

SINGLE DEPOSIT

EFFECTIVE ANNUAL YIELD

NUMBER OF MONTHS	9.00%	9.05%	9.10%	9.15%	9.20%	9.25%	9.30%	9.35%
1	1.00721	1.00725	1.00728	1.00732	1.00736	1.00740	1.00744	1.00748
2	1.01447	1.01454	1.01462	1.01470	1.01478	1.01485	1.01493	1.01501
3	1.02178	1.02190	1.02201	1.02213	1.02225	1.02236	1.02248	1.02260
4	1.02914	1.02930	1.02946	1.02961	1.02977	1.02993	1.03009	1.03024
5	1.03656	1.03676	1.03696	1.03715	1.03735	1.03755	1.03775	1.03795
6	1.04403	1.04427	1.04451	1.04475	1.04499	1.04523	1.04547	1.04571
7	1.05156	1.05184	1.05212	1.05240	1.05268	1.05296	1.05324	1.05352
8	1.05913	1.05946	1.05978	1.06011	1.06043	1.06075	1.06108	1.06140
9	1.06677	1.06713	1.06750	1.06787	1.06824	1.06860	1.06897	1.06934
10	1.07446	1.07487	1.07528	1.07569	1.07610	1.07651	1.07692	1.07733
11	1.08220	1.08266	1.08311	1.08357	1.08402	1.08448	1.08493	1.08539
12	1.09000	1.09050	1.09100	1.09150	1.09200	1.09250	1.09300	1.09350
13	1.09786	1.09840	1.09895	1.09949	1.10004	1.10058	1.10113	1.10168
14	1.10577	1.10636	1.10695	1.10754	1.10814	1.10873	1.10932	1.10991
15	1.11374	1.11438	1.11502	1.11565	1.11629	1.11693	1.11757	1.11821
16	1.12177	1.12245	1.12314	1.12382	1.12451	1.12520	1.12588	1.12657
17	1.12985	1.13058	1.13132	1.13205	1.13279	1.13352	1.13426	1.13499
18	1.13799	1.13878	1.13956	1.14034	1.14113	1.14191	1.14269	1.14348
19	1.14620	1.14703	1.14786	1.14869	1.14953	1.15036	1.15119	1.15203
20	1.15446	1.15534	1.15622	1.15711	1.15799	1.15887	1.15976	1.16064
21	1.16278	1.16371	1.16464	1.16558	1.16651	1.16745	1.16838	1.16932
22	1.17116	1.17214	1.17313	1.17411	1.17510	1.17609	1.17707	1.17806
23	1.17960	1.18064	1.18167	1.18271	1.18375	1.18479	1.18583	1.18687
24	1.18810	1.18919	1.19028	1.19137	1.19246	1.19356	1.19465	1.19574
25	1.19666	1.19781	1.19895	1.20010	1.20124	1.20239	1.20353	1.20468
26	1.20529	1.20649	1.20768	1.20888	1.21008	1.21129	1.21249	1.21369
27	1.21397	1.21523	1.21648	1.21774	1.21899	1.22025	1.22151	1.22276
28	1.22272	1.22403	1.22534	1.22665	1.22797	1.22928	1.23059	1.23190
29	1.23154	1.23290	1.23427	1.23564	1.23700	1.23837	1.23974	1.24112
30	1.24041	1.24184	1.24326	1.24468	1.24611	1.24754	1.24897	1.25039
31	1.24935	1.25083	1.25232	1.25380	1.25528	1.25677	1.25826	1.25974
32	1.25836	1.25990	1.26144	1.26298	1.26452	1.26607	1.26761	1.26916
33	1.26743	1.26903	1.27063	1.27223	1.27383	1.27544	1.27704	1.27865
34	1.27656	1.27822	1.27988	1.28155	1.28321	1.28487	1.28654	1.28821
35	1.28576	1.28748	1.28921	1.29093	1.29266	1.29438	1.29611	1.29784
36	1.29503	1.29681	1.29860	1.30038	1.30217	1.30396	1.30575	1.30754
37	1.30436	1.30621	1.30806	1.30991	1.31176	1.31361	1.31546	1.31732
38	1.31376	1.31567	1.31758	1.31950	1.32141	1.32333	1.32525	1.32717
39	1.32323	1.32521	1.32718	1.32916	1.33114	1.33312	1.33511	1.33709
40	1.33277	1.33481	1.33685	1.33889	1.34094	1.34299	1.34504	1.34709
41	1.34238	1.34448	1.34659	1.34870	1.35081	1.35292	1.35504	1.35716
42	1.35205	1.35422	1.35640	1.35857	1.36075	1.36293	1.36512	1.36731
43	1.36179	1.36403	1.36628	1.36852	1.37077	1.37302	1.37527	1.37753
44	1.37161	1.37392	1.37623	1.37854	1.38086	1.38318	1.38550	1.38783
45	1.38150	1.38387	1.38625	1.38864	1.39102	1.39341	1.39581	1.39820
46	1.39145	1.39390	1.39635	1.39881	1.40126	1.40373	1.40619	1.40866
47	1.40148	1.40400	1.40652	1.40905	1.41158	1.41411	1.41665	1.41919
48	1.41158	1.41417	1.41677	1.41937	1.42197	1.42458	1.42719	1.42980
60	1.53862	1.54216	1.54569	1.54924	1.55279	1.55635	1.55991	1.56349
72	1.67710	1.68172	1.68635	1.69100	1.69565	1.70031	1.70499	1.70967
84	1.82804	1.83392	1.83981	1.84572	1.85165	1.85759	1.86355	1.86953
96	1.99256	1.99989	2.00723	2.01461	2.02200	2.02942	2.03686	2.04433
108	2.17189	2.18088	2.18989	2.19894	2.20802	2.21714	2.22629	2.23547
120	2.36736	2.37825	2.38917	2.40014	2.41116	2.42222	2.43333	2.44449
132	2.58043	2.59348	2.60659	2.61976	2.63299	2.64628	2.65963	2.67305
144	2.81266	2.82819	2.84379	2.85947	2.87522	2.89106	2.90698	2.92298
156	3.06580	3.08414	3.10257	3.12111	3.13974	3.15848	3.17733	3.19628
168	3.34173	3.36325	3.38491	3.40669	3.42860	3.45064	3.47282	3.49513
180	3.64248	3.66763	3.69293	3.71840	3.74403	3.76983	3.79579	3.82192
192	3.97031	3.99955	4.02899	4.05863	4.08848	4.11854	4.14880	4.17927
204	4.32763	4.36151	4.39563	4.43000	4.46462	4.49950	4.53464	4.57003
216	4.71712	4.75622	4.79563	4.83534	4.87537	4.91571	4.95636	4.99733
228	5.14166	5.18666	5.23203	5.27778	5.32390	5.37041	5.41730	5.46458
240	5.60441	5.65605	5.70815	5.76069	5.81370	5.86717	5.92111	5.97552
252	6.10881	6.16792	6.22759	6.28780	6.34856	6.40989	6.47177	6.53423
264	6.65860	6.72612	6.79430	6.86313	6.93263	7.00280	7.07365	7.14518
276	7.25787	7.33484	7.41258	7.49111	7.57043	7.65056	7.73150	7.81326
288	7.91108	7.99964	8.08712	8.17654	8.26691	8.35824	8.45053	8.54380
300	8.62308	8.72252	8.82305	8.92470	9.02747	9.13137	9.23643	9.34264
312	9.39916	9.51190	9.62595	9.74131	9.85800	9.97603	10.09542	10.21618
324	10.24508	10.37273	10.50191	10.63264	10.76493	10.89881	11.03429	11.17139
336	11.16714	11.31146	11.45758	11.60552	11.75530	11.90695	12.06048	12.21592
348	12.17218	12.33515	12.50022	12.66743	12.83679	13.00834	13.18210	13.35810
360	13.26768	13.45148	13.63774	13.82650	14.01778	14.21161	14.40804	14.60709
420	20.41397	20.74428	21.07979	21.42056	21.76669	22.11824	22.47531	22.83797
480	31.40942	31.99092	32.58292	33.18559	33.79913	34.42372	35.05956	35.70685

18

SINGLE DEPOSIT

NUMBER OF MONTHS	EFFECTIVE ANNUAL YIELD							
	9.40%	9.45%	9.50%	9.55%	9.60%	9.65%	9.70%	9.75%
1	1.00751	1.00755	1.00759	1.00763	1.00767	1.00771	1.00774	1.00778
2	1.01509	1.01516	1.01524	1.01532	1.01540	1.01547	1.01555	1.01563
3	1.02271	1.02283	1.02295	1.02306	1.02318	1.02330	1.02341	1.02353
4	1.03040	1.03056	1.03071	1.03087	1.03103	1.03118	1.03134	1.03150
5	1.03814	1.03834	1.03854	1.03874	1.03893	1.03913	1.03933	1.03953
6	1.04594	1.04618	1.04642	1.04666	1.04690	1.04714	1.04738	1.04762
7	1.05380	1.05409	1.05437	1.05465	1.05493	1.05521	1.05549	1.05577
8	1.06172	1.06205	1.06237	1.06269	1.06302	1.06334	1.06366	1.06399
9	1.06970	1.07007	1.07044	1.07080	1.07117	1.07154	1.07190	1.07227
10	1.07774	1.07815	1.07856	1.07897	1.07938	1.07979	1.08020	1.08061
11	1.08584	1.08630	1.08675	1.08720	1.08766	1.08811	1.08857	1.08902
12	1.09400	1.09450	1.09500	1.09550	1.09600	1.09650	1.09700	1.09750
13	1.10222	1.10277	1.10331	1.10386	1.10440	1.10495	1.10550	1.10604
14	1.11050	1.11110	1.11169	1.11228	1.11287	1.11347	1.11406	1.11465
15	1.11885	1.11949	1.12013	1.12077	1.12141	1.12205	1.12269	1.12333
16	1.12726	1.12794	1.12863	1.12932	1.13001	1.13069	1.13138	1.13207
17	1.13573	1.13646	1.13720	1.13794	1.13867	1.13941	1.14014	1.14088
18	1.14426	1.14505	1.14583	1.14662	1.14740	1.14819	1.14897	1.14976
19	1.15286	1.15370	1.15453	1.15537	1.15620	1.15704	1.15787	1.15871
20	1.16153	1.16241	1.16330	1.16418	1.16507	1.16595	1.16684	1.16773
21	1.17025	1.17119	1.17213	1.17306	1.17400	1.17494	1.17588	1.17681
22	1.17905	1.18004	1.18103	1.18201	1.18300	1.18399	1.18498	1.18597
23	1.18791	1.18895	1.18999	1.19103	1.19207	1.19312	1.19416	1.19520
24	1.19684	1.19793	1.19902	1.20012	1.20122	1.20231	1.20341	1.20451
25	1.20583	1.20698	1.20813	1.20928	1.21043	1.21158	1.21273	1.21388
26	1.21489	1.21609	1.21730	1.21850	1.21971	1.22091	1.22212	1.22333
27	1.22402	1.22528	1.22654	1.22780	1.22906	1.23032	1.23159	1.23285
28	1.23322	1.23454	1.23585	1.23717	1.23849	1.23981	1.24112	1.24245
29	1.24249	1.24386	1.24523	1.24661	1.24798	1.24936	1.25074	1.25212
30	1.25182	1.25325	1.25469	1.25612	1.25755	1.25899	1.26042	1.26186
31	1.26123	1.26272	1.26421	1.26570	1.26720	1.26869	1.27019	1.27168
32	1.27071	1.27226	1.27381	1.27536	1.27691	1.27847	1.28002	1.28158
33	1.28026	1.28187	1.28348	1.28509	1.28671	1.28832	1.28994	1.29155
34	1.28988	1.29155	1.29322	1.29490	1.29657	1.29825	1.29993	1.30161
35	1.29957	1.30131	1.30304	1.30478	1.30651	1.30825	1.30999	1.31174
36	1.30934	1.31113	1.31293	1.31473	1.31653	1.31834	1.32014	1.32195
37	1.31918	1.32104	1.32290	1.32476	1.32663	1.32850	1.33036	1.33223
38	1.32909	1.33102	1.33294	1.33487	1.33680	1.33873	1.34067	1.34260
39	1.33908	1.34107	1.34306	1.34506	1.34705	1.34905	1.35105	1.35305
40	1.34914	1.35120	1.35326	1.35532	1.35738	1.35945	1.36151	1.36358
41	1.35928	1.36140	1.36353	1.36566	1.36779	1.36992	1.37206	1.37420
42	1.36950	1.37169	1.37388	1.37608	1.37828	1.38048	1.38268	1.38489
43	1.37979	1.38205	1.38431	1.38658	1.38885	1.39112	1.39339	1.39567
44	1.39016	1.39249	1.39482	1.39716	1.39950	1.40184	1.40418	1.40653
45	1.40060	1.40300	1.40541	1.40782	1.41023	1.41264	1.41506	1.41748
46	1.41113	1.41360	1.41608	1.41856	1.42104	1.42353	1.42602	1.42851
47	1.42173	1.42428	1.42683	1.42938	1.43194	1.43450	1.43706	1.43963
48	1.43242	1.43504	1.43766	1.44029	1.44292	1.44555	1.44819	1.45084
60	1.56706	1.57065	1.57424	1.57784	1.58144	1.58505	1.58867	1.59229
72	1.71437	1.71907	1.72379	1.72852	1.73326	1.73801	1.74277	1.74754
84	1.87552	1.88153	1.88755	1.89359	1.89965	1.90573	1.91182	1.91793
96	2.05182	2.05933	2.06687	2.07443	2.08202	2.08963	2.09726	2.10492
108	2.24469	2.25394	2.26322	2.27254	2.28189	2.29128	2.30070	2.31015
120	2.45569	2.46693	2.47823	2.48957	2.50095	2.51239	2.52387	2.53539
132	2.68652	2.70006	2.71366	2.72732	2.74104	2.75483	2.76868	2.78259
144	2.93906	2.95522	2.97146	2.98778	3.00418	3.02067	3.03724	3.05390
156	3.21533	3.23448	3.25375	3.27311	3.29259	3.31217	3.33186	3.35165
168	3.51757	3.54014	3.56285	3.58570	3.60867	3.63179	3.65505	3.67844
180	3.84822	3.87469	3.90132	3.92813	3.95511	3.98226	4.00958	4.03709
192	4.20995	4.24084	4.27195	4.30327	4.33480	4.36655	4.39851	4.43070
204	4.60569	4.64160	4.67778	4.71423	4.75094	4.78792	4.82517	4.86269
216	5.03862	5.08023	5.12217	5.16444	5.20703	5.24995	5.29321	5.33681
228	5.51225	5.56032	5.60878	5.65764	5.70690	5.75657	5.80665	5.85715
240	6.03040	6.08577	6.14161	6.19794	6.25477	6.31208	6.36990	6.42822
252	6.59726	6.66087	6.72507	6.78985	6.85522	6.92120	6.98778	7.05497
264	7.21741	7.29032	7.36395	7.43828	7.51333	7.58910	7.66559	7.74283
276	7.89584	7.97926	8.06352	8.14863	8.23460	8.32144	8.40916	8.49775
288	8.63805	8.73330	8.82956	8.92683	9.02513	9.12446	9.22484	9.32629
300	9.45003	9.55860	9.66836	9.77934	9.89154	10.00497	10.11965	10.23560
312	10.33833	10.46188	10.58686	10.71327	10.84113	10.97045	11.10126	11.23357
324	11.31013	11.45053	11.59261	11.73638	11.88187	12.02910	12.17808	12.32884
336	12.37328	12.53261	12.69391	12.85721	13.02253	13.18991	13.35936	13.53090
348	13.53637	13.71694	13.89983	14.08507	14.27270	14.46274	14.65522	14.85017
360	14.80879	15.01319	15.22031	15.43020	15.64288	15.85839	16.07677	16.29806
420	23.20632	23.58043	23.96041	24.34632	24.73827	25.13635	25.54065	25.95126
480	36.36578	37.03656	37.71940	38.41451	39.12210	39.84240	40.57561	41.32198

19

SINGLE DEPOSIT

EFFECTIVE ANNUAL YIELD

NUMBER OF MONTHS	9.80%	9.85%	9.90%	9.95%	10.00%	10.05%	10.10%	10.15%
1	1.00782	1.00786	1.00790	1.00794	1.00797	1.00801	1.00805	1.00809
2	1.01570	1.01578	1.01586	1.01593	1.01601	1.01609	1.01617	1.01624
3	1.02365	1.02376	1.02388	1.02400	1.02411	1.02423	1.02435	1.02446
4	1.03165	1.03181	1.03197	1.03212	1.03228	1.03244	1.03259	1.03275
5	1.03972	1.03992	1.04012	1.04031	1.04051	1.04071	1.04091	1.04110
6	1.04785	1.04809	1.04833	1.04857	1.04881	1.04905	1.04929	1.04952
7	1.05605	1.05633	1.05661	1.05689	1.05717	1.05745	1.05773	1.05801
8	1.06431	1.06463	1.06496	1.06528	1.06560	1.06593	1.06625	1.06657
9	1.07263	1.07300	1.07337	1.07373	1.07410	1.07447	1.07483	1.07520
10	1.08102	1.08143	1.08184	1.08225	1.08266	1.08307	1.08348	1.08389
11	1.08948	1.08993	1.09039	1.09084	1.09130	1.09175	1.09221	1.09266
12	1.09800	1.09850	1.09900	1.09950	1.10000	1.10050	1.10100	1.10150
13	1.10659	1.10713	1.10768	1.10823	1.10877	1.10932	1.10986	1.11041
14	1.11524	1.11584	1.11643	1.11702	1.11761	1.11821	1.11880	1.11939
15	1.12397	1.12461	1.12525	1.12589	1.12653	1.12717	1.12781	1.12845
16	1.13276	1.13344	1.13413	1.13482	1.13551	1.13620	1.13688	1.13757
17	1.14162	1.14235	1.14309	1.14383	1.14456	1.14530	1.14604	1.14677
18	1.15054	1.15133	1.15212	1.15290	1.15369	1.15448	1.15526	1.15605
19	1.15954	1.16038	1.16122	1.16205	1.16289	1.16373	1.16456	1.16540
20	1.16861	1.16950	1.17039	1.17127	1.17216	1.17305	1.17394	1.17483
21	1.17775	1.17869	1.17963	1.18057	1.18151	1.18245	1.18339	1.18433
22	1.18696	1.18796	1.18895	1.18994	1.19093	1.19192	1.19292	1.19391
23	1.19625	1.19729	1.19834	1.19938	1.20043	1.20147	1.20252	1.20357
24	1.20560	1.20670	1.20780	1.20890	1.21000	1.21110	1.21220	1.21330
25	1.21503	1.21619	1.21734	1.21849	1.21965	1.22080	1.22196	1.22312
26	1.22454	1.22575	1.22695	1.22816	1.22937	1.23059	1.23180	1.23301
27	1.23411	1.23538	1.23664	1.23791	1.23918	1.24045	1.24171	1.24298
28	1.24377	1.24509	1.24641	1.24773	1.24906	1.25038	1.25171	1.25304
29	1.25349	1.25487	1.25625	1.25764	1.25902	1.26040	1.26179	1.26317
30	1.26330	1.26474	1.26618	1.26762	1.26906	1.27050	1.27194	1.27339
31	1.27318	1.27468	1.27618	1.27768	1.27918	1.28068	1.28218	1.28369
32	1.28314	1.28470	1.28626	1.28782	1.28938	1.29094	1.29251	1.29407
33	1.29317	1.29479	1.29641	1.29804	1.29966	1.30129	1.30291	1.30454
34	1.30329	1.30497	1.30665	1.30834	1.31002	1.31171	1.31340	1.31509
35	1.31348	1.31523	1.31697	1.31872	1.32047	1.32222	1.32397	1.32573
36	1.32375	1.32556	1.32737	1.32919	1.33100	1.33282	1.33463	1.33645
37	1.33411	1.33598	1.33786	1.33973	1.34161	1.34349	1.34538	1.34726
38	1.34454	1.34648	1.34842	1.35037	1.35231	1.35426	1.35621	1.35816
39	1.35506	1.35706	1.35907	1.36108	1.36310	1.36511	1.36713	1.36915
40	1.36566	1.36773	1.36981	1.37188	1.37396	1.37605	1.37813	1.38022
41	1.37634	1.37848	1.38062	1.38277	1.38492	1.38707	1.38923	1.39138
42	1.38710	1.38931	1.39153	1.39374	1.39596	1.39819	1.40041	1.40264
43	1.39795	1.40023	1.40252	1.40481	1.40710	1.40939	1.41169	1.41398
44	1.40888	1.41124	1.41359	1.41595	1.41832	1.42068	1.42305	1.42542
45	1.41990	1.42233	1.42476	1.42719	1.42963	1.43206	1.43451	1.43695
46	1.43101	1.43351	1.43601	1.43852	1.44103	1.44354	1.44605	1.44857
47	1.44220	1.44478	1.44735	1.44993	1.45252	1.45511	1.45770	1.46029
48	1.45348	1.45613	1.45878	1.46144	1.46410	1.46676	1.46943	1.47210
60	1.59592	1.59956	1.60320	1.60685	1.61051	1.61417	1.61784	1.62152
72	1.75232	1.75712	1.76192	1.76673	1.77156	1.77640	1.78125	1.78611
84	1.92405	1.93019	1.93635	1.94253	1.94872	1.95493	1.96115	1.96739
96	2.11261	2.12032	2.12805	2.13581	2.14359	2.15140	2.15923	2.16709
108	2.31964	2.32917	2.33873	2.34832	2.35795	2.36761	2.37731	2.38704
120	2.54697	2.55859	2.57026	2.58198	2.59374	2.60556	2.61742	2.62933
132	2.79657	2.81061	2.82471	2.83888	2.85312	2.86741	2.88178	2.89621
144	3.07063	3.08746	3.10436	3.12135	3.13843	3.15559	3.17284	3.19017
156	3.37156	3.39157	3.41169	3.43193	3.45227	3.47273	3.49329	3.51397
168	3.70197	3.72564	3.74945	3.77340	3.79750	3.82174	3.84612	3.87064
180	4.06476	4.09262	4.12065	4.14886	4.17725	4.20582	4.23457	4.26351
192	4.46311	4.49574	4.52859	4.56167	4.59497	4.62851	4.66227	4.69626
204	4.90049	4.93857	4.97692	5.01555	5.05447	5.09367	5.13316	5.17293
216	5.38074	5.42502	5.46964	5.51460	5.55992	5.60558	5.65160	5.69798
228	5.90805	5.95938	6.01113	6.06331	6.11591	6.16894	6.22242	6.27633
240	6.48704	6.54638	6.60623	6.66660	6.72750	6.78892	6.85088	6.91337
252	7.12277	7.19120	7.26025	7.32993	7.40025	7.47121	7.54282	7.61508
264	7.82081	7.89953	7.97901	8.05926	8.14027	8.22207	8.30464	8.38801
276	8.58724	8.67764	8.76894	8.86116	8.95430	9.04839	9.14341	9.23939
288	9.42879	9.53238	9.63706	9.74284	9.84973	9.95775	10.06690	10.17719
300	10.35282	10.47132	10.59113	10.71225	10.83471	10.95850	11.08365	11.21018
312	11.36739	11.50275	11.63965	11.77812	11.91818	12.05983	12.20310	12.34801
324	12.48140	12.63577	12.79198	12.95005	13.10999	13.27184	13.43562	13.60134
336	13.70457	13.88039	14.05838	14.23858	14.42099	14.60566	14.79261	14.98187
348	15.04762	15.24761	15.45016	15.65531	15.86309	16.07353	16.28667	16.50253
360	16.52229	16.74950	16.97973	17.21302	17.44940	17.68892	17.93162	18.17754
420	26.36829	26.79182	27.22195	27.65879	28.10244	28.55299	29.01056	29.47525
480	42.08173	42.85509	43.64231	44.44361	45.25926	46.08949	46.93456	47.79474

SINGLE DEPOSIT

NUMBER OF MONTHS	EFFECTIVE ANNUAL YIELD							
	10.20%	10.25%	10.30%	10.35%	10.40%	10.45%	10.50%	10.55%
1	1.00813	1.00816	1.00820	1.00824	1.00828	1.00832	1.00836	1.00839
2	1.01632	1.01640	1.01647	1.01655	1.01663	1.01670	1.01678	1.01686
3	1.02458	1.02470	1.02481	1.02493	1.02504	1.02516	1.02528	1.02539
4	1.03291	1.03306	1.03322	1.03337	1.03353	1.03369	1.03384	1.03400
5	1.04130	1.04150	1.04169	1.04189	1.04209	1.04228	1.04248	1.04268
6	1.04976	1.05000	1.05024	1.05048	1.05071	1.05095	1.05119	1.05143
7	1.05829	1.05857	1.05885	1.05913	1.05941	1.05969	1.05997	1.06025
8	1.06689	1.06722	1.06754	1.06786	1.06818	1.06851	1.06883	1.06915
9	1.07556	1.07593	1.07630	1.07666	1.07703	1.07739	1.07776	1.07812
10	1.08430	1.08471	1.08512	1.08553	1.08594	1.08635	1.08676	1.08717
11	1.09312	1.09357	1.09403	1.09448	1.09493	1.09539	1.09584	1.09630
12	1.10200	1.10250	1.10300	1.10350	1.10400	1.10450	1.10500	1.10550
13	1.11096	1.11150	1.11205	1.11259	1.11314	1.11369	1.11423	1.11478
14	1.11998	1.12058	1.12117	1.12176	1.12236	1.12295	1.12354	1.12414
15	1.12909	1.12973	1.13037	1.13101	1.13165	1.13229	1.13293	1.13357
16	1.13826	1.13895	1.13964	1.14033	1.14102	1.14171	1.14240	1.14308
17	1.14751	1.14825	1.14899	1.14973	1.15046	1.15120	1.15194	1.15268
18	1.15684	1.15762	1.15841	1.15920	1.15999	1.16078	1.16156	1.16235
19	1.16624	1.16708	1.16791	1.16875	1.16959	1.17043	1.17127	1.17211
20	1.17572	1.17661	1.17750	1.17839	1.17928	1.18017	1.18106	1.18195
21	1.18527	1.18621	1.18715	1.18810	1.18904	1.18998	1.19092	1.19187
22	1.19490	1.19590	1.19689	1.19789	1.19888	1.19988	1.20087	1.20187
23	1.20461	1.20566	1.20671	1.20776	1.20881	1.20986	1.21091	1.21196
24	1.21440	1.21551	1.21661	1.21771	1.21882	1.21992	1.22103	1.22213
25	1.22427	1.22543	1.22659	1.22775	1.22891	1.23007	1.23123	1.23239
26	1.23422	1.23544	1.23665	1.23787	1.23908	1.24030	1.24151	1.24273
27	1.24425	1.24552	1.24679	1.24807	1.24934	1.25061	1.25189	1.25316
28	1.25436	1.25569	1.25702	1.25835	1.25968	1.26101	1.26235	1.26368
29	1.26456	1.26595	1.26733	1.26872	1.27011	1.27150	1.27289	1.27429
30	1.27484	1.27628	1.27773	1.27918	1.28063	1.28208	1.28353	1.28498
31	1.28520	1.28670	1.28821	1.28972	1.29123	1.29274	1.29425	1.29577
32	1.29564	1.29721	1.29878	1.30035	1.30192	1.30349	1.30507	1.30664
33	1.30617	1.30780	1.30943	1.31106	1.31270	1.31433	1.31597	1.31761
34	1.31678	1.31848	1.32017	1.32187	1.32357	1.32527	1.32697	1.32867
35	1.32749	1.32924	1.33100	1.33276	1.33452	1.33629	1.33805	1.33982
36	1.33827	1.34010	1.34192	1.34375	1.34557	1.34740	1.34923	1.35106
37	1.34915	1.35104	1.35293	1.35482	1.35671	1.35861	1.36051	1.36240
38	1.36011	1.36207	1.36403	1.36598	1.36795	1.36991	1.37187	1.37384
39	1.37117	1.37319	1.37521	1.37724	1.37927	1.38130	1.38334	1.38537
40	1.38231	1.38440	1.38650	1.38859	1.39069	1.39279	1.39489	1.39700
41	1.39354	1.39570	1.39787	1.40003	1.40220	1.40437	1.40655	1.40872
42	1.40487	1.40710	1.40934	1.41157	1.41381	1.41605	1.41830	1.42055
43	1.41629	1.41859	1.42090	1.42321	1.42552	1.42783	1.43015	1.43247
44	1.42779	1.43017	1.43255	1.43493	1.43732	1.43971	1.44210	1.44449
45	1.43940	1.44185	1.44430	1.44676	1.44922	1.45168	1.45415	1.45662
46	1.45110	1.45362	1.45615	1.45868	1.46122	1.46376	1.46630	1.46884
47	1.46289	1.46549	1.46809	1.47070	1.47331	1.47593	1.47855	1.48117
48	1.47478	1.47746	1.48014	1.48282	1.48551	1.48821	1.49090	1.49360
60	1.62520	1.62889	1.63259	1.63630	1.64001	1.64372	1.64745	1.65118
72	1.79098	1.79586	1.80075	1.80565	1.81057	1.81549	1.82043	1.82538
84	1.97365	1.97993	1.98623	1.99254	1.99887	2.00521	2.01157	2.01795
96	2.17497	2.18287	2.19081	2.19876	2.20675	2.21476	2.22279	2.23085
108	2.39681	2.40662	2.41646	2.42634	2.43625	2.44620	2.45618	2.46620
120	2.64129	2.65330	2.66536	2.67746	2.68962	2.70182	2.71408	2.72639
132	2.91070	2.92526	2.93989	2.95458	2.96934	2.98417	2.99906	3.01402
144	3.20759	3.22510	3.24270	3.26038	3.27815	3.29601	3.31396	3.33200
156	3.53477	3.55567	3.57669	3.59783	3.61908	3.64044	3.66193	3.68353
168	3.89531	3.92013	3.94509	3.97020	3.99546	4.02087	4.04643	4.07214
180	4.29263	4.32194	4.35144	4.38112	4.41099	4.44105	4.47130	4.50175
192	4.73048	4.76494	4.79963	4.83456	4.86973	4.90514	4.94079	4.97668
204	5.21299	5.25335	5.29400	5.33494	5.37619	5.41773	5.45957	5.50172
216	5.74472	5.79182	5.83928	5.88711	5.93531	5.98388	6.03283	6.08215
228	6.33068	6.38548	6.44072	6.49642	6.55258	6.60920	6.66628	6.72382
240	6.97641	7.03999	7.10412	7.16880	7.23405	7.29986	7.36623	7.43318
252	7.68800	7.76159	7.83584	7.91078	7.98639	8.06269	8.13969	8.21739
264	8.47218	8.55715	8.64294	8.72954	8.81698	8.90524	8.99436	9.08432
276	9.33634	9.43426	9.53316	9.63305	9.73394	9.83584	9.93876	10.04272
288	10.28865	10.40127	10.51507	10.63007	10.74627	10.86369	10.98233	11.10222
300	11.33809	11.46740	11.59813	11.73028	11.86388	11.99894	12.13548	12.27351
312	12.49457	12.64281	12.79273	12.94437	13.09773	13.25283	13.40971	13.56836
324	13.76902	13.93870	14.11038	14.28411	14.45989	14.63775	14.81772	14.99982
336	15.17346	15.36741	15.56375	15.76251	15.96372	16.16740	16.37359	16.58231
348	16.72115	16.94257	17.16682	17.39393	17.62394	17.85689	18.09281	18.33174
360	18.42671	18.67919	18.93500	19.19420	19.45684	19.72294	19.99256	20.26574
420	29.94717	30.42643	30.91313	31.40739	31.90932	32.41904	32.93667	33.46233
480	48.67027	49.56144	50.46851	51.39176	52.33147	53.28792	54.26142	55.25224

SINGLE DEPOSIT

EFFECTIVE ANNUAL YIELD

NUMBER OF MONTHS	10.60%	10.65%	10.70%	10.75%	10.80%	10.85%	10.90%	10.95%
1	1.00843	1.00847	1.00851	1.00855	1.00858	1.00862	1.00866	1.00870
2	1.01693	1.01701	1.01709	1.01716	1.01724	1.01732	1.01739	1.01747
3	1.02551	1.02562	1.02574	1.02585	1.02597	1.02609	1.02620	1.02632
4	1.03415	1.03431	1.03447	1.03462	1.03478	1.03493	1.03509	1.03524
5	1.04287	1.04307	1.04327	1.04346	1.04366	1.04385	1.04405	1.04425
6	1.05167	1.05190	1.05214	1.05238	1.05262	1.05285	1.05309	1.05333
7	1.06053	1.06081	1.06109	1.06137	1.06165	1.06193	1.06221	1.06249
8	1.06947	1.06980	1.07012	1.07044	1.07076	1.07108	1.07141	1.07173
9	1.07849	1.07886	1.07922	1.07959	1.07995	1.08032	1.08068	1.08105
10	1.08758	1.08799	1.08840	1.08881	1.08922	1.08963	1.09004	1.09045
11	1.09675	1.09721	1.09766	1.09812	1.09857	1.09903	1.09948	1.09993
12	1.10600	1.10650	1.10700	1.10750	1.10800	1.10850	1.10900	1.10950
13	1.11532	1.11587	1.11642	1.11696	1.11751	1.11806	1.11860	1.11915
14	1.12473	1.12532	1.12591	1.12651	1.12710	1.12769	1.12829	1.12888
15	1.13421	1.13485	1.13549	1.13613	1.13678	1.13742	1.13806	1.13870
16	1.14377	1.14446	1.14515	1.14584	1.14653	1.14722	1.14791	1.14860
17	1.15342	1.15416	1.15489	1.15563	1.15637	1.15711	1.15785	1.15859
18	1.16314	1.16393	1.16472	1.16551	1.16630	1.16709	1.16788	1.16867
19	1.17295	1.17379	1.17463	1.17547	1.17631	1.17715	1.17799	1.17883
20	1.18284	1.18373	1.18462	1.18551	1.18640	1.18730	1.18819	1.18908
21	1.19281	1.19375	1.19470	1.19564	1.19659	1.19753	1.19848	1.19942
22	1.20287	1.20386	1.20486	1.20586	1.20686	1.20786	1.20886	1.20986
23	1.21301	1.21406	1.21511	1.21616	1.21722	1.21827	1.21932	1.22038
24	1.22324	1.22434	1.22545	1.22656	1.22766	1.22877	1.22988	1.23099
25	1.23355	1.23471	1.23587	1.23704	1.23820	1.23937	1.24053	1.24170
26	1.24395	1.24517	1.24639	1.24761	1.24883	1.25005	1.25127	1.25249
27	1.25444	1.25571	1.25699	1.25827	1.25955	1.26083	1.26211	1.26339
28	1.26501	1.26635	1.26768	1.26902	1.27036	1.27170	1.27303	1.27437
29	1.27568	1.27707	1.27847	1.27986	1.28126	1.28266	1.28406	1.28546
30	1.28643	1.28789	1.28934	1.29080	1.29226	1.29372	1.29518	1.29664
31	1.29728	1.29880	1.30031	1.30183	1.30335	1.30487	1.30639	1.30791
32	1.30822	1.30980	1.31138	1.31296	1.31454	1.31612	1.31770	1.31929
33	1.31925	1.32089	1.32253	1.32417	1.32582	1.32747	1.32911	1.33076
34	1.33037	1.33208	1.33378	1.33549	1.33720	1.33891	1.34062	1.34233
35	1.34159	1.34336	1.34513	1.34690	1.34868	1.35045	1.35223	1.35401
36	1.35290	1.35473	1.35657	1.35841	1.36025	1.36209	1.36394	1.36578
37	1.36431	1.36621	1.36811	1.37002	1.37193	1.37384	1.37575	1.37766
38	1.37581	1.37778	1.37975	1.38173	1.38370	1.38568	1.38766	1.38964
39	1.38741	1.38945	1.39149	1.39353	1.39558	1.39763	1.39968	1.40173
40	1.39911	1.40121	1.40333	1.40544	1.40756	1.40967	1.41180	1.41392
41	1.41090	1.41308	1.41526	1.41745	1.41964	1.42183	1.42402	1.42621
42	1.42280	1.42505	1.42730	1.42956	1.43182	1.43409	1.43635	1.43862
43	1.43479	1.43712	1.43945	1.44178	1.44411	1.44645	1.44879	1.45113
44	1.44689	1.44929	1.45169	1.45410	1.45651	1.45892	1.46133	1.46375
45	1.45909	1.46156	1.46404	1.46652	1.46901	1.47150	1.47399	1.47648
46	1.47139	1.47394	1.47650	1.47905	1.48162	1.48418	1.48675	1.48932
47	1.48380	1.48643	1.48906	1.49169	1.49433	1.49698	1.49962	1.50227
48	1.49631	1.49901	1.50173	1.50444	1.50716	1.50988	1.51261	1.51534
60	1.65491	1.65866	1.66241	1.66617	1.66993	1.67370	1.67748	1.68127
72	1.83034	1.83531	1.84029	1.84528	1.85028	1.85530	1.86033	1.86537
84	2.02435	2.03077	2.03720	2.04365	2.05012	2.05660	2.06310	2.06962
96	2.23893	2.24704	2.25518	2.26334	2.27153	2.27974	2.28798	2.29625
108	2.47626	2.48635	2.49648	2.50665	2.51685	2.52709	2.53737	2.54769
120	2.73874	2.75115	2.76361	2.77611	2.78867	2.80128	2.81394	2.82666
132	3.02905	3.04415	3.05931	3.07455	3.08985	3.10522	3.12066	3.13618
144	3.35013	3.36835	3.38666	3.40506	3.42355	3.44214	3.46082	3.47959
156	3.70524	3.72708	3.74903	3.77110	3.79330	3.81561	3.83805	3.86060
168	4.09800	4.12401	4.15018	4.17650	4.20297	4.22960	4.25639	4.28334
180	4.53239	4.56322	4.59425	4.62547	4.65689	4.68852	4.72034	4.75236
192	5.01282	5.04920	5.08583	5.12271	5.15984	5.19722	5.23486	5.27275
204	5.54418	5.58694	5.63002	5.67340	5.71710	5.76112	5.80546	5.85011
216	6.13186	6.18195	6.23243	6.28329	6.33455	6.38620	6.43825	6.49070
228	6.78184	6.84033	6.89930	6.95875	7.01868	7.07910	7.14002	7.20143
240	7.50071	7.56882	7.63752	7.70681	7.77670	7.84719	7.91828	7.98999
252	8.29579	8.37490	8.45474	8.53529	8.61658	8.69861	8.78137	8.86489
264	9.17514	9.26683	9.35939	9.45284	9.54717	9.64240	9.73854	9.83560
276	10.14771	10.25375	10.36085	10.46902	10.57827	10.68861	10.80004	10.91260
288	11.22336	11.34577	11.46946	11.59444	11.72072	11.84832	11.97725	12.10752
300	12.41304	12.55410	12.69669	12.84084	12.98656	13.13386	13.28277	13.43330
312	13.72882	13.89111	14.05524	14.22123	14.38910	14.55889	14.73059	14.90424
324	15.18408	15.37051	15.55915	15.75001	15.94313	16.13852	16.33623	16.53626
336	16.79359	17.00747	17.22397	17.44314	17.66499	17.88955	18.11688	18.34698
348	18.57371	18.81877	19.06694	19.31827	19.57280	19.83057	20.09161	20.35597
360	20.54252	20.82296	21.10710	21.39499	21.68667	21.98219	22.28160	22.58495
420	33.99613	34.53820	35.08866	35.64763	36.21526	36.79166	37.37697	37.97132
480	56.26069	57.28709	58.33173	59.39493	60.47702	61.57833	62.69918	63.83991

22

NUMBER OF MONTHS	EFFECTIVE ANNUAL YIELD							
	11.00%	11.05%	11.10%	11.15%	11.20%	11.25%	11.30%	11.35%
1	1.00873	1.00877	1.00881	1.00885	1.00889	1.00892	1.00896	1.00900
2	1.01755	1.01762	1.01770	1.01777	1.01785	1.01793	1.01800	1.01808
3	1.02643	1.02655	1.02666	1.02678	1.02690	1.02701	1.02713	1.02724
4	1.03540	1.03555	1.03571	1.03586	1.03602	1.03618	1.03633	1.03649
5	1.04444	1.04464	1.04483	1.04503	1.04523	1.04542	1.04562	1.04581
6	1.05357	1.05380	1.05404	1.05428	1.05451	1.05475	1.05499	1.05523
7	1.06277	1.06305	1.06333	1.06361	1.06388	1.06416	1.06444	1.06472
8	1.07205	1.07237	1.07269	1.07302	1.07334	1.07366	1.07398	1.07430
9	1.08141	1.08178	1.08215	1.08251	1.08288	1.08324	1.08361	1.08397
10	1.09086	1.09127	1.09168	1.09209	1.09250	1.09291	1.09332	1.09373
11	1.10039	1.10084	1.10130	1.10175	1.10221	1.10266	1.10311	1.10357
12	1.11000	1.11050	1.11100	1.11150	1.11200	1.11250	1.11300	1.11350
13	1.11970	1.12024	1.12079	1.12133	1.12188	1.12243	1.12297	1.12352
14	1.12948	1.13007	1.13066	1.13126	1.13185	1.13244	1.13304	1.13363
15	1.13934	1.13998	1.14062	1.14127	1.14191	1.14255	1.14319	1.14383
16	1.14929	1.14998	1.15067	1.15136	1.15205	1.15275	1.15344	1.15413
17	1.15933	1.16007	1.16081	1.16155	1.16229	1.16303	1.16377	1.16451
18	1.16946	1.17025	1.17104	1.17183	1.17262	1.17341	1.17420	1.17499
19	1.17967	1.18051	1.18136	1.18220	1.18304	1.18388	1.18472	1.18557
20	1.18998	1.19087	1.19176	1.19266	1.19355	1.19445	1.19534	1.19624
21	1.20037	1.20132	1.20226	1.20321	1.20416	1.20511	1.20605	1.20700
22	1.21085	1.21186	1.21286	1.21386	1.21486	1.21586	1.21686	1.21786
23	1.22143	1.22249	1.22354	1.22460	1.22565	1.22671	1.22777	1.22882
24	1.23210	1.23321	1.23432	1.23543	1.23654	1.23766	1.23877	1.23988
25	1.24286	1.24403	1.24520	1.24636	1.24753	1.24870	1.24987	1.25104
26	1.25372	1.25494	1.25617	1.25739	1.25862	1.25984	1.26107	1.26230
27	1.26467	1.26595	1.26723	1.26852	1.26980	1.27109	1.27237	1.27366
28	1.27571	1.27706	1.27840	1.27974	1.28108	1.28243	1.28377	1.28512
29	1.28686	1.28826	1.28966	1.29106	1.29247	1.29387	1.29528	1.29669
30	1.29810	1.29956	1.30102	1.30249	1.30395	1.30542	1.30689	1.30835
31	1.30944	1.31096	1.31249	1.31401	1.31554	1.31707	1.31860	1.32013
32	1.32087	1.32246	1.32405	1.32564	1.32723	1.32882	1.33041	1.33201
33	1.33241	1.33406	1.33571	1.33737	1.33902	1.34068	1.34234	1.34400
34	1.34405	1.34577	1.34748	1.34920	1.35092	1.35264	1.35437	1.35609
35	1.35579	1.35757	1.35935	1.36114	1.36293	1.36471	1.36650	1.36830
36	1.36763	1.36948	1.37133	1.37318	1.37504	1.37689	1.37875	1.38061
37	1.37958	1.38149	1.38341	1.38533	1.38726	1.38918	1.39111	1.39303
38	1.39163	1.39361	1.39560	1.39759	1.39958	1.40158	1.40357	1.40557
39	1.40378	1.40584	1.40790	1.40996	1.41202	1.41408	1.41615	1.41822
40	1.41604	1.41817	1.42030	1.42243	1.42457	1.42670	1.42884	1.43098
41	1.42841	1.43061	1.43281	1.43502	1.43722	1.43943	1.44165	1.44386
42	1.44089	1.44316	1.44544	1.44772	1.45000	1.45228	1.45456	1.45685
43	1.45347	1.45582	1.45817	1.46052	1.46288	1.46524	1.46760	1.46996
44	1.46617	1.46859	1.47102	1.47345	1.47588	1.47831	1.48075	1.48319
45	1.47898	1.48148	1.48398	1.48648	1.48899	1.49151	1.49402	1.49654
46	1.49189	1.49447	1.49705	1.49964	1.50223	1.50482	1.50741	1.51001
47	1.50493	1.50758	1.51024	1.51291	1.51557	1.51824	1.52092	1.52360
48	1.51807	1.52081	1.52355	1.52629	1.52904	1.53179	1.53455	1.53731
60	1.68506	1.68886	1.69266	1.69647	1.70029	1.70412	1.70795	1.71179
72	1.87041	1.87548	1.88055	1.88563	1.89073	1.89583	1.90095	1.90608
84	2.07616	2.08272	2.08929	2.09588	2.10249	2.10911	2.11576	2.12242
96	2.30454	2.31286	2.32120	2.32957	2.33797	2.34639	2.35484	2.36332
108	2.55804	2.56843	2.57885	2.58932	2.59982	2.61036	2.62094	2.63155
120	2.83942	2.85224	2.86511	2.87803	2.89100	2.90402	2.91710	2.93023
132	3.15176	3.16741	3.18313	3.19893	3.21479	3.23073	3.24673	3.26281
144	3.49845	3.51741	3.53646	3.55561	3.57485	3.59418	3.61362	3.63314
156	3.88328	3.90608	3.92901	3.95206	3.97523	3.99853	4.02195	4.04551
168	4.31044	4.33770	4.36513	4.39271	4.42046	4.44836	4.47644	4.50467
180	4.78459	4.81702	4.84966	4.88250	4.91555	4.94880	4.98227	5.01595
192	5.31089	5.34930	5.38797	5.42690	5.46609	5.50554	5.54527	5.58526
204	5.89509	5.94040	5.98603	6.03199	6.07829	6.12492	6.17188	6.21919
216	6.54355	6.59681	6.65048	6.70456	6.75906	6.81397	6.86931	6.92507
228	7.26334	7.32576	7.38868	7.45212	7.51607	7.58054	7.64554	7.71106
240	8.06231	8.13526	8.20883	8.28303	8.35787	8.43336	8.50949	8.58627
252	8.94917	9.03420	9.12001	9.20659	9.29395	9.38211	9.47106	9.56081
264	9.93357	10.03248	10.13233	10.23312	10.33488	10.43759	10.54129	10.64596
276	11.02627	11.14107	11.25702	11.37412	11.49238	11.61182	11.73245	11.85428
288	12.23916	12.37216	12.50655	12.64233	12.77953	12.91815	13.05822	13.19974
300	13.58546	13.73928	13.89477	14.05195	14.21084	14.37145	14.53380	14.69791
312	15.01760	15.25747	15.43709	15.61875	15.80245	15.98823	16.17612	16.36612
324	16.73865	16.94342	17.15061	17.36024	17.57233	17.78691	18.00402	18.22368
336	18.57909	18.81567	19.05433	19.29590	19.54043	19.78794	20.03847	20.29206
348	20.62369	20.89481	21.16936	21.44739	21.72895	22.01408	22.30282	22.59521
360	22.89230	23.20368	23.51916	23.83878	24.16260	24.49067	24.82304	25.15977
420	38.57485	39.18769	39.80999	40.44188	41.08351	41.73503	42.39657	43.06830
480	65.00087	66.18240	67.38486	68.60862	69.85403	71.12148	72.41134	73.72399

23

SINGLE DEPOSIT

EFFECTIVE ANNUAL YIELD

NUMBER OF MONTHS	11.40%	11.45%	11.50%	11.55%	11.60%	11.65%	11.70%	11.75%
1	1.00904	1.00907	1.00911	1.00915	1.00919	1.00923	1.00926	1.00930
2	1.01816	1.01823	1.01831	1.01838	1.01846	1.01854	1.01861	1.01869
3	1.02736	1.02747	1.02759	1.02770	1.02782	1.02793	1.02805	1.02816
4	1.03664	1.03680	1.03695	1.03711	1.03726	1.03742	1.03757	1.03773
5	1.04601	1.04620	1.04640	1.04660	1.04679	1.04699	1.04718	1.04738
6	1.05546	1.05570	1.05594	1.05617	1.05641	1.05665	1.05688	1.05712
7	1.06500	1.06528	1.06556	1.06584	1.06612	1.06639	1.06667	1.06695
8	1.07462	1.07495	1.07527	1.07559	1.07591	1.07623	1.07655	1.07687
9	1.08434	1.08470	1.08507	1.08543	1.08580	1.08616	1.08653	1.08689
10	1.09414	1.09454	1.09495	1.09536	1.09577	1.09618	1.09659	1.09700
11	1.10402	1.10448	1.10493	1.10539	1.10584	1.10629	1.10675	1.10720
12	1.11400	1.11450	1.11500	1.11550	1.11600	1.11650	1.11700	1.11750
13	1.12407	1.12461	1.12516	1.12571	1.12625	1.12680	1.12735	1.12789
14	1.13423	1.13482	1.13541	1.13601	1.13660	1.13720	1.13779	1.13838
15	1.14448	1.14512	1.14576	1.14640	1.14704	1.14769	1.14833	1.14897
16	1.15482	1.15551	1.15620	1.15689	1.15758	1.15827	1.15897	1.15966
17	1.16525	1.16600	1.16674	1.16748	1.16822	1.16896	1.16970	1.17044
18	1.17578	1.17658	1.17737	1.17816	1.17895	1.17974	1.18054	1.18133
19	1.18641	1.18725	1.18810	1.18894	1.18978	1.19063	1.19147	1.19232
20	1.19713	1.19803	1.19892	1.19982	1.20072	1.20161	1.20251	1.20341
21	1.20795	1.20890	1.20985	1.21080	1.21175	1.21270	1.21365	1.21460
22	1.21887	1.21987	1.22087	1.22188	1.22288	1.22389	1.22489	1.22590
23	1.22988	1.23094	1.23200	1.23306	1.23412	1.23518	1.23624	1.23730
24	1.24100	1.24211	1.24323	1.24434	1.24546	1.24657	1.24769	1.24881
25	1.25221	1.25338	1.25455	1.25573	1.25690	1.25807	1.25925	1.26042
26	1.26353	1.26476	1.26599	1.26722	1.26845	1.26968	1.27091	1.27214
27	1.27495	1.27623	1.27752	1.27881	1.28010	1.28139	1.28268	1.28398
28	1.28647	1.28782	1.28916	1.29051	1.29186	1.29321	1.29457	1.29592
29	1.29809	1.29950	1.30091	1.30232	1.30373	1.30514	1.30656	1.30797
30	1.30982	1.31129	1.31277	1.31424	1.31571	1.31719	1.31866	1.32014
31	1.32166	1.32319	1.32473	1.32626	1.32780	1.32934	1.33088	1.33241
32	1.33360	1.33520	1.33680	1.33840	1.34000	1.34160	1.34320	1.34481
33	1.34566	1.34732	1.34898	1.35065	1.35231	1.35398	1.35565	1.35732
34	1.35782	1.35954	1.36127	1.36300	1.36474	1.36647	1.36820	1.36994
35	1.37009	1.37188	1.37368	1.37548	1.37727	1.37908	1.38088	1.38268
36	1.38247	1.38433	1.38620	1.38806	1.38993	1.39180	1.39367	1.39554
37	1.39496	1.39689	1.39883	1.40076	1.40270	1.40464	1.40658	1.40852
38	1.40757	1.40957	1.41157	1.41358	1.41559	1.41760	1.41961	1.42162
39	1.42029	1.42236	1.42444	1.42651	1.42859	1.43067	1.43276	1.43484
40	1.43312	1.43527	1.43742	1.43957	1.44172	1.44387	1.44603	1.44819
41	1.44608	1.44829	1.45052	1.45274	1.45497	1.45719	1.45942	1.46166
42	1.45914	1.46144	1.46373	1.46603	1.46833	1.47064	1.47294	1.47525
43	1.47233	1.47470	1.47707	1.47945	1.48182	1.48420	1.48659	1.48897
44	1.48564	1.48808	1.49053	1.49298	1.49544	1.49790	1.50036	1.50282
45	1.49906	1.50159	1.50411	1.50664	1.50918	1.51172	1.51426	1.51680
46	1.51261	1.51521	1.51782	1.52043	1.52305	1.52566	1.52828	1.53091
47	1.52628	1.52896	1.53165	1.53434	1.53704	1.53974	1.54244	1.54515
48	1.54007	1.54284	1.54561	1.54838	1.55116	1.55394	1.55673	1.55952
60	1.71564	1.71949	1.72335	1.72722	1.73110	1.73498	1.73886	1.74276
72	1.91122	1.91637	1.92154	1.92671	1.93190	1.93710	1.94231	1.94753
84	2.12910	2.13580	2.14252	2.14925	2.15600	2.16277	2.16956	2.17637
96	2.37182	2.38035	2.38891	2.39749	2.40610	2.41474	2.42340	2.43209
108	2.64221	2.65290	2.66363	2.67440	2.68521	2.69605	2.70694	2.71786
120	2.94342	2.95666	2.96995	2.98329	2.99669	3.01014	3.02365	3.03721
132	3.27897	3.29519	3.31149	3.32786	3.34431	3.36083	3.37742	3.39409
144	3.65277	3.67249	3.69231	3.71223	3.73225	3.75236	3.77258	3.79289
156	4.06919	4.09299	4.11693	4.14099	4.16519	4.18951	4.21397	4.23856
168	4.53307	4.56164	4.59037	4.61928	4.64835	4.67759	4.70700	4.73659
180	5.04984	5.08395	5.11827	5.15280	5.18756	5.22253	5.25772	5.29314
192	5.62552	5.66606	5.70687	5.74795	5.78931	5.83095	5.87288	5.91508
204	6.26683	6.31482	6.36316	6.41184	6.46087	6.51026	6.56000	6.61010
216	6.98125	7.03787	7.09492	7.15241	7.21034	7.26871	7.32752	7.38679
228	7.77712	7.84371	7.91084	7.97851	8.04673	8.11551	8.18484	8.25473
240	8.66371	8.74181	8.82058	8.90003	8.98016	9.06097	9.14247	9.22467
252	9.65137	9.74275	9.83495	9.92798	10.02185	10.11657	10.21214	10.30856
264	10.75163	10.85829	10.96597	11.07467	11.18439	11.29515	11.40696	11.51982
276	11.97731	12.10157	12.22706	12.35379	12.48178	12.61103	12.74157	12.87340
288	13.34273	13.48720	13.63317	13.78065	13.92966	14.08022	14.23233	14.38602
300	14.86380	15.03148	15.20098	15.37232	15.54551	15.72057	15.89752	16.07638
312	16.55827	16.75259	16.94910	17.14782	17.34878	17.55201	17.75753	17.96536
324	18.44591	18.67076	18.89824	19.12839	19.36124	19.59682	19.83516	20.07629
336	20.54875	20.80856	21.07154	21.33772	21.60715	21.87985	22.15587	22.43525
348	22.89130	23.19114	23.49477	23.80223	24.11358	24.42885	24.74811	25.07139
360	25.50091	25.84653	26.19667	26.55139	26.91075	27.27482	27.64364	28.01728
420	43.75036	44.44292	45.14611	45.86011	46.58508	47.32117	48.06855	48.82740
480	75.05984	76.41927	77.80270	79.21054	80.64321	82.10112	83.58473	85.09446

NUMBER OF MONTHS	EFFECTIVE ANNUAL YIELD							
	11.80%	11.85%	11.90%	11.95%	12.00%	12.05%	12.10%	12.15%
1	1.00934	1.00938	1.00941	1.00945	1.00949	1.00953	1.00956	1.00960
2	1.01876	1.01884	1.01892	1.01899	1.01907	1.01914	1.01922	1.01929
3	1.02828	1.02839	1.02851	1.02862	1.02874	1.02885	1.02897	1.02908
4	1.03788	1.03803	1.03819	1.03834	1.03850	1.03865	1.03881	1.03896
5	1.04757	1.04777	1.04796	1.04816	1.04835	1.04855	1.04874	1.04894
6	1.05736	1.05759	1.05783	1.05806	1.05830	1.05854	1.05877	1.05901
7	1.06723	1.06751	1.06779	1.06806	1.06834	1.06862	1.06890	1.06918
8	1.07720	1.07752	1.07784	1.07816	1.07848	1.07880	1.07912	1.07944
9	1.08725	1.08762	1.08798	1.08835	1.08871	1.08908	1.08944	1.08981
10	1.09741	1.09782	1.09823	1.09863	1.09904	1.09945	1.09986	1.10027
11	1.10766	1.10811	1.10856	1.10902	1.10947	1.10993	1.11038	1.11083
12	1.11800	1.11850	1.11900	1.11950	1.12000	1.12050	1.12100	1.12150
13	1.12844	1.12899	1.12953	1.13008	1.13063	1.13117	1.13172	1.13227
14	1.13898	1.13957	1.14017	1.14076	1.14136	1.14195	1.14254	1.14314
15	1.14961	1.15026	1.15090	1.15154	1.15219	1.15283	1.15347	1.15412
16	1.16035	1.16104	1.16173	1.16243	1.16312	1.16381	1.16450	1.16520
17	1.17119	1.17193	1.17267	1.17341	1.17416	1.17490	1.17564	1.17638
18	1.18212	1.18292	1.18371	1.18450	1.18530	1.18609	1.18688	1.18768
19	1.19316	1.19401	1.19485	1.19570	1.19654	1.19739	1.19824	1.19908
20	1.20430	1.20520	1.20610	1.20700	1.20790	1.20880	1.20970	1.21059
21	1.21555	1.21650	1.21745	1.21841	1.21936	1.22031	1.22126	1.22222
22	1.22690	1.22791	1.22891	1.22992	1.23093	1.23194	1.23294	1.23395
23	1.23836	1.23942	1.24048	1.24155	1.24261	1.24367	1.24474	1.24580
24	1.24992	1.25104	1.25216	1.25328	1.25440	1.25552	1.25664	1.25776
25	1.26160	1.26277	1.26395	1.26513	1.26630	1.26748	1.26866	1.26984
26	1.27338	1.27461	1.27585	1.27708	1.27832	1.27956	1.28079	1.28203
27	1.28527	1.28656	1.28786	1.28915	1.29045	1.29174	1.29304	1.29434
28	1.29727	1.29863	1.29999	1.30134	1.30269	1.30405	1.30541	1.30677
29	1.30939	1.31080	1.31222	1.31364	1.31505	1.31647	1.31789	1.31931
30	1.32161	1.32309	1.32457	1.32605	1.32753	1.32901	1.33050	1.33198
31	1.33396	1.33550	1.33704	1.33858	1.34013	1.34167	1.34322	1.34477
32	1.34641	1.34802	1.34963	1.35124	1.35285	1.35446	1.35607	1.35768
33	1.35899	1.36066	1.36233	1.36401	1.36568	1.36736	1.36904	1.37072
34	1.37168	1.37342	1.37516	1.37690	1.37864	1.38039	1.38213	1.38388
35	1.38449	1.38629	1.38810	1.38991	1.39172	1.39354	1.39535	1.39717
36	1.39742	1.39929	1.40117	1.40305	1.40493	1.40681	1.40869	1.41058
37	1.41046	1.41241	1.41436	1.41631	1.41826	1.42021	1.42217	1.42412
38	1.42364	1.42565	1.42767	1.42969	1.43172	1.43374	1.43577	1.43780
39	1.43693	1.43902	1.44111	1.44321	1.44530	1.44740	1.44950	1.45160
40	1.45035	1.45251	1.45468	1.45685	1.45902	1.46119	1.46336	1.46554
41	1.46389	1.46613	1.46837	1.47062	1.47286	1.47511	1.47736	1.47961
42	1.47756	1.47988	1.48219	1.48451	1.48684	1.48916	1.49149	1.49382
43	1.49136	1.49375	1.49615	1.49854	1.50094	1.50335	1.50575	1.50816
44	1.50529	1.50776	1.51023	1.51271	1.51519	1.51767	1.52015	1.52264
45	1.51935	1.52190	1.52445	1.52700	1.52956	1.53213	1.53469	1.53726
46	1.53353	1.53617	1.53880	1.54144	1.54408	1.54672	1.54937	1.55202
47	1.54786	1.55057	1.55329	1.55601	1.55873	1.56146	1.56419	1.56692
48	1.56231	1.56511	1.56791	1.57071	1.57352	1.57633	1.57915	1.58197
60	1.74666	1.75057	1.75449	1.75841	1.76234	1.76628	1.77022	1.77417
72	1.95277	1.95801	1.96327	1.96854	1.97382	1.97912	1.98442	1.98974
84	2.18320	2.19004	2.19690	2.20378	2.21068	2.21760	2.22454	2.23149
96	2.44081	2.44956	2.45833	2.46713	2.47596	2.48482	2.49370	2.50262
108	2.72883	2.73983	2.75087	2.76196	2.77308	2.78424	2.79544	2.80668
120	3.05083	3.06450	3.07823	3.09201	3.10585	3.11974	3.13369	3.14770
132	3.41083	3.42765	3.44454	3.46151	3.47855	3.49567	3.51287	3.53014
144	3.81331	3.83382	3.85444	3.87516	3.89598	3.91690	3.93792	3.95905
156	4.26328	4.28813	4.31312	4.33824	4.36349	4.38888	4.41441	4.44008
168	4.76634	4.79627	4.82638	4.85666	4.88711	4.91775	4.94856	4.97955
180	5.32877	5.36463	5.40072	5.43703	5.47357	5.51033	5.54733	5.58456
192	5.95757	6.00034	6.04340	6.08675	6.13039	6.17433	6.21856	6.26309
204	6.66056	6.71138	6.76257	6.81412	6.86604	6.91834	6.97101	7.02405
216	7.44650	7.50668	7.56731	7.62841	7.68997	7.75200	7.81450	7.87747
228	8.32519	8.39622	8.46782	8.54000	8.61276	8.68611	8.76005	8.83459
240	9.30756	9.39117	9.47549	9.56053	9.64629	9.73279	9.82002	9.90799
252	10.40586	10.50403	10.60307	10.70301	10.80385	10.90559	11.00824	11.11181
264	11.63375	11.74875	11.86484	11.98202	12.10031	12.21971	12.34024	12.46190
276	13.00653	13.14098	13.27676	13.41387	13.55235	13.69219	13.83340	13.97602
288	14.54130	14.69819	14.85669	15.01683	15.17863	15.34209	15.50725	15.67410
300	16.25718	16.43992	16.62464	16.81134	17.00006	17.19082	17.38362	17.57851
312	18.17552	18.38805	18.60297	18.82030	19.04007	19.26231	19.48704	19.71429
324	20.32023	20.56704	20.81672	21.06933	21.32488	21.58342	21.84497	22.10958
336	22.71802	23.00423	23.29391	23.58711	23.88387	24.18422	24.48822	24.79589
348	25.39875	25.73023	26.06589	26.40577	26.74993	27.09842	27.45129	27.80860
360	28.39580	28.77926	29.16773	29.56126	29.95992	30.36378	30.77290	31.18734
420	49.59788	50.38017	51.17443	51.98086	52.79962	53.63091	54.47490	55.33179
480	86.63076	88.19410	89.78493	91.40373	93.05097	94.72714	96.43274	98.16827

SINGLE DEPOSIT

EFFECTIVE ANNUAL YIELD

NUMBER OF MONTHS	12.20%	12.25%	12.30%	12.35%	12.40%	12.45%	12.50%	12.55%
1	1.00964	1.00968	1.00971	1.00975	1.00979	1.00983	1.00986	1.00990
2	1.01937	1.01945	1.01952	1.01960	1.01967	1.01975	1.01982	1.01990
3	1.02920	1.02931	1.02943	1.02954	1.02965	1.02977	1.02988	1.03000
4	1.03912	1.03927	1.03943	1.03958	1.03973	1.03989	1.04004	1.04020
5	1.04913	1.04933	1.04952	1.04972	1.04991	1.05011	1.05030	1.05049
6	1.05925	1.05948	1.05972	1.05995	1.06019	1.06042	1.06066	1.06090
7	1.06945	1.06973	1.07001	1.07029	1.07057	1.07084	1.07112	1.07140
8	1.07976	1.08008	1.08040	1.08073	1.08105	1.08137	1.08169	1.08201
9	1.09017	1.09054	1.09090	1.09126	1.09163	1.09199	1.09236	1.09272
10	1.10068	1.10109	1.10150	1.10191	1.10231	1.10272	1.10313	1.10354
11	1.11129	1.11174	1.11220	1.11265	1.11310	1.11356	1.11401	1.11447
12	1.12200	1.12250	1.12300	1.12350	1.12400	1.12450	1.12500	1.12550
13	1.13281	1.13336	1.13391	1.13446	1.13500	1.13555	1.13610	1.13664
14	1.14373	1.14433	1.14492	1.14552	1.14611	1.14671	1.14730	1.14790
15	1.15476	1.15540	1.15604	1.15669	1.15733	1.15798	1.15862	1.15926
16	1.16589	1.16658	1.16727	1.16797	1.16866	1.16935	1.17005	1.17074
17	1.17713	1.17787	1.17861	1.17936	1.18010	1.18084	1.18159	1.18233
18	1.18847	1.18927	1.19006	1.19086	1.19165	1.19245	1.19324	1.19404
19	1.19993	1.20078	1.20162	1.20247	1.20332	1.20416	1.20501	1.20586
20	1.21149	1.21239	1.21329	1.21420	1.21510	1.21600	1.21690	1.21780
21	1.22317	1.22413	1.22508	1.22604	1.22699	1.22795	1.22890	1.22986
22	1.23496	1.23597	1.23698	1.23799	1.23900	1.24001	1.24102	1.24203
23	1.24687	1.24793	1.24900	1.25006	1.25113	1.25220	1.25326	1.25433
24	1.25888	1.26001	1.26113	1.26225	1.26338	1.26450	1.26562	1.26675
25	1.27102	1.27220	1.27338	1.27456	1.27574	1.27693	1.27811	1.27929
26	1.28327	1.28451	1.28575	1.28699	1.28823	1.28947	1.29072	1.29196
27	1.29564	1.29694	1.29824	1.29954	1.30084	1.30214	1.30345	1.30475
28	1.30813	1.30949	1.31085	1.31221	1.31357	1.31494	1.31630	1.31767
29	1.32074	1.32216	1.32358	1.32501	1.32643	1.32786	1.32929	1.33071
30	1.33347	1.33495	1.33644	1.33793	1.33942	1.34091	1.34240	1.34389
31	1.34632	1.34787	1.34942	1.35097	1.35253	1.35408	1.35564	1.35720
32	1.35930	1.36091	1.36253	1.36415	1.36577	1.36739	1.36901	1.37063
33	1.37240	1.37408	1.37577	1.37745	1.37914	1.38082	1.38251	1.38420
34	1.38563	1.38738	1.38913	1.39088	1.39264	1.39439	1.39615	1.39791
35	1.39898	1.40080	1.40262	1.40445	1.40627	1.40809	1.40992	1.41175
36	1.41247	1.41436	1.41625	1.41814	1.42003	1.42193	1.42383	1.42573
37	1.42608	1.42804	1.43001	1.43197	1.43393	1.43590	1.43787	1.43984
38	1.43983	1.44186	1.44390	1.44593	1.44797	1.45001	1.45205	1.45410
39	1.45371	1.45581	1.45792	1.46003	1.46215	1.46426	1.46638	1.46850
40	1.46772	1.46990	1.47208	1.47427	1.47646	1.47865	1.48084	1.48304
41	1.48187	1.48412	1.48638	1.48865	1.49091	1.49318	1.49545	1.49772
42	1.49615	1.49848	1.50082	1.50316	1.50550	1.50785	1.51020	1.51255
43	1.51057	1.51298	1.51540	1.51782	1.52024	1.52267	1.52509	1.52752
44	1.52513	1.52762	1.53012	1.53262	1.53512	1.53763	1.54014	1.54265
45	1.53983	1.54241	1.54498	1.54757	1.55015	1.55274	1.55533	1.55792
46	1.55467	1.55733	1.55999	1.56266	1.56532	1.56799	1.57067	1.57335
47	1.56966	1.57240	1.57515	1.57789	1.58065	1.58340	1.58616	1.58892
48	1.58479	1.58762	1.59045	1.59328	1.59612	1.59896	1.60181	1.60466
60	1.77813	1.78210	1.78607	1.79005	1.79404	1.79803	1.80203	1.80604
72	1.99507	2.00041	2.00576	2.01112	2.01650	2.02189	2.02729	2.03270
84	2.23846	2.24546	2.25247	2.25950	2.26654	2.27361	2.28070	2.28780
96	2.51156	2.52052	2.52952	2.53854	2.54760	2.55668	2.56578	2.57492
108	2.81797	2.82929	2.84065	2.85205	2.86350	2.87498	2.88651	2.89807
120	3.16176	3.17588	3.19005	3.20428	3.21857	3.23292	3.24732	3.26178
132	3.54749	3.56492	3.58243	3.60001	3.61767	3.63542	3.65324	3.67114
144	3.98029	4.00162	4.02307	4.04461	4.06627	4.08802	4.10989	4.13186
156	4.46588	4.49182	4.51790	4.54412	4.57048	4.59698	4.62363	4.65041
168	5.01072	5.04207	5.07360	5.10532	5.13722	5.16931	5.20158	5.23404
180	5.62203	5.65766	5.69766	5.73583	5.77424	5.81289	5.85178	5.89091
192	6.30791	6.35304	6.39847	6.44420	6.49024	6.53659	6.58325	6.63022
204	7.07748	7.13129	7.18548	7.24006	7.29503	7.35040	7.40616	7.46231
216	7.94093	8.00487	8.06930	8.13421	8.19962	8.26552	8.33193	8.39883
228	8.90972	8.98547	9.06182	9.13878	9.21637	9.29458	9.37342	9.45289
240	9.99671	10.08619	10.17642	10.26742	10.35920	10.45175	10.54509	10.63922
252	11.21631	11.32174	11.42812	11.53545	11.64374	11.75300	11.86323	11.97445
264	12.58470	12.70866	12.83378	12.96008	13.08756	13.21625	13.34613	13.47724
276	14.12003	14.26547	14.41234	14.56065	14.71042	14.86167	15.01440	15.16863
288	15.84268	16.01299	16.18505	16.35889	16.53452	16.71195	16.89120	17.07230
300	17.77548	17.97458	18.17582	18.37921	18.58480	18.79258	19.00260	19.21487
312	19.94409	20.17647	20.41144	20.64905	20.88931	21.13226	21.37793	21.62634
324	22.37727	22.64808	22.92205	23.19920	23.47958	23.76323	24.05017	24.34044
336	25.10730	25.42247	25.74146	26.06431	26.39105	26.72175	27.05644	27.39517
348	28.17039	28.53673	28.90766	29.28325	29.66354	30.04861	30.43849	30.83326
360	31.60718	32.03247	32.46330	32.89973	33.34182	33.78966	34.24330	34.70284
420	56.20177	57.08503	57.98177	58.89219	59.81649	60.75487	61.70755	62.67473
480	99.93423	101.73116	103.55957	105.42001	107.31303	109.23917	111.19900	113.19311

26

SINGLE DEPOSIT

NUMBER OF MONTHS	EFFECTIVE ANNUAL YIELD							
	12.60%	12.65%	12.70%	12.75%	12.80%	12.85%	12.90%	12.95%
1	1.00994	1.00998	1.01001	1.01005	1.01009	1.01013	1.01016	1.01020
2	1.01998	1.02005	1.02013	1.02020	1.02028	1.02035	1.02043	1.02050
3	1.03011	1.03023	1.03034	1.03046	1.03057	1.03068	1.03080	1.03091
4	1.04035	1.04050	1.04066	1.04081	1.04097	1.04112	1.04127	1.04143
5	1.05069	1.05088	1.05108	1.05127	1.05147	1.05166	1.05185	1.05205
6	1.06113	1.06137	1.06160	1.06184	1.06207	1.06231	1.06254	1.06278
7	1.07168	1.07195	1.07223	1.07251	1.07279	1.07306	1.07334	1.07362
8	1.08233	1.08265	1.08297	1.08329	1.08361	1.08393	1.08425	1.08457
9	1.09308	1.09345	1.09381	1.09418	1.09454	1.09490	1.09527	1.09563
10	1.10395	1.10436	1.10477	1.10517	1.10558	1.10599	1.10640	1.10681
11	1.11492	1.11537	1.11583	1.11628	1.11673	1.11719	1.11764	1.11810
12	1.12600	1.12650	1.12700	1.12750	1.12800	1.12850	1.12900	1.12950
13	1.13719	1.13774	1.13828	1.13883	1.13938	1.13993	1.14047	1.14102
14	1.14849	1.14909	1.14968	1.15028	1.15087	1.15147	1.15206	1.15266
15	1.15991	1.16055	1.16119	1.16184	1.16248	1.16313	1.16377	1.16442
16	1.17143	1.17213	1.17282	1.17352	1.17421	1.17490	1.17560	1.17629
17	1.18308	1.18382	1.18456	1.18531	1.18605	1.18680	1.18754	1.18829
18	1.19483	1.19563	1.19643	1.19722	1.19802	1.19882	1.19961	1.20041
19	1.20671	1.20756	1.20841	1.20925	1.21010	1.21095	1.21180	1.21265
20	1.21870	1.21960	1.22051	1.22141	1.22231	1.22321	1.22412	1.22502
21	1.23081	1.23177	1.23273	1.23368	1.23464	1.23560	1.23656	1.23752
22	1.24305	1.24406	1.24507	1.24608	1.24710	1.24811	1.24912	1.25014
23	1.25540	1.25647	1.25754	1.25861	1.25968	1.26075	1.26182	1.26289
24	1.26788	1.26900	1.27013	1.27126	1.27238	1.27351	1.27464	1.27577
25	1.28048	1.28166	1.28285	1.28403	1.28522	1.28641	1.28759	1.28878
26	1.29320	1.29445	1.29569	1.29694	1.29818	1.29943	1.30068	1.30193
27	1.30605	1.30736	1.30867	1.30997	1.31128	1.31259	1.31390	1.31521
28	1.31903	1.32040	1.32177	1.32314	1.32451	1.32588	1.32725	1.32862
29	1.33214	1.33357	1.33500	1.33644	1.33787	1.33930	1.34074	1.34217
30	1.34538	1.34688	1.34837	1.34987	1.35137	1.35286	1.35436	1.35586
31	1.35875	1.36031	1.36187	1.36343	1.36500	1.36656	1.36813	1.36969
32	1.37226	1.37388	1.37551	1.37714	1.37877	1.38040	1.38203	1.38366
33	1.38590	1.38759	1.38928	1.39098	1.39268	1.39437	1.39607	1.39777
34	1.39967	1.40143	1.40319	1.40496	1.40672	1.40849	1.41026	1.41203
35	1.41358	1.41541	1.41724	1.41908	1.42092	1.42275	1.42459	1.42643
36	1.42763	1.42953	1.43144	1.43334	1.43525	1.43716	1.43907	1.44098
37	1.44182	1.44379	1.44577	1.44775	1.44973	1.45171	1.45369	1.45568
38	1.45615	1.45819	1.46025	1.46230	1.46435	1.46641	1.46847	1.47053
39	1.47062	1.47274	1.47487	1.47699	1.47912	1.48126	1.48339	1.48553
40	1.48523	1.48743	1.48963	1.49184	1.49404	1.49625	1.49846	1.50068
41	1.49999	1.50227	1.50455	1.50683	1.50912	1.51140	1.51369	1.51598
42	1.51490	1.51726	1.51962	1.52198	1.52434	1.52671	1.52908	1.53145
43	1.52996	1.53239	1.53483	1.53727	1.53972	1.54216	1.54461	1.54707
44	1.54516	1.54768	1.55020	1.55272	1.55525	1.55778	1.56031	1.56285
45	1.56052	1.56312	1.56572	1.56833	1.57094	1.57355	1.57617	1.57879
46	1.57603	1.57871	1.58140	1.58409	1.58679	1.58948	1.59218	1.59489
47	1.59169	1.59446	1.59723	1.60001	1.60279	1.60558	1.60836	1.61116
48	1.60751	1.61037	1.61323	1.61609	1.61896	1.62183	1.62471	1.62759
60	1.81006	1.81408	1.81811	1.82214	1.82619	1.83024	1.83430	1.83836
72	2.03812	2.04356	2.04901	2.05447	2.05994	2.06542	2.07092	2.07643
84	2.29493	2.30207	2.30923	2.31641	2.32361	2.33083	2.33807	2.34533
96	2.58409	2.59328	2.60250	2.61175	2.62103	2.63034	2.63968	2.64905
108	2.90968	2.92133	2.93302	2.94475	2.95653	2.96834	2.98020	2.99210
120	3.27630	3.29088	3.30552	3.32021	3.33496	3.34977	3.36465	3.37958
132	3.68912	3.70718	3.72532	3.74354	3.76184	3.78022	3.79869	3.81723
144	4.15394	4.17613	4.19843	4.22084	4.24335	4.26598	4.28872	4.31156
156	4.67734	4.70441	4.73163	4.75899	4.78650	4.81416	4.84196	4.86991
168	5.26669	5.29952	5.33255	5.36577	5.39917	5.43278	5.46657	5.50056
180	5.93029	5.96991	6.00978	6.04990	6.09027	6.13089	6.17176	6.21289
192	6.67751	6.72511	6.77302	6.82126	6.86982	6.91871	6.96792	7.01746
204	7.51887	7.57583	7.63320	7.69097	7.74916	7.80776	7.86678	7.92622
216	8.46625	8.53417	8.60262	8.67157	8.74105	8.81106	8.88159	8.95266
228	9.53300	9.61375	9.69515	9.77720	9.85991	9.94328	10.02732	10.11203
240	10.73415	10.82989	10.92643	11.02379	11.12198	11.22099	11.32084	11.42154
252	12.08666	12.19987	12.31409	12.42933	12.54559	12.66289	12.78123	12.90063
264	13.60958	13.74315	13.87798	14.01406	14.15143	14.29007	14.43001	14.57126
276	15.32438	15.48166	15.64048	15.80086	15.96281	16.12635	16.29148	16.45824
288	17.25525	17.44009	17.62682	17.81547	18.00605	18.19858	18.39309	18.58958
300	19.42942	19.64626	19.86543	20.08694	20.31082	20.53710	20.76579	20.99693
312	21.87752	22.13151	22.38834	22.64802	22.91061	23.17612	23.44458	23.71604
324	24.63409	24.93115	25.23165	25.53565	25.84316	26.15425	26.46893	26.78726
336	27.73799	28.08494	28.43607	28.79144	29.15109	29.51507	29.88343	30.25621
348	31.23297	31.63768	32.04746	32.46235	32.88243	33.30775	33.73839	34.17439
360	35.16833	35.63985	36.11748	36.60130	37.09138	37.58780	38.09064	38.59998
420	63.65663	64.65347	65.66547	66.69285	67.73583	68.79466	69.86955	70.96076
480	115.22206	117.28645	119.38689	121.52399	123.69837	125.91067	128.16153	130.45160

SINGLE DEPOSIT

EFFECTIVE ANNUAL YIELD

NUMBER OF MONTHS	13.00%	13.05%	13.10%	13.15%	13.20%	13.25%	13.30%	13.35%
1	1.01024	1.01027	1.01031	1.01035	1.01039	1.01042	1.01046	1.01050
2	1.02058	1.02065	1.02073	1.02080	1.02088	1.02095	1.02103	1.02110
3	1.03103	1.03114	1.03125	1.03137	1.03148	1.03160	1.03171	1.03182
4	1.04158	1.04173	1.04189	1.04204	1.04219	1.04235	1.04250	1.04265
5	1.05224	1.05244	1.05263	1.05282	1.05302	1.05321	1.05341	1.05360
6	1.06301	1.06325	1.06348	1.06372	1.06395	1.06419	1.06442	1.06466
7	1.07390	1.07417	1.07445	1.07473	1.07500	1.07528	1.07556	1.07584
8	1.08489	1.08521	1.08553	1.08585	1.08617	1.08649	1.08681	1.08713
9	1.09600	1.09636	1.09672	1.09709	1.09745	1.09781	1.09818	1.09854
10	1.10722	1.10762	1.10803	1.10844	1.10885	1.10926	1.10966	1.11007
11	1.11855	1.11900	1.11946	1.11991	1.12036	1.12082	1.12127	1.12172
12	1.13000	1.13050	1.13100	1.13150	1.13200	1.13250	1.13300	1.13350
13	1.14157	1.14211	1.14266	1.14321	1.14376	1.14430	1.14485	1.14540
14	1.15325	1.15385	1.15444	1.15504	1.15564	1.15623	1.15683	1.15742
15	1.16506	1.16570	1.16635	1.16699	1.16764	1.16828	1.16893	1.16957
16	1.17699	1.17768	1.17837	1.17907	1.17976	1.18046	1.18115	1.18185
17	1.18903	1.18978	1.19053	1.19127	1.19202	1.19276	1.19351	1.19426
18	1.20121	1.20200	1.20280	1.20360	1.20440	1.20519	1.20599	1.20679
19	1.21350	1.21435	1.21520	1.21605	1.21691	1.21776	1.21861	1.21946
20	1.22593	1.22683	1.22773	1.22864	1.22954	1.23045	1.23135	1.23226
21	1.23848	1.23943	1.24039	1.24135	1.24231	1.24327	1.24423	1.24520
22	1.25115	1.25217	1.25318	1.25420	1.25522	1.25623	1.25725	1.25827
23	1.26396	1.26503	1.26611	1.26718	1.26825	1.26933	1.27040	1.27148
24	1.27690	1.27803	1.27916	1.28029	1.28142	1.28256	1.28369	1.28482
25	1.28997	1.29116	1.29235	1.29354	1.29473	1.29592	1.29712	1.29831
26	1.30318	1.30443	1.30568	1.30693	1.30818	1.30943	1.31068	1.31194
27	1.31652	1.31783	1.31914	1.32045	1.32177	1.32308	1.32439	1.32571
28	1.32999	1.33137	1.33274	1.33412	1.33549	1.33687	1.33825	1.33963
29	1.34361	1.34505	1.34648	1.34792	1.34936	1.35080	1.35225	1.35369
30	1.35736	1.35887	1.36037	1.36187	1.36338	1.36488	1.36639	1.36790
31	1.37126	1.37283	1.37440	1.37597	1.37754	1.37911	1.38068	1.38226
32	1.38530	1.38693	1.38857	1.39020	1.39184	1.39348	1.39512	1.39677
33	1.39948	1.40118	1.40289	1.40459	1.40630	1.40801	1.40972	1.41143
34	1.41380	1.41558	1.41735	1.41913	1.42090	1.42268	1.42446	1.42625
35	1.42828	1.43012	1.43197	1.43381	1.43566	1.43751	1.43936	1.44122
36	1.44290	1.44481	1.44673	1.44865	1.45057	1.45249	1.45442	1.45635
37	1.45767	1.45966	1.46165	1.46364	1.46564	1.46763	1.46963	1.47163
38	1.47259	1.47465	1.47672	1.47879	1.48086	1.48293	1.48501	1.48708
39	1.48766	1.48980	1.49195	1.49409	1.49624	1.49839	1.50054	1.50269
40	1.50289	1.50511	1.50733	1.50955	1.51178	1.51401	1.51623	1.51847
41	1.51828	1.52057	1.52287	1.52518	1.52748	1.52979	1.53209	1.53441
42	1.53382	1.53620	1.53858	1.54096	1.54334	1.54573	1.54812	1.55051
43	1.54952	1.55198	1.55444	1.55691	1.55937	1.56184	1.56431	1.56679
44	1.56538	1.56793	1.57047	1.57302	1.57557	1.57812	1.58068	1.58324
45	1.58141	1.58403	1.58666	1.58930	1.59193	1.59457	1.59721	1.59986
46	1.59760	1.60031	1.60302	1.60574	1.60846	1.61119	1.61392	1.61665
47	1.61395	1.61675	1.61955	1.62236	1.62517	1.62798	1.63080	1.63362
48	1.63047	1.63336	1.63625	1.63915	1.64205	1.64495	1.64786	1.65077
60	1.84244	1.84651	1.85060	1.85470	1.85880	1.86291	1.86702	1.87115
72	2.08195	2.08749	2.09303	2.09859	2.10416	2.10974	2.11534	2.12094
84	2.35261	2.35990	2.36722	2.37455	2.38191	2.38928	2.39668	2.40409
96	2.65844	2.66787	2.67732	2.68681	2.69632	2.70586	2.71543	2.72504
108	3.00404	3.01603	3.02805	3.04012	3.05223	3.06439	3.07659	3.08883
120	3.39457	3.40962	3.42473	3.43990	3.45513	3.47042	3.48577	3.50119
132	3.83586	3.85457	3.87337	3.89224	3.91121	3.93025	3.94938	3.96859
144	4.33452	4.35759	4.38078	4.40407	4.42749	4.45101	4.47465	4.49840
156	4.89801	4.92626	4.95466	4.98321	5.01191	5.04077	5.06978	5.09894
168	5.53475	5.56914	5.60372	5.63850	5.67349	5.70867	5.74406	5.77965
180	6.25427	6.29591	6.33781	6.37997	6.42239	6.46507	6.50802	6.55123
192	7.06733	7.11753	7.16806	7.21893	7.27014	7.32169	7.37358	7.42582
204	7.98608	8.04636	8.10708	8.16822	8.22980	8.29181	8.35427	8.41717
216	9.02427	9.09641	9.16910	9.24234	9.31613	9.39048	9.46539	9.54086
228	10.19742	10.28350	10.37026	10.45771	10.54586	10.63472	10.72428	10.81456
240	11.52309	11.62549	11.72876	11.83290	11.93792	12.04382	12.15061	12.25831
252	13.02109	13.14262	13.26523	13.38893	13.51372	13.63962	13.76664	13.89479
264	14.71383	14.85773	15.00297	15.14957	15.29753	15.44688	15.59761	15.74975
276	16.62663	16.79666	16.96836	17.14174	17.31681	17.49359	17.67209	17.85234
288	18.78809	18.98863	19.19122	19.39588	19.60263	19.81149	20.02248	20.23562
300	21.23054	21.46664	21.70527	21.94643	22.19017	22.43651	22.68547	22.93708
312	23.99051	24.26804	24.54866	24.83239	25.11927	25.40935	25.70264	25.99918
324	27.10928	27.43502	27.76453	28.09785	28.43502	28.77608	29.12109	29.47007
336	30.63349	31.01529	31.40168	31.79272	32.18844	32.58891	32.99419	33.40432
348	34.61584	35.06279	35.51530	35.97346	36.43732	36.90695	37.38242	37.86380
360	39.11590	39.63848	40.16781	40.70397	41.24704	41.79712	42.35428	42.91862
420	72.06851	73.19305	74.33463	75.49350	76.66991	77.86412	79.07639	80.30699
480	132.78155	135.15206	137.56381	140.01750	142.51385	145.05357	147.63740	150.26609

28

SINGLE DEPOSIT

EFFECTIVE ANNUAL YIELD

NUMBER OF MONTHS	13.40%	13.45%	13.50%	13.55%	13.60%	13.65%	13.70%	13.75%
1	1.01053	1.01057	1.01061	1.01065	1.01068	1.01072	1.01076	1.01079
2	1.02118	1.02125	1.02132	1.02140	1.02148	1.02155	1.02163	1.02170
3	1.03194	1.03205	1.03216	1.03228	1.03239	1.03251	1.03262	1.03273
4	1.04281	1.04296	1.04311	1.04327	1.04342	1.04357	1.04373	1.04388
5	1.05379	1.05399	1.05418	1.05437	1.05457	1.05476	1.05495	1.05515
6	1.06489	1.06513	1.06536	1.06560	1.06583	1.06607	1.06630	1.06654
7	1.07611	1.07639	1.07667	1.07694	1.07722	1.07750	1.07777	1.07805
8	1.08745	1.08777	1.08809	1.08841	1.08873	1.08905	1.08937	1.08968
9	1.09890	1.09927	1.09963	1.09999	1.10036	1.10072	1.10108	1.10145
10	1.11048	1.11089	1.11130	1.11170	1.11211	1.11252	1.11293	1.11334
11	1.12218	1.12263	1.12309	1.12354	1.12399	1.12445	1.12490	1.12535
12	1.13400	1.13450	1.13500	1.13550	1.13600	1.13650	1.13700	1.13750
13	1.14595	1.14649	1.14704	1.14759	1.14814	1.14868	1.14923	1.14978
14	1.15802	1.15861	1.15921	1.15981	1.16040	1.16100	1.16159	1.16219
15	1.17022	1.17086	1.17151	1.17215	1.17280	1.17344	1.17409	1.17473
16	1.18254	1.18324	1.18393	1.18463	1.18533	1.18602	1.18672	1.18741
17	1.19500	1.19575	1.19649	1.19724	1.19799	1.19874	1.19948	1.20023
18	1.20759	1.20839	1.20919	1.20999	1.21079	1.21159	1.21239	1.21319
19	1.22031	1.22116	1.22202	1.22287	1.22372	1.22457	1.22543	1.22628
20	1.23317	1.23407	1.23498	1.23589	1.23679	1.23770	1.23861	1.23952
21	1.24616	1.24712	1.24808	1.24904	1.25001	1.25097	1.25193	1.25290
22	1.25928	1.26030	1.26132	1.26234	1.26336	1.26438	1.26540	1.26642
23	1.27255	1.27363	1.27470	1.27578	1.27686	1.27793	1.27901	1.28009
24	1.28596	1.28709	1.28822	1.28936	1.29050	1.29163	1.29277	1.29391
25	1.29950	1.30070	1.30189	1.30309	1.30428	1.30548	1.30668	1.30787
26	1.31319	1.31445	1.31570	1.31696	1.31822	1.31947	1.32073	1.32199
27	1.32703	1.32834	1.32966	1.33098	1.33230	1.33362	1.33494	1.33626
28	1.34101	1.34239	1.34377	1.34515	1.34653	1.34791	1.34930	1.35068
29	1.35513	1.35658	1.35802	1.35947	1.36091	1.36236	1.36381	1.36526
30	1.36941	1.37092	1.37243	1.37394	1.37545	1.37697	1.37848	1.38000
31	1.38383	1.38541	1.38699	1.38857	1.39015	1.39173	1.39331	1.39489
32	1.39841	1.40006	1.40170	1.40335	1.40500	1.40665	1.40830	1.40995
33	1.41314	1.41486	1.41657	1.41829	1.42001	1.42173	1.42345	1.42517
34	1.42803	1.42981	1.43160	1.43339	1.43518	1.43697	1.43876	1.44055
35	1.44307	1.44493	1.44679	1.44865	1.45051	1.45237	1.45424	1.45610
36	1.45827	1.46020	1.46214	1.46407	1.46600	1.46794	1.46988	1.47182
37	1.47364	1.47564	1.47765	1.47965	1.48166	1.48368	1.48569	1.48771
38	1.48916	1.49124	1.49332	1.49541	1.49749	1.49958	1.50167	1.50376
39	1.50485	1.50700	1.50916	1.51133	1.51349	1.51566	1.51782	1.51999
40	1.52070	1.52294	1.52517	1.52742	1.52966	1.53190	1.53415	1.53640
41	1.53672	1.53904	1.54135	1.54368	1.54600	1.54833	1.55065	1.55299
42	1.55291	1.55531	1.55771	1.56011	1.56251	1.56492	1.56733	1.56975
43	1.56927	1.57175	1.57423	1.57672	1.57921	1.58170	1.58419	1.58669
44	1.58580	1.58836	1.59093	1.59350	1.59608	1.59865	1.60123	1.60382
45	1.60250	1.60515	1.60781	1.61047	1.61313	1.61579	1.61846	1.62113
46	1.61938	1.62212	1.62487	1.62761	1.63036	1.63311	1.63587	1.63863
47	1.63644	1.63927	1.64210	1.64494	1.64778	1.65062	1.65347	1.65632
48	1.65368	1.65660	1.65952	1.66245	1.66538	1.66831	1.67125	1.67419
60	1.87528	1.87941	1.88356	1.88771	1.89187	1.89604	1.90021	1.90439
72	2.12656	2.13220	2.13784	2.14350	2.14917	2.15485	2.16054	2.16625
84	2.41152	2.41898	2.42645	2.43394	2.44145	2.44898	2.45654	2.46411
96	2.73467	2.74433	2.75402	2.76374	2.77349	2.78327	2.79308	2.80292
108	3.10111	3.11344	3.12581	3.13823	3.15068	3.16319	3.17573	3.18833
120	3.51666	3.53220	3.54780	3.56346	3.57919	3.59496	3.61081	3.62672
132	3.98789	4.00728	4.02675	4.04630	4.06595	4.08568	4.10549	4.12539
144	4.52227	4.54626	4.57036	4.59458	4.61892	4.64337	4.66794	4.69264
156	5.12626	5.15773	5.18736	5.21714	5.24709	5.27719	5.30745	5.33787
168	5.81544	5.85144	5.88765	5.92407	5.96069	5.99753	6.03457	6.07183
180	6.59471	6.63846	6.68248	6.72678	6.77135	6.81619	6.86131	6.90671
192	7.47840	7.53134	7.58462	7.63826	7.69225	7.74660	7.80131	7.85638
204	8.48051	8.54430	8.60854	8.67324	8.73839	8.80401	8.87009	8.93663
216	9.61690	9.69351	9.77070	9.84846	9.92682	10.00576	10.08529	10.16542
228	10.90556	10.99729	11.08974	11.18293	11.27686	11.37154	11.46697	11.56316
240	12.36691	12.47642	12.58686	12.69822	12.81052	12.92376	13.03795	13.15310
252	14.02407	14.15450	14.28608	14.41883	14.55275	14.68785	14.82415	14.96165
264	15.90330	16.05828	16.21470	16.37258	16.53192	16.69274	16.85506	17.01888
276	18.03434	18.21812	18.40369	18.59106	18.78026	18.97130	19.16420	19.35897
288	20.45094	20.66845	20.88818	21.11015	21.33438	21.56088	21.78970	22.02083
300	23.19137	23.44836	23.70809	23.97058	24.23585	24.50394	24.77488	25.04870
312	26.29901	26.60217	26.90868	27.21859	27.53193	27.84873	28.16904	28.49289
324	29.82308	30.18016	30.54135	30.90671	31.27627	31.65009	32.02820	32.41067
336	33.81937	34.23939	34.66443	35.09457	35.52984	35.97032	36.41606	36.86713
348	38.35117	38.84459	39.34413	39.84988	40.36190	40.88027	41.40507	41.93636
360	43.49022	44.06918	44.65559	45.24954	45.85112	46.46043	47.07756	47.70261
420	81.55619	82.82425	84.11146	85.41809	86.74443	88.09077	89.45740	90.84461
480	152.94039	155.66107	158.42892	161.24473	164.10932	167.02351	169.98813	173.00403

29

SINGLE DEPOSIT

EFFECTIVE ANNUAL YIELD

NUMBER OF MONTHS	13.80%	13.85%	13.90%	13.95%	14.00%	14.05%	14.10%	14.15%
1	1.01083	1.01087	1.01090	1.01094	1.01098	1.01102	1.01105	1.01109
2	1.02178	1.02185	1.02193	1.02200	1.02208	1.02215	1.02223	1.02230
3	1.03285	1.03296	1.03307	1.03319	1.03330	1.03341	1.03353	1.03364
4	1.04403	1.04419	1.04434	1.04449	1.04464	1.04480	1.04495	1.04510
5	1.05534	1.05553	1.05573	1.05592	1.05611	1.05631	1.05650	1.05669
6	1.06677	1.06701	1.06724	1.06747	1.06771	1.06794	1.06818	1.06841
7	1.07832	1.07860	1.07888	1.07915	1.07943	1.07971	1.07998	1.08026
8	1.09000	1.09032	1.09064	1.09096	1.09128	1.09160	1.09192	1.09224
9	1.10181	1.10217	1.10254	1.10290	1.10326	1.10362	1.10399	1.10435
10	1.11374	1.11415	1.11456	1.11497	1.11537	1.11578	1.11619	1.11660
11	1.12581	1.12626	1.12671	1.12717	1.12762	1.12807	1.12853	1.12898
12	1.13800	1.13850	1.13900	1.13950	1.14000	1.14050	1.14100	1.14150
13	1.15033	1.15087	1.15142	1.15197	1.15252	1.15306	1.15361	1.15416
14	1.16278	1.16338	1.16398	1.16457	1.16517	1.16577	1.16636	1.16696
15	1.17538	1.17602	1.17667	1.17732	1.17796	1.17861	1.17925	1.17990
16	1.18811	1.18881	1.18950	1.19020	1.19089	1.19159	1.19229	1.19298
17	1.20098	1.20173	1.20247	1.20322	1.20397	1.20472	1.20547	1.20621
18	1.21399	1.21479	1.21559	1.21639	1.21719	1.21799	1.21879	1.21959
19	1.22713	1.22799	1.22884	1.22970	1.23055	1.23140	1.23226	1.23311
20	1.24042	1.24133	1.24224	1.24315	1.24406	1.24497	1.24588	1.24679
21	1.25386	1.25482	1.25579	1.25675	1.25772	1.25868	1.25965	1.26062
22	1.26744	1.26846	1.26948	1.27050	1.27153	1.27255	1.27357	1.27460
23	1.28117	1.28225	1.28333	1.28441	1.28549	1.28657	1.28765	1.28873
24	1.29504	1.29618	1.29732	1.29846	1.29960	1.30074	1.30188	1.30302
25	1.30907	1.31027	1.31147	1.31267	1.31387	1.31507	1.31627	1.31747
26	1.32325	1.32451	1.32577	1.32703	1.32829	1.32956	1.33082	1.33208
27	1.33758	1.33890	1.34023	1.34155	1.34288	1.34420	1.34553	1.34685
28	1.35207	1.35345	1.35484	1.35623	1.35762	1.35901	1.36040	1.36179
29	1.36671	1.36816	1.36962	1.37107	1.37252	1.37398	1.37544	1.37689
30	1.38152	1.38303	1.38455	1.38607	1.38759	1.38912	1.39064	1.39216
31	1.39648	1.39806	1.39965	1.40124	1.40283	1.40442	1.40601	1.40760
32	1.41160	1.41326	1.41491	1.41657	1.41823	1.41989	1.42155	1.42321
33	1.42689	1.42862	1.43034	1.43207	1.43380	1.43553	1.43726	1.43899
34	1.44235	1.44414	1.44594	1.44774	1.44954	1.45134	1.45315	1.45495
35	1.45797	1.45984	1.46171	1.46358	1.46545	1.46733	1.46921	1.47109
36	1.47376	1.47570	1.47765	1.47960	1.48154	1.48349	1.48545	1.48740
37	1.48972	1.49174	1.49376	1.49579	1.49781	1.49984	1.50186	1.50389
38	1.50586	1.50795	1.51005	1.51215	1.51425	1.51636	1.51846	1.52057
39	1.52217	1.52434	1.52652	1.52870	1.53088	1.53306	1.53525	1.53743
40	1.53865	1.54091	1.54317	1.54542	1.54769	1.54995	1.55222	1.55448
41	1.55532	1.55765	1.55999	1.56233	1.56468	1.56702	1.56937	1.57172
42	1.57216	1.57458	1.57700	1.57943	1.58186	1.58429	1.58672	1.58915
43	1.58919	1.59170	1.59420	1.59671	1.59922	1.60174	1.60426	1.60678
44	1.60640	1.60899	1.61159	1.61418	1.61678	1.61938	1.62199	1.62459
45	1.62380	1.62648	1.62916	1.63184	1.63453	1.63722	1.63991	1.64261
46	1.64139	1.64416	1.64693	1.64970	1.65248	1.65526	1.65804	1.66083
47	1.65917	1.66203	1.66489	1.66775	1.67062	1.67349	1.67637	1.67924
48	1.67714	1.68009	1.68304	1.68600	1.68896	1.69193	1.69489	1.69787
60	1.90858	1.91278	1.91698	1.92120	1.92541	1.92964	1.93387	1.93812
72	2.17197	2.17770	2.18345	2.18920	2.19497	2.20076	2.20655	2.21236
84	2.47170	2.47931	2.48694	2.49460	2.50227	2.50996	2.51767	2.52541
96	2.81280	2.82270	2.83263	2.84259	2.85259	2.86261	2.87267	2.88275
108	3.20096	3.21364	3.22637	3.23913	3.25195	3.26481	3.27771	3.29066
120	3.64269	3.65873	3.67483	3.69099	3.70722	3.72351	3.73987	3.75629
132	4.14539	4.16546	4.18563	4.20589	4.22623	4.24667	4.26719	4.28781
144	4.71745	4.74238	4.76743	4.79261	4.81790	4.84332	4.86887	4.89453
156	5.36846	5.39920	5.43011	5.46118	5.49241	5.52381	5.55537	5.58711
168	6.10930	6.14699	6.18489	6.22301	6.26135	6.29991	6.33868	6.37768
180	6.95239	6.99835	7.04459	7.09112	7.13794	7.18504	7.23244	7.28012
192	7.91182	7.96762	8.02379	8.08033	8.13725	8.19454	8.25221	8.31026
204	9.00365	9.07113	9.13910	9.20754	9.27646	9.34587	9.41577	9.48616
216	10.24615	10.32749	10.40943	10.49199	10.57517	10.65897	10.74340	10.82845
228	11.66012	11.75784	11.85634	11.95562	12.05569	12.15655	12.25822	12.36068
240	13.26922	13.38630	13.50437	13.62343	13.74349	13.86455	13.98662	14.10972
252	15.10037	15.24031	15.38148	15.52390	15.66758	15.81252	15.95874	16.10624
264	17.18422	17.35109	17.51951	17.68949	17.86104	18.03418	18.20892	18.38528
276	19.55564	19.75422	19.95472	20.15717	20.36158	20.56798	20.77638	20.98679
288	22.25432	22.49018	22.72843	22.96910	23.21221	23.45778	23.70585	23.95642
300	25.32541	25.60506	25.88768	26.17329	26.46192	26.75360	27.04837	27.34626
312	28.82032	29.15137	29.48607	29.82446	30.16658	30.51248	30.86219	31.21575
324	32.79753	33.18883	33.58463	33.98497	34.38991	34.79949	35.21376	35.63278
336	37.32358	37.78548	38.25289	38.72587	39.20449	39.68881	40.17890	40.67482
348	42.47424	43.01877	43.57004	44.12813	44.69312	45.26509	45.84413	46.43031
360	48.33568	48.97687	49.62628	50.28401	50.95016	51.62484	52.30815	53.00020
420	92.25272	93.68201	95.13281	96.60543	98.10018	99.61738	101.15738	102.72048
480	176.07207	179.19315	182.36814	185.59795	188.88351	192.22576	195.62564	199.08413

SINGLE DEPOSIT

NUMBER OF MONTHS	EFFECTIVE ANNUAL YIELD							
	14.20%	14.25%	14.30%	14.35%	14.40%	14.45%	14.50%	14.55%
1	1.01113	1.01116	1.01120	1.01124	1.01127	1.01131	1.01135	1.01138
2	1.02238	1.02245	1.02253	1.02260	1.02268	1.02275	1.02282	1.02290
3	1.03375	1.03387	1.03398	1.03409	1.03420	1.03432	1.03443	1.03454
4	1.04525	1.04541	1.04556	1.04571	1.04586	1.04602	1.04617	1.04632
5	1.05688	1.05708	1.05727	1.05746	1.05766	1.05785	1.05804	1.05823
6	1.06864	1.06888	1.06911	1.06935	1.06958	1.06981	1.07005	1.07028
7	1.08053	1.08081	1.08109	1.08136	1.08164	1.08191	1.08219	1.08246
8	1.09256	1.09288	1.09319	1.09351	1.09383	1.09415	1.09447	1.09479
9	1.10471	1.10508	1.10544	1.10580	1.10616	1.10653	1.10689	1.10725
10	1.11700	1.11741	1.11782	1.11823	1.11863	1.11904	1.11945	1.11986
11	1.12943	1.12989	1.13034	1.13079	1.13125	1.13170	1.13215	1.13261
12	1.14200	1.14250	1.14300	1.14350	1.14400	1.14450	1.14500	1.14550
13	1.15471	1.15525	1.15580	1.15635	1.15690	1.15745	1.15799	1.15854
14	1.16755	1.16815	1.16875	1.16934	1.16994	1.17054	1.17113	1.17173
15	1.18055	1.18119	1.18184	1.18248	1.18313	1.18378	1.18442	1.18507
16	1.19368	1.19438	1.19507	1.19577	1.19647	1.19717	1.19786	1.19856
17	1.20696	1.20771	1.20846	1.20921	1.20996	1.21071	1.21146	1.21221
18	1.22039	1.22119	1.22199	1.22280	1.22360	1.22440	1.22520	1.22601
19	1.23397	1.23483	1.23568	1.23654	1.23739	1.23825	1.23911	1.23996
20	1.24770	1.24861	1.24952	1.25043	1.25134	1.25226	1.25317	1.25408
21	1.26158	1.26255	1.26352	1.26448	1.26545	1.26642	1.26739	1.26836
22	1.27562	1.27664	1.27767	1.27869	1.27972	1.28074	1.28177	1.28280
23	1.28981	1.29090	1.29198	1.29306	1.29415	1.29523	1.29631	1.29740
24	1.30416	1.30531	1.30645	1.30759	1.30874	1.30988	1.31102	1.31217
25	1.31867	1.31988	1.32108	1.32229	1.32349	1.32470	1.32590	1.32711
26	1.33335	1.33461	1.33588	1.33714	1.33841	1.33968	1.34095	1.34222
27	1.34818	1.34951	1.35084	1.35217	1.35350	1.35483	1.35616	1.35750
28	1.36318	1.36458	1.36597	1.36736	1.36876	1.37016	1.37155	1.37295
29	1.37835	1.37981	1.38127	1.38273	1.38419	1.38565	1.38712	1.38858
30	1.39369	1.39521	1.39674	1.39827	1.39980	1.40133	1.40286	1.40439
31	1.40919	1.41079	1.41238	1.41398	1.41558	1.41718	1.41878	1.42038
32	1.42487	1.42654	1.42820	1.42987	1.43154	1.43321	1.43488	1.43655
33	1.44073	1.44246	1.44420	1.44594	1.44768	1.44942	1.45116	1.45290
34	1.45676	1.45857	1.46037	1.46219	1.46400	1.46581	1.46763	1.46944
35	1.47297	1.47485	1.47673	1.47862	1.48050	1.48239	1.48428	1.48617
36	1.48936	1.49131	1.49327	1.49523	1.49719	1.49916	1.50112	1.50309
37	1.50593	1.50796	1.51000	1.51203	1.51407	1.51611	1.51816	1.52020
38	1.52268	1.52479	1.52691	1.52902	1.53114	1.53326	1.53539	1.53751
39	1.53962	1.54182	1.54401	1.54621	1.54841	1.55061	1.55281	1.55501
40	1.55676	1.55903	1.56130	1.56358	1.56586	1.56814	1.57043	1.57272
41	1.57408	1.57643	1.57879	1.58115	1.58352	1.58588	1.58825	1.59062
42	1.59159	1.59403	1.59647	1.59892	1.60137	1.60382	1.60627	1.60873
43	1.60930	1.61183	1.61435	1.61689	1.61942	1.62196	1.62450	1.62704
44	1.62721	1.62982	1.63244	1.63506	1.63768	1.64030	1.64293	1.64557
45	1.64531	1.64801	1.65072	1.65343	1.65614	1.65886	1.66158	1.66430
46	1.66362	1.66641	1.66921	1.67201	1.67481	1.67762	1.68043	1.68325
47	1.68213	1.68501	1.68790	1.69080	1.69370	1.69660	1.69950	1.70241
48	1.70084	1.70382	1.70681	1.70980	1.71279	1.71579	1.71879	1.72179
60	1.94236	1.94662	1.95088	1.95515	1.95943	1.96372	1.96801	1.97231
72	2.21818	2.22401	2.22986	2.23572	2.24159	2.24747	2.25337	2.25928
84	2.53316	2.54093	2.54873	2.55654	2.56438	2.57223	2.58011	2.58801
96	2.89287	2.90302	2.91320	2.92341	2.93365	2.94392	2.95423	2.96456
108	3.30366	3.31670	3.32978	3.34292	3.35609	3.36932	3.38259	3.39591
120	3.77278	3.78933	3.80594	3.82262	3.83937	3.85619	3.87307	3.89001
132	4.30851	4.32931	4.35019	4.37117	4.39224	4.41340	4.43466	4.45601
144	4.92032	4.94623	4.97227	4.99843	5.02472	5.05114	5.07769	5.10436
156	5.61900	5.65107	5.68331	5.71571	5.74829	5.78103	5.81395	5.84704
168	6.41690	6.45635	6.49602	6.53591	6.57604	6.61639	6.65697	6.69779
180	7.32810	7.37638	7.42495	7.47382	7.52299	7.57246	7.62223	7.67231
192	8.36869	8.42751	8.48672	8.54631	8.60630	8.66668	8.72746	8.78864
204	9.55705	9.62843	9.70032	9.77271	9.84561	9.91902	9.99294	10.06738
216	10.91415	11.00048	11.08746	11.17509	11.26337	11.35231	11.44192	11.53219
228	12.46396	12.56805	12.67297	12.77872	12.88530	12.99272	13.10099	13.21012
240	14.23384	14.35900	14.48520	14.61246	14.74078	14.87017	15.00064	15.13219
252	16.25505	16.40516	16.55659	16.70935	16.86345	17.01891	17.17573	17.33393
264	18.56326	18.74289	18.92418	19.10714	19.29179	19.47814	19.66621	19.85601
276	21.19924	21.41375	21.63034	21.84902	22.06981	22.29273	22.51781	22.74506
288	24.20954	24.46521	24.72348	24.98435	25.24786	25.51403	25.78290	26.05447
300	27.64729	27.95151	28.25893	28.56960	28.88355	29.20081	29.52141	29.84540
312	31.57321	31.93460	32.29996	32.66934	33.04278	33.42033	33.80202	34.18790
324	36.05660	36.48528	36.91885	37.35739	37.80095	38.24957	38.70331	39.16224
336	41.17664	41.68443	42.19825	42.71818	43.24428	43.77663	44.31529	44.86035
348	47.02372	47.62446	48.23260	48.84824	49.47146	50.10235	50.74101	51.38753
360	53.70109	54.41094	55.12986	55.85796	56.59535	57.34214	58.09846	58.86441
420	104.30704	105.91740	107.55189	109.21088	110.89472	112.60376	114.33838	116.09895
480	202.60220	206.18086	209.82113	213.52403	217.29062	221.12196	225.01914	228.98326

31

SINGLE DEPOSIT

NUMBER OF MONTHS	EFFECTIVE ANNUAL YIELD							
	14.60%	14.65%	14.70%	14.75%	14.80%	14.85%	14.90%	14.95%
1	1.01142	1.01146	1.01149	1.01153	1.01157	1.01160	1.01164	1.01168
2	1.02297	1.02305	1.02312	1.02320	1.02327	1.02334	1.02342	1.02349
3	1.03466	1.03477	1.03488	1.03499	1.03511	1.03522	1.03533	1.03545
4	1.04647	1.04663	1.04678	1.04693	1.04708	1.04723	1.04739	1.04754
5	1.05843	1.05862	1.05881	1.05900	1.05919	1.05939	1.05958	1.05977
6	1.07051	1.07075	1.07098	1.07121	1.07145	1.07168	1.07191	1.07215
7	1.08274	1.08302	1.08329	1.08357	1.08384	1.08412	1.08439	1.08467
8	1.09511	1.09543	1.09574	1.09606	1.09638	1.09670	1.09702	1.09734
9	1.10761	1.10798	1.10834	1.10870	1.10906	1.10943	1.10979	1.11015
10	1.12026	1.12067	1.12108	1.12149	1.12189	1.12230	1.12271	1.12311
11	1.13306	1.13351	1.13397	1.13442	1.13487	1.13532	1.13578	1.13623
12	1.14600	1.14650	1.14700	1.14750	1.14800	1.14850	1.14900	1.14950
13	1.15909	1.15964	1.16018	1.16073	1.16128	1.16183	1.16238	1.16292
14	1.17233	1.17292	1.17352	1.17412	1.17471	1.17531	1.17591	1.17651
15	1.18572	1.18636	1.18701	1.18766	1.18830	1.18895	1.18960	1.19024
16	1.19926	1.19996	1.20065	1.20135	1.20205	1.20275	1.20345	1.20414
17	1.21296	1.21371	1.21446	1.21521	1.21596	1.21671	1.21746	1.21821
18	1.22681	1.22761	1.22842	1.22922	1.23002	1.23083	1.23163	1.23243
19	1.24082	1.24168	1.24254	1.24339	1.24425	1.24511	1.24597	1.24683
20	1.25499	1.25590	1.25682	1.25773	1.25864	1.25956	1.26047	1.26139
21	1.26933	1.27030	1.27126	1.27223	1.27320	1.27418	1.27515	1.27612
22	1.28382	1.28485	1.28588	1.28691	1.28793	1.28896	1.28999	1.29102
23	1.29849	1.29957	1.30066	1.30175	1.30283	1.30392	1.30501	1.30610
24	1.31332	1.31446	1.31561	1.31676	1.31790	1.31905	1.32020	1.32135
25	1.32832	1.32952	1.33073	1.33194	1.33315	1.33436	1.33557	1.33678
26	1.34349	1.34476	1.34603	1.34730	1.34857	1.34984	1.35112	1.35239
27	1.35883	1.36017	1.36150	1.36284	1.36417	1.36551	1.36685	1.36819
28	1.37435	1.37575	1.37715	1.37855	1.37995	1.38136	1.38276	1.38416
29	1.39005	1.39151	1.39298	1.39445	1.39592	1.39739	1.39886	1.40033
30	1.40592	1.40746	1.40899	1.41053	1.41207	1.41360	1.41514	1.41668
31	1.42198	1.42358	1.42519	1.42679	1.42840	1.43001	1.43162	1.43323
32	1.43822	1.43990	1.44157	1.44325	1.44492	1.44660	1.44828	1.44996
33	1.45465	1.45639	1.45814	1.45989	1.46164	1.46339	1.46514	1.46690
34	1.47126	1.47308	1.47490	1.47672	1.47855	1.48037	1.48220	1.48403
35	1.48806	1.48996	1.49186	1.49375	1.49565	1.49755	1.49945	1.50136
36	1.50506	1.50703	1.50900	1.51098	1.51295	1.51493	1.51691	1.51889
37	1.52225	1.52430	1.52635	1.52840	1.53046	1.53251	1.53457	1.53663
38	1.53964	1.54176	1.54389	1.54603	1.54816	1.55030	1.55243	1.55458
39	1.55722	1.55943	1.56164	1.56385	1.56607	1.56829	1.57051	1.57273
40	1.57501	1.57730	1.57959	1.58189	1.58419	1.58649	1.58879	1.59110
41	1.59299	1.59537	1.59775	1.60013	1.60251	1.60490	1.60729	1.60968
42	1.61119	1.61365	1.61611	1.61858	1.62105	1.62352	1.62600	1.62848
43	1.62959	1.63214	1.63469	1.63725	1.63980	1.64236	1.64493	1.64749
44	1.64820	1.65084	1.65348	1.65613	1.65877	1.66142	1.66408	1.66673
45	1.66703	1.66975	1.67249	1.67522	1.67796	1.68070	1.68345	1.68620
46	1.68607	1.68889	1.69171	1.69454	1.69737	1.70021	1.70305	1.70589
47	1.70532	1.70824	1.71116	1.71408	1.71701	1.71994	1.72287	1.72581
48	1.72480	1.72781	1.73083	1.73385	1.73687	1.73990	1.74293	1.74597
60	1.97662	1.98094	1.98526	1.98959	1.99393	1.99827	2.00263	2.00699
72	2.26521	2.27114	2.27709	2.28305	2.28903	2.29502	2.30102	2.30703
84	2.59593	2.60386	2.61182	2.61980	2.62781	2.63583	2.64387	2.65193
96	2.97493	2.98533	2.99576	3.00623	3.01672	3.02725	3.03781	3.04840
108	3.40927	3.42268	3.43614	3.44964	3.46320	3.47679	3.49044	3.50413
120	3.90702	3.92410	3.94125	3.95847	3.97575	3.99310	4.01052	4.02800
132	4.47745	4.49899	4.52062	4.54234	4.56416	4.58607	4.60808	4.63019
144	5.13116	5.15809	5.18515	5.21234	5.23965	5.26711	5.29469	5.32240
156	5.88031	5.91375	5.94736	5.98115	6.01512	6.04927	6.08360	6.11810
168	6.73883	6.78011	6.82163	6.86337	6.90536	6.94759	6.99005	7.03276
180	7.72270	7.77340	7.82440	7.87572	7.92736	7.97930	8.03157	8.08416
192	8.85022	8.91220	8.97459	9.03739	9.10060	9.16423	9.22827	9.29274
204	10.14235	10.21784	10.29386	10.37041	10.44749	10.52512	10.60329	10.68200
216	11.62313	11.71475	11.80705	11.90004	11.99372	12.08810	12.18318	12.27896
228	13.32011	13.43096	13.54269	13.65530	13.76879	13.88318	13.99847	14.11466
240	15.26484	15.39860	15.53347	15.66945	15.80657	15.94483	16.08424	16.22481
252	17.49351	17.65449	17.81688	17.98070	18.14595	18.31264	18.48079	18.65041
264	20.04756	20.24088	20.43597	20.63285	20.83155	21.03207	21.23443	21.43865
276	22.97451	23.20616	23.44005	23.67620	23.91462	24.15533	24.39836	24.64373
288	26.32879	26.60587	26.88574	27.16844	27.45398	27.74240	28.03372	28.32797
300	30.17279	30.50363	30.83795	31.17578	31.51717	31.86214	32.21074	32.56300
312	34.57802	34.97241	35.37112	35.77421	36.18171	36.59367	37.01014	37.43117
324	39.62641	40.09587	40.57068	41.05091	41.53660	42.02783	42.52465	43.02713
336	45.41186	45.96991	46.53457	47.10591	47.68402	48.26897	48.86083	49.45968
348	52.04199	52.70450	53.37515	54.05404	54.74126	55.43691	56.14109	56.85390
360	59.64012	60.42571	61.22130	62.02701	62.84296	63.66929	64.50611	65.35356
420	117.88583	119.69943	121.54011	123.40828	125.30433	127.22867	129.18170	131.16385
480	233.01544	237.11682	241.28855	245.53181	249.84780	254.23772	258.70281	263.24433

SINGLE DEPOSIT

NUMBER OF MONTHS	EFFECTIVE ANNUAL YIELD							
	15.00%	15.05%	15.10%	15.15%	15.20%	15.25%	15.30%	15.35%
1	1.01171	1.01175	1.01179	1.01182	1.01186	1.01190	1.01193	1.01197
2	1.02357	1.02364	1.02372	1.02379	1.02386	1.02394	1.02401	1.02409
3	1.03556	1.03567	1.03578	1.03590	1.03601	1.03612	1.03623	1.03635
4	1.04769	1.04784	1.04799	1.04814	1.04830	1.04845	1.04860	1.04875
5	1.05996	1.06016	1.06035	1.06054	1.06073	1.06092	1.06111	1.06131
6	1.07238	1.07261	1.07285	1.07308	1.07331	1.07355	1.07378	1.07401
7	1.08494	1.08522	1.08549	1.08577	1.08604	1.08632	1.08659	1.08687
8	1.09765	1.09797	1.09829	1.09861	1.09893	1.09924	1.09956	1.09988
9	1.11051	1.11087	1.11124	1.11160	1.11196	1.11232	1.11268	1.11305
10	1.12352	1.12393	1.12434	1.12474	1.12515	1.12556	1.12596	1.12637
11	1.13668	1.13714	1.13759	1.13804	1.13850	1.13895	1.13940	1.13985
12	1.15000	1.15050	1.15100	1.15150	1.15200	1.15250	1.15300	1.15350
13	1.16347	1.16402	1.16457	1.16512	1.16566	1.16621	1.16676	1.16731
14	1.17710	1.17770	1.17830	1.17889	1.17949	1.18009	1.18069	1.18128
15	1.19089	1.19154	1.19219	1.19283	1.19348	1.19413	1.19478	1.19542
16	1.20484	1.20554	1.20624	1.20694	1.20764	1.20834	1.20904	1.20973
17	1.21896	1.21971	1.22046	1.22121	1.22196	1.22271	1.22346	1.22422
18	1.23324	1.23404	1.23485	1.23565	1.23646	1.23726	1.23807	1.23887
19	1.24768	1.24854	1.24940	1.25026	1.25112	1.25198	1.25284	1.25370
20	1.26230	1.26322	1.26413	1.26505	1.26596	1.26688	1.26779	1.26871
21	1.27709	1.27806	1.27903	1.28001	1.28098	1.28195	1.28293	1.28390
22	1.29205	1.29308	1.29411	1.29514	1.29617	1.29720	1.29824	1.29927
23	1.30719	1.30828	1.30937	1.31046	1.31155	1.31264	1.31373	1.31482
24	1.32250	1.32365	1.32480	1.32595	1.32710	1.32826	1.32941	1.33056
25	1.33799	1.33921	1.34042	1.34163	1.34285	1.34406	1.34527	1.34649
26	1.35367	1.35494	1.35622	1.35750	1.35877	1.36005	1.36133	1.36261
27	1.36953	1.37087	1.37221	1.37355	1.37489	1.37623	1.37758	1.37892
28	1.38557	1.38698	1.38838	1.38979	1.39120	1.39261	1.39402	1.39543
29	1.40180	1.40327	1.40475	1.40622	1.40770	1.40918	1.41066	1.41213
30	1.41822	1.41977	1.42131	1.42285	1.42440	1.42594	1.42749	1.42904
31	1.43484	1.43645	1.43806	1.43968	1.44129	1.44291	1.44453	1.44615
32	1.45165	1.45333	1.45502	1.45670	1.45839	1.46008	1.46177	1.46346
33	1.46865	1.47041	1.47217	1.47393	1.47569	1.47745	1.47921	1.48098
34	1.48586	1.48769	1.48952	1.49136	1.49319	1.49503	1.49687	1.49871
35	1.50326	1.50517	1.50708	1.50899	1.51090	1.51282	1.51473	1.51665
36	1.52088	1.52286	1.52485	1.52683	1.52882	1.53082	1.53281	1.53480
37	1.53869	1.54076	1.54282	1.54489	1.54696	1.54903	1.55110	1.55318
38	1.55672	1.55886	1.56101	1.56316	1.56531	1.56746	1.56961	1.57177
39	1.57495	1.57718	1.57941	1.58164	1.58387	1.58611	1.58835	1.59059
40	1.59340	1.59572	1.59803	1.60034	1.60266	1.60498	1.60730	1.60963
41	1.61207	1.61447	1.61687	1.61927	1.62167	1.62408	1.62649	1.62890
42	1.63096	1.63344	1.63593	1.63841	1.64091	1.64340	1.64590	1.64840
43	1.65006	1.65264	1.65521	1.65779	1.66037	1.66295	1.66554	1.66813
44	1.66939	1.67206	1.67472	1.67739	1.68006	1.68274	1.68542	1.68810
45	1.68895	1.69171	1.69446	1.69723	1.69999	1.70276	1.70553	1.70831
46	1.70874	1.71159	1.71444	1.71730	1.72016	1.72302	1.72589	1.72876
47	1.72875	1.73170	1.73465	1.73760	1.74056	1.74352	1.74648	1.74945
48	1.74901	1.75205	1.75510	1.75815	1.76121	1.76426	1.76733	1.77040
60	2.01136	2.01573	2.02012	2.02451	2.02891	2.03332	2.03773	2.04215
72	2.31306	2.31910	2.32516	2.33122	2.33730	2.34340	2.34950	2.35562
84	2.66002	2.66813	2.67625	2.68440	2.69257	2.70076	2.70898	2.71721
96	3.05902	3.06968	3.08037	3.09109	3.10184	3.11263	3.12345	3.13430
108	3.51788	3.53167	3.54550	3.55939	3.57332	3.58731	3.60134	3.61542
120	4.04556	4.06318	4.08087	4.09864	4.11647	4.13437	4.15234	4.17038
132	4.65239	4.67469	4.69709	4.71958	4.74217	4.76486	4.78765	4.81054
144	5.35025	5.37823	5.40635	5.43460	5.46298	5.49150	5.52016	5.54895
156	6.15279	6.18766	6.22270	6.25794	6.29335	6.32896	6.36474	6.40072
168	7.07571	7.11890	7.16233	7.20602	7.24994	7.29412	7.33855	7.38323
180	8.13706	8.19029	8.24385	8.29773	8.35194	8.40648	8.46135	8.51656
192	9.35762	9.42293	9.48867	9.55483	9.62143	9.68846	9.75594	9.82385
204	10.76126	10.84108	10.92146	11.00239	11.08389	11.16596	11.24859	11.33181
216	12.37545	12.47266	12.57059	12.66925	12.76864	12.86876	12.96963	13.07124
228	14.23177	14.34980	14.46875	14.58864	14.70947	14.83125	14.95398	15.07768
240	16.36654	16.50944	16.65354	16.79882	16.94531	17.09302	17.24194	17.39210
252	18.82152	18.99412	19.16822	19.34384	19.52100	19.69970	19.87996	20.06179
264	21.64475	21.85273	22.06262	22.27444	22.48819	22.70390	22.92159	23.14127
276	24.89146	25.14157	25.39408	25.64901	25.90640	26.16625	26.42859	26.69345
288	28.62518	28.92537	29.22858	29.53484	29.84417	30.15660	30.47217	30.79090
300	32.91865	33.27864	33.64210	34.00937	34.38048	34.75548	35.13441	35.51730
312	37.85680	38.28708	38.72206	39.16179	39.60632	40.05570	40.50998	40.96921
324	43.53531	44.04928	44.56909	45.09480	45.62648	46.16419	46.70800	47.25798
336	50.06561	50.67870	51.29902	51.92666	52.56170	53.20423	53.85433	54.51208
348	57.57545	58.30584	59.04517	59.79355	60.55108	61.31787	62.09404	62.87969
360	66.21177	67.08087	67.96099	68.85227	69.75484	70.66885	71.59443	72.53172
420	133.17552	135.21716	137.28919	139.39204	141.52617	143.69203	145.89008	148.12077
480	267.86355	272.56176	277.34028	282.20044	287.14361	292.17117	297.28452	302.48508

SINGLE DEPOSIT

EFFECTIVE ANNUAL YIELD

NUMBER OF MONTHS	15.40%	15.45%	15.50%	15.55%	15.60%	15.65%	15.70%	15.75%
1	1.01201	1.01204	1.01208	1.01212	1.01215	1.01219	1.01223	1.01226
2	1.02416	1.02423	1.02431	1.02438	1.02446	1.02453	1.02460	1.02468
3	1.03646	1.03657	1.03668	1.03679	1.03691	1.03702	1.03713	1.03724
4	1.04890	1.04905	1.04921	1.04936	1.04951	1.04966	1.04981	1.04996
5	1.06150	1.06169	1.06188	1.06207	1.06226	1.06246	1.06265	1.06284
6	1.07424	1.07448	1.07471	1.07494	1.07517	1.07541	1.07564	1.07587
7	1.08714	1.08742	1.08769	1.08797	1.08824	1.08852	1.08879	1.08907
8	1.10020	1.10051	1.10083	1.10115	1.10147	1.10179	1.10210	1.10242
9	1.11341	1.11377	1.11413	1.11449	1.11485	1.11522	1.11558	1.11594
10	1.12678	1.12718	1.12759	1.12800	1.12840	1.12881	1.12922	1.12962
11	1.14031	1.14076	1.14121	1.14167	1.14212	1.14257	1.14302	1.14348
12	1.15400	1.15450	1.15500	1.15550	1.15600	1.15650	1.15700	1.15750
13	1.16786	1.16841	1.16895	1.16950	1.17005	1.17060	1.17115	1.17169
14	1.18188	1.18248	1.18308	1.18367	1.18427	1.18487	1.18547	1.18606
15	1.19607	1.19672	1.19737	1.19802	1.19866	1.19931	1.19996	1.20061
16	1.21043	1.21113	1.21183	1.21253	1.21323	1.21393	1.21463	1.21533
17	1.22497	1.22572	1.22647	1.22722	1.22798	1.22873	1.22948	1.23024
18	1.23968	1.24048	1.24129	1.24210	1.24290	1.24371	1.24451	1.24532
19	1.25456	1.25542	1.25628	1.25715	1.25801	1.25887	1.25973	1.26059
20	1.26963	1.27054	1.27146	1.27238	1.27330	1.27422	1.27513	1.27605
21	1.28487	1.28585	1.28682	1.28780	1.28877	1.28975	1.29072	1.29170
22	1.30030	1.30133	1.30237	1.30340	1.30444	1.30547	1.30651	1.30754
23	1.31591	1.31701	1.31810	1.31920	1.32029	1.32138	1.32248	1.32358
24	1.33172	1.33287	1.33402	1.33518	1.33634	1.33749	1.33865	1.33981
25	1.34771	1.34892	1.35014	1.35136	1.35258	1.35380	1.35502	1.35624
26	1.36389	1.36517	1.36645	1.36773	1.36902	1.37030	1.37158	1.37287
27	1.38027	1.38161	1.38296	1.38431	1.38566	1.38700	1.38835	1.38970
28	1.39684	1.39825	1.39967	1.40108	1.40250	1.40391	1.40533	1.40675
29	1.41361	1.41509	1.41658	1.41806	1.41954	1.42103	1.42251	1.42400
30	1.43059	1.43214	1.43369	1.43524	1.43679	1.43835	1.43990	1.44146
31	1.44777	1.44939	1.45101	1.45263	1.45426	1.45588	1.45751	1.45914
32	1.46515	1.46684	1.46854	1.47023	1.47193	1.47363	1.47533	1.47703
33	1.48274	1.48451	1.48628	1.48805	1.48982	1.49159	1.49337	1.49514
34	1.50055	1.50239	1.50423	1.50608	1.50793	1.50978	1.51163	1.51348
35	1.51857	1.52049	1.52241	1.52433	1.52625	1.52818	1.53011	1.53204
36	1.53680	1.53880	1.54080	1.54280	1.54480	1.54681	1.54882	1.55083
37	1.55525	1.55733	1.55941	1.56150	1.56358	1.56567	1.56775	1.56984
38	1.57393	1.57609	1.57825	1.58042	1.58258	1.58475	1.58692	1.58909
39	1.59283	1.59507	1.59732	1.59957	1.60182	1.60407	1.60632	1.60858
40	1.61195	1.61428	1.61662	1.61895	1.62129	1.62362	1.62597	1.62831
41	1.63131	1.63373	1.63614	1.63857	1.64099	1.64342	1.64585	1.64828
42	1.65090	1.65340	1.65591	1.65842	1.66093	1.66345	1.66597	1.66849
43	1.67072	1.67332	1.67592	1.67852	1.68112	1.68373	1.68634	1.68895
44	1.69078	1.69347	1.69616	1.69886	1.70155	1.70425	1.70696	1.70966
45	1.71109	1.71387	1.71665	1.71944	1.72223	1.72503	1.72783	1.73063
46	1.73163	1.73451	1.73739	1.74028	1.74316	1.74606	1.74895	1.75185
47	1.75242	1.75540	1.75838	1.76136	1.76435	1.76734	1.77034	1.77333
48	1.77347	1.77654	1.77962	1.78271	1.78579	1.78889	1.79198	1.79508
60	2.04658	2.05102	2.05546	2.05992	2.06438	2.06885	2.07332	2.07781
72	2.36176	2.36790	2.37406	2.38023	2.38642	2.39262	2.39883	2.40506
84	2.72547	2.73374	2.74204	2.75036	2.75870	2.76707	2.77545	2.78386
96	3.14519	3.15611	3.16706	3.17804	3.18906	3.20011	3.21120	3.22232
108	3.62955	3.64372	3.65795	3.67223	3.68655	3.70093	3.71535	3.72983
120	4.18850	4.20668	4.22493	4.24326	4.26166	4.28012	4.29866	4.31728
132	4.83352	4.85661	4.87980	4.90309	4.92647	4.94996	4.97356	4.99725
144	5.57789	5.60696	5.63617	5.66552	5.69500	5.72463	5.75440	5.78432
156	6.43688	6.47323	6.50977	6.54650	6.58342	6.62054	6.65784	6.69535
168	7.42816	7.47335	7.51879	7.56448	7.61044	7.65665	7.70313	7.74986
180	8.57210	8.62798	8.68420	8.74076	8.79767	8.85492	8.91252	8.97047
192	9.89220	9.96100	10.03025	10.09995	10.17010	10.24071	10.31178	10.38331
204	11.41560	11.49998	11.58494	11.67049	11.75664	11.84338	11.93073	12.01869
216	13.17360	13.27672	13.38060	13.48525	13.59067	13.69687	13.80386	13.91163
228	15.20234	15.32798	15.45460	15.58221	15.71082	15.84044	15.97106	16.10271
240	17.54350	17.69615	17.85006	18.00524	18.16171	18.31946	18.47852	18.63889
252	20.24520	20.43020	20.61682	20.80506	20.99493	21.18646	21.37965	21.57451
264	23.36296	23.58667	23.81243	24.04025	24.27014	24.50214	24.73625	24.97250
276	26.96085	27.23081	27.50335	27.77850	28.05629	28.33672	28.61984	28.90567
288	31.11282	31.43797	31.76637	32.09806	32.43307	32.77142	33.11316	33.45831
300	35.90420	36.29514	36.69016	37.08931	37.49263	37.90015	38.31192	38.72799
312	41.43344	41.90273	42.37713	42.85670	43.34147	43.83152	44.32690	44.82765
324	47.81419	48.37671	48.94559	49.52091	50.10274	50.69116	51.28622	51.88801
336	55.17758	55.85091	56.53216	57.22142	57.91877	58.62432	59.33816	60.06037
348	63.67493	64.47987	65.29464	66.11935	66.95410	67.79903	68.65425	69.51988
360	73.48087	74.44201	75.41531	76.40090	77.39894	78.40958	79.43296	80.46926
420	150.38458	152.68199	155.01347	157.37953	159.78065	162.21735	164.69013	167.19951
480	307.77430	313.15366	318.62465	324.18879	329.84763	335.60273	341.45569	347.40814

34

SINGLE DEPOSIT

EFFECTIVE ANNUAL YIELD

NUMBER OF MONTHS	15.80%	15.85%	15.90%	15.95%	16.00%	16.05%	16.10%	16.15%
1	1.01230	1.01234	1.01237	1.01241	1.01245	1.01248	1.01252	1.01255
2	1.02475	1.02482	1.02490	1.02497	1.02505	1.02512	1.02519	1.02527
3	1.03735	1.03747	1.03758	1.03769	1.03780	1.03791	1.03803	1.03814
4	1.05011	1.05026	1.05042	1.05057	1.05072	1.05087	1.05102	1.05117
5	1.06303	1.06322	1.06341	1.06360	1.06379	1.06398	1.06418	1.06437
6	1.07610	1.07634	1.07657	1.07680	1.07703	1.07727	1.07750	1.07773
7	1.08934	1.08961	1.08989	1.09016	1.09044	1.09071	1.09099	1.09126
8	1.10274	1.10306	1.10337	1.10369	1.10401	1.10432	1.10464	1.10496
9	1.11630	1.11666	1.11702	1.11739	1.11775	1.11811	1.11847	1.11883
10	1.13003	1.13044	1.13084	1.13125	1.13166	1.13206	1.13247	1.13288
11	1.14393	1.14438	1.14484	1.14529	1.14574	1.14619	1.14665	1.14710
12	1.15800	1.15850	1.15900	1.15950	1.16000	1.16050	1.16100	1.16150
13	1.17224	1.17279	1.17334	1.17389	1.17444	1.17498	1.17553	1.17608
14	1.18666	1.18726	1.18786	1.18845	1.18905	1.18965	1.19025	1.19085
15	1.20126	1.20190	1.20255	1.20320	1.20385	1.20450	1.20515	1.20580
16	1.21603	1.21673	1.21743	1.21813	1.21883	1.21953	1.22023	1.22093
17	1.23099	1.23174	1.23249	1.23325	1.23400	1.23475	1.23551	1.23626
18	1.24613	1.24694	1.24774	1.24855	1.24936	1.25017	1.25097	1.25178
19	1.26146	1.26232	1.26318	1.26404	1.26491	1.26577	1.26663	1.26750
20	1.27697	1.27789	1.27881	1.27973	1.28065	1.28157	1.28249	1.28341
21	1.29268	1.29365	1.29463	1.29561	1.29659	1.29756	1.29854	1.29952
22	1.30858	1.30961	1.31065	1.31169	1.31272	1.31376	1.31480	1.31584
23	1.32467	1.32577	1.32686	1.32796	1.32906	1.33016	1.33126	1.33236
24	1.34096	1.34212	1.34328	1.34444	1.34560	1.34676	1.34792	1.34908
25	1.35746	1.35868	1.35990	1.36112	1.36235	1.36357	1.36479	1.36602
26	1.37415	1.37544	1.37673	1.37801	1.37930	1.38059	1.38188	1.38317
27	1.39105	1.39241	1.39376	1.39511	1.39647	1.39782	1.39918	1.40053
28	1.40816	1.40958	1.41100	1.41242	1.41385	1.41527	1.41669	1.41812
29	1.42548	1.42697	1.42846	1.42995	1.43144	1.43293	1.43443	1.43592
30	1.44302	1.44458	1.44613	1.44769	1.44926	1.45082	1.45238	1.45395
31	1.46077	1.46240	1.46403	1.46566	1.46729	1.46893	1.47056	1.47220
32	1.47873	1.48044	1.48214	1.48385	1.48555	1.48726	1.48897	1.49068
33	1.49692	1.49870	1.50048	1.50226	1.50404	1.50582	1.50761	1.50939
34	1.51533	1.51719	1.51904	1.52090	1.52276	1.52462	1.52648	1.52834
35	1.53397	1.53590	1.53784	1.53977	1.54171	1.54365	1.54559	1.54753
36	1.55284	1.55485	1.55686	1.55888	1.56090	1.56292	1.56494	1.56696
37	1.57194	1.57403	1.57612	1.57822	1.58032	1.58242	1.58453	1.58663
38	1.59127	1.59345	1.59563	1.59781	1.59999	1.60217	1.60436	1.60655
39	1.61084	1.61310	1.61537	1.61763	1.61990	1.62217	1.62444	1.62672
40	1.63065	1.63300	1.63535	1.63771	1.64006	1.64242	1.64478	1.64714
41	1.65071	1.65315	1.65559	1.65803	1.66047	1.66292	1.66537	1.66782
42	1.67101	1.67354	1.67607	1.67860	1.68114	1.68367	1.68621	1.68876
43	1.69157	1.69418	1.69681	1.69943	1.70206	1.70469	1.70732	1.70996
44	1.71237	1.71508	1.71780	1.72052	1.72324	1.72597	1.72869	1.73143
45	1.73343	1.73624	1.73905	1.74187	1.74469	1.74751	1.75033	1.75316
46	1.75475	1.75766	1.76057	1.76348	1.76640	1.76932	1.77224	1.77517
47	1.77634	1.77934	1.78235	1.78537	1.78838	1.79140	1.79443	1.79746
48	1.79818	1.80129	1.80440	1.80752	1.81064	1.81376	1.81689	1.82002
60	2.08230	2.08680	2.09130	2.09582	2.10034	2.10487	2.10941	2.11396
72	2.41130	2.41755	2.42382	2.43010	2.43640	2.44270	2.44903	2.45536
84	2.79229	2.80074	2.80921	2.81770	2.82622	2.83476	2.84332	2.85190
96	3.23347	3.24465	3.25587	3.26713	3.27841	3.28974	3.30109	3.31248
108	3.74436	3.75893	3.77356	3.78823	3.80296	3.81774	3.83257	3.84745
120	4.33596	4.35472	4.37355	4.39246	4.41144	4.43049	4.44961	4.46881
132	5.02105	5.04494	5.06895	5.09305	5.11726	5.14158	5.16600	5.19053
144	5.81437	5.84457	5.87491	5.90540	5.93603	5.96680	5.99773	6.02880
156	6.73304	6.77093	6.80902	6.84731	6.88579	6.92448	6.96336	7.00245
168	7.79686	7.84413	7.89166	7.93945	7.98752	8.03585	8.08446	8.13334
180	9.02877	9.08742	9.14643	9.20579	9.26552	9.32561	9.38606	9.44688
192	10.45531	10.52778	10.60071	10.67412	10.74800	10.82237	10.89721	10.97255
204	12.10725	12.19643	12.28622	12.37664	12.46768	12.55936	12.65167	12.74461
216	14.02020	14.12956	14.23973	14.35072	14.46251	14.57514	14.68858	14.80287
228	16.23539	16.36910	16.50385	16.63965	16.77652	16.91444	17.05345	17.19353
240	18.80058	18.96360	19.12796	19.29368	19.46076	19.62921	19.79905	19.97029
252	21.77107	21.96933	22.16931	22.37102	22.57448	22.77970	22.98670	23.19549
264	25.21090	25.45147	25.69423	25.93920	26.18640	26.43584	26.68756	26.94156
276	29.19422	29.48553	29.77961	30.07650	30.37622	30.67880	30.98425	31.29262
288	33.80691	34.15898	34.51457	34.87370	35.23642	35.60274	35.97272	36.34638
300	39.14840	39.57318	40.00239	40.43606	40.87424	41.31698	41.76433	42.21632
312	45.33384	45.84553	46.36277	46.88561	47.41412	47.94836	48.48838	49.03425
324	52.49659	53.11205	53.73445	54.36387	55.00038	55.64407	56.29501	56.95329
336	60.79105	61.53030	62.27822	63.03490	63.80044	64.57495	65.35851	66.15124
348	70.39604	71.28286	72.18046	73.08897	74.00851	74.93923	75.88123	76.83467
360	81.51861	82.58119	83.65715	84.74666	85.84988	86.96697	88.09811	89.24347
420	169.74601	172.33018	174.95254	177.61366	180.31407	183.05436	185.83508	188.65681
480	353.46171	359.61809	365.87896	372.24607	378.72116	385.30602	392.00246	398.81232

SINGLE DEPOSIT

EFFECTIVE ANNUAL YIELD

NUMBER OF MONTHS	16.20%	16.25%	16.30%	16.35%	16.40%	16.45%	16.50%	16.55%
1	1.01259	1.01263	1.01266	1.01270	1.01274	1.01277	1.01281	1.01284
2	1.02534	1.02541	1.02549	1.02556	1.02563	1.02571	1.02578	1.02585
3	1.03825	1.03836	1.03847	1.03858	1.03870	1.03881	1.03892	1.03903
4	1.05132	1.05147	1.05162	1.05177	1.05192	1.05207	1.05223	1.05238
5	1.06456	1.06475	1.06494	1.06513	1.06532	1.06551	1.06570	1.06589
6	1.07796	1.07819	1.07842	1.07866	1.07889	1.07912	1.07935	1.07958
7	1.09153	1.09181	1.09208	1.09235	1.09263	1.09290	1.09318	1.09345
8	1.10528	1.10559	1.10591	1.10623	1.10654	1.10686	1.10718	1.10749
9	1.11919	1.11955	1.11991	1.12028	1.12064	1.12100	1.12136	1.12172
10	1.13328	1.13369	1.13410	1.13450	1.13491	1.13531	1.13572	1.13613
11	1.14755	1.14800	1.14846	1.14891	1.14936	1.14981	1.15027	1.15072
12	1.16200	1.16250	1.16300	1.16350	1.16400	1.16450	1.16500	1.16550
13	1.17663	1.17718	1.17773	1.17828	1.17882	1.17937	1.17992	1.18047
14	1.19144	1.19204	1.19264	1.19324	1.19384	1.19444	1.19503	1.19563
15	1.20645	1.20709	1.20774	1.20839	1.20904	1.20969	1.21034	1.21099
16	1.22164	1.22234	1.22304	1.22374	1.22444	1.22514	1.22584	1.22654
17	1.23702	1.23777	1.23852	1.23928	1.24003	1.24079	1.24154	1.24230
18	1.25259	1.25340	1.25421	1.25502	1.25583	1.25664	1.25744	1.25825
19	1.26836	1.26923	1.27009	1.27095	1.27182	1.27268	1.27355	1.27442
20	1.28433	1.28525	1.28617	1.28710	1.28802	1.28894	1.28986	1.29078
21	1.30050	1.30148	1.30246	1.30344	1.30442	1.30540	1.30638	1.30736
22	1.31688	1.31791	1.31895	1.31999	1.32103	1.32207	1.32311	1.32416
23	1.33346	1.33456	1.33566	1.33676	1.33786	1.33896	1.34006	1.34116
24	1.35024	1.35141	1.35257	1.35373	1.35490	1.35606	1.35722	1.35839
25	1.36724	1.36847	1.36970	1.37092	1.37215	1.37338	1.37461	1.37584
26	1.38446	1.38575	1.38704	1.38833	1.38963	1.39092	1.39221	1.39351
27	1.40189	1.40325	1.40461	1.40596	1.40732	1.40868	1.41005	1.41141
28	1.41954	1.42097	1.42239	1.42382	1.42525	1.42668	1.42811	1.42954
29	1.43741	1.43891	1.44040	1.44190	1.44340	1.44490	1.44640	1.44790
30	1.45551	1.45708	1.45864	1.46021	1.46178	1.46335	1.46492	1.46650
31	1.47384	1.47547	1.47711	1.47876	1.48040	1.48204	1.48369	1.48533
32	1.49239	1.49411	1.49582	1.49754	1.49925	1.50097	1.50269	1.50441
33	1.51118	1.51297	1.51476	1.51655	1.51835	1.52014	1.52194	1.52373
34	1.53021	1.53208	1.53394	1.53581	1.53768	1.53956	1.54143	1.54330
35	1.54947	1.55142	1.55337	1.55532	1.55727	1.55922	1.56117	1.56313
36	1.56898	1.57101	1.57304	1.57507	1.57710	1.57913	1.58117	1.58320
37	1.58874	1.59085	1.59296	1.59507	1.59718	1.59930	1.60142	1.60354
38	1.60874	1.61093	1.61313	1.61533	1.61753	1.61973	1.62193	1.62414
39	1.62900	1.63127	1.63356	1.63584	1.63813	1.64041	1.64270	1.64500
40	1.64951	1.65187	1.65424	1.65661	1.65899	1.66136	1.66374	1.66613
41	1.67027	1.67273	1.67519	1.67765	1.68012	1.68258	1.68505	1.68753
42	1.69130	1.69385	1.69640	1.69896	1.70151	1.70407	1.70664	1.70920
43	1.71260	1.71524	1.71788	1.72053	1.72318	1.72584	1.72849	1.73115
44	1.73416	1.73690	1.73964	1.74238	1.74513	1.74788	1.75063	1.75339
45	1.75599	1.75883	1.76167	1.76451	1.76735	1.77020	1.77306	1.77591
46	1.77810	1.78104	1.78398	1.78692	1.78986	1.79281	1.79576	1.79872
47	1.80049	1.80353	1.80657	1.80961	1.81266	1.81571	1.81876	1.82182
48	1.82316	1.82630	1.82944	1.83259	1.83574	1.83890	1.84206	1.84522
60	2.11851	2.12307	2.12764	2.13222	2.13681	2.14140	2.14600	2.15061
72	2.46171	2.46807	2.47445	2.48084	2.48724	2.49366	2.50009	2.50653
84	2.86051	2.86913	2.87778	2.88645	2.89515	2.90387	2.91260	2.92137
96	3.32391	3.33537	3.34686	3.35839	3.36995	3.38155	3.39318	3.40485
108	3.86238	3.87736	3.89240	3.90749	3.92263	3.93782	3.95306	3.96835
120	4.48809	4.50744	4.52686	4.54636	4.56594	4.58559	4.60531	4.62512
132	5.21516	5.23989	5.26474	5.28969	5.31475	5.33992	5.36519	5.39057
144	6.06001	6.09138	6.12289	6.15455	6.18637	6.21833	6.25045	6.28271
156	7.04173	7.08123	7.12092	7.16082	7.20093	7.24125	7.28177	7.32250
168	8.18250	8.23193	8.28163	8.33162	8.38189	8.43243	8.48326	8.53438
180	9.50806	9.56961	9.63154	9.69384	9.75651	9.81957	9.88300	9.94682
192	11.04837	11.12468	11.20148	11.27878	11.35658	11.43489	11.51370	11.59302
204	12.83820	12.93244	13.02732	13.12286	13.21906	13.31593	13.41346	13.51166
216	14.91799	15.03396	15.15078	15.26845	15.38699	15.50640	15.62668	15.74784
228	17.33470	17.47698	17.62035	17.76484	17.91046	18.05720	18.20508	18.35411
240	20.14293	20.31698	20.49247	20.66939	20.84777	21.02761	21.20892	21.39171
252	23.40608	23.61849	23.83274	24.04884	24.26680	24.48665	24.70839	24.93204
264	27.19787	27.45650	27.71748	27.98083	28.24656	28.51470	28.78527	29.05829
276	31.60392	31.91818	32.23543	32.55569	32.87900	33.20537	33.53484	33.86744
288	36.72375	37.10488	37.48980	37.87855	38.27115	38.66765	39.06809	39.47250
300	42.67300	43.13443	43.60064	44.07169	44.54762	45.02848	45.51433	46.00520
312	49.58603	50.14377	50.70754	51.27741	51.85343	52.43567	53.02419	53.61906
324	57.61897	58.29214	58.97287	59.66127	60.35739	61.06134	61.77318	62.49302
336	66.95324	67.76461	68.58545	69.41588	70.25600	71.10593	71.96576	72.83561
348	77.79966	78.77636	79.76488	80.76538	81.77799	82.80285	83.84011	84.88991
360	90.40321	91.57751	92.76656	93.97052	95.18958	96.42392	97.67373	98.93919
420	191.52015	194.42569	197.37403	200.36579	203.40157	206.48202	209.60777	212.77947
480	405.73748	412.77982	419.94130	427.22387	434.62951	442.16027	449.81819	457.60537

SINGLE DEPOSIT

EFFECTIVE ANNUAL YIELD

NUMBER OF MONTHS	16.60%	16.65%	16.70%	16.75%	16.80%	16.85%	16.90%	16.95%
1	1.01288	1.01292	1.01295	1.01299	1.01303	1.01306	1.01310	1.01313
2	1.02593	1.02600	1.02607	1.02615	1.02622	1.02629	1.02637	1.02644
3	1.03914	1.03925	1.03936	1.03948	1.03959	1.03970	1.03981	1.03992
4	1.05253	1.05268	1.05283	1.05298	1.05313	1.05328	1.05343	1.05358
5	1.06608	1.06627	1.06646	1.06665	1.06684	1.06703	1.06723	1.06742
6	1.07981	1.08005	1.08028	1.08051	1.08074	1.08097	1.08120	1.08143
7	1.09372	1.09400	1.09427	1.09454	1.09482	1.09509	1.09536	1.09564
8	1.10781	1.10813	1.10844	1.10876	1.10908	1.10939	1.10971	1.11003
9	1.12208	1.12244	1.12280	1.12316	1.12352	1.12388	1.12424	1.12461
10	1.13653	1.13694	1.13735	1.13775	1.13816	1.13856	1.13897	1.13938
11	1.15117	1.15162	1.15208	1.15253	1.15298	1.15343	1.15389	1.15434
12	1.16600	1.16650	1.16700	1.16750	1.16800	1.16850	1.16900	1.16950
13	1.18102	1.18157	1.18212	1.18266	1.18321	1.18376	1.18431	1.18486
14	1.19623	1.19683	1.19743	1.19803	1.19862	1.19922	1.19982	1.20042
15	1.21164	1.21229	1.21294	1.21359	1.21424	1.21489	1.21554	1.21619
16	1.22725	1.22795	1.22865	1.22935	1.23005	1.23076	1.23146	1.23216
17	1.24305	1.24381	1.24456	1.24532	1.24607	1.24683	1.24759	1.24834
18	1.25906	1.25987	1.26068	1.26149	1.26230	1.26312	1.26393	1.26474
19	1.27528	1.27615	1.27701	1.27788	1.27875	1.27961	1.28048	1.28135
20	1.29171	1.29263	1.29355	1.29448	1.29540	1.29633	1.29725	1.29818
21	1.30835	1.30933	1.31031	1.31129	1.31228	1.31326	1.31424	1.31523
22	1.32520	1.32624	1.32728	1.32832	1.32937	1.33041	1.33146	1.33250
23	1.34227	1.34337	1.34447	1.34558	1.34668	1.34779	1.34889	1.35000
24	1.35956	1.36072	1.36189	1.36306	1.36422	1.36539	1.36656	1.36773
25	1.37707	1.37830	1.37953	1.38076	1.38199	1.38323	1.38446	1.38569
26	1.39481	1.39610	1.39740	1.39870	1.39999	1.40129	1.40259	1.40389
27	1.41277	1.41413	1.41550	1.41686	1.41823	1.41960	1.42096	1.42233
28	1.43097	1.43240	1.43383	1.43527	1.43670	1.43814	1.43957	1.44101
29	1.44940	1.45090	1.45241	1.45391	1.45542	1.45692	1.45843	1.45994
30	1.46807	1.46964	1.47122	1.47279	1.47437	1.47595	1.47753	1.47911
31	1.48698	1.48863	1.49027	1.49192	1.49358	1.49523	1.49688	1.49854
32	1.50613	1.50785	1.50958	1.51130	1.51303	1.51476	1.51649	1.51822
33	1.52553	1.52733	1.52913	1.53093	1.53274	1.53454	1.53635	1.53816
34	1.54518	1.54706	1.54894	1.55082	1.55270	1.55459	1.55647	1.55836
35	1.56508	1.56704	1.56900	1.57096	1.57293	1.57489	1.57686	1.57882
36	1.58524	1.58728	1.58932	1.59137	1.59341	1.59546	1.59751	1.59956
37	1.60566	1.60778	1.60991	1.61204	1.61417	1.61630	1.61843	1.62057
38	1.62634	1.62855	1.63076	1.63298	1.63519	1.63741	1.63963	1.64185
39	1.64729	1.64959	1.65189	1.65419	1.65649	1.65880	1.66111	1.66342
40	1.66851	1.67089	1.67328	1.67567	1.67807	1.68046	1.68286	1.68526
41	1.69000	1.69248	1.69496	1.69744	1.69992	1.70241	1.70490	1.70740
42	1.71177	1.71434	1.71691	1.71949	1.72207	1.72465	1.72723	1.72982
43	1.73382	1.73648	1.73915	1.74182	1.74450	1.74717	1.74985	1.75254
44	1.75615	1.75891	1.76168	1.76445	1.76722	1.76999	1.77277	1.77556
45	1.77877	1.78163	1.78450	1.78737	1.79024	1.79311	1.79599	1.79887
46	1.80168	1.80464	1.80761	1.81058	1.81356	1.81653	1.81951	1.82250
47	1.82489	1.82795	1.83102	1.83410	1.83718	1.84026	1.84335	1.84644
48	1.84839	1.85157	1.85474	1.85792	1.86111	1.86430	1.86749	1.87069
60	2.15523	2.15985	2.16448	2.16912	2.17377	2.17843	2.18309	2.18777
72	2.51299	2.51947	2.52595	2.53245	2.53897	2.54550	2.55204	2.55859
84	2.93015	2.93896	2.94779	2.95664	2.96551	2.97441	2.98333	2.99228
96	3.41655	3.42829	3.44007	3.45188	3.46372	3.47560	3.48752	3.49947
108	3.98370	3.99910	4.01456	4.03006	4.04562	4.06124	4.07691	4.09263
120	4.64500	4.66495	4.68499	4.70510	4.72529	4.74556	4.76590	4.78633
132	5.41607	5.44167	5.46738	5.49320	5.51914	5.54518	5.57134	5.59761
144	6.31513	6.34771	6.38043	6.41332	6.44635	6.47955	6.51290	6.54640
156	7.36345	7.40460	7.44597	7.48755	7.52934	7.57135	7.61358	7.65602
168	8.58578	8.63747	8.68944	8.74171	8.79427	8.84712	8.90027	8.95371
180	10.01102	10.07561	10.14058	10.20595	10.27171	10.33786	10.40442	10.47137
192	11.67285	11.75319	11.83406	11.91544	11.99735	12.07979	12.16276	12.24626
204	13.61054	13.71010	13.81035	13.91128	14.01291	14.11524	14.21827	14.32201
216	15.86989	15.99283	16.11667	16.24142	16.36708	16.49365	16.62116	16.74959
228	18.50429	18.65564	18.80816	18.96186	19.11675	19.27284	19.43013	19.58864
240	21.57600	21.76180	21.94912	22.13797	22.32836	22.52031	22.71382	22.90892
252	25.15762	25.38514	25.61462	25.84608	26.07953	26.31498	26.55246	26.79198
264	29.33379	29.61177	29.89227	30.17530	30.46089	30.74905	31.03982	31.33322
276	34.20319	34.54213	34.88427	35.22966	35.57832	35.93027	36.28555	36.64420
288	39.88092	40.29339	40.70995	41.13063	41.55547	41.98452	42.41781	42.85539
300	46.50116	47.00224	47.50851	48.02001	48.53679	49.05891	49.58642	50.11938
312	54.22035	54.82812	55.44243	56.06336	56.69097	57.32534	57.96653	58.61461
324	63.22093	63.95700	64.70132	65.45397	66.21506	66.98466	67.76287	68.54979
336	73.71560	74.60584	75.50644	76.41751	77.33919	78.27157	79.21480	80.16898
348	85.95239	87.02771	88.11601	89.21745	90.33217	91.46033	92.60210	93.75762
360	100.22049	101.51782	102.83138	104.16137	105.50797	106.87140	108.25185	109.64953
420	215.99777	219.26333	222.57683	225.93896	229.35040	232.81185	236.32403	239.88766
480	465.52394	473.57604	481.76389	490.08969	498.55573	507.16429	515.91772	524.81839

SINGLE DEPOSIT

EFFECTIVE ANNUAL YIELD

NUMBER OF MONTHS	17.00%	17.05%	17.10%	17.15%	17.20%	17.25%	17.30%	17.35%
1	1.01317	1.01321	1.01324	1.01328	1.01331	1.01335	1.01339	1.01342
2	1.02651	1.02659	1.02666	1.02673	1.02680	1.02688	1.02695	1.02702
3	1.04003	1.04014	1.04025	1.04036	1.04048	1.04059	1.04070	1.04081
4	1.05373	1.05388	1.05403	1.05418	1.05433	1.05448	1.05463	1.05478
5	1.06761	1.06780	1.06799	1.06818	1.06837	1.06856	1.06875	1.06893
6	1.08167	1.08190	1.08213	1.08236	1.08259	1.08282	1.08305	1.08328
7	1.09591	1.09618	1.09646	1.09673	1.09700	1.09728	1.09755	1.09782
8	1.11034	1.11066	1.11098	1.11129	1.11161	1.11192	1.11224	1.11256
9	1.12497	1.12533	1.12569	1.12605	1.12641	1.12677	1.12713	1.12749
10	1.13978	1.14019	1.14059	1.14100	1.14140	1.14181	1.14222	1.14262
11	1.15479	1.15524	1.15570	1.15615	1.15660	1.15705	1.15751	1.15796
12	1.17000	1.17050	1.17100	1.17150	1.17200	1.17250	1.17300	1.17350
13	1.18541	1.18596	1.18651	1.18705	1.18760	1.18815	1.18870	1.18925
14	1.20102	1.20162	1.20222	1.20282	1.20342	1.20401	1.20461	1.20521
15	1.21684	1.21749	1.21814	1.21879	1.21944	1.22009	1.22074	1.22139
16	1.23286	1.23356	1.23427	1.23497	1.23567	1.23638	1.23708	1.23778
17	1.24910	1.24985	1.25061	1.25137	1.25212	1.25288	1.25364	1.25440
18	1.26555	1.26636	1.26717	1.26798	1.26879	1.26961	1.27042	1.27123
19	1.28222	1.28308	1.28395	1.28482	1.28569	1.28656	1.28742	1.28829
20	1.29910	1.30003	1.30095	1.30188	1.30280	1.30373	1.30466	1.30559
21	1.31621	1.31719	1.31818	1.31916	1.32015	1.32114	1.32212	1.32311
22	1.33354	1.33459	1.33563	1.33668	1.33773	1.33877	1.33982	1.34087
23	1.35111	1.35221	1.35332	1.35443	1.35554	1.35665	1.35775	1.35886
24	1.36890	1.37007	1.37124	1.37241	1.37358	1.37476	1.37593	1.37710
25	1.38693	1.38816	1.38940	1.39063	1.39187	1.39311	1.39435	1.39559
26	1.40519	1.40649	1.40780	1.40910	1.41040	1.41171	1.41301	1.41432
27	1.42370	1.42507	1.42644	1.42781	1.42918	1.43055	1.43193	1.43330
28	1.44245	1.44389	1.44533	1.44677	1.44821	1.44965	1.45109	1.45254
29	1.46145	1.46295	1.46447	1.46598	1.46749	1.46900	1.47052	1.47203
30	1.48069	1.48227	1.48386	1.48544	1.48703	1.48861	1.49020	1.49179
31	1.50019	1.50185	1.50351	1.50517	1.50683	1.50849	1.51015	1.51181
32	1.51995	1.52168	1.52342	1.52515	1.52689	1.52862	1.53036	1.53210
33	1.53997	1.54178	1.54359	1.54540	1.54722	1.54903	1.55085	1.55267
34	1.56025	1.56214	1.56403	1.56592	1.56782	1.56971	1.57161	1.57351
35	1.58079	1.58277	1.58474	1.58671	1.58869	1.59067	1.59265	1.59463
36	1.60161	1.60367	1.60572	1.60778	1.60984	1.61190	1.61396	1.61603
37	1.62271	1.62484	1.62699	1.62913	1.63127	1.63342	1.63557	1.63772
38	1.64408	1.64630	1.64853	1.65076	1.65299	1.65523	1.65746	1.65970
39	1.66573	1.66804	1.67036	1.67268	1.67500	1.67732	1.67965	1.68198
40	1.68766	1.69007	1.69248	1.69489	1.69730	1.69972	1.70213	1.70455
41	1.70989	1.71239	1.71489	1.71739	1.71990	1.72241	1.72492	1.72743
42	1.73241	1.73500	1.73760	1.74020	1.74280	1.74540	1.74801	1.75062
43	1.75522	1.75791	1.76061	1.76330	1.76600	1.76870	1.77141	1.77411
44	1.77834	1.78113	1.78392	1.78671	1.78951	1.79231	1.79512	1.79792
45	1.80176	1.80465	1.80754	1.81044	1.81334	1.81624	1.81915	1.82206
46	1.82549	1.82848	1.83148	1.83448	1.83748	1.84049	1.84350	1.84651
47	1.84953	1.85263	1.85573	1.85883	1.86194	1.86506	1.86817	1.87129
48	1.87389	1.87709	1.88030	1.88352	1.88673	1.88995	1.89318	1.89641
60	2.19245	2.19714	2.20183	2.20654	2.21125	2.21597	2.22070	2.22544
72	2.56516	2.57175	2.57835	2.58496	2.59159	2.59823	2.60488	2.61155
84	3.00124	3.01023	3.01924	3.02828	3.03734	3.04642	3.05553	3.06466
96	3.51145	3.52348	3.53554	3.54763	3.55976	3.57193	3.58413	3.59637
108	4.10840	4.12423	4.14011	4.15605	4.17204	4.18809	4.20419	4.22034
120	4.80683	4.82741	4.84807	4.86881	4.88963	4.91053	4.93151	4.95257
132	5.62399	5.65048	5.67709	5.70381	5.73065	5.75760	5.78466	5.81185
144	6.58007	6.61389	6.64787	6.68202	6.71632	6.75078	6.78541	6.82020
156	7.69868	7.74156	7.78466	7.82798	7.87153	7.91529	7.95929	8.00351
168	9.00745	9.06149	9.11584	9.17048	9.22543	9.28068	9.33624	9.39211
180	10.53872	10.60648	10.67464	10.74322	10.81220	10.88160	10.95141	11.02164
192	12.33020	12.41488	12.50001	12.58568	12.67190	12.75868	12.84601	12.93390
204	14.42646	14.53162	14.63751	14.74412	14.85147	14.95955	15.06837	15.17793
216	16.87895	17.00926	17.14052	17.27274	17.40592	17.54007	17.67520	17.81130
228	19.74838	19.90934	20.07155	20.23502	20.39974	20.56573	20.73300	20.90156
240	23.10560	23.30389	23.50379	23.70532	23.90849	24.11332	24.31981	24.52799
252	27.03355	27.27720	27.52294	27.77078	28.02076	28.27287	28.52714	28.78359
264	31.62925	31.92796	32.22936	32.53347	32.84033	33.14994	33.46234	33.77754
276	37.00623	37.37168	37.74058	38.11297	38.48886	38.86830	39.25132	39.63795
288	43.29729	43.74355	44.19422	44.64934	45.10895	45.57309	46.04180	46.51513
300	50.65783	51.20183	51.75143	52.30670	52.86768	53.43444	54.00703	54.58551
312	59.26966	59.93174	60.60093	61.27730	61.96093	62.65188	63.35025	64.05609
324	69.34550	70.15010	70.96369	71.78636	72.61821	73.45933	74.30984	75.16982
336	81.13423	82.11069	83.09848	84.09772	85.10854	86.13107	87.16544	88.21179
348	94.92705	96.11056	97.30832	98.52047	99.74721	100.98868	102.24506	103.51653
360	111.06465	112.49741	113.94804	115.41674	116.90373	118.40923	119.93346	121.47665
420	243.50347	247.17220	250.89461	254.67145	258.50345	262.39152	266.33634	270.33874
480	533.86871	543.07114	552.42815	561.94229	571.61612	581.45225	591.45333	601.62207

38

SINGLE DEPOSIT

NUMBER OF MONTHS	EFFECTIVE ANNUAL YIELD							
	17.40%	17.45%	17.50%	17.55%	17.60%	17.65%	17.70%	17.75%
1	1.01346	1.01349	1.01353	1.01357	1.01360	1.01364	1.01367	1.01371
2	1.02710	1.02717	1.02724	1.02732	1.02739	1.02746	1.02753	1.02761
3	1.04092	1.04103	1.04114	1.04125	1.04136	1.04147	1.04158	1.04169
4	1.05493	1.05508	1.05523	1.05538	1.05553	1.05568	1.05583	1.05598
5	1.06912	1.06931	1.06950	1.06969	1.06988	1.07007	1.07026	1.07045
6	1.08351	1.08374	1.08397	1.08420	1.08444	1.08467	1.08490	1.08513
7	1.09809	1.09837	1.09864	1.09891	1.09919	1.09946	1.09973	1.10000
8	1.11287	1.11319	1.11350	1.11382	1.11414	1.11445	1.11477	1.11508
9	1.12785	1.12821	1.12857	1.12893	1.12929	1.12965	1.13001	1.13037
10	1.14303	1.14343	1.14384	1.14424	1.14465	1.14506	1.14546	1.14587
11	1.15841	1.15886	1.15931	1.15977	1.16022	1.16067	1.16112	1.16158
12	1.17400	1.17450	1.17500	1.17550	1.17600	1.17650	1.17700	1.17750
13	1.18980	1.19035	1.19090	1.19145	1.19200	1.19254	1.19309	1.19364
14	1.20581	1.20641	1.20701	1.20761	1.20821	1.20881	1.20941	1.21001
15	1.22204	1.22269	1.22334	1.22399	1.22464	1.22529	1.22594	1.22659
16	1.23849	1.23919	1.23989	1.24060	1.24130	1.24200	1.24271	1.24341
17	1.25515	1.25591	1.25667	1.25742	1.25818	1.25894	1.25970	1.26046
18	1.27204	1.27286	1.27367	1.27448	1.27530	1.27611	1.27692	1.27774
19	1.28916	1.29003	1.29090	1.29177	1.29264	1.29351	1.29438	1.29525
20	1.30651	1.30744	1.30837	1.30930	1.31022	1.31115	1.31208	1.31301
21	1.32410	1.32508	1.32607	1.32706	1.32805	1.32903	1.33002	1.33101
22	1.34191	1.34296	1.34401	1.34506	1.34611	1.34716	1.34821	1.34926
23	1.35997	1.36108	1.36219	1.36331	1.36442	1.36553	1.36664	1.36776
24	1.37828	1.37945	1.38062	1.38180	1.38298	1.38415	1.38533	1.38651
25	1.39682	1.39806	1.39930	1.40055	1.40179	1.40303	1.40427	1.40551
26	1.41562	1.41693	1.41824	1.41954	1.42085	1.42216	1.42347	1.42478
27	1.43467	1.43605	1.43743	1.43880	1.44018	1.44156	1.44294	1.44432
28	1.45398	1.45543	1.45687	1.45832	1.45977	1.46122	1.46267	1.46412
29	1.47355	1.47507	1.47658	1.47810	1.47962	1.48114	1.48267	1.48419
30	1.49338	1.49497	1.49656	1.49815	1.49975	1.50134	1.50294	1.50453
31	1.51348	1.51514	1.51681	1.51848	1.52015	1.52182	1.52349	1.52516
32	1.53385	1.53559	1.53733	1.53908	1.54082	1.54257	1.54432	1.54607
33	1.55449	1.55631	1.55813	1.55996	1.56178	1.56361	1.56544	1.56727
34	1.57541	1.57731	1.57921	1.58112	1.58302	1.58493	1.58684	1.58875
35	1.59661	1.59859	1.60058	1.60257	1.60456	1.60655	1.60854	1.61053
36	1.61810	1.62016	1.62223	1.62431	1.62638	1.62846	1.63053	1.63261
37	1.63987	1.64203	1.64418	1.64634	1.64850	1.65066	1.65283	1.65499
38	1.66194	1.66418	1.66643	1.66867	1.67092	1.67317	1.67543	1.67768
39	1.68431	1.68664	1.68897	1.69131	1.69365	1.69599	1.69834	1.70068
40	1.70697	1.70940	1.71183	1.71426	1.71669	1.71912	1.72156	1.72400
41	1.72995	1.73247	1.73499	1.73751	1.74004	1.74257	1.74510	1.74763
42	1.75323	1.75584	1.75846	1.76108	1.76370	1.76633	1.76896	1.77159
43	1.77682	1.77954	1.78225	1.78497	1.78769	1.79042	1.79315	1.79588
44	1.80073	1.80355	1.80637	1.80919	1.81201	1.81483	1.81766	1.82050
45	1.82497	1.82788	1.83080	1.83373	1.83665	1.83958	1.84252	1.84545
46	1.84953	1.85255	1.85557	1.85860	1.86164	1.86467	1.86771	1.87075
47	1.87442	1.87755	1.88068	1.88382	1.88696	1.89010	1.89325	1.89640
48	1.89964	1.90288	1.90613	1.90937	1.91262	1.91588	1.91914	1.92240
60	2.23018	2.23494	2.23970	2.24447	2.24924	2.25403	2.25882	2.26363
72	2.61823	2.62493	2.63164	2.63837	2.64511	2.65187	2.65864	2.66542
84	3.07381	3.08298	3.09218	3.10140	3.11065	3.11992	3.12921	3.13853
96	3.60865	3.62096	3.63331	3.64570	3.65813	3.67059	3.68308	3.69562
108	4.23656	4.25282	4.26914	4.28552	4.30196	4.31844	4.33499	4.35159
120	4.97372	4.99494	5.01624	5.03763	5.05910	5.08065	5.10228	5.12400
132	5.83914	5.86656	5.89409	5.92173	5.94949	5.97739	6.00539	6.03351
144	6.85515	6.89027	6.92555	6.96100	6.99661	7.03239	7.06834	7.10446
156	8.04795	8.09262	8.13752	8.18265	8.22802	8.27361	8.31944	8.36550
168	9.44829	9.50478	9.56159	9.61871	9.67615	9.73390	9.79198	9.85038
180	11.09230	11.16337	11.23487	11.30679	11.37915	11.45194	11.52516	11.59882
192	13.02236	13.11138	13.20097	13.29114	13.38188	13.47320	13.56511	13.65761
204	15.28825	15.39931	15.51114	15.62373	15.73709	15.85123	15.96614	16.08183
216	17.94840	18.08649	18.22559	18.36570	18.50682	18.64897	18.79214	18.93636
228	21.07142	21.24259	21.41507	21.58888	21.76402	21.94051	22.11835	22.29756
240	24.73785	24.94942	25.16271	25.37772	25.59449	25.81301	26.03330	26.25538
252	29.04223	29.30309	29.56618	29.83151	30.09912	30.36900	30.64120	30.91571
264	34.09558	34.41648	34.74026	35.06695	35.39656	35.72913	36.06469	36.40325
276	40.02822	40.42216	40.81981	41.22119	41.62636	42.03533	42.44814	42.86483
288	46.99312	47.47582	47.96327	48.45551	48.95260	49.45456	49.96146	50.47333
300	55.16993	55.76035	56.35684	56.95946	57.56825	58.18329	58.80464	59.43235
312	64.76900	65.49054	66.21929	66.95584	67.70026	68.45264	69.21306	69.98159
324	76.03939	76.91864	77.80767	78.70659	79.61551	80.53453	81.46377	82.40332
336	89.27024	90.34094	91.42401	92.51960	93.62784	94.74888	95.88286	97.02991
348	104.80326	106.10543	107.42321	108.75679	110.10634	111.47206	112.85412	114.25272
360	123.03903	124.62083	126.22227	127.84360	129.48506	131.14687	132.82930	134.53258
420	274.39955	278.51958	282.69969	286.94071	291.24351	295.60897	300.03796	304.53138
480	611.96118	622.47347	633.16174	644.02887	655.07778	666.31143	677.73281	689.34500

39

EFFECTIVE ANNUAL YIELD

NUMBER OF MONTHS	17.80%	17.85%	17.90%	18.00%	18.10%	18.20%	18.30%	18.40%
1	1.01375	1.01378	1.01382	1.01389	1.01396	1.01403	1.01410	1.01417
2	1.02768	1.02775	1.02782	1.02797	1.02811	1.02826	1.02840	1.02855
3	1.04180	1.04192	1.04203	1.04225	1.04247	1.04269	1.04291	1.04313
4	1.05612	1.05627	1.05642	1.05672	1.05702	1.05732	1.05762	1.05791
5	1.07064	1.07083	1.07102	1.07140	1.07178	1.07215	1.07253	1.07291
6	1.08536	1.08559	1.08582	1.08628	1.08674	1.08720	1.08766	1.08812
7	1.10028	1.10055	1.10082	1.10136	1.10191	1.10245	1.10300	1.10354
8	1.11540	1.11571	1.11603	1.11666	1.11729	1.11792	1.11855	1.11918
9	1.13073	1.13109	1.13145	1.13217	1.13289	1.13361	1.13433	1.13505
10	1.14627	1.14668	1.14708	1.14789	1.14870	1.14951	1.15033	1.15114
11	1.16203	1.16248	1.16293	1.16384	1.16474	1.16564	1.16655	1.16745
12	1.17800	1.17850	1.17900	1.18000	1.18100	1.18200	1.18300	1.18400
13	1.19419	1.19474	1.19529	1.19639	1.19749	1.19859	1.19968	1.20078
14	1.21061	1.21121	1.21181	1.21300	1.21420	1.21540	1.21660	1.21780
15	1.22725	1.22790	1.22855	1.22985	1.23115	1.23246	1.23376	1.23506
16	1.24411	1.24482	1.24552	1.24693	1.24834	1.24975	1.25116	1.25257
17	1.26122	1.26197	1.26273	1.26425	1.26577	1.26729	1.26881	1.27033
18	1.27855	1.27936	1.28018	1.28181	1.28344	1.28507	1.28670	1.28833
19	1.29612	1.29700	1.29787	1.29961	1.30135	1.30310	1.30485	1.30659
20	1.31394	1.31487	1.31580	1.31766	1.31952	1.32138	1.32325	1.32511
21	1.33200	1.33299	1.33398	1.33596	1.33794	1.33993	1.34191	1.34390
22	1.35031	1.35136	1.35241	1.35451	1.35662	1.35873	1.36083	1.36294
23	1.36887	1.36998	1.37110	1.37333	1.37556	1.37779	1.38003	1.38226
24	1.38768	1.38886	1.39004	1.39240	1.39476	1.39712	1.39949	1.40186
25	1.40676	1.40800	1.40925	1.41174	1.41423	1.41673	1.41923	1.42173
26	1.42609	1.42741	1.42872	1.43135	1.43397	1.43661	1.43924	1.44188
27	1.44570	1.44708	1.44846	1.45122	1.45399	1.45676	1.45954	1.46232
28	1.46557	1.46702	1.46847	1.47138	1.47429	1.47721	1.48012	1.48304
29	1.48571	1.48724	1.48876	1.49181	1.49487	1.49793	1.50100	1.50407
30	1.50613	1.50773	1.50933	1.51253	1.51574	1.51895	1.52217	1.52538
31	1.52683	1.52851	1.53019	1.53354	1.53690	1.54026	1.54363	1.54701
32	1.54782	1.54957	1.55133	1.55484	1.55835	1.56188	1.56540	1.56893
33	1.56910	1.57093	1.57276	1.57643	1.58011	1.58379	1.58748	1.59117
34	1.59066	1.59258	1.59449	1.59833	1.60217	1.60601	1.60987	1.61373
35	1.61253	1.61452	1.61652	1.62053	1.62453	1.62855	1.63257	1.63660
36	1.63469	1.63677	1.63886	1.64303	1.64721	1.65140	1.65560	1.65980
37	1.65716	1.65933	1.66150	1.66585	1.67021	1.67457	1.67894	1.68332
38	1.67994	1.68220	1.68448	1.68899	1.69352	1.69807	1.70262	1.70718
39	1.70303	1.70538	1.70773	1.71244	1.71717	1.72190	1.72663	1.73138
40	1.72644	1.72888	1.73133	1.73623	1.74114	1.74606	1.75099	1.75592
41	1.75017	1.75271	1.75525	1.76034	1.76544	1.77056	1.77568	1.78081
42	1.77422	1.77686	1.77950	1.78479	1.79009	1.79540	1.80072	1.80605
43	1.79861	1.80135	1.80409	1.80958	1.81508	1.82059	1.82612	1.83165
44	1.82333	1.82617	1.82902	1.83471	1.84042	1.84614	1.85187	1.85762
45	1.84840	1.85134	1.85429	1.86019	1.86611	1.87204	1.87799	1.88395
46	1.87380	1.87685	1.87991	1.88603	1.89216	1.89831	1.90447	1.91065
47	1.89956	1.90272	1.90588	1.91222	1.91857	1.92495	1.93133	1.93773
48	1.92567	1.92894	1.93221	1.93878	1.94536	1.95196	1.95857	1.96520
60	2.26844	2.27325	2.27808	2.28776	2.29747	2.30721	2.31699	2.32680
72	2.67222	2.67903	2.68586	2.69955	2.71331	2.72712	2.74100	2.75493
84	3.14787	3.15724	3.16662	3.18547	3.20442	3.22346	3.24260	3.26183
96	3.70819	3.72080	3.73345	3.75886	3.78442	3.81013	3.83599	3.86201
108	4.36825	4.38497	4.40174	4.43545	4.46940	4.50357	4.53798	4.57262
120	5.14580	5.16768	5.18965	5.23384	5.27836	5.32322	5.36843	5.41398
132	6.06175	6.09011	6.11860	6.17593	6.23374	6.29205	6.35085	6.41016
144	7.14074	7.17720	7.21383	7.28759	7.36205	7.43720	7.51306	7.58963
156	8.41180	8.45833	8.50510	8.59936	8.69458	8.79078	8.88795	8.98612
168	9.90910	9.96814	10.02751	10.14724	10.26830	10.39070	10.51445	10.63956
180	11.67292	11.74746	11.82244	11.97375	12.12686	12.28180	12.43859	12.59724
192	13.75069	13.84438	13.93866	14.12902	14.32182	14.51709	14.71485	14.91514
204	16.19832	16.31560	16.43367	16.67225	16.91408	17.15920	17.40767	17.65952
216	19.08162	19.22793	19.37530	19.67325	19.97552	20.28218	20.59327	20.90887
228	22.47815	22.66012	22.84348	23.21444	23.59109	23.97353	24.36184	24.75611
240	26.47926	26.70495	26.93246	27.39303	27.86108	28.33672	28.82006	29.31123
252	31.19257	31.47178	31.75338	32.32378	32.90394	33.49400	34.09413	34.70450
264	36.74484	37.08949	37.43723	38.14206	38.85955	39.58991	40.33336	41.09012
276	43.28542	43.70997	44.13849	45.00763	45.89313	46.79527	47.71436	48.65071
288	50.99023	51.51220	52.03929	53.10901	54.19978	55.31201	56.44609	57.60244
300	60.06649	60.70713	61.35432	62.66863	64.00994	65.37880	66.77573	68.20129
312	70.75833	71.54335	72.33674	73.94898	75.59574	77.27774	78.99568	80.75032
324	83.35331	84.31284	85.28502	87.25980	89.27857	91.34228	93.45189	95.60838
336	98.19020	99.36385	100.55103	102.96656	105.43799	107.96658	110.55359	113.20032
348	115.66805	117.10030	118.54967	121.50054	124.52227	127.61650	130.78490	134.02918
360	136.25697	138.00271	139.77006	143.37064	147.06080	150.84270	154.71853	158.69055
420	309.09015	313.71518	318.40742	327.99729	337.86750	348.02599	358.48093	369.24072
480	701.15110	713.15425	725.35766	750.37834	776.23980	802.96952	830.59590	859.14822

SINGLE DEPOSIT

EFFECTIVE ANNUAL YIELD

NUMBER OF MONTHS	18.50%	18.60%	18.70%	18.80%	18.90%	19.00%	19.10%	19.20%
1	1.01425	1.01432	1.01439	1.01446	1.01453	1.01460	1.01467	1.01474
2	1.02869	1.02884	1.02898	1.02913	1.02927	1.02942	1.02956	1.02970
3	1.04335	1.04357	1.04379	1.04401	1.04423	1.04445	1.04467	1.04489
4	1.05821	1.05851	1.05881	1.05910	1.05940	1.05970	1.06000	1.06029
5	1.07329	1.07366	1.07404	1.07442	1.07480	1.07517	1.07555	1.07592
6	1.08858	1.08904	1.08950	1.08995	1.09041	1.09087	1.09133	1.09179
7	1.10408	1.10463	1.10517	1.10571	1.10626	1.10680	1.10734	1.10788
8	1.11981	1.12044	1.12107	1.12170	1.12233	1.12296	1.12359	1.12422
9	1.13577	1.13648	1.13720	1.13792	1.13864	1.13936	1.14008	1.14079
10	1.15195	1.15276	1.15357	1.15438	1.15519	1.15599	1.15680	1.15761
11	1.16836	1.16926	1.17016	1.17107	1.17197	1.17287	1.17378	1.17468
12	1.18500	1.18600	1.18700	1.18800	1.18900	1.19000	1.19100	1.19200
13	1.20188	1.20298	1.20408	1.20518	1.20628	1.20738	1.20848	1.20957
14	1.21900	1.22020	1.22140	1.22260	1.22380	1.22501	1.22621	1.22741
15	1.23637	1.23767	1.23898	1.24028	1.24159	1.24289	1.24420	1.24550
16	1.25398	1.25539	1.25680	1.25822	1.25963	1.26104	1.26245	1.26387
17	1.27185	1.27337	1.27489	1.27641	1.27793	1.27945	1.28098	1.28250
18	1.28996	1.29160	1.29323	1.29487	1.29650	1.29814	1.29977	1.30141
19	1.30834	1.31009	1.31184	1.31359	1.31534	1.31709	1.31884	1.32060
20	1.32698	1.32885	1.33071	1.33258	1.33445	1.33632	1.33820	1.34007
21	1.34588	1.34787	1.34986	1.35185	1.35384	1.35584	1.35783	1.35983
22	1.36506	1.36717	1.36928	1.37140	1.37351	1.37563	1.37775	1.37988
23	1.38450	1.38674	1.38898	1.39123	1.39347	1.39572	1.39797	1.40022
24	1.40423	1.40660	1.40897	1.41134	1.41372	1.41610	1.41848	1.42086
25	1.42423	1.42673	1.42924	1.43175	1.43426	1.43678	1.43929	1.44181
26	1.44452	1.44716	1.44981	1.45245	1.45510	1.45776	1.46041	1.46307
27	1.46510	1.46788	1.47067	1.47346	1.47625	1.47904	1.48184	1.48464
28	1.48597	1.48890	1.49183	1.49476	1.49770	1.50064	1.50358	1.50653
29	1.50714	1.51021	1.51329	1.51637	1.51946	1.52255	1.52564	1.52874
30	1.52861	1.53183	1.53507	1.53830	1.54154	1.54478	1.54803	1.55128
31	1.55038	1.55377	1.55715	1.56054	1.56394	1.56734	1.57074	1.57415
32	1.57247	1.57601	1.57956	1.58311	1.58666	1.59022	1.59379	1.59736
33	1.59487	1.59857	1.60228	1.60600	1.60972	1.61344	1.61718	1.62091
34	1.61759	1.62146	1.62534	1.62922	1.63311	1.63700	1.64090	1.64481
35	1.64063	1.64468	1.64872	1.65278	1.65684	1.66091	1.66498	1.66906
36	1.66401	1.66822	1.67245	1.67668	1.68091	1.68516	1.68941	1.69367
37	1.68771	1.69211	1.69651	1.70092	1.70534	1.70977	1.71420	1.71864
38	1.71175	1.71633	1.72092	1.72551	1.73012	1.73473	1.73935	1.74398
39	1.73614	1.74091	1.74568	1.75047	1.75526	1.76006	1.76487	1.76969
40	1.76087	1.76583	1.77080	1.77578	1.78076	1.78576	1.79077	1.79578
41	1.78596	1.79111	1.79628	1.80145	1.80664	1.81184	1.81704	1.82226
42	1.81140	1.81676	1.82212	1.82750	1.83289	1.83829	1.84370	1.84913
43	1.83720	1.84277	1.84834	1.85393	1.85952	1.86513	1.87076	1.87639
44	1.86338	1.86915	1.87493	1.88073	1.88654	1.89237	1.89821	1.90406
45	1.88992	1.89591	1.90191	1.90793	1.91396	1.92000	1.92606	1.93213
46	1.91685	1.92305	1.92928	1.93551	1.94177	1.94803	1.95432	1.96061
47	1.94415	1.95059	1.95704	1.96350	1.96998	1.97648	1.98299	1.98952
48	1.97185	1.97851	1.98519	1.99189	1.99861	2.00534	2.01209	2.01885
60	2.33664	2.34652	2.35642	2.36637	2.37634	2.38635	2.39640	2.40647
72	2.76892	2.78297	2.79708	2.81124	2.82547	2.83976	2.85411	2.86852
84	3.28117	3.30060	3.32013	3.33976	3.35949	3.37932	3.39924	3.41927
96	3.88818	3.91451	3.94099	3.96763	3.99443	4.02139	4.04850	4.07577
108	4.60750	4.64261	4.67796	4.71355	4.74938	4.78545	4.82176	4.85832
120	5.45989	5.50614	5.55274	5.59970	5.64701	5.69468	5.74272	5.79112
132	6.46996	6.53028	6.59110	6.65244	6.71429	6.77667	6.83958	6.90301
144	7.66691	7.74491	7.82364	7.90310	7.98330	8.06424	8.14594	8.22839
156	9.08528	9.18546	9.28666	9.38888	9.49214	9.59645	9.70181	9.80825
168	10.76606	10.89396	11.02326	11.15399	11.28615	11.41977	11.55486	11.69143
180	12.75776	12.92023	13.08461	13.25094	13.41924	13.58953	13.76184	13.93618
192	15.11797	15.32340	15.53143	15.74211	15.95547	16.17154	16.39035	16.61193
204	17.91480	18.17355	18.43581	18.70163	18.97106	19.24413	19.52090	19.80142
216	21.22904	21.55383	21.88331	22.21754	22.55659	22.90052	23.24940	23.60329
228	25.15641	25.56284	25.97548	26.39444	26.81978	27.25162	27.69003	28.13513
240	29.81035	30.31753	30.83290	31.35659	31.88872	32.42942	32.97883	33.53707
252	35.32526	35.95659	36.59865	37.25163	37.91569	38.59101	39.27779	39.97619
264	41.86043	42.64451	43.44260	44.25493	45.08175	45.92331	46.77984	47.65161
276	49.60461	50.57639	51.56637	52.57486	53.60221	54.64873	55.71479	56.80072
288	58.78147	59.98360	61.20928	62.45894	63.73302	65.03199	66.35632	67.70646
300	69.65604	71.14055	72.65541	74.20121	75.77856	77.38807	79.03037	80.70610
312	82.54240	84.37269	86.24197	88.15104	90.10071	92.09181	94.12518	96.20168
324	97.81275	100.06601	102.36922	104.72344	107.12975	109.58925	112.10308	114.67240
336	115.90811	118.67829	121.51227	124.41145	127.37727	130.41121	133.51477	136.68950
348	137.35111	140.75246	144.23506	147.80080	151.45157	155.18934	159.01609	162.93388
360	162.76106	166.93241	171.20702	175.58735	180.07592	184.67531	189.38817	194.21719
420	380.31396	391.70951	403.43648	415.50420	427.92229	440.70061	453.84928	467.37872
480	888.65669	919.15248	950.66774	983.23567	1016.89049	1051.66751	1087.60316	1124.73502

SINGLE DEPOSIT

EFFECTIVE ANNUAL YIELD

NUMBER OF MONTHS	19.30%	19.40%	19.50%	19.60%	19.70%	19.80%	19.90%	20.00%
1	1.01481	1.01489	1.01496	1.01503	1.01510	1.01517	1.01524	1.01531
2	1.02985	1.02999	1.03014	1.03028	1.03042	1.03057	1.03071	1.03085
3	1.04511	1.04532	1.04554	1.04576	1.04598	1.04620	1.04642	1.04664
4	1.06059	1.06088	1.06118	1.06148	1.06177	1.06207	1.06236	1.06266
5	1.07630	1.07668	1.07705	1.07743	1.07780	1.07818	1.07855	1.07893
6	1.09225	1.09270	1.09316	1.09362	1.09407	1.09453	1.09499	1.09545
7	1.10843	1.10897	1.10951	1.11005	1.11059	1.11113	1.11168	1.11222
8	1.12485	1.12548	1.12610	1.12673	1.12736	1.12799	1.12862	1.12924
9	1.14151	1.14223	1.14295	1.14366	1.14438	1.14510	1.14581	1.14653
10	1.15842	1.15923	1.16004	1.16085	1.16166	1.16247	1.16328	1.16408
11	1.17558	1.17649	1.17739	1.17829	1.17920	1.18010	1.18100	1.18191
12	1.19300	1.19400	1.19500	1.19600	1.19700	1.19800	1.19900	1.20000
13	1.21067	1.21177	1.21287	1.21397	1.21507	1.21617	1.21727	1.21837
14	1.22861	1.22981	1.23101	1.23221	1.23342	1.23462	1.23582	1.23702
15	1.24681	1.24812	1.24942	1.25073	1.25204	1.25335	1.25465	1.25596
16	1.26528	1.26670	1.26811	1.26953	1.27094	1.27236	1.27377	1.27519
17	1.28403	1.28555	1.28708	1.28860	1.29013	1.29166	1.29318	1.29471
18	1.30305	1.30469	1.30633	1.30797	1.30961	1.31125	1.31289	1.31453
19	1.32235	1.32411	1.32586	1.32762	1.32938	1.33114	1.33290	1.33466
20	1.34194	1.34382	1.34569	1.34757	1.34945	1.35133	1.35321	1.35509
21	1.36182	1.36382	1.36582	1.36782	1.36982	1.37183	1.37383	1.37584
22	1.38200	1.38412	1.38625	1.38838	1.39051	1.39264	1.39477	1.39690
23	1.40247	1.40473	1.40698	1.40924	1.41150	1.41376	1.41602	1.41829
24	1.42325	1.42564	1.42803	1.43042	1.43281	1.43520	1.43760	1.44000
25	1.44433	1.44686	1.44938	1.45191	1.45444	1.45697	1.45951	1.46205
26	1.46573	1.46839	1.47106	1.47373	1.47640	1.47907	1.48175	1.48443
27	1.48745	1.49025	1.49306	1.49587	1.49869	1.50151	1.50433	1.50715
28	1.50948	1.51244	1.51539	1.51835	1.52132	1.52428	1.52725	1.53023
29	1.53184	1.53495	1.53806	1.54117	1.54429	1.54740	1.55053	1.55366
30	1.55454	1.55780	1.56106	1.56433	1.56760	1.57088	1.57416	1.57744
31	1.57757	1.58099	1.58441	1.58784	1.59127	1.59470	1.59815	1.60159
32	1.60094	1.60452	1.60811	1.61170	1.61529	1.61889	1.62250	1.62611
33	1.62466	1.62840	1.63216	1.63592	1.63968	1.64345	1.64722	1.65101
34	1.64872	1.65264	1.65657	1.66050	1.66443	1.66838	1.67233	1.67628
35	1.67315	1.67724	1.68134	1.68545	1.68956	1.69368	1.69781	1.70194
36	1.69794	1.70221	1.70649	1.71078	1.71507	1.71937	1.72368	1.72800
37	1.72309	1.72755	1.73201	1.73649	1.74097	1.74545	1.74995	1.75445
38	1.74862	1.75326	1.75792	1.76258	1.76725	1.77193	1.77662	1.78131
39	1.77452	1.77936	1.78421	1.78907	1.79393	1.79881	1.80369	1.80859
40	1.80081	1.80585	1.81089	1.81595	1.82102	1.82609	1.83118	1.83627
41	1.82749	1.83273	1.83798	1.84324	1.84851	1.85379	1.85908	1.86439
42	1.85456	1.86001	1.86547	1.87094	1.87642	1.88191	1.88741	1.89293
43	1.88204	1.88770	1.89337	1.89905	1.90475	1.91046	1.91618	1.92191
44	1.90992	1.91580	1.92169	1.92759	1.93350	1.93943	1.94538	1.95133
45	1.93821	1.94431	1.95043	1.95655	1.96270	1.96885	1.97502	1.98121
46	1.96693	1.97326	1.97960	1.98596	1.99233	1.99872	2.00512	2.01154
47	1.99607	2.00263	2.00921	2.01580	2.02241	2.02903	2.03568	2.04233
48	2.02564	2.03244	2.03926	2.04609	2.05294	2.05981	2.06670	2.07360
60	2.41659	2.42673	2.43691	2.44712	2.45737	2.46765	2.47797	2.48832
72	2.88229	2.89752	2.91211	2.92676	2.94147	2.95625	2.97109	2.98598
84	3.43940	3.45964	3.47997	3.50040	3.52094	3.54159	3.56233	3.58318
96	4.10321	4.13218	4.15856	4.18648	4.21457	4.24282	4.27123	4.29982
108	4.89513	4.93218	4.96948	5.00703	5.04484	5.08290	5.12121	5.15978
120	5.83989	5.88902	5.93853	5.98841	6.03867	6.08931	6.14033	6.19174
132	6.96699	7.03149	7.09654	7.16214	7.22829	7.29500	7.36226	7.43008
144	8.31161	8.39560	8.48037	8.56592	8.65226	8.73940	8.82735	8.91610
156	9.91575	10.02435	10.13404	10.24484	10.35676	10.46981	10.58399	10.69932
168	11.82950	11.96907	12.11018	12.25283	12.39704	12.54283	12.69020	12.83918
180	14.11259	14.29108	14.47167	14.65439	14.83926	15.02631	15.21555	15.40702
192	16.83632	17.06354	17.29364	17.52665	17.76259	18.00152	18.24345	18.48843
204	20.08573	20.37387	20.66590	20.96187	21.26183	21.56582	21.87389	22.18611
216	23.96227	24.32640	24.69575	25.07040	25.45041	25.83585	26.22680	26.62333
228	28.58699	29.04572	29.51143	29.98420	30.46414	30.95135	31.44593	31.94800
240	34.10428	34.68059	35.26615	35.86110	36.46557	37.07971	37.70367	38.33760
252	40.68640	41.40863	42.14305	42.88987	43.64929	44.42150	45.20670	46.00512
264	48.53888	49.44190	50.36095	51.29629	52.24820	53.21695	54.20284	55.20614
276	57.90689	59.03363	60.18134	61.35036	62.54109	63.75391	64.98920	66.24737
288	69.08291	70.48616	71.91670	73.37503	74.86169	76.37718	77.92205	79.49685
300	82.41592	84.16047	85.94045	87.75654	89.60944	91.49986	93.42854	95.39622
312	98.32219	100.48761	102.69894	104.95682	107.26250	109.61684	112.02082	114.47546
324	117.29837	119.98220	122.72511	125.52836	128.39321	131.32097	134.31297	137.37055
336	139.93696	143.25875	146.65651	150.13192	153.68667	157.32252	161.04125	164.84466
348	166.94479	171.05094	175.25453	179.55777	183.96295	188.47238	193.08846	197.81359
360	199.16513	204.23483	209.42916	214.75110	220.20365	225.78992	231.51306	237.37631
420	481.29963	495.62298	510.36007	525.52247	541.12209	557.17116	573.68224	590.66823
480	1163.10185	1202.74365	1243.70165	1286.01841	1329.73781	1374.90510	1421.56697	1469.77157

42

TABLE 2. MONTHLY DEPOSITS

MONTHLY DEPOSITS

EFFECTIVE ANNUAL YIELD

NUMBER OF MONTHLY DEPOSITS	5.00%	5.05%	5.10%	5.15%	5.20%	5.25%	5.30%	5.35%
1	1.00407	1.00411	1.00415	1.00419	1.00423	1.00427	1.00431	1.00435
2	2.01224	2.01236	2.01248	2.01260	2.01272	2.01284	2.01296	2.01308
3	3.02451	3.02475	3.02499	3.02523	3.02547	3.02571	3.02595	3.02619
4	4.04091	4.04131	4.04171	4.04211	4.04251	4.04291	4.04332	4.04372
5	5.06144	5.06205	5.06265	5.06326	5.06386	5.06446	5.06507	5.06567
6	6.08614	6.08699	6.08784	6.08868	6.08953	6.09038	6.09122	6.09207
7	7.11501	7.11614	7.11728	7.11841	7.11954	7.12068	7.12181	7.12294
8	8.14807	8.14953	8.15099	8.15246	8.15392	8.15538	8.15684	8.15830
9	9.18534	9.18717	9.18901	9.19084	9.19267	9.19450	9.19633	9.19816
10	10.22684	10.22908	10.23133	10.23357	10.23582	10.23806	10.24030	10.24255
11	11.27258	11.27528	11.27798	11.28068	11.28338	11.28608	11.28878	11.29148
12	12.32258	12.32578	12.32898	12.33218	12.33538	12.33858	12.34178	12.34498
13	13.37686	13.38060	13.38435	13.38809	13.39184	13.39558	13.39932	13.40307
14	14.43543	14.43976	14.44410	14.44843	14.45276	14.45709	14.46143	14.46576
15	15.49831	15.50328	15.50825	15.51321	15.51818	15.52314	15.52811	15.53307
16	16.56553	16.57117	16.57682	16.58246	16.58811	16.59375	16.59939	16.60504
17	17.63709	17.64346	17.64983	17.65620	17.66256	17.66893	17.67530	17.68166
18	18.71302	18.72016	18.72730	18.73443	18.74157	18.74870	18.75584	18.76298
19	19.79334	19.80129	19.80924	19.81719	19.82514	19.83309	19.84105	19.84900
20	20.87805	20.88686	20.89568	20.90449	20.91330	20.92212	20.93093	20.93975
21	21.96719	21.97691	21.98663	21.99635	22.00607	22.01579	22.02552	22.03524
22	23.06076	23.07143	23.08211	23.09278	23.10346	23.11414	23.12482	23.13550
23	24.15878	24.17046	24.18214	24.19382	24.20550	24.21718	24.22887	24.24056
24	25.26128	25.27401	25.28674	25.29947	25.31220	25.32494	25.33768	25.35042
25	26.36828	26.38210	26.39593	26.40976	26.42359	26.43743	26.45127	26.46511
26	27.47978	27.49475	27.50973	27.52470	27.53969	27.55467	27.56966	27.58466
27	28.59581	28.61198	28.62815	28.64433	28.66051	28.67669	28.69288	28.70907
28	29.71638	29.73380	29.75122	29.76864	29.78607	29.80350	29.82094	29.83839
29	30.84153	30.86024	30.87895	30.89767	30.91640	30.93513	30.95387	30.97261
30	31.97125	31.99131	32.01137	32.03144	32.05151	32.07159	32.09168	32.11178
31	33.10558	33.12703	33.14849	33.16996	33.19143	33.21291	33.23440	33.25590
32	34.24453	34.26743	34.29034	34.31325	34.33618	34.35911	34.38205	34.40500
33	35.38812	35.41252	35.43692	35.46134	35.48577	35.51020	35.53465	35.55911
34	36.53637	36.56232	36.58828	36.61424	36.64022	36.66622	36.69222	36.71823
35	37.68930	37.71685	37.74441	37.77198	37.79957	37.82717	37.85478	37.88241
36	38.84693	38.87613	38.90534	38.93458	38.96382	38.99308	39.02236	39.05165
37	40.00927	40.04018	40.07110	40.10204	40.13300	40.16398	40.19497	40.22598
38	41.17634	41.20901	41.24170	41.27441	41.30713	41.33988	41.37264	41.40542
39	42.34818	42.38266	42.41717	42.45169	42.48624	42.52080	42.55539	42.58999
40	43.52478	43.56113	43.59751	43.63391	43.67033	43.70677	43.74323	43.77972
41	44.70618	44.74446	44.78276	44.82108	44.85943	44.89781	44.93621	44.97463
42	45.89239	45.93265	45.97293	46.01324	46.05357	46.09394	46.13432	46.17474
43	47.08344	47.12573	47.16805	47.21039	47.25277	47.29517	47.33761	47.38007
44	48.27934	48.32371	48.36812	48.41257	48.45704	48.50155	48.54608	48.59065
45	49.48011	49.52663	49.57319	49.61978	49.66641	49.71307	49.75977	49.80650
46	50.68577	50.73449	50.78326	50.83206	50.88090	50.92978	50.97869	51.02764
47	51.89634	51.94733	51.99835	52.04942	52.10053	52.15168	52.20287	52.25410
48	53.11185	53.16515	53.21850	53.27189	53.32532	53.37880	53.43232	53.48589
60	68.09002	68.17577	68.26162	68.34757	68.43362	68.51977	68.60602	68.69237
72	83.81710	83.94443	84.07195	84.19965	84.32755	84.45564	84.58392	84.71239
84	100.33053	100.50940	100.68860	100.86812	101.04797	101.22815	101.40865	101.58949
96	117.66963	117.91090	118.15270	118.39501	118.63784	118.88121	119.12509	119.36950
108	135.87569	136.19118	136.50746	136.82453	137.14239	137.46105	137.78050	138.10075
120	154.99206	155.39462	155.79832	156.20318	156.60918	157.01634	157.42465	157.83412
132	175.06424	175.56783	176.07302	176.57982	177.08824	177.59828	178.10994	178.62323
144	196.14003	196.75978	197.38173	198.00587	198.63221	199.26077	199.89155	200.52456
156	218.26960	219.02193	219.77717	220.53535	221.29647	222.06054	222.82758	223.59760
168	241.50566	242.40832	243.31479	244.22510	245.13927	246.05730	246.97923	247.90505
180	265.90352	266.97572	268.05283	269.13488	270.22189	271.31390	272.41091	273.51296
192	291.52128	292.78377	294.05250	295.32751	296.60881	297.89646	299.19047	300.49088
204	318.41992	319.89513	321.37816	322.86905	324.36785	325.87460	327.38935	328.91212
216	346.66349	348.37561	350.09743	351.82899	353.57037	355.32160	357.08276	358.85390
228	376.31924	378.29436	380.28138	382.28037	384.29141	386.31457	388.34993	390.39757
240	407.45778	409.72400	412.00471	414.29999	416.60994	418.93467	421.27426	423.62882
252	440.15325	442.74085	445.34593	447.96862	450.60904	453.26732	455.94358	458.63794
264	474.48349	477.42504	480.38755	483.37118	486.37609	489.40244	492.45037	495.52005
276	510.53024	513.86078	517.21630	520.59698	524.00303	527.43465	530.89202	534.37536
288	548.37933	552.13653	555.92331	559.73991	563.58657	567.46355	571.37108	575.30942
300	588.12088	592.34520	596.60438	600.89870	605.22846	609.59397	613.99553	618.43345
312	629.84950	634.58442	639.36018	644.17716	649.03572	653.93623	658.87907	663.86463
324	673.66455	678.95671	684.29653	689.68447	695.12096	700.60647	706.14145	711.72636
336	719.67035	725.56980	731.52464	737.53540	743.60263	749.72689	755.90873	762.14871
348	767.97645	774.53686	781.16137	787.85065	794.60535	801.42613	808.31367	815.26864
360	818.69785	825.97675	833.32959	840.75714	848.26021	855.83959	863.49608	871.23050
420	1112.97899	1124.86701	1136.89905	1149.07694	1161.40250	1173.87761	1186.50414	1199.28400
480	1488.56458	1507.24426	1526.18763	1545.39858	1564.88102	1584.63894	1604.67639	1624.99747

MONTHLY DEPOSITS

NUMBER OF MONTHLY DEPOSITS	EFFECTIVE ANNUAL YIELD							
	5.40%	5.45%	5.50%	5.55%	5.60%	5.65%	5.70%	5.75%
1	1.00439	1.00443	1.00447	1.00451	1.00455	1.00459	1.00463	1.00467
2	2.01320	2.01332	2.01344	2.01355	2.01367	2.01379	2.01391	2.01403
3	3.02643	3.02667	3.02691	3.02715	3.02739	3.02763	3.02787	3.02811
4	4.04412	4.04452	4.04492	4.04532	4.04572	4.04612	4.04652	4.04692
5	5.06627	5.06687	5.06748	5.06808	5.06868	5.06928	5.06988	5.07049
6	6.09292	6.09376	6.09461	6.09545	6.09630	6.09714	6.09799	6.09883
7	7.12407	7.12520	7.12633	7.12746	7.12859	7.12972	7.13085	7.13198
8	8.15975	8.16121	8.16267	8.16413	8.16559	8.16705	8.16850	8.16996
9	9.19999	9.20182	9.20364	9.20547	9.20730	9.20913	9.21095	9.21278
10	10.24479	10.24703	10.24927	10.25151	10.25375	10.25599	10.25823	10.26047
11	11.29418	11.29688	11.29958	11.30227	11.30497	11.30767	11.31036	11.31306
12	12.34818	12.35138	12.35458	12.35777	12.36097	12.36417	12.36736	12.37056
13	13.40681	13.41055	13.41429	13.41803	13.42178	13.42552	13.42926	13.43300
14	14.47009	14.47442	14.47875	14.48308	14.48741	14.49174	14.49607	14.50040
15	15.53804	15.54300	15.54797	15.55293	15.55789	15.56286	15.56782	15.57278
16	16.61068	16.61632	16.62196	16.62761	16.63325	16.63889	16.64453	16.65017
17	17.68803	17.69440	17.70076	17.70713	17.71350	17.71986	17.72623	17.73260
18	18.77011	18.77725	18.78439	18.79153	18.79866	18.80580	18.81294	18.82007
19	19.85695	19.86490	19.87286	19.88081	19.88877	19.89672	19.90468	19.91263
20	20.94856	20.95738	20.96619	20.97501	20.98383	20.99265	21.00147	21.01029
21	22.04497	22.05469	22.06442	22.07415	22.08388	22.09361	22.10334	22.11307
22	23.14619	23.15687	23.16756	23.17825	23.18893	23.19962	23.21032	23.22101
23	24.25225	24.26394	24.27563	24.28732	24.29902	24.31072	24.32242	24.33412
24	25.36316	25.37591	25.38865	25.40140	25.41415	25.42691	25.43966	25.45242
25	26.47896	26.49280	26.50666	26.52051	26.53437	26.54822	26.56209	26.57595
26	27.59965	27.61465	27.62966	27.64466	27.65967	27.67469	27.68971	27.70473
27	28.72527	28.74147	28.75768	28.77389	28.79010	28.80632	28.82255	28.83877
28	29.85584	29.87329	29.89075	29.90821	29.92568	29.94315	29.96063	29.97812
29	30.99136	31.01012	31.02888	31.04765	31.06642	31.08520	31.10399	31.12278
30	32.13188	32.15199	32.17211	32.19223	32.21236	32.23249	32.25264	32.27279
31	33.27741	33.29892	33.32044	33.34197	33.36351	33.38505	33.40660	33.42816
32	34.42796	34.45093	34.47391	34.49690	34.51990	34.54290	34.56592	34.58894
33	35.58357	35.60805	35.63254	35.65704	35.68155	35.70607	35.73059	35.75513
34	36.74426	36.77030	36.79635	36.82241	36.84848	36.87457	36.90067	36.92677
35	37.91005	37.93770	37.96536	37.99304	38.02073	38.04844	38.07616	38.10389
36	39.08095	39.11027	39.13961	39.16895	39.19832	39.22769	39.25709	39.28649
37	40.25700	40.28804	40.31910	40.35017	40.38126	40.41237	40.44349	40.47463
38	41.43821	41.47103	41.50386	41.53672	41.56959	41.60247	41.63538	41.66831
39	42.62462	42.65926	42.69393	42.72861	42.76332	42.79805	42.83279	42.86756
40	43.81623	43.85276	43.88931	43.92589	43.96249	43.99911	44.03575	44.07241
41	45.01308	45.05155	45.09005	45.12857	45.16711	45.20568	45.24428	45.28290
42	46.21518	46.25565	46.29615	46.33667	46.37722	46.41780	46.45840	46.49903
43	47.42257	47.46509	47.50764	47.55022	47.59283	47.63547	47.67814	47.72084
44	48.63525	48.67989	48.72455	48.76925	48.81398	48.85874	48.90353	48.94836
45	49.85327	49.90007	49.94691	49.99378	50.04068	50.08762	50.13460	50.18161
46	51.07663	51.12566	51.17472	51.22383	51.27297	51.32215	51.37137	51.42062
47	52.30537	52.35668	52.40803	52.45943	52.51086	52.56234	52.61386	52.66542
48	53.53950	53.59316	53.64686	53.70060	53.75439	53.80823	53.86210	53.91603
60	68.77882	68.86536	68.95201	69.03876	69.12561	69.21256	69.29961	69.38676
72	84.84105	84.96990	85.09895	85.22818	85.35761	85.48723	85.61705	85.74705
84	101.77065	101.95214	102.13397	102.31612	102.49861	102.68143	102.86458	103.04806
96	119.61444	119.85991	120.10591	120.35244	120.59950	120.84710	121.09522	121.34389
108	138.42180	138.74366	139.06631	139.38977	139.71404	140.03912	140.36501	140.69172
120	158.24476	158.65656	159.06953	159.48368	159.89900	160.31550	160.73318	161.15205
132	179.13816	179.65472	180.17294	180.69280	181.21431	181.73749	182.26234	182.78885
144	201.15980	201.79728	202.43702	203.07902	203.72329	204.36983	205.01865	205.66977
156	224.37061	225.14661	225.92563	226.70768	227.49276	228.28089	229.07208	229.86634
168	248.83480	249.76848	250.70612	251.64773	252.59332	253.54292	254.49655	255.45421
180	274.62006	275.73224	276.84953	277.97195	279.09952	280.23227	281.37021	282.51338
192	301.79772	303.11103	304.43083	305.75717	307.09006	308.42956	309.77568	311.12846
204	330.44298	331.98196	333.52910	335.08446	336.64808	338.21999	339.80025	341.38890
216	360.63508	362.42635	364.22778	366.03942	367.86134	369.69359	371.53623	373.38932
228	392.45755	394.52997	396.61489	398.71238	400.82254	402.94544	405.08116	407.22977
240	425.99844	428.38323	430.78328	433.19870	435.62958	438.07603	440.53814	443.01604
252	461.35054	464.08149	466.83094	469.59900	472.38580	475.19149	478.01618	480.86002
264	498.61165	501.72531	504.86121	508.01951	511.20038	514.40397	517.63047	520.88003
276	537.88485	541.42072	544.98316	548.57237	552.18857	555.83196	559.50276	563.20119
288	579.27882	583.27953	587.31181	591.37591	595.47210	599.60064	603.76178	607.95581
300	622.90805	627.41964	631.96853	636.55505	641.17951	645.84224	650.54357	655.28383
312	668.89327	673.96539	679.08138	684.24162	689.44653	694.69649	699.99191	705.33321
324	717.36168	723.04788	728.78543	734.57481	740.41650	746.31101	752.25882	758.26042
336	768.44739	774.80537	781.22320	787.70148	794.24080	800.84175	807.50493	814.23096
348	822.29173	829.38364	836.54505	843.77669	851.07925	858.45347	865.90007	873.41979
360	879.04367	886.93642	894.90961	902.96407	911.10066	919.32026	927.62374	936.01199
420	1212.21914	1225.31150	1238.56308	1251.97587	1265.55191	1279.29327	1293.20202	1307.28028
480	1645.60634	1666.50723	1687.70442	1709.20227	1731.00520	1753.11769	1775.54429	1798.28961

45

EFFECTIVE ANNUAL YIELD

NUMBER OF MONTHLY DEPOSITS	5.80%	5.85%	5.90%	5.95%	6.00%	6.05%	6.10%	6.15%
1	1.00471	1.00475	1.00479	1.00483	1.00487	1.00491	1.00495	1.00499
2	2.01415	2.01427	2.01439	2.01451	2.01463	2.01475	2.01486	2.01498
3	3.02835	3.02858	3.02882	3.02906	3.02930	3.02954	3.02978	3.03002
4	4.04732	4.04772	4.04812	4.04851	4.04891	4.04931	4.04971	4.05011
5	5.07109	5.07169	5.07229	5.07289	5.07349	5.07409	5.07469	5.07529
6	6.09968	6.10052	6.10137	6.10221	6.10305	6.10389	6.10474	6.10558
7	7.13311	7.13424	7.13537	7.13650	7.13763	7.13875	7.13988	7.14101
8	8.17142	8.17287	8.17433	8.17578	8.17724	8.17869	8.18015	8.18160
9	9.21461	9.21643	9.21826	9.22008	9.22191	9.22373	9.22555	9.22738
10	10.26271	10.26495	10.26719	10.26943	10.27166	10.27390	10.27614	10.27837
11	11.31575	11.31845	11.32114	11.32384	11.32653	11.32922	11.33191	11.33461
12	12.37375	12.37695	12.38014	12.38334	12.38653	12.38972	12.39291	12.39611
13	13.43674	13.44047	13.44421	13.44795	13.45169	13.45543	13.45916	13.46290
14	14.50472	14.50905	14.51338	14.51771	14.52203	14.52636	14.53068	14.53501
15	15.57774	15.58270	15.58766	15.59263	15.59759	15.60255	15.60751	15.61247
16	16.65581	16.66145	16.66710	16.67274	16.67838	16.68402	16.68966	16.69530
17	17.73896	17.74533	17.75169	17.75806	17.76443	17.77079	17.77716	17.78352
18	18.82721	18.83435	18.84149	18.84863	18.85576	18.86290	18.87004	18.87718
19	19.92059	19.92854	19.93650	19.94446	19.95241	19.96037	19.96833	19.97629
20	21.01911	21.02793	21.03675	21.04558	21.05440	21.06322	21.07205	21.08087
21	22.12281	22.13254	22.14228	22.15201	22.16175	22.17149	22.18123	22.19097
22	23.23170	23.24240	23.25309	23.26379	23.27449	23.28519	23.29589	23.30660
23	24.34582	24.35752	24.36923	24.38094	24.39265	24.40436	24.41607	24.42779
24	25.46518	25.47795	25.49071	25.50348	25.51625	25.52902	25.54179	25.55457
25	26.58982	26.60369	26.61756	26.63144	26.64532	26.65920	26.67308	26.68697
26	27.71975	27.73478	27.74981	27.76484	27.77988	27.79492	27.80997	27.82502
27	28.85500	28.87124	28.88748	28.90372	28.91997	28.93622	28.95248	28.96874
28	29.99560	30.01310	30.03060	30.04810	30.06561	30.08312	30.10064	30.11816
29	31.14157	31.16038	31.17919	31.19800	31.21682	31.23565	31.25448	31.27332
30	32.29294	32.31311	32.33328	32.35345	32.37364	32.39383	32.41403	32.43423
31	33.44973	33.47131	33.49289	33.51449	33.53609	33.55769	33.57931	33.60093
32	34.61197	34.63501	34.65806	34.68112	34.70419	34.72727	34.75036	34.77345
33	35.77968	35.80424	35.82881	35.85339	35.87798	35.90258	35.92720	35.95182
34	36.95289	36.97903	37.00517	37.03132	37.05749	37.08367	37.10986	37.13606
35	38.13163	38.15939	38.18716	38.21494	38.24274	38.27054	38.29837	38.32620
36	39.31592	39.34535	39.37480	39.40427	39.43375	39.46325	39.49276	39.52228
37	40.50578	40.53695	40.56814	40.59934	40.63056	40.66180	40.69306	40.72433
38	41.70125	41.73421	41.76719	41.80019	41.83320	41.86624	41.89929	41.93236
39	42.90235	42.93715	42.97198	43.00683	43.04170	43.07658	43.11149	43.14642
40	44.10910	44.14581	44.18254	44.21930	44.25607	44.29287	44.32969	44.36653
41	45.32154	45.36021	45.39890	45.43762	45.47636	45.51512	45.55391	45.59273
42	46.53969	46.58037	46.62108	46.66182	46.70258	46.74338	46.78419	46.82504
43	47.76357	47.80633	47.84912	47.89193	47.93478	47.97765	48.02056	48.06349
44	48.99322	49.03811	49.08303	49.12798	49.17297	49.21799	49.26304	49.30812
45	50.22866	50.27574	50.32285	50.37000	50.41719	50.46441	50.51167	50.55896
46	51.46991	51.51925	51.56861	51.61802	51.66747	51.71695	51.76647	51.81603
47	52.71702	52.76866	52.82034	52.87206	52.92383	52.97563	53.02748	53.07937
48	53.96999	54.02400	54.07806	54.13216	54.18631	54.24049	54.29473	54.34901
60	69.47401	69.56136	69.64881	69.73636	69.82401	69.91177	69.99962	70.08758
72	85.87725	86.00764	86.13823	86.26901	86.39998	86.53115	86.66251	86.79407
84	103.23188	103.41604	103.60052	103.78535	103.97051	104.15600	104.34184	104.52801
96	121.59309	121.84282	122.09310	122.34391	122.59527	122.84716	123.09960	123.35259
108	141.01924	141.34757	141.67673	142.00671	142.33751	142.66914	143.00159	143.33488
120	161.57211	161.99336	162.41580	162.83944	163.26429	163.69034	164.11760	164.54608
132	183.31704	183.84691	184.37847	184.91173	185.44668	185.98333	186.52169	187.06176
144	206.32318	206.97891	207.63695	208.29731	208.96000	209.62504	210.29243	210.96217
156	230.66368	231.46412	232.26767	233.07433	233.88413	234.69708	235.51318	236.33245
168	256.41593	257.38172	258.35160	259.32559	260.30371	261.28597	262.27239	263.26300
180	283.66180	284.81550	285.97449	287.13880	288.30846	289.48349	290.66392	291.84978
192	312.48794	313.85415	315.22712	316.60689	317.99350	319.38697	320.78734	322.19464
204	342.98599	344.59156	346.20566	347.82834	349.45963	351.09960	352.74828	354.40572
216	375.25293	377.12012	379.01194	380.90746	382.81374	384.73085	386.65884	388.59778
228	409.39136	411.56600	413.75379	415.95479	418.16909	420.39678	422.63794	424.89264
240	445.50981	448.01956	450.54540	453.08743	455.64577	458.22051	460.81177	463.41965
252	483.72313	486.60565	489.50772	492.42947	495.37104	498.33257	501.31420	504.31606
264	524.15282	527.44903	530.76882	534.11236	537.47983	540.87141	544.28728	547.72760
276	566.92744	570.68175	574.46432	578.27538	582.11515	585.98385	589.88171	593.80896
288	612.18299	616.44358	620.73786	625.06610	629.42859	633.82560	638.25741	642.72431
300	660.06335	664.88247	669.74153	674.64087	679.58083	684.56177	689.58403	694.64796
312	710.72078	716.15504	721.63642	727.16534	732.74221	738.36748	744.04157	749.76779
324	764.31634	770.42706	776.59311	782.81501	789.09327	795.42843	801.82102	808.27157
336	821.02044	827.87399	834.79225	841.77584	848.82540	855.94157	863.12501	870.37637
348	881.01337	888.68157	896.42513	904.24483	912.14145	920.11576	928.16855	936.30062
360	944.48590	953.04639	961.69436	970.43074	979.25646	988.17248	997.17974	1006.27922
420	1321.53019	1335.95392	1350.55365	1365.33162	1380.29006	1395.43126	1410.75753	1426.27120
480	1821.35834	1844.75523	1868.48510	1892.55286	1916.96347	1941.72198	1966.83349	1992.30321

NUMBER OF MONTHLY DEPOSITS	EFFECTIVE ANNUAL YIELD							
	6.20%	6.25%	6.30%	6.35%	6.40%	6.45%	6.50%	6.55%
1	1.00503	1.00506	1.00510	1.00514	1.00518	1.00522	1.00526	1.00530
2	2.01510	2.01522	2.01534	2.01546	2.01558	2.01569	2.01581	2.01593
3	3.03025	3.03049	3.03073	3.03097	3.03121	3.03144	3.03168	3.03192
4	4.05051	4.05091	4.05130	4.05170	4.05210	4.05250	4.05289	4.05329
5	5.07589	5.07649	5.07709	5.07769	5.07828	5.07888	5.07948	5.08008
6	6.10642	6.10726	6.10811	6.10895	6.10979	6.11063	6.11147	6.11231
7	7.14213	7.14326	7.14439	7.14551	7.14664	7.14776	7.14889	7.15001
8	8.18305	8.18451	8.18596	8.18741	8.18886	8.19031	8.19177	8.19322
9	9.22920	9.23102	9.23285	9.23467	9.23649	9.23831	9.24013	9.24195
10	10.28061	10.28284	10.28508	10.28731	10.28954	10.29178	10.29401	10.29624
11	11.33730	11.33999	11.34268	11.34537	11.34806	11.35075	11.35344	11.35612
12	12.39930	12.40249	12.40568	12.40887	12.41206	12.41525	12.41844	12.42162
13	13.46663	13.47037	13.47410	13.47784	13.48157	13.48531	13.48904	13.49277
14	14.53933	14.54366	14.54798	14.55231	14.55663	14.56095	14.56528	14.56960
15	15.61743	15.62238	15.62734	15.63230	15.63726	15.64222	15.64718	15.65213
16	16.70094	16.70657	16.71221	16.71785	16.72349	16.72913	16.73477	16.74041
17	17.78989	17.79626	17.80262	17.80899	17.81535	17.82172	17.82808	17.83445
18	18.88432	18.89146	18.89859	18.90573	18.91287	18.92001	18.92715	18.93429
19	19.98424	19.99220	20.00016	20.00812	20.01608	20.02404	20.03200	20.03996
20	21.08970	21.09852	21.10735	21.11618	21.12501	21.13384	21.14267	21.15150
21	22.20071	22.21045	22.22019	22.22994	22.23968	22.24943	22.25917	22.26892
22	23.31730	23.32801	23.33871	23.34942	23.36013	23.37084	23.38156	23.39227
23	24.43951	24.45122	24.46294	24.47467	24.48639	24.49812	24.50984	24.52157
24	25.56735	25.58013	25.59291	25.60570	25.61849	25.63128	25.64407	25.65686
25	26.70086	26.71475	26.72865	26.74255	26.75645	26.77035	26.78426	26.79817
26	27.84007	27.85513	27.87018	27.88525	27.90031	27.91538	27.93045	27.94553
27	28.98500	29.00127	29.01754	29.03382	29.05010	29.06639	29.08268	29.09897
28	30.13569	30.15322	30.17076	30.18830	30.20585	30.22341	30.24096	30.25853
29	31.29216	31.31101	31.32986	31.34873	31.36759	31.38647	31.40534	31.42423
30	32.45444	32.47466	32.49488	32.51512	32.53535	32.55560	32.57585	32.59611
31	33.62256	33.64420	33.66585	33.68750	33.70917	33.73084	33.75252	33.77420
32	34.79656	34.81967	34.84279	34.86592	34.88906	34.91221	34.93537	34.95854
33	35.97645	36.00109	36.02574	36.05041	36.07508	36.09976	36.12445	36.14916
34	37.16227	37.18849	37.21473	37.24098	37.26724	37.29351	37.31979	37.34609
35	38.35405	38.38191	38.40979	38.43768	38.46558	38.49349	38.52142	38.54936
36	39.55182	39.58138	39.61095	39.64053	39.67013	39.69974	39.72937	39.75901
37	40.75561	40.78691	40.81823	40.84957	40.88092	40.91229	40.94367	40.97508
38	41.96545	41.99856	42.03168	42.06483	42.09799	42.13117	42.16437	42.19759
39	43.18137	43.21634	43.25133	43.28634	43.32137	43.35642	43.39149	43.42658
40	44.40340	44.44029	44.47720	44.51413	44.55108	44.58806	44.62506	44.66208
41	45.63157	45.67043	45.70932	45.74824	45.78718	45.82614	45.86513	45.90414
42	46.86591	46.90681	46.94774	46.98869	47.02967	47.07068	47.11172	47.15278
43	48.10646	48.14945	48.19248	48.23553	48.27861	48.32172	48.36487	48.40804
44	49.35324	49.39839	49.44357	49.48878	49.53402	49.57930	49.62461	49.66995
45	50.60628	50.65365	50.70104	50.74847	50.79594	50.84344	50.89098	50.93855
46	51.86563	51.91526	51.96494	52.01465	52.06440	52.11419	52.16401	52.21388
47	53.13130	53.18327	53.23528	53.28734	53.33943	53.39157	53.44375	53.49597
48	54.40333	54.45770	54.51211	54.56657	54.62107	54.67562	54.73021	54.78485
60	70.17563	70.26379	70.35205	70.44042	70.52888	70.61744	70.70611	70.79488
72	86.92582	87.05777	87.18991	87.32225	87.45479	87.58752	87.72044	87.85357
84	104.71452	104.90137	105.08855	105.27608	105.46395	105.65216	105.84071	106.02960
96	123.60611	123.86019	124.11481	124.36998	124.62570	124.88197	125.13879	125.39616
108	143.66899	144.00394	144.33972	144.67634	145.01380	145.35210	145.69125	146.03124
120	164.97576	165.40667	165.83880	166.27216	166.70674	167.14256	167.57961	168.01791
132	187.60356	188.14708	188.69232	189.23931	189.78803	190.33850	190.89072	191.44470
144	211.63428	212.30876	212.98562	213.66487	214.34652	215.03058	215.71706	216.40595
156	237.15490	237.98054	238.80939	239.64146	240.47676	241.31530	242.15710	243.00217
168	264.25780	265.25681	266.26006	267.26756	268.27933	269.29538	270.31575	271.34043
180	293.04108	294.23785	295.44012	296.64792	297.86126	299.08018	300.30471	301.53486
192	323.60892	325.03020	326.45853	327.89393	329.33644	330.78610	332.24295	333.70701
204	356.07197	357.74708	359.43109	361.12406	362.82603	364.53705	366.25717	367.98645
216	390.54773	392.50876	394.48093	396.46431	398.45895	400.46494	402.48233	404.51118
228	427.16098	429.44304	431.73891	434.04866	436.37239	438.71017	441.06211	443.42829
240	466.04426	468.68572	471.34414	474.01962	476.71228	479.42223	482.14959	484.89446
252	507.33830	510.38107	513.44449	516.52873	519.63392	522.76021	525.90774	529.07667
264	551.19257	554.68237	558.19718	561.73717	565.30255	568.89349	572.51018	576.15282
276	597.76581	601.75251	605.76928	609.81635	613.89397	618.00236	622.14178	626.31245
288	647.22659	651.76453	656.33842	660.94856	665.59524	670.27876	674.99943	679.75754
300	699.75393	704.90230	710.09342	715.32766	720.60539	725.92699	731.29283	736.70328
312	755.53797	761.36118	767.23498	773.15983	779.13620	785.16453	791.24530	797.37897
324	814.78062	821.34874	827.97646	834.66435	841.41297	848.22289	855.09468	862.02892
336	877.69632	885.08552	892.54466	900.07440	907.67546	915.34851	923.09427	930.91344
348	944.51279	952.80585	961.18065	969.63800	978.17874	986.80374	995.51383	1004.30989
360	1015.47188	1024.75871	1034.14071	1043.61888	1053.19424	1062.86782	1072.64066	1082.51381
420	1441.97464	1457.87025	1473.96044	1490.24769	1506.73448	1523.42332	1540.31678	1557.41743
480	2018.13641	2044.33842	2070.91468	2097.87070	2125.21206	2152.94444	2181.07359	2209.60535

MONTHLY DEPOSITS

NUMBER OF MONTHLY DEPOSITS	EFFECTIVE ANNUAL YIELD							
	6.60%	6.65%	6.70%	6.75%	6.80%	6.85%	6.90%	6.95%
1	1.00534	1.00538	1.00542	1.00546	1.00550	1.00554	1.00558	1.00561
2	2.01605	2.01617	2.01629	2.01640	2.01652	2.01664	2.01676	2.01688
3	3.03216	3.03239	3.03263	3.03287	3.03311	3.03334	3.03358	3.03382
4	4.05369	4.05409	4.05448	4.05488	4.05528	4.05567	4.05607	4.05647
5	5.08068	5.08128	5.08187	5.08247	5.08307	5.08366	5.08426	5.08486
6	6.11315	6.11399	6.11483	6.11567	6.11651	6.11735	6.11819	6.11902
7	7.15114	7.15226	7.15338	7.15451	7.15563	7.15675	7.15788	7.15900
8	8.19467	8.19612	8.19757	8.19902	8.20046	8.20191	8.20336	8.20481
9	9.24377	9.24559	9.24741	9.24923	9.25104	9.25286	9.25468	9.25649
10	10.29847	10.30071	10.30294	10.30517	10.30740	10.30963	10.31186	10.31408
11	11.35881	11.36150	11.36419	11.36687	11.36956	11.37224	11.37493	11.37761
12	12.42481	12.42800	12.43119	12.43437	12.43756	12.44074	12.44393	12.44711
13	13.49650	13.50024	13.50397	13.50770	13.51143	13.51516	13.51889	13.52262
14	14.57392	14.57824	14.58256	14.58688	14.59120	14.59552	14.59984	14.60416
15	15.65709	15.66205	15.66700	15.67196	15.67691	15.68187	15.68682	15.69178
16	16.74604	16.75168	16.75732	16.76296	16.76859	16.77423	16.77987	16.78550
17	17.84081	17.84718	17.85354	17.85991	17.86627	17.87264	17.87900	17.88537
18	18.94143	18.94857	18.95571	18.96285	18.96999	18.97713	18.98427	18.99141
19	20.04792	20.05588	20.06385	20.07181	20.07977	20.08773	20.09570	20.10366
20	21.16033	21.16916	21.17799	21.18682	21.19565	21.20449	21.21332	21.22216
21	22.27867	22.28842	22.29817	22.30792	22.31767	22.32743	22.33718	22.34693
22	23.40298	23.41370	23.42442	23.43514	23.44586	23.45658	23.46730	23.47803
23	24.53330	24.54504	24.55677	24.56851	24.58025	24.59199	24.60373	24.61547
24	25.66966	25.68246	25.69526	25.70806	25.72087	25.73368	25.74649	25.75930
25	26.81208	26.82600	26.83992	26.85384	26.86776	26.88169	26.89562	26.90955
26	27.96061	27.97569	27.99078	28.00587	28.02096	28.03606	28.05116	28.06626
27	29.11527	29.13157	29.14788	29.16419	29.18050	29.19682	29.21314	29.22947
28	30.27609	30.29367	30.31124	30.32883	30.34642	30.36401	30.38161	30.39921
29	31.44312	31.46201	31.48092	31.49982	31.51874	31.53766	31.55658	31.57551
30	32.61638	32.63665	32.65693	32.67721	32.69751	32.71781	32.73811	32.75843
31	33.79590	33.81760	33.83931	33.86103	33.88275	33.90449	33.92623	33.94798
32	34.98172	35.00490	35.02810	35.05130	35.07452	35.09774	35.12097	35.14421
33	36.17387	36.19860	36.22333	36.24808	36.27283	36.29760	36.32237	36.34716
34	37.37239	37.39871	37.42504	37.45138	37.47773	37.50410	37.53047	37.55686
35	38.57731	38.60528	38.63326	38.66125	38.68926	38.71728	38.74531	38.77336
36	39.78867	39.81834	39.84803	39.87773	39.90745	39.93718	39.96692	39.99668
37	41.00649	41.03793	41.06938	41.10085	41.13233	41.16383	41.19535	41.22688
38	42.23082	42.26408	42.29735	42.33064	42.36395	42.39727	42.43062	42.46398
39	43.46169	43.49682	43.53197	43.56714	43.60233	43.63755	43.67278	43.70803
40	44.69913	44.73619	44.77328	44.81040	44.84753	44.88469	44.92187	44.95907
41	45.94318	45.98224	46.02132	46.06043	46.09957	46.13873	46.17792	46.21713
42	47.19387	47.23498	47.27613	47.31730	47.35849	47.39972	47.44097	47.48225
43	48.45124	48.49447	48.53773	48.58102	48.62434	48.66769	48.71107	48.75448
44	49.71532	49.76073	49.80617	49.85164	49.89714	49.94268	49.98825	50.03385
45	50.98616	51.03380	51.08148	51.12919	51.17694	51.22473	51.27254	51.32040
46	52.26378	52.31372	52.36370	52.41372	52.46378	52.51387	52.56401	52.61418
47	53.54823	53.60053	53.65287	53.70526	53.75769	53.81016	53.86267	53.91522
48	54.83953	54.89426	54.94903	55.00385	55.05871	55.11362	55.16857	55.22357
60	70.88375	70.97273	71.06180	71.15098	71.24026	71.32964	71.41913	71.50872
72	87.98689	88.12041	88.25413	88.38804	88.52216	88.65647	88.79098	88.92569
84	106.21884	106.40842	106.59834	106.78861	106.97922	107.17018	107.36148	107.55314
96	125.65409	125.91258	126.17161	126.43121	126.69137	126.95208	127.21335	127.47519
108	146.37207	146.71376	147.05630	147.39969	147.74394	148.08904	148.43500	148.78183
120	168.45744	168.89822	169.34026	169.78354	170.22808	170.67388	171.12095	171.56928
132	192.00044	192.55795	193.11724	193.67830	194.24115	194.80579	195.37222	195.94046
144	217.09729	217.79106	218.48728	219.18596	219.88711	220.59073	221.29683	222.00543
156	243.85052	244.70216	245.55711	246.41538	247.27699	248.14194	249.01024	249.88192
168	272.36946	273.40285	274.44062	275.48279	276.52938	277.58040	278.63588	279.69583
180	302.77066	304.01214	305.25933	306.51225	307.77093	309.03540	310.30568	311.58180
192	335.17833	336.65695	338.14289	339.63620	341.13692	342.64507	344.16070	345.68385
204	369.72492	371.47263	373.22965	374.99602	376.77178	378.55700	380.35172	382.15599
216	406.55157	408.60356	410.66722	412.74262	414.82982	416.92890	419.03992	421.16295
228	445.80879	448.20370	450.61311	453.03712	455.47581	457.92927	460.39760	462.88088
240	487.65698	490.43724	493.23538	496.05150	498.88572	501.73817	504.60896	507.49822
252	532.26715	535.47932	538.71333	541.96935	545.24751	548.54798	551.87091	555.21646
264	579.82159	583.51669	587.23831	590.98665	594.76190	598.56426	602.39393	606.25112
276	630.51463	634.74855	639.01446	643.31262	647.64326	652.00665	656.40304	660.83268
288	684.55340	689.38733	694.25962	699.17059	704.12056	709.10985	714.13878	719.20766
300	742.15874	747.65958	753.20620	758.79898	764.43832	770.12462	775.85828	781.63971
312	803.56603	809.80694	816.10220	822.45208	828.85768	835.31890	841.83643	848.41078
324	869.02620	876.08710	883.21223	890.40218	897.65756	904.97899	912.36707	919.82245
336	938.80674	946.77489	954.81864	962.93870	971.13584	979.41079	987.76433	996.19722
348	1013.19279	1022.16342	1031.22267	1040.37144	1049.61063	1058.94118	1068.36400	1077.88004
360	1092.48833	1102.56529	1112.74577	1123.03088	1133.42171	1143.91939	1154.52504	1165.23981
420	1574.72790	1592.25083	1609.98891	1627.94486	1646.12143	1664.52141	1683.14762	1702.00292
480	2238.54566	2267.90052	2297.67605	2327.87842	2358.51394	2389.58899	2421.11003	2453.08363

MONTHLY DEPOSITS

NUMBER OF MONTHLY DEPOSITS	EFFECTIVE ANNUAL YIELD							
	7.00%	7.05%	7.10%	7.15%	7.20%	7.25%	7.30%	7.35%
1	1.00565	1.00569	1.00573	1.00577	1.00581	1.00585	1.00589	1.00593
2	2.01699	2.01711	2.01723	2.01735	2.01747	2.01758	2.01770	2.01782
3	3.03405	3.03429	3.03453	3.03476	3.03500	3.03524	3.03547	3.03571
4	4.05686	4.05726	4.05765	4.05805	4.05845	4.05884	4.05924	4.05963
5	5.08545	5.08605	5.08665	5.08724	5.08784	5.08843	5.08903	5.08962
6	6.11986	6.12070	6.12154	6.12238	6.12321	6.12405	6.12489	6.12572
7	7.16012	7.16124	7.16236	7.16348	7.16460	7.16572	7.16684	7.16796
8	8.20626	8.20770	8.20915	8.21060	8.21204	8.21349	8.21494	8.21638
9	9.25831	9.26013	9.26194	9.26376	9.26557	9.26739	9.26920	9.27101
10	10.31631	10.31854	10.32077	10.32300	10.32522	10.32745	10.32967	10.33190
11	11.38030	11.38298	11.38566	11.38835	11.39103	11.39371	11.39639	11.39907
12	12.45030	12.45348	12.45666	12.45985	12.46303	12.46621	12.46939	12.47257
13	13.52635	13.53008	13.53380	13.53753	13.54126	13.54499	13.54871	13.55244
14	14.60848	14.61280	14.61712	14.62144	14.62575	14.63007	14.63439	14.63870
15	15.69673	15.70169	15.70664	15.71160	15.71655	15.72150	15.72645	15.73141
16	16.79114	16.79678	16.80241	16.80805	16.81368	16.81932	16.82495	16.83059
17	17.89173	17.89810	17.90446	17.91083	17.91719	17.92356	17.92992	17.93628
18	18.99855	19.00569	19.01283	19.01997	19.02711	19.03425	19.04140	19.04854
19	20.11162	20.11959	20.12755	20.13552	20.14348	20.15145	20.15942	20.16738
20	21.23099	21.23983	21.24867	21.25750	21.26634	21.27518	21.28402	21.29286
21	22.35669	22.36645	22.37620	22.38596	22.39572	22.40548	22.41525	22.42501
22	23.48875	23.49948	23.51021	23.52094	23.53167	23.54240	23.55313	23.56387
23	24.62722	24.63896	24.65071	24.66246	24.67421	24.68597	24.69772	24.70948
24	25.77212	25.78493	25.79775	25.81057	25.82340	25.83622	25.84905	25.86188
25	26.92349	26.93743	26.95137	26.96531	26.97926	26.99321	27.00716	27.02112
26	28.08137	28.09648	28.11160	28.12671	28.14184	28.15696	28.17209	28.18722
27	29.24580	29.26214	29.27848	29.29482	29.31117	29.32752	29.34388	29.36024
28	30.41682	30.43443	30.45205	30.46967	30.48730	30.50493	30.52257	30.54021
29	31.59445	31.61339	31.63234	31.65130	31.67026	31.68923	31.70820	31.72718
30	32.77875	32.79907	32.81941	32.83975	32.86009	32.88045	32.90081	32.92118
31	33.96974	33.99150	34.01327	34.03505	34.05684	34.07864	34.10045	34.12226
32	35.16746	35.19072	35.21399	35.23726	35.26055	35.28384	35.30715	35.33046
33	36.37196	36.39676	36.42158	36.44641	36.47124	36.49609	36.52095	36.54582
34	37.58326	37.60967	37.63610	37.66253	37.68898	37.71543	37.74190	37.76839
35	38.80142	38.82949	38.85757	38.88567	38.91379	38.94191	38.97005	38.99820
36	40.02646	40.05625	40.08606	40.11588	40.14571	40.17556	40.20542	40.23530
37	41.25843	41.29000	41.32158	41.35318	41.38479	41.41643	41.44808	41.47974
38	42.49737	42.53077	42.56418	42.59762	42.63108	42.66455	42.69804	42.73155
39	43.74331	43.77860	43.81391	43.84925	43.88460	43.91998	43.95537	43.99079
40	44.99629	45.03354	45.07081	45.10810	45.14541	45.18275	45.22011	45.25749
41	46.25636	46.29562	46.33490	46.37421	46.41355	46.45291	46.49229	46.53170
42	47.52355	47.56489	47.60625	47.64764	47.68905	47.73049	47.77196	47.81346
43	48.79791	48.84138	48.88488	48.92841	48.97197	49.01555	49.05917	49.10282
44	50.07948	50.12514	50.17084	50.21657	50.26234	50.30813	50.35396	50.39982
45	51.36829	51.41621	51.46418	51.51217	51.56020	51.60827	51.65637	51.70451
46	52.66439	52.71464	52.76492	52.81525	52.86561	52.91602	52.96646	53.01694
47	53.96781	54.02045	54.07313	54.12585	54.17861	54.23141	54.28425	54.33714
48	55.27861	55.33370	55.38883	55.44401	55.49923	55.55450	55.60981	55.66517
60	71.59841	71.68820	71.77810	71.86810	71.95820	72.04841	72.13872	72.22914
72	89.06060	89.19570	89.33101	89.46652	89.60222	89.73813	89.87424	90.01055
84	107.74513	107.93748	108.13018	108.32322	108.51661	108.71036	108.90445	109.09890
96	127.73759	128.00055	128.26408	128.52818	128.79284	129.05807	129.32387	129.59024
108	149.12952	149.47807	149.82750	150.17779	150.52895	150.88099	151.23391	151.58770
120	172.01888	172.46976	172.92191	173.37535	173.83007	174.28608	174.74337	175.20197
132	196.51050	197.08236	197.65603	198.23153	198.80886	199.38803	199.96903	200.55189
144	222.71653	223.43015	224.14628	224.86493	225.58613	226.30987	227.03617	227.76503
156	250.75699	251.63545	252.51733	253.40262	254.29136	255.18355	256.07920	256.97833
168	280.76027	281.82923	282.90272	283.98076	285.06337	286.15057	287.24237	288.33881
180	312.86379	314.15167	315.44548	316.74523	318.05096	319.36269	320.68046	322.00429
192	347.21455	348.75285	350.29877	351.85236	353.41366	354.98270	356.55953	358.14417
204	383.96987	385.79340	387.62665	389.46965	391.32247	393.18516	395.05776	396.94034
216	423.29806	425.44532	427.60480	429.77658	431.96072	434.15729	436.36637	438.58803
228	465.37922	467.89269	470.42141	472.96545	475.52492	478.09991	480.69051	483.29683
240	510.40606	513.33261	516.27799	519.24233	522.22574	525.22836	528.25031	531.29172
252	558.58478	561.97604	565.39039	568.82800	572.28902	575.77363	579.28198	582.81423
264	610.13601	614.04883	617.98977	621.95905	625.95686	629.98343	634.03895	638.12365
276	665.29583	669.79276	674.32371	678.88897	683.48879	688.12344	692.79319	697.49832
288	724.31684	729.46663	734.65736	739.88938	745.16301	750.47860	755.83648	761.23702
300	787.46931	793.34750	799.27470	805.25131	811.27777	817.35451	823.48194	829.66051
312	855.04246	861.73198	868.47986	875.28663	882.15280	889.07892	896.06551	903.11313
324	927.34573	934.93757	942.59860	950.32947	958.13083	966.00335	973.94769	981.96452
336	1004.71023	1013.30415	1021.97976	1030.73787	1039.57928	1048.50481	1057.51526	1066.61149
348	1087.49024	1097.19557	1106.99699	1116.89548	1126.89202	1136.98762	1147.18327	1157.48000
360	1176.06486	1187.00134	1198.05044	1209.21335	1220.49128	1231.88543	1243.39704	1255.02736
420	1721.09021	1740.41242	1759.97251	1779.77350	1799.81842	1820.11037	1840.65247	1861.44787
480	2485.51646	2518.41530	2551.78700	2585.63853	2619.97696	2654.80947	2690.14333	2725.98595

49

MONTHLY DEPOSITS

EFFECTIVE ANNUAL YIELD

NUMBER OF MONTHLY DEPOSITS	7.40%	7.45%	7.50%	7.55%	7.60%	7.65%	7.70%	7.75%
1	1.00597	1.00601	1.00604	1.00608	1.00612	1.00616	1.00620	1.00624
2	2.01794	2.01805	2.01817	2.01829	2.01841	2.01852	2.01864	2.01876
3	3.03594	3.03618	3.03642	3.03665	3.03689	3.03712	3.03736	3.03759
4	4.06003	4.06042	4.06082	4.06121	4.06160	4.06200	4.06239	4.06279
5	5.09022	5.09081	5.09141	5.09200	5.09260	5.09319	5.09378	5.09438
6	6.12656	6.12739	6.12823	6.12907	6.12990	6.13074	6.13157	6.13240
7	7.16908	7.17020	7.17132	7.17244	7.17356	7.17467	7.17579	7.17691
8	8.21783	8.21927	8.22071	8.22216	8.22360	8.22504	8.22649	8.22793
9	9.27283	9.27464	9.27645	9.27827	9.28008	9.28189	9.28370	9.28551
10	10.33412	10.33635	10.33857	10.34080	10.34302	10.34524	10.34747	10.34969
11	11.40175	11.40443	11.40711	11.40979	11.41247	11.41515	11.41783	11.42051
12	12.47575	12.47893	12.48211	12.48529	12.48847	12.49165	12.49483	12.49801
13	13.55616	13.55989	13.56361	13.56734	13.57106	13.57478	13.57851	13.58223
14	14.64302	14.64733	14.65165	14.65596	14.66028	14.66459	14.66890	14.67322
15	15.73636	15.74131	15.74626	15.75121	15.75616	15.76111	15.76606	15.77101
16	16.83622	16.84186	16.84749	16.85313	16.85876	16.86439	16.87003	16.87566
17	17.94265	17.94901	17.95538	17.96174	17.96811	17.97447	17.98083	17.98720
18	19.05568	19.06282	19.06996	19.07710	19.08425	19.09139	19.09853	19.10567
19	20.17535	20.18332	20.19128	20.19925	20.20722	20.21519	20.22316	20.23112
20	21.30170	21.31054	21.31938	21.32822	21.33707	21.34591	21.35476	21.36360
21	22.43477	22.44454	22.45430	22.46407	22.47383	22.48360	22.49337	22.50314
22	23.57460	23.58534	23.59608	23.60682	23.61756	23.62830	23.63905	23.64979
23	24.72124	24.73300	24.74476	24.75653	24.76829	24.78006	24.79183	24.80360
24	25.87471	25.88755	25.90039	25.91323	25.92607	25.93891	25.95176	25.96461
25	27.03507	27.04903	27.06300	27.07696	27.09093	27.10491	27.11888	27.13286
26	28.20236	28.21749	28.23264	28.24778	28.26293	28.27808	28.29324	28.30840
27	29.37660	29.39297	29.40934	29.42572	29.44210	29.45849	29.47488	29.49127
28	30.55786	30.57551	30.59317	30.61083	30.62850	30.64617	30.66385	30.68153
29	31.74616	31.76515	31.78415	31.80315	31.82215	31.84117	31.86019	31.87921
30	32.94155	32.96193	32.98232	33.00272	33.02312	33.04353	33.06394	33.08437
31	34.14408	34.16591	34.18774	34.20959	34.23144	34.25330	34.27517	34.29704
32	35.35378	35.37711	35.40045	35.42380	35.44716	35.47052	35.49390	35.51728
33	36.57070	36.59559	36.62049	36.64540	36.67032	36.69525	36.72019	36.74514
34	37.79488	37.82138	37.84790	37.87443	37.90097	37.92752	37.95408	37.98066
35	39.02636	39.05454	39.08273	39.11094	39.13915	39.16739	39.19563	39.22389
36	40.26520	40.29511	40.32503	40.35497	40.38492	40.41489	40.44487	40.47487
37	41.51142	41.54312	41.57484	41.60657	41.63832	41.67008	41.70186	41.73366
38	42.76508	42.79863	42.83220	42.86578	42.89939	42.93301	42.96665	43.00030
39	44.02623	44.06168	44.09716	44.13266	44.16818	44.20371	44.23927	44.27485
40	45.29489	45.33232	45.36977	45.40724	45.44473	45.48225	45.51979	45.55735
41	46.57113	46.61059	46.65007	46.68958	46.72911	46.76867	46.80825	46.84786
42	47.85498	47.89653	47.93811	47.97972	48.02135	48.06301	48.10470	48.14641
43	49.14649	49.19020	49.23394	49.27770	49.32150	49.36533	49.40918	49.45307
44	50.44571	50.49164	50.53760	50.58359	50.62961	50.67567	50.72176	50.76788
45	51.75268	51.80089	51.84914	51.89742	51.94573	51.99409	52.04247	52.09090
46	53.06745	53.11801	53.16861	53.21924	53.26991	53.32063	53.37138	53.42217
47	54.39007	54.44304	54.49605	54.54911	54.60220	54.65534	54.70852	54.76174
48	55.72058	55.77603	55.83152	55.88706	55.94265	55.99828	56.05396	56.10968
60	72.31965	72.41027	72.50100	72.59183	72.68276	72.77380	72.86494	72.95618
72	90.14706	90.28377	90.42069	90.55780	90.69512	90.83264	90.97037	91.10829
84	109.29370	109.48885	109.68435	109.88021	110.07642	110.27299	110.46991	110.66719
96	129.85719	130.12470	130.39279	130.66146	130.93070	131.20053	131.47093	131.74191
108	151.94237	152.29793	152.65437	153.01170	153.36991	153.72902	154.08902	154.44991
120	175.66186	176.12306	176.58556	177.04937	177.51450	177.98094	178.44870	178.91778
132	201.13659	201.72316	202.31159	202.90189	203.49407	204.08813	204.68408	205.28192
144	228.49646	229.23047	229.96707	230.70628	231.44809	232.19252	232.93958	233.68927
156	257.88095	258.78708	259.69672	260.60990	261.52662	262.44690	263.37075	264.29820
168	289.43989	290.54565	291.65609	292.77124	293.89111	295.01574	296.14513	297.27931
180	323.33420	324.67023	326.01241	327.36076	328.71531	330.07609	331.44313	332.81647
192	359.73669	361.33710	362.94545	364.56179	366.18615	367.81856	369.45908	371.10775
204	398.83295	400.73565	402.64848	404.57150	406.50476	408.44833	410.40226	412.36660
216	440.82235	443.06939	445.32923	447.60194	449.88760	452.18628	454.49806	456.82302
228	485.91896	488.55699	491.21103	493.88118	496.56753	499.27018	501.98924	504.72481
240	534.35271	537.43342	540.53397	543.65450	546.79513	549.95600	553.13724	556.33899
252	586.37057	589.95114	593.55614	597.18571	600.84003	604.51929	608.22364	611.95327
264	642.23774	646.38144	650.55496	654.75852	658.99235	663.25666	667.55169	671.87765
276	702.23909	707.01579	711.82870	716.67808	721.56424	726.48745	731.44800	736.44617
288	766.68054	772.16740	777.69796	783.27257	788.89159	794.55539	800.26432	806.01876
300	835.89065	842.17281	848.50742	854.89495	861.33583	867.83053	874.37950	880.98322
312	910.22231	917.39362	924.62759	931.92481	939.28582	946.71121	954.20155	961.75742
324	990.05452	998.21838	1006.45678	1014.77042	1023.16002	1031.62627	1040.16990	1048.79163
336	1075.79431	1085.06458	1094.42315	1103.87088	1113.40865	1123.03733	1132.75781	1142.57099
348	1167.87884	1178.38082	1188.98700	1199.69843	1210.51618	1221.44134	1232.47499	1243.61825
360	1266.77763	1278.64913	1290.64314	1302.76095	1315.00388	1327.37325	1339.87039	1352.49666
420	1882.49978	1903.81144	1925.38614	1947.22720	1969.33799	1991.72191	2014.38243	2037.32304
480	2762.34481	2799.22752	2836.64181	2874.59550	2913.09657	2952.15306	2991.77317	3031.96521

MONTHLY DEPOSITS

EFFECTIVE ANNUAL YIELD

NUMBER OF MONTHLY DEPOSITS	7.80%	7.85%	7.90%	7.95%	8.00%	8.05%	8.10%	8.15%
1	1.00628	1.00632	1.00636	1.00640	1.00643	1.00647	1.00651	1.00655
2	2.01888	2.01899	2.01911	2.01923	2.01934	2.01946	2.01958	2.01969
3	3.03783	3.03806	3.03830	3.03854	3.03877	3.03900	3.03924	3.03947
4	4.06318	4.06358	4.06397	4.06436	4.06476	4.06515	4.06554	4.06593
5	5.09497	5.09556	5.09616	5.09675	5.09734	5.09793	5.09853	5.09912
6	6.13324	6.13407	6.13491	6.13574	6.13657	6.13741	6.13824	6.13907
7	7.17803	7.17914	7.18026	7.18137	7.18249	7.18361	7.18472	7.18584
8	8.22937	8.23081	8.23225	8.23370	8.23514	8.23658	8.23802	8.23946
9	9.28732	9.28913	9.29094	9.29275	9.29456	9.29636	9.29817	9.29998
10	10.35191	10.35413	10.35635	10.35857	10.36079	10.36301	10.36523	10.36745
11	11.42318	11.42586	11.42854	11.43121	11.43389	11.43656	11.43924	11.44191
12	12.50118	12.50436	12.50754	12.51071	12.51389	12.51706	12.52024	12.52341
13	13.58595	13.58967	13.59339	13.59711	13.60084	13.60456	13.60827	13.61199
14	14.67753	14.68184	14.68615	14.69047	14.69478	14.69909	14.70340	14.70771
15	15.77596	15.78091	15.78586	15.79081	15.79576	15.80071	15.80565	15.81060
16	16.88129	16.88693	16.89256	16.89819	16.90382	16.90945	16.91509	16.92072
17	17.99356	17.99993	18.00629	18.01265	18.01902	18.02538	18.03174	18.03811
18	19.11281	19.11996	19.12710	19.13424	19.14139	19.14853	19.15567	19.16281
19	20.23909	20.24706	20.25503	20.26300	20.27098	20.27895	20.28692	20.29489
20	21.37245	21.38129	21.39014	21.39899	21.40783	21.41668	21.42553	21.43438
21	22.51291	22.52268	22.53246	22.54223	22.55201	22.56178	22.57156	22.58134
22	23.66054	23.67129	23.68204	23.69279	23.70354	23.71429	23.72505	23.73580
23	24.81537	24.82715	24.83893	24.85070	24.86248	24.87427	24.88605	24.89783
24	25.97746	25.99031	26.00317	26.01602	26.02888	26.04175	26.05461	26.06748
25	27.14684	27.16082	27.17481	27.18880	27.20279	27.21678	27.23078	27.24478
26	28.32356	28.33873	28.35390	28.36907	28.38425	28.39943	28.41461	28.42980
27	29.50767	29.52407	29.54048	29.55689	29.57331	29.58972	29.60615	29.62257
28	30.69922	30.71691	30.73461	30.75231	30.77001	30.78773	30.80544	30.82317
29	31.89824	31.91728	31.93632	31.95537	31.97442	31.99348	32.01255	32.03162
30	33.10480	33.12523	33.14568	33.16613	33.18658	33.20705	33.22752	33.24799
31	34.31893	34.34082	34.36272	34.38462	34.40654	34.42846	34.45039	34.47233
32	35.54068	35.56408	35.58749	35.61092	35.63435	35.65779	35.68123	35.70469
33	36.77010	36.79507	36.82006	36.84505	36.87005	36.89507	36.92009	36.94512
34	38.00725	38.03384	38.06045	38.08708	38.11371	38.14036	38.16701	38.19368
35	39.25216	39.28044	39.30874	39.33705	39.36537	39.39371	39.42206	39.45042
36	40.50488	40.53491	40.56495	40.59501	40.62508	40.65517	40.68527	40.71539
37	41.76547	41.79731	41.82915	41.86102	41.89290	41.92480	41.95671	41.98864
38	43.03398	43.06768	43.10139	43.13512	43.16887	43.20264	43.23643	43.27023
39	44.31045	44.34607	44.38171	44.41737	44.45306	44.48876	44.52448	44.56022
40	45.59494	45.63254	45.67017	45.70783	45.74550	45.78320	45.82092	45.85866
41	46.88749	46.92714	46.96683	47.00653	47.04626	47.08602	47.12580	47.16561
42	48.18815	48.22992	48.27172	48.31354	48.35540	48.39727	48.43918	48.48111
43	49.49699	49.54093	49.58491	49.62891	49.67295	49.71702	49.76111	49.80524
44	50.81404	50.86022	50.90644	50.95270	50.99898	51.04530	51.09165	51.13803
45	52.13935	52.18785	52.23638	52.28494	52.33354	52.38218	52.43085	52.47956
46	53.47299	53.52386	53.57477	53.62571	53.67669	53.72772	53.77878	53.82988
47	54.81501	54.86831	54.92166	54.97505	55.02849	55.08196	55.13548	55.18904
48	56.16545	56.22126	56.27712	56.33302	56.38897	56.44497	56.50101	56.55710
60	73.04753	73.13899	73.23055	73.32221	73.41398	73.50585	73.59783	73.68991
72	91.24642	91.38476	91.52330	91.66204	91.80098	91.94013	92.07949	92.21905
84	110.86483	111.06282	111.26117	111.45988	111.65895	111.85838	112.05816	112.25831
96	132.01347	132.28651	132.55834	132.83165	133.10555	133.38004	133.65511	133.93077
108	154.81170	155.17439	155.53798	155.90248	156.26788	156.63419	157.00141	157.36954
120	179.38820	179.85994	180.33302	180.80744	181.28320	181.76030	182.23876	182.71857
132	205.88166	206.48331	207.08686	207.69234	208.29974	208.90907	209.52034	210.13354
144	234.44161	235.19660	235.95426	236.71459	237.47761	238.24331	239.01172	239.78284
156	265.22924	266.16390	267.10218	268.04411	268.98970	269.93896	270.89190	271.84855
168	298.41830	299.56212	300.71079	301.86433	303.02276	304.18611	305.35438	306.52761
180	334.19611	335.58211	336.97448	338.37326	339.77847	341.19015	342.60832	344.03302
192	372.76459	374.42966	376.10300	377.78464	379.47464	381.17302	382.87983	384.59512
204	414.34141	416.32675	418.32267	420.32923	422.34649	424.37451	426.41334	428.46303
216	459.16123	461.51276	463.87770	466.25612	468.64810	471.05372	473.47305	475.90618
228	507.47699	510.24587	513.03157	515.83419	518.65383	521.49060	524.34460	527.21594
240	559.56137	562.80453	566.06860	569.35372	572.66003	575.98766	579.33675	582.70745
252	615.70834	619.48905	623.29556	627.12805	630.98671	634.87172	638.78326	642.72152
264	676.23478	680.62330	685.04344	689.49545	693.97954	698.49596	703.04494	707.62673
276	741.48227	746.55659	751.66941	756.82104	762.01179	767.24195	772.51182	777.82172
288	811.81907	817.66564	823.55883	829.49903	835.48662	841.52198	847.60551	853.73760
300	887.64214	894.35675	901.12751	907.95491	914.83943	921.78156	928.78180	935.84603
312	969.37941	977.06811	984.82412	992.64804	1000.54047	1008.50204	1016.53336	1024.63505
324	1057.49219	1066.27232	1075.13276	1084.07427	1093.09760	1102.20352	1111.39280	1120.66621
336	1152.47777	1162.47906	1172.57579	1182.76889	1193.05929	1203.44796	1213.93585	1224.52392
348	1254.87221	1266.23802	1277.71681	1289.30972	1301.01792	1312.84258	1324.78489	1336.84603
360	1365.25343	1378.14207	1391.16397	1404.32056	1417.61324	1431.04347	1444.61270	1458.32339
420	2060.54727	2084.05873	2107.86102	2131.95785	2156.35292	2181.05001	2206.05294	2231.36557
480	3072.73761	3114.09893	3156.05785	3198.62318	3241.80387	3285.60898	3330.04772	3375.12944

51

MONTHLY DEPOSITS

EFFECTIVE ANNUAL YIELD

NUMBER OF MONTHLY DEPOSITS	8.20%	8.25%	8.30%	8.35%	8.40%	8.45%	8.50%	8.55%
1	1.00659	1.00663	1.00667	1.00671	1.00674	1.00678	1.00682	1.00686
2	2.01981	2.01993	2.02004	2.02016	2.02028	2.02039	2.02051	2.02063
3	3.03971	3.03994	3.04018	3.04041	3.04065	3.04088	3.04112	3.04135
4	4.06633	4.06672	4.06711	4.06751	4.06790	4.06829	4.06868	4.06907
5	5.09971	5.10030	5.10089	5.10149	5.10208	5.10267	5.10326	5.10385
6	6.13990	6.14074	6.14157	6.14240	6.14323	6.14406	6.14489	6.14572
7	7.18695	7.18806	7.18918	7.19029	7.19140	7.19252	7.19363	7.19474
8	8.24090	8.24233	8.24377	8.24521	8.24665	8.24809	8.24952	8.25096
9	9.30179	9.30359	9.30540	9.30720	9.30901	9.31081	9.31262	9.31442
10	10.36967	10.37188	10.37410	10.37632	10.37853	10.38075	10.38297	10.38518
11	11.44458	11.44726	11.44993	11.45260	11.45527	11.45794	11.46061	11.46329
12	12.52658	12.52976	12.53293	12.53610	12.53927	12.54244	12.54561	12.54879
13	13.61571	13.61943	13.62315	13.62687	13.63058	13.63430	13.63802	13.64173
14	14.71202	14.71633	14.72064	14.72495	14.72925	14.73356	14.73787	14.74218
15	15.81555	15.82050	15.82544	15.83039	15.83533	15.84028	15.84522	15.85017
16	16.92635	16.93198	16.93761	16.94324	16.94887	16.95450	16.96013	16.96576
17	18.04447	18.05083	18.05720	18.06356	18.06992	18.07629	18.08265	18.08901
18	19.16996	19.17710	19.18425	19.19139	19.19853	19.20568	19.21282	19.21997
19	20.30286	20.31083	20.31881	20.32678	20.33475	20.34273	20.35070	20.35868
20	21.44323	21.45208	21.46093	21.46979	21.47864	21.48749	21.49635	21.50520
21	22.59111	22.60089	22.61067	22.62046	22.63024	22.64002	22.64981	22.65959
22	23.74656	23.75732	23.76808	23.77884	23.78960	23.80037	23.81113	23.82190
23	24.90962	24.92141	24.93320	24.94499	24.95679	24.96858	24.98038	24.99218
24	26.08035	26.09322	26.10609	26.11897	26.13184	26.14472	26.15761	26.17049
25	27.25878	27.27279	27.28680	27.30081	27.31482	27.32884	27.34286	27.35688
26	28.44499	28.46018	28.47538	28.49058	28.50578	28.52099	28.53620	28.55142
27	29.63901	29.65544	29.67188	29.68833	29.70477	29.72123	29.73768	29.75414
28	30.84089	30.85863	30.87636	30.89410	30.91185	30.92960	30.94736	30.96512
29	32.05070	32.06978	32.08887	32.10797	32.12707	32.14618	32.16529	32.18441
30	33.26848	33.28897	33.30947	33.32997	33.35048	33.37100	33.39153	33.41206
31	34.49428	34.51623	34.53820	34.56017	34.58215	34.60413	34.62613	34.64813
32	35.72816	35.75164	35.77512	35.79861	35.82212	35.84563	35.86915	35.89268
33	36.97017	36.99522	37.02029	37.04536	37.07045	37.09555	37.12065	37.14577
34	38.22036	38.24706	38.27376	38.30048	38.32720	38.35394	38.38069	38.40746
35	39.47879	39.50718	39.53559	39.56400	39.59243	39.62087	39.64933	39.67780
36	40.74552	40.77566	40.80582	40.83600	40.86619	40.89640	40.92662	40.95685
37	42.02059	42.05255	42.08453	42.11653	42.14854	42.18057	42.21262	42.24468
38	43.30406	43.33790	43.37176	43.40564	43.43954	43.47346	43.50739	43.54135
39	44.59599	44.63177	44.66758	44.70340	44.73925	44.77511	44.81100	44.84691
40	45.89643	45.93422	45.97203	46.00986	46.04772	46.08560	46.12350	46.16143
41	47.20544	47.24530	47.28518	47.32508	47.36502	47.40497	47.44495	47.48496
42	48.52308	48.56506	48.60708	48.64912	48.69120	48.73329	48.77542	48.81757
43	49.84939	49.89358	49.93780	49.98204	50.02632	50.07063	50.11496	50.15933
44	51.18445	51.23090	51.27738	51.32390	51.37045	51.41703	51.46364	51.51029
45	52.52831	52.57709	52.62590	52.67475	52.72364	52.77256	52.82152	52.87052
46	53.88102	53.93219	53.98341	54.03467	54.08596	54.13729	54.18867	54.24008
47	55.24264	55.29628	55.34997	55.40370	55.45747	55.51128	55.56514	55.61903
48	56.61323	56.66941	56.72564	56.78191	56.83822	56.89459	56.95099	57.00745
60	73.78210	73.87439	73.96679	74.05930	74.15191	74.24462	74.33744	74.43037
72	92.35882	92.49879	92.63897	92.77935	92.91994	93.06074	93.20174	93.34295
84	112.45882	112.65969	112.86093	113.06253	113.26449	113.46681	113.66950	113.87256
96	134.20703	134.48387	134.76131	135.03935	135.31798	135.59720	135.87703	136.15745
108	157.73859	158.10855	158.47943	158.85123	159.22396	159.59761	159.97219	160.34770
120	183.19974	183.68226	184.16615	184.65141	185.13804	185.62605	186.11544	186.60621
132	210.74870	211.36580	211.98487	212.60591	213.22891	213.85390	214.48087	215.10983
144	240.55667	241.33324	242.11255	242.89460	243.67941	244.46700	245.25735	246.05050
156	272.80890	273.77299	274.74082	275.71240	276.68776	277.66690	278.64984	279.63660
168	307.70582	308.88902	310.07723	311.27049	312.46880	313.67220	314.88070	316.09432
180	345.46428	346.90212	348.34657	349.79767	351.25545	352.71994	354.19117	355.66917
192	386.31893	388.05130	389.79227	391.54188	393.30018	395.06722	396.84303	398.62767
204	430.52366	432.59528	434.67795	436.77173	438.87667	440.99284	443.12031	445.25912
216	478.35319	480.81415	483.28915	485.77827	488.28159	490.79918	493.33115	495.87756
228	530.10473	533.01107	535.93508	538.87685	541.83651	544.81416	547.80991	550.82387
240	586.09990	589.51424	592.95062	596.40917	599.89005	603.39340	606.91936	610.46810
252	646.66668	650.57893	654.69845	658.74544	662.82009	666.92258	671.05313	675.21190
264	712.24157	716.88969	721.57135	726.28678	731.03625	735.81999	740.63826	745.49131
276	783.17196	788.56285	793.99470	799.46783	804.98256	810.53922	816.13812	821.77960
288	859.91865	866.14904	872.42919	878.75950	885.14037	891.57223	898.05548	904.59054
300	942.95856	950.13609	957.37374	964.67201	972.03144	979.45252	986.93581	994.48182
312	1032.80774	1041.05207	1049.36869	1057.75823	1066.22135	1074.75871	1083.37097	1092.05880
324	1130.02456	1139.46863	1148.99922	1158.61774	1168.33155	1178.11826	1188.00311	1197.97861
336	1235.21316	1246.00455	1256.89908	1267.89777	1279.00164	1290.21170	1301.52899	1312.95456
348	1349.02722	1361.32968	1373.75463	1386.30334	1398.97705	1411.77703	1424.70457	1437.76096
360	1472.17403	1486.16913	1500.30920	1514.59577	1529.03039	1543.61463	1558.35007	1573.23831
420	2256.99183	2282.93566	2309.20110	2335.79221	2362.71310	2389.96794	2417.56096	2445.49643
480	3420.86362	3467.25988	3514.32798	3562.07783	3610.51948	3659.66314	3709.51915	3760.09803

MONTHLY DEPOSITS

NUMBER OF MONTHLY DEPOSITS	EFFECTIVE ANNUAL YIELD							
	8.60%	8.65%	8.70%	8.75%	8.80%	8.85%	8.90%	8.95%
1	1.00690	1.00694	1.00698	1.00701	1.00705	1.00709	1.00713	1.00717
2	2.02074	2.02086	2.02098	2.02109	2.02121	2.02133	2.02144	2.02156
3	3.04158	3.04182	3.04205	3.04228	3.04252	3.04275	3.04299	3.04322
4	4.06947	4.06986	4.07025	4.07064	4.07103	4.07142	4.07181	4.07220
5	5.10444	5.10503	5.10562	5.10621	5.10680	5.10739	5.10798	5.10857
6	6.14655	6.14738	6.14821	6.14904	6.14987	6.15070	6.15153	6.15236
7	7.19585	7.19697	7.19808	7.19919	7.20030	7.20141	7.20252	7.20363
8	8.25240	8.25383	8.25527	8.25670	8.25814	8.25957	8.26101	8.26244
9	9.31623	9.31803	9.31983	9.32164	9.32344	9.32524	9.32704	9.32884
10	10.38740	10.38961	10.39182	10.39404	10.39625	10.39846	10.40068	10.40289
11	11.46595	11.46862	11.47129	11.47396	11.47663	11.47930	11.48197	11.48463
12	12.55195	12.55512	12.55829	12.56146	12.56463	12.56780	12.57097	12.57413
13	13.64545	13.64916	13.65288	13.65659	13.66030	13.66402	13.66773	13.67144
14	14.74648	14.75079	14.75510	14.75940	14.76371	14.76801	14.77232	14.77662
15	15.85511	15.86006	15.86500	15.86995	15.87489	15.87983	15.88478	15.88972
16	16.97139	16.97702	16.98265	16.98828	16.99391	16.99954	17.00517	17.01080
17	18.09538	18.10174	18.10810	18.11446	18.12083	18.12719	18.13355	18.13991
18	19.22711	19.23425	19.24140	19.24854	19.25569	19.26283	19.26998	19.27713
19	20.36665	20.37463	20.38260	20.39058	20.39856	20.40653	20.41451	20.42249
20	21.51406	21.52291	21.53177	21.54063	21.54948	21.55834	21.56720	21.57606
21	22.66938	22.67916	22.68895	22.69874	22.70853	22.71832	22.72811	22.73791
22	23.83267	23.84344	23.85421	23.86498	23.87575	23.88653	23.89730	23.90808
23	25.00398	25.01578	25.02759	25.03940	25.05120	25.06301	25.07483	25.08664
24	26.18338	26.19627	26.20916	26.22205	26.23495	26.24785	26.26075	26.27365
25	27.37091	27.38494	27.39897	27.41300	27.42704	27.44108	27.45512	27.46917
26	28.56664	28.58186	28.59708	28.61231	28.62754	28.64278	28.65802	28.67326
27	29.77061	29.78708	30.80355	29.82003	29.83651	29.85300	29.86949	29.88598
28	30.98289	31.00066	31.01844	31.03622	31.05401	31.07180	31.08960	31.10740
29	32.20353	32.22266	32.24180	32.26094	32.28009	32.29924	32.31840	32.33757
30	33.43260	33.45314	33.47369	33.49425	33.51482	33.53539	33.55597	33.57656
31	34.67014	34.69216	34.71418	34.73622	34.75826	34.78031	34.80237	34.82443
32	35.91622	35.93977	35.96333	35.98689	36.01047	36.03405	36.05765	36.08125
33	37.17090	37.19604	37.22118	37.24634	37.27151	37.29669	37.32188	37.34708
34	38.43423	38.46102	38.48782	38.51463	38.54145	38.56828	38.59513	38.62198
35	39.70628	39.73477	39.76328	39.79181	39.82034	39.84889	39.87745	39.90603
36	40.98710	41.01737	41.04765	41.07794	41.10825	41.13858	41.16892	41.19927
37	42.27676	42.30886	42.34097	42.37310	42.40525	42.43742	42.46960	42.50179
38	43.57532	43.60931	43.64332	43.67735	43.71140	43.74546	43.77955	43.81365
39	44.88284	44.91879	44.95475	44.99074	45.02675	45.06279	45.09884	45.13491
40	46.19937	46.23734	46.27534	46.31335	46.35139	46.38945	46.42754	46.46564
41	47.52499	47.56505	47.60513	47.64524	47.68537	47.72553	47.76571	47.80591
42	48.85976	48.90196	48.94420	48.98646	49.02876	49.07107	49.11342	49.15579
43	50.20373	50.24815	50.29261	50.33710	50.38162	50.42617	50.47074	50.51535
44	51.55697	51.60368	51.65043	51.69721	51.74402	51.79087	51.83774	51.88466
45	52.91955	52.96862	53.01772	53.06686	53.11603	53.16525	53.21449	53.26378
46	54.29153	54.34302	54.39455	54.44612	54.49773	54.54937	54.60106	54.65278
47	55.67297	55.72696	55.78098	55.83505	55.88916	55.94331	55.99751	56.05175
48	57.06395	57.12050	57.17709	57.23373	57.29041	57.34714	57.40392	57.46074
60	74.52340	74.61654	74.70979	74.80314	74.89660	74.99016	75.08383	75.17761
72	93.48437	93.62600	93.76783	93.90988	94.05213	94.19459	94.33726	94.48014
84	114.07598	114.27977	114.48393	114.68845	114.89335	115.09861	115.30424	115.51024
96	136.43847	136.72010	137.00232	137.28515	137.56859	137.85263	138.13728	138.42254
108	160.72414	161.10151	161.47982	161.85907	162.23926	162.62039	163.00247	163.38549
120	187.09837	187.59191	188.08686	188.58320	189.08094	189.58009	190.08065	190.58263
132	215.74078	216.37374	217.00871	217.64569	218.28470	218.92573	219.56880	220.21390
144	246.84644	247.64519	248.44676	249.25115	250.05838	250.86845	251.68138	252.49718
156	280.62719	281.62163	282.61992	283.62209	284.62815	285.63811	286.65199	287.66981
168	317.31309	318.53702	319.76615	321.00048	322.24005	323.48488	324.73499	325.99039
180	357.15397	358.64560	360.14410	361.64949	363.16181	364.68109	366.20736	367.74066
192	400.42116	402.22357	404.03493	405.85528	407.68468	409.52317	411.37079	413.22758
204	447.40934	449.57103	451.74426	453.92908	456.12556	458.33376	460.55375	462.78559
216	498.43849	501.01405	503.60430	506.20934	508.82924	511.46410	514.11400	516.77903
228	553.85616	556.90689	559.97617	563.06412	566.17085	569.29647	572.44111	575.60488
240	614.03975	617.63446	621.25239	624.89369	628.55851	632.24701	635.95934	639.69565
252	679.39912	683.61496	687.85964	692.13335	696.43629	700.76867	705.13068	709.52255
264	750.37940	755.30278	760.26172	765.25648	770.28731	775.35449	780.45828	785.59895
276	827.46398	833.19160	838.96279	844.77788	850.63723	856.54116	862.49003	868.48418
288	911.17784	917.81780	924.51084	931.25741	938.05793	944.91285	951.82261	958.78765
300	1002.09109	1009.76416	1017.50158	1025.30390	1033.17166	1041.10544	1049.10579	1057.17328
312	1100.82288	1109.66388	1118.58251	1127.57945	1136.65540	1145.81107	1155.04717	1164.36442
324	1208.04560	1218.20493	1228.45748	1238.80411	1249.24570	1259.78314	1270.41733	1281.14917
336	1324.48947	1336.13479	1347.89158	1359.76093	1371.74396	1383.84175	1396.05544	1408.38615
348	1450.94752	1464.26557	1477.71644	1491.30148	1505.02205	1518.87954	1532.87534	1547.01084
360	1588.28097	1603.47967	1618.83606	1634.35182	1650.02863	1665.86818	1681.87221	1698.04244
420	2473.77867	2502.41209	2531.40110	2560.75022	2590.46398	2620.54701	2651.00396	2681.83957
480	3811.41042	3863.46716	3916.27921	3969.85771	4024.21397	4079.35945	4135.30579	4192.06481

MONTHLY DEPOSITS

EFFECTIVE ANNUAL YIELD

NUMBER OF MONTHLY DEPOSITS	9.00%	9.05%	9.10%	9.15%	9.20%	9.25%	9.30%	9.35%
1	1.00721	1.00725	1.00728	1.00732	1.00736	1.00740	1.00744	1.00748
2	2.02167	2.02179	2.02191	2.02202	2.02214	2.02225	2.02237	2.02249
3	3.04345	3.04369	3.04392	3.04415	3.04438	3.04462	3.04485	3.04508
4	4.07259	4.07299	4.07338	4.07377	4.07416	4.07455	4.07494	4.07533
5	5.10915	5.10974	5.11033	5.11092	5.11151	5.11210	5.11268	5.11327
6	6.15319	6.15401	6.15484	6.15567	6.15650	6.15732	6.15815	6.15898
7	7.20474	7.20585	7.20696	7.20807	7.20918	7.21028	7.21139	7.21250
8	8.26387	8.26531	8.26674	8.26817	8.26961	8.27104	8.27247	8.27390
9	9.33064	9.33244	9.33424	9.33604	9.33784	9.33964	9.34144	9.34324
10	10.40510	10.40731	10.40952	10.41173	10.41394	10.41615	10.41836	10.42057
11	11.48730	11.48996	11.49263	11.49530	11.49796	11.50062	11.50329	11.50595
12	12.57730	12.58046	12.58363	12.58680	12.58996	12.59312	12.59629	12.59945
13	13.67515	13.67887	13.68258	13.68629	13.69000	13.69371	13.69742	13.70113
14	14.78092	14.78523	14.78953	14.79383	14.79813	14.80244	14.80674	14.81104
15	15.89466	15.89960	15.90455	15.90949	15.91443	15.91937	15.92431	15.92925
16	17.01643	17.02206	17.02768	17.03331	17.03894	17.04457	17.05019	17.05582
17	18.14628	18.15264	18.15900	18.16536	18.17173	18.17809	18.18445	18.19081
18	19.28427	19.29142	19.29856	19.30571	19.31285	19.32000	19.32715	19.33429
19	20.43047	20.43844	20.44642	20.45440	20.46238	20.47036	20.47834	20.48632
20	21.58492	21.59378	21.60264	21.61151	21.62037	21.62923	21.63810	21.64696
21	22.74770	22.75749	22.76729	22.77709	22.78688	22.79668	22.80648	22.81628
22	23.91886	23.92964	23.94042	23.95120	23.96198	23.97277	23.98355	23.99434
23	25.09845	25.11027	25.12209	25.13391	25.14573	25.15756	25.16938	25.18121
24	26.28655	26.29946	26.31237	26.32528	26.33820	26.35111	26.36403	26.37695
25	27.48322	27.49727	27.51132	27.52538	27.53944	27.55350	27.56757	27.58163
26	28.68851	28.70375	28.71901	28.73426	28.74952	28.76479	28.78005	28.79532
27	29.90248	29.91898	29.93549	29.95200	29.96852	29.98504	30.00156	30.01809
28	31.12520	31.14302	31.16083	31.17865	31.19648	31.21431	31.23215	31.24999
29	32.35674	32.37592	32.39510	32.41429	32.43349	32.45269	32.47189	32.49111
30	33.59715	33.61775	33.63836	33.65898	33.67960	33.70022	33.72086	33.74150
31	34.84651	34.86859	34.89068	34.91277	34.93488	34.95699	34.97911	35.00124
32	36.10486	36.12849	36.15212	36.17576	36.19940	36.22306	36.24673	36.27040
33	37.37229	37.39751	37.42274	37.44798	37.47324	37.49850	37.52377	37.54905
34	38.64885	38.67573	38.70263	38.72953	38.75645	38.78337	38.81031	38.83726
35	39.93461	39.96322	39.99183	40.02046	40.04910	40.07776	40.10642	40.13510
36	41.22964	41.26003	41.29043	41.32084	41.35127	41.38172	41.41217	41.44265
37	42.53401	42.56624	42.59848	42.63075	42.66303	42.69532	42.72764	42.75997
38	43.84777	43.88191	43.91607	43.95024	43.98444	44.01865	44.05289	44.08714
39	45.17100	45.20712	45.24325	45.27940	45.31558	45.35178	45.38799	45.42423
40	46.50377	46.54192	46.58010	46.61830	46.65652	46.69476	46.73303	46.77132
41	47.84615	47.88640	47.92669	47.96699	48.00733	48.04768	48.08807	48.12848
42	49.19820	49.24063	49.28308	49.32557	49.36808	49.41062	49.45319	49.49578
43	50.55999	50.60466	50.64936	50.69409	50.73885	50.78364	50.82846	50.87331
44	51.93160	51.97858	52.02559	52.07263	52.11971	52.16682	52.21396	52.26114
45	53.31310	53.36245	53.41184	53.46127	53.51073	53.56023	53.60977	53.65934
46	54.70455	54.75635	54.80819	54.86008	54.91200	54.96396	55.01596	55.06800
47	56.10603	56.16035	56.21472	56.26913	56.32358	56.37807	56.43261	56.48719
48	57.51761	57.57453	57.63149	57.68849	57.74555	57.80265	57.85980	57.91699
60	75.27149	75.36548	75.45958	75.55379	75.64810	75.74252	75.83704	75.93168
72	94.62323	94.76653	94.91003	95.05375	95.19768	95.34183	95.48618	95.63074
84	115.71662	115.92336	116.13048	116.33797	116.54583	116.75407	116.96268	117.17167
96	138.70841	138.99489	139.28198	139.56969	139.85802	140.14695	140.43650	140.72667
108	163.76947	164.15439	164.54027	164.92711	165.31491	165.70366	166.09338	166.48407
120	191.08602	191.59083	192.09707	192.60474	193.11384	193.62438	194.13635	194.64978
132	220.86106	221.51027	222.16153	222.81487	223.47027	224.12775	224.78732	225.44899
144	253.31585	254.13741	254.96186	255.78922	256.61950	257.45270	258.28883	259.12792
156	288.69158	289.71731	290.74702	291.78073	292.81845	293.86020	294.90598	295.95583
168	327.25112	328.51719	329.78863	331.06546	332.34771	333.63539	334.92853	336.22715
180	369.28102	370.82846	372.38303	373.94475	375.51366	377.08979	378.67317	380.26384
192	415.09361	416.96890	418.85351	420.74749	422.65087	424.56372	426.48606	428.41796
204	465.02933	467.28505	469.55281	471.83268	474.12471	476.42898	478.74556	481.07449
216	519.45927	522.15481	524.86575	527.59216	530.33415	533.09179	535.86518	538.65441
228	578.78790	581.99029	585.21216	588.45364	591.71485	594.99591	598.29693	601.61805
240	643.45611	647.24088	651.05010	654.88395	658.74258	662.62615	666.53483	670.46879
252	713.94446	718.39664	722.87929	727.39262	731.93685	736.51219	741.11886	745.75707
264	790.77676	795.99200	801.24494	806.53584	811.86500	817.23270	822.63920	828.08481
276	874.52397	880.60974	886.74186	892.92067	899.14655	905.41985	911.74094	918.11019
288	965.80843	972.88539	980.01899	987.20971	994.45799	1001.76431	1009.12913	1016.55295
300	1065.30848	1073.51198	1081.78435	1090.12619	1098.53808	1107.02063	1115.57443	1124.20010
312	1173.76355	1183.24528	1192.81036	1202.45953	1212.19355	1222.01316	1231.91914	1241.91226
324	1291.97956	1302.90944	1313.93973	1325.07138	1336.30531	1347.64250	1359.08391	1370.63051
336	1420.83502	1433.40321	1446.09188	1458.90220	1471.83536	1484.89256	1498.07500	1511.38391
348	1561.28747	1575.70667	1590.26987	1604.97855	1619.83418	1634.83825	1649.99227	1665.29776
360	1714.38064	1730.88859	1747.56806	1764.42088	1781.44888	1798.65391	1816.03784	1833.60255
420	2713.05862	2744.66596	2776.66649	2809.06518	2841.86708	2875.07726	2908.70090	2942.74321
480	4249.64848	4308.06897	4367.33861	4427.46992	4488.47562	4550.36858	4613.16190	4676.86885

MONTHLY DEPOSITS

NUMBER OF MONTHLY DEPOSITS	EFFECTIVE ANNUAL YIELD							
	9.40%	9.45%	9.50%	9.55%	9.60%	9.65%	9.70%	9.75%
1	1.00751	1.00755	1.00759	1.00763	1.00767	1.00771	1.00774	1.00778
2	2.02260	2.02272	2.02283	2.02295	2.02306	2.02318	2.02329	2.02341
3	3.04532	3.04555	3.04578	3.04601	3.04624	3.04648	3.04671	3.04694
4	4.07572	4.07610	4.07649	4.07688	4.07727	4.07766	4.07805	4.07844
5	5.11386	5.11445	5.11503	5.11562	5.11621	5.11679	5.11738	5.11796
6	6.15980	6.16063	6.16145	6.16228	6.16311	6.16393	6.16476	6.16558
7	7.21361	7.21471	7.21582	7.21693	7.21803	7.21914	7.22025	7.22135
8	8.27533	8.27676	8.27819	8.27962	8.28105	8.28248	8.28391	8.28534
9	9.34503	9.34683	9.34863	9.35042	9.35222	9.35402	9.35581	9.35761
10	10.42277	10.42498	10.42719	10.42940	10.43160	10.43381	10.43601	10.43822
11	11.50861	11.51128	11.51394	11.51660	11.51926	11.52192	11.52458	11.52724
12	12.60261	12.60578	12.60894	12.61210	12.61526	12.61842	12.62158	12.62474
13	13.70484	13.70854	13.71225	13.71596	13.71967	13.72337	13.72708	13.73079
14	14.81534	14.81964	14.82394	14.82824	14.83254	14.83684	14.84114	14.84544
15	15.93419	15.93913	15.94407	15.94901	15.95395	15.95889	15.96382	15.96876
16	17.06145	17.06707	17.07270	17.07833	17.08395	17.08958	17.09520	17.10083
17	18.19718	18.20354	18.20990	18.21626	18.22262	18.22899	18.23535	18.24171
18	19.34144	19.34859	19.35573	19.36288	19.37003	19.37717	19.38432	19.39147
19	20.49430	20.50228	20.51026	20.51825	20.52623	20.53421	20.54219	20.55018
20	21.65583	21.66469	21.67356	21.68243	21.69129	21.70016	21.70903	21.71790
21	22.82608	22.83588	22.84569	22.85549	22.86530	22.87510	22.88491	22.89472
22	24.00513	24.01592	24.02671	24.03750	24.04830	24.05909	24.06989	24.08069
23	25.19304	25.20487	25.21670	25.22854	25.24037	25.25221	25.26405	25.27589
24	26.38988	26.40280	26.41573	26.42866	26.44159	26.45452	26.46746	26.48040
25	27.59571	27.60978	27.62386	27.63793	27.65202	27.66610	27.68019	27.69428
26	28.81060	28.82587	28.84115	28.85644	28.87173	28.88702	28.90231	28.91761
27	30.03462	30.05115	30.06769	30.08424	30.10079	30.11734	30.13390	30.15046
28	31.26784	31.28569	31.30355	31.32141	31.33927	31.35715	31.37502	31.39290
29	32.51032	32.52955	32.54878	32.56802	32.58726	32.60651	32.62576	32.64502
30	33.76215	33.78280	33.80347	33.82414	33.84481	33.86549	33.88618	33.90688
31	35.02338	35.04553	35.06768	35.08984	35.11201	35.13418	35.15637	35.17856
32	36.29409	36.31778	36.34149	36.36520	36.38892	36.41265	36.43639	36.46014
33	37.57435	37.59965	37.62497	37.65029	37.67563	37.70097	37.72633	37.75169
34	38.86423	38.89120	38.91819	38.94519	38.97220	38.99922	39.02625	39.05330
35	40.16380	40.19251	40.22123	40.24996	40.27871	40.30747	40.33625	40.36504
36	41.47314	41.50364	41.53416	41.56470	41.59524	41.62581	41.65639	41.68698
37	42.79232	42.82468	42.85706	42.88946	42.92187	42.95430	42.98675	43.01922
38	44.12141	44.15570	44.19000	44.22433	44.25867	44.29304	44.32742	44.36182
39	45.46049	45.49677	45.53306	45.56938	45.60573	45.64209	45.67847	45.71487
40	46.80963	46.84796	46.88632	46.92470	46.96311	47.00153	47.03998	47.07846
41	48.16891	48.20937	48.24985	48.29036	48.33090	48.37146	48.41204	48.45265
42	49.53841	49.58106	49.62373	49.66644	49.70918	49.75194	49.79473	49.83754
43	50.91819	50.96310	51.00805	51.05302	51.09802	51.14306	51.18812	51.23321
44	52.30835	52.35559	52.40287	52.45018	52.49752	52.54490	52.59230	52.63975
45	53.70895	53.75860	53.80828	53.85799	53.90775	53.95754	54.00736	54.05723
46	55.12008	55.17220	55.22436	55.27655	55.32879	55.38107	55.43338	55.48574
47	56.54181	56.59648	56.65119	56.70594	56.76073	56.81557	56.87045	56.92537
48	57.97423	58.03151	58.08885	58.14623	58.20365	58.26112	58.31864	58.37621
60	76.02642	76.12127	76.21623	76.31129	76.40646	76.50174	76.59713	76.69263
72	95.77552	95.92051	96.06571	96.21112	96.35675	96.50259	96.64864	96.79490
84	117.38103	117.59077	117.80089	118.01138	118.22226	118.43351	118.64514	118.85715
96	141.01746	141.30888	141.60091	141.89357	142.18685	142.48076	142.77530	143.07047
108	166.87572	167.26834	167.66194	168.05651	168.45206	168.84858	169.24609	169.64458
120	195.16465	195.68098	196.19876	196.71801	197.23871	197.76089	198.28454	198.80967
132	226.11274	226.77861	227.44658	228.11668	228.78889	229.46324	230.13973	230.81836
144	259.96996	260.81496	261.66295	262.51392	263.36789	264.22487	265.08486	265.94789
156	297.00975	298.06776	299.12987	300.19610	301.26647	302.34099	303.41968	304.50255
168	337.53128	338.84094	340.15614	341.47693	342.80331	344.13532	345.47297	346.81629
180	381.86183	383.46718	385.07992	386.70008	388.32769	389.96280	391.60543	393.25563
192	430.35946	432.31061	434.27145	436.24204	438.22241	440.21263	442.21274	444.22279
204	483.41587	485.76974	488.13618	490.51525	492.90703	495.31158	497.72896	500.15926
216	541.45957	544.28076	547.11805	549.97156	552.84136	555.72757	558.63026	561.54953
228	604.95939	608.32106	611.70321	615.10594	618.52940	621.97370	625.43897	628.92535
240	674.42818	678.41318	682.42395	686.46066	690.52348	694.61258	698.72814	702.87032
252	750.42705	755.09397	759.86317	764.62976	769.42900	774.26112	779.12635	784.02492
264	833.56980	839.09447	844.65911	850.26400	855.90945	861.59574	867.32319	873.09209
276	924.52798	930.99468	937.51066	944.07631	950.69201	957.35816	964.07512	970.84331
288	1024.03623	1031.57945	1039.18311	1046.84770	1054.57371	1062.36164	1070.21199	1078.12528
300	1132.89825	1141.66949	1150.51445	1159.43376	1168.42805	1177.49796	1186.64414	1195.86724
312	1251.99330	1262.16303	1272.42226	1282.77178	1293.21240	1303.74494	1314.37021	1325.08904
324	1382.28328	1394.04322	1405.91731	1417.88859	1429.97606	1442.17475	1454.48570	1466.90996
336	1524.82052	1538.38608	1552.08183	1565.90905	1579.86902	1593.96303	1608.19240	1622.55842
348	1680.75627	1696.36934	1712.13854	1728.06547	1744.15171	1760.39889	1776.80864	1793.38261
360	1851.34997	1869.28202	1887.40064	1905.70782	1924.20553	1942.89581	1961.78066	1980.86216
420	2977.20949	3012.10509	3047.43544	3083.20603	3119.42242	3156.09025	3193.21522	3230.80310
480	4741.50290	4807.07771	4873.60715	4941.10531	5009.58645	5079.06506	5149.55586	5221.07375

55

MONTHLY DEPOSITS

EFFECTIVE ANNUAL YIELD

NUMBER OF MONTHLY DEPOSITS	9.80%	9.85%	9.90%	9.95%	10.00%	10.05%	10.10%	10.15%
1	1.00782	1.00786	1.00790	1.00794	1.00797	1.00801	1.00805	1.00809
2	2.02353	2.02364	2.02376	2.02387	2.02399	2.02410	2.02422	2.02433
3	3.04717	3.04740	3.04764	3.04787	3.04810	3.04833	3.04856	3.04879
4	4.07883	4.07922	4.07960	4.07999	4.08038	4.08077	4.08116	4.08154
5	5.11855	5.11914	5.11972	5.12031	5.12089	5.12148	5.12206	5.12265
6	6.16640	6.16723	6.16805	6.16888	6.16970	6.17052	6.17135	6.17217
7	7.22246	7.22356	7.22466	7.22577	7.22687	7.22798	7.22908	7.23018
8	8.28677	8.28819	8.28962	8.29105	8.29247	8.29390	8.29533	8.29675
9	9.35940	9.36119	9.36299	9.36478	9.36657	9.36837	9.37016	9.37195
10	10.44042	10.44263	10.44483	10.44704	10.44924	10.45144	10.45364	10.45585
11	11.52990	11.53256	11.53522	11.53788	11.54054	11.54319	11.54585	11.54851
12	12.62790	12.63106	12.63422	12.63738	12.64054	12.64369	12.64685	12.65001
13	13.73449	13.73820	13.74190	13.74560	13.74931	13.75301	13.75671	13.76042
14	14.84973	14.85403	14.85833	14.86262	14.86692	14.87122	14.87551	14.87981
15	15.97370	15.97864	15.98357	15.98851	15.99345	15.99838	16.00332	16.00825
16	17.10645	17.11208	17.11771	17.12333	17.12895	17.13458	17.14020	17.14583
17	18.24807	18.25443	18.26079	18.26716	18.27352	18.27988	18.28624	18.29260
18	19.39862	19.40576	19.41291	19.42006	19.42721	19.43436	19.44150	19.44865
19	20.55816	20.56614	20.57413	20.58211	20.59010	20.59808	20.60607	20.61405
20	21.72677	21.73564	21.74451	21.75339	21.76226	21.77113	21.78001	21.78888
21	22.90452	22.91433	22.92414	22.93396	22.94377	22.95358	22.96340	22.97321
22	24.09149	24.10229	24.11309	24.12389	24.13470	24.14551	24.15631	24.16712
23	25.28774	25.29958	25.31143	25.32328	25.33513	25.34698	25.35883	25.37069
24	26.49334	26.50628	26.51923	26.53218	26.54513	26.55808	26.57103	26.58399
25	27.70837	27.72247	27.73657	27.75067	27.76478	27.77888	27.79299	27.80711
26	28.93291	28.94821	28.96352	28.97883	28.99415	29.00947	29.02479	29.04012
27	30.16702	30.18359	30.20017	30.21675	30.23333	30.24991	30.26650	30.28310
28	31.41079	31.42868	31.44658	31.46448	31.48239	31.50030	31.51821	31.53614
29	32.66428	32.68356	32.70283	32.72212	32.74141	32.76070	32.78000	32.79931
30	33.92758	33.94829	33.96901	33.98973	34.01046	34.03120	34.05195	34.07270
31	35.20076	35.22297	35.24519	35.26741	35.28964	35.31188	35.33413	35.35639
32	36.48390	36.50767	36.53144	36.55523	36.57902	36.60282	36.62664	36.65046
33	37.77707	37.80246	37.82786	37.85326	37.87868	37.90411	37.92955	37.95500
34	39.08036	39.10743	39.13451	39.16160	39.18871	39.21582	39.24295	39.27009
35	40.39384	40.42265	40.45148	40.48032	40.50918	40.53804	40.56693	40.59582
36	41.71759	41.74821	41.77885	41.80951	41.84018	41.87086	41.90156	41.93227
37	43.05170	43.08420	43.11671	43.14924	43.18179	43.21435	43.24694	43.27954
38	44.39624	44.43068	44.46513	44.49961	44.53410	44.56861	44.60315	44.63770
39	45.75130	45.78774	45.82420	45.86069	45.89720	45.93372	45.97027	46.00684
40	47.11695	47.15547	47.19401	47.23257	47.27116	47.30977	47.34840	47.38706
41	48.49329	48.53395	48.57463	48.61535	48.65608	48.69684	48.73763	48.77845
42	49.88039	49.92326	49.96616	50.00909	50.05205	50.09503	50.13804	50.18108
43	51.27834	51.32349	51.36868	51.41390	51.45914	51.50442	51.54973	51.59507
44	52.68722	52.73473	52.78227	52.82985	52.87746	52.92510	52.97278	53.02049
45	54.10713	54.15706	54.20703	54.25704	54.30709	54.35717	54.40729	54.45744
46	55.53814	55.59057	55.64304	55.69556	55.74811	55.80071	55.85334	55.90601
47	56.98034	57.03535	57.09040	57.14549	57.20063	57.25581	57.31104	57.36630
48	58.43382	58.49148	58.54918	58.60693	58.66473	58.72258	58.78047	58.83841
60	76.78823	76.88395	76.97977	77.07570	77.17174	77.26789	77.36415	77.46051
72	96.94138	97.08808	97.23499	97.38211	97.52945	97.67701	97.82477	97.97276
84	119.06954	119.28232	119.49547	119.70901	119.92293	120.13724	120.35193	120.56700
96	143.36626	143.66269	143.95974	144.25744	144.55576	144.85472	145.15432	145.45456
108	170.04406	170.44452	170.84598	171.24843	171.65188	172.05632	172.46176	172.86821
120	199.33628	199.86437	200.39395	200.92503	201.45760	201.99167	202.52725	203.06434
132	231.49914	232.18207	232.86717	233.55445	234.24390	234.93553	235.62935	236.32538
144	266.81395	267.68307	268.55525	269.43049	270.30882	271.19024	272.07477	272.96241
156	305.58962	306.68091	307.77644	308.87621	309.98024	311.08856	312.20117	313.31810
168	348.16531	349.52005	350.88052	352.24677	353.61880	354.99665	356.38034	357.76989
180	394.91341	396.57883	398.25192	399.93270	401.62122	403.31751	405.02161	406.73355
192	446.24283	448.27291	450.31308	452.36338	454.42388	456.49461	458.57564	460.66701
204	502.60253	505.05885	507.52829	510.01092	512.50680	515.01601	517.53863	520.07472
216	564.48548	567.43821	570.40781	573.39438	576.39802	579.41882	582.45688	585.51231
228	632.43296	635.96194	639.51241	643.08450	646.67836	650.29410	653.93188	657.59181
240	707.03930	711.23525	715.45836	719.70079	723.98673	728.29235	732.62585	736.98739
252	788.95705	793.92298	798.92295	803.95719	809.02594	814.12943	819.26791	824.44162
264	878.90274	884.75546	890.65055	896.58831	902.56907	908.59313	914.66082	920.77245
276	977.66312	984.53494	991.45917	998.43623	1005.46651	1012.55044	1019.68841	1026.88086
288	1086.10200	1094.14269	1102.24785	1110.41801	1118.65370	1126.95545	1135.32379	1143.75928
300	1205.16790	1214.54681	1224.00461	1233.54198	1243.15961	1252.85816	1262.63855	1272.50085
312	1335.90226	1346.81073	1357.81528	1368.91679	1380.11610	1391.41410	1402.81167	1414.30969
324	1479.44859	1492.10265	1504.87322	1517.76139	1530.76825	1543.89492	1557.14250	1570.51214
336	1637.06245	1651.70582	1666.48989	1681.41602	1696.48561	1711.70005	1727.06075	1742.56912
348	1810.12247	1827.02990	1844.10661	1861.35430	1878.77471	1896.36960	1914.14073	1932.08990
360	2000.14238	2019.62341	2039.30738	2059.19643	2079.29272	2099.59844	2120.11580	2140.84703
420	3268.85975	3307.39107	3346.40307	3385.90181	3425.89345	3466.38421	3507.38039	3548.88837
480	5293.63389	5367.25162	5441.94253	5517.72744	5594.60740	5672.61369	5751.75784	5832.05660

56

MONTHLY DEPOSITS

NUMBER OF MONTHLY DEPOSITS	EFFECTIVE ANNUAL YIELD							
	10.20%	10.25%	10.30%	10.35%	10.40%	10.45%	10.50%	10.55%
1	1.00813	1.00816	1.00820	1.00824	1.00828	1.00832	1.00836	1.00839
2	2.02445	2.02456	2.02468	2.02479	2.02491	2.02502	2.02514	2.02525
3	3.04903	3.04926	3.04949	3.04972	3.04995	3.05018	3.05041	3.05064
4	4.08193	4.08232	4.08271	4.08309	4.08348	4.08387	4.08425	4.08464
5	5.12323	5.12381	5.12440	5.12498	5.12557	5.12615	5.12673	5.12732
6	6.17299	6.17381	6.17464	6.17546	6.17628	6.17710	6.17792	6.17874
7	7.23128	7.23239	7.23349	7.23459	7.23569	7.23679	7.23789	7.23900
8	8.29818	8.29960	8.30103	8.30245	8.30388	8.30530	8.30672	8.30815
9	9.37374	9.37553	9.37732	9.37911	9.38090	9.38269	9.38448	9.38627
10	10.45805	10.46025	10.46245	10.46465	10.46685	10.46905	10.47125	10.47345
11	11.55116	11.55382	11.55647	11.55913	11.56178	11.56444	11.56709	11.56974
12	12.65316	12.65632	12.65947	12.66263	12.66578	12.66894	12.67209	12.67524
13	13.76412	13.76782	13.77152	13.77522	13.77892	13.78262	13.78632	13.79002
14	14.88410	14.88840	14.89269	14.89699	14.90128	14.90557	14.90987	14.91416
15	16.01319	16.01812	16.02306	16.02799	16.03293	16.03786	16.04279	16.04773
16	17.15145	17.15707	17.16270	17.16832	17.17394	17.17957	17.18519	17.19081
17	18.29896	18.30532	18.31169	18.31805	18.32441	18.33077	18.33713	18.34349
18	19.45580	19.46295	19.47010	19.47725	19.48440	19.49155	19.49869	19.50584
19	20.62204	20.63003	20.63801	20.64600	20.65399	20.66198	20.66996	20.67795
20	21.79776	21.80663	21.81551	21.82439	21.83326	21.84214	21.85102	21.85990
21	22.98303	22.99284	23.00266	23.01248	23.02230	23.03212	23.04194	23.05177
22	24.17793	24.18874	24.19955	24.21037	24.22118	24.23200	24.24282	24.25364
23	25.38255	25.39440	25.40627	25.41813	25.42999	25.44186	25.45373	25.46560
24	26.59695	26.60991	26.62287	26.63584	26.64881	26.66178	26.67475	26.68773
25	27.82122	27.83534	27.84946	27.86359	27.87771	27.89185	27.90598	27.92011
26	29.05545	29.07078	29.08611	29.10145	29.11680	29.13214	29.14749	29.16285
27	30.29970	30.31630	30.33291	30.34952	30.36614	30.38275	30.39938	30.41601
28	31.55406	31.57199	31.58993	31.60787	31.62582	31.64377	31.66173	31.67969
29	32.81862	32.83794	32.85726	32.87659	32.89593	32.91527	32.93462	32.95397
30	34.09346	34.11422	34.13499	34.15577	34.17656	34.19735	34.21815	34.23895
31	35.37865	35.40092	35.42320	35.44549	35.46779	35.49009	35.51240	35.53472
32	36.67429	36.69813	36.72198	36.74584	36.76971	36.79358	36.81747	36.84136
33	37.98046	38.00593	38.03141	38.05690	38.08240	38.10792	38.13344	38.15897
34	39.29724	39.32441	39.35158	39.37877	39.40597	39.43318	39.46041	39.48764
35	40.62473	40.65365	40.68258	40.71153	40.74049	40.76947	40.79846	40.82746
36	41.96300	41.99375	42.02450	42.05528	42.08607	42.11687	42.14769	42.17852
37	43.31215	43.34478	43.37743	43.41010	43.44278	43.47548	43.50820	43.54093
38	44.67226	44.70685	44.74146	44.77608	44.81073	44.84539	44.88007	44.91477
39	46.04343	46.08004	46.11667	46.15332	46.19000	46.22669	46.26340	46.30014
40	47.42574	47.46444	47.50317	47.54192	47.58069	47.61948	47.65830	47.69714
41	48.81928	48.86015	48.90104	48.94195	48.98289	49.02385	49.06485	49.10586
42	50.22415	50.26725	50.31037	50.35352	50.39670	50.43991	50.48314	50.52641
43	51.64044	51.68584	51.73127	51.77673	51.82222	51.86774	51.91329	51.95888
44	53.06823	53.11601	53.16382	53.21166	53.25954	53.30745	53.35539	53.40337
45	54.50763	54.55786	54.60812	54.65842	54.70876	54.75913	54.80954	54.85999
46	55.95873	56.01148	56.06427	56.11710	56.16997	56.22289	56.27584	56.32883
47	57.42161	57.47697	57.53237	57.58781	57.64329	57.69882	57.75439	57.81000
48	58.89639	58.95442	59.01250	59.07063	59.12880	59.18702	59.24529	59.30360
60	77.55699	77.65357	77.75027	77.84707	77.94398	78.04100	78.13814	78.23538
72	98.12096	98.26938	98.41802	98.56687	98.71594	98.86523	99.01473	99.16445
84	120.78246	120.99831	121.21455	121.43117	121.64818	121.86558	122.08337	122.30155
96	145.75544	146.05696	146.35912	146.66192	146.96537	147.26947	147.57421	147.87960
108	173.27566	173.68412	174.09358	174.50406	174.91556	175.32807	175.74160	176.15615
120	203.60294	204.14306	204.68470	205.22786	205.77256	206.31879	206.86655	207.41586
132	237.02360	237.72404	238.42669	239.13157	239.83869	240.54804	241.25963	241.97348
144	273.85317	274.74707	275.64412	276.54432	277.44769	278.35424	279.26398	280.17693
156	314.43936	315.56497	316.69494	317.82929	318.96804	320.11120	321.25879	322.41084
168	359.16534	360.56669	361.97399	363.38725	364.80650	366.23176	367.66306	369.10042
180	408.45336	410.18110	411.91678	413.66046	415.41215	417.17191	418.93977	420.71576
192	462.76877	464.88098	467.00369	469.13694	471.28080	473.43531	475.60054	477.77652
204	522.62435	525.18760	527.76454	530.35525	532.95979	535.57824	538.21068	540.85719
216	588.58520	591.67565	594.78376	597.90964	601.05339	604.21511	607.39490	610.59286
228	661.27405	664.97872	668.70596	672.45592	676.22873	680.02452	683.84345	687.68565
240	741.37717	745.79536	750.24215	754.71774	759.22230	763.75602	768.31910	772.91173
252	829.65080	834.89570	840.17657	845.49365	850.84720	856.23746	861.66470	867.12916
264	926.92835	933.12883	939.37423	945.66487	952.00109	958.38322	964.81158	971.28654
276	1034.12820	1041.43085	1048.78925	1056.20362	1063.67499	1071.20320	1078.78889	1086.43251
288	1152.26244	1160.83384	1169.47402	1178.18354	1186.96297	1195.81287	1204.73382	1213.72638
300	1282.44637	1292.47562	1302.58931	1312.78817	1323.07290	1333.44425	1343.90296	1354.44976
312	1425.90907	1437.61069	1449.41549	1461.32437	1473.33827	1485.45511	1497.68486	1510.01945
324	1584.00495	1597.62211	1611.36476	1625.23407	1639.23123	1653.35742	1667.61386	1682.00175
336	1758.22662	1774.03649	1789.99480	1806.10843	1822.37706	1838.80221	1855.38541	1872.12818
348	1950.21890	1968.52957	1987.02374	2005.70328	2024.57006	2043.62598	2062.87296	2082.31294
360	2161.79439	2182.96017	2204.34666	2225.95620	2247.79113	2269.85383	2292.14672	2314.67220
420	3590.91461	3633.46566	3676.54815	3720.16877	3764.33432	3809.05169	3854.32783	3900.16980
480	5913.52699	5996.18627	6080.05195	6165.14180	6251.47386	6339.06643	6427.93805	6518.10758

MONTHLY DEPOSITS

EFFECTIVE ANNUAL YIELD

NUMBER OF MONTHLY DEPOSITS	10.60%	10.65%	10.70%	10.75%	10.80%	10.85%	10.90%	10.95%
1	1.00843	1.00847	1.00851	1.00855	1.00858	1.00862	1.00866	1.00870
2	2.02536	2.02548	2.02559	2.02571	2.02582	2.02594	2.02605	2.02617
3	3.05087	3.05110	3.05133	3.05156	3.05179	3.05202	3.05225	3.05248
4	4.08503	4.08541	4.08580	4.08618	4.08657	4.08696	4.08734	4.08773
5	5.12790	5.12848	5.12906	5.12965	5.13023	5.13081	5.13139	5.13197
6	6.17956	6.18038	6.18120	6.18202	6.18284	6.18366	6.18448	6.18530
7	7.24010	7.24120	7.24230	7.24339	7.24449	7.24559	7.24669	7.24779
8	8.30957	8.31099	8.31241	8.31384	8.31526	8.31668	8.31810	8.31952
9	9.38806	9.38985	9.39164	9.39342	9.39521	9.39700	9.39878	9.40057
10	10.47564	10.47784	10.48004	10.48224	10.48443	10.48663	10.48882	10.49102
11	11.57240	11.57505	11.57770	11.58035	11.58300	11.58565	11.58830	11.59095
12	12.67840	12.68155	12.68470	12.68785	12.69100	12.69415	12.69730	12.70045
13	13.79372	13.79742	13.80112	13.80482	13.80851	13.81221	13.81591	13.81960
14	14.91845	14.92274	14.92703	14.93132	14.93561	14.93990	14.94419	14.94848
15	16.05266	16.05759	16.06253	16.06746	16.07239	16.07732	16.08225	16.08718
16	17.19643	17.20206	17.20768	17.21330	17.21892	17.22454	17.23016	17.23579
17	18.34985	18.35621	18.36257	18.36893	18.37530	18.38166	18.38802	18.39438
18	19.51299	19.52014	19.52729	19.53444	19.54159	19.54874	19.55589	19.56304
19	20.68594	20.69393	20.70192	20.70991	20.71790	20.72589	20.73388	20.74188
20	21.86878	21.87766	21.88654	21.89542	21.90431	21.91319	21.92207	21.93096
21	23.06159	23.07142	23.08124	23.09107	23.10090	23.11072	23.12055	23.13038
22	24.26446	24.27528	24.28610	24.29693	24.30775	24.31858	24.32941	24.34024
23	25.47747	25.48934	25.50121	25.51309	25.52497	25.53685	25.54873	25.56062
24	26.70070	26.71368	26.72666	26.73965	26.75263	26.76562	26.77861	26.79161
25	27.93425	27.94839	27.96254	27.97668	27.99083	28.00499	28.01914	28.03330
26	29.17820	29.19356	29.20893	29.22429	29.23966	29.25504	29.27041	29.28580
27	30.43264	30.44928	30.46592	30.48256	30.49921	30.51586	30.53252	30.54918
28	31.69765	31.71562	31.73360	31.75158	31.76957	31.78756	31.80556	31.82356
29	32.97333	32.99270	33.01207	33.03145	33.05083	33.07022	33.08961	33.10901
30	34.25977	34.28059	34.30141	34.32225	34.34309	34.36394	34.38479	34.40565
31	35.55705	35.57938	35.60173	35.62408	35.64644	35.66881	35.69118	35.71356
32	36.86527	36.88918	36.91310	36.93703	36.96098	36.98492	37.00888	37.03285
33	38.18452	38.21007	38.23563	38.26121	38.28679	38.31239	38.33800	38.36361
34	39.51489	39.54215	39.56942	39.59670	39.62399	39.65130	39.67862	39.70595
35	40.85647	40.88550	40.91455	40.94360	40.97267	41.00175	41.03085	41.05996
36	42.20937	42.24024	42.27112	42.30201	42.33292	42.36385	42.39478	42.42574
37	43.57368	43.60645	43.63923	43.67203	43.70485	43.73768	43.77053	43.80340
38	44.94949	44.98423	45.01898	45.05376	45.08855	45.12336	45.15819	45.19304
39	46.33690	46.37367	46.41047	46.44729	46.48413	46.52099	46.55787	46.59477
40	47.73600	47.77489	47.81380	47.85273	47.89168	47.93066	47.96967	48.00869
41	49.14690	49.18797	49.22906	49.27018	49.31132	49.35249	49.39369	49.43490
42	50.56970	50.61302	50.65637	50.69974	50.74314	50.78658	50.83004	50.87352
43	52.00449	52.05014	52.09581	52.14152	52.18726	52.23302	52.27882	52.32465
44	53.45138	53.49943	53.54751	53.59562	53.64376	53.69194	53.74016	53.78840
45	54.91047	54.96099	55.01155	55.06214	55.11277	55.16344	55.21414	55.26488
46	56.38186	56.43493	56.48804	56.54120	56.59439	56.64762	56.70089	56.75420
47	57.86566	57.92136	57.97710	58.03289	58.08872	58.14459	58.20051	58.25647
48	59.36196	59.42037	59.47883	59.53733	59.59588	59.65448	59.71312	59.77181
60	78.33273	78.43019	78.52776	78.62544	78.72324	78.82114	78.91915	79.01728
72	99.31439	99.46455	99.61493	99.76553	99.91635	100.06739	100.21864	100.37012
84	122.52012	122.73908	122.95843	123.17818	123.39832	123.61885	123.83978	124.06110
96	148.18565	148.49234	148.79968	149.10768	149.41634	149.72565	150.03562	150.34625
108	176.57172	176.98832	177.40595	177.82461	178.24431	178.66504	179.08680	179.50961
120	207.96672	208.51913	209.07309	209.62861	210.18569	210.74435	211.30457	211.86637
132	242.68959	243.40796	244.12861	244.85154	245.57675	246.30426	247.03407	247.76619
144	281.09308	282.01246	282.93507	283.86093	284.79004	285.72243	286.65809	287.59704
156	323.56734	324.72833	325.89382	327.06383	328.23837	329.41746	330.60112	331.78937
168	370.54388	371.99345	373.44916	374.91104	376.37912	377.85341	379.33395	380.82076
180	422.49993	424.29230	426.09292	427.90183	429.71907	431.54466	433.37865	435.22108
192	479.96332	482.16098	484.36957	486.58913	488.81973	491.06141	493.31423	495.57825
204	543.51782	546.19267	548.88181	551.58532	554.30326	557.03572	559.78278	562.54452
216	613.80911	617.04374	620.29687	623.56859	626.85902	630.16825	633.49641	636.84360
228	691.55127	695.44045	699.35333	703.29006	707.25079	711.23566	715.24482	719.27842
240	777.53410	782.18641	786.86884	791.58160	796.32488	801.09888	805.90381	810.73986
252	872.63111	878.17081	883.74851	889.36447	895.01897	900.71227	906.44463	912.21633
264	977.80841	984.37755	990.99430	997.65900	1004.37202	1011.13370	1017.94440	1024.80447
276	1094.13450	1101.89530	1109.71539	1117.59520	1125.53520	1133.53586	1141.59764	1149.72101
288	1222.79115	1231.92870	1241.13963	1250.42453	1259.78401	1269.21865	1278.72909	1288.31592
300	1365.08541	1375.81066	1386.62627	1397.53302	1408.53168	1419.62303	1430.80786	1442.08696
312	1522.46086	1535.01604	1547.67999	1560.45568	1573.34411	1586.34636	1599.46322	1612.69594
324	1696.52232	1711.17680	1725.96644	1740.89251	1755.95627	1771.15901	1786.50201	1801.98660
336	1889.03208	1906.09868	1923.32955	1940.72631	1958.29055	1976.02391	1993.92804	2012.00453
348	2101.94787	2121.77973	2141.81052	2162.04224	2182.47694	2203.11666	2223.96350	2245.01954
360	2337.43275	2360.43082	2383.66894	2407.14963	2430.87545	2454.84897	2479.07282	2503.54963
420	3946.58473	3993.57986	4041.16250	4089.34007	4138.12007	4187.51011	4237.51787	4288.15114
480	6609.59413	6702.41708	6796.59612	6892.15121	6989.10261	7087.47087	7187.27684	7288.54170

MONTHLY DEPOSITS

EFFECTIVE ANNUAL YIELD

NUMBER OF MONTHLY DEPOSITS	11.00%	11.05%	11.10%	11.15%	11.20%	11.25%	11.30%	11.35%
1	1.00873	1.00877	1.00881	1.00885	1.00889	1.00892	1.00896	1.00900
2	2.02628	2.02639	2.02651	2.02662	2.02674	2.02685	2.02696	2.02708
3	3.05271	3.05294	3.05317	3.05340	3.05363	3.05386	3.05409	3.05432
4	4.08811	4.08850	4.08888	4.08927	4.08965	4.09004	4.09042	4.09081
5	5.13255	5.13314	5.13372	5.13430	5.13488	5.13546	5.13604	5.13662
6	6.18612	6.18694	6.18776	6.18858	6.18939	6.19021	6.19103	6.19184
7	7.24889	7.24999	7.25108	7.25218	7.25328	7.25437	7.25547	7.25657
8	8.32094	8.32236	8.32378	8.32520	8.32662	8.32803	8.32945	8.33087
9	9.40235	9.40414	9.40592	9.40771	9.40949	9.41127	9.41306	9.41484
10	10.49321	10.49541	10.49760	10.49980	10.50199	10.50418	10.50637	10.50857
11	11.59360	11.59625	11.59890	11.60155	11.60419	11.60684	11.60949	11.61213
12	12.70360	12.70675	12.70990	12.71305	12.71619	12.71934	12.72249	12.72563
13	13.82330	13.82699	13.83069	13.83438	13.83808	13.84177	13.84546	13.84916
14	14.95277	14.95706	14.96135	14.96564	14.96994	14.97421	14.97850	14.98279
15	16.09211	16.09704	16.10197	16.10690	16.11183	16.11676	16.12169	16.12662
16	17.24141	17.24703	17.25265	17.25827	17.26389	17.26951	17.27513	17.28075
17	18.40074	18.40710	18.41346	18.41982	18.42618	18.43254	18.43890	18.44526
18	19.57020	19.57735	19.58450	19.59165	19.59880	19.60595	19.61310	19.62025
19	20.74987	20.75786	20.76585	20.77385	20.78184	20.78983	20.79783	20.80582
20	21.93984	21.94873	21.95762	21.96650	21.97539	21.98428	21.99317	22.00206
21	23.14021	23.15005	23.15988	23.16971	23.17955	23.18938	23.19922	23.20906
22	24.35107	24.36190	24.37274	24.38357	24.39441	24.40524	24.41608	24.42692
23	25.57250	25.58439	25.59628	25.60817	25.62006	25.63195	25.64385	25.65575
24	26.80460	26.81760	26.83060	26.84360	26.85660	26.86961	26.88262	26.89563
25	28.04746	28.06163	28.07579	28.08996	28.10414	28.11831	28.13249	28.14667
26	29.30118	29.31657	29.33196	29.34735	29.36275	29.37815	29.39356	29.40897
27	30.56585	30.58252	30.59919	30.61587	30.63255	30.64924	30.66593	30.68263
28	31.84156	31.85957	31.87759	31.89561	31.91364	31.93167	31.94971	31.96775
29	33.12842	33.14783	33.16725	33.18668	33.20611	33.22554	33.24499	33.26443
30	34.42652	34.44739	34.46828	34.48916	34.51006	34.53096	34.55187	34.57279
31	35.73596	35.75835	35.78076	35.80318	35.82560	35.84803	35.87047	35.89292
32	37.05683	37.08082	37.10481	37.12882	37.15283	37.17685	37.20088	37.22493
33	38.38924	38.41488	38.44053	38.46618	38.49185	38.51753	38.54322	38.56892
34	39.73329	39.76064	39.78801	39.81539	39.84278	39.87018	39.89759	39.92501
35	41.08908	41.11821	41.14736	41.17653	41.20570	41.23489	41.26409	41.29331
36	42.45671	42.48769	42.51869	42.54971	42.58074	42.61178	42.64284	42.67392
37	43.83629	43.86919	43.90211	43.93504	43.96799	44.00096	44.03395	44.06695
38	45.22791	45.26280	45.29771	45.33263	45.36758	45.40254	45.43752	45.47252
39	46.63169	46.66864	46.70560	46.74259	46.77959	46.81662	46.85367	46.89074
40	48.04774	48.08681	48.12590	48.16502	48.20416	48.24332	48.28251	48.32172
41	49.47615	49.51742	49.55872	49.60004	49.64139	49.68276	49.72416	49.76558
42	50.91704	50.96058	51.00415	51.04775	51.09138	51.13504	51.17872	51.22243
43	52.37051	52.41640	52.46233	52.50828	52.55426	52.60028	52.64632	52.69240
44	53.83668	53.88500	53.93334	53.98173	54.03014	54.07859	54.12707	54.17559
45	55.31566	55.36647	55.41732	55.46821	55.51914	55.57010	55.62110	55.67213
46	56.80755	56.86094	56.91438	56.96785	57.02136	57.07491	57.12851	57.18214
47	58.31248	58.36853	58.42462	58.48075	58.53693	58.59316	58.64942	58.70573
48	59.83055	59.88933	59.94817	60.00705	60.06598	60.12495	60.18397	60.24304
60	79.11551	79.21386	79.31231	79.41088	79.50956	79.60835	79.70725	79.80626
72	100.52182	100.67374	100.82588	100.97824	101.13083	101.28363	101.43666	101.58991
84	124.28282	124.50494	124.72745	124.95036	125.17367	125.39738	125.62149	125.84600
96	150.65754	150.96649	151.28210	151.59538	151.90932	152.22393	152.53921	152.85515
108	179.93347	180.35836	180.78431	181.21131	181.63936	182.06846	182.49863	182.92985
120	212.42975	212.99471	213.56127	214.12942	214.69916	215.27051	215.84346	216.41802
132	248.50062	249.23738	249.97647	250.71789	251.46166	252.20778	252.95626	253.70710
144	288.53930	289.48486	290.43376	291.38599	292.34156	293.30050	294.26280	295.22849
156	332.98222	334.17969	335.38180	336.58857	337.80001	339.01615	340.23699	341.46256
168	382.31387	383.81330	385.31908	386.83124	388.34981	389.87480	391.40626	392.94420
180	437.07199	438.93142	440.79940	442.67597	444.56118	446.45506	448.35765	450.26900
192	497.85352	500.14009	502.43803	504.74739	507.06823	509.40060	511.74456	514.10017
204	565.32100	568.11232	570.91855	573.73977	576.57606	579.42751	582.29418	585.17617
216	640.20992	643.59549	647.00041	650.42481	653.86878	657.33244	660.81591	664.31930
228	723.33661	727.41954	731.52736	735.66022	739.81828	744.00169	748.21060	752.44517
240	815.60724	820.50615	825.43679	830.39938	835.39412	840.42122	845.48089	850.57334
252	918.02764	923.87883	929.77018	935.70196	941.67445	947.68795	953.74271	959.83905
264	1031.71428	1038.67419	1045.68457	1052.74577	1059.85819	1067.02218	1074.23813	1081.50641
276	1157.90645	1166.15444	1174.46545	1182.83998	1191.27850	1199.78152	1208.34953	1216.98302
288	1297.97977	1307.72126	1317.54102	1327.43968	1337.41789	1347.47628	1357.61551	1367.83623
300	1453.46114	1464.93121	1476.49797	1488.16225	1499.92489	1511.78671	1523.74855	1535.81128
312	1626.04547	1639.51285	1653.09914	1666.80539	1680.63267	1694.58205	1708.65463	1722.85150
324	1817.61407	1833.38578	1849.30305	1865.36724	1881.57972	1897.94187	1914.45509	1931.12078
336	2030.25522	2048.68166	2067.28558	2086.06873	2105.03284	2124.17968	2143.51100	2163.02862
348	2266.28690	2287.76773	2309.46418	2331.37844	2353.51272	2375.86923	2398.45024	2421.25800
360	2528.28206	2553.27281	2578.52461	2604.04019	2629.82234	2655.87386	2682.19760	2708.79642
420	4339.41782	4391.32589	4443.88344	4497.09865	4550.97981	4605.53533	4660.77370	4716.70353
480	7391.28690	7495.53423	7601.30581	7708.62404	7817.51170	7927.99186	8040.08796	8153.82375

MONTHLY DEPOSITS

EFFECTIVE ANNUAL YIELD

NUMBER OF MONTHLY DEPOSITS	11.40%	11.45%	11.50%	11.55%	11.60%	11.65%	11.70%	11.75%
1	1.00904	1.00907	1.00911	1.00915	1.00919	1.00923	1.00926	1.00930
2	2.02719	2.02731	2.02742	2.02753	2.02765	2.02776	2.02788	2.02799
3	3.05455	3.05478	3.05501	3.05524	3.05547	3.05569	3.05592	3.05615
4	4.09119	4.09157	4.09196	4.09234	4.09273	4.09311	4.09349	4.09388
5	5.13720	5.13778	5.13836	5.13894	5.13952	5.14010	5.14068	5.14125
6	6.19266	6.19348	6.19429	6.19511	6.19593	6.19674	6.19756	6.19837
7	7.25766	7.25876	7.25985	7.26095	7.26204	7.26314	7.26423	7.26532
8	8.33229	8.33370	8.33512	8.33654	8.33795	8.33937	8.34078	8.34220
9	9.41662	9.41840	9.42019	9.42197	9.42375	9.42553	9.42731	9.42909
10	10.51076	10.51295	10.51514	10.51733	10.51952	10.52171	10.52390	10.52609
11	11.61478	11.61743	11.62007	11.62272	11.62536	11.62800	11.63065	11.63329
12	12.72878	12.73193	12.73507	12.73822	12.74136	12.74450	12.74765	12.75079
13	13.85285	13.85654	13.86023	13.86392	13.86761	13.87130	13.87499	13.87868
14	14.98707	14.99136	14.99564	14.99993	15.00422	15.00850	15.01278	15.01707
15	16.13155	16.13648	16.14140	16.14633	16.15126	16.15619	16.16111	16.16604
16	17.28637	17.29199	17.29761	17.30322	17.30884	17.31446	17.32008	17.32570
17	18.45162	18.45798	18.46434	18.47070	18.47706	18.48342	18.48978	18.49614
18	19.62741	19.63456	19.64171	19.64886	19.65601	19.66317	19.67032	19.67747
19	20.81382	20.82181	20.82981	20.83780	20.84580	20.85380	20.86179	20.86979
20	22.01095	22.01984	22.02873	22.03762	22.04651	22.05541	22.06430	22.07320
21	23.21890	23.22874	23.23858	23.24842	23.25826	23.26811	23.27795	23.28780
22	24.43776	24.44861	24.45945	24.47030	24.48114	24.49199	24.50284	24.51369
23	25.66765	25.67955	25.69145	25.70336	25.71526	25.72717	25.73908	25.75099
24	26.90864	26.92166	26.93468	26.94770	26.96072	26.97374	26.98677	26.99980
25	28.16085	28.17504	28.18923	28.20342	28.21762	28.23181	28.24602	28.26022
26	29.42438	29.43980	29.45522	29.47064	29.48606	29.50149	29.51693	29.53236
27	30.69933	30.71603	30.73274	30.74945	30.76617	30.78289	30.79961	30.81634
28	31.98579	32.00384	32.02190	32.03996	32.05803	32.07610	32.09418	32.11226
29	33.28389	33.30335	33.32281	33.34228	33.36176	33.38124	33.40073	33.42023
30	34.59371	34.61464	34.63558	34.65652	34.67747	34.69843	34.71939	34.74036
31	35.91537	35.93783	35.96031	35.98278	36.00527	36.02777	36.05027	36.07278
32	37.24898	37.27304	37.29711	37.32118	37.34527	37.36937	37.39347	37.41759
33	38.59463	38.62035	38.64609	38.67183	38.69758	38.72334	38.74912	38.77490
34	39.95245	39.97990	40.00736	40.03483	40.06232	40.08981	40.11732	40.14484
35	41.32254	41.35178	41.38104	41.41031	41.43959	41.46889	41.49820	41.52752
36	42.70501	42.73611	42.76723	42.79837	42.82952	42.86069	42.89187	42.92306
37	44.09997	44.13301	44.16606	44.19913	44.23222	44.26532	44.29845	44.33158
38	45.50754	45.54258	45.57764	45.61271	45.64781	45.68292	45.71805	45.75321
39	46.92783	46.96494	47.00207	47.03923	47.07640	47.11360	47.15081	47.18805
40	48.36095	48.40021	48.43949	48.47879	48.51812	48.55747	48.59684	48.63624
41	49.80703	49.84851	49.89001	49.93153	49.97308	50.01466	50.05627	50.09789
42	51.26617	51.30994	51.35374	51.39757	51.44142	51.48530	51.52921	51.57315
43	52.73851	52.78464	52.83081	52.87701	52.92324	52.96950	53.01580	53.06212
44	54.22414	54.27273	54.32134	54.37000	54.41868	54.46740	54.51616	54.56494
45	55.72320	55.77431	55.82546	55.87664	55.92786	55.97912	56.03041	56.08174
46	57.23581	57.28952	57.34328	57.39707	57.45091	57.50478	57.55869	57.61265
47	58.76209	58.81849	58.87493	58.93141	58.98794	59.04452	59.10113	59.15780
48	60.30216	60.36133	60.42054	60.47980	60.53910	60.59846	60.65786	60.71731
60	79.90539	80.00462	80.10397	80.20343	80.30300	80.40268	80.50248	80.60239
72	101.74338	101.89708	102.05100	102.20514	102.35951	102.51410	102.66892	102.82396
84	126.07091	126.29622	126.52193	126.74805	126.97457	127.20150	127.42883	127.65656
96	153.17177	153.48906	153.80703	154.12567	154.44498	154.76497	155.08565	155.40700
108	183.36214	183.79549	184.22991	184.66540	185.10196	185.53960	185.97831	186.41811
120	216.99420	217.57200	218.15142	218.73247	219.31515	219.89946	220.48542	221.07303
132	254.46032	255.21592	255.97390	256.73428	257.49706	258.26226	259.02986	259.79990
144	296.19758	297.17007	298.14597	299.12531	300.10808	301.09431	302.08401	303.07718
156	342.69288	343.92796	345.16783	346.41250	347.66198	348.91630	350.17548	351.43953
168	394.48865	396.03964	397.59720	399.16135	400.73213	402.30956	403.89366	405.48447
180	452.18914	454.11811	456.05595	458.00271	459.95842	461.92312	463.89686	465.87968
192	516.46748	518.84656	521.23746	523.64023	526.05495	528.48167	530.92044	533.37134
204	588.07355	590.98641	593.91483	596.85890	599.81869	602.79429	605.78578	608.79326
216	667.84272	671.38628	674.95011	678.53432	682.13902	685.76433	689.41037	693.07726
228	756.70557	760.99194	765.30444	769.64324	774.00850	778.40037	782.81903	787.26462
240	855.69878	860.85744	866.04953	871.27526	876.53485	881.82852	887.15650	892.51901
252	965.97723	972.15755	978.38029	984.64576	990.95425	997.30605	1003.70146	1010.14078
264	1088.82741	1096.20151	1103.62910	1111.11056	1118.64630	1126.23671	1133.88218	1141.58311
276	1225.68252	1234.44851	1243.28152	1252.18205	1261.15063	1270.18779	1279.29404	1288.46992
288	1378.13910	1388.52479	1398.99396	1409.54729	1420.18547	1430.90917	1441.71909	1452.61592
300	1547.95574	1560.24281	1572.61334	1585.08822	1597.66834	1610.35459	1623.14787	1636.04908
312	1737.17376	1751.62253	1766.19894	1780.90413	1795.73923	1810.70540	1825.80381	1841.03564
324	1947.94035	1964.91524	1982.04689	1999.33677	2016.78634	2034.39708	2052.17051	2070.10812
336	2182.73433	2202.62996	2222.71736	2242.99838	2263.47491	2284.14885	2305.02210	2326.09661
348	2444.29482	2467.56302	2491.06492	2514.80291	2538.77936	2562.99669	2587.45733	2612.16375
360	2735.67321	2762.83091	2790.27246	2818.00086	2846.01913	2874.33031	2902.93749	2931.84378
420	4773.33352	4830.67250	4888.72941	4947.51329	5007.03329	5067.29869	5128.31887	5190.10335
480	8269.22336	8386.31126	8505.11226	8625.65156	8747.95471	8872.04764	8997.95667	9125.70847

MONTHLY DEPOSITS

EFFECTIVE ANNUAL YIELD

NUMBER OF MONTHLY DEPOSITS	11.80%	11.85%	11.90%	11.95%	12.00%	12.05%	12.10%	12.15%
1	1.00934	1.00938	1.00941	1.00945	1.00949	1.00953	1.00956	1.00960
2	2.02810	2.02822	2.02833	2.02844	2.02856	2.02867	2.02878	2.02890
3	3.05638	3.05661	3.05684	3.05707	3.05729	3.05752	3.05775	3.05798
4	4.09426	4.09464	4.09503	4.09541	4.09579	4.09618	4.09656	4.09694
5	5.14183	5.14241	5.14299	5.14357	5.14415	5.14472	5.14530	5.14588
6	6.19919	6.20000	6.20082	6.20163	6.20245	6.20326	6.20407	6.20489
7	7.26642	7.26751	7.26860	7.26970	7.27079	7.27188	7.27297	7.27406
8	8.34361	8.34503	8.34644	8.34786	8.34927	8.35068	8.35209	8.35351
9	9.43087	9.43265	9.43443	9.43620	9.43798	9.43976	9.44154	9.44331
10	10.52828	10.53046	10.53265	10.53484	10.53703	10.53921	10.54140	10.54358
11	11.63593	11.63857	11.64122	11.64386	11.64650	11.64914	11.65178	11.65442
12	12.75393	12.75707	12.76022	12.76336	12.76650	12.76964	12.77278	12.77592
13	13.88237	13.88606	13.88975	13.89344	13.89713	13.90081	13.90450	13.90819
14	15.02135	15.02563	15.02992	15.03420	15.03848	15.04276	15.04704	15.05133
15	16.17097	16.17589	16.18082	16.18574	16.19067	16.19559	16.20052	16.20544
16	17.33132	17.33693	17.34255	17.34817	17.35379	17.35940	17.36502	17.37064
17	18.50250	18.50886	18.51522	18.52158	18.52794	18.53430	18.54066	18.54702
18	19.68462	19.69178	19.69893	19.70608	19.71324	19.72039	19.72754	19.73470
19	20.87779	20.88579	20.89378	20.90178	20.90978	20.91778	20.92578	20.93378
20	22.08209	22.09099	22.09988	22.10878	22.11768	22.12658	22.13548	22.14438
21	23.29764	23.30749	23.31734	23.32719	23.33704	23.34689	23.35674	23.36659
22	24.52454	24.53540	24.54625	24.55711	24.56797	24.57883	24.58969	24.60055
23	25.76290	25.77482	25.78674	25.79866	25.81058	25.82250	25.83442	25.84635
24	27.01283	27.02586	27.03890	27.05194	27.06498	27.07802	27.09106	27.10411
25	28.27442	28.28863	28.30285	28.31706	28.33128	28.34550	28.35972	28.37395
26	29.54780	29.56325	29.57869	29.59414	29.60960	29.62505	29.64051	29.65598
27	30.83307	30.84981	30.86655	30.88330	30.90004	30.91680	30.93356	30.95032
28	32.13034	32.14843	32.16653	32.18463	32.20274	32.22085	32.23897	32.25709
29	33.43973	33.45924	33.47875	33.49827	33.51779	33.53732	33.55686	33.57640
30	34.76134	34.78233	34.80332	34.82432	34.84532	34.86634	34.88736	34.90838
31	36.09530	36.11782	36.14036	36.16290	36.18545	36.20801	36.23058	36.25315
32	37.44171	37.46584	37.48999	37.51414	37.53830	37.56247	37.58665	37.61083
33	38.80070	38.82650	38.85232	38.87814	38.90398	38.92983	38.95568	38.98155
34	40.17237	40.19992	40.22747	40.25504	40.28262	40.31021	40.33782	40.36543
35	41.55686	41.58621	41.61557	41.64495	41.67434	41.70375	41.73316	41.76260
36	42.95427	42.98550	43.01674	43.04800	43.07927	43.11056	43.14186	43.17318
37	44.36474	44.39791	44.43110	44.46431	44.49753	44.53077	44.56403	44.59730
38	45.78838	45.82356	45.85877	45.89400	45.92925	45.96451	45.99980	46.03510
39	47.22531	47.26259	47.29989	47.33721	47.37455	47.41191	47.44930	47.48670
40	48.67566	48.71510	48.75456	48.79405	48.83356	48.87310	48.91266	48.95224
41	50.13955	50.18123	50.22294	50.26467	50.30642	50.34821	50.39002	50.43185
42	51.61711	51.66111	51.70513	51.74918	51.79326	51.83737	51.88150	51.92567
43	53.10848	53.15486	53.20128	53.24773	53.29420	53.34071	53.38726	53.43383
44	54.61376	54.66262	54.71151	54.76043	54.80939	54.85838	54.90741	54.95647
45	56.13311	56.18452	56.23596	56.28744	56.33896	56.39051	56.44210	56.49373
46	57.66665	57.72068	57.77476	57.82888	57.88303	57.93723	57.99147	58.04575
47	59.21450	59.27125	59.32804	59.38488	59.44176	59.49869	59.55566	59.61267
48	60.77681	60.83636	60.89595	60.95559	61.01528	61.07502	61.13480	61.19464
60	80.70241	80.80254	80.90278	81.00314	81.10361	81.20420	81.30489	81.40570
72	102.97922	103.13471	103.29043	103.44637	103.60254	103.75894	103.91556	104.07241
84	127.88470	128.11325	128.34221	128.57157	128.80135	129.03153	129.26212	129.49313
96	155.72903	156.05175	156.37515	156.69923	157.02401	157.34947	157.67562	158.00246
108	186.85899	187.30095	187.74401	188.18815	188.63339	189.07972	189.52715	189.97568
120	221.66228	222.25319	222.84576	223.43999	224.03589	224.63346	225.23271	225.83364
132	260.57236	261.34727	262.12462	262.90443	263.68669	264.47143	265.25865	266.04834
144	304.07383	305.07399	306.07767	307.08486	308.09560	309.10988	310.12772	311.14914
156	352.70848	353.98234	355.26112	356.54486	357.83356	359.12726	360.42595	361.72967
168	407.08201	408.68632	410.29741	411.91533	413.54009	415.17173	416.81027	418.45575
180	467.87162	469.87272	471.88302	473.90257	475.93140	477.96956	480.01709	482.07404
192	535.83441	538.30971	540.79732	543.29728	545.80967	548.33453	550.87194	553.42195
204	611.81680	614.85649	617.91241	620.98466	624.07332	627.17848	630.30022	633.43864
216	696.76511	700.47406	704.20421	707.95569	711.72862	715.52312	719.33933	723.17735
228	791.73733	796.23731	800.76472	805.31975	809.90255	814.51330	819.15216	823.81931
240	897.91627	903.34850	908.81594	914.31882	919.85736	925.43179	931.04235	936.68928
252	1016.62432	1023.15237	1029.72526	1036.34327	1043.00674	1049.71596	1056.47126	1063.27294
264	1149.33992	1157.15300	1165.02278	1172.94965	1180.93404	1188.97637	1197.07706	1205.23652
276	1297.71596	1307.03271	1316.42070	1325.88049	1335.41263	1345.01766	1354.69616	1364.44868
288	1463.60038	1474.67316	1485.83498	1497.08657	1508.42864	1519.86193	1531.38717	1543.00511
300	1649.05915	1662.17900	1675.40956	1688.75177	1702.20657	1715.77493	1729.45780	1743.25615
312	1856.40207	1871.90429	1887.54352	1903.32096	1919.23786	1935.29544	1951.49497	1967.83769
324	2088.21144	2106.48202	2124.92141	2143.53118	2162.31290	2181.26818	2200.39864	2219.70589
336	2347.37432	2368.85722	2390.54727	2412.44651	2434.55695	2456.88064	2479.41965	2502.17607
348	2637.11843	2662.32387	2687.78261	2713.49722	2739.47028	2765.70439	2792.20221	2818.96638
360	2961.05233	2990.56632	3020.38896	3050.52350	3080.97321	3111.74141	3142.83145	3174.24671
420	5252.66173	5316.00378	5380.13935	5445.07842	5510.83113	5577.40769	5644.81849	5713.07401
480	9255.33014	9386.84914	9520.29337	9655.69109	9793.07101	9932.46225	10073.89434	10217.39725

NUMBER OF MONTHLY DEPOSITS	EFFECTIVE ANNUAL YIELD							
	12.20%	12.25%	12.30%	12.35%	12.40%	12.45%	12.50%	12.55%
1	1.00964	1.00968	1.00971	1.00975	1.00979	1.00983	1.00986	1.00990
2	2.02901	2.02912	2.02924	2.02935	2.02946	2.02958	2.02969	2.02980
3	3.05821	3.05843	3.05866	3.05889	3.05912	3.05934	3.05957	3.05980
4	4.09732	4.09770	4.09809	4.09847	4.09885	4.09923	4.09961	4.09999
5	5.14646	5.14703	5.14761	5.14819	5.14876	5.14934	5.14991	5.15049
6	6.20570	6.20651	6.20733	6.20814	6.20895	6.20976	6.21057	6.21139
7	7.27516	7.27625	7.27734	7.27843	7.27952	7.28061	7.28170	7.28279
8	8.35492	8.35633	8.35774	8.35915	8.36056	8.36197	8.36338	8.36479
9	9.44509	9.44687	9.44864	9.45042	9.45219	9.45397	9.45574	9.45751
10	10.54577	10.54795	10.55014	10.55232	10.55451	10.55669	10.55887	10.56105
11	11.65706	11.65970	11.66233	11.66497	11.66761	11.67025	11.67288	11.67552
12	12.77906	12.78220	12.78533	12.78847	12.79161	12.79475	12.79788	12.80102
13	13.91187	13.91556	13.91924	13.92293	13.92661	13.93030	13.93398	13.93766
14	15.05561	15.05989	15.06417	15.06845	15.07272	15.07700	15.08128	15.08556
15	16.21036	16.21529	16.22021	16.22513	16.23006	16.23498	16.23990	16.24482
16	17.37625	17.38187	17.38749	17.39310	17.39872	17.40433	17.40995	17.41556
17	18.55338	18.55974	18.56610	18.57246	18.57882	18.58518	18.59154	18.59790
18	19.74185	19.74901	19.75616	19.76331	19.77047	19.77762	19.78478	19.79193
19	20.94178	20.94978	20.95778	20.96578	20.97379	20.98179	20.98979	20.99779
20	22.15328	22.16218	22.17108	22.17998	22.18888	22.19779	22.20669	22.21559
21	23.37645	23.38630	23.39616	23.40601	23.41587	23.42573	23.43559	23.44545
22	24.61141	24.62227	24.63314	24.64400	24.65487	24.66574	24.67661	24.68748
23	25.85827	25.87020	25.88213	25.89407	25.90600	25.91794	25.92988	25.94182
24	27.11716	27.13021	27.14326	27.15632	27.16938	27.18244	27.19550	27.20857
25	28.38818	28.40241	28.41664	28.43088	28.44512	28.45936	28.47361	28.48786
26	29.67145	29.68692	29.70239	29.71787	29.73335	29.74884	29.76432	29.77982
27	30.96709	30.98386	31.00063	31.01741	31.03419	31.05098	31.06777	31.08457
28	32.27521	32.29334	32.31148	32.32962	32.34777	32.36592	32.38407	32.40224
29	33.59595	33.61550	33.63506	33.65463	33.67420	33.69378	33.71336	33.73295
30	34.92942	34.95046	34.97150	34.99256	35.01362	35.03468	35.05576	35.07684
31	36.27573	36.29833	36.32092	36.34353	36.36614	36.38877	36.41140	36.43404
32	37.63503	37.65924	37.68345	37.70768	37.73191	37.75616	37.78041	37.80467
33	39.00743	39.03332	39.05922	39.08513	39.11105	39.13698	39.16292	39.18887
34	40.39306	40.42070	40.44835	40.47601	40.50369	40.53137	40.55907	40.58678
35	41.79204	41.82150	41.85097	41.88046	41.90996	41.93947	41.96899	41.99853
36	43.20451	43.23586	43.26722	43.29860	43.32999	43.36140	43.39282	43.42426
37	44.63059	44.66390	44.69722	44.73057	44.76392	44.79730	44.83069	44.86410
38	46.07042	46.10576	46.14112	46.17650	46.21190	46.24731	46.28275	46.31820
39	47.52413	47.56157	47.59904	47.63653	47.67404	47.71157	47.74913	47.78670
40	48.99185	49.03147	49.07113	49.11080	49.15050	49.19022	49.22997	49.26973
41	50.47371	50.51560	50.55751	50.59945	50.64141	50.68340	50.72541	50.76745
42	51.96986	52.01408	52.05833	52.10261	52.14691	52.19125	52.23561	52.28000
43	53.48043	53.52707	53.57373	53.62043	53.66716	53.71391	53.76071	53.80753
44	55.00556	55.05469	55.10385	55.15305	55.20228	55.25154	55.30084	55.35017
45	56.54539	56.59710	56.64884	56.70061	56.75243	56.80428	56.85617	56.90810
46	58.10007	58.15443	58.20883	58.26327	58.31775	58.37228	58.42684	58.48144
47	59.66973	59.72683	59.78397	59.84116	59.89840	59.95568	60.01300	60.07037
48	61.25452	61.31444	61.37442	61.43445	61.49452	61.55464	61.61481	61.67502
60	81.50662	81.60766	81.70881	81.81007	81.91145	82.01294	82.11454	82.21626
72	104.22949	104.38679	104.54433	104.70209	104.86008	105.01829	105.17674	105.33542
84	129.72454	129.95637	130.18861	130.42127	130.65433	130.88782	131.12172	131.35603
96	158.32999	158.65822	158.98714	159.31676	159.64708	159.97810	160.30981	160.64223
108	190.42531	190.87605	191.32790	191.78086	192.23493	192.69012	193.14642	193.60385
120	226.43626	227.04056	227.64656	228.25426	228.86367	229.47478	230.08761	230.70215
132	266.84054	267.63523	268.43242	269.23214	270.03437	270.83914	271.64644	272.45629
144	312.17414	313.20274	314.23495	315.27078	316.31024	317.35336	318.40013	319.45058
156	363.03844	364.35227	365.67118	366.99519	368.32432	369.65860	370.99803	372.34264
168	420.10819	421.76762	423.43407	425.10757	426.78815	428.47584	430.17067	431.87266
180	484.14044	486.21634	488.30179	490.39682	492.50149	494.61582	496.73988	498.87370
192	555.98463	558.56004	561.14824	563.74930	566.36328	568.99024	571.63025	574.28337
204	636.59381	639.76584	642.95481	646.16081	649.38394	652.62427	655.88191	659.15695
216	727.03732	730.91935	734.82359	738.75015	742.69915	746.67074	750.66504	754.68217
228	828.51492	833.23917	837.99222	842.77426	847.58546	852.42599	857.29605	862.19580
240	942.37280	948.09316	953.85060	959.64535	965.47766	971.34778	977.25594	983.20239
252	1070.12134	1077.01677	1083.95956	1090.95003	1097.98850	1105.07532	1112.21081	1119.39531
264	1213.45520	1221.73352	1230.07192	1238.47083	1246.93069	1255.45194	1264.03504	1272.68044
276	1374.27579	1384.17807	1394.15610	1404.21044	1414.34170	1424.55046	1434.83731	1445.20285
288	1554.71650	1566.52208	1578.42263	1590.41891	1602.51168	1614.70174	1626.98985	1639.37683
300	1757.17097	1771.20323	1785.35395	1799.62411	1814.01474	1828.52685	1843.16147	1857.91964
312	1984.32488	2000.95782	2017.73782	2034.66616	2051.74417	2068.97319	2086.35454	2103.88957
324	2239.19157	2258.85735	2278.70490	2298.73590	2318.95206	2339.35509	2359.94673	2380.72873
336	2525.15200	2548.34958	2571.77094	2595.41826	2619.29373	2643.39955	2667.73796	2692.31121
348	2845.99960	2873.30459	2900.88410	2928.74089	2956.87776	2985.29754	3014.00309	3042.99728
360	3205.99061	3238.06660	3270.47818	3303.22886	3336.32221	3369.76183	3403.55136	3437.69446
420	5782.18489	5852.16188	5923.01587	5994.75791	6067.39915	6140.95089	6215.42460	6290.83185
480	10363.00139	10510.73761	10660.63721	10812.73194	10967.05403	11123.63616	11282.51149	11443.71366

MONTHLY DEPOSITS

EFFECTIVE ANNUAL YIELD

NUMBER OF MONTHLY DEPOSITS	12.60%	12.65%	12.70%	12.75%	12.80%	12.85%	12.90%	12.95%
1	1.00994	1.00998	1.01001	1.01005	1.01009	1.01013	1.01016	1.01020
2	2.02991	2.03003	2.03014	2.03025	2.03036	2.03048	2.03059	2.03070
3	3.06003	3.06025	3.06048	3.06071	3.06093	3.06116	3.06139	3.06161
4	4.10038	4.10076	4.10114	4.10152	4.10190	4.10228	4.10266	4.10304
5	5.15107	5.15164	5.15222	5.15279	5.15337	5.15394	5.15452	5.15509
6	6.21220	6.21301	6.21382	6.21463	6.21544	6.21625	6.21706	6.21787
7	7.28387	7.28496	7.28605	7.28714	7.28823	7.28931	7.29040	7.29149
8	8.36620	8.36761	8.36902	8.37043	8.37184	8.37324	8.37465	8.37606
9	9.45929	9.46106	9.46283	9.46461	9.46638	9.46815	9.46992	9.47169
10	10.56324	10.56542	10.56760	10.56978	10.57196	10.57414	10.57632	10.57850
11	11.67815	11.68079	11.68343	11.68606	11.68869	11.69133	11.69396	11.69659
12	12.80415	12.80729	12.81043	12.81356	12.81669	12.81983	12.82296	12.82609
13	13.94135	13.94503	13.94871	13.95239	13.95607	13.95975	13.96343	13.96711
14	15.08984	15.09412	15.09839	15.10267	15.10695	15.11122	15.11550	15.11977
15	16.24974	16.25467	16.25959	16.26451	16.26943	16.27435	16.27927	16.28419
16	17.42118	17.42679	17.43241	17.43802	17.44364	17.44925	17.45487	17.46048
17	18.60425	18.61061	18.61697	18.62333	18.62969	18.63605	18.64241	18.64877
18	19.79909	19.80624	19.81340	19.82055	19.82771	19.83487	19.84202	19.84918
19	21.00580	21.01380	21.02180	21.02981	21.03781	21.04582	21.05382	21.06183
20	22.22450	22.23340	22.24231	22.25122	22.26013	22.26903	22.27794	22.28685
21	23.45531	23.46517	23.47504	23.48490	23.49477	23.50463	23.51450	23.52437
22	24.69836	24.70923	24.72011	24.73098	24.74186	24.75274	24.76362	24.77451
23	25.95376	25.96570	25.97765	25.98959	26.00154	26.01349	26.02544	26.03740
24	27.22163	27.23470	27.24777	27.26085	27.27392	27.28700	27.30008	27.31317
25	28.50211	28.51636	28.53062	28.54488	28.55914	28.57341	28.58768	28.60195
26	29.79531	29.81081	29.82631	29.84182	29.85733	29.87284	29.88836	29.90388
27	31.10137	31.11817	31.13498	31.15179	31.16861	31.18543	31.20225	31.21908
28	32.42040	32.43857	32.45675	32.47493	32.49312	32.51131	32.52950	32.54770
29	33.75255	33.77215	33.79175	33.81137	33.83099	33.85061	33.87024	33.88988
30	35.09793	35.11902	35.14013	35.16123	35.18235	35.20347	35.22460	35.24574
31	36.45668	36.47934	36.50200	36.52467	36.54735	36.57003	36.59273	36.61543
32	37.82894	37.85322	37.87751	37.90181	37.92612	37.95043	37.97476	37.99909
33	39.21484	39.24081	39.26679	39.29279	39.31879	39.34481	39.37083	39.39687
34	40.61451	40.64224	40.66999	40.69775	40.72552	40.75330	40.78109	40.80890
35	42.02809	42.05765	42.08723	42.11682	42.14643	42.17605	42.20568	42.23533
36	43.45571	43.48718	43.51867	43.55017	43.58168	43.61321	43.64475	43.67631
37	44.89753	44.93097	44.96443	44.99791	45.03141	45.06492	45.09845	45.13199
38	46.35368	46.38917	46.42468	46.46021	46.49576	46.53133	46.56692	46.60252
39	47.82429	47.86191	47.89955	47.93720	47.97488	48.01258	48.05031	48.08805
40	49.30953	49.34934	49.38918	49.42904	49.46893	49.50884	49.54877	49.58873
41	50.80952	50.85161	50.89373	50.93588	50.97805	51.02024	51.06246	51.10471
42	52.32442	52.36887	52.41335	52.45785	52.50239	52.54695	52.59154	52.63616
43	53.85438	53.90126	53.94818	53.99512	54.04210	54.08911	54.13615	54.18322
44	55.39954	55.44894	55.49838	55.54785	55.59735	55.64689	55.69646	55.74607
45	56.96006	57.01206	57.06410	57.11618	57.16829	57.22044	57.27263	57.32486
46	58.53609	58.59077	58.64550	58.70027	58.75508	58.80992	58.86481	58.91974
47	60.12778	60.18523	60.24273	60.30028	60.35787	60.41550	60.47318	60.53090
48	61.73529	61.79560	61.85596	61.91637	61.97683	62.03733	62.09789	62.15849
60	82.31809	82.42003	82.52209	82.62427	82.72656	82.82896	82.93148	83.03411
72	105.49432	105.65346	105.81283	105.97242	106.13225	106.29231	106.45260	106.61312
84	131.59076	131.82591	132.06148	132.29747	132.53387	132.77070	133.00794	133.24561
96	160.97535	161.30918	161.64371	161.97895	162.31490	162.65156	162.98893	163.32701
108	194.06240	194.52208	194.98289	195.44483	195.90790	196.37211	196.83746	197.30395
120	231.31842	231.93641	232.55614	233.17760	233.80081	234.42576	235.05246	235.68091
132	273.26870	274.08366	274.90120	275.72131	276.54400	277.36929	278.19718	279.02768
144	320.50471	321.56253	322.62407	323.68933	324.75833	325.83107	326.90758	327.98786
156	373.69245	375.04748	376.40775	377.77328	379.14409	380.52019	381.90162	383.28838
168	433.58186	435.29828	437.02196	438.75294	440.49123	442.23687	443.98989	445.75032
180	501.01733	503.17080	505.33418	507.50749	509.69080	511.88413	514.08754	516.30108
192	576.94966	579.62920	582.32204	585.02826	587.74791	590.48107	593.22780	595.98816
204	662.44948	665.75959	669.08737	672.43292	675.79634	679.17771	682.57714	685.99472
216	758.72227	762.78546	766.87189	770.98168	775.11496	779.27188	783.45256	787.65713
228	867.12543	872.08511	877.07504	882.09540	887.14637	892.22814	897.34090	902.48483
240	989.18738	995.21117	1001.27400	1007.37613	1013.51780	1019.69929	1025.92083	1032.18271
252	1126.62915	1133.91267	1141.24622	1148.63014	1156.06478	1163.55047	1171.08758	1178.67646
264	1281.38858	1290.15992	1298.99492	1307.89404	1316.85776	1325.88653	1334.98084	1344.14115
276	1455.64769	1466.17244	1476.77770	1487.46410	1498.23225	1509.08278	1520.01633	1531.03353
288	1651.86346	1664.45054	1677.13889	1689.92933	1702.82267	1715.81975	1728.92140	1742.12846
300	1872.80241	1887.81082	1902.94596	1918.20888	1933.60066	1949.12241	1964.77522	1980.56019
312	2121.57966	2139.42618	2157.43052	2175.59407	2193.91824	2212.40447	2231.05418	2249.86883
324	2401.70286	2422.87089	2444.23462	2465.79587	2487.55647	2509.51827	2531.68313	2554.05294
336	2717.12517	2742.17134	2767.46284	2792.99840	2818.78039	2844.81120	2871.09322	2897.62889
348	3072.28304	3101.86331	3131.74105	3161.91926	3192.40098	3223.18926	3254.28720	3285.69792
360	3472.19486	3507.05631	3542.28258	3577.87752	3613.84500	3650.18891	3686.91321	3724.02190
420	6367.18438	6444.49407	6522.77295	6602.03319	6682.28713	6763.54724	6845.82616	6929.13669
480	11607.27682	11773.23559	11941.62511	12112.48103	12285.83950	12461.73723	12640.21142	12821.29985

63

MONTHLY DEPOSITS

EFFECTIVE ANNUAL YIELD

NUMBER OF MONTHLY DEPOSITS	13.00%	13.05%	13.10%	13.15%	13.20%	13.25%	13.30%	13.35%
1	1.01024	1.01027	1.01031	1.01035	1.01039	1.01042	1.01046	1.01050
2	2.03082	2.03093	2.03104	2.03115	2.03127	2.03138	2.03149	2.03160
3	3.06184	3.06207	3.06207	3.06252	3.06275	3.06297	3.06320	3.06343
4	4.10342	4.10380	4.10418	4.10456	4.10494	4.10532	4.10570	4.10608
5	5.15566	5.15624	5.15681	5.15739	5.15796	5.15853	5.15911	5.15968
6	6.21868	6.21949	6.22030	6.22111	6.22191	6.22272	6.22353	6.22434
7	7.29258	7.29366	7.29475	7.29583	7.29692	7.29801	7.29909	7.30017
8	8.37747	8.37887	8.38028	8.38168	8.38309	8.38449	8.38590	8.38730
9	9.47346	9.47523	9.47700	9.47877	9.48054	9.48231	9.48408	9.48584
10	10.58068	10.58285	10.58503	10.58721	10.58939	10.59156	10.59374	10.59592
11	11.69923	11.70186	11.70449	11.70712	11.70975	11.71238	11.71501	11.71764
12	12.82923	12.83236	12.83549	12.83862	12.84175	12.84488	12.84801	12.85114
13	13.97079	13.97447	13.97815	13.98183	13.98551	13.98919	13.99286	13.99654
14	15.12405	15.12832	15.13260	15.13687	15.14114	15.14542	15.14969	15.15396
15	16.28911	16.29403	16.29894	16.30386	16.30878	16.31370	16.31862	16.32353
16	17.46609	17.47171	17.47732	17.48293	17.48855	17.49416	17.49977	17.50538
17	18.65513	18.66149	18.66784	18.67420	18.68056	18.68692	18.69328	18.69964
18	19.85633	19.86349	19.87065	19.87780	19.88496	19.89212	19.89927	19.90643
19	21.06984	21.07784	21.08585	21.09386	21.10186	21.10987	21.11788	21.12589
20	22.29576	22.30467	22.31358	22.32250	22.33141	22.34032	22.34924	22.35815
21	23.53424	23.54411	23.55398	23.56385	23.57372	23.58360	23.59347	23.60335
22	24.78539	24.79628	24.80716	24.81805	24.82894	24.83983	24.85072	24.86161
23	26.04935	26.06131	26.07327	26.08523	26.09719	26.10915	26.12112	26.13309
24	27.32625	27.33934	27.35243	27.36552	27.37861	27.39171	27.40481	27.41791
25	28.61622	28.63050	28.64478	28.65906	28.67335	28.68764	28.70193	28.71622
26	29.91940	29.93493	29.95046	29.96599	29.98153	29.99707	30.01261	30.02816
27	31.23592	31.25275	31.26960	31.28644	31.30329	31.32015	31.33700	31.35387
28	32.56591	32.58412	32.60234	32.62056	32.63879	32.65702	32.67525	32.69349
29	33.90952	33.92917	33.94882	33.96848	33.98815	34.00782	34.02750	34.04718
30	35.26688	35.28803	35.30919	35.33035	35.35153	35.37270	35.39389	35.41508
31	36.63814	36.66086	36.68359	36.70632	36.72906	36.75181	36.77457	36.79734
32	38.02344	38.04779	38.07215	38.09653	38.12091	38.14530	38.16970	38.19411
33	39.42291	39.44897	39.47504	39.50112	39.52721	39.55330	39.57941	39.60553
34	40.83672	40.86455	40.89239	40.92024	40.94811	40.97599	41.00388	41.03178
35	42.26499	42.29467	42.32436	42.35406	42.38377	42.41350	42.44324	42.47300
36	43.70789	43.73948	43.77109	43.80271	43.83434	43.86599	43.89766	43.92934
37	45.16556	45.19914	45.23274	45.26635	45.29998	45.33363	45.36729	45.40098
38	46.63815	46.67379	46.70946	46.74514	46.78084	46.81656	46.85230	46.88806
39	48.12581	48.16360	48.20140	48.23923	48.27708	48.31495	48.35284	48.39075
40	49.62870	49.66871	49.70873	49.74878	49.78886	49.82895	49.86907	49.90922
41	51.14698	51.18928	51.23161	51.27396	51.31634	51.35874	51.40117	51.44362
42	52.68080	52.72548	52.77018	52.81492	52.85968	52.90447	52.94929	52.99414
43	54.23033	54.27746	54.32463	54.37182	54.41905	54.46631	54.51360	54.56092
44	55.79571	55.84539	55.89510	55.94484	55.99462	56.04443	56.09428	56.14416
45	57.37712	57.42942	57.48176	57.53413	57.58655	57.63900	57.69149	57.74402
46	58.97472	59.02973	59.08478	59.13988	59.19501	59.25019	59.30541	59.36066
47	60.58867	60.64648	60.70434	60.76224	60.82018	60.87817	60.93621	60.99428
48	62.21914	62.27984	62.34059	62.40138	62.46223	62.52312	62.58406	62.64505
60	83.13686	83.23972	83.34270	83.44579	83.54899	83.65232	83.75575	83.85931
72	106.77387	106.93486	107.09608	107.25753	107.41921	107.58113	107.74328	107.90567
84	133.48370	133.72222	133.96115	134.20051	134.44030	134.68051	134.92115	135.16222
96	163.66581	164.00532	164.34555	164.68650	165.02817	165.37056	165.71368	166.05751
108	197.77159	198.24038	198.71031	199.18140	199.65364	200.12704	200.60161	201.07733
120	236.31112	236.94310	237.57685	238.21237	238.84968	239.48876	240.12963	240.77230
132	279.86080	280.69654	281.53491	282.37592	283.21958	284.06590	284.91489	285.76654
144	329.07193	330.15979	331.25147	332.34698	333.44632	334.54952	335.65658	336.76752
156	384.68050	386.07800	387.48090	388.88923	390.30299	391.72221	393.14692	394.57712
168	447.51819	449.29354	451.07639	452.86678	454.66473	456.47029	458.28347	460.10431
180	518.52479	520.75871	523.00289	525.25738	527.52223	529.79748	532.08318	534.37938
192	598.76223	601.55008	604.35175	607.16735	609.99692	612.84053	615.69826	618.57017
204	689.43055	692.88472	696.35733	699.84848	703.35826	706.88678	710.43414	714.00042
216	791.88575	796.13853	800.41563	804.71717	809.04330	813.39416	817.76989	822.17062
228	907.66012	912.86697	918.10557	923.37610	928.67877	934.01377	939.38129	944.78154
240	1038.48516	1044.82847	1051.21288	1057.63868	1064.10612	1070.61548	1077.16702	1083.76102
252	1186.31746	1194.01094	1201.75726	1209.55679	1217.40988	1225.31691	1233.27824	1241.29426
264	1353.36796	1362.66173	1372.02295	1381.45212	1390.94974	1400.51628	1410.15226	1419.85818
276	1542.13502	1553.32144	1564.59345	1575.95170	1587.39685	1598.92957	1610.55053	1622.26039
288	1755.44179	1768.68224	1782.03068	1796.02797	1809.77499	1823.63262	1837.60176	1851.68330
300	1996.47845	2012.53113	2028.71935	2045.04427	2061.50704	2078.10883	2094.85080	2111.73416
312	2268.84988	2287.99880	2307.31707	2326.80621	2346.46772	2366.30313	2386.31397	2406.50181
324	2576.62959	2599.41500	2622.41110	2645.61985	2669.04321	2692.68317	2716.54174	2740.62094
336	2924.42066	2951.47101	2978.78244	3006.35748	3034.19866	3062.30858	3090.68981	3119.34498
348	3317.42457	3349.47034	3381.83843	3414.53211	3447.55464	3480.90934	3514.59956	3548.62868
360	3761.51899	3799.40857	3837.69476	3876.38170	3915.47360	3954.97471	3994.88932	4035.22175
420	7013.49177	7098.90454	7185.38825	7272.95635	7361.62246	7451.40034	7542.30395	7634.34742
480	13005.04083	13191.47323	13380.63648	13572.57058	13767.31613	13964.91430	14165.40686	14368.83619

MONTHLY DEPOSITS

NUMBER OF MONTHLY DEPOSITS	EFFECTIVE ANNUAL YIELD							
	13.40%	13.45%	13.50%	13.55%	13.60%	13.65%	13.70%	13.75%
1	1.01053	1.01057	1.01061	1.01065	1.01068	1.01072	1.01076	1.01079
2	2.03171	2.03183	2.03194	2.03205	2.03216	2.03227	2.03239	2.03250
3	3.06365	3.06388	3.06410	3.06433	3.06455	3.06478	3.06501	3.06523
4	4.10646	4.10684	4.10722	4.10760	4.10798	4.10835	4.10873	4.10911
5	5.16025	5.16083	5.16140	5.16197	5.16254	5.16311	5.16369	5.16426
6	6.22515	6.22595	6.22676	6.22757	6.22838	6.22918	6.22999	6.23079
7	7.30126	7.30234	7.30343	7.30451	7.30559	7.30668	7.30776	7.30884
8	8.38871	8.39011	8.39152	8.39292	8.39432	8.39572	8.39713	8.39853
9	9.48761	9.48938	9.49115	9.49291	9.49468	9.49644	9.49821	9.49997
10	10.59809	10.60027	10.60244	10.60462	10.60679	10.60896	10.61114	10.61331
11	11.72027	11.72290	11.72553	11.72816	11.73078	11.73341	11.73604	11.73866
12	12.85427	12.85740	12.86053	12.86366	12.86678	12.86991	12.87304	12.87616
13	14.00022	14.00389	14.00757	14.01124	14.01492	14.01859	14.02227	14.02594
14	15.15823	15.16251	15.16678	15.17105	15.17532	15.17959	15.18386	15.18813
15	16.32845	16.33337	16.33828	16.34320	16.34812	16.35303	16.35795	16.36286
16	17.51100	17.51661	17.52222	17.52783	17.53344	17.53905	17.54467	17.55028
17	18.70600	18.71236	18.71871	18.72507	18.73143	18.73779	18.74415	18.75051
18	19.91359	19.92074	19.92790	19.93506	19.94222	19.94938	19.95653	19.96369
19	21.13390	21.14191	21.14992	21.15793	21.16594	21.17395	21.18196	21.18997
20	22.36707	22.37598	22.38490	22.39381	22.40273	22.41165	22.42057	22.42949
21	23.61322	23.62310	23.63298	23.64286	23.65274	23.66262	23.67250	23.68238
22	24.87251	24.88340	24.89430	24.90520	24.91610	24.92700	24.93790	24.94880
23	26.14506	26.15703	26.16900	26.18098	26.19295	26.20493	26.21691	26.22889
24	27.43101	27.44412	27.45723	27.47034	27.48345	27.49656	27.50968	27.52280
25	28.73052	28.74482	28.75912	28.77342	28.78773	28.80204	28.81636	28.83067
26	30.04371	30.05926	30.07482	30.09038	30.10595	30.12151	30.13709	30.15266
27	31.37073	31.38761	31.40448	31.42136	31.43824	31.45513	31.47202	31.48892
28	32.71174	32.72999	32.74825	32.76651	32.78477	32.80305	32.82132	32.83960
29	34.06687	34.08657	34.10627	34.12598	34.14569	34.16541	34.18513	34.20486
30	35.43628	35.45748	35.47870	35.49992	35.52114	35.54238	35.56362	35.58486
31	36.82011	36.84289	36.86568	36.88848	36.91129	36.93410	36.95693	36.97976
32	38.21852	38.24295	38.26739	38.29183	38.31629	38.34075	38.36522	38.38971
33	39.63167	39.65781	39.68396	39.71012	39.73629	39.76248	39.78867	39.81488
34	41.05969	41.08762	41.11556	41.14351	41.17147	41.19944	41.22743	41.25543
35	42.50277	42.53255	42.56235	42.59215	42.62198	42.65181	42.68167	42.71153
36	43.96104	43.99275	44.02448	44.05622	44.08798	44.11975	44.15154	44.18335
37	45.43468	45.46839	45.50213	45.53588	45.56965	45.60343	45.63723	45.67105
38	46.92384	46.95963	46.99545	47.03128	47.06714	47.10301	47.13890	47.17482
39	48.42868	48.46664	48.50461	48.54261	48.58063	48.61867	48.65673	48.69481
40	49.94938	49.98957	50.02979	50.07003	50.11029	50.15057	50.19088	50.23121
41	51.48610	51.52861	51.57114	51.61370	51.65629	51.69890	51.74153	51.78420
42	53.03901	53.08392	53.12885	53.17381	53.21880	53.26382	53.30887	53.35394
43	54.60828	54.65566	54.70308	54.75053	54.79801	54.84552	54.89306	54.94064
44	56.19408	56.24403	56.29401	56.34403	56.39409	56.44417	56.49430	56.54445
45	57.79658	57.84918	57.90182	57.95450	58.00721	58.05997	58.11276	58.16558
46	59.41596	59.47130	59.52669	59.58211	59.63757	59.69308	59.74862	59.80421
47	61.05241	61.11058	61.16879	61.22705	61.28535	61.34370	61.40209	61.46053
48	62.70609	62.76718	62.82831	62.88950	62.95073	63.01201	63.07334	63.13472
60	83.96298	84.06676	84.17066	84.27468	84.37881	84.48306	84.58743	84.69191
72	108.06829	108.23114	108.39423	108.55756	108.72111	108.88491	109.04894	109.21321
84	135.40371	135.64563	135.88798	136.13076	136.37397	136.61761	136.86168	137.10619
96	166.40208	166.74737	167.09339	167.44013	167.78761	168.13583	168.48477	168.83445
108	201.55423	202.03229	202.51152	202.99193	203.47351	203.95628	204.44022	204.92535
120	241.41676	242.06303	242.71110	243.36099	244.01269	244.66622	245.32157	245.97875
132	286.62088	287.47791	288.33763	289.20006	290.06520	290.93307	291.80366	292.67700
144	337.88235	339.00108	340.12374	341.25032	342.38085	343.51534	344.65380	345.79625
156	396.01285	397.45413	398.90097	400.35340	401.81143	403.27510	404.74441	406.21939
168	461.93285	463.76911	465.61313	467.46494	469.32457	471.19206	473.06743	474.95072
180	536.68612	539.00345	541.33143	543.67009	546.01950	548.37968	550.75071	553.13261
192	621.45633	624.35682	627.27170	630.20105	633.14493	636.10342	639.07659	642.06451
204	717.58575	721.19021	724.81391	728.45694	732.11942	735.80145	739.50312	743.22454
216	826.59651	831.04719	835.52431	840.02652	844.55445	849.10826	853.68808	858.29408
228	950.21471	955.68101	961.18062	966.71377	972.28064	977.88144	983.51639	989.18568
240	1090.36976	1097.07750	1103.80054	1110.56714	1117.37759	1124.23217	1131.13117	1138.07488
252	1249.36533	1257.49183	1265.67414	1273.91264	1282.20772	1290.55977	1298.96918	1307.43633
264	1429.63455	1439.48188	1449.40067	1459.39146	1469.45476	1479.59109	1489.80099	1500.08499
276	1634.05985	1645.94959	1657.93029	1670.00266	1682.16739	1694.42519	1706.77677	1719.22284
288	1865.87814	1880.18721	1894.61141	1909.15167	1923.80893	1938.58413	1953.47822	1968.49215
300	2128.76008	2145.92978	2163.24448	2180.70538	2198.31373	2216.07078	2233.97777	2252.03598
312	2426.86821	2447.41474	2468.14301	2489.05461	2510.15118	2531.43435	2552.90576	2574.56709
324	2764.92282	2789.44942	2814.20284	2839.18517	2864.39853	2889.84505	2915.52689	2941.44623
336	3148.27674	3177.48777	3206.98075	3236.75842	3266.82351	3297.17881	3327.82711	3358.77125
348	3583.00010	3617.71727	3652.78368	3688.20284	3723.97829	3760.11363	3796.61246	3833.47846
360	4075.97638	4117.15765	4158.77001	4200.81798	4243.30612	4286.23905	4329.62141	4373.45791
420	7727.54503	7821.91126	7917.46077	8014.20839	8112.16914	8211.35822	8311.79104	8413.48318
480	14575.24528	14784.67776	14997.17787	15212.79049	15431.56118	15653.53614	15878.76222	16107.28699

65

MONTHLY DEPOSITS

EFFECTIVE ANNUAL YIELD

NUMBER OF MONTHLY DEPOSITS	13.80%	13.85%	13.90%	13.95%	14.00%	14.05%	14.10%	14.15%
1	1.01083	1.01087	1.01090	1.01094	1.01098	1.01102	1.01105	1.01109
2	2.03261	2.03272	2.03283	2.03295	2.03306	2.03317	2.03328	2.03339
3	3.06546	3.06568	3.06591	3.06613	3.06636	3.06658	3.06681	3.06703
4	4.10949	4.10987	4.11024	4.11062	4.11100	4.11138	4.11176	4.11213
5	5.16483	5.16540	5.16597	5.16654	5.16711	5.16768	5.16825	5.16882
6	6.23160	6.23241	6.23321	6.23402	6.23482	6.23563	6.23643	6.23723
7	7.30993	7.31101	7.31209	7.31317	7.31425	7.31533	7.31641	7.31749
8	8.39993	8.40133	8.40273	8.40413	8.40553	8.40693	8.40833	8.40973
9	9.50174	9.50350	9.50527	9.50703	9.50879	9.51056	9.51232	9.51408
10	10.61548	10.61765	10.61983	10.62200	10.62417	10.62634	10.62851	10.63068
11	11.74129	11.74391	11.74654	11.74916	11.75179	11.75441	11.75704	11.75966
12	12.87929	12.88241	12.88554	12.88866	12.89179	12.89491	12.89804	12.90116
13	14.02961	14.03329	14.03696	14.04063	14.04430	14.04798	14.05165	14.05532
14	15.19240	15.19667	15.20094	15.20521	15.20947	15.21374	15.21801	15.22228
15	16.36778	16.37269	16.37761	16.38252	16.38744	16.39235	16.39726	16.40217
16	17.55589	17.56150	17.56711	17.57272	17.57833	17.58394	17.58955	17.59516
17	18.75686	18.76322	18.76958	18.77594	18.78230	18.78866	18.79501	18.80137
18	19.97085	19.97801	19.98517	19.99233	19.99948	20.00664	20.01380	20.02096
19	21.19798	21.20600	21.21401	21.22202	21.23004	21.23805	21.24606	21.25408
20	22.43841	22.44733	22.45625	22.46517	22.47410	22.48302	22.49194	22.50087
21	23.69227	23.70215	23.71204	23.72193	23.73181	23.74170	23.75159	23.76148
22	24.95971	24.97061	24.98152	24.99243	25.00334	25.01425	25.02516	25.03608
23	26.24088	26.25286	26.26485	26.27684	26.28883	26.30082	26.31281	26.32481
24	27.53592	27.54904	27.56217	27.57530	27.58843	27.60156	27.61469	27.62783
25	28.84499	28.85931	28.87364	28.88797	28.90230	28.91663	28.93097	28.94530
26	30.16824	30.18382	30.19941	30.21500	30.23059	30.24618	30.26178	30.27739
27	31.50582	31.52273	31.53963	31.55655	31.57346	31.59039	31.60731	31.62424
28	32.85789	32.87618	32.89448	32.91278	32.93108	32.94940	32.96771	32.98603
29	34.22460	34.24434	34.26409	34.28385	34.30361	34.32337	34.34315	34.36293
30	35.60612	35.62738	35.64865	35.66992	35.69120	35.71249	35.73379	35.75509
31	37.00260	37.02544	37.04830	37.07116	37.09403	37.11691	37.13979	37.16269
32	38.41420	38.43870	38.46321	38.48773	38.51226	38.53680	38.56134	38.58590
33	39.84109	39.86732	39.89355	39.91980	39.94606	39.97232	39.99860	40.02489
34	41.28344	41.31146	41.33949	41.36754	41.39560	41.42367	41.45175	41.47984
35	42.74141	42.77130	42.80120	42.83112	42.86105	42.89100	42.92096	42.95093
36	44.21517	44.24700	44.27885	44.31072	44.34260	44.37449	44.40640	44.43833
37	45.70489	45.73874	45.77261	45.80650	45.84041	45.87433	45.90827	45.94222
38	47.21075	47.24670	47.28266	47.31865	47.35466	47.39069	47.42673	47.46280
39	48.73291	48.77104	48.80918	48.84735	48.88554	48.92375	48.96198	49.00023
40	50.27157	50.31195	50.35235	50.39277	50.43322	50.47370	50.51419	50.55472
41	51.82689	51.86960	51.91234	51.95511	51.99790	52.04072	52.08357	52.12644
42	53.39905	53.44418	53.48935	53.53454	53.57976	53.62501	53.67028	53.71559
43	54.98824	55.03588	55.08355	55.13125	55.17898	55.22675	55.27454	55.32237
44	56.59465	56.64487	56.69514	56.74543	56.79576	56.84613	56.89653	56.94696
45	58.21845	58.27135	58.32430	58.37728	58.43029	58.48335	58.53644	58.58957
46	59.85984	59.91551	59.97122	60.02698	60.08277	60.13861	60.19448	60.25040
47	61.51901	61.57754	61.63611	61.69473	61.75339	61.81210	61.87085	61.92964
48	63.19615	63.25763	63.31915	63.38073	63.44235	63.50402	63.56574	63.62751
60	84.79651	84.90122	85.00605	85.11100	85.21607	85.32125	85.42655	85.53196
72	109.37771	109.54246	109.70743	109.87265	110.03810	110.20380	110.36973	110.53590
84	137.35113	137.59650	137.84231	138.08855	138.33523	138.58234	138.82989	139.07788
96	169.18487	169.53603	169.88793	170.24057	170.59395	170.94807	171.30294	171.65856
108	205.41167	205.89919	206.38789	206.87779	207.36889	207.86119	208.35470	208.84941
120	246.63777	247.29864	247.96135	248.62591	249.29232	249.96060	250.63074	251.30276
132	293.55308	294.43191	295.31351	296.19788	297.08504	297.97498	298.86771	299.76326
144	346.94269	348.09315	349.24763	350.40615	351.56873	352.73537	353.90610	355.08092
156	407.70007	409.18646	410.67859	412.17648	413.68014	415.18961	416.70489	418.22603
168	476.84197	478.74120	480.64845	482.56376	484.48715	486.41866	488.35832	490.30617
180	555.52545	557.92927	560.34413	562.77007	565.20714	567.65539	570.11488	572.58565
192	645.06725	648.08489	651.11750	654.16516	657.22793	660.30589	663.39911	666.50768
204	746.96582	750.72707	754.50838	758.30986	762.13162	765.97378	769.83642	773.71967
216	862.92640	867.58518	872.27058	876.98275	881.72184	886.48800	891.28139	896.10217
228	994.88953	1000.62814	1006.40173	1012.21051	1018.05469	1023.93448	1029.85011	1035.80178
240	1145.06357	1152.09755	1159.17711	1166.30254	1173.47413	1180.69219	1187.95701	1195.26889
252	1315.96164	1324.54548	1333.18827	1341.89041	1350.65230	1359.47435	1368.35698	1377.30060
264	1510.44363	1520.87744	1531.38698	1541.97278	1552.63541	1563.37541	1574.19335	1585.08979
276	1731.76414	1744.40139	1757.13531	1769.96665	1782.89615	1795.92457	1809.05265	1822.28116
288	1983.62688	1998.88339	2014.26266	2029.76566	2045.39341	2061.14689	2077.02711	2093.03510
300	2270.24668	2288.61116	2307.13071	2325.80664	2344.64027	2363.63294	2382.78597	2402.10073
312	2596.42001	2618.46622	2640.70741	2663.14533	2685.78170	2708.61827	2731.65683	2754.89914
324	2967.60526	2994.00620	3020.65128	3047.54277	3074.68292	3102.07406	3129.71848	3157.61853
336	3390.01408	3421.55848	3453.40735	3485.56365	3518.03032	3550.81037	3583.90682	3617.32271
348	3870.71531	3908.32674	3946.31652	3984.68844	4023.44636	4062.59414	4102.13571	4142.07503
360	4417.75331	4462.51241	4507.74005	4553.44114	4599.62064	4646.28353	4693.43489	4741.07981
420	8516.45041	8620.70870	8726.27424	8833.16338	8941.39271	9050.97900	9161.93924	9274.29062
480	16339.15867	16574.42621	16813.13924	17055.34814	17301.10398	17550.45859	17803.46457	18060.17523

66

MONTHLY DEPOSITS

NUMBER OF MONTHLY DEPOSITS	EFFECTIVE ANNUAL YIELD							
	14.20%	14.25%	14.30%	14.35%	14.40%	14.45%	14.50%	14.55%
1	1.01113	1.01116	1.01120	1.01124	1.01127	1.01131	1.01135	1.01138
2	2.03350	2.03361	2.03373	2.03384	2.03395	2.03406	2.03417	2.03428
3	3.06726	3.06748	3.06770	3.06793	3.06815	3.06838	3.06860	3.06883
4	4.11251	4.11289	4.11326	4.11364	4.11402	4.11439	4.11477	4.11515
5	5.16939	5.16996	5.17053	5.17110	5.17167	5.17224	5.17281	5.17338
6	6.23804	6.23884	6.23965	6.24045	6.24125	6.24206	6.24286	6.24366
7	7.31857	7.31965	7.32073	7.32181	7.32289	7.32397	7.32505	7.32613
8	8.41113	8.41253	8.41393	8.41533	8.41672	8.41812	8.41952	8.42091
9	9.51584	9.51760	9.51937	9.52113	9.52289	9.52465	9.52641	9.52817
10	10.63285	10.63502	10.63719	10.63935	10.64152	10.64369	10.64586	10.64802
11	11.76228	11.76490	11.76753	11.77015	11.77277	11.77539	11.77801	11.78063
12	12.90428	12.90740	12.91053	12.91365	12.91677	12.91989	12.92301	12.92613
13	14.05899	14.06266	14.06633	14.07000	14.07367	14.07733	14.08100	14.08467
14	15.22654	15.23081	15.23507	15.23934	15.24361	15.24787	15.25214	15.25640
15	16.40709	16.41200	16.41691	16.42182	16.42674	16.43165	16.43656	16.44147
16	17.60077	17.60638	17.61199	17.61760	17.62320	17.62881	17.63442	17.64003
17	18.80773	18.81409	18.82045	18.82680	18.83316	18.83952	18.84588	18.85224
18	20.02812	20.03528	20.04244	20.04960	20.05676	20.06392	20.07108	20.07824
19	21.26209	21.27011	21.27812	21.28614	21.29415	21.30217	21.31019	21.31821
20	22.50979	22.51872	22.52764	22.53657	22.54550	22.55443	22.56336	22.57229
21	23.77137	23.78127	23.79116	23.80105	23.81095	23.82085	23.83074	23.84064
22	25.04699	25.05791	25.06883	25.07975	25.09067	25.10159	25.11251	25.12344
23	26.33681	26.34881	26.36081	26.37281	26.38481	26.39682	26.40883	26.42084
24	27.64097	27.65411	27.66726	27.68040	27.69355	27.70670	27.71985	27.73301
25	28.95965	28.97399	28.98834	29.00269	29.01704	29.03140	29.04576	29.06012
26	30.29299	30.30860	30.32422	30.33983	30.35545	30.37108	30.38670	30.40233
27	31.64118	31.65811	31.67506	31.69200	31.70895	31.72591	31.74287	31.75983
28	33.00436	33.02269	33.04103	33.05937	33.07772	33.09607	33.11442	33.13278
29	34.38271	34.40250	34.42230	34.44210	34.46191	34.48172	34.50154	34.52136
30	35.77640	35.79771	35.81904	35.84037	35.86170	35.88305	35.90440	35.92575
31	37.18559	37.20850	37.23142	37.25435	37.27728	37.30022	37.32317	37.34613
32	38.61046	38.63504	38.65962	38.68422	38.70882	38.73343	38.75805	38.78268
33	40.05119	40.07750	40.10382	40.13015	40.15650	40.18285	40.20921	40.23558
34	41.50795	41.53607	41.56420	41.59234	41.62049	41.64866	41.67684	41.70503
35	42.98092	43.01091	43.04093	43.07096	43.10100	43.13105	43.16112	43.19120
36	44.47027	44.50223	44.53420	44.56619	44.59819	44.63021	44.66224	44.69429
37	45.97620	46.01019	46.04420	46.07822	46.11226	46.14632	46.18040	46.21449
38	47.49888	47.53498	47.57110	47.60725	47.64341	47.67959	47.71578	47.75200
39	49.03850	49.07680	49.11514	49.15345	49.19181	49.23019	49.26859	49.30702
40	50.59526	50.63583	50.67642	50.71703	50.75767	50.79834	50.83902	50.87973
41	52.16934	52.21226	52.25521	52.29819	52.34119	52.38422	52.42727	52.47035
42	53.76093	53.80629	53.85168	53.89711	53.94256	53.98804	54.03354	54.07908
43	55.37023	55.41812	55.46604	55.51399	55.56198	55.60999	55.65804	55.70612
44	56.99743	57.04794	57.09847	57.14905	57.19966	57.25030	57.30098	57.35169
45	58.64274	58.69595	58.74919	58.80248	58.85580	58.90916	58.96255	59.01599
46	60.30636	60.36236	60.41840	60.47449	60.53061	60.58678	60.64299	60.69924
47	61.98849	62.04737	62.10631	62.16528	62.22431	62.28338	62.34249	62.40165
48	63.68933	63.75120	63.81312	63.87508	63.93710	63.99916	64.06127	64.12344
60	85.63750	85.74315	85.84892	85.95480	86.06081	86.16693	86.27317	86.37953
72	110.70230	110.86895	111.03584	111.20296	111.37033	111.53794	111.70579	111.87388
84	139.32631	139.57518	139.82449	140.07424	140.32443	140.57506	140.82613	141.07765
96	172.01493	172.37205	172.72991	173.08854	173.44791	173.80804	174.16893	174.53058
108	209.34533	209.84247	210.34082	210.84039	211.34118	211.84319	212.34644	212.85091
120	251.97665	252.65242	253.33008	254.00963	254.69108	255.37442	256.05968	256.74684
132	300.66162	301.56280	302.46681	303.37366	304.28336	305.19592	306.11134	307.02964
144	356.25985	357.44290	358.63009	359.82143	361.01693	362.21662	363.42049	364.62858
156	419.75303	421.28591	422.82471	424.36945	425.92014	427.47680	429.03947	430.60816
168	492.26224	494.22656	496.19917	498.18011	500.16940	502.16709	504.17320	506.18778
180	575.06776	577.56125	580.06618	582.58260	585.11057	587.65012	590.20133	592.76423
192	669.63166	672.77113	675.92617	679.09685	682.28326	685.48546	688.70353	691.93755
204	777.62364	781.54842	785.49414	789.46090	793.44881	797.45799	801.48855	805.54060
216	900.95048	905.82648	910.73033	915.66219	920.62221	925.61056	930.62740	935.67288
228	1041.78972	1047.81415	1053.87529	1059.97336	1066.10858	1072.28118	1078.49138	1084.73942
240	1202.62815	1210.03507	1217.48998	1224.99318	1232.54498	1240.14569	1247.79564	1255.49513
252	1386.30562	1395.37248	1404.50157	1413.69335	1422.94822	1432.26664	1441.64901	1451.09580
264	1596.06531	1607.12046	1618.25583	1629.47199	1640.76954	1652.14905	1663.61113	1675.15637
276	1835.61086	1849.04623	1862.57693	1876.21487	1889.95712	1903.80448	1917.75775	1931.81774
288	2109.17188	2125.43849	2141.83596	2158.36535	2175.02771	2191.82412	2208.75564	2225.82336
300	2421.57857	2441.22088	2461.02903	2481.00442	2501.14847	2521.46259	2541.94821	2562.60678
312	2778.34701	2802.00226	2825.86671	2849.94221	2874.23062	2898.73382	2923.45371	2948.39220
324	3185.77657	3214.19498	3242.87617	3271.82256	3301.03659	3330.52075	3360.27751	3390.30939
336	3651.06112	3685.12517	3719.51799	3754.24274	3789.30263	3824.70088	3860.44075	3896.52553
348	4182.41608	4223.16291	4264.31959	4305.89022	4347.87898	4390.29005	4433.12767	4476.39613
360	4789.22345	4837.87103	4887.02781	4936.69912	4986.89032	5037.60685	5088.85419	5140.63789
420	9388.05056	9503.23667	9619.86681	9737.95903	9857.53161	9978.60308	10101.19217	10225.31784
480	18320.64470	18584.92787	18853.08041	19125.15882	19401.22040	19681.32328	19965.52643	20253.88967

MONTHLY DEPOSITS

EFFECTIVE ANNUAL YIELD

NUMBER OF MONTHLY DEPOSITS	14.60%	14.65%	14.70%	14.75%	14.80%	14.85%	14.90%	14.95%
1	1.01142	1.01146	1.01149	1.01153	1.01157	1.01160	1.01164	1.01168
2	2.03439	2.03451	2.03462	2.03473	2.03484	2.03495	2.03506	2.03517
3	3.06905	3.06927	3.06950	3.06972	3.06995	3.07017	3.07039	3.07062
4	4.11552	4.11590	4.11628	4.11665	4.11703	4.11740	4.11778	4.11815
5	5.17395	5.17452	5.17509	5.17565	5.17622	5.17679	5.17736	5.17793
6	6.24446	6.24527	6.24607	6.24687	6.24767	6.24847	6.24927	6.25007
7	7.32720	7.32828	7.32936	7.33044	7.33151	7.33259	7.33367	7.33474
8	8.42231	8.42371	8.42510	8.42650	8.42789	8.42929	8.43068	8.43208
9	9.52992	9.53168	9.53344	9.53520	9.53696	9.53871	9.54047	9.54223
10	10.65019	10.65235	10.65452	10.65668	10.65885	10.66101	10.66318	10.66534
11	11.78325	11.78587	11.78849	11.79110	11.79372	11.79634	11.79896	11.80157
12	12.92925	12.93237	12.93549	12.93860	12.94172	12.94484	12.94796	12.95107
13	14.08834	14.09200	14.09567	14.09934	14.10300	14.10667	14.11033	14.11400
14	15.26066	15.26493	15.26919	15.27345	15.27772	15.28198	15.28624	15.29050
15	16.44638	16.45129	16.45620	16.46111	16.46602	16.47093	16.47584	16.48075
16	17.64564	17.65125	17.65685	17.66246	17.66807	17.67368	17.67928	17.68489
17	18.85859	18.86495	18.87131	18.87767	18.88402	18.89038	18.89674	18.90310
18	20.08540	20.09256	20.09972	20.10689	20.11405	20.12121	20.12837	20.13553
19	21.32622	21.33424	21.34226	21.35028	21.35830	21.36632	21.37434	21.38236
20	22.58122	22.59015	22.59908	22.60801	22.61694	22.62588	22.63481	22.64374
21	23.85054	23.86044	23.87034	23.88024	23.89015	23.90005	23.90996	23.91986
22	25.13436	25.14529	25.15622	25.16715	25.17808	25.18901	25.19995	25.21088
23	26.43285	26.44486	26.45688	26.46889	26.48091	26.49293	26.50496	26.51698
24	27.74617	27.75933	27.77249	27.78565	27.79882	27.81199	27.82516	27.83833
25	29.07448	29.08885	29.10322	29.11759	29.13197	29.14635	29.16073	29.17511
26	30.41797	30.43361	30.44925	30.46489	30.48054	30.49619	30.51184	30.52750
27	31.77680	31.79377	31.81075	31.82773	31.84471	31.86170	31.87869	31.89569
28	33.15115	33.16952	33.18790	33.20628	33.22466	33.24306	33.26145	33.27985
29	34.54120	34.56103	34.58088	34.60073	34.62058	34.64044	34.66031	34.68018
30	35.94712	35.96849	35.98987	36.01125	36.03265	36.05405	36.07545	36.09686
31	37.36910	37.39207	37.41506	37.43805	37.46105	37.48405	37.50707	37.53009
32	38.80732	38.83197	38.85663	38.88129	38.90597	38.93066	38.95535	38.98006
33	40.26197	40.28836	40.31477	40.34118	40.36761	40.39405	40.42049	40.44695
34	41.73323	41.76144	41.78967	41.81791	41.84616	41.87442	41.90269	41.93098
35	43.22129	43.25140	43.28152	43.31166	43.34181	43.37197	43.40215	43.43234
36	44.72635	44.75843	44.79053	44.82264	44.85476	44.88690	44.91906	44.95123
37	46.24860	46.28273	46.31688	46.35104	46.38522	46.41942	46.45363	46.48786
38	47.78824	47.82450	47.86077	47.89707	47.93338	47.96971	48.00607	48.04244
39	49.34546	49.38392	49.42241	49.46092	49.49945	49.53800	49.57657	49.61517
40	50.92046	50.96122	51.00200	51.04281	51.08364	51.12449	51.16536	51.20626
41	52.51346	52.55659	52.59975	52.64294	52.68615	52.72939	52.77265	52.81594
42	54.12465	54.17024	54.21586	54.26152	54.30720	54.35291	54.39865	54.44442
43	55.75424	55.80238	55.85056	55.89876	55.94700	55.99527	56.04358	56.09191
44	57.40244	57.45322	57.50404	57.55489	57.60578	57.65670	57.70765	57.75865
45	59.06946	59.12297	59.17652	59.23011	59.28374	59.33740	59.39110	59.44484
46	60.75553	60.81186	60.86824	60.92465	60.98111	61.03761	61.09415	61.15073
47	62.46085	62.52010	62.57939	62.63873	62.69812	62.75755	62.81702	62.87655
48	64.18565	64.24791	64.31022	64.37258	64.43499	64.49745	64.55996	64.62251
60	86.48600	86.59260	86.69931	86.80614	86.91309	87.02016	87.12734	87.23465
72	112.04221	112.21078	112.37959	112.54865	112.71795	112.88749	113.05727	113.22730
84	141.32962	141.58202	141.83488	142.08818	142.34192	142.59612	142.85076	143.10586
96	174.89299	175.25616	175.62009	175.98479	176.35025	176.71648	177.08348	177.45125
108	213.35661	213.86355	214.37173	214.88115	215.39181	215.90372	216.41688	216.93129
120	257.43592	258.12693	258.81986	259.51472	260.21152	260.91026	261.61095	262.31359
132	307.95082	308.87489	309.80186	310.73174	311.66454	312.60027	313.53893	314.48054
144	365.84088	367.05743	368.27822	369.50328	370.73262	371.96625	373.20419	374.44645
156	432.18290	433.76371	435.35060	436.94362	438.54277	440.14808	441.75957	443.37727
168	508.21085	510.24246	512.28263	514.33140	516.38882	518.45490	520.52970	522.61324
180	595.33888	597.92534	600.52366	603.13389	605.75608	608.39030	611.03658	613.69500
192	695.18761	698.45377	701.73612	705.03474	708.34970	711.68109	715.02899	718.39347
204	809.61425	813.70962	817.82682	821.96597	826.12718	830.31057	834.51626	838.74437
216	940.74718	945.85044	950.98285	956.14455	961.33573	966.55653	971.80714	977.08772
228	1091.02551	1097.34990	1103.71281	1110.11448	1116.55513	1123.03502	1129.55436	1136.11341
240	1263.24448	1271.04403	1278.89408	1286.79497	1294.74702	1302.75055	1310.80592	1318.91343
252	1460.60743	1470.18434	1479.82699	1489.53583	1499.31129	1509.15385	1519.06395	1529.04206
264	1686.78536	1698.49872	1710.29705	1722.18097	1734.15109	1746.20804	1758.35244	1770.58492
276	1945.98527	1960.26115	1974.64620	1989.14126	2003.74717	2018.46477	2033.29491	2048.23844
288	2243.02837	2260.37177	2277.85468	2295.47820	2313.24347	2331.15162	2349.20380	2367.40116
300	2583.43976	2604.44860	2625.63480	2646.99984	2668.54523	2690.27248	2712.18313	2734.27871
312	2973.55121	2998.93269	3024.53860	3050.37092	3076.43164	3102.72278	3129.24637	3156.00445
324	3420.61893	3451.20869	3482.08126	3513.23923	3544.68525	3576.42195	3608.45203	3640.77818
336	3932.95854	3969.74313	4006.88269	4044.38062	4082.24038	4120.46545	4159.05934	4198.02559
348	4520.09974	4564.24287	4608.82993	4653.86537	4699.35368	4745.29941	4791.70713	4838.58149
360	5192.96355	5245.83682	5299.26341	5353.24911	5407.79975	5462.92121	5518.61945	5574.90049
420	10350.99932	10478.25603	10607.10766	10737.57414	10869.67564	11003.43257	11138.86561	11275.99568
480	20546.47369	20843.34004	21144.55118	21450.17045	21760.26211	22074.89134	22394.12427	22718.02799

MONTHLY DEPOSITS

NUMBER OF MONTHLY DEPOSITS	EFFECTIVE ANNUAL YIELD							
	15.00%	15.05%	15.10%	15.15%	15.20%	15.25%	15.30%	15.35%
1	1.01171	1.01175	1.01179	1.01182	1.01186	1.01190	1.01193	1.01197
2	2.03528	2.03539	2.03550	2.03561	2.03572	2.03584	2.03595	2.03606
3	3.07084	3.07106	3.07129	3.07151	3.07173	3.07196	3.07218	3.07240
4	4.11853	4.11890	4.11928	4.11965	4.12003	4.12040	4.12078	4.12115
5	5.17849	5.17906	5.17963	5.18019	5.18076	5.18133	5.18189	5.18246
6	6.25087	6.25167	6.25247	6.25327	6.25407	6.25487	6.25567	6.25647
7	7.33582	7.33689	7.33797	7.33904	7.34012	7.34119	7.34227	7.34334
8	8.43347	8.43486	8.43626	8.43765	8.43904	8.44043	8.44183	8.44322
9	9.54398	9.54574	9.54749	9.54925	9.55100	9.55276	9.55451	9.55626
10	10.66750	10.66967	10.67183	10.67399	10.67615	10.67831	10.68047	10.68264
11	11.80419	11.80680	11.80942	11.81203	11.81465	11.81726	11.81988	11.82249
12	12.95419	12.95730	12.96042	12.96353	12.96665	12.96976	12.97288	12.97599
13	14.11766	14.12132	14.12499	14.12865	14.13231	14.13598	14.13964	14.14330
14	15.29476	15.29902	15.30328	15.30754	15.31180	15.31606	15.32032	15.32458
15	16.48565	16.49056	16.49547	16.50038	16.50529	16.51019	16.51510	16.52001
16	17.69050	17.69610	17.70171	17.70731	17.71292	17.71853	17.72413	17.72974
17	18.90945	18.91581	18.92217	18.92853	18.93488	18.94124	18.94760	18.95396
18	20.14269	20.14985	20.15702	20.16418	20.17134	20.17850	20.18567	20.19283
19	21.39038	21.39840	21.40642	21.41444	21.42246	21.43049	21.43851	21.44653
20	22.65268	22.66161	22.67055	22.67949	22.68843	22.69736	22.70630	22.71524
21	23.92977	23.93968	23.94958	23.95949	23.96940	23.97932	23.98923	23.99914
22	25.22182	25.23276	25.24369	25.25463	25.26558	25.27652	25.28746	25.29841
23	26.52900	26.54103	26.55306	26.56509	26.57712	26.58916	26.60119	26.61323
24	27.85150	27.86468	27.87786	27.89104	27.90423	27.91741	27.93060	27.94379
25	29.18950	29.20389	29.21828	29.23267	29.24707	29.26147	29.27588	29.29028
26	30.54316	30.55883	30.57450	30.59017	30.60585	30.62153	30.63721	30.65289
27	31.91269	31.92970	31.94671	31.96372	31.98074	31.99776	32.01479	32.03182
28	33.29826	33.31667	33.33509	33.35351	33.37194	33.39037	33.40880	33.42724
29	34.70006	34.71995	34.73984	34.75973	34.77964	34.79954	34.81946	34.83938
30	36.11828	36.13971	36.16114	36.18259	36.20403	36.22549	36.24695	36.26842
31	37.55312	37.57616	37.59921	37.62226	37.64533	37.66840	37.69148	37.71456
32	39.00477	39.02949	39.05422	39.07896	39.10371	39.12847	39.15324	39.17802
33	40.47342	40.49990	40.52639	40.55289	40.57940	40.60592	40.63246	40.65900
34	41.95928	41.98759	42.01591	42.04425	42.07259	42.10095	42.12932	42.15770
35	43.46254	43.49276	43.52299	43.55324	43.58350	43.61377	43.64405	43.67435
36	44.98342	45.01562	45.04784	45.08007	45.11232	45.14458	45.17686	45.20916
37	46.52211	46.55638	46.59066	46.62496	46.65928	46.69361	46.72796	46.76233
38	48.07883	48.11524	48.15167	48.18812	48.22458	48.26107	48.29758	48.33410
39	49.65378	49.69242	49.73108	49.76976	49.80846	49.84718	49.88592	49.92469
40	51.24719	51.28813	51.32911	51.37010	51.41112	51.45216	51.49323	51.53432
41	52.85926	52.90260	52.94597	52.98937	53.03279	53.07624	53.11971	53.16321
42	54.49022	54.53604	54.58190	54.62778	54.67369	54.71964	54.76561	54.81161
43	56.14028	56.18868	56.23711	56.28557	56.33406	56.38259	56.43115	56.47974
44	57.80967	57.86073	57.91183	57.96296	58.01413	58.06533	58.11657	58.16784
45	59.49862	59.55244	59.60629	59.66019	59.71412	59.76809	59.82210	59.87614
46	61.20736	61.26403	61.32073	61.37748	61.43428	61.49111	61.54798	61.60490
47	62.93611	62.99573	63.05538	63.11509	63.17484	63.23463	63.29447	63.35436
48	64.68512	64.74778	64.81048	64.87324	64.93604	64.99889	65.06180	65.12475
60	87.34208	87.44962	87.55728	87.66506	87.77297	87.88099	87.98913	88.09739
72	113.39757	113.56809	113.73885	113.90986	114.08111	114.25260	114.42434	114.59633
84	143.36140	143.61739	143.87384	144.13073	144.38808	144.64589	144.90414	145.16286
96	177.81980	178.18911	178.55921	178.93007	179.30172	179.67415	180.04735	180.42134
108	217.44695	217.96388	218.48206	219.00151	219.52223	220.04422	220.56748	221.09201
120	263.01819	263.72475	264.43328	265.14378	265.85626	266.57072	267.28718	268.00562
132	315.42510	316.37842	317.32312	318.27659	319.23306	320.19252	321.15499	322.12048
144	375.69305	376.94401	378.19933	379.45903	380.72313	381.99164	383.26458	384.54196
156	445.00120	446.63139	448.26785	449.91061	451.55970	453.21513	454.87694	456.54514
168	524.70557	526.80671	528.91671	531.03560	533.16342	535.30020	537.44598	539.60081
180	616.36559	619.04843	621.74355	624.45103	627.17091	629.90324	632.64810	635.40552
192	721.77462	725.17252	728.58725	732.01889	735.46753	738.93325	742.41613	745.91626
204	842.99500	847.26829	851.56434	855.88329	860.22525	864.59033	868.97868	873.39039
216	982.39844	987.73947	993.11098	998.51314	1003.94613	1009.41012	1014.90529	1020.43181
228	1142.71239	1149.35156	1156.03116	1162.75142	1169.51259	1176.31493	1183.15868	1190.04408
240	1327.07344	1335.28628	1343.55228	1351.87179	1360.24516	1368.67272	1377.15483	1385.69184
252	1539.08864	1549.20416	1559.38909	1569.64390	1579.96907	1590.36507	1600.83240	1611.37153
264	1782.90613	1795.31669	1807.81726	1820.40849	1833.09102	1845.86551	1858.73263	1871.69304
276	2063.29624	2078.46916	2093.75809	2109.16391	2124.68750	2140.32976	2156.09160	2171.97392
288	2385.74486	2404.23607	2422.87598	2441.66577	2460.60665	2479.69981	2498.94649	2518.34790
300	2756.56078	2779.03091	2801.69067	2824.54167	2847.58551	2870.82380	2894.25818	2917.89030
312	3182.39069	3210.23236	3237.70638	3265.42327	3293.38515	3321.59419	3350.05256	3378.76245
324	3673.40313	3706.32964	3739.56047	3773.09843	3806.94634	3841.10706	3875.58347	3910.37847
336	4237.36779	4277.08955	4317.19452	4357.68637	4398.56883	4439.84566	4481.52062	4523.59756
348	4885.92715	4933.74883	4982.05131	5030.83939	5080.11795	5129.89188	5180.16615	5230.94577
360	5631.77041	5689.23533	5747.30147	5805.97509	5865.26252	5925.17015	5985.70445	6046.87194
420	11414.84396	11555.43191	11697.78123	11841.91389	11987.85214	12135.61850	12285.23577	12436.72702
480	23046.67053	23380.12091	23718.44916	24061.72630	24410.02437	24763.41645	25121.97669	25485.78028

EFFECTIVE ANNUAL YIELD

NUMBER OF MONTHLY DEPOSITS	15.40%	15.45%	15.50%	15.55%	15.60%	15.65%	15.70%	15.75%
1	1.01201	1.01204	1.01208	1.01212	1.01215	1.01219	1.01223	1.01226
2	2.03617	2.03628	2.03639	2.03650	2.03661	2.03672	2.03683	2.03694
3	3.07262	3.07285	3.07307	3.07329	3.07352	3.07374	3.07396	3.07418
4	4.12153	4.12190	4.12228	4.12265	4.12302	4.12340	4.12377	4.12414
5	5.18303	5.18359	5.18416	5.18472	5.18529	5.18585	5.18642	5.18698
6	6.25727	6.25807	6.25887	6.25966	6.26046	6.26126	6.26206	6.26285
7	7.34441	7.34549	7.34656	7.34763	7.34870	7.34978	7.35085	7.35192
8	8.44461	8.44600	8.44739	8.44878	8.45017	8.45156	8.45295	8.45434
9	9.55802	9.55977	9.56152	9.56327	9.56503	9.56678	9.56853	9.57028
10	10.68480	10.68695	10.68911	10.69127	10.69343	10.69559	10.69775	10.69990
11	11.82510	11.82772	11.83033	11.83294	11.83555	11.83816	11.84077	11.84338
12	12.97910	12.98222	12.98533	12.98844	12.99155	12.99466	12.99777	13.00088
13	14.14696	14.15062	14.15428	14.15794	14.16160	14.16526	14.16892	14.17258
14	15.32884	15.33310	15.33736	15.34161	15.34587	15.35013	15.35438	15.35864
15	16.52491	16.52982	16.53472	16.53963	16.54453	16.54944	16.55434	16.55925
16	17.73535	17.74095	17.74656	17.75216	17.75777	17.76337	17.76897	17.77458
17	18.96031	18.96667	18.97303	18.97939	18.98574	18.99210	18.99846	19.00481
18	20.19999	20.20715	20.21432	20.22148	20.22864	20.23581	20.24297	20.25014
19	21.45455	21.46258	21.47060	21.47863	21.48665	21.49468	21.50270	21.51073
20	22.72418	22.73312	22.74206	22.75101	22.75995	22.76889	22.77784	22.78678
21	24.00905	24.01897	24.02889	24.03880	24.04872	24.05864	24.06856	24.07848
22	25.30936	25.32030	25.33125	25.34220	25.35316	25.36411	25.37507	25.38602
23	26.62527	26.63731	26.64936	26.66140	26.67345	26.68549	26.69754	26.70960
24	27.95699	27.97018	27.98338	27.99658	28.00978	28.02299	28.03619	28.04940
25	29.30469	29.31911	29.33352	29.34794	29.36236	29.37678	29.39121	29.40564
26	30.66858	30.68428	30.69997	30.71567	30.73138	30.74708	30.76279	30.77851
27	32.04865	32.06589	32.08293	32.09998	32.11703	32.13409	32.15115	32.16821
28	33.44569	33.46414	33.48260	33.50106	33.51953	33.53800	33.55648	33.57496
29	34.85930	34.87924	34.89917	34.91912	34.93907	34.95902	34.97899	34.99895
30	36.28989	36.31137	36.33286	36.35436	36.37586	36.39737	36.41889	36.44041
31	37.73766	37.76076	37.78387	37.80699	37.83012	37.85326	37.87640	37.89955
32	39.20281	39.22761	39.25241	39.27723	39.30205	39.32688	39.35173	39.37658
33	40.68555	40.71212	40.73869	40.76528	40.79187	40.81848	40.84510	40.87172
34	42.18610	42.21451	42.24293	42.27136	42.29980	42.32825	42.35672	42.38520
35	43.70467	43.73499	43.76533	43.79569	43.82605	43.85644	43.88683	43.91724
36	45.24147	45.27379	45.30613	45.33849	45.37086	45.40325	45.43565	45.46807
37	46.79672	46.83112	46.86554	46.89998	46.93444	46.96891	47.00340	47.03791
38	48.37065	48.40721	48.44380	48.48040	48.51702	48.55366	48.59032	48.62700
39	49.96348	50.00228	50.04111	50.07997	50.11884	50.15773	50.19665	50.23559
40	51.57543	51.61657	51.65773	51.69891	51.74012	51.78136	51.82261	51.86389
41	53.20674	53.25029	53.29387	53.33748	53.38111	53.42477	53.46846	53.51217
42	54.85764	54.90370	54.94979	54.99590	55.04205	55.08822	55.13443	55.18066
43	56.52836	56.57701	56.62570	56.67442	56.72317	56.77195	56.82076	56.86961
44	58.21914	58.27049	58.32186	58.37327	58.42472	58.47620	58.52772	58.57927
45	59.93023	59.98435	60.03852	60.09272	60.14695	60.20123	60.25555	60.30990
46	61.66186	61.71886	61.77591	61.83299	61.89012	61.94729	62.00450	62.06175
47	63.41429	63.47426	63.53429	63.59435	63.65447	63.71463	63.77484	63.83509
48	65.18775	65.25081	65.31391	65.37706	65.44026	65.50351	65.56682	65.63017
60	88.20577	88.31427	88.42289	88.53163	88.64049	88.74948	88.85858	88.96780
72	114.76856	114.94104	115.11377	115.28674	115.45996	115.63343	115.80715	115.98111
84	145.42202	145.68165	145.94173	146.20227	146.46327	146.72472	146.98664	147.24902
96	180.79612	181.17168	181.54802	181.92516	182.30309	182.68180	183.06131	183.44162
108	221.61782	222.14492	222.67330	223.20296	223.73392	224.26617	224.79971	225.33456
120	268.72607	269.44852	270.17298	270.89946	271.62796	272.35848	273.09104	273.82563
132	323.08899	324.06053	325.03512	326.01277	326.99347	327.97725	328.96410	329.95405
144	385.82379	387.11010	388.40090	389.69619	390.99600	392.30035	393.60924	394.92270
156	458.21976	459.90083	461.58836	463.28239	464.98293	466.69001	468.40366	470.12390
168	541.76471	543.93772	546.11988	548.31124	550.51182	552.72166	554.94081	557.16930
180	638.17557	640.95831	643.75379	646.56207	649.38321	652.21726	655.06429	657.92434
192	749.43372	752.96859	756.52096	760.09092	763.67854	767.28393	770.90715	774.54831
204	877.82561	882.28445	886.76703	891.27349	895.80395	900.35852	904.93735	909.54055
216	1025.93986	1031.57961	1037.20125	1042.85496	1048.54091	1054.25929	1060.01028	1065.79407
228	1196.97140	1203.94088	1210.95277	1218.00734	1225.10484	1232.24553	1239.42967	1246.65752
240	1394.28410	1402.93196	1411.63578	1420.39592	1429.21275	1438.08662	1447.01790	1456.00696
252	1621.98295	1632.66716	1643.42465	1654.25593	1665.16149	1676.14184	1687.19748	1698.32894
264	1884.74743	1897.89645	1911.14080	1924.48117	1937.91823	1951.45269	1965.08526	1978.81663
276	2187.97763	2204.10367	2220.35296	2236.72643	2253.22502	2269.84970	2286.60141	2303.48113
288	2537.90529	2557.61990	2577.49299	2597.52582	2617.71968	2638.07584	2658.59561	2679.28028
300	2941.72181	2965.75439	2989.98973	3014.42953	3039.07550	3063.92937	3088.99289	3114.26781
312	3407.72607	3436.94566	3466.42347	3496.16176	3526.16283	3556.42898	3586.96255	3617.76587
324	3945.49499	3980.93598	4016.70443	4052.80335	4089.23578	4126.00478	4163.11344	4200.56488
336	4566.08032	4608.97280	4652.27895	4696.00271	4740.14811	4784.71919	4829.72002	4875.15473
348	5282.23579	5334.04132	5386.36751	5439.21957	5492.60277	5546.52240	5600.98383	5655.99248
360	6108.67920	6171.13292	6234.23980	6298.00666	6362.44035	6427.54782	6493.33607	6559.81218
420	12590.11562	12745.42521	12902.67974	13061.90343	13223.12081	13386.35672	13551.63630	13718.98498
480	25854.90349	26229.42371	26609.41942	26994.97025	27386.15693	27783.06141	28185.76676	28594.35727

MONTHLY DEPOSITS

EFFECTIVE ANNUAL YIELD

NUMBER OF MONTHLY DEPOSITS	15.80%	15.85%	15.90%	15.95%	16.00%	16.05%	16.10%	16.15%
1	1.01230	1.01234	1.01237	1.01241	1.01245	1.01248	1.01252	1.01255
2	2.03705	2.03716	2.03727	2.03738	2.03749	2.03760	2.03771	2.03782
3	3.07440	3.07463	3.07485	3.07507	3.07529	3.07551	3.07574	3.07596
4	4.12452	4.12489	4.12526	4.12564	4.12601	4.12638	4.12676	4.12713
5	5.18755	5.18811	5.18868	5.18924	5.18980	5.19037	5.19093	5.19149
6	6.26365	6.26445	6.26524	6.26604	6.26684	6.26763	6.26843	6.26922
7	7.35299	7.35406	7.35513	7.35620	7.35727	7.35834	7.35941	7.36048
8	8.45573	8.45712	8.45851	8.45989	8.46128	8.46267	8.46406	8.46544
9	9.57203	9.57378	9.57553	9.57728	9.57903	9.58078	9.58252	9.58427
10	10.70206	10.70422	10.70637	10.70853	10.71069	10.71284	10.71500	10.71715
11	11.84599	11.84860	11.85121	11.85382	11.85643	11.85903	11.86164	11.86425
12	13.00399	13.00710	13.01021	13.01332	13.01643	13.01953	13.02264	13.02575
13	14.17623	14.17989	14.18355	14.18721	14.19086	14.19452	14.19817	14.20183
14	15.36290	15.36715	15.37141	15.37566	15.37992	15.38417	15.38842	15.39268
15	16.56415	16.56906	16.57396	16.57886	16.58377	16.58867	16.59357	16.59847
16	17.78018	17.78579	17.79139	17.79699	17.80260	17.80820	17.81380	17.81941
17	19.01117	19.01753	19.02388	19.03024	19.03660	19.04296	19.04931	19.05567
18	20.25730	20.26446	20.27163	20.27879	20.28596	20.29312	20.30029	20.30745
19	21.51875	21.52678	21.53481	21.54284	21.55086	21.55889	21.56692	21.57495
20	22.79573	22.80467	22.81362	22.82256	22.83151	22.84046	22.84941	22.85836
21	24.08840	24.09833	24.10825	24.11817	24.12810	24.13803	24.14795	24.15788
22	25.39698	25.40794	25.41890	25.42986	25.44082	25.45179	25.46275	25.47372
23	26.72165	26.73370	26.74576	26.75782	26.76988	26.78194	26.79401	26.80607
24	28.06261	28.07583	28.08904	28.10226	28.11548	28.12870	28.14193	28.15516
25	29.42007	29.43451	29.44894	29.46338	29.47783	29.49227	29.50672	29.52117
26	30.79422	30.80995	30.82567	30.84140	30.85713	30.87286	30.88860	30.90434
27	32.18528	32.20235	32.21943	32.23651	32.25359	32.27068	32.28778	32.30487
28	33.59344	33.61194	33.63043	33.64893	33.66744	33.68595	33.70447	33.72299
29	35.01893	35.03891	35.05889	35.07888	35.09888	35.11888	35.13889	35.15891
30	36.46194	36.48348	36.50503	36.52658	36.54814	36.56970	36.59127	36.61285
31	37.92271	37.94588	37.96905	37.99224	38.01543	38.03863	38.06184	38.08505
32	39.40144	39.42631	39.45119	39.47608	39.50098	39.52589	39.55081	39.57573
33	40.89836	40.92501	40.95167	40.97834	41.00502	41.03171	41.05841	41.08513
34	42.41369	42.44220	42.47071	42.49924	42.52778	42.55633	42.58490	42.61347
35	43.94766	43.97810	44.00855	44.03901	44.06949	44.09998	44.13048	44.16100
36	45.50050	45.53295	45.56541	45.59789	45.63038	45.66289	45.69542	45.72796
37	47.07243	47.10698	47.14154	47.17611	47.21071	47.24532	47.27995	47.31459
38	48.66370	48.70042	48.73716	48.77392	48.81069	48.84749	48.88431	48.92114
39	50.27454	50.31353	50.35253	50.39155	50.43060	50.46966	50.50875	50.54786
40	51.90520	51.94653	51.98788	52.02926	52.07066	52.11208	52.15353	52.19500
41	53.55591	53.59967	53.64347	53.68728	53.73113	53.77500	53.81890	53.86282
42	55.22692	55.27321	55.31954	55.36589	55.41226	55.45867	55.50511	55.55158
43	56.91849	56.96740	57.01634	57.06532	57.11432	57.16336	57.21243	57.26154
44	58.63086	58.68248	58.73414	58.78584	58.83756	58.88933	58.94113	58.99296
45	60.36429	60.41873	60.47320	60.52770	60.58225	60.63684	60.69146	60.74612
46	62.11905	62.17639	62.23376	62.29119	62.34865	62.40616	62.46370	62.52130
47	63.89538	63.95573	64.01612	64.07655	64.13703	64.19756	64.25813	64.31875
48	65.69357	65.75702	65.82052	65.88407	65.94767	66.01132	66.07502	66.13878
60	89.07714	89.18661	89.29619	89.40590	89.51573	89.62567	89.73574	89.84594
72	116.15532	116.32979	116.50450	116.67946	116.85467	117.03013	117.20584	117.38180
84	147.51186	147.77516	148.03892	148.30315	148.56784	148.83300	149.09862	149.36471
96	183.82272	184.20462	184.58732	184.97082	185.35512	185.74023	186.12614	186.51286
108	225.87070	226.40816	226.94691	227.48699	228.02837	228.57107	229.11509	229.66044
120	274.56227	275.30095	276.04168	276.78448	277.52934	278.27626	279.02526	279.77635
132	330.94710	331.94325	332.94252	333.94492	334.95046	335.95914	336.97097	337.98597
144	396.24073	397.56336	398.89059	400.22245	401.55896	402.90011	404.24594	405.59646
156	471.85076	473.58425	475.32441	477.07125	478.82481	480.58511	482.35218	484.12603
168	559.40717	561.65445	563.91120	566.17744	568.45321	570.73856	573.03352	575.33814
180	660.79749	663.68378	666.58329	669.49606	672.42215	675.36163	678.31456	681.28100
192	778.20749	781.88477	785.58024	789.29400	793.02612	796.77671	800.54585	804.33362
204	914.16826	918.82060	923.49771	928.19971	932.92673	937.67891	942.45637	947.25925
216	1071.61084	1077.46077	1083.34405	1089.26088	1095.21143	1101.19590	1107.21449	1113.26737
228	1253.92934	1261.24540	1268.60597	1276.01131	1283.46169	1290.95738	1298.49866	1306.08580
240	1465.05417	1474.15990	1483.32452	1492.54843	1501.83198	1511.17557	1520.57959	1530.04441
252	1709.53672	1720.82134	1732.18333	1743.62322	1755.14153	1766.73879	1778.41554	1790.17230
264	1992.64751	2006.57863	2020.61069	2034.74444	2048.98060	2063.31990	2077.76308	2092.31090
276	2320.48981	2337.62844	2354.89800	2372.29950	2389.83392	2407.50227	2425.30558	2443.24486
288	2700.13119	2721.14965	2742.33700	2763.69459	2785.22377	2806.92592	2828.80242	2850.85466
300	3139.75591	3165.45897	3191.37879	3217.51719	3243.87600	3270.45707	3297.26225	3324.29343
312	3648.46533	3680.19131	3711.81823	3743.72450	3775.91259	3808.38496	3841.14412	3874.19257
324	4238.36226	4276.50874	4315.00753	4353.86188	4393.07503	4432.65028	4472.59096	4512.90042
336	4921.02748	4967.34247	5014.10394	5061.31616	5108.98346	5157.11019	5205.70075	5254.75958
348	5711.55382	5767.67336	5824.35668	5881.60941	5939.43724	5997.84591	6056.84121	6116.42901
360	6626.98331	6694.85668	6763.43960	6832.73943	6902.76362	6973.51971	7045.01529	7117.25804
420	13888.42854	14059.99303	14233.70486	14409.59074	14587.67772	14767.99317	14950.56480	15135.42067
480	29008.91845	29429.53700	29856.30091	30289.29938	30728.62293	31174.36335	31626.61377	32085.46864

EFFECTIVE ANNUAL YIELD

NUMBER OF MONTHLY DEPOSITS	16.20%	16.25%	16.30%	16.35%	16.40%	16.45%	16.50%	16.55%
1	1.01259	1.01263	1.01266	1.01270	1.01274	1.01277	1.01281	1.01284
2	2.03793	2.03804	2.03815	2.03826	2.03837	2.03848	2.03859	2.03870
3	3.07618	3.07640	3.07662	3.07684	3.07706	3.07729	3.07751	3.07773
4	4.12750	4.12787	4.12824	4.12862	4.12899	4.12936	4.12973	4.13010
5	5.19206	5.19262	5.19318	5.19375	5.19431	5.19487	5.19543	5.19600
6	6.27002	6.27081	6.27161	6.27240	6.27320	6.27399	6.27479	6.27558
7	7.36155	7.36262	7.36369	7.36476	7.36583	7.36689	7.36796	7.36903
8	8.46683	8.46821	8.46960	8.47099	8.47237	8.47375	8.47514	8.47652
9	9.58602	9.58777	9.58951	9.59126	9.59301	9.59475	9.59650	9.59824
10	10.71930	10.72146	10.72361	10.72576	10.72791	10.73007	10.73222	10.73437
11	11.86685	11.86946	11.87207	11.87467	11.87728	11.87988	11.88249	11.88509
12	13.02885	13.03196	13.03507	13.03817	13.04128	13.04438	13.04749	13.05059
13	14.20549	14.20914	14.21279	14.21645	14.22010	14.22375	14.22741	14.23106
14	15.39693	15.40118	15.40543	15.40969	15.41394	15.41819	15.42244	15.42669
15	16.60337	16.60828	16.61318	16.61808	16.62298	16.62788	16.63278	16.63768
16	17.82501	17.83061	17.83622	17.84182	17.84742	17.85302	17.85862	17.86423
17	19.06203	19.06838	19.07474	19.08110	19.08745	19.09381	19.10017	19.10652
18	20.31462	20.32178	20.32895	20.33611	20.34328	20.35044	20.35761	20.36478
19	21.58298	21.59101	21.59904	21.60707	21.61510	21.62313	21.63116	21.63919
20	22.86731	22.87626	22.88521	22.89416	22.90312	22.91207	22.92102	22.92998
21	24.16781	24.17774	24.18767	24.19760	24.20754	24.21747	24.22741	24.23734
22	25.48469	25.49565	25.50663	25.51760	25.52857	25.53954	25.55052	25.56150
23	26.81814	26.83021	26.84228	26.85435	26.86643	26.87850	26.89058	26.90266
24	28.16838	28.18162	28.19485	28.20809	28.22132	28.23456	28.24781	28.26105
25	29.53563	29.55009	29.56455	29.57901	29.59348	29.60794	29.62242	29.63689
26	30.92009	30.93584	30.95159	30.96734	30.98310	30.99886	31.01463	31.03040
27	32.32198	32.33908	32.35619	32.37331	32.39043	32.40755	32.42468	32.44181
28	33.74152	33.76005	33.77859	33.79713	33.81567	33.83423	33.85278	33.87134
29	35.17893	35.19896	35.21899	35.23903	35.25907	35.27912	35.29918	35.31924
30	36.63444	36.65603	36.67763	36.69924	36.72085	36.74247	36.76410	36.78574
31	38.10828	38.13151	38.15475	38.17800	38.20125	38.22452	38.24779	38.27107
32	39.60067	39.62561	39.65057	39.67553	39.70050	39.72549	39.75048	39.77548
33	41.11185	41.13858	41.16533	41.19208	41.21885	41.24563	41.27241	41.29921
34	42.64206	42.67066	42.69927	42.72790	42.75653	42.78518	42.81384	42.84251
35	44.19153	44.22208	44.25264	44.28321	44.31380	44.34440	44.37501	44.40564
36	45.76052	45.79309	45.82568	45.85828	45.89090	45.92353	45.95618	45.98885
37	47.34926	47.38394	47.41863	47.45335	47.48808	47.52283	47.55760	47.59238
38	48.95800	48.99487	49.03176	49.06868	49.10561	49.14256	49.17953	49.21652
39	50.58699	50.62614	50.66532	50.70452	50.74373	50.78297	50.82223	50.86152
40	52.23650	52.27802	52.31956	52.36113	52.40272	52.44434	52.48598	52.52764
41	53.90677	53.95075	53.99475	54.03878	54.08284	54.12692	54.17103	54.21517
42	55.59807	55.64460	55.69115	55.73774	55.78435	55.83099	55.87767	55.92437
43	57.31067	57.35984	57.40904	57.45827	57.50753	57.55683	57.60616	57.65552
44	59.04483	59.09674	59.14868	59.20065	59.25266	59.30471	59.35679	59.40891
45	60.80083	60.85557	60.91034	60.96516	61.02002	61.07491	61.12985	61.18482
46	62.57893	62.63660	62.69432	62.75208	62.80988	62.86773	62.92561	62.98354
47	64.37942	64.44013	64.50089	64.56169	64.62254	64.68343	64.74438	64.80536
48	66.20258	66.26643	66.33033	66.39428	66.45828	66.52233	66.58644	66.65059
60	89.95625	90.06668	90.17724	90.28792	90.39872	90.50964	90.62068	90.73185
72	117.55802	117.73448	117.91120	118.08816	118.26538	118.44286	118.62058	118.79856
84	149.63127	149.89829	150.16579	150.43375	150.70218	150.97109	151.24046	151.51031
96	186.90039	187.28873	187.67788	188.06784	188.45862	188.85021	189.24263	189.63586
108	230.20711	230.75511	231.30444	231.85511	232.40711	232.96046	233.51515	234.07118
120	280.52951	281.28477	282.04213	282.80159	283.56315	284.32683	285.09263	285.86055
132	339.00415	340.02551	341.05006	342.07782	343.10879	344.14298	345.18040	346.22107
144	406.95168	408.31162	409.67629	411.04572	412.41991	413.79888	415.18265	416.57124
156	485.90670	487.69422	489.48859	491.28986	493.09805	494.91318	496.73528	498.56437
168	577.65245	579.97649	582.31030	584.65393	587.00741	589.37078	591.74408	594.12736
180	684.26100	687.25463	690.26195	693.28302	696.31790	699.36665	702.42934	705.50603
192	808.14013	811.96546	815.80971	819.67296	823.55531	827.45685	831.37767	835.31787
204	952.08769	956.94181	961.82176	966.72766	971.65966	976.61788	981.60247	986.61357
216	1119.35475	1125.47682	1131.63377	1137.82581	1144.05312	1150.31590	1156.61437	1162.94870
228	1313.71908	1321.39876	1329.12514	1336.89850	1344.71911	1352.58725	1360.50322	1368.46730
240	1539.57042	1549.15802	1558.80761	1568.51957	1578.29432	1588.13224	1598.03374	1607.99923
252	1802.00968	1813.92816	1825.92832	1838.01070	1850.17586	1862.42437	1874.75679	1887.17350
264	2106.96411	2121.72345	2136.58970	2151.56362	2166.64598	2181.83756	2197.13915	2212.55153
276	2461.32115	2479.53547	2497.88889	2516.38244	2535.01720	2553.79422	2572.71459	2591.77940
288	2873.08403	2895.49195	2918.07984	2940.84914	2963.80129	2986.93775	3010.25999	3033.76948
300	3351.55250	3379.04135	3406.76192	3434.71615	3462.90598	3491.33040	3520.00037	3548.90892
312	3907.53286	3941.16753	3975.09918	4009.33041	4043.86384	4078.70212	4113.84792	4149.30393
324	4553.58203	4594.63922	4636.07542	4677.89411	4720.09879	4762.69300	4805.68031	4849.06432
336	5304.29118	5354.30005	5404.79078	5455.76797	5507.23627	5559.20038	5611.66505	5664.63506
348	6176.61520	6237.40577	6298.80674	6360.82420	6423.46429	6486.73323	6550.63727	6615.18275
360	7190.25572	7264.01617	7338.54731	7413.85713	7489.95371	7566.84522	7644.53990	7723.04608
420	15322.58917	15512.09905	15703.97939	15898.25965	16094.96964	16294.13954	16495.79989	16699.98160
480	32551.02375	33023.37629	33502.62481	33988.86929	34482.21114	34982.75321	35490.59984	36005.85682

MONTHLY DEPOSITS

NUMBER OF MONTHLY DEPOSITS	EFFECTIVE ANNUAL YIELD							
	16.60%	16.65%	16.70%	16.75%	16.80%	16.85%	16.90%	16.95%
1	1.01288	1.01292	1.01295	1.01299	1.01303	1.01306	1.01310	1.01313
2	2.03881	2.03892	2.03903	2.03914	2.03925	2.03935	2.03946	2.03957
3	3.07795	3.07817	3.07839	3.07861	3.07883	3.07905	3.07927	3.07949
4	4.13047	4.13085	4.13122	4.13159	4.13196	4.13233	4.13270	4.13307
5	5.19656	5.19712	5.19768	5.19824	5.19880	5.19937	5.19993	5.20049
6	6.27637	6.27717	6.27796	6.27875	6.27954	6.28034	6.28113	6.28192
7	7.37010	7.37116	7.37223	7.37330	7.37436	7.37543	7.37649	7.37756
8	8.47791	8.47929	8.48067	8.48206	8.48344	8.48482	8.48620	8.48759
9	9.59999	9.60173	9.60348	9.60522	9.60696	9.60871	9.61045	9.61219
10	10.73652	10.73867	10.74082	10.74297	10.74512	10.74727	10.74942	10.75157
11	11.88769	11.89030	11.89290	11.89550	11.89810	11.90070	11.90330	11.90591
12	13.05369	13.05680	13.05990	13.06300	13.06610	13.06920	13.07230	13.07541
13	14.23471	14.23836	14.24201	14.24567	14.24932	14.25297	14.25662	14.26027
14	15.43094	15.43519	15.43944	15.44369	15.44794	15.45219	15.45644	15.46069
15	16.64258	16.64748	16.65238	16.65728	16.66218	16.66708	16.67197	16.67687
16	17.86983	17.87543	17.88103	17.88663	17.89223	17.89783	17.90343	17.90903
17	19.11288	19.11924	19.12559	19.13195	19.13831	19.14466	19.15102	19.15737
18	20.37194	20.37911	20.38628	20.39344	20.40061	20.40778	20.41494	20.42211
19	21.64722	21.65526	21.66329	21.67132	21.67936	21.68739	21.69543	21.70346
20	22.93893	22.94789	22.95684	22.96580	22.97476	22.98372	22.99268	23.00164
21	24.24728	24.25722	24.26715	24.27709	24.28703	24.29696	24.30692	24.31686
22	25.57248	25.58346	25.59444	25.60542	25.61640	25.62739	25.63837	25.64936
23	26.91474	26.92683	26.93891	26.95100	26.96309	26.97518	26.98727	26.99936
24	28.27430	28.28755	28.30080	28.31405	28.32731	28.34057	28.35383	28.36709
25	29.65137	29.66585	29.68033	29.69481	29.70930	29.72379	29.73829	29.75279
26	31.04617	31.06195	31.07773	31.09351	31.10930	31.12509	31.14088	31.15668
27	32.45894	32.47608	32.49323	32.51037	32.52753	32.54468	32.56184	32.57901
28	33.88991	33.90848	33.92706	33.94564	33.96423	33.98282	34.00142	34.02002
29	35.33931	35.35938	35.37947	35.39955	35.41964	35.43974	35.45985	35.47996
30	36.80738	36.82903	36.85068	36.87235	36.89402	36.91569	36.93738	36.95907
31	38.29436	38.31765	38.34096	38.36427	38.38759	38.41092	38.43426	38.45760
32	39.80049	39.82551	39.85054	39.87557	39.90062	39.92568	39.95074	39.97582
33	41.32602	41.35284	41.37967	41.40651	41.43336	41.46022	41.48709	41.51398
34	42.87120	42.89990	42.92861	42.95733	42.98606	43.01481	43.04356	43.07233
35	44.43628	44.46694	44.49761	44.52829	44.55899	44.58970	44.62042	44.65116
36	46.02153	46.05422	46.08693	46.11966	46.15240	46.18516	46.21793	46.25072
37	47.62719	47.66201	47.69684	47.73170	47.76657	47.80146	47.83636	47.87129
38	49.25353	49.29056	49.32761	49.36467	49.40176	49.43887	49.47599	49.51314
39	50.90082	50.94015	50.97949	51.01886	51.05825	51.09767	51.13710	51.17656
40	52.56933	52.61104	52.65278	52.69454	52.73632	52.77813	52.81996	52.86182
41	54.25933	54.30352	54.34773	54.39198	54.43625	54.48054	54.52486	54.56921
42	55.97110	56.01786	56.06465	56.11146	56.15831	56.20519	56.25210	56.29903
43	57.70491	57.75434	57.80380	57.85329	57.90281	57.95236	58.00195	58.05157
44	59.46106	59.51325	59.56547	59.61773	59.67003	59.72236	59.77472	59.82713
45	61.23983	61.29488	61.34997	61.40510	61.46027	61.51547	61.57072	61.62600
46	63.04151	63.09953	63.15758	63.21568	63.27382	63.33201	63.39023	63.44850
47	64.86640	64.92748	64.98861	65.04978	65.11100	65.17227	65.23358	65.29494
48	66.71479	66.77904	66.84335	66.90770	66.97211	67.03656	67.10107	67.16562
60	90.84314	90.95455	91.06609	91.17774	91.28952	91.40143	91.51345	91.62560
72	118.97679	119.15528	119.33402	119.51302	119.69227	119.87177	120.05153	120.23155
84	151.78063	152.05143	152.32270	152.59445	152.86667	153.13937	153.41254	153.68620
96	190.02991	190.42479	190.82049	191.21702	191.61437	192.01255	192.41157	192.81141
108	234.62857	235.18731	235.74741	236.30887	236.87169	237.43587	238.00143	238.56835
120	286.63061	287.40280	288.17713	288.95360	289.73223	290.51302	291.29597	292.08110
132	347.26498	348.31216	349.36260	350.41633	351.47335	352.53367	353.59730	354.66425
144	417.96466	419.36293	420.76606	422.17407	423.58698	425.00480	426.42755	427.85524
156	500.40049	502.24365	504.09389	505.95123	507.81569	509.68731	511.56611	513.45211
168	596.52066	598.92402	601.33747	603.76106	606.19483	608.63882	611.09308	613.55765
180	708.59678	711.70166	714.82072	717.95404	721.10166	724.26367	727.44012	730.63108
192	839.27754	843.25678	847.25568	851.27434	855.31285	859.37130	863.44980	867.54845
204	991.65291	996.71583	1001.80728	1006.92579	1012.07151	1017.24457	1022.44513	1027.67332
216	1169.31912	1175.72581	1182.16899	1188.64886	1195.16562	1201.71948	1208.31066	1214.93935
228	1376.47979	1384.54096	1392.65111	1400.81054	1409.01955	1417.27842	1425.58746	1433.94697
240	1618.02912	1628.12382	1638.28375	1648.50931	1658.80093	1669.15904	1679.58405	1690.07639
252	1899.67565	1912.26324	1924.93703	1937.69762	1950.54559	1963.48154	1976.50606	1989.61974
264	2228.07550	2243.71186	2259.46141	2275.32497	2291.30336	2307.39738	2323.60789	2339.93570
276	2610.98973	2630.34668	2649.85137	2669.50491	2689.30842	2709.26305	2729.36992	2749.63020
288	3057.46771	3081.35620	3105.43645	3129.70998	3154.17834	3178.84307	3203.70574	3228.76793
300	3578.06105	3607.45880	3637.10423	3666.99940	3697.14640	3727.54734	3758.20432	3789.11950
312	4185.07287	4221.15749	4257.56053	4294.28480	4331.33310	4368.70827	4406.41316	4444.45066
324	4892.84867	4937.03701	4981.63304	5026.64051	5072.06316	5117.90481	5164.16928	5210.86045
336	5718.11524	5772.11046	5826.62566	5881.66579	5937.23588	5993.34098	6049.98620	6107.17670
348	6680.37606	6746.22365	6812.73204	6879.90781	6947.75761	7016.28813	7085.50617	7155.41855
360	7802.37218	7882.52668	7963.51819	8045.35537	8128.04699	8211.60189	8296.02902	8381.33740
420	16906.71598	17116.03471	17327.96984	17542.55385	17759.81957	17979.80028	18202.52962	18428.04167
480	36528.63150	37059.03275	37597.17096	38143.15815	38697.10790	39259.13544	39829.35761	40407.89294

73

MONTHLY DEPOSITS

EFFECTIVE ANNUAL YIELD

NUMBER OF MONTHLY DEPOSITS	17.00%	17.05%	17.10%	17.15%	17.20%	17.25%	17.30%	17.35%
1	1.01317	1.01321	1.01324	1.01328	1.01331	1.01335	1.01339	1.01342
2	2.03968	2.03979	2.03990	2.04001	2.04012	2.04023	2.04034	2.04045
3	3.07971	3.07993	3.08015	3.08037	3.08059	3.08081	3.08103	3.08125
4	4.13344	4.13381	4.13418	4.13455	4.13492	4.13529	4.13566	4.13603
5	5.20105	5.20161	5.20217	5.20273	5.20329	5.20385	5.20441	5.20497
6	6.28271	6.28350	6.28430	6.28509	6.28588	6.28667	6.28746	6.28825
7	7.37862	7.37969	7.38075	7.38182	7.38288	7.38394	7.38501	7.38607
8	8.48897	8.49035	8.49173	8.49311	8.49449	8.49587	8.49725	8.49863
9	9.61393	9.61567	9.61742	9.61916	9.62090	9.62264	9.62438	9.62612
10	10.75371	10.75586	10.75801	10.76016	10.76230	10.76445	10.76659	10.76874
11	11.90851	11.91111	11.91370	11.91630	11.91890	11.92150	11.92410	11.92670
12	13.07851	13.08161	13.08470	13.08780	13.09090	13.09400	13.09710	13.10020
13	14.26391	14.26756	14.27121	14.27486	14.27851	14.28215	14.28580	14.28945
14	15.46493	15.46918	15.47343	15.47768	15.48192	15.48617	15.49041	15.49466
15	16.68177	16.68667	16.69157	16.69646	16.70136	16.70626	16.71115	16.71605
16	17.91463	17.92023	17.92583	17.93143	17.93703	17.94263	17.94823	17.95383
17	19.16373	19.17009	19.17644	19.18280	19.18916	19.19551	19.20187	19.20822
18	20.42928	20.43645	20.44362	20.45078	20.45795	20.46512	20.47229	20.47946
19	21.71149	21.71953	21.72757	21.73560	21.74364	21.75168	21.75971	21.76775
20	23.01060	23.01956	23.02852	23.03748	23.04644	23.05541	23.06437	23.07334
21	24.32681	24.33675	24.34670	24.35665	24.36659	24.37654	24.38649	24.39644
22	25.66035	25.67134	25.68233	25.69333	25.70432	25.71532	25.72631	25.73731
23	27.01146	27.02355	27.03565	27.04775	27.05986	27.07196	27.08407	27.09617
24	28.38036	28.39362	28.40689	28.42017	28.43344	28.44672	28.46000	28.47328
25	29.76729	29.78179	29.79629	29.81080	29.82531	29.83983	29.85434	29.86886
26	31.17248	31.18828	31.20409	31.21990	31.23571	31.25153	31.26735	31.28318
27	32.59618	32.61335	32.63053	32.64771	32.66490	32.68209	32.69928	32.71648
28	34.03863	34.05724	34.07585	34.09448	34.11310	34.13174	34.15037	34.16902
29	35.50007	35.52019	35.54032	35.56045	35.58059	35.60074	35.62089	35.64105
30	36.98076	37.00247	37.02418	37.04590	37.06762	37.08935	37.11109	37.13284
31	38.48095	38.50432	38.52768	38.55106	38.57445	38.59784	38.62124	38.64465
32	40.00090	40.02600	40.05110	40.07621	40.10133	40.12647	40.15161	40.17675
33	41.54087	41.56777	41.59469	41.62161	41.64855	41.67550	41.70245	41.72942
34	43.10112	43.12991	43.15872	43.18753	43.21637	43.24521	43.27406	43.30293
35	44.68191	44.71268	44.74346	44.77425	44.80506	44.83587	44.86671	44.89756
36	46.28352	46.31634	46.34918	46.38203	46.41489	46.44778	46.48067	46.51359
37	47.90623	47.94119	47.97616	48.01116	48.04617	48.08120	48.11624	48.15131
38	49.55031	49.58749	49.62469	49.66192	49.69916	49.73642	49.77370	49.81101
39	51.21603	51.25553	51.29505	51.33460	51.37416	51.41375	51.45335	51.49298
40	52.90370	52.94560	52.98753	53.02948	53.07146	53.11346	53.15549	53.19754
41	54.61359	54.65799	54.70242	54.74688	54.79136	54.83587	54.88040	54.92497
42	56.34600	56.39299	56.44002	56.48707	56.53415	56.58127	56.62841	56.67558
43	58.10122	58.15091	58.20062	58.25037	58.30015	58.34997	58.39982	58.44969
44	59.87956	59.93204	59.98454	60.03709	60.08967	60.14228	60.19493	60.24762
45	61.68132	61.73668	61.79209	61.84752	61.90300	61.95852	62.01408	62.06967
46	63.50681	63.56517	63.62356	63.68200	63.74048	63.79901	63.85757	63.91618
47	65.35634	65.41779	65.47929	65.54084	65.60243	65.66406	65.72575	65.78748
48	67.23023	67.29489	67.35959	67.42435	67.48916	67.55402	67.61893	67.68389
60	91.73787	91.85027	91.96279	92.07543	92.18820	92.30109	92.41410	92.52724
72	120.41182	120.59235	120.77313	120.95417	121.13547	121.31703	121.49884	121.68091
84	153.96033	154.23495	154.51004	154.78562	155.06167	155.33821	155.61524	155.89275
96	193.21209	193.61361	194.01596	194.41915	194.82318	195.22806	195.63377	196.04034
108	239.13666	239.70633	240.27740	240.84984	241.42367	241.99890	242.57552	243.15353
120	292.86839	293.65787	294.44954	295.24339	296.03945	296.83771	297.63818	298.44086
132	355.73452	356.80814	357.88511	358.96544	360.04914	361.13621	362.22668	363.32055
144	429.28790	430.72554	432.16817	433.61582	435.06849	436.52621	437.98900	439.45686
156	515.34535	517.24585	519.15363	521.06873	522.99117	524.92098	526.85819	528.80282
168	616.03256	618.51787	621.01361	623.51982	626.03656	628.56386	631.10176	633.65031
180	733.83660	737.05677	740.29164	743.54128	746.80575	750.08512	753.37946	756.68883
192	871.66733	875.80656	879.96621	884.14641	888.34724	892.56881	896.81121	901.07454
204	1032.92928	1038.21318	1043.52514	1048.86532	1054.23387	1059.63092	1065.05664	1070.51117
216	1221.60577	1228.31013	1235.05265	1241.83353	1248.65300	1255.51126	1262.40854	1269.34506
228	1442.35726	1450.81861	1459.33135	1467.89578	1476.51221	1485.18095	1493.90232	1502.67662
240	1700.63649	1711.26479	1721.96172	1732.72772	1743.56322	1754.46867	1765.44467	1776.49121
252	2002.82320	2016.11705	2029.50188	2042.97832	2056.54699	2070.20852	2083.96352	2097.81263
264	2356.38165	2372.94661	2389.63141	2406.43691	2423.36398	2440.41349	2457.58630	2474.88332
276	2770.04504	2790.61561	2811.34308	2832.22864	2853.27349	2874.47881	2895.84583	2917.37577
288	3254.03120	3279.49718	3305.16745	3331.04366	3357.12743	3383.42041	3409.92426	3436.64066
300	3820.29501	3851.73305	3883.43579	3915.40545	3947.64425	3980.15643	4012.93826	4045.99801
312	4482.82367	4521.53514	4560.58802	4599.98529	4639.72996	4679.82507	4720.27368	4761.07887
324	5257.98220	5305.53849	5353.53327	5401.97057	5450.85442	5500.18889	5549.97812	5600.22625
336	6164.91768	6223.21441	6282.07217	6341.49633	6401.49228	6462.06548	6523.22143	6584.96569
348	7226.03219	7297.35407	7369.39122	7442.15075	7515.63985	7589.86578	7664.83584	7740.55744
360	8467.53617	8554.63454	8642.64182	8731.56741	8821.42081	8912.21162	9003.94954	9096.64435
420	18656.37092	18887.55228	19121.62109	19358.61309	19598.56451	19841.51198	20087.49258	20336.54386
480	40994.86166	41590.38569	42194.58870	42807.59612	43429.53517	44060.53489	44700.72613	45350.24164

74

MONTHLY DEPOSITS

NUMBER OF MONTHLY DEPOSITS	EFFECTIVE ANNUAL YIELD							
	17.40%	17.45%	17.50%	17.55%	17.60%	17.65%	17.70%	17.75%
1	1.01346	1.01349	1.01353	1.01357	1.01360	1.01364	1.01367	1.01371
2	2.04055	2.04066	2.04077	2.04088	2.04099	2.04110	2.04121	2.04132
3	3.08147	3.08169	3.08191	3.08213	3.08235	3.08257	3.08279	3.08301
4	4.13640	4.13674	4.13714	4.13751	4.13788	4.13825	4.13862	4.13898
5	5.20553	5.20609	5.20664	5.20720	5.20776	5.20832	5.20888	5.20944
6	6.28904	6.28983	6.29062	6.29141	6.29220	6.29299	6.29377	6.29456
7	7.38713	7.38820	7.38926	7.39032	7.39138	7.39244	7.39351	7.39457
8	8.50001	8.50138	8.50276	8.50414	8.50552	8.50690	8.50827	8.50965
9	9.62786	9.62959	9.63133	9.63307	9.63481	9.63655	9.63828	9.64002
10	10.77088	10.77303	10.77517	10.77732	10.77946	10.78160	10.78374	10.78589
11	11.92929	11.93189	11.93449	11.93708	11.93968	11.94227	11.94487	11.94746
12	13.10329	13.10639	13.10949	13.11258	13.11568	13.11877	13.12187	13.12496
13	14.29309	14.29674	14.30038	14.30403	14.30767	14.31132	14.31496	14.31860
14	15.49890	15.50315	15.50739	15.51164	15.51588	15.52013	15.52437	15.52861
15	16.72094	16.72584	16.73073	16.73563	16.74052	16.74542	16.75031	16.75521
16	17.95943	17.96503	17.97063	17.97622	17.98182	17.98742	17.99302	17.99862
17	19.21458	19.22094	19.22729	19.23365	19.24001	19.24636	19.25272	19.25907
18	20.48663	20.49379	20.50096	20.50813	20.51530	20.52247	20.52964	20.53681
19	21.77579	21.78383	21.79186	21.79990	21.80794	21.81598	21.82402	21.83206
20	23.08230	23.09127	23.10023	23.10920	23.11817	23.12714	23.13610	23.14507
21	24.40640	24.41635	24.42630	24.43626	24.44621	24.45617	24.46613	24.47609
22	25.74831	25.75931	25.77031	25.78132	25.79232	25.80333	25.81433	25.82534
23	27.10828	27.12039	27.13251	27.14462	27.15674	27.16886	27.18098	27.19310
24	28.48656	28.49985	28.51313	28.52642	28.53971	28.55301	28.56631	28.57960
25	29.88338	29.89791	29.91244	29.92697	29.94150	29.95604	29.97058	29.98512
26	31.29901	31.31484	31.33067	31.34651	31.36235	31.37820	31.39405	31.40990
27	32.73368	32.75089	32.76810	32.78531	32.80253	32.81976	32.83699	32.85422
28	34.18766	34.20631	34.22497	34.24363	34.26230	34.28097	34.29965	34.31833
29	35.66121	35.68138	35.70156	35.72174	35.74192	35.76212	35.78232	35.80252
30	37.15459	37.17635	37.19812	37.21989	37.24167	37.26346	37.28525	37.30706
31	38.66807	38.69149	38.71493	38.73837	38.76182	38.78528	38.80874	38.83222
32	40.20191	40.22708	40.25226	40.27745	40.30264	40.32785	40.35306	40.37829
33	41.75640	41.78339	41.81039	41.83740	41.86442	41.89146	41.91850	41.94555
34	43.33181	43.36070	43.38960	43.41852	43.44745	43.47639	43.50534	43.53430
35	44.92842	44.95929	44.99018	45.02109	45.05200	45.08293	45.11388	45.14484
36	46.54651	46.57946	46.61242	46.64539	46.67838	46.71139	46.74441	46.77745
37	48.18639	48.22148	48.25660	48.29173	48.32688	48.36205	48.39724	48.43244
38	49.84833	49.88567	49.92303	49.96041	49.99781	50.03523	50.07266	50.11012
39	51.53263	51.57231	51.61200	51.65172	51.69146	51.73122	51.77100	51.81080
40	53.23961	53.28171	53.32383	53.36597	53.40814	53.45034	53.49256	53.53480
41	54.96956	55.01417	55.05881	55.10348	55.14818	55.19290	55.23765	55.28243
42	56.72278	56.77001	56.81727	56.86456	56.91188	56.95923	57.00661	57.05402
43	58.49961	58.54955	58.59953	58.64954	58.69958	58.74965	58.79976	58.84990
44	60.30034	60.35310	60.40589	60.45872	60.51159	60.56449	60.61742	60.67039
45	62.12531	62.18098	62.23670	62.29245	62.34824	62.40407	62.45994	62.51585
46	63.97484	64.03353	64.09227	64.15105	64.20988	64.26874	64.32765	64.38660
47	65.84926	65.91108	65.97295	66.03487	66.09683	66.15884	66.22090	66.28301
48	67.74890	67.81396	67.87908	67.94424	68.00946	68.07472	68.14004	68.20541
60	92.64050	92.75389	92.86740	92.98104	93.09480	93.20868	93.32269	93.43683
72	121.86324	122.04583	122.22868	122.41179	122.59516	122.77879	122.96268	123.14683
84	156.17074	156.44922	156.72819	157.00764	157.28758	157.56802	157.84894	158.13035
96	196.44774	196.85600	197.26511	197.67507	198.08588	198.49754	198.91007	199.32345
108	243.73294	244.31376	244.89599	245.47962	246.06467	246.65113	247.23902	247.82832
120	299.24577	300.05290	300.86227	301.67388	302.48773	303.30383	304.12219	304.94281
132	364.41783	365.51853	366.62266	367.73023	368.84125	369.95573	371.07368	372.19512
144	440.92982	442.40790	443.89111	445.37946	446.87298	448.37169	449.87559	451.38472
156	530.75491	532.71447	534.68154	536.65614	538.63831	540.62806	542.62544	544.63047
168	636.20955	638.77953	641.36029	643.95188	646.55433	649.16769	651.79201	654.42734
180	760.01331	763.35295	766.70783	770.07801	773.46357	776.86456	780.28107	783.71315
192	905.35892	909.66443	913.99119	918.33929	922.70883	927.09993	931.51268	935.94720
204	1075.99466	1081.50726	1087.04913	1092.62041	1098.22126	1103.85184	1109.51230	1115.20278
216	1276.32103	1283.33667	1290.39221	1297.48788	1304.62388	1311.80046	1319.01784	1326.27624
228	1511.50418	1520.38531	1529.32034	1538.30958	1547.35337	1556.45202	1565.60586	1574.81524
240	1787.60920	1798.79894	1810.06088	1821.39549	1832.80324	1844.28457	1855.83979	1867.46990
252	2111.75649	2125.79574	2139.93102	2154.16299	2168.49228	2182.91957	2197.44551	2212.07077
264	2492.30542	2509.85349	2527.52844	2545.33117	2563.26260	2581.32365	2599.51523	2617.83830
276	2939.06985	2960.92931	2982.95540	3005.14937	3027.51250	3050.04604	3072.75130	3095.62955
288	3463.57130	3490.71787	3518.08208	3545.66567	3573.47037	3601.49794	3629.75015	3658.22876
300	4079.33600	4112.95452	4146.85593	4181.04258	4215.51684	4250.28110	4285.33379	4320.68933
312	4802.24375	4843.77148	4885.66521	4927.92813	4970.56348	5013.57449	5056.96445	5100.73665
324	5650.93746	5702.11599	5753.76611	5805.89210	5858.49833	5911.58916	5965.16902	6019.24236
336	6647.30387	6710.24162	6773.78466	6837.93875	6902.70971	6968.10342	7034.12581	7100.78285
348	7817.03804	7894.28518	7972.30646	8051.10958	8130.70230	8211.09245	8292.28794	8374.29676
360	9190.30595	9284.44433	9380.56958	9477.19190	9574.82158	9673.46904	9773.14477	9873.85940
420	20588.70382	20844.01092	21102.50408	21364.22271	21629.20668	21897.49637	22169.13263	22444.15682
480	46009.21602	46677.78583	47356.08953	48044.26758	48742.46242	49450.81852	50169.48240	50898.60268

MONTHLY DEPOSITS

NUMBER OF MONTHLY DEPOSITS	EFFECTIVE ANNUAL YIELD							
	17.80%	17.85%	17.90%	18.00%	18.10%	18.20%	18.30%	18.40%
1	1.01375	1.01378	1.01382	1.01389	1.01396	1.01403	1.01410	1.01417
2	2.04142	2.04153	2.04164	2.04186	2.04207	2.04229	2.04251	2.04272
3	3.08323	3.08345	3.08367	3.08410	3.08454	3.08498	3.08542	3.08585
4	4.13935	4.13971	4.14009	4.14083	4.14156	4.14230	4.14303	4.14377
5	5.20999	5.21055	5.21111	5.21222	5.21334	5.21445	5.21557	5.21668
6	6.29535	6.29614	6.29693	6.29850	6.30008	6.30165	6.30322	6.30479
7	7.39563	7.39669	7.39775	7.39987	7.40199	7.40410	7.40622	7.40834
8	8.51103	8.51240	8.51378	8.51653	8.51928	8.52203	8.52477	8.52752
9	9.64176	9.64349	9.64523	9.64870	9.65217	9.65563	9.65910	9.66257
10	10.78803	10.79017	10.79231	10.79659	10.80087	10.80515	10.80943	10.81370
11	11.95006	11.95265	11.95524	11.96043	11.96561	11.97079	11.97597	11.98115
12	13.12806	13.13115	13.13424	13.14043	13.14661	13.15279	13.15897	13.16515
13	14.32225	14.32589	14.32953	14.33682	14.34410	14.35138	14.35866	14.36594
14	15.53285	15.53710	15.54134	15.54982	15.55830	15.56678	15.57526	15.58374
15	16.76010	16.76499	16.76989	16.77967	16.78946	16.79924	16.80902	16.81880
16	18.00421	18.00981	18.01541	18.02660	18.03780	18.04899	18.06018	18.07137
17	19.26543	19.27179	19.27814	19.29085	19.30356	19.31628	19.32899	19.34170
18	20.54398	20.55115	20.55832	20.57266	20.58700	20.60134	20.61569	20.63003
19	21.84010	21.84815	21.85619	21.87227	21.88836	21.90444	21.92053	21.93662
20	23.15404	23.16302	23.17199	23.18993	23.20788	23.22583	23.24378	23.26174
21	24.48604	24.49600	24.50597	24.52589	24.54582	24.56575	24.58569	24.60563
22	25.83635	25.84736	25.85838	25.88041	25.90244	25.92448	25.94653	25.96858
23	27.20522	27.21735	27.22947	27.25373	27.27800	27.30227	27.32655	27.35084
24	28.59291	28.60621	28.61951	28.64613	28.67276	28.69940	28.72604	28.75269
25	29.99966	30.01421	30.02876	30.05787	30.08699	30.11612	30.14527	30.17442
26	31.42576	31.44162	31.45748	31.48922	31.52097	31.55273	31.58451	31.61630
27	32.87145	32.88869	32.90594	32.94044	32.97496	33.00949	33.04405	33.07862
28	34.33702	34.35571	34.37441	34.41182	34.44925	34.48670	34.52417	34.56166
29	35.82273	35.84295	35.86317	35.90363	35.94412	35.98463	36.02517	36.06572
30	37.32886	37.35068	37.37250	37.41617	37.45986	37.50358	37.54733	37.59111
31	38.85570	38.87919	38.90269	38.94971	38.99676	39.04385	39.09096	39.13811
32	40.40352	40.42876	40.45401	40.50455	40.55512	40.60572	40.65637	40.70705
33	41.97262	41.99969	42.02678	42.08098	42.13523	42.18951	42.24385	42.29822
34	43.56328	43.59227	43.62127	43.67931	43.73739	43.79553	43.85371	43.91195
35	45.17581	45.20679	45.23779	45.29983	45.36193	45.42408	45.48628	45.54855
36	46.81050	46.84357	46.87665	46.94286	47.00914	47.07548	47.14188	47.20834
37	48.46766	48.50290	48.53815	48.60872	48.67935	48.75005	48.82082	48.89167
38	50.14760	50.18510	50.22261	50.29770	50.37287	50.44812	50.52345	50.59885
39	51.85063	51.89048	51.93034	52.01015	52.09004	52.17002	52.25008	52.33023
40	53.57707	53.61936	53.66167	53.74638	53.83118	53.91607	54.00107	54.08616
41	55.32723	55.37206	55.41692	55.50672	55.59662	55.68663	55.77675	55.86697
42	57.10146	57.14893	57.19642	57.29151	57.38671	57.48203	57.57747	57.67303
43	58.90007	58.95027	59.00051	59.10108	59.20179	59.30262	59.40359	59.50468
44	60.72340	60.77645	60.82953	60.93579	61.04220	61.14876	61.25546	61.36230
45	62.57180	62.62779	62.68381	62.79598	62.90831	63.02080	63.13344	63.24625
46	64.44560	64.50464	64.56372	64.68201	64.80047	64.91911	65.03792	65.15690
47	66.34516	66.40735	66.46960	66.59423	66.71905	66.84405	66.96925	67.09463
48	68.27082	68.33629	68.40181	68.53301	68.66441	68.79601	68.92782	69.05983
60	93.55109	93.66547	93.77998	94.00938	94.23928	94.46968	94.70058	94.93199
72	123.33124	123.51591	123.70084	124.07149	124.44320	124.81595	125.18976	125.56463
84	158.41225	158.69465	158.97753	159.54479	160.11403	160.68525	161.25847	161.83368
96	199.73769	200.15279	200.56875	201.40328	202.24128	203.08276	203.92774	204.77623
108	248.41905	249.01121	249.60480	250.79630	251.99356	253.19662	254.40549	255.62021
120	305.76570	306.59086	307.41831	309.08006	310.75101	312.43119	314.12067	315.81948
132	373.32005	374.44848	375.58043	377.85490	380.14355	382.44646	384.76373	387.09542
144	452.89907	454.41869	455.94357	459.00921	462.09614	465.20451	468.33446	471.48613
156	546.64317	548.66357	550.69171	554.77129	558.88216	563.02453	567.19864	571.40473
168	657.07371	659.73117	662.39976	667.77055	673.18644	678.64779	684.15497	689.70836
180	787.16088	790.62433	794.10357	801.10968	808.17980	815.31448	822.51430	829.77985
192	940.40357	944.88192	949.38235	958.44985	967.60695	976.85451	986.19339	995.62450
204	1120.92347	1126.67449	1132.45603	1144.11125	1155.89042	1167.79482	1179.82576	1191.98456
216	1333.57590	1340.91704	1348.29990	1363.19171	1378.25320	1393.48627	1408.89285	1424.47487
228	1584.08046	1593.40188	1602.77983	1621.70664	1640.86364	1660.25357	1679.87921	1699.74340
240	1879.17484	1890.95527	1902.81166	1926.75427	1951.00671	1975.57251	2000.45608	2025.66133
252	2226.79602	2241.62193	2256.54919	2286.71046	2317.28537	2348.27950	2379.69852	2411.54817
264	2636.29377	2654.88260	2673.60573	2711.45877	2749.86063	2788.81916	2828.34232	2868.43819
276	3118.68211	3141.91029	3165.31540	3212.66178	3260.73202	3309.53704	3359.08794	3409.39597
288	3686.93559	3715.87243	3745.04110	3804.08133	3864.07112	3925.02558	3986.96001	4049.88998
300	4356.33818	4392.28680	4428.53770	4501.95640	4576.61461	4652.53302	4729.73266	4808.23489
312	5144.89443	5189.44115	5234.38019	5325.44897	5418.12846	5512.44683	5608.43272	5706.11527
324	6073.81369	6128.08754	6184.46849	6297.17022	6411.95633	6528.86494	6647.93488	6769.20563
336	7168.08058	7236.02512	7304.62259	7443.80129	7585.66703	7730.27116	7877.66593	8027.90462
348	8457.12698	8540.78675	8625.28428	8796.82594	8971.81938	9150.33330	9332.43778	9518.20422
360	9975.62364	10078.44833	10182.34441	10393.39504	10608.86530	10828.84676	11053.43286	11282.71895
420	22722.61078	23004.53690	23289.97803	23871.57951	24467.76877	25078.90801	25705.36826	26347.52961
480	51638.33007	52388.81742	53150.21976	54706.40056	56308.15725	57956.81131	59653.72197	61400.28722

76

MONTHLY DEPOSITS

NUMBER OF MONTHLY DEPOSITS	EFFECTIVE ANNUAL YIELD							
	18.50%	18.60%	18.70%	18.80%	18.90%	19.00%	19.10%	19.20%
1	1.01425	1.01432	1.01439	1.01446	1.01453	1.01460	1.01467	1.01474
2	2.04294	2.04316	2.04337	2.04359	2.04380	2.04402	2.04423	2.04445
3	3.08629	3.08673	3.08716	3.08760	3.08803	3.08847	3.08890	3.08933
4	4.14450	4.14523	4.14597	4.14670	4.14743	4.14816	4.14890	4.14963
5	5.21779	5.21890	5.22001	5.22112	5.22223	5.22334	5.22444	5.22555
6	6.30637	6.30794	6.30951	6.31107	6.31264	6.31421	6.31577	6.31734
7	7.41045	7.41256	7.41468	7.41679	7.41890	7.42101	7.42312	7.42522
8	8.53026	8.53301	8.53575	8.53849	8.54123	8.54397	8.54671	8.54944
9	9.66603	9.66949	9.67295	9.67641	9.67987	9.68333	9.68678	9.69024
10	10.81797	10.82225	10.82652	10.83079	10.83505	10.83932	10.84359	10.84785
11	11.98633	11.99151	11.99668	12.00185	12.00703	12.01220	12.01736	12.02253
12	13.17133	13.17751	13.18368	13.18985	13.19603	13.20220	13.20836	13.21453
13	14.37321	14.38049	14.38776	14.39503	14.40230	14.40957	14.41684	14.42410
14	15.59221	15.60069	15.60916	15.61764	15.62611	15.63458	15.64305	15.65151
15	16.82858	16.83836	16.84814	16.85792	16.86769	16.87747	16.88724	16.89702
16	18.08256	18.09376	18.10495	18.11613	18.12732	18.13851	18.14970	18.16088
17	19.35441	19.36712	19.37983	19.39254	19.40525	19.41797	19.43068	19.44339
18	20.64437	20.65872	20.67306	20.68741	20.70176	20.71610	20.73045	20.74480
19	21.95271	21.96881	21.98490	22.00100	22.01710	22.03319	22.04929	22.06540
20	23.27969	23.29765	23.31562	23.33358	23.35155	23.36952	23.38749	23.40546
21	24.62558	24.64552	24.66548	24.68543	24.70539	24.72535	24.74532	24.76529
22	25.99063	26.01269	26.03476	26.05683	26.07891	26.10099	26.12307	26.14517
23	27.37513	27.39943	27.42374	27.44806	27.47238	27.49671	27.52104	27.54539
24	28.77936	28.80603	28.83271	28.85940	28.88610	28.91281	28.93952	28.96625
25	30.20359	30.23276	30.26195	30.29115	30.32036	30.34958	30.37882	30.40806
26	31.64811	31.67992	31.71176	31.74361	31.77547	31.80734	31.83923	31.87113
27	33.11320	33.14780	33.18242	33.21706	33.25171	33.28638	33.32107	33.35577
28	34.59917	34.63670	34.67425	34.71182	34.74941	34.78702	34.82465	34.86230
29	36.10631	36.14691	36.18754	36.22820	36.26887	36.30957	36.35030	36.39105
30	37.63491	37.67875	37.72261	37.76650	37.81041	37.85436	37.89833	37.94233
31	39.18530	39.23251	39.27976	39.32704	39.37435	39.42170	39.46907	39.51648
32	40.75777	40.80852	40.85932	40.91015	40.96102	41.01192	41.06286	41.11384
33	42.35264	42.40710	42.46160	42.51615	42.57073	42.62537	42.68004	42.73476
34	43.97023	44.02856	44.08694	44.14537	44.20384	44.26237	44.32094	44.37957
35	45.61086	45.67323	45.73566	45.79814	45.86068	45.92328	45.98593	46.04863
36	47.27487	47.34146	47.40811	47.47482	47.54160	47.60844	47.67534	47.74230
37	48.96258	49.03356	49.10462	49.17574	49.24694	49.31820	49.38954	49.46094
38	50.67434	50.74990	50.82554	50.90126	50.97705	51.05293	51.12889	51.20492
39	52.41048	52.49080	52.57122	52.65172	52.73231	52.81299	52.89376	52.97461
40	54.17135	54.25663	54.34202	54.42750	54.51308	54.59875	54.68453	54.77040
41	55.95730	56.04775	56.13829	56.22895	56.31972	56.41059	56.50157	56.59266
42	57.76870	57.86450	57.96042	58.05645	58.15261	58.24888	58.34527	58.44179
43	59.60591	59.70727	59.80876	59.91038	60.01213	60.11401	60.21603	60.31818
44	61.46928	61.57641	61.68369	61.79111	61.89867	62.00638	62.11423	62.22223
45	63.35921	63.47232	63.58560	63.69904	63.81263	63.92638	64.04029	64.15436
46	65.27605	65.39538	65.51488	65.63455	65.75440	65.87441	65.99461	66.11498
47	67.22020	67.34596	67.47191	67.59805	67.72438	67.85090	67.97760	68.10450
48	69.19205	69.32448	69.45711	69.58994	69.72298	69.85623	69.98969	70.12335
60	95.16391	95.39633	95.62927	95.86271	96.09665	96.33111	96.56608	96.80157
72	125.94057	126.31756	126.69562	127.07475	127.45495	127.83622	128.21857	128.60200
84	162.41090	162.99013	163.57138	164.15465	164.73996	165.32730	165.91668	166.50811
96	205.62825	206.48380	207.34291	208.20558	209.07183	209.94168	210.81513	211.69220
108	256.84081	258.06730	259.29972	260.53809	261.78244	263.03279	264.28918	265.55163
120	317.52768	319.24532	320.97244	322.70910	324.45534	326.21122	327.97678	329.75207
132	389.44164	391.80246	394.17797	396.56827	398.97343	401.39364	403.82870	406.27900
144	474.65967	477.85522	481.07293	484.31295	487.57543	490.86051	494.16835	497.49909
156	575.64304	579.91380	584.21725	588.55364	592.92321	597.32620	601.76287	606.23345
168	695.30833	700.95527	706.64956	712.39158	718.18172	724.02038	729.90794	735.84480
180	837.11171	844.51046	851.97671	859.51105	867.11409	874.78644	882.52872	890.34154
192	1005.14870	1014.76691	1024.48004	1034.28898	1044.19468	1054.19806	1064.30007	1074.50164
204	1204.27254	1216.69107	1229.24148	1241.92517	1254.74350	1267.69789	1280.78974	1294.02049
216	1440.23429	1456.17311	1472.29332	1488.59695	1505.08605	1521.76268	1538.62894	1555.68695
228	1719.84897	1740.19982	1760.79585	1781.64303	1802.74334	1824.09979	1845.71544	1867.59337
240	2051.19236	2077.05330	2103.24836	2129.78178	2156.65785	2183.88094	2211.45545	2239.38583
252	2443.83428	2476.56272	2509.73948	2543.37060	2577.46221	2612.02052	2647.05180	2682.56244
264	2909.11495	2950.38090	2992.24445	3034.71413	3077.79860	3121.50661	3165.84706	3210.82896
276	3460.47255	3512.32925	3564.97784	3618.43024	3672.69856	3727.79506	3783.73221	3840.52265
288	4113.83130	4178.80000	4244.81238	4311.88498	4380.03461	4449.27832	4519.63343	4591.11753
300	4888.06142	4969.23431	5051.77597	5135.70921	5221.05717	5307.84339	5396.09177	5485.82663
312	5805.52411	5906.68939	6009.64176	6114.41240	6221.03301	6329.53583	6439.95367	6552.31987
324	6892.71740	7018.51113	7146.62845	7277.11178	7410.00427	7545.34983	7683.19318	7823.57981
336	8181.04145	8337.13170	8496.23166	8658.39865	8823.69103	8992.16850	9163.89144	9338.92167
348	9707.70545	9901.01571	10098.21066	10299.36745	10504.56474	10713.88271	10927.40307	11145.20916
360	11516.80229	11755.78213	11999.75973	12248.83839	12503.12351	12762.72261	13027.74542	13298.30384
420	27005.78140	27680.52246	28372.16134	29081.11653	29807.81669	30552.70093	31316.21901	32098.83161
480	63197.94494	65048.17400	66952.49541	68912.47349	70929.71709	73005.88081	75142.66632	77341.82362

77

MONTHLY DEPOSITS

EFFECTIVE ANNUAL YIELD

NUMBER OF MONTHLY DEPOSITS	19.30%	19.40%	19.50%	19.60%	19.70%	19.80%	19.90%	20.00%
1	1.01481	1.01489	1.01496	1.01503	1.01510	1.01517	1.01524	1.01531
2	2.04466	2.04488	2.04509	2.04531	2.04552	2.04574	2.04595	2.04616
3	3.08977	3.09020	3.09064	3.09107	3.09150	3.09193	3.09237	3.09280
4	4.15036	4.15109	4.15182	4.15255	4.15327	4.15400	4.15473	4.15546
5	5.22666	5.22776	5.22887	5.22997	5.23108	5.23218	5.23328	5.23438
6	6.31890	6.32047	6.32203	6.32359	6.32515	6.32671	6.32827	6.32983
7	7.42733	7.42943	7.43154	7.43364	7.43574	7.43785	7.43995	7.44204
8	8.55218	8.55491	8.55764	8.56037	8.56310	8.56583	8.56856	8.57129
9	9.69369	9.69714	9.70059	9.70404	9.70749	9.71093	9.71438	9.71782
10	10.85211	10.85637	10.86063	10.86489	10.86914	10.87340	10.87765	10.88190
11	12.02770	12.03286	12.03802	12.04318	12.04834	12.05350	12.05865	12.06381
12	13.22070	13.22686	13.23302	13.23918	13.24534	13.25150	13.25765	13.26381
13	14.43137	14.43863	14.44589	14.45315	14.46041	14.46767	14.47493	14.48218
14	15.65998	15.66844	15.67691	15.68537	15.69383	15.70229	15.71075	15.71920
15	16.90679	16.91656	16.92633	16.93610	16.94587	16.95564	16.96540	16.97517
16	18.17207	18.18326	18.19444	18.20563	18.21681	18.22799	18.23918	18.25036
17	19.45610	19.46881	19.48152	19.49423	19.50694	19.51965	19.53236	19.54507
18	20.75915	20.77350	20.78785	20.80220	20.81655	20.83090	20.84525	20.85960
19	22.08150	22.09760	22.11371	22.12982	22.14593	22.16204	22.17815	22.19426
20	23.42344	23.44142	23.45940	23.47739	23.49538	23.51337	23.53136	23.54935
21	24.78527	24.80524	24.82523	24.84521	24.86520	24.88519	24.90519	24.92519
22	26.16726	26.18937	26.21147	26.23359	26.25571	26.27783	26.29996	26.32209
23	27.56974	27.59409	27.61846	27.64283	27.66720	27.69159	27.71598	27.74038
24	28.99298	29.01973	29.04648	29.07324	29.10001	29.12679	29.15358	29.18038
25	30.43732	30.46659	30.49586	30.52515	30.55445	30.58377	30.61309	30.64243
26	31.90305	31.93498	31.96692	31.99888	32.03085	32.06284	32.09484	32.12685
27	33.39049	33.42523	33.45999	33.49476	33.52954	33.56435	33.59917	33.63401
28	34.89998	34.93767	34.97538	35.01311	35.05086	35.08863	35.12643	35.16424
29	36.43182	36.47262	36.51344	36.55428	36.59515	36.63604	36.67695	36.71789
30	37.98636	38.03041	38.07450	38.11861	38.16275	38.20691	38.25111	38.29533
31	39.56392	39.61140	39.65890	39.70644	39.75402	39.80162	39.84926	39.89692
32	41.16486	41.21592	41.26701	41.31814	41.36931	41.42051	41.47175	41.52303
33	42.78952	42.84432	42.89917	42.95405	43.00899	43.06396	43.11898	43.17404
34	44.43824	44.49696	44.55573	44.61455	44.67342	44.73234	44.79131	44.85032
35	46.11139	46.17421	46.23708	46.30000	46.36299	46.42602	46.48912	46.55227
36	47.80933	47.87641	47.94357	48.01078	48.07806	48.14540	48.21280	48.28027
37	49.53242	49.60396	49.67558	49.74727	49.81902	49.89085	49.96275	50.03472
38	51.28103	51.35723	51.43350	51.50985	51.58627	51.66278	51.73937	51.81603
39	53.05556	53.13659	53.21770	53.29891	53.38021	53.46159	53.54306	53.62462
40	54.85637	54.94243	55.02860	55.11486	55.20122	55.28768	55.37424	55.46089
41	56.68386	56.77516	56.86658	56.95810	57.04973	57.14147	57.23332	57.32528
42	58.53842	58.63517	58.73204	58.82904	58.92615	59.02338	59.12074	59.21821
43	60.42046	60.52287	60.62541	60.72809	60.83090	60.93384	61.03691	61.14012
44	62.33038	62.43866	62.54710	62.65568	62.76440	62.87327	62.98229	63.09145
45	64.26859	64.38298	64.49752	64.61223	64.72710	64.84212	64.95731	65.07266
46	66.23552	66.35623	66.47712	66.59819	66.71943	66.84084	66.96243	67.08419
47	68.23158	68.35886	68.48633	68.61399	68.74183	68.86987	68.99810	69.12653
48	70.25722	70.39130	70.52558	70.66008	70.79478	70.92968	71.06480	71.20013
60	97.03756	97.27407	97.51109	97.74863	97.98669	98.22526	98.46435	98.70396
72	128.98650	129.32210	129.75878	130.14655	130.53541	130.92536	131.31641	131.70856
84	167.10160	167.69714	168.29476	168.89445	169.49622	170.10008	170.70603	171.31408
96	212.57290	213.45725	214.34526	215.23694	216.13232	217.03139	217.93419	218.84071
108	266.82016	269.09481	269.37560	270.66257	271.95572	273.25511	274.56075	275.87266
120	331.53715	333.33207	335.13687	336.95161	338.77634	340.61112	342.45599	344.31100
132	408.74451	411.22534	413.72158	416.23331	418.76062	421.30362	423.86238	426.43701
144	500.85290	504.22992	507.63031	511.05422	514.50181	517.97323	521.46865	524.98823
156	610.73821	615.27738	619.85124	624.46003	629.10400	633.78343	638.49857	643.24968
168	741.83138	747.86806	753.95525	760.09337	766.28283	772.52405	778.81744	785.16343
180	898.22553	906.18132	914.20955	922.31086	930.48589	938.73531	947.05976	955.45992
192	1084.80375	1095.20735	1105.71343	1116.32297	1127.03696	1137.85640	1148.78231	1159.81571
204	1307.39157	1320.90444	1334.56057	1348.36145	1362.30858	1376.40347	1390.64765	1405.04266
216	1572.93883	1590.38676	1608.03290	1625.87948	1643.92871	1662.18285	1680.64418	1699.31501
228	1889.73672	1912.14865	1934.83234	1957.79104	1981.02800	2004.54655	2028.35003	2052.44182
240	2267.67661	2296.33234	2325.35767	2354.75726	2384.53586	2414.69827	2445.24934	2476.19399
252	2718.55889	2755.04768	2792.03543	2829.52886	2867.53477	2906.06003	2945.11161	2984.69659
264	3256.46145	3302.75379	3349.71536	3397.35570	3445.68446	3494.71141	3544.44648	3594.89972
276	3898.17920	3956.71488	4016.14288	4076.47660	4137.72964	4199.91577	4263.04898	4327.14348
288	4663.74848	4737.54442	4812.52376	4888.70520	4966.10772	5044.75059	5124.65338	5205.83598
300	5577.07264	5669.85490	5764.19892	5860.13060	5957.67628	6056.86270	6157.71706	6260.26699
312	6666.66835	6783.03361	6901.45073	7021.95538	7144.58384	7269.37301	7396.36041	7525.58419
324	7966.55604	8112.16899	8260.46664	8411.49782	8565.31220	8721.96037	8881.49379	9043.96484
336	9517.32205	9699.15663	9884.49066	10073.39057	10265.91430	10462.16002	10662.16871	10866.02162
348	11367.38590	11594.01998	11825.19936	12061.04150	12301.55642	12546.91920	12797.19793	13052.48975
360	13574.51207	13856.48660	14144.34626	14438.21229	14738.20838	15044.46071	15357.09798	15676.25151
420	32901.01061	33723.23933	34566.01281	35429.83809	36315.23450	37222.73393	38152.88115	39106.23411
480	79605.15245	81934.50361	84331.78041	86798.94014	89337.99558	91951.01649	94640.13124	97407.52843

TABLE 3. QUARTERLY DEPOSITS

QUARTERLY DEPOSITS

EFFECTIVE ANNUAL YIELD

NUMBER OF QUARTLRY DEPOSITS	5.00%	5.05%	5.10%	5.15%	5.20%	5.25%	5.30%	5.35%
1	1.01227	1.01239	1.01251	1.01263	1.01275	1.01287	1.01299	1.01311
2	2.03697	2.03733	2.03770	2.03806	2.03842	2.03879	2.03915	2.03952
3	3.07424	3.07497	3.07571	3.07644	3.07718	3.07791	3.07864	3.07938
4	4.12424	4.12547	4.12671	4.12794	4.12918	4.13041	4.13164	4.13288
5	5.18712	5.18899	5.19086	5.19273	5.19459	5.19646	5.19833	5.20020
6	6.26305	6.26569	6.26833	6.27096	6.27360	6.27624	6.27887	6.28151
7	7.35219	7.35573	7.35928	7.36282	7.36637	7.36991	7.37346	7.37700
8	8.45469	8.45928	8.46388	8.46847	8.47307	8.47767	8.48227	8.48687
9	9.57072	9.57651	9.58230	9.58809	9.59389	9.59969	9.60548	9.61128
10	10.70044	10.70758	10.71472	10.72186	10.72900	10.73615	10.74330	10.75045
11	11.84403	11.85267	11.86131	11.86995	11.87859	11.88724	11.89590	11.90455
12	13.00166	13.01195	13.02224	13.03254	13.04285	13.05316	13.06347	13.07379
13	14.17349	14.18559	14.19770	14.20982	14.22195	14.23408	14.24622	14.25837
14	15.35970	15.37378	15.38788	15.40198	15.41609	15.43021	15.44434	15.45848
15	16.56047	16.57670	16.59294	16.60919	16.62546	16.64173	16.65802	16.67432
16	17.77598	17.79452	17.81308	17.83166	17.85025	17.86886	17.88748	17.90612
17	19.00640	19.02744	19.04849	19.06957	19.09066	19.11178	19.13291	19.15407
18	20.25193	20.27563	20.29936	20.32312	20.34690	20.37070	20.39453	20.41838
19	21.51274	21.53930	21.56589	21.59251	21.61916	21.64583	21.67254	21.69928
20	22.78902	22.81862	22.84826	22.87793	22.90764	22.93738	22.96716	22.99698
21	24.08096	24.11380	24.14667	24.17959	24.21256	24.24556	24.27860	24.31169
22	25.38876	25.42503	25.46134	25.49770	25.53411	25.57058	25.60709	25.64365
23	26.71261	26.75250	26.79245	26.83246	26.87253	26.91265	26.95283	26.99307
24	28.05271	28.09643	28.14023	28.18409	28.22801	28.27201	28.31607	28.36019
25	29.40925	29.45702	29.50486	29.55279	29.60078	29.64886	29.69701	29.74524
26	30.78244	30.83446	30.88657	30.93878	30.99106	31.04344	31.09591	31.14846
27	32.17248	32.22898	32.28558	32.34228	32.39908	32.45598	32.51298	32.57008
28	33.57958	33.64077	33.70208	33.76351	33.82505	33.88670	33.94846	34.01034
29	35.00395	35.07007	35.13632	35.20270	35.26920	35.33584	35.40260	35.46949
30	36.44580	36.51707	36.58850	36.66006	36.73178	36.80363	36.87563	36.94778
31	37.90534	37.98201	38.05885	38.13585	38.21300	38.29033	38.36781	38.44546
32	39.38279	39.46511	39.54760	39.63027	39.71312	39.79616	39.87937	39.96277
33	40.87838	40.96658	41.05498	41.14358	41.23238	41.32138	41.41058	41.49999
34	42.39232	42.48666	42.58122	42.67600	42.77100	42.86623	42.96169	43.05737
35	43.92484	44.02558	44.12656	44.22778	44.32926	44.43098	44.53295	44.63517
36	45.47617	45.58357	45.69123	45.79917	45.90738	46.01587	46.12463	46.23366
37	47.04654	47.16086	47.27549	47.39041	47.50564	47.62116	47.73699	47.85312
38	48.63618	48.75771	48.87957	49.00176	49.12427	49.24712	49.37030	49.49381
39	50.24532	50.37434	50.50372	50.63346	50.76355	50.89402	51.02484	51.15603
40	51.87422	52.01101	52.14819	52.28577	52.42374	52.56211	52.70088	52.84004
41	53.52310	53.66796	53.81325	53.95896	54.10511	54.25168	54.39869	54.54614
42	55.19222	55.34545	55.49913	55.65329	55.80791	55.96301	56.11857	56.27461
43	56.88183	57.04372	57.20612	57.36902	57.53244	57.69636	57.86080	58.02575
44	58.59217	58.76304	58.93446	59.10643	59.27895	59.45203	59.62567	59.79986
45	60.32350	60.50366	60.68443	60.86579	61.04775	61.23031	61.41347	61.59723
46	62.07607	62.26586	62.45630	62.64737	62.83910	63.03147	63.22450	63.41818
47	63.85016	64.04990	64.25034	64.45147	64.65330	64.85583	65.05907	65.26301
48	65.64601	65.85604	66.06682	66.27835	66.49064	66.70367	66.91747	67.13203
50	69.30411	69.53576	69.76827	70.00166	70.23591	70.47104	70.70704	70.94393
52	73.05255	73.30725	73.56294	73.81963	74.07733	74.33603	74.59574	74.85647
54	76.89356	77.17279	77.45316	77.73468	78.01735	78.30118	78.58616	78.87231
56	80.82942	81.13474	81.44136	81.74928	82.05852	82.36908	82.68096	82.99417
58	84.86247	85.19549	85.52998	85.86596	86.20343	86.54240	86.88287	87.22486
60	88.99513	89.35571	89.72157	90.08731	90.45474	90.82387	91.19470	91.56724
62	93.22983	93.62333	94.01872	94.41600	94.81519	95.21629	95.61931	96.02427
64	97.56912	97.99554	98.42408	98.85475	99.28756	99.72253	100.15966	100.59897
66	102.01556	102.47678	102.94038	103.40637	103.87475	104.34555	104.81878	105.29444
68	106.57181	107.06979	107.57041	108.07371	108.57969	109.08837	109.59977	110.11389
70	111.24058	111.77733	112.31705	112.85974	113.40542	113.95410	114.50582	115.06058
72	116.02464	116.60228	117.18321	117.76745	118.35501	118.94592	119.54020	120.13786
74	120.92685	121.54756	122.17192	122.79995	123.43167	124.06711	124.70627	125.34920
76	125.95011	126.61617	127.28626	127.96042	128.63865	129.32100	130.00748	130.69812
78	131.09743	131.81119	132.52940	133.25209	133.97930	134.71104	135.44735	136.18826
80	136.37185	137.13576	137.90457	138.67832	139.45704	140.24076	141.02952	141.82334
82	141.77653	142.59312	143.41511	144.24252	145.07540	145.91378	146.75770	147.60721
84	147.31468	148.18659	149.06441	149.94819	150.83798	151.73381	152.63573	153.54377
86	152.98960	153.91955	154.85598	155.79895	156.74849	157.70466	158.66751	159.63707
88	158.80466	159.79548	160.79340	161.79847	162.81073	163.83025	164.85706	165.89124
90	164.76332	165.81796	166.88035	167.95054	169.02859	170.11457	171.20853	172.31053
92	170.86913	171.99063	173.12057	174.25903	175.40607	176.56174	177.72613	178.89930
96	183.53682	184.80163	186.07643	187.36131	188.65636	189.96165	191.27726	192.60329
100	196.83790	198.25958	199.69304	201.13836	202.59566	204.06504	205.54660	207.04045
104	210.80403	212.39716	214.00409	215.62493	217.25982	218.90887	220.57222	222.24999
108	225.46847	227.24869	229.04500	230.85756	232.68650	234.53199	236.39419	238.27325
112	240.86613	242.85022	244.85301	246.87466	248.91538	250.97533	253.05473	255.15374
116	257.03368	259.23963	261.46722	263.71665	265.98815	268.28195	270.59827	272.93735
120	274.00960	276.45671	278.92875	281.42600	283.94871	286.49716	289.07163	291.67237
140	372.50242	376.49611	380.53831	384.62965	388.77073	392.96220	397.20468	401.49881
160	498.20698	504.47883	510.83943	517.29009	523.83213	530.46689	537.19574	544.02006

QUARTERLY DEPOSITS

EFFECTIVE ANNUAL YIELD

NUMBER OF QUARTRLY DEPOSITS	5.40%	5.45%	5.50%	5.55%	5.60%	5.65%	5.70%	5.75%
1	1.01323	1.01336	1.01348	1.01360	1.01372	1.01384	1.01396	1.01408
2	2.03988	2.04024	2.04061	2.04097	2.04133	2.04170	2.04206	2.04242
3	3.08011	3.08085	3.08158	3.08231	3.08305	3.08378	3.08451	3.08525
4	4.13411	4.13535	4.13658	4.13781	4.13905	4.14028	4.14151	4.14275
5	5.20206	5.20393	5.20580	5.20766	5.20953	5.21140	5.21326	5.21513
6	6.28415	6.28678	6.28942	6.29206	6.29470	6.29733	6.29997	6.30261
7	7.38055	7.38410	7.38765	7.39119	7.39474	7.39829	7.40184	7.40539
8	8.49147	8.49607	8.50067	8.50528	8.50988	8.51449	8.51909	8.52370
9	9.61709	9.62289	9.62869	9.63450	9.64031	9.64612	9.65193	9.65775
10	10.75760	10.76476	10.77192	10.77908	10.78624	10.79341	10.80058	10.80775
11	11.91321	11.92188	11.93055	11.93922	11.94790	11.95658	11.96526	11.97395
12	13.08412	13.09445	13.10479	13.11513	13.12548	13.13583	13.14619	13.15656
13	14.27052	14.28268	14.29485	14.30703	14.31921	14.33141	14.34360	14.35581
14	15.47263	15.48678	15.50095	15.51513	15.52932	15.54352	15.55773	15.57194
15	16.69064	16.70697	16.72331	16.73966	16.75602	16.77240	16.78879	16.80520
16	17.92477	17.94344	17.96213	17.98083	17.99955	18.01829	18.03704	18.05580
17	19.17524	19.19644	19.21765	19.23888	19.26014	19.28141	19.30270	19.32402
18	20.44226	20.46616	20.49009	20.51404	20.53801	20.56201	20.58603	20.61008
19	21.72605	21.75284	21.77967	21.80652	21.83341	21.86032	21.88727	21.91424
20	23.02682	23.05671	23.08663	23.11658	23.14657	23.17660	23.20666	23.23676
21	24.34482	24.37799	24.41120	24.44445	24.47775	24.51109	24.54447	24.57789
22	25.68025	25.71691	25.75362	25.79038	25.82718	25.86404	25.90095	25.93790
23	27.03337	27.07372	27.11413	27.15460	27.19513	27.23571	27.27635	27.31705
24	28.40439	28.44865	28.49297	28.53737	28.58183	28.62636	28.67095	28.71562
25	29.79355	29.84193	29.89040	29.93893	29.98755	30.03624	30.08502	30.13387
26	31.20110	31.25383	31.30665	31.35956	31.41255	31.46564	31.51881	31.57208
27	32.62728	32.68458	32.74199	32.79949	32.85710	32.91481	32.97262	33.03053
28	34.07233	34.13444	34.19667	34.25900	34.32146	34.38403	34.44671	34.50951
29	35.53651	35.60367	35.67095	35.73836	35.80590	35.87357	35.94138	36.00931
30	37.02007	37.09251	37.16509	37.23783	37.31070	37.38373	37.45690	37.53022
31	38.52327	38.60124	38.67938	38.75768	38.83614	38.91477	38.99357	39.07253
32	40.04635	40.13012	40.21406	40.29819	40.38251	40.46700	40.55169	40.63655
33	41.58960	41.67941	41.76943	41.85965	41.95008	42.04071	42.13155	42.22259
34	43.15327	43.24940	43.34575	43.44234	43.53915	43.63619	43.73345	43.83095
35	44.73763	44.84035	44.94332	45.04654	45.15001	45.25374	45.35772	45.46195
36	46.34297	46.45255	46.56242	46.67256	46.78297	46.89365	47.00464	47.11590
37	47.96955	48.08629	48.20333	48.32067	48.43833	48.55629	48.67456	48.79313
38	49.61766	49.74184	49.86635	49.99120	50.11639	50.24191	50.36777	50.49397
39	51.28758	51.41950	51.55178	51.68444	51.81746	51.95085	52.08462	52.21875
40	52.97960	53.11956	53.25993	53.40070	53.54187	53.68344	53.82542	53.96781
41	54.69402	54.84234	54.99109	55.14029	55.28992	55.44000	55.59052	55.74148
42	56.43112	56.58811	56.74558	56.90353	57.06195	57.22086	57.38025	57.54012
43	58.19122	58.35721	58.52371	58.69074	58.85829	59.02636	59.19495	59.36408
44	59.97461	60.14993	60.32580	60.50225	60.67926	60.85684	61.03498	61.21371
45	61.78161	61.96659	62.15218	62.33838	62.52520	62.71264	62.90069	63.08937
46	63.61252	63.80751	64.00317	64.19948	64.39647	64.59412	64.79244	64.99143
47	65.46766	65.67302	65.87910	66.08589	66.29340	66.50163	66.71058	66.92026
48	67.34735	67.56344	67.78030	67.99794	68.21634	68.43553	68.65549	68.87624
50	71.18171	71.42037	71.65992	71.90037	72.14172	72.38396	72.62712	72.87118
52	75.11822	75.38100	75.64480	75.90963	76.17550	76.44241	76.71037	76.97937
54	79.15963	79.44812	79.73780	80.02865	80.32070	80.61394	80.90838	81.20402
56	83.30872	83.62461	83.94184	84.26043	84.58038	84.90169	85.22437	85.54843
58	87.56836	87.91339	88.25996	88.60806	88.95770	89.30890	89.66167	90.01599
60	91.94150	92.31750	92.69523	93.07470	93.45593	93.83891	94.22367	94.61021
62	96.43117	96.84002	97.25083	97.66362	98.07838	98.49514	98.91389	99.33466
64	101.04046	101.48415	101.93004	102.37816	102.82850	103.28109	103.73593	104.19304
66	105.77296	106.25315	106.73621	107.22176	107.70982	108.20039	108.69350	109.18915
68	110.63076	111.15038	111.67277	112.19796	112.72595	113.25675	113.79039	114.32688
70	115.61839	116.17929	116.74328	117.31038	117.88061	118.45399	119.03054	119.61027
72	120.73893	121.34342	121.95136	122.56276	123.17765	123.79604	124.41796	125.04343
74	125.99590	126.64641	127.30074	127.95892	128.62097	129.28692	129.95679	130.63060
76	131.39294	132.09198	132.79526	133.50281	134.21464	134.93080	135.65130	136.37617
78	136.93379	137.68398	138.43886	139.19845	139.96280	140.73192	141.50584	142.28461
80	142.62227	143.42634	144.23558	145.05002	145.86971	146.69466	147.52493	148.36054
82	148.46233	149.32311	150.18958	151.06178	151.93976	152.82355	153.71319	154.60872
84	154.45799	155.37842	156.30512	157.23811	158.17746	159.12319	160.07537	161.03402
86	160.61341	161.59656	162.58658	163.58352	164.58743	165.59836	166.61635	167.64147
88	166.93283	167.98189	169.03848	170.10264	171.17444	172.25393	173.34117	174.43622
90	173.42064	174.53892	175.66543	176.80022	177.94337	179.09495	180.25500	181.42360
92	180.08132	181.27225	182.47217	183.68115	184.89926	186.12656	187.36313	188.60905
96	193.93982	195.28694	196.64472	198.01327	199.39266	200.78299	202.18435	203.59682
100	208.54669	210.06542	211.59676	213.14082	214.69770	216.26751	217.85037	219.44638
104	223.94422	225.64033	227.37117	229.10795	230.85981	232.62690	234.40935	236.20729
108	240.16932	242.08257	244.01316	245.96125	247.92701	249.91060	251.91219	253.93196
112	257.27257	259.41142	261.57046	263.74991	265.94997	268.17083	270.41270	272.67579
116	275.29941	277.68468	280.09342	282.52585	284.98221	287.46276	289.96774	292.49739
120	294.29969	296.95585	299.63514	302.34385	305.08027	307.84469	310.63741	313.45874
140	405.84527	410.24470	414.69777	419.20516	423.76757	428.38568	433.06021	437.79186
160	550.94126	557.96077	565.08003	572.30050	579.62369	587.05110	594.58427	602.22475

81

QUARTERLY DEPOSITS

NUMBER OF QUARTRLY DEPOSITS	EFFECTIVE ANNUAL YIELD							
	5.80%	5.85%	5.90%	5.95%	6.00%	6.05%	6.10%	6.15%
1	1.01419	1.01431	1.01443	1.01455	1.01467	1.01479	1.01491	1.01503
2	2.04279	2.04315	2.04351	2.04387	2.04424	2.04460	2.04496	2.04532
3	3.08598	3.08671	3.08744	3.08818	3.08891	3.08964	3.09037	3.09110
4	4.14398	4.14521	4.14644	4.14768	4.14891	4.15014	4.15137	4.15260
5	5.21700	5.21886	5.22073	5.22260	5.22446	5.22633	5.22819	5.23006
6	6.30525	6.30788	6.31052	6.31316	6.31580	6.31844	6.32108	6.32371
7	7.40894	7.41249	7.41605	7.41960	7.42315	7.42670	7.43026	7.43381
8	8.52831	8.53292	8.53753	8.54214	8.54675	8.55136	8.55598	8.56059
9	9.66356	9.66938	9.67520	9.68102	9.68684	9.69266	9.69849	9.70431
10	10.81493	10.82211	10.82929	10.83647	10.84365	10.85084	10.85803	10.86523
11	11.98264	11.99134	12.00004	12.00874	12.01745	12.02616	12.03487	12.04359
12	13.16693	13.17730	13.18768	13.19807	13.20846	13.21886	13.22926	13.23967
13	14.36802	14.38025	14.39248	14.40471	14.41695	14.42921	14.44146	14.45373
14	15.58617	15.60041	15.61466	15.62891	15.64318	15.65746	15.67174	15.68604
15	16.82161	16.83804	16.85448	16.87093	16.88740	16.90388	16.92037	16.93688
16	18.07459	18.09339	18.11220	18.13103	18.14988	18.16874	18.18762	18.20651
17	19.34535	19.36670	19.38807	19.40947	19.43088	19.45231	19.47376	19.49524
18	20.63415	20.65824	20.68236	20.70651	20.73068	20.75487	20.77909	20.80333
19	21.94124	21.96828	21.99534	22.02243	22.04955	22.07670	22.10388	22.13110
20	23.26689	23.29706	23.32726	23.35750	23.38778	23.41809	23.44843	23.47882
21	24.61136	24.64486	24.67841	24.71201	24.74564	24.77932	24.81304	24.84680
22	25.97491	26.01196	26.04907	26.08622	26.12343	26.16068	26.19799	26.23534
23	27.35781	27.39863	27.43951	27.48044	27.52143	27.56248	27.60359	27.64476
24	28.76035	28.80515	28.85001	28.89495	28.93995	28.98502	29.03016	29.07537
25	30.18279	30.23180	30.28088	30.33005	30.37929	30.42860	30.47800	30.52748
26	31.62543	31.67887	31.73241	31.78603	31.83974	31.89354	31.94744	32.00142
27	33.08854	33.14666	33.20488	33.26320	33.32163	33.38015	33.43878	33.49752
28	34.57243	34.63546	34.69861	34.76187	34.82526	34.88876	34.95237	35.01611
29	36.07737	36.14557	36.21390	36.28236	36.35095	36.41967	36.48853	36.55752
30	37.60368	37.67730	37.75106	37.82497	37.89903	37.97324	38.04760	38.12211
31	39.15166	39.23095	39.31041	39.39004	39.46983	39.54979	39.62992	39.71022
32	40.72161	40.80684	40.89227	40.97788	41.06368	41.14966	41.23584	41.32220
33	42.31384	42.40530	42.49696	42.58883	42.68092	42.77320	42.86570	42.95841
34	43.92867	44.02663	44.12482	44.22323	44.32188	44.42076	44.51988	44.61922
35	45.56643	45.67117	45.77617	45.88142	45.98693	46.09269	46.19872	46.30500
36	47.22744	47.33926	47.45136	47.56374	47.67641	47.78936	47.90260	48.01612
37	48.91202	49.03122	49.15073	49.27055	49.39068	49.51112	49.63188	49.75296
38	50.62052	50.74740	50.87462	51.00219	51.13010	51.25836	51.38696	51.51591
39	52.35326	52.48815	52.62341	52.75904	52.89505	53.03144	53.16821	53.30536
40	54.11061	54.25381	54.39743	54.54146	54.68590	54.83075	54.97602	55.12171
41	55.89290	56.04475	56.19706	56.34982	56.50303	56.65669	56.81080	56.96537
42	57.70048	57.86133	58.02267	58.18450	58.34682	58.50963	58.67294	58.83674
43	59.53373	59.70391	59.87463	60.04588	60.21766	60.38998	60.56284	60.73624
44	61.39300	61.57287	61.75332	61.93435	62.11596	62.29815	62.48093	62.66430
45	63.27866	63.46858	63.65913	63.85031	64.04211	64.23455	64.42763	64.62134
46	65.19109	65.39143	65.59245	65.79415	65.99653	66.19960	66.40336	66.60780
47	67.13067	67.34180	67.55368	67.76628	67.97963	68.19372	68.40855	68.62412
48	69.09777	69.32010	69.54321	69.76712	69.99183	70.21733	70.44364	70.67076
50	73.11615	73.36204	73.60885	73.85658	74.10523	74.35482	74.60533	74.85678
52	77.24942	77.52053	77.79270	78.06594	78.34024	78.61562	78.89208	79.16961
54	81.50087	81.79893	82.09821	82.39872	82.70045	83.00342	83.30763	83.61308
56	85.87387	86.20069	86.52892	86.85854	87.18957	87.52201	87.85586	88.19115
58	90.37190	90.72938	91.08845	91.44912	91.81139	92.17527	92.54077	92.90789
60	94.99853	95.38865	95.78056	96.17430	96.56985	96.96723	97.36644	97.76750
62	99.75744	100.18226	100.60911	101.03802	101.46898	101.90201	102.33712	102.77433
64	104.65242	105.11409	105.57806	106.04434	106.51294	106.98388	107.45717	107.93281
66	109.68735	110.18813	110.69149	111.19745	111.70603	112.21722	112.73106	113.24755
68	114.86624	115.40848	115.95361	116.50166	117.05263	117.60655	118.16343	118.72328
70	120.19320	120.77935	121.36873	121.96138	122.55729	123.15650	123.75903	124.36488
72	125.67246	126.30508	126.94132	127.58118	128.22469	128.87188	129.52277	130.17736
74	131.30838	131.99015	132.67593	133.36575	134.05964	134.75761	135.45970	136.16592
76	137.10544	137.83914	138.57730	139.31993	140.06708	140.81877	141.57503	142.33588
78	143.06825	143.85678	144.65026	145.44869	146.25213	147.06059	147.87411	148.69273
80	149.20154	150.04794	150.89980	151.75715	152.62002	153.48845	154.36247	155.24213
82	155.51018	156.41762	157.33106	158.25057	159.17616	160.10789	161.04580	161.98993
84	161.99920	162.97096	163.94933	164.93437	165.92612	166.92464	167.92996	168.94213
86	168.67375	169.71326	170.76004	171.81415	172.87564	173.94456	175.02097	176.10492
88	175.53913	176.64997	177.76879	178.89564	180.03060	181.17372	182.32505	183.48467
90	182.60081	183.78669	184.98133	186.18477	187.39708	188.61834	189.84862	191.08797
92	189.86438	191.12920	192.40359	193.68761	194.98134	196.28487	197.59825	198.92158
96	205.02049	206.45547	207.90184	209.35970	210.82913	212.31024	213.80312	215.30786
100	221.05566	222.67833	224.31449	225.96427	227.62779	229.30515	230.99648	232.70190
104	238.02087	239.85022	241.69549	243.55682	245.43436	247.32825	249.23864	251.16557
108	255.97006	258.02667	260.10197	262.19613	264.30933	266.44175	268.59357	270.76496
112	274.96030	277.26644	279.59443	281.94448	284.31680	286.71161	289.12914	291.56961
116	295.05197	297.63174	300.23694	302.86785	305.52471	308.20781	310.91739	313.65374
120	316.30897	319.18841	322.09737	325.03616	328.00510	331.00452	334.03473	337.09605
140	442.58135	447.42943	452.33683	457.30430	462.33260	467.42250	472.57479	477.79024
160	609.97413	617.83402	625.80603	633.89183	642.09308	650.41150	658.84881	667.40676

QUARTERLY DEPOSITS

EFFECTIVE ANNUAL YIELD

NUMBER OF QUARTRLY DEPOSITS	6.20%	6.25%	6.30%	6.35%	6.40%	6.45%	6.50%	6.55%
1	1.01515	1.01527	1.01539	1.01551	1.01563	1.01575	1.01587	1.01599
2	2.04569	2.04605	2.04641	2.04677	2.04713	2.04750	2.04786	2.04822
3	3.09183	3.09257	3.09330	3.09403	3.09476	3.09549	3.09622	3.09695
4	4.15383	4.15507	4.15630	4.15753	4.15876	4.15999	4.16122	4.16245
5	5.23193	5.23379	5.23566	5.23752	5.23939	5.24126	5.24312	5.24499
6	6.32635	6.32899	6.33163	6.33427	6.33691	6.33955	6.34219	6.34483
7	7.43736	7.44092	7.44447	7.44803	7.45158	7.45514	7.45870	7.46225
8	8.56521	8.56982	8.57444	8.57906	8.58368	8.58830	8.59292	8.59754
9	9.71014	9.71597	9.72180	9.72763	9.73347	9.73931	9.74514	9.75098
10	10.87242	10.87962	10.88682	10.89402	10.90123	10.90844	10.91565	10.92287
11	12.05231	12.06104	12.06977	12.07851	12.08724	12.09599	12.10473	12.11348
12	13.25008	13.26050	13.27093	13.28136	13.29179	13.30224	13.31268	13.32313
13	14.46600	14.47828	14.49057	14.50287	14.51517	14.52748	14.53980	14.55213
14	15.70035	15.71466	15.72899	15.74332	15.75767	15.77202	15.78639	15.80076
15	16.95339	16.96992	16.98646	17.00302	17.01959	17.03617	17.05276	17.06937
16	18.22542	18.24435	18.26329	18.28225	18.30123	18.32022	18.33923	18.35825
17	19.51673	19.53824	19.55978	19.58133	19.60290	19.62449	19.64611	19.66774
18	20.82760	20.85189	20.87621	20.90055	20.92492	20.94931	20.97373	20.99817
19	22.15834	22.18561	22.21291	22.24024	22.26760	22.29499	22.32241	22.34986
20	23.50924	23.53969	23.57018	23.60070	23.63127	23.66186	23.69250	23.72317
21	24.88060	24.91445	24.94834	24.98227	25.01625	25.05026	25.08433	25.11843
22	26.27275	26.31020	26.34771	26.38527	26.42287	26.46053	26.49824	26.53600
23	27.68599	27.72727	27.76862	27.81002	27.85149	27.89301	27.93459	27.97623
24	29.12064	29.16599	29.21140	29.25688	29.30243	29.34804	29.39373	29.43949
25	30.57703	30.62667	30.67638	30.72617	30.77605	30.82600	30.87603	30.92614
26	32.05549	32.10966	32.16391	32.21826	32.27270	32.32723	32.38185	32.43656
27	33.55535	33.61530	33.67434	33.73349	33.79274	33.85210	33.91156	33.97112
28	35.07996	35.14393	35.20801	35.27222	35.33654	35.40098	35.46554	35.53022
29	36.62664	36.69590	36.76529	36.83481	36.90447	36.97426	37.04419	37.11425
30	38.19677	38.27158	38.34654	38.42165	38.49691	38.57232	38.64789	38.72360
31	39.79068	39.87132	39.95212	40.03309	40.11424	40.19555	40.27703	40.35868
32	41.40875	41.49549	41.58241	41.66953	41.75684	41.84434	41.93203	42.01991
33	43.05133	43.14446	43.23780	43.33135	43.42512	43.51909	43.61328	43.70769
34	44.71880	44.81862	44.91867	45.01895	45.11947	45.22023	45.32122	45.42245
35	46.41154	46.51834	46.62540	46.73272	46.84031	46.94815	47.05626	47.16463
36	48.12993	48.24402	48.35840	48.47308	48.58804	48.70329	48.81883	48.93466
37	49.87435	49.99606	50.11808	50.24042	50.36308	50.48607	50.60937	50.73299
38	51.64520	51.77485	51.90484	52.03518	52.16588	52.29692	52.42832	52.56007
39	53.44289	53.58080	53.71910	53.85778	53.99684	54.13630	54.27614	54.41636
40	55.26782	55.41434	55.56128	55.70864	55.85643	56.00464	56.15327	56.30233
41	57.12039	57.27588	57.43182	57.58822	57.74508	57.90241	58.06020	58.21845
42	59.00104	59.16584	59.33114	59.49694	59.66325	59.83006	59.99738	60.16521
43	60.91018	61.08467	61.25970	61.43528	61.61140	61.78808	61.96531	62.14309
44	62.84825	63.03280	63.21794	63.40367	63.59000	63.77693	63.96446	64.15259
45	64.81569	65.01068	65.20632	65.40260	65.59953	65.79710	65.99533	66.19421
46	66.81294	67.01877	67.22530	67.43253	67.64046	67.84909	68.05843	68.26848
47	68.84045	69.05753	69.27536	69.49394	69.71329	69.93340	70.15427	70.37591
48	70.89868	71.12742	71.35697	71.58733	71.81852	72.05053	72.28337	72.51703
50	75.10918	75.36251	75.61679	75.87202	76.12821	76.38535	76.64345	76.90252
52	79.44823	79.72795	80.00875	80.29066	80.57367	80.85778	81.14301	81.42935
54	83.91978	84.22773	84.53695	84.84742	85.15917	85.47219	85.78650	86.10208
56	88.52786	88.86601	89.20560	89.54664	89.88914	90.23310	90.57852	90.92542
58	93.27664	93.64703	94.01907	94.39276	94.76812	95.14514	95.52384	95.90422
60	98.17042	98.57520	98.98185	99.39038	99.80080	100.21312	100.62735	101.04349
62	103.21363	103.65504	104.09857	104.54423	104.99204	105.44199	105.89411	106.34840
64	108.41082	108.89122	109.37401	109.85920	110.34681	110.83686	111.32935	111.82429
66	113.76671	114.28854	114.81308	115.34032	115.87029	116.40299	116.93845	117.47667
68	119.28613	119.85198	120.42086	120.99279	121.56777	122.14583	122.72698	123.31123
70	124.97408	125.58664	126.20260	126.82196	127.44475	128.07097	128.70067	129.33385
72	130.83570	131.49780	132.16368	132.83336	133.50687	134.18422	134.86545	135.55057
74	136.87630	137.59088	138.30966	139.03268	139.75997	140.49154	141.22743	141.96766
76	143.10135	143.87148	144.64629	145.42581	146.21007	146.99910	147.79293	148.59158
78	149.51647	150.34537	151.17947	152.01879	152.86337	153.71324	154.56844	155.42900
80	156.12747	157.01851	157.91530	158.81787	159.72627	160.64053	161.56069	162.48678
82	162.94033	163.89702	164.86007	165.82951	166.80538	167.78773	168.77661	169.77205
84	169.96121	170.98723	172.02026	173.06034	174.10751	175.16183	176.22335	177.29212
86	177.19646	178.29565	179.40255	180.51721	181.63968	182.77003	183.90831	185.05457
88	184.65263	185.82900	187.01383	188.20720	189.40915	190.61976	191.83909	193.06721
90	192.33648	193.59420	194.86121	196.13758	197.42338	198.71869	200.02357	201.33809
92	200.25493	201.59838	202.95200	204.31588	205.69009	207.07472	208.46985	209.87556
96	216.82457	218.35334	219.89428	221.44747	223.01302	224.59103	226.18161	227.78486
100	234.42153	236.15549	237.90391	239.66691	241.44461	243.23715	245.04464	246.86722
104	253.10950	255.07028	257.04816	259.04329	261.05583	263.08593	265.13376	267.19947
108	272.95612	275.16724	277.39849	279.65006	281.92216	284.21497	286.52868	288.86349
112	294.03324	296.52026	299.03089	301.56537	304.12394	306.70682	309.31426	311.94650
116	316.41713	319.20784	322.02613	324.87230	327.74663	330.64940	333.58091	336.54145
120	340.18883	343.31339	346.47008	349.65922	352.88117	356.13628	359.42489	362.74737
140	483.06967	488.41388	493.82370	499.29994	504.84346	510.45511	516.13575	521.88625
160	676.08713	684.89172	693.82238	702.88096	712.06934	721.38944	730.84320	740.43260

QUARTERLY DEPOSITS

EFFECTIVE ANNUAL YIELD

NUMBER OF QUARTRLY DEPOSITS	6.60%	6.65%	6.70%	6.75%	6.80%	6.85%	6.90%	6.95%
1	1.01611	1.01623	1.01634	1.01646	1.01658	1.01670	1.01682	1.01694
2	2.04858	2.04894	2.04930	2.04966	2.05002	2.05038	2.05075	2.05111
3	3.09768	3.09841	3.09914	3.09987	3.10060	3.10133	3.10206	3.10279
4	4.16368	4.16491	4.16614	4.16737	4.16860	4.16983	4.17106	4.17229
5	5.24665	5.24872	5.25058	5.25245	5.25431	5.25618	5.25804	5.25991
6	6.34747	6.35011	6.35275	6.35539	6.35803	6.36067	6.36331	6.36595
7	7.46581	7.46937	7.47293	7.47649	7.48005	7.48360	7.48717	7.49073
8	8.60217	8.60679	8.61142	8.61604	8.62067	8.62530	8.62993	8.63456
9	9.75683	9.76267	9.76851	9.77436	9.78021	9.78606	9.79191	9.79776
10	10.93008	10.93730	10.94452	10.95175	10.95898	10.96621	10.97344	10.98067
11	12.12224	12.13099	12.13976	12.14852	12.15729	12.16606	12.17484	12.18362
12	13.33359	13.34405	13.35452	13.36500	13.37548	13.38596	13.39645	13.40695
13	14.56446	14.57680	14.58915	14.60150	14.61386	14.62623	14.63861	14.65100
14	15.81515	15.82954	15.84395	15.85836	15.87279	15.88722	15.90167	15.91612
15	17.08599	17.10262	17.11926	17.13592	17.15259	17.16927	17.18597	17.20267
16	18.37729	18.39635	18.41542	18.43451	18.45361	18.47273	18.49187	18.51102
17	19.68939	19.71107	19.73276	19.75448	19.77621	19.79796	19.81974	19.84153
18	21.02263	21.04712	21.07164	21.09618	21.12074	21.14533	21.16994	21.19458
19	22.37734	22.40485	22.43239	22.45997	22.48757	22.51520	22.54286	22.57055
20	23.75387	23.78462	23.81539	23.84621	23.87706	23.90795	23.93887	23.96983
21	25.15258	25.18677	25.22100	25.25527	25.28959	25.32396	25.35836	25.39281
22	26.57381	26.61167	26.64958	26.68754	26.72555	26.76362	26.80173	26.83990
23	28.01793	28.05969	28.10151	28.14339	28.18532	28.22732	28.26938	28.31150
24	29.48531	29.53120	29.57717	29.62320	29.66930	29.71547	29.76171	29.80802
25	30.97633	31.02660	31.07695	31.12738	31.17789	31.22848	31.27915	31.32990
26	32.49136	32.54625	32.60124	32.65632	32.71149	32.76676	32.82211	32.87756
27	34.03079	34.09057	34.15045	34.21044	34.27053	34.33072	34.39103	34.45143
28	35.59502	35.65994	35.72498	35.79014	35.85542	35.92081	35.98633	36.05197
29	37.18445	37.25478	37.32525	37.39585	37.46659	37.53746	37.60847	37.67962
30	38.79947	38.87549	38.95167	39.02799	39.10448	39.18111	39.25790	39.33484
31	40.44051	40.52250	40.60467	40.68701	40.76953	40.85221	40.93507	41.01810
32	42.10798	42.19624	42.28470	42.37334	42.46219	42.55122	42.64045	42.72987
33	43.80230	43.89713	43.99218	44.08744	44.18292	44.27861	44.37452	44.47064
34	45.52392	45.62563	45.72757	45.82976	45.93218	46.03485	46.13775	46.24090
35	47.27326	47.38216	47.49133	47.60076	47.71045	47.82042	47.93065	48.04115
36	49.05079	49.16720	49.28391	49.40092	49.51822	49.63581	49.75370	49.87189
37	50.85694	50.98121	51.10580	51.23071	51.35596	51.48153	51.60742	51.73364
38	52.69218	52.82644	52.95746	53.09064	53.22417	53.35807	53.49232	53.62694
39	54.55698	54.69799	54.83939	54.98118	55.12337	55.26595	55.40893	55.55230
40	56.45182	56.60173	56.75208	56.90285	57.05406	57.20570	57.35777	57.51028
41	58.37718	58.53637	58.69603	58.85616	59.01676	59.17784	59.33939	59.50142
42	60.33354	60.50239	60.67175	60.84163	61.01202	61.18293	61.35435	61.52630
43	62.32142	62.50032	62.67977	62.85978	63.04036	63.22150	63.40320	63.58548
44	64.34132	64.53066	64.72061	64.91117	65.10234	65.29412	65.48652	65.67953
45	66.39375	66.59479	66.79480	66.99632	67.19851	67.40136	67.60487	67.80906
46	68.47924	68.69071	68.90290	69.11581	69.32944	69.54379	69.75886	69.97467
47	70.59832	70.82150	71.04546	71.27019	71.49571	71.72200	71.94909	72.17696
48	72.75153	72.98686	73.22303	73.46004	73.69790	73.93660	74.17615	74.41655
50	77.16255	77.42356	77.68554	77.94850	78.21244	78.47737	78.74329	79.01020
52	81.71681	82.00540	82.29512	82.58597	82.87796	83.17109	83.46536	83.76079
54	86.41896	86.73714	87.05661	87.37740	87.69949	88.02290	88.34764	88.67370
56	91.27380	91.62367	91.97503	92.32789	92.68226	93.03814	93.39554	93.75446
58	96.28630	96.67007	97.05555	97.44274	97.83166	98.22230	98.61468	99.00881
60	101.46156	101.88156	102.30350	102.72740	103.15325	103.58108	104.01089	104.44268
62	106.80487	107.26354	107.72441	108.18750	108.65281	109.12036	109.59016	110.06221
64	112.32170	112.82159	113.32398	113.82887	114.33628	114.84622	115.35870	115.87374
66	118.01768	118.56148	119.10809	119.65753	120.20980	120.76494	121.32294	121.88383
68	123.89862	124.48914	125.08283	125.67969	126.27975	126.88302	127.48951	128.09926
70	129.97053	130.61073	131.25447	131.90178	132.55267	133.20717	133.86528	134.52705
72	136.23961	136.93258	137.62952	138.33044	139.03537	139.74433	140.45735	141.17445
74	142.71226	143.46125	144.21467	144.97253	145.73486	146.50169	147.27305	148.04897
76	149.39510	150.20351	151.01684	151.83512	152.65838	153.48665	154.31997	155.15836
78	156.29495	157.16634	158.04319	158.92559	159.81343	160.70689	161.60595	162.51066
80	163.41886	164.33696	165.30111	166.25136	167.20775	168.17032	169.13911	170.11416
82	170.77410	171.78281	172.79823	173.82039	174.84935	175.88514	176.92782	177.97744
84	178.36819	179.45161	180.54243	181.64070	182.74648	183.85982	184.98077	186.10938
86	186.20888	187.37128	188.54185	189.72064	190.90770	192.10311	193.30691	194.51916
88	194.30417	195.55005	196.80491	198.06882	199.34184	200.62405	201.91550	203.21628
90	202.66234	203.99639	205.34030	206.69415	208.05803	209.43200	210.81614	212.21054
92	211.29193	212.71904	214.15698	215.60584	217.06569	218.53663	220.01873	221.51210
96	229.40088	231.02977	232.67164	234.32660	235.99476	237.67622	239.37109	241.07948
100	248.70502	250.55816	252.42679	254.31102	256.21101	258.12687	260.05876	262.00679
104	269.28323	271.38519	273.50552	275.64439	277.80196	279.97839	282.17387	284.38856
108	291.21960	293.59722	295.99653	298.41776	300.86109	303.32675	305.81493	308.32585
112	314.60378	317.28635	319.99445	322.72833	325.48825	328.27446	331.08722	333.92679
116	339.53131	342.55080	345.60022	348.67986	351.79005	354.93109	358.10330	361.30699
120	366.10406	369.49534	372.92157	376.38313	379.88038	383.41370	386.98349	390.59012
140	527.70749	533.60039	539.56583	545.60474	551.71806	557.90672	564.17169	570.51391
160	750.15964	760.02635	770.03479	780.18706	790.48527	800.93158	811.52818	822.27728

QUARTERLY DEPOSITS

EFFECTIVE ANNUAL YIELD

NUMBER OF QUARTERLY DEPOSITS	7.00%	7.05%	7.10%	7.15%	7.20%	7.25%	7.30%	7.35%
1	1.01706	1.01718	1.01730	1.01741	1.01753	1.01765	1.01777	1.01789
2	2.05147	2.05183	2.05219	2.05255	2.05291	2.05327	2.05363	2.05399
3	3.10352	3.10425	3.10498	3.10571	3.10644	3.10716	3.10789	3.10862
4	4.17352	4.17475	4.17598	4.17721	4.17844	4.17966	4.18089	4.18212
5	5.26177	5.26364	5.26550	5.26737	5.26923	5.27110	5.27296	5.27483
6	6.36859	6.37123	6.37387	6.37651	6.37915	6.38179	6.38444	6.38708
7	7.49429	7.49785	7.50141	7.50497	7.50853	7.51210	7.51566	7.51923
8	8.63919	8.64382	8.64845	8.65308	8.65772	8.66235	8.66699	8.67163
9	9.80362	9.80947	9.81533	9.82119	9.82705	9.83292	9.83878	9.84465
10	10.98791	10.99515	11.00239	11.00964	11.01689	11.02414	11.03139	11.03865
11	12.19241	12.20120	12.20999	12.21878	12.22759	12.23639	12.24520	12.25401
12	13.41745	13.42796	13.43847	13.44899	13.45951	13.47004	13.48057	13.49111
13	14.66339	14.67579	14.68820	14.70061	14.71304	14.72547	14.73790	14.75035
14	15.93058	15.94506	15.95954	15.97404	15.98854	16.00305	16.01758	16.03211
15	17.21940	17.23613	17.25288	17.26964	17.28641	17.30319	17.31999	17.33680
16	18.53019	18.54938	18.56858	18.58780	18.60703	18.62628	18.64555	18.66483
17	19.86335	19.88518	19.90704	19.92891	19.95081	19.97273	19.99466	20.01662
18	21.21925	21.24393	21.26865	21.29339	21.31815	21.34294	21.36775	21.39259
19	22.59827	22.62603	22.65381	22.68162	22.70946	22.73734	22.76524	22.79318
20	24.00082	24.03186	24.06293	24.09403	24.12517	24.15635	24.18757	24.21882
21	25.42730	25.46184	25.49642	25.53104	25.56570	25.60041	25.63517	25.66996
22	26.87811	26.91638	26.95470	26.99307	27.03149	27.06997	27.10849	27.14707
23	28.35367	28.39591	28.43821	28.48056	28.52298	28.56546	28.60800	28.65060
24	29.85440	29.90085	29.94737	29.99396	30.04062	30.08735	30.13415	30.18102
25	31.38073	31.43165	31.48264	31.53371	31.58487	31.63611	31.68743	31.73883
26	32.93310	32.98873	33.04446	33.10028	33.15620	33.21220	33.26830	33.32450
27	34.51195	34.57257	34.63330	34.69413	34.75507	34.81612	34.87727	34.93854
28	36.11773	36.18361	36.24961	36.31574	36.38198	36.44835	36.51484	36.58145
29	37.75090	37.82233	37.89389	37.96558	38.03742	38.10939	38.18150	38.25375
30	39.41194	39.48919	39.56660	39.64416	39.72188	39.79975	39.87778	39.95597
31	41.10131	41.18469	41.26824	41.35197	41.43587	41.51995	41.60421	41.68864
32	42.81949	42.90931	42.99931	43.08952	43.17992	43.27052	43.36131	43.45231
33	44.56699	44.66355	44.76033	44.85733	44.95455	45.05199	45.14964	45.24752
34	46.34429	46.44793	46.55180	46.65592	46.76029	46.86490	46.96975	47.07485
35	48.15192	48.26296	48.37426	48.48584	48.59769	48.70980	48.82221	48.93488
36	49.99038	50.10916	50.22824	50.34763	50.46731	50.58730	50.70758	50.82817
37	51.86020	51.98708	52.11429	52.24183	52.36971	52.49792	52.62646	52.75534
38	53.76191	53.89726	54.03296	54.16903	54.30547	54.44227	54.57944	54.71698
39	55.69607	55.84024	55.98481	56.12979	56.27516	56.42094	56.56712	56.71371
40	57.66322	57.81661	57.97043	58.12469	58.27939	58.43454	58.59013	58.74616
41	59.66393	59.82692	59.99038	60.15433	60.31877	60.48368	60.64908	60.81498
42	61.69877	61.87176	62.04528	62.21932	62.39389	62.56900	62.74463	62.92080
43	63.76832	63.95173	64.13571	64.32027	64.50541	64.69112	64.87741	65.06429
44	65.87317	66.06743	66.26231	66.45781	66.65392	66.85071	67.04810	67.24613
45	68.01393	68.21946	68.42568	68.63257	68.84015	69.04841	69.25736	69.46700
46	70.19120	70.40847	70.62647	70.84521	71.06469	71.28491	71.50588	71.72760
47	72.40562	72.63508	72.86533	73.09638	73.32823	73.56089	73.79436	74.02864
48	74.65781	74.89993	75.14291	75.38675	75.63146	75.87705	76.12350	76.37084
50	79.27811	79.54702	79.81693	80.08785	80.35978	80.63273	80.90670	81.18170
52	84.05738	84.35512	84.65403	84.95411	85.25537	85.55780	85.86141	86.16622
54	89.00109	89.32983	89.65991	89.99134	90.32412	90.65827	90.99379	91.33067
56	94.11491	94.47691	94.84045	95.20554	95.57219	95.94040	96.31019	96.68155
58	99.40469	99.80233	100.20174	100.60293	101.00590	101.41066	101.81722	102.22560
60	104.87648	105.31228	105.75010	106.18994	106.63182	107.07575	107.52173	107.96977
62	110.53654	111.01315	111.49204	111.97324	112.45676	112.94260	113.43077	113.92130
64	116.39135	116.91154	117.43433	117.95973	118.48775	119.01840	119.55170	120.08767
66	122.44762	123.01432	123.58396	124.15654	124.73208	125.31060	125.89211	126.47664
68	128.71227	129.32856	129.94815	130.57106	131.19730	131.82690	132.45987	133.09623
70	135.19247	135.86158	136.53440	137.21094	137.89123	138.57528	139.26313	139.95479
72	141.89565	142.62097	143.35044	144.08409	144.82194	145.56402	146.31034	147.06093
74	148.82946	149.61457	150.40432	151.19873	151.99783	152.80166	153.61023	154.42359
76	156.00186	156.85050	157.70430	158.56331	159.42756	160.29707	161.17188	162.05203
78	163.42105	164.33715	165.25900	166.18664	167.12011	168.05944	169.00467	169.95584
80	171.09551	172.08321	173.07729	174.07780	175.08478	176.09827	177.11832	178.14497
82	179.03404	180.09767	181.16837	182.24619	183.33119	184.42341	185.52291	186.62972
84	187.24572	188.38982	189.54175	190.70157	191.86932	193.04506	194.22885	195.42075
86	195.73994	196.96930	198.20730	199.45400	200.70948	201.97378	203.24697	204.52912
88	204.52644	205.84605	207.17520	208.51394	209.86235	211.22049	212.58845	213.96630
90	213.61526	215.03038	216.45600	217.89217	219.33899	220.79654	222.26489	223.74414
92	223.01681	224.53295	226.06061	227.59989	229.15087	230.71364	232.28830	233.87494
96	242.80150	244.53727	246.28690	248.05049	249.82817	251.62005	253.42624	255.24687
100	263.97113	265.95190	267.94924	269.96331	271.99423	274.04217	276.10725	278.18963
104	286.62263	288.87626	291.14962	293.44289	295.75625	298.08989	300.44397	302.81869
108	310.85973	313.41678	315.99722	318.60126	321.22914	323.88107	326.55727	329.25799
112	336.79343	339.68741	342.60900	345.55846	348.53607	351.54211	354.57685	357.64057
116	364.54249	367.81013	371.11022	374.44310	377.80911	381.20858	384.64185	388.10928
120	394.23399	397.91549	401.63502	405.39299	409.18980	413.02586	416.90160	420.81743
140	576.93439	583.43410	590.01405	596.67526	603.41876	610.24560	617.15681	624.15349
160	833.18115	844.24206	855.46233	866.84432	878.39042	890.10304	901.98466	914.03776

QUARTERLY DEPOSITS

EFFECTIVE ANNUAL YIELD

NUMBER OF QUARTERLY DEPOSITS	7.40%	7.45%	7.50%	7.55%	7.60%	7.65%	7.70%	7.75%
1	1.01801	1.01813	1.01824	1.01836	1.01848	1.01860	1.01872	1.01884
2	2.05435	2.05471	2.05507	2.05543	2.05579	2.05614	2.05650	2.05686
3	3.10935	3.11008	3.11081	3.11153	3.11226	3.11299	3.11372	3.11444
4	4.18335	4.18458	4.18581	4.18703	4.18826	4.18949	4.19072	4.19194
5	5.27669	5.27855	5.28042	5.28228	5.28415	5.28601	5.28787	5.28974
6	6.38972	6.39236	6.39500	6.39764	6.40029	6.40293	6.40557	6.40821
7	7.52279	7.52636	7.52992	7.53349	7.53705	7.54062	7.54419	7.54775
8	8.67627	8.68091	8.68555	8.69019	8.69483	8.69947	8.70412	8.70876
9	9.85051	9.85638	9.86225	9.86813	9.87400	9.87988	9.88576	9.89164
10	11.04591	11.05317	11.06043	11.06770	11.07497	11.08224	11.08951	11.09679
11	12.26283	12.27165	12.28047	12.28930	12.29813	12.30696	12.31580	12.32465
12	13.50166	13.51221	13.52277	13.53333	13.54390	13.55447	13.56505	13.57563
13	14.76280	14.77526	14.78773	14.80020	14.81269	14.82518	14.83767	14.85018
14	16.04665	16.06121	16.07577	16.09034	16.10493	16.11952	16.13412	16.14873
15	17.35362	17.37046	17.38731	17.40417	17.42105	17.43794	17.45484	17.47175
16	18.68413	18.70345	18.72278	18.74213	18.76149	18.78087	18.80027	18.81969
17	20.03860	20.06060	20.08261	20.10465	20.12671	20.14879	20.17089	20.19301
18	21.41745	21.44234	21.46726	21.49220	21.51716	21.54215	21.56716	21.59220
19	22.82114	22.84914	22.87716	22.90522	22.93331	22.96143	22.98957	23.01775
20	24.25011	24.28143	24.31279	24.34419	24.37563	24.40710	24.43861	24.47015
21	25.70480	25.73969	25.77461	25.80959	25.84460	25.87966	25.91476	25.94991
22	27.18570	27.22438	27.26311	27.30189	27.34073	27.37961	27.41855	27.45754
23	28.69326	28.73598	28.77876	28.82160	28.86450	28.90746	28.95049	28.99357
24	30.22796	30.27498	30.32206	30.36921	30.41643	30.46373	30.51110	30.55853
25	31.79031	31.84187	31.89352	31.94524	31.99705	32.04894	32.10092	32.15297
26	33.38079	33.43717	33.49365	33.55022	33.60688	33.66364	33.72050	33.77744
27	34.99991	35.06138	35.12297	35.18466	35.24646	35.30837	35.37039	35.43252
28	36.64818	36.71504	36.78202	36.84912	36.91634	36.98369	37.05117	37.11876
29	38.32614	38.39867	38.47133	38.54413	38.61709	38.69018	38.76340	38.83677
30	40.03431	40.11282	40.19147	40.27029	40.34926	40.42840	40.50769	40.58714
31	41.77325	41.85803	41.94300	42.02814	42.11345	42.19895	42.28462	42.37048
32	43.54350	43.63489	43.72647	43.81826	43.91025	44.00243	44.09482	44.18741
33	45.34562	45.44395	45.54249	45.64126	45.74025	45.83946	45.93890	46.03856
34	47.18020	47.28580	47.39164	47.49773	47.60407	47.71066	47.81750	47.92458
35	49.04782	49.16103	49.27453	49.38829	49.50234	49.61666	49.73126	49.84613
36	50.94906	51.07026	51.19176	51.31357	51.43569	51.55811	51.68084	51.80387
37	52.88455	53.01410	53.14398	53.27421	53.40477	53.53567	53.66691	53.79849
38	54.85489	54.99317	55.13182	55.27084	55.41024	55.55001	55.69016	55.83068
39	56.86071	57.00811	57.15592	57.30414	57.45277	57.60182	57.75128	57.90115
40	58.90264	59.05957	59.21695	59.37478	59.53306	59.69179	59.85098	60.01062
41	60.98135	61.14822	61.31559	61.48344	61.65179	61.82063	61.98998	62.15982
42	63.09750	63.27473	63.45251	63.63082	63.80968	63.98907	64.16902	64.34950
43	65.25175	65.43979	65.62842	65.81764	66.00745	66.19785	66.38884	66.58043
44	67.44479	67.64409	67.84403	68.04461	68.24583	68.44770	68.65022	68.85338
45	69.67732	69.88834	70.10006	70.31247	70.52559	70.73940	70.95392	71.16915
46	71.95006	72.17328	72.39725	72.62198	72.84747	73.07373	73.30075	73.52853
47	74.26373	74.49963	74.73636	74.97390	75.21227	75.45147	75.69150	75.93236
48	76.61905	76.86815	77.11814	77.36901	77.62078	77.87344	78.12700	78.38146
50	81.45772	81.73477	82.01285	82.29198	82.57214	82.85335	83.13562	83.41893
52	86.47221	86.77941	87.08780	87.39740	87.70821	88.02024	88.33349	88.64797
54	91.66894	92.00858	92.34962	92.69205	93.03588	93.38112	93.72778	94.07584
56	97.05451	97.42905	97.80519	98.18294	98.56230	98.94328	99.32589	99.71013
58	102.63579	103.04780	103.46165	103.87734	104.29487	104.71427	105.13553	105.55867
60	108.41989	108.87209	109.32639	109.78278	110.24129	110.70193	111.16470	111.62960
62	114.41418	114.90944	115.40708	115.90711	116.40954	116.91440	117.42168	117.93140
64	120.62631	121.16764	121.71167	122.25842	122.80789	123.36011	123.91509	124.47284
66	127.06418	127.65477	128.24841	128.84513	129.44493	130.04784	130.65387	131.26303
68	133.73601	134.37920	135.02585	135.67596	136.32955	136.98665	137.64727	138.31143
70	140.65028	141.34963	142.05285	142.75997	143.47100	144.18598	144.90493	145.62786
72	147.81582	148.57503	149.33859	150.10653	150.87886	151.65562	152.43682	153.22251
74	155.24175	156.06475	156.89262	157.72538	158.56306	159.40570	160.25332	161.10596
76	162.93754	163.82845	164.72479	165.62660	166.53391	167.44676	168.36518	169.28919
78	170.91299	171.87615	172.84537	173.82068	174.80211	175.78972	176.78354	177.78361
80	179.17827	180.21825	181.26496	182.31844	183.37875	184.44593	185.52001	186.60105
82	187.74390	188.86550	189.99457	191.13117	192.27534	193.42713	194.58659	195.75379
84	196.62081	197.82908	199.04563	200.27052	201.50380	202.74553	203.99577	205.25457
86	205.82030	207.12056	208.42997	209.74861	211.07652	212.41379	213.76047	215.11665
88	215.35410	216.75193	218.15986	219.57798	221.00635	222.44505	223.89415	225.35374
90	225.23435	226.73562	228.24803	229.77166	231.30660	232.85293	234.41075	235.98013
92	235.47365	237.08452	238.70766	240.34315	241.99109	243.65158	245.32472	247.01060
96	257.08205	258.93190	260.79654	262.67609	264.57067	266.48042	268.40544	270.34587
100	280.28947	282.40690	284.54208	286.69517	288.86631	291.05565	293.26337	295.48961
104	305.21424	307.63079	310.06854	312.52768	315.00840	317.51090	320.03537	322.58200
108	331.98344	334.73386	337.50949	340.31056	343.13730	345.98997	348.86881	351.77405
112	360.73357	363.85611	367.00851	370.19104	373.40400	376.64769	379.92242	383.22848
116	391.61120	395.14797	398.71995	402.32749	405.97096	409.65073	413.36716	417.12063
120	424.77378	428.77107	432.80975	436.89025	441.01302	445.17850	449.38715	453.63942
140	631.23671	638.40756	645.66716	653.01664	660.45733	667.98978	675.61577	683.33628
160	926.26488	938.66860	951.25151	964.01627	976.96556	990.10212	1003.42870	1016.94812

QUARTERLY DEPOSITS

NUMBER OF QUARTERLY DEPOSITS	7.80%	7.85%	7.90%	7.95%	8.00%	8.05%	8.10%	8.15%
				EFFECTIVE ANNUAL YIELD				
1	1.01895	1.01907	1.01919	1.01931	1.01943	1.01954	1.01966	1.01978
2	2.05722	2.05758	2.05794	2.05830	2.05866	2.05902	2.05937	2.05973
3	3.11517	3.11590	3.11662	3.11735	3.11808	3.11880	3.11953	3.12025
4	4.19317	4.19440	4.19562	4.19685	4.19808	4.19930	4.20053	4.20175
5	5.29160	5.29347	5.29533	5.29719	5.29906	5.30092	5.30278	5.30465
6	6.41085	6.41350	6.41614	6.41878	6.42143	6.42407	6.42671	6.42936
7	7.55132	7.55489	7.55846	7.56203	7.56560	7.56917	7.57274	7.57631
8	8.71341	8.71805	8.72270	8.72735	8.73200	8.73665	8.74130	8.74595
9	9.89752	9.90340	9.90928	9.91517	9.92106	9.92695	9.93284	9.93873
10	11.10407	11.11135	11.11864	11.12593	11.13322	11.14051	11.14780	11.15510
11	12.33349	12.34235	12.35120	12.36006	12.36892	12.37779	12.38666	12.39553
12	13.58622	13.59682	13.60742	13.61802	13.62863	13.63925	13.64987	13.66050
13	14.86269	14.87521	14.88774	14.90028	14.91282	14.92537	14.93793	14.95049
14	16.16336	16.17799	16.19263	16.20729	16.22195	16.23662	16.25131	16.26600
15	17.48868	17.50562	17.52257	17.53953	17.55651	17.57350	17.59051	17.60753
16	18.83912	18.85856	18.87803	18.89751	18.91700	18.93651	18.95604	18.97559
17	20.21515	20.23731	20.25949	20.28170	20.30392	20.32616	20.34843	20.37071
18	21.61727	21.64236	21.66747	21.69262	21.71778	21.74297	21.76819	21.79343
19	23.04596	23.07420	23.10247	23.13078	23.15911	23.18747	23.21587	23.24429
20	24.50174	24.53336	24.56501	24.59671	24.62844	24.66021	24.69201	24.72385
21	25.98510	26.02034	26.05562	26.09094	26.12631	26.16172	26.19718	26.23268
22	27.49659	27.53568	27.57483	27.61403	27.65328	27.69258	27.73194	27.77135
23	29.03672	29.07992	29.12319	29.16652	29.20991	29.25337	29.29688	29.34046
24	30.60604	30.65362	30.70127	30.74899	30.79679	30.84465	30.89259	30.94060
25	32.20511	32.25733	32.30963	32.36202	32.41449	32.46704	32.51968	32.57240
26	33.83449	33.89163	33.94886	34.00619	34.06362	34.12114	34.17876	34.23647
27	35.49475	35.55710	35.61955	35.68211	35.74478	35.80757	35.87046	35.93346
28	37.18648	37.25433	37.32230	37.39039	37.45861	37.52695	37.59542	37.66402
29	38.91028	38.98393	39.05772	39.13165	39.20573	39.27994	39.35430	39.42880
30	40.66675	40.74652	40.82645	40.90654	40.98678	41.06719	41.14777	41.22850
31	42.45651	42.54272	42.62912	42.71569	42.80244	42.88938	42.97649	43.06379
32	44.28020	44.37319	44.46638	44.55978	44.65337	44.74717	44.84118	44.93539
33	46.13845	46.23856	46.33890	46.43947	46.54026	46.64128	46.74253	46.84401
34	48.03192	48.13952	48.24736	48.35545	48.46380	48.57241	48.68126	48.79038
35	49.96129	50.07672	50.19244	50.30844	50.42471	50.54128	50.65812	50.77525
36	51.92722	52.05088	52.17485	52.29913	52.42372	52.54862	52.67384	52.79938
37	53.93042	54.06269	54.19530	54.32826	54.46156	54.59521	54.72920	54.86355
38	55.97168	56.11286	56.25452	56.39656	56.53898	56.68179	56.82497	56.96855
39	58.05144	58.20214	58.35327	58.50481	58.65677	58.80915	58.96195	59.11518
40	60.17071	60.33127	60.49228	60.65376	60.81569	60.97809	61.14095	61.30428
41	62.33016	62.50100	62.67235	62.84420	63.01656	63.18942	63.36280	63.53668
42	64.53054	64.71212	64.89425	65.07694	65.26018	65.44397	65.62833	65.81324
43	66.77262	66.96541	67.15880	67.35279	67.54739	67.74259	67.93840	68.13482
44	69.05720	69.26167	69.46680	69.67258	69.87902	70.08613	70.29390	70.50233
45	71.38508	71.60173	71.81909	72.03716	72.25596	72.47547	72.69571	72.91667
46	73.75709	73.98642	74.21652	74.44741	74.67907	74.91152	75.14475	75.37877
47	76.17405	76.41659	76.65996	76.90418	77.14925	77.39517	77.64194	77.88957
48	78.63683	78.89311	79.15030	79.40840	79.66742	79.92737	80.18823	80.45003
50	83.70331	83.98875	84.27525	84.56282	84.85147	85.14120	85.43200	85.72390
52	88.96367	89.28061	89.59879	89.91822	90.23889	90.56082	90.88401	91.20846
54	94.42534	94.77626	95.12862	95.48242	95.83766	96.19436	96.55252	96.91215
56	100.09601	100.48354	100.87272	101.26357	101.65608	102.05027	102.44614	102.84371
58	105.98368	106.41059	106.83940	107.27012	107.70275	108.13731	108.57381	109.01224
60	112.09667	112.56589	113.03729	113.51087	113.98664	114.46462	114.94481	115.42722
62	118.44358	118.95822	119.47534	119.99494	120.51705	121.04167	121.56881	122.09849
64	125.03338	125.59671	126.16286	126.73183	127.30365	127.87832	128.45587	129.03630
66	131.87535	132.49084	133.10951	133.73139	134.35649	134.98483	135.61642	136.25128
68	138.97915	139.65045	140.32535	141.00386	141.68602	142.37183	143.06132	143.75451
70	146.35480	147.08577	147.82079	148.55989	149.30309	150.05041	150.80187	151.55751
72	154.01269	154.80741	155.60667	156.41052	157.21898	158.03207	158.84982	159.67226
74	161.96364	162.82639	163.69425	164.56725	165.44541	166.32877	167.21736	168.11120
76	170.21885	171.15418	172.09522	173.04201	173.99457	174.95295	175.91718	176.88730
78	178.78997	179.80266	180.82172	181.84719	182.87912	183.91754	184.96249	186.01402
80	187.68909	188.78418	189.88637	190.99570	192.11221	193.23596	194.36700	195.50537
82	196.92876	198.11157	199.30226	200.50090	201.70752	202.92220	204.14498	205.37592
84	206.52201	207.79814	209.08301	210.37670	211.67927	212.99076	214.31126	215.64081
86	216.48237	217.85772	219.24276	220.63757	222.04220	223.45674	224.88125	226.31581
88	226.82390	228.30469	229.79620	231.29850	232.81168	234.33582	235.87100	237.41729
90	237.56117	239.15395	240.75856	242.37510	244.00365	245.64431	247.29716	248.96230
92	248.70933	250.42100	252.14572	253.88358	255.63469	257.39916	259.17708	260.96856
96	272.30183	274.27345	276.26085	278.26418	280.28355	282.31909	284.37095	286.43925
100	297.73454	299.99831	302.28108	304.58303	306.90430	309.24508	311.60553	313.98580
104	325.15100	327.74257	330.35691	332.99423	335.65473	338.33861	341.04610	343.77740
108	354.70595	357.66476	360.65073	363.66412	366.70518	369.77417	372.87136	375.99701
112	386.56618	389.93584	393.33776	396.77227	400.23967	403.74030	407.27447	410.84223
116	420.91152	424.74020	428.60707	432.51251	436.45692	440.44069	444.46423	448.52795
120	457.93578	462.27670	466.66265	471.09410	475.57155	480.09547	484.66637	489.28473
140	691.15251	699.06566	707.07697	715.18769	723.39907	731.71239	740.12894	748.65003
160	1030.66323	1044.57691	1058.69211	1073.01180	1087.53900	1102.27678	1117.22826	1132.39659

QUARTERLY DEPOSITS

EFFECTIVE ANNUAL YIELD

NUMBER OF QUARTRLY DEPOSITS	8.20%	8.25%	8.30%	8.35%	8.40%	8.45%	8.50%	8.55%
1	1.01990	1.02002	1.02013	1.02025	1.02037	1.02049	1.02060	1.02072
2	2.06009	2.06045	2.06081	2.06116	2.06152	2.06188	2.06224	2.06260
3	3.12098	3.12171	3.12243	3.12316	3.12388	3.12461	3.12533	3.12606
4	4.20298	4.20421	4.20543	4.20666	4.20788	4.20911	4.21033	4.21156
5	5.30651	5.30837	5.31024	5.31210	5.31396	5.31583	5.31769	5.31955
6	6.43200	6.43464	6.43729	6.43993	6.44257	6.44522	6.44786	6.45051
7	7.57988	7.58345	7.58703	7.59060	7.59417	7.59775	7.60132	7.60489
8	8.75061	8.75526	8.75992	8.76457	8.76923	8.77389	8.77854	8.78320
9	9.94463	9.95052	9.95642	9.96232	9.96822	9.97412	9.98003	9.98593
10	11.16240	11.16971	11.17701	11.18432	11.19163	11.19895	11.20626	11.21358
11	12.40441	12.41330	12.42218	12.43107	12.43997	12.44886	12.45777	12.46667
12	13.67114	13.68178	13.69242	13.70307	13.71373	13.72439	13.73505	13.74573
13	14.96307	14.97565	14.98823	15.00083	15.01343	15.02604	15.03866	15.05129
14	16.28070	16.29541	16.31014	16.32487	16.33961	16.35437	16.36913	16.38390
15	17.62456	17.64160	17.65865	17.67572	17.69281	17.70990	17.72701	17.74413
16	18.99515	19.01473	19.03432	19.05393	19.07356	19.09321	19.11287	19.13254
17	20.39302	20.41534	20.43769	20.46006	20.48244	20.50485	20.52728	20.54973
18	21.81870	21.84399	21.86931	21.89465	21.92002	21.94542	21.97084	21.99628
19	23.27275	23.30124	23.32975	23.35830	23.38688	23.41550	23.44414	23.47281
20	24.75573	24.78765	24.81960	24.85160	24.88362	24.91569	24.94779	24.97994
21	26.26823	26.30381	26.33945	26.37513	26.41085	26.44662	26.48243	26.51829
22	27.81081	27.85033	27.88989	27.92951	27.96919	28.00891	28.04869	28.08852
23	29.38410	29.42780	29.47156	29.51538	29.55927	29.60321	29.64722	29.69129
24	30.98868	31.03684	31.08506	31.13336	31.18173	31.23017	31.27869	31.32728
25	32.62520	32.67809	32.73106	32.78411	32.83725	32.89047	32.94377	32.99716
26	34.29428	34.35219	34.41019	34.46829	34.52648	34.58477	34.64316	34.70165
27	35.99657	36.05979	36.12313	36.18657	36.25013	36.31379	36.37757	36.44146
28	37.73274	37.80158	37.87056	37.93965	38.00888	38.07823	38.14771	38.21732
29	39.50345	39.57823	39.65317	39.72824	39.80346	39.87882	39.95433	40.02998
30	41.30939	41.39045	41.47167	41.55305	41.63459	41.71630	41.79817	41.88020
31	43.15127	43.23893	43.32678	43.41481	43.50302	43.59142	43.68000	43.76876
32	45.02980	45.12442	45.21924	45.31427	45.40951	45.50495	45.60060	45.69646
33	46.94571	47.04765	47.14981	47.25221	47.35483	47.45769	47.56078	47.66410
34	48.89974	49.00937	49.11925	49.22938	49.33978	49.45043	49.56134	49.67252
35	50.89266	51.01035	51.12833	51.24660	51.36516	51.48400	51.60313	51.72255
36	52.92523	53.05139	53.17787	53.30467	53.43179	53.55923	53.68699	53.81506
37	54.99824	55.13328	55.26868	55.40445	55.54052	55.67697	55.81378	55.95094
38	57.11250	57.25685	57.40158	57.54669	57.69220	57.83810	57.98439	58.13107
39	59.26884	59.42291	59.57742	59.73235	59.88771	60.04351	60.19973	60.35639
40	61.46808	61.63234	61.79707	61.96227	62.12794	62.29409	62.46071	62.62781
41	63.71108	63.88599	64.06141	64.23735	64.41381	64.59078	64.76828	64.94630
42	65.99871	66.18474	66.37134	66.55850	66.74623	66.93453	67.12340	67.31284
43	68.33186	68.52951	68.72778	68.92666	69.12616	69.32629	69.52704	69.72841
44	70.71144	70.92121	71.13166	71.34278	71.55457	71.76705	71.98021	72.19405
45	73.13836	73.36079	73.58394	73.80783	74.03245	74.25781	74.48392	74.71077
46	75.61358	75.84919	76.08559	76.32279	76.56080	76.79961	77.03922	77.27964
47	78.13805	78.38740	78.63761	78.88869	79.14064	79.39347	79.64717	79.90175
48	80.71276	80.97642	81.24102	81.50656	81.77304	82.04047	82.30886	82.57819
50	86.01688	86.31095	86.60613	86.90240	87.19979	87.49828	87.79789	88.09861
52	91.53418	91.86118	92.18945	92.51901	92.84986	93.18200	93.51544	93.85019
54	97.27324	97.63581	97.99987	98.36541	98.73245	99.10099	99.47104	99.84260
56	103.24297	103.64393	104.04661	104.45101	104.85713	105.26499	105.67459	106.08594
58	109.45263	109.89498	110.33929	110.78558	111.23386	111.68413	112.13641	112.59070
60	115.91187	116.39876	116.88791	117.37932	117.87301	118.36899	118.86726	119.36784
62	122.63073	123.16552	123.70288	124.24284	124.78539	125.33055	125.87834	126.42877
64	129.61963	130.20587	130.79504	131.38716	131.98223	132.58028	133.18131	133.78535
66	136.88943	137.53088	138.17566	138.82377	139.47524	140.13009	140.78833	141.44998
68	144.45142	145.15206	145.85646	146.56464	147.27662	147.99242	148.71206	149.43556
70	152.31734	153.08138	153.84967	154.62221	155.39905	156.18019	156.96567	157.75552
72	160.49941	161.33131	162.16798	163.00945	163.85574	164.70689	165.56292	166.42386
74	169.01034	169.91480	170.82462	171.73983	172.66045	173.58653	174.51809	175.45517
76	177.86334	178.84535	179.83335	180.82739	181.82750	182.83373	183.84610	184.86465
78	187.07217	188.13698	189.20850	190.28676	191.37181	192.46370	193.56246	194.66815
80	196.65112	197.80430	198.96495	200.13314	201.30890	202.49228	203.68335	204.88214
82	206.61507	207.86249	209.11823	210.38236	211.65493	212.93599	214.22560	215.52383
84	216.97949	218.32736	219.68448	221.05091	222.42673	223.81199	225.20677	226.61112
86	227.76048	229.21535	230.68048	232.15595	233.64182	235.13819	236.64511	238.16268
88	238.97479	240.54357	242.12372	243.71522	245.31846	246.93321	248.55968	250.19793
90	250.63983	252.32982	254.03239	255.74762	257.47562	259.21647	260.97028	262.73714
92	262.77370	264.59262	266.42542	268.27221	270.13309	272.00818	273.89758	275.80141
96	288.52413	290.62572	292.74416	294.87959	297.03215	299.20198	301.38921	303.59399
100	316.38609	318.80655	321.24736	323.70870	326.19074	328.69365	331.21763	333.76284
104	346.53273	349.31230	352.11632	354.94503	357.79864	360.67737	363.58146	366.51112
108	379.15139	382.33477	385.54741	388.78960	392.06161	395.36372	398.69621	402.05938
112	414.44479	418.08159	421.75328	425.46019	429.20267	432.98106	436.79572	440.64701
116	452.63224	456.77753	460.96423	465.19277	469.46357	473.77707	478.13309	482.53389
120	493.95106	498.66588	503.42970	508.24303	513.10640	518.02034	522.98539	528.00209
140	757.27699	766.01115	774.85388	783.80656	792.87057	802.04734	811.33828	820.74484
160	1147.78497	1163.39666	1179.23497	1195.30323	1211.60485	1228.14328	1244.92202	1261.94463

QUARTERLY DEPOSITS

NUMBER OF QUARTERLY DEPOSITS	EFFECTIVE ANNUAL YIELD							
	8.60%	8.65%	8.70%	8.75%	8.80%	8.85%	8.90%	8.95%
1	1.02084	1.02096	1.02107	1.02119	1.02131	1.02143	1.02154	1.02166
2	2.06295	2.06331	2.06367	2.06402	2.06438	2.06474	2.06510	2.06545
3	3.12678	3.12751	3.12823	3.12896	3.12968	3.13041	3.13113	3.13185
4	4.21278	4.21401	4.21523	4.21646	4.21768	4.21891	4.22013	4.22135
5	5.32141	5.32328	5.32514	5.32700	5.32887	5.33073	5.33259	5.33445
6	6.45315	6.45579	6.45844	6.46108	6.46373	6.46637	6.46902	6.47166
7	7.60847	7.61204	7.61562	7.61920	7.62277	7.62635	7.62993	7.63351
8	8.78787	8.79253	8.79719	8.80185	8.80652	8.81118	8.81585	8.82052
9	9.99184	9.99775	10.00366	10.00957	10.01549	10.02140	10.02732	10.03324
10	11.22090	11.22823	11.23556	11.24288	11.25022	11.25755	11.26489	11.27223
11	12.47558	12.48449	12.49341	12.50233	12.51126	12.52019	12.52912	12.53806
12	13.75640	13.76709	13.77778	13.78847	13.79917	13.80988	13.82059	13.83131
13	15.06392	15.07656	15.08921	15.10187	15.11453	15.12720	15.13988	15.15257
14	16.39868	16.41348	16.42828	16.44309	16.45792	16.47275	16.48759	16.50245
15	17.76126	17.77841	17.79557	17.81274	17.82993	17.84713	17.86434	17.88157
16	19.15224	19.17195	19.19168	19.21142	19.23118	19.25096	19.27075	19.29056
17	20.57220	20.59469	20.61720	20.63974	20.66229	20.68486	20.70746	20.73007
18	22.02175	22.04725	22.07277	22.09832	22.12389	22.14949	22.17512	22.20077
19	23.50152	23.53025	23.55902	23.58782	23.61665	23.64551	23.67440	23.70332
20	25.01211	25.04433	25.07658	25.10888	25.14121	25.17357	25.20598	25.23842
21	26.55419	26.59014	26.62613	26.66217	26.69825	26.73438	26.77055	26.80677
22	28.12841	28.16835	28.20834	28.24838	28.28848	28.32863	28.36883	28.40909
23	29.73543	29.77963	29.82388	29.86821	29.91259	29.95704	30.00155	30.04612
24	31.37594	31.42467	31.47348	31.52236	31.57131	31.62034	31.66944	31.71851
25	33.05064	33.10420	33.15784	33.21157	33.26538	33.31928	33.37326	33.42733
26	34.76023	34.81892	34.87769	34.93657	34.99555	35.05462	35.11379	35.17306
27	36.50546	36.56957	36.63380	36.69813	36.76258	36.82714	36.89181	36.95660
28	38.28705	38.35691	38.42690	38.49702	38.56727	38.63764	38.70815	38.77878
29	40.10577	40.18172	40.25780	40.33404	40.41041	40.48694	40.56361	40.64043
30	41.96240	42.04476	42.12729	42.20998	42.29283	42.37586	42.45904	42.54240
31	43.85771	43.94685	44.03617	44.12567	44.21537	44.30525	44.39532	44.48557
32	45.79252	45.88880	45.98528	46.08197	46.17887	46.27598	46.37330	46.47083
33	47.76765	47.87144	47.97546	48.07972	48.18421	48.28894	48.39390	48.49910
34	49.78395	49.89564	50.00759	50.11981	50.23228	50.34502	50.45803	50.57130
35	51.84226	51.96226	52.08255	52.20313	52.32400	52.44517	52.56663	52.68838
36	53.94346	54.07218	54.20123	54.33060	54.46029	54.59031	54.72065	54.85132
37	56.08846	56.22633	56.36456	56.50315	56.64210	56.78141	56.92108	57.06112
38	58.27815	58.42562	58.57348	58.72175	58.87041	59.01946	59.16892	59.31878
39	60.51347	60.67100	60.82896	60.98736	61.14619	61.30547	61.46519	61.62534
40	62.79538	62.96344	63.13197	63.30098	63.47048	63.64046	63.81092	63.98187
41	65.12485	65.30391	65.48351	65.66363	65.84429	66.02547	66.20719	66.38944
42	67.50285	67.69344	67.88461	68.07636	68.26868	68.46159	68.65508	68.84916
43	69.93042	70.13305	70.33631	70.54021	70.74474	70.94991	71.15572	71.36217
44	72.40857	72.62378	72.83968	73.05627	73.27356	73.49154	73.71022	73.92960
45	74.93837	75.16671	75.39581	75.62566	75.85627	76.08763	76.31976	76.55265
46	77.52088	77.76293	78.00580	78.24949	78.49401	78.73935	78.98552	79.23252
47	80.15722	80.41357	80.67080	80.92893	81.18796	81.44788	81.70870	81.97043
48	82.84849	83.11975	83.39197	83.66515	83.93931	84.21445	84.49056	84.76765
50	88.40046	88.70344	89.00754	89.31278	89.61916	89.92669	90.23536	90.54518
52	94.18624	94.52361	94.86230	95.20231	95.54365	95.88633	96.23035	96.57571
54	100.21568	100.59029	100.96643	101.34411	101.72333	102.10410	102.48643	102.87033
56	106.49904	106.91391	107.33055	107.74897	108.16918	108.59118	109.01498	109.44059
58	113.04701	113.50536	113.96574	114.42817	114.89266	115.35922	115.82785	116.29857
60	119.87074	120.37597	120.88354	121.39346	121.90575	122.42040	122.93744	123.45688
62	126.98184	127.53758	128.09599	128.65709	129.22090	129.78742	130.35666	130.92865
64	134.39241	135.00250	135.61564	136.23185	136.85113	137.47351	138.09900	138.72762
66	142.11506	142.78359	143.45558	144.13105	144.81002	145.49251	146.17853	146.86812
68	150.16294	150.89423	151.62944	152.36859	153.11171	153.85882	154.60994	155.36509
70	158.54974	159.34838	160.15144	160.95897	161.77098	162.58750	163.40855	164.23416
72	167.28974	168.16058	169.03643	169.91730	170.80322	171.69423	172.59036	173.49162
74	176.39780	177.34602	178.29985	179.25934	180.22451	181.19540	182.17204	183.15448
76	185.88944	186.92048	187.95783	189.00152	190.05159	191.10808	192.17103	193.24048
78	195.78080	196.90046	198.02717	199.16099	200.30195	201.45010	202.60548	203.76815
80	206.08871	207.30311	208.52539	209.75561	210.99381	212.24005	213.49438	214.75685
82	216.83073	218.14635	219.47077	220.80403	222.14620	223.49733	224.85750	226.22676
84	228.02512	229.44884	230.88234	232.32568	233.77895	235.24220	236.71551	238.19894
86	239.69095	241.23002	242.77996	244.34084	245.91274	247.49575	249.08995	250.69540
88	251.84807	253.51017	255.18433	256.87063	258.56917	260.28004	262.00331	263.73910
90	264.51716	266.31042	268.11704	269.93712	271.77075	273.61803	275.47908	277.35400
92	277.71978	279.65281	281.60060	283.56327	285.54094	287.53372	289.54174	291.56510
96	305.81647	308.05678	310.31508	312.59151	314.88623	317.19936	319.53108	321.88153
100	336.32947	338.91770	341.52773	344.15973	346.81389	349.49041	352.18948	354.91128
104	369.46659	372.44809	375.45587	378.49016	381.55120	384.63922	387.75447	390.89719
108	405.45350	408.87886	412.33577	415.82451	419.34538	422.89870	426.48475	430.10385
112	444.53528	448.46089	452.42421	456.42561	460.46546	464.54414	468.66202	472.81949
116	486.97810	491.44676	496.00035	500.57931	505.20410	509.87520	514.59307	519.35819
120	533.07099	538.19265	543.36761	548.59645	553.87974	559.21806	564.61198	570.06210
140	830.26850	839.91074	849.67305	859.55696	869.56402	879.69578	889.95382	900.33975
160	1279.21469	1296.73588	1314.51191	1332.54654	1350.84359	1369.40695	1388.24054	1407.34838

EFFECTIVE ANNUAL YIELD

NUMBER OF QUARTRLY DEPOSITS	9.00%	9.05%	9.10%	9.15%	9.20%	9.25%	9.30%	9.35%
1	1.02178	1.02190	1.02201	1.02213	1.02225	1.02236	1.02248	1.02260
2	2.06581	2.06617	2.06652	2.06688	2.06723	2.06759	2.06795	2.06830
3	3.13258	3.13330	3.13402	3.13475	3.13547	3.13619	3.13692	3.13764
4	4.22258	4.22380	4.22502	4.22625	4.22747	4.22869	4.22992	4.23114
5	5.33631	5.33818	5.34004	5.34190	5.34376	5.34563	5.34749	5.34935
6	6.47431	6.47695	6.47960	6.48224	6.48489	6.48754	6.49018	6.49283
7	7.63709	7.64066	7.64424	7.64782	7.65140	7.65498	7.65857	7.66215
8	8.82519	8.82985	8.83452	8.83920	8.84387	8.84854	8.85321	8.85789
9	10.03916	10.04508	10.05101	10.05693	10.06286	10.06879	10.07472	10.08065
10	11.27957	11.28692	11.29427	11.30162	11.30897	11.31633	11.32368	11.33105
11	12.54700	12.55594	12.56489	12.57385	12.58280	12.59176	12.60073	12.60970
12	13.84203	13.85276	13.86349	13.87423	13.88497	13.89572	13.90648	13.91724
13	15.16526	15.17796	15.19067	15.20339	15.21611	15.22884	15.24158	15.25433
14	16.51731	16.53218	16.54707	16.56196	16.57687	16.59178	16.60670	16.62164
15	17.89881	17.91606	17.93332	17.95060	17.96789	17.98519	18.00251	18.01984
16	19.31039	19.33023	19.35009	19.36997	19.38986	19.40977	19.42970	19.44964
17	20.75271	20.77537	20.79805	20.82075	20.84347	20.86621	20.88897	20.91175
18	22.22645	22.25215	22.27787	22.30363	22.32941	22.35521	22.38104	22.40690
19	23.73227	23.76126	23.79028	23.81933	23.84841	23.87752	23.90666	23.93584
20	25.27090	25.30342	25.33597	25.36857	25.40120	25.43387	25.46658	25.49932
21	26.84303	26.87934	26.91569	26.95209	26.98853	27.02502	27.06156	27.09814
22	28.44940	28.48977	28.53018	28.57066	28.61118	28.65176	28.69240	28.73308
23	30.09076	30.13545	30.18022	30.22504	30.26993	30.31488	30.35990	30.40497
24	31.76786	31.81718	31.86657	31.91604	31.96558	32.01519	32.06488	32.11465
25	33.48148	33.53572	33.59004	33.64445	33.69895	33.75353	33.80820	33.86295
26	35.23242	35.29189	35.35146	35.41112	35.47088	35.53074	35.59070	35.65077
27	37.02150	37.08651	37.15164	37.21688	37.28223	37.34770	37.41328	37.47898
28	38.84954	38.92043	38.99145	39.06260	39.13388	39.20529	39.27683	39.34850
29	40.71739	40.79450	40.87176	40.94917	41.02672	41.10443	41.18228	41.26028
30	42.62592	42.70961	42.79346	42.87748	42.96167	43.04603	43.13056	43.21525
31	44.57601	44.66664	44.75746	44.84847	44.93967	45.03106	45.12263	45.21440
32	46.56858	46.66653	46.76470	46.86308	46.96167	47.06047	47.15949	47.25873
33	48.60453	48.71020	48.81611	48.92226	49.02865	49.13528	49.24214	49.34925
34	50.68483	50.79863	50.91269	51.02702	51.14162	51.25648	51.37161	51.48701
35	52.81043	52.93277	53.05542	53.17835	53.30159	53.42512	53.54895	53.67309
36	54.98232	55.11365	55.24531	55.37729	55.50961	55.64226	55.77524	55.90856
37	57.20152	57.34228	57.48340	57.62490	57.76676	57.90898	58.05158	58.19454
38	59.46904	59.61970	59.77077	59.92224	60.07412	60.22640	60.37909	60.53219
39	61.78595	61.94699	62.10848	62.27042	62.43280	62.59564	62.75892	62.92266
40	64.15331	64.32524	64.49765	64.67056	64.84397	65.01786	65.19226	65.36715
41	66.57223	66.75555	66.93942	67.12382	67.30877	67.49426	67.68029	67.86687
42	69.04383	69.23909	69.43493	69.63137	69.82840	70.02603	70.22426	70.42309
43	71.56926	71.77669	71.98508	72.19441	72.40409	72.61443	72.82542	73.03707
44	74.14968	74.37047	74.59196	74.81417	75.03708	75.26071	75.48505	75.71011
45	76.78631	77.02073	77.25593	77.49190	77.72865	77.96617	78.20448	78.44356
46	79.48035	79.72902	79.97853	80.22889	80.48009	80.73213	80.98503	81.23879
47	82.23307	82.49661	82.76107	83.02644	83.29274	83.55996	83.82810	84.09717
48	85.04573	85.32480	85.60486	85.88591	86.16796	86.45102	86.73508	87.02015
50	90.85616	91.16830	91.48160	91.79608	92.11173	92.42855	92.74656	93.06575
52	96.92242	97.27049	97.61992	97.97072	98.32289	98.67643	99.03136	99.38767
54	103.25579	103.64283	104.03145	104.42167	104.81347	105.20688	105.60190	105.99854
56	109.86802	110.29727	110.72836	111.16129	111.59606	112.03269	112.47119	112.91156
58	116.77139	117.24631	117.72334	118.20250	118.68378	119.16721	119.65280	120.14054
60	123.97872	124.50298	125.02966	125.55879	126.09037	126.62441	127.16092	127.69993
62	131.50339	132.08090	132.66119	133.24427	133.83016	134.41887	135.01042	135.60482
64	139.35938	139.99430	140.63239	141.27367	141.91815	142.56586	143.21681	143.87101
66	147.56127	148.25802	148.95838	149.66237	150.37001	151.08131	151.79631	152.51501
68	156.12430	156.88758	157.65496	158.42645	159.20209	159.98190	160.76589	161.55409
70	165.06436	165.89917	166.73861	167.58272	168.43152	169.28503	170.14328	171.00630
72	174.39806	175.30970	176.22658	177.14872	178.07616	179.00891	179.94703	180.89053
74	184.14273	185.13684	186.13685	187.14279	188.15469	189.17259	190.19652	191.22653
76	194.31646	195.39903	196.48822	197.58408	198.68663	199.79593	200.91202	202.03493
78	204.93815	206.11553	207.30033	208.49260	209.69239	210.89974	212.11471	213.33735
80	216.02752	217.30645	218.59368	219.88927	221.19327	222.50575	223.82675	225.15634
82	227.60516	228.99279	230.38968	231.79592	233.21156	234.63666	236.07130	237.51553
84	239.69258	241.19648	242.71072	244.23538	245.77052	247.31622	248.87256	250.43960
86	252.31221	253.94043	255.58017	257.23149	258.89449	260.56925	262.25584	263.95437
88	265.48748	267.24856	269.02242	270.80916	272.60888	274.42167	276.24762	278.08684
90	279.24288	281.14584	283.06299	284.99442	286.94025	288.90059	290.87555	292.86524
92	293.60393	295.65836	297.72849	299.81445	301.91637	304.03436	306.16856	308.31909
96	324.25087	326.63924	329.04680	331.47372	333.92014	336.38624	338.87216	341.37807
100	357.65602	360.42389	363.21509	366.02981	368.86827	371.73066	374.61718	377.52806
104	394.06764	397.26605	400.49268	403.74779	407.03162	410.34443	413.68650	417.05807
108	433.75630	437.44243	441.16254	444.91696	448.70600	452.52999	456.38926	460.28414
112	477.01695	481.25477	485.53335	489.85310	494.21442	498.61771	503.06337	507.55184
116	524.17105	529.03212	533.94191	538.90091	543.90961	548.96854	554.07818	559.23908
120	575.56902	581.13333	586.75565	592.43659	598.17677	603.97682	609.83737	615.75907
140	910.85518	921.50176	932.28115	943.19502	954.24510	965.43310	976.76077	988.22987
160	1426.73450	1446.40302	1466.35811	1486.60402	1507.14504	1527.98553	1549.12991	1570.58268

QUARTERLY DEPOSITS

NUMBER OF QUARTRLY DEPOSITS	EFFECTIVE ANNUAL YIELD							
	9.40%	9.45%	9.50%	9.55%	9.60%	9.65%	9.70%	9.75%
1	1.02271	1.02283	1.02295	1.02306	1.02318	1.02330	1.02341	1.02353
2	2.06866	2.06901	2.06937	2.06973	2.07008	2.07044	2.07079	2.07115
3	3.13836	3.13908	3.13981	3.14053	3.14125	3.14197	3.14269	3.14342
4	4.23236	4.23358	4.23481	4.23603	4.23725	4.23847	4.23969	4.24092
5	5.35121	5.35307	5.35493	5.35680	5.35866	5.36052	5.36238	5.36424
6	6.49547	6.49812	6.50077	6.50341	6.50606	6.50871	6.51135	6.51400
7	7.66573	7.66931	7.67289	7.67648	7.68006	7.68364	7.68723	7.69081
8	8.86256	8.86724	8.87192	8.87660	8.88128	8.88596	8.89064	8.89532
9	10.08659	10.09252	10.09846	10.10440	10.11034	10.11628	10.12223	10.12817
10	11.33841	11.34578	11.35315	11.36052	11.36789	11.37527	11.38265	11.39003
11	12.61867	12.62764	12.63662	12.64561	12.65460	12.66359	12.67258	12.68158
12	13.92801	13.93878	13.94956	13.96034	13.97113	13.98192	13.99272	14.00353
13	15.26709	15.27985	15.29262	15.30540	15.31818	15.33097	15.34377	15.35658
14	16.63658	16.65154	16.66650	16.68148	16.69646	16.71145	16.72646	16.74147
15	18.03718	18.05454	18.07191	18.08929	18.10669	18.12410	18.14152	18.15896
16	19.46960	19.48958	19.50957	19.52958	19.54961	19.56965	19.58971	19.60979
17	20.93455	20.95738	20.98022	21.00309	21.02598	21.04889	21.07182	21.09477
18	22.43278	22.45869	22.48442	22.51058	22.53657	22.56258	22.58862	22.61468
19	23.96504	23.99428	24.02355	24.05285	24.08218	24.11155	24.14094	24.17037
20	25.53210	25.56493	25.59779	25.63068	25.66362	25.69660	25.72961	25.76266
21	27.13476	27.17143	27.20815	27.24491	27.28172	27.31858	27.35548	27.39242
22	28.77382	28.81462	28.85547	28.89637	28.93733	28.97834	29.01941	29.06053
23	30.45012	30.49532	30.54059	30.58592	30.63132	30.67678	30.72231	30.76790
24	32.16448	32.21440	32.26438	32.31444	32.36458	32.41479	32.46508	32.51544
25	33.91779	33.97272	34.02773	34.08283	34.13802	34.19329	34.24865	34.30410
26	35.71093	35.77119	35.83155	35.89201	35.95257	36.01323	36.07399	36.13485
27	37.54479	37.61071	37.67675	37.74291	37.80918	37.87556	37.94206	38.00868
28	39.42031	39.49224	39.56431	39.63650	39.70883	39.78129	39.85388	39.92661
29	41.33843	41.41672	41.49517	41.57377	41.65252	41.73142	41.81046	41.88966
30	43.30011	43.38515	43.47035	43.55572	43.64126	43.72698	43.81286	43.89891
31	45.30636	45.39851	45.49085	45.58338	45.67611	45.76903	45.86214	45.95544
32	47.35818	47.45784	47.55772	47.65782	47.75813	47.85866	47.95940	48.06037
33	49.45660	49.56419	49.67202	49.78009	49.88841	49.99697	50.10577	50.21482
34	51.60269	51.71863	51.83484	51.95132	52.06807	52.18510	52.30240	52.41997
35	53.79752	53.92225	54.04729	54.17263	54.29827	54.42421	54.55046	54.67702
36	56.04221	56.17619	56.31051	56.44517	56.58016	56.71549	56.85116	56.98717
37	58.33788	58.48159	58.62567	58.77012	58.91495	59.06015	59.20573	59.35168
38	60.68570	60.83962	60.99395	61.14870	61.30386	61.45944	61.61543	61.77184
39	63.08685	63.25149	63.41659	63.58214	63.74815	63.91462	64.08155	64.24894
40	65.54254	65.71842	65.89481	66.07171	66.24910	66.42701	66.60542	66.78433
41	68.05400	68.24168	68.42991	68.61870	68.80803	68.99793	69.18838	69.37939
42	70.62252	70.82255	71.02319	71.22443	71.42628	71.62874	71.83182	72.03551
43	73.24937	73.46234	73.67597	73.89026	74.10522	74.32085	74.53715	74.75413
44	75.93590	76.16240	76.38963	76.61758	76.84627	77.07568	77.30583	77.53672
45	78.68344	78.92410	79.16556	79.40781	79.65085	79.89470	80.13934	80.38479
46	81.49339	81.74886	82.00519	82.26239	82.52045	82.77939	83.03920	83.29988
47	84.36717	84.63811	84.90999	85.18281	85.45658	85.73129	86.00695	86.28357
48	87.30623	87.59333	87.88145	88.17059	88.46076	88.75196	89.04419	89.33747
50	93.38613	93.70771	94.03049	94.35448	94.67967	95.00607	95.33369	95.66254
52	99.74538	100.10448	100.46499	100.82691	101.19024	101.55500	101.92118	102.28879
54	106.39679	106.79668	107.19820	107.60136	108.00617	108.41263	108.82076	109.23055
56	113.35380	113.79794	114.24397	114.69191	115.14176	115.59353	116.04722	116.50286
58	120.63045	121.12255	121.61683	122.11332	122.61201	123.11292	123.61606	124.12145
60	128.24142	128.78543	129.33196	129.88101	130.43262	130.98677	131.54350	132.10280
62	136.20208	136.80221	137.40524	138.01117	138.62001	139.23179	139.84652	140.46420
64	144.52848	145.18924	145.85330	146.52068	147.19140	147.86547	148.54291	149.22374
66	153.23743	153.96360	154.69354	155.42726	156.16478	156.90613	157.65132	158.40038
68	162.34652	163.14320	163.94417	164.74943	165.55902	166.37296	167.19127	168.01397
70	171.87411	172.74675	173.62423	174.50659	175.39385	176.28605	177.18320	178.08533
72	181.83945	182.79382	183.75367	184.71903	185.68994	186.66642	187.64852	188.63625
74	192.26264	193.30490	194.35334	195.40800	196.46891	197.53612	198.60966	199.68957
76	203.16472	204.30142	205.44507	206.59573	207.75342	208.91821	210.09012	211.26920
78	214.56769	215.80580	217.05171	218.30549	219.56718	220.83683	222.11449	223.40022
80	226.49457	227.84149	229.19716	230.56165	231.93500	233.31728	234.70855	236.10886
82	238.96941	240.43303	241.90643	243.38969	244.88288	246.38606	247.89929	249.42265
84	252.01742	253.60609	255.20570	256.81631	258.43801	260.07087	261.71498	263.37039
86	265.66490	267.38753	269.12235	270.86944	272.62889	274.40078	276.18522	277.98228
88	279.93941	281.80545	283.68505	285.57830	287.48531	289.40619	291.34102	293.28992
90	294.86976	296.88924	298.92378	300.97350	303.03851	305.11893	307.21488	309.32646
92	310.48608	312.66965	314.86993	317.08706	319.32115	321.57236	323.84080	326.12661
96	343.90413	346.45052	349.01738	351.60490	354.21324	356.84256	359.49305	362.16487
100	380.46348	383.42367	386.40884	389.41919	392.45496	395.51634	398.60357	401.71686
104	420.45941	423.89079	427.35248	430.84476	434.36788	437.92214	441.50781	445.12517
108	464.21496	468.18206	472.18578	476.22646	480.30445	484.42010	488.57376	492.76578
112	512.08352	516.65885	521.27823	525.94211	530.65093	535.40511	540.20511	545.05136
116	564.45174	569.71669	575.03447	580.40561	585.83067	591.31018	596.84470	602.43479
120	621.74256	627.78850	633.89755	640.07038	646.30766	652.61008	658.97833	665.41310
140	999.84221	1011.59960	1023.50387	1035.55688	1047.76053	1060.11671	1072.62736	1085.29444
160	1592.34840	1614.43168	1636.83723	1659.56980	1682.63423	1706.03542	1729.77834	1753.86805

QUARTERLY DEPOSITS

NUMBER OF QUARTRLY DEPOSITS	EFFECTIVE ANNUAL YIELD							
	9.80%	9.85%	9.90%	9.95%	10.00%	10.05%	10.10%	10.15%
1	1.02365	1.02376	1.02388	1.02400	1.02411	1.02423	1.02435	1.02446
2	2.07150	2.07186	2.07221	2.07257	2.07292	2.07328	2.07363	2.07399
3	3.14414	3.14486	3.14558	3.14630	3.14702	3.14774	3.14846	3.14918
4	4.24214	4.24336	4.24458	4.24580	4.24702	4.24824	4.24946	4.25068
5	5.36610	5.36796	5.36983	5.37169	5.37355	5.37541	5.37727	5.37913
6	6.51665	6.51929	6.52194	6.52459	6.52724	6.52988	6.53253	6.53518
7	7.69440	7.69799	7.70157	7.70516	7.70875	7.71233	7.71592	7.71951
8	8.90000	8.90469	8.90937	8.91406	8.91875	8.92343	8.92812	8.93281
9	10.13412	10.14007	10.14602	10.15197	10.15792	10.16388	10.16984	10.17580
10	11.39742	11.40480	11.41219	11.41959	11.42698	11.43438	11.44178	11.44919
11	12.69059	12.69960	12.70861	12.71762	12.72664	12.73567	12.74469	12.75373
12	14.01434	14.02516	14.03598	14.04681	14.05764	14.06848	14.07933	14.09018
13	15.36940	15.38222	15.39505	15.40789	15.42074	15.43359	15.44645	15.45932
14	16.75650	16.77154	16.78658	16.80164	16.81670	16.83178	16.84687	16.86196
15	18.17640	18.19387	18.21134	18.22883	18.24633	18.26384	18.28137	18.29891
16	19.62988	19.65000	19.67012	19.69027	19.71043	19.73061	19.75080	19.77101
17	21.11774	21.14073	21.16374	21.18678	21.20983	21.23291	21.25601	21.27913
18	22.64077	22.66689	22.69303	22.71920	22.74540	22.77162	22.79786	22.82413
19	24.19983	24.22932	24.25884	24.28840	24.31798	24.34760	24.37725	24.40694
20	25.79575	25.82888	25.86205	25.89525	25.92849	25.96178	25.99510	26.02846
21	27.42941	27.46645	27.50353	27.54066	27.57784	27.61506	27.65233	27.68964
22	29.10171	29.14294	29.18422	29.22556	29.26696	29.30841	29.34991	29.39147
23	30.81355	30.85927	30.90505	30.95089	30.99680	31.04278	31.08882	31.13492
24	32.56587	32.61638	32.66697	32.71763	32.76837	32.81918	32.87007	32.92103
25	34.35963	34.41525	34.47096	34.52676	34.58265	34.63862	34.69468	34.75083
26	36.19581	36.25688	36.31804	36.37931	36.44067	36.50214	36.56371	36.62539
27	38.07541	38.14226	38.20923	38.27631	38.34351	38.41082	38.47825	38.54580
28	39.99946	40.07245	40.14558	40.21883	40.29222	40.36575	40.43941	40.51320
29	41.96901	42.04852	42.12817	42.20797	42.28793	42.36804	42.44830	42.52872
30	43.98514	44.07154	44.15811	44.24485	44.33176	44.41885	44.50611	44.59355
31	46.04894	46.14263	46.23652	46.33060	46.42488	46.51935	46.61402	46.70889
32	48.16155	48.26295	48.36457	48.46641	48.56847	48.67075	48.77325	48.87597
33	50.32411	50.43365	50.54344	50.65347	50.76375	50.87427	50.98505	51.09607
34	52.53782	52.65594	52.77434	52.89301	53.01196	53.13119	53.25069	53.37048
35	54.80388	54.93104	55.05852	55.18630	55.31439	55.44279	55.57150	55.70052
36	57.12352	57.26021	57.39724	57.53462	57.67234	57.81040	57.94881	58.08757
37	59.49802	59.64473	59.79182	59.93929	60.08714	60.23538	60.38400	60.53300
38	61.92866	62.08597	62.24358	62.40167	62.56018	62.71912	62.87848	63.03826
39	64.41679	64.58511	64.75389	64.92314	65.09285	65.26303	65.43369	65.60481
40	66.96376	67.14370	67.32415	67.50511	67.68659	67.86859	68.05110	68.23414
41	69.57096	69.76309	69.95579	70.14905	70.34288	70.53728	70.73225	70.92779
42	72.23981	72.44473	72.65027	72.85644	73.06322	73.27063	73.47867	73.68733
43	74.97178	75.19010	75.40910	75.62879	75.84916	76.07021	76.29195	76.51438
44	77.76835	78.00071	78.23382	78.46767	78.70227	78.93763	79.17373	79.41059
45	80.63105	80.87811	81.12599	81.37468	81.62419	81.87452	82.12567	82.37764
46	83.56145	83.82390	84.08723	84.35145	84.61656	84.88257	85.14948	85.41728
47	86.56115	86.83968	87.11919	87.39966	87.68110	87.96351	88.24690	88.53128
48	89.63178	89.92714	90.22355	90.52101	90.81952	91.11910	91.41974	91.72145
50	95.99261	96.32391	96.65645	96.99022	97.32524	97.66151	97.99904	98.33782
52	102.65783	103.02832	103.40026	103.77365	104.14850	104.52481	104.90260	105.28186
54	109.64202	110.05517	110.47001	110.88655	111.30479	111.72474	112.14640	112.56979
56	116.96044	117.41997	117.88146	118.34493	118.81037	119.27780	119.74722	120.21865
58	124.62908	125.13897	125.65113	126.16556	126.68229	127.20132	127.72265	128.24631
60	132.66470	133.22920	133.79631	134.36605	134.93843	135.51346	136.09116	136.67153
62	141.08486	141.70751	142.33517	142.96484	143.59754	144.23329	144.87211	145.51399
64	149.90798	150.59563	151.28672	151.98127	152.67929	153.38081	154.08583	154.79437
66	159.15332	159.91016	160.67093	161.43564	162.20432	162.97698	163.75365	164.53435
68	168.84109	169.67266	170.50869	171.34921	172.19425	173.04382	173.89796	174.75669
70	178.99248	179.90467	180.82193	181.74429	182.67177	183.60441	184.54223	185.48527
72	189.62966	190.62877	191.63363	192.64426	193.66069	194.68297	195.71112	196.74517
74	200.77588	201.86864	202.96788	204.07365	205.18597	206.30490	207.43046	208.56271
76	212.45550	213.64907	214.84994	216.05816	217.27378	218.49685	219.72740	220.96549
78	224.69405	225.99606	227.30628	228.62477	229.95159	231.28678	232.63040	233.98251
80	237.51828	238.93686	240.36466	241.80175	243.24818	244.70403	246.16933	247.64417
82	250.95621	252.50003	254.05418	255.61874	257.19377	258.77935	260.37554	261.98242
84	265.03721	266.71550	268.40534	270.10683	271.82003	273.54502	275.28190	277.03074
86	279.79205	281.61464	283.45013	285.29861	287.16017	289.03491	290.92293	292.82432
88	295.25299	297.23033	299.22205	301.22826	303.24905	305.28454	307.33484	309.40005
90	311.45381	313.59704	315.75627	317.93162	320.12321	322.33117	324.55561	326.79667
92	328.42992	330.75088	333.08962	335.44627	337.82098	340.21388	342.62512	345.05484
96	364.85819	367.57320	370.31007	373.06897	375.85010	378.65362	381.47972	384.32859
100	404.85643	408.02252	411.21535	414.43514	417.68213	420.95655	424.25863	427.58862
104	448.77450	452.45610	456.17024	459.91724	463.69736	467.51093	471.35822	475.23955
108	496.99654	501.26638	505.57568	509.92480	514.31412	518.74402	523.21486	527.72705
112	549.94434	554.88448	559.87225	564.90812	569.99256	575.12603	580.30903	585.54203
116	608.08102	613.78396	619.54418	625.36228	631.23883	637.17444	643.16970	649.22523
120	671.91510	678.48504	685.12364	691.83163	698.60974	705.45872	712.37931	719.37227
140	1098.11993	1111.10583	1124.25418	1137.56703	1151.04647	1164.69460	1178.51356	1192.50552
160	1778.30966	1803.10839	1828.26949	1853.79833	1879.70034	1905.98102	1932.64598	1959.70088

QUARTERLY DEPOSITS

EFFECTIVE ANNUAL YIELD

NUMBER OF QUARTERLY DEPOSITS	10.20%	10.25%	10.30%	10.35%	10.40%	10.45%	10.50%	10.55%
1	1.02458	1.02470	1.02481	1.02493	1.02504	1.02516	1.02528	1.02539
2	2.07434	2.07470	2.07505	2.07540	2.07576	2.07611	2.07647	2.07682
3	3.14990	3.15062	3.15135	3.15207	3.15279	3.15350	3.15422	3.15494
4	4.25190	4.25312	4.25435	4.25557	4.25679	4.25800	4.25922	4.26044
5	5.38099	5.38285	5.38471	5.38657	5.38843	5.39029	5.39215	5.39401
6	6.53783	6.54048	6.54312	6.54577	6.54842	6.55107	6.55372	6.55637
7	7.72310	7.72669	7.73028	7.73387	7.73746	7.74105	7.74464	7.74823
8	8.93750	8.94220	8.94689	8.95158	8.95628	8.96097	8.96567	8.97036
9	10.18176	10.18772	10.19368	10.19965	10.20561	10.21158	10.21755	10.22353
10	11.45659	11.46400	11.47141	11.47883	11.48624	11.49366	11.50108	11.50851
11	12.76276	12.77180	12.78084	12.78989	12.79894	12.80800	12.81705	12.82612
12	14.10103	14.11190	14.12276	14.13363	14.14451	14.15540	14.16629	14.17718
13	15.47220	15.48508	15.49798	15.51088	15.52378	15.53670	15.54962	15.56255
14	16.87707	16.89218	16.90731	16.92245	16.93760	16.95275	16.96792	16.98310
15	18.31647	18.33403	18.35161	18.36921	18.38682	18.40444	18.42207	18.43972
16	19.79124	19.81149	19.83175	19.85203	19.87233	19.89264	19.91297	19.93332
17	21.30227	21.32543	21.34861	21.37182	21.39504	21.41829	21.44156	21.46485
18	22.85043	22.87676	22.90311	22.92949	22.95589	22.98232	23.00878	23.03526
19	24.43665	24.46640	24.49618	24.52599	24.55583	24.58570	24.61561	24.64555
20	26.06185	26.09529	26.12877	26.16228	26.19583	26.22943	26.26306	26.29673
21	27.72700	27.76441	27.80187	27.83937	27.87691	27.91450	27.95214	27.98983
22	29.43308	29.47475	29.51648	29.55825	29.60009	29.64198	29.68392	29.72592
23	31.18109	31.22733	31.27363	31.31999	31.36642	31.41291	31.45947	31.50610
24	32.97207	33.02318	33.07438	33.12564	33.17699	33.22841	33.27990	33.33148
25	34.80706	34.86339	34.91980	34.97630	35.03290	35.08958	35.14634	35.20320
26	36.68716	36.74904	36.81102	36.87310	36.93528	36.99757	37.05996	37.12245
27	38.61347	38.68125	38.74916	38.81718	38.88531	38.95357	39.02194	39.09044
28	40.58712	40.66119	40.73538	40.80971	40.88418	40.95878	41.03352	41.10839
29	42.60929	42.69001	42.77089	42.85192	42.93310	43.01444	43.09593	43.17758
30	44.68116	44.76894	44.85690	44.94503	45.03334	45.12182	45.21048	45.29932
31	46.80395	46.89921	46.99466	47.09032	47.18617	47.28222	47.37847	47.47492
32	48.97892	49.08208	49.18547	49.28908	49.39292	49.49698	49.60126	49.70577
33	51.20734	51.31886	51.43063	51.54266	51.65493	51.76745	51.88023	51.99326
34	53.49054	53.61088	53.73150	53.85241	53.97359	54.09506	54.21681	54.33884
35	55.82986	55.95950	56.08946	56.21973	56.35032	56.48122	56.61244	56.74397
36	58.22667	58.36612	58.50592	58.64607	58.78657	58.92742	59.06862	59.21017
37	60.68239	60.83217	60.98233	61.13289	61.28383	61.43516	61.58688	61.73900
38	63.19848	63.35912	63.52019	63.68169	63.84363	64.00599	64.16879	64.33203
39	65.77641	65.94847	66.12102	66.29404	66.46754	66.64151	66.81597	66.99090
40	68.41769	68.60177	68.78637	68.97150	69.15715	69.34334	69.53005	69.71729
41	71.12390	71.32059	71.51786	71.71571	71.91413	72.11314	72.31273	72.51290
42	73.89663	74.10656	74.31712	74.52832	74.74015	74.95263	75.16574	75.37950
43	76.73750	76.96132	77.18583	77.41104	77.63694	77.86355	78.09087	78.31889
44	79.64820	79.88658	80.12572	80.36562	80.60628	80.84772	81.08993	81.33291
45	82.63045	82.88408	83.13854	83.39385	83.64998	83.90696	84.16479	84.42346
46	85.68599	85.95560	86.22613	86.49756	86.76991	87.04318	87.31737	87.59248
47	88.81663	89.10298	89.39031	89.67864	89.96797	90.25830	90.54963	90.84197
48	92.02423	92.32808	92.63301	92.93902	93.24612	93.55431	93.86359	94.17397
50	98.67786	99.01918	99.36176	99.70562	100.05077	100.39720	100.74492	101.09393
52	105.66260	106.04483	106.42855	106.81378	107.20050	107.58874	107.97850	108.36977
54	112.99491	113.42177	113.85037	114.28072	114.71283	115.14671	115.58236	116.01979
56	120.69209	121.16755	121.64504	122.12457	122.60614	123.08977	123.57546	124.06323
58	128.77230	129.30062	129.83130	130.36434	130.89975	131.43754	131.97773	132.52032
60	137.25459	137.84035	138.42882	139.02003	139.61396	140.21065	140.81011	141.41234
62	146.15898	146.80706	147.45827	148.11261	148.77011	149.43077	150.09462	150.76166
64	155.50646	156.22211	156.94134	157.66416	158.39060	159.12067	159.85440	160.59179
66	165.31910	166.10791	166.90082	167.69784	168.49899	169.30429	170.11378	170.92746
68	175.62002	176.48800	177.36064	178.23797	179.12001	180.00679	180.89833	181.79466
70	186.43355	187.38710	188.34595	189.31013	190.27967	191.25460	192.23495	193.22075
72	197.78517	198.83115	199.88313	200.94116	202.00528	203.07550	204.15188	205.23444
74	209.70167	210.84740	211.99992	213.15929	214.32554	215.49871	216.67884	217.86598
76	222.21116	223.46446	224.72544	225.99414	227.27061	228.55490	229.84705	231.14712
78	235.34315	236.71238	238.09026	239.47684	240.87218	242.27633	243.68934	245.11128
80	249.12861	250.62270	252.12651	253.64010	255.16354	256.69689	258.24022	259.79359
82	263.60006	265.22853	266.86790	268.51826	270.17967	271.85221	273.53595	275.23097
84	278.79163	280.56465	282.34988	284.14741	285.95733	287.77972	289.61466	291.46226
86	294.73917	296.66758	298.60964	300.56546	302.53514	304.51877	306.51645	308.52828
88	311.48028	313.57565	315.68626	317.81224	319.95368	322.11070	324.28343	326.47197
90	329.05447	331.32913	333.62078	335.92956	338.25558	340.59898	342.95990	345.33846
92	347.50317	349.97028	352.45629	354.96137	357.48564	360.02928	362.59241	365.17520
96	387.20040	390.09536	393.01364	395.95543	398.92094	401.91034	404.92384	407.96163
100	430.94675	434.33326	437.74839	441.19239	444.66550	448.16798	451.70007	455.26203
104	479.15522	483.10534	487.09082	491.11136	495.16750	499.25953	503.38780	507.55262
108	532.28096	536.87698	541.51551	546.19695	550.92170	555.69016	560.50274	565.35986
112	590.82552	596.16000	601.54596	606.98390	612.47434	618.01779	623.61476	629.26577
116	655.34163	661.51952	667.75954	674.06230	680.42846	686.85865	693.35353	699.91375
120	726.43838	733.57840	740.79311	748.08332	755.44980	762.89339	770.41487	778.01510
140	1206.67266	1221.01720	1235.54140	1250.24751	1265.13785	1280.21474	1295.48055	1310.93767
160	1987.15149	2015.00365	2043.26329	2071.93643	2101.02916	2130.54769	2160.49830	2190.88737

QUARTERLY DEPOSITS

EFFECTIVE ANNUAL YIELD

NUMBER OF QUARTRLY DEPOSITS	10.60%	10.65%	10.70%	10.75%	10.80%	10.85%	10.90%	10.95%
1	1.02551	1.02562	1.02574	1.02585	1.02597	1.02609	1.02620	1.02632
2	2.07717	2.07753	2.07788	2.07823	2.07859	2.07894	2.07929	2.07965
3	3.15566	3.15638	3.15710	3.15782	3.15854	3.15926	3.15998	3.16070
4	4.26166	4.26288	4.26410	4.26532	4.26654	4.26776	4.26898	4.27020
5	5.39587	5.39773	5.39959	5.40145	5.40331	5.40517	5.40703	5.40869
6	6.55902	6.56167	6.56431	6.56696	6.56961	6.57226	6.57491	6.57756
7	7.75183	7.75542	7.75901	7.76261	7.76620	7.76980	7.77339	7.77699
8	8.97506	8.97976	8.98446	8.98916	8.99386	8.99857	9.00327	9.00798
9	10.22950	10.23548	10.24145	10.24743	10.25341	10.25939	10.26538	10.27136
10	11.51594	11.52337	11.53080	11.53823	11.54567	11.55311	11.56055	11.56800
11	12.83518	12.84425	12.85333	12.86241	12.87149	12.88058	12.88967	12.89876
12	14.18808	14.19899	14.20990	14.22082	14.23174	14.24267	14.25360	14.26454
13	15.57549	15.58844	15.60139	15.61435	15.62732	15.64030	15.65328	15.66627
14	16.99829	17.01349	17.02869	17.04391	17.05914	17.07438	17.08963	17.10489
15	18.45738	18.47505	18.49274	18.51044	18.52815	18.54588	18.56362	18.58137
16	19.95368	19.97406	19.99446	20.01488	20.03531	20.05576	20.07622	20.09671
17	21.48816	21.51149	21.53484	21.55821	21.58161	21.60503	21.62847	21.65192
18	23.06177	23.08830	23.11487	23.14145	23.16807	23.19471	23.22138	23.24807
19	24.67552	24.70553	24.73556	24.76563	24.79573	24.82586	24.85603	24.88623
20	26.33044	26.36418	26.39797	26.43180	26.46566	26.49957	26.53351	26.56749
21	28.02756	28.06534	28.10317	28.14104	28.17896	28.21693	28.25494	28.29301
22	29.76798	29.81009	29.85226	29.89448	29.93676	29.97909	30.02148	30.06393
23	31.55279	31.59955	31.64637	31.69326	31.74021	31.78723	31.83431	31.88146
24	33.38313	33.43485	33.48666	33.53854	33.59049	33.64253	33.69464	33.74683
25	35.26015	35.31718	35.37431	35.43153	35.48883	35.54623	35.60371	35.66128
26	37.18505	37.24775	37.31055	37.37346	37.43647	37.49958	37.56280	37.62613
27	39.15905	39.22778	39.29663	39.36560	39.43469	39.50390	39.57323	39.64268
28	41.18340	41.25855	41.33383	41.40925	41.48481	41.56050	41.63633	41.71230
29	43.25939	43.34135	43.42346	43.50574	43.58816	43.67075	43.75349	43.83639
30	45.38833	45.47752	45.56688	45.65643	45.74615	45.83605	45.92613	46.01638
31	47.57157	47.66842	47.76547	47.86272	47.96018	48.05783	48.15569	48.25375
32	49.81050	49.91546	50.02065	50.12606	50.23170	50.33757	50.44367	50.54999
33	52.10655	52.22008	52.33388	52.44792	52.56222	52.67678	52.79160	52.90667
34	54.46115	54.58375	54.70664	54.82981	54.95327	55.07702	55.20105	55.32537
35	56.87582	57.00799	57.14048	57.27329	57.40641	57.53986	57.67363	57.80773
36	59.35208	59.49434	59.63696	59.77994	59.92327	60.06696	60.21100	60.35541
37	61.89150	62.04440	62.19770	62.35139	62.50548	62.65997	62.81486	62.97015
38	64.49570	64.65981	64.82435	64.98934	65.15476	65.32063	65.48694	65.65369
39	67.16632	67.34222	67.51861	67.69549	67.87285	68.05070	68.22904	68.40787
40	69.90506	70.09337	70.28222	70.47160	70.66152	70.85198	71.04298	71.23452
41	72.71367	72.91502	73.11696	73.31949	73.52262	73.72634	73.93066	74.13557
42	75.59391	75.80896	76.02466	76.24101	76.45802	76.67568	76.89399	77.11297
43	78.54762	78.77705	79.00720	79.23807	79.46965	79.70195	79.93498	80.16872
44	81.57666	81.82120	82.06652	82.31262	82.55950	82.80718	83.05564	83.30490
45	84.68298	84.94335	85.20457	85.46666	85.72960	85.99340	86.25807	86.52361
46	87.86852	88.14550	88.42340	88.70224	88.98202	89.26275	89.54442	89.82703
47	91.13533	91.42969	91.72508	92.02148	92.31891	92.61737	92.91687	93.21739
48	94.48545	94.79804	95.11174	95.42654	95.74247	96.05951	96.37768	96.69698
50	101.44425	101.79587	102.14881	102.50305	102.85862	103.21551	103.57373	103.93329
52	108.76258	109.15691	109.55279	109.95022	110.34919	110.74973	111.15183	111.55549
54	116.45900	116.90002	117.34283	117.78745	118.23389	118.68215	119.13225	119.58418
56	124.55307	125.04501	125.53904	126.03519	126.53345	127.03383	127.53635	128.04102
58	133.06532	133.61275	134.16261	134.71492	135.26969	135.82692	136.38664	136.94884
60	142.01736	142.62518	143.23582	143.84929	144.46560	145.08476	145.70679	146.33170
62	151.43191	152.10539	152.78212	153.46210	154.14536	154.83190	155.52176	156.21493
64	161.33286	162.07765	162.82616	163.57841	164.33442	165.09422	165.85781	166.62522
66	171.74536	172.56750	173.39390	174.22459	175.05959	175.89892	176.74261	177.59066
68	182.69581	183.60180	184.51266	185.42841	186.34908	187.27470	188.20529	189.14088
70	194.21023	195.20882	196.21115	197.21906	198.23257	199.25172	200.27653	201.30704
72	206.32323	207.41828	208.51961	209.62728	210.74132	211.86176	212.98864	214.12200
74	219.06017	220.26144	221.46985	222.68543	223.90823	225.13828	226.37565	227.62035
76	232.45516	233.77120	235.09531	236.42754	237.76792	239.11652	240.47338	241.83855
78	246.54221	247.98217	249.43122	250.88943	252.35685	253.83355	255.31957	256.81498
80	261.35707	262.93072	264.51461	266.10882	267.71340	269.32842	270.95395	272.59007
82	276.93734	278.65515	280.38447	282.12537	283.87793	285.64224	287.41838	289.20641
84	293.32258	295.19572	297.08178	298.98084	300.89298	302.81831	304.75691	306.70887
86	310.55436	312.59481	314.64970	316.71916	318.80329	320.90219	323.01596	325.14471
88	328.67644	330.89695	333.13363	335.38660	337.65596	339.94185	342.24439	344.56369
90	347.73479	350.14903	352.58132	355.03180	357.50058	359.98783	362.49367	365.01825
92	367.77780	370.40036	373.04303	375.70598	378.38935	381.09330	383.81800	386.56361
96	411.02391	414.11088	417.22274	420.35969	423.52194	426.70968	429.92314	433.16252
100	458.85411	462.47657	466.12967	469.81368	473.52884	477.27544	481.05374	484.86401
104	511.75431	515.99321	520.26965	524.58397	528.93650	533.32759	537.75758	542.22682
108	570.26193	575.20937	580.20260	585.24206	590.32818	595.46139	600.64213	605.87085
112	634.97136	640.73205	646.54838	652.42091	658.35016	664.33671	670.38110	676.48390
116	706.53998	713.23289	719.99316	726.82147	733.71852	740.68500	747.72161	754.82908
120	785.69488	793.45508	801.29653	809.22010	817.22666	825.31708	833.49225	841.75306
140	1326.58851	1342.43554	1358.48122	1374.72808	1391.17866	1407.83553	1424.70131	1441.77863
160	2221.72138	2253.00688	2284.75054	2316.95913	2349.63950	2382.79862	2416.44355	2450.58145

QUARTERLY DEPOSITS

EFFECTIVE ANNUAL YIELD

NUMBER OF QUARTRLY DEPOSITS	11.00%	11.05%	11.10%	11.15%	11.20%	11.25%	11.30%	11.35%
1	1.02643	1.02655	1.02666	1.02678	1.02690	1.02701	1.02713	1.02724
2	2.08000	2.08035	2.08070	2.08106	2.08141	2.08176	2.08211	2.08247
3	3.16141	3.16213	3.16285	3.16357	3.16429	3.16500	3.16572	3.16644
4	4.27141	4.27263	4.27385	4.27507	4.27629	4.27750	4.27872	4.27994
5	5.41075	5.41261	5.41447	5.41633	5.41819	5.42005	5.42191	5.42377
6	6.58021	6.58286	6.58551	6.58816	6.59081	6.59346	6.59611	6.59876
7	7.78058	7.78418	7.78778	7.79137	7.79497	7.79857	7.80217	7.80577
8	9.01268	9.01739	9.02210	9.02680	9.03151	9.03622	9.04094	9.04565
9	10.27735	10.28334	10.28933	10.29532	10.30132	10.30731	10.31331	10.31931
10	11.57545	11.58290	11.59035	11.59781	11.60527	11.61273	11.62019	11.62766
11	12.90786	12.91696	12.92607	12.93518	12.94429	12.95341	12.96253	12.97166
12	14.27549	14.28644	14.29740	14.30836	14.31933	14.33030	14.34128	14.35227
13	15.67927	15.69228	15.70529	15.71832	15.73135	15.74439	15.75743	15.77049
14	17.12016	17.13544	17.15073	17.16603	17.18134	17.19667	17.21200	17.22734
15	18.59914	18.61692	18.63471	18.65252	18.67034	18.68817	18.70602	18.72388
16	20.11721	20.13772	20.15826	20.17881	20.19938	20.21996	20.24057	20.26119
17	21.67541	21.69891	21.72243	21.74598	21.76954	21.79313	21.81674	21.84037
18	23.27479	23.30154	23.32831	23.35511	23.38194	23.40879	23.43567	23.46258
19	24.91646	24.94672	24.97701	25.00734	25.03770	25.06809	25.09852	25.12898
20	26.60151	26.63557	26.66968	26.70382	26.73799	26.77221	26.80647	26.84076
21	28.33111	28.36927	28.40747	28.44572	28.48402	28.52236	28.56075	28.59919
22	30.10643	30.14899	30.19160	30.23428	30.27700	30.31978	30.36262	30.40552
23	31.92868	31.97596	32.02331	32.07073	32.11821	32.16576	32.21337	32.26105
24	33.79909	33.85144	33.90386	33.95636	34.00893	34.06159	34.11432	34.16713
25	35.71895	35.77670	35.83455	35.89249	35.95051	36.00863	36.06684	36.12514
26	37.68955	37.75309	37.81672	37.88046	37.94431	38.00826	38.07232	38.13648
27	39.71225	39.78194	39.85175	39.92168	39.99173	40.06191	40.13220	40.20262
28	41.78841	41.86465	41.94104	42.01756	42.09422	42.17102	42.24796	42.32504
29	43.91945	44.00266	44.08603	44.16957	44.25326	44.33710	44.42111	44.50527
30	46.10682	46.19743	46.28823	46.37920	46.47036	46.56170	46.65321	46.74491
31	48.35201	48.45047	48.54914	48.64801	48.74709	48.84637	48.94586	49.04555
32	50.65655	50.76333	50.87034	50.97758	51.08506	51.19276	51.30070	51.40887
33	53.02200	53.13759	53.25343	53.36954	53.48591	53.60253	53.71942	53.83657
34	55.44998	55.57488	55.70007	55.82555	55.95132	56.07739	56.20375	56.33040
35	57.94214	58.07688	58.21195	58.34734	58.48305	58.61909	58.75546	58.89216
36	60.50018	60.64531	60.79080	60.93665	61.08287	61.22945	61.37640	61.52372
37	63.12583	63.28192	63.43841	63.59531	63.75261	63.91032	64.06843	64.22695
38	65.82089	65.98854	66.15663	66.32517	66.49416	66.66360	66.83349	67.00383
39	68.58719	68.76701	68.94732	69.12813	69.30944	69.49125	69.67355	69.85636
40	71.42661	71.61925	71.81243	72.00616	72.20044	72.39527	72.59065	72.78659
41	74.34109	74.54721	74.75393	74.96126	75.16919	75.37773	75.58689	75.79665
42	77.33260	77.55290	77.77386	77.99549	78.21779	78.44076	78.66439	78.88871
43	80.40320	80.63839	80.87432	81.11099	81.34838	81.58651	81.82538	82.06500
44	83.55495	83.80580	84.05746	84.30991	84.56317	84.81724	85.07212	85.32781
45	86.79002	87.05730	87.32546	87.59450	87.86442	88.13523	88.40692	88.67951
46	90.11060	90.39513	90.68061	90.96706	91.25447	91.54284	91.83219	92.12251
47	93.51896	93.82157	94.12522	94.42993	94.73568	95.04250	95.35037	95.65931
48	97.01741	97.33898	97.66168	97.98553	98.31053	98.63668	98.96399	99.29245
50	104.29418	104.65642	105.02001	105.38495	105.75125	106.11892	106.48795	106.85836
52	111.96074	112.36756	112.77598	113.18599	113.59760	114.01081	114.42564	114.84209
54	120.03796	120.49359	120.95108	121.41044	121.87168	122.33480	122.79981	123.26672
56	128.54783	129.05681	129.56796	130.08129	130.59681	131.11453	131.63446	132.15660
58	137.51355	138.08076	138.65050	139.22277	139.79759	140.37496	140.95491	141.53743
60	146.95951	147.59022	148.22386	148.86042	149.49994	150.14242	150.78787	151.43631
62	156.91145	157.61132	158.31455	159.02118	159.73121	160.44465	161.16153	161.88186
64	167.39647	168.17157	168.95055	169.73343	170.52022	171.31094	172.10562	172.90427
66	178.44312	179.30000	180.16132	181.02711	181.89739	182.77218	183.65150	184.53539
68	190.08149	191.02716	191.97791	192.93377	193.89477	194.86093	195.83228	196.80884
70	202.34328	203.38528	204.43308	205.48670	206.54618	207.61155	208.68284	209.76010
72	215.26187	216.40830	217.56131	218.72096	219.88727	221.06028	222.24004	223.42658
74	228.87245	230.13198	231.39900	232.67353	233.95563	235.24535	236.54273	237.84781
76	243.21209	244.59404	245.98447	247.38341	248.79093	250.20707	251.63189	253.06544
78	258.31983	259.83420	261.35813	262.89170	264.43495	265.98796	267.55077	269.12347
80	274.23683	275.89432	277.56259	279.24173	280.93180	282.63287	284.34501	286.06830
82	291.00643	292.81851	294.64274	296.47919	298.32795	300.18910	302.06273	303.94892
84	308.67430	310.65327	312.64589	314.65225	316.67244	318.70657	320.75472	322.81699
86	327.28855	329.44759	331.62193	333.81169	336.01697	338.23788	340.47454	342.72706
88	346.89988	349.25309	351.62343	354.01104	356.41604	358.83856	361.27872	363.73666
90	367.56170	370.12418	372.70581	375.30676	377.92715	380.56714	383.22688	385.90652
92	389.33028	392.11819	394.92748	397.75834	400.61092	403.48540	406.38194	409.30071
96	436.42803	439.71988	443.03828	446.38346	449.75603	453.15501	456.58182	460.03628
100	488.70652	492.58156	496.48938	500.43028	504.40455	508.41245	512.45428	516.53033
104	546.73566	551.28445	555.87355	560.50333	565.17414	569.88635	574.64034	579.43646
108	611.14799	616.47401	621.84937	627.27452	632.74993	638.27607	643.85341	649.48244
112	682.64568	688.86702	695.14850	701.49069	707.89421	714.35963	720.88757	727.47863
116	762.00812	769.25946	776.58383	783.98197	791.45464	799.00259	806.62659	814.32740
120	850.10043	858.53526	867.05848	875.67103	884.37385	893.16789	902.05411	911.03349
140	1459.07017	1476.57865	1494.30679	1512.25739	1530.43324	1548.83721	1567.47216	1586.34103
160	2485.21961	2520.36539	2556.02629	2592.20990	2628.92394	2666.17622	2703.97467	2742.32737

QUARTERLY DEPOSITS

EFFECTIVE ANNUAL YIELD

NUMBER OF QUARTRLY DEPOSITS	11.40%	11.45%	11.50%	11.55%	11.60%	11.65%	11.70%	11.75%
1	1.02736	1.02747	1.02759	1.02770	1.02782	1.02793	1.02805	1.02816
2	2.08282	2.08317	2.08352	2.08387	2.08423	2.08458	2.08493	2.08528
3	3.16715	3.16751	3.16787	3.16859	3.17002	3.17074	3.17146	3.17217
4	4.28115	4.28237	4.28359	4.28481	4.28602	4.28724	4.28846	4.28967
5	5.42563	5.42749	5.42935	5.43121	5.43307	5.43493	5.43678	5.43864
6	6.60141	6.60407	6.60672	6.60937	6.61202	6.61467	6.61732	6.61997
7	7.80937	7.81297	7.81657	7.82017	7.82377	7.82737	7.83097	7.83457
8	9.05036	9.05508	9.05979	9.06451	9.06922	9.07394	9.07866	9.08338
9	10.32531	10.33131	10.33731	10.34332	10.34932	10.35533	10.36134	10.36736
10	11.63513	11.64260	11.65008	11.65756	11.66504	11.67252	11.68000	11.68749
11	12.98079	12.98992	12.99906	13.00820	13.01735	13.02650	13.03565	13.04481
12	14.36326	14.37425	14.38526	14.39626	14.40728	14.41829	14.42932	14.44035
13	15.78355	15.79662	15.80969	15.82278	15.83587	15.84897	15.86208	15.87519
14	17.24269	17.25805	17.27343	17.28881	17.30420	17.31961	17.33502	17.35044
15	18.74175	18.75964	18.77754	18.79545	18.81338	18.83132	18.84928	18.86724
16	20.28182	20.30248	20.32315	20.34384	20.36454	20.38526	20.40600	20.42676
17	21.86403	21.88770	21.91140	21.93511	21.95885	21.98261	22.00639	22.03020
18	23.48951	23.51647	23.54346	23.57047	23.59751	23.62458	23.65167	23.67879
19	25.15947	25.18999	25.22055	25.25113	25.28176	25.31241	25.34310	25.37382
20	26.87511	26.90948	26.94390	26.97836	27.01285	27.04739	27.08196	27.11658
21	28.63768	28.67621	28.71480	28.75342	28.79210	28.83083	28.86960	28.90842
22	30.44847	30.49148	30.53455	30.57767	30.62085	30.66408	30.70737	30.75072
23	32.30880	32.35662	32.40450	32.45245	32.50046	32.54854	32.59669	32.64491
24	34.22002	34.27299	34.32604	34.37916	34.43236	34.48565	34.53901	34.59245
25	36.18353	36.24201	36.30059	36.35925	36.41801	36.47686	36.53580	36.59483
26	38.20075	38.26513	38.32961	38.39419	38.45889	38.52369	38.58859	38.65360
27	40.27316	40.34382	40.41460	40.48551	40.55654	40.62769	40.69896	40.77036
28	42.40226	42.47962	42.55712	42.63476	42.71254	42.79046	42.86853	42.94673
29	44.58961	44.67409	44.75874	44.84355	44.92852	45.01365	45.09894	45.18439
30	46.83679	46.92886	47.02110	47.11353	47.20614	47.29893	47.39191	47.48507
31	49.14545	49.24556	49.34587	49.44639	49.54712	49.64805	49.74920	49.85055
32	51.51727	51.62591	51.73478	51.84388	51.95322	52.06279	52.17260	52.28264
33	53.95398	54.07165	54.18959	54.30779	54.42625	54.54498	54.66397	54.78323
34	56.45734	56.58458	56.71212	56.83995	56.96807	57.09650	57.22522	57.35424
35	59.02919	59.16655	59.30424	59.44226	59.58061	59.71929	59.85831	59.99766
36	61.67140	61.81945	61.96787	62.11665	62.26581	62.41534	62.56525	62.71553
37	64.38589	64.54523	64.70498	64.86514	65.02572	65.18671	65.34811	65.50993
38	67.17463	67.34589	67.51760	67.68977	67.86239	68.03548	68.20903	68.38304
39	70.03967	70.22349	70.40781	70.59264	70.77798	70.96383	71.15019	71.33706
40	72.98309	73.18015	73.37776	73.57593	73.77467	73.97397	74.17384	74.37427
41	76.00703	76.21803	76.42964	76.64187	76.85472	77.06820	77.28230	77.49702
42	79.11370	79.33936	79.56571	79.79274	80.02045	80.24885	80.47794	80.70772
43	82.30535	82.54645	82.78830	83.03090	83.27425	83.51835	83.76321	84.00883
44	85.58432	85.84164	86.09979	86.35876	86.61855	86.87918	87.14063	87.40292
45	88.95299	89.22736	89.50264	89.77881	90.05589	90.33388	90.61278	90.89259
46	92.41381	92.70609	92.99936	93.29361	93.58885	93.88508	94.18231	94.48055
47	95.96932	96.28039	96.59254	96.90577	97.22008	97.53548	97.85197	98.16954
48	99.62209	99.95288	100.28485	100.61800	100.95233	101.28784	101.62454	101.96243
50	107.23014	107.60331	107.97787	108.35382	108.73118	109.10993	109.49010	109.87168
52	115.26016	115.67986	116.10120	116.52419	116.94882	117.37511	117.80307	118.23269
54	123.73553	124.20626	124.67892	125.15350	125.63002	126.10848	126.58890	127.07127
56	132.68097	133.20758	133.73643	134.26754	134.80091	135.33655	135.87448	136.41471
58	142.12254	142.71025	143.30058	143.89353	144.48912	145.08736	145.68825	146.29182
60	152.08776	152.74222	153.39971	154.06024	154.72384	155.39050	156.06025	156.73311
62	162.60566	163.33295	164.06374	164.79804	165.53588	166.27727	167.02223	167.77078
64	173.70692	174.51357	175.32426	176.13901	176.95782	177.78073	178.60776	179.43892
66	185.42386	186.31694	187.21465	188.11702	189.02407	189.93581	190.85229	191.77352
68	197.79066	198.77775	199.77014	200.76787	201.77095	202.77943	203.79332	204.81266
70	210.84334	211.93261	213.02793	214.12934	215.23688	216.35058	217.47046	218.59658
72	224.61995	225.82017	227.02730	228.24136	229.46241	230.69047	231.92559	233.16782
74	239.16064	240.48126	241.80973	243.14609	244.49038	245.84266	247.20296	248.57135
76	254.50778	255.95895	257.41902	258.88804	260.36607	261.85315	263.34934	264.85471
78	270.70610	272.29874	273.90144	275.51426	277.13729	278.77057	280.41417	282.06816
80	287.80282	289.54863	291.30580	293.07442	294.85455	296.64628	298.44967	300.26481
82	305.84775	307.75931	309.68369	311.62097	313.57123	315.53457	317.51108	319.50084
84	324.89349	326.98432	329.08956	331.20932	333.34370	335.49281	337.65674	339.83560
86	344.99555	347.28013	349.58090	351.89800	354.23152	356.58159	358.94833	361.33186
88	366.21251	368.70639	371.21845	373.74880	376.29760	378.86496	381.45103	384.05595
90	388.60620	391.32607	394.06630	396.82702	399.60840	402.41059	405.23374	408.07802
92	412.24189	415.20565	418.19216	421.20159	424.23414	427.28997	430.36926	433.47220
96	463.51862	467.02906	470.56784	474.13518	477.73132	481.35649	485.01092	488.69485
100	520.64090	524.78626	528.96673	533.18260	537.43418	541.72176	546.04565	550.40617
104	584.27511	589.15666	594.08150	599.05000	604.06256	609.11958	614.22145	619.36857
108	655.16363	660.89747	666.68446	672.52508	678.41984	684.36925	690.37381	696.43405
112	734.13344	740.85261	747.63676	754.48653	761.40257	768.38551	775.43601	782.55472
116	822.10581	829.96260	837.89858	845.91453	854.01129	862.18966	870.45047	878.79457
120	920.10702	929.27569	938.54050	947.90247	957.36262	966.92199	976.58163	986.34260
140	1605.44676	1624.79235	1644.38083	1664.21527	1684.29877	1704.63448	1725.22558	1746.07531
160	2781.24246	2820.72825	2860.79314	2901.44567	2942.69450	2984.54842	3027.01635	3070.10731

QUARTERLY DEPOSITS

NUMBER OF QUARTERLY DEPOSITS	EFFECTIVE ANNUAL YIELD							
	11.80%	11.85%	11.90%	11.95%	12.00%	12.05%	12.10%	12.15%
1	1.02828	1.02839	1.02851	1.02862	1.02874	1.02885	1.02897	1.02908
2	2.08563	2.08598	2.08634	2.08669	2.08704	2.08739	2.08774	2.08809
3	3.17289	3.17360	3.17432	3.17504	3.17575	3.17647	3.17718	3.17790
4	4.29089	4.29210	4.29332	4.29454	4.29575	4.29697	4.29818	4.29940
5	5.44050	5.44236	5.44422	5.44608	5.44794	5.44980	5.45165	5.45351
6	6.62263	6.62528	6.62793	6.63058	6.63323	6.63589	6.63854	6.64119
7	7.83818	7.84178	7.84538	7.84899	7.85259	7.85620	7.85980	7.86341
8	9.08810	9.09282	9.09754	9.10227	9.10699	9.11172	9.11644	9.12117
9	10.37337	10.37938	10.38540	10.39142	10.39744	10.40346	10.40949	10.41551
10	11.69498	11.70248	11.70997	11.71747	11.72497	11.73248	11.73998	11.74749
11	13.05397	13.06313	13.07230	13.08148	13.09065	13.09984	13.10902	13.11821
12	14.45138	14.46243	14.47347	14.48452	14.49558	14.50665	14.51772	14.52879
13	15.88831	15.90145	15.91458	15.92773	15.94088	15.95405	15.96722	15.98039
14	17.36588	17.38132	17.39678	17.41224	17.42772	17.44321	17.45870	17.47421
15	18.88523	18.90322	18.92123	18.93925	18.95728	18.97533	18.99339	19.01147
16	20.44754	20.46833	20.48913	20.50996	20.53080	20.55166	20.57254	20.59344
17	22.05402	22.07787	22.10174	22.12563	22.14954	22.17348	22.19743	22.22141
18	23.70594	23.73311	23.76032	23.78754	23.81480	23.84208	23.86939	23.89672
19	25.40457	25.43536	25.46617	25.49703	25.52791	25.55883	25.58978	25.62076
20	27.15123	27.18593	27.22066	27.25544	27.29025	27.32511	27.36000	27.39494
21	28.94729	28.98620	29.02517	29.06418	29.10324	29.14235	29.18150	29.22071
22	30.79413	30.83759	30.88111	30.92469	30.96833	31.01202	31.05577	31.09957
23	32.69320	32.74155	32.78997	32.83846	32.88701	32.93563	32.98432	33.03308
24	34.64597	34.69956	34.75324	34.80700	34.86083	34.91475	34.96874	35.02282
25	36.65395	36.71317	36.77248	36.83188	36.89138	36.95097	37.01065	37.07042
26	38.71872	38.78395	38.84929	38.91473	38.98028	39.04593	39.11170	39.17757
27	40.84188	40.91353	40.98529	41.05719	41.12920	41.20134	41.27361	41.34600
28	43.02508	43.10357	43.18220	43.26097	43.33988	43.41894	43.49814	43.57749
29	45.27001	45.35579	45.44173	45.52783	45.61409	45.70052	45.78712	45.87387
30	47.57842	47.67195	47.76567	47.85957	47.95366	48.04793	48.14239	48.23704
31	49.95211	50.05388	50.15586	50.25806	50.36046	50.46307	50.56590	50.66893
32	52.39292	52.50344	52.61420	52.72519	52.83642	52.94789	53.05960	53.17155
33	54.90276	55.02255	55.14261	55.26294	55.38354	55.50440	55.62554	55.74695
34	57.48356	57.61318	57.74310	57.87333	58.00385	58.13468	58.26581	58.39724
35	60.13735	60.27737	60.41773	60.55843	60.69946	60.84084	60.98255	61.12461
36	62.86618	63.01720	63.16861	63.32039	63.47254	63.62508	63.77799	63.93129
37	65.67217	65.83483	65.99790	66.16140	66.32531	66.48965	66.65441	66.81960
38	68.55751	68.73245	68.90785	69.08372	69.26006	69.43687	69.61415	69.79190
39	71.52444	71.71234	71.90076	72.08970	72.27915	72.46913	72.65962	72.85064
40	74.57527	74.77685	74.97899	75.18171	75.38500	75.58887	75.79331	75.99834
41	77.71237	77.92836	78.14497	78.36222	78.58010	78.79862	79.01778	79.23757
42	80.93819	81.16935	81.40121	81.63376	81.86702	82.10098	82.33564	82.57101
43	84.25522	84.50236	84.75027	84.99895	85.24840	85.49862	85.74962	86.00139
44	87.66604	87.93001	88.19481	88.46046	88.72695	88.99429	89.26249	89.53153
45	91.17332	91.45497	91.73754	92.02104	92.30546	92.59082	92.87711	93.16434
46	94.77978	95.08002	95.38127	95.68353	95.98682	96.29112	96.59644	96.90279
47	98.48822	98.80799	99.12887	99.45086	99.77396	100.09817	100.42350	100.74996
48	102.30152	102.64182	102.98331	103.32602	103.66993	104.01507	104.36143	104.70901
50	110.25468	110.63911	111.02496	111.41225	111.80098	112.19116	112.58279	112.97587
52	118.66399	119.09067	119.51934	119.96801	120.40608	120.84585	121.28734	121.73056
54	127.55562	128.04194	128.53025	129.02055	129.51285	130.00716	130.50349	131.00184
56	136.95723	137.50207	138.04923	138.59872	139.15056	139.70475	140.26129	140.82022
58	146.89807	147.50702	148.11867	148.73304	149.35015	149.96999	150.59259	151.21796
60	157.40907	158.08817	158.77041	159.45581	160.14438	160.83613	161.53109	162.22927
62	168.52293	169.27870	170.03811	170.80118	171.56792	172.33834	173.11248	173.89034
64	180.27423	181.11372	181.95741	182.80531	183.65745	184.51385	185.37454	186.23952
66	192.69953	193.63033	194.56597	195.50645	196.45182	197.40208	198.35727	199.31741
68	205.83748	206.86780	207.90366	208.94508	209.99210	211.04474	212.10304	213.16702
70	219.72896	220.86763	222.01264	223.16401	224.32179	225.48600	226.65668	227.83388
72	234.41719	235.67374	236.93751	238.20855	239.48690	240.77260	242.06569	243.36621
74	249.94786	251.33255	252.72546	254.12665	255.53615	256.95403	258.38032	259.81509
76	266.36930	267.89318	269.42640	270.96901	272.52108	274.08266	275.65382	277.23460
78	283.73260	285.40756	287.09311	288.78932	290.49624	292.21395	293.94253	295.68202
80	302.09177	303.93063	305.78146	307.64434	309.51936	311.40659	313.30611	315.21800
82	321.50393	323.52046	325.55051	327.59417	329.65154	331.72270	333.80775	335.90679
84	342.02949	344.23651	346.46277	348.70238	350.95744	353.22805	355.51433	357.81639
86	363.73229	366.14974	368.58434	371.03621	373.50548	375.99225	378.49667	381.01886
88	386.67985	389.32288	391.98516	394.66685	397.36808	400.08900	402.82975	405.59048
90	410.94358	413.83059	416.73920	419.66958	422.62189	425.59629	428.59295	431.61205
92	436.59896	439.74974	442.92471	446.12407	449.34800	452.59669	455.87033	459.16912
96	492.40853	496.15219	499.92608	503.73043	507.56551	511.43156	515.32882	519.25756
100	554.80362	559.23833	563.71060	568.22076	572.76912	577.35603	581.98179	586.64675
104	624.56134	629.80017	635.08548	640.41767	645.79717	651.22640	656.69977	662.22373
108	702.55047	708.72360	714.95397	721.24212	727.58858	733.99390	740.45863	746.98331
112	789.74231	796.99945	804.32681	811.72509	819.19496	826.73713	834.35230	842.04118
116	887.22279	895.73599	904.33502	913.02077	921.79411	930.65592	939.60711	948.64858
120	996.20597	1006.17280	1016.24421	1026.42129	1036.70515	1047.09569	1057.59776	1068.20878
140	1767.18692	1788.56372	1810.20906	1832.12633	1854.31896	1876.79042	1899.54424	1922.58397
160	3113.83051	3158.19524	3203.21096	3248.88725	3295.23384	3342.26061	3389.97755	3438.39483

QUARTERLY DEPOSITS

EFFECTIVE ANNUAL YIELD

NUMBER OF QUARTRLY DEPOSITS	12.20%	12.25%	12.30%	12.35%	12.40%	12.45%	12.50%	12.55%
1	1.02920	1.02931	1.02943	1.02954	1.02965	1.02977	1.02988	1.03000
2	2.08844	2.08879	2.08914	2.08949	2.08984	2.09019	2.09054	2.09089
3	3.17861	3.17933	3.18004	3.18076	3.18147	3.18219	3.18290	3.18361
4	4.30061	4.30183	4.30304	4.30426	4.30547	4.30669	4.30790	4.30911
5	5.45537	5.45723	5.45909	5.46095	5.46280	5.46466	5.46652	5.46838
6	6.64384	6.64650	6.64915	6.65180	6.65446	6.65711	6.65976	6.66242
7	7.86702	7.87062	7.87423	7.87784	7.88145	7.88505	7.88866	7.89227
8	9.12590	9.13063	9.13536	9.14009	9.14482	9.14955	9.15429	9.15902
9	10.42154	10.42757	10.43360	10.43963	10.44566	10.45170	10.45773	10.46377
10	11.75500	11.76252	11.77004	11.77756	11.78508	11.79260	11.80013	11.80766
11	13.12740	13.13660	13.14580	13.15501	13.16422	13.17343	13.18265	13.19187
12	14.53987	14.55096	14.56205	14.57315	14.58425	14.59536	14.60647	14.61759
13	15.99358	16.00677	16.01997	16.03318	16.04640	16.05962	16.07285	16.08609
14	17.48973	17.50526	17.52079	17.53634	17.55190	17.56747	17.58305	17.59864
15	19.02956	19.04766	19.06578	19.08391	19.10205	19.12021	19.13838	19.15656
16	20.61435	20.63528	20.65622	20.67719	20.69817	20.71917	20.74018	20.76122
17	22.24541	22.26943	22.29347	22.31753	22.34162	22.36573	22.38986	22.41401
18	23.92409	23.95148	23.97889	24.00634	24.03381	24.06131	24.08883	24.11638
19	25.65178	25.68283	25.71391	25.74503	25.77618	25.80736	25.83857	25.86982
20	27.42991	27.46493	27.49998	27.53508	27.57021	27.60539	27.64061	27.67586
21	29.25996	29.29926	29.33861	29.37801	29.41745	29.45695	29.49649	29.53608
22	31.14344	31.18736	31.23134	31.27538	31.31947	31.36362	31.40783	31.45210
23	33.08191	33.13080	33.17976	33.22879	33.27789	33.32706	33.37630	33.42560
24	35.07697	35.13121	35.18552	35.23992	35.29439	35.34895	35.40358	35.45830
25	37.13029	37.19025	37.25030	37.31045	37.37069	37.43102	37.49145	37.55197
26	39.24355	39.30964	39.37584	39.44214	39.50856	39.57508	39.64171	39.70846
27	41.41851	41.49115	41.56392	41.63681	41.70982	41.78297	41.85623	41.92963
28	43.65698	43.73661	43.81638	43.89630	43.97637	44.05658	44.13693	44.21743
29	45.96079	46.04788	46.13513	46.22254	46.31013	46.39787	46.48578	46.57386
30	48.33187	48.42690	48.52211	48.61750	48.71309	48.80886	48.90483	49.00098
31	50.77218	50.87565	50.97932	51.08321	51.18731	51.29163	51.39616	51.50091
32	53.28374	53.39617	53.50884	53.62175	53.73491	53.84831	53.96195	54.07583
33	55.86862	55.99057	56.11279	56.23529	56.35805	56.48109	56.60441	56.72800
34	58.52898	58.66102	58.79337	58.92602	59.05898	59.19225	59.32583	59.45972
35	61.26700	61.40974	61.55282	61.69624	61.84001	61.98412	62.12858	62.27339
36	64.08497	64.23903	64.39347	64.54830	64.70351	64.85911	65.01509	65.17146
37	66.98521	67.15124	67.31771	67.48460	67.65192	67.81967	67.98786	68.15647
38	69.97012	70.14882	70.32799	70.50764	70.68777	70.86838	71.04946	71.23103
39	73.04219	73.23426	73.42686	73.61999	73.81364	74.00783	74.20256	74.39781
40	76.20395	76.41014	76.61691	76.82427	77.03222	77.24075	77.44988	77.65960
41	79.45801	79.67910	79.90083	80.12321	80.34623	80.56991	80.79424	81.01923
42	82.80709	83.04388	83.28138	83.51959	83.75852	83.99817	84.23854	84.47964
43	86.25395	86.50728	86.76140	87.01631	87.27201	87.52850	87.78578	88.04385
44	89.80144	90.07220	90.34383	90.61632	90.88968	91.16391	91.43901	91.71499
45	93.45251	93.74162	94.03167	94.32268	94.61464	94.90755	95.20142	95.49625
46	97.21017	97.51858	97.82803	98.13852	98.45005	98.76263	99.07626	99.39095
47	101.07754	101.40625	101.73610	102.06708	102.39921	102.73248	103.06690	103.40247
48	105.05783	105.40788	105.75916	106.11170	106.46547	106.82050	107.17679	107.53434
50	113.37042	113.76643	114.16392	114.56288	114.96333	115.36527	115.76870	116.17362
52	122.17549	122.62217	123.07058	123.52075	123.97266	124.42634	124.88179	125.33901
54	131.50222	132.00465	132.50913	133.01566	133.52426	134.03493	134.54768	135.06253
56	141.38152	141.94521	142.51131	143.07982	143.65075	144.22411	144.79991	145.37817
58	151.84611	152.47705	153.11079	153.74735	154.38674	155.02896	155.67404	156.32199
60	162.93067	163.63533	164.34324	165.05443	165.76891	166.48670	167.20780	167.93225
62	174.67195	175.45731	176.24646	177.03940	177.83616	178.63675	179.44120	180.24952
64	187.10883	187.98248	188.86050	189.74291	190.62973	191.52097	192.41668	193.31686
66	200.28254	201.25266	202.22782	203.20803	204.19332	205.18372	206.17925	207.17994
68	214.23672	215.31216	216.39339	217.48041	218.57328	219.67202	220.77666	221.88724
70	229.01762	230.20794	231.40488	232.60847	233.81876	235.03578	236.25956	237.49014
72	244.67421	245.98973	247.31281	248.64350	249.98184	251.32787	252.68165	254.04320
74	261.25838	262.71024	264.17072	265.63988	267.11776	268.60442	270.09990	271.60427
76	278.82508	280.42530	282.03533	283.65523	285.28506	286.92488	288.57475	290.23473
78	297.43251	299.19407	300.96676	302.75066	304.54583	306.35235	308.17029	309.99972
80	317.14235	319.07923	321.02872	322.99091	324.96588	326.95371	328.95450	330.96831
82	338.01989	340.14717	342.28872	344.44462	346.61499	348.79990	350.99948	353.21380
84	360.13433	362.46826	364.81829	367.18454	369.56712	371.96614	374.38171	376.81395
86	383.55893	386.11703	388.69327	391.28779	393.90072	396.53218	399.18231	401.85124
88	408.37133	411.17245	413.99399	416.83609	419.69892	422.58261	425.48732	428.41321
90	434.65374	437.71819	440.80559	443.91609	447.04988	450.20712	453.38800	456.59269
92	462.49324	465.84290	469.21829	472.61961	476.04705	479.50083	482.98114	486.48818
96	523.21803	527.21048	531.23518	535.29239	539.38236	543.50537	547.66168	551.85156
100	591.35124	596.09560	600.88015	605.70525	610.57124	615.47847	620.42729	625.41805
104	667.79671	673.41913	679.09145	684.81411	690.58755	696.41223	702.28860	708.21713
108	753.56852	760.21480	766.92274	773.69291	780.52588	787.42224	794.38258	801.40749
112	849.80449	857.64295	865.55728	873.54824	881.61656	889.76299	897.99830	906.29325
116	957.78125	967.00603	976.32387	985.73570	995.24248	1004.84517	1014.54474	1024.34216
120	1078.93117	1089.76610	1100.71475	1111.77832	1122.95802	1134.25508	1145.67073	1157.20622
140	1945.91322	1969.53565	1993.45495	2017.67487	2042.19920	2067.03176	2092.17646	2117.63722
160	3487.52277	3537.37181	3587.95258	3639.27583	3691.35249	3744.19364	3797.81052	3852.21455

QUARTERLY DEPOSITS

EFFECTIVE ANNUAL YIELD

NUMBER OF QUARTERLY DEPOSITS	12.60%	12.65%	12.70%	12.75%	12.80%	12.85%	12.90%	12.95%
1	1.03011	1.03023	1.03034	1.03046	1.03057	1.03068	1.03080	1.03091
2	2.09124	2.09159	2.09194	2.09229	2.09264	2.09299	2.09334	2.09369
3	3.18433	3.18504	3.18576	3.18647	3.18718	3.18790	3.18861	3.18932
4	4.31033	4.31154	4.31276	4.31397	4.31518	4.31640	4.31761	4.31882
5	5.47023	5.47209	5.47395	5.47581	5.47767	5.47952	5.48138	5.48324
6	6.66507	6.66772	6.67038	6.67303	6.67568	6.67834	6.68099	6.68365
7	7.89588	7.89949	7.90310	7.90671	7.91033	7.91394	7.91755	7.92116
8	9.16376	9.16849	9.17323	9.17797	9.18271	9.18745	9.19219	9.19693
9	10.46981	10.47585	10.48190	10.48794	10.49399	10.50004	10.50609	10.51214
10	11.81520	11.82273	11.83027	11.83781	11.84536	11.85290	11.86045	11.86800
11	13.20109	13.21032	13.21955	13.22879	13.23803	13.24728	13.25652	13.26578
12	14.62872	14.63985	14.65099	14.66213	14.67328	14.68443	14.69559	14.70676
13	16.09924	16.11259	16.12586	16.13913	16.15240	16.16569	16.17898	16.19229
14	17.61424	17.62985	17.64547	17.66110	17.67674	17.69240	17.70806	17.72373
15	19.17476	19.19297	19.21119	19.22943	19.24768	19.26595	19.28423	19.30252
16	20.78227	20.80334	20.82442	20.84552	20.86664	20.88778	20.90904	20.93011
17	22.43818	22.46238	22.48660	22.51083	22.53510	22.55938	22.58368	22.60801
18	24.14396	24.17157	24.19920	24.22686	24.25455	24.28227	24.31001	24.33778
19	25.90111	25.93242	25.96377	25.99515	26.02657	26.05802	26.08950	26.12102
20	27.71116	27.74650	27.78188	27.81730	27.85276	27.88826	27.92380	27.95938
21	29.57572	29.61541	29.65515	29.69494	29.73477	29.77466	29.81459	29.85457
22	31.49643	31.54081	31.58526	31.62976	31.67432	31.71893	31.76361	31.80834
23	33.47497	33.52442	33.57393	33.62351	33.67315	33.72287	33.77266	33.82251
24	35.51310	35.56797	35.62293	35.67797	35.73309	35.78830	35.84358	35.89894
25	37.61259	37.67330	37.73411	37.79501	37.85601	37.91710	37.97828	38.03956
26	39.77531	39.84227	39.90934	39.97652	40.04381	40.11121	40.17873	40.24635
27	42.00315	42.07680	42.15057	42.22447	42.29850	42.37266	42.44694	42.52135
28	44.29808	44.37887	44.45980	44.54088	44.62211	44.70349	44.78501	44.86668
29	46.66211	46.75052	46.83910	46.92784	47.01676	47.10584	47.19509	47.28451
30	49.09733	49.19386	49.29058	49.38750	49.48460	49.58190	49.67939	49.77707
31	51.60587	51.71105	51.81645	51.92206	52.02789	52.13394	52.24021	52.34669
32	54.18996	54.30433	54.41895	54.53382	54.64893	54.76428	54.87989	54.99574
33	56.85186	56.97600	57.10042	57.22511	57.35009	57.47534	57.60087	57.72667
34	59.59392	59.72842	59.86324	59.99837	60.13382	60.26957	60.40564	60.54203
35	62.41854	62.56404	62.70989	62.85610	63.00265	63.14955	63.29680	63.44441
36	65.32822	65.48558	65.64292	65.80085	65.95917	66.11789	66.27700	66.43651
37	68.32552	68.49501	68.66493	68.83529	69.00608	69.17731	69.34899	69.52110
38	71.41308	71.59651	71.77863	71.96214	72.14613	72.33061	72.51558	72.70104
39	74.59361	74.78994	74.98681	75.18422	75.38217	75.58066	75.77970	75.97928
40	77.86697	78.08082	78.29232	78.50443	78.71713	78.93044	79.14435	79.35886
41	81.24487	81.47117	81.69813	81.92575	82.15404	82.38300	82.61262	82.84291
42	84.72146	84.96400	85.20727	85.45128	85.69602	85.94149	86.18770	86.43465
43	88.30273	88.56241	88.82289	89.08417	89.34627	89.60917	89.87289	90.13743
44	91.99185	92.26958	92.54820	92.82771	93.10811	93.38940	93.67158	93.95466
45	95.79205	96.08881	96.38655	96.68526	96.98494	97.28561	97.58725	97.88989
46	99.70669	100.02349	100.34135	100.66029	100.98029	101.30137	101.62353	101.94676
47	103.73920	104.07710	104.41615	104.75638	105.09778	105.44035	105.78411	106.12905
48	107.89315	108.25323	108.61458	108.97721	109.34113	109.70633	110.07282	110.44061
50	116.58006	116.98800	117.39746	117.80844	118.22095	118.63499	119.05057	119.46769
52	125.79801	126.25880	126.72139	127.18578	127.65198	128.11999	128.58983	129.06149
54	135.57947	136.09853	136.61970	137.14299	137.66842	138.19599	138.72570	139.25758
56	145.95889	146.54209	147.12776	147.71594	148.30661	148.89980	149.49552	150.09378
58	156.97282	157.62653	158.28315	158.94269	159.60516	160.27057	160.93893	161.61026
60	168.66004	169.39120	170.12575	170.86369	171.60504	172.34983	173.09806	173.84974
62	181.06172	181.87783	182.69787	183.52185	184.34980	185.18173	186.01766	186.85761
64	194.22153	195.13073	196.04447	196.96278	197.88567	198.81318	199.74531	200.68211
66	208.18583	209.19692	210.21326	211.23486	212.26176	213.29398	214.33155	215.37450
68	223.00378	224.12631	225.25488	226.38950	227.53022	228.67707	229.83007	230.98927
70	238.72757	239.97187	241.22310	242.48127	243.74645	245.01865	246.29793	247.58432
72	255.41258	256.78983	258.17500	259.56813	260.96927	262.37847	263.79576	265.22120
74	273.11757	274.63986	276.17119	277.71161	279.26118	280.81995	282.38797	283.96531
76	291.90489	293.58529	295.27598	296.97704	298.68852	300.41050	302.14302	303.88617
78	311.84071	313.69334	315.55768	317.43381	319.32179	321.22171	323.13363	325.05764
80	332.99524	335.03537	337.08879	339.15558	341.23584	343.32964	345.43708	347.55825
82	355.44297	357.68709	359.94626	362.22059	364.51016	366.81509	369.13548	371.47143
84	379.26297	381.72889	384.21182	386.71189	389.22921	391.76390	394.31608	396.88587
86	404.53911	407.24605	409.97220	412.71768	415.48265	418.26723	421.07157	423.89580
88	431.36043	434.32913	437.31948	440.33162	443.36573	446.42195	449.50046	452.60141
90	459.82137	463.07422	466.35142	469.65316	472.97961	476.33097	479.70741	483.10913
92	490.02217	493.58331	497.17181	500.78788	504.43173	508.10357	511.80363	515.53212
96	556.07529	560.33314	564.62538	568.95230	573.31417	577.71128	582.14391	586.61235
100	630.45111	635.52682	640.64556	645.80769	651.01357	656.26357	661.55808	666.89747
104	714.19828	720.23251	726.32031	732.46214	738.65849	744.90984	751.21668	757.57952
108	808.49759	815.65347	822.87574	830.16503	837.52196	844.94715	852.44125	860.00489
112	914.67861	923.14517	931.69372	940.32504	949.03995	957.83026	966.72378	975.69434
116	1034.23845	1044.23458	1054.33157	1064.53045	1074.83225	1085.23800	1095.74875	1106.36558
120	1168.86282	1180.64179	1192.54444	1204.57206	1216.72596	1229.00748	1241.41795	1253.95875
140	2143.41803	2169.52292	2195.95598	2222.72133	2249.82317	2277.26573	2305.05331	2333.19025
160	3907.41731	3963.43052	4020.26611	4077.93617	4136.45296	4195.82893	4256.07670	4317.20907

EFFECTIVE ANNUAL YIELD

NUMBER OF QUARTRLY DEPOSITS	13.00%	13.05%	13.10%	13.15%	13.20%	13.25%	13.30%	13.35%
1	1.03103	1.03114	1.03125	1.03137	1.03148	1.03160	1.03171	1.03182
2	2.09404	2.09439	2.09474	2.09509	2.09544	2.09579	2.09613	2.09648
3	3.19004	3.19075	3.19146	3.19217	3.19289	3.19360	3.19431	3.19502
4	4.32004	4.32125	4.32246	4.32367	4.32489	4.32610	4.32731	4.32852
5	5.48510	5.48695	5.48881	5.49067	5.49252	5.49438	5.49624	5.49810
6	6.68630	6.68896	6.69161	6.69427	6.69692	6.69958	6.70223	6.70489
7	7.92478	7.92839	7.93201	7.93562	7.93924	7.94285	7.94647	7.95008
8	9.20168	9.20642	9.21117	9.21591	9.22066	9.22541	9.23016	9.23491
9	10.51819	10.52425	10.53031	10.53636	10.54242	10.54849	10.55455	10.56061
10	11.87556	11.88311	11.89067	11.89824	11.90580	11.91337	11.92094	11.92851
11	13.27503	13.28430	13.29356	13.30283	13.31210	13.32138	13.33066	13.33994
12	14.71793	14.72911	14.74029	14.75148	14.76267	14.77387	14.78508	14.79629
13	16.20560	16.21891	16.23224	16.24557	16.25891	16.27226	16.28562	16.29898
14	17.73942	17.75511	17.77081	17.78653	17.80225	17.81799	17.83374	17.84949
15	19.32083	19.33914	19.35748	19.37582	19.39419	19.41256	19.43095	19.44935
16	20.95130	20.97251	20.99373	21.01497	21.03623	21.05751	21.07880	21.10012
17	22.63236	22.65673	22.68112	22.70554	22.72998	22.75443	22.77892	22.80342
18	24.36558	24.39340	24.42125	24.44913	24.47704	24.50497	24.53294	24.56092
19	26.15257	26.18415	26.21577	26.24742	26.27910	26.31082	26.34257	26.37436
20	27.99500	28.03067	28.06637	28.10212	28.13790	28.17373	28.20960	28.24551
21	29.89460	29.93468	29.97481	30.01499	30.05522	30.09550	30.13582	30.17620
22	31.85314	31.89799	31.94290	31.98787	32.03290	32.07798	32.12313	32.16833
23	33.87244	33.92243	33.97250	34.02263	34.07283	34.12311	34.17345	34.22386
24	35.95439	36.00992	36.06553	36.12122	36.17699	36.23285	36.28879	36.34481
25	38.10094	38.16241	38.22397	38.28564	38.34739	38.40925	38.47120	38.53324
26	40.31408	40.38193	40.44988	40.51795	40.58612	40.65441	40.72281	40.79133
27	42.59589	42.67056	42.74536	42.82028	42.89533	42.97052	43.04583	43.12127
28	44.94850	45.03046	45.11257	45.19483	45.27724	45.35980	45.44251	45.52536
29	47.37409	47.46385	47.55378	47.64387	47.73414	47.82457	47.91518	48.00596
30	49.87495	49.97302	50.07128	50.16973	50.26838	50.36722	50.46626	50.56549
31	52.45339	52.56032	52.66746	52.77482	52.88241	52.99021	53.09824	53.20648
32	55.11184	55.22819	55.34478	55.46163	55.57873	55.69607	55.81367	55.93152
33	57.85276	57.97913	58.10578	58.23272	58.35993	58.48743	58.61521	58.74328
34	60.67873	60.81574	60.95308	61.09073	61.22869	61.36698	61.50558	61.64451
35	63.59237	63.74069	63.88936	64.03839	64.18777	64.33751	64.48761	64.63807
36	66.59641	66.75671	66.91741	67.07851	67.24000	67.40190	67.56420	67.72690
37	69.69366	69.86666	70.04010	70.21399	70.38833	70.56311	70.73834	70.91403
38	72.88700	73.07345	73.26039	73.44783	73.63577	73.82420	74.01314	74.20258
39	76.17942	76.38010	76.58133	76.78311	76.98544	77.18833	77.39178	77.59578
40	79.57398	79.78971	80.00605	80.22301	80.44057	80.65875	80.87755	81.09697
41	83.07387	83.30551	83.53782	83.77081	84.00447	84.23882	84.47386	84.70957
42	86.68235	86.93078	87.17996	87.42990	87.68058	87.93201	88.18420	88.43714
43	90.40278	90.66895	90.93594	91.20376	91.47241	91.74189	92.01219	92.28334
44	94.23864	94.52352	94.80931	95.09601	95.38361	95.67214	95.96158	96.25193
45	98.19351	98.49812	98.80373	99.11034	99.41795	99.72657	100.03619	100.34682
46	102.27109	102.59650	102.92300	103.25060	103.57930	103.90910	104.24001	104.57203
47	106.47517	106.82249	107.17101	107.52073	107.87165	108.22378	108.57713	108.93169
48	110.80970	111.18009	111.55179	111.92481	112.29914	112.67479	113.05178	113.43009
50	119.88636	120.30659	120.72838	121.15173	121.57665	122.00316	122.43124	122.86092
52	129.53499	130.01034	130.48754	130.96659	131.44751	131.93030	132.41497	132.90153
54	139.79163	140.32785	140.86626	141.40686	141.94966	142.49467	143.04191	143.59137
56	150.69458	151.29794	151.90387	152.51237	153.12347	153.73717	154.35348	154.97241
58	162.28458	162.96188	163.64220	164.32553	165.01190	165.70132	166.39379	167.08934
60	174.60491	175.36557	176.12573	176.89142	177.66066	178.43344	179.20980	179.98975
62	187.70161	188.54966	189.40179	190.25801	191.11836	191.98284	192.85148	193.72429
64	201.62358	202.56976	203.52067	204.47632	205.43675	206.40197	207.37202	208.34691
66	216.42285	217.47664	218.53588	219.60062	220.67087	221.74667	222.82804	223.91501
68	232.15469	233.32637	234.50434	235.68863	236.87929	238.07633	239.27981	240.48974
70	248.87786	250.17859	251.48655	252.80177	254.12431	255.45420	256.79148	258.13619
72	266.65483	268.09671	269.54687	271.00536	272.47224	273.94755	275.43133	276.92365
74	285.55202	287.14814	288.75374	290.36888	291.99361	293.62798	295.27206	296.92589
76	305.64000	307.40458	309.17997	310.96624	312.76346	314.57170	316.39101	318.22148
78	326.99381	328.94222	330.90295	332.87606	334.86165	336.85979	338.87055	340.89402
80	349.69323	351.84212	354.00501	356.18198	358.37313	360.57855	362.79833	365.03257
82	373.82305	376.19043	378.57369	380.97294	383.38827	385.81981	388.26765	390.73190
84	399.47339	402.07877	404.70212	407.34358	410.00327	412.68130	415.37782	418.09294
86	426.74008	429.60453	432.48931	435.39456	438.32041	441.26703	444.23455	447.22313
88	455.72497	458.87130	462.04056	465.23294	468.44858	471.68767	474.95038	478.23687
90	486.53653	489.98917	493.46787	496.97261	500.50360	504.06101	507.64506	511.25594
92	519.28925	523.07525	526.89034	530.73474	534.60868	538.51239	542.44609	546.41002
96	591.11689	595.65782	600.23544	604.85003	609.50192	614.19138	618.91873	623.68428
100	672.28212	677.71241	683.18874	688.71149	694.28106	699.89784	705.56223	711.27465
104	763.99883	770.47513	777.00893	783.60072	790.25104	796.96040	803.72932	810.55834
108	867.63871	875.34338	883.11956	890.96789	898.88907	906.88375	914.95264	923.09640
112	984.75178	993.89695	1003.13068	1012.45385	1021.86731	1031.37195	1040.96865	1050.65830
116	1117.08955	1127.92175	1138.86326	1149.91520	1161.07868	1172.35483	1183.74479	1195.24970
120	1266.63123	1279.43678	1292.37681	1305.45272	1318.66596	1332.01795	1345.51016	1359.14406
140	2361.68094	2390.52984	2419.74147	2449.32038	2479.27119	2509.59859	2540.30732	2571.40217
160	4379.23905	4442.17981	4506.04474	4570.84741	4636.60158	4703.32121	4771.02050	4839.71380

QUARTERLY DEPOSITS

NUMBER OF QUARTRLY DEPOSITS	EFFECTIVE ANNUAL YIELD							
	13.40%	13.45%	13.50%	13.55%	13.60%	13.65%	13.70%	13.75%
1	1.03194	1.03205	1.03216	1.03228	1.03239	1.03251	1.03262	1.03273
2	2.09683	2.09718	2.09753	2.09788	2.09822	2.09857	2.09892	2.09927
3	3.19574	3.19645	3.19716	3.19787	3.19858	3.19929	3.20000	3.20072
4	4.32974	4.33095	4.33216	4.33337	4.33458	4.33579	4.33700	4.33822
5	5.49995	5.50181	5.50367	5.50552	5.50738	5.50924	5.51109	5.51295
6	6.70754	6.71020	6.71285	6.71551	6.71817	6.72082	6.72348	6.72613
7	7.95370	7.95732	7.96093	7.96455	7.96817	7.97179	7.97541	7.97903
8	9.23966	9.24441	9.24916	9.25391	9.25867	9.26342	9.26818	9.27294
9	10.56668	10.57275	10.57882	10.58489	10.59097	10.59704	10.60312	10.60920
10	11.93609	11.94367	11.95125	11.95883	11.96642	11.97401	11.98160	11.98919
11	13.34923	13.35852	13.36782	13.37712	13.38643	13.39573	13.40505	13.41436
12	14.80751	14.81873	14.82996	14.84119	14.85243	14.86367	14.87492	14.88618
13	16.31235	16.32573	16.33912	16.35252	16.36592	16.37933	16.39275	16.40618
14	17.86526	17.88104	17.89683	17.91262	17.92843	17.94425	17.96008	17.97592
15	19.46776	19.48619	19.50464	19.52309	19.54156	19.56004	19.57854	19.59705
16	21.12145	21.14279	21.16416	21.18554	21.20694	21.22836	21.24979	21.27125
17	22.82794	22.85249	22.87706	22.90165	22.92627	22.95090	22.97556	23.00024
18	24.58894	24.61699	24.64506	24.67316	24.70128	24.72944	24.75762	24.78583
19	26.40618	26.43803	26.46992	26.50184	26.53380	26.56578	26.59781	26.62986
20	28.28146	28.31745	28.35348	28.38955	28.42567	28.46182	28.49802	28.53426
21	30.21662	30.25710	30.29762	30.33820	30.37882	30.41949	30.46022	30.50099
22	32.21359	32.25892	32.30430	32.34974	32.39524	32.44080	32.48642	32.53210
23	34.27434	34.32490	34.37552	34.42621	34.47697	34.52781	34.57871	34.62969
24	36.40091	36.45709	36.51336	36.56971	36.62614	36.68266	36.73925	36.79594
25	38.59539	38.65763	38.71996	38.78239	38.84492	38.90755	38.97027	39.03309
26	40.85995	40.92869	40.99754	41.06650	41.13557	41.20476	41.27406	41.34348
27	43.19684	43.27254	43.34837	43.42433	43.50043	43.57665	43.65300	43.72948
28	45.60836	45.69152	45.77482	45.85827	45.94188	46.02563	46.10954	46.19359
29	48.09690	48.18802	48.27932	48.37078	48.46241	48.55422	48.64620	48.73836
30	50.66492	50.76455	50.86437	50.96438	51.06459	51.16501	51.26561	51.36642
31	53.31495	53.42365	53.53256	53.64170	53.75107	53.86065	53.97047	54.08050
32	56.04962	56.16797	56.28658	56.40544	56.52456	56.64392	56.76355	56.88343
33	58.87163	59.00026	59.12918	59.25839	59.38788	59.51767	59.64774	59.77810
34	61.78376	61.92332	62.06321	62.20343	62.34396	62.48482	62.62601	62.76752
35	64.78889	64.94007	65.09162	65.24352	65.39579	65.54843	65.70142	65.85479
36	67.89001	68.05351	68.21743	68.38175	68.54648	68.71161	68.87716	69.04311
37	71.09016	71.26674	71.44378	71.62127	71.79922	71.97762	72.15648	72.33580
38	74.39252	74.58296	74.77391	74.96536	75.15732	75.34979	75.54277	75.73627
39	77.80034	78.00546	78.21115	78.41739	78.62420	78.83158	79.03952	79.24804
40	81.31700	81.53766	81.75894	81.98085	82.20338	82.42654	82.65033	82.87476
41	84.94598	85.18307	85.42085	85.65933	85.89849	86.13836	86.37893	86.62019
42	88.69085	88.94531	89.20054	89.45654	89.71330	89.97083	90.22914	90.48822
43	92.55532	92.82814	93.10181	93.37632	93.65168	93.92788	94.20494	94.48286
44	96.54322	96.83542	97.12856	97.42262	97.71762	98.01356	98.31043	98.60825
45	100.65847	100.97114	101.28482	101.59953	101.91527	102.23204	102.54984	102.86868
46	104.90516	105.23941	105.57478	105.91127	106.24889	106.58765	106.92754	107.26857
47	109.28747	109.64448	110.00271	110.36218	110.72289	111.08483	111.44803	111.81247
48	113.80974	114.19073	114.57307	114.95676	115.34180	115.72820	116.11597	116.50510
50	123.29218	123.72505	124.15953	124.59562	125.03332	125.47265	125.91361	126.35621
52	133.38998	133.88034	134.37260	134.86677	135.36287	135.86090	136.36086	136.86277
54	144.14307	144.69702	145.25323	145.81169	146.37244	146.93546	147.50078	148.06840
56	155.59398	156.21819	156.84505	157.47459	158.10680	158.74170	159.37930	160.01962
58	167.78798	168.48972	169.19457	169.90255	170.61367	171.32795	172.04540	172.76602
60	180.77331	181.56048	182.35130	183.14577	183.94391	184.74574	185.55127	186.36053
62	194.60131	195.48253	196.36800	197.25772	198.15171	199.05001	199.95262	200.85957
64	209.32666	210.31131	211.30088	212.29539	213.29486	214.29933	215.30880	216.32332
66	225.00762	226.10588	227.20984	228.31951	229.43493	230.55613	231.68313	232.81598
68	241.70617	242.92913	244.15866	245.39478	246.63755	247.88698	249.14311	250.40599
70	259.48837	260.84807	262.21532	263.59017	264.97266	266.36283	267.76073	269.16639
72	278.42454	279.93405	281.45224	282.97915	284.51483	286.05934	287.61273	289.17503
74	298.58955	300.26308	301.94655	303.64001	305.34353	307.05715	308.78095	310.51498
76	320.06316	321.91613	323.78045	325.65619	327.54343	329.44224	331.35267	333.27482
78	342.93028	344.97941	347.04149	349.11660	351.20483	353.30625	355.42095	357.54901
80	367.28136	369.54479	371.82297	374.11598	376.42392	378.74690	381.08499	383.43832
82	393.21268	395.71009	398.22425	400.75527	403.30327	405.86834	408.45062	411.05021
84	420.82680	423.57951	426.35123	429.14207	431.95216	434.78164	437.63064	440.49930
86	450.23291	453.26405	456.31669	459.39098	462.48709	465.60517	468.74536	471.90783
88	481.54732	484.88191	488.24080	491.62419	495.03223	498.46513	501.92305	505.40617
90	514.89386	518.55901	522.25160	525.97183	529.71992	533.49607	537.30048	541.13338
92	550.40440	554.42947	558.48547	562.57263	566.69120	570.84141	575.02351	579.23774
96	628.48832	633.33118	638.21317	643.13460	648.09579	653.09706	658.13873	663.22114
100	717.03549	722.84517	728.70411	734.61271	740.57139	746.58060	752.64075	758.75227
104	817.44799	824.39880	831.41132	838.48610	845.62369	852.82464	860.08953	867.41892
108	931.31575	939.61138	947.98401	956.43433	964.96309	973.57100	982.25880	991.02724
112	1060.44180	1070.32006	1080.29401	1090.36456	1100.53265	1110.79924	1121.16526	1131.63170
116	1206.87073	1218.60906	1230.46586	1242.44233	1254.53968	1266.75913	1279.10191	1291.56927
120	1372.92115	1386.84292	1400.91091	1415.12663	1429.49165	1444.00754	1458.67588	1473.49826
140	2602.88799	2634.76971	2667.05230	2699.74081	2732.84033	2766.35602	2800.29313	2834.65694
160	4909.41571	4980.14103	5051.90477	5124.72216	5198.60865	5273.57993	5349.65190	5426.84070

EFFECTIVE ANNUAL YIELD

NUMBER OF QUARTERLY DEPOSITS	13.80%	13.85%	13.90%	13.95%	14.00%	14.05%	14.10%	14.15%
1	1.03285	1.03296	1.03307	1.03319	1.03330	1.03341	1.03353	1.03364
2	2.09962	2.09996	2.10031	2.10066	2.10101	2.10135	2.10170	2.10205
3	3.20143	3.20214	3.20285	3.20356	3.20427	3.20498	3.20569	3.20640
4	4.33943	4.34064	4.34185	4.34306	4.34427	4.34548	4.34669	4.34790
5	5.51481	5.51666	5.51852	5.52037	5.52223	5.52409	5.52594	5.52780
6	6.72879	6.73145	6.73410	6.73676	6.73942	6.74207	6.74473	6.74739
7	7.98265	7.98627	7.98989	7.99351	7.99714	8.00076	8.00438	8.00801
8	9.27769	9.28245	9.28721	9.29197	9.29674	9.30150	9.30626	9.31103
9	10.61528	10.62136	10.62744	10.63353	10.63961	10.64570	10.65179	10.65788
10	11.99679	12.00439	12.01199	12.01960	12.02721	12.03482	12.04243	12.05004
11	13.42368	13.43301	13.44234	13.45167	13.46100	13.47034	13.47969	13.48904
12	14.89744	14.90871	14.91998	14.93126	14.94255	14.95384	14.96514	14.97644
13	16.41961	16.43305	16.44650	16.45996	16.47343	16.48690	16.50038	16.51387
14	17.99177	18.00764	18.02351	18.03939	18.05528	18.07119	18.08710	18.10303
15	19.61558	19.63412	19.65267	19.67123	19.68981	19.70841	19.72702	19.74564
16	21.29272	21.31420	21.33571	21.35723	21.37877	21.40033	21.42191	21.44350
17	23.02494	23.04967	23.07442	23.09918	23.12398	23.14879	23.17363	23.19849
18	24.81407	24.84233	24.87062	24.89894	24.92729	24.95567	24.98407	25.01250
19	26.66195	26.69408	26.72624	26.75843	26.79066	26.82292	26.85521	26.88754
20	28.57054	28.60686	28.64322	28.67963	28.71607	28.75256	28.78909	28.82566
21	30.54181	30.58268	30.62361	30.66458	30.70560	30.74667	30.78780	30.82897
22	32.57783	32.62363	32.66949	32.71541	32.76138	32.80742	32.85352	32.89967
23	34.68073	34.73185	34.78303	34.83429	34.88562	34.93702	34.98849	35.04003
24	36.85270	36.90955	36.96648	37.02349	37.08059	37.13777	37.19504	37.25239
25	39.09601	39.15902	39.22214	39.28535	39.34866	39.41206	39.47557	39.53917
26	41.41300	41.48264	41.55240	41.62226	41.69225	41.76234	41.83255	41.90288
27	43.80610	43.88285	43.95972	44.03673	44.11387	44.19115	44.26856	44.34609
28	46.27780	46.36216	46.44667	46.53133	46.61614	46.70111	46.78623	46.87150
29	48.83069	48.92319	49.01586	49.10871	49.20174	49.29494	49.38831	49.48186
30	51.46742	51.56863	51.67003	51.77163	51.87343	51.97543	52.07763	52.18003
31	54.19077	54.30126	54.41197	54.52292	54.63409	54.74549	54.85711	54.96897
32	57.00356	57.12395	57.24460	57.36551	57.48667	57.60810	57.72978	57.85172
33	59.90875	60.03969	60.17092	60.30244	60.43425	60.56635	60.69875	60.83144
34	62.90935	63.05152	63.19401	63.33683	63.47998	63.62346	63.76727	63.91141
35	66.00852	66.16262	66.31709	66.47192	66.62713	66.78271	66.93865	67.09498
36	69.20948	69.37626	69.54345	69.71106	69.87908	70.04751	70.21637	70.38564
37	72.51558	72.69582	72.87652	73.05769	73.23931	73.42141	73.60397	73.78699
38	75.93027	76.12479	76.31982	76.51538	76.71144	76.90803	77.10514	77.30277
39	79.45712	79.66678	79.87701	80.08781	80.29920	80.51115	80.72369	80.93681
40	83.09982	83.32551	83.55184	83.77881	84.00642	84.23467	84.46356	84.69310
41	86.86216	87.10483	87.34821	87.59229	87.83709	88.08259	88.32882	88.57575
42	90.74808	91.00871	91.27013	91.53233	91.79532	92.05909	92.32365	92.58901
43	94.76163	95.04127	95.32176	95.60312	95.88535	96.16845	96.45242	96.73727
44	98.90702	99.20673	99.50739	99.80901	100.11158	100.41512	100.71962	101.02508
45	103.18856	103.50948	103.83145	104.15447	104.47855	104.80368	105.12987	105.45712
46	107.61074	107.95406	108.29852	108.64415	108.99093	109.33887	109.68798	110.03826
47	112.17816	112.54512	112.91333	113.28282	113.65357	114.02560	114.39891	114.77350
48	116.89561	117.28750	117.68077	118.07543	118.47148	118.86892	119.26777	119.66803
50	126.80045	127.24633	127.69387	128.14307	128.59393	129.04646	129.50067	129.95657
52	137.36663	137.87245	138.38024	138.89001	139.40175	139.91549	140.43122	140.94895
54	148.63833	149.21058	149.78516	150.36208	150.94135	151.52297	152.10696	152.69332
56	160.66266	161.30843	161.95695	162.60822	163.26227	163.91909	164.57871	165.24113
58	173.48985	174.21689	174.94715	175.68065	176.41741	177.15743	177.90073	178.64733
60	187.17353	187.99028	188.81081	189.63513	190.46325	191.29520	192.13100	192.97065
62	201.77088	202.68656	203.60665	204.53116	205.46011	206.39353	207.33142	208.27383
64	217.34290	218.36757	219.39736	220.43229	221.47238	222.51766	223.56816	224.62390
66	233.95469	235.09929	236.24983	237.40632	238.56880	239.73730	240.91184	242.09247
68	251.67565	252.95212	254.23544	255.52565	256.82278	258.12687	259.43796	260.75608
70	270.57986	272.00118	273.43040	274.86756	276.31270	277.76586	279.22710	280.69646
72	290.74632	292.32663	293.91602	295.51453	297.12224	298.73917	300.36540	302.00096
74	312.25931	314.01398	315.77907	317.55464	319.34074	321.13745	322.94481	324.76291
76	335.20874	337.15450	339.11219	341.08187	343.06362	345.05751	347.06361	349.08200
78	359.69052	361.84556	364.01421	366.19657	368.39272	370.60274	372.82672	375.06476
80	385.80697	388.19104	390.59063	393.00585	395.43679	397.88357	400.34627	402.82500
82	413.66723	416.30180	418.95404	421.62405	424.31197	427.01790	429.74198	432.48432
84	443.38776	446.29613	449.22458	452.17323	455.14222	458.13169	461.14178	464.17264
86	475.09274	478.30024	481.53050	484.78367	488.05991	491.35940	494.68229	498.02875
88	508.91469	512.44879	516.00864	519.59445	523.20639	526.84467	530.50946	534.20096
90	544.99496	548.88546	552.80508	556.75405	560.73257	564.74087	568.77918	572.84772
92	583.48435	587.76358	592.07569	596.42093	600.79906	605.21182	609.65798	614.13830
96	668.34461	673.50948	678.71606	683.96471	689.25577	694.58956	699.96645	705.38677
100	764.91560	771.13118	777.39944	783.72085	790.09584	796.52488	803.00841	809.54690
104	874.81338	882.27348	889.79982	897.39297	905.05353	912.78210	920.57928	928.44568
108	999.87705	1008.80900	1017.82384	1026.92235	1036.10529	1045.37347	1054.72765	1064.16865
112	1142.19951	1152.86968	1163.64320	1174.52107	1185.50430	1196.59392	1207.79094	1219.09641
116	1304.16247	1316.88277	1329.73145	1342.70982	1355.81918	1369.06084	1382.43615	1395.94645
120	1488.47631	1503.61167	1518.90597	1534.36090	1549.97813	1565.75937	1581.70634	1597.82077
140	2869.45282	2904.68620	2940.36256	2976.48747	3013.06657	3050.10555	3087.61019	3125.58633
160	5505.16269	5584.63448	5665.27292	5747.09511	5830.11838	5914.36033	5999.83880	6086.57191

QUARTERLY DEPOSITS

EFFECTIVE ANNUAL YIELD

NUMBER OF QUARTRLY DEPOSITS	14.20%	14.25%	14.30%	14.35%	14.40%	14.45%	14.50%	14.55%
1	1.03375	1.03387	1.03398	1.03409	1.03420	1.03432	1.03443	1.03454
2	2.10240	2.10274	2.10309	2.10344	2.10378	2.10413	2.10448	2.10482
3	3.20711	3.20782	3.20853	3.20924	3.20995	3.21066	3.21137	3.21208
4	4.34911	4.35032	4.35153	4.35274	4.35395	4.35516	4.35637	4.35758
5	5.52965	5.53151	5.53337	5.53522	5.53708	5.53893	5.54079	5.54265
6	6.75005	6.75270	6.75536	6.75802	6.76068	6.76333	6.76599	6.76865
7	8.01163	8.01525	8.01888	8.02250	8.02613	8.02975	8.03338	8.03701
8	9.31579	9.32056	9.32533	9.33010	9.33486	9.33963	9.34441	9.34918
9	10.66398	10.67007	10.67617	10.68227	10.68837	10.69447	10.70057	10.70668
10	12.05766	12.06528	12.07291	12.08053	12.08816	12.09579	12.10343	12.11107
11	13.49839	13.50775	13.51711	13.52647	13.53584	13.54521	13.55459	13.56397
12	14.98775	14.99906	15.01038	15.02170	15.03303	15.04437	15.05571	15.06706
13	16.52737	16.54088	16.55439	16.56791	16.58144	16.59498	16.60852	16.62207
14	18.11896	18.13491	18.15086	18.16683	18.18281	18.19879	18.21479	18.23080
15	19.76427	19.78292	19.80158	19.82026	19.83895	19.85765	19.87637	19.89510
16	21.46511	21.48674	21.50839	21.53006	21.55174	21.57344	21.59516	21.61689
17	23.22337	23.24827	23.27319	23.29814	23.32311	23.34811	23.37312	23.39816
18	25.04096	25.06945	25.09796	25.12651	25.15508	25.18368	25.21230	25.24096
19	26.91991	26.95231	26.98474	27.01720	27.04970	27.08224	27.11481	27.14741
20	28.86227	28.89892	28.93562	28.97236	29.00914	29.04596	29.08282	29.11972
21	30.87019	30.91147	30.95279	30.99417	31.03559	31.07706	31.11859	31.16017
22	32.94589	32.99217	33.03850	33.08490	33.13136	33.17788	33.22445	33.27109
23	35.09164	35.14333	35.19508	35.24691	35.29881	35.35078	35.40282	35.45494
24	37.30982	37.36734	37.42494	37.48263	37.54040	37.59826	37.65620	37.71422
25	39.60287	39.66667	39.73057	39.79457	39.85866	39.92286	39.98715	40.05155
26	41.97331	42.04387	42.11454	42.18532	42.25622	42.32724	42.39837	42.46961
27	44.42377	44.50157	44.57951	44.65758	44.73579	44.81413	44.89260	44.97121
28	46.95693	47.04251	47.12824	47.21413	47.30017	47.38636	47.47271	47.55921
29	49.57559	49.66949	49.76357	49.85783	49.95226	50.04687	50.14166	50.23662
30	52.28264	52.38544	52.48845	52.59165	52.69506	52.79868	52.90250	53.00652
31	55.08105	55.19337	55.30591	55.41868	55.53169	55.64492	55.75839	55.87209
32	57.97392	58.09638	58.21911	58.34209	58.46534	58.58885	58.71262	58.83666
33	60.96443	61.09771	61.23129	61.36516	61.49933	61.63380	61.76856	61.90363
34	64.05588	64.20068	64.34582	64.49129	64.63710	64.78325	64.92972	65.07654
35	67.25167	67.40874	67.56618	67.72400	67.88220	68.04077	68.19973	68.35906
36	70.55533	70.72544	70.89597	71.06692	71.23829	71.41009	71.58232	71.75497
37	73.97049	74.15446	74.33889	74.52380	74.70918	74.89504	75.08137	75.26818
38	77.50092	77.69960	77.89880	78.09853	78.29879	78.49958	78.70090	78.90275
39	81.15052	81.36480	81.57968	81.79514	82.01118	82.22782	82.44505	82.66288
40	84.92329	85.15413	85.38562	85.61776	85.85056	86.08401	86.31812	86.55289
41	88.82341	89.07179	89.32088	89.57071	89.82125	90.07253	90.32454	90.57727
42	92.85516	93.12211	93.38986	93.65841	93.92777	94.19793	94.46890	94.74068
43	97.02300	97.30961	97.59710	97.88548	98.17474	98.46490	98.75595	99.04790
44	101.33151	101.63891	101.94729	102.25665	102.56698	102.87831	103.19061	103.50391
45	105.78544	106.11483	106.44530	106.77684	107.10946	107.44317	107.77796	108.11384
46	110.38971	110.74233	111.09614	111.45113	111.80731	112.16469	112.52325	112.88302
47	115.14938	115.52655	115.90501	116.28478	116.66585	117.04824	117.43193	117.81695
48	120.06969	120.47278	120.87728	121.28322	121.69058	122.09938	122.50962	122.92130
50	130.41416	130.87344	131.33442	131.79711	132.26151	132.72764	133.19549	133.66508
52	141.46870	141.99047	142.51426	143.04010	143.56797	144.09789	144.62988	145.16393
54	153.28207	153.87322	154.46677	155.06273	155.66112	156.26194	156.86521	157.47092
56	165.90637	166.57443	167.24533	167.91909	168.59571	169.27520	169.95758	170.64286
58	179.39724	180.15047	180.90705	181.66697	182.43027	183.19695	183.96703	184.74052
60	193.81418	194.66161	195.51295	196.36822	197.22744	198.09062	198.95779	199.82897
62	209.22076	210.17224	211.12828	212.08892	213.05418	214.02407	214.99861	215.97784
64	225.68490	226.75120	227.82283	228.89979	229.98213	231.06987	232.16304	233.26166
66	243.27921	244.47210	245.67116	246.87642	248.08793	249.30570	250.52978	251.76019
68	262.08127	263.41357	264.75302	266.09965	267.45351	268.81463	270.18305	271.55880
70	282.17397	283.65969	285.15366	286.65593	288.16654	289.68553	291.21296	292.74887
72	303.64592	305.30032	306.96423	308.63769	310.32076	312.01350	313.71595	315.42818
74	326.59179	328.43152	330.28217	332.14379	334.01647	335.90025	337.79521	339.70144
76	351.11275	353.15594	355.21164	357.27994	359.36090	361.45461	363.56113	365.68056
78	377.31693	379.58333	381.86404	384.15917	386.46879	388.79299	391.13188	393.48554
80	405.31987	407.83098	410.35844	412.90235	415.46282	418.03995	420.63388	423.24466
82	435.24504	438.02427	440.82213	443.63875	446.47424	449.32874	452.20237	455.09526
84	467.22440	470.29721	473.39122	476.50657	479.64341	482.80189	485.98214	489.18433
86	501.39895	504.79305	508.21123	511.65364	515.12048	518.61190	522.12808	525.66919
88	537.91937	541.66489	545.43770	549.23801	553.06601	556.92192	560.80592	564.71823
90	576.94671	581.07638	585.23696	589.42868	593.65177	597.90647	602.19302	606.51164
92	618.65304	623.20245	627.78682	632.40640	637.06147	641.75229	646.47914	651.24230
96	710.85088	716.35912	721.91186	727.50946	733.15227	738.84065	744.57499	750.35563
100	816.14081	822.79062	829.49679	836.25980	843.08014	849.95828	856.89472	863.88995
104	936.38191	944.48269	952.46636	960.61582	968.83763	977.13241	985.50083	993.94352
108	1073.69726	1083.31429	1093.02058	1102.81693	1112.70419	1122.68320	1132.75481	1142.91987
112	1230.51138	1242.03690	1253.67405	1265.42390	1277.28755	1289.26608	1301.36063	1313.57229
116	1409.59310	1423.37748	1437.30097	1451.36497	1465.57090	1479.92019	1494.41428	1509.05464
120	1614.10443	1630.55909	1647.18653	1663.98858	1680.96706	1698.12382	1715.46072	1732.97966
140	3164.03988	3202.97685	3242.40329	3282.32534	3322.74922	3363.68122	3405.12770	3447.09513
160	6174.57801	6263.87575	6354.48403	6446.42202	6539.70918	6634.36524	6730.41024	6827.86448

103

QUARTERLY DEPOSITS

EFFECTIVE ANNUAL YIELD

NUMBER OF QUARTRLY DEPOSITS	14.60%	14.65%	14.70%	14.75%	14.80%	14.85%	14.90%	14.95%
1	1.03466	1.03477	1.03488	1.03499	1.03511	1.03522	1.03533	1.03545
2	2.10517	2.10552	2.10586	2.10621	2.10656	2.10690	2.10725	2.10759
3	3.21278	3.21349	3.21420	3.21491	3.21562	3.21633	3.21704	3.21774
4	4.35878	4.35999	4.36120	4.36241	4.36362	4.36483	4.36604	4.36724
5	5.54450	5.54636	5.54821	5.55007	5.55192	5.55378	5.55563	5.55749
6	6.77131	6.77397	6.77663	6.77929	6.78194	6.78460	6.78726	6.78992
7	8.04064	8.04426	8.04789	8.05152	8.05515	8.05878	8.06241	8.06604
8	9.35395	9.35873	9.36350	9.36828	9.37305	9.37783	9.38261	9.38739
9	10.71278	10.71889	10.72500	10.73111	10.73723	10.74334	10.74946	10.75558
10	12.11871	12.12635	12.13399	12.14164	12.14929	12.15694	12.16460	12.17226
11	13.57335	13.58274	13.59213	13.60153	13.61093	13.62033	13.62974	13.63915
12	15.07841	15.08977	15.10114	15.11251	15.12388	15.13527	15.14665	15.15805
13	16.63563	16.64920	16.66278	16.67636	16.68995	16.70355	16.71716	16.73078
14	18.24682	18.26285	18.27889	18.29494	18.31100	18.32708	18.34316	18.35925
15	19.91385	19.93261	19.95138	19.97017	19.98897	20.00778	20.02661	20.04545
16	21.63865	21.66042	21.68221	21.70401	21.72584	21.74768	21.76954	21.79142
17	23.42322	23.44830	23.47341	23.49853	23.52369	23.54886	23.57405	23.59927
18	25.26964	25.29835	25.32709	25.35586	25.38465	25.41347	25.44233	25.47120
19	27.18005	27.21273	27.24543	27.27817	27.31095	27.34376	27.37661	27.40949
20	29.15667	29.19366	29.23069	29.26776	29.30488	29.34204	29.37924	29.41648
21	31.20179	31.24347	31.28520	31.32698	31.36881	31.41069	31.45262	31.49460
22	33.31179	33.36455	33.41137	33.45826	33.50520	33.55220	33.59927	33.64639
23	35.50712	35.55938	35.61171	35.66412	35.71659	35.76914	35.82176	35.87445
24	37.77233	37.83052	37.88880	37.94717	38.00562	38.06416	38.12278	38.18148
25	40.11604	40.18063	40.24533	40.31012	40.37501	40.44000	40.50510	40.57029
26	42.54097	42.61245	42.68405	42.75576	42.82759	42.89953	42.97159	43.04377
27	45.04995	45.12883	45.20784	45.28698	45.36627	45.44568	45.52524	45.60492
28	47.64587	47.73269	47.81966	47.90679	47.99407	48.08151	48.16911	48.25686
29	50.33177	50.42709	50.52259	50.61827	50.71413	50.81017	50.90639	51.00279
30	53.11074	53.21517	53.31980	53.42464	53.52969	53.63494	53.74039	53.84606
31	55.98603	56.10019	56.21459	56.32922	56.44409	56.55919	56.67453	56.79010
32	58.96096	59.08552	59.21035	59.33545	59.46081	59.58644	59.71234	59.83850
33	62.03899	62.17465	62.31061	62.44688	62.58344	62.72031	62.85748	62.99495
34	65.22369	65.37119	65.51902	65.66719	65.81570	65.96455	66.11375	66.26329
35	68.51877	68.67886	68.83934	69.00019	69.16144	69.32306	69.48507	69.64747
36	71.92804	72.10154	72.27548	72.44984	72.62463	72.79985	72.97551	73.15160
37	75.45547	75.64323	75.83148	76.02020	76.20941	76.39910	76.58928	76.77994
38	79.10514	79.30806	79.51151	79.71551	79.92004	80.12512	80.33073	80.53689
39	82.88129	83.10031	83.31992	83.54013	83.76095	83.98236	84.20438	84.42701
40	86.78832	87.02441	87.26117	87.49860	87.73669	87.97546	88.21490	88.45501
41	90.83075	91.08496	91.33990	91.59559	91.85202	92.10920	92.36712	92.62579
42	95.01327	95.28668	95.56091	95.83596	96.11183	96.38852	96.66605	96.94440
43	99.34075	99.63450	99.92915	100.22471	100.52118	100.81857	101.11687	101.41609
44	103.81820	104.13348	104.44977	104.76705	105.08534	105.40464	105.72495	106.04628
45	108.45082	108.78890	109.12807	109.46835	109.80974	110.15224	110.49585	110.84058
46	113.24399	113.60617	113.96956	114.33417	114.70000	115.06705	115.43532	115.80483
47	118.20328	118.59094	118.97994	119.37027	119.76194	120.15495	120.54932	120.94504
48	123.33444	123.74903	124.16508	124.58260	125.00159	125.42206	125.84401	126.26744
50	134.13640	134.60947	135.08429	135.56087	136.03921	136.51933	137.00122	137.48489
52	145.70005	146.23826	146.77855	147.32095	147.86545	148.41206	148.96080	149.51166
54	158.07910	158.68975	159.30288	159.91851	160.53664	161.15728	161.78044	162.40613
56	171.33104	172.02216	172.71620	173.41320	174.11315	174.81608	175.52199	176.23090
58	185.51743	186.29779	187.08161	187.86890	188.65968	189.45396	190.25176	191.05309
60	200.70416	201.58340	202.46669	203.35406	204.24552	205.14109	206.04080	206.94466
62	216.96176	217.95041	218.94381	219.94197	220.94493	221.95270	222.96530	223.98277
64	234.36575	235.47536	236.59049	237.71119	238.83747	239.96937	241.10692	242.25013
66	252.99697	254.24014	255.48975	256.74583	258.00840	259.27750	260.55317	261.83544
68	272.94194	274.33249	275.73050	277.13600	278.54904	279.96965	281.39788	282.83377
70	294.29331	295.84632	297.40795	298.97824	300.55726	302.14504	303.74163	305.34708
72	317.15024	318.88219	320.62408	322.37597	324.13791	325.90997	327.69220	329.48466
74	341.61891	343.54779	345.48812	347.43995	349.40335	351.37840	353.36516	355.36371
76	367.81296	369.95843	372.11702	374.28884	376.47394	378.67243	380.88438	383.10986
78	395.85406	398.23754	400.63607	403.04975	405.47867	407.92292	410.38261	412.85783
80	425.87244	428.51733	431.17943	433.85885	436.55571	439.27011	442.00218	444.75203
82	458.00754	460.93933	463.89078	466.86200	469.85313	472.86430	475.89565	478.94731
84	492.40860	495.65511	498.92400	502.21544	505.52957	508.86655	512.22654	515.60970
86	529.23542	532.82694	536.44392	540.08655	543.75501	547.44948	551.17014	554.91718
88	568.65904	572.62858	576.62703	580.65463	584.71157	588.79806	592.91433	597.06059
90	610.86258	615.24608	619.66238	624.11173	628.59437	633.11055	637.66053	642.24454
92	656.04205	660.87866	665.75241	670.66359	675.61250	680.59940	685.62460	690.68839
96	756.18297	762.05737	767.97922	773.94889	779.96676	786.03324	792.14870	798.31355
100	870.94447	878.05877	885.23336	892.46876	899.76546	907.12400	914.54490	922.02867
104	1002.46115	1011.05437	1019.72387	1028.47031	1037.29437	1046.19674	1055.17812	1064.23920
108	1153.17926	1163.53383	1173.98448	1184.53209	1195.17756	1205.92179	1216.76570	1227.71020
112	1325.90221	1338.35153	1350.92140	1363.61298	1376.42745	1389.36600	1402.42982	1415.62012
116	1523.84272	1538.78002	1553.86805	1569.10831	1584.50234	1600.05168	1615.75790	1631.62257
120	1750.68254	1768.57129	1786.64785	1804.91419	1823.37230	1842.02418	1860.87186	1879.91739
140	3489.59002	3532.61899	3576.18873	3620.30601	3664.97770	3710.21072	3756.01212	3802.38901
160	6926.74856	7027.08339	7128.89019	7232.19044	7337.00600	7443.35898	7551.27184	7660.76738

104

QUARTERLY DEPOSITS

EFFECTIVE ANNUAL YIELD

NUMBER OF QUARTRLY DEPOSITS	15.00%	15.05%	15.10%	15.15%	15.20%	15.25%	15.30%	15.35%
1	1.03556	1.03567	1.03578	1.03590	1.03601	1.03612	1.03623	1.03635
2	2.10794	2.10828	2.10863	2.10898	2.10932	2.10967	2.11001	2.11036
3	3.21845	3.21916	3.21987	3.22057	3.22128	3.22199	3.22270	3.22340
4	4.36845	4.36966	4.37087	4.37207	4.37328	4.37449	4.37570	4.37690
5	5.55934	5.56120	5.56305	5.56491	5.56676	5.56862	5.57047	5.57233
6	6.79258	6.79524	6.79790	6.80056	6.80322	6.80588	6.80854	6.81120
7	8.06967	8.07330	8.07693	8.08056	8.08420	8.08783	8.09146	8.09510
8	9.39217	9.39695	9.40173	9.40652	9.41130	9.41609	9.42087	9.42566
9	10.76170	10.76782	10.77394	10.78006	10.78619	10.79232	10.79845	10.80458
10	12.17992	12.18758	12.19525	12.20292	12.21059	12.21826	12.22594	12.23362
11	13.64857	13.65799	13.66742	13.67684	13.68628	13.69571	13.70515	13.71460
12	15.16945	15.18085	15.19226	15.20368	15.21510	15.22653	15.23796	15.24940
13	16.74440	16.75803	16.77167	16.78532	16.79897	16.81264	16.82631	16.83999
14	18.37536	18.39147	18.40760	18.42373	18.43988	18.45604	18.47220	18.48838
15	20.06431	20.08318	20.10206	20.12096	20.13987	20.15880	20.17774	20.19669
16	21.81331	21.83523	21.85716	21.87911	21.90108	21.92306	21.94507	21.96709
17	23.62451	23.64977	23.67506	23.70037	23.72570	23.75105	23.77643	23.80183
18	25.50011	25.52905	25.55801	25.58700	25.61602	25.64507	25.67415	25.70325
19	27.44240	27.47535	27.50834	27.54136	27.57441	27.60750	27.64063	27.67378
20	29.45376	29.49109	29.52846	29.56587	29.60332	29.64082	29.67836	29.71594
21	31.53664	31.57872	31.62086	31.66305	31.70529	31.74758	31.78992	31.83231
22	33.69358	33.74083	33.78814	33.83551	33.88294	33.93043	33.97799	34.02560
23	35.92722	35.98005	36.03296	36.08595	36.13900	36.19213	36.24534	36.29861
24	38.24028	38.29916	38.35812	38.41717	38.47631	38.53553	38.59484	38.65424
25	40.63559	40.70098	40.76648	40.83207	40.89777	40.96357	41.02947	41.09547
26	43.11607	43.18848	43.26101	43.33366	43.40643	43.47931	43.55232	43.62544
27	45.68475	45.76471	45.84481	45.92504	46.00541	46.08592	46.16657	46.24735
28	48.34477	48.43284	48.52106	48.60945	48.69799	48.78669	48.87555	48.96456
29	51.09937	51.19614	51.29308	51.39021	51.48751	51.58500	51.68268	51.78053
30	53.95193	54.05801	54.16429	54.27078	54.37748	54.48440	54.59151	54.69884
31	56.90591	57.02196	57.13824	57.25476	57.37152	57.48852	57.60575	57.72322
32	59.96494	60.09164	60.21861	60.34585	60.47336	60.60114	60.72920	60.85753
33	63.13273	63.27081	63.40920	63.54790	63.68690	63.82620	63.96582	64.10574
34	66.41317	66.56339	66.71396	66.86488	67.01614	67.16775	67.31971	67.47202
35	69.81025	69.97342	70.13698	70.30093	70.46527	70.63000	70.79513	70.96064
36	73.32813	73.50509	73.68249	73.86032	74.03859	74.21731	74.39646	74.57606
37	76.97109	77.16273	77.35486	77.54748	77.74059	77.93419	78.12829	78.32288
38	80.74359	80.95084	81.15864	81.36698	81.57588	81.78532	81.99532	82.20588
39	84.65024	84.87408	85.09853	85.32360	85.54927	85.77557	86.00247	86.23000
40	88.69580	88.93726	89.17941	89.42223	89.66574	89.90994	90.15482	90.40039
41	92.88521	93.14538	93.40631	93.66799	93.93044	94.19364	94.45761	94.72234
42	97.22358	97.50360	97.78446	98.06616	98.34869	98.63208	98.91630	99.20138
43	101.71623	102.01729	102.31928	102.62219	102.92604	103.23083	103.53655	103.84321
44	106.36862	106.69198	107.01636	107.34177	107.66822	107.99569	108.32420	108.65375
45	111.18644	111.53342	111.88153	112.23077	112.58114	112.93266	113.28532	113.63912
46	116.17557	116.54755	116.92078	117.29525	117.67098	118.04796	118.42619	118.80570
47	121.34211	121.74055	122.14035	122.54153	122.94408	123.34802	123.75334	124.16005
48	126.69236	127.11878	127.54670	127.97613	128.40707	128.83952	129.27350	129.70900
50	137.97036	138.45762	138.94668	139.43756	139.93025	140.42476	140.92110	141.41927
52	150.06467	150.61981	151.17712	151.73658	152.29822	152.86204	153.42804	153.99623
54	163.03436	163.66515	164.29850	164.93442	165.57292	166.21402	166.85772	167.50403
56	176.94282	177.65774	178.37573	179.09675	179.82083	180.54798	181.27822	182.01156
58	191.85797	192.66641	193.47844	194.29406	195.11329	195.93615	196.76265	197.59280
60	207.85269	208.76491	209.68133	210.60198	211.52688	212.45604	213.38949	214.32724
62	225.00512	226.03237	227.06455	228.10168	229.14379	230.19090	231.24303	232.30020
64	243.39904	244.55368	245.71408	246.88026	248.05225	249.23007	250.41377	251.60337
66	263.12433	264.41990	265.72216	267.03116	268.34693	269.66950	270.99891	272.33519
68	284.27735	285.72867	287.18777	288.65469	290.12947	291.61215	293.10278	294.60139
70	306.96144	308.58475	310.21708	311.85846	313.50894	315.16858	316.83743	318.51554
72	331.28741	333.10050	334.92399	336.75795	338.60243	340.45749	342.32320	344.19960
74	357.37410	359.39642	361.43072	363.47709	365.53558	367.60628	369.68926	371.78458
76	385.34897	387.60178	389.86838	392.14885	394.44328	396.75175	399.07434	401.41115
78	415.34867	417.85524	420.37763	422.91594	425.47027	428.04073	430.62741	433.23041
80	447.51976	450.30551	453.10937	455.93148	458.77194	461.63088	464.50841	467.40466
82	482.01942	485.11211	488.22551	491.35978	494.51504	497.69143	500.88910	504.10818
84	519.01618	522.44614	525.89975	529.37717	532.87855	536.40407	539.95389	543.52818
86	558.69078	562.49114	566.31843	570.17286	574.05460	577.96386	581.90082	585.86569
88	601.23706	605.44395	609.68148	613.94988	618.24937	622.58018	626.94253	631.33665
90	646.86285	651.51571	656.20338	660.92612	665.68418	670.47784	675.30735	680.17298
92	695.79107	700.93292	706.11425	711.33536	716.59656	721.89815	727.24044	732.62373
96	804.52818	810.79298	817.10837	823.47474	829.89252	836.36211	842.88392	849.45838
100	929.57585	937.18698	944.86260	952.60324	960.40946	968.28181	976.22085	984.22714
104	1073.38068	1082.60328	1091.90772	1101.29471	1110.76498	1120.31928	1129.95834	1139.68291
108	1238.75624	1249.90474	1261.15665	1272.51293	1283.97454	1295.54246	1307.21766	1319.00114
112	1428.93812	1442.38506	1455.96217	1469.67071	1483.51195	1497.48711	1511.59766	1525.84472
116	1647.64729	1663.83367	1680.18332	1696.69790	1713.37905	1730.22845	1747.24780	1764.43879
120	1899.16284	1918.61029	1938.26187	1958.11970	1978.18595	1998.46278	2018.95241	2039.65704
140	3849.34858	3896.89814	3945.04507	3993.79683	4043.16099	4093.14522	4143.75727	4195.00498
160	7771.86870	7884.59924	7998.98280	8115.04348	8232.80578	8352.29450	8473.53485	8596.55236

QUARTERLY DEPOSITS

EFFECTIVE ANNUAL YIELD

NUMBER OF QUARTERLY DEPOSITS	15.40%	15.45%	15.50%	15.55%	15.60%	15.65%	15.70%	15.75%
1	1.03646	1.03657	1.03668	1.03679	1.03691	1.03702	1.03713	1.03724
2	2.11070	2.11105	2.11139	2.11174	2.11208	2.11243	2.11277	2.11311
3	3.22411	3.22482	3.22552	3.22623	3.22694	3.22764	3.22835	3.22905
4	4.37811	4.37932	4.38052	4.38173	4.38294	4.38414	4.38535	4.38655
5	5.57418	5.57604	5.57789	5.57974	5.58160	5.58345	5.58531	5.58716
6	6.81386	6.81652	6.81918	6.82184	6.82450	6.82716	6.82982	6.83248
7	8.09873	8.10237	8.10600	8.10964	8.11327	8.11691	8.12055	8.12418
8	9.43045	9.43524	9.44003	9.44482	9.44961	9.45440	9.45920	9.46399
9	10.81071	10.81685	10.82299	10.82912	10.83526	10.84141	10.84755	10.85369
10	12.24130	12.24899	12.25667	12.26437	12.27206	12.27975	12.28745	12.29515
11	13.72405	13.73350	13.74295	13.75241	13.76188	13.77135	13.78082	13.79030
12	15.26085	15.27230	15.28375	15.29522	15.30668	15.31816	15.32964	15.34112
13	16.85367	16.86737	16.88107	16.89478	16.90850	16.92223	16.93596	16.94970
14	18.50457	18.52077	18.53698	18.55320	18.56943	18.58568	18.60193	18.61819
15	20.21566	20.23464	20.25363	20.27264	20.29167	20.31071	20.32976	20.34882
16	21.98913	22.01118	22.03326	22.05535	22.07746	22.09959	22.12174	22.14390
17	23.82725	23.85269	23.87816	23.90365	23.92916	23.95470	23.98026	24.00584
18	25.73239	25.76155	25.79074	25.81996	25.84920	25.87848	25.90778	25.93711
19	27.70698	27.74021	27.77347	27.80677	27.84010	27.87347	27.90688	27.94032
20	29.75336	29.79123	29.82894	29.86669	29.90448	29.94232	29.98020	30.01812
21	31.87475	31.91725	31.95980	32.00240	32.04505	32.08775	32.13050	32.17331
22	34.07328	34.12102	34.16882	34.21668	34.26461	34.31260	34.36065	34.40876
23	36.35196	36.40539	36.45888	36.51245	36.56610	36.61981	36.67360	36.72747
24	38.71372	38.77329	38.83294	38.89269	38.95252	39.01243	39.07244	39.13253
25	41.16158	41.22778	41.29409	41.36050	41.42701	41.49362	41.56034	41.62716
26	43.69868	43.77204	43.84551	43.91911	43.99283	44.06667	44.14062	44.21470
27	46.32827	46.40933	46.49053	46.57187	46.65334	46.73496	46.81671	46.89860
28	49.05374	49.14308	49.23257	49.32223	49.41204	49.50202	49.59216	49.68246
29	51.87857	51.97679	52.07520	52.17379	52.27256	52.37152	52.47066	52.56999
30	54.80638	54.91413	55.02209	55.13026	55.23865	55.34724	55.45605	55.56507
31	57.84094	57.95889	58.07709	58.19552	58.31420	58.43312	58.55228	58.67168
32	60.98612	61.11500	61.24414	61.37356	61.50326	61.63323	61.76347	61.89400
33	64.24598	64.38652	64.52737	64.66854	64.81001	64.95180	65.09390	65.23632
34	67.62468	67.77768	67.93104	68.08475	68.23881	68.39322	68.54799	68.70312
35	71.12655	71.29286	71.45956	71.62665	71.79415	71.96204	72.13033	72.29903
36	74.75610	74.93658	75.11751	75.29888	75.48070	75.66297	75.84569	76.02886
37	78.51797	78.71355	78.90964	79.10623	79.30331	79.50090	79.69900	79.89759
38	82.41698	82.62865	82.84087	83.05366	83.26700	83.48091	83.69538	83.91041
39	86.45815	86.68692	86.91631	87.14633	87.37697	87.60824	87.84014	88.07268
40	90.64665	90.89360	91.14124	91.38959	91.63863	91.88837	92.13881	92.38995
41	94.98784	95.25411	95.52116	95.78897	96.05756	96.32693	96.59709	96.86802
42	99.48731	99.77409	100.06173	100.35023	100.63959	100.92981	101.22090	101.51286
43	104.15081	104.45936	104.76886	105.07931	105.39072	105.70308	106.01640	106.33068
44	108.98434	109.31598	109.64866	109.98240	110.31719	110.65304	110.98995	111.32793
45	113.99408	114.35019	114.70746	115.06589	115.42548	115.78624	116.14813	116.51128
46	119.18646	119.56851	119.95182	120.33642	120.72230	121.10947	121.49793	121.88768
47	124.56815	124.97765	125.38856	125.80087	126.21460	126.62975	127.04632	127.46431
48	130.14604	130.58461	131.02473	131.46639	131.90961	132.35438	132.80072	133.24863
50	141.91929	142.42116	142.92488	143.43046	143.93791	144.44724	144.95845	145.47155
52	154.56664	155.13925	155.71408	156.29114	156.87044	157.45198	158.03578	158.62184
54	168.15297	168.80454	169.45876	170.11563	170.77516	171.43737	172.10227	172.76987
56	182.74801	183.48758	184.23029	184.97614	185.72516	186.47736	187.23275	187.99134
58	198.42664	199.26416	200.10539	200.95034	201.79902	202.65147	203.50768	204.36768
60	215.26693	216.21572	217.16650	218.12166	219.08123	220.04521	221.01364	221.98652
62	233.36245	234.42979	235.50224	236.57984	237.66261	238.75056	239.84373	240.94214
64	252.79889	254.00037	255.20783	256.42131	257.64083	258.86643	260.09812	261.33596
66	273.67837	275.02850	276.38561	277.74974	279.12091	280.49917	281.88455	283.27708
68	296.10803	297.62274	299.14557	300.67655	302.21574	303.76316	305.31888	306.88292
70	320.20295	321.89972	323.60591	325.32155	327.04671	328.78143	330.52577	332.27978
72	346.08678	347.98477	349.89366	351.81349	353.74433	355.68624	357.63929	359.60354
74	373.89232	376.01255	378.14534	380.29078	382.44893	384.61986	386.80366	389.00040
76	403.76225	406.12774	408.50770	410.90221	413.31138	415.73528	418.17401	420.62765
78	435.84984	438.48580	441.13840	443.80772	446.49390	449.19701	451.91718	454.65451
80	470.31974	473.25379	476.20691	479.17924	482.17089	485.18199	488.21267	491.26306
82	507.34883	510.61118	513.89537	517.20156	520.52988	523.88049	527.25353	530.64915
84	547.12709	550.75081	554.39950	558.07334	561.77248	565.49712	569.24741	573.02354
86	589.85866	593.87992	597.92967	602.00813	606.11548	610.25193	614.41768	618.61295
88	635.76278	640.22113	644.71195	649.23547	653.79193	658.38156	663.00460	667.66130
90	685.07500	690.01368	694.98930	700.00212	705.05243	710.14049	715.26661	720.43104
92	738.04835	743.51461	749.02283	754.57332	760.16640	765.80241	771.48167	777.20451
96	856.08591	862.76694	869.50189	876.29119	883.13530	890.03463	896.98964	904.00078
100	992.30125	1000.44374	1008.65520	1016.93620	1025.28734	1033.70919	1042.20237	1050.76745
104	1149.49375	1159.39162	1169.37728	1179.45151	1189.61510	1199.86882	1210.21349	1220.64988
108	1330.89390	1342.89694	1355.01128	1367.23795	1379.57799	1392.03244	1404.60235	1417.28879
112	1540.22967	1554.75383	1569.41855	1584.22518	1599.17509	1614.26966	1629.51027	1644.89833
116	1781.80315	1799.34262	1817.05895	1834.95393	1853.02934	1871.28700	1889.72873	1908.35637
120	2060.57894	2081.72037	2103.08361	2124.67100	2146.48486	2168.52756	2190.80148	2213.30905
140	4246.89630	4299.43927	4352.64205	4406.51286	4461.06007	4516.29210	4572.21752	4628.84498
160	8721.37296	8848.02292	8976.52893	9106.91802	9239.21764	9373.45563	9509.66022	9647.86005

QUARTERLY DEPOSITS

EFFECTIVE ANNUAL YIELD

NUMBER OF QUARTERLY DEPOSITS	15.80%	15.85%	15.90%	15.95%	16.00%	16.05%	16.10%	16.15%
1	1.03735	1.03747	1.03758	1.03769	1.03780	1.03791	1.03803	1.03814
2	2.11346	2.11380	2.11415	2.11449	2.11483	2.11518	2.11552	2.11587
3	3.22976	3.23047	3.23117	3.23188	3.23258	3.23329	3.23399	3.23470
4	4.38776	4.38897	4.39017	4.39138	4.39258	4.39379	4.39499	4.39620
5	5.58902	5.59087	5.59272	5.59458	5.59643	5.59829	5.60014	5.60199
6	6.83514	6.83781	6.84047	6.84313	6.84579	6.84845	6.85111	6.85378
7	8.12782	8.13146	8.13510	8.13874	8.14238	8.14602	8.14966	8.15330
8	9.46879	9.47358	9.47838	9.48318	9.48798	9.49278	9.49758	9.50238
9	10.85984	10.86599	10.87214	10.87829	10.88444	10.89060	10.89675	10.90291
10	12.30286	12.31056	12.31827	12.32598	12.33370	12.34142	12.34914	12.35686
11	13.79978	13.80926	13.81875	13.82824	13.83774	13.84724	13.85674	13.86625
12	15.35261	15.36411	15.37561	15.38712	15.39864	15.41015	15.42168	15.43321
13	16.96345	16.97721	16.99098	17.00475	17.01854	17.03233	17.04612	17.05993
14	18.63447	18.65075	18.66705	18.68336	18.69967	18.71600	18.73234	18.74869
15	20.36790	20.38699	20.40610	20.42522	20.44436	20.46351	20.48267	20.50185
16	22.16609	22.18829	22.21051	22.23274	22.25500	22.27727	22.29956	22.32187
17	24.03144	24.05707	24.08272	24.10839	24.13408	24.15980	24.18554	24.21131
18	25.96647	25.99586	26.02528	26.05473	26.08420	26.11371	26.14324	26.17280
19	27.97379	28.00730	28.04084	28.07442	28.10804	28.14169	28.17537	28.20910
20	30.05069	30.09410	30.13215	30.17024	30.20838	30.24656	30.28479	30.32305
21	32.21617	32.25908	32.30204	32.34505	32.38812	32.43124	32.47441	32.51763
22	34.45694	34.50517	34.55347	34.60183	34.65026	34.69874	34.74729	34.79590
23	36.78141	36.83542	36.88951	36.94367	36.99791	37.05222	37.10660	37.16106
24	39.19271	39.25298	39.31333	39.37377	39.43430	39.49492	39.55563	39.61642
25	41.69408	41.76111	41.82823	41.89547	41.96280	42.03024	42.09778	42.16542
26	44.28889	44.36321	44.43764	44.51220	44.58688	44.66168	44.73660	44.81164
27	46.98063	47.06280	47.14511	47.22756	47.31015	47.39289	47.47576	47.55877
28	49.77292	49.86354	49.95432	50.04527	50.13637	50.22764	50.31908	50.41067
29	52.66951	52.76921	52.86909	52.96917	53.06943	53.16988	53.27051	53.37134
30	55.67430	55.78374	55.89340	56.00327	56.11336	56.22366	56.33418	56.44491
31	58.79133	58.91122	59.03136	59.15174	59.27236	59.39323	59.51435	59.63571
32	62.02480	62.15587	62.28723	62.41886	62.55077	62.68297	62.81544	62.94819
33	65.37905	65.52209	65.66545	65.80913	65.95312	66.09743	66.24206	66.38701
34	68.85860	69.01443	69.17062	69.32717	69.48408	69.64135	69.79898	69.95697
35	72.46812	72.63761	72.80751	72.97781	73.14852	73.31963	73.49115	73.66307
36	76.21247	76.39655	76.58107	76.76605	76.95148	77.13737	77.32372	77.51052
37	80.09670	80.29631	80.49643	80.69706	80.89820	81.09986	81.30202	81.50470
38	84.12601	84.34218	84.55892	84.77623	84.99412	85.21257	85.43160	85.65121
39	88.30584	88.53964	88.77408	89.00915	89.24486	89.48122	89.71822	89.95586
40	92.64181	92.89436	93.14763	93.40161	93.65630	93.91171	94.16783	94.42467
41	97.13974	97.41224	97.68553	97.95962	98.23450	98.51017	98.78664	99.06391
42	101.80568	102.09939	102.39396	102.68942	102.98576	103.28298	103.58108	103.88008
43	106.64592	106.96214	107.27933	107.59749	107.91662	108.23674	108.55784	108.87993
44	111.66697	112.00709	112.34827	112.69054	113.03389	113.37832	113.72384	114.07045
45	116.87557	117.24105	117.60770	117.97555	118.34460	118.71484	119.08628	119.45893
46	122.27874	122.67110	123.06477	123.45976	123.85606	124.25368	124.65263	125.05291
47	127.88374	128.30461	128.72691	129.15066	129.57587	130.00253	130.43065	130.86023
48	133.69811	134.14917	134.60182	135.05606	135.51189	135.96933	136.42837	136.88903
50	145.98654	146.50344	147.02224	147.54297	148.06561	148.59019	149.11670	149.64515
52	159.21017	159.80078	160.39368	160.98888	161.58638	162.18619	162.78833	163.39280
54	173.44018	174.11320	174.78895	175.46745	176.14869	176.83270	177.51948	178.20904
56	188.75314	189.51817	190.28645	191.05798	191.83278	192.61087	193.39225	194.17694
58	205.23148	206.09911	206.97057	207.84588	208.72506	209.60813	210.49511	211.38600
60	222.96390	223.94577	224.93217	225.92310	226.91861	227.91870	228.92339	229.93271
62	242.04582	243.15478	244.26906	245.38867	246.51366	247.64403	248.77981	249.92104
64	262.57995	263.83014	265.08655	266.34922	267.61817	268.89343	270.17505	271.46304
66	284.67682	286.08378	287.49801	288.91954	290.34842	291.78468	293.22835	294.67948
68	308.45534	310.03618	311.62548	313.22329	314.82966	316.44462	318.06822	319.70052
70	334.04351	335.81702	337.60036	339.39359	341.19675	343.00991	344.83311	346.66641
72	361.57905	363.56588	365.56411	367.57378	369.59498	371.62777	373.67220	375.72835
74	391.21015	393.43299	395.66899	397.91824	400.18081	402.45678	404.74623	407.04924
76	423.09630	425.58004	428.07897	430.59318	433.12276	435.66781	438.22841	440.80467
78	457.40911	460.18108	462.97053	465.77758	468.60233	471.44489	474.30537	477.18389
80	494.33327	497.42344	500.53370	503.66417	506.81499	509.98628	513.17818	516.39082
82	534.06751	537.50875	540.97302	544.46048	547.97128	551.50558	555.06352	558.64528
84	576.82569	580.65402	584.50873	588.38998	592.29797	596.23286	600.19486	604.18414
86	622.83794	627.09285	631.37790	635.69330	640.03927	644.41601	648.82374	653.26269
88	672.35190	677.07665	681.83578	686.62956	691.45822	696.32203	701.22122	706.15607
90	725.63409	730.87603	736.15716	741.47776	746.83813	752.23856	757.67936	763.16081
92	782.97127	788.78226	794.63784	800.53835	806.48412	812.47550	818.51283	824.59648
96	911.06848	918.19322	925.37543	932.61559	939.91416	947.27160	954.68839	962.16501
100	1059.40506	1068.11581	1076.90030	1085.75916	1094.69301	1103.70248	1112.78822	1121.95085
104	1231.17882	1241.80113	1252.51762	1263.32912	1274.23647	1285.24052	1296.34211	1307.54215
108	1430.09284	1443.01557	1456.05809	1469.22149	1482.50689	1495.91541	1509.44818	1523.10636
112	1660.43527	1676.12251	1691.96510	1707.95369	1724.10057	1740.40362	1756.86433	1773.48423
116	1927.17180	1946.17689	1965.37354	1984.76368	2004.34924	2024.13219	2044.11448	2064.29813
120	2236.05270	2259.03489	2282.25811	2305.72487	2329.43771	2353.39919	2377.61191	2402.07848
140	4686.18325	4744.24119	4803.02779	4862.55214	4922.82343	4983.85099	5045.64425	5108.21275
160	9788.08418	9930.36208	10074.72365	10221.19920	10369.81951	10520.61577	10673.61963	10828.86321

QUARTERLY DEPOSITS

EFFECTIVE ANNUAL YIELD

NUMBER OF QUARTRLY DEPOSITS	16.20%	16.25%	16.30%	16.35%	16.40%	16.45%	16.50%	16.55%
1	1.03825	1.03836	1.03847	1.03858	1.03870	1.03881	1.03892	1.03903
2	2.11621	2.11655	2.11690	2.11724	2.11758	2.11793	2.11827	2.11861
3	3.23540	3.23611	3.23681	3.23752	3.23822	3.23892	3.23963	3.24033
4	4.39740	4.39861	4.39981	4.40102	4.40222	4.40342	4.40463	4.40583
5	5.60385	5.60570	5.60755	5.60941	5.61126	5.61312	5.61497	5.61682
6	6.85644	6.85910	6.86176	6.86443	6.86709	6.86975	6.87241	6.87508
7	8.15694	8.16058	8.16422	8.16787	8.17151	8.17515	8.17880	8.18244
8	9.50718	9.51199	9.51679	9.52160	9.52640	9.53121	9.53602	9.54083
9	10.90907	10.91523	10.92140	10.92756	10.93373	10.93990	10.94607	10.95224
10	12.36458	12.37231	12.38004	12.38777	12.39551	12.40325	12.41099	12.41873
11	13.87577	13.88528	13.89480	13.90433	13.91386	13.92339	13.93293	13.94247
12	15.44475	15.45629	15.46784	15.47939	15.49096	15.50252	15.51409	15.52567
13	17.07374	17.08757	17.10140	17.11523	17.12908	17.14293	17.15680	17.17067
14	18.76505	18.78142	18.79780	18.81419	18.83059	18.84701	18.86343	18.87987
15	20.52104	20.54025	20.55947	20.57870	20.59795	20.61721	20.63649	20.65578
16	22.34420	22.36655	22.38891	22.41129	22.43369	22.45611	22.47855	22.50100
17	24.23709	24.26290	24.28874	24.31459	24.34047	24.36637	24.39230	24.41824
18	26.20239	26.23201	26.26165	26.29133	26.32103	26.35077	26.38053	26.41032
19	28.24285	28.27664	28.31047	28.34433	28.37823	28.41217	28.44614	28.48014
20	30.36136	30.39972	30.43811	30.47655	30.51504	30.55356	30.59214	30.63075
21	32.56090	32.60423	32.64761	32.69104	32.73453	32.77806	32.82165	32.86530
22	34.84458	34.89331	34.94211	34.99098	35.03990	35.08889	35.13794	35.18706
23	37.21560	37.27021	37.32489	37.37965	37.43448	37.48939	37.54438	37.59944
24	39.67731	39.73828	39.79934	39.86049	39.92172	39.98305	40.04447	40.10597
25	42.23317	42.30103	42.36898	42.43704	42.50521	42.57348	42.64186	42.71034
26	44.88680	44.96208	45.03749	45.11302	45.18867	45.26444	45.34033	45.41635
27	47.64193	47.72522	47.80866	47.89224	47.97596	48.05982	48.14383	48.22798
28	50.50243	50.59435	50.68644	50.77869	50.87111	50.96369	51.05643	51.14934
29	53.47235	53.57355	53.67494	53.77652	53.87828	53.98024	54.08239	54.18473
30	56.55586	56.66703	56.77841	56.89001	57.00183	57.11386	57.22611	57.33859
31	59.75732	59.87918	60.00128	60.12363	60.24624	60.36909	60.49219	60.61554
32	63.08123	63.21454	63.34814	63.48202	63.61619	63.75064	63.88537	64.02039
33	66.53227	66.67786	66.82377	66.96999	67.11654	67.26342	67.41061	67.55813
34	70.11532	70.27403	70.43310	70.59254	70.75235	70.91252	71.07305	71.23395
35	73.83541	74.00815	74.18130	74.35486	74.52884	74.70323	74.87803	75.05324
36	77.69779	77.88551	78.07370	78.26235	78.45146	78.64104	78.83109	79.02160
37	81.70790	81.91162	82.11585	82.32060	82.52588	82.73167	82.93799	83.14484
38	85.87140	86.09216	86.31351	86.53544	86.75795	86.98105	87.20473	87.42901
39	90.19414	90.43308	90.67266	90.91290	91.15379	91.39533	91.63753	91.88039
40	94.68223	94.94052	95.19953	95.45926	95.71972	95.98092	96.24284	96.50550
41	99.34198	99.62086	99.90055	100.18104	100.46234	100.74446	101.02739	101.31114
42	104.17997	104.48075	104.78242	105.08500	105.38848	105.69286	105.99814	106.30434
43	109.20300	109.52706	109.85212	110.17818	110.50523	110.83329	111.16235	111.49242
44	114.41816	114.76696	115.11686	115.46787	115.81998	116.17320	116.52754	116.88300
45	119.83279	120.20786	120.58415	120.96165	121.34039	121.72035	122.10154	122.48397
46	125.45452	125.85748	126.26177	126.66741	127.07441	127.48276	127.89247	128.30354
47	131.29129	131.72382	132.15783	132.59332	133.03031	133.46879	133.90877	134.35025
48	137.35130	137.81519	138.28072	138.74788	139.21668	139.68712	140.15922	140.63297
50	150.17556	150.70792	151.24225	151.77855	152.31683	152.85709	153.39935	153.94361
52	163.99961	164.60877	165.22029	165.83417	166.45043	167.06908	167.69011	168.31356
54	178.90140	179.59657	180.29455	180.99536	181.69901	182.40551	183.11487	183.82711
56	194.96495	195.75630	196.55101	197.34907	198.15052	198.95536	199.76361	200.57528
58	212.28083	213.17962	214.08237	214.98912	215.89987	216.81464	217.73346	218.65633
60	230.94667	231.96531	232.98863	234.01666	235.04943	236.08695	237.12924	238.17632
62	251.06773	252.21991	253.37761	254.54085	255.70967	256.88407	258.06411	259.24978
64	272.75744	274.05828	275.36559	276.67940	277.99976	279.32667	280.66019	282.00034
66	296.13810	297.60425	299.07797	300.55930	302.04827	303.54493	305.04931	306.56146
68	321.34154	322.99135	324.64999	326.31750	327.99394	329.67934	331.37375	333.07723
70	348.50988	350.36355	352.22749	354.10176	355.98641	357.88149	359.78708	361.70321
72	377.79628	379.87606	381.96775	384.07143	386.18716	388.31501	390.45505	392.60734
74	409.36588	411.69623	414.04039	416.39841	418.77040	421.15643	423.55657	425.97092
76	443.39668	446.00452	448.62831	451.26813	453.92408	456.59625	459.28476	461.98969
78	480.08055	482.99548	485.92878	488.88057	491.85097	494.84008	497.84803	500.87494
80	519.62434	522.87886	526.15453	529.45148	532.76984	536.10976	539.47137	542.85481
82	562.25100	565.88085	569.53498	573.21356	576.91674	580.64470	584.39759	588.17558
84	608.20088	612.24529	616.31753	620.41781	624.54632	628.70324	632.88878	637.10312
86	657.73307	662.23509	666.76900	671.33499	675.93331	680.56418	685.22782	689.92447
88	711.12683	716.13375	721.17710	726.25714	731.37414	736.52835	741.72005	746.94952
90	768.68323	774.24690	779.85215	785.49928	791.18859	796.92041	802.69504	808.51280
92	830.72678	836.90409	843.12878	849.40120	855.72171	862.09069	868.50849	874.97549
96	969.70192	977.29962	984.95858	992.67931	1000.46230	1008.30803	1016.21702	1024.18977
100	1131.19103	1140.50941	1149.90664	1159.38340	1168.94033	1178.57813	1188.29746	1198.09901
104	1318.84138	1330.24080	1341.74124	1353.34360	1365.04877	1376.85765	1388.77117	1400.79023
108	1536.89109	1550.80353	1564.84487	1579.01629	1593.31898	1607.75416	1622.32304	1637.02684
112	1790.26484	1807.20771	1824.31440	1841.58647	1859.02552	1876.63314	1894.41097	1912.36062
116	2084.68515	2105.27757	2126.07746	2147.08687	2168.30792	2189.74272	2211.39341	2233.26213
120	2426.80155	2451.78379	2477.02789	2502.53659	2528.31264	2554.35882	2580.67795	2607.27285
140	5171.56615	5235.71424	5300.66692	5366.43421	5433.02626	5500.45334	5568.72585	5637.85431
160	10986.37905	11146.20021	11308.36018	11472.89295	11639.83300	11809.21530	11981.07531	12155.44901

108

QUARTERLY DEPOSITS

EFFECTIVE ANNUAL YIELD

NUMBER OF QUARTERLY DEPOSITS	16.60%	16.65%	16.70%	16.75%	16.80%	16.85%	16.90%	16.95%
1	1.03914	1.03925	1.03936	1.03948	1.03959	1.03970	1.03981	1.03992
2	2.11896	2.11930	2.11964	2.11998	2.12033	2.12067	2.12101	2.12135
3	3.24104	3.24174	3.24244	3.24315	3.24385	3.24455	3.24526	3.24596
4	4.40704	4.40824	4.40944	4.41065	4.41185	4.41305	4.41426	4.41546
5	5.61868	5.62053	5.62238	5.62423	5.62609	5.62794	5.62979	5.63165
6	6.87774	6.88040	6.88307	6.88573	6.88839	6.89106	6.89372	6.89638
7	8.18608	8.18973	8.19338	8.19702	8.20067	8.20432	8.20796	8.21161
8	9.54564	9.55045	9.55526	9.56008	9.56489	9.56971	9.57452	9.57934
9	10.95841	10.96459	10.97076	10.97694	10.98312	10.98930	10.99549	11.00167
10	12.42648	12.43423	12.44198	12.44974	12.45749	12.46525	12.47302	12.48078
11	13.95201	13.96156	13.97111	13.98067	13.99023	13.99980	14.00936	14.01894
12	15.53725	15.54884	15.56044	15.57204	15.58364	15.59526	15.60687	15.61850
13	17.18454	17.19843	17.21232	17.22623	17.24014	17.25405	17.26798	17.28191
14	18.89631	18.91277	18.92924	18.94571	18.96220	18.97870	18.99521	19.01173
15	20.67508	20.69440	20.71373	20.73308	20.75244	20.77182	20.79120	20.81061
16	22.52347	22.54597	22.56847	22.59100	22.61355	22.63611	22.65869	22.68129
17	24.44422	24.47021	24.49623	24.52227	24.54833	24.57442	24.60053	24.62666
18	26.44014	26.46999	26.49986	26.52977	26.55970	26.58967	26.61966	26.64968
19	28.51418	28.54826	28.58237	28.61652	28.65070	28.68492	28.71918	28.75347
20	30.66941	30.70811	30.74685	30.78564	30.82447	30.86335	30.90227	30.94123
21	32.90899	32.95274	32.99654	33.04039	33.08430	33.12826	33.17227	33.21634
22	35.23624	35.28548	35.33478	35.38415	35.43358	35.48308	35.53264	35.58226
23	37.65457	37.70978	37.76507	37.82043	37.87587	37.93138	37.98697	38.04264
24	40.16757	40.22925	40.29102	40.35288	40.41484	40.47688	40.53901	40.60123
25	42.77892	42.84761	42.91641	42.98531	43.05431	43.12342	43.19264	43.26197
26	45.49249	45.56875	45.64514	45.72164	45.79828	45.87503	45.95191	46.02892
27	48.31227	48.39670	48.48128	48.56600	48.65087	48.73587	48.82103	48.90633
28	51.24242	51.33566	51.42907	51.52264	51.61638	51.71029	51.80436	51.89860
29	54.28726	54.38998	54.49289	54.59599	54.69929	54.80278	54.90646	55.01033
30	57.45128	57.56419	57.67732	57.79067	57.90424	58.01803	58.13204	58.24628
31	60.73914	60.86299	60.98710	61.11145	61.23606	61.36092	61.48604	61.61141
32	64.15570	64.29129	64.42716	64.56333	64.69978	64.83652	64.97355	65.11087
33	67.70598	67.85415	68.00265	68.15147	68.30062	68.45010	68.59990	68.75004
34	71.39523	71.55686	71.71887	71.88125	72.04400	72.20712	72.37062	72.53448
35	75.22887	75.40492	75.58139	75.75827	75.93557	76.11329	76.29144	76.47000
36	79.21258	79.40403	79.59594	79.78833	79.98120	80.17453	80.36834	80.56263
37	83.35221	83.56011	83.76853	83.97749	84.18697	84.39699	84.60754	84.81863
38	87.65387	87.87932	88.10537	88.33201	88.55924	88.78708	89.01551	89.24454
39	92.12390	92.36808	92.61292	92.85843	93.10460	93.35144	93.59895	93.84713
40	96.76890	97.03304	97.29791	97.56353	97.82989	98.09699	98.36485	98.63345
41	101.59571	101.88110	102.16732	102.45436	102.74224	103.03094	103.32048	103.61085
42	106.61145	106.91947	107.22841	107.53827	107.84905	108.16075	108.47338	108.78695
43	111.82351	112.15561	112.48872	112.82286	113.15802	113.49421	113.83142	114.16967
44	117.23958	117.59728	117.95611	118.31606	118.67716	119.03939	119.40276	119.76728
45	122.86764	123.25255	123.63871	124.02612	124.41478	124.80471	125.19589	125.58835
46	128.71598	129.12980	129.54500	129.96157	130.37954	130.79889	131.21964	131.64179
47	134.79325	135.23776	135.68378	136.13134	136.58042	137.03104	137.48319	137.93689
48	141.10838	141.58546	142.06422	142.54465	143.02677	143.51058	143.99609	144.48330
50	154.48987	155.03815	155.58845	156.14078	156.69515	157.25156	157.81002	158.37054
52	168.93941	169.56768	170.19839	170.83153	171.46712	172.10517	172.74568	173.38868
54	184.54223	185.26025	185.98117	186.70501	187.43179	188.16150	188.89417	189.62980
56	201.39039	202.20894	203.03096	203.85646	204.68545	205.51794	206.35396	207.19352
58	219.58328	220.51432	221.44947	222.38875	223.33218	224.27977	225.23154	226.18751
60	239.22823	240.28497	241.34658	242.41306	243.48445	244.56077	245.64204	246.72828
62	260.44114	261.63819	262.84098	264.04951	265.26383	266.48396	267.70993	268.94176
64	283.34715	284.70068	286.06090	287.42790	288.80169	290.18231	291.56980	292.96418
66	308.08140	309.60919	311.14486	312.68845	314.24001	315.79956	317.36716	318.94285
68	334.78981	336.51156	338.24251	339.98272	341.73223	343.49109	345.25935	347.03707
70	363.62995	365.56736	367.51550	369.47442	371.44418	373.42484	375.41647	377.41912
72	394.77196	396.94897	399.13845	401.34047	403.55509	405.78239	408.02244	410.27531
74	428.39956	430.84257	433.30003	435.77203	438.25865	440.75999	443.27611	445.80712
76	464.71114	467.44922	470.20402	472.97564	475.76420	478.56978	481.39249	484.23244
78	503.92092	506.98610	510.07058	513.17449	516.29796	519.44110	522.60403	525.78689
80	546.26023	549.68775	553.13753	556.60971	560.10443	563.62184	567.16208	570.72529
82	591.97883	595.80752	599.66181	603.54187	607.44786	611.37998	615.33837	619.32322
84	641.34646	645.61900	649.92095	654.25249	658.61383	663.00517	667.42672	671.87869
86	694.65436	699.41771	704.21477	709.04578	713.91096	718.81055	723.74481	728.71397
88	752.21701	757.52281	762.86719	768.25043	773.67280	779.13460	784.63610	790.17759
90	814.37401	820.27900	826.22808	832.22159	838.25985	844.34319	850.47194	856.64645
92	881.49207	888.05860	894.67545	901.34302	908.06168	914.83183	921.65386	928.52815
96	1032.22679	1040.32859	1048.49570	1056.72862	1065.02790	1073.39405	1081.82761	1090.32913
100	1207.98347	1217.95154	1228.00392	1238.14131	1248.36443	1258.67400	1269.07074	1279.55538
104	1412.91577	1425.14871	1437.49002	1449.94063	1462.50151	1475.17362	1487.95795	1500.85547
108	1651.86682	1666.84422	1681.96030	1697.21633	1712.61361	1728.15343	1743.83710	1759.66594
112	1930.48375	1948.78202	1967.25711	1985.91072	2004.74405	2023.76034	2042.95983	2062.34477
116	2255.35109	2277.66246	2300.19849	2322.96141	2345.95349	2369.17701	2392.63430	2416.32767
120	2634.14640	2661.30150	2688.74108	2716.46809	2744.48552	2772.79639	2801.40375	2830.31067
140	5707.84937	5778.72182	5850.48257	5923.14268	5996.71333	6071.20584	6146.63167	6223.00243
160	12332.37291	12511.88401	12694.01986	12878.81855	13066.31871	13256.55950	13449.58069	13645.42258

QUARTERLY DEPOSITS

EFFECTIVE ANNUAL YIELD

NUMBER OF QUARTERLY DEPOSITS	17.00%	17.05%	17.10%	17.15%	17.20%	17.25%	17.30%	17.35%
1	1.04003	1.04014	1.04025	1.04036	1.04048	1.04059	1.04070	1.04081
2	2.12170	2.12204	2.12238	2.12272	2.12307	2.12341	2.12375	2.12409
3	3.24666	3.24737	3.24807	3.24877	3.24947	3.25018	3.25088	3.25158
4	4.41666	4.41787	4.41907	4.42027	4.42147	4.42268	4.42388	4.42508
5	5.63350	5.63535	5.63721	5.63906	5.64091	5.64276	5.64462	5.64647
6	6.89905	6.90171	6.90438	6.90704	6.90971	6.91237	6.91503	6.91770
7	8.21526	8.21891	8.22256	8.22621	8.22986	8.23351	8.23716	8.24081
8	9.58416	9.58898	9.59380	9.59862	9.60344	9.60826	9.61309	9.61791
9	11.00786	11.01405	11.02024	11.02643	11.03262	11.03881	11.04501	11.05121
10	12.48855	12.49632	12.50409	12.51187	12.51965	12.52743	12.53521	12.54300
11	14.02852	14.03810	14.04768	14.05727	14.06686	14.07646	14.08606	14.09567
12	15.63013	15.64176	15.65340	15.66505	15.67670	15.68836	15.70003	15.71170
13	17.29586	17.30981	17.32376	17.33773	17.35170	17.36569	17.37968	17.39367
14	19.02827	19.04481	19.06136	19.07793	19.09450	19.11109	19.12768	19.14429
15	20.83003	20.84946	20.86890	20.88836	20.90784	20.92733	20.94683	20.96635
16	22.70391	22.72655	22.74920	22.77188	22.79457	22.81728	22.84001	22.86276
17	24.65281	24.67899	24.70520	24.73142	24.75767	24.78394	24.81024	24.83656
18	26.67973	26.70981	26.73992	26.77006	26.80023	26.83042	26.86065	26.89090
19	28.78779	28.82216	28.85655	28.89099	28.92546	28.95996	28.99451	29.02909
20	30.98024	31.01929	31.05839	31.09753	31.13671	31.17594	31.21521	31.25452
21	33.26046	33.30463	33.34885	33.39313	33.43746	33.48185	33.52629	33.57078
22	35.63195	35.68170	35.73152	35.78140	35.83134	35.88135	35.93142	35.98155
23	38.09838	38.15420	38.21009	38.26606	38.32211	38.37823	38.43443	38.49071
24	40.66354	40.72595	40.78844	40.85102	40.91370	40.97646	41.03932	41.10226
25	43.33140	43.40093	43.47057	43.54032	43.61018	43.68014	43.75021	43.82039
26	46.10605	46.18330	46.26067	46.33818	46.41580	46.49355	46.57143	46.64943
27	48.99177	49.07735	49.16309	49.24896	49.33499	49.42115	49.50747	49.59393
28	51.99301	52.08759	52.18233	52.27724	52.37233	52.46758	52.56300	52.65858
29	55.11440	55.21866	55.32311	55.42776	55.53260	55.63764	55.74287	55.84830
30	58.36074	58.47542	58.59032	58.70544	58.82079	58.93637	59.05217	59.16819
31	61.73703	61.86201	61.98904	62.11543	62.24208	62.36898	62.49614	62.62356
32	65.24848	65.38639	65.52458	65.66306	65.80184	65.94091	66.08027	66.21993
33	68.90051	69.05130	69.20243	69.35389	69.50568	69.65781	69.81027	69.96306
34	72.69872	72.86334	73.02833	73.19370	73.35944	73.52557	73.69207	73.85895
35	76.64899	76.82840	77.00824	77.18850	77.36919	77.55030	77.73185	77.91382
36	80.75739	80.95263	81.14835	81.34455	81.54123	81.73839	81.93604	82.13417
37	85.03025	85.24242	85.45511	85.66835	85.88213	86.09646	86.31132	86.52673
38	89.47417	89.70440	89.93524	90.16669	90.39874	90.63140	90.86467	91.09856
39	94.09598	94.34551	94.59571	94.84660	95.09816	95.35041	95.60333	95.85695
40	98.90281	99.17292	99.44378	99.71541	99.98779	100.26094	100.53485	100.80952
41	103.90206	104.19411	104.48701	104.78075	105.07533	105.37077	105.66706	105.96420
42	109.10144	109.41687	109.73324	110.05055	110.36880	110.68799	111.00814	111.32924
43	114.50896	114.84928	115.19065	115.53306	115.87652	116.22103	116.56659	116.91321
44	120.13295	120.49977	120.86774	121.23687	121.60716	121.97862	122.35125	122.72505
45	125.98207	126.37707	126.77335	127.17092	127.56976	127.96990	128.37134	128.77407
46	132.06535	132.49031	132.91669	133.34449	133.77370	134.20435	134.63643	135.06994
47	138.39215	138.84895	139.30732	139.76725	140.22875	140.69183	141.15649	141.62273
48	144.97221	145.46284	145.95519	146.44927	146.94507	147.44261	147.94190	148.44293
50	158.93312	159.49778	160.06451	160.63334	161.20425	161.77727	162.35240	162.92965
52	174.03415	174.68212	175.33260	175.98558	176.64110	177.29914	177.95972	178.62286
54	190.36841	191.11001	191.85461	192.60222	193.35286	194.10653	194.86325	195.62303
56	208.03662	208.88329	209.73354	210.58738	211.44484	212.30592	213.17063	214.03900
58	227.14771	228.11214	229.08082	230.05377	231.03102	232.01258	232.99847	233.98870
60	247.81951	248.91576	250.01704	251.12339	252.23482	253.35136	254.47303	255.59985
62	270.71948	271.42312	272.67271	273.92827	275.18983	276.45743	277.73108	279.01082
64	294.36549	295.77376	297.18902	298.61132	300.04068	301.47715	302.92074	304.37150
66	320.52665	322.11863	323.71881	325.32724	326.94396	328.56901	330.20243	331.84428
68	348.82428	350.62105	352.42742	354.24343	356.06916	357.90463	359.74991	361.60504
70	379.43285	381.45772	383.49379	385.54113	387.59979	389.66984	391.75133	393.84434
72	412.54107	414.81980	417.11157	419.41645	421.73452	424.06585	426.41052	428.76859
74	448.35310	450.91413	453.49030	456.08170	458.68843	461.31056	463.94819	466.60141
76	487.08972	489.96445	492.85672	495.76665	498.69433	501.63989	504.60341	507.58502
78	528.98978	532.21285	535.45621	538.71999	542.00431	545.30931	548.63511	551.98184
80	574.31163	577.92125	581.55429	585.21090	588.89123	592.59544	596.32368	600.07610
82	623.33471	627.37301	631.43829	635.53073	639.65052	643.79784	647.97286	652.17576
84	676.36127	680.87469	685.41914	689.99484	694.60200	699.24083	703.91156	708.61439
86	733.71827	738.75797	743.83330	748.94453	754.09189	759.27564	764.49600	769.75334
88	795.75935	801.38169	807.04488	812.74922	818.49501	824.28255	830.11213	835.98406
90	862.86704	869.13407	875.44787	881.80878	888.21716	894.67336	901.17773	907.73062
92	935.45511	942.43513	949.46862	956.55599	963.69763	970.89397	978.14541	985.45238
96	1098.88914	1107.53819	1116.24682	1125.02561	1133.87509	1142.79585	1151.78844	1160.85345
100	1290.12865	1300.79131	1311.54410	1322.38777	1333.32308	1344.35081	1355.47172	1366.68660
104	1513.86719	1526.99410	1540.23721	1553.59754	1567.07613	1580.67400	1594.39221	1608.23180
108	1775.64127	1791.70446	1808.03684	1824.45979	1841.03469	1857.76294	1874.64594	1891.68510
112	2081.91695	2101.67816	2121.63021	2141.77492	2162.11414	2182.64972	2203.38356	2224.31754
116	2440.25950	2464.43215	2488.84804	2513.50959	2538.41924	2563.57948	2588.99279	2614.66172
120	2859.52028	2889.03570	2918.86012	2948.99675	2979.44882	3010.21961	3041.31243	3072.73060
140	6300.32985	6378.62583	6457.90239	6538.17172	6619.44614	6701.73813	6785.06032	6869.42551
160	13844.12605	14045.73258	14250.28423	14457.82366	14668.39415	14882.03959	15098.80450	15318.73403

QUARTERLY DEPOSITS

EFFECTIVE ANNUAL YIELD

NUMBER OF QUARTRLY DEPOSITS	17.40%	17.45%	17.50%	17.55%	17.60%	17.65%	17.70%	17.75%
1	1.04092	1.04103	1.04114	1.04125	1.04136	1.04147	1.04158	1.04169
2	2.12443	2.12477	2.12511	2.12546	2.12580	2.12614	2.12648	2.12682
3	3.25228	3.25298	3.25368	3.25439	3.25509	3.25579	3.25649	3.25719
4	4.42628	4.42748	4.42868	4.42989	4.43109	4.43229	4.43349	4.43469
5	5.64832	5.65017	5.65203	5.65388	5.65573	5.65758	5.65943	5.66129
6	6.92036	6.92303	6.92569	6.92836	6.93103	6.93369	6.93636	6.93902
7	8.24446	8.24811	8.25176	8.25542	8.25907	8.26272	8.26638	8.27003
8	9.62274	9.62756	9.63239	9.63722	9.64205	9.64688	9.65171	9.65654
9	11.05741	11.06361	11.06981	11.07602	11.08223	11.08843	11.09464	11.10086
10	12.55079	12.55858	12.56638	12.57417	12.58197	12.58978	12.59758	12.60539
11	14.10528	14.11489	14.12451	14.13413	14.14375	14.15338	14.16302	14.17266
12	15.72337	15.73505	15.74674	15.75844	15.77013	15.78184	15.79355	15.80527
13	17.40768	17.42169	17.43572	17.44975	17.46378	17.47783	17.49189	17.50595
14	19.16091	19.17754	19.19418	19.21083	19.22749	19.24416	19.26084	19.27754
15	20.98588	21.00542	21.02498	21.04456	21.06414	21.08375	21.10336	21.12299
16	22.88552	22.90830	22.93111	22.95393	22.97677	22.99962	23.02250	23.04539
17	24.86290	24.88926	24.91565	24.94206	24.96850	24.99496	25.02144	25.04794
18	26.92119	26.95150	26.98184	27.01221	27.04261	27.07304	27.10350	27.13399
19	29.06370	29.09835	29.13304	29.16776	29.20252	29.23732	29.27215	29.30702
20	31.29388	31.33329	31.37273	31.41223	31.45176	31.49135	31.53097	31.57064
21	33.61532	33.65992	33.70458	33.74928	33.79404	33.83886	33.88372	33.92865
22	36.03176	36.08202	36.13235	36.18274	36.23320	36.28373	36.33431	36.38497
23	38.54707	38.60350	38.66000	38.71659	38.77325	38.82999	38.88681	38.94370
24	41.16530	41.22843	41.29165	41.35496	41.41836	41.48186	41.54544	41.60912
25	43.89067	43.96106	44.03156	44.10217	44.17288	44.24370	44.31463	44.38567
26	46.72756	46.80582	46.88420	46.96270	47.04133	47.12009	47.19898	47.27799
27	49.68054	49.76729	49.85419	49.94124	50.02843	50.11577	50.20326	50.29090
28	52.75434	52.85027	52.94637	53.04264	53.13908	53.23569	53.33248	53.42943
29	55.95393	56.05975	56.16577	56.27198	56.37840	56.48501	56.59181	56.69882
30	59.28444	59.40091	59.51761	59.63454	59.75170	59.86908	59.98669	60.10452
31	62.75123	62.87916	63.00736	63.13581	63.26452	63.39350	63.52273	63.65223
32	66.35988	66.50013	66.64067	66.78151	66.92265	67.06408	67.20581	67.34785
33	70.11619	70.26966	70.42346	70.57760	70.73208	70.88690	71.04205	71.19755
34	74.02621	74.19386	74.36188	74.53029	74.69908	74.86826	75.03782	75.20777
35	78.09623	78.27906	78.46233	78.64603	78.83017	79.01474	79.19974	79.38519
36	82.33278	82.53188	82.73147	82.93155	83.13212	83.33318	83.53473	83.73678
37	86.74269	86.95920	87.17625	87.39386	87.61201	87.83072	88.04999	88.26981
38	91.33305	91.56817	91.80390	92.04024	92.27721	92.51479	92.75300	92.99184
39	96.11125	96.36624	96.62192	96.87830	97.13536	97.39313	97.65159	97.91075
40	101.08497	101.36118	101.63817	101.91593	102.19446	102.47378	102.75387	103.03475
41	106.26220	106.56106	106.86078	107.16137	107.46282	107.76514	108.06833	108.37239
42	111.65129	111.97429	112.29826	112.62319	112.94908	113.27594	113.60378	113.93258
43	117.26089	117.60963	117.95944	118.31032	118.66227	119.01530	119.36941	119.72460
44	123.10003	123.47619	123.85353	124.23206	124.61177	124.99269	125.37480	125.75811
45	129.17811	129.58345	129.99010	130.39807	130.80736	131.21797	131.62991	132.04318
46	135.50489	135.94129	136.37914	136.81845	137.25921	137.70144	138.14513	138.59030
47	142.09057	142.56000	143.03103	143.50367	143.97792	144.45379	144.93128	145.41040
48	148.94572	149.45027	149.95658	150.46467	150.97453	151.48618	151.99963	152.51486
50	163.50903	164.09053	164.67418	165.25997	165.84792	166.43803	167.03031	167.62477
52	179.28856	179.95682	180.62767	181.30111	181.97714	182.65579	183.33705	184.02094
54	196.38588	197.15181	197.92084	198.69298	199.46824	200.24663	201.02817	201.81286
56	214.91104	215.78677	216.66620	217.54934	218.43621	219.32682	220.22120	221.11935
58	234.98330	235.98229	236.98567	237.99348	239.00574	240.02245	241.04364	242.06934
60	256.73185	257.86904	259.01146	260.15913	261.31206	262.47029	263.63384	264.80272
62	280.29668	281.58868	282.88685	284.19123	285.50183	286.81870	288.14186	289.47133
64	305.82947	307.29468	308.76716	310.24694	311.73408	313.22859	314.73052	316.23990
66	333.49458	335.15339	336.82074	338.49667	340.18125	341.87449	343.57646	345.28719
68	363.47008	365.34508	367.23009	369.12517	371.03036	372.94572	374.87131	376.80717
70	395.94892	398.06513	400.19305	402.33273	404.48423	406.64763	408.82298	411.01035
72	431.14016	433.52528	435.92404	438.33652	440.76279	443.20293	445.65702	448.12514
74	469.27031	471.95498	474.65552	477.37201	480.10454	482.85322	485.61814	488.39938
76	510.58482	513.60292	516.63944	519.69447	522.76813	525.86054	528.97180	532.10204
78	555.34963	558.73861	562.14892	565.58068	569.03403	572.50911	576.00604	579.52496
80	603.85286	607.65412	611.48002	615.33073	619.20641	623.10721	627.03330	630.98484
82	656.40674	660.66598	664.95366	669.26998	673.61511	677.98925	682.39260	686.82533
84	713.34954	718.11724	722.91771	727.75116	732.61783	737.51793	742.45159	747.41934
86	775.04780	780.37968	785.74924	791.15674	796.60246	802.08664	807.60958	813.17152
88	841.89665	847.85619	853.85699	859.90138	865.98965	872.12213	878.29913	884.52097
90	914.33240	920.98341	927.68404	934.43464	941.23558	948.08723	954.98996	961.94416
92	992.81529	1000.23457	1007.71065	1015.24395	1022.83492	1030.48397	1038.19156	1045.95813
96	1169.99143	1179.20299	1188.48870	1197.84915	1207.28495	1216.79668	1226.38496	1236.05039
100	1377.99623	1389.40140	1400.90291	1412.50157	1424.19819	1435.99359	1447.88859	1459.88403
104	1622.19385	1636.27942	1650.48960	1664.82548	1679.28816	1693.87874	1708.59836	1723.44813
108	1908.88186	1926.23766	1943.75397	1961.43224	1979.27396	1997.28063	2015.45376	2033.79487
112	2245.45359	2266.79362	2288.33960	2310.09348	2332.05726	2354.23295	2376.62256	2399.22815
116	2640.58879	2666.77659	2693.22771	2719.94477	2746.93043	2774.18735	2801.71825	2829.52583
120	3104.47702	3136.55659	3168.97124	3201.72497	3234.82127	3268.26371	3302.05587	3336.20136
140	6954.84662	7041.33675	7128.90918	7217.57731	7307.35474	7398.25521	7490.29265	7583.48113
160	15541.87399	15768.27081	15997.97162	16231.04200	16467.44701	16707.37922	16950.78068	17197.73196

111

QUARTERLY DEPOSITS

EFFECTIVE ANNUAL YIELD

NUMBER OF QUARTRLY DEPOSITS	17.80%	17.85%	17.90%	18.00%	18.10%	18.20%	18.30%	18.40%
1	1.04180	1.04192	1.04203	1.04225	1.04247	1.04269	1.04291	1.04313
2	2.12716	2.12750	2.12784	2.12852	2.12921	2.12989	2.13057	2.13125
3	3.25789	3.25859	3.25929	3.26069	3.26209	3.26349	3.26489	3.26629
4	4.43589	4.43709	4.43829	4.44069	4.44309	4.44549	4.44789	4.45029
5	5.66314	5.66499	5.66684	5.67055	5.67425	5.67795	5.68165	5.68536
6	6.94169	6.94435	6.94702	6.95235	6.95769	6.96302	6.96835	6.97369
7	8.27369	8.27734	8.28100	8.28831	8.29563	8.30295	8.31026	8.31758
8	9.66137	9.66621	9.67104	9.68071	9.69039	9.70007	9.70975	9.71944
9	11.10707	11.11328	11.11950	11.13194	11.14438	11.15683	11.16929	11.18176
10	12.61320	12.62101	12.62883	12.64447	12.66012	12.67578	12.69146	12.70714
11	14.18230	14.19194	14.20159	14.22090	14.24023	14.25958	14.27894	14.29831
12	15.81699	15.82872	15.84045	15.86394	15.88745	15.91098	15.93453	15.95811
13	17.52002	17.53410	17.54818	17.57638	17.60461	17.63287	17.66117	17.68949
14	19.29424	19.31096	19.32768	19.36117	19.39470	19.42827	19.46189	19.49555
15	21.14264	21.16230	21.18197	21.22136	21.26081	21.30031	21.33988	21.37950
16	23.06830	23.09124	23.11419	23.16014	23.20617	23.25227	23.29845	23.34470
17	25.07447	25.10103	25.12760	25.18082	25.23414	25.28755	25.34105	25.39465
18	27.16451	27.19506	27.22563	27.28688	27.34824	27.40971	27.47131	27.53302
19	29.34192	29.37686	29.41184	29.48190	29.55211	29.62247	29.69297	29.76362
20	31.61036	31.65011	31.68992	31.76966	31.84958	31.92968	32.00996	32.09041
21	33.97362	34.01865	34.06374	34.15407	34.24461	34.33538	34.42636	34.51756
22	36.43568	36.48647	36.53732	36.63921	36.74136	36.84378	36.94645	37.04939
23	39.00067	39.05772	39.11485	39.22934	39.34414	39.45925	39.57468	39.69042
24	41.67289	41.73675	41.80071	41.92889	42.05745	42.18637	42.31567	42.44534
25	44.45682	44.52807	44.59944	44.74249	44.88598	45.02991	45.17428	45.31909
26	47.35713	47.43639	47.51579	47.67496	47.83464	47.99484	48.15555	48.31677
27	50.37868	50.46662	50.55470	50.73131	50.90852	51.08633	51.26474	51.44374
28	53.52656	53.62386	53.72133	53.91679	54.11294	54.30979	54.50733	54.70558
29	56.80602	56.91343	57.02103	57.23684	57.45344	57.67085	57.88907	58.10809
30	60.22259	60.34088	60.45941	60.69715	60.93581	61.17539	61.41591	61.65735
31	63.78198	63.91200	64.04229	64.30364	64.56606	64.82953	65.09408	65.35969
32	67.49018	67.63281	67.77574	68.06250	68.35048	68.63966	68.93007	69.22170
33	71.35339	71.50957	71.66609	71.98016	72.29561	72.61244	72.93066	73.25028
34	75.37810	75.54882	75.71994	76.06333	76.40828	76.75481	77.10291	77.45260
35	79.57107	79.75739	79.94415	80.31899	80.69561	81.07400	81.45419	81.83616
36	83.93932	84.14235	84.34589	84.75445	85.16501	85.57758	85.99217	86.40879
37	88.49018	88.71112	88.93261	89.37728	89.82421	90.27340	90.72487	91.17862
38	93.23130	93.47138	93.71208	94.19542	94.68128	95.16968	95.66064	96.15417
39	98.17061	98.43117	98.69244	99.21771	99.74461	100.27497	100.80820	101.34431
40	103.31641	103.59886	103.88209	104.45094	105.02297	105.59819	106.17663	106.75829
41	108.67733	108.98315	109.28984	109.90589	110.52549	111.14865	111.77541	112.40578
42	114.26236	114.59312	114.92486	115.59129	116.26168	116.93605	117.61443	118.29683
43	120.08087	120.43823	120.79669	121.51688	122.24148	122.97051	123.70399	124.44196
44	126.14262	126.52835	126.91528	127.69281	128.47522	129.26256	130.05485	130.85211
45	132.45778	132.87373	133.29102	134.12964	134.97369	135.82320	136.67821	137.53873
46	139.03695	139.48508	139.93470	140.83642	141.74814	142.66391	143.58576	144.51374
47	145.89116	146.37355	146.85759	147.83061	148.81028	149.79663	150.78972	151.78957
48	153.03190	153.55075	154.07141	155.11820	156.17233	157.23384	158.30278	159.37920
50	168.22142	168.82026	169.42130	170.63003	171.84765	173.07424	174.30985	175.55456
52	184.70747	185.39665	186.08849	187.48018	188.88262	190.29589	191.72008	193.15526
54	202.60072	203.39177	204.18601	205.78412	207.39517	209.01924	210.65645	212.30689
56	222.02129	222.92705	223.83662	225.66730	227.51347	229.37524	231.25275	233.14612
58	243.09955	244.13429	245.17360	247.26596	249.37679	251.50624	253.65448	255.82166
60	265.97698	267.15662	268.34167	270.72811	273.13650	275.56703	278.01989	280.49530
62	290.80716	292.14936	293.49797	296.21453	298.95708	301.72587	304.52114	307.34313
64	317.75677	319.28116	320.81312	323.89987	327.01730	330.16572	333.34543	336.55673
66	347.00672	348.73511	350.47240	353.97384	357.51141	361.08547	364.69640	368.34456
68	378.75337	380.70995	382.67696	386.64254	390.65052	394.70138	398.79554	402.93346
70	413.20981	415.42142	417.64525	422.12982	426.66407	431.24852	435.88374	440.57026
72	450.60736	453.10376	455.61443	460.67889	465.80136	470.98252	476.22301	481.52352
74	491.19705	494.01124	496.84204	502.55389	508.33336	514.18125	520.09835	526.08548
76	535.25136	538.41988	541.60771	548.04178	554.55451	561.14683	567.81972	574.57414
78	583.06602	586.62934	590.21506	597.45428	604.78479	612.20773	619.72425	627.33550
80	634.96199	638.96492	642.99378	651.12999	659.37197	667.72105	676.17862	684.74607
82	691.28766	695.77977	700.30185	709.43674	718.69393	728.07503	737.58168	747.21552
84	752.42112	757.45725	762.52796	772.77409	783.16139	793.69178	804.36721	815.18964
86	818.77275	824.41355	830.09418	841.57605	853.22063	865.03019	877.00702	889.15347
88	890.78797	897.10046	903.45876	916.31412	929.35669	942.58918	956.01430	969.63483
90	968.95020	976.00846	983.11933	997.50044	1012.09666	1026.91117	1041.94720	1057.20801
92	1053.78412	1061.66999	1069.61617	1085.69315	1102.01335	1118.58590	1135.41281	1152.49793
96	1245.79359	1255.61517	1265.51576	1285.55649	1305.92086	1326.61403	1347.64125	1369.00784
100	1471.98074	1484.17957	1496.48138	1521.39735	1546.73563	1572.50328	1598.70749	1625.35557
104	1738.42920	1753.54272	1768.78984	1799.68957	1831.13787	1863.14437	1895.71886	1928.87129
108	2052.30549	2070.98719	2089.84151	2128.07439	2167.01692	2206.68214	2247.08330	2288.23390
112	2422.05176	2445.09549	2468.36144	2515.56847	2563.69008	2612.74378	2662.74744	2713.71924
116	2857.61287	2885.98213	2914.63643	2972.81149	3032.16108	3092.70865	3154.47811	3217.49387
120	3370.70385	3405.56703	3440.79464	3512.35826	3585.45333	3660.02712	3736.19550	3813.96303
140	7677.83493	7773.36846	7870.09635	8067.19451	8269.24987	8476.38585	8688.72888	8906.40850
160	17448.28435	17702.48986	17960.40125	18487.55647	19030.18727	19588.74345	20163.68766	20755.49580

112

QUARTERLY DEPOSITS

EFFECTIVE ANNUAL YIELD

NUMBER OF QUARTRLY DEPOSITS	18.50%	18.60%	18.70%	18.80%	18.90%	19.00%	19.10%	19.20%
1	1.04335	1.04357	1.04379	1.04401	1.04423	1.04445	1.04467	1.04489
2	2.13193	2.13261	2.13328	2.13396	2.13464	2.13532	2.13600	2.13667
3	3.26769	3.26909	3.27049	3.27188	3.27328	3.27468	3.27607	3.27747
4	4.45269	4.45509	4.45749	4.45988	4.46228	4.46468	4.46707	4.46947
5	5.68906	5.69276	5.69646	5.70017	5.70387	5.70757	5.71127	5.71497
6	6.97902	6.98436	6.98970	6.99503	7.00037	7.00571	7.01104	7.01638
7	8.32491	8.33223	8.33956	8.34688	8.35421	8.36154	8.36888	8.37621
8	9.72913	9.73883	9.74852	9.75823	9.76793	9.77764	9.78736	9.79707
9	11.19423	11.20671	11.21919	11.23168	11.24418	11.25669	11.26920	11.28171
10	12.72284	12.73854	12.75426	12.76998	12.78572	12.80147	12.81723	12.83300
11	14.31771	14.33711	14.35654	14.37598	14.39544	14.41491	14.43440	14.45391
12	15.98171	16.00534	16.02899	16.05266	16.07635	16.10007	16.12381	16.14758
13	17.71785	17.74624	17.77467	17.80312	17.83161	17.86013	17.88869	17.91727
14	19.52925	19.56300	19.59679	19.63062	19.66450	19.69842	19.73239	19.76640
15	21.41917	21.45891	21.49870	21.53855	21.57846	21.61842	21.65845	21.69853
16	23.39102	23.43742	23.48389	23.53044	23.57707	23.62376	23.67054	23.71738
17	25.44835	25.50213	25.55602	25.60999	25.66407	25.71823	25.77250	25.82686
18	27.59485	27.65661	27.71888	27.78107	27.84337	27.90580	27.96835	28.03102
19	29.83441	29.90535	29.97644	30.04768	30.11907	30.19060	30.26228	30.33411
20	32.17105	32.25187	32.33287	32.41405	32.49541	32.57695	32.65868	32.74059
21	34.60898	34.70062	34.79248	34.88456	34.97686	35.06938	35.16212	35.25508
22	37.15259	37.25606	37.35979	37.46379	37.56805	37.67258	37.77738	37.88244
23	39.80647	39.92284	40.03953	40.15653	40.27385	40.39149	40.50945	40.62773
24	42.57539	42.70581	42.83660	42.96778	43.09932	43.23125	43.36356	43.49625
25	45.46434	45.61003	45.75616	45.90274	46.04976	46.19724	46.34515	46.49352
26	48.47852	48.64078	48.80356	48.96687	49.13070	49.29505	49.45993	49.62534
27	51.62336	51.80358	51.98441	52.16584	52.34789	52.53055	52.71383	52.89772
28	54.90453	55.10418	55.30454	55.50560	55.70738	55.90987	56.11307	56.31700
29	58.32793	58.54858	58.77005	58.99234	59.21545	59.43937	59.66415	59.88975
30	61.89973	62.14305	62.38732	62.63252	62.87868	63.12578	63.37385	63.62287
31	65.62637	65.89413	66.16298	66.43291	66.70392	66.97603	67.24924	67.52355
32	69.51456	69.80864	70.10397	70.40054	70.69835	70.99742	71.29774	71.59933
33	73.57129	73.89371	74.21754	74.54278	74.86945	75.19755	75.52708	75.85805
34	77.80388	78.15675	78.51123	78.86732	79.22503	79.58436	79.94532	80.30793
35	82.21994	82.60553	82.99294	83.38218	83.77325	84.16616	84.56092	84.95754
36	86.82744	87.24814	87.67090	88.09572	88.52262	88.95161	89.38268	89.81587
37	91.63467	92.09303	92.55370	93.01671	93.48206	93.94976	94.41982	94.89226
38	96.65029	97.14900	97.65032	98.15426	98.66084	99.17007	99.68195	100.19651
39	101.88332	102.42525	102.97011	103.51791	104.06867	104.62241	105.17913	105.73886
40	107.34321	107.93139	108.52285	109.11761	109.71568	110.31709	110.92185	111.52998
41	113.03977	113.67742	114.31873	114.96374	115.61245	116.26489	116.92108	117.58104
42	118.98328	119.67380	120.36842	121.06715	121.77002	122.47706	123.18828	123.90371
43	125.18443	125.93144	126.68301	127.43916	128.19993	128.96534	129.73542	130.51019
44	131.65439	132.46171	133.27411	134.09160	134.91423	135.74201	136.57500	137.41320
45	138.40482	139.27651	140.15382	141.03680	141.92548	142.81990	143.72008	144.62607
46	145.44788	146.38822	147.33480	148.28766	149.24683	150.21237	151.18431	152.16269
47	152.79624	153.80978	154.83022	155.85761	156.89200	157.93343	158.98195	160.03761
48	160.46315	161.55468	162.65385	163.76070	164.87529	165.99767	167.12789	168.26601
50	176.80843	178.07152	179.34389	180.62562	181.91677	183.21740	184.52759	185.84740
52	194.60152	196.05894	197.52761	199.00760	200.49901	202.00191	203.51639	205.04255
54	213.97068	215.64791	217.33869	219.04312	220.76132	222.49339	224.23943	225.99957
56	235.05550	236.98100	238.92276	240.88092	242.85560	244.84695	246.85510	248.88018
58	258.00795	260.21351	262.43851	264.68311	266.94749	269.23181	271.53624	273.86095
60	282.99345	285.51455	288.05880	290.62641	293.21759	295.83254	298.47149	301.13465
62	310.19211	313.06831	315.97199	318.90342	321.86284	324.85053	327.86673	330.91172
64	339.79994	343.07535	346.38329	349.72406	353.09799	356.50541	359.94662	363.42197
66	372.03034	375.75410	379.51624	383.31715	387.15720	391.03680	394.95635	398.91624
68	407.11562	411.34245	415.61445	419.93207	424.29580	428.70611	433.16350	437.66845
70	445.30864	450.09946	454.94327	459.84065	464.79219	469.79847	474.86008	479.97763
72	486.88470	492.30724	497.79184	503.33918	508.94998	514.62495	520.36480	526.17026
74	532.14343	538.27305	544.47515	550.75058	557.10020	563.52486	570.02543	576.60280
76	581.41106	588.33148	595.33640	602.42683	609.60381	616.86836	624.22155	631.66442
78	635.04266	642.84692	650.74949	658.75158	666.85442	675.05926	683.36736	691.78001
80	693.42479	702.21622	711.12179	720.14296	729.28121	738.53803	747.91493	757.41346
82	756.97824	766.87154	776.89713	787.05676	797.35218	807.78519	818.35760	829.07124
84	826.16107	837.28353	848.55905	859.98972	871.57764	883.32493	895.23376	907.30631
86	901.47191	913.96474	926.63438	939.48331	952.51403	965.72906	979.13098	992.72238
88	983.45356	997.47335	1011.69708	1026.12768	1040.76810	1055.62135	1070.69048	1085.97859
90	1072.69691	1088.41727	1104.37250	1120.56606	1137.00146	1153.68226	1170.61207	1187.79455
92	1169.84516	1187.45849	1205.34193	1223.49956	1241.93555	1260.65408	1279.65944	1298.95594
96	1390.71921	1412.78086	1435.19835	1457.97737	1481.12365	1504.64303	1528.54146	1552.82495
100	1652.45496	1680.01319	1708.03793	1736.53699	1765.51830	1794.98989	1824.95995	1855.43681
104	1962.61182	1996.95073	2031.89851	2067.46583	2103.66353	2140.50264	2177.99437	2216.15014
108	2330.14769	2372.83865	2416.32102	2460.60930	2505.71822	2551.66282	2598.45837	2646.12044
112	2765.67771	2818.64173	2872.63054	2927.66373	2983.76125	3040.94343	3099.23099	3158.64503
116	3281.78078	3347.36418	3414.26994	3482.52439	3552.15440	3623.18736	3695.65119	3769.57434
120	3893.36291	3974.42901	4057.19591	4141.69886	4227.97387	4316.05764	4405.98764	4497.80209
140	9129.55741	9358.31154	9592.81014	9833.19589	10079.61490	10332.21690	10591.15521	10856.58693
160	21364.65736	21991.67584	22637.06911	23301.36982	23985.12581	24688.90056	25413.27361	26158.84098

113

NUMBER OF QUARTRLY DEPOSITS	EFFECTIVE ANNUAL YIELD							
	19.30%	19.40%	19.50%	19.60%	19.70%	19.80%	19.90%	20.00%
1	1.04511	1.04532	1.04554	1.04576	1.04598	1.04620	1.04642	1.04664
2	2.13735	2.13803	2.13870	2.13938	2.14006	2.14073	2.14141	2.14208
3	3.27886	3.28026	3.28165	3.28304	3.28444	3.28583	3.28722	3.28861
4	4.47186	4.47426	4.47665	4.47904	4.48144	4.48383	4.48622	4.48861
5	5.71867	5.72237	5.72607	5.72977	5.73347	5.73717	5.74087	5.74457
6	7.02172	7.02706	7.03240	7.03774	7.04308	7.04842	7.05377	7.05911
7	8.38355	8.39088	8.39822	8.40556	8.41291	8.42025	8.42760	8.43495
8	9.80679	9.81652	9.82625	9.83598	9.84572	9.85546	9.86520	9.87495
9	11.29424	11.30677	11.31931	11.33185	11.34441	11.35696	11.36953	11.38210
10	12.84878	12.86457	12.88037	12.89618	12.91201	12.92784	12.94369	12.95954
11	14.47343	14.49297	14.51253	14.53210	14.55169	14.57129	14.59091	14.61055
12	16.17137	16.19518	16.21902	16.24288	16.26676	16.29066	16.31459	16.33855
13	17.94589	17.97454	18.00322	18.03194	18.06069	18.08947	18.11829	18.14713
14	19.80045	19.83455	19.86869	19.90288	19.93711	19.97138	20.00570	20.04006
15	21.73867	21.77886	21.81912	21.85943	21.89980	21.94023	21.98072	22.02127
16	23.76430	23.81130	23.85837	23.90552	23.95275	24.00004	24.04742	24.09487
17	25.88131	25.93586	25.99050	26.04524	26.10008	26.15501	26.21004	26.26517
18	28.09380	28.15671	28.21974	28.28289	28.34615	28.40954	28.47305	28.53668
19	30.40609	30.47822	30.55050	30.62292	30.69550	30.76823	30.84110	30.91413
20	32.82268	32.90495	32.98741	33.07005	33.15287	33.23588	33.31907	33.40245
21	35.34826	35.44167	35.53530	35.62916	35.72323	35.81754	35.91206	36.00682
22	37.98777	38.09337	38.19924	38.30537	38.41178	38.51846	38.62541	38.73263
23	40.74633	40.86525	40.98449	41.10406	41.22395	41.34417	41.46470	41.58557
24	43.62932	43.76277	43.89660	44.03082	44.16542	44.30041	44.43579	44.57155
25	46.64234	46.79161	46.94134	47.09151	47.24215	47.39324	47.54478	47.69679
26	49.79127	49.95774	50.12474	50.29227	50.46034	50.62895	50.79809	50.96777
27	53.08223	53.26737	53.45312	53.63950	53.82651	54.01414	54.20240	54.39130
28	56.52164	56.72700	56.93309	57.13991	57.34745	57.55572	57.76473	57.97448
29	60.11618	60.34344	60.57155	60.80050	61.03029	61.26093	61.49242	61.72476
30	63.87285	64.12380	64.37571	64.62860	64.88246	65.13730	65.39313	65.64994
31	67.79897	68.07549	68.35313	68.63189	68.91176	69.19277	69.47490	69.75817
32	71.90218	72.20630	72.51169	72.81837	73.12633	73.43559	73.74613	74.05798
33	76.19046	76.52433	76.85965	77.19644	77.53469	77.87442	78.21563	78.55832
34	80.67217	81.03807	81.40563	81.77485	82.14574	82.51832	82.89258	83.26854
35	85.35603	85.75639	86.15864	86.56278	86.96882	87.37676	87.78662	88.19841
36	90.25116	90.68658	91.12812	91.56981	92.01366	92.45966	92.90784	93.35819
37	95.36708	95.84430	96.32393	96.80598	97.29046	97.77738	98.26676	98.75860
38	100.71376	101.23371	101.75637	102.28176	102.80989	103.34078	103.87443	104.41086
39	106.30161	106.86739	107.43623	108.00813	108.58311	109.16119	109.74238	110.32671
40	112.14149	112.75642	113.37476	113.99654	114.62178	115.25050	115.88272	116.51844
41	118.24479	118.91235	119.58375	120.25900	120.93812	121.62113	122.30806	122.99893
42	124.62338	125.34731	126.07552	126.80803	127.54488	128.28608	129.03166	129.78164
43	131.28968	132.07392	132.86294	133.65676	134.45542	135.25893	136.06734	136.88066
44	138.25667	139.10542	139.95949	140.81891	141.68371	142.55393	143.42960	144.31074
45	145.53790	146.45561	147.37923	148.30880	149.24436	150.18594	151.13359	152.08733
46	153.14756	154.13894	155.13689	156.14145	157.15265	158.17055	159.19518	160.22658
47	161.10045	162.17052	163.24787	164.33253	165.42457	166.52403	167.63096	168.74540
48	169.41206	170.56612	171.72824	172.89846	174.07684	175.26344	176.45831	177.66150
50	187.17690	188.51615	189.86524	191.22422	192.59316	193.97215	195.36124	196.76050
52	206.58046	208.13021	209.69189	211.26560	212.85141	214.44943	216.05973	217.68241
54	227.77390	229.56255	231.36561	233.18321	235.01545	236.86246	238.72434	240.60122
56	250.92235	252.98173	255.05846	257.15270	259.26458	261.39424	263.54184	265.70751
58	276.20613	278.57194	280.95855	283.36616	285.79493	288.24506	290.71671	293.21007
60	303.82222	306.53444	309.27151	312.03367	314.82113	317.63413	320.47288	323.33762
62	333.98577	337.08915	340.22212	343.38497	346.57797	349.80140	353.05555	356.34070
64	366.93177	370.47637	374.05611	377.67131	381.32233	385.00951	388.73320	392.49376
66	402.91689	406.95870	411.04209	415.16747	419.33527	423.54591	427.79983	432.09745
68	442.22147	446.82305	451.47370	456.17394	460.92427	465.72523	470.57733	475.48112
70	485.15171	490.38294	495.67194	501.01934	506.42575	511.89183	517.41821	523.00555
72	532.04207	537.98098	543.98772	550.06307	556.20779	562.42265	568.70844	575.06596
74	583.25785	589.99149	596.80462	603.69817	610.67306	617.73024	624.87066	632.09527
76	639.19806	646.82354	654.54198	662.35448	670.26216	678.26616	686.36764	694.56776
78	700.29848	708.92410	717.65818	726.50206	735.45709	744.52466	753.70614	763.00294
80	767.03514	776.78157	786.65431	796.65500	806.78524	817.04669	827.44102	837.96992
82	839.92795	850.92963	862.07817	873.37550	884.82358	896.42437	908.17988	920.09214
84	919.54479	931.95145	944.52856	957.27842	970.20337	983.30577	996.58801	1010.05252
86	1006.50591	1020.48423	1034.66006	1049.03614	1063.61526	1078.40022	1093.39390	1108.59918
88	1101.48879	1117.22428	1133.18827	1149.38403	1165.81487	1182.48414	1199.39524	1216.55163
90	1205.23341	1222.93243	1240.89543	1259.12627	1277.62890	1296.40729	1315.46550	1334.80762
92	1318.54799	1338.44005	1358.63664	1379.14235	1399.96183	1421.09982	1442.56111	1464.35057
96	1577.45992	1602.57168	1628.04743	1653.93329	1680.23575	1706.96142	1734.11700	1761.70930
100	1886.42891	1917.94484	1949.99333	1982.58326	2015.72363	2049.42361	2083.69250	2118.53977
104	2254.98155	2294.50039	2334.71868	2375.64962	2417.30262	2459.69331	2502.83353	2546.73653
108	2694.66485	2744.10773	2794.46548	2845.75479	2897.99267	2951.19641	3005.38362	3060.57221
112	3219.20703	3280.93888	3343.86289	3408.00177	3473.37866	3540.01713	3607.94118	3677.17526
116	3844.98585	3921.91528	4000.39281	4080.44917	4162.11570	4245.42435	4330.40769	4417.09893
120	4591.53998	4687.24111	4784.94606	4884.69625	4986.53330	5090.50220	5196.64504	5305.00733
140	11128.67297	11407.57814	11693.47128	11986.52531	12286.91739	12594.82893	12910.44578	13233.95828
160	26926.21569	27716.02820	28528.92688	29365.57855	30226.66895	31112.90333	32025.00692	32963.72553

TABLE 4. ANNUAL DEPOSITS

ANNUAL DEPOSITS

NUMBER OF ANNUAL DEPOSITS	EFFECTIVE ANNUAL YIELD							
	5.00%	5.05%	5.10%	5.15%	5.20%	5.25%	5.30%	5.35%
1	1.05000	1.05050	1.05100	1.05150	1.05200	1.05250	1.05300	1.05350
2	2.15250	2.15405	2.15560	2.15715	2.15870	2.16026	2.16181	2.16336
3	3.31013	3.31333	3.31654	3.31975	3.32296	3.32617	3.32938	3.33260
4	4.52563	4.53115	4.53668	4.54221	4.54775	4.55329	4.55884	4.56440
5	5.80191	5.81048	5.81905	5.82764	5.83623	5.84484	5.85346	5.86209
6	7.14201	7.15441	7.16682	7.17926	7.19172	7.20420	7.21669	7.22921
7	8.54911	8.56620	8.58333	8.60049	8.61769	8.63492	8.65218	8.66948
8	10.02656	10.04930	10.07208	10.09492	10.11781	10.14075	10.16374	10.18679
9	11.57789	11.60729	11.63676	11.66631	11.69593	11.72564	11.75542	11.78529
10	13.20679	13.24395	13.28123	13.31862	13.35612	13.39373	13.43146	13.46930
11	14.91713	14.96327	15.00957	15.05603	15.10264	15.14941	15.19633	15.24341
12	16.71298	16.76942	16.82606	16.88291	16.93998	16.99725	17.05473	17.11243
13	18.59863	18.66677	18.73519	18.80388	18.87286	18.94210	19.01163	19.08144
14	20.57856	20.65995	20.74169	20.82378	20.90624	20.98907	21.07225	21.15580
15	22.65749	22.75377	22.85051	22.94771	23.04537	23.14349	23.24208	23.34114
16	24.84037	24.95334	25.06689	25.18102	25.29573	25.41102	25.52691	25.64339
17	27.13238	27.26398	27.39630	27.52934	27.66311	27.79760	27.93284	28.06881
18	29.53900	29.69131	29.84451	29.99860	30.15359	30.30948	30.46628	30.62399
19	32.06595	32.24122	32.41758	32.59503	32.77357	32.95323	33.13399	33.31587
20	34.71925	34.91991	35.12188	35.32517	35.52980	35.73577	35.94309	36.15177
21	37.50521	37.73386	37.96409	38.19592	38.42935	38.66440	38.90107	39.13939
22	40.43048	40.68992	40.95126	41.21451	41.47967	41.74678	42.01583	42.28685
23	43.50200	43.79526	44.09078	44.38855	44.68862	44.99098	45.29567	45.60270
24	46.72710	47.05742	47.39041	47.72607	48.06443	48.40551	48.74934	49.09594
25	50.11345	50.48432	50.85832	51.23546	51.61578	51.99930	52.38606	52.77607
26	53.66913	54.08428	54.50309	54.92558	55.35180	55.78176	56.21552	56.65309
27	57.40258	57.86604	58.33375	58.80575	59.28209	59.76281	60.24794	60.73753
28	61.32271	61.83877	62.35977	62.88575	63.41676	63.95285	64.49408	65.04049
29	65.43885	66.01213	66.59112	67.17586	67.76643	68.36288	68.96527	69.57366
30	69.76079	70.39624	71.03826	71.68692	72.34228	73.00443	73.67343	74.34935
31	74.29883	75.00175	75.71222	76.43030	77.15608	77.88966	78.63112	79.38054
32	79.06377	79.83984	80.62454	81.41796	82.22020	83.03137	83.85157	84.68090
33	84.06696	84.92225	85.78739	86.66248	87.54765	88.44302	89.34870	90.26483
34	89.32031	90.26133	91.21355	92.17710	93.15213	94.13877	95.13718	96.14750
35	94.83632	95.87003	96.91644	97.97572	99.04804	100.13356	101.23245	102.34489
36	100.62814	101.76196	102.91018	104.07297	105.25054	106.44307	107.65077	108.87384
37	106.70955	107.95144	109.20959	110.48423	111.77556	113.08383	114.40926	115.75209
38	113.09502	114.45349	115.83028	117.22567	118.63989	120.07323	121.52595	122.99833
39	119.79977	121.28389	122.78863	124.31429	125.86117	127.42958	129.01983	130.63224
40	126.83976	128.45923	130.10185	131.76797	133.45795	135.17213	136.91088	138.67456
41	134.23175	135.99692	137.78804	139.60552	141.44976	143.32117	145.22016	147.14715
42	141.99334	143.91526	145.86623	147.84671	149.85715	151.89803	153.96983	156.07302
43	150.14301	152.23348	154.35641	156.51231	158.70172	160.92518	163.18323	165.47643
44	158.70016	160.97177	163.27959	165.62420	168.00621	170.42625	172.88494	175.38292
45	167.68516	170.15135	172.65785	175.20534	177.79453	180.42613	183.10084	185.81940
46	177.11942	179.79449	182.51440	185.27992	188.09185	190.95100	193.85818	196.81424
47	187.02539	189.92461	192.87363	195.87333	198.92463	202.02843	205.18567	208.39730
48	197.42666	200.56631	203.76119	207.01231	210.32071	213.68742	217.11351	220.60006
49	208.34800	211.74540	215.20401	218.72495	222.30938	225.95851	229.67352	233.45566
50	219.81540	223.48905	227.23041	231.04078	234.92147	238.87383	242.89922	246.99904

ANNUAL DEPOSITS

NUMBER OF ANNUAL DEPOSITS	EFFECTIVE ANNUAL YIELD							
	5.40%	5.45%	5.50%	5.55%	5.60%	5.65%	5.70%	5.75%
1	1.05400	1.05450	1.05500	1.05550	1.05600	1.05650	1.05700	1.05750
2	2.16492	2.16647	2.16802	2.16958	2.17114	2.17269	2.17425	2.17581
3	3.33582	3.33904	3.34227	3.34549	3.34872	3.35195	3.35518	3.35842
4	4.56996	4.57552	4.58109	4.58667	4.59225	4.59783	4.60343	4.60902
5	5.87073	5.87939	5.88805	5.89673	5.90541	5.91411	5.92282	5.93154
6	7.24175	7.25431	7.26689	7.27950	7.29212	7.30476	7.31742	7.33011
7	8.68681	8.70417	8.72157	8.73901	8.75648	8.77398	8.79152	8.80909
8	10.20990	10.23305	10.25626	10.27952	10.30284	10.32621	10.34963	10.37311
9	11.81523	11.84525	11.87535	11.90554	11.93580	11.96614	11.99656	12.02706
10	13.50725	13.54532	13.58350	13.62179	13.66020	13.69873	13.73737	13.77612
11	15.29064	15.33804	15.38559	15.43330	15.48117	15.52920	15.57740	15.62575
12	17.17034	17.22846	17.28680	17.34535	17.40412	17.46310	17.52231	17.58173
13	19.15154	19.22191	19.29257	19.36352	19.43475	19.50627	19.57808	19.65018
14	21.23972	21.32401	21.40866	21.49369	21.57910	21.66487	21.75103	21.83756
15	23.44066	23.54066	23.64114	23.74209	23.84352	23.94544	24.04784	24.15072
16	25.76046	25.87813	25.99640	26.11528	26.23476	26.35486	26.47556	26.59689
17	28.20553	28.34299	28.48120	28.62018	28.75991	28.90041	29.04167	29.18371
18	30.78262	30.94218	31.10267	31.26410	31.42646	31.58978	31.75405	31.91927
19	33.49889	33.68303	33.86832	34.05475	34.24235	34.43110	34.62103	34.81213
20	36.36183	36.57326	36.78608	37.00029	37.21592	37.43296	37.65143	37.87133
21	39.37936	39.62100	39.86431	40.10931	40.35601	40.60442	40.85456	41.10643
22	42.55985	42.83484	43.11185	43.39088	43.67194	43.95507	44.24027	44.52755
23	45.91208	46.22384	46.53800	46.85457	47.17357	47.49503	47.81896	48.14538
24	49.44533	49.79754	50.15259	50.51050	50.87129	51.23500	51.60164	51.97124
25	53.16938	53.56601	53.96598	54.36933	54.77609	55.18628	55.59994	56.01709
26	57.09453	57.53985	57.98911	58.44233	58.89955	59.36080	59.82613	60.29557
27	61.23163	61.73028	62.23351	62.74138	63.25392	63.77119	64.29322	64.82007
28	65.59214	66.14908	66.71135	67.27902	67.85214	68.43076	69.01494	69.60472
29	70.18812	70.80870	71.43548	72.06851	72.70786	73.35360	74.00579	74.66449
30	75.03227	75.72228	76.41943	77.12381	77.83550	78.55458	79.28112	80.01520
31	80.13802	80.90364	81.67750	82.45968	83.25029	84.04941	84.85714	85.67358
32	85.51947	86.36739	87.22476	88.09170	88.96831	89.85470	90.75100	91.65731
33	91.19152	92.12891	93.07712	94.03628	95.00653	95.98799	96.98080	97.98510
34	97.16986	98.20444	99.25136	100.31080	101.38290	102.46781	103.56511	104.67674
35	103.47104	104.61108	105.76519	106.93355	108.11634	109.31375	110.52596	111.75316
36	110.11247	111.36688	112.63727	113.92386	115.22685	116.54647	117.88293	119.23646
37	117.11255	118.49088	119.88732	121.30213	122.73556	124.18785	125.65926	127.15006
38	124.49062	126.00313	127.53613	129.08990	130.66475	132.26096	133.87884	135.51869
39	132.26712	133.92480	135.60561	137.30989	139.03797	140.79021	142.56693	144.36851
40	140.46354	142.27820	144.11892	145.98609	147.88010	149.80135	151.75025	153.72720
41	149.10257	151.08686	153.10046	155.14382	157.21739	159.32163	161.45701	163.62402
42	158.20811	160.37560	162.57599	164.80980	167.07756	169.37980	171.71706	174.08990
43	167.80535	170.17057	172.57267	175.01225	177.48990	180.00626	182.56194	185.15757
44	177.92084	180.49936	183.11917	185.78092	188.48534	191.23311	194.02497	196.86163
45	188.58256	191.39108	194.24572	197.14727	200.09652	203.09428	206.14139	209.23867
46	199.82002	202.87639	205.98423	209.14444	212.35792	215.62561	218.94845	222.32740
47	211.66430	214.98766	218.36837	221.80746	225.30597	228.86496	232.48551	236.16872
48	224.14818	227.75898	231.43363	235.17327	238.97910	242.85233	246.79418	250.80592
49	237.30618	241.22635	245.21748	249.28089	253.41793	257.62998	261.91845	266.28476
50	251.17471	255.42769	259.75944	264.17148	268.66533	273.24258	277.90480	282.65364

ANNUAL DEPOSITS

EFFECTIVE ANNUAL YIELD

NUMBER OF ANNUAL DEPOSITS	5.80%	5.85%	5.90%	5.95%	6.00%	6.05%	6.10%	6.15%
1	1.05800	1.05850	1.05900	1.05950	1.06000	1.06050	1.06100	1.06150
2	2.17736	2.17892	2.18048	2.18204	2.18360	2.18516	2.18672	2.18828
3	3.36165	3.36489	3.36813	3.37137	3.37462	3.37786	3.38111	3.38436
4	4.61463	4.62024	4.62585	4.63147	4.63709	4.64272	4.64836	4.65400
5	5.94028	5.94902	5.95777	5.96654	5.97532	5.98411	5.99291	6.00172
6	7.34281	7.35554	7.36828	7.38105	7.39384	7.40665	7.41948	7.43233
7	8.82669	8.84434	8.86201	8.87972	8.89747	8.91525	8.93306	8.95091
8	10.39664	10.42023	10.44387	10.46757	10.49132	10.51512	10.53898	10.56290
9	12.05765	12.08831	12.11906	12.14989	12.18079	12.21179	12.24286	12.27401
10	13.81499	13.85398	13.89308	13.93230	13.97164	14.01110	14.05067	14.09037
11	15.67426	15.72294	15.77177	15.82078	15.86994	15.91927	15.96876	16.01842
12	17.64137	17.70123	17.76131	17.82161	17.88214	17.94289	18.00386	18.06506
13	19.72257	19.79525	19.86823	19.94150	20.01507	20.08893	20.16309	20.23756
14	21.92448	22.01177	22.09945	22.18752	22.27597	22.36481	22.45404	22.54367
15	24.25410	24.35796	24.46232	24.56717	24.67253	24.77838	24.88474	24.99160
16	26.71883	26.84140	26.96460	27.08842	27.21288	27.33797	27.46371	27.59009
17	29.32653	29.47012	29.61451	29.75968	29.90565	30.05242	30.20000	30.34838
18	32.08546	32.25263	32.42076	32.58988	32.75999	32.93109	33.10319	33.27630
19	35.00442	35.19790	35.39259	35.58848	35.78559	35.98392	36.18349	36.38429
20	38.09268	38.31548	38.53975	38.76550	38.99273	39.22145	39.45168	39.68343
21	41.36005	41.61544	41.87260	42.13154	42.39229	42.65485	42.91924	43.18546
22	44.81694	45.10844	45.40208	45.69787	45.99583	46.29597	46.59831	46.90287
23	48.47432	48.80578	49.13980	49.47639	49.81558	50.15737	50.50181	50.84889
24	52.34383	52.71942	53.09805	53.47974	53.86451	54.25240	54.64342	55.03760
25	56.43777	56.86201	57.28984	57.72128	58.15638	58.59517	59.03766	59.48391
26	60.76916	61.24694	61.72894	62.21520	62.70577	63.20067	63.69996	64.20367
27	65.35177	65.88838	66.42994	66.97650	67.52811	68.08481	68.64666	69.21370
28	70.20018	70.80135	71.40831	72.02111	72.63980	73.26444	73.89511	74.53184
29	75.32979	76.00173	76.68040	77.36586	78.05819	78.75744	79.46371	80.17705
30	80.75691	81.50633	82.26354	83.02863	83.80168	84.58277	85.37199	86.16944
31	86.49881	87.33295	88.17609	89.02833	89.88978	90.76053	91.64068	92.53036
32	92.57375	93.50043	94.43748	95.38502	96.34316	97.31204	98.29177	99.28247
33	99.00102	100.02871	101.06829	102.11993	103.18375	104.25992	105.34856	106.44984
34	105.80108	106.93889	108.09032	109.25557	110.43478	111.62814	112.83583	114.05801
35	112.99554	114.25331	115.52665	116.81577	118.12087	119.44214	120.77981	122.13408
36	120.60729	121.99563	123.40173	124.82581	126.26812	127.72889	129.20838	130.70682
37	128.66051	130.19087	131.74143	133.31245	134.90421	136.51699	138.15109	139.80679
38	137.18082	138.86554	140.57317	142.30404	144.05846	145.83677	147.63931	149.46641
39	146.19531	148.04767	149.92599	151.83063	153.76197	155.72039	157.70631	159.72010
40	155.73263	157.76696	159.83062	161.92405	164.04768	166.20198	168.38739	170.60438
41	165.82313	168.05483	170.31963	172.61803	174.95054	177.31770	179.72002	182.15805
42	176.49887	178.94454	181.42749	183.94830	186.50758	189.10592	191.74394	194.42227
43	187.79380	190.47129	193.19071	195.95273	198.75803	201.60733	204.50132	207.44074
44	199.74384	202.67236	205.64796	208.67141	211.74351	214.86507	218.03690	221.25985
45	212.38699	215.58720	218.84019	222.14686	225.50812	228.92491	232.39815	235.92883
46	225.76343	229.25755	232.81076	236.42410	240.09861	243.83536	247.63544	251.49995
47	239.91571	243.72762	247.60560	251.55083	255.56453	259.64790	263.80220	268.02870
48	254.88882	259.04418	263.27333	267.57761	271.95840	276.41710	280.95514	285.57396
49	270.73037	275.25677	279.86545	284.55798	289.33590	294.20084	299.15440	304.19826
50	287.49073	292.41779	297.43652	302.54868	307.75606	313.06049	318.46382	323.96795

ANNUAL DEPOSITS

EFFECTIVE ANNUAL YIELD

NUMBER OF ANNUAL DEPOSITS	6.20%	6.25%	6.30%	6.35%	6.40%	6.45%	6.50%	6.55%
1	1.06200	1.06250	1.06300	1.06350	1.06400	1.06450	1.06500	1.06550
2	2.18984	2.19141	2.19297	2.19453	2.19610	2.19766	2.19922	2.20079
3	3.38761	3.39087	3.39413	3.39739	3.40065	3.40391	3.40717	3.41044
4	4.65965	4.66530	4.67096	4.67662	4.68229	4.68796	4.69364	4.69933
5	6.01054	6.01938	6.02823	6.03708	6.04595	6.05484	6.06373	6.07263
6	7.44520	7.45809	7.47100	7.48394	7.49689	7.50987	7.52287	7.53589
7	8.96980	8.98672	9.00468	9.02267	9.04070	9.05876	9.07686	9.09499
8	10.58687	10.61089	10.63497	10.65911	10.68330	10.70755	10.73185	10.75621
9	12.30525	12.33657	12.36798	12.39946	12.43103	12.46269	12.49442	12.52624
10	14.13018	14.17011	14.21016	14.25033	14.29062	14.33103	14.37156	14.41221
11	16.06825	16.11824	16.16840	16.21872	16.26922	16.31988	16.37071	16.42171
12	18.12648	18.18813	18.25001	18.31211	18.37445	18.43701	18.49981	18.56283
13	20.31232	20.38739	20.46276	20.53843	20.61441	20.69070	20.76730	20.84420
14	22.63369	22.72410	22.81491	22.90612	22.99773	23.08975	23.18217	23.27500
15	25.09897	25.20686	25.31525	25.42416	25.53359	25.64354	25.75401	25.86501
16	27.71711	27.84478	27.97311	28.10210	28.23174	28.36205	28.49302	28.62467
17	30.49757	30.64758	30.79842	30.95008	31.10257	31.25590	31.41007	31.56508
18	33.45042	33.62556	33.80172	33.97891	34.15714	34.33640	34.51672	34.69809
19	36.58635	36.78965	36.99423	37.20007	37.40719	37.61560	37.82531	38.03632
20	39.91670	40.15151	40.38786	40.62577	40.86525	41.10631	41.34895	41.59320
21	43.45354	43.72348	43.99530	44.26901	44.54463	44.82217	45.10164	45.38305
22	47.20966	47.51869	47.83000	48.14359	48.45948	48.77770	49.09824	49.42114
23	51.19865	51.55111	51.90629	52.26421	52.62489	52.98836	53.35463	53.72373
24	55.43497	55.83556	56.23939	56.64649	57.05688	57.47061	57.88768	58.30813
25	59.93394	60.38778	60.84547	61.30704	61.77253	62.24196	62.71538	63.19281
26	64.71184	65.22452	65.74173	66.26354	66.78997	67.32107	67.85688	68.39744
27	69.78598	70.36355	70.94646	71.53477	72.12852	72.72777	73.33257	73.94298
28	75.17471	75.82377	76.47909	77.14073	77.80875	78.48322	79.16419	79.85174
29	80.89754	81.62526	82.36027	83.10267	83.85251	84.60988	85.37486	86.14753
30	86.97519	87.78933	88.61197	89.44319	90.28307	91.13172	91.98923	92.85569
31	93.42965	94.33867	95.25752	96.18633	97.12519	98.07422	99.03353	100.00324
32	100.28429	101.29733	102.32175	103.35766	104.40520	105.46450	106.53571	107.61895
33	107.56391	108.69092	109.83102	110.98437	112.15113	113.33146	114.52553	115.73350
34	115.29487	116.54660	117.81337	119.09538	120.39280	121.70584	123.03469	124.37954
35	123.50516	124.89326	126.29862	127.72143	129.16194	130.62037	132.09695	133.59190
36	132.22448	133.76159	135.31843	136.89525	138.49231	140.10989	141.74825	143.40767
37	141.48439	143.18419	144.90649	146.65159	148.41982	150.21147	152.02688	153.86637
38	151.31843	153.19570	155.09860	157.02747	158.98268	160.96461	162.97363	165.01012
39	161.76217	163.83294	165.93281	168.06221	170.22158	172.41133	174.63192	176.88378
40	172.85342	175.13499	177.44958	179.79766	182.17976	184.59636	187.04799	189.53517
41	184.63234	187.14343	189.69190	192.27832	194.90326	197.56733	200.27111	203.01522
42	197.14154	199.90240	202.70549	205.55149	208.44107	211.37492	214.35373	217.37822
43	210.42632	213.45879	216.53894	219.66751	222.84530	226.07310	229.35172	232.68199
44	224.53475	227.86247	231.24089	234.67990	238.17140	241.71932	245.32459	248.98816
45	239.51790	243.16637	246.87525	250.64557	254.47837	258.37471	262.33568	266.36239
46	255.43001	259.42677	263.49139	267.62506	271.82898	276.10438	280.45250	284.87462
47	272.32867	276.70345	281.15435	285.68275	290.29004	294.97761	299.74692	304.59941
48	290.27505	295.05991	299.93008	304.88711	309.93260	315.06817	320.29547	325.61617
49	309.33410	314.56366	319.88867	325.31094	330.83229	336.45457	342.17967	348.00953
50	329.57482	335.28638	341.10466	347.03169	353.06955	359.22039	365.48635	371.86966

NUMBER OF ANNUAL DEPOSITS	EFFECTIVE ANNUAL YIELD							
	6.60%	6.65%	6.70%	6.75%	6.80%	6.85%	6.90%	6.95%
1	1.06600	1.06650	1.06700	1.06750	1.06800	1.06850	1.06900	1.06950
2	2.20236	2.20392	2.20549	2.20706	2.20862	2.21019	2.21176	2.21333
3	3.41371	3.41698	3.42026	3.42353	3.42681	3.43009	3.43337	3.43666
4	4.70502	4.71071	4.71641	4.72212	4.72783	4.73355	4.73928	4.74500
5	6.08155	6.09047	6.09941	6.10836	6.11733	6.12630	6.13529	6.14428
6	7.54893	7.56199	7.57507	7.58818	7.60130	7.61445	7.62762	7.64081
7	9.11316	9.13136	9.14960	9.16788	9.18619	9.20454	9.22293	9.24135
8	10.78063	10.80510	10.82963	10.85421	10.87885	10.90355	10.92831	10.95312
9	12.55815	12.59014	12.62221	12.65437	12.68662	12.71895	12.75136	12.78386
10	14.45299	14.49388	14.53490	14.57604	14.61731	14.65869	14.70020	14.74184
11	16.47288	16.52423	16.57574	16.62743	16.67928	16.73131	16.78352	16.83590
12	18.62609	18.68959	18.75331	18.81728	18.88147	18.94591	19.01058	19.07549
13	20.92142	20.99894	21.07679	21.15494	21.23341	21.31220	21.39131	21.47074
14	23.36823	23.46187	23.55593	23.65040	23.74529	23.84059	23.93631	24.03246
15	25.97653	26.08859	26.20118	26.31430	26.42797	26.54217	26.65692	26.77221
16	28.75698	28.88998	29.02366	29.15802	29.29307	29.42881	29.56525	29.70238
17	31.72095	31.87766	32.03524	32.19368	32.35300	32.51318	32.67425	32.83620
18	34.88053	35.06403	35.24860	35.43426	35.62100	35.80884	35.99777	36.18781
19	38.24864	38.46229	38.67726	38.89357	39.11123	39.33024	39.55062	39.77236
20	41.83905	42.08653	42.33564	42.58639	42.83879	43.09286	43.34861	43.60604
21	45.66643	45.95178	46.23912	46.52847	46.81983	47.11322	47.40866	47.70616
22	49.74641	50.07408	50.40415	50.73664	51.07158	51.40898	51.74886	52.09124
23	54.09568	54.47050	54.84822	55.22886	55.61245	55.99899	56.38853	56.78108
24	58.73199	59.15929	59.59005	60.02431	60.46209	60.90342	61.34834	61.79687
25	63.67430	64.15988	64.64959	65.14345	65.64151	66.14381	66.65038	67.16125
26	68.94281	69.49302	70.04811	70.60814	71.17314	71.74316	72.31825	72.89846
27	74.55903	75.18080	75.80833	76.44168	77.08091	77.72607	78.37721	79.03440
28	80.54593	81.24682	81.95449	82.66900	83.39041	84.11880	84.85424	85.59679
29	86.92796	87.71624	88.51244	89.31666	90.12896	90.94944	91.77818	92.61527
30	93.73121	94.61587	95.50978	96.41303	97.32573	98.24798	99.17988	100.12153
31	100.98347	101.97432	102.97593	103.98841	105.01188	106.04646	107.09229	108.14948
32	108.71438	109.82212	110.94232	112.07513	113.22069	114.37915	115.55065	116.73536
33	116.95552	118.19179	119.44245	120.70770	121.98769	123.28262	124.59265	125.91797
34	125.74059	127.11804	128.51210	129.92297	131.35086	132.79598	134.25854	135.73877
35	135.10547	136.63789	138.18941	139.76027	141.35072	142.96100	144.59138	146.24211
36	145.08843	146.79081	148.51510	150.26159	152.03056	153.82233	155.63719	157.47544
37	155.73026	157.61890	159.53261	161.47174	163.43664	165.42766	167.44515	169.48949
38	167.07446	169.16706	171.28830	173.43859	175.61833	177.82795	180.06787	182.33850
39	179.16738	181.48317	183.83161	186.21319	188.62838	191.07767	193.56155	196.08053
40	192.05842	194.61830	197.21533	199.85008	202.52311	205.23499	207.98630	210.77763
41	205.80028	208.62691	211.49576	214.40746	217.36268	220.36209	223.40635	226.49617
42	220.44910	223.56710	226.73297	229.94746	233.21134	236.52539	239.89039	243.30716
43	236.06474	239.50081	242.99108	246.53642	250.13772	253.79588	257.51183	261.28650
44	252.71101	256.49412	260.33848	264.24513	268.21508	272.24940	276.34915	280.51542
45	270.45594	274.61748	278.84816	283.14917	287.52171	291.96698	296.48624	301.08074
46	289.37203	293.94604	298.59799	303.32924	308.14118	313.03522	318.01279	323.07535
47	309.53658	314.55995	319.67105	324.87147	330.16278	335.54663	341.02467	346.59858
48	331.03200	336.54469	342.15602	347.86779	353.68185	359.60008	365.62437	371.75669
49	353.94611	359.99141	366.14747	372.41637	378.80022	385.30118	391.92145	398.66328
50	378.37255	384.99734	391.74635	398.62197	405.62663	412.76281	420.03303	427.43987

ANNUAL DEPOSITS

NUMBER OF ANNUAL DEPOSITS	EFFECTIVE ANNUAL YIELD							
	7.00%	7.05%	7.10%	7.15%	7.20%	7.25%	7.30%	7.35%
1	1.07000	1.07050	1.07100	1.07150	1.07200	1.07250	1.07300	1.07350
2	2.21490	2.21647	2.21804	2.21961	2.22118	2.22276	2.22433	2.22590
3	3.43994	3.44323	3.44652	3.44981	3.45311	3.45641	3.45971	3.46301
4	4.75074	4.75648	4.76222	4.76798	4.77373	4.77950	4.78526	4.79104
5	6.15329	6.16231	6.17134	6.18039	6.18944	6.19851	6.20759	6.21668
6	7.65402	7.66725	7.68051	7.69378	7.70708	7.72040	7.73374	7.74710
7	9.25980	9.27830	9.29682	9.31539	9.33399	9.35263	9.37130	9.39002
8	10.97799	11.00292	11.02790	11.05294	11.07804	11.10320	11.12841	11.15368
9	12.81645	12.84912	12.88188	12.91473	12.94766	12.98068	13.01378	13.04698
10	14.78360	14.82548	14.86749	14.90963	14.95189	14.99428	15.03679	15.07943
11	16.88845	16.94118	16.99409	17.04717	17.10043	17.15386	17.20748	17.26127
12	19.14064	19.20603	19.27167	19.33754	19.40366	19.47002	19.53662	19.60347
13	21.55049	21.63056	21.71095	21.79167	21.87272	21.95409	22.03579	22.11783
14	24.12902	24.22601	24.32343	24.42128	24.51955	24.61826	24.71741	24.81699
15	26.88805	27.00445	27.12139	27.23890	27.35696	27.47559	27.59478	27.71454
16	29.84022	29.97876	30.11801	30.25798	30.39866	30.54007	30.68220	30.82506
17	32.99903	33.16276	33.32739	33.49293	33.65937	33.82672	33.99500	34.16420
18	36.37896	36.57124	36.76464	36.95917	37.15484	37.35166	37.54963	37.74877
19	39.99549	40.22001	40.44593	40.67325	40.90199	41.13216	41.36376	41.59680
20	43.86518	44.12602	44.38859	44.65289	44.91893	45.18674	45.45631	45.72766
21	48.00574	48.30741	48.61118	48.91707	49.22510	49.53528	49.84762	50.16215
22	52.43614	52.78358	53.13357	53.48614	53.84130	54.19908	54.55950	54.92257
23	57.17667	57.57532	57.97705	58.38190	58.78988	59.20102	59.61534	60.03287
24	62.24904	62.70488	63.16443	63.62771	64.09475	64.56559	65.04026	65.51879
25	67.67647	68.19607	68.72010	69.24859	69.78157	70.31910	70.86120	71.40792
26	73.48382	74.07440	74.67023	75.27136	75.87784	76.48973	77.10707	77.72990
27	79.69769	80.36714	81.04281	81.72476	82.41305	83.10774	83.80888	84.51655
28	86.34653	87.10353	87.86785	88.63958	89.41879	90.20555	90.99993	91.80202
29	93.46079	94.31482	95.17747	96.04881	96.92894	97.81795	98.71593	99.62297
30	101.07304	102.03452	103.00607	103.98780	104.97983	105.98225	106.99519	108.01875
31	109.21815	110.29845	111.39050	112.49443	113.61037	114.73846	115.87884	117.03163
32	117.93343	119.14499	120.37023	121.60928	122.86232	124.12950	125.41099	126.70696
33	127.25876	128.61522	129.98751	131.37585	132.78041	134.20139	135.63900	137.09342
34	137.23688	138.75309	140.28763	141.84072	143.41260	145.00349	146.61364	148.24328
35	147.91346	149.60568	151.31905	153.05383	154.81030	156.58875	158.38944	160.21267
36	159.33740	161.22338	163.13370	165.06868	167.02865	169.01393	171.02487	173.06180
37	171.56102	173.66013	175.78719	177.94259	180.12671	182.33994	184.58268	186.85534
38	184.64029	186.97367	189.33908	191.73699	194.16783	196.63209	199.13022	201.66271
39	198.63511	201.22581	203.85316	206.51768	209.21992	211.96041	214.73972	217.55842
40	213.60957	216.48273	219.39773	222.35519	225.35575	228.40004	231.48872	234.62246
41	229.63224	232.81527	236.04597	239.32509	242.65336	246.03154	249.46040	252.94071
42	246.77650	250.29924	253.87624	257.50833	261.19641	264.94133	268.74401	272.60535
43	265.12085	269.01584	272.97245	276.99168	281.07455	285.22208	289.43532	293.71535
44	284.74931	289.05196	293.42449	297.86809	302.38391	306.97318	311.63710	316.37692
45	305.75176	310.50062	315.32863	320.23715	325.22756	330.30123	335.45961	340.70413
46	328.22439	333.46141	338.78797	344.20561	349.71594	355.32057	361.02116	366.81938
47	352.27009	358.04094	363.91291	369.88781	375.96749	382.15381	388.44871	394.85411
48	377.99900	384.35333	390.82173	397.40629	404.10915	410.93247	417.87846	424.94938
49	405.52893	412.52074	419.64107	426.89234	434.27700	441.79757	449.45659	457.25666
50	434.98595	442.67395	450.50659	458.48664	466.61695	474.90039	483.33992	491.93853

121

EFFECTIVE ANNUAL YIELD

NUMBER OF ANNUAL DEPOSITS	7.40%	7.45%	7.50%	7.55%	7.60%	7.65%	7.70%	7.75%
1	1.07400	1.07450	1.07500	1.07550	1.07600	1.07650	1.07700	1.07750
2	2.22748	2.22905	2.23062	2.23220	2.23378	2.23535	2.23693	2.23851
3	3.46631	3.46961	3.47292	3.47623	3.47954	3.48286	3.48617	3.48949
4	4.79682	4.80260	4.80839	4.81419	4.81999	4.82580	4.83161	4.83743
5	6.22578	6.23489	6.24402	6.25316	6.26231	6.27147	6.28064	6.28983
6	7.76049	7.77389	7.78732	7.80077	7.81424	7.82774	7.84125	7.85479
7	9.40876	9.42755	9.44637	9.46523	9.48413	9.50306	9.52203	9.54103
8	11.17901	11.20440	11.22985	11.25535	11.28092	11.30654	11.33222	11.35796
9	13.08026	13.11363	13.14709	13.18063	13.21427	13.24799	13.28180	13.31571
10	15.12220	15.16510	15.20812	15.25127	15.29455	15.33796	15.38150	15.42517
11	17.31524	17.36939	17.42373	17.47824	17.53294	17.58782	17.64288	17.69812
12	19.67057	19.73791	19.80551	19.87335	19.94144	20.00979	20.07838	20.14723
13	22.20019	22.28289	22.36592	22.44929	22.53299	22.61703	22.70142	22.78614
14	24.91701	25.01746	25.11836	25.21971	25.32150	25.42374	25.52643	25.62957
15	27.83486	27.95577	28.07724	28.19930	28.32193	28.44515	28.56896	28.69336
16	30.96864	31.11297	31.25804	31.40384	31.55040	31.69771	31.84577	31.99459
17	34.33432	34.50539	34.67739	34.85033	35.02423	35.19908	35.37489	35.55167
18	37.94906	38.15054	38.35319	38.55703	38.76207	38.96831	39.17576	39.38443
19	41.83130	42.06725	42.30468	42.54359	42.78399	43.02589	43.26930	43.51422
20	46.00081	46.27576	46.55253	46.83113	47.11157	47.39387	47.67803	47.96407
21	50.47887	50.79781	51.11897	51.44238	51.76805	52.09600	52.42624	52.75879
22	55.28831	55.65674	56.02790	56.40178	56.77842	57.15784	57.54006	57.92509
23	60.45364	60.87767	61.30499	61.73562	62.16958	62.60692	63.04764	63.49179
24	66.00121	66.48756	66.97786	67.47216	67.97047	68.47285	68.97931	69.48990
25	71.95930	72.51538	73.07620	73.64180	74.21223	74.78752	75.36772	75.95287
26	78.35829	78.99228	79.63192	80.27726	80.92836	81.58527	82.24803	82.91672
27	85.23080	85.95170	86.67931	87.41369	88.15491	88.90304	89.65813	90.42026
28	92.61188	93.42960	94.25526	95.08893	95.93069	96.78062	97.63881	98.50533
29	100.53916	101.46461	102.39940	103.34364	104.29742	105.26084	106.23400	107.21700
30	109.05306	110.09822	111.15436	112.22158	113.30002	114.38979	115.49102	116.60381
31	118.19699	119.37504	120.56593	121.76981	122.98682	124.21711	125.46082	126.71811
32	128.01756	129.34298	130.68338	132.03894	133.40982	134.79622	136.19831	137.61626
33	138.56486	140.05353	141.55963	143.08338	144.62497	146.18463	147.76258	149.35902
34	149.89266	151.56202	153.25161	154.96167	156.69247	158.44426	160.21729	162.01185
35	162.05872	163.92789	165.82048	167.73678	169.67710	171.64174	173.63103	175.64527
36	175.12506	177.21502	179.33201	181.47640	183.64855	185.84883	188.07762	190.33528
37	189.15832	191.49204	193.85691	196.25337	198.68184	201.14277	203.63659	206.16376
38	204.23004	206.83269	209.47118	212.14600	214.85766	217.60669	220.39361	223.21895
39	220.41706	223.31623	226.25652	229.23852	232.26285	235.33010	238.44092	241.59592
40	237.80192	241.02779	244.30076	247.62153	250.99082	254.40936	257.87787	261.39710
41	256.47326	260.05886	263.69832	267.39246	271.14213	274.94817	278.81146	282.73288
42	276.52628	280.50774	284.55069	288.65609	292.82493	297.05821	301.35695	305.72218
43	298.06323	302.48007	306.96699	311.52512	316.15562	320.85966	325.63843	330.49314
44	321.19391	326.08934	331.06452	336.12077	341.25945	346.48193	351.78959	357.18386
45	346.03626	351.45749	356.96935	362.57339	368.27117	374.06429	379.95439	385.94311
46	372.71694	378.71558	384.81706	391.02318	397.33578	403.75671	410.28788	416.93120
47	401.37199	408.00439	414.75333	421.62093	428.60930	435.72060	442.95704	450.32087
48	432.14752	439.47521	446.93483	454.52881	462.25960	470.12973	478.14174	486.29824
49	465.20044	473.29062	481.52995	489.92123	498.46733	507.17115	516.03565	525.06385
50	500.69927	509.62527	518.71969	527.98579	537.42685	547.04624	556.84739	566.83380

ANNUAL DEPOSITS

NUMBER OF ANNUAL DEPOSITS	EFFECTIVE ANNUAL YIELD							
	7.80%	7.85%	7.90%	7.95%	8.00%	8.05%	8.10%	8.15%
1	1.07800	1.07850	1.07900	1.07950	1.08000	1.08050	1.08100	1.08150
2	2.24008	2.24166	2.24324	2.24482	2.24640	2.24798	2.24956	2.25114
3	3.49281	3.49613	3.49946	3.50278	3.50611	3.50944	3.51278	3.51611
4	4.84325	4.84908	4.85491	4.86075	4.86660	4.87245	4.87831	4.88417
5	6.29902	6.30823	6.31745	6.32668	6.33593	6.34519	6.35445	6.36373
6	7.86835	7.88193	7.89553	7.90916	7.92280	7.93647	7.95016	7.96388
7	9.56008	9.57916	9.59828	9.61743	9.63663	9.65586	9.67513	9.69443
8	11.38376	11.40962	11.43554	11.46152	11.48756	11.51366	11.53981	11.56603
9	13.34970	13.38378	13.41795	13.45221	13.48656	13.52100	13.55554	13.59016
10	15.46897	15.51291	15.55697	15.60116	15.64549	15.68995	15.73454	15.77926
11	17.75355	17.80917	17.86497	17.92095	17.97713	18.03349	18.09003	18.14677
12	20.21633	20.28569	20.35530	20.42517	20.49530	20.56568	20.63633	20.70723
13	22.87121	22.95661	23.04237	23.12847	23.21492	23.30172	23.38887	23.47637
14	25.73316	25.83721	25.94172	26.04668	26.15211	26.25801	26.36437	26.47119
15	28.81835	28.94393	29.07011	29.19690	29.32428	29.45228	29.58088	29.71010
16	32.14418	32.29453	32.44565	32.59755	32.75023	32.90369	33.05793	33.21297
17	35.72942	35.90815	36.08786	36.26855	36.45024	36.63293	36.81662	37.00133
18	39.59432	39.80544	40.01780	40.23140	40.44626	40.66238	40.87977	41.09844
19	43.76067	44.00867	44.25820	44.50930	44.76196	45.01620	45.27203	45.52946
20	48.25201	48.54185	48.83360	49.12729	49.42292	49.72051	50.02007	50.32161
21	53.09366	53.43088	53.77046	54.11241	54.45676	54.80351	55.15269	55.50432
22	58.31297	58.70371	59.09732	59.49385	59.89330	60.29569	60.70106	61.10942
23	63.93938	64.39045	64.84501	65.30311	65.76476	66.23000	66.69885	67.17134
24	70.00465	70.52360	71.04677	71.57420	72.10594	72.64201	73.18245	73.72730
25	76.54302	77.13820	77.73846	78.34385	78.95442	79.57019	80.19123	80.81758
26	83.59137	84.27205	84.95880	85.65169	86.35077	87.05609	87.76772	88.48571
27	91.18950	91.96590	92.74955	93.54050	94.33883	95.14461	95.95791	96.77880
28	99.38028	100.26373	101.15576	102.05647	102.96594	103.88425	104.81150	105.74777
29	108.20994	109.21293	110.22607	111.24946	112.28321	113.32743	114.38223	115.44770
30	117.72832	118.86464	120.01293	121.17329	122.34587	123.53079	124.72819	125.93820
31	127.98912	129.27402	130.57295	131.88607	133.21354	134.55552	135.91217	137.28366
32	139.05028	140.50053	141.96721	143.45051	144.95062	146.46774	148.00206	149.55378
33	150.97420	152.60832	154.26162	155.93432	157.62667	159.33889	161.07123	162.82392
34	163.82818	165.66657	167.52729	169.41060	171.31680	173.24617	175.19900	177.17556
35	177.68478	179.74990	181.84094	183.95825	186.10215	188.27299	190.47111	192.69687
36	192.62220	194.93877	197.28538	199.66243	202.07032	204.50946	206.98027	209.48317
37	208.72473	211.31996	213.94992	216.61509	219.31595	222.05298	224.82668	227.63755
38	226.08326	228.98708	231.93096	234.91549	237.94122	241.00874	244.11864	247.27151
39	244.79575	248.04106	251.33251	254.67077	258.05652	261.49044	264.97325	268.50563
40	264.96782	268.59078	272.26678	275.99660	279.78104	283.62093	287.51708	291.47034
41	286.71331	290.75366	294.85485	299.01783	303.24352	307.53291	311.88696	316.30668
42	310.15495	314.65632	319.22739	323.86924	328.58301	333.36981	338.23081	343.16717
43	335.42503	340.43534	345.52535	350.69635	355.94965	361.28658	366.70850	372.21680
44	362.66618	368.23802	373.90085	379.65621	385.50562	391.45065	397.49289	403.63396
45	392.03215	398.22320	404.51802	410.91838	417.42607	424.04293	430.77082	437.61163
46	423.68865	430.56222	437.55395	444.66589	451.90015	459.25888	466.74425	474.35848
47	457.81437	465.43986	473.19971	481.09633	489.13216	497.30972	505.63154	514.10020
48	494.60189	503.05539	511.66148	520.42298	529.34274	538.42365	547.66869	557.08086
49	534.25884	543.62374	553.16174	562.87611	572.77016	582.84726	593.11085	603.56445
50	577.00903	587.37670	597.94052	608.70426	619.67177	630.84696	642.23383	653.83646

ANNUAL DEPOSITS

EFFECTIVE ANNUAL YIELD

NUMBER OF ANNUAL DEPOSITS	8.20%	8.25%	8.30%	8.35%	8.40%	8.45%	8.50%	8.55%
1	1.08200	1.08250	1.08300	1.08350	1.08400	1.08450	1.08500	1.08550
2	2.25272	2.25431	2.25589	2.25747	2.25906	2.26064	2.26222	2.26381
3	3.51945	3.52279	3.52613	3.52947	3.53282	3.53616	3.53951	3.54287
4	4.89004	4.89592	4.90180	4.90768	4.91357	4.91947	4.92537	4.93128
5	6.37303	6.38233	6.39165	6.40097	6.41031	6.41967	6.42903	6.43841
6	7.97761	7.99137	8.00515	8.01895	8.03278	8.04663	8.06050	8.07439
7	9.71378	9.73316	9.75258	9.77204	9.79153	9.81107	9.83064	9.85025
8	11.59231	11.61865	11.64504	11.67150	11.69802	11.72460	11.75124	11.77795
9	13.62488	13.65968	13.69458	13.72957	13.76466	13.79983	13.83510	13.87046
10	15.82412	15.86911	15.91423	15.95949	16.00489	16.05042	16.09608	16.14188
11	18.20369	18.26081	18.31811	18.37561	18.43330	18.49118	18.54925	18.60752
12	20.77840	20.84983	20.92152	20.99347	21.06569	21.13818	21.21094	21.28396
13	23.56423	23.65244	23.74100	23.82993	23.91921	24.00886	24.09887	24.18924
14	26.57849	26.68626	26.79451	26.90323	27.01243	27.12211	27.23227	27.34292
15	29.83993	29.97038	30.10145	30.23315	30.36547	30.49842	30.63201	30.76624
16	33.36880	33.52544	33.68287	33.84111	34.00017	34.16004	34.32073	34.48225
17	37.18704	37.37378	37.56155	37.75035	37.94018	38.13107	38.32300	38.51598
18	41.31838	41.53962	41.76216	41.98600	42.21116	42.43764	42.66545	42.89460
19	45.78849	46.04914	46.31142	46.57533	46.84090	47.10812	47.37701	47.64759
20	50.62515	50.93069	51.23827	51.54787	51.85953	52.17326	52.48906	52.80695
21	55.85841	56.21498	56.57404	56.93562	57.29973	57.66640	58.03563	58.40745
22	61.52080	61.93521	62.35269	62.77325	63.19691	63.62371	64.05366	64.48679
23	67.64750	68.12737	68.61096	69.09831	69.58945	70.08441	70.58322	71.08591
24	74.27660	74.83037	75.38867	75.95152	76.51897	77.09104	77.66779	78.24925
25	81.44928	82.08638	82.72893	83.37697	84.03056	84.68974	85.35455	86.02506
26	89.21012	89.94101	90.67843	91.42245	92.17313	92.93052	93.69469	94.46570
27	97.60735	98.44364	99.28774	100.13972	100.99967	101.86765	102.74374	103.62802
28	106.69315	107.64774	108.61162	109.58489	110.56764	111.55996	112.56196	113.57372
29	116.52399	117.61118	118.70939	119.81873	120.93932	122.07128	123.21473	124.36977
30	127.16096	128.39660	129.64527	130.90709	132.18223	133.47080	134.77298	136.08889
31	138.67016	140.07182	141.48882	142.92134	144.36953	145.83359	147.31368	148.80999
32	151.12311	152.71025	154.31539	155.93877	157.58057	159.24103	160.92034	162.61874
33	164.59720	166.39134	168.20657	170.04315	171.90134	173.78139	175.68357	177.60814
34	179.17618	181.20113	183.25072	185.32526	187.42505	189.55042	191.70168	193.87914
35	194.95062	197.23272	199.54353	201.88342	204.25276	206.65193	209.08132	211.54131
36	212.01857	214.58692	217.18864	219.82418	222.49399	225.19852	227.93823	230.71359
37	230.48610	233.37284	236.29830	239.26300	242.26748	245.31229	248.39798	251.52510
38	250.46796	253.70860	256.99406	260.32496	263.70195	267.12568	270.59681	274.11600
39	272.08833	275.72206	279.40756	283.14560	286.93692	290.78230	294.68254	298.63841
40	295.48157	299.55163	303.68139	307.87175	312.12362	316.43791	320.81555	325.25750
41	320.79306	325.34714	329.96995	334.66254	339.42600	344.26141	349.16987	354.15251
42	348.18009	353.27078	358.44045	363.69037	369.02179	374.43600	379.93431	385.51805
43	377.81286	383.49811	389.27401	395.14201	401.10362	405.88032	413.31373	419.56535
44	409.87551	416.21921	422.66675	429.21987	435.88032	442.64989	449.53040	456.52368
45	444.56731	451.63979	458.83109	466.14323	473.57827	481.13831	488.82548	496.64196
46	482.10382	489.98258	497.99707	506.14969	514.44284	522.87899	531.46065	540.19035
47	522.71834	531.48864	540.41383	549.49669	558.74004	568.14677	577.71980	587.46212
48	566.66324	576.41895	586.35118	596.46316	606.75820	617.23967	627.91098	638.77563
49	614.21163	625.05602	636.10133	647.35134	658.80989	670.48092	682.36842	694.47645
50	665.65898	677.70564	689.98074	702.48867	715.23392	728.22106	741.45473	754.93968

ANNUAL DEPOSITS

EFFECTIVE ANNUAL YIELD

NUMBER OF ANNUAL DEPOSITS	8.60%	8.65%	8.70%	8.75%	8.80%	8.85%	8.90%	8.95%
1	1.08600	1.08650	1.08700	1.08750	1.08800	1.08850	1.08900	1.08950
2	2.26540	2.26698	2.26857	2.27016	2.27174	2.27333	2.27492	2.27651
3	3.54622	3.54958	3.55293	3.55629	3.55966	3.56302	3.56639	3.56976
4	4.93719	4.94311	4.94904	4.95497	4.96091	4.96685	4.97280	4.97875
5	6.44779	6.45719	6.46661	6.47603	6.48547	6.49492	6.50438	6.51385
6	8.08830	8.10224	8.11620	8.13018	8.14419	8.15822	8.17227	8.18634
7	9.86990	9.88959	9.90931	9.92907	9.94888	9.96872	9.98860	10.00852
8	11.80471	11.83153	11.85842	11.88537	11.91238	11.93945	11.96658	11.99378
9	13.90591	13.94146	13.97710	14.01284	14.04867	14.08459	14.12061	14.15672
10	16.18782	16.23390	16.28011	16.32646	16.37295	16.41958	16.46634	16.51325
11	18.66598	18.72463	18.78348	18.84253	18.90177	18.96121	19.02085	19.08068
12	21.35725	21.43081	21.50464	21.57875	21.65313	21.72778	21.80270	21.87791
13	24.27997	24.37108	24.46255	24.55439	24.64660	24.73918	24.83214	24.92548
14	27.45405	27.56567	27.67779	27.79040	27.90350	28.01710	28.13120	28.24581
15	30.90110	31.03661	31.17276	31.30956	31.44701	31.58512	31.72388	31.86331
16	34.64459	34.80777	34.97179	35.13664	35.30235	35.46890	35.63631	35.80457
17	38.71003	38.90514	39.10133	39.29860	39.49695	39.69640	39.89694	40.09858
18	43.12509	43.35694	43.59015	43.82473	44.06068	44.29803	44.53677	44.77691
19	47.91985	48.19381	48.46949	48.74689	49.02602	49.30690	49.58954	49.87394
20	53.12696	53.44908	53.77334	54.09974	54.42831	54.75906	55.09201	55.42716
21	58.78187	59.15892	59.53862	59.92097	60.30601	60.69374	61.08420	61.47739
22	64.92312	65.36267	65.80548	66.25156	66.70094	67.15364	67.60969	68.06911
23	71.59250	72.10304	72.61755	73.13607	73.65862	74.18523	74.71595	75.25080
24	78.83546	79.42646	80.02228	80.62297	81.22858	81.83913	82.45467	83.07525
25	86.70131	87.38334	88.07122	88.76498	89.46469	90.17039	90.88214	91.59998
26	95.24362	96.02850	96.82041	97.61942	98.42558	99.23897	100.05965	100.88768
27	104.52057	105.42147	106.33079	107.24862	108.17503	109.11012	110.05396	111.00663
28	114.59534	115.62693	116.66857	117.72037	118.78244	119.85486	120.93776	122.03122
29	125.53654	126.71515	127.90573	129.10841	130.32329	131.55052	132.79022	134.04251
30	137.41868	138.76252	140.12053	141.49289	142.87974	144.28124	145.69755	147.12882
31	150.32269	151.85197	153.39802	154.96102	156.54116	158.13863	159.75363	161.38635
32	164.33644	166.07367	167.83065	169.60761	171.40478	173.22240	175.06070	176.91993
33	179.55538	181.52554	183.51891	185.53577	187.57640	189.64108	191.73010	193.84376
34	196.08314	198.31400	200.57206	202.85765	205.17112	207.51282	209.88308	212.28228
35	214.03229	216.55466	219.10883	221.69520	224.31418	226.96620	229.65168	232.37104
36	233.52506	236.37314	239.25830	242.18103	245.14183	248.14121	251.17968	254.25775
37	254.69422	257.90592	261.16077	264.45937	267.80231	271.19021	274.62367	278.10332
38	277.68392	281.30128	284.96876	288.68706	292.45692	296.27904	300.15417	304.08306
39	302.65074	306.72034	310.84804	315.03468	319.28113	323.58824	327.95690	332.38800
40	329.76470	334.33815	338.97882	343.68772	348.46586	353.31430	358.23406	363.22622
41	359.21047	364.34490	369.55697	374.84789	380.21886	385.67111	391.20589	396.82447
42	391.18857	396.94723	402.79543	408.73458	414.76612	420.89150	427.11222	433.42976
43	425.91679	432.36967	438.92563	445.58636	452.35354	459.22890	466.21420	473.31122
44	463.63163	470.85614	478.19916	485.66266	493.24865	500.95916	508.79627	516.76208
45	504.58995	512.67170	520.88949	529.24565	537.74253	546.38255	555.16814	564.10178
46	549.07069	558.10430	567.29388	576.64214	586.15187	595.82590	605.66710	615.67839
47	597.37676	607.46682	617.73544	628.18583	638.82124	649.64499	660.66047	671.87111
48	649.83717	661.09920	672.56543	684.23959	696.12551	708.22708	720.54825	733.09307
49	706.80916	719.37078	732.16562	745.19805	758.47255	771.99367	785.76605	799.79440
50	768.68075	782.68286	796.95103	811.49038	826.30614	841.40361	856.78823	872.46550

ANNUAL DEPOSITS

EFFECTIVE ANNUAL YIELD

NUMBER OF ANNUAL DEPOSITS	9.00%	9.05%	9.10%	9.15%	9.20%	9.25%	9.30%	9.35%
1	1.09000	1.09050	1.09100	1.09150	1.09200	1.09250	1.09300	1.09350
2	2.27810	2.27969	2.28128	2.28287	2.28446	2.28606	2.28765	2.28924
3	3.57313	3.57650	3.57988	3.58326	3.58663	3.59002	3.59340	3.59679
4	4.98471	4.99068	4.99665	5.00262	5.00861	5.01459	5.02059	5.02659
5	6.52333	6.53283	6.54234	6.55186	6.56140	6.57094	6.58050	6.59007
6	8.20043	8.21455	8.22869	8.24286	8.25705	8.27126	8.28549	8.29974
7	10.02847	10.04847	10.06851	10.08858	10.10869	10.12885	10.14904	10.16927
8	12.02104	12.04836	12.07574	12.10318	12.13069	12.15826	12.18590	12.21360
9	14.19293	14.22923	14.26563	14.30213	14.33872	14.37540	14.41219	14.44907
10	16.56029	16.60748	16.65480	16.70227	16.74988	16.79763	16.84552	16.89356
11	19.14072	19.20096	19.26139	19.32203	19.38287	19.44391	19.50515	19.56660
12	21.95338	22.02914	22.10518	22.18149	22.25809	22.33497	22.41213	22.48958
13	25.01919	25.11328	25.20775	25.30260	25.39784	25.49346	25.58946	25.68586
14	28.36092	28.47653	28.59265	28.70929	28.82644	28.94410	29.06228	29.18098
15	32.00340	32.14416	32.28559	32.42769	32.57047	32.71393	32.85807	33.00291
16	35.97370	36.14370	36.31457	36.48632	36.65895	36.83247	37.00687	37.18218
17	40.30134	40.50521	40.71020	40.91632	41.12358	41.33197	41.54151	41.75221
18	45.01846	45.26143	45.50583	45.75166	45.99894	46.24768	46.49787	46.74954
19	50.16012	50.44809	50.73786	51.02944	51.32285	51.61809	51.91518	52.21412
20	55.76453	56.10414	56.44600	56.79014	57.13655	57.48526	57.83629	58.18964
21	61.87334	62.27207	62.67359	63.07793	63.48511	63.89515	64.30806	64.72388
22	68.53194	68.99819	69.46789	69.94106	70.41774	70.89795	71.38171	71.86906
23	75.78981	76.33302	76.88047	77.43217	77.98818	78.54851	79.11321	79.68232
24	83.70090	84.33166	84.96759	85.60872	86.25509	86.90675	87.56374	88.22611
25	92.32398	93.05418	93.79064	94.53341	95.28256	96.03812	96.80017	97.56875
26	101.72313	102.56608	103.41659	104.27472	105.14055	106.01415	106.89559	107.78493
27	111.96822	112.93881	113.91850	114.90736	115.90548	116.91296	117.92988	118.95632
28	123.13536	124.25027	125.37608	126.51288	127.66079	128.81991	129.99035	131.17224
29	135.30754	136.58542	137.87630	139.18031	140.49758	141.82825	143.17246	144.53034
30	148.57522	150.03690	151.51405	153.00681	154.51535	156.03986	157.58049	159.13743
31	163.03699	164.70574	166.39282	168.09843	169.82277	171.56605	173.32848	175.11028
32	178.80032	180.70211	182.62557	184.57094	186.53846	188.52841	190.54103	192.57659
33	195.98234	198.14616	200.33550	202.55068	204.79200	207.05978	209.35435	211.67600
34	214.71075	217.16888	219.65703	222.17556	224.72486	227.30531	229.91730	232.56121
35	235.12472	237.91317	240.73682	243.59613	246.49155	249.42356	252.39261	255.39918
36	257.37595	260.53481	263.73487	266.97667	270.26077	273.58774	276.95812	280.37251
37	281.62978	285.20371	288.82574	292.49654	296.21677	299.98710	303.80823	307.68084
38	308.06646	312.10514	316.19988	320.35147	324.56071	328.82841	333.15539	337.54249
39	336.88245	341.44116	346.06507	350.75513	355.51229	360.33754	365.23184	370.19622
40	368.29187	373.43208	378.64799	383.94073	389.31142	394.76126	400.29140	405.90306
41	402.52813	408.31819	414.19596	420.16280	426.22008	432.36917	438.61150	444.94850
42	439.84566	446.36148	452.97879	459.69920	466.52432	473.45582	480.49537	487.64469
43	480.52177	487.84770	495.29086	502.85317	510.53656	518.34299	526.27444	534.33296
44	524.85873	533.08841	541.45333	549.95574	558.59792	567.38221	576.31097	585.38660
45	573.18602	582.42342	591.81659	601.36819	611.08093	620.95757	631.00089	641.21374
46	625.86276	636.22324	646.76290	657.48488	668.39238	679.48864	690.77697	702.26073
47	683.28041	694.89194	706.70932	718.73625	730.97648	743.43384	756.11223	769.01561
48	745.86565	758.87016	772.11087	785.59211	799.31831	813.29397	827.52367	842.01206
49	814.08356	828.63841	843.46396	858.56529	873.94760	889.61616	905.57637	921.83369
50	888.44108	904.72068	921.31018	938.21552	955.44278	972.99816	990.88797	1009.11864

ANNUAL DEPOSITS

EFFECTIVE ANNUAL YIELD

NUMBER OF ANNUAL DEPOSITS	9.40%	9.45%	9.50%	9.55%	9.60%	9.65%	9.70%	9.75%
1	1.09400	1.09450	1.09500	1.09550	1.09600	1.09650	1.09700	1.09750
2	2.29084	2.29243	2.29402	2.29562	2.29722	2.29881	2.30041	2.30201
3	3.60017	3.60356	3.60696	3.61035	3.61375	3.61715	3.62055	3.62395
4	5.03259	5.03860	5.04462	5.05064	5.05667	5.06270	5.06874	5.07479
5	6.59965	6.60925	6.61886	6.62848	6.63811	6.64775	6.65741	6.66708
6	8.31402	8.32832	8.34265	8.35700	8.37137	8.38576	8.40018	8.41462
7	10.18954	10.20985	10.23020	10.25059	10.27102	10.29149	10.31200	10.33254
8	12.24136	12.26918	12.29707	12.32502	12.35304	12.38112	12.40926	12.43747
9	14.48604	14.52312	14.56029	14.59756	14.63493	14.67239	14.70996	14.74762
10	16.94173	16.99005	17.03852	17.08713	17.13588	17.18478	17.23382	17.28301
11	19.62826	19.69011	19.75218	19.81445	19.87693	19.93961	20.00250	20.06561
12	22.56731	22.64533	22.72363	22.80223	22.88111	22.96028	23.03975	23.11950
13	25.78264	25.87981	25.97738	26.07534	26.17370	26.27245	26.37160	26.47116
14	29.30021	29.41996	29.54023	29.66104	29.78237	29.90424	30.02665	30.14959
15	33.14843	33.29464	33.44155	33.58916	33.73748	33.88650	34.03623	34.18668
16	37.35838	37.53548	37.71350	37.89243	38.07228	38.25305	38.43475	38.61738
17	41.96407	42.17709	42.39128	42.60666	42.82322	43.04097	43.25992	43.48007
18	47.00269	47.25732	47.51345	47.77109	48.03024	48.29092	48.55313	48.81688
19	52.51494	52.81764	53.12223	53.42873	53.73715	54.04750	54.35978	54.67403
20	58.54535	58.90341	59.26384	59.62668	59.99191	60.35958	60.72968	61.10225
21	65.14261	65.56428	65.98891	66.41652	66.84714	67.28078	67.71746	68.15721
22	72.36001	72.85460	73.35286	73.85480	74.36046	74.86987	75.38306	75.90004
23	80.25585	80.83386	81.41638	82.00343	82.59507	83.19132	83.79221	84.39780
24	88.89300	89.56716	90.24593	90.93026	91.62019	92.31578	93.01706	93.72408
25	98.34393	99.12576	99.91430	100.70960	101.51173	102.32075	103.13671	103.95968
26	108.68226	109.58764	110.50116	111.42287	112.35286	113.29120	114.23797	115.19325
27	119.99239	121.03818	122.09377	123.15925	124.23473	125.32030	126.41606	127.52209
28	132.36568	133.57078	134.78767	136.01646	137.25727	138.51021	139.77541	141.05300
29	145.90205	147.28772	148.68750	150.10153	151.52997	152.97295	154.43063	155.90316
30	160.71085	162.30091	163.90781	165.53173	167.17284	168.83134	170.50740	172.20122
31	176.91166	178.73285	180.57406	182.43551	184.31744	186.22006	188.14362	190.08834
32	194.63536	196.71760	198.82359	200.95360	203.10791	205.28680	207.49055	209.71945
33	214.02509	216.40192	218.80683	221.24017	223.70227	226.19347	228.71413	231.26460
34	235.23744	237.94640	240.68848	243.46411	246.27369	249.11764	251.99602	254.91040
35	258.44376	261.52683	264.64889	267.81043	271.01196	274.25400	277.53705	280.86166
36	283.83148	287.33562	290.88553	294.48183	298.12511	301.81601	305.55515	309.34317
37	311.60564	315.58334	319.61466	323.70034	327.84112	332.03775	336.29100	340.60163
38	341.99056	346.50046	351.07305	355.70922	360.40987	365.17589	370.00823	374.90779
39	375.23168	380.33925	385.51999	390.77495	396.10521	401.51187	406.99602	412.55880
40	411.59746	417.37581	423.23939	429.18946	435.22732	441.35426	447.57164	453.88079
41	451.38162	457.91233	464.54213	471.27256	478.10514	485.04145	492.08309	499.23166
42	494.90549	502.27954	509.76864	517.37458	525.09923	532.94445	540.91215	549.00425
43	542.52060	550.83946	559.29166	567.87936	576.60476	585.47009	594.47762	603.62966
44	594.61154	603.98829	613.51936	623.20734	633.05481	643.06445	653.23895	663.58105
45	651.59903	662.15968	672.89870	683.81914	694.92408	706.21667	717.70013	729.37771
46	713.94333	725.82827	737.91908	750.21936	762.73279	775.46308	788.41404	801.58953
47	782.14801	795.51354	809.11639	822.96081	837.05114	851.39177	865.98721	880.84201
48	856.76392	871.78407	887.07745	902.64907	918.50404	934.64758	951.08497	967.82161
49	938.39373	955.26217	972.44481	989.94756	1007.77643	1025.93757	1044.43721	1063.28172
50	1027.69674	1046.62894	1065.92206	1085.58305	1105.61897	1126.03704	1146.84462	1168.04918

ANNUAL DEPOSITS

NUMBER OF ANNUAL DEPOSITS	EFFECTIVE ANNUAL YIELD							
	9.80%	9.85%	9.90%	9.95%	10.00%	10.05%	10.10%	10.15%
1	1.09800	1.09850	1.09900	1.09950	1.10000	1.10050	1.10100	1.10150
2	2.30360	2.30520	2.30680	2.30840	2.31000	2.31160	2.31320	2.31480
3	3.62736	3.63076	3.63417	3.63759	3.64100	3.64442	3.64783	3.65125
4	5.08084	5.08689	5.09296	5.09903	5.10510	5.11118	5.11727	5.12336
5	6.67676	6.68645	6.69616	6.70588	6.71561	6.72535	6.73511	6.74488
6	8.42908	8.44357	8.45808	8.47261	8.48717	8.50175	8.51636	8.53098
7	10.35313	10.37376	10.39443	10.41514	10.43589	10.45668	10.47751	10.49838
8	12.46574	12.49408	12.52248	12.55095	12.57948	12.60807	12.63674	12.66546
9	14.78538	14.82324	14.86120	14.89926	14.93742	14.97569	15.01405	15.05251
10	17.33235	17.38183	17.43146	17.48124	17.53117	17.58124	17.63146	17.68184
11	20.12892	20.19244	20.25618	20.32012	20.38428	20.44866	20.51324	20.57804
12	23.19955	23.27990	23.36054	23.44148	23.52271	23.60425	23.68608	23.76821
13	26.57111	26.67147	26.77223	26.87340	26.97498	27.07697	27.17937	27.28219
14	30.27308	30.39711	30.52168	30.64681	30.77248	30.89871	31.02549	31.15283
15	34.33784	34.48972	34.64233	34.79567	34.94973	35.10453	35.26007	35.41634
16	38.80095	38.98546	39.17092	39.35733	39.54470	39.73303	39.92233	40.11260
17	43.70144	43.92403	44.14784	44.37289	44.59917	44.82670	45.05549	45.28553
18	49.08218	49.34905	49.61748	49.88749	50.15909	50.43229	50.70709	50.98351
19	54.99024	55.30843	55.62861	55.95080	56.27500	56.60123	56.92951	57.25984
20	61.47728	61.85481	62.23484	62.61740	63.00250	63.39016	63.78039	64.17321
21	68.60006	69.04601	69.49509	69.94733	70.40275	70.86137	71.32321	71.78829
22	76.42086	76.94554	77.47411	78.00659	78.54302	79.08343	79.62785	80.17631
23	85.00811	85.62317	86.24304	86.86775	87.49733	88.13182	88.77126	89.41570
24	94.43690	95.15556	95.88010	96.61059	97.34706	98.08957	98.83816	99.59289
25	104.78972	105.62688	106.47123	107.32284	108.18177	109.04807	109.92182	110.80307
26	116.15711	117.12963	118.11089	119.10096	120.09994	121.10790	122.12492	123.15108
27	128.63850	129.76540	130.90286	132.05101	133.20994	134.37974	135.56054	136.75242
28	142.34308	143.64579	144.96125	146.28959	147.63093	148.98541	150.35315	151.73429
29	157.39070	158.89340	160.41141	161.94490	163.49402	165.05894	166.63982	168.23682
30	173.91299	175.64290	177.39114	179.15792	180.94342	182.74787	184.57144	186.41436
31	192.05446	194.04222	196.05186	198.08363	200.13777	202.21453	204.31416	206.43692
32	211.97380	214.25388	216.56000	218.89245	221.25154	223.63759	226.05089	228.49176
33	233.84523	236.45639	239.09844	241.77175	244.47670	247.21366	249.98303	252.78518
34	257.86006	260.84584	263.86818	266.92754	270.02437	273.15914	276.33231	279.54437
35	284.22835	287.63766	291.09013	294.58633	298.12681	301.71213	305.34287	309.01963
36	313.18073	317.06847	321.00706	324.99717	329.03949	333.13470	337.28351	341.48662
37	344.97044	349.39821	353.88576	358.43389	363.04343	367.71524	372.45014	377.24901
38	379.87554	384.91244	390.01945	395.19756	400.44778	405.77112	411.16860	416.64128
39	418.20135	423.92481	429.73037	435.61922	441.59256	447.65161	453.79763	460.03187
40	460.28308	466.77990	473.37268	480.06283	486.85181	493.74110	500.73219	507.82661
41	506.48882	513.85622	521.33557	528.92858	536.63699	544.46258	552.40714	560.47251
42	557.22272	565.56956	574.04679	582.65647	591.40069	600.28157	609.30127	618.46197
43	612.92855	622.37666	631.97643	641.73029	651.64076	661.71037	671.94169	682.33736
44	674.09355	684.77927	695.64109	706.68196	717.90484	729.31276	740.90881	752.69610
45	741.25272	753.32852	765.60856	778.09631	790.79532	803.70919	816.84159	830.19626
46	814.99348	828.62988	842.50281	856.61639	870.97485	885.58247	900.44360	915.56268
47	895.96084	911.34843	927.00959	942.94923	959.17234	975.68400	992.48940	1009.59379
48	984.86301	1002.21475	1019.88254	1037.87217	1056.18957	1074.84075	1093.83183	1113.16906
49	1082.47758	1102.03140	1121.94991	1142.23996	1162.90853	1183.96274	1205.40984	1227.25722
50	1189.65838	1211.67999	1234.12195	1256.99233	1280.29938	1304.05150	1328.25724	1352.92532

128

ANNUAL DEPOSITS

NUMBER OF ANNUAL DEPOSITS	EFFECTIVE ANNUAL YIELD							
	10.20%	10.25%	10.30%	10.35%	10.40%	10.45%	10.50%	10.55%
1	1.10200	1.10250	1.10300	1.10350	1.10400	1.10450	1.10500	1.10550
2	2.31640	2.31801	2.31961	2.32121	2.32282	2.32442	2.32602	2.32763
3	3.65468	3.65810	3.66153	3.66496	3.66839	3.67182	3.67526	3.67870
4	5.12945	5.13556	5.14167	5.14778	5.15390	5.16003	5.16616	5.17230
5	6.75466	6.76445	6.77426	6.78408	6.79391	6.80375	6.81361	6.82347
6	8.54563	8.56031	8.57501	8.58973	8.60447	8.61924	8.63404	8.64885
7	10.51929	10.54024	10.56123	10.58226	10.60334	10.62445	10.64561	10.66681
8	12.69426	12.72311	12.75204	12.78103	12.81009	12.83921	12.86840	12.89765
9	15.09107	15.12973	15.16850	15.20737	15.24633	15.28541	15.32458	15.36386
10	17.73236	17.78303	17.83385	17.88483	17.93595	17.98723	18.03866	18.09024
11	20.64306	20.70829	20.77374	20.83941	20.90529	20.97140	21.03772	21.10426
12	23.85065	23.93339	24.01644	24.09979	24.18344	24.26741	24.35168	24.43626
13	27.38542	27.48906	27.59313	27.69761	27.80252	27.90785	28.01361	28.11979
14	31.28073	31.40919	31.53822	31.66782	31.79798	31.92872	32.06004	32.19193
15	35.57337	35.73114	35.88966	36.04894	36.20897	36.36977	36.53134	36.69367
16	40.30385	40.49608	40.68929	40.88350	41.07871	41.27491	41.47213	41.67036
17	45.51684	45.74943	45.98329	46.21844	46.45489	46.69264	46.93170	47.17208
18	51.26156	51.54124	51.82257	52.10555	52.39020	52.67652	52.96453	53.25423
19	57.59224	57.92672	58.26329	58.60198	58.94278	59.28572	59.63081	59.97806
20	64.56865	64.96671	65.36741	65.77078	66.17683	66.58558	66.99704	67.41124
21	72.25665	72.72830	73.20326	73.68156	74.16322	74.64827	75.13673	75.62863
22	80.72883	81.28545	81.84619	82.41110	82.98020	83.55352	84.13109	84.71295
23	90.06517	90.71970	91.37935	92.04415	92.71414	93.38936	94.06985	94.75566
24	100.35381	101.12097	101.89442	102.67422	103.46041	104.25305	105.05219	105.85789
25	111.69190	112.58837	113.49255	114.40450	115.32429	116.25199	117.18767	118.13139
26	124.18648	125.23118	126.28528	127.34887	128.42202	129.50482	130.59737	131.69975
27	137.95550	139.16988	140.39567	141.63297	142.88191	144.14258	145.41510	146.69958
28	153.12896	154.53729	155.95942	157.39549	158.84562	160.30998	161.78868	163.28188
29	169.85011	171.47986	173.12624	174.78942	176.46957	178.16687	179.88149	181.61362
30	188.27682	190.15905	192.06124	193.98362	195.92641	197.88981	199.87405	201.87936
31	208.58306	210.75285	212.94655	215.16443	217.40675	219.67379	221.96583	224.28313
32	230.96053	233.45752	235.98305	238.53745	241.12105	243.73420	246.37724	249.05050
33	255.62051	258.48941	261.39230	264.32957	267.30164	270.30893	273.35185	276.43083
34	282.79580	286.08708	289.41871	292.79118	296.20501	299.66071	303.15879	306.69978
35	312.74297	316.51350	320.33183	324.19857	328.11434	332.07975	336.09547	340.16211
36	345.74475	350.05864	354.42901	358.85662	363.34223	367.88659	372.49049	377.15471
37	382.11272	387.04215	392.03820	397.10178	402.23382	407.43524	412.70699	418.05004
38	422.19021	427.81647	433.52114	439.30532	445.17013	451.11672	457.14622	463.25982
39	466.35562	472.77016	479.27681	485.87692	492.57183	499.36292	506.25158	513.23923
40	515.02589	522.33160	529.74532	537.26868	544.90330	552.65084	560.51299	568.49146
41	568.66053	576.97309	585.41209	593.97949	602.67724	611.50736	620.47186	629.57281
42	627.76590	637.21533	646.81254	656.55986	666.45967	676.51437	686.72640	697.09825
43	692.90003	703.63240	714.53723	725.61731	736.87548	748.31463	759.93768	771.74761
44	764.67783	776.85722	789.23756	801.82220	814.61453	827.61800	840.83613	854.27248
45	843.77697	857.58759	871.63203	885.91430	900.43844	915.20859	930.22893	945.50373
46	930.94422	946.59281	962.51313	978.70993	995.18804	1011.95238	1029.00796	1046.35987
47	1027.00253	1044.72108	1062.75499	1081.10991	1099.79160	1118.80591	1138.15880	1157.85634
48	1132.85878	1152.90749	1173.32175	1194.10828	1215.27392	1236.82562	1258.77047	1281.11568
49	1249.51238	1272.18300	1295.27689	1318.80199	1342.76641	1367.17840	1392.04637	1417.37889
50	1378.06464	1403.68426	1429.79341	1456.40150	1483.51812	1511.15305	1539.31624	1568.01786

ANNUAL DEPOSITS

EFFECTIVE ANNUAL YIELD

NUMBER OF ANNUAL DEPOSITS	10.60%	10.65%	10.70%	10.75%	10.80%	10.85%	10.90%	10.95%
1	1.10600	1.10650	1.10700	1.10750	1.10800	1.10850	1.10900	1.10950
2	2.32924	2.33084	2.33245	2.33406	2.33566	2.33727	2.33888	2.34049
3	3.68214	3.68558	3.68902	3.69247	3.69592	3.69937	3.70282	3.70627
4	5.17844	5.18459	5.19075	5.19691	5.20307	5.20925	5.21543	5.22161
5	6.83336	6.84325	6.85316	6.86308	6.87301	6.88295	6.89291	6.90288
6	8.66369	8.67856	8.69344	8.70836	8.72329	8.73825	8.75323	8.76824
7	10.68804	10.70932	10.73064	10.75200	10.77341	10.79485	10.81634	10.83786
8	12.92698	12.95636	12.98582	13.01534	13.04493	13.07459	13.10432	13.13411
9	15.40324	15.44272	15.48230	15.52199	15.56179	15.60169	15.64169	15.68180
10	18.14198	18.19387	18.24591	18.29811	18.35046	18.40297	18.45563	18.50845
11	21.17103	21.23801	21.30522	21.37265	21.44031	21.50819	21.57630	21.64463
12	24.52116	24.60636	24.69188	24.77772	24.86386	24.95033	25.03711	25.12422
13	28.22640	28.33344	28.44091	28.54882	28.65716	28.76594	28.87516	28.98482
14	32.32440	32.45745	32.59109	32.72532	32.86013	32.99555	33.13155	33.26815
15	36.85678	37.02067	37.18534	37.35079	37.51703	37.68406	37.85189	38.02052
16	41.86960	42.06987	42.27117	42.47350	42.67687	42.88128	43.08675	43.29326
17	47.41378	47.65681	47.90118	48.14690	48.39397	48.64240	48.89220	49.14338
18	53.54564	53.83876	54.13361	54.43019	54.72852	55.02860	55.33045	55.63408
19	60.32748	60.67909	61.03291	61.38894	61.74720	62.10771	62.47047	62.83551
20	67.82819	68.24792	68.67043	69.09575	69.52390	69.95489	70.38875	70.82550
21	76.12398	76.62282	77.12516	77.63104	78.14048	78.65350	79.17013	79.69039
22	85.29912	85.88965	86.48456	87.08388	87.68765	88.29590	88.90867	89.52598
23	95.44683	96.14340	96.84540	97.55290	98.26592	98.98451	99.70871	100.43858
24	106.67019	107.48917	108.31486	109.14733	109.98663	110.83283	111.68596	112.54610
25	119.08323	120.04326	121.01155	121.98817	122.97319	123.96669	124.96873	125.97940
26	132.81206	133.93437	135.06679	136.20940	137.36230	138.52557	139.69933	140.88365
27	147.99614	149.30488	150.62593	151.95941	153.30542	154.66410	156.03555	157.41991
28	164.78973	166.31235	167.84991	169.40254	170.97041	172.55365	174.15243	175.76689
29	183.36344	185.13112	186.91685	188.72082	190.54321	192.38422	194.24404	196.12286
30	203.90596	205.95408	208.02395	210.11581	212.22988	214.36641	216.52564	218.70781
31	226.62599	228.99469	231.38951	233.81076	236.25871	238.73367	241.23594	243.76582
32	251.75435	254.48913	257.25519	260.05291	262.88265	265.74477	268.63965	271.56768
33	279.54631	282.69872	285.88850	289.11610	292.38197	295.68658	299.03038	302.41384
34	310.28422	313.91263	317.58557	321.30308	325.06723	328.87707	332.73369	336.63765
35	344.28034	348.45083	352.67422	356.95122	361.28249	365.66873	370.11066	374.60898
36	381.88006	386.66734	391.51737	396.43097	401.40900	406.45229	411.56172	416.73816
37	423.46535	428.95391	434.51672	440.15480	445.86917	451.66087	457.53095	463.48049
38	469.45867	475.74400	482.11701	488.57894	495.13104	501.77457	508.51082	515.34110
39	520.32729	527.51724	534.81053	542.20868	549.71319	557.32561	565.04750	572.88045
40	576.58799	584.80432	593.14226	601.60361	610.19021	618.90394	627.74668	636.72036
41	638.81231	648.19248	657.71548	667.38350	677.19876	687.16352	697.28007	707.55074
42	707.63242	718.33148	729.19804	740.23472	751.44422	762.82926	774.39260	786.13705
43	783.74746	795.94029	808.32923	820.91746	833.70820	846.70473	859.91039	873.32855
44	867.93069	881.81443	895.92746	910.27358	924.85669	939.68070	954.74962	970.06753
45	961.03734	976.83416	992.89869	1009.23550	1025.84921	1042.74455	1059.92633	1077.39943
46	1064.01330	1081.97350	1100.24585	1118.83581	1137.74892	1156.99084	1176.56730	1196.48416
47	1177.90471	1198.31018	1219.07916	1240.21816	1261.73381	1283.63284	1305.92214	1328.60868
48	1303.86860	1327.03671	1350.62763	1374.64911	1399.10906	1424.01551	1449.37665	1475.20083
49	1443.18468	1469.47262	1496.25179	1523.53139	1551.32083	1579.62969	1608.46770	1637.84482
50	1597.26825	1627.07796	1657.45773	1688.41852	1719.97148	1752.12801	1784.89968	1818.29833

ANNUAL DEPOSITS

NUMBER OF ANNUAL DEPOSITS	EFFECTIVE ANNUAL YIELD							
	11.00%	11.05%	11.10%	11.15%	11.20%	11.25%	11.30%	11.35%
1	1.11000	1.11050	1.11100	1.11150	1.11200	1.11250	1.11300	1.11350
2	2.34210	2.34371	2.34532	2.34693	2.34854	2.35016	2.35177	2.35338
3	3.70973	3.71319	3.71665	3.72012	3.72358	3.72705	3.73052	3.73399
4	5.22780	5.23400	5.24020	5.24641	5.25262	5.25884	5.26507	5.27130
5	6.91286	6.92285	6.93286	6.94288	6.95292	6.96296	6.97302	6.98309
6	8.78327	8.79833	8.81341	8.82851	8.84364	8.85879	8.87397	8.88917
7	10.85943	10.88105	10.90270	10.92439	10.94613	10.96791	10.98973	11.01159
8	13.16397	13.19390	13.22390	13.25396	13.28410	13.31430	13.34457	13.37491
9	15.72201	15.76233	15.80275	15.84328	15.88392	15.92466	15.96551	16.00646
10	18.56143	18.61456	18.66786	18.72131	18.77491	18.82868	18.88261	18.93670
11	21.71319	21.78197	21.85099	21.92023	21.98970	22.05941	22.12934	22.19951
12	25.21164	25.29938	25.38745	25.47584	25.56455	25.65359	25.74296	25.83265
13	29.09492	29.20546	29.31645	29.42789	29.53978	29.65212	29.76491	29.87816
14	33.40536	33.54317	33.68158	33.82060	33.96024	34.10048	34.24135	34.38283
15	38.18995	38.36019	38.53124	38.70310	38.87578	39.04929	39.22362	39.39878
16	43.50084	43.70949	43.91920	44.13000	44.34187	44.55483	44.76889	44.98405
17	49.39594	49.64989	49.90523	50.16199	50.42016	50.67975	50.94077	51.20323
18	55.93949	56.24670	56.55572	56.86655	57.17922	57.49372	57.81008	58.12830
19	63.20283	63.57246	63.94440	64.31867	64.69529	65.07427	65.45562	65.83936
20	71.26514	71.70771	72.15323	72.60170	73.05316	73.50762	73.96511	74.42563
21	80.21431	80.74192	81.27324	81.80830	82.34712	82.88973	83.43616	83.98644
22	90.14788	90.77440	91.40557	92.04142	92.68199	93.32733	93.97745	94.63240
23	101.17415	101.91547	102.66258	103.41554	104.17438	104.93915	105.70990	106.48668
24	113.41331	114.28763	115.16913	116.05787	116.95391	117.85730	118.76812	119.68642
25	126.99877	128.02691	129.06390	130.10982	131.16475	132.22875	133.30192	134.38433
26	142.07864	143.28439	144.50100	145.72857	146.96720	148.21699	149.47803	150.75045
27	158.81729	160.22781	161.65161	163.08880	164.53952	166.00390	167.48205	168.97412
28	177.39719	179.04348	180.70594	182.38471	184.07995	185.79184	187.52052	189.26618
29	198.02088	199.93829	201.87530	203.83210	205.80891	207.80592	209.82334	211.86140
30	220.91317	223.14197	225.39445	227.67088	229.97150	232.29658	234.64638	237.02117
31	246.32362	248.90966	251.52424	254.16768	256.84031	259.54245	262.27442	265.03657
32	274.52922	277.52468	280.55443	283.61888	286.71843	289.85347	293.02443	296.23172
33	305.83744	309.30165	312.80697	316.35388	319.94289	323.57449	327.24919	330.96752
34	340.58955	344.58999	348.63954	352.73884	356.88849	361.08912	365.34135	369.64583
35	379.16441	383.77768	388.44953	393.18072	397.97200	402.82415	407.73793	412.71413
36	421.98249	427.29561	432.67843	438.13187	443.65687	449.25436	454.92531	460.67069
37	469.51056	475.62228	481.81674	488.09508	494.45844	500.90798	507.44487	514.07031
38	522.26673	529.28904	536.40940	543.62918	550.94978	558.37263	565.89914	573.53079
39	580.82607	588.88598	597.06184	605.35533	613.76816	622.30205	630.95874	639.74003
40	645.82693	655.06838	664.44670	673.96395	683.62219	693.42353	703.37008	713.46403
41	717.97790	728.56393	739.31129	750.22243	761.29988	772.54617	783.96390	795.55570
42	798.06547	810.18075	822.48584	834.98373	847.67746	860.57012	873.66482	886.96477
43	886.96267	900.81622	914.89277	929.19592	943.72934	958.49675	973.50195	988.74877
44	985.63856	1001.46691	1017.55687	1033.91273	1050.53903	1067.44014	1084.62067	1102.08525
45	1095.16880	1113.23951	1131.61668	1150.30554	1169.31140	1188.63966	1208.29580	1228.28543
46	1216.74737	1237.36297	1258.33713	1279.67611	1301.38627	1323.47412	1345.94623	1368.80933
47	1351.69958	1375.20208	1399.12355	1423.47149	1448.25354	1473.47745	1499.15115	1525.28269
48	1501.49653	1528.27241	1555.53727	1583.30006	1611.56993	1640.35617	1669.66823	1699.51577
49	1667.77115	1698.25701	1729.31290	1760.94952	1793.17777	1826.00874	1859.45375	1893.52431
50	1852.33598	1887.02491	1922.37764	1958.40689	1995.12567	2032.54722	2070.68502	2109.55282

ANNUAL DEPOSITS

EFFECTIVE ANNUAL YIELD

NUMBER OF ANNUAL DEPOSITS	11.40%	11.45%	11.50%	11.55%	11.60%	11.65%	11.70%	11.75%
1	1.11400	1.11450	1.11500	1.11550	1.11600	1.11650	1.11700	1.11750
2	2.35500	2.35661	2.35822	2.35984	2.36146	2.36307	2.36469	2.36631
3	3.73747	3.74094	3.74442	3.74790	3.75138	3.75487	3.75836	3.76185
4	5.27754	5.28378	5.29003	5.29628	5.30255	5.30881	5.31509	5.32136
5	6.99318	7.00327	7.01338	7.02351	7.03364	7.04379	7.05395	7.06412
6	8.90440	8.91965	8.93492	8.95022	8.96554	8.98089	8.99626	9.01166
7	11.03350	11.05545	11.07744	11.09947	11.12155	11.14366	11.16583	11.18803
8	13.40532	13.43580	13.46634	13.49696	13.52765	13.55840	13.58923	13.62012
9	16.04752	16.08869	16.12997	16.17136	16.21285	16.25446	16.29617	16.33799
10	18.99094	19.04535	19.09992	19.15465	19.20954	19.26460	19.31982	19.37520
11	22.26991	22.34054	22.41141	22.48251	22.55385	22.62542	22.69724	22.76929
12	25.92268	26.01303	26.10372	26.19474	26.28610	26.37779	26.46981	26.56218
13	29.99186	30.10603	30.22065	30.33574	30.45128	30.56730	30.68378	30.80073
14	34.52494	34.66767	34.81102	34.95501	35.09963	35.24489	35.39078	35.53732
15	39.57478	39.75162	39.92929	40.10782	40.28719	40.46742	40.64851	40.83045
16	45.20030	45.41768	45.63616	45.85577	46.07650	46.29837	46.52138	46.74553
17	51.46714	51.73250	51.99932	52.26761	52.53738	52.80863	53.08138	53.35563
18	58.44839	58.77037	59.09424	59.42002	59.74772	60.07734	60.40890	60.74242
19	66.22551	66.61408	67.00508	67.39853	67.79445	68.19285	68.59375	68.99715
20	74.88922	75.35589	75.82566	76.29856	76.77461	77.25382	77.73621	78.22182
21	84.54059	85.09864	85.66062	86.22655	86.79646	87.37039	87.94835	88.53038
22	95.29222	95.95693	96.62659	97.30121	97.98085	98.66554	99.35531	100.05020
23	107.26953	108.05850	108.85364	109.65500	110.46263	111.27657	112.09688	112.92360
24	120.61226	121.54570	122.48681	123.43566	124.39229	125.35679	126.32921	127.30963
25	135.47605	136.57718	137.68780	138.80797	139.93780	141.07736	142.22673	143.38601
26	152.03432	153.32977	154.63689	155.95579	157.28658	158.62937	159.98426	161.35136
27	170.48024	172.00053	173.53513	175.08419	176.64783	178.22619	179.81942	181.42765
28	191.02898	192.80909	194.60668	196.42191	198.25498	200.10604	201.97529	203.86290
29	213.92029	216.00023	218.10144	220.22414	222.36855	224.53490	226.72340	228.93429
30	239.42120	241.84676	244.29811	246.77553	249.27931	251.80971	254.36704	256.95157
31	267.82922	270.65271	273.50739	276.39361	279.31171	282.26204	285.24498	288.26088
32	299.47575	302.75695	306.07574	309.43257	312.82786	316.26207	319.73564	323.24903
33	334.72998	338.53712	342.38945	346.28753	350.23190	354.22310	358.26171	362.34829
34	374.00320	378.41412	382.87924	387.39924	391.97480	396.60660	401.29533	406.04172
35	417.75357	422.85703	428.02535	433.25935	438.55987	443.92776	449.36389	454.86912
36	466.49147	472.38866	478.36327	484.41631	490.54882	496.76185	503.05646	509.43374
37	520.78550	527.59166	534.49004	541.48189	548.56848	555.75110	563.03107	570.40970
38	581.26905	589.11541	597.07140	605.13855	613.31842	621.61261	630.02270	638.55034
39	648.64772	657.68362	666.84691	676.14755	685.57936	695.14698	704.85236	714.69751
40	723.70756	734.10290	744.65231	755.35809	766.22257	777.24810	788.43709	799.79196
41	807.32422	819.27218	831.40233	843.71745	856.22038	868.91400	881.80123	894.88502
42	900.47318	914.19335	928.12860	942.28232	956.65795	971.25898	986.08897	1001.15151
43	1004.24112	1019.98298	1035.97838	1052.23142	1068.74627	1085.52716	1102.57838	1119.90431
44	1119.83861	1137.88553	1156.23090	1174.87965	1193.83684	1213.10757	1232.69705	1252.61057
45	1248.61421	1269.28793	1290.31245	1311.69375	1333.43791	1355.55110	1378.03961	1400.90981
46	1392.07023	1415.73590	1439.81338	1464.30988	1489.23271	1514.58930	1540.38724	1566.63421
47	1551.88024	1578.95216	1606.50692	1634.55317	1663.09970	1692.15546	1721.72955	1751.83124
48	1729.90859	1760.85668	1792.37022	1824.45957	1857.13527	1890.40807	1924.28890	1958.78891
49	1928.23217	1963.58927	1999.60779	2036.30014	2073.67896	2111.75711	2150.54770	2190.06410
50	2149.16463	2189.53474	2230.67769	2272.60831	2315.34172	2358.89331	2403.27879	2448.51413

ANNUAL DEPOSITS

EFFECTIVE ANNUAL YIELD

NUMBER OF ANNUAL DEPOSITS	11.80%	11.85%	11.90%	11.95%	12.00%	12.05%	12.10%	12.15%
1	1.11800	1.11850	1.11900	1.11950	1.12000	1.12050	1.12100	1.12150
2	2.36792	2.36954	2.37116	2.37278	2.37440	2.37602	2.37764	2.37926
3	3.76534	3.76883	3.77233	3.77583	3.77933	3.78283	3.78634	3.78984
4	5.32765	5.33394	5.34024	5.34654	5.35285	5.35916	5.36548	5.37181
5	7.07431	7.08451	7.09472	7.10495	7.11519	7.12544	7.13571	7.14598
6	9.02708	9.04253	9.05800	9.07349	9.08901	9.10456	9.12013	9.13572
7	11.21028	11.23257	11.25490	11.27727	11.29969	11.32216	11.34466	11.36721
8	13.65109	13.68212	13.71323	13.74441	13.77566	13.80698	13.83837	13.86983
9	16.37992	16.42196	16.46411	16.50637	16.54874	16.59122	16.63381	16.67651
10	19.43075	19.48646	19.54233	19.59838	19.65458	19.71096	19.76750	19.82421
11	22.84158	22.91410	22.98687	23.05988	23.13313	23.20663	23.28037	23.35435
12	26.65488	26.74792	26.84131	26.93504	27.02911	27.12353	27.21829	27.31340
13	30.91816	31.03605	31.15443	31.27327	31.39260	31.51241	31.63270	31.75348
14	35.68450	35.83233	35.98080	36.12993	36.27971	36.43016	36.58126	36.73303
15	41.01327	41.19696	41.38152	41.56696	41.75328	41.94049	42.12859	42.31759
16	46.97084	47.19730	47.42492	47.65371	47.88367	48.11482	48.34715	48.58068
17	53.63140	53.90868	54.18748	54.46783	54.74971	55.03316	55.31816	55.60473
18	61.07790	61.41535	61.75479	62.09623	62.43968	62.78515	63.13265	63.48220
19	69.40309	69.81157	70.22261	70.63623	71.05244	71.47126	71.89270	72.31679
20	78.71066	79.20274	79.69811	80.19676	80.69874	81.20405	81.71272	82.22478
21	89.11651	89.70677	90.30118	90.89978	91.50258	92.10964	92.72096	93.33659
22	100.75026	101.45552	102.16602	102.88180	103.60289	104.32935	105.06120	105.79849
23	113.75679	114.59650	115.44278	116.29567	117.15524	118.02153	118.89460	119.77450
24	128.29810	129.29469	130.29947	131.31251	132.33387	133.36363	134.40185	135.44860
25	144.55527	145.73461	146.92410	148.12385	149.33393	150.55445	151.78547	153.02711
26	162.73079	164.12266	165.52707	166.94415	168.37401	169.81676	171.27252	172.74140
27	183.05103	184.68969	186.34379	188.01348	189.69889	191.40017	193.11749	194.85098
28	205.76905	207.69392	209.63771	211.60059	213.58275	215.58440	217.60571	219.64688
29	231.16780	233.42415	235.70359	238.00636	240.33268	242.68282	245.05700	247.45547
30	259.56360	262.20341	264.87132	267.56762	270.29261	273.04660	275.82989	278.64282
31	291.31010	294.39302	297.51001	300.66145	303.84772	307.06921	310.32631	313.61942
32	326.80269	330.39709	334.03270	337.70999	341.42945	345.19155	348.99679	352.84568
33	366.48341	370.66765	374.90159	379.18583	383.52098	387.90763	392.34641	396.83793
34	410.84645	415.71026	420.63388	425.61804	430.66350	435.77100	440.94132	446.17523
35	460.44433	466.09043	471.80831	477.59890	483.46312	489.40191	495.41622	501.50702
36	515.89476	522.44064	529.07250	535.79147	542.59869	549.49534	556.48258	563.56163
37	577.88835	585.46836	593.15113	600.93805	608.83053	616.83002	624.93798	633.15587
38	647.19717	655.96486	664.85511	673.86964	683.01020	692.27854	701.67647	711.20580
39	724.68444	734.81520	745.09187	755.51657	766.09142	776.81861	787.70033	798.73881
40	811.31520	823.00930	834.87680	846.92029	859.14239	871.54575	884.13306	896.90707
41	908.16839	921.65440	935.34614	949.24677	963.35948	977.68751	992.23417	1007.00278
42	1016.45026	1031.98895	1047.77133	1063.80126	1080.08262	1096.61936	1113.41550	1130.47512
43	1137.50940	1155.39814	1173.57512	1192.04501	1210.81253	1229.88249	1249.25977	1268.94935
44	1272.85350	1293.43132	1314.34956	1335.61389	1357.23003	1379.20383	1401.54121	1424.24820
45	1424.16822	1447.82143	1471.87616	1496.33925	1521.21764	1546.51839	1572.24869	1598.41585
46	1593.33807	1620.50677	1648.14842	1676.27129	1704.88375	1733.99436	1763.61179	1793.74488
47	1782.46996	1813.65532	1845.39709	1877.70521	1910.58980	1944.06118	1978.12981	2012.80638
48	1993.91941	2029.69197	2066.11834	2103.21048	2140.98058	2179.44105	2218.60452	2258.48385
49	2230.31990	2271.32897	2313.10542	2355.66363	2399.01825	2443.18419	2488.17667	2534.01114
50	2494.61565	2541.59996	2589.48397	2638.28494	2688.02044	2738.70839	2790.36704	2843.01500

ANNUAL DEPOSITS

NUMBER OF ANNUAL DEPOSITS	12.20%	12.25%	12.30%	12.35%	12.40%	12.45%	12.50%	12.55%
1	1.12200	1.12250	1.12300	1.12350	1.12400	1.12450	1.12500	1.12550
2	2.38088	2.38251	2.38413	2.38575	2.38738	2.38900	2.39063	2.39225
3	3.79335	3.79686	3.80038	3.80389	3.80741	3.81093	3.81445	3.81798
4	5.37814	5.38448	5.39082	5.39717	5.40353	5.40989	5.41626	5.42263
5	7.15627	7.16658	7.17689	7.18722	7.19757	7.20792	7.21829	7.22867
6	9.15134	9.16698	9.18265	9.19835	9.21407	9.22981	9.24558	9.26137
7	11.38980	11.41244	11.43512	11.45784	11.48061	11.50342	11.52628	11.54918
8	13.90136	13.93296	13.96464	13.99639	14.02821	14.06010	14.09206	14.12410
9	16.71932	16.76225	16.80529	16.84844	16.89170	16.93508	16.97857	17.02217
10	19.88108	19.93813	19.99534	20.05272	20.11027	20.16800	20.22589	20.28395
11	23.42857	23.50305	23.57777	23.65273	23.72795	23.80341	23.87913	23.95509
12	27.40886	27.50467	27.60083	27.69735	27.79421	27.89144	27.98902	28.08695
13	31.87474	31.99649	32.11873	32.24147	32.36470	32.48842	32.61264	32.73737
14	36.88546	37.03856	37.19234	37.34679	37.50192	37.65773	37.81422	37.97141
15	42.50749	42.69829	42.89000	43.08262	43.27616	43.47062	43.66600	43.86232
16	48.81540	49.05133	49.28846	49.52682	49.76640	50.00721	50.24925	50.49254
17	55.89288	56.18261	56.47395	56.76688	57.06143	57.35760	57.65541	57.95485
18	63.83381	64.18748	64.54324	64.90109	65.26105	65.62313	65.98733	66.35368
19	72.74353	73.17295	73.60506	74.03988	74.47742	74.91771	75.36075	75.80657
20	82.74024	83.25914	83.78148	84.30730	84.83662	85.36946	85.90584	86.44580
21	93.95655	94.58088	95.20960	95.84275	96.48036	97.12246	97.76908	98.42024
22	106.54125	107.28954	108.04339	108.80283	109.56793	110.33870	111.11521	111.89749
23	120.66129	121.55501	122.45572	123.36348	124.27835	125.20037	126.12961	127.06612
24	136.50396	137.56800	138.64078	139.72238	140.81286	141.91232	143.02081	144.13842
25	154.27945	155.54258	156.81659	158.10159	159.39766	160.70490	162.02341	163.35329
26	174.22354	175.71904	177.22803	178.75063	180.28697	181.83716	183.40134	184.97963
27	196.60081	198.36712	200.15008	201.94984	203.76655	205.60039	207.45151	209.32007
28	221.70811	223.78960	225.89154	228.01414	230.15761	232.32214	234.50795	236.71524
29	249.87850	252.32632	254.79920	257.29739	259.82115	262.37075	264.94644	267.54850
30	281.48568	284.35880	287.26250	290.19712	293.16297	296.16040	299.18974	302.25134
31	316.94893	320.31525	323.71879	327.15996	330.63918	334.15687	337.71346	341.30938
32	356.73870	360.67637	364.65920	368.68772	372.76244	376.88390	381.05265	385.26921
33	401.38282	405.98172	410.63528	415.34415	420.10898	424.93045	429.80923	434.74600
34	451.47352	456.83698	462.26642	467.76265	473.32650	478.95879	484.66038	490.43212
35	507.67529	513.92202	520.24819	526.65484	533.14298	539.71366	546.36793	553.10685
36	570.73368	577.99996	585.36172	592.82021	600.37671	608.03251	615.78892	623.64726
37	641.48519	649.92746	658.48421	667.15701	675.94742	684.85706	693.88753	703.04049
38	720.86838	730.66607	740.60077	750.67440	760.88890	771.24626	781.74847	792.39757
39	809.93632	821.29517	832.81767	844.50619	856.36313	868.39092	880.59203	892.96896
40	909.87055	923.02632	936.37724	949.92620	963.67616	977.63009	991.79104	1006.16207
41	1021.99676	1037.21955	1052.67464	1068.36559	1084.29600	1100.46954	1116.88992	1133.56091
42	1147.80237	1165.40144	1183.27662	1201.43224	1219.87270	1238.60250	1257.62616	1276.94830
43	1288.95626	1309.28562	1329.94264	1350.93262	1372.26092	1393.93301	1415.95443	1438.33082
44	1447.33092	1470.79561	1494.64859	1518.89630	1543.54527	1568.60217	1594.07373	1619.96683
45	1625.02729	1652.09057	1679.61336	1707.60349	1736.06889	1765.01764	1794.45795	1824.39817
46	1824.40262	1855.59416	1887.32881	1919.61602	1952.46543	1985.88683	2019.89019	2054.48564
47	2048.10174	2084.02695	2120.59325	2157.81210	2195.69514	2234.25424	2273.50146	2313.44909
48	2299.09215	2340.44275	2382.54922	2425.42539	2469.08534	2513.54339	2558.81415	2604.91245
49	2580.70340	2628.26949	2676.72578	2726.08893	2776.37592	2827.60405	2879.79091	2932.95446
50	2896.67121	2951.35500	3007.08605	3063.88441	3121.77054	3180.76525	3240.88978	3302.16575

ANNUAL DEPOSITS

NUMBER OF ANNUAL DEPOSITS	EFFECTIVE ANNUAL YIELD							
	12.60%	12.65%	12.70%	12.75%	12.80%	12.85%	12.90%	12.95%
1	1.12600	1.12650	1.12700	1.12750	1.12800	1.12850	1.12900	1.12950
2	2.39388	2.39550	2.39713	2.39876	2.40038	2.40201	2.40364	2.40527
3	3.82150	3.82503	3.82856	3.83210	3.83563	3.83917	3.84271	3.84625
4	5.42901	5.43540	5.44179	5.44819	5.45459	5.46100	5.46742	5.47384
5	7.23907	7.24948	7.25990	7.27033	7.28078	7.29124	7.30172	7.31221
6	9.27719	9.29304	9.30891	9.32480	9.34072	9.35667	9.37264	9.38864
7	11.57212	11.59511	11.61814	11.64121	11.66433	11.68750	11.71071	11.73396
8	14.15621	14.18839	14.22064	14.25297	14.28537	14.31784	14.35039	14.38301
9	17.06589	17.10972	17.15366	17.19772	17.24190	17.28619	17.33059	17.37511
10	20.34219	20.40060	20.45918	20.51793	20.57686	20.63596	20.69524	20.75469
11	24.03131	24.10777	24.18449	24.26147	24.33870	24.41618	24.49392	24.57192
12	28.18525	28.28391	28.38292	28.48231	28.58205	28.68216	28.78264	28.88349
13	32.86259	32.98832	33.11456	33.24130	33.36855	33.49632	33.62460	33.75340
14	38.12928	38.28784	38.44710	38.60707	38.76773	38.92910	39.09117	39.25396
15	44.05957	44.25776	44.45689	44.65697	44.85800	45.05999	45.26294	45.46685
16	50.73707	50.98286	51.22991	51.47823	51.72782	51.97869	52.23085	52.48431
17	58.25594	58.55869	58.86311	59.16920	59.47698	59.78646	60.09763	60.41052
18	66.72219	67.09287	67.46573	67.84078	68.21804	68.59752	68.97923	69.36319
19	76.25519	76.70662	77.16087	77.61798	78.07795	78.54080	79.00655	79.47522
20	86.98934	87.53650	88.08730	88.64177	89.19992	89.76179	90.32739	90.89676
21	99.07600	99.73637	100.40139	101.07109	101.74551	102.42468	103.10863	103.79739
22	112.68557	113.47952	114.27937	115.08516	115.89694	116.71475	117.53864	118.36865
23	128.00996	128.96118	129.91985	130.88602	131.85975	132.84110	133.83013	134.82690
24	145.26521	146.40127	147.54667	148.70148	149.86579	151.03968	152.22321	153.41648
25	164.69463	166.04753	167.41209	168.78842	170.17662	171.57678	172.98901	174.41341
26	186.57215	188.17904	189.80043	191.43645	193.08722	194.75289	196.43359	198.12945
27	211.20624	213.11019	215.03209	216.97209	218.93039	220.90714	222.90252	224.91671
28	238.94423	241.19513	243.46816	245.76354	248.08148	250.42220	252.78595	255.17293
29	270.17720	272.83282	275.51562	278.22589	280.96390	283.72996	286.52433	289.34732
30	305.34553	308.47267	311.63310	314.82719	318.05528	321.31776	324.61497	327.94730
31	344.94507	348.62096	352.33750	356.09515	359.89436	363.73559	367.61930	371.54597
32	389.53415	393.84801	398.21137	402.62478	407.08884	411.60411	416.17119	420.79068
33	439.74145	444.79628	449.91121	455.08694	460.32421	465.62374	470.98628	476.41257
34	496.27487	502.18951	508.17693	514.23803	520.37371	526.58489	532.87251	539.23750
35	559.93150	566.84299	573.84241	580.93088	588.10954	595.37955	602.74206	610.19825
36	631.60887	639.67512	647.84739	656.12707	664.51557	673.01432	681.62479	690.34843
37	712.31759	721.72053	731.25101	740.91077	750.70156	760.62516	770.68338	780.87805
38	803.19561	814.14468	825.24689	836.50439	847.91936	859.49400	871.23054	883.13126
39	905.52425	918.26048	931.18024	944.28620	957.58104	971.06747	984.74828	998.62626
40	1020.74631	1035.54693	1050.56713	1065.81019	1081.27941	1096.97814	1112.90981	1129.07786
41	1150.48635	1167.67011	1185.11616	1202.82849	1220.81117	1239.06834	1257.60417	1276.42294
42	1296.57363	1316.50688	1336.75291	1357.31662	1378.20300	1399.41712	1420.96411	1442.84921
43	1461.06790	1484.17150	1507.64753	1531.50199	1555.74099	1580.37072	1605.39748	1630.82768
44	1646.28846	1673.04570	1700.24577	1727.89600	1756.00383	1784.57685	1813.62276	1843.14936
45	1854.84680	1885.81248	1917.30398	1949.33023	1981.90032	2015.02348	2048.70909	2082.96671
46	2089.68350	2125.49426	2161.92858	2198.99734	2236.71157	2275.08250	2314.12157	2353.84040
47	2354.10962	2395.49578	2437.62052	2480.49700	2524.13865	2568.55910	2613.77225	2659.79223
48	2651.85343	2699.65250	2748.32532	2797.88787	2848.35639	2899.74744	2952.07787	3005.36482
49	2987.11297	3042.28504	3098.48964	3155.74607	3214.07401	3273.49349	3334.02491	3395.68907
50	3364.61520	3428.26060	3493.12482	3559.23119	3626.60348	3695.26590	3765.24313	3836.56030

ANNUAL DEPOSITS

EFFECTIVE ANNUAL YIELD

NUMBER OF ANNUAL DEPOSITS	13.00%	13.05%	13.10%	13.15%	13.20%	13.25%	13.30%	13.35%
1	1.13000	1.13050	1.13100	1.13150	1.13200	1.13250	1.13300	1.13350
2	2.40690	2.40853	2.41016	2.41179	2.41342	2.41506	2.41669	2.41832
3	3.84980	3.85334	3.85689	3.86044	3.86400	3.86755	3.87111	3.87467
4	5.48027	5.48670	5.49314	5.49959	5.50604	5.51250	5.51897	5.52544
5	7.32271	7.33322	7.34375	7.35429	7.36484	7.37541	7.38599	7.39658
6	9.40466	9.42070	9.43678	9.45288	9.46900	9.48515	9.50133	9.51753
7	11.75726	11.78061	11.80400	11.82743	11.85091	11.87443	11.89800	11.92162
8	14.41571	14.44848	14.48132	14.51424	14.54723	14.58029	14.61344	14.64665
9	17.41975	17.46450	17.50937	17.55436	17.59946	17.64468	17.69002	17.73548
10	20.81432	20.87412	20.93410	20.99426	21.05459	21.11510	21.17580	21.23667
11	24.65018	24.72869	24.80747	24.88650	24.96580	25.04536	25.12518	25.20526
12	28.98470	29.08629	29.18824	29.29058	29.39328	29.49636	29.59982	29.70366
13	33.88271	34.01255	34.14290	34.27379	34.40520	34.53713	34.66960	34.80260
14	39.41746	39.58168	39.74663	39.91229	40.07868	40.24580	40.41366	40.58225
15	45.67173	45.87759	46.08443	46.29226	46.50107	46.71087	46.92167	47.13348
16	52.73906	52.99512	53.25249	53.51119	53.77121	54.03256	54.29526	54.55930
17	60.72514	61.04148	61.35957	61.67941	62.00101	62.32438	62.64953	62.97647
18	69.74941	70.13790	70.52867	70.92175	71.31714	71.71486	72.11491	72.51732
19	79.94683	80.42139	80.89893	81.37946	81.86300	82.34958	82.83920	83.33189
20	91.46992	92.04688	92.62769	93.21236	93.80092	94.39339	94.98981	95.59019
21	104.49101	105.18950	105.89292	106.60129	107.31464	108.03302	108.75646	109.48498
22	119.20484	120.04723	120.89589	121.75086	122.61217	123.47989	124.35406	125.23473
23	135.83147	136.84390	137.86425	138.89259	139.92898	140.97348	142.02615	143.08707
24	154.61956	155.83253	157.05547	158.28847	159.53161	160.78497	162.04863	163.32269
25	175.85010	177.29917	178.76074	180.23490	181.72178	183.22148	184.73410	186.25977
26	199.84061	201.56721	203.30939	205.06729	206.84105	208.63082	210.43674	212.25895
27	226.94989	229.00223	231.07392	233.16514	235.27607	237.40690	239.55782	241.72902
28	257.58338	260.01753	262.47561	264.95786	267.46451	269.99582	272.55201	275.13334
29	292.19922	295.08031	297.99091	300.93132	303.90183	306.90277	309.93443	312.99714
30	331.31511	334.71879	338.15872	341.63528	345.14887	348.69988	352.28871	355.91576
31	375.51608	379.53010	383.58851	387.69182	391.84052	396.03512	400.27611	404.56401
32	425.46317	430.18927	434.96961	439.80480	444.69547	449.64227	454.64583	459.70681
33	481.90338	487.45947	493.08163	498.77063	504.52728	510.35237	516.24673	522.21117
34	545.68082	552.20343	558.80632	565.49047	572.25688	579.10656	586.04054	593.05986
35	617.74933	625.39648	633.14095	640.98396	648.92678	656.97068	665.11693	673.36685
36	699.18674	708.14122	717.21341	726.40486	735.71712	745.15179	754.71048	764.39483
37	791.21101	801.68415	812.29937	823.05859	833.96378	845.01690	856.21998	867.57504
38	895.19845	907.43443	919.84159	932.42230	945.17900	958.11414	971.23024	984.52980
39	1012.70424	1026.98513	1041.47184	1056.16733	1071.07462	1086.19677	1101.53686	1117.09803
40	1145.48579	1162.13719	1179.03565	1196.18484	1213.58848	1231.25034	1249.17426	1267.36412
41	1295.52895	1314.92659	1334.62032	1354.61464	1374.91415	1395.52351	1416.44744	1437.69073
42	1465.07771	1487.65501	1510.58658	1533.87797	1557.53482	1581.56288	1605.96795	1630.75594
43	1656.66781	1682.92449	1709.60442	1736.71442	1764.26142	1792.25246	1820.69468	1849.59536
44	1873.16463	1903.67664	1934.69360	1966.22386	1998.27593	2030.85841	2063.98008	2097.64984
45	2117.80603	2153.23694	2189.26946	2225.91380	2263.18035	2301.07965	2339.62243	2378.81960
46	2394.25082	2435.36486	2477.19476	2519.75297	2563.05215	2607.10520	2651.92521	2697.52551
47	2706.63342	2754.31047	2802.83827	2852.23198	2902.50704	2953.67914	3005.76426	3058.77867
48	3059.62577	3114.87849	3171.14108	3228.43199	3286.76997	3346.17412	3406.66391	3468.25912
49	3458.50712	3522.50063	3587.69157	3654.10230	3721.75560	3790.67469	3860.88321	3932.40521
50	3909.24304	3983.31746	4058.81016	4135.74825	4214.15934	4294.07159	4375.51367	4458.51481

ANNUAL DEPOSITS

NUMBER OF ANNUAL DEPOSITS	EFFECTIVE ANNUAL YIELD							
	13.40%	13.45%	13.50%	13.55%	13.60%	13.65%	13.70%	13.75%
1	1.13400	1.13450	1.13500	1.13550	1.13600	1.13650	1.13700	1.13750
2	2.41996	2.42159	2.42323	2.42486	2.42650	2.42813	2.42977	2.43141
3	3.87823	3.88179	3.88536	3.88893	3.89250	3.89607	3.89965	3.90322
4	5.53191	5.53840	5.54488	5.55138	5.55788	5.56439	5.57090	5.57742
5	7.40719	7.41781	7.42844	7.43909	7.44975	7.46042	7.47111	7.48181
6	9.53375	9.55001	9.56628	9.58259	9.59892	9.61527	9.63165	9.64806
7	11.94528	11.96898	11.99273	12.01653	12.04037	12.06426	12.08819	12.11217
8	14.67994	14.71331	14.74675	14.78027	14.81386	14.84753	14.88127	14.91509
9	17.78105	17.82675	17.87256	17.91849	17.96455	18.01072	18.05701	18.10342
10	21.29772	21.35895	21.42036	21.48195	21.54372	21.60568	21.66782	21.73014
11	25.28561	25.36622	25.44711	25.52825	25.60967	25.69135	25.77331	25.85553
12	29.80788	29.91248	30.01746	30.12283	30.22858	30.33472	30.44125	30.54817
13	34.93614	35.07021	35.20482	35.33998	35.47567	35.61191	35.74870	35.88604
14	40.75158	40.92165	41.09247	41.26404	41.43636	41.60944	41.78328	41.95787
15	47.34629	47.56012	47.77496	47.99082	48.20771	48.42563	48.64459	48.86458
16	54.82470	55.09145	55.35958	55.62908	55.89996	56.17223	56.44589	56.72096
17	63.30520	63.63575	63.96812	64.30232	64.63835	64.97624	65.31598	65.65759
18	72.92210	73.32926	73.73882	74.15078	74.56517	74.98199	75.40127	75.82301
19	83.82766	84.32655	84.82856	85.33371	85.84203	86.35353	86.86824	87.38618
20	96.19457	96.80297	97.41541	98.03193	98.65255	99.27729	99.90619	100.53928
21	110.21864	110.95747	111.70149	112.45075	113.20529	113.96514	114.73034	115.50093
22	126.12194	127.01575	127.91619	128.82333	129.73721	130.65788	131.58540	132.51981
23	144.15628	145.23386	146.31988	147.41439	148.51747	149.62919	150.74960	151.87878
24	164.60722	165.90232	167.20806	168.52454	169.85185	171.19007	172.53929	173.89961
25	187.79859	189.35068	190.91615	192.49512	194.08770	195.69401	197.31418	198.94831
26	214.09760	215.95285	217.82483	219.71371	221.61963	223.54275	225.48322	227.44120
27	243.92068	246.13300	248.36618	250.62042	252.89590	255.19283	257.51142	259.85187
28	277.74005	280.37239	283.03062	285.71498	288.42574	291.16315	293.92749	296.71900
29	316.09122	319.21698	322.37475	325.56486	328.78764	332.04343	335.33255	338.65536
30	359.58144	363.28616	367.03034	370.81440	374.63876	378.50385	382.41011	386.35797
31	408.89915	413.28265	417.71444	422.19525	426.72563	431.30613	435.93730	440.61969
32	464.82587	470.00367	475.24089	480.53821	485.89632	491.31592	496.79770	502.34240
33	528.24653	534.35366	540.53341	546.78664	553.11422	559.51704	565.99599	572.55198
34	600.16557	607.35873	614.64042	622.01172	629.47375	637.02761	644.67444	652.41538
35	681.72176	690.18298	698.75188	707.42981	716.21818	725.11838	734.13184	743.25999
36	774.20647	784.14709	794.21838	804.42205	814.75985	825.23354	835.84490	846.59574
37	879.08414	890.74937	902.57286	914.55674	926.70319	939.01442	951.49265	964.14016
38	998.01541	1011.68966	1025.55520	1039.61468	1053.87083	1068.32639	1082.98415	1097.84693
39	1132.88348	1148.89642	1165.14015	1181.61797	1198.33326	1215.28944	1232.48997	1249.93838
40	1285.82386	1304.55749	1323.56907	1342.86270	1362.44258	1382.31295	1402.47810	1422.94241
41	1459.25826	1481.15498	1503.38589	1525.95610	1548.87078	1572.13517	1595.75460	1619.73449
42	1655.93287	1681.50482	1707.47799	1733.85865	1760.65320	1787.86812	1815.50998	1843.58548
43	1878.96187	1908.80172	1939.12251	1969.93200	2001.23804	2033.04861	2065.37185	2098.21599
44	2131.87677	2166.67005	2202.03905	2237.99328	2274.54241	2311.69625	2349.46479	2387.85818
45	2418.68225	2459.22167	2500.44933	2542.37687	2585.01618	2628.37929	2672.47847	2717.32618
46	2743.91967	2791.12149	2839.14498	2888.00444	2937.71438	2988.28956	3039.74502	3092.09603
47	3112.73891	3167.66183	3223.56456	3280.46454	3338.37953	3397.32759	3457.32709	3518.39674
48	3530.97992	3594.84684	3659.88077	3726.10299	3793.53515	3862.19930	3932.11790	4003.31379
49	4005.26523	4079.48824	4155.09968	4232.12544	4310.59193	4390.52601	4471.95505	4554.90694
50	4543.10477	4629.31391	4717.17313	4806.71394	4897.96843	4990.96931	5085.74989	5182.34414

137

NUMBER OF ANNUAL DEPOSITS	EFFECTIVE ANNUAL YIELD							
	13.80%	13.85%	13.90%	13.95%	14.00%	14.05%	14.10%	14.15%
1	1.13800	1.13850	1.13900	1.13950	1.14000	1.14050	1.14100	1.14150
2	2.43304	2.43468	2.43632	2.43796	2.43960	2.44124	2.44288	2.44452
3	3.90680	3.91039	3.91397	3.91756	3.92114	3.92473	3.92833	3.93192
4	5.58394	5.59047	5.59701	5.60355	5.61010	5.61666	5.62322	5.62979
5	7.49253	7.50325	7.51400	7.52475	7.53552	7.54630	7.55710	7.56790
6	9.66450	9.68096	9.69744	9.71395	9.73049	9.74706	9.76365	9.78026
7	12.13620	12.16027	12.18439	12.20855	12.23276	12.25702	12.28132	12.30567
8	14.94899	14.98297	15.01702	15.05114	15.08535	15.11963	15.15399	15.18842
9	18.14995	18.19661	18.24338	18.29028	18.33730	18.38444	18.43170	18.47908
10	21.79265	21.85534	21.91821	21.98127	22.04452	22.10795	22.17157	22.23537
11	25.93803	26.02080	26.10384	26.18716	26.27075	26.35462	26.43876	26.52318
12	30.65548	30.76318	30.87128	30.97977	31.08865	31.19794	31.30762	31.41771
13	36.02394	36.16238	36.30138	36.44094	36.58107	36.72175	36.86300	37.00482
14	42.13324	42.30937	42.48628	42.66396	42.84241	43.02166	43.20168	43.38250
15	49.08563	49.30772	49.53087	49.75508	49.98035	50.20670	50.43412	50.66262
16	56.99744	57.27534	57.55466	57.83541	58.11760	58.40124	58.68633	58.97288
17	66.00109	66.34647	66.69376	67.04295	67.39407	67.74711	68.10210	68.45904
18	76.24724	76.67396	77.10319	77.53494	77.96923	78.40608	78.84550	79.28750
19	87.90736	88.43180	88.95953	89.49057	90.02493	90.56264	91.10371	91.64818
20	101.17657	101.81811	102.46391	103.11400	103.76842	104.42719	105.09034	105.75790
21	116.27694	117.05841	117.84539	118.63790	119.43600	120.23971	121.04907	121.86414
22	133.46116	134.40950	135.36490	136.32739	137.29704	138.27389	139.25799	140.24942
23	153.01680	154.16372	155.31962	156.48456	157.65862	158.84187	160.03437	161.23621
24	175.27112	176.65390	178.04804	179.45366	180.87083	182.29965	183.74022	185.19263
25	200.59653	202.25896	203.93572	205.62694	207.33274	209.05325	210.78859	212.53889
26	229.41685	231.41033	233.42179	235.45140	237.49933	239.56573	241.65078	243.75464
27	262.21438	264.59916	267.00642	269.43637	271.88923	274.36522	276.86454	279.38742
28	299.53796	302.38464	305.25931	308.16225	311.09373	314.05403	317.04344	320.06224
29	342.01220	345.40341	348.82935	352.29038	355.78685	359.31912	362.88756	366.49255
30	390.34788	394.38028	398.45563	402.57439	406.73701	410.94396	415.19571	419.49275
31	445.35389	450.14045	454.97997	459.87301	464.82019	469.82208	474.87931	479.99247
32	507.95072	513.62341	519.36118	525.16480	531.03501	536.97259	542.97829	549.05290
33	579.18592	585.89875	592.69139	599.56479	606.51991	613.55773	620.67923	627.88539
34	660.25158	668.18422	676.21449	684.34358	692.57270	700.90309	709.33600	717.87267
35	752.50430	761.86624	771.34730	780.94901	790.67288	800.52048	810.49337	820.59316
36	857.48789	868.52321	879.70358	891.03089	902.50708	914.13411	925.91394	937.84859
37	976.95922	989.95218	1003.12137	1016.46920	1029.99808	1043.71045	1057.60881	1071.69566
38	1112.91760	1128.19905	1143.69425	1159.40615	1175.33781	1191.49227	1207.87265	1224.48210
39	1267.63822	1285.59312	1303.80675	1322.28281	1341.02510	1360.03743	1379.32369	1398.88782
40	1443.71030	1464.78627	1486.17488	1507.88077	1529.90861	1552.26319	1574.94933	1597.97194
41	1644.08032	1668.79767	1693.89219	1719.36963	1745.23582	1771.49667	1798.15819	1825.22647
42	1872.10141	1901.06465	1930.48221	1960.36120	1990.70883	2021.53245	2052.83949	2084.63752
43	2131.58940	2165.50060	2199.95823	2234.97108	2270.54807	2306.69826	2343.43086	2380.75523
44	2426.88674	2466.56093	2506.89143	2547.88905	2589.56480	2631.92986	2674.99561	2718.77359
45	2762.93511	2809.31812	2856.48834	2904.45907	2953.24387	3002.85651	3053.31099	3104.62156
46	3145.35815	3199.54718	3254.67922	3310.77061	3367.83801	3425.89835	3484.96884	3545.06701
47	3580.55557	3643.82297	3708.21863	3773.76261	3840.47534	3908.37757	3977.49045	4047.83549
48	4075.81024	4149.63095	4224.80002	4301.34200	4379.28188	4458.64512	4539.45760	4621.74571
49	4639.41006	4725.49333	4813.18622	4902.51871	4993.52135	5086.22526	5180.66212	5276.86423
50	5280.78665	5381.11266	5483.35810	5587.55956	5693.75433	5801.98040	5912.27648	6024.68201

ANNUAL DEPOSITS

NUMBER OF ANNUAL DEPOSITS	EFFECTIVE ANNUAL YIELD							
	14.20%	14.25%	14.30%	14.35%	14.40%	14.45%	14.50%	14.55%
1	1.14200	1.14250	1.14300	1.14350	1.14400	1.14450	1.14500	1.14550
2	2.44616	2.44781	2.44945	2.45109	2.45274	2.45438	2.45603	2.45767
3	3.93552	3.93912	3.94272	3.94632	3.94993	3.95354	3.95715	3.96076
4	5.63636	5.64294	5.64953	5.65612	5.66272	5.66932	5.67594	5.68255
5	7.57873	7.58956	7.60041	7.61127	7.62215	7.63304	7.64395	7.65486
6	9.79691	9.81358	9.83027	9.84699	9.86374	9.88052	9.89732	9.91415
7	12.33007	12.35451	12.37900	12.40354	12.42812	12.45275	12.47743	12.50215
8	15.22294	15.25753	15.29220	15.32694	15.36177	15.39667	15.43166	15.46672
9	18.52659	18.57422	18.62198	18.66986	18.71786	18.76599	18.81425	18.86263
10	22.29937	22.36355	22.42792	22.49249	22.55724	22.62218	22.68731	22.75264
11	26.60788	26.69286	26.77812	26.86366	26.94948	27.03558	27.12197	27.20865
12	31.52820	31.63909	31.75039	31.86209	31.97420	32.08673	32.19966	32.31300
13	37.14720	37.29016	37.43369	37.57780	37.72249	37.86776	38.01361	38.16005
14	43.56410	43.74651	43.92971	44.11372	44.29853	44.48415	44.67058	44.85783
15	50.89221	51.12289	51.35466	51.58753	51.82152	52.05661	52.29282	52.53015
16	59.26090	59.55040	59.84138	60.13385	60.42781	60.72329	61.02027	61.31878
17	68.81795	69.17883	69.54169	69.90655	70.27342	70.64230	71.01321	71.38617
18	79.73210	80.17931	80.62915	81.08164	81.53679	81.99462	82.45513	82.91835
19	92.19606	92.74736	93.30212	93.86036	94.42209	94.98734	95.55612	96.12847
20	106.42990	107.10636	107.78733	108.47282	109.16287	109.85751	110.55676	111.26067
21	122.68494	123.51152	124.34392	125.18217	126.02632	126.87642	127.73249	128.59459
22	141.24820	142.25441	143.26810	144.28931	145.31811	146.35456	147.39871	148.45061
23	162.44745	163.66816	164.89843	166.13833	167.38792	168.64729	169.91652	171.19567
24	186.65699	188.13338	189.62191	191.12268	192.63578	194.16133	195.69941	197.25014
25	214.30428	216.08488	217.88084	219.69228	221.51934	223.36214	225.22083	227.09554
26	245.87748	248.01948	250.18080	252.36162	254.56212	256.78247	259.02285	261.28344
27	281.93409	284.50476	287.09966	289.71902	292.36307	295.03203	297.72616	300.44568
28	323.11073	326.18918	329.29791	332.43720	335.60735	338.80866	342.04145	345.30602
29	370.13445	373.81364	377.53051	381.28543	385.07880	388.91102	392.78246	396.69355
30	423.83554	428.22459	432.66037	437.14339	441.67415	446.25316	450.88092	455.55796
31	485.16219	490.38909	495.67381	501.01697	506.41923	511.88124	517.40365	522.98714
32	555.19722	561.41204	567.69816	574.05641	580.48760	586.99258	593.57218	600.22727
33	635.17723	642.55575	650.02200	657.57700	665.22181	672.95751	680.78515	688.70584
34	726.51439	735.26245	744.11814	753.08280	762.15776	771.34437	780.64400	790.05804
35	830.82144	841.17985	851.67004	862.29368	873.05247	883.94813	894.98238	906.15699
36	949.94008	962.19047	974.60185	987.17632	999.91603	1012.82313	1025.89982	1039.14833
37	1085.97357	1100.44512	1115.11292	1129.97963	1145.04794	1160.32057	1175.80030	1191.48991
38	1241.32382	1258.40104	1275.71706	1293.27520	1311.07884	1329.13139	1347.43634	1365.99719
39	1418.73380	1438.86569	1459.28760	1480.00369	1501.01819	1522.33538	1543.95961	1565.89528
40	1621.33600	1645.04656	1669.10873	1693.52772	1718.30881	1743.45734	1768.97875	1794.87855
41	1852.70771	1880.60819	1908.93428	1937.69245	1966.88928	1996.53143	2026.62567	2057.17888
42	2116.93421	2149.73736	2183.05488	2216.89482	2251.26534	2286.17472	2321.63139	2357.64390
43	2418.68087	2457.21743	2496.37473	2536.16273	2576.59154	2617.67147	2659.41295	2701.82659
44	2763.27555	2808.51341	2854.49931	2901.24558	2948.76473	2997.06950	3046.17282	3096.08786
45	3156.80268	3209.86907	3263.83572	3318.71782	3374.53085	3431.29054	3489.01288	3547.71414
46	3606.21066	3668.41792	3731.70722	3796.09732	3861.60729	3928.25652	3996.06475	4065.05205
47	4119.43457	4192.30997	4266.48436	4341.98079	4418.82274	4497.03409	4576.63914	4657.66262
48	4705.53628	4790.85664	4877.73462	4966.19853	5056.27721	5148.00002	5241.39682	5336.49803
49	5374.86443	5474.69621	5576.39367	5679.99152	5785.52513	5893.03052	6002.54435	6114.10400
50	6139.23718	6255.98292	6374.96096	6496.21381	6619.78475	6745.71793	6874.05829	7004.85163

ANNUAL DEPOSITS

NUMBER OF ANNUAL DEPOSITS	EFFECTIVE ANNUAL YIELD							
	14.60%	14.65%	14.70%	14.75%	14.80%	14.85%	14.90%	14.95%
1	1.14600	1.14650	1.14700	1.14750	1.14800	1.14850	1.14900	1.14950
2	2.45932	2.46096	2.46261	2.46426	2.46590	2.46755	2.46920	2.47085
3	3.96438	3.96799	3.97161	3.97523	3.97886	3.98248	3.98611	3.98974
4	5.68918	5.69580	5.70244	5.70908	5.71573	5.72238	5.72904	5.73571
5	7.66579	7.67674	7.68770	7.69867	7.70966	7.72066	7.73167	7.74270
6	9.93100	9.94788	9.96479	9.98172	9.99869	10.01567	10.03269	10.04973
7	12.52693	12.55175	12.57661	12.60153	12.62649	12.65150	12.67656	12.70167
8	15.50186	15.53708	15.57238	15.60775	15.64321	15.67875	15.71437	15.75006
9	18.91113	18.95976	19.00852	19.05740	19.10641	19.15554	19.20481	19.25420
10	22.81815	22.88386	22.94977	23.01586	23.08216	23.14864	23.21532	23.28220
11	27.29560	27.38285	27.47038	27.55820	27.64631	27.73472	27.82341	27.91239
12	32.42676	32.54094	32.65553	32.77054	32.88597	33.00182	33.11809	33.23479
13	38.30707	38.45469	38.60289	38.75169	38.90109	39.05109	39.20169	39.35289
14	45.04590	45.23480	45.42452	45.61507	45.80645	45.99868	46.19174	46.38565
15	52.76860	53.00819	53.24892	53.49079	53.73381	53.97798	54.22331	54.46981
16	61.61882	61.92039	62.22351	62.52818	62.83441	63.14221	63.45159	63.76254
17	71.76117	72.13823	72.51737	72.89859	73.28191	73.66733	74.05487	74.44454
18	83.38430	83.85298	84.32442	84.79863	85.27563	85.75543	86.23805	86.72350
19	96.70441	97.28395	97.86711	98.45393	99.04442	99.63861	100.23652	100.83817
20	111.96925	112.68254	113.40058	114.12339	114.85100	115.58344	116.32076	117.06297
21	129.46276	130.33704	131.21746	132.10408	132.99694	133.89608	134.80155	135.71339
22	149.51032	150.57791	151.65343	152.73694	153.82849	154.92815	156.03598	157.15204
23	172.48483	173.78408	175.09348	176.41314	177.74311	179.08348	180.43434	181.79577
24	198.81362	200.38994	201.97923	203.58157	205.19709	206.82588	208.46806	210.12374
25	228.98640	230.89357	232.81717	234.75735	236.71426	238.68803	240.67880	242.68673
26	263.56442	265.86598	268.18830	270.53156	272.89597	275.28170	277.68894	280.11790
27	303.19082	305.96184	308.75898	311.58247	314.43257	317.30953	320.21360	323.14503
28	348.60268	351.93175	355.29355	358.68838	362.11659	365.57849	369.07442	372.60471
29	400.64468	404.63626	408.66870	412.74242	416.85785	421.01540	425.21551	429.45861
30	460.28480	465.06197	469.89000	474.76943	479.70081	484.68469	489.72162	494.81218
31	528.63238	534.34004	540.11083	545.94542	551.84453	557.80886	563.83914	569.93610
32	606.95871	613.76736	620.65412	627.61987	634.66552	641.79198	649.00018	656.29104
33	696.72068	704.83078	713.03727	721.34130	729.74401	738.24659	746.85020	755.55605
34	799.58790	809.23499	819.00075	828.88664	838.89413	849.02471	859.27988	869.66118
35	917.47373	928.93441	940.54086	952.29492	964.19846	976.25338	988.46159	1000.82503
36	1052.57090	1066.16981	1079.94737	1093.90592	1108.04783	1122.37550	1136.89136	1151.59787
37	1207.39225	1223.51018	1239.84663	1256.40454	1273.18691	1290.19676	1307.43717	1324.91126
38	1384.81751	1403.90092	1423.25109	1442.87171	1462.76657	1482.93948	1503.39431	1524.13499
39	1588.14687	1610.71891	1633.61600	1656.84279	1680.40403	1704.30450	1728.54907	1753.14267
40	1821.16232	1847.83573	1874.90455	1902.37460	1930.25182	1958.54221	1987.25188	2016.38700
41	2088.19801	2119.69017	2151.66252	2184.12236	2217.07709	2250.53423	2284.50141	2318.98635
42	2394.22092	2431.37127	2469.10391	2507.42790	2546.35250	2585.88707	2626.04112	2666.82431
43	2744.92318	2788.71367	2833.20918	2878.42102	2924.36067	2971.03980	3018.47024	3066.66405
44	3146.82796	3198.40672	3250.83793	3304.13562	3358.31405	3413.38771	3469.37131	3526.27983
45	3607.41084	3668.11980	3729.85810	3792.64313	3856.49253	3921.42428	3987.45663	4054.60816
46	4135.23883	4206.64585	4279.29425	4353.20549	4428.40142	4504.90429	4582.73667	4661.92158
47	4740.12970	4824.06597	4909.49570	4996.45080	5084.95284	5175.03107	5266.71344	5360.02836
48	5433.33463	5531.93814	5632.34063	5734.57479	5838.67386	5944.67169	6052.60274	6162.50209
49	6227.74749	6343.51357	6461.44171	6581.57207	6703.94559	6828.60393	6955.58955	7084.94566
50	7138.14462	7273.98481	7412.42064	7553.50145	7697.27753	7843.80012	7993.12139	8145.29453

ANNUAL DEPOSITS

EFFECTIVE ANNUAL YIELD

NUMBER OF ANNUAL DEPOSITS	15.00%	15.05%	15.10%	15.15%	15.20%	15.25%	15.30%	15.35%
1	1.15000	1.15050	1.15100	1.15150	1.15200	1.15250	1.15300	1.15350
2	2.47250	2.47415	2.47580	2.47745	2.47910	2.48076	2.48241	2.48406
3	3.99337	3.99701	4.00065	4.00429	4.00793	4.01157	4.01522	4.01887
4	5.74238	5.74906	5.75574	5.76244	5.76913	5.77584	5.78255	5.78926
5	7.75374	7.76479	7.77586	7.78694	7.79804	7.80915	7.82028	7.83141
6	10.06680	10.08389	10.10102	10.11817	10.13534	10.15255	10.16978	10.18704
7	12.72682	12.75202	12.77727	12.80257	12.82792	12.85331	12.87875	12.90425
8	15.78584	15.82170	15.85764	15.89366	15.92976	15.96594	16.00220	16.03855
9	19.30372	19.35337	19.40314	19.45305	19.50308	19.55325	19.60354	19.65396
10	23.34928	23.41655	23.48402	23.55168	23.61955	23.68762	23.75588	23.82435
11	28.00167	28.09124	28.18110	28.27126	28.36172	28.45248	28.54353	28.63488
12	33.35192	33.46947	33.58745	33.70586	33.82470	33.94398	34.06369	34.18384
13	39.50471	39.65712	39.81015	39.96380	40.11806	40.27294	40.42844	40.58456
14	46.58041	46.77602	46.97249	47.16981	47.36800	47.56706	47.76699	47.96779
15	54.71747	54.96631	55.21633	55.46754	55.71994	55.97354	56.22834	56.48434
16	64.07509	64.38924	64.70500	65.02237	65.34137	65.66200	65.98427	66.30819
17	74.83636	75.23032	75.62646	76.02476	76.42526	76.82796	77.23287	77.64000
18	87.21181	87.70299	88.19705	88.69401	89.19390	89.69672	90.20249	90.71124
19	101.44358	102.05279	102.66580	103.28266	103.90337	104.52797	105.15647	105.78891
20	117.81012	118.56223	119.31934	120.08148	120.84868	121.62098	122.39842	123.18101
21	136.63164	137.55635	138.48756	139.42532	140.36968	141.32068	142.27837	143.24280
22	158.27638	159.40908	160.55018	161.69976	162.85788	164.02459	165.19996	166.38407
23	183.16784	184.55064	185.94426	187.34878	188.76427	190.19084	191.62856	193.07752
24	211.79302	213.47602	215.17284	216.88362	218.60844	220.34744	222.10073	223.86842
25	244.71197	246.75466	248.81494	250.89298	252.98893	255.10293	257.23514	259.38572
26	282.56877	285.04173	287.53700	290.05477	292.59524	295.15862	297.74512	300.35493
27	326.10408	329.09101	332.10609	335.14957	338.22172	341.32281	344.45312	347.61291
28	376.16969	379.76971	383.40511	387.07623	390.78342	394.52704	398.30745	402.12499
29	433.74515	438.07555	442.45028	446.86978	451.33640	455.84492	460.40149	465.00468
30	499.95692	505.15642	510.41127	515.72205	521.08935	526.51377	531.99591	537.53640
31	576.10046	582.33296	588.63437	595.00544	601.44693	607.95961	614.54429	621.20173
32	663.66552	671.12458	678.66916	686.30026	694.01886	701.82596	709.72256	717.70970
33	764.36535	773.27932	782.29920	791.42625	800.66172	810.00691	819.46311	829.03164
34	880.17016	890.80836	901.57738	912.47883	923.51431	934.68547	945.99397	957.44150
35	1013.34568	1026.02552	1038.86657	1051.87087	1065.04048	1078.37750	1091.88405	1105.56227
36	1166.49753	1181.59286	1196.88642	1212.38080	1228.07863	1243.98257	1260.09531	1276.41957
37	1342.62216	1360.57309	1378.76727	1397.20800	1415.89859	1434.84241	1454.04289	1473.50348
38	1545.16549	1566.48984	1588.11213	1610.03651	1632.26717	1654.80838	1677.66445	1700.83976
39	1778.09031	1803.39706	1829.06806	1855.10854	1881.52378	1908.31916	1935.50011	1963.07217
40	2045.95385	2075.95881	2106.40834	2137.30898	2168.66740	2200.49033	2232.78463	2265.55724
41	2353.99693	2389.54112	2425.62700	2462.26279	2499.45684	2537.21761	2575.55368	2614.47378
42	2708.24647	2750.31755	2793.04767	2836.44711	2880.52628	2925.29579	2970.76639	3016.94900
43	3115.63344	3165.39084	3215.94887	3267.32034	3319.51828	3372.55590	3426.44665	3481.20418
44	3584.12846	3642.93267	3702.70815	3763.47087	3825.23705	3888.02318	3951.84599	4016.72252
45	4122.89773	4192.34453	4262.96808	4334.78821	4407.82509	4482.09921	4557.63143	4634.44292
46	4742.48239	4824.44289	4907.82726	4992.66013	5078.96650	5166.77184	5256.10203	5346.98341
47	5455.00475	5551.67204	5650.06018	5750.19963	5852.12141	5955.85704	6061.43864	6168.89887
48	6274.40546	6388.34918	6504.37027	6622.50638	6742.79586	6865.27774	6989.99176	7116.97834
49	7216.71628	7350.94623	7487.68118	7626.96760	7768.85283	7913.38510	8060.61350	8210.58802
50	8300.37372	8458.41414	8619.47203	8783.60469	8950.87046	9121.32883	9295.04036	9472.06678

ANNUAL DEPOSITS

EFFECTIVE ANNUAL YIELD

NUMBER OF ANNUAL DEPOSITS	15.40%	15.45%	15.50%	15.55%	15.60%	15.65%	15.70%	15.75%
1	1.15400	1.15450	1.15500	1.15550	1.15600	1.15650	1.15700	1.15750
2	2.48572	2.48737	2.48903	2.49068	2.49234	2.49399	2.49565	2.49731
3	4.02252	4.02617	4.02982	4.03348	4.03714	4.04080	4.04447	4.04813
4	5.79598	5.80271	5.80945	5.81619	5.82293	5.82969	5.83645	5.84321
5	7.84257	7.85373	7.86491	7.87610	7.88731	7.89853	7.90977	7.92102
6	10.20432	10.22163	10.23897	10.25634	10.27373	10.29115	10.30860	10.32608
7	12.92979	12.95537	12.98101	13.00670	13.03244	13.05822	13.08405	13.10994
8	16.07497	16.11148	16.14807	16.18474	16.22149	16.25833	16.29525	16.33225
9	19.70452	19.75520	19.80602	19.85697	19.90805	19.95926	20.01060	20.06208
10	23.89301	23.96188	24.03095	24.10023	24.16970	24.23938	24.30927	24.37936
11	28.72654	28.81849	28.91075	29.00331	29.09618	29.18935	29.28282	29.37661
12	34.30443	34.42545	34.54692	34.66883	34.79118	34.91398	35.03723	35.16092
13	40.74131	40.89868	41.05669	41.21533	41.37461	41.53452	41.69507	41.85627
14	48.16947	48.37203	48.57548	48.77981	48.98504	49.19117	49.39820	49.60613
15	56.74157	57.00001	57.25968	57.52057	57.78271	58.04609	58.31072	58.57660
16	66.63377	66.96101	67.28993	67.62052	67.95281	68.28680	68.62250	68.95991
17	78.04937	78.46099	78.87486	79.29102	79.70945	80.13019	80.55323	80.97860
18	91.22297	91.73771	92.25547	92.77627	93.30013	93.82706	94.35709	94.89023
19	106.42531	107.06568	107.71007	108.35848	109.01095	109.66750	110.32815	110.99294
20	123.96881	124.76183	125.56013	126.36372	127.17265	127.98696	128.80667	129.63183
21	144.21400	145.19203	146.17695	147.16878	148.16759	149.17342	150.18632	151.20634
22	167.57696	168.77870	169.98937	171.20903	172.43773	173.67556	174.92257	176.17884
23	194.53781	196.00951	197.49272	198.98753	200.49402	202.01228	203.54241	205.08450
24	225.65063	227.44748	229.25910	231.08559	232.92709	234.78371	236.65557	238.54281
25	261.55483	263.74262	265.94926	268.17490	270.41971	272.68386	274.96750	277.27081
26	302.98827	305.64536	308.32639	311.03160	313.76119	316.51538	319.29440	322.09846
27	350.80247	354.02206	357.27198	360.55251	363.86393	367.20654	370.58062	373.98647
28	405.98005	409.87297	413.80414	417.77392	421.78270	425.83086	429.91877	434.04683
29	469.65497	474.35285	479.09878	483.89327	488.73681	493.62989	498.57302	503.56671
30	543.13584	548.79486	554.51409	560.29417	566.13575	572.03946	578.00598	584.03597
31	627.93276	634.73817	641.61878	648.57542	655.60892	662.72014	669.90992	677.17913
32	725.78840	733.95971	742.22469	750.58439	759.03992	767.59234	776.24278	784.99235
33	838.71382	848.51099	858.42451	868.45577	878.60614	888.87705	899.26990	909.78614
34	969.02974	980.76044	992.63531	1004.65614	1016.82470	1029.14280	1041.61227	1054.23496
35	1119.41432	1133.44242	1147.64879	1162.03567	1176.60536	1191.36015	1206.30240	1221.43446
36	1292.95813	1309.71378	1326.68935	1343.88772	1361.31179	1378.96451	1396.84887	1414.96789
37	1493.22768	1513.21906	1533.48120	1554.01776	1574.83243	1595.92896	1617.31115	1638.98283
38	1724.33874	1748.16590	1772.32578	1796.82302	1821.66229	1846.84834	1872.38600	1898.28013
39	1991.04091	2019.41203	2048.19128	2077.38450	2106.99761	2137.03661	2167.50760	2198.41675
40	2298.81521	2332.56569	2366.81593	2401.57329	2436.84523	2472.63934	2508.96329	2545.82489
41	2653.98675	2694.10159	2734.82740	2776.17343	2818.14909	2860.76390	2904.02753	2947.94981
42	3063.85471	3111.49478	3159.88064	3209.02390	3258.93635	3309.62995	3361.11685	3413.40940
43	3536.84234	3593.37523	3650.81714	3709.18262	3768.48642	3828.74353	3889.96920	3952.17888
44	4082.67006	4149.70620	4217.84880	4287.11602	4357.52630	4429.09839	4501.85136	4575.80456
45	4712.55525	4791.99031	4872.77036	4954.91806	5038.45640	5123.40879	5209.79902	5297.65127
46	5439.44276	5533.50731	5629.20477	5726.56331	5825.61160	5926.37877	6028.89447	6133.18885
47	6278.27094	6389.58869	6502.88651	6618.19941	6735.56301	6855.01355	6976.58790	7100.32359
48	7246.27867	7377.93464	7511.98892	7648.48492	7787.46684	7928.97967	8073.06920	8219.78206
49	8363.35959	8518.98005	8677.50220	8838.97982	9003.46766	9171.02149	9341.69807	9515.55523
50	9652.47096	9836.31696	10023.67004	10214.59668	10409.16462	10607.44285	10809.50167	11015.41268

ANNUAL DEPOSITS

EFFECTIVE ANNUAL YIELD

NUMBER OF ANNUAL DEPOSITS	15.80%	15.85%	15.90%	15.95%	16.00%	16.05%	16.10%	16.15%
1	1.15800	1.15850	1.15900	1.15950	1.16000	1.16050	1.16100	1.16150
2	2.49896	2.50062	2.50228	2.50394	2.50560	2.50726	2.50892	2.51058
3	4.05180	4.05547	4.05914	4.06282	4.06650	4.07018	4.07386	4.07754
4	5.84998	5.85676	5.86355	5.87034	5.87714	5.88394	5.89075	5.89756
5	7.93228	7.94356	7.95485	7.96616	7.97748	7.98881	8.00016	8.01152
6	10.34358	10.36111	10.37867	10.39626	10.41387	10.43151	10.44918	10.46688
7	13.13587	13.16185	13.18788	13.21396	13.24009	13.26627	13.29250	13.31878
8	16.36934	16.40650	16.44376	16.48109	16.51851	16.55601	16.59360	16.63127
9	20.11369	20.16544	20.21731	20.26932	20.32147	20.37375	20.42616	20.47872
10	24.44965	24.52016	24.59086	24.66178	24.73290	24.80424	24.87578	24.94753
11	29.47070	29.56510	29.65981	29.75483	29.85017	29.94582	30.04178	30.13805
12	35.28507	35.40967	35.53472	35.66023	35.78620	35.91262	36.03950	36.16685
13	42.01811	42.18060	42.34374	42.50754	42.67199	42.83710	43.00286	43.16930
14	49.81497	50.02473	50.23540	50.44699	50.65951	50.87295	51.08733	51.30264
15	58.84374	59.11215	59.38183	59.65278	59.92503	60.19856	60.47338	60.74951
16	69.29905	69.63992	69.98254	70.32690	70.67303	71.02093	71.37060	71.72206
17	81.40630	81.83635	82.26876	82.70355	83.14072	83.58028	84.02227	84.46667
18	95.42650	95.96591	96.50849	97.05426	97.60323	98.15542	98.71085	99.26954
19	111.66188	112.33501	113.01234	113.69392	114.37975	115.06987	115.76430	116.46307
20	130.46246	131.29861	132.14031	132.98759	133.84051	134.69908	135.56335	136.43336
21	152.23353	153.26794	154.30962	155.35862	156.41499	157.47878	158.55005	159.62884
22	177.44443	178.71941	180.00385	181.29782	182.60138	183.91463	185.23761	186.57040
23	206.63865	208.20493	209.78346	211.37432	212.97761	214.59342	216.22186	217.86302
24	240.44555	242.36391	244.29803	246.24802	248.21402	250.19617	252.19458	254.20940
25	279.59395	281.93709	284.30041	286.68408	289.08827	291.51315	293.95891	296.42572
26	324.92779	327.78262	330.66318	333.56969	336.50239	339.46151	342.44729	345.45997
27	377.42438	380.89467	384.39762	387.93356	391.50277	395.10558	398.74231	402.41326
28	438.21544	442.42497	446.67585	450.96846	455.30322	459.68053	464.10082	468.56450
29	508.61147	513.70783	518.85631	524.05743	529.31173	534.61976	539.98205	545.39916
30	590.13009	596.28902	602.51346	608.80409	615.16161	621.58673	628.08016	634.64263
31	684.52864	691.95933	699.47210	707.06784	714.74746	722.51190	730.36207	738.29891
32	793.84217	802.79339	811.84716	821.00466	830.26706	839.63556	849.11136	858.69569
33	920.42723	931.19464	942.08986	953.11440	964.26979	975.55756	986.97929	998.53654
34	1067.01273	1079.94749	1093.04115	1106.29565	1119.71295	1133.29505	1147.04395	1160.96169
35	1236.75874	1252.27767	1267.99369	1283.90931	1300.02703	1316.34941	1332.87903	1349.61851
36	1433.32462	1451.92218	1470.76369	1489.85234	1509.19135	1528.78399	1548.63355	1568.74340
37	1660.94792	1683.21034	1705.77412	1728.64329	1751.82197	1775.31432	1799.12456	1823.25695
38	1924.53569	1951.15768	1978.15120	2005.52139	2033.27348	2061.41277	2089.94461	2118.87445
39	2229.77032	2261.57467	2293.83624	2326.56155	2359.75724	2393.43002	2427.58669	2462.23418
40	2583.23204	2621.19276	2659.71520	2698.80762	2738.47840	2778.73603	2819.58915	2861.04650
41	2992.54070	3037.81031	3083.76892	3130.42694	3177.79494	3225.88367	3274.70400	3324.26701
42	3466.52013	3520.46175	3575.24718	3630.88953	3687.40213	3744.79850	3803.09235	3862.29763
43	4015.38831	4079.61343	4144.87048	4211.17592	4278.54648	4346.99915	4416.55121	4487.22019
44	4650.97766	4727.39066	4805.06089	4884.01797	4964.27391	5045.85302	5128.77066	5213.06775
45	5386.99013	5477.84058	5570.22804	5664.17834	5759.71774	5856.87293	5955.67105	6056.13970
46	6239.29257	6347.23682	6457.05330	6568.77429	6682.43257	6798.06153	6915.69509	7035.36776
47	7226.25880	7354.43235	7484.88378	7617.65329	7752.78179	7890.31091	8030.28300	8172.74115
48	8369.16569	8521.26838	8676.13930	8833.82848	8994.38687	9157.86631	9324.31956	9493.80035
49	9692.65186	9873.04792	10056.80445	10243.98363	10434.64877	10628.86435	10826.69601	11028.21060
50	11225.24886	11439.08451	11656.99535	11879.05852	12105.35258	12335.95758	12570.95507	12810.42812

ANNUAL DEPOSITS

EFFECTIVE ANNUAL YIELD

NUMBER OF ANNUAL DEPOSITS	16.20%	16.25%	16.30%	16.35%	16.40%	16.45%	16.50%	16.55%
1	1.16200	1.16250	1.16300	1.16350	1.16400	1.16450	1.16500	1.16550
2	2.51224	2.51391	2.51557	2.51723	2.51890	2.52056	2.52223	2.52389
3	4.08123	4.08492	4.08861	4.09230	4.09599	4.09969	4.10339	4.10709
4	5.90439	5.91121	5.91805	5.92489	5.93174	5.93859	5.94545	5.95232
5	8.02290	8.03429	8.04569	8.05711	8.06854	8.07999	8.09145	8.10293
6	10.48461	10.50236	10.52014	10.53795	10.55578	10.57365	10.59154	10.60946
7	13.34511	13.37149	13.39792	13.42440	13.45093	13.47751	13.50415	13.53083
8	16.66902	16.70686	16.74478	16.78279	16.82089	16.85906	16.89733	16.93568
9	20.53140	20.58422	20.63718	20.69028	20.74351	20.79688	20.85039	20.90403
10	25.01949	25.09166	25.16404	25.23664	25.30945	25.38247	25.45570	25.52915
11	30.23465	30.33156	30.42878	30.52633	30.62420	30.72238	30.82089	30.91973
12	36.29466	36.42293	36.55168	36.68088	36.81056	36.94072	37.07134	37.20244
13	43.33639	43.50416	43.67260	43.84171	44.01150	44.18196	44.35311	44.52494
14	51.51889	51.73609	51.95423	52.17333	52.39338	52.61440	52.83638	53.05932
15	61.02695	61.30570	61.58577	61.86717	62.14990	62.43396	62.71938	63.00614
16	72.07532	72.43038	72.78725	73.14595	73.50648	73.86885	74.23307	74.59916
17	84.91352	85.36281	85.81457	86.26881	86.72554	87.18478	87.64653	88.11082
18	99.83151	100.39677	100.96535	101.53726	102.11253	102.69117	103.27321	103.85866
19	117.16621	117.87375	118.58570	119.30211	120.02299	120.74837	121.47829	122.21277
20	137.30914	138.19073	139.07817	139.97150	140.87076	141.77598	142.68721	143.60448
21	160.71522	161.80922	162.91091	164.02034	165.13756	166.26263	167.39560	168.53652
22	187.91308	189.26572	190.62839	192.00117	193.38412	194.77733	196.18087	197.59481
23	219.51700	221.18390	222.86382	224.55686	226.26312	227.98270	229.71571	231.46225
24	256.24076	258.28879	260.35362	262.43540	264.53427	266.65036	268.78381	270.93476
25	298.91376	301.42321	303.95426	306.50709	309.08189	311.67884	314.29813	316.93996
26	348.49979	351.56698	354.66181	357.78450	360.93532	364.11451	367.32233	370.55902
27	406.11875	409.85912	413.63468	417.44577	421.29271	425.17585	429.09551	433.05204
28	473.07199	477.62373	482.22014	486.86165	491.54872	496.28177	501.06127	505.88766
29	550.87165	556.40008	561.98502	567.62703	573.32671	579.08462	584.90138	590.77756
30	641.27486	647.97760	654.75157	661.59755	668.51629	675.50854	682.57510	689.71675
31	746.32339	754.43645	762.63908	770.93225	779.31696	787.79420	796.36500	805.03037
32	868.38978	878.19488	888.11225	898.14317	908.28894	918.55085	928.93022	939.42840
33	1010.23092	1022.06405	1034.03755	1046.15308	1058.41232	1070.81696	1083.36871	1096.06930
34	1175.05033	1189.31195	1203.74867	1218.36261	1233.15594	1248.13085	1263.28954	1278.63427
35	1366.57049	1383.73765	1401.12270	1418.72840	1436.55752	1454.61288	1472.89732	1491.41374
36	1589.11690	1609.75751	1630.66870	1651.85399	1673.31695	1695.06119	1717.09038	1739.40821
37	1847.71584	1872.50561	1897.63070	1923.09563	1948.90493	1975.06326	2001.57529	2028.44577
38	2148.20781	2177.95027	2208.10751	2238.68525	2269.68934	2301.12567	2333.00021	2365.31904
39	2497.37948	2533.02969	2569.19203	2605.87379	2643.08239	2680.82534	2719.11025	2757.94485
40	2903.01695	2945.80952	2989.13333	3033.09766	3077.71190	3122.98561	3168.92844	3215.55022
41	3374.58390	3425.66606	3477.52506	3530.17263	3583.62066	3637.88124	3692.96663	3748.88928
42	3922.42849	3983.49930	4045.52465	4108.51935	4172.49844	4237.47720	4303.47112	4370.49596
43	4559.02390	4631.98043	4706.10817	4781.42576	4857.95219	4935.70670	5014.70886	5094.97854
44	5298.74777	5385.83975	5474.34680	5564.35238	5655.82035	5748.79495	5843.30082	5939.36298
45	6158.30691	6262.20121	6367.85158	6475.28749	6584.53889	6695.63622	6808.61046	6923.49306
46	7157.11463	7280.97141	7406.97439	7535.16049	7665.56726	7798.23288	7933.19618	8070.49666
47	8317.72921	8465.29177	8615.47422	8768.32274	8923.88429	9082.20669	9243.33855	9407.32936
48	9666.36334	9842.06418	10020.95952	10203.10700	10388.56532	10577.39419	10769.65441	10965.40786
49	11233.47620	11442.56211	11655.53892	11872.47850	12093.45403	12318.54004	12547.81239	12781.34837
50	13054.46134	13303.14095	13556.55476	13814.79223	14077.94449	14346.10437	14619.36644	14897.82702

ANNUAL DEPOSITS

NUMBER OF ANNUAL DEPOSITS	EFFECTIVE ANNUAL YIELD							
	16.60%	16.65%	16.70%	16.75%	16.80%	16.85%	16.90%	16.95%
1	1.16600	1.16650	1.16700	1.16750	1.16800	1.16850	1.16900	1.16950
2	2.52556	2.52722	2.52889	2.53056	2.53222	2.53389	2.53556	2.53723
3	4.11080	4.11450	4.11821	4.12192	4.12564	4.12935	4.13307	4.13679
4	5.95919	5.96607	5.97296	5.97985	5.98674	5.99365	6.00056	6.00748
5	8.11442	8.12592	8.13744	8.14897	8.16052	8.17208	8.18365	8.19524
6	10.62741	10.64539	10.66339	10.68142	10.69948	10.71757	10.73569	10.75384
7	13.55756	13.58434	13.61118	13.63806	13.66500	13.69199	13.71902	13.74611
8	16.97411	17.01264	17.05124	17.08994	17.12872	17.16759	17.20654	17.24558
9	20.95782	21.01174	21.06580	21.12000	21.17434	21.22882	21.28344	21.33821
10	25.60282	25.67669	25.75079	25.82510	25.89963	25.97438	26.04935	26.12453
11	31.01888	31.11836	31.21817	31.31831	31.41877	31.51956	31.62069	31.72214
12	37.33402	37.46607	37.59861	37.73162	37.86512	37.99911	38.13358	38.26854
13	44.69746	44.87067	45.04457	45.21917	45.39446	45.57046	45.74716	45.92456
14	53.28324	53.50814	53.73402	53.96088	54.18873	54.41758	54.64743	54.87827
15	63.29426	63.58375	63.87460	64.16683	64.46044	64.75544	65.05184	65.34964
16	74.96711	75.33694	75.70866	76.08227	76.45780	76.83524	77.21460	77.59590
17	88.57765	89.04704	89.51900	89.99355	90.47071	90.95047	91.43287	91.91791
18	104.44754	105.03987	105.63568	106.23497	106.83779	107.44413	108.05403	108.66750
19	122.95183	123.69551	124.44383	125.19683	125.95453	126.71696	127.48416	128.25614
20	144.52783	145.45731	146.39296	147.33480	148.28289	149.23727	150.19798	151.16505
21	169.68545	170.84245	172.00758	173.18088	174.36242	175.55225	176.75044	177.95703
22	199.01924	200.45422	201.89984	203.35618	204.82331	206.30131	207.79026	209.29024
23	233.22243	234.99635	236.78412	238.58584	240.40162	242.23158	244.07581	245.93444
24	273.10336	275.28974	277.49407	279.71647	281.95713	284.21610	286.49363	288.78983
25	319.60451	322.29199	325.00258	327.73648	330.49389	333.27501	336.08005	338.90920
26	373.82486	377.12010	380.44501	383.79984	387.18486	390.60035	394.04658	397.52381
27	437.04579	441.07710	445.14632	449.25381	453.39992	457.58501	461.80945	466.07360
28	510.76139	515.68294	520.65276	525.67132	530.73910	535.85658	541.02425	546.24258
29	596.71378	602.71065	608.76877	614.88877	621.07127	627.31692	633.62634	640.00019
30	696.93427	704.22847	711.60015	719.05014	726.57925	734.18832	741.87819	749.64972
31	813.79136	822.64901	831.60438	840.65853	849.81256	859.06755	868.42461	877.88485
32	950.04673	960.78657	971.64931	982.63634	993.74907	1004.98893	1016.35737	1027.85583
33	1108.92048	1121.92403	1135.08174	1148.39542	1161.86691	1175.49807	1189.29076	1203.24690
34	1294.16728	1309.89088	1325.80739	1341.91916	1358.22856	1374.73799	1391.44990	1408.36675
35	1510.16505	1529.15421	1548.38423	1567.85812	1587.57895	1607.54985	1627.77394	1648.25441
36	1762.01845	1784.92489	1808.13139	1831.64185	1855.46022	1879.59049	1904.03673	1928.80304
37	2055.67951	2083.28139	2111.25634	2139.60936	2168.34554	2197.46999	2226.98794	2256.90465
38	2398.08831	2431.31424	2465.00314	2499.16143	2533.79558	2568.91219	2604.51790	2640.61949
39	2797.33697	2837.29456	2877.82567	2918.93847	2960.64124	3002.94239	3045.85043	3089.37399
40	3262.86091	3310.87060	3359.58955	3409.02816	3459.19697	3510.10668	3561.76815	3614.19238
41	3805.66182	3863.29706	3921.80801	3981.20788	4041.51006	4102.72816	4164.87597	4227.96749
42	4438.56768	4507.70252	4577.91695	4649.22770	4721.65175	4795.20635	4869.90900	4945.77748
43	5176.53591	5259.40149	5343.59608	5429.14084	5516.05725	5604.36712	5694.09263	5785.25626
44	6037.00687	6136.25833	6237.14362	6339.68941	6443.92287	6549.87148	6657.56328	6767.02670
45	7040.31601	7159.11185	7279.91361	7402.75491	7527.66991	7654.69333	7783.86047	7915.20723
46	8210.17447	8352.27047	8496.82618	8643.88386	8793.48645	8945.67766	9100.50189	9258.00435
47	9574.22943	9744.09000	9916.96315	10092.90190	10271.96018	10454.19284	10639.65572	10828.40559
48	11164.71752	11367.64749	11574.26300	11784.63047	11998.81749	12216.89283	12438.92653	12664.98984
49	13019.22663	13261.52729	13508.33192	13759.72358	14015.78682	14276.60778	14542.27411	14812.87511
50	15181.58425	15470.73809	15765.39035	16065.64477	16371.60701	16683.38469	17001.08744	17324.82694

ANNUAL DEPOSITS

NUMBER OF ANNUAL DEPOSITS	EFFECTIVE ANNUAL YIELD							
	17.00%	17.05%	17.10%	17.15%	17.20%	17.25%	17.30%	17.35%
1	1.17000	1.17050	1.17100	1.17150	1.17200	1.17250	1.17300	1.17350
2	2.53890	2.54057	2.54224	2.54391	2.54558	2.54726	2.54893	2.55060
3	4.14051	4.14424	4.14796	4.15169	4.15542	4.15916	4.16289	4.16663
4	6.01440	6.02133	6.02827	6.03521	6.04216	6.04911	6.05607	6.06304
5	8.20685	8.21847	8.23010	8.24175	8.25341	8.26508	8.27678	8.28848
6	10.77201	10.79022	10.80845	10.82671	10.84499	10.86331	10.88166	10.90003
7	13.77325	13.80045	13.82769	13.85499	13.88233	13.90973	13.93718	13.96469
8	17.28471	17.32392	17.36323	17.40262	17.44210	17.48166	17.52132	17.56106
9	21.39311	21.44815	21.50334	21.55867	21.61414	21.66975	21.72550	21.78140
10	26.19994	26.27556	26.35141	26.42748	26.50377	26.58028	26.65702	26.73398
11	31.82393	31.92605	32.02850	32.13129	32.23442	32.33788	32.44168	32.54582
12	38.40399	38.53994	38.67637	38.81331	38.95073	39.08866	39.22709	39.36602
13	46.10267	46.28150	46.46103	46.64129	46.82226	47.00396	47.18638	47.36953
14	55.11013	55.34299	55.57687	55.81177	56.04769	56.28464	56.52262	56.76164
15	65.64885	65.94947	66.25151	66.55499	66.85989	67.16624	67.47404	67.78329
16	77.97915	78.36435	78.75152	79.14067	79.53179	79.92492	80.32004	80.71719
17	92.40561	92.89598	93.38903	93.88479	94.38326	94.88446	95.38841	95.89512
18	109.28456	109.90524	110.52956	111.15753	111.78918	112.42453	113.06361	113.70642
19	129.03294	129.81458	130.60111	131.39255	132.18892	132.99027	133.79661	134.60798
20	152.13854	153.11847	154.10490	155.09787	156.09742	157.10359	158.11642	159.13597
21	179.17209	180.39567	181.62784	182.86865	184.11817	185.37646	186.64357	187.91956
22	210.80134	212.32363	213.85720	215.40213	216.95850	218.52640	220.10590	221.69711
23	247.80757	249.69531	251.59778	253.51509	255.44736	257.39470	259.35722	261.33505
24	291.10486	293.43886	295.79200	298.16443	300.55631	302.96778	305.39902	307.85018
25	341.76268	344.64069	347.54344	350.47113	353.42399	356.40223	359.40605	362.43569
26	401.03234	404.57243	408.14436	411.74843	415.38492	419.05411	422.75630	426.49178
27	470.37783	474.72253	479.10805	483.53479	488.00312	492.51345	497.06614	501.66161
28	551.51207	556.83322	562.20653	567.63250	573.11166	578.64451	584.23158	589.87340
29	646.43912	652.94378	659.51484	666.15298	672.85887	679.63319	686.47665	693.38993
30	757.50377	765.44119	773.46288	781.56972	789.76259	798.04242	806.41011	814.86658
31	887.44941	897.11942	906.89603	916.78042	926.77376	936.87724	947.09206	957.41944
32	1039.48581	1051.24878	1063.14626	1075.17976	1087.35085	1099.66106	1112.11198	1124.70521
33	1217.36839	1231.65720	1246.11526	1260.74459	1275.54719	1290.52509	1305.68036	1321.01506
34	1425.49102	1442.82525	1460.37198	1478.13379	1496.11331	1514.31317	1532.73606	1551.38468
35	1668.99450	1689.99745	1711.26658	1732.80524	1754.61680	1776.70469	1799.07240	1821.72342
36	1953.89356	1979.31252	2005.06417	2031.15283	2057.58289	2084.35875	2111.48492	2138.96593
37	2287.22547	2317.95580	2349.10114	2380.66704	2412.65914	2445.08314	2477.94481	2511.25002
38	2677.22379	2714.33776	2751.96844	2790.12294	2828.80851	2868.03248	2907.80226	2948.12540
39	3133.52184	3178.30285	3223.72604	3269.80053	3316.53558	3363.94058	3412.02506	3460.79866
40	3667.39055	3721.37399	3776.15419	3831.74282	3888.15170	3945.39283	4003.47839	4062.42072
41	4292.01695	4357.03876	4423.04756	4490.05821	4558.08579	4627.14559	4697.25315	4768.42422
42	5022.82983	5101.08436	5180.55969	5261.27469	5343.24855	5426.50071	5511.05095	5596.91932
43	5877.88090	5971.98975	6067.60640	6164.75480	6263.45930	6363.74458	6465.63576	6569.15832
44	6878.29065	6991.38403	7106.33809	7223.18175	7341.94629	7462.66302	7585.36375	7710.08079
45	8048.77006	8184.58606	8322.69291	8463.12892	8605.93306	8751.14489	8898.80467	9048.95331
46	9418.23097	9581.22848	9747.04439	9915.72703	10087.32554	10261.88989	10439.47088	10620.12021
47	11020.50024	11215.99844	11414.95999	11617.44572	11823.51754	12033.23839	12246.67235	12463.88457
48	12895.15528	13129.49667	13368.08914	13611.00916	13858.33455	14110.14451	14366.51966	14627.54204
49	15088.50167	15369.24635	15655.20339	15946.46873	16243.14009	16545.31694	16853.10056	17166.59408
50	17654.71696	17990.87335	18333.41417	18682.45962	19038.13219	19400.55661	19769.85996	20146.17165

ANNUAL DEPOSITS

NUMBER OF ANNUAL DEPOSITS	EFFECTIVE ANNUAL YIELD							
	17.40%	17.45%	17.50%	17.55%	17.60%	17.65%	17.70%	17.75%
1	1.17400	1.17450	1.17500	1.17550	1.17600	1.17650	1.17700	1.17750
2	2.55228	2.55395	2.55563	2.55730	2.55898	2.56065	2.56233	2.56401
3	4.17037	4.17411	4.17786	4.18161	4.18536	4.18911	4.19286	4.19662
4	6.07002	6.07700	6.08398	6.09098	6.09798	6.10498	6.11200	6.11902
5	8.30020	8.31193	8.32368	8.33545	8.34722	8.35901	8.37082	8.38264
6	10.91843	10.93687	10.95533	10.97382	10.99233	11.01088	11.02946	11.04806
7	13.99224	14.01985	14.04751	14.07522	14.10298	14.13080	14.15867	14.18659
8	17.60089	17.64081	17.68082	17.72092	17.76111	17.80139	17.84176	17.88221
9	21.83745	21.89363	21.94997	22.00644	22.06307	22.11983	22.17675	22.23381
10	26.81116	26.88857	26.96621	27.04407	27.12216	27.20048	27.27903	27.35781
11	32.65031	32.75513	32.86030	32.96581	33.07167	33.17787	33.28442	33.39132
12	39.50546	39.64540	39.78585	39.92681	40.06828	40.21026	40.35276	40.49577
13	47.55341	47.73802	47.92337	48.10946	48.29630	48.48387	48.67220	48.86127
14	57.00170	57.24281	57.48496	57.72817	57.97244	58.21778	58.46418	58.71165
15	68.09400	68.40618	68.71983	69.03497	69.35159	69.66971	69.98934	70.31047
16	81.11635	81.51756	81.92080	82.32611	82.73347	83.14292	83.55445	83.96808
17	96.40460	96.91687	97.43194	97.94984	98.47057	98.99414	99.52059	100.04991
18	114.35300	115.00336	115.65753	116.31553	116.97739	117.64311	118.31273	118.98627
19	135.42442	136.24595	137.07260	137.90441	138.74141	139.58362	140.43108	141.28383
20	160.16227	161.19537	162.23531	163.28213	164.33589	165.39663	166.46439	167.53921
21	189.20451	190.49846	191.80149	193.11365	194.43501	195.76563	197.10558	198.45492
22	223.30009	224.91494	226.54175	228.18059	229.83157	231.49477	233.17027	234.85817
23	263.32830	265.33710	267.36155	269.40179	271.45793	273.53009	275.61841	277.72300
24	310.32143	312.81292	315.32482	317.85730	320.41052	322.98466	325.57987	328.19633
25	365.49136	368.57328	371.68167	374.81676	377.97878	381.16795	384.38450	387.62868
26	430.26085	434.06381	437.90096	441.77260	445.67904	449.62059	453.59756	457.61027
27	506.30024	510.98245	515.70863	520.47919	525.29455	530.15512	535.06133	540.01359
28	595.57049	601.32338	607.13264	612.99879	618.92239	624.90400	630.94419	637.04351
29	700.37375	707.42882	714.55585	721.75558	729.02873	736.37606	743.79831	751.29623
30	823.41278	832.04964	840.77812	849.59918	858.51379	867.52293	876.62761	885.82881
31	967.86061	978.41681	989.08929	999.87934	1010.78822	1021.81723	1032.96769	1044.24093
32	1137.44235	1150.32504	1163.35492	1176.53366	1189.86294	1203.34447	1216.97998	1230.77119
33	1336.53132	1352.23126	1368.11703	1384.19082	1400.45482	1416.91127	1433.56243	1450.41058
34	1570.26177	1589.37011	1608.71251	1628.29180	1648.11087	1668.17261	1688.47998	1709.03595
35	1844.66132	1867.88970	1891.41220	1915.23252	1939.35438	1963.78158	1988.51794	2013.56734
36	2166.80639	2195.01095	2223.58433	2252.53132	2281.85675	2311.56553	2341.66261	2372.15304
37	2545.00470	2579.21486	2613.88659	2649.02607	2684.63954	2720.73335	2757.31390	2794.38770
38	2989.00952	3030.46235	3072.49175	3115.10565	3158.31210	3202.11928	3246.53546	3291.56902
39	3510.27117	3560.45253	3611.35280	3662.98219	3715.35103	3768.46983	3822.34923	3877.00002
40	4122.23236	4182.92600	4244.51454	4307.01106	4370.42881	4434.78126	4500.08205	4566.34502
41	4840.67479	4914.02109	4988.47959	5064.06700	5140.80028	5218.69665	5297.77357	5378.04876
42	5684.12620	5772.69227	5862.63852	5953.98626	6046.75713	6140.97311	6236.65649	6333.82992
43	6674.33816	6781.20157	6889.77526	7000.08635	7112.16239	7226.03137	7341.72169	7459.26223
44	7836.84700	7965.69574	8096.66093	8229.77700	8365.07897	8502.60240	8642.38343	8784.45878
45	9201.63238	9356.88415	9514.75159	9675.27837	9838.50887	10004.48823	10173.26230	10344.87771
46	10803.89041	10990.83494	11181.00812	11374.46522	11571.26243	11771.45690	11975.10672	12182.27100
47	12684.94135	12909.91013	13138.85954	13371.85936	13608.98062	13850.29554	14095.87762	14345.80161
48	14893.29514	15163.86395	15439.33496	15719.79618	16005.33721	16296.04920	16592.02495	16893.35889
49	17485.90250	17811.13271	18142.39358	18479.79591	18823.45256	19173.47839	19529.99037	19893.10759
50	20529.62353	20920.34987	21318.48745	21724.17560	22137.55621	22558.77382	22987.97567	23425.31169

ANNUAL DEPOSITS

NUMBER OF ANNUAL DEPOSITS	EFFECTIVE ANNUAL YIELD							
	17.80%	17.85%	17.90%	18.00%	18.10%	18.20%	18.30%	18.40%
1	1.17800	1.17850	1.17900	1.18000	1.18100	1.18200	1.18300	1.18400
2	2.56568	2.56736	2.56904	2.57240	2.57576	2.57912	2.58249	2.58586
3	4.20038	4.20414	4.20790	4.21543	4.22297	4.23052	4.23808	4.24565
4	6.12604	6.13307	6.14011	6.15421	6.16833	6.18248	6.19665	6.21085
5	8.39448	8.40633	8.41819	8.44197	8.46580	8.48969	8.51364	8.53765
6	11.06670	11.08536	11.10405	11.14152	11.17911	11.21682	11.25464	11.29258
7	14.21457	14.24259	14.27068	14.32700	14.38353	14.44028	14.49724	14.55441
8	17.92276	17.96340	18.00413	18.08585	18.16795	18.25041	18.33323	18.41643
9	22.29101	22.34836	22.40586	22.52131	22.63735	22.75398	22.87121	22.98905
10	27.43681	27.51605	27.59551	27.75514	27.91571	28.07720	28.23964	28.40303
11	33.49856	33.60616	33.71411	33.93107	34.14945	34.36926	34.59050	34.81319
12	40.63931	40.78336	40.92794	41.21866	41.51150	41.80646	42.10356	42.40282
13	49.05111	49.24169	49.43304	49.81802	50.20608	50.59724	50.99151	51.38894
14	58.96020	59.20983	59.46055	59.96527	60.47438	60.98793	61.50596	62.02850
15	70.63312	70.95729	71.28299	71.93901	72.60124	73.26974	73.94455	74.62574
16	84.38381	84.80167	85.22165	86.06804	86.92307	87.78683	88.65940	89.54088
17	100.58213	101.11726	101.65532	102.74028	103.83714	104.94603	106.06707	107.20040
18	119.66375	120.34519	121.03062	122.41353	123.81267	125.22821	126.66035	128.10928
19	142.14190	143.00531	143.87411	145.62797	147.40376	149.20174	151.02219	152.86538
20	168.62116	169.71026	170.80657	173.02100	175.26484	177.53846	179.84225	182.17661
21	199.81372	201.18204	202.55995	205.34479	208.16877	211.03246	213.93638	216.88111
22	236.55856	238.27153	239.99718	243.48685	247.02832	250.62236	254.26974	257.97123
23	279.84399	281.98150	284.13567	288.49448	292.92145	297.41763	301.98410	306.62194
24	330.83422	333.49370	336.17496	341.60349	347.12123	352.72964	358.43019	364.22438
25	390.90071	394.20083	397.52927	404.27211	411.13117	418.10844	425.20592	432.42566
26	461.65904	465.74418	469.86601	478.22109	486.72692	495.38618	504.20160	513.17598
27	545.01234	550.05801	555.15103	565.48089	576.00549	586.72846	597.65350	608.78437
28	643.20254	649.42187	655.70206	668.44745	681.44348	694.69504	708.20709	721.98469
29	758.87059	766.52217	774.25173	789.94799	805.96575	822.31154	838.99198	856.01387
30	895.12756	904.52488	914.02179	933.31863	953.02656	973.15424	993.71052	1014.70442
31	1055.63827	1067.16107	1078.81070	1102.49598	1126.70536	1151.45031	1176.74254	1202.59404
32	1244.71988	1258.82782	1273.09681	1302.12526	1331.82003	1362.19626	1393.26943	1425.05534
33	1467.45801	1484.70708	1502.16014	1537.68781	1574.06046	1611.29798	1649.42073	1688.44952
34	1729.84354	1750.90580	1772.22580	1815.65161	1860.14640	1905.73622	1952.44772	2000.30823
35	2038.93369	2064.62098	2090.63322	2143.64890	2198.01390	2253.76221	2310.92866	2369.54895
36	2403.04189	2434.33433	2466.03557	2530.68570	2597.03542	2665.12893	2735.01160	2806.72996
37	2831.96134	2870.04150	2908.63494	2987.38913	3068.27983	3151.36439	3236.70173	3324.35227
38	3337.22846	3383.52241	3430.45959	3526.29918	3624.81947	3726.09471	3830.20114	3937.21709
39	3932.43313	3988.65966	4045.69086	4162.21303	4282.09280	4405.42595	4532.31095	4662.84903
40	4633.58423	4701.81391	4771.04852	4912.59137	5058.33260	5208.39547	5362.90686	5521.99725
41	5459.54022	5542.26619	5626.24521	5798.03782	5975.07179	6157.50545	6345.50181	6539.22875
42	6432.51638	6532.73921	6634.52210	6842.86463	7057.74079	7279.35344	7507.91164	7743.63084
43	7578.68230	7700.01166	7823.28055	8075.76026	8336.37287	8605.37777	8883.04247	9169.64291
44	8928.86574	9075.64224	9224.82677	9530.57711	9846.43736	10172.73852	10509.82224	10858.04121
45	10519.38185	10696.82288	10877.24977	11247.26098	11629.82353	12025.35893	12434.30271	12857.10479
46	12393.00982	12607.38426	12825.45647	13272.94796	13736.00258	14215.15626	14710.96311	15223.99607
47	14600.14356	14858.98085	15122.39218	15663.25859	16223.40005	16803.49670	17404.25236	18026.39534
48	17200.14712	17512.48744	17830.47938	18483.82514	19161.01646	19862.91510	20590.41354	21344.43609
49	20262.95130	20639.64494	21023.31419	21812.09367	22630.34144	23479.14765	24359.64222	25272.99633
50	23870.93464	24325.00007	24787.66643	25739.45053	26727.61424	27753.53452	28818.63975	29924.41165

ANNUAL DEPOSITS

NUMBER OF ANNUAL DEPOSITS	EFFECTIVE ANNUAL YIELD							
	18.50%	18.60%	18.70%	18.80%	18.90%	19.00%	19.10%	19.20%
1	1.18500	1.18600	1.18700	1.18800	1.18900	1.19000	1.19100	1.19200
2	2.58923	2.59260	2.59597	2.59934	2.60272	2.60610	2.60948	2.61286
3	4.25323	4.26082	4.26842	4.27602	4.28364	4.29126	4.29889	4.30653
4	6.22508	6.23933	6.25361	6.26791	6.28224	6.29660	6.31098	6.32539
5	8.56172	8.58585	8.61003	8.63428	8.65859	8.68295	8.70738	8.73186
6	11.33064	11.36881	11.40711	11.44552	11.48406	11.52271	11.56149	11.60038
7	14.61181	14.66941	14.72724	14.78528	14.84355	14.90203	14.96073	15.01965
8	18.49999	18.58392	18.66823	18.75292	18.83798	18.92341	19.00923	19.09543
9	23.10749	23.22653	23.34619	23.46647	23.58735	23.70886	23.83099	23.95375
10	28.56737	28.73267	28.89893	29.06616	29.23436	29.40355	29.57371	29.74487
11	35.03734	35.26295	35.49003	35.71860	35.94866	36.18022	36.41329	36.64788
12	42.70424	43.00785	43.31367	43.62170	43.93195	44.24446	44.55923	44.87628
13	51.78953	52.19332	52.60032	53.01057	53.42409	53.84091	54.26104	54.68452
14	62.55559	63.08727	63.62358	64.16456	64.71025	65.26068	65.81590	66.37595
15	75.31338	76.00751	76.70819	77.41550	78.12948	78.85021	79.57774	80.31213
16	90.43135	91.33090	92.23963	93.15761	94.08496	95.02175	95.96809	96.92406
17	108.34615	109.50445	110.67544	111.85924	113.05601	114.26588	115.48899	116.72548
18	129.57519	131.05828	132.55874	134.07678	135.61260	137.16640	138.73839	140.32878
19	154.73160	156.62112	158.53423	160.47122	162.43238	164.41802	166.42842	168.46390
20	184.54194	186.93864	189.36713	191.82781	194.32110	196.84744	199.40725	202.00097
21	219.86720	222.89523	225.96578	229.07943	232.23679	235.43846	238.68504	241.97716
22	261.72763	265.53974	269.40838	273.33437	277.31855	281.36176	285.46488	289.62877
23	311.33225	316.11614	320.97475	325.90923	330.92075	336.01050	341.17967	346.42950
24	370.11371	376.09974	382.18403	388.36816	394.65377	401.04249	407.53599	414.13596
25	439.76975	447.24029	454.83944	462.56938	470.43234	478.43056	486.56636	494.84207
26	522.31215	531.61298	541.08141	550.72042	560.53305	570.52237	580.69154	591.04374
27	620.12490	631.67900	643.45064	655.44386	667.66279	680.11162	692.79462	705.71614
28	736.03300	750.35729	764.96291	779.85531	795.04006	810.52283	826.30940	842.40564
29	873.38411	891.10975	909.19797	927.65611	946.49163	965.71217	985.32549	1005.33952
30	1036.14517	1058.04216	1080.40499	1103.24345	1126.56755	1150.38748	1174.71366	1199.55671
31	1229.01703	1256.02400	1283.62772	1311.84122	1340.67782	1370.15110	1400.27497	1431.06360
32	1457.57018	1490.83047	1524.85311	1559.65537	1595.25493	1631.66981	1668.91849	1707.01981
33	1728.40566	1769.31093	1811.18764	1854.05858	1897.94711	1942.87708	1988.87292	2035.95961
34	2049.34571	2099.58877	2151.06673	2203.80960	2257.84811	2313.21372	2369.93864	2428.05586
35	2429.65966	2491.29828	2554.50320	2619.31380	2685.77040	2753.91433	2823.78793	2895.43458
36	2880.33170	2955.86576	3033.38230	3112.93280	3194.57001	3278.34805	3364.32242	3452.55002
37	3414.37806	3506.84279	3601.81179	3699.35216	3799.53274	3902.42418	4008.09900	4116.63163
38	4047.22300	4160.30154	4276.53760	4396.01837	4518.83343	4645.07477	4774.83691	4908.21690
39	4797.14426	4935.30363	5077.43713	5223.65782	5374.08194	5528.82898	5688.02176	5851.78654
40	5685.80095	5854.45611	6028.10487	6206.89349	6390.97243	6580.49649	6775.62492	6976.52156
41	6738.85912	6944.57094	7156.54748	7374.97747	7600.05522	7831.98082	8070.96028	8317.20570
42	7986.73306	8237.44714	8496.00886	8762.66123	9037.65466	9321.24718	9613.70469	9915.30119
43	9465.46368	9770.79830	10085.94952	10411.22955	10746.96039	11093.47414	11451.11329	11820.23102
44	11217.75946	11589.35279	11973.20908	12369.72870	12779.32490	13202.42423	13639.46692	14090.92548
45	13294.22996	13746.15841	14213.38618	14696.42569	15195.80631	15712.07483	16245.79611	16797.55359
46	15754.84750	16304.12987	16872.47639	17460.54173	18069.00270	18698.55905	19349.93416	20023.87588
47	18670.67929	19337.88403	20028.81648	20744.31157	21485.23321	22252.47527	23046.96259	23869.65205
48	22125.93996	22935.91646	23775.39216	24645.43015	25547.13129	26481.63557	27450.12344	28453.81725
49	26220.42385	27203.18292	28222.57749	29279.95901	30376.72810	31514.33633	32694.28802	33918.14216
50	31072.38726	32264.16094	33501.38648	34785.77931	36119.11871	37503.25023	38940.08803	40431.61745

ANNUAL DEPOSITS

NUMBER OF ANNUAL DEPOSITS	EFFECTIVE ANNUAL YIELD							
	19.30%	19.40%	19.50%	19.60%	19.70%	19.80%	19.90%	20.00%
1	1.19300	1.19400	1.19500	1.19600	1.19700	1.19800	1.19900	1.20000
2	2.61625	2.61964	2.62303	2.62642	2.62981	2.63320	2.63660	2.64000
3	4.31419	4.32185	4.32951	4.33719	4.34488	4.35258	4.36028	4.36800
4	6.33982	6.35428	6.36877	6.38328	6.39782	6.41239	6.42698	6.44160
5	8.75641	8.78101	8.80568	8.83041	8.85519	8.88004	8.90495	8.92992
6	11.63940	11.67853	11.71779	11.75717	11.79667	11.83629	11.87604	11.91590
7	15.07880	15.13817	15.19776	15.25757	15.31761	15.37788	15.43837	15.49908
8	19.18201	19.26897	19.35632	19.44406	19.53218	19.62070	19.70960	19.79890
9	24.07713	24.20115	24.32580	24.45109	24.57702	24.70359	24.83081	24.95868
10	29.91702	30.09017	30.26433	30.43950	30.61569	30.79290	30.97114	31.15042
11	36.88401	37.12167	37.36088	37.60165	37.84398	38.08790	38.33340	38.58050
12	45.19562	45.51727	45.84125	46.16757	46.49625	46.82730	47.16075	47.49660
13	55.11137	55.54162	55.97529	56.41241	56.85301	57.29711	57.74474	58.19592
14	66.94087	67.51070	68.08547	68.66525	69.25005	69.83994	70.43494	71.03511
15	81.05346	81.80177	82.55714	83.31963	84.08931	84.86624	85.65049	86.44213
16	97.88977	98.86532	99.85079	100.84628	101.85191	102.86776	103.89394	104.93056
17	117.97550	119.23919	120.51669	121.80815	123.11373	124.43358	125.76784	127.11667
18	141.93777	143.56559	145.21244	146.87855	148.56414	150.26943	151.99464	153.74000
19	170.52476	172.61131	174.72387	176.86275	179.02827	181.22077	183.44057	185.68800
20	204.62904	207.29191	209.99002	212.72385	215.49384	218.30048	221.14424	224.02560
21	245.31545	248.70054	252.13308	255.61372	259.14313	262.72198	266.35095	270.03072
22	293.85433	298.14244	302.49403	306.91001	311.39133	315.93893	320.55378	325.23686
23	351.76121	357.17608	362.67536	368.26037	373.93242	379.69284	385.54299	391.48424
24	420.84413	427.66223	434.59206	441.63541	448.79411	456.07002	463.46504	470.98108
25	503.26004	511.82271	520.53251	529.39195	538.40355	547.56989	556.89358	566.37730
26	601.58223	612.31031	623.23135	634.34877	645.66605	657.18673	668.91441	680.85276
27	718.88060	732.29251	745.95647	759.87713	774.05926	788.50770	803.22738	818.22331
28	858.81756	875.55126	892.61298	910.00905	927.74593	945.83022	964.26862	983.06797
29	1025.76235	1046.60221	1067.86751	1089.56682	1111.70888	1134.30260	1157.35708	1180.88157
30	1224.92748	1250.83703	1277.29667	1304.31791	1331.91253	1360.09252	1388.87014	1418.25788
31	1462.53148	1494.69342	1527.56452	1561.16023	1595.49630	1630.58884	1666.45430	1703.10946
32	1745.99306	1785.85794	1826.63460	1868.34363	1911.00607	1954.64343	1999.27770	2044.93135
33	2084.16272	2133.50838	2184.02335	2235.73498	2288.67126	2342.86083	2398.33296	2455.11762
34	2487.59912	2548.60301	2611.10290	2675.13501	2740.73650	2807.94527	2876.80022	2947.34115
35	2968.89875	3044.22599	3121.46297	3200.65750	3281.85859	3365.11644	3450.48247	3538.00937
36	3543.08921	3635.99983	3731.34325	3829.18238	3929.58174	4032.60749	4138.32748	4246.81125
37	4228.09843	4342.57780	4460.15018	4580.89812	4704.90634	4832.26178	4963.05365	5097.37350
38	5045.31443	5186.23190	5331.07447	5479.95015	5632.96989	5790.24761	5951.90032	6118.04820
39	6020.25311	6193.55488	6371.82899	6555.21638	6743.86196	6937.91463	7137.52748	7342.85784
40	7183.35496	7396.29853	7615.53064	7841.23479	8073.59976	8312.81973	8559.09445	8812.62941
41	8570.93547	8832.37445	9101.75411	9379.31281	9665.29592	9959.95604	10263.55325	10576.35529
42	10226.31902	10547.04909	10877.79117	11218.85412	11570.55621	11933.22533	12307.19935	12692.82635
43	12201.19159	12594.37061	13000.15544	13418.94553	13851.15278	14297.20195	14757.53102	15232.59162
44	14557.21457	15038.87251	15536.38076	16050.25486	16581.02688	17129.24594	17695.47869	18280.30994
45	17367.54998	17957.60778	18567.17000	19197.30081	19848.68618	20522.03463	21218.00795	21937.57193
46	20721.15732	21442.57769	22188.96315	22961.16777	23760.07436	24586.59549	25441.67446	26326.28631
47	24721.53368	25603.63176	26517.00597	27462.75265	28442.00600	29455.93940	30505.76668	31592.74358
48	29493.98269	30571.93032	31689.01713	32846.64817	34046.27819	35289.41340	36577.61325	37912.49229
49	35187.51434	36504.07880	37869.57047	39285.78721	40754.59199	42277.91525	43857.75729	45496.19075
50	41979.89761	43587.06409	45255.33172	46986.99750	48784.44361	50650.14047	52586.64998	54596.62890

WITHDRAWAL TABLES
INSTRUCTIONS

These sections of the book are designed to solve problems concerning the receipt of money from fixed interest rate investments. All calculations are based on withdrawals made at the end of each period. However, you can adjust the results to solve problems in which the withdrawals are made at the beginning of each period. The second example below demonstrates how you would make this adjustment. The table entries are based on an initial investment of $1,000. Be sure to read the Effective Annual Yield (EAY) Table instructions starting on page 263 before you attempt to solve any problems. And remember that most problems start with finding the EAY on the investment.

The Withdrawal Tables consists of three tables: Monthly Withdrawals, Quarterly Withdrawals, and Annual Withdrawals. Four basic problems can be solved with these tables.

1. How much can be withdrawn periodically from an initial fund for a certain period of time.
2. How big an initial fund is required to allow periodic withdrawals for a certain period of time.
3. How many periodic withdrawals can be made from an initial fund, if the periodic withdrawal amount is known.
4. What EAY must be earned to achieve a specific financial result.

EXAMPLE: At retirement you have $200,000 to invest in an account that pays 8% interest, compounded monthly. How much can be withdrawn monthly to exhaust the fund in 10 years (120) months? First turn to page 268 of the EAY Table to find the EAY on the account. Move down the nominal annual rate (NAR) column on the left-hand side of the page to the 8% row. Move across the page to find the 8.3% EAY under the monthly compounding method.

Turn to page 164 of the Monthly Withdrawals Table and move down the Number of Monthly Withdrawals to 120 months. Then move across this row until you find the table entry 12.132784 under the 8.3% EAY column. Divide $200,000 by $1,000 to get 200, the number of thousand dollar units in your initial fund. Multiply 200 by 12.132784 to get $2,426.56, the amount of the monthly stipend you can expect to receive.

EXAMPLE: The initial fund available for retirement is $200,000, the same as in the previous example. However, you choose to begin withdrawing your monthly stipend at the time you set up the account. How much can you withdraw to make the fund last for 120 monthly payments?

This problem is solved exactly as the previous problem with one difference. Rather than dividing the initial fund by $1,000 to get the number of $1,000 units in the initial fund, go to the first table entry beneath the 8.3% EAY and use that table entry as the divisor. In the previous example the first table entry is 1006.666705. Thus $200,000 divided by 1006.666705 equals 198.67549. Multiplying this result by 12.132784 (120 months entry) gives $2,410.49 as the amount of the monthly stipend.

EXAMPLE: You estimate that you will live for 15 years after your retirement. You wish to place your money in a passbook account that pays 5% compounded continuously 365/360. You estimate that you will need to withdraw $5,000 every three months. How much must you deposit in the passbook account to ensure that you will receive your quarterly stipend? First turn to page 265 of the EAY Table to find the EAY. Move down the NAR column at the left-hand side of the page to the 5% row. Move across the page to find the 5.2% EAY under the continuously 365/360 compounding method.

Turn to page 192 of the Quarterly Withdrawals Table and move down the Number of Quarterly Withdrawals column to 60 quarters (15 years). Then move across this row until you find the table entry 23.950175 under the 5.20% EAY column. Divide $5,000 by the table entry to get 208.76674. Multiply this result by $1,000 to get $208,766.74, the amount of the initial fund.

EXAMPLE: You start with an initial fund of $200,000 that you can invest in an account earning 7% interest, compounded daily 365/365. You wish to make monthly withdrawals of $4,800. How long will the fund last? Turn to page 267 of the EAY Table to find the EAY. Move down the NAR column at the left-hand side of the page to the 7% row. Move across this row to find the EAY of 7.25% under the daily 365/365 compounding method.

Next, turn to page 161 of the Monthly Withdrawals Table. Calculate your monthly withdrawal factor per $1,000 of initial fund by dividing $4,800 by $200,000 and then multiplying the result by $1,000 to get 24. Move down the 7.25% column until you find the first table entry that is less than the calculated monthly withdrawal factor. This entry is 23.955380. Move across the row to the left-hand column and find 48 as the Number of Monthly Withdrawals. This is the number of monthly withdrawals you can make. The last withdrawal will be somewhat less than $4,800.

EXAMPLE: What EAY must I earn on my funds to make $250,000 last for 20 years if I wish to withdraw $3,750 monthly for seven (7) years?

Calculate the withdrawal factor per $1,000 by dividing the $3,750 monthly stipend by $250,000 and multiplying the result by $1,000 to get 15. Starting from the first page of the Monthly Withdrawals Table (page 156) along the 84 months row, begin to move across each column until you find the first table entry that exceeds 15. On page 161 of the Monthly Withdrawals Table you find the table entry 15.010667. Read up the column to the EAY of 7.05%. In order to withdraw at least $3,750 per month for 7 years, the account must earn 7.05% EAY.

The previous five examples are typical of the problems that can be solved using the Withdrawal Tables in conjunction with the EAY Table. Remember the most important rule. Be sure to convert the nominal rate of interest to the effective annual yield before you start most problems.

One further problem requires using a combination of both these Withdrawal Tables and the Deposit Tables in the previous section.

EXAMPLE: You are going to make defined contributions to your pension plan for the next 20 years (80 quarters) until retirement. You then have a life expectancy of 15 years (60 quarters). If you can earn 6.3% compounded quarterly throughout the whole 35-year period, what amount should you contribute quarterly so that you can have a defined quarterly benefit of $7,500 beginning three months after retirement?

First turn to page 266 of the EAY Table to find the EAY. Read down the NAR column at the left-hand side of the page to the 6.3% row. Then read across this row to find 6.45% EAY under the quarterly compounding column.

This is a two-part problem. First you find the amount of the retirement fund that will ensure you the defined quarterly benefit. Turn to page 195 of the Quarterly Withdrawals Table and read down to 60 in the Number of Quarterly Withdrawals column. Read across the row to get the table entry of 25.884919 under the 6.45% EAY column. If you divide the $7,500 quarterly benefit by this table entry and multiply the result by $1,000, you get the amount of the initial retirement fund, $289,744.

Next, turn to page 83 of the Quarterly Deposits Table and read down to 80 in the Number of Quarterly Deposits column. Read across the row to get the table entry of 160.64053 under the 6.45% EAY column. If you divide the retirement fund ($289,744) by the table entry, you get the quarterly contribution of $1803.68. This is the amount you must begin to deposit today to ensure you will be able to receive the defined benefit after you retire.

The Simple Interest Approximation to Withdrawal Tables Problems.
This book does not contain simple interest tables. However, some problems require using simple interest rates to find the answer. These are problems where periodic withdrawals from an account are made more frequently than interest is compounded.

In order to solve such problems you must convert the stated problem to one in which the withdrawals are refigured as equivalent withdrawals for the compounding period. Then you use the tables to solve the equivalent problem. For example, let's say that you wish to withdraw $100 each month from an account paying interest at 6.30% compounded quarterly. What initial amount would be required to permit 36 such withdrawals?

First turn to page 266 of the Effective Annual Yield Table and find the EAY of 6.45%. Next, figure out what one quarterly withdrawal is equivalent to 3 months of $100 withdrawals at 6.30% *simple interest*. The first month's withdrawal earns two months interest to the end of the quarter, the second month's withdrawal earns one month interest to the end of the quarter, and the third month's withdrawal earns no interest to the end of the quarter. Thus the total interest earned in one quarter for the three withdrawals is 3 months interest, or 1.575% on a $100 withdrawal. This equals $101.575 which, when combined with the other two $100 monthly withdrawals, gives a total equivalent quarterly withdrawal of $301.575.

In the Quarterly Withdrawals Table, on page 195, for 12 quarterly withdrawals, we read across the row to the 6.45% EAY column to find the table entry 92.108304. Divide $301.575 by this table entry, and multiply the result by $1,000, to get $3,274.13 as the balance initially required to provide for the desired withdrawals.

The same simple interest approximation can be applied to any other type of Withdrawal Tables problem. Simply remember to convert the more frequent withdrawals to the equivalent withdrawal by figuring simple interest for the duration of the specified compounding period. Then use the table entries for the applicable EAY to solve the remainder of the problem.

TABLE 5. MONTHLY WITHDRAWALS PER $1,000

MONTHLY WITHDRAWALS PER $1000

NUMBER OF MONTHLY WTHDRWLS	EFFECTIVE ANNUAL YIELD							
	5.00%	5.05%	5.10%	5.15%	5.20%	5.25%	5.30%	5.35%
1	1004.074124	1004.113959	1004.153777	1004.193578	1004.233362	1004.273128	1004.312877	1004.352608
2	503.057663	503.087581	503.117485	503.147377	503.177257	503.207123	503.236978	503.266819
3	336.053097	336.079726	336.106345	336.132952	336.159549	336.186134	336.212709	336.239273
4	252.551504	252.576503	252.601492	252.626471	252.651440	252.676399	252.701348	252.726288
5	202.451100	202.475132	202.499154	202.523167	202.547170	202.571165	202.595150	202.619126
6	169.051291	169.074687	169.098073	169.121451	169.144821	169.168182	169.191534	169.214877
7	145.194679	145.217628	145.240569	145.263501	145.286426	145.309342	145.332250	145.355150
8	127.302565	127.325186	127.347799	127.370404	127.393002	127.415591	127.438173	127.460748
9	113.386783	113.409155	113.431519	113.453876	113.476225	113.498567	113.520902	113.543229
10	102.254434	102.276611	102.298782	102.320946	102.343102	102.365252	102.387394	102.409530
11	93.146399	93.168423	93.190440	93.212451	93.234454	93.256452	93.278442	93.300426
12	85.556599	85.578500	85.600394	85.622282	85.644163	85.666038	85.687906	85.709768
13	79.134674	79.156474	79.178268	79.200056	79.221838	79.243613	79.265383	79.287146
14	73.630364	73.652082	73.673794	73.695500	73.717200	73.738895	73.760584	73.782267
15	68.860145	68.881796	68.903440	68.925079	68.946713	68.968341	68.989964	69.011581
16	64.686377	64.707971	64.729560	64.751144	64.772723	64.794297	64.815865	64.837428
17	61.003802	61.025351	61.046894	61.068432	61.089966	61.111495	61.133018	61.154537
18	57.730556	57.752066	57.773572	57.795073	57.816570	57.838061	57.859549	57.881031
19	54.802007	54.823486	54.844961	54.866432	54.887898	54.909360	54.930817	54.952270
20	52.166451	52.187905	52.209355	52.230801	52.252243	52.273680	52.295114	52.316543
21	49.782032	49.803465	49.824895	49.846322	49.867744	49.889162	49.910577	49.931988
22	47.614503	47.635921	47.657335	47.678746	47.700153	47.721557	47.742957	47.764353
23	45.635575	45.656981	45.678383	45.699782	45.721178	45.742570	45.763959	45.785345
24	43.821673	43.843070	43.864463	43.885854	43.907241	43.928626	43.950007	43.971386
25	42.152993	42.174384	42.195772	42.217157	42.238539	42.259918	42.281295	42.302669
26	40.612779	40.634167	40.655551	40.676933	40.698313	40.719690	40.741064	40.762436
27	39.186758	39.208144	39.229527	39.250908	39.272287	39.293664	39.315039	39.336411
28	37.862693	37.884080	37.905464	37.926847	37.948228	37.969606	37.990983	38.012357
29	36.630039	36.651428	36.672815	36.694201	36.715585	36.736967	36.758347	36.779726
30	35.479653	35.501046	35.522438	35.543828	35.565217	35.586605	35.607991	35.629375
31	34.403575	34.424974	34.446371	34.467768	34.489163	34.510557	34.531950	34.553342
32	33.394837	33.416243	33.437648	33.459052	33.480455	33.501858	33.523259	33.544659
33	32.447319	32.468733	32.490147	32.511559	32.532971	32.554383	32.575794	32.597204
34	31.555618	31.577042	31.598465	31.619887	31.641310	31.662731	31.684153	31.705573
35	30.714950	30.736384	30.757818	30.779251	30.800685	30.822118	30.843551	30.864983
36	29.921063	29.942508	29.963953	29.985398	30.006844	30.028289	30.049735	30.071180
37	29.170163	29.191620	29.213078	29.234535	29.255994	29.277452	29.298911	29.320370
38	28.458856	28.480326	28.501797	28.523268	28.544740	28.566212	28.587685	28.609159
39	27.784097	27.805581	27.827066	27.848551	27.870037	27.891524	27.913012	27.934501
40	27.143145	27.164643	27.186143	27.207643	27.229144	27.250646	27.272150	27.293654
41	26.533527	26.555040	26.576554	26.598069	26.619586	26.641104	26.662624	26.684145
42	25.953003	25.974531	25.996061	26.017593	26.039126	26.060661	26.082197	26.103735
43	25.399544	25.421088	25.442635	25.464183	25.485733	25.507284	25.528838	25.550393
44	24.871305	24.892866	24.914429	24.935994	24.957561	24.979131	25.000702	25.022275
45	24.366605	24.388183	24.409763	24.431345	24.452930	24.474517	24.496107	24.517699
46	23.883908	23.905503	23.927101	23.948701	23.970304	23.991910	24.013518	24.035129
47	23.421809	23.443422	23.465038	23.486657	23.508278	23.529903	23.551530	23.573160
48	22.979022	23.000653	23.022288	23.043925	23.065566	23.087209	23.108856	23.130506
60	18.820398	18.842270	18.864148	18.886032	18.907923	18.929819	18.951721	18.973630
72	16.053491	16.075611	16.097599	16.119917	16.142083	16.164259	16.186444	16.208638
84	14.081787	14.104209	14.126642	14.149088	14.171546	14.194016	14.216498	14.238992
96	12.601016	12.629830	12.652558	12.675301	12.698058	12.720831	12.743618	12.766420
108	11.463776	11.486786	11.509813	11.532858	11.555921	11.579002	11.602100	11.625216
120	10.552353	10.575663	10.598993	10.622344	10.645715	10.669106	10.692518	10.715951
132	9.809585	9.833396	9.856831	9.880488	9.904169	9.927874	9.951601	9.975352
144	9.193294	9.217207	9.241147	9.265113	9.289104	9.313122	9.337165	9.361235
156	8.674279	8.698495	8.722740	8.747014	8.771316	8.795647	8.820007	8.844394
168	8.231683	8.256202	8.280751	8.305332	8.329945	8.354588	8.379263	8.403968
180	7.850208	7.875028	7.899881	7.924769	7.949690	7.974645	7.999634	8.024656
192	7.518381	7.543500	7.568657	7.593849	7.619078	7.644343	7.669644	7.694981
204	7.227426	7.252844	7.278301	7.303798	7.329332	7.354906	7.380517	7.406167
216	6.970518	6.996233	7.021990	7.047788	7.073626	7.099506	7.125426	7.151387
228	6.742268	6.768278	6.794332	6.820429	6.846570	6.872753	6.898979	6.925249
240	6.538365	6.564667	6.591016	6.617410	6.643850	6.670335	6.696865	6.723440
252	6.355316	6.381909	6.408550	6.435239	6.461975	6.488759	6.515590	6.542467
264	6.190265	6.217146	6.244077	6.271057	6.298088	6.325167	6.352296	6.379474
276	6.040852	6.068018	6.095236	6.122505	6.149826	6.177199	6.204623	6.232097
288	5.905108	5.932557	5.960059	5.987614	6.015223	6.042886	6.070601	6.098369
300	5.781382	5.809109	5.836892	5.864731	5.892625	5.920574	5.948577	5.976635
312	5.668273	5.696277	5.724338	5.752456	5.780631	5.808863	5.837152	5.865496
324	5.564590	5.592866	5.621202	5.649597	5.678050	5.706562	5.735131	5.763758
336	5.469310	5.497856	5.526464	5.555131	5.583859	5.612646	5.641493	5.670399
348	5.381552	5.410365	5.439240	5.468177	5.497176	5.526235	5.555356	5.584536
360	5.300552	5.329628	5.358767	5.387970	5.417236	5.446564	5.475954	5.505406
420	4.976274	5.006611	5.037017	5.067491	5.098035	5.128646	5.159324	5.190068
480	4.748649	4.780151	4.811727	4.843374	4.875093	4.906883	4.938743	4.970672

156

MONTHLY WITHDRAWALS PER $1000

EFFECTIVE ANNUAL YIELD

NUMBER OF MONTHLY WTHDRWLS	5.40%	5.45%	5.50%	5.55%	5.60%	5.65%	5.70%	5.75%
1	1004.392322	1004.432019	1004.471699	1004.511361	1004.551007	1004.590635	1004.630246	1004.669839
2	503.296648	503.326464	503.356268	503.386059	503.415838	503.445604	503.475358	503.505099
3	336.265826	336.292368	336.318900	336.345420	336.371930	336.398429	336.424917	336.451394
4	252.751217	252.776137	252.801047	252.825947	252.850837	252.875717	252.900588	252.925448
5	202.643093	202.667051	202.691000	202.714939	202.738870	202.762791	202.786703	202.810606
6	169.238212	169.261539	169.284856	169.308165	169.331466	169.354758	169.378041	169.401316
7	145.378041	145.400925	145.423800	145.446667	145.469526	145.492377	145.515220	145.538055
8	127.483314	127.505873	127.528424	127.550967	127.573502	127.596030	127.618550	127.641062
9	113.565549	113.587862	113.610167	113.632465	113.654755	113.677038	113.699313	113.721582
10	102.431658	102.453780	102.475894	102.498001	102.520101	102.542195	102.564281	102.586360
11	93.322403	93.344373	93.366336	93.388293	93.410243	93.432187	93.454124	93.476054
12	85.731624	85.753473	85.775316	85.797152	85.818982	85.840806	85.862623	85.884434
13	79.308903	79.330655	79.352400	79.374139	79.395872	79.417599	79.439320	79.461035
14	73.803944	73.825615	73.847281	73.868941	73.890595	73.912243	73.933886	73.955522
15	69.033193	69.054799	69.076399	69.097995	69.119584	69.141168	69.162747	69.184320
16	64.858986	64.880538	64.902086	64.923628	64.945165	64.966697	64.988224	65.009745
17	61.176051	61.197560	61.219064	61.240563	61.262057	61.283546	61.305030	61.326509
18	57.902509	57.923982	57.945451	57.966914	57.988374	58.009828	58.031278	58.052723
19	54.973719	54.995163	55.016603	55.038039	55.059470	55.080897	55.102319	55.123737
20	52.337969	52.359390	52.380807	52.402220	52.423629	52.445034	52.466434	52.487831
21	49.953395	49.974798	49.996197	50.017592	50.038984	50.060372	50.081756	50.103136
22	47.785746	47.807135	47.828521	47.849903	47.871281	47.892656	47.914028	47.935396
23	45.806728	45.828107	45.849483	45.870855	45.892223	45.913590	45.934953	45.956312
24	43.992761	44.014133	44.035503	44.056869	44.078232	44.099592	44.120949	44.142303
25	42.324040	42.345408	42.366774	42.388137	42.409497	42.430854	42.452208	42.473560
26	40.783805	40.805172	40.826537	40.847899	40.869258	40.890615	40.911969	40.933321
27	39.357781	39.379149	39.400514	39.421877	39.443238	39.464597	39.485953	39.507308
28	38.033730	38.055100	38.076469	38.097836	38.119201	38.140563	38.161923	38.183282
29	36.801103	36.822478	36.843852	36.865223	36.886593	36.907962	36.929328	36.950693
30	35.650758	35.672140	35.693520	35.714498	35.736275	35.757651	35.779025	35.800397
31	34.574732	34.596122	34.617510	34.638896	34.660282	34.681666	34.703049	34.724431
32	33.566058	33.587456	33.608854	33.630250	33.651645	33.673040	33.694433	33.715825
33	32.618613	32.640021	32.661429	32.682836	32.704243	32.725648	32.747053	32.768457
34	31.726994	31.748414	31.769833	31.791252	31.812671	31.834089	31.855506	31.876923
35	30.886416	30.907848	30.929280	30.950712	30.972144	30.993575	31.015006	31.036437
36	30.092626	30.114071	30.135517	30.156962	30.178408	30.199854	30.221300	30.242745
37	29.341829	29.363289	29.384749	29.406209	29.427670	29.449131	29.470592	29.492053
38	28.630633	28.652108	28.673583	28.695059	28.716535	28.738012	28.759489	28.780967
39	27.955990	27.977481	27.998972	28.020464	28.041956	28.063450	28.084944	28.106439
40	27.315160	27.336666	27.358174	27.379683	27.401192	27.422703	27.444215	27.465727
41	26.705667	26.727191	26.748715	26.770241	26.791769	26.813297	26.834827	26.856359
42	26.125274	26.146815	26.168358	26.189902	26.211447	26.232994	26.254543	26.276093
43	25.571951	25.593510	25.615070	25.636633	25.658197	25.679763	25.701331	25.722901
44	25.043851	25.065428	25.087008	25.108589	25.130173	25.151759	25.173346	25.194936
45	24.539293	24.560889	24.582488	24.604089	24.625693	24.647298	24.668906	24.690516
46	24.056742	24.078358	24.099976	24.121597	24.143221	24.164847	24.186475	24.208106
47	23.594793	23.616429	23.638067	23.659709	23.681353	23.702999	23.724649	23.746301
48	23.152159	23.173815	23.195473	23.217135	23.238800	23.260468	23.282139	23.303813
60	18.995544	19.017465	19.039391	19.061324	19.083262	19.105207	19.127157	19.149113
72	16.230840	16.253052	16.275272	16.297502	16.319740	16.341987	16.364244	16.386508
84	14.261497	14.284014	14.306544	14.329085	14.351637	14.374202	14.396778	14.419366
96	12.789237	12.812069	12.834915	12.857775	12.880651	12.903541	12.926446	12.949365
108	11.648349	11.671500	11.694668	11.717854	11.741057	11.764277	11.787515	11.810770
120	10.739403	10.762876	10.786369	10.809883	10.833416	10.856970	10.880543	10.904137
132	9.999125	10.022922	10.046741	10.070583	10.094448	10.118336	10.142247	10.166180
144	9.385329	9.409450	9.433596	9.457768	9.481965	9.506187	9.530435	9.554708
156	8.868810	8.893254	8.917727	8.942227	8.966756	8.991312	9.015897	9.040509
168	8.428704	8.453471	8.478269	8.503098	8.527957	8.552846	8.577766	8.602716
180	8.049711	8.074800	8.099921	8.125076	8.150264	8.175485	8.200738	8.226024
192	7.720354	7.745762	7.771206	7.796685	7.822200	7.847750	7.873335	7.898955
204	7.431855	7.457581	7.483345	7.509147	7.534986	7.560863	7.586777	7.612729
216	7.177388	7.203429	7.229511	7.255632	7.281794	7.307995	7.334236	7.360516
228	6.951560	6.977915	7.004311	7.030750	7.057230	7.083753	7.110317	7.136923
240	6.750059	6.776724	6.803432	6.830185	6.856982	6.883823	6.910707	6.937635
252	6.569392	6.596363	6.623381	6.650445	6.677554	6.704710	6.731911	6.759158
264	6.406700	6.433975	6.461299	6.488670	6.516089	6.543556	6.571071	6.598632
276	6.259622	6.287198	6.314823	6.342499	6.370224	6.397999	6.425822	6.453695
288	6.126189	6.154062	6.181986	6.209962	6.237989	6.266068	6.294197	6.322377
300	6.004747	6.032913	6.061132	6.089405	6.117730	6.146108	6.174539	6.203022
312	5.893896	5.922351	5.950861	5.979427	6.008046	6.036720	6.065448	6.094230
324	5.792442	5.821183	5.849981	5.878835	5.907744	5.936710	5.965730	5.994806
336	5.699363	5.728386	5.757467	5.786605	5.815801	5.845053	5.874362	5.903727
348	5.613777	5.643078	5.672437	5.701856	5.731333	5.760868	5.790461	5.820111
360	5.534919	5.564493	5.594127	5.623821	5.653575	5.683388	5.713260	5.743191
420	5.220879	5.251755	5.282697	5.313702	5.344772	5.375905	5.407100	5.438358
480	5.002670	5.034736	5.066869	5.099069	5.131335	5.163666	5.196061	5.228520

MONTHLY WITHDRAWALS PER $1000

EFFECTIVE ANNUAL YIELD

NUMBER OF MONTHLY WTHDRWLS	5.80%	5.85%	5.90%	5.95%	6.00%	6.05%	6.10%	6.15%
1	1004.709416	1004.748975	1004.788517	1004.828043	1004.867551	1004.907042	1004.946515	1004.985972
2	503.534828	503.564544	503.594247	503.623939	503.653617	503.683284	503.712938	503.742579
3	336.477861	336.504317	336.530762	336.557196	336.583619	336.610032	336.636434	336.662826
4	252.950299	252.975140	252.999972	253.024793	253.049605	253.074407	253.099200	253.123982
5	202.834500	202.858385	202.882260	202.906127	202.929984	202.953833	202.977672	203.001503
6	169.424582	169.447839	169.471088	169.494329	169.517561	169.540784	169.563999	169.587205
7	145.560881	145.583699	145.606510	145.629312	145.652106	145.674892	145.697670	145.720440
8	127.663567	127.686063	127.708552	127.731034	127.753508	127.775974	127.798432	127.820883
9	113.743843	113.766096	113.788343	113.810582	113.832813	113.855037	113.877254	113.899464
10	102.608432	102.630498	102.652556	102.674607	102.696651	102.718689	102.740719	102.762742
11	93.497977	93.519894	93.541804	93.563708	93.585604	93.607494	93.629378	93.651255
12	85.906239	85.928037	85.949829	85.971614	85.993393	86.015166	86.036933	86.058693
13	79.482743	79.504446	79.526143	79.547833	79.569518	79.591196	79.612869	79.634535
14	73.977153	73.998779	74.020398	74.042012	74.063620	74.085222	74.106819	74.128409
15	69.205888	69.227450	69.249007	69.270558	69.292104	69.313645	69.335179	69.356709
16	65.031261	65.052772	65.074278	65.095779	65.117274	65.138764	65.160249	65.181729
17	61.347984	61.369453	61.390918	61.412377	61.433832	61.455282	61.476727	61.498167
18	58.074164	58.095600	58.117031	58.138458	58.159880	58.181297	58.202710	58.224118
19	55.145151	55.166560	55.187965	55.209366	55.230762	55.252153	55.273541	55.294924
20	52.509223	52.530612	52.551996	52.573376	52.594752	52.616124	52.637492	52.658856
21	50.124512	50.145884	50.167253	50.188617	50.209978	50.231335	50.252688	50.274038
22	47.956760	47.978120	47.999478	48.020831	48.042181	48.063527	48.084870	48.106209
23	45.977668	45.999021	46.020370	46.041716	46.063059	46.084398	46.105734	46.127067
24	44.163654	44.185002	44.206347	44.227689	44.249028	44.270363	44.291696	44.313026
25	42.494909	42.516255	42.537598	42.558939	42.580276	42.601611	42.622943	42.644272
26	40.954670	40.976017	40.997361	41.018702	41.040042	41.061378	41.082712	41.104044
27	39.528659	39.550009	39.571356	39.592701	39.614044	39.635384	39.656723	39.678059
28	38.204638	38.225993	38.247345	38.268695	38.290044	38.311390	38.332735	38.354077
29	36.972056	36.993417	37.014776	37.036134	37.057490	37.078844	37.100196	37.121547
30	35.821768	35.843138	35.864505	35.885872	35.907237	35.928600	35.949962	35.971323
31	34.745811	34.767190	34.788568	34.809945	34.831321	34.852695	34.874068	34.895439
32	33.737217	33.758607	33.779996	33.801385	33.822772	33.844158	33.865544	33.886928
33	32.789861	32.811263	32.832665	32.854066	32.875467	32.896866	32.918265	32.939663
34	31.898340	31.919756	31.941171	31.962586	31.984001	32.005415	32.026828	32.048241
35	31.057868	31.079298	31.100728	31.122158	31.143588	31.165017	31.186446	31.207875
36	30.264191	30.285637	30.307082	30.328528	30.349974	30.371420	30.392865	30.414311
37	29.513515	29.534977	29.556439	29.577901	29.599364	29.620827	29.642290	29.663753
38	28.802445	28.823924	28.845403	28.866883	28.888363	28.909844	28.931325	28.952807
39	28.127934	28.149431	28.170928	28.192426	28.213925	28.235424	28.256924	28.278425
40	27.487241	27.508756	27.530272	27.551788	27.573306	27.594825	27.616345	27.637865
41	26.877891	26.899425	26.920960	26.942496	26.964033	26.985572	27.007112	27.028653
42	26.297645	26.319198	26.340753	26.362309	26.383866	26.405426	26.426986	26.448548
43	25.744472	25.766046	25.787621	25.809197	25.830776	25.852356	25.873937	25.895521
44	25.216528	25.238121	25.259717	25.281315	25.302914	25.324516	25.346119	25.367725
45	24.712129	24.733743	24.755360	24.776979	24.798601	24.820224	24.841850	24.863478
46	24.229740	24.251376	24.273014	24.294655	24.316299	24.337945	24.359593	24.381244
47	23.767056	23.788614	23.811275	23.832938	23.854604	23.876273	23.897944	23.919618
48	23.325490	23.347170	23.368853	23.390539	23.412228	23.433920	23.455615	23.477312
60	19.171075	19.193043	19.215017	19.236997	19.258983	19.280975	19.302972	19.324975
72	16.408782	16.431065	16.453356	16.475656	16.497965	16.520282	16.542608	16.564943
84	14.441965	14.464576	14.487199	14.509833	14.532479	14.555137	14.577806	14.600486
96	12.972299	12.995246	13.018209	13.041186	13.064177	13.087182	13.110202	13.133235
108	11.834042	11.857332	11.880638	11.903962	11.927303	11.950660	11.974035	11.997427
120	10.927750	10.951384	10.975037	10.998710	11.022403	11.046115	11.069847	11.093599
132	10.190136	10.214114	10.238115	10.262138	10.286184	10.310252	10.334342	10.358454
144	9.579006	9.603330	9.627678	9.652051	9.676450	9.700873	9.725321	9.749793
156	9.065149	9.089816	9.114511	9.139234	9.163984	9.188761	9.213565	9.238397
168	8.627696	8.652706	8.677746	8.702816	8.727916	8.753046	8.778205	8.803394
180	8.251343	8.276694	8.302077	8.327493	8.352941	8.378421	8.403933	8.429477
192	7.924610	7.950304	7.976024	8.001783	8.027576	8.053404	8.079265	8.105161
204	7.638717	7.664743	7.690805	7.716904	7.743040	7.769212	7.795421	7.821666
216	7.386835	7.413193	7.439591	7.466027	7.492502	7.519016	7.545568	7.572158
228	7.163570	7.190258	7.216987	7.243757	7.270568	7.297419	7.324311	7.351243
240	6.964606	6.991620	7.018678	7.045778	7.072921	7.100106	7.127333	7.154603
252	6.786450	6.813787	6.841168	6.868595	6.896065	6.923580	6.951140	6.978742
264	6.626241	6.653897	6.681599	6.709347	6.737142	6.764982	6.792869	6.820800
276	6.481617	6.509587	6.537605	6.565671	6.593786	6.621947	6.650156	6.678412
288	6.350607	6.378887	6.407218	6.435597	6.464026	6.492505	6.521031	6.549607
300	6.231557	6.260202	6.288780	6.317469	6.346208	6.374998	6.403838	6.432728
312	6.123064	6.151952	6.180892	6.209885	6.238930	6.268027	6.297175	6.326374
324	6.023936	6.053121	6.082359	6.111651	6.140996	6.170395	6.199846	6.229349
336	5.933148	5.962625	5.992156	6.021743	6.051384	6.081079	6.110827	6.140629
348	5.849818	5.879581	5.909401	5.939277	5.969208	5.999194	6.029235	6.059331
360	5.773179	5.803225	5.833328	5.863488	5.893704	5.923976	5.954304	5.984687
420	5.469678	5.501059	5.532500	5.564001	5.595562	5.627182	5.658861	5.690597
480	5.261042	5.293627	5.326273	5.358980	5.391748	5.424575	5.457462	5.490407

158

MONTHLY WITHDRAWALS PER $1000

NUMBER OF MONTHLY WITHDRWLS	EFFECTIVE ANNUAL YIELD							
	6.20%	6.25%	6.30%	6.35%	6.40%	6.45%	6.50%	6.55%
1	1005.025412	1005.064835	1005.104241	1005.143630	1005.183001	1005.222356	1005.261694	1005.301015
2	503.772208	503.801825	503.831429	503.861021	503.890600	503.920167	503.949722	503.979265
3	336.689206	336.715576	336.741935	336.768284	336.794622	336.820949	336.847266	336.873572
4	253.148755	253.173518	253.198271	253.223015	253.247749	253.272473	253.297188	253.321893
5	203.025324	203.049136	203.072939	203.096733	203.120518	203.144294	203.168062	203.191820
6	169.610403	169.633592	169.656773	169.679945	169.703109	169.726264	169.749411	169.772549
7	145.743202	145.765956	145.788701	145.811439	145.834169	145.856890	145.879604	145.902309
8	127.843326	127.865761	127.888189	127.910609	127.933021	127.955426	127.977823	128.000213
9	113.921666	113.943862	113.966049	113.988230	114.010403	114.032569	114.054728	114.076879
10	102.784759	102.806768	102.828771	102.850766	102.872755	102.894737	102.916711	102.938679
11	93.673125	93.694989	93.716846	93.738696	93.760540	93.782377	93.804207	93.826031
12	86.080447	86.102194	86.123935	86.145670	86.167399	86.189121	86.210837	86.232547
13	79.656195	79.677850	79.699498	79.721141	79.742777	79.764407	79.786032	79.807650
14	74.149994	74.171574	74.193147	74.214715	74.236277	74.257833	74.279384	74.300929
15	69.378233	69.399752	69.421265	69.442772	69.464275	69.485771	69.507263	69.528749
16	65.203204	65.224674	65.246138	65.267597	65.289051	65.310500	65.331944	65.353383
17	61.519602	61.541032	61.562457	61.583878	61.605293	61.626704	61.648110	61.669511
18	58.245522	58.266921	58.288315	58.309705	58.331090	58.352470	58.373846	58.395217
19	55.316303	55.337677	55.359047	55.380413	55.401774	55.423131	55.444484	55.465832
20	52.680215	52.701571	52.722922	52.744270	52.765613	52.786952	52.808287	52.829618
21	50.295383	50.316725	50.338063	50.359397	50.380727	50.402054	50.423376	50.444695
22	48.127545	48.148877	48.170206	48.191531	48.212852	48.234170	48.255484	48.276795
23	46.148397	46.169723	46.191046	46.212365	46.233682	46.254995	46.276304	46.297611
24	44.334352	44.355676	44.376996	44.398314	44.419628	44.440939	44.462248	44.483553
25	42.665599	42.686923	42.708244	42.729562	42.750877	42.772190	42.793499	42.814806
26	41.125373	41.146699	41.168023	41.189344	41.210663	41.231979	41.253293	41.274604
27	39.699392	39.720724	39.742053	39.763379	39.784704	39.806026	39.827346	39.848663
28	38.375417	38.396756	38.418092	38.439426	38.460758	38.482088	38.503416	38.524742
29	37.142895	37.164242	37.185588	37.206931	37.228273	37.249613	37.270951	37.292287
30	35.992681	36.014039	36.035394	36.056749	36.078101	36.099453	36.120802	36.142150
31	34.916810	34.938179	34.959547	34.980913	35.002279	35.023643	35.045005	35.066367
32	33.908311	33.929693	33.951075	33.972455	33.993834	34.015212	34.036589	34.057965
33	32.961060	32.982457	33.003853	33.025248	33.046642	33.068035	33.089428	33.110820
34	32.069654	32.091065	32.112477	32.133888	32.155298	32.176708	32.198117	32.219526
35	31.229304	31.250732	31.272160	31.293588	31.315015	31.336442	31.357869	31.379296
36	30.435756	30.457202	30.478648	30.500093	30.521539	30.542984	30.564429	30.585875
37	29.685217	29.706680	29.728144	29.749609	29.771073	29.792537	29.814002	29.835467
38	28.974289	28.995772	29.017255	29.038738	29.060222	29.081707	29.103192	29.124677
39	28.299927	28.321429	28.342932	28.364435	28.385940	28.407445	28.428951	28.450457
40	27.659387	27.680909	27.702433	27.723957	27.745483	27.767009	27.788536	27.810064
41	27.050195	27.071738	27.093283	27.114829	27.136376	27.157924	27.179473	27.201024
42	26.470111	26.491676	26.513243	26.534810	26.556380	26.577950	26.599522	26.621096
43	25.917106	25.938693	25.960281	25.981872	26.003464	26.025057	26.046652	26.068249
44	25.389332	25.410941	25.432553	25.454166	25.475781	25.497398	25.519017	25.540638
45	24.885108	24.906740	24.928374	24.950011	24.971650	24.993291	25.014934	25.036579
46	24.402897	24.424553	24.446211	24.467871	24.489534	24.511199	24.532866	24.554536
47	23.941295	23.962974	23.984656	24.006341	24.028028	24.049718	24.071410	24.093105
48	23.499013	23.520716	23.542422	23.564132	23.585844	23.607559	23.629277	23.650997
60	19.346984	19.368999	19.391020	19.413046	19.435078	19.457116	19.479160	19.501209
72	16.587286	16.609639	16.631999	16.654369	16.676746	16.699133	16.721528	16.743931
84	14.623178	14.645881	14.668596	14.691322	14.714059	14.736808	14.759568	14.782339
96	13.156283	13.179346	13.202422	13.225513	13.248617	13.271736	13.294868	13.318015
108	12.020836	12.044261	12.067703	12.091162	12.114638	12.138131	12.161640	12.185166
120	11.117370	11.141161	11.164971	11.188801	11.212650	11.236518	11.260405	11.284312
132	10.382589	10.406745	10.430924	10.455125	10.479347	10.503591	10.527857	10.552145
144	9.774290	9.798812	9.823359	9.847929	9.872525	9.897144	9.921788	9.946456
156	9.263256	9.288142	9.313054	9.337994	9.362960	9.387954	9.412973	9.438020
168	8.828613	8.853860	8.879138	8.904444	8.929779	8.955143	8.980537	9.005959
180	8.455052	8.480659	8.506298	8.531968	8.557670	8.583403	8.609167	8.634962
192	8.131091	8.157055	8.183052	8.209083	8.235148	8.261246	8.287377	8.313541
204	7.847947	7.874263	7.900616	7.927004	7.953428	7.979888	8.006382	8.032912
216	7.598786	7.625453	7.652157	7.678898	7.705678	7.732495	7.759349	7.786240
228	7.378215	7.405226	7.432278	7.459369	7.486500	7.513669	7.540878	7.568126
240	7.181914	7.209267	7.236662	7.264098	7.291575	7.319093	7.346652	7.374252
252	7.006389	7.034079	7.061812	7.089588	7.117407	7.145269	7.173173	7.201120
264	6.848777	6.876800	6.904867	6.932978	6.961134	6.989334	7.017579	7.045867
276	6.706715	6.735065	6.763460	6.791902	6.820390	6.848923	6.877502	6.906126
288	6.578231	6.606902	6.635622	6.664389	6.693203	6.722064	6.750972	6.779926
300	6.461668	6.490656	6.519694	6.548781	6.577916	6.607099	6.636331	6.665609
312	6.355624	6.384924	6.414275	6.443676	6.473126	6.502626	6.532175	6.561772
324	6.258904	6.288511	6.318169	6.347878	6.377638	6.407449	6.437309	6.467219
336	6.170484	6.200392	6.230352	6.260364	6.290427	6.320542	6.350707	6.380923
348	6.089480	6.119682	6.149938	6.180247	6.210608	6.241021	6.271486	6.302002
360	6.015125	6.045617	6.076163	6.106762	6.137415	6.168121	6.198878	6.229688
420	5.722391	5.754241	5.786148	5.818110	5.850128	5.882201	5.914327	5.946508
480	5.523409	5.556468	5.589584	5.622755	5.655982	5.689262	5.722597	5.755984

MONTHLY WITHDRAWALS PER $1000

EFFECTIVE ANNUAL YIELD

NUMBER OF MONTHLY WTHDRWLS	6.60%	6.65%	6.70%	6.75%	6.80%	6.85%	6.90%	6.95%
1	1005.340319	1005.379607	1005.418877	1005.458130	1005.497367	1005.536587	1005.575790	1005.614976
2	504.008795	504.038313	504.067818	504.097312	504.126793	504.156261	504.185718	504.215162
3	336.899867	336.926152	336.952426	336.978689	337.004942	337.031184	337.057416	337.083637
4	253.346588	253.371274	253.395950	253.420616	253.445273	253.469920	253.494557	253.519185
5	203.215569	203.239309	203.263040	203.286762	203.310475	203.334180	203.357875	203.381561
6	169.795679	169.818801	169.841914	169.865018	169.888114	169.911202	169.934281	169.957352
7	145.925007	145.947696	145.970378	145.993051	146.015717	146.038374	146.061024	146.083666
8	128.022595	128.044969	128.067336	128.089695	128.112047	128.134391	128.156727	128.179056
9	114.099023	114.121160	114.143290	114.165412	114.187528	114.209636	114.231736	114.253830
10	102.960640	102.982594	103.004541	103.026481	103.048415	103.070341	103.092261	103.114173
11	93.847848	93.869659	93.891463	93.913261	93.935052	93.956836	93.978614	94.000385
12	86.254250	86.275947	86.297638	86.319322	86.341001	86.362673	86.384338	86.405998
13	79.829262	79.850868	79.872469	79.894063	79.915652	79.937234	79.958810	79.980381
14	74.322468	74.344002	74.365529	74.387052	74.408568	74.430079	74.451584	74.473083
15	69.550229	69.571704	69.593174	69.614638	69.636097	69.657550	69.678998	69.700441
16	65.374816	65.396244	65.417668	65.439086	65.460499	65.481906	65.503309	65.524706
17	61.690907	61.712298	61.733684	61.755066	61.776442	61.797814	61.819181	61.840543
18	58.416584	58.437946	58.459303	58.480656	58.502004	58.523348	58.544687	58.566021
19	55.487176	55.508515	55.529851	55.551182	55.572508	55.593830	55.615148	55.636462
20	52.850945	52.872268	52.893587	52.914902	52.936213	52.957519	52.978822	53.000120
21	50.466010	50.487321	50.508628	50.529932	50.551232	50.572527	50.593819	50.615108
22	48.298102	48.319406	48.340706	48.362002	48.383295	48.404584	48.425870	48.447152
23	46.318914	46.340214	46.361510	46.382803	46.404093	46.425379	46.446663	46.467943
24	44.504855	44.526154	44.547450	44.568743	44.590033	44.611320	44.632604	44.653885
25	42.836110	42.857412	42.878710	42.900006	42.921299	42.942589	42.963876	42.985161
26	41.295913	41.317219	41.338522	41.359823	41.381122	41.402417	41.423711	41.445001
27	39.869979	39.891292	39.912602	39.933911	39.955217	39.976521	39.997822	40.019122
28	38.546066	38.567388	38.588708	38.610026	38.631342	38.652656	38.673967	38.695277
29	37.313621	37.334954	37.356285	37.377614	37.398941	37.420267	37.441590	37.462912
30	36.163497	36.184842	36.206185	36.227527	36.248868	36.270206	36.291544	36.312879
31	35.087727	35.109085	35.130443	35.151799	35.173154	35.194508	35.215860	35.237211
32	34.079340	34.100714	34.122086	34.143458	34.164829	34.186199	34.207567	34.228935
33	33.132210	33.153601	33.174990	33.196379	33.217766	33.239153	33.260539	33.281925
34	32.240934	32.262341	32.283748	32.305155	32.326560	32.347966	32.369370	32.390774
35	31.400722	31.422148	31.443573	31.464999	31.486424	31.507848	31.529272	31.550696
36	30.607320	30.628765	30.650210	30.671655	30.693100	30.714545	30.735990	30.757434
37	29.856932	29.878397	29.899863	29.921328	29.942794	29.964260	29.985726	30.007192
38	29.146163	29.167649	29.189135	29.210622	29.232110	29.253597	29.275086	29.296574
39	28.471964	28.493473	28.514980	28.536489	28.557999	28.579509	28.601020	28.622531
40	27.831343	27.853123	27.874654	27.896186	27.917718	27.939252	27.960786	27.982321
41	27.222575	27.244128	27.265682	27.287237	27.308793	27.330350	27.351909	27.373468
42	26.642670	26.664247	26.685824	26.707403	26.728983	26.750565	26.772148	26.793732
43	26.089848	26.111448	26.133049	26.154653	26.176258	26.197864	26.219472	26.241082
44	25.562260	25.583885	25.605511	25.627139	25.648769	25.670401	25.692035	25.713670
45	25.058226	25.079875	25.101527	25.123180	25.144836	25.166494	25.188153	25.209815
46	24.576209	24.597883	24.619560	24.641240	24.662921	24.684605	24.706291	24.727980
47	24.114083	24.136503	24.158206	24.179912	24.201620	24.223330	24.245043	24.266759
48	23.672721	23.694447	23.716176	23.737908	23.759643	23.781381	23.803121	23.824864
60	19.523264	19.545324	19.567391	19.589463	19.611540	19.633623	19.655712	19.677806
72	16.766343	16.788764	16.811193	16.833630	16.856076	16.878530	16.900992	16.923463
84	14.805122	14.827916	14.850721	14.873537	14.896364	14.919202	14.942052	14.964912
96	13.341176	13.364350	13.387538	13.410741	13.433957	13.457186	13.480430	13.503687
108	12.208708	12.232267	12.255843	12.279435	12.303043	12.326668	12.350309	12.373967
120	11.308228	11.332183	11.356147	11.380130	11.404133	11.428154	11.452193	11.476252
132	10.576455	10.600786	10.625139	10.649513	10.673909	10.698326	10.722764	10.747224
144	9.971148	9.995864	10.020604	10.045368	10.070156	10.094968	10.119803	10.144662
156	9.463092	9.488192	9.513317	9.538469	9.563647	9.588851	9.614081	9.639337
168	9.031410	9.056889	9.082398	9.107934	9.133499	9.159093	9.184714	9.210364
180	8.660788	8.686644	8.712532	8.738450	8.764399	8.790378	8.816387	8.842427
192	8.339739	8.365969	8.392232	8.418528	8.444856	8.471217	8.497610	8.524036
204	8.059477	8.086077	8.112711	8.139381	8.166084	8.192822	8.219595	8.246401
216	7.813168	7.840132	7.867134	7.894172	7.921246	7.948357	7.975503	8.002686
228	7.595413	7.622738	7.650101	7.677503	7.704943	7.732421	7.759936	7.787490
240	7.401892	7.429573	7.457293	7.485053	7.512853	7.540693	7.568572	7.596490
252	7.229108	7.257139	7.285211	7.313324	7.341479	7.369675	7.397911	7.426188
264	7.074198	7.102573	7.130991	7.159452	7.187955	7.216501	7.245089	7.273719
276	6.934795	6.963509	6.992267	7.021069	7.049915	7.078805	7.107739	7.136715
288	6.808927	6.837973	6.867066	6.896203	6.925386	6.954613	6.983886	7.013202
300	6.694936	6.724309	6.753729	6.783196	6.812708	6.842267	6.871872	6.901521
312	6.591418	6.621112	6.650854	6.680643	6.710479	6.740363	6.770292	6.800269
324	6.497178	6.527186	6.557243	6.587348	6.617502	6.647703	6.677951	6.708247
336	6.411190	6.441506	6.471872	6.502286	6.532750	6.563262	6.593822	6.624430
348	6.332569	6.363187	6.393854	6.424572	6.455339	6.486155	6.517019	6.547932
360	6.260549	6.291467	6.322425	6.353438	6.384501	6.415614	6.446776	6.477987
420	5.978741	6.011027	6.043365	6.075755	6.108195	6.140686	6.173228	6.205818
480	5.789424	5.822915	5.856458	5.890051	5.923694	5.957386	5.991127	6.024915

160

MONTHLY WITHDRAWALS PER $1000

NUMBER OF MONTHLY WTHDRWLS	EFFECTIVE ANNUAL YIELD							
	7.00%	7.05%	7.10%	7.15%	7.20%	7.25%	7.30%	7.35%
1	1005.654145	1005.693298	1005.732434	1005.771553	1005.810655	1005.849741	1005.888810	1005.927862
2	504.244594	504.274014	504.303421	504.332817	504.362200	504.391571	504.420929	504.450276
3	337.109848	337.136048	337.162237	337.188416	337.214585	337.240743	337.266890	337.293027
4	253.543803	253.568412	253.593011	253.617600	253.642180	253.666750	253.691311	253.715862
5	203.405239	203.428907	203.452567	203.476218	203.499859	203.523492	203.547116	203.570731
6	169.980415	170.003469	170.026514	170.049552	170.072581	170.095601	170.118613	170.141617
7	146.106299	146.128925	146.151543	146.174153	146.196754	146.219348	146.241934	146.264513
8	128.201377	128.223691	128.245997	128.268295	128.290586	128.312870	128.335145	128.357414
9	114.275916	114.297995	114.320067	114.342132	114.364190	114.386240	114.408283	114.430319
10	103.136079	103.157978	103.179870	103.201755	103.223633	103.245505	103.267369	103.289227
11	94.022150	94.043908	94.065659	94.087404	94.109143	94.130875	94.152600	94.174319
12	86.427651	86.449298	86.470939	86.492573	86.514201	86.535823	86.557439	86.579048
13	80.001945	80.023504	80.045056	80.066603	80.088144	80.109678	80.131207	80.152730
14	74.494577	74.516065	74.537547	74.559024	74.580495	74.601960	74.623420	74.644874
15	69.721878	69.743310	69.764736	69.786157	69.807573	69.828983	69.850388	69.871788
16	65.546099	65.567486	65.588868	65.610245	65.631617	65.652984	65.674345	65.695702
17	61.861900	61.883252	61.904599	61.925942	61.947279	61.968612	61.989940	62.011263
18	58.587351	58.608676	58.629997	58.651313	58.672624	58.693931	58.715233	58.736531
19	55.657771	55.679076	55.700377	55.721673	55.742965	55.764252	55.785536	55.806814
20	53.021414	53.042705	53.063991	53.085273	53.106551	53.127825	53.149095	53.170361
21	50.636392	50.657673	50.678949	50.700222	50.721492	50.742757	50.764018	50.785276
22	48.468431	48.489706	48.510978	48.532246	48.553510	48.574771	48.596028	48.617282
23	46.489219	46.510492	46.531762	46.553029	46.574293	46.595553	46.616809	46.638063
24	44.675163	44.696437	44.717709	44.738978	44.760243	44.781506	44.802765	44.824021
25	43.006443	43.027722	43.048998	43.070271	43.091542	43.112809	43.134074	43.155336
26	41.466290	41.487575	41.508858	41.530139	41.551417	41.572692	41.593965	41.615236
27	40.040419	40.061713	40.083005	40.104295	40.125583	40.146869	40.168152	40.189432
28	38.716585	38.737890	38.759194	38.780495	38.801794	38.823092	38.844387	38.865680
29	37.484232	37.505551	37.526867	37.548182	37.569494	37.590805	37.612115	37.633422
30	36.334214	36.355546	36.376877	36.398207	36.419534	36.440861	36.462185	36.483508
31	35.258560	35.279909	35.301256	35.322601	35.343946	35.365289	35.386630	35.407971
32	34.250301	34.271666	34.293031	34.314394	34.335756	34.357117	34.378477	34.399836
33	33.303309	33.324693	33.346075	33.367457	33.388838	33.410219	33.431598	33.452976
34	32.412178	32.433581	32.454983	32.476385	32.497786	32.519187	32.540586	32.561986
35	31.572120	31.593543	31.614965	31.636389	31.657811	31.679232	31.700654	31.722075
36	30.778879	30.800323	30.821768	30.843212	30.864656	30.886100	30.907544	30.928987
37	30.028659	30.050125	30.071592	30.093058	30.114525	30.135992	30.157459	30.178927
38	29.318063	29.339552	29.361042	29.382532	29.404022	29.425513	29.447004	29.468495
39	28.644044	28.665556	28.687070	28.708584	28.730098	28.751614	28.773129	28.794646
40	28.003858	28.025394	28.046932	28.068471	28.090010	28.111551	28.133092	28.154634
41	27.395029	27.416591	27.438153	27.459717	27.481282	27.502848	27.524415	27.545983
42	26.815318	26.836905	26.858493	26.880082	26.901674	26.923266	26.944860	26.966455
43	26.262693	26.284306	26.305920	26.327536	26.349154	26.370773	26.392394	26.414016
44	25.735308	25.756947	25.778588	25.800231	25.821875	25.843522	25.865170	25.886820
45	25.231479	25.253145	25.274813	25.296483	25.318155	25.339829	25.361505	25.383183
46	24.749671	24.771364	24.793059	24.814757	24.836457	24.858159	24.879863	24.901570
47	24.288477	24.310198	24.331921	24.353647	24.375375	24.397106	24.418839	24.440575
48	23.846610	23.868359	23.890110	23.911864	23.933621	23.955380	23.977143	23.998908
60	19.699906	19.722012	19.744123	19.766240	19.788362	19.810489	19.832622	19.854761
72	16.945942	16.968430	16.990925	17.013426	17.035942	17.058462	17.080991	17.103528
84	14.987784	15.010667	15.033560	15.056465	15.079380	15.102307	15.125244	15.148192
96	13.526958	13.550243	13.573541	13.596853	13.620178	13.643517	13.666870	13.690236
108	12.397640	12.421330	12.445036	12.468759	12.492497	12.516252	12.540022	12.563809
120	11.500330	11.524426	11.548541	11.572675	11.596829	11.620998	11.645187	11.669395
132	10.771705	10.796207	10.820730	10.845274	10.869840	10.894426	10.919033	10.943661
144	10.169545	10.194451	10.219381	10.244334	10.269310	10.294310	10.319332	10.344378
156	9.664618	9.689926	9.715259	9.740618	9.766003	9.791413	9.816848	9.842308
168	9.236042	9.261747	9.287481	9.313242	9.339031	9.364848	9.390692	9.416563
180	8.868497	8.894597	8.920726	8.946886	8.973075	8.999294	9.025542	9.051820
192	8.550493	8.576983	8.603524	8.630057	8.656642	8.683259	8.709906	8.736585
204	8.273242	8.300116	8.327024	8.353966	8.380941	8.407950	8.434992	8.462066
216	8.029904	8.057158	8.084448	8.111772	8.139132	8.166527	8.193957	8.221422
228	7.815080	7.842708	7.870373	7.898075	7.925814	7.953589	7.981401	8.009249
240	7.624448	7.652444	7.680478	7.708551	7.736663	7.764812	7.793000	7.821225
252	7.454506	7.482864	7.511262	7.539700	7.568177	7.596694	7.625251	7.653846
264	7.302391	7.331105	7.359860	7.388655	7.417492	7.446370	7.475288	7.504246
276	7.165735	7.194797	7.223902	7.253049	7.282239	7.311470	7.340742	7.370056
288	7.042563	7.071967	7.101415	7.130907	7.160441	7.190019	7.219639	7.249301
300	6.931216	6.960956	6.990740	7.020569	7.050441	7.080357	7.110317	7.140319
312	6.830291	6.860358	6.890472	6.920630	6.950833	6.981080	7.011372	7.041707
324	6.738589	6.768978	6.799412	6.829893	6.860419	6.890990	6.921605	6.952266
336	6.655085	6.685787	6.716536	6.747331	6.778172	6.809059	6.839991	6.870968
348	6.578893	6.609901	6.640957	6.672059	6.703208	6.734403	6.765643	6.796929
360	6.509246	6.540553	6.571908	6.603310	6.634758	6.666253	6.697794	6.729381
420	6.238458	6.271146	6.303882	6.336665	6.369495	6.402372	6.435295	6.468263
480	6.058751	6.092634	6.126563	6.160537	6.194556	6.228619	6.262726	6.296877

MONTHLY WITHDRAWALS PER $1000

NUMBER OF MONTHLY WTHDRWLS	EFFECTIVE ANNUAL YIELD							
	7.40%	7.45%	7.50%	7.55%	7.60%	7.65%	7.70%	7.75%
1	1005.966898	1006.005917	1006.044919	1006.083905	1006.122874	1006.161826	1006.200762	1006.239681
2	504.479611	504.508933	504.538243	504.567541	504.596827	504.626101	504.655363	504.684613
3	337.319154	337.345270	337.371375	337.397470	337.423555	337.449629	337.475693	337.501746
4	253.740404	253.764936	253.789459	253.813972	253.838476	253.862970	253.887455	253.911930
5	203.594338	203.617935	203.641524	203.665103	203.688674	203.712236	203.735789	203.759334
6	170.164613	170.187600	170.210579	170.233549	170.256511	170.279465	170.302410	170.325348
7	146.287083	146.309645	146.332199	146.354746	146.377285	146.399815	146.422338	146.444853
8	128.379675	128.401928	128.424174	128.446412	128.468643	128.490866	128.513082	128.535291
9	114.452348	114.474370	114.496384	114.518391	114.540392	114.562385	114.584371	114.606349
10	103.311078	103.332922	103.354759	103.376590	103.398413	103.420230	103.442040	103.463843
11	94.196031	94.217737	94.239436	94.261129	94.282815	94.304495	94.326168	94.347835
12	86.600652	86.622249	86.643839	86.665424	86.687002	86.708575	86.730141	86.751700
13	80.174247	80.195758	80.217263	80.238762	80.260255	80.281742	80.303224	80.324699
14	74.666322	74.687765	74.709202	74.730633	74.752059	74.773479	74.794894	74.816303
15	69.893182	69.914570	69.935954	69.957332	69.978704	70.000072	70.021433	70.042790
16	65.717053	65.738399	65.759741	65.781077	65.802408	65.823734	65.845055	65.866370
17	62.032582	62.053895	62.075204	62.096507	62.117806	62.139101	62.160390	62.181674
18	58.757824	58.779113	58.800397	58.821676	58.842951	58.864221	58.885487	58.906748
19	55.828089	55.849359	55.870625	55.891887	55.913144	55.934397	55.955646	55.976891
20	53.191623	53.212881	53.234134	53.255384	53.276630	53.297871	53.319109	53.340342
21	50.806530	50.827780	50.849027	50.870269	50.891508	50.912743	50.933974	50.955201
22	48.638532	48.659779	48.681022	48.702262	48.723498	48.744730	48.765959	48.787184
23	46.659313	46.680560	46.701803	46.723044	46.744281	46.765514	46.786745	46.807972
24	44.845275	44.866525	44.887772	44.909016	44.930257	44.951496	44.972731	44.993962
25	43.176596	43.197852	43.219106	43.240357	43.261605	43.282850	43.304092	43.325332
26	41.636503	41.657769	41.679031	41.700291	41.721549	41.742804	41.764056	41.785306
27	40.210711	40.231987	40.253261	40.274532	40.295801	40.317068	40.338333	40.359595
28	38.886971	38.908260	38.929547	38.950832	38.972115	38.993396	39.014674	39.035951
29	37.654728	37.676031	37.697333	37.718633	37.739931	37.761228	37.782522	37.803815
30	36.504830	36.526150	36.547468	36.568785	36.590100	36.611414	36.632726	36.654036
31	35.429310	35.450647	35.471984	35.493319	35.514652	35.535984	35.557315	35.578645
32	34.421194	34.442550	34.463906	34.485260	34.506614	34.527966	34.549317	34.570667
33	33.474234	33.495731	33.517107	33.538482	33.559856	33.581230	33.602602	33.623974
34	32.583384	32.604782	32.626180	32.647577	32.668973	32.690368	32.711763	32.733158
35	31.744946	31.764916	31.786336	31.807755	31.829174	31.850592	31.872012	31.893429
36	30.950431	30.971874	30.993318	31.014761	31.036204	31.057647	31.079089	31.100532
37	30.200394	30.221861	30.243329	30.264796	30.286264	30.307732	30.329199	30.350667
38	29.489987	29.511479	29.532972	29.554465	29.575958	29.597451	29.618945	29.640439
39	28.816163	28.837680	28.859198	28.880717	28.902236	28.923756	28.945276	28.966797
40	28.176177	28.197720	28.219264	28.240810	28.262356	28.283902	28.305450	28.326998
41	27.567553	27.589123	27.610694	27.632266	27.653840	27.675414	27.696989	27.718566
42	26.988051	27.009648	27.031247	27.052847	27.074448	27.096051	27.117655	27.139259
43	26.435639	26.457265	26.478891	26.500519	26.522149	26.543780	26.565413	26.587047
44	25.908471	25.930125	25.951780	25.973437	25.995095	26.016755	26.038417	26.060081
45	25.404863	25.426547	25.448229	25.469915	25.491603	25.513293	25.534985	25.556679
46	24.923279	24.944990	24.966703	24.988419	25.010137	25.031856	25.053578	25.075303
47	24.462313	24.484053	24.505796	24.527542	24.549289	24.571040	24.592792	24.614547
48	24.020675	24.042446	24.064219	24.085995	24.107773	24.129554	24.151338	24.173124
60	19.876905	19.899054	19.921209	19.943370	19.965536	19.987707	20.009883	20.032065
72	17.126073	17.148627	17.171188	17.193758	17.216335	17.238921	17.261515	17.284117
84	15.171151	15.194121	15.217102	15.240093	15.263095	15.286108	15.309131	15.332165
96	13.713615	13.737008	13.760414	13.783833	13.807266	13.830712	13.854171	13.877644
108	12.587611	12.611430	12.635264	12.659114	12.682980	12.706861	12.730759	12.754672
120	11.693621	11.717666	11.742128	11.766410	11.790709	11.815026	11.839362	11.863715
132	10.968309	10.992979	11.017669	11.042379	11.067111	11.091862	11.116634	11.141427
144	10.369447	10.394539	10.419654	10.444791	10.469952	10.495135	10.520340	10.545569
156	9.867794	9.893305	9.918841	9.944402	9.969988	9.995599	10.021235	10.046895
168	9.442462	9.468388	9.494341	9.520321	9.546328	9.572362	9.598423	9.624511
180	9.078127	9.104464	9.130829	9.157223	9.183647	9.210099	9.236579	9.263089
192	8.763296	8.790037	8.816809	8.843612	8.870446	8.897310	8.924205	8.951130
204	8.489174	8.516315	8.543488	8.570694	8.597932	8.625202	8.652505	8.679839
216	8.248921	8.276455	8.304023	8.331625	8.359261	8.386931	8.414635	8.442372
228	8.037134	8.065054	8.093010	8.121002	8.149029	8.177091	8.205189	8.233322
240	7.849487	7.877788	7.906125	7.934499	7.962910	7.991358	8.019842	8.048362
252	7.682480	7.711153	7.739864	7.768613	7.797401	7.826226	7.855089	7.883990
264	7.533244	7.562282	7.591360	7.620477	7.649633	7.678828	7.708062	7.737335
276	7.399411	7.428807	7.458244	7.487720	7.517237	7.546794	7.576391	7.606027
288	7.279005	7.308751	7.338538	7.368367	7.398236	7.428147	7.458098	7.488089
300	7.170365	7.200453	7.230583	7.260756	7.290970	7.321225	7.351522	7.381859
312	7.072086	7.102508	7.132973	7.163481	7.194031	7.224623	7.255257	7.285932
324	6.982970	7.013718	7.044510	7.075345	7.106222	7.137142	7.168105	7.199109
336	6.901990	6.933056	6.964166	6.995319	7.026516	7.057755	7.089037	7.120362
348	6.828260	6.859636	6.891055	6.922519	6.954026	6.985576	7.017169	7.048804
360	6.761013	6.792689	6.824410	6.856175	6.887984	6.919836	6.951731	6.983668
420	6.501276	6.534334	6.567435	6.600580	6.633768	6.666998	6.700270	6.733584
480	6.331069	6.365304	6.399580	6.433896	6.468253	6.502649	6.537085	6.571559

MONTHLY WITHDRAWALS PER $1000

NUMBER OF MONTHLY WTHDRWLS	EFFECTIVE ANNUAL YIELD							
	7.80%	7.85%	7.90%	7.95%	8.00%	8.05%	8.10%	8.15%
1	1006.278584	1006.317470	1006.356340	1006.395193	1006.434030	1006.472850	1006.511654	1006.550441
2	504.713850	504.743076	504.772290	504.801491	504.830681	504.859858	504.889024	504.918177
3	337.527789	337.553821	337.579843	337.605855	337.631856	337.657847	337.683828	337.709798
4	253.936395	253.960852	253.985298	254.009736	254.034164	254.058582	254.082991	254.107391
5	203.782869	203.806396	203.829914	203.853423	203.876923	203.900415	203.923898	203.947372
6	170.348277	170.371197	170.394110	170.417014	170.439909	170.462797	170.485676	170.508547
7	146.467360	146.489859	146.512351	146.534834	146.557309	146.579778	146.602238	146.624690
8	128.557491	128.579685	128.601871	128.624049	128.646220	128.668384	128.690540	128.712689
9	114.628321	114.650286	114.672243	114.694193	114.716137	114.738073	114.760002	114.781924
10	103.485640	103.507429	103.529212	103.550988	103.572757	103.594520	103.616275	103.638024
11	94.369495	94.391149	94.412796	94.434437	94.456072	94.477699	94.499321	94.520936
12	86.773254	86.794801	86.816343	86.837878	86.859406	86.880929	86.902446	86.923956
13	80.346169	80.367632	80.389090	80.410542	80.431988	80.453428	80.474862	80.496290
14	74.837706	74.859103	74.880496	74.901882	74.923263	74.944638	74.966007	74.987371
15	70.064141	70.085487	70.106827	70.128163	70.149492	70.170817	70.192136	70.213450
16	65.887681	65.908987	65.930287	65.951582	65.972872	65.994158	66.015438	66.036713
17	62.202954	62.224229	62.245499	62.266764	62.288024	62.309280	62.330531	62.351777
18	58.928004	58.949256	58.970504	58.991747	59.012985	59.034219	59.055448	59.076673
19	55.998131	56.019367	56.040598	56.061825	56.083048	56.104267	56.125481	56.146691
20	53.361572	53.382797	53.404018	53.425235	53.446449	53.467658	53.488863	53.510064
21	50.976425	50.997644	51.018860	51.040072	51.061281	51.082485	51.103686	51.124883
22	48.808406	48.829625	48.850839	48.872050	48.893258	48.914462	48.935663	48.956860
23	46.829196	46.850416	46.871633	46.892847	46.914058	46.935265	46.956469	46.977669
24	45.015191	45.036417	45.057640	45.078860	45.100076	45.121290	45.142501	45.163708
25	43.346569	43.367803	43.389034	43.410263	43.431488	43.452711	43.473931	43.495148
26	41.806553	41.827798	41.849040	41.870280	41.891517	41.912751	41.933983	41.955212
27	40.380855	40.402113	40.423368	40.444621	40.465871	40.487120	40.508366	40.529609
28	39.057225	39.078498	39.099768	39.121036	39.142303	39.163567	39.184829	39.206089
29	37.825106	37.846395	37.867682	37.888967	37.910251	37.931533	37.952812	37.974090
30	36.675345	36.696652	36.717958	36.739262	36.760565	36.781865	36.803164	36.824462
31	35.599973	35.621300	35.642625	35.663949	35.685272	35.706594	35.727914	35.749232
32	34.592016	34.613363	34.634710	34.656056	34.677400	34.698743	34.720085	34.741426
33	33.645344	33.666714	33.688083	33.709451	33.730818	33.752184	33.773550	33.794914
34	32.754551	32.775944	32.797337	32.818728	32.840119	32.861510	32.882899	32.904288
35	31.914847	31.936264	31.957681	31.979097	32.000513	32.021928	32.043343	32.064758
36	31.121974	31.143416	31.164858	31.186300	31.207741	31.229183	31.250624	31.272065
37	30.372135	30.393603	30.415071	30.436539	30.458007	30.479476	30.500944	30.522412
38	29.661933	29.683427	29.704922	29.726418	29.747913	29.769409	29.790905	29.812401
39	28.988318	29.009840	29.031363	29.052885	29.074409	29.095933	29.117457	29.138982
40	28.348547	28.370097	28.391648	28.413199	28.434751	28.456304	28.477857	28.499412
41	27.740143	27.761722	27.783301	27.804881	27.826462	27.848045	27.869628	27.891212
42	27.160866	27.182473	27.204082	27.225692	27.247303	27.268915	27.290528	27.312143
43	26.608683	26.630320	26.651958	26.673598	26.695239	26.716882	26.738526	26.760172
44	26.081747	26.103414	26.125082	26.146753	26.168425	26.190099	26.211774	26.233451
45	25.578374	25.600072	25.621771	25.643473	25.665176	25.686881	25.708589	25.730298
46	25.097029	25.118758	25.140488	25.162221	25.183956	25.205693	25.227432	25.249174
47	24.636305	24.658065	24.679827	24.701591	24.723358	24.745128	24.766899	24.788673
48	24.194913	24.216704	24.238498	24.260295	24.282094	24.303896	24.325701	24.347508
60	20.054252	20.076445	20.098643	20.120846	20.143055	20.165268	20.187488	20.209712
72	17.306727	17.329345	17.351968	17.374605	17.397246	17.419896	17.442554	17.465219
84	15.355210	15.378266	15.401332	15.424408	15.447495	15.470593	15.493701	15.516819
96	13.901129	13.924628	13.948140	13.971665	13.995203	14.018754	14.042318	14.065894
108	12.778601	12.802545	12.826505	12.850480	12.874471	12.898477	12.922499	12.946536
120	11.888087	11.912477	11.936884	11.961310	11.985753	12.010214	12.034692	12.059189
132	11.166240	11.191073	11.215926	11.240799	11.265693	11.290606	11.315539	11.340493
144	10.570820	10.596093	10.621389	10.646706	10.672047	10.697409	10.722793	10.748200
156	10.072580	10.098289	10.124023	10.149781	10.175564	10.201371	10.227201	10.253056
168	9.650625	9.676765	9.702932	9.729126	9.755345	9.781591	9.807862	9.834160
180	9.289626	9.316193	9.342787	9.369409	9.396060	9.422739	9.449445	9.476179
192	8.978086	9.005071	9.032087	9.059132	9.086207	9.113312	9.140447	9.167610
204	8.707206	8.734604	8.762034	8.789496	8.816988	8.844512	8.872067	8.899653
216	8.470143	8.497946	8.525783	8.553653	8.581556	8.609492	8.637460	8.665460
228	8.261489	8.289691	8.317928	8.346199	8.374504	8.402843	8.431216	8.459622
240	8.076919	8.105511	8.134139	8.162803	8.191502	8.220236	8.249006	8.277810
252	7.912927	7.941902	7.970913	7.999962	8.029046	8.058167	8.087324	8.116517
264	7.766645	7.795994	7.825380	7.854804	7.884266	7.913765	7.943300	7.972873
276	7.635702	7.665416	7.695169	7.724960	7.754789	7.784657	7.814562	7.844505
288	7.518120	7.548190	7.578301	7.608450	7.638638	7.668865	7.699131	7.729434
300	7.412238	7.442656	7.473115	7.503613	7.534151	7.564728	7.595344	7.625999
312	7.316649	7.347406	7.378204	7.409042	7.439920	7.470838	7.501795	7.532792
324	7.230155	7.261242	7.292370	7.323539	7.354748	7.385996	7.417285	7.448613
336	7.151728	7.183136	7.214584	7.246074	7.277604	7.309175	7.340785	7.372435
348	7.080481	7.112201	7.143961	7.175762	7.207604	7.239487	7.271409	7.303371
360	7.015648	7.047669	7.079732	7.111835	7.143980	7.176164	7.208389	7.240653
420	6.766939	6.800335	6.833770	6.867246	6.900760	6.934313	6.967904	7.001533
480	6.606070	6.640619	6.675205	6.709827	6.744485	6.779178	6.813906	6.848667

MONTHLY WITHDRAWALS PER $1000

NUMBER OF MONTHLY WTHDRWLS	EFFECTIVE ANNUAL YIELD							
	8.20%	8.25%	8.30%	8.35%	8.40%	8.45%	8.50%	8.55%
1	1006.589212	1006.627967	1006.666705	1006.705427	1006.744132	1006.782821	1006.821493	1006.860150
2	504.947319	504.976448	505.005566	505.034671	505.063765	505.092847	505.121917	505.150975
3	337.735758	337.761708	337.787647	337.813576	337.839495	337.865403	337.891301	337.917189
4	254.131781	254.156162	254.180533	254.204895	254.229248	254.253591	254.277925	254.302250
5	203.970837	203.994294	204.017742	204.041181	204.064611	204.088033	204.111446	204.134850
6	170.531410	170.554264	170.577111	170.599949	170.622779	170.645600	170.668414	170.691219
7	146.647135	146.669572	146.692000	146.714421	146.736835	146.759240	146.781638	146.804028
8	128.734830	128.756964	128.779090	128.801209	128.823321	128.845425	128.867522	128.889611
9	114.803839	114.825746	114.847647	114.869541	114.891427	114.913307	114.935179	114.957045
10	103.659766	103.681502	103.703230	103.724952	103.746667	103.768376	103.790078	103.811773
11	94.542544	94.564147	94.585742	94.607331	94.628914	94.650490	94.672060	94.693624
12	86.945460	86.966958	86.988450	87.009936	87.031416	87.052889	87.074356	87.095818
13	80.517713	80.539129	80.560540	80.581945	80.603344	80.624737	80.646124	80.667506
14	75.008730	75.030083	75.051430	75.072771	75.094107	75.115438	75.136763	75.158082
15	70.234758	70.256061	70.277359	70.298652	70.319939	70.341221	70.362497	70.383769
16	66.057983	66.079248	66.100508	66.121763	66.143013	66.164258	66.185498	66.206732
17	62.373018	62.394254	62.415486	62.436712	62.457934	62.479152	62.500364	62.521571
18	59.097893	59.119108	59.140320	59.161526	59.182728	59.203925	59.225118	59.246307
19	56.167897	56.189099	56.210296	56.231489	56.252677	56.273862	56.295042	56.316217
20	53.531261	53.552454	53.573643	53.594828	53.616009	53.637185	53.658358	53.679527
21	51.146076	51.167265	51.188451	51.209633	51.230810	51.251984	51.273155	51.294322
22	48.978053	48.999243	49.020429	49.041612	49.062791	49.083967	49.105139	49.126308
23	46.999867	47.020061	47.041252	47.062439	47.083623	47.104804	47.125982	47.147156
24	45.184913	45.206114	45.227312	45.248508	45.269700	45.290889	45.312075	45.333258
25	43.516363	43.537574	43.558783	43.579989	43.601192	43.622392	43.643590	43.664784
26	41.976439	41.997663	42.018885	42.040104	42.061320	42.082534	42.103745	42.124954
27	40.550851	40.572089	40.593326	40.614560	40.635792	40.657022	40.678249	40.699474
28	39.227346	39.248602	39.269856	39.291107	39.312357	39.333604	39.354849	39.376092
29	37.995366	38.016641	38.037913	38.059183	38.080452	38.101719	38.122984	38.144247
30	36.845758	36.867052	36.888345	36.909636	36.930925	36.952213	36.973499	36.994784
31	35.770549	35.791865	35.813180	35.834493	35.855804	35.877115	35.898424	35.919731
32	34.762766	34.784104	34.805442	34.826778	34.848114	34.869448	34.890780	34.912112
33	33.816278	33.837640	33.859002	33.880363	33.901723	33.923082	33.944440	33.965797
34	32.925677	32.947064	32.968451	32.989837	33.011223	33.032608	33.053992	33.075376
35	32.086172	32.107586	32.128999	32.150412	32.171824	32.193236	32.214647	32.236058
36	31.293506	31.314946	31.336387	31.357827	31.379267	31.400706	31.422146	31.443585
37	30.543880	30.565348	30.586817	30.608285	30.629753	30.651222	30.672690	30.694158
38	29.833897	29.855394	29.876891	29.898388	29.919886	29.941383	29.962881	29.984379
39	29.160508	29.182033	29.203560	29.225087	29.246614	29.268142	29.289670	29.311199
40	28.520967	28.542522	28.564079	28.585636	28.607193	28.628752	28.650311	28.671871
41	27.912797	27.934383	27.955970	27.977558	27.999147	28.020737	28.042328	28.063919
42	27.333759	27.355376	27.376994	27.398613	27.420234	27.441856	27.463479	27.485102
43	26.781819	26.803468	26.825117	26.846769	26.868421	26.890075	26.911731	26.933387
44	26.255130	26.276810	26.298492	26.320176	26.341861	26.363548	26.385236	26.406926
45	25.752008	25.773721	25.795436	25.817152	25.838870	25.860590	25.882312	25.904036
46	25.270917	25.292662	25.314410	25.336160	25.357911	25.379665	25.401421	25.423178
47	24.810450	24.832228	24.854009	24.875792	24.897578	24.919366	24.941156	24.962948
48	24.369317	24.391129	24.412944	24.434761	24.456581	24.478403	24.500227	24.522055
60	20.231941	20.254176	20.276416	20.298661	20.320912	20.343167	20.365428	20.387694
72	17.487893	17.510574	17.533263	17.555960	17.578665	17.601377	17.624097	17.646825
84	15.539948	15.563088	15.586237	15.609397	15.632568	15.655748	15.678939	15.702141
96	14.089484	14.113087	14.136703	14.160331	14.183972	14.207626	14.231293	14.254972
108	12.970588	12.994656	13.018739	13.042837	13.066950	13.091078	13.115222	13.139380
120	12.083703	12.108235	12.132784	12.157350	12.181934	12.206536	12.231155	12.255791
132	11.365466	11.390426	11.415472	11.440504	11.465556	11.490628	11.515719	11.540829
144	10.773628	10.799079	10.824551	10.850045	10.875561	10.901098	10.926657	10.952237
156	10.278935	10.304838	10.330764	10.356715	10.382689	10.408686	10.434707	10.460752
168	9.860484	9.886833	9.913208	9.939609	9.966035	9.992486	10.018963	10.045465
180	9.502941	9.529731	9.556547	9.583391	9.610263	9.637161	9.664087	9.691039
192	9.194804	9.222026	9.249277	9.276557	9.303867	9.331204	9.358571	9.385966
204	8.927270	8.954918	8.982596	9.010304	9.038043	9.065812	9.093611	9.121440
216	8.693493	8.721557	8.749654	8.777782	8.805942	8.834134	8.862357	8.890611
228	8.488062	8.516535	8.545042	8.573581	8.602154	8.630759	8.659396	8.688066
240	8.306649	8.335522	8.364429	8.393371	8.422346	8.451355	8.480398	8.509474
252	8.145745	8.175009	8.204308	8.233643	8.263012	8.292416	8.321854	8.351326
264	8.002482	8.032127	8.061808	8.091526	8.121279	8.151067	8.180890	8.210749
276	7.874485	7.904502	7.934556	7.964646	7.994773	8.024936	8.055134	8.085369
288	7.759776	7.790155	7.820571	7.851025	7.881515	7.912043	7.942606	7.973206
300	7.656692	7.687423	7.718193	7.748999	7.779843	7.810724	7.841642	7.872597
312	7.563827	7.594900	7.626012	7.657161	7.688349	7.719573	7.750835	7.782133
324	7.479980	7.511386	7.542830	7.574312	7.605832	7.637389	7.668984	7.700616
336	7.404124	7.435851	7.467618	7.499422	7.531265	7.563145	7.595062	7.627016
348	7.335372	7.367411	7.399490	7.431606	7.463761	7.495952	7.528181	7.560447
360	7.272956	7.305297	7.337678	7.370096	7.402552	7.435045	7.467575	7.500142
420	7.035199	7.068903	7.102642	7.136418	7.170228	7.204074	7.237955	7.271870
480	6.883462	6.918291	6.953151	6.988044	7.022968	7.057923	7.092909	7.127925

MONTHLY WITHDRAWALS PER $1000

NUMBER OF MONTHLY WTHDRWLS	EFFECTIVE ANNUAL YIELD							
	8.60%	8.65%	8.70%	8.75%	8.80%	8.85%	8.90%	8.95%
1	1006.898790	1006.937413	1006.976021	1007.014612	1007.053186	1007.091745	1007.130287	1007.168813
2	505.180021	505.209055	505.238077	505.267088	505.296086	505.325073	505.354048	505.383011
3	337.943066	337.968933	337.994790	338.020637	338.046474	338.072300	338.098116	338.123922
4	254.326565	254.350871	254.375168	254.399455	254.423733	254.448001	254.472261	254.496511
5	204.158245	204.181632	204.205010	204.228380	204.251741	204.275093	204.298436	204.321771
6	170.714016	170.736805	170.759586	170.782358	170.805123	170.827879	170.850627	170.873367
7	146.826410	146.848784	146.871151	146.893510	146.915861	146.938205	146.960540	146.982868
8	128.911693	128.933768	128.955835	128.977895	128.999948	129.021993	129.044031	129.066061
9	114.978903	115.000754	115.022599	115.044436	115.066266	115.088089	115.109906	115.131715
10	103.833461	103.855142	103.876817	103.898485	103.920147	103.941801	103.963449	103.985091
11	94.715181	94.736732	94.758276	94.779814	94.801345	94.822870	94.844389	94.865901
12	87.117273	87.138722	87.160165	87.181601	87.203032	87.224457	87.245875	87.267287
13	80.688881	80.710251	80.731615	80.752973	80.774325	80.795672	80.817012	80.838347
14	75.179396	75.200704	75.222006	75.243303	75.264595	75.285881	75.307161	75.328436
15	70.405034	70.426295	70.447550	70.468800	70.490045	70.511285	70.532519	70.553748
16	66.227962	66.249187	66.270406	66.291621	66.312830	66.334035	66.355234	66.376429
17	62.542774	62.563972	62.585166	62.606354	62.627538	62.648717	62.669891	62.691060
18	59.267490	59.288670	59.309845	59.331015	59.352181	59.373342	59.394498	59.415651
19	56.337389	56.358556	56.379719	56.400878	56.422032	56.443182	56.464328	56.485469
20	53.700692	53.721853	53.743009	53.764162	53.785310	53.806455	53.827596	53.848732
21	51.315485	51.336644	51.357799	51.378950	51.400098	51.421242	51.442382	51.463519
22	49.147473	49.168634	49.189792	49.210947	49.232098	49.253245	49.274389	49.295529
23	47.168327	47.189495	47.210659	47.231820	47.252978	47.274132	47.295284	47.316431
24	45.354438	45.375615	45.396789	45.417960	45.439128	45.460293	45.481454	45.502613
25	43.685976	43.707165	43.728351	43.749535	43.770715	43.791893	43.813068	43.834240
26	42.146160	42.167364	42.188565	42.209763	42.230959	42.252152	42.273343	42.294531
27	40.720697	40.741917	40.763135	40.784351	40.805564	40.826775	40.847983	40.869189
28	39.397333	39.418572	39.439809	39.461044	39.482276	39.503507	39.524735	39.545962
29	38.165508	38.186767	38.208025	38.229280	38.250534	38.271786	38.293036	38.314284
30	37.016067	37.037348	37.058628	37.079906	37.101182	37.122457	37.143730	37.165002
31	35.941037	35.962342	35.983645	36.004947	36.026247	36.047546	36.068844	36.090140
32	34.933443	34.954772	34.976100	34.997427	35.018753	35.040078	35.061401	35.082723
33	33.987153	34.008508	34.029862	34.051216	34.072568	34.093919	34.115270	34.136619
34	33.096758	33.118141	33.139522	33.160903	33.182283	33.203662	33.225040	33.246418
35	32.257468	32.278878	32.300288	32.321697	32.343105	32.364513	32.385921	32.407328
36	31.465024	31.486463	31.507901	31.529339	31.550777	31.572215	31.593652	31.615089
37	30.715627	30.737095	30.758563	30.780031	30.801499	30.822968	30.844436	30.865904
38	30.005878	30.027376	30.048875	30.070374	30.091873	30.113373	30.134872	30.156372
39	29.332728	29.354257	29.375787	29.397318	29.418849	29.440380	29.461912	29.483444
40	28.693432	28.714993	28.736555	28.758117	28.779680	28.801244	28.822808	28.844374
41	28.085512	28.107105	28.128699	28.150295	28.171891	28.193488	28.215085	28.236684
42	27.506727	27.528353	27.549981	27.571609	27.593239	27.614869	27.636501	27.658134
43	26.955045	26.976705	26.998365	27.020028	27.041691	27.063356	27.085022	27.106689
44	26.428618	26.450311	26.472006	26.493702	26.515400	26.537099	26.558800	26.580503
45	25.925761	25.947489	25.969218	25.990949	26.012681	26.034416	26.056152	26.077890
46	25.444938	25.466700	25.488464	25.510230	25.531998	25.553768	25.575540	25.597313
47	24.984742	25.006539	25.028338	25.050139	25.071943	25.093749	25.115557	25.137367
48	24.543884	24.565716	24.587551	24.609388	24.631227	24.653069	24.674914	24.696760
60	20.409965	20.432241	20.454522	20.476809	20.499100	20.521397	20.543698	20.566005
72	17.669561	17.692304	17.715055	17.737814	17.760580	17.783354	17.806136	17.828925
84	15.725352	15.748574	15.771806	15.795048	15.818300	15.841562	15.864834	15.888116
96	14.278664	14.302369	14.326086	14.349816	14.373558	14.397313	14.421080	14.444860
108	13.163554	13.187742	13.211945	13.236164	13.260397	13.284645	13.308907	13.333185
120	12.280444	12.305115	12.329802	12.354507	12.379229	12.403968	12.428724	12.453497
132	11.565959	11.591108	11.616277	11.641465	11.666671	11.691898	11.717143	11.742407
144	10.977839	11.003462	11.029106	11.054772	11.080459	11.106167	11.131895	11.157645
156	10.486820	10.512911	10.539025	10.565162	10.591323	10.617506	10.643712	10.669941
168	10.071992	10.098545	10.125122	10.151724	10.178351	10.205003	10.231679	10.258379
180	9.718018	9.745024	9.772057	9.799116	9.826202	9.853313	9.880451	9.907615
192	9.413389	9.440840	9.468320	9.495828	9.523363	9.550926	9.578517	9.606136
204	9.149299	9.177187	9.205105	9.233052	9.261028	9.289034	9.317069	9.345132
216	8.918896	8.947212	8.975559	9.003936	9.032344	9.060782	9.089250	9.117749
228	8.716768	8.745503	8.774269	8.803066	8.831895	8.860756	8.889648	8.918571
240	8.538584	8.567726	8.596901	8.626109	8.655349	8.684622	8.713927	8.743263
252	8.380833	8.410373	8.439947	8.469555	8.499195	8.528869	8.558576	8.588316
264	8.240642	8.270570	8.300533	8.330529	8.360560	8.390624	8.420722	8.450853
276	8.115639	8.145944	8.176284	8.206658	8.237067	8.267511	8.297988	8.328499
288	8.003841	8.034513	8.065219	8.095961	8.126738	8.157549	8.188394	8.219274
300	7.903587	7.934614	7.965676	7.996774	8.027907	8.059074	8.090277	8.121513
312	7.813468	7.844839	7.876246	7.907688	7.939166	7.970678	8.002226	8.033808
324	7.732284	7.763988	7.795728	7.827504	7.859315	7.891162	7.923043	7.954958
336	7.659006	7.691033	7.723095	7.755194	7.787327	7.819496	7.851699	7.883936
348	7.592749	7.625087	7.657461	7.689871	7.722315	7.754794	7.787308	7.819855
360	7.532745	7.565383	7.598058	7.630767	7.663511	7.696290	7.729102	7.761949
420	7.305818	7.339800	7.373814	7.407861	7.441940	7.476051	7.510193	7.544365
480	7.162970	7.198044	7.233146	7.268277	7.303435	7.338620	7.373832	7.409069

NUMBER OF MONTHLY WTHDRWLS	9.00%	9.05%	9.10%	9.15%	9.20%	9.25%	9.30%	9.35%
				EFFECTIVE ANNUAL YIELD				
1	1007.207323	1007.245817	1007.284295	1007.322756	1007.361201	1007.399630	1007.438043	1007.476440
2	505.411962	505.440902	505.469829	505.498745	505.527649	505.556542	505.585422	505.614291
3	338.149717	338.175503	338.201278	338.227043	338.252798	338.278543	338.304278	338.330002
4	254.520752	254.544983	254.569205	254.593418	254.617622	254.641816	254.666002	254.690178
5	204.345097	204.368415	204.391724	204.415024	204.438316	204.461599	204.484873	204.508139
6	170.896099	170.919822	170.941538	170.964245	170.986944	171.009636	171.032319	171.054994
7	147.005189	147.027501	147.049806	147.072103	147.094393	147.116675	147.138949	147.161215
8	129.088084	129.110100	129.132109	129.154110	129.176104	129.198090	129.220070	129.242041
9	115.153517	115.175312	115.197101	115.218882	115.240656	115.262423	115.284184	115.305937
10	104.006725	104.028353	104.049975	104.071589	104.093197	104.114799	104.136393	104.157981
11	94.887407	94.908907	94.930400	94.951887	94.973367	94.994841	95.016309	95.037770
12	87.288693	87.310094	87.331488	87.352876	87.374258	87.395633	87.417003	87.438367
13	80.859676	80.880999	80.902316	80.923628	80.944934	80.966234	80.987528	81.008816
14	75.349705	75.370969	75.392227	75.413479	75.434727	75.455968	75.477204	75.498435
15	70.574971	70.596190	70.617403	70.638611	70.659813	70.681010	70.702202	70.723389
16	66.397618	66.418802	66.439982	66.461156	66.482326	66.503490	66.524649	66.545804
17	62.712225	62.733385	62.754540	62.775690	62.796836	62.817976	62.839112	62.860244
18	59.436798	59.457941	59.479080	59.500214	59.521344	59.542469	59.563589	59.584706
19	56.506607	56.527740	56.548868	56.569993	56.591113	56.612229	56.633341	56.654448
20	53.869865	53.890993	53.912118	53.933238	53.954355	53.975467	53.996576	54.017680
21	51.484651	51.505780	51.526905	51.548026	51.569144	51.590257	51.611367	51.632474
22	49.316666	49.337800	49.358929	49.380055	49.401178	49.422297	49.443413	49.464525
23	47.337576	47.358717	47.379855	47.400990	47.422121	47.443250	47.464374	47.485496
24	45.523768	45.544921	45.566070	45.587217	45.608360	45.629500	45.650638	45.671772
25	43.855409	43.876576	43.897740	43.918900	43.940058	43.961214	43.982366	44.003515
26	42.315716	42.336899	42.358080	42.379257	42.400433	42.421605	42.442775	42.463942
27	40.890393	40.911595	40.932794	40.953991	40.975185	40.996377	41.017567	41.038754
28	39.567186	39.588408	39.609628	39.630845	39.652061	39.673275	39.694486	39.715695
29	38.335530	38.356774	38.378017	38.399257	38.420496	38.441733	38.462968	38.484201
30	37.186271	37.207539	37.228806	37.250071	37.271334	37.292595	37.313855	37.335113
31	36.111435	36.132729	36.154020	36.175311	36.196600	36.217888	36.239174	36.260459
32	35.104045	35.125364	35.146683	35.168001	35.189317	35.210632	35.231946	35.253259
33	34.157968	34.179315	34.200662	34.222008	34.243352	34.264696	34.286039	34.307381
34	33.267795	33.289171	33.310547	33.331922	33.353296	33.374669	33.396042	33.417414
35	32.428734	32.450140	32.471546	32.492951	32.514355	32.535759	32.557163	32.578566
36	31.636526	31.657963	31.679399	31.700835	31.722271	31.743706	31.765141	31.786576
37	30.887372	30.908840	30.930308	30.951776	30.973243	30.994711	31.016179	31.037646
38	30.177872	30.199372	30.220872	30.242373	30.263873	30.285374	30.306875	30.328377
39	29.504976	29.526509	29.548042	29.569576	29.591110	29.612645	29.634179	29.655714
40	28.865939	28.887506	28.909073	28.930640	28.952208	28.973777	28.995346	29.016916
41	28.258284	28.279884	28.301485	28.323087	28.344690	28.366294	28.387898	28.409503
42	27.679767	27.701402	27.723038	27.744675	27.766313	27.787952	27.809593	27.831234
43	27.128358	27.150028	27.171699	27.193371	27.215045	27.236720	27.258397	27.280074
44	26.602206	26.623912	26.645619	26.667327	26.689037	26.710749	26.732462	26.754176
45	26.099629	26.121371	26.143114	26.164859	26.186605	26.208354	26.230104	26.251855
46	25.619089	25.640867	25.662647	25.684428	25.706212	25.727997	25.749785	25.771574
47	25.159179	25.180993	25.202809	25.224629	25.246450	25.268273	25.290098	25.311926
48	24.718609	24.740461	24.762315	24.784171	24.806030	24.827891	24.849754	24.871620
60	20.588316	20.610633	20.632954	20.655281	20.677612	20.699949	20.722290	20.744637
72	17.851722	17.874526	17.897338	17.920157	17.942984	17.965818	17.988660	18.011509
84	15.911409	15.934711	15.958024	15.981346	16.004678	16.028020	16.051372	16.074734
96	14.468652	14.492456	14.516273	14.540102	14.563944	14.587797	14.611663	14.635541
108	13.357477	13.381783	13.406105	13.430440	13.454791	13.479156	13.503535	13.527929
120	12.478286	12.503093	12.527916	12.552756	12.577612	12.602486	12.627375	12.652282
132	11.767690	11.792991	11.818312	11.843652	11.869010	11.894387	11.919782	11.945196
144	11.183416	11.209208	11.235020	11.260853	11.286707	11.312581	11.338475	11.364390
156	10.696193	10.722467	10.748746	10.775084	10.801426	10.827790	10.854176	10.880585
168	10.285104	10.311854	10.338628	10.365425	10.392247	10.419093	10.445963	10.472856
180	9.934805	9.962021	9.989263	10.016530	10.043823	10.071142	10.098485	10.125854
192	9.633782	9.661455	9.689155	9.716883	9.744637	9.772418	9.800226	9.828061
204	9.373224	9.401345	9.429494	9.457671	9.485877	9.514110	9.542372	9.570661
216	9.146277	9.174835	9.203422	9.232039	9.260685	9.289360	9.318065	9.346798
228	8.947524	8.976509	9.005524	9.034569	9.063645	9.092751	9.121886	9.151052
240	8.772632	8.802032	8.831463	8.860926	8.890419	8.919944	8.949499	8.979085
252	8.618088	8.647892	8.677728	8.707596	8.737496	8.767428	8.797391	8.827385
264	8.481017	8.511214	8.541444	8.571706	8.602000	8.632326	8.662685	8.693075
276	8.359044	8.389622	8.420233	8.450877	8.481554	8.512263	8.543004	8.573777
288	8.250188	8.281135	8.312116	8.343130	8.374176	8.405256	8.436367	8.467511
300	8.152784	8.184089	8.215427	8.246798	8.278203	8.309640	8.341110	8.372612
312	8.065424	8.097074	8.128758	8.160475	8.192225	8.224007	8.255823	8.287670
324	7.986908	8.018891	8.050908	8.082959	8.115042	8.147158	8.179306	8.211486
336	7.916207	7.948512	7.980851	8.013222	8.045626	8.078063	8.110532	8.143032
348	7.852437	7.885051	7.917699	7.950380	7.983093	8.015838	8.048615	8.081423
360	7.794828	7.827741	7.860687	7.893664	7.926674	7.959716	7.992788	8.025892
420	7.578568	7.612800	7.647062	7.681353	7.715673	7.750021	7.784397	7.818800
480	7.444333	7.479622	7.514935	7.550273	7.585634	7.621019	7.656427	7.691857

MONTHLY WITHDRAWALS PER $1000

EFFECTIVE ANNUAL YIELD

NUMBER OF MONTHLY WTHDRWLS	9.40%	9.45%	9.50%	9.55%	9.60%	9.65%	9.70%	9.75%
1	1007.514821	1007.553186	1007.591534	1007.629867	1007.668183	1007.706484	1007.744769	1007.783037
2	505.643148	505.671994	505.700827	505.729649	505.758460	505.787258	505.816045	505.844820
3	338.355716	338.381421	338.407115	338.432799	338.458473	338.484136	338.509790	338.535434
4	254.714344	254.738502	254.762650	254.786790	254.810920	254.835040	254.859152	254.883254
5	204.531397	204.554645	204.577886	204.601117	204.624340	204.647555	204.670761	204.693958
6	171.077661	171.100319	171.122970	171.145613	171.168247	171.190874	171.213493	171.236103
7	147.183474	147.205725	147.227969	147.250205	147.272433	147.294653	147.316866	147.339072
8	129.264006	129.285963	129.307913	129.329856	129.351792	129.373720	129.395641	129.417555
9	115.327684	115.349423	115.371156	115.392881	115.414600	115.436311	115.458016	115.479714
10	104.179563	104.201138	104.222706	104.244267	104.265822	104.287370	104.308912	104.330447
11	95.059225	95.080674	95.102116	95.123552	95.144982	95.166405	95.187822	95.209233
12	87.459724	87.481076	87.502422	87.523761	87.545094	87.566422	87.587743	87.609059
13	81.030099	81.051375	81.072646	81.093912	81.115171	81.136425	81.157673	81.178915
14	75.519660	75.540879	75.562093	75.583302	75.604505	75.625702	75.646894	75.668081
15	70.744571	70.765747	70.786918	70.808084	70.829244	70.850399	70.871549	70.892694
16	66.566953	66.588097	66.609237	66.630371	66.651500	66.672624	66.693744	66.714858
17	62.881370	62.902492	62.923609	62.944722	62.965829	62.986932	63.008030	63.029124
18	59.605817	59.626949	59.648027	59.669125	59.690219	59.711308	59.732392	59.753473
19	56.675552	56.696651	56.717745	56.738836	56.759922	56.781004	56.802082	56.823155
20	54.038781	54.059877	54.080969	54.102058	54.123142	54.144223	54.165299	54.186371
21	51.653576	51.674665	51.695770	51.716861	51.737948	51.759032	51.780111	51.801188
22	49.485633	49.506738	49.527840	49.548938	49.570032	49.591123	49.612211	49.633294
23	47.506614	47.527729	47.548841	47.569949	47.591054	47.612156	47.633255	47.654350
24	45.692903	45.714031	45.735156	45.756278	45.777397	45.798513	45.819625	45.840735
25	44.024662	44.045806	44.066947	44.088085	44.109221	44.130353	44.151483	44.172610
26	42.485107	42.506269	42.527429	42.548586	42.569740	42.590892	42.612041	42.633188
27	41.059939	41.081122	41.102302	41.123480	41.144656	41.165829	41.187000	41.208168
28	39.736903	39.758108	39.779310	39.800511	39.821710	39.842906	39.864101	39.885293
29	38.505432	38.526661	38.547888	38.569113	38.590337	38.611558	38.632778	38.653996
30	37.356370	37.377625	37.398878	37.420129	37.441379	37.462627	37.483874	37.505119
31	36.281742	36.303024	36.324305	36.345584	36.366861	36.388137	36.409412	36.430685
32	35.274570	35.295880	35.317189	35.338497	35.359804	35.381109	35.402413	35.423716
33	34.328721	34.350061	34.371400	34.392738	34.414074	34.435409	34.456745	34.478079
34	33.438785	33.460155	33.481525	33.502893	33.524261	33.545629	33.566995	33.588361
35	32.599968	32.621370	32.642771	32.664172	32.685572	32.706971	32.728371	32.749769
36	31.808011	31.829445	31.850879	31.872312	31.893746	31.915178	31.936611	31.958043
37	31.059114	31.080581	31.102048	31.123515	31.144983	31.166449	31.187916	31.209383
38	30.349877	30.371378	30.392880	30.414381	30.435882	30.457385	30.478887	30.500389
39	29.677250	29.698786	29.720322	29.741859	29.763396	29.784933	29.806470	29.828008
40	29.038487	29.060058	29.081630	29.103202	29.124775	29.146348	29.167922	29.189496
41	28.431109	28.452716	28.474324	28.495932	28.517542	28.539152	28.560763	28.582374
42	27.852876	27.874519	27.896163	27.917809	27.939455	27.961102	27.982750	28.004400
43	27.301753	27.323433	27.345114	27.366797	27.388481	27.410166	27.431852	27.453539
44	26.775892	26.797609	26.819328	26.841048	26.862770	26.884493	26.906218	26.927944
45	26.273609	26.295364	26.317120	26.338879	26.360639	26.382401	26.404164	26.425929
46	25.793365	25.815159	25.836954	25.858750	25.880549	25.902350	25.924152	25.945957
47	25.333755	25.355587	25.377420	25.399256	25.421094	25.442934	25.464776	25.486620
48	24.893488	24.915359	24.937231	24.959106	24.980984	25.002864	25.024746	25.046630
60	20.766988	20.789344	20.811705	20.834071	20.856442	20.878818	20.901198	20.923583
72	18.034365	18.057229	18.080101	18.102979	18.125865	18.148759	18.171659	18.194567
84	16.098106	16.121487	16.144878	16.168279	16.191690	16.215111	16.238541	16.261980
96	14.659431	14.683333	14.707248	14.731174	14.755113	14.779063	14.803026	14.827000
108	13.552337	13.576759	13.601196	13.625647	13.650112	13.674592	13.699085	13.723593
120	12.677205	12.702144	12.727099	12.752071	12.777060	12.802064	12.827085	12.852122
132	11.970628	11.996079	12.021548	12.047036	12.072541	12.098065	12.123607	12.149167
144	11.390326	11.416281	11.442257	11.468253	11.494269	11.520306	11.546362	11.572437
156	10.907015	10.933468	10.959943	10.986439	11.012957	11.039497	11.066059	11.092642
168	10.499773	10.526714	10.553678	10.580666	10.607677	10.634711	10.661769	10.688849
180	10.153249	10.180668	10.208112	10.235581	10.263075	10.290593	10.318136	10.345704
192	9.855922	9.883809	9.911723	9.939662	9.967628	9.995620	10.023637	10.051680
204	9.598978	9.627323	9.655695	9.684094	9.712521	9.740974	9.769454	9.797961
216	9.375560	9.404350	9.433169	9.462016	9.490891	9.519794	9.548725	9.577684
228	9.180246	9.209471	9.238724	9.268007	9.297319	9.326659	9.356028	9.385426
240	9.008701	9.038347	9.068023	9.097729	9.127465	9.157230	9.187024	9.216848
252	8.857410	8.887465	8.917551	8.947668	8.977815	9.007991	9.038198	9.068434
264	8.723496	8.753948	8.784432	8.814946	8.845490	8.876066	8.906671	8.937306
276	8.604582	8.635419	8.666286	8.697185	8.728115	8.759075	8.790065	8.821086
288	8.498687	8.529895	8.561134	8.592404	8.623705	8.655037	8.686400	8.717792
300	8.404146	8.435712	8.467309	8.498938	8.530597	8.562287	8.594008	8.625759
312	8.319550	8.351461	8.383403	8.415377	8.447381	8.479416	8.511482	8.543577
324	8.243698	8.275942	8.308216	8.340522	8.372858	8.405225	8.437622	8.470048
336	8.175564	8.208127	8.240721	8.273346	8.306001	8.338686	8.371401	8.404144
348	8.114262	8.147132	8.180033	8.212964	8.245925	8.278915	8.311934	8.344982
360	8.059026	8.092191	8.125386	8.158610	8.191864	8.225146	8.258457	8.291797
420	7.853230	7.887687	7.922170	7.956679	7.991214	8.025774	8.060358	8.094967
480	7.727309	7.762783	7.798279	7.833795	7.869331	7.904888	7.940464	7.976059

MONTHLY WITHDRAWALS PER $1000

EFFECTIVE ANNUAL YIELD

NUMBER OF MONTHLY WTHDRWLS	9.80%	9.85%	9.90%	9.95%	10.00%	10.05%	10.10%	10.15%
1	1007.821290	1007.859526	1007.897747	1007.935952	1007.974140	1008.012313	1008.050470	1008.088611
2	505.873584	505.902336	505.931076	505.959805	505.988522	506.017228	506.045922	506.074604
3	338.561067	338.586691	338.612304	338.637908	338.663501	338.689085	338.714658	338.740221
4	254.907348	254.931432	254.955507	254.979573	255.003630	255.027677	255.051716	255.075745
5	204.717147	204.740327	204.763499	204.786663	204.809817	204.832964	204.856102	204.879231
6	171.258706	171.281300	171.303886	171.326465	171.349035	171.371597	171.394152	171.416698
7	147.361269	147.383459	147.405642	147.427817	147.449984	147.472144	147.494296	147.516440
8	129.439461	129.461360	129.483252	129.505137	129.527015	129.548885	129.570748	129.592604
9	115.501405	115.523089	115.544766	115.566436	115.588100	115.609756	115.631406	115.653048
10	104.351975	104.373497	104.395012	104.416521	104.438023	104.459518	104.481007	104.502489
11	95.230637	95.252035	95.273427	95.294813	95.316192	95.337565	95.358931	95.380292
12	87.630368	87.651671	87.672968	87.694260	87.715545	87.736824	87.758097	87.779364
13	81.200151	81.221382	81.242607	81.263826	81.285039	81.306247	81.327449	81.348645
14	75.689262	75.710437	75.731607	75.752772	75.773931	75.795084	75.816232	75.837375
15	70.913834	70.934968	70.956097	70.977221	70.998339	71.019453	71.040561	71.061664
16	66.735968	66.757072	66.778172	66.799266	66.820356	66.841440	66.862520	66.883595
17	63.050212	63.071296	63.092375	63.113450	63.134520	63.155585	63.176645	63.197701
18	59.774548	59.795619	59.816686	59.837748	59.858806	59.879859	59.900908	59.921953
19	56.844224	56.865289	56.886350	56.907407	56.928459	56.949507	56.970551	56.991591
20	54.207440	54.228504	54.249565	54.270621	54.291673	54.312722	54.333766	54.354807
21	51.822260	51.843328	51.864393	51.885454	51.906511	51.927565	51.948615	51.969661
22	49.654375	49.675452	49.696525	49.717595	49.738661	49.759724	49.780783	49.801838
23	47.675442	47.696530	47.717616	47.738698	47.759777	47.780852	47.801924	47.822993
24	45.861842	45.882945	45.904046	45.925143	45.946238	45.967329	45.988417	46.009503
25	44.193734	44.214856	44.235974	44.257090	44.278203	44.299313	44.320420	44.341524
26	42.654332	42.675474	42.696612	42.717749	42.738882	42.760013	42.781142	42.802268
27	41.229334	41.250498	41.271659	41.292818	41.313975	41.335129	41.356281	41.377431
28	39.906483	39.927671	39.948857	39.970041	39.991222	40.012402	40.033579	40.054754
29	38.675212	38.696426	38.717638	38.738848	38.760056	38.781262	38.802466	38.823669
30	37.526362	37.547603	37.568843	37.590081	37.611317	37.632552	37.653785	37.675016
31	36.451957	36.473277	36.494496	36.515763	36.537029	36.558294	36.579557	36.600818
32	35.445018	35.466318	35.487618	35.508916	35.530212	35.551508	35.572802	35.594095
33	34.499411	34.520743	34.542074	34.563404	34.584732	34.606060	34.627387	34.648712
34	33.609726	33.631090	33.652453	33.673815	33.695177	33.716538	33.737898	33.759257
35	32.771167	32.792564	32.813961	32.835357	32.856753	32.878148	32.899543	32.920937
36	31.979475	32.000907	32.022338	32.043769	32.065199	32.086629	32.108059	32.129488
37	31.230850	31.252316	31.273783	31.295249	31.316715	31.338181	31.359647	31.381112
38	30.521891	30.543393	30.564895	30.586397	30.607900	30.629402	30.650905	30.672408
39	29.849547	29.871085	29.892624	29.914163	29.935703	29.957242	29.978782	30.000323
40	29.211071	29.232647	29.254223	29.275799	29.297376	29.318954	29.340532	29.362111
41	28.603986	28.625600	28.647213	28.668828	28.690443	28.712059	28.733676	28.755293
42	28.026050	28.047701	28.069353	28.091006	28.112660	28.134315	28.155971	28.177628
43	27.475228	27.496917	27.518608	27.540300	27.561993	27.583688	27.605383	27.627080
44	26.949671	26.971400	26.993130	27.014861	27.036594	27.058329	27.080064	27.101801
45	26.447695	26.469464	26.491233	26.513005	26.534778	26.556552	26.578329	26.600106
46	25.967763	25.989571	26.011381	26.033193	26.055006	26.076821	26.098638	26.120457
47	25.508467	25.530315	25.552165	25.574017	25.595872	25.617728	25.639586	25.661447
48	25.068516	25.090405	25.112296	25.134189	25.156085	25.177983	25.199883	25.221785
60	20.945973	20.968368	20.990768	21.013172	21.035582	21.057995	21.080414	21.102838
72	18.217482	18.240405	18.263334	18.286271	18.309215	18.332166	18.355124	18.378090
84	16.285430	16.308889	16.332357	16.355835	16.379323	16.402820	16.426327	16.449843
96	14.850986	14.874944	14.898994	14.923016	14.947049	14.971094	14.995151	15.019220
108	13.748114	13.772650	13.797199	13.821763	13.846340	13.870932	13.895537	13.920156
120	12.877175	12.902244	12.927329	12.952429	12.977546	13.002678	13.027828	13.052992
132	12.174746	12.200342	12.225956	12.251588	12.277237	12.302905	12.328590	12.354292
144	11.598533	11.624649	11.650784	11.676939	11.703113	11.729307	11.755520	11.781752
156	11.119246	11.145872	11.172519	11.199188	11.225877	11.252588	11.279319	11.306072
168	10.715953	10.743079	10.770228	10.797400	10.824594	10.851811	10.879051	10.906312
180	10.373295	10.400911	10.428551	10.456216	10.483904	10.511615	10.539351	10.567110
192	10.079749	10.107843	10.135963	10.164107	10.192277	10.220471	10.248691	10.276935
204	9.826495	9.855055	9.883642	9.912254	9.940893	9.969558	9.998249	10.026965
216	9.606670	9.635684	9.664724	9.693792	9.722887	9.752009	9.781157	9.810332
228	9.414852	9.444306	9.473788	9.503298	9.532835	9.562400	9.591992	9.621612
240	9.246700	9.276581	9.306491	9.336429	9.366395	9.396390	9.426412	9.456462
252	9.098699	9.128994	9.159318	9.189670	9.220051	9.250461	9.280899	9.311365
264	8.967971	8.998665	9.029389	9.060142	9.090924	9.121734	9.152573	9.183441
276	8.852137	8.883217	8.914327	8.945466	8.976634	9.007831	9.039057	9.070311
288	8.749215	8.780667	8.812149	8.843660	8.875200	8.906770	8.938367	8.969993
300	8.657539	8.689350	8.721190	8.753059	8.784957	8.816883	8.848839	8.880822
312	8.575702	8.607857	8.640041	8.672253	8.704495	8.736765	8.769063	8.801389
324	8.502504	8.534989	8.567503	8.600045	8.632616	8.665215	8.697842	8.730497
336	8.436918	8.469719	8.502550	8.535408	8.568295	8.601209	8.634150	8.667119
348	8.378059	8.411164	8.444298	8.477458	8.510647	8.543862	8.577104	8.610372
360	8.325164	8.358560	8.391982	8.425432	8.458908	8.492411	8.525940	8.559494
420	8.129599	8.164256	8.198935	8.233638	8.268363	8.303110	8.337879	8.372669
480	8.011673	8.047306	8.082956	8.118624	8.154309	8.190011	8.225730	8.261464

MONTHLY WITHDRAWALS PER $1000

NUMBER OF MONTHLY WTHDRWLS	EFFECTIVE ANNUAL YIELD							
	10.20%	10.25%	10.30%	10.35%	10.40%	10.45%	10.50%	10.55%
1	1008.126737	1008.164846	1008.202940	1008.241017	1008.279079	1008.317125	1008.355156	1008.393170
2	506.103275	506.131934	506.160581	506.189217	506.217842	506.246455	506.275057	506.303647
3	338.765775	338.791318	338.816852	338.842375	338.867888	338.893392	338.918886	338.944369
4	255.099765	255.123777	255.147779	255.171772	255.195756	255.219731	255.243696	255.267653
5	204.902352	204.925464	204.948568	204.971664	204.994751	205.017830	205.040900	205.063962
6	171.439237	171.461767	171.484290	171.506804	171.529311	171.551809	171.574300	171.596783
7	147.538577	147.560707	147.582828	147.604943	147.627049	147.649149	147.671240	147.693324
8	129.614452	129.636294	129.658128	129.679955	129.701775	129.723588	129.745393	129.767192
9	115.674684	115.696313	115.717935	115.739550	115.761159	115.782760	115.804355	115.825942
10	104.523965	104.545434	104.566897	104.588353	104.609802	104.631245	104.652682	104.674112
11	95.401646	95.422993	95.444335	95.465670	95.486999	95.508322	95.529638	95.550949
12	87.800626	87.821881	87.843130	87.864373	87.885610	87.906842	87.928067	87.949286
13	81.369836	81.391020	81.412199	81.433373	81.454540	81.475702	81.496858	81.518009
14	75.858512	75.879644	75.900770	75.921891	75.943006	75.964116	75.985221	76.006320
15	71.082762	71.103854	71.124942	71.146024	71.167101	71.188173	71.209239	71.230301
16	66.904664	66.925729	66.946789	66.967844	66.988894	67.009938	67.030978	67.052014
17	63.218752	63.239798	63.260839	63.281876	63.302908	63.323936	63.344958	63.365976
18	59.942993	59.964028	59.985059	60.006085	60.027107	60.048125	60.069138	60.090147
19	57.012626	57.033657	57.054684	57.075707	57.096725	57.117740	57.138750	57.159756
20	54.375843	54.396876	54.417904	54.438928	54.459949	54.480965	54.501978	54.522987
21	51.990703	52.011741	52.032776	52.053807	52.074834	52.095858	52.116878	52.137894
22	49.822891	49.843939	49.864984	49.886026	49.907064	49.928098	49.949130	49.970157
23	47.844059	47.865121	47.886180	47.907236	47.928288	47.949338	47.970383	47.991426
24	46.030585	46.051664	46.072740	46.093813	46.114883	46.135950	46.157014	46.178075
25	44.362626	44.383724	44.404820	44.425913	44.447003	44.468091	44.489175	44.510257
26	42.823391	42.844512	42.865630	42.886745	42.907858	42.928968	42.950076	42.971181
27	41.398578	41.419723	41.440865	41.462005	41.483143	41.504278	41.525411	41.546541
28	40.075927	40.097098	40.118266	40.139433	40.160597	40.181759	40.202919	40.224077
29	38.844869	38.866068	38.887264	38.908459	38.929652	38.950843	38.972032	38.993219
30	37.696246	37.717473	37.738700	37.759924	37.781147	37.802368	37.823587	37.844805
31	36.622078	36.643337	36.664594	36.685849	36.707103	36.728356	36.749607	36.770857
32	35.615387	35.636677	35.657966	35.679254	35.700541	35.721826	35.743110	35.764393
33	34.670037	34.691360	34.712683	34.734004	34.755325	34.776644	34.797962	34.819279
34	33.780616	33.801973	33.823330	33.844686	33.866041	33.887396	33.908749	33.930102
35	32.942330	32.963722	32.985115	33.006506	33.027897	33.049287	33.070677	33.092066
36	32.150917	32.172346	32.193774	32.215202	32.236629	32.258057	32.279483	32.300909
37	31.402578	31.424043	31.445508	31.466973	31.488438	31.509903	31.531367	31.552831
38	30.693910	30.715413	30.736916	30.758419	30.779922	30.801425	30.822927	30.844430
39	30.021863	30.043404	30.064945	30.086487	30.108028	30.129570	30.151112	30.172655
40	29.383690	29.405269	29.426850	29.448430	29.470011	29.491593	29.513174	29.534757
41	28.776912	28.798530	28.820150	28.841770	28.863391	28.885013	28.906635	28.928258
42	28.199286	28.220944	28.242603	28.264264	28.285926	28.307588	28.329251	28.350915
43	27.648778	27.670477	27.692177	27.713878	27.735581	27.757284	27.778989	27.800694
44	27.123540	27.145279	27.167020	27.188763	27.210506	27.232251	27.253998	27.275745
45	26.621886	26.643667	26.665449	26.687233	26.709018	26.730806	26.752594	26.774384
46	26.142278	26.164100	26.185925	26.207751	26.229578	26.251408	26.273239	26.295072
47	25.683309	25.705174	25.727040	25.748908	25.770778	25.792651	25.814525	25.836401
48	25.243689	25.265596	25.287505	25.309416	25.331329	25.353244	25.375161	25.397081
60	21.125266	21.147698	21.170136	21.192578	21.215025	21.237476	21.259932	21.282393
72	18.401062	18.424042	18.447029	18.470023	18.493023	18.516031	18.539046	18.562068
84	16.473368	16.496903	16.520447	16.544001	16.567564	16.591136	16.614718	16.638309
96	15.043300	15.067392	15.091495	15.115610	15.139737	15.163875	15.188024	15.212185
108	13.944788	13.969435	13.994095	14.018768	14.043456	14.068156	14.092871	14.117598
120	13.078172	13.103367	13.128581	13.153806	13.179048	13.204306	13.229579	13.254868
132	12.380012	12.405750	12.431505	12.457278	12.483068	12.508875	12.534699	12.560541
144	11.808004	11.834275	11.860565	11.886874	11.913202	11.939549	11.965915	11.992300
156	11.332845	11.359639	11.386454	11.413290	11.440145	11.467022	11.493919	11.520835
168	10.933596	10.960903	10.988231	11.015581	11.042953	11.070347	11.097762	11.125200
180	10.594893	10.622699	10.650528	10.678381	10.706257	10.734156	10.762077	10.790022
192	10.305204	10.333498	10.361815	10.390157	10.418524	10.446914	10.475328	10.503766
204	10.055707	10.084474	10.113267	10.142085	10.170928	10.199795	10.228688	10.257605
216	9.839533	9.868761	9.898014	9.927294	9.956599	9.985930	10.015287	10.044669
228	9.651259	9.680932	9.710632	9.740359	9.770112	9.799891	9.829697	9.859528
240	9.486539	9.516644	9.546776	9.576935	9.607121	9.637334	9.667573	9.697838
252	9.341858	9.372380	9.402929	9.433505	9.464109	9.494739	9.525396	9.556080
264	9.214336	9.245259	9.276210	9.307189	9.338195	9.369228	9.400287	9.431374
276	9.101593	9.132903	9.164241	9.195607	9.227000	9.258419	9.289866	9.321339
288	9.001647	9.033329	9.065039	9.096776	9.128541	9.160332	9.192150	9.223994
300	8.912833	8.944872	8.976939	9.009032	9.041153	9.073300	9.105474	9.137674
312	8.833743	8.866124	8.898532	8.930968	8.963429	8.995917	9.028432	9.060972
324	8.763178	8.795887	8.828622	8.861384	8.894172	8.926986	8.959825	8.992690
336	8.700114	8.733135	8.766183	8.799257	8.832356	8.865481	8.898630	8.931805
348	8.643667	8.676987	8.710333	8.743704	8.777101	8.810521	8.843967	8.877436
360	8.593075	8.626680	8.660310	8.693965	8.727644	8.761347	8.795073	8.828823
420	8.407480	8.442313	8.477165	8.512038	8.546930	8.581841	8.616772	8.651721
480	8.297215	8.332980	8.368761	8.404556	8.440366	8.476189	8.512026	8.547877

MONTHLY WITHDRAWALS PER $1000

EFFECTIVE ANNUAL YIELD

NUMBER OF MONTHLY WTHDRWLS	10.60%	10.65%	10.70%	10.75%	10.80%	10.85%	10.90%	10.95%
1	1008.431169	1008.469152	1008.507119	1008.545071	1008.583007	1008.620927	1008.658832	1008.696721
2	506.332225	506.360792	506.389348	506.417892	506.446424	506.474946	506.503455	506.531954
3	338.969843	338.995307	339.020761	339.046205	339.071639	339.097063	339.122477	339.147882
4	255.291601	255.315540	255.339469	255.363390	255.387302	255.411205	255.435098	255.458983
5	205.087015	205.110060	205.133097	205.156125	205.179145	205.202156	205.225159	205.248154
6	171.619257	171.641724	171.664183	171.686634	171.709077	171.731512	171.753940	171.776359
7	147.715401	147.737470	147.759531	147.781586	147.803632	147.825671	147.847703	147.869727
8	129.788983	129.810767	129.832544	129.854313	129.876076	129.897831	129.919580	129.941321
9	115.847523	115.869098	115.890665	115.912225	115.933779	115.955326	115.976866	115.998399
10	104.695535	104.716952	104.738362	104.759766	104.781163	104.802554	104.823938	104.845316
11	95.572253	95.593550	95.614842	95.636127	95.657406	95.678679	95.699946	95.721206
12	87.970500	87.991707	88.012908	88.034104	88.055294	88.076477	88.097655	88.118826
13	81.539154	81.560293	81.581426	81.602554	81.623676	81.644792	81.665903	81.687008
14	76.027413	76.048501	76.069584	76.090661	76.111733	76.132800	76.153861	76.174916
15	71.251357	71.272408	71.293454	71.314494	71.335530	71.356560	71.377585	71.398605
16	67.073044	67.094069	67.115089	67.136104	67.157115	67.178120	67.199121	67.220116
17	63.386990	63.407998	63.429002	63.450001	63.470996	63.491986	63.512971	63.533951
18	60.111151	60.132151	60.153146	60.174137	60.195123	60.216105	60.237083	60.258056
19	57.180757	57.201755	57.222748	57.243737	57.264722	57.285702	57.306679	57.327651
20	54.543991	54.564992	54.585988	54.606981	54.627970	54.648954	54.669935	54.690912
21	52.158906	52.179914	52.200919	52.221920	52.242917	52.263911	52.284901	52.305887
22	49.991181	50.012202	50.033219	50.054232	50.075242	50.096248	50.117251	50.138251
23	48.012465	48.033501	48.054534	48.075564	48.096590	48.117613	48.138632	48.159649
24	46.199132	46.220187	46.241239	46.262287	46.283333	46.304375	46.325414	46.346451
25	44.531336	44.552412	44.573485	44.594556	44.615623	44.636688	44.657750	44.678809
26	42.992283	43.013383	43.034480	43.055575	43.076667	43.097756	43.118843	43.139927
27	41.567670	41.588795	41.609919	41.631040	41.652158	41.673274	41.694388	41.715500
28	40.245233	40.266387	40.287538	40.308687	40.329834	40.350979	40.372122	40.393262
29	39.014404	39.035587	39.056768	39.077947	39.099124	39.120300	39.141473	39.162644
30	37.866020	37.887235	37.908447	37.929658	37.950867	37.972074	37.993279	38.014483
31	36.792105	36.813351	36.834596	36.855840	36.877082	36.898323	36.919562	36.940799
32	35.785675	35.806955	35.828234	35.849512	35.870788	35.892063	35.913337	35.934610
33	34.840596	34.861911	34.883225	34.904538	34.925850	34.947161	34.968470	34.989779
34	33.951454	33.972805	33.994155	34.015504	34.036853	34.058200	34.079547	34.100893
35	33.113454	33.134842	33.156229	33.177616	33.199002	33.220387	33.241771	33.263155
36	32.322335	32.343761	32.365186	32.386610	32.408034	32.429458	32.450882	32.472304
37	31.574295	31.595759	31.617223	31.638686	31.660150	31.681613	31.703075	31.724538
38	30.865933	30.887437	30.908940	30.930443	30.951946	30.973449	30.994952	31.016455
39	30.194197	30.215740	30.237283	30.258827	30.280370	30.301914	30.323458	30.345002
40	29.556340	29.577923	29.599507	29.621091	29.642676	29.664261	29.685846	29.707432
41	28.949882	28.971506	28.993131	29.014757	29.036383	29.058010	29.079637	29.101265
42	28.372580	28.394246	28.415913	28.437580	28.459249	28.480918	28.502587	28.524259
43	27.822401	27.844109	27.865818	27.887528	27.909239	27.930951	27.952664	27.974378
44	27.297494	27.319245	27.340996	27.362749	27.384503	27.406258	27.428015	27.449773
45	26.796176	26.817969	26.839763	26.861560	26.883357	26.905156	26.926957	26.948759
46	26.316906	26.338743	26.360581	26.382421	26.404262	26.426105	26.447950	26.469796
47	25.858279	25.880159	25.902041	25.923924	25.945810	25.967697	25.989587	26.011478
48	25.419003	25.440927	25.462852	25.484781	25.506711	25.528643	25.550577	25.572514
60	21.304858	21.327328	21.349802	21.372281	21.394764	21.417252	21.439745	21.462242
72	18.585097	18.608132	18.631175	18.654225	18.677281	18.700344	18.723414	18.746491
84	16.661909	16.685518	16.709136	16.732764	16.756400	16.780046	16.803701	16.827365
96	15.236357	15.260541	15.284735	15.308942	15.333159	15.357388	15.381628	15.405879
108	14.142339	14.167094	14.191862	14.216643	14.241437	14.266245	14.291066	14.315900
120	13.280172	13.305491	13.330825	13.356175	13.381540	13.406920	13.432315	13.457725
132	12.586400	12.612275	12.638168	12.664078	12.690004	12.715947	12.741907	12.767884
144	12.018704	12.045126	12.071567	12.098026	12.124504	12.151000	12.177514	12.204047
156	11.547773	11.574730	11.601707	11.628705	11.655722	11.682759	11.709816	11.736892
168	11.152658	11.180138	11.207640	11.235163	11.262707	11.290272	11.317858	11.345465
180	10.817989	10.845979	10.873991	10.902025	10.930082	10.958161	10.986263	11.014386
192	10.532228	10.560713	10.589222	10.617754	10.646310	10.674885	10.703490	10.732114
204	10.286547	10.315514	10.344504	10.373519	10.402558	10.431621	10.460707	10.489817
216	10.074076	10.103508	10.132965	10.162447	10.191954	10.221485	10.251041	10.280621
228	9.889385	9.919268	9.949176	9.979110	10.009068	10.039052	10.069060	10.099094
240	9.728130	9.758449	9.788791	9.819160	9.849554	9.879974	9.910419	9.940889
252	9.586790	9.617527	9.648289	9.679078	9.709891	9.740731	9.771596	9.802485
264	9.462487	9.493626	9.524791	9.555983	9.587200	9.618442	9.649710	9.681003
276	9.352839	9.384365	9.415917	9.447495	9.479099	9.510728	9.542382	9.574061
288	9.255865	9.287762	9.319685	9.351633	9.383607	9.415606	9.447630	9.479678
300	9.169900	9.202152	9.234429	9.266732	9.299060	9.331412	9.363789	9.396191
312	9.093537	9.126128	9.158745	9.191386	9.224051	9.256741	9.289455	9.322193
324	9.025580	9.058495	9.091434	9.124397	9.157385	9.190397	9.223432	9.256490
336	8.965004	8.998227	9.031474	9.064745	9.098039	9.131357	9.164697	9.198060
348	8.910929	8.944446	8.977986	9.011549	9.045135	9.078743	9.112373	9.146025
360	8.862596	8.896392	8.930210	8.964050	8.997912	9.031796	9.065701	9.099627
420	8.686689	8.721675	8.756678	8.791699	8.826737	8.861791	8.896862	8.931949
480	8.583740	8.619616	8.655504	8.691403	8.727315	8.763238	8.799171	8.835115

MONTHLY WITHDRAWALS PER $1000

NUMBER OF MONTHLY WTHDRWLS	EFFECTIVE ANNUAL YIELD							
	11.00%	11.05%	11.10%	11.15%	11.20%	11.25%	11.30%	11.35%
1	1008.734594	1008.772451	1008.810293	1008.848120	1008.885931	1008.923726	1008.961505	1008.999269
2	506.560441	506.588916	506.617380	506.645833	506.674274	506.702704	506.731123	506.759530
3	339.173276	339.198661	339.224036	339.249401	339.274756	339.300101	339.325437	339.350763
4	255.482859	255.506725	255.530583	255.554432	255.578272	255.602103	255.625925	255.649738
5	205.271140	205.294118	205.317088	205.340049	205.363002	205.385946	205.408882	205.431810
6	171.798771	171.821174	171.843570	171.865958	171.888338	171.910710	171.933075	171.955431
7	147.891743	147.913752	147.935754	147.957748	147.979735	148.001714	148.023686	148.045651
8	129.963055	129.984782	130.006502	130.028214	130.049920	130.071619	130.093310	130.114994
9	116.019925	116.041445	116.062958	116.084464	116.105963	116.127456	116.148942	116.170421
10	104.866687	104.888052	104.909410	104.930762	104.952107	104.973446	104.994779	105.016105
11	95.742460	95.763708	95.784950	95.806186	95.827415	95.848639	95.869856	95.891066
12	88.139992	88.161152	88.182306	88.203454	88.224596	88.245732	88.266862	88.287987
13	81.708107	81.729201	81.750289	81.771371	81.792448	81.813519	81.834584	81.855644
14	76.195966	76.217011	76.238050	76.259084	76.280113	76.301136	76.322154	76.343166
15	71.419620	71.440630	71.461634	71.482634	71.503628	71.524617	71.545601	71.566580
16	67.241107	67.262033	67.283074	67.304050	67.325021	67.345987	67.366948	67.387905
17	63.554927	63.575898	63.596865	63.617827	63.638784	63.659736	63.680684	63.701627
18	60.279025	60.299989	60.320949	60.341904	60.362855	60.383802	60.404744	60.425681
19	57.348619	57.369582	57.390542	57.411497	57.432449	57.453396	57.474338	57.495277
20	54.711885	54.732853	54.753818	54.774779	54.795736	54.816689	54.837638	54.858583
21	52.326869	52.347848	52.368822	52.389794	52.410761	52.431725	52.452684	52.473641
22	50.159247	50.180239	50.201228	50.222213	50.243195	50.264174	50.285148	50.306120
23	48.180662	48.201671	48.222678	48.243681	48.264681	48.285678	48.306671	48.327661
24	46.367484	46.388514	46.409541	46.430566	46.451587	46.472605	46.493619	46.514631
25	44.699865	44.720918	44.741969	44.763017	44.784061	44.805103	44.826143	44.847179
26	43.161009	43.182088	43.203164	43.224238	43.245309	43.266377	43.287443	43.308507
27	41.736609	41.757715	41.778819	41.799921	41.821021	41.842118	41.863212	41.884305
28	40.414401	40.435537	40.456671	40.477803	40.498933	40.520060	40.541186	40.562309
29	39.183814	39.204981	39.226147	39.247311	39.268472	39.289632	39.310790	39.331945
30	38.035685	38.056886	38.078084	38.099281	38.120476	38.141670	38.162861	38.184051
31	36.962035	36.983270	37.004503	37.025734	37.046964	37.068193	37.089420	37.110645
32	35.955881	35.977151	35.998420	36.019687	36.040953	36.062218	36.083481	36.104743
33	35.011087	35.032393	35.053699	35.075003	35.096306	35.117608	35.138909	35.160209
34	34.122238	34.143582	34.164925	34.186267	34.207609	34.228949	34.250289	34.271628
35	33.284539	33.305921	33.327303	33.348684	33.370065	33.391445	33.412824	33.434203
36	32.493727	32.515149	32.536570	32.557991	32.579412	32.600832	32.622252	32.643671
37	31.746000	31.767463	31.788925	31.810386	31.831848	31.853309	31.874770	31.896230
38	31.037958	31.059461	31.080964	31.102467	31.123970	31.145473	31.166975	31.188478
39	30.366546	30.388091	30.409635	30.431180	30.452725	30.474271	30.495816	30.517362
40	29.729018	29.750605	29.772192	29.793779	29.815367	29.836955	29.858544	29.880133
41	29.122894	29.144523	29.166153	29.187784	29.209415	29.231047	29.252679	29.274312
42	28.545930	28.567603	28.589276	28.610951	28.632626	28.654301	28.675978	28.697655
43	27.996093	28.017809	28.039527	28.061245	28.082964	28.104684	28.126406	28.148128
44	27.471532	27.493292	27.515054	27.536817	27.558581	27.580346	27.602112	27.623880
45	26.970562	26.992367	27.014173	27.035980	27.057790	27.079601	27.101413	27.123226
46	26.491644	26.513494	26.535346	26.557199	26.579053	26.600910	26.622767	26.644627
47	26.033371	26.055266	26.077163	26.099062	26.120962	26.142865	26.164769	26.186675
48	25.594452	25.616393	25.638336	25.660280	25.682227	25.704176	25.726126	25.748079
60	21.484743	21.507249	21.529760	21.552274	21.574794	21.597318	21.619846	21.642378
72	18.769575	18.792666	18.815763	18.838817	18.861978	18.885096	18.908220	18.931351
84	16.851038	16.874720	16.898411	16.922111	16.945820	16.969538	16.993264	17.017000
96	15.430141	15.454414	15.478698	15.502994	15.527300	15.551618	15.575946	15.600285
108	14.340747	14.365607	14.390481	14.415367	14.440266	14.465178	14.490103	14.515041
120	13.483150	13.508590	13.534045	13.559514	13.584998	13.610497	13.636011	13.661540
132	12.793878	12.819888	12.845914	12.871958	12.898017	12.924093	12.950185	12.976294
144	12.230598	12.257167	12.283754	12.310359	12.336983	12.363623	12.390282	12.416959
156	11.763989	11.791104	11.818239	11.845394	11.872567	11.899760	11.926972	11.954203
168	11.373092	11.400741	11.428410	11.456100	11.483810	11.511540	11.539291	11.567062
180	11.042531	11.070698	11.098886	11.127096	11.155328	11.183581	11.211855	11.240150
192	10.760761	10.789431	10.818124	10.846839	10.875576	10.904335	10.933117	10.961921
204	10.518951	10.548108	10.577289	10.606492	10.635719	10.664968	10.694240	10.723535
216	10.310225	10.339853	10.369505	10.399180	10.428879	10.458602	10.488347	10.518116
228	10.129151	10.159234	10.189340	10.219470	10.249625	10.279803	10.310005	10.340230
240	9.971383	10.001903	10.032447	10.063015	10.093607	10.124223	10.154864	10.185527
252	9.833400	9.864340	9.895304	9.926292	9.957305	9.988342	10.019402	10.050487
264	9.712321	9.743663	9.775030	9.806422	9.837837	9.869277	9.900740	9.932227
276	9.605765	9.637493	9.669246	9.701023	9.732824	9.764649	9.796497	9.828368
288	9.511751	9.543849	9.575970	9.608115	9.640284	9.672476	9.704692	9.736930
300	9.428616	9.461066	9.493539	9.526035	9.558555	9.591097	9.623663	9.656251
312	9.354954	9.387739	9.420547	9.453378	9.486232	9.519108	9.552006	9.584926
324	9.289571	9.322675	9.355802	9.388951	9.422121	9.455314	9.488528	9.521764
336	9.231445	9.264852	9.298281	9.331732	9.365204	9.398697	9.432210	9.465745
348	9.179698	9.213393	9.247109	9.280846	9.314603	9.348380	9.382178	9.415995
360	9.133574	9.167541	9.201529	9.235536	9.269563	9.303610	9.337675	9.371759
420	8.967052	9.002171	9.037304	9.072453	9.107616	9.142793	9.177985	9.213190
480	8.871070	8.907035	8.943009	8.978992	9.014985	9.050987	9.086997	9.123015

MONTHLY WITHDRAWALS PER $1000

EFFECTIVE ANNUAL YIELD

NUMBER OF MONTHLY WTHDRWLS	11.40%	11.45%	11.50%	11.55%	11.60%	11.65%	11.70%	11.75%
1	1009.037018	1009.074751	1009.112468	1009.150170	1009.187857	1009.225528	1009.263184	1009.300824
2	506.787926	506.816311	506.844684	506.873046	506.901397	506.929736	506.958064	506.986381
3	339.376079	339.401385	339.426681	339.451968	339.477245	339.502512	339.527769	339.553017
4	255.673542	255.697337	255.721124	255.744901	255.768670	255.792429	255.816180	255.839922
5	205.454730	205.477641	205.500544	205.523439	205.546325	205.569204	205.592073	205.614935
6	171.977780	172.000121	172.022454	172.044779	172.067096	172.089406	172.111708	172.134002
7	148.067608	148.089557	148.111499	148.133434	148.155361	148.177281	148.199194	148.221099
8	130.136672	130.158342	130.180005	130.201661	130.223310	130.244952	130.266587	130.288215
9	116.191893	116.213358	116.234817	116.256269	116.277714	116.299153	116.320585	116.342010
10	105.037424	105.058737	105.080044	105.101344	105.122637	105.143925	105.165205	105.186480
11	95.912271	95.933470	95.954662	95.975848	95.997028	96.018202	96.039370	96.060532
12	88.309105	88.330218	88.351324	88.372425	88.393520	88.414609	88.435692	88.456769
13	81.876698	81.897747	81.918790	81.939827	81.960858	81.981884	82.002905	82.023919
14	76.364173	76.385175	76.406171	76.427162	76.448147	76.469127	76.490102	76.511071
15	71.587553	71.608522	71.629485	71.650443	71.671396	71.692344	71.713287	71.734225
16	67.408856	67.429803	67.450744	67.471681	67.492613	67.513540	67.534462	67.555379
17	63.722566	63.743500	63.764429	63.785353	63.806273	63.827189	63.848099	63.869005
18	60.446648	60.467543	60.488468	60.509388	60.530303	60.551214	60.572121	60.593023
19	57.516211	57.537142	57.558068	57.578989	57.599907	57.620821	57.641730	57.662635
20	54.879524	54.900461	54.921394	54.942324	54.963249	54.984170	55.005087	55.026001
21	52.494593	52.515514	52.536487	52.557428	52.578366	52.599299	52.620229	52.641156
22	50.327088	50.348052	50.369013	50.389970	50.410924	50.431874	50.452821	50.473765
23	48.348648	48.369631	48.390612	48.411588	48.432562	48.453533	48.474500	48.495464
24	46.535640	46.556646	46.577649	46.598648	46.619645	46.640638	46.661629	46.682616
25	44.868213	44.889243	44.910271	44.931296	44.952318	44.973338	44.994354	45.015368
26	43.329567	43.350625	43.371681	43.392733	43.413784	43.434831	43.455876	43.476918
27	41.905395	41.926482	41.947567	41.968650	41.989730	42.010808	42.031883	42.052957
28	40.583430	40.604549	40.625665	40.646780	40.667892	40.689002	40.710110	40.731216
29	39.353099	39.374251	39.395401	39.416549	39.437695	39.458839	39.479981	39.501121
30	38.205239	38.226426	38.247610	38.268793	38.289974	38.311154	38.332331	38.353507
31	37.131869	37.153091	37.174312	37.195531	37.216749	37.237965	37.259180	37.280393
32	36.126004	36.147264	36.168522	36.189779	36.211034	36.232288	36.253541	36.274792
33	35.181508	35.202806	35.224103	35.245398	35.266692	35.287986	35.309278	35.330569
34	34.292966	34.314303	34.335639	34.356974	34.378309	34.399642	34.420974	34.442306
35	33.455581	33.476958	33.498335	33.519711	33.541086	33.562460	33.583834	33.605207
36	32.665090	32.686508	32.707926	32.729343	32.750760	32.772177	32.793593	32.815008
37	31.917691	31.939151	31.960611	31.982070	32.003530	32.024989	32.046448	32.067906
38	31.209981	31.231484	31.252986	31.274489	31.295991	31.317494	31.338996	31.360498
39	30.538907	30.560453	30.581999	30.603546	30.625092	30.646638	30.668185	30.689732
40	29.901722	29.923312	29.944902	29.966492	29.988083	30.009674	30.031266	30.052857
41	29.295945	29.317579	29.339214	29.360849	29.382485	29.404121	29.425758	29.447395
42	28.719333	28.741012	28.762692	28.784372	28.806053	28.827735	28.849418	28.871101
43	28.169851	28.191575	28.213301	28.235027	28.256754	28.278482	28.300211	28.321941
44	27.645649	27.667419	27.689190	27.710962	27.732736	27.754510	27.776286	27.798063
45	27.145041	27.166857	27.188674	27.210493	27.232314	27.254135	27.275958	27.297783
46	26.666488	26.688351	26.710215	26.732081	26.753948	26.775817	26.797688	26.819560
47	26.208583	26.230492	26.252404	26.274317	26.296232	26.318148	26.340067	26.361987
48	25.770034	25.791991	25.813950	25.835910	25.857873	25.879838	25.901804	25.923773
60	21.664915	21.687456	21.710002	21.732552	21.755107	21.777665	21.800228	21.822795
72	18.954489	18.977633	19.000784	19.023942	19.047106	19.070276	19.093454	19.116637
84	17.040744	17.064497	17.088259	17.112030	17.135809	17.159598	17.183394	17.207200
96	15.624635	15.648996	15.673368	15.697751	15.722144	15.746548	15.770963	15.795388
108	14.539992	14.564955	14.589931	14.614920	14.639922	14.664936	14.689962	14.715002
120	13.687082	13.712640	13.738212	13.763798	13.789399	13.815014	13.840643	13.866287
132	13.002418	13.028559	13.054716	13.080889	13.107078	13.133283	13.159503	13.185740
144	12.443653	12.470365	12.497094	12.523841	12.550605	12.577386	12.604185	12.631001
156	11.981453	12.008722	12.036010	12.063316	12.090642	12.117985	12.145348	12.172728
168	11.594853	11.622664	11.650496	11.678346	11.706217	11.734108	11.762017	11.789947
180	11.268467	11.296804	11.325163	11.353542	11.381942	11.410362	11.438803	11.467265
192	10.990746	11.019593	11.048462	11.077353	11.106265	11.135198	11.164152	11.193128
204	10.752853	10.782192	10.811555	10.840939	10.870345	10.899773	10.929223	10.958695
216	10.547908	10.577723	10.607560	10.637420	10.667303	10.697208	10.727135	10.757084
228	10.370478	10.400750	10.431045	10.461363	10.491703	10.522066	10.552451	10.582859
240	10.216214	10.246932	10.277670	10.308415	10.339195	10.369997	10.400822	10.431669
252	10.081594	10.112725	10.143880	10.175057	10.206257	10.237480	10.268725	10.299992
264	9.963737	9.995270	10.026827	10.058406	10.090008	10.121632	10.153279	10.184947
276	9.860263	9.892181	9.924121	9.956084	9.988069	10.020076	10.052105	10.084156
288	9.769192	9.801475	9.833781	9.866110	9.898460	9.930832	9.963225	9.995640
300	9.688861	9.721493	9.754147	9.786823	9.819520	9.852238	9.884977	9.917737
312	9.617868	9.650831	9.683815	9.716821	9.749847	9.782894	9.815961	9.849048
324	9.555020	9.588297	9.621595	9.654913	9.688251	9.721609	9.754986	9.788383
336	9.499299	9.532874	9.566468	9.600082	9.633715	9.667367	9.701038	9.734727
348	9.449831	9.483687	9.517561	9.551454	9.585366	9.619296	9.653243	9.687209
360	9.405862	9.439983	9.474122	9.508279	9.542453	9.576645	9.610853	9.645078
420	9.248408	9.283640	9.318885	9.354142	9.389411	9.424692	9.459985	9.495290
480	9.159041	9.195075	9.231116	9.267165	9.303220	9.339281	9.375349	9.411423

MONTHLY WITHDRAWALS PER $1000

NUMBER OF MONTHLY WTHDRWLS	EFFECTIVE ANNUAL YIELD							
	11.80%	11.85%	11.90%	11.95%	12.00%	12.05%	12.10%	12.15%
1	1009.338448	1009.376058	1009.413651	1009.451230	1009.488793	1009.526341	1009.563873	1009.601390
2	507.014686	507.042981	507.071264	507.099536	507.127796	507.156046	507.184284	507.212511
3	339.578255	339.603483	339.628701	339.653910	339.679109	339.704298	339.729478	339.754648
4	255.863655	255.887379	255.911095	255.934801	255.958499	255.982188	256.005868	256.029539
5	205.637788	205.660634	205.683470	205.706299	205.729119	205.751932	205.774736	205.797531
6	172.156288	172.178566	172.200837	172.223100	172.245355	172.267603	172.289842	172.312074
7	148.242997	148.264887	148.286770	148.308645	148.330514	148.352375	148.374228	148.396074
8	130.309836	130.331449	130.353056	130.374656	130.396249	130.417834	130.439413	130.460985
9	116.363428	116.384840	116.406245	116.427643	116.449034	116.470419	116.491797	116.513169
10	105.207748	105.229009	105.250264	105.271513	105.292755	105.313991	105.335221	105.356444
11	96.081687	96.102836	96.123979	96.145117	96.166247	96.187372	96.208491	96.229604
12	88.477841	88.498906	88.519966	88.541019	88.562067	88.583109	88.604146	88.625176
13	82.044928	82.065932	82.086930	82.107922	82.128909	82.149890	82.170865	82.191835
14	76.532035	76.552994	76.573947	76.594895	76.615838	76.636775	76.657707	76.678633
15	71.755157	71.776085	71.797007	71.817925	71.838837	71.859744	71.880646	71.901543
16	67.576292	67.597199	67.618102	67.639000	67.659893	67.680781	67.701664	67.722542
17	63.889907	63.910803	63.931695	63.952583	63.973466	63.994344	64.015217	64.036086
18	60.613921	60.634815	60.655704	60.676589	60.697469	60.718345	60.739217	60.760084
19	57.683536	57.704433	57.725325	57.746214	57.767098	57.787978	57.808854	57.829726
20	55.046910	55.067816	55.088717	55.109615	55.130509	55.151398	55.172284	55.193166
21	52.662078	52.682997	52.703912	52.724824	52.745731	52.766636	52.787536	52.808433
22	50.494704	50.515641	50.536574	50.557503	50.578429	50.599351	50.620270	50.641185
23	48.516424	48.537381	48.558335	48.579286	48.600234	48.621178	48.642119	48.663056
24	46.703600	46.724582	46.745560	46.766535	46.787507	46.808476	46.829442	46.850405
25	45.036379	45.057387	45.078392	45.099394	45.120394	45.141390	45.162384	45.183375
26	43.497958	43.518995	43.540030	43.561061	43.582090	43.603117	43.624141	43.645162
27	42.074027	42.095095	42.116161	42.137225	42.158286	42.179344	42.200401	42.221454
28	40.752319	40.773420	40.794520	40.815618	40.836711	40.857804	40.878894	40.899982
29	39.522259	39.543395	39.564529	39.585661	39.606791	39.627919	39.649046	39.670170
30	38.374681	38.395854	38.417024	38.438193	38.459360	38.480525	38.501689	38.522850
31	37.301604	37.322814	37.344022	37.365229	37.386435	37.407638	37.428840	37.450041
32	36.296043	36.317291	36.338539	36.359785	36.381030	36.402273	36.423515	36.444756
33	35.351859	35.373148	35.394435	35.415722	35.437007	35.458291	35.479574	35.500856
34	34.463637	34.484966	34.506295	34.527623	34.548950	34.570276	34.591601	34.612925
35	33.626579	33.647951	33.669322	33.690692	33.712062	33.733430	33.754798	33.776166
36	32.836423	32.857837	32.879251	32.900664	32.922077	32.943490	32.964901	32.986313
37	32.089364	32.110822	32.132280	32.153737	32.175194	32.196650	32.218107	32.239563
38	31.382001	31.403503	31.425005	31.446506	31.468008	31.489510	31.511011	31.532513
39	30.711278	30.732825	30.754372	30.775919	30.797467	30.819014	30.840561	30.862109
40	30.074449	30.096042	30.117634	30.139227	30.160821	30.182414	30.204008	30.225602
41	29.469033	29.490671	29.512310	29.533950	29.555590	29.577230	29.598871	29.620512
42	28.892786	28.914470	28.936156	28.957842	28.979529	29.001217	29.022905	29.044595
43	28.343672	28.365404	28.387136	28.408870	28.430605	28.452340	28.474076	28.495814
44	27.819841	27.841620	27.863401	27.885182	27.906965	27.928749	27.950533	27.972319
45	27.319608	27.341435	27.363264	27.385093	27.406924	27.428756	27.450590	27.472425
46	26.841434	26.863309	26.885185	26.907064	26.928943	26.950825	26.972707	26.994591
47	26.383909	26.405833	26.427758	26.449685	26.471614	26.493544	26.515477	26.537410
48	25.945744	25.967716	25.989690	26.011667	26.033645	26.055625	26.077607	26.099591
60	21.845367	21.867943	21.890523	21.913107	21.935696	21.958289	21.980886	22.003487
72	19.139828	19.163025	19.186228	19.209438	19.232654	19.255877	19.279106	19.302341
84	17.231014	17.254837	17.278668	17.302508	17.326357	17.350214	17.374079	17.397953
96	15.819825	15.844271	15.868729	15.893196	15.917675	15.942164	15.966663	15.991173
108	14.740053	14.765117	14.790194	14.815283	14.840384	14.865498	14.890624	14.915762
120	13.891945	13.917617	13.943303	13.969003	13.994717	14.020446	14.046188	14.071944
132	13.211992	13.238260	13.264544	13.290843	13.317157	13.343488	13.369833	13.396194
144	12.657834	12.684685	12.711552	12.738436	12.765337	12.792255	12.819189	12.846141
156	12.200127	12.227545	12.254979	12.282434	12.309906	12.337395	12.364903	12.392428
168	11.817896	11.845864	11.873851	11.901858	11.929883	11.957928	11.985992	12.014074
180	11.495746	11.524248	11.552770	11.581312	11.609873	11.638455	11.667056	11.695677
192	11.222124	11.251142	11.280180	11.309239	11.338318	11.367418	11.396538	11.425679
204	10.988188	11.017703	11.047238	11.076795	11.106373	11.135972	11.165592	11.195232
216	10.787055	10.817047	10.847062	10.877098	10.907155	10.937233	10.967333	10.997453
228	10.613288	10.643740	10.674213	10.704709	10.735225	10.765763	10.796323	10.826903
240	10.462538	10.493429	10.524342	10.555277	10.586234	10.617211	10.648210	10.679230
252	10.331282	10.362593	10.393926	10.425281	10.456657	10.488054	10.519473	10.550912
264	10.216638	10.248350	10.280084	10.311839	10.343615	10.375412	10.407230	10.439069
276	10.116229	10.148323	10.180438	10.212574	10.244731	10.276908	10.309106	10.341324
288	10.028075	10.060532	10.093009	10.125507	10.158025	10.190563	10.223121	10.255699
300	9.950518	9.983318	10.016139	10.048980	10.081840	10.114720	10.147619	10.180537
312	9.882155	9.915282	9.948428	9.981593	10.014777	10.047980	10.081201	10.114441
324	9.821799	9.855234	9.888687	9.922159	9.955649	9.989157	10.022683	10.056226
336	9.768434	9.802160	9.835904	9.869665	9.903443	9.937238	9.971050	10.004879
348	9.721191	9.755191	9.789208	9.823241	9.857291	9.891357	9.925438	9.959536
360	9.679320	9.713578	9.747851	9.782141	9.816446	9.850766	9.885100	9.919450
420	9.530606	9.565933	9.601270	9.636618	9.671976	9.707343	9.742721	9.778108
480	9.447503	9.483588	9.519679	9.555775	9.591875	9.627980	9.664089	9.700202

173

MONTHLY WITHDRAWALS PER $1000

NUMBER OF MONTHLY WTHDRWLS	EFFECTIVE ANNUAL YIELD							
	12.20%	12.25%	12.30%	12.35%	12.40%	12.45%	12.50%	12.55%
1	1009.638892	1009.676378	1009.713849	1009.751305	1009.788745	1009.826171	1009.863581	1009.900975
2	507.240727	507.268931	507.297125	507.325307	507.353478	507.381638	507.409787	507.437925
3	339.779808	339.804959	339.830100	339.855231	339.880353	339.905465	339.930567	339.955660
4	256.053201	256.076855	256.100500	256.124136	256.147763	256.171382	256.194991	256.218592
5	205.820319	205.843098	205.865869	205.888632	205.911387	205.934134	205.956872	205.979602
6	172.334298	172.356515	172.378724	172.400925	172.423118	172.445303	172.467481	172.489652
7	148.417913	148.439745	148.461569	148.483386	148.505195	148.526997	148.548792	148.570580
8	130.482550	130.504107	130.525658	130.547202	130.568739	130.590268	130.611791	130.633307
9	116.534534	116.555892	116.577243	116.598588	116.619926	116.641258	116.662582	116.683901
10	105.377661	105.398871	105.420075	105.441273	105.462464	105.483649	105.504828	105.526000
11	96.250710	96.271810	96.292905	96.313993	96.335075	96.356151	96.377221	96.398285
12	88.646200	88.667219	88.688232	88.709239	88.730240	88.751235	88.772225	88.793209
13	82.212799	82.233758	82.254711	82.275659	82.296601	82.317537	82.338468	82.359393
14	76.699554	76.720470	76.741381	76.762286	76.783186	76.804081	76.824970	76.845854
15	71.922434	71.943321	71.964203	71.985079	72.005951	72.026817	72.047678	72.068535
16	67.743416	67.764284	67.785148	67.806007	67.826861	67.847710	67.868555	67.889394
17	64.056950	64.077810	64.098665	64.119516	64.140362	64.161203	64.182039	64.202871
18	60.780946	60.801805	60.822659	60.843508	60.864354	60.885194	60.906031	60.926863
19	57.850594	57.871457	57.892316	57.913171	57.934022	57.954869	57.975712	57.996550
20	55.214044	55.234918	55.255788	55.276654	55.297516	55.318374	55.339229	55.360079
21	52.829325	52.850215	52.871100	52.891982	52.912860	52.933734	52.954605	52.975472
22	50.662097	50.683006	50.703910	50.724812	50.745710	50.766604	50.787495	50.808382
23	48.683991	48.704922	48.725849	48.746774	48.767695	48.788613	48.809528	48.830439
24	46.871365	46.892322	46.913276	46.934226	46.955174	46.976119	46.997060	47.017999
25	45.204363	45.225348	45.246331	45.267310	45.288287	45.309261	45.330232	45.351200
26	43.666181	43.687197	43.708211	43.729221	43.750230	43.771235	43.792238	43.813238
27	42.242506	42.263555	42.284601	42.305645	42.326687	42.347726	42.368763	42.389798
28	40.921068	40.942152	40.963233	40.984313	41.005390	41.026465	41.047538	41.068608
29	39.691292	39.712412	39.733530	39.754646	39.775761	39.796873	39.817983	39.839091
30	38.544010	38.565169	38.586325	38.607479	38.628632	38.649783	38.670932	38.692080
31	37.471240	37.492438	37.513633	37.534828	37.556020	37.577212	37.598401	37.619589
32	36.465995	36.487233	36.508470	36.529705	36.550939	36.572171	36.593403	36.614632
33	35.522137	35.543417	35.564695	35.585972	35.607248	35.628522	35.649795	35.671070
34	34.634248	34.655571	34.676892	34.698212	34.719532	34.740850	34.762168	34.783484
35	33.797532	33.818898	33.840263	33.861627	33.882991	33.904354	33.925716	33.947077
36	33.007723	33.029133	33.050543	33.071952	33.093361	33.114769	33.136176	33.157583
37	32.261018	32.282474	32.303929	32.325383	32.346838	32.368292	32.389745	32.411198
38	31.554014	31.575515	31.597016	31.618517	31.640018	31.661519	31.683019	31.704519
39	30.883657	30.905204	30.926752	30.948300	30.969848	30.991396	31.012943	31.034491
40	30.247197	30.268791	30.290386	30.311982	30.333577	30.355173	30.376769	30.398365
41	29.642154	29.663796	29.685439	29.707083	29.728726	29.750371	29.772015	29.793660
42	29.066284	29.087975	29.109666	29.131358	29.153050	29.174743	29.196437	29.218131
43	28.517552	28.539291	28.561031	28.582772	28.604513	28.626256	28.647999	28.669743
44	27.994106	28.015894	28.037683	28.059473	28.081265	28.103057	28.124850	28.146645
45	27.494261	27.516098	27.537937	27.559777	27.581618	27.603461	27.625304	27.647149
46	27.016477	27.038364	27.060253	27.082143	27.104035	27.125927	27.147822	27.169718
47	26.559346	26.581283	26.603222	26.625163	26.647105	26.669049	26.690994	26.712941
48	26.121577	26.143564	26.165554	26.187545	26.209538	26.231533	26.253530	26.275529
60	22.026092	22.048702	22.071315	22.093933	22.116555	22.139181	22.161812	22.184446
72	19.325583	19.348831	19.372086	19.395347	19.418614	19.441887	19.465167	19.488453
84	17.421836	17.445727	17.469626	17.493534	17.517450	17.541374	17.565307	17.589248
96	16.015693	16.040023	16.064764	16.089315	16.113877	16.138448	16.163030	16.187622
108	14.940912	14.966075	14.991249	15.016436	15.041634	15.066845	15.092068	15.117302
120	14.097713	14.123497	14.149294	14.175105	14.200930	14.226768	14.252620	14.278485
132	13.422571	13.448462	13.475369	13.501791	13.528228	13.554680	13.581147	13.607628
144	12.873109	12.900093	12.927094	12.954111	12.981145	13.008195	13.035261	13.062344
156	12.419972	12.447532	12.475111	12.502707	12.530320	12.557951	12.585599	12.613265
168	12.042175	12.070294	12.098433	12.126589	12.154764	12.182957	12.211169	12.239398
180	11.724317	11.752977	11.781656	11.810354	11.839072	11.867808	11.896563	11.925337
192	11.454839	11.484020	11.513220	11.542440	11.571680	11.600939	11.630218	11.659517
204	11.224893	11.254575	11.284276	11.313998	11.343740	11.373502	11.403284	11.433085
216	11.027595	11.057757	11.087939	11.118142	11.148366	11.178609	11.208872	11.239156
228	10.857504	10.888127	10.918769	10.949433	10.980116	11.010820	11.041544	11.072288
240	10.710271	10.741333	10.772415	10.803518	10.834641	10.865784	10.896947	10.928130
252	10.582372	10.613853	10.645354	10.676875	10.708417	10.739978	10.771559	10.803160
264	10.470928	10.502807	10.534707	10.566626	10.598565	10.630523	10.662501	10.694498
276	10.373561	10.405819	10.438096	10.470393	10.502709	10.535044	10.567398	10.599771
288	10.288296	10.320912	10.353547	10.386201	10.418874	10.451565	10.484275	10.517003
300	10.213474	10.246429	10.279403	10.312395	10.345405	10.378433	10.411478	10.444541
312	10.147699	10.180975	10.214268	10.247579	10.280906	10.314251	10.347613	10.380991
324	10.089786	10.123363	10.156958	10.190569	10.224196	10.257839	10.291499	10.325174
336	10.038725	10.072586	10.106463	10.140356	10.174265	10.208189	10.242127	10.276081
348	9.993649	10.027777	10.061920	10.096078	10.130250	10.164437	10.198638	10.232852
360	9.953814	9.988193	10.022585	10.056991	10.091411	10.125843	10.160289	10.194748
420	9.813504	9.848909	9.884322	9.919744	9.955174	9.990612	10.026058	10.061511
480	9.736319	9.772439	9.808563	9.844690	9.880820	9.916953	9.953088	9.989225

174

MONTHLY WITHDRAWALS PER $1000

NUMBER OF MONTHLY WTHDRWLS	EFFECTIVE ANNUAL YIELD							
	12.60%	12.65%	12.70%	12.75%	12.80%	12.85%	12.90%	12.95%
1	1009.938355	1009.975719	1010.013068	1010.050402	1010.087721	1010.125024	1010.162313	1010.199586
2	507.466051	507.494167	507.522271	507.550365	507.578447	507.606518	507.634578	507.662628
3	339.980744	340.005817	340.030881	340.055936	340.080981	340.106016	340.131042	340.156058
4	256.242184	256.265768	256.289343	256.312909	256.336466	256.360015	256.383554	256.407086
5	206.002325	206.025039	206.047744	206.070442	206.093132	206.115813	206.138486	206.161152
6	172.511814	172.533969	172.556116	172.578255	172.600387	172.622511	172.644628	172.666737
7	148.592360	148.614133	148.635899	148.657657	148.679408	148.701152	148.722889	148.744618
8	130.654816	130.676318	130.697813	130.719301	130.740783	130.762257	130.783724	130.805185
9	116.705212	116.726517	116.747815	116.769107	116.790392	116.811670	116.832942	116.854207
10	105.547166	105.568325	105.589478	105.610625	105.631765	105.652900	105.674027	105.695149
11	96.419342	96.440394	96.461440	96.482479	96.503513	96.524540	96.545562	96.566577
12	88.814187	88.835159	88.856125	88.877085	88.898040	88.918989	88.939932	88.960869
13	82.380313	82.401227	82.422136	82.443039	82.463936	82.484828	82.505715	82.526596
14	76.866732	76.887606	76.908474	76.929336	76.950194	76.971046	76.991893	77.012734
15	72.089386	72.110232	72.131073	72.151909	72.172739	72.193565	72.214386	72.235202
16	67.910229	67.931059	67.951884	67.972704	67.993519	68.014330	68.035136	68.055937
17	64.223699	64.244522	64.265340	64.286153	64.306962	64.327767	64.348567	64.369362
18	60.947691	60.968514	60.989333	61.010147	61.030958	61.051763	61.072565	61.093362
19	58.017385	58.038215	58.059041	58.079863	58.100680	58.121494	58.142304	58.163109
20	55.380926	55.401768	55.422607	55.443441	55.464272	55.485099	55.505922	55.526741
21	52.996335	53.017194	53.038050	53.058902	53.079750	53.100595	53.121436	53.142273
22	50.829266	50.850147	50.871024	50.891897	50.912767	50.933634	50.954497	50.975356
23	48.851347	48.872252	48.893154	48.914052	48.934947	48.955839	48.976728	48.997613
24	47.038934	47.059867	47.080796	47.101722	47.122645	47.143565	47.164483	47.185397
25	45.372166	45.393128	45.414088	45.435045	45.455999	45.476950	45.497898	45.518843
26	43.834236	43.855231	43.876223	43.897213	43.918200	43.939185	43.960167	43.981146
27	42.410830	42.431859	42.452887	42.473911	42.494934	42.515954	42.536971	42.557986
28	41.089676	41.110743	41.131806	41.152868	41.173927	41.194985	41.216040	41.237093
29	39.860198	39.881302	39.902404	39.923504	39.944602	39.965699	39.986793	40.007885
30	38.713226	38.734369	38.755511	38.776652	38.797790	38.818927	38.840062	38.861195
31	37.640776	37.661960	37.683144	37.704325	37.725505	37.746684	37.767860	37.789036
32	36.635861	36.657088	36.678313	36.699537	36.720760	36.741982	36.763202	36.784420
33	35.692341	35.713611	35.734881	35.756148	35.777415	35.798681	35.819945	35.841208
34	34.804800	34.826114	34.847428	34.868740	34.890052	34.911363	34.932672	34.953981
35	33.968437	33.989797	34.011156	34.032543	34.053872	34.075228	34.096584	34.117939
36	33.178989	33.200395	33.221800	33.243205	33.264609	33.286012	33.307415	33.328817
37	32.432651	32.454104	32.475556	32.497008	32.518459	32.539910	32.561361	32.582811
38	31.726020	31.747520	31.769019	31.790517	31.812018	31.833518	31.855017	31.876516
39	31.056040	31.077588	31.099136	31.120684	31.142232	31.163780	31.185328	31.206877
40	30.419962	30.441559	30.463156	30.484753	30.506350	30.527948	30.549546	30.571144
41	29.815306	29.836952	29.858598	29.880245	29.901892	29.923540	29.945188	29.966836
42	29.239827	29.261522	29.283219	29.304915	29.326613	29.348311	29.370010	29.391709
43	28.691488	28.713234	28.734981	28.756728	28.778476	28.800225	28.821975	28.843726
44	28.168440	28.190236	28.212034	28.233832	28.255632	28.277432	28.299233	28.321036
45	27.668995	27.690843	27.712691	27.734541	27.756392	27.778244	27.800098	27.821952
46	27.191615	27.213514	27.235414	27.257315	27.279218	27.301122	27.323028	27.344935
47	26.734890	26.756840	26.778792	26.800746	26.822701	26.844658	26.866616	26.888576
48	26.297529	26.319532	26.341536	26.363542	26.385549	26.407559	26.429570	26.451583
60	22.207084	22.229727	22.252373	22.275024	22.297678	22.320337	22.342999	22.365666
72	19.511745	19.535044	19.558348	19.581659	19.604976	19.628299	19.651629	19.674964
84	17.613197	17.637155	17.661120	17.685094	17.709076	17.733066	17.757065	17.781071
96	16.212224	16.236837	16.261459	16.286091	16.310734	16.335386	16.360049	16.384721
108	15.142549	15.167807	15.193077	15.218359	15.243652	15.268958	15.294275	15.319603
120	14.304364	14.330256	14.356162	14.382081	14.408013	14.433958	14.459917	14.485888
132	13.634125	13.660637	13.687163	13.713704	13.740260	13.766830	13.793415	13.820014
144	13.089442	13.116557	13.143687	13.170834	13.197996	13.225174	13.252368	13.279577
156	12.640947	12.668647	12.696363	12.724097	12.751847	12.779614	12.807398	12.835199
168	12.267646	12.295911	12.324195	12.352496	12.380815	12.409151	12.437505	12.465876
180	11.954130	11.982942	12.011771	12.040620	12.069487	12.098371	12.127275	12.156196
192	11.688834	11.718171	11.747526	11.776901	11.806294	11.835706	11.865137	11.894586
204	11.462906	11.492747	11.522607	11.552486	11.582384	11.612301	11.642237	11.672192
216	11.269459	11.299782	11.330124	11.360486	11.390867	11.421267	11.451686	11.482123
228	11.103052	11.133835	11.164638	11.195460	11.226302	11.257162	11.288041	11.318940
240	10.959333	10.990555	11.021796	11.053057	11.084337	11.115635	11.146953	11.178288
252	10.834780	10.866419	10.898077	10.929754	10.961450	10.993165	11.024898	11.056649
264	10.726514	10.758549	10.790602	10.822674	10.854765	10.886873	10.919000	10.951144
276	10.632162	10.664571	10.696999	10.729444	10.761907	10.794388	10.826886	10.859402
288	10.549748	10.582511	10.615292	10.648090	10.680905	10.713737	10.746586	10.779451
300	10.477621	10.510717	10.543831	10.576961	10.610108	10.643271	10.676449	10.709644
312	10.414386	10.447797	10.481224	10.514666	10.548124	10.581598	10.615086	10.648590
324	10.358864	10.392570	10.426291	10.460027	10.493777	10.527542	10.561321	10.595114
336	10.310049	10.344032	10.378028	10.412039	10.446063	10.480101	10.514152	10.548216
348	10.267080	10.301322	10.335577	10.369844	10.404125	10.438417	10.472723	10.507040
360	10.229219	10.263703	10.298199	10.332706	10.367226	10.401757	10.436299	10.470852
420	10.096971	10.132438	10.167912	10.203393	10.238880	10.274373	10.309872	10.345376
480	10.025364	10.061505	10.097647	10.133791	10.169936	10.206083	10.242229	10.278377

MONTHLY WITHDRAWALS PER $1000

NUMBER OF MONTHLY WTHDRWLS	EFFECTIVE ANNUAL YIELD							
	13.00%	13.05%	13.10%	13.15%	13.20%	13.25%	13.30%	13.35%
1	1010.236844	1010.274087	1010.311315	1010.348528	1010.385726	1010.422909	1010.460077	1010.497229
2	507.690666	507.718693	507.746709	507.774714	507.802708	507.830691	507.858663	507.886624
3	340.181065	340.206062	340.231050	340.256028	340.280996	340.305955	340.330905	340.355845
4	256.430608	256.454122	256.477627	256.501123	256.524611	256.548090	256.571561	256.595023
5	206.183809	206.206458	206.229099	206.251732	206.274356	206.296973	206.319582	206.342182
6	172.688838	172.710932	172.733018	172.755096	172.777167	172.799230	172.821285	172.843333
7	148.766340	148.788055	148.809763	148.831463	148.853156	148.874842	148.896521	148.918192
8	130.826638	130.848085	130.869524	130.890957	130.912383	130.933802	130.955214	130.976619
9	116.875466	116.896718	116.917963	116.939202	116.960434	116.981660	117.002879	117.024091
10	105.716264	105.737373	105.758476	105.779572	105.800662	105.821745	105.842823	105.863894
11	96.587586	96.608590	96.629587	96.650578	96.671563	96.692542	96.713515	96.734482
12	88.981801	89.002727	89.023647	89.044561	89.065469	89.086372	89.107269	89.128160
13	82.547471	82.568341	82.589205	82.610064	82.630917	82.651765	82.672608	82.693444
14	77.033570	77.054401	77.075227	77.096047	77.116862	77.137672	77.158477	77.179276
15	72.256012	72.276818	72.297619	72.318414	72.339205	72.359990	72.380770	72.401546
16	68.076733	68.097524	68.118310	68.139092	68.159869	68.180641	68.201408	68.222171
17	64.390152	64.410938	64.431720	64.452497	64.473269	64.494037	64.514800	64.535559
18	61.114155	61.134943	61.155727	61.176507	61.197282	61.218053	61.238820	61.259582
19	58.183910	58.204707	58.225500	58.246289	58.267074	58.287854	58.308631	58.329403
20	55.547556	55.568367	55.589174	55.609978	55.630777	55.651572	55.672364	55.693152
21	53.163107	53.183937	53.204763	53.225585	53.246404	53.267219	53.288030	53.308838
22	50.996212	51.017065	51.037914	51.058760	51.079602	51.100440	51.121275	51.142107
23	49.018495	49.039374	49.060249	49.081121	49.101990	49.122856	49.143718	49.164577
24	47.206308	47.227215	47.248120	47.269022	47.289921	47.310817	47.331709	47.352599
25	45.539786	45.560726	45.581663	45.602597	45.623528	45.644456	45.665382	45.686305
26	44.002122	44.023096	44.044068	44.065036	44.086003	44.106966	44.127927	44.148885
27	42.578999	42.600009	42.621017	42.642022	42.663025	42.684026	42.705024	42.725020
28	41.258143	41.279192	41.300238	41.321282	41.342323	41.363363	41.384400	41.405435
29	40.028975	40.050063	40.071149	40.092234	40.113316	40.134396	40.155474	40.176550
30	38.882326	38.903455	38.924583	38.945709	38.966833	38.987955	39.009075	39.030194
31	37.810209	37.831381	37.852552	37.873721	37.894888	37.916053	37.937217	37.958380
32	36.805638	36.826854	36.848068	36.869281	36.890493	36.911703	36.932912	36.954119
33	35.862470	35.883731	35.904991	35.926249	35.947506	35.968762	35.990017	36.011270
34	34.975288	34.996595	35.017901	35.039205	35.060509	35.081812	35.103113	35.124414
35	34.139293	34.160647	34.182000	34.203351	34.224702	34.246053	34.267402	34.288751
36	33.350219	33.371620	33.393021	33.414421	33.435820	33.457219	33.478617	33.500014
37	32.604261	32.625710	32.647159	32.668608	32.690056	32.711504	32.732952	32.754399
38	31.898014	31.919513	31.941011	31.962509	31.984007	32.005505	32.027002	32.048500
39	31.228425	31.249973	31.271521	31.293069	31.314617	31.336166	31.357714	31.379262
40	30.592742	30.614341	30.635939	30.657538	30.679137	30.700736	30.722336	30.743935
41	29.988485	30.010135	30.031784	30.053434	30.075085	30.096735	30.118386	30.140038
42	29.413409	29.435110	29.456811	29.478512	29.500215	29.521917	29.543621	29.565325
43	28.865478	28.887230	28.908983	28.930737	28.952491	28.974246	28.996002	29.017759
44	28.342839	28.364644	28.386449	28.408255	28.430063	28.451871	28.473680	28.495490
45	27.843808	27.865665	27.887523	27.909382	27.931242	27.953104	27.974967	27.996830
46	27.366844	27.388753	27.410664	27.432577	27.454491	27.476406	27.498322	27.520240
47	26.910537	26.932500	26.954465	26.976431	26.998398	27.020367	27.042338	27.064310
48	26.473597	26.495614	26.517632	26.539652	26.561674	26.583697	26.605722	26.627749
60	22.388336	22.411011	22.433689	22.456372	22.479058	22.501748	22.524443	22.547141
72	19.698305	19.721653	19.745007	19.768366	19.791732	19.815103	19.838481	19.861865
84	17.805085	17.829108	17.853138	17.877177	17.901223	17.925278	17.949340	17.973411
96	16.409403	16.434095	16.458797	16.483509	16.508231	16.532962	16.557703	16.582454
108	15.344943	15.370295	15.395658	15.421033	15.446419	15.471816	15.497225	15.522645
120	14.511873	14.537871	14.563882	14.589905	14.615942	14.641992	14.668054	14.694129
132	13.846628	13.873256	13.899898	13.926555	13.953226	13.979911	14.006610	14.033323
144	13.306802	13.334042	13.361298	13.388570	13.415856	13.443158	13.470475	13.497807
156	12.863016	12.890849	12.918699	12.946565	12.974448	13.002346	13.030261	13.058192
168	12.494265	12.522671	12.551094	12.579534	12.607992	12.636466	12.664957	12.693464
180	12.185135	12.214092	12.243066	12.272059	12.301069	12.330096	12.359141	12.388202
192	11.924053	11.953539	11.983043	12.012565	12.042105	12.071662	12.101238	12.130831
204	11.702165	11.732157	11.762167	11.792196	11.822243	11.852307	11.882390	11.912491
216	11.512580	11.543055	11.573549	11.604061	11.634591	11.665139	11.695705	11.726290
228	11.349857	11.380792	11.411746	11.442718	11.473708	11.504716	11.535742	11.566786
240	11.209643	11.241016	11.272406	11.303815	11.335242	11.366686	11.398148	11.429628
252	11.088418	11.120205	11.152010	11.183833	11.215673	11.247531	11.279405	11.311297
264	10.983306	11.015485	11.047682	11.079895	11.112126	11.144373	11.176638	11.208918
276	10.891934	10.924483	10.957049	10.989632	11.022231	11.054846	11.087477	11.120124
288	10.812333	10.845231	10.878145	10.911074	10.944020	10.976980	11.009956	11.042947
300	10.742854	10.776079	10.809320	10.842576	10.875846	10.909131	10.942431	10.975745
312	10.682108	10.715641	10.749188	10.782749	10.816325	10.849914	10.883516	10.917132
324	10.628921	10.662742	10.696576	10.730423	10.764283	10.798156	10.832042	10.865940
336	10.582293	10.616383	10.650485	10.684599	10.718725	10.752864	10.787013	10.821175
348	10.541369	10.575709	10.610062	10.644425	10.678799	10.713184	10.747580	10.781986
360	10.505416	10.539990	10.574575	10.609170	10.643776	10.678390	10.713015	10.747649
420	10.380886	10.416402	10.451922	10.487447	10.522977	10.558511	10.594049	10.629591
480	10.314525	10.350673	10.386821	10.422969	10.459116	10.495263	10.531410	10.567555

MONTHLY WITHDRAWALS PER $1000

NUMBER OF MONTHLY WTHDRWLS	EFFECTIVE ANNUAL YIELD							
	13.40%	13.45%	13.50%	13.55%	13.60%	13.65%	13.70%	13.75%
1	1010.534367	1010.571490	1010.608597	1010.645690	1010.682768	1010.719830	1010.756878	1010.793911
2	507.914574	507.942513	507.970442	507.998359	508.026265	508.054161	508.082045	508.109919
3	340.380776	340.405697	340.430609	340.455511	340.480404	340.505287	340.530161	340.555026
4	256.618476	256.641920	256.665356	256.688784	256.712202	256.735613	256.759014	256.782407
5	206.364775	206.387360	206.409936	206.432504	206.455065	206.477617	206.500162	206.522698
6	172.865373	172.887406	172.909431	172.931449	172.953459	172.975461	172.997456	173.019443
7	148.939857	148.961514	148.983164	149.004806	149.026442	149.048070	149.069691	149.091305
8	130.998018	131.019409	131.040794	131.062172	131.083543	131.104907	131.126264	131.147615
9	117.045297	117.066496	117.087689	117.108875	117.130055	117.151228	117.172395	117.193555
10	105.884959	105.906017	105.927070	105.948116	105.969155	105.990189	106.011216	106.032237
11	96.755444	96.776399	96.797348	96.818291	96.839228	96.860159	96.881084	96.902003
12	89.149046	89.169925	89.190799	89.211667	89.232530	89.253386	89.274237	89.295083
13	82.714276	82.735101	82.755922	82.776736	82.797546	82.818349	82.839148	82.859941
14	77.200070	77.220859	77.241642	77.262421	77.283194	77.303962	77.324724	77.345481
15	72.422316	72.443082	72.463842	72.484597	72.505347	72.526093	72.546833	72.567568
16	68.242928	68.263681	68.284429	68.305173	68.325911	68.346645	68.367374	68.388098
17	64.556313	64.577062	64.597807	64.618547	64.639283	64.660014	64.680741	64.701463
18	61.280340	61.301093	61.321843	61.342587	61.363328	61.384064	61.404796	61.425524
19	58.350171	58.370935	58.391695	58.412451	58.433202	58.453950	58.474693	58.495433
20	55.713936	55.734715	55.755491	55.776263	55.797032	55.817796	55.838556	55.859313
21	53.329642	53.350443	53.371239	53.392032	53.412821	53.433607	53.454389	53.475167
22	51.162935	51.183760	51.204581	51.225399	51.246213	51.267024	51.287831	51.308635
23	49.185433	49.206286	49.227135	49.247981	49.268824	49.289664	49.310500	49.331333
24	47.373485	47.394369	47.415249	47.436127	47.457001	47.477872	47.498740	47.519605
25	45.707224	45.728141	45.749056	45.769967	45.790875	45.811781	45.832684	45.853584
26	44.169840	44.190793	44.211743	44.232691	44.253636	44.274578	44.295518	44.316455
27	42.747013	42.768004	42.788992	42.809978	42.830961	42.851942	42.872921	42.893897
28	41.426468	41.447498	41.468527	41.489553	41.510577	41.531598	41.552618	41.573635
29	40.197624	40.218696	40.239766	40.260834	40.281900	40.302964	40.324025	40.345085
30	39.051311	39.072425	39.093538	39.114650	39.135759	39.156867	39.177972	39.199076
31	37.979541	38.000700	38.021857	38.043013	38.064167	38.085320	38.106471	38.127620
32	36.975325	36.996530	37.017733	37.038934	37.060135	37.081334	37.102531	37.123727
33	36.032522	36.053774	36.075023	36.096272	36.117519	36.138766	36.160011	36.181254
34	35.145714	35.167012	35.188310	35.209606	35.230902	35.252196	35.273490	35.294782
35	34.310099	34.331445	34.352789	34.374137	34.395481	34.416825	34.438168	34.459510
36	33.521411	33.542807	33.564203	33.585597	33.606992	33.628385	33.649778	33.671171
37	32.775845	32.797291	32.818737	32.840182	32.861627	32.883071	32.904515	32.925959
38	32.069997	32.091493	32.112990	32.134486	32.155982	32.177478	32.198973	32.220469
39	31.400810	31.422358	31.443906	31.465454	31.487002	31.508549	31.530097	31.551645
40	30.765535	30.787135	30.808735	30.830335	30.851935	30.873535	30.895136	30.916737
41	30.161690	30.183342	30.204994	30.226647	30.248300	30.269954	30.291608	30.313262
42	29.587029	29.608734	29.630440	29.652146	29.673852	29.695560	29.717267	29.738975
43	29.039517	29.061275	29.083034	29.104794	29.126554	29.148315	29.170077	29.191840
44	28.517301	28.539113	28.560926	28.582740	28.604554	28.626370	28.648186	28.670004
45	28.018695	28.040561	28.062428	28.084297	28.106166	28.128036	28.149908	28.171780
46	27.542159	27.564079	27.586001	27.607924	27.629848	27.651774	27.673701	27.695629
47	27.086284	27.108259	27.130235	27.152213	27.174193	27.196174	27.218156	27.240140
48	26.649777	26.671807	26.693839	26.715872	26.737907	26.759944	26.781982	26.804022
60	22.569842	22.592548	22.615258	22.637971	22.660689	22.683410	22.706135	22.728864
72	19.885254	19.908650	19.932051	19.955458	19.978871	20.002290	20.025715	20.049146
84	17.997489	18.021575	18.045669	18.069770	18.093880	18.117997	18.142122	18.166254
96	16.607214	16.631984	16.656764	16.681553	16.706352	16.731160	16.755978	16.780805
108	15.548077	15.573519	15.598973	15.624438	15.649914	15.675402	15.700900	15.726409
120	14.720217	14.746317	14.772431	14.798557	14.824695	14.850845	14.877009	14.903184
132	14.060050	14.086791	14.113546	14.140315	14.167097	14.193893	14.220703	14.247527
144	13.525155	13.552517	13.579894	13.607286	13.634693	13.662115	13.689551	13.717002
156	13.086139	13.114101	13.142080	13.170074	13.198084	13.226109	13.254150	13.282207
168	12.721989	12.750530	12.779087	12.807661	12.836251	12.864858	12.893480	12.922119
180	12.417282	12.446378	12.475492	12.504622	12.533769	12.562933	12.592113	12.621310
192	12.160442	12.190070	12.219715	12.249378	12.279057	12.308754	12.338468	12.368198
204	11.942609	11.972745	12.002898	12.033069	12.063257	12.093462	12.123684	12.153923
216	11.756891	11.787511	11.818147	11.848802	11.879473	11.910161	11.940867	11.971589
228	11.597847	11.628926	11.660021	11.691135	11.722265	11.753412	11.784575	11.815756
240	11.461124	11.492638	11.524169	11.555717	11.587281	11.618862	11.650459	11.682072
252	11.343205	11.375130	11.407072	11.439030	11.471004	11.502994	11.535000	11.567022
264	11.241215	11.273528	11.305857	11.338202	11.370562	11.402938	11.435329	11.467736
276	11.152786	11.185464	11.218158	11.250866	11.283589	11.316328	11.349080	11.381848
288	11.075953	11.108974	11.142009	11.175059	11.208123	11.241201	11.274292	11.307397
300	11.009073	11.042414	11.075770	11.109139	11.142521	11.175917	11.209325	11.242747
312	10.950761	10.984403	11.018058	11.051726	11.085406	11.119098	11.152802	11.186518
324	10.899851	10.933773	10.967707	11.001653	11.035611	11.069579	11.103559	11.137549
336	10.855347	10.889531	10.923725	10.957930	10.992145	11.026371	11.060607	11.094853
348	10.816403	10.850829	10.885265	10.919711	10.954166	10.988631	11.023104	11.057586
360	10.782291	10.816943	10.851604	10.886273	10.920950	10.955636	10.990330	11.025031
420	10.665137	10.700687	10.736240	10.771797	10.807356	10.842918	10.878483	10.914051
480	10.603699	10.639842	10.675984	10.712124	10.748262	10.784399	10.820533	10.856665

MONTHLY WITHDRAWALS PER $1000

NUMBER OF MONTHLY WTHDRWLS	EFFECTIVE ANNUAL YIELD							
	13.80%	13.85%	13.90%	13.95%	14.00%	14.05%	14.10%	14.15%
1	1010.830929	1010.867932	1010.904920	1010.941894	1010.978852	1011.015796	1011.052724	1011.089638
2	508.137781	508.165633	508.193474	508.221304	508.249124	508.276932	508.304730	508.332516
3	340.579881	340.604726	340.629563	340.654390	340.679207	340.704015	340.728814	340.753603
4	256.805791	256.829167	256.852534	256.875893	256.899243	256.922585	256.945918	256.969242
5	206.545226	206.567747	206.590259	206.612764	206.635260	206.657748	206.680229	206.702702
6	173.041423	173.063395	173.085360	173.107317	173.129267	173.151209	173.173144	173.195071
7	149.112912	149.134512	149.156104	149.177689	149.199268	149.220839	149.242403	149.263959
8	131.168958	131.190295	131.211625	131.232948	131.254264	131.275574	131.296876	131.318172
9	117.214709	117.235856	117.256996	117.278130	117.299258	117.320379	117.341493	117.362601
10	106.053252	106.074260	106.095263	106.116259	106.137248	106.158232	106.179209	106.200180
11	96.922917	96.943824	96.964725	96.985620	97.006509	97.027393	97.048270	97.069142
12	89.315922	89.336756	89.357584	89.378406	89.399223	89.420034	89.440839	89.461639
13	82.880728	82.901510	82.922286	82.943057	82.963823	82.984583	83.005337	83.026086
14	77.366233	77.386980	77.407722	77.428458	77.449189	77.469915	77.490636	77.511351
15	72.588298	72.609024	72.629744	72.650459	72.671169	72.691875	72.712575	72.733270
16	68.408817	68.429532	68.450242	68.470947	68.491647	68.512343	68.533034	68.553720
17	64.722181	64.742894	64.763602	64.784306	64.805005	64.825700	64.846390	64.867076
18	61.446247	61.466966	61.487680	61.508391	61.529096	61.549798	61.570495	61.591188
19	58.516168	58.536899	58.557626	58.578349	58.599068	58.619782	58.640493	58.661199
20	55.880065	55.900814	55.921559	55.942299	55.963036	55.983769	56.004499	56.025224
21	53.495941	53.516712	53.537479	53.558243	53.579003	53.599759	53.620511	53.641260
22	51.329436	51.350233	51.371026	51.391816	51.412603	51.433386	51.454165	51.474941
23	49.352163	49.372989	49.393812	49.414632	49.435449	49.456262	49.477072	49.497879
24	47.540647	47.561326	47.582182	47.603035	47.623885	47.644732	47.665576	47.686416
25	45.874481	45.895375	45.916266	45.937155	45.958040	45.978923	45.999803	46.020680
26	44.337389	44.358321	44.379250	44.400176	44.421100	44.442021	44.462940	44.483856
27	42.914871	42.935842	42.956811	42.977777	42.998741	43.019703	43.040662	43.061619
28	41.594650	41.615663	41.636673	41.657681	41.678687	41.699691	41.720692	41.741692
29	40.366143	40.387199	40.408252	40.429304	40.450354	40.471401	40.492447	40.513490
30	39.220178	39.241279	39.262377	39.283474	39.304568	39.325661	39.346752	39.367841
31	38.148768	38.169914	38.191058	38.212201	38.233342	38.254482	38.275620	38.296756
32	37.144922	37.166115	37.187306	37.208497	37.229685	37.250873	37.272059	37.293243
33	36.202497	36.223738	36.244977	36.266217	36.287454	36.308690	36.329925	36.351159
34	35.316073	35.337364	35.358653	35.379941	35.401228	35.422514	35.443799	35.465083
35	34.480851	34.502191	34.523531	34.544869	34.566207	34.587544	34.608880	34.630215
36	33.692562	33.713953	33.735344	33.756733	33.778123	33.799511	33.820899	33.842286
37	32.947402	32.968844	32.990286	33.011728	33.033169	33.054610	33.076050	33.097490
38	32.241964	32.263459	32.284953	32.306447	32.327941	32.349435	32.370928	32.392421
39	31.573192	31.594740	31.616287	31.637835	31.659382	31.680929	31.702476	31.724023
40	30.938337	30.959938	30.981539	31.003140	31.024742	31.046343	31.067944	31.089546
41	30.334916	30.356571	30.378226	30.399882	30.421537	30.443193	30.464849	30.486506
42	29.760684	29.782393	29.804103	29.825813	29.847523	29.869234	29.890946	29.912658
43	29.213603	29.235367	29.257131	29.278897	29.300663	29.322429	29.344196	29.365964
44	28.691822	28.713641	28.735461	28.757282	28.779103	28.800926	28.822749	28.844574
45	28.193654	28.215528	28.237404	28.259281	28.281159	28.303037	28.324917	28.346798
46	27.717558	27.739488	27.761420	27.783353	27.805288	27.827223	27.849160	27.871097
47	27.262125	27.284112	27.306100	27.328090	27.350081	27.372073	27.394067	27.416062
48	26.826064	26.848107	26.870152	26.892198	26.914246	26.936296	26.958347	26.980400
60	22.751596	22.774332	22.797072	22.819816	22.842564	22.865315	22.888070	22.910829
72	20.072582	20.096025	20.119473	20.142927	20.166386	20.189852	20.213323	20.236799
84	18.190395	18.214543	18.238699	18.262862	18.287033	18.311211	18.335397	18.359591
96	16.805641	16.830487	16.855343	16.880207	16.905081	16.929965	16.954857	16.979759
108	15.751929	15.777461	15.803003	15.828556	15.854120	15.879694	15.905280	15.930876
120	14.929372	14.955573	14.981785	15.008010	15.034247	15.060496	15.086757	15.113031
132	14.274364	14.301215	14.328079	14.354956	14.381847	14.408751	14.435668	14.462599
144	13.744468	13.771948	13.799442	13.826951	13.854474	13.882012	13.909563	13.937129
156	13.310278	13.338366	13.366468	13.394585	13.422718	13.450866	13.479028	13.507206
168	12.950774	12.979444	13.008131	13.036833	13.065551	13.094284	13.123033	13.151798
180	12.650523	12.679753	12.708999	12.738261	12.767539	12.796833	12.826144	12.855469
192	12.397945	12.427709	12.457489	12.487286	12.517099	12.546928	12.576773	12.606634
204	12.184178	12.214451	12.244740	12.275045	12.305367	12.335705	12.366059	12.396429
216	12.002328	12.033083	12.063855	12.094644	12.125448	12.156269	12.187105	12.217958
228	11.846952	11.878165	11.909395	11.940640	11.971902	12.003179	12.034472	12.065780
240	11.713702	11.745347	11.777009	11.808686	11.840378	11.872086	11.903809	11.935548
252	11.599060	11.631113	11.663181	11.695265	11.727364	11.759477	11.791605	11.823748
264	11.500157	11.532593	11.565044	11.597509	11.629989	11.662483	11.694991	11.727513
276	11.414629	11.447425	11.480234	11.513058	11.545895	11.578746	11.611609	11.644486
288	11.340516	11.373648	11.406794	11.439952	11.473123	11.506307	11.539503	11.572712
300	11.276181	11.309627	11.343086	11.376556	11.410039	11.443534	11.477040	11.510557
312	11.220246	11.253986	11.287736	11.321498	11.355271	11.389054	11.422849	11.456653
324	11.171551	11.205563	11.239585	11.273617	11.307659	11.341712	11.375773	11.409844
336	11.129108	11.163373	11.197647	11.231930	11.266223	11.300524	11.334833	11.369151
348	11.092077	11.126577	11.161084	11.195600	11.230124	11.264655	11.299194	11.333740
360	11.059740	11.094456	11.129180	11.163911	11.198648	11.233392	11.268143	11.302900
420	10.949621	10.985193	11.020766	11.056342	11.091919	11.127498	11.163078	11.198659
480	10.892795	10.928922	10.965046	11.001168	11.037286	11.073402	11.109514	11.145623

EFFECTIVE ANNUAL YIELD

NUMBER OF MONTHLY WTHDRWLS	14.20%	14.25%	14.30%	14.35%	14.40%	14.45%	14.50%	14.55%
1	1011.126537	1011.163421	1011.200291	1011.237146	1011.273985	1011.310811	1011.347621	1011.384417
2	508.360292	508.388057	508.415812	508.443555	508.471288	508.499010	508.526721	508.554421
3	340.778383	340.803154	340.827915	340.852667	340.877410	340.902143	340.926868	340.951582
4	256.992558	257.015866	257.039165	257.062455	257.085737	257.109010	257.132275	257.155532
5	206.725166	206.747623	206.770072	206.792512	206.814945	206.837370	206.859787	206.882196
6	173.216990	173.238902	173.260807	173.282704	173.304594	173.326476	173.348351	173.370218
7	149.285509	149.307052	149.328587	149.350115	149.371636	149.393151	149.414658	149.436158
8	131.339461	131.360744	131.382019	131.403288	131.424550	131.445805	131.467054	131.488295
9	117.383703	117.404798	117.425886	117.446968	117.468044	117.489113	117.510175	117.531232
10	106.221145	106.242104	106.263057	106.284003	106.304943	106.325877	106.346805	106.367726
11	97.090007	97.110867	97.131720	97.152568	97.173410	97.194245	97.215075	97.235899
12	89.482433	89.503221	89.524003	89.544780	89.565551	89.586317	89.607076	89.627831
13	83.046830	83.067568	83.088301	83.109028	83.129750	83.150467	83.171178	83.191883
14	77.532062	77.552767	77.573466	77.594161	77.614851	77.635535	77.656214	77.676888
15	72.753960	72.774646	72.795326	72.816001	72.836672	72.857337	72.877998	72.898653
16	68.574401	68.595077	68.615749	68.636416	68.657078	68.677736	68.698389	68.719037
17	64.887757	64.908434	64.929106	64.949774	64.970437	64.991095	65.011749	65.032399
18	61.611877	61.632561	61.653241	61.673917	61.694588	61.715255	61.735918	61.756577
19	58.681902	58.702660	58.723294	58.743984	58.764670	58.785352	58.806030	58.826703
20	56.045945	56.066663	56.087377	56.108086	56.128792	56.149494	56.170192	56.190886
21	53.662005	53.682746	53.703484	53.724218	53.744948	53.765675	53.786398	53.807117
22	51.495714	51.516483	51.537249	51.558011	51.578770	51.599525	51.620277	51.641025
23	49.518683	49.539483	49.560280	49.581074	49.601865	49.622652	49.643436	49.664217
24	47.707254	47.728089	47.748920	47.769749	47.790574	47.811396	47.832216	47.853032
25	46.041554	46.062426	46.083294	46.104160	46.125023	46.145883	46.166740	46.187594
26	44.504769	44.525679	44.546587	44.567492	44.588395	44.609295	44.630192	44.651087
27	43.082573	43.103525	43.124474	43.145421	43.166365	43.187307	43.208246	43.229183
28	41.762689	41.783683	41.804676	41.825666	41.846654	41.867640	41.888623	41.909604
29	40.534532	40.555571	40.576608	40.597644	40.618677	40.639708	40.660737	40.681764
30	39.388929	39.410014	39.431098	39.452180	39.473260	39.494338	39.515414	39.536488
31	38.317891	38.339023	38.360155	38.381284	38.402412	38.423539	38.444663	38.465786
32	37.314426	37.335607	37.356787	37.377966	37.399143	37.420319	37.441493	37.462666
33	36.372391	36.393623	36.414852	36.436081	36.457308	36.478535	36.499759	36.520983
34	35.486366	35.507648	35.528929	35.550208	35.571487	35.592764	35.614041	35.635316
35	34.651549	34.672882	34.694215	34.715546	34.736877	34.758207	34.779536	34.800864
36	33.863672	33.885058	33.906443	33.927827	33.949211	33.970593	33.991976	34.013357
37	33.118929	33.140368	33.161806	33.183244	33.204681	33.226117	33.247554	33.268989
38	32.413914	32.435406	32.456898	32.478390	32.499882	32.521373	32.542864	32.564354
39	31.745570	31.767117	31.788664	31.810210	31.831756	31.853303	31.874849	31.896395
40	31.111147	31.132749	31.154351	31.175952	31.197554	31.219156	31.240758	31.262360
41	30.508163	30.529820	30.551477	30.573135	30.594792	30.616450	30.638109	30.659767
42	29.934370	29.956083	29.977797	29.999510	30.021224	30.042939	30.064654	30.086370
43	29.387733	29.409502	29.431272	29.453042	29.474813	29.496585	29.518357	29.540130
44	28.866399	28.888224	28.910051	28.931879	28.953707	28.975536	28.997366	29.019196
45	28.368680	28.390563	28.412447	28.434332	28.456218	28.478104	28.499992	28.521881
46	27.893037	27.914977	27.936918	27.958861	27.980805	28.002750	28.024696	28.046643
47	27.438059	27.460057	27.482056	27.504057	27.526059	27.548062	27.570067	27.592073
48	27.002454	27.024510	27.046568	27.068627	27.090687	27.112749	27.134813	27.156878
60	22.933591	22.956357	22.979127	23.001900	23.024677	23.047457	23.070242	23.093029
72	20.262022	20.283770	20.307263	20.330762	20.354267	20.377778	20.401294	20.424815
84	18.383792	18.408000	18.432216	18.456440	18.480671	18.504909	18.529155	18.553408
96	17.004670	17.029590	17.054519	17.079457	17.104404	17.129361	17.154326	17.179300
108	15.956483	15.982100	16.007728	16.033367	16.059016	16.084676	16.110346	16.136026
120	15.139316	15.165613	15.191922	15.218243	15.244576	15.270921	15.297277	15.323645
132	14.489542	14.516499	14.543469	14.570451	14.597447	14.624455	14.651477	14.678510
144	13.964709	13.992302	14.019910	14.047532	14.075167	14.102816	14.130479	14.158155
156	13.535398	13.563605	13.591826	13.620062	13.648313	13.676578	13.704858	13.733152
168	13.180578	13.209373	13.238183	13.267008	13.295848	13.324704	13.353574	13.382459
180	12.884811	12.914168	12.943541	12.972929	13.002332	13.031751	13.061185	13.090634
192	12.636511	12.666404	12.696313	12.726237	12.756176	12.786131	12.816101	12.846087
204	12.426815	12.457216	12.487634	12.518067	12.548515	12.578979	12.609458	12.639952
216	12.248826	12.279710	12.310609	12.341524	12.372453	12.403398	12.434358	12.465333
228	12.097104	12.128443	12.159797	12.191167	12.222551	12.253950	12.285364	12.316792
240	11.967301	11.999069	12.030852	12.062650	12.094462	12.126288	12.158128	12.189983
252	11.855905	11.888076	11.920262	11.952461	11.984675	12.016902	12.049142	12.081396
264	11.760049	11.792599	11.825161	11.857737	11.890327	11.922929	11.955544	11.988172
276	11.677376	11.710279	11.743195	11.776123	11.809063	11.842016	11.874980	11.907957
288	11.605932	11.639165	11.672409	11.705665	11.738933	11.772212	11.805502	11.838803
300	11.544086	11.577625	11.611176	11.644737	11.678309	11.711892	11.745484	11.779087
312	11.490468	11.524293	11.558128	11.591973	11.625827	11.659691	11.693564	11.727446
324	11.443925	11.478014	11.512113	11.546220	11.580336	11.614460	11.648592	11.682733
336	11.403478	11.437812	11.472154	11.506504	11.540861	11.575226	11.609598	11.643977
348	11.368294	11.402854	11.437421	11.471995	11.506576	11.541162	11.575755	11.610354
360	11.337663	11.372431	11.407206	11.441986	11.476772	11.511563	11.546359	11.581160
420	11.234241	11.269823	11.305407	11.340990	11.376574	11.412159	11.447743	11.483327
480	11.181728	11.217829	11.253927	11.290020	11.326110	11.362195	11.398276	11.434352

MONTHLY WITHDRAWALS PER $1000

NUMBER OF MONTHLY WTHDRWLS	EFFECTIVE ANNUAL YIELD							
	14.60%	**14.65%**	**14.70%**	**14.75%**	**14.80%**	**14.85%**	**14.90%**	**14.95%**
1	1011.421198	1011.457964	1011.494715	1011.531452	1011.568175	1011.604882	1011.641575	1011.678253
2	508.582111	508.609790	508.637458	508.665116	508.692763	508.720399	508.748024	508.775639
3	340.976288	341.000984	341.025671	341.050348	341.075017	341.099676	341.124326	341.148966
4	257.178780	257.202019	257.225250	257.248473	257.271687	257.294893	257.318090	257.341279
5	206.904597	206.926991	206.949376	206.971754	206.994124	207.016485	207.038839	207.061185
6	173.392078	173.413930	173.435775	173.457612	173.479443	173.501265	173.523080	173.544888
7	149.457650	149.479136	149.500615	149.522087	149.543551	149.565009	149.586459	149.607903
8	131.509530	131.530759	131.551980	131.573195	131.594403	131.615604	131.636799	131.657986
9	117.552281	117.573325	117.594362	117.615392	117.636416	117.657433	117.678444	117.699449
10	106.388642	106.409551	106.430454	106.451351	106.472242	106.493126	106.514005	106.534877
11	97.256717	97.277529	97.298336	97.319136	97.339930	97.360719	97.381502	97.402278
12	89.648579	89.669322	89.690059	89.710790	89.731516	89.752236	89.772951	89.793660
13	83.212583	83.233278	83.253967	83.274651	83.295330	83.316003	83.336671	83.357333
14	77.697556	77.718220	77.738878	77.759531	77.780179	77.800822	77.821459	77.842092
15	72.919304	72.939949	72.960590	72.981226	73.001856	73.022482	73.043103	73.063719
16	68.739680	68.760318	68.780952	68.801581	68.822206	68.842825	68.863440	68.884050
17	65.053044	65.073684	65.094320	65.114952	65.135579	65.156201	65.176819	65.197433
18	61.777231	61.797881	61.818526	61.839167	61.859804	61.880437	61.901065	61.921690
19	58.847373	58.868038	58.888700	58.909357	58.930010	58.950660	58.971305	58.991946
20	56.211577	56.232263	56.252946	56.273625	56.294299	56.314970	56.335638	56.356301
21	53.827833	53.848545	53.869253	53.889958	53.910659	53.931356	53.952050	53.972740
22	51.661770	51.682512	51.703250	51.723984	51.744715	51.765443	51.786167	51.806888
23	49.684995	49.705769	49.726540	49.747308	49.768072	49.788834	49.809592	49.830346
24	47.873845	47.894655	47.915462	47.936266	47.957067	47.977865	47.998660	48.019452
25	46.208446	46.229294	46.250140	46.270983	46.291823	46.312660	46.333494	46.354326
26	44.671979	44.692868	44.713755	44.734639	44.755520	44.776399	44.797275	44.818148
27	43.250118	43.271050	43.291980	43.312907	43.333832	43.354754	43.375674	43.396591
28	41.930583	41.951560	41.972535	41.993507	42.014477	42.035444	42.056409	42.077373
29	40.702789	40.723812	40.744833	40.765852	40.786869	40.807883	40.828896	40.849907
30	39.557561	39.578631	39.599700	39.620767	39.641832	39.662895	39.683957	39.705016
31	38.486907	38.508027	38.529145	38.550261	38.571376	38.592489	38.613600	38.634709
32	37.483837	37.505007	37.526175	37.547342	37.568507	37.589671	37.610833	37.631994
33	36.542205	36.563426	36.584646	36.605864	36.627081	36.648297	36.669512	36.690725
34	35.656590	35.677864	35.699136	35.720407	35.741677	35.762945	35.784213	35.805480
35	34.822911	34.843517	34.864842	34.886167	34.907490	34.928812	34.950135	34.971455
36	34.034738	34.056118	34.077497	34.098876	34.120254	34.141631	34.163007	34.184383
37	33.290424	33.311859	33.333293	33.354727	33.376160	33.397592	33.419024	33.440456
38	32.585844	32.607334	32.628824	32.650313	32.671802	32.693290	32.714778	32.736266
39	31.917941	31.939486	31.961032	31.982577	32.004123	32.025668	32.047212	32.068757
40	31.283962	31.305564	31.327166	31.348768	31.370371	31.391973	31.413575	31.435177
41	30.681426	30.703085	30.724744	30.746403	30.768063	30.789723	30.811383	30.833043
42	30.108086	30.129802	30.151519	30.173236	30.194953	30.216671	30.238389	30.260108
43	29.561904	29.583678	29.605452	29.627228	29.649003	29.670780	29.692557	29.714334
44	29.041028	29.062860	29.084693	29.106527	29.128361	29.150197	29.172033	29.193869
45	28.543771	28.565661	28.587553	28.609446	28.631339	28.653234	28.675129	28.697025
46	28.068591	28.090541	28.112492	28.134443	28.156396	28.178350	28.200305	28.222262
47	27.614080	27.636089	27.658099	27.680110	27.702122	27.724136	27.746151	27.768168
48	27.178944	27.201012	27.223082	27.245153	27.267225	27.289299	27.311375	27.333452
60	23.115821	23.138616	23.161414	23.184216	23.207022	23.229831	23.252644	23.275460
72	20.448242	20.471875	20.495413	20.518957	20.542506	20.566060	20.589620	20.613185
84	18.577668	18.601936	18.626210	18.650493	18.674782	18.699079	18.723382	18.747693
96	17.204284	17.228709	17.254277	17.279287	17.304306	17.329333	17.354370	17.379415
108	16.161717	16.187419	16.213130	16.238852	16.264584	16.290327	16.316079	16.341842
120	15.350025	15.376416	15.402819	15.429233	15.455659	15.482096	15.508545	15.535005
132	14.705557	14.732617	14.759688	14.786773	14.813870	14.840979	14.868101	14.895235
144	14.185845	14.213549	14.241266	14.268996	14.296740	14.324497	14.352267	14.380050
156	13.761460	13.789782	13.818118	13.846468	13.874833	13.903211	13.931603	13.960008
168	13.411358	13.440272	13.469201	13.498144	13.527102	13.556074	13.585060	13.614060
180	13.120098	13.149576	13.179070	13.208578	13.238101	13.267639	13.297191	13.326757
192	12.876087	12.906103	12.936133	12.966178	12.996238	13.026312	13.056401	13.086504
204	12.670461	12.700985	12.731523	12.762077	12.792645	12.823227	12.853824	12.884435
216	12.496323	12.527327	12.558346	12.589380	12.620427	12.651489	12.682565	12.713655
228	12.348235	12.379692	12.411163	12.442648	12.474147	12.505660	12.537186	12.568726
240	12.221851	12.253733	12.285629	12.317538	12.349461	12.381397	12.413346	12.445308
252	12.113664	12.145944	12.178238	12.210544	12.242863	12.275195	12.307539	12.339895
264	12.020812	12.053465	12.086130	12.118807	12.151496	12.184197	12.216910	12.249634
276	11.940945	11.973945	12.006956	12.039979	12.073013	12.106058	12.139113	12.172179
288	11.872115	11.905438	11.938771	11.972115	12.005469	12.038833	12.072207	12.105590
300	11.812699	11.846322	11.879954	11.913595	11.947246	11.980905	12.014573	12.048251
312	11.761337	11.795237	11.829145	11.863062	11.896987	11.930920	11.964861	11.998810
324	11.716881	11.751037	11.785201	11.819372	11.853551	11.887736	11.921928	11.956127
336	11.678363	11.712756	11.747155	11.781560	11.815972	11.850390	11.884813	11.919242
348	11.644958	11.679569	11.714184	11.748805	11.783431	11.818063	11.852698	11.887339
360	11.615965	11.650775	11.685590	11.720409	11.755232	11.790059	11.824889	11.859723
420	11.518910	11.554493	11.590076	11.625657	11.661238	11.696818	11.732396	11.767973
480	11.470424	11.506491	11.542553	11.578610	11.614662	11.650708	11.686749	11.722785

MONTHLY WITHDRAWALS PER $1000

NUMBER OF MONTHLY WTHDRWLS	EFFECTIVE ANNUAL YIELD							
	15.00%	15.05%	15.10%	15.15%	15.20%	15.25%	15.30%	15.35%
1	1011.714917	1011.751566	1011.788200	1011.824820	1011.861426	1011.898016	1011.934592	1011.971154
2	508.803243	508.830836	508.858419	508.885991	508.913552	508.941103	508.968643	508.996173
3	341.173598	341.198220	341.222833	341.247436	341.272031	341.296616	341.321192	341.345759
4	257.364459	257.387631	257.410795	257.433950	257.457097	257.480236	257.503366	257.526487
5	207.083524	207.105854	207.128177	207.150491	207.172798	207.195097	207.217388	207.239672
6	173.566688	173.588481	173.610267	173.632045	173.653816	173.675579	173.697335	173.719084
7	149.629339	149.650768	149.672191	149.693606	149.715014	149.736415	149.757810	149.779197
8	131.679167	131.700342	131.721510	131.742671	131.763825	131.784972	131.806113	131.827248
9	117.720447	117.741439	117.762425	117.783404	117.804376	117.825343	117.846302	117.867256
10	106.555743	106.576603	106.597457	106.618305	106.639146	106.659982	106.680811	106.701634
11	97.423049	97.443814	97.464573	97.485327	97.506074	97.526815	97.547551	97.568281
12	89.814363	89.835061	89.855753	89.876439	89.897120	89.917795	89.938464	89.959128
13	83.377990	83.398641	83.419287	83.439928	83.460563	83.481193	83.501818	83.522437
14	77.862719	77.883341	77.903958	77.924570	77.945176	77.965778	77.986374	78.006965
15	73.084330	73.104936	73.125537	73.146133	73.166724	73.187310	73.207892	73.228468
16	68.904656	68.925257	68.945853	68.966444	68.987031	69.007613	69.028190	69.048762
17	65.218042	65.238646	65.259246	65.279841	65.300432	65.321019	65.341601	65.362178
18	61.942309	61.962925	61.983536	62.004143	62.024746	62.045344	62.065938	62.086528
19	59.012583	59.033216	59.053844	59.074469	59.095090	59.115706	59.136319	59.156927
20	56.376960	56.397616	56.418267	56.438915	56.459559	56.480199	56.500835	56.521468
21	53.993426	54.014109	54.034788	54.055463	54.076135	54.096803	54.117468	54.138128
22	51.827605	51.848319	51.869029	51.889736	51.910439	51.931139	51.951836	51.972529
23	49.851098	49.871846	49.892591	49.913333	49.934072	49.954807	49.975539	49.996268
24	48.040241	48.061026	48.081809	48.102589	48.123365	48.144139	48.164909	48.185677
25	46.375155	46.395980	46.416803	46.437623	46.458440	46.479255	46.500066	46.520875
26	44.839019	44.859887	44.880753	44.901615	44.922476	44.943333	44.964188	44.985040
27	43.417506	43.438419	43.459329	43.480236	43.501141	43.522044	43.542944	43.563842
28	42.098334	42.119293	42.140249	42.161203	42.182155	42.203104	42.224052	42.244997
29	40.870915	40.891921	40.912926	40.933928	40.954928	40.975926	40.996922	41.017916
30	39.726073	39.747129	39.768183	39.789235	39.810285	39.831333	39.852379	39.873423
31	38.655817	38.676923	38.698028	38.719131	38.740232	38.761331	38.782429	38.803525
32	37.653154	37.674311	37.695466	37.716623	37.737776	37.758928	37.780078	37.801227
33	36.711937	36.733148	36.754357	36.775565	36.796772	36.817977	36.839181	36.860384
34	35.826745	35.848009	35.869272	35.890535	35.911796	35.933055	35.954314	35.975572
35	34.992775	35.014094	35.035412	35.056729	35.078045	35.099360	35.120674	35.141988
36	34.205758	34.227132	34.248506	34.269879	34.291251	34.312622	34.333992	34.355362
37	33.461887	33.483317	33.504747	33.526176	33.547604	33.569032	33.590460	33.611887
38	32.757754	32.779241	32.800727	32.822214	32.843699	32.865185	32.886670	32.908155
39	32.090302	32.111846	32.133390	32.154934	32.176478	32.198021	32.219565	32.241108
40	31.456779	31.478382	31.499984	31.521586	31.543188	31.564790	31.586392	31.607995
41	30.854703	30.876364	30.898025	30.919686	30.941347	30.963008	30.984669	31.006331
42	30.281827	30.303546	30.325266	30.346986	30.368706	30.390427	30.412148	30.433870
43	29.736112	29.757891	29.779670	29.801449	29.823230	29.845010	29.866792	29.888573
44	29.215707	29.237545	29.259384	29.281223	29.303064	29.324905	29.346746	29.368589
45	28.718923	28.740821	28.762720	28.784620	28.806520	28.828422	28.850325	28.872228
46	28.244219	28.266177	28.288137	28.310097	28.332059	28.354021	28.375985	28.397950
47	27.790185	27.812204	27.834225	27.856246	27.878269	27.900293	27.922318	27.944344
48	27.355530	27.377610	27.399691	27.421773	27.443857	27.465943	27.488030	27.510118
60	23.298279	23.321103	23.343929	23.366759	23.389593	23.412429	23.435270	23.458114
72	20.636756	20.660332	20.683914	20.707500	20.731093	20.754690	20.778293	20.801901
84	18.772011	18.796336	18.820669	18.845008	18.869354	18.893708	18.918068	18.942436
96	17.404469	17.429531	17.454602	17.479682	17.504770	17.529867	17.554973	17.580087
108	16.367614	16.393397	16.419190	16.444993	16.470806	16.496628	16.522461	16.548303
120	15.561476	15.587958	15.614452	15.640957	15.667473	15.694000	15.720538	15.747087
132	14.922382	14.949649	14.976711	15.003894	15.031089	15.058296	15.085515	15.112746
144	14.407846	14.435656	14.463478	14.491313	14.519161	14.547022	14.574895	14.602781
156	13.988427	14.016680	14.045307	14.073767	14.102240	14.130726	14.159226	14.187739
168	13.643074	13.672103	13.701145	13.730201	13.759270	13.788354	13.817451	13.846561
180	13.356337	13.385932	13.415612	13.445163	13.474800	13.504450	13.534114	13.563792
192	13.116622	13.146753	13.176899	13.207059	13.237233	13.267420	13.297621	13.327836
204	12.915060	12.945700	12.976353	13.007020	13.037700	13.068395	13.099103	13.129824
216	12.744759	12.775876	12.807007	12.838152	12.869310	12.900481	12.931665	12.962863
228	12.600280	12.631846	12.663426	12.695019	12.726625	12.758243	12.789875	12.821518
240	12.477282	12.509270	12.541270	12.573282	12.605307	12.637344	12.669393	12.701454
252	12.372264	12.404644	12.437037	12.469441	12.501857	12.534284	12.566723	12.599173
264	12.282370	12.315116	12.347874	12.380643	12.413423	12.446213	12.479014	12.511826
276	12.205256	12.238343	12.271441	12.304548	12.337666	12.370793	12.403930	12.437076
288	12.138984	12.172386	12.205798	12.239220	12.272650	12.306089	12.339537	12.372993
300	12.081938	12.115632	12.149335	12.183046	12.216766	12.250493	12.284228	12.317970
312	12.032766	12.066743	12.100702	12.134680	12.168666	12.202659	12.236658	12.270663
324	11.990333	12.024545	12.058764	12.092988	12.127219	12.161455	12.195698	12.229945
336	11.953677	11.988117	12.022563	12.057013	12.091469	12.125929	12.160394	12.194863
348	11.921984	11.956633	11.991287	12.025945	12.060606	12.095271	12.129940	12.164613
360	11.894561	11.929402	11.964246	11.999093	12.033943	12.068796	12.103651	12.138509
420	11.803548	11.839122	11.874694	11.910265	11.945833	11.981399	12.016962	12.052524
480	11.758815	11.794840	11.830859	11.866871	11.902878	11.938879	11.974873	12.010861

MONTHLY WITHDRAWALS PER $1000

EFFECTIVE ANNUAL YIELD

NUMBER OF MONTHLY WTHDRWLS	15.40%	15.45%	15.50%	15.55%	15.60%	15.65%	15.70%	15.75%
1	1012.007701	1012.044234	1012.080752	1012.117255	1012.153745	1012.190219	1012.226679	1012.263125
2	509.023691	509.051200	509.078697	509.106185	509.133661	509.161127	509.188583	509.216027
3	341.370317	341.394865	341.419405	341.443935	341.468456	341.492968	341.517471	341.541965
4	257.549601	257.572706	257.595802	257.618891	257.641971	257.665042	257.688106	257.711161
5	207.261948	207.284215	207.306475	207.328728	207.350972	207.373209	207.395438	207.417659
6	173.740825	173.762559	173.784286	173.806005	173.827717	173.849421	173.871119	173.892809
7	149.800577	149.821951	149.843317	149.864676	149.886028	149.907374	149.928712	149.950044
8	131.848375	131.869496	131.890610	131.911718	131.932819	131.953913	131.975001	131.996082
9	117.888203	117.909144	117.930078	117.951006	117.971928	117.992843	118.013752	118.034654
10	106.722451	106.743262	106.764067	106.784866	106.805659	106.826445	106.847226	106.868000
11	97.589005	97.609723	97.630435	97.651142	97.671842	97.692537	97.713226	97.733909
12	89.979787	90.000439	90.021086	90.041728	90.062364	90.082994	90.103619	90.124238
13	83.543051	83.563660	83.584263	83.604860	83.625453	83.646040	83.666621	83.687198
14	78.027551	78.048132	78.068708	78.089279	78.109844	78.130404	78.150960	78.171510
15	73.249040	73.269606	73.290168	73.310725	73.331277	73.351824	73.372366	73.392903
16	69.069330	69.089893	69.110452	69.131005	69.151554	69.172099	69.192638	69.213173
17	65.382751	65.403320	65.423884	65.444443	65.464998	65.485549	65.506095	65.526637
18	62.107114	62.127695	62.148272	62.168845	62.189413	62.209978	62.230538	62.251093
19	59.177532	59.198132	59.218728	59.239321	59.259909	59.280493	59.301073	59.321649
20	56.542096	56.562721	56.583342	56.603958	56.624572	56.645181	56.665786	56.686388
21	54.158785	54.179439	54.200089	54.220735	54.241377	54.262016	54.282651	54.303283
22	51.993218	52.013905	52.034587	52.055267	52.075942	52.096615	52.117284	52.137949
23	50.016993	50.037715	50.058434	50.079150	50.099863	50.120572	50.141278	50.161981
24	48.206441	48.227202	48.247960	48.268716	48.289468	48.310217	48.330963	48.351706
25	46.541681	46.562484	46.583284	46.604081	46.624875	46.645667	46.666455	46.687241
26	45.005890	45.026736	45.047581	45.068422	45.089261	45.110097	45.130931	45.151761
27	43.584737	43.605630	43.626520	43.647408	43.668293	43.689176	43.710056	43.730934
28	42.265940	42.286880	42.307818	42.328754	42.349688	42.370619	42.391548	42.412475
29	41.038908	41.059898	41.080886	41.101872	41.122855	41.143837	41.164816	41.185793
30	39.894466	39.915507	39.936545	39.957582	39.978617	39.999650	40.020681	40.041710
31	38.824619	38.845712	38.866803	38.887892	38.908980	38.930065	38.951149	38.972232
32	37.822374	37.843520	37.864665	37.885807	37.906949	37.928088	37.949227	37.970363
33	36.881585	36.902785	36.923984	36.945181	36.966377	36.987572	37.008766	37.029958
34	35.996828	36.018083	36.039338	36.060591	36.081842	36.103093	36.124342	36.145591
35	35.163300	35.184611	35.205922	35.227231	35.248540	35.269847	35.291154	35.312459
36	34.376731	34.398099	34.419467	34.440833	34.462199	34.483564	34.504929	34.526292
37	33.633313	33.654739	33.676164	33.697589	33.719013	33.740436	33.761859	33.783281
38	32.929639	32.951123	32.972607	32.994090	33.015572	33.037055	33.058537	33.080018
39	32.262651	32.284194	32.305736	32.327278	32.348820	32.370362	32.391904	32.413445
40	31.629597	31.651199	31.672801	31.694403	31.716004	31.737606	31.759208	31.780810
41	31.027992	31.049654	31.071316	31.092978	31.114641	31.136303	31.157965	31.179628
42	30.455591	30.477313	30.499036	30.520759	30.542482	30.564205	30.585928	30.607652
43	29.910356	29.932138	29.953921	29.975705	29.997489	30.019274	30.041059	30.062845
44	29.390432	29.412276	29.434120	29.455965	29.477811	29.499657	29.521504	29.543352
45	28.894132	28.916037	28.937943	28.959850	28.981758	29.003666	29.025576	29.047486
46	28.419916	28.441882	28.463850	28.485819	28.507789	28.529760	28.551732	28.573705
47	27.966722	27.988600	28.010430	28.032461	28.054494	28.076527	28.098562	28.120598
48	27.532207	27.554298	27.576391	27.598484	27.620579	27.642676	27.664774	27.686873
60	23.480961	23.503811	23.526665	23.549522	23.572383	23.595247	23.618114	23.640985
72	20.825514	20.849132	20.872756	20.896385	20.920019	20.943659	20.967303	20.990953
84	18.966810	18.991191	19.015580	19.039975	19.064377	19.088785	19.113201	19.137624
96	17.605209	17.630340	17.655479	17.680627	17.705783	17.730947	17.756120	17.781301
108	16.574156	16.600018	16.625889	16.651771	16.677662	16.703563	16.729473	16.755393
120	15.773647	15.800217	15.826799	15.853392	15.879995	15.906609	15.933233	15.959869
132	15.139989	15.167244	15.194510	15.221788	15.249078	15.276379	15.303692	15.331016
144	14.630680	14.658591	14.686515	14.714451	14.742400	14.770360	14.798333	14.826318
156	14.216265	14.244804	14.273356	14.301921	14.330499	14.359090	14.387693	14.416309
168	13.875685	13.904822	13.933973	13.963136	13.992313	14.021503	14.050706	14.079922
180	13.593484	13.623189	13.652907	13.682638	13.712383	13.742141	13.771912	13.801696
192	13.358064	13.388306	13.418561	13.448829	13.479111	13.509405	13.539713	13.570033
204	13.160558	13.191306	13.222067	13.252841	13.283628	13.314427	13.345239	13.376064
216	12.994073	13.025296	13.056532	13.087781	13.119042	13.150315	13.181601	13.212899
228	12.853175	12.884843	12.916524	12.948217	12.979922	13.011639	13.043367	13.075107
240	12.733527	12.765612	12.797708	12.829815	12.861934	12.894064	12.926205	12.958358
252	12.631634	12.664105	12.696588	12.729082	12.761586	12.794100	12.826625	12.859160
264	12.544647	12.577479	12.610321	12.643172	12.676034	12.708905	12.741785	12.774675
276	12.470232	12.503397	12.536572	12.569755	12.602947	12.636148	12.669357	12.702575
288	12.406458	12.439931	12.473413	12.506902	12.540399	12.573904	12.607417	12.640937
300	12.351720	12.385477	12.419242	12.453013	12.486791	12.520576	12.554368	12.588166
312	12.304676	12.338694	12.372719	12.406749	12.440786	12.474828	12.508876	12.542929
324	12.264198	12.298456	12.332720	12.366988	12.401261	12.435539	12.469821	12.504108
336	12.229337	12.263815	12.298297	12.332783	12.367272	12.401766	12.436262	12.470762
348	12.199288	12.233967	12.268649	12.303333	12.338020	12.372710	12.407402	12.442097
360	12.173368	12.208230	12.243094	12.277960	12.312827	12.347696	12.382566	12.417438
420	12.088082	12.123638	12.159191	12.194742	12.230289	12.265833	12.301374	12.336911
480	12.046843	12.082818	12.118787	12.154748	12.190703	12.226651	12.262592	12.298526

MONTHLY WITHDRAWALS PER $1000

NUMBER OF MONTHLY WTHDRWLS	EFFECTIVE ANNUAL YIELD							
	15.80%	15.85%	15.90%	15.95%	16.00%	16.05%	16.10%	16.15%
1	1012.299557	1012.335974	1012.372376	1012.408764	1012.445138	1012.481497	1012.517842	1012.554173
2	509.243462	509.270886	509.298299	509.325702	509.353094	509.380476	509.407847	509.435208
3	341.566449	341.590925	341.615391	341.639849	341.664297	341.688736	341.713166	341.737587
4	257.734207	257.757246	257.780276	257.803297	257.826311	257.849316	257.872313	257.895302
5	207.439873	207.462078	207.484276	207.506466	207.528649	207.550824	207.572991	207.595150
6	173.914491	173.936166	173.957834	173.979495	174.001148	174.022794	174.044433	174.066065
7	149.971368	149.992686	150.013996	150.035300	150.056597	150.077886	150.099169	150.120445
8	132.017156	132.038224	132.059285	132.080339	132.101387	132.122428	132.143463	132.164491
9	118.055550	118.076440	118.097324	118.118201	118.139072	118.159936	118.180794	118.201646
10	106.888769	106.909531	106.930287	106.951038	106.971782	106.992520	107.013252	107.033978
11	97.754586	97.775257	97.795923	97.816583	97.837237	97.857885	97.878527	97.899164
12	90.144851	90.165459	90.186062	90.206659	90.227250	90.247836	90.268416	90.288990
13	83.707769	83.728334	83.748895	83.769450	83.789999	83.810544	83.831083	83.851616
14	78.192055	78.212595	78.233129	78.253659	78.274184	78.294703	78.315217	78.335727
15	73.413435	73.433962	73.454485	73.475002	73.495515	73.516023	73.536526	73.557024
16	69.233704	69.254229	69.274750	69.295267	69.315778	69.336285	69.356787	69.377285
17	65.547174	65.567707	65.588235	65.608759	65.629278	65.649793	65.670303	65.690809
18	62.271645	62.292192	62.312735	62.333274	62.353808	62.374338	62.394664	62.415386
19	59.342221	59.362789	59.383352	59.403912	59.424468	59.445020	59.465567	59.486111
20	56.706985	56.727579	56.748169	56.768755	56.789338	56.809916	56.830491	56.851061
21	54.323911	54.344535	54.365156	54.385773	54.406386	54.426996	54.447602	54.468204
22	52.158611	52.179270	52.199925	52.220577	52.241225	52.261870	52.282511	52.303149
23	50.182680	50.203376	50.224069	50.244759	50.265446	50.286129	50.306809	50.327486
24	48.372446	48.393183	48.413916	48.434647	48.455375	48.476100	48.496821	48.517540
25	46.708024	46.728804	46.749581	46.770356	46.791127	46.811896	46.832662	46.853425
26	45.172590	45.193415	45.214238	45.235058	45.255876	45.276691	45.297503	45.318312
27	43.751810	43.772683	43.793553	43.814421	43.835287	43.856150	43.877011	43.897869
28	42.433400	42.454322	42.475242	42.496160	42.517075	42.537988	42.558899	42.579808
29	41.206768	41.227742	41.248713	41.269682	41.290648	41.311613	41.332576	41.353536
30	40.062737	40.083763	40.104786	40.125808	40.146828	40.167845	40.188861	40.209875
31	38.993313	39.014391	39.035469	39.056544	39.077618	39.098690	39.119760	39.140829
32	37.991499	38.012632	38.033764	38.054895	38.076024	38.097152	38.118278	38.139402
33	37.051149	37.072338	37.093526	37.114713	37.135898	37.157082	37.178265	37.199446
34	36.166838	36.188084	36.209329	36.230573	36.251816	36.273057	36.294297	36.315536
35	35.333764	35.355068	35.376370	35.397672	35.418972	35.440272	35.461571	35.482869
36	34.547655	34.569017	34.590378	34.611738	34.633098	34.654456	34.675814	34.697171
37	33.804702	33.826123	33.847544	33.868963	33.890383	33.911801	33.933219	33.954636
38	33.101499	33.122980	33.144460	33.165939	33.187419	33.208897	33.230376	33.251854
39	32.434986	32.456527	32.478067	32.499608	32.521148	32.542687	32.564227	32.585766
40	31.802411	31.824013	31.845614	31.867216	31.888817	31.910418	31.932019	31.953620
41	31.201291	31.222953	31.244616	31.266279	31.287942	31.309605	31.331269	31.352932
42	30.629377	30.651101	30.672826	30.694551	30.716276	30.738001	30.759727	30.781453
43	30.084631	30.106417	30.128204	30.149992	30.171780	30.193568	30.215356	30.237146
44	29.565200	29.587049	29.608899	29.630749	29.652600	29.674451	29.696303	29.718156
45	29.069397	29.091308	29.113221	29.135134	29.157048	29.178963	29.200879	29.222795
46	28.595678	28.617653	28.639629	28.661605	28.683583	28.705562	28.727541	28.749522
47	28.142635	28.164673	28.186712	28.208752	28.230794	28.252837	28.274880	28.296925
48	27.708973	27.731075	27.753178	27.775282	27.797388	27.819495	27.841603	27.863712
60	23.663858	23.686736	23.709616	23.732500	23.755387	23.778277	23.801170	23.824067
72	21.014607	21.038267	21.061932	21.085602	21.109277	21.132957	21.156643	21.180333
84	19.162053	19.186489	19.210931	19.235381	19.259837	19.284300	19.308769	19.333245
96	17.806490	17.831688	17.856893	17.882107	17.907329	17.932559	17.957797	17.983043
108	16.781322	16.807261	16.833209	16.859167	16.885134	16.911111	16.937097	16.963092
120	15.986515	16.013171	16.039838	16.066515	16.093203	16.119901	16.146610	16.173329
132	15.358352	15.385700	15.413058	15.440428	15.467809	15.495202	15.522605	15.550020
144	14.854316	14.882325	14.910346	14.938379	14.966424	14.994481	15.022550	15.050630
156	14.444937	14.473578	14.502232	14.530897	14.559575	14.588266	14.616968	14.645682
168	14.109150	14.138391	14.167645	14.196912	14.226191	14.255482	14.284786	14.314102
180	13.831493	13.861302	13.891125	13.920959	13.950807	13.980667	14.010539	14.040423
192	13.600366	13.630712	13.661070	13.691441	13.721824	13.752219	13.782627	13.813046
204	13.406901	13.437751	13.468613	13.499487	13.530373	13.561272	13.592182	13.623103
216	13.244209	13.275531	13.306864	13.338210	13.369567	13.400935	13.432315	13.463707
228	13.106859	13.138621	13.170396	13.202181	13.233977	13.265785	13.297603	13.329432
240	12.990520	13.022694	13.054878	13.087073	13.119278	13.151493	13.183719	13.215954
252	12.891705	12.924260	12.956825	12.989399	13.021983	13.054577	13.087179	13.119791
264	12.807574	12.840482	12.873399	12.906325	12.939259	12.972202	13.005154	13.038114
276	12.735800	12.769035	12.802277	12.835527	12.868785	12.902050	12.935323	12.968603
288	12.674464	12.707999	12.741540	12.775089	12.808644	12.842206	12.875774	12.909349
300	12.621970	12.655781	12.689597	12.723419	12.757248	12.791081	12.824921	12.858765
312	12.576987	12.611051	12.645119	12.679192	12.713270	12.747353	12.781440	12.815532
324	12.538399	12.572694	12.606993	12.641295	12.675602	12.709912	12.744225	12.778542
336	12.505266	12.539772	12.574281	12.608793	12.643308	12.677825	12.712344	12.746866
348	12.476794	12.511492	12.546193	12.580895	12.615599	12.650305	12.685012	12.719720
360	12.452311	12.487185	12.522059	12.556934	12.591810	12.626687	12.661563	12.696440
420	12.372445	12.407975	12.443501	12.479024	12.514542	12.550056	12.585567	12.621073
480	12.334453	12.370372	12.406284	12.442189	12.478086	12.513975	12.549857	12.585731

MONTHLY WITHDRAWALS PER $1000

EFFECTIVE ANNUAL YIELD

NUMBER OF MONTHLY WTHDRWLS	16.20%	16.25%	16.30%	16.35%	16.40%	16.45%	16.50%	16.55%
1	1012.590489	1012.626791	1012.663079	1012.699353	1012.735612	1012.771856	1012.808087	1012.844303
2	509.462558	509.489898	509.517227	509.544546	509.571855	509.599153	509.626441	509.653718
3	341.761999	341.786402	341.810796	341.835180	341.859556	341.883923	341.908281	341.932629
4	257.918282	257.941254	257.964218	257.987174	258.010121	258.033060	258.055991	258.078914
5	207.617302	207.639446	207.661582	207.683710	207.705831	207.727944	207.750050	207.772148
6	174.087689	174.109306	174.130915	174.152518	174.174113	174.195701	174.217282	174.238855
7	150.141714	150.162976	150.184231	150.205480	150.226721	150.247956	150.269183	150.290404
8	132.185512	132.206527	132.227535	132.248537	132.269532	132.290521	132.311503	132.332478
9	118.222492	118.243331	118.264164	118.284991	118.305811	118.326625	118.347433	118.368235
10	107.054698	107.075412	107.096120	107.116821	107.137517	107.158207	107.178891	107.199568
11	97.919795	97.940420	97.961039	97.981652	98.002260	98.022862	98.043458	98.064049
12	90.309559	90.330123	90.350681	90.371233	90.391780	90.412321	90.432857	90.453388
13	83.872145	83.892668	83.913185	83.933698	83.954205	83.974707	83.995203	84.015694
14	78.356231	78.376730	78.397224	78.417713	78.438196	78.458675	78.479149	78.499617
15	73.577517	73.598005	73.618489	73.638967	73.659441	73.679910	73.700374	73.720833
16	69.397778	69.418266	69.438750	69.459229	69.479703	69.500173	69.520638	69.541098
17	65.711311	65.731808	65.752301	65.772789	65.793273	65.813752	65.834227	65.854697
18	62.435903	62.456417	62.476926	62.497430	62.517931	62.538427	62.558919	62.579407
19	59.506651	59.527186	59.547718	59.568245	59.588768	59.609288	59.629803	59.650315
20	56.871628	56.892191	56.912751	56.933306	56.953858	56.974405	56.994949	57.015489
21	54.488803	54.509398	54.529990	54.550577	54.571162	54.591742	54.612319	54.632893
22	52.323783	52.344414	52.365042	52.385666	52.406287	52.426904	52.447518	52.468128
23	50.348159	50.368829	50.389497	50.410160	50.430821	50.451478	50.472132	50.492783
24	48.538255	48.558968	48.579677	48.600384	48.621087	48.641787	48.662484	48.683179
25	46.874185	46.894942	46.915696	46.936448	46.957196	46.977942	46.998685	47.019425
26	45.339119	45.359923	45.380725	45.401524	45.422320	45.443114	45.463904	45.484693
27	43.918725	43.939578	43.960429	43.981277	44.002123	44.022966	44.043807	44.064645
28	42.600714	42.621618	42.642520	42.663419	42.684316	42.705211	42.726103	42.746994
29	41.374495	41.395451	41.416405	41.437357	41.458307	41.479255	41.500201	41.521145
30	40.230887	40.251897	40.272906	40.293912	40.314916	40.335919	40.356919	40.377918
31	39.161896	39.182961	39.204025	39.225086	39.246146	39.267204	39.288261	39.309316
32	38.160525	38.181646	38.202766	38.223884	38.245001	38.266116	38.287230	38.308342
33	37.220626	37.241804	37.262982	37.284158	37.305332	37.326505	37.347677	37.368847
34	36.336774	36.358011	36.379247	36.400481	36.421714	36.442946	36.464177	36.485406
35	35.504165	35.525461	35.546756	35.568049	35.589342	35.610634	35.631924	35.653214
36	34.718528	34.739883	34.761238	34.782592	34.803945	34.825297	34.846648	34.867998
37	33.976052	33.997468	34.018884	34.040298	34.061712	34.083125	34.104538	34.125950
38	33.273331	33.294808	33.316285	33.337761	33.359236	33.380711	33.402186	33.423660
39	32.607305	32.628844	32.650382	32.671920	32.693458	32.714995	32.736532	32.758069
40	31.975221	31.996822	32.018423	32.040023	32.061624	32.083224	32.104824	32.126424
41	31.374595	31.396259	31.417922	31.439586	31.461249	31.482913	31.504576	31.526240
42	30.803179	30.824906	30.846633	30.868360	30.890087	30.911814	30.933542	30.955269
43	30.258935	30.280725	30.302515	30.324306	30.346097	30.367889	30.389681	30.411473
44	29.740009	29.761863	29.783717	29.805572	29.827427	29.849283	29.871140	29.892997
45	29.244712	29.266630	29.288549	29.310468	29.332388	29.354309	29.376231	29.398153
46	28.771503	28.793485	28.815469	28.837453	28.859438	28.881424	28.903411	28.925398
47	28.318971	28.341018	28.363066	28.385115	28.407166	28.429217	28.451269	28.473323
48	27.885823	27.907935	27.930048	27.952163	27.974278	27.996395	28.018513	28.040633
60	23.846967	23.869870	23.892776	23.915686	23.938598	23.961514	23.984433	24.007355
72	21.204028	21.227728	21.251433	21.275143	21.298858	21.322578	21.346302	21.370032
84	19.357728	19.382217	19.406713	19.431215	19.455724	19.480239	19.504760	19.529289
96	18.008298	18.033560	18.058830	18.084108	18.109394	18.134688	18.159990	18.185299
108	16.989096	17.015109	17.041132	17.067164	17.093205	17.119255	17.145314	17.171382
120	16.200508	16.226797	16.253547	16.280306	16.307076	16.333855	16.360645	16.387445
132	15.577445	15.604882	15.632330	15.659788	15.687257	15.714738	15.742228	15.769730
144	15.078722	15.106826	15.134941	15.163067	15.191205	15.219354	15.247515	15.275687
156	14.674409	14.703147	14.731898	14.760660	14.789434	14.818219	14.847016	14.875825
168	14.343430	14.372770	14.402123	14.431487	14.460863	14.490252	14.519651	14.549063
180	14.070320	14.100229	14.130150	14.160083	14.190027	14.219984	14.249952	14.279932
192	13.843478	13.873922	13.904377	13.934844	13.965323	13.995814	14.026316	14.056829
204	13.654037	13.684982	13.715938	13.746906	13.777886	13.808876	13.839878	13.870890
216	13.495109	13.526523	13.557947	13.589383	13.620829	13.652286	13.683753	13.715231
228	13.361271	13.393121	13.424981	13.456852	13.488732	13.520623	13.552523	13.584434
240	13.248199	13.280454	13.312719	13.344993	13.377276	13.409569	13.441871	13.474182
252	13.152412	13.185042	13.217681	13.250328	13.282984	13.315649	13.348321	13.381002
264	13.071082	13.104058	13.137041	13.170033	13.203033	13.236039	13.269054	13.302075
276	13.001891	13.035185	13.068487	13.101795	13.135110	13.168432	13.201760	13.235095
288	12.942930	12.976517	13.010110	13.043709	13.077313	13.110923	13.144539	13.178160
300	12.892615	12.926470	12.960330	12.994195	13.028064	13.061938	13.095817	13.129699
312	12.849627	12.883727	12.917831	12.951938	12.986049	13.020164	13.054282	13.088403
324	12.812862	12.847184	12.881510	12.915839	12.950170	12.984503	13.018839	13.053178
336	12.781390	12.815915	12.850443	12.884972	12.919503	12.954036	12.988570	13.023105
348	12.754429	12.789139	12.823850	12.858561	12.893274	12.927986	12.962699	12.997412
360	12.731318	12.766195	12.801071	12.835948	12.870824	12.905700	12.940575	12.975449
420	12.656574	12.692071	12.727564	12.763051	12.798534	12.834012	12.869485	12.904953
480	12.621597	12.657455	12.693305	12.729148	12.764981	12.800807	12.836624	12.872433

184

MONTHLY WITHDRAWALS PER $1000

NUMBER OF MONTHLY WTHDRWLS	\multicolumn{8}{c}{EFFECTIVE ANNUAL YIELD}							
	16.60%	16.65%	16.70%	16.75%	16.80%	16.85%	16.90%	16.95%
1	1012.880506	1012.916693	1012.952867	1012.989027	1013.025172	1013.061303	1013.097420	1013.133523
2	509.680985	509.708241	509.735487	509.762723	509.789949	509.817163	509.844368	509.871562
3	341.956969	341.981300	342.005621	342.029934	342.054238	342.078533	342.102818	342.127095
4	258.101829	258.124735	258.147633	258.170523	258.193405	258.216278	258.239144	258.262001
5	207.794238	207.816320	207.838395	207.860462	207.882522	207.904574	207.926618	207.948655
6	174.260421	174.281980	174.303532	174.325077	174.346614	174.368144	174.389667	174.411183
7	150.311618	150.332825	150.354025	150.375218	150.396405	150.417584	150.438757	150.459923
8	132.353447	132.374409	132.395365	132.416314	132.437256	132.458192	132.479122	132.500045
9	118.389030	118.409819	118.430602	118.451378	118.472148	118.492912	118.513670	118.534421
10	107.220240	107.240906	107.261566	107.282219	107.302867	107.323509	107.344145	107.364774
11	98.084633	98.105212	98.125785	98.146352	98.166914	98.187470	98.208020	98.228564
12	90.473912	90.494432	90.514945	90.535453	90.555956	90.576453	90.596945	90.617431
13	84.036180	84.056661	84.077136	84.097606	84.118071	84.138530	84.158984	84.179433
14	78.520081	78.540539	78.560993	78.581441	78.601884	78.622322	78.642755	78.663184
15	73.741287	73.761737	73.782181	73.802621	73.823056	73.843486	73.863911	73.884332
16	69.561554	69.582005	69.602451	69.622893	69.643330	69.663763	69.684191	69.704614
17	65.875163	65.895625	65.916082	65.936535	65.956983	65.977427	65.997866	66.018301
18	62.599891	62.620370	62.640845	62.661316	62.681783	62.702245	62.722703	62.743157
19	59.670822	59.691325	59.711824	59.732320	59.752811	59.773298	59.793781	59.814260
20	57.036026	57.056558	57.077087	57.097612	57.118133	57.138650	57.159163	57.179673
21	54.653462	54.674028	54.694591	54.715150	54.735705	54.756256	54.776804	54.797349
22	52.488735	52.509339	52.529939	52.550536	52.571129	52.591719	52.612305	52.632888
23	50.513431	50.534075	50.554716	50.575353	50.595989	50.616620	50.637248	50.657873
24	48.703870	48.724558	48.745243	48.765925	48.786604	48.807280	48.827952	48.848622
25	47.040162	47.060897	47.081628	47.102357	47.123082	47.143805	47.164525	47.185243
26	45.505478	45.526261	45.547041	45.567818	45.588594	45.609366	45.630135	45.650902
27	44.085481	44.106314	44.127145	44.147974	44.168799	44.189623	44.210444	44.231262
28	42.767862	42.788767	42.809651	42.830532	42.851410	42.872287	42.893161	42.914033
29	41.542086	41.563026	41.583963	41.604899	41.625832	41.646763	41.667692	41.688618
30	40.398914	40.419909	40.440902	40.461893	40.482882	40.503869	40.524854	40.545337
31	39.330369	39.351420	39.372469	39.393517	39.414563	39.435607	39.456650	39.477691
32	38.329452	38.350561	38.371668	38.392774	38.413878	38.434981	38.456082	38.477181
33	37.390016	37.411184	37.432350	37.453515	37.474678	37.495840	37.517001	37.538160
34	36.506635	36.527862	36.549088	36.570313	36.591536	36.612758	36.633979	36.655199
35	35.674503	35.695790	35.717077	35.738362	35.759647	35.780930	35.802213	35.823494
36	34.889348	34.910697	34.932045	34.953392	34.974738	34.996083	35.017428	35.038771
37	34.147361	34.168772	34.190182	34.211591	34.233000	34.254408	34.275815	34.297221
38	33.445134	33.466607	33.488079	33.509551	33.531023	33.552494	33.573965	33.595435
39	32.779605	32.801142	32.822677	32.844213	32.865748	32.887283	32.908817	32.930352
40	32.148024	32.169624	32.191223	32.212822	32.234422	32.256021	32.277620	32.299218
41	31.547904	31.569568	31.591231	31.612895	31.634559	31.656223	31.677886	31.699550
42	30.976997	30.998726	31.020454	31.042183	31.063911	31.085640	31.107369	31.129099
43	30.433266	30.455059	30.476852	30.498646	30.520440	30.542234	30.564029	30.585824
44	29.914855	29.936713	29.958572	29.980431	30.002291	30.024151	30.046012	30.067873
45	29.420076	29.442000	29.463924	29.485849	29.507775	29.529701	29.551628	29.573556
46	28.947387	28.969377	28.991367	29.013358	29.035350	29.057343	29.079337	29.101331
47	28.495377	28.517433	28.539489	28.561547	28.583606	28.605665	28.627726	28.649787
48	28.062753	28.084875	28.106998	28.129122	28.151248	28.173374	28.195502	28.217631
60	24.030280	24.053208	24.076139	24.099074	24.122011	24.144952	24.167895	24.190842
72	21.393767	21.417506	21.441250	21.464999	21.488753	21.512511	21.536275	21.560043
84	19.553824	19.578365	19.602912	19.627466	19.652026	19.676593	19.701165	19.725744
96	18.210616	18.235941	18.261274	18.286615	18.311963	18.337319	18.362682	18.388053
108	17.197458	17.223544	17.249639	17.275743	17.301855	17.327976	17.354106	17.380245
120	16.414254	16.441073	16.467901	16.494742	16.521590	16.548449	16.575317	16.602195
132	15.797242	15.824765	15.852298	15.879842	15.907396	15.934961	15.962536	15.990121
144	15.303870	15.332064	15.360269	15.388485	15.416712	15.444950	15.473198	15.501458
156	14.904645	14.933477	14.962320	14.991174	15.020040	15.048916	15.077804	15.106703
168	14.578486	14.607921	14.637367	14.666824	14.696293	14.725773	14.755264	14.784767
180	14.309923	14.339926	14.369940	14.399965	14.430002	14.460049	14.490108	14.520178
192	14.087354	14.117889	14.148436	14.178994	14.209563	14.240143	14.270733	14.301335
204	13.901913	13.932948	13.963993	13.995048	14.026114	14.057191	14.088277	14.119374
216	13.746719	13.778218	13.809727	13.841245	13.872774	13.904313	13.935861	13.967419
228	13.616354	13.648284	13.680223	13.712171	13.744129	13.776096	13.808072	13.840057
240	13.506502	13.538831	13.571168	13.603514	13.635869	13.668232	13.700603	13.732983
252	13.413692	13.446389	13.479094	13.511806	13.544527	13.577254	13.609990	13.642732
264	13.335104	13.368140	13.401183	13.434233	13.467289	13.500352	13.533422	13.566497
276	13.268435	13.301782	13.335135	13.368494	13.401858	13.435228	13.468603	13.501984
288	13.211786	13.245418	13.279054	13.312695	13.346341	13.379992	13.413647	13.447306
300	13.163586	13.197477	13.231372	13.265271	13.299174	13.333080	13.366989	13.400902
312	13.122528	13.156655	13.190786	13.224919	13.259055	13.293193	13.327334	13.361477
324	13.087518	13.121860	13.156205	13.190551	13.224898	13.259247	13.293598	13.327950
336	13.057641	13.092178	13.126716	13.161255	13.195794	13.230334	13.264874	13.299415
348	13.032126	13.066839	13.101552	13.136265	13.170978	13.205690	13.240401	13.275112
360	13.010323	13.045195	13.080066	13.114936	13.149805	13.184672	13.219538	13.254402
420	12.940415	12.975873	13.011325	13.046771	13.082212	13.117647	13.153077	13.188500
480	12.908234	12.944026	12.979809	13.015584	13.051350	13.087107	13.122856	13.158595

MONTHLY WITHDRAWALS PER $1000

EFFECTIVE ANNUAL YIELD

NUMBER OF MONTHLY WTHDRWLS	17.00%	17.05%	17.10%	17.15%	17.20%	17.25%	17.30%	17.35%
1	1013.169611	1013.205686	1013.241746	1013.277792	1013.313824	1013.349842	1013.385846	1013.421836
2	509.898746	509.925920	509.953083	509.980236	510.007379	510.034511	510.061633	510.088745
3	342.151363	342.175622	342.199872	342.224114	342.248346	342.272569	342.296784	342.320989
4	258.284850	258.307691	258.330524	258.353349	258.376165	258.398973	258.421774	258.444566
5	207.970684	207.992706	208.014720	208.036726	208.058725	208.080716	208.102699	208.124675
6	174.432691	174.454192	174.475687	174.497174	174.518653	174.540126	174.561592	174.583050
7	150.481082	150.502234	150.523379	150.544518	150.565650	150.586775	150.607893	150.629004
8	132.520961	132.541871	132.562775	132.583672	132.604562	132.625446	132.646324	132.667195
9	118.555166	118.575905	118.596638	118.617365	118.638085	118.658799	118.679507	118.700208
10	107.385398	107.406016	107.426628	107.447234	107.467833	107.488427	107.509015	107.529597
11	98.249103	98.269636	98.290163	98.310685	98.331200	98.351710	98.372215	98.392713
12	90.637912	90.658387	90.678857	90.699321	90.719780	90.740233	90.760681	90.781123
13	84.199877	84.220315	84.240748	84.261176	84.281599	84.302016	84.322428	84.342835
14	78.683607	78.704025	78.724437	78.744845	78.765248	78.785646	78.806039	78.826427
15	73.904747	73.925158	73.945564	73.965965	73.986361	74.006752	74.027139	74.047521
16	69.725033	69.745447	69.765856	69.786261	69.806661	69.827057	69.847448	69.867834
17	66.038732	66.059158	66.079580	66.099997	66.120410	66.140818	66.161223	66.181622
18	62.763607	62.784053	62.804494	62.824931	62.845364	62.865793	62.886218	62.906638
19	59.834736	59.855207	59.875674	59.896137	59.916596	59.937051	59.957502	59.977949
20	57.200178	57.220680	57.241178	57.261672	57.282163	57.302650	57.323132	57.343611
21	54.817889	54.838426	54.858960	54.879490	54.900016	54.920538	54.941057	54.961573
22	52.653468	52.674044	52.694616	52.715186	52.735751	52.756314	52.776873	52.797428
23	50.678495	50.699113	50.719728	50.740340	50.760949	50.781555	50.802157	50.822756
24	48.869289	48.889953	48.910613	48.931271	48.951925	48.972577	48.993225	49.013871
25	47.205957	47.226668	47.247377	47.268083	47.288786	47.309486	47.330183	47.350877
26	45.671666	45.692428	45.713187	45.733943	45.754696	45.775447	45.796195	45.816940
27	44.252078	44.272892	44.293703	44.314511	44.335317	44.356121	44.376922	44.397720
28	42.934902	42.955769	42.976634	42.997497	43.018357	43.039215	43.060071	43.080924
29	41.709543	41.730466	41.751386	41.772304	41.793220	41.814134	41.835046	41.855956
30	40.566818	40.587797	40.608775	40.629750	40.650723	40.671695	40.692664	40.713632
31	39.498730	39.519767	39.540802	39.561836	39.582868	39.603898	39.624926	39.645953
32	38.498279	38.519376	38.540470	38.561563	38.582655	38.603745	38.624833	38.645920
33	37.559318	37.580474	37.601629	37.622783	37.643935	37.665086	37.686235	37.707383
34	36.676418	36.697635	36.718852	36.740067	36.761280	36.782493	36.803704	36.824914
35	35.844774	35.866053	35.887332	35.908609	35.929885	35.951160	35.972434	35.993707
36	35.060114	35.081456	35.102797	35.124137	35.145476	35.166814	35.188152	35.209488
37	34.318627	34.340032	34.361437	34.382840	34.404243	34.425646	34.447047	34.468448
38	33.616904	33.638373	33.659842	33.681309	33.702777	33.724244	33.745710	33.767176
39	32.951885	32.973419	32.994952	33.016484	33.038017	33.059549	33.081080	33.102612
40	32.320817	32.342415	32.364013	32.385611	32.407209	32.428807	32.450404	32.472001
41	31.721214	31.742878	31.764541	31.786205	31.807869	31.829533	31.851196	31.872860
42	31.150828	31.172558	31.194287	31.216017	31.237747	31.259477	31.281207	31.302938
43	30.607620	30.629415	30.651211	30.673008	30.694804	30.716601	30.738399	30.760196
44	30.089735	30.111597	30.133460	30.155323	30.177187	30.199051	30.220916	30.242781
45	29.595485	29.617414	29.639344	29.661274	29.683205	29.705137	29.727069	29.749002
46	29.123327	29.145323	29.167320	29.189318	29.211316	29.233316	29.255316	29.277317
47	28.671850	28.693914	28.715978	28.738044	28.760110	28.782178	28.804246	28.826315
48	28.239761	28.261892	28.284024	28.306158	28.328292	28.350428	28.372565	28.394703
60	24.213791	24.236744	24.259700	24.282658	24.305620	24.328585	24.351552	24.374523
72	21.583815	21.607593	21.631375	21.655162	21.678953	21.702749	21.726550	21.750356
84	19.750330	19.774921	19.799519	19.824123	19.848733	19.873349	19.897971	19.922599
96	18.413432	18.438818	18.464212	18.489613	18.515022	18.540438	18.565861	18.591292
108	17.406392	17.432548	17.458713	17.484886	17.511067	17.537257	17.563456	17.589663
120	16.629082	16.655979	16.682885	16.709801	16.736726	16.763660	16.790604	16.817557
132	16.017717	16.045323	16.072939	16.100565	16.128201	16.155847	16.183503	16.211169
144	15.529728	15.558009	15.586300	15.614602	15.642915	15.671238	15.699571	15.727914
156	15.135612	15.164533	15.193464	15.222407	15.251360	15.280323	15.309297	15.338282
168	14.814280	14.843804	14.873339	14.902885	14.932442	14.962009	14.991587	15.021176
180	14.550259	14.580350	14.610452	14.640565	14.670688	14.700822	14.730966	14.761121
192	14.331946	14.362569	14.393201	14.423844	14.454497	14.485161	14.515834	14.546518
204	14.150481	14.181599	14.212726	14.243863	14.275009	14.306166	14.337332	14.368507
216	13.998986	14.030563	14.062150	14.093745	14.125350	14.156964	14.188586	14.220218
228	13.872051	13.904054	13.936065	13.968085	14.000113	14.032150	14.064194	14.096247
240	13.765310	13.797766	13.830169	13.862580	13.894998	13.927425	13.959858	13.992299
252	13.675482	13.708239	13.741002	13.773773	13.806550	13.839334	13.872124	13.904921
264	13.599580	13.632668	13.665762	13.698862	13.731968	13.765079	13.798196	13.831319
276	13.535370	13.568762	13.602158	13.635559	13.668965	13.702376	13.735791	13.769211
288	13.480969	13.514637	13.548309	13.581984	13.615664	13.649347	13.683034	13.716724
300	13.434818	13.468738	13.502660	13.536585	13.570513	13.604443	13.638376	13.672311
312	13.395623	13.429770	13.463919	13.498071	13.532224	13.566378	13.600534	13.634692
324	13.362303	13.396657	13.431012	13.465368	13.499724	13.534081	13.568439	13.602797
336	13.333956	13.368496	13.403037	13.437577	13.472118	13.506658	13.541197	13.575736
348	13.309822	13.344531	13.379239	13.413946	13.448652	13.483356	13.518059	13.552760
360	13.289265	13.324125	13.358983	13.393840	13.428694	13.463546	13.498395	13.533242
420	13.223918	13.259330	13.294735	13.330135	13.365528	13.400915	13.436295	13.471669
480	13.194326	13.230047	13.265760	13.301463	13.337157	13.372841	13.408517	13.444183

MONTHLY WITHDRAWALS PER $1000

NUMBER OF MONTHLY WTHDRWLS	EFFECTIVE ANNUAL YIELD							
	17.40%	17.45%	17.50%	17.55%	17.60%	17.65%	17.70%	17.75%
1	1013.457812	1013.493774	1013.529722	1013.565655	1013.601575	1013.637481	1013.673373	1013.709251
2	510.115847	510.142938	510.170019	510.197090	510.224151	510.251201	510.278241	510.305271
3	342.345186	342.369374	342.393552	342.417722	342.441884	342.466036	342.490179	342.514314
4	258.467350	258.490126	258.512894	258.535654	258.558405	258.581149	258.603884	258.626612
5	208.146644	208.168604	208.190558	208.212504	208.234442	208.256372	208.278296	208.300211
6	174.604501	174.625945	174.647382	174.668812	174.690235	174.711650	174.733059	174.754460
7	150.650109	150.671206	150.692297	150.713382	150.734459	150.755530	150.776594	150.797651
8	132.688059	132.708917	132.729769	132.750614	132.771452	132.792284	132.813110	132.833929
9	118.720904	118.741593	118.762276	118.782952	118.803623	118.824288	118.844946	118.865598
10	107.550174	107.570744	107.591308	107.611866	107.632419	107.652965	107.673505	107.694040
11	98.413206	98.433693	98.454175	98.474651	98.495121	98.515585	98.536044	98.556497
12	90.801560	90.821991	90.842417	90.862838	90.883253	90.903662	90.924066	90.944465
13	84.363237	84.383633	84.404024	84.424410	84.444791	84.465166	84.485536	84.505901
14	78.846809	78.867187	78.887560	78.907927	78.928290	78.948648	78.969000	78.989348
15	74.067897	74.088270	74.108637	74.128999	74.149357	74.169710	74.190058	74.210402
16	69.888216	69.908593	69.928966	69.949334	69.969697	69.990056	70.010410	70.030760
17	66.202018	66.222409	66.242795	66.263177	66.283555	66.303928	66.324297	66.344662
18	62.927054	62.947466	62.967874	62.988277	63.008677	63.029072	63.049463	63.069850
19	59.998392	60.018832	60.039267	60.059698	60.080125	60.100548	60.120967	60.141382
20	57.364087	57.384558	57.405026	57.425489	57.445949	57.466405	57.486858	57.507306
21	54.982085	55.002593	55.023097	55.043598	55.064095	55.084589	55.105079	55.125566
22	52.817980	52.838529	52.859074	52.879616	52.900155	52.920690	52.941221	52.961750
23	50.843352	50.863944	50.884534	50.905120	50.925703	50.946282	50.966859	50.987432
24	49.034513	49.055152	49.075789	49.096422	49.117052	49.137679	49.158303	49.178924
25	47.371569	47.392257	47.412943	47.433626	47.454306	47.474983	47.495657	47.516329
26	45.837683	45.858423	45.879161	45.899895	45.920628	45.941357	45.962084	45.982808
27	44.418516	44.439310	44.460101	44.480889	44.501676	44.522459	44.543240	44.564019
28	43.101775	43.122624	43.143471	43.164315	43.185157	43.205996	43.226833	43.247668
29	41.876864	41.897769	41.918673	41.939574	41.960473	41.981370	42.002265	42.023158
30	40.734598	40.755561	40.776523	40.797483	40.818440	40.839396	40.860350	40.881302
31	39.666978	39.688001	39.709022	39.730042	39.751059	39.772075	39.793090	39.814102
32	38.667005	38.688089	38.709171	38.730251	38.751330	38.772407	38.793483	38.814557
33	37.728529	37.749674	37.770818	37.791960	37.813101	37.834241	37.855379	37.876515
34	36.846123	36.867330	36.888537	36.909742	36.930945	36.952148	36.973349	36.994549
35	36.014979	36.036249	36.057519	36.078788	36.100055	36.121322	36.142587	36.163851
36	35.230824	35.252159	35.273493	35.294826	35.316158	35.337489	35.358819	35.380148
37	34.489848	34.511248	34.532646	34.554044	34.575441	34.596838	34.618233	34.639628
38	33.788641	33.810106	33.831570	33.853033	33.874496	33.895958	33.917420	33.938881
39	33.124142	33.145673	33.167203	33.188732	33.210262	33.231791	33.253319	33.274847
40	32.493598	32.515195	32.536791	32.558388	32.579984	32.601580	32.623175	32.644770
41	31.894523	31.916187	31.937850	31.959513	31.981177	32.002840	32.024503	32.046166
42	31.324668	31.346399	31.368130	31.389860	31.411591	31.433322	31.455053	31.476785
43	30.781994	30.803792	30.825591	30.847389	30.869188	30.890987	30.912787	30.934586
44	30.264646	30.286512	30.308379	30.330245	30.352113	30.373980	30.395848	30.417717
45	29.770935	29.792869	29.814804	29.836739	29.858675	29.880612	29.902549	29.924487
46	29.299319	29.321321	29.343325	29.365329	29.387334	29.409339	29.431345	29.453352
47	28.848386	28.870457	28.892529	28.914602	28.936675	28.958751	28.980826	29.002903
48	28.416842	28.438982	28.461123	28.483265	28.505408	28.527553	28.549698	28.571845
60	24.397496	24.420472	24.443452	24.466434	24.489419	24.512407	24.535397	24.558391
72	21.774166	21.797980	21.821799	21.845623	21.869451	21.893284	21.917121	21.940963
84	19.947234	19.971874	19.996521	20.021173	20.045832	20.070496	20.095167	20.119843
96	18.616730	18.642176	18.667628	18.693088	18.718556	18.744030	18.769512	18.795001
108	17.615879	17.642103	17.668335	17.694575	17.720824	17.747081	17.773346	17.799619
120	16.844519	16.871491	16.898472	16.925461	16.952460	16.979468	17.006485	17.033511
132	16.238845	16.266530	16.294226	16.321931	16.349645	16.377370	16.405103	16.432847
144	15.756268	15.784632	15.813006	15.841391	15.869785	15.898189	15.926603	15.955027
156	15.367277	15.396282	15.425298	15.454324	15.483360	15.512407	15.541463	15.570530
168	15.050774	15.080384	15.110003	15.139633	15.169273	15.198923	15.228583	15.258253
180	14.791286	14.821461	14.851646	14.881841	14.912046	14.942261	14.972486	15.002720
192	14.577211	14.607914	14.638627	14.669350	14.700082	14.730823	14.761574	14.792334
204	14.399692	14.430886	14.462090	14.493302	14.524524	14.555754	14.586993	14.618242
216	14.251858	14.283507	14.315165	14.346831	14.378505	14.410188	14.441879	14.473578
228	14.128308	14.160377	14.192454	14.224538	14.256630	14.288730	14.320837	14.352951
240	14.024747	14.057202	14.089664	14.122133	14.154609	14.187091	14.219580	14.252076
252	13.937724	13.970534	14.003349	14.036170	14.068998	14.101830	14.134669	14.167513
264	13.864447	13.897580	13.930718	13.963861	13.997009	14.030162	14.063320	14.096482
276	13.802635	13.836063	13.869495	13.902932	13.936372	13.969816	14.003264	14.036715
288	13.750417	13.784114	13.817813	13.851516	13.885222	13.918930	13.952641	13.986354
300	13.706249	13.740189	13.774131	13.808075	13.842021	13.875968	13.909917	13.943868
312	13.668851	13.703010	13.737171	13.771333	13.805496	13.839660	13.873824	13.907988
324	13.637155	13.671514	13.705872	13.740231	13.774589	13.808947	13.843305	13.877662
336	13.610274	13.644811	13.679347	13.713882	13.748416	13.782949	13.817481	13.852011
348	13.587459	13.622157	13.656853	13.691547	13.726239	13.760928	13.795616	13.830301
360	13.568087	13.602928	13.637767	13.672603	13.707436	13.742266	13.777093	13.811917
420	13.507036	13.542397	13.577751	13.613098	13.648438	13.683771	13.719097	13.754416
480	13.479839	13.515486	13.551124	13.586752	13.622370	13.657979	13.693578	13.729167

MONTHLY WITHDRAWALS PER $1000

EFFECTIVE ANNUAL YIELD

NUMBER OF MONTHLY WTHDRWLS	17.80%	17.85%	17.90%	18.00%	18.10%	18.20%	18.30%	18.40%
1	1013.745114	1013.780964	1013.816800	1013.888430	1013.960005	1014.031524	1014.102987	1014.174395
2	510.332291	510.359300	510.386299	510.440268	510.494195	510.548082	510.601928	510.655734
3	342.538440	342.562557	342.586665	342.634855	342.683009	342.731129	342.779213	342.827263
4	258.649331	258.672043	258.694746	258.740129	258.785479	258.830798	258.876084	258.921338
5	208.322119	208.344020	208.365913	208.409676	208.453410	208.497114	208.540788	208.584432
6	174.775854	174.797241	174.818621	174.861360	174.904071	174.946753	174.989407	175.032033
7	150.818701	150.839745	150.860782	150.902835	150.944862	150.986861	151.028834	151.070780
8	132.854742	132.875548	132.896348	132.937928	132.979483	133.021012	133.062515	133.103993
9	118.886244	118.906884	118.927517	118.968766	119.009990	119.051190	119.092365	119.133515
10	107.714569	107.735091	107.755608	107.796624	107.837617	107.878585	107.919531	107.960453
11	98.576945	98.597386	98.617822	98.658678	98.699510	98.740320	98.781108	98.821873
12	90.964858	90.985246	91.005628	91.046377	91.087103	91.127808	91.168492	91.209154
13	84.526261	84.546616	84.566965	84.607648	84.648310	84.688952	84.729573	84.770172
14	79.009691	79.030028	79.050361	79.091011	79.131641	79.172252	79.212842	79.253413
15	74.230740	74.251074	74.271403	74.312046	74.352671	74.393276	74.433862	74.474429
16	70.051105	70.071445	70.091781	70.132439	70.173079	70.213700	70.254303	70.294888
17	66.365022	66.385378	66.405729	66.446419	66.487091	66.527746	66.568383	66.609003
18	63.090232	63.110611	63.130985	63.171721	63.212440	63.253143	63.293828	63.334498
19	60.161793	60.182200	60.202603	60.243398	60.284176	60.324939	60.365685	60.406416
20	57.527751	57.548192	57.568629	57.609492	57.650340	57.691173	57.731990	57.772793
21	55.146049	55.166528	55.187004	55.227944	55.268870	55.309782	55.350679	55.391562
22	52.982274	53.002796	53.023314	53.064339	53.105351	53.146349	53.187334	53.228305
23	51.008002	51.028568	51.049132	51.090249	51.131354	51.172445	51.213524	51.254589
24	49.199542	49.220157	49.240769	49.281984	49.323186	49.364377	49.405555	49.446721
25	47.536997	47.557663	47.578326	47.619643	47.660948	47.702242	47.743525	47.784796
26	46.003529	46.024248	46.044964	46.086387	46.127801	46.169203	46.210595	46.251976
27	44.584795	44.605568	44.626339	44.667874	44.709399	44.750913	44.792418	44.833913
28	43.268501	43.289331	43.310159	43.351808	43.393447	43.435077	43.476698	43.518310
29	42.044048	42.064937	42.085823	42.127589	42.169347	42.211096	42.252836	42.294568
30	40.902252	40.923200	40.944146	40.986032	41.027911	41.069781	41.111644	41.153498
31	39.835113	39.856121	39.877128	39.919137	39.961139	40.003133	40.045120	40.087100
32	38.835629	38.856700	38.877769	38.919902	38.962029	39.004150	39.046263	39.088371
33	37.897650	37.918784	37.939916	37.982176	38.024430	38.066679	38.108921	38.151158
34	37.015748	37.036945	37.058141	37.100530	37.142913	37.185292	37.227665	37.270033
35	36.185114	36.206377	36.227637	36.270156	36.312670	36.355180	36.397685	36.440186
36	35.401476	35.422804	35.444130	35.486781	35.529427	35.572070	35.614708	35.657344
37	34.661022	34.682416	34.703809	34.746592	34.789372	34.832148	34.874922	34.917693
38	33.960342	33.981802	34.003261	34.046179	34.089093	34.132005	34.174915	34.217822
39	33.296375	33.317902	33.339428	33.382481	33.425531	33.468580	33.511627	33.554672
40	32.666365	32.687900	32.709555	32.752743	32.795930	32.839116	32.882301	32.925485
41	32.067829	32.089492	32.111155	32.154480	32.197805	32.241129	32.284453	32.327776
42	31.498516	31.520247	31.541979	31.585442	31.628905	31.672368	31.715832	31.759295
43	30.956386	30.978187	30.999987	31.043588	31.087191	31.130794	31.174398	31.218002
44	30.439586	30.461455	30.483325	30.527065	30.570808	30.614551	30.658296	30.702042
45	29.946425	29.968363	29.990303	30.034183	30.078065	30.121950	30.165836	30.209725
46	29.475360	29.497369	29.519378	29.563398	29.607421	29.651447	29.695476	29.739507
47	29.024981	29.047059	29.069138	29.113299	29.157464	29.201632	29.245803	29.289977
48	28.593992	28.616141	28.638290	28.682592	28.726899	28.771209	28.815523	28.859841
60	24.581387	24.604387	24.627389	24.673402	24.719425	24.765460	24.811506	24.857563
72	21.964089	21.988660	22.012515	22.060238	22.107979	22.155738	22.203514	22.251307
84	20.144525	20.169214	20.193908	20.243313	20.292742	20.342193	20.391668	20.441165
96	18.820497	18.846000	18.871510	18.922551	18.973620	19.024717	19.075842	19.126994
108	17.825901	17.852190	17.878488	17.931107	17.983758	18.036441	18.089155	18.141900
120	17.060546	17.087589	17.114642	17.168773	17.222939	17.277139	17.331374	17.385643
132	16.460600	16.488362	16.516134	16.571705	16.627313	16.682958	16.738639	16.794355
144	15.983461	16.011905	16.040358	16.097293	16.154267	16.211278	16.268327	16.325412
156	15.599606	15.628692	15.657788	15.716009	15.774269	15.832567	15.890902	15.949275
168	15.287932	15.317622	15.347321	15.406749	15.466215	15.525718	15.585258	15.644835
180	15.032964	15.063108	15.093481	15.154035	15.214627	15.275254	15.335918	15.396617
192	14.823104	14.853882	14.884670	14.946272	15.007910	15.069582	15.131288	15.193027
204	14.649498	14.680764	14.712037	14.774610	14.837216	14.899854	14.962524	15.025224
216	14.505285	14.537000	14.568723	14.632191	14.695690	14.759218	14.822774	14.886359
228	14.385072	14.417201	14.449337	14.513629	14.577948	14.642293	14.706663	14.771059
240	14.284577	14.317085	14.349600	14.414646	14.479716	14.544809	14.609923	14.675059
252	14.200363	14.233218	14.266078	14.331813	14.397569	14.463343	14.529135	14.594945
264	14.129649	14.162820	14.195995	14.262358	14.328736	14.395130	14.461538	14.527959
276	14.070170	14.103628	14.137090	14.204022	14.270966	14.337921	14.404886	14.471860
288	14.020070	14.053789	14.087509	14.154957	14.222412	14.289874	14.357342	14.424816
300	13.977820	14.011771	14.045728	14.113641	14.181557	14.249476	14.317398	14.385320
312	13.942153	13.976319	14.010484	14.078816	14.147147	14.215477	14.283805	14.352130
324	13.912019	13.946375	13.980730	14.049437	14.118141	14.186839	14.255531	14.324217
336	13.886539	13.921066	13.955591	14.024636	14.093673	14.162701	14.231719	14.300727
348	13.864983	13.899663	13.934340	14.003687	14.073021	14.142343	14.211652	14.280947
360	13.846737	13.881553	13.916366	13.985982	14.055582	14.125165	14.194733	14.264283
420	13.789728	13.825033	13.860330	13.930903	14.001445	14.071957	14.142438	14.212888
480	13.764746	13.800315	13.835875	13.906964	13.978012	14.049020	14.119987	14.190913

188

MONTHLY WITHDRAWALS PER $1000

NUMBER OF MONTHLY WTHDRWLS	EFFECTIVE ANNUAL YIELD							
	18.50%	18.60%	18.70%	18.80%	18.90%	19.00%	19.10%	19.20%
1	1014.245748	1014.317046	1014.388289	1014.459476	1014.530609	1014.601687	1014.672710	1014.743679
2	510.709500	510.763225	510.816910	510.870554	510.924159	510.977723	511.031248	511.084732
3	342.875277	342.923257	342.971202	343.019111	343.066987	343.114827	343.162633	343.210404
4	258.966561	259.011752	259.056910	259.102035	259.147133	259.192197	259.237229	259.282229
5	208.628046	208.671630	208.715185	208.758710	208.802206	208.845672	208.889108	208.932515
6	175.074630	175.117200	175.159742	175.202255	175.244741	175.287198	175.329628	175.372030
7	151.112700	151.154592	151.196458	151.238297	151.280110	151.321896	151.363655	151.405388
8	133.145445	133.186872	133.228273	133.269649	133.310999	133.352324	133.393624	133.434898
9	119.174641	119.215743	119.256820	119.297873	119.338901	119.379905	119.420885	119.461841
10	108.001351	108.042226	108.083077	108.123906	108.164710	108.205492	108.246250	108.286985
11	98.862615	98.903335	98.944032	98.984707	99.025360	99.065990	99.106598	99.147184
12	91.249794	91.290412	91.331009	91.371585	91.412139	91.452672	91.493183	91.533672
13	84.810752	84.851310	84.891848	84.932365	84.972862	85.013338	85.053793	85.094228
14	79.293964	79.334495	79.375006	79.415497	79.455968	79.496420	79.536852	79.577264
15	74.514978	74.555507	74.596017	74.636508	74.676980	74.717433	74.757868	74.798283
16	70.335544	70.376003	70.416533	70.457035	70.497539	70.538015	70.578472	70.618912
17	66.649605	66.690190	66.730758	66.771308	66.811841	66.852356	66.892854	66.933335
18	63.375150	63.415786	63.456405	63.497008	63.537594	63.578163	63.618716	63.659253
19	60.447131	60.487829	60.528512	60.569180	60.609831	60.650467	60.691086	60.731690
20	57.813580	57.854352	57.895109	57.935851	57.976578	58.017290	58.057987	58.098668
21	55.432431	55.473285	55.514125	55.554950	55.595761	55.636558	55.677340	55.718109
22	53.269262	53.310206	53.351136	53.392053	53.432956	53.473845	53.514721	53.555583
23	51.295642	51.336682	51.377709	51.418723	51.459724	51.500712	51.541688	51.582650
24	49.487874	49.529016	49.570145	49.611263	49.652368	49.693461	49.734542	49.775610
25	47.826056	47.867305	47.908542	47.949767	47.990981	48.032184	48.073375	48.114555
26	46.293346	46.334706	46.376054	46.417392	46.458720	46.500036	46.541342	46.582637
27	44.875397	44.916872	44.958336	44.999791	45.041235	45.082670	45.124094	45.165508
28	43.559912	43.601505	43.643089	43.684663	43.726228	43.767784	43.809330	43.850867
29	42.336291	42.378005	42.419711	42.461408	42.503097	42.544777	42.586448	42.628111
30	41.195345	41.237184	41.279014	41.320837	41.362652	41.404459	41.446258	41.488049
31	40.129072	40.171038	40.212996	40.254947	40.296890	40.338827	40.380756	40.422677
32	39.130472	39.172566	39.214653	39.256734	39.298809	39.340877	39.382938	39.424992
33	38.193389	38.235614	38.277833	38.320046	38.362254	38.404455	38.446650	38.488840
34	37.312396	37.354753	37.397106	37.439453	37.481794	37.524131	37.566462	37.608788
35	36.482682	36.525174	36.567661	36.610144	36.652622	36.695095	36.737564	36.780028
36	35.699975	35.742602	35.785225	35.827845	35.870460	35.913072	35.955679	35.998283
37	34.960460	35.003224	35.045985	35.088743	35.131497	35.174248	35.216996	35.259740
38	34.260727	34.303629	34.346528	34.389426	34.432320	34.475212	34.518101	34.560987
39	33.597715	33.640756	33.683795	33.726832	33.769868	33.812901	33.855932	33.898961
40	32.968667	33.011849	33.055029	33.098207	33.141384	33.184560	33.227735	33.270907
41	32.371099	32.414421	32.457742	32.501063	32.544383	32.587702	32.631021	32.674338
42	31.802759	31.846223	31.889686	31.933150	31.976613	32.020077	32.063540	32.107003
43	31.261608	31.305214	31.348820	31.392428	31.436035	31.479643	31.523252	31.566861
44	30.745790	30.789539	30.833289	30.877040	30.920793	30.964546	31.008301	31.052057
45	30.253615	30.297508	30.341402	30.385298	30.429196	30.473095	30.516997	30.560900
46	29.783541	29.827577	29.871616	29.915657	29.959701	30.003747	30.047795	30.091846
47	29.334155	29.378336	29.422519	29.466706	29.510896	29.555089	29.599285	29.643483
48	28.904163	28.948488	28.992817	29.037150	29.081487	29.125827	29.170170	29.214517
60	24.903631	24.949709	24.995798	25.041897	25.088007	25.134127	25.180258	25.226399
72	22.299117	22.346944	22.394787	22.442647	22.490525	22.538418	22.586328	22.634254
84	20.490685	20.540227	20.589791	20.639377	20.688985	20.738615	20.788266	20.837939
96	19.178173	19.229378	19.280611	19.331870	19.383155	19.434466	19.485803	19.537165
108	18.194676	18.247482	18.300319	18.353185	18.406082	18.459007	18.511962	18.564946
120	17.439945	17.494280	17.548648	17.603049	17.657482	17.711947	17.766444	17.820972
132	16.850107	16.905894	16.961716	17.017572	17.073462	17.129385	17.185342	17.241331
144	16.382534	16.439691	16.496884	16.554113	16.611376	16.668673	16.726004	16.783368
156	16.007684	16.066129	16.124609	16.183125	16.241675	16.300259	16.358877	16.417528
168	15.704448	15.764096	15.823779	15.883496	15.943247	16.003031	16.062848	16.122697
180	15.457350	15.518117	15.578918	15.639751	15.700617	15.761515	15.822444	15.883403
192	15.254799	15.316603	15.378438	15.440304	15.502201	15.564126	15.626081	15.688064
204	15.087955	15.150715	15.213504	15.276321	15.339165	15.402037	15.464935	15.527858
216	14.949971	15.013610	15.077274	15.140963	15.204677	15.268415	15.332176	15.395959
228	14.835478	14.899920	14.964385	15.028872	15.093380	15.157908	15.222455	15.287022
240	14.740215	14.805390	14.870585	14.935797	15.001027	15.066274	15.131536	15.196814
252	14.660771	14.726613	14.792469	14.858341	14.924225	14.990123	15.056032	15.121953
264	14.594392	14.660838	14.727295	14.793761	14.860238	14.926723	14.993216	15.059717
276	14.538843	14.605834	14.672831	14.739835	14.806845	14.873859	14.940877	15.007899
288	14.492294	14.559775	14.627260	14.694747	14.762235	14.829724	14.897214	14.964702
300	14.453243	14.521165	14.589087	14.657007	14.724924	14.792838	14.860749	14.928654
312	14.420452	14.488770	14.557082	14.625389	14.693690	14.761983	14.830269	14.898547
324	14.392896	14.461566	14.530228	14.598881	14.667523	14.736154	14.804774	14.873382
336	14.369724	14.438709	14.507681	14.576641	14.645587	14.714519	14.783435	14.852336
348	14.350227	14.419492	14.488741	14.557974	14.627189	14.696387	14.765566	14.834726
360	14.333815	14.403329	14.472823	14.542297	14.611751	14.681184	14.750596	14.819985
420	14.283305	14.353690	14.424042	14.494360	14.564645	14.634895	14.705111	14.775292
480	14.261797	14.332639	14.403440	14.474197	14.544912	14.615585	14.686214	14.756799

NUMBER OF MONTHLY WTHDRWLS	EFFECTIVE ANNUAL YIELD							
	19.30%	19.40%	19.50%	19.60%	19.70%	19.80%	19.90%	20.00%
1	1014.814593	1014.885452	1014.956257	1015.027008	1015.097705	1015.168347	1015.238936	1015.309470
2	511.138177	511.191582	511.244947	511.298272	511.351558	511.404804	511.458011	511.511178
3	343.258141	343.305843	343.353511	343.401144	343.448743	343.496308	343.543838	343.591335
4	259.327198	259.372136	259.417042	259.461917	259.506760	259.551572	259.596353	259.641103
5	208.975892	209.019241	209.062559	209.105849	209.149109	209.192340	209.235542	209.278715
6	175.414404	175.456750	175.499068	175.541359	175.583622	175.625858	175.668066	175.710246
7	151.447095	151.488775	151.530429	151.572056	151.613657	151.655232	151.696780	151.738303
8	133.476147	133.517371	133.558569	133.599743	133.640891	133.682014	133.723112	133.764185
9	119.502772	119.543680	119.584563	119.625422	119.666257	119.707068	119.747854	119.788617
10	108.327697	108.368386	108.409051	108.449694	108.490313	108.530909	108.571482	108.612032
11	99.187748	99.228289	99.268808	99.309304	99.349779	99.390231	99.430662	99.471070
12	91.574141	91.614588	91.655014	91.695418	91.735801	91.776163	91.816504	91.856823
13	85.134643	85.175037	85.215410	85.255763	85.296095	85.336408	85.376699	85.416971
14	79.617657	79.658030	79.698383	79.738717	79.779031	79.819325	79.859600	79.899856
15	74.838680	74.879058	74.919416	74.959756	75.000078	75.040380	75.080664	75.120929
16	70.659333	70.699737	70.740122	70.780489	70.820838	70.861170	70.901483	70.941778
17	66.973798	67.014245	67.054674	67.095085	67.135480	67.175857	67.216217	67.256559
18	63.699772	63.740276	63.780762	63.821233	63.861686	63.902124	63.942544	63.982949
19	60.772278	60.812851	60.853407	60.893948	60.934473	60.974982	61.015476	61.055954
20	58.139335	58.179986	58.220623	58.261245	58.301851	58.342443	58.383019	58.423581
21	55.758862	55.799602	55.840327	55.881038	55.921735	55.962417	56.003085	56.043739
22	53.596431	53.637266	53.678087	53.718895	53.759689	53.800470	53.841237	53.881991
23	51.623600	51.664537	51.705460	51.746372	51.787270	51.828155	51.869028	51.909887
24	49.816667	49.857711	49.898743	49.939763	49.980771	50.021767	50.062750	50.103722
25	48.155723	48.196879	48.238025	48.279159	48.320281	48.361392	48.402491	48.443579
26	46.623922	46.665195	46.706458	46.747710	46.788951	46.830182	46.871401	46.912610
27	45.206912	45.248307	45.289691	45.331065	45.372429	45.413782	45.455126	45.496460
28	43.892395	43.933913	43.975422	44.016921	44.058411	44.099892	44.141363	44.182824
29	42.669765	42.711410	42.753046	42.794674	42.836293	42.877903	42.919505	42.961097
30	41.529832	41.571606	41.613373	41.655132	41.696883	41.738625	41.780360	41.822086
31	40.464591	40.506498	40.548398	40.590290	40.632175	40.674052	40.715922	40.757785
32	39.467040	39.509081	39.551116	39.593144	39.635165	39.677179	39.719186	39.761187
33	38.531023	38.573200	38.615371	38.657537	38.699696	38.741849	38.783996	38.826136
34	37.651109	37.693424	37.735734	37.778038	37.820337	37.862630	37.904918	37.947201
35	36.822487	36.864942	36.907391	36.949836	36.992277	37.034712	37.077143	37.119569
36	36.040882	36.083478	36.126069	36.168656	36.211239	36.253818	36.296393	36.338963
37	35.302481	35.345218	35.387952	35.430683	35.473410	35.516133	35.558853	35.601569
38	34.603870	34.646751	34.689628	34.732503	34.775375	34.818245	34.861111	34.903974
39	33.941988	33.985013	34.028036	34.071056	34.114074	34.157090	34.200103	34.243115
40	33.314079	33.357249	33.400417	33.443584	33.486749	33.529912	33.573074	33.616234
41	32.717655	32.760971	32.804285	32.847599	32.890912	32.934224	32.977535	33.020844
42	32.150466	32.193928	32.237390	32.280852	32.324313	32.367774	32.411235	32.454695
43	31.610470	31.654080	31.697690	31.741300	31.784911	31.828521	31.872132	31.915743
44	31.095813	31.139571	31.183329	31.227089	31.270849	31.314610	31.358371	31.402134
45	30.604804	30.648710	30.692617	30.736526	30.780437	30.824348	30.868261	30.912176
46	30.135898	30.179953	30.224010	30.268069	30.312130	30.356193	30.400258	30.444324
47	29.687684	29.731888	29.776095	29.820305	29.864516	29.908731	29.952948	29.997167
48	29.258867	29.303221	29.347578	29.391938	29.436301	29.480668	29.525037	29.569409
60	25.272549	25.318710	25.364881	25.411062	25.457252	25.503452	25.549662	25.595881
72	22.682196	22.730154	22.778127	22.826117	22.874122	22.922142	22.970178	23.018229
84	20.887632	20.937347	20.987083	21.036839	21.086615	21.136413	21.186230	21.236067
96	19.588553	19.639622	19.691404	19.742867	19.794354	19.845866	19.897402	19.948961
108	18.617958	18.670999	18.724068	18.777165	18.830289	18.883441	18.936620	18.989826
120	17.875531	17.930120	17.984740	18.039390	18.094070	18.148780	18.203518	18.258286
132	17.297353	17.353407	17.409492	17.465609	17.521757	17.577936	17.634145	17.690384
144	16.840766	16.898196	16.955658	17.013152	17.070677	17.128233	17.185820	17.243437
156	16.476212	16.534929	16.593677	16.652456	16.711266	16.770107	16.828977	16.887877
168	16.182578	16.242490	16.302433	16.362406	16.422409	16.482440	16.542501	16.602589
180	15.944392	16.005411	16.066458	16.127534	16.188638	16.249769	16.310926	16.372110
192	15.750075	15.812113	15.874177	15.936268	15.998383	16.060524	16.122688	16.184876
204	15.590806	15.653778	15.716775	15.779794	15.842835	15.905899	15.968984	16.032089
216	15.459764	15.523590	15.587436	15.651302	15.715188	15.779092	15.843013	15.906952
228	15.351607	15.416209	15.480828	15.545464	15.610115	15.674780	15.739460	15.804154
240	15.262106	15.327412	15.392731	15.458062	15.523405	15.588760	15.654124	15.719499
252	15.187884	15.253825	15.319776	15.385735	15.451702	15.517676	15.583656	15.649642
264	15.126224	15.192737	15.259255	15.325778	15.392305	15.458834	15.525367	15.591901
276	15.074923	15.141949	15.208977	15.276004	15.343032	15.410059	15.477085	15.544108
288	15.032189	15.099674	15.167156	15.234635	15.302110	15.369580	15.437045	15.504503
300	14.996555	15.064449	15.132337	15.200217	15.268090	15.335954	15.403809	15.471654
312	14.966815	15.035073	15.103322	15.171559	15.239784	15.307998	15.376198	15.444385
324	14.941977	15.010559	15.079127	15.147680	15.216218	15.284740	15.353245	15.421734
336	14.921221	14.990089	15.058939	15.127771	15.196585	15.265380	15.334155	15.402909
348	14.903867	14.972988	15.042087	15.111166	15.180223	15.249257	15.318269	15.387257
360	14.889352	14.958695	15.028014	15.097310	15.166580	15.235825	15.305045	15.374238
420	14.845437	14.915547	14.985620	15.055657	15.125657	15.195620	15.265546	15.335433
480	14.827341	14.897839	14.968293	15.038702	15.109067	15.179388	15.249663	15.319894

TABLE 6. QUARTERLY WITHDRAWALS PER $1,000

QUARTERLY WITHDRAWALS PER $1000

EFFECTIVE ANNUAL YIELD

NUMBER OF QUARTERLY WTHDRWLS	5.00%	5.05%	5.10%	5.15%	5.20%	5.25%	5.30%	5.35%
1	1012.272234	1012.392722	1012.513166	1012.633567	1012.753925	1012.874240	1012.994513	1013.114742
2	509.222887	509.313620	509.404325	509.495001	509.585648	509.676266	509.766855	509.857416
3	341.548087	341.629066	341.710022	341.790956	341.871868	341.952757	342.033623	342.114467
4	257.716923	257.793148	257.869354	257.945542	258.021711	258.097863	258.173996	258.250111
5	207.423213	207.496683	207.570138	207.643579	207.717004	207.790415	207.863811	207.937192
6	173.898230	173.969945	174.041649	174.113340	174.185021	174.256689	174.328345	174.399990
7	149.955375	150.025907	150.096430	150.166945	150.237450	150.307946	150.378434	150.448912
8	132.001351	132.071057	132.140756	132.210449	132.280137	132.349818	132.419492	132.489161
9	118.039879	118.108996	118.178110	118.247221	118.316328	118.385431	118.454530	118.523626
10	106.873193	106.941889	107.010584	107.079278	107.147971	107.216662	107.285353	107.354043
11	97.739079	97.807474	97.875871	97.944269	98.012669	98.081070	98.149473	98.217877
12	90.129392	90.197578	90.265767	90.333961	90.402159	90.470360	90.538565	90.606774
13	83.692341	83.760387	83.828440	83.896498	83.964563	84.032634	84.100712	84.168796
14	78.176646	78.244608	78.312578	78.380556	78.448543	78.516539	78.584544	78.652557
15	73.398036	73.465956	73.533887	73.601830	73.669783	73.737747	73.805722	73.873709
16	69.218306	69.286221	69.354149	69.422090	69.490045	69.558013	69.625995	69.693990
17	65.531771	65.599710	65.667664	65.735634	65.803620	65.871621	65.939638	66.007671
18	62.256232	62.324218	62.392223	62.460246	62.528286	62.596345	62.664422	62.732517
19	59.326792	59.394847	59.462923	59.531019	59.599136	59.667272	59.735430	59.803607
20	56.691537	56.759679	56.827843	56.896030	56.964239	57.032471	57.100726	57.169003
21	54.308440	54.376683	54.444950	54.513242	54.581560	54.649902	54.718269	54.786661
22	52.143115	52.211471	52.279855	52.348265	52.416703	52.485169	52.553661	52.622180
23	50.167156	50.235637	50.304148	50.372688	50.441258	50.509857	50.578486	50.647144
24	48.356891	48.425507	48.494155	48.562834	48.631545	48.700288	48.769063	48.837869
25	46.692437	46.761196	46.829989	46.898816	46.967678	47.036573	47.105502	47.174465
26	45.156969	45.225878	45.294825	45.363807	45.432826	45.501881	45.570972	45.640099
27	43.736154	43.805221	43.874326	43.943471	44.012653	44.081875	44.151134	44.220432
28	42.417707	42.486937	42.556208	42.625520	42.694873	42.764266	42.833700	42.903175
29	41.191037	41.260436	41.329878	41.399363	41.468891	41.538462	41.608075	41.677732
30	40.046967	40.116539	40.186157	40.255819	40.325527	40.395280	40.465078	40.534921
31	38.977502	39.047212	39.117049	39.186933	39.256785	39.325798	39.396711	39.466745
32	37.975647	38.045578	38.115559	38.185589	38.255669	38.325798	38.395977	38.466205
33	37.035256	37.105371	37.175539	37.245758	37.316029	37.386352	37.456726	37.527152
34	36.150903	36.221206	36.291564	36.361975	36.432441	36.502960	36.573533	36.644160
35	35.317786	35.388280	35.458830	35.529436	35.600099	35.670818	35.741592	35.812423
36	34.531633	34.602320	34.673066	34.743870	34.814732	34.885653	34.956631	35.027668
37	33.788636	33.859519	33.930462	34.001466	34.072531	34.143655	34.214840	34.286085
38	33.085388	33.156469	33.227612	33.298817	33.370086	33.441417	33.512810	33.584265
39	32.418830	32.490110	32.561455	32.632864	32.704339	32.775878	32.847481	32.919149
40	31.786210	31.857691	31.929239	32.000854	32.072536	32.144285	32.216100	32.287982
41	31.185044	31.256727	31.328481	31.400303	31.472194	31.544154	31.616183	31.688280
42	30.613083	30.684972	30.756931	30.828962	30.901064	30.973236	31.045480	31.117794
43	30.068291	30.140385	30.212552	30.284793	30.357107	30.429493	30.501953	30.574485
44	29.548814	29.621115	29.693491	29.765942	29.838469	29.911071	29.983748	30.056500
45	29.052963	29.125472	29.198058	29.270722	29.343463	29.416281	29.489176	29.562148
46	28.579198	28.651915	28.724712	28.797589	28.870545	28.943581	29.016695	29.089889
47	28.126107	28.199034	28.272043	28.345134	28.418306	28.491560	28.564894	28.638310
48	27.692398	27.765536	27.838757	27.912063	27.985452	28.058924	28.132480	28.206118
50	26.878470	26.952032	27.025681	27.099418	27.173243	27.247155	27.321155	27.395241
52	26.120902	26.202989	26.277069	26.351240	26.425503	26.499857	26.574302	26.648839
54	25.436825	25.511241	25.585752	25.660359	25.735062	25.809860	25.884753	25.959741
56	24.795797	24.870641	24.945586	25.020630	25.095774	25.171018	25.246360	25.321801
58	24.200619	24.275894	24.351274	24.426756	24.502343	24.578032	24.653824	24.729719
60	23.646703	23.722409	23.798224	23.874146	23.950175	24.026311	24.102554	24.178904
62	23.130049	23.206187	23.282438	23.358799	23.435272	23.511856	23.588550	23.665354
64	22.647159	22.723730	22.800416	22.877218	22.954134	23.031165	23.108310	23.185569
66	22.194958	22.271961	22.349084	22.426325	22.503685	22.581163	22.658759	22.736472
68	21.770733	21.848169	21.925727	22.003408	22.081211	22.159136	22.237183	22.315350
70	21.372081	21.449949	21.527943	21.606063	21.684309	21.762680	21.841177	21.919798
72	20.996866	21.075165	21.153594	21.232153	21.310841	21.389658	21.468603	21.547677
74	20.643182	20.721911	20.800775	20.879772	20.958901	21.038163	21.117556	21.197082
76	20.309323	20.388483	20.467780	20.547214	20.626784	20.706489	20.786330	20.866306
78	19.993761	20.073350	20.153079	20.232949	20.312958	20.393106	20.473393	20.553818
80	19.695117	19.775134	19.855295	19.935599	20.016046	20.096636	20.177367	20.258240
82	19.412148	19.492592	19.573183	19.653921	19.734805	19.815834	19.897009	19.978328
84	19.143730	19.224600	19.305620	19.386790	19.468109	19.549577	19.631193	19.712957
86	18.888843	18.970136	19.051584	19.133184	19.214937	19.296842	19.378898	19.461105
88	18.646558	18.728274	18.810148	18.892177	18.974362	19.056702	19.139196	19.221844
90	18.416031	18.498168	18.580466	18.662923	18.745538	18.828311	18.911242	18.994329
92	18.196489	18.279046	18.361767	18.444649	18.527693	18.610898	18.694263	18.777787
96	17.787598	17.870989	17.954549	18.038277	18.122172	18.206234	18.290461	18.374853
100	17.414904	17.499121	17.583513	17.668079	17.752817	17.837727	17.922809	18.008060
104	17.074193	17.159229	17.244445	17.329840	17.415412	17.501162	17.587088	17.673189
108	16.761874	16.847721	16.933752	17.019967	17.106364	17.192944	17.279705	17.366645
112	16.474869	16.561516	16.648353	16.735379	16.822592	16.909992	16.997578	17.085347
116	16.210521	16.297960	16.385594	16.473421	16.561440	16.649650	16.738049	16.826637
120	15.966529	16.054751	16.143172	16.231790	16.320604	16.409613	16.498815	16.588211
140	14.989726	15.081707	15.173905	15.266316	15.358941	15.451776	15.544821	15.638074
160	14.304065	14.399531	14.495223	14.591141	14.687281	14.783642	14.880221	14.977017

192

QUARTERLY WITHDRAWALS PER $1000

EFFECTIVE ANNUAL YIELD

NUMBER OF QUARTRLY WTHDRWLS	5.40%	5.45%	5.50%	5.55%	5.60%	5.65%	5.70%	5.75%
1	1013.234929	1013.355073	1013.475174	1013.595233	1013.715249	1013.835223	1013.955153	1014.075042
2	509.947948	510.038452	510.128926	510.219373	510.309790	510.400179	510.490540	510.580872
3	342.195288	342.276087	342.356863	342.437618	342.518349	342.599058	342.679745	342.760410
4	258.326207	258.402286	258.478346	258.554385	258.630412	258.706418	258.782405	258.858374
5	208.010558	208.083909	208.157246	208.230568	208.303875	208.377168	208.450446	208.523709
6	174.471623	174.543245	174.614854	174.686452	174.758038	174.829613	174.901176	174.972727
7	150.519382	150.589843	150.660294	150.730737	150.801171	150.871597	150.942013	151.012420
8	132.558823	132.628479	132.698129	132.767773	132.837410	132.907041	132.976666	133.046285
9	118.592719	118.661807	118.730892	118.799974	118.869051	118.938125	119.007196	119.076262
10	107.422731	107.491418	107.560105	107.628790	107.697473	107.766156	107.834838	107.903518
11	98.286282	98.354689	98.423097	98.491506	98.559917	98.628329	98.696742	98.765157
12	90.674987	90.743204	90.811424	90.879648	90.947876	91.016107	91.084343	91.152581
13	84.236886	84.304982	84.373084	84.441192	84.509307	84.577427	84.645554	84.713687
14	78.720578	78.788609	78.856647	78.924695	78.992750	79.060814	79.128887	79.196968
15	73.941706	74.009714	74.077733	74.145763	74.213803	74.281855	74.349917	74.417990
16	69.761998	69.830019	69.898054	69.966101	70.034162	70.102236	70.170323	70.238424
17	66.075719	66.143783	66.211862	66.279957	66.348067	66.416193	66.484334	66.552490
18	62.800630	62.868760	62.936908	63.005075	63.073259	63.141460	63.209680	63.277917
19	59.871804	59.940022	60.008260	60.076518	60.144796	60.213094	60.281412	60.349749
20	57.237303	57.305625	57.373966	57.442337	57.510726	57.579137	57.647571	57.716027
21	54.855078	54.923519	54.991985	55.060476	55.128991	55.197531	55.266096	55.334684
22	52.690727	52.759300	52.827901	52.896528	52.965182	53.033863	53.102571	53.171305
23	50.715831	50.784548	50.853293	50.922068	50.990872	51.059705	51.128567	51.197458
24	48.906707	48.975576	49.044477	49.113409	49.182372	49.251367	49.320393	49.389450
25	47.243462	47.312492	47.381556	47.450654	47.519785	47.588950	47.658148	47.727379
26	45.709262	45.778461	45.847696	45.916967	45.986273	46.055615	46.124993	46.194406
27	44.289768	44.359142	44.428555	44.498005	44.567493	44.637019	44.706583	44.776185
28	42.972690	43.042245	43.111840	43.181476	43.251152	43.320868	43.390624	43.460420
29	41.747431	41.817172	41.886956	41.956783	42.026651	42.096562	42.166515	42.236511
30	40.604809	40.674741	40.744718	40.814740	40.884806	40.954916	41.025071	41.095270
31	39.536825	39.606953	39.677127	39.747348	39.817615	39.887930	39.958291	40.028698
32	38.536482	38.606808	38.677184	38.747608	38.818081	38.888603	38.959173	39.029792
33	37.597629	37.668158	37.738737	37.809368	37.880050	37.950782	38.021565	38.092399
34	36.714840	36.785574	36.856361	36.927201	36.998094	37.069041	37.140040	37.211092
35	35.883309	35.954250	36.025247	36.096300	36.167407	36.238570	36.309788	36.381060
36	35.098762	35.169914	35.241124	35.312391	35.383715	35.455097	35.526535	35.598031
37	34.357390	34.428754	34.500179	34.571663	34.643206	34.714809	34.786471	34.858192
38	33.655783	33.727362	33.799003	33.870706	33.942470	34.014296	34.086183	34.158132
39	32.990881	33.062676	33.134536	33.206460	33.278447	33.350498	33.422612	33.494789
40	32.359930	32.431944	32.504024	32.576170	32.648382	32.720659	32.793002	32.865410
41	31.760445	31.832679	31.904981	31.977351	32.049789	32.122294	32.194867	32.267507
42	31.190179	31.262634	31.335159	31.407754	31.480419	31.553154	31.625958	31.698831
43	30.647090	30.719768	30.792517	30.865339	30.938232	31.011197	31.084234	31.157342
44	30.129326	30.202227	30.275200	30.348251	30.421374	30.494571	30.567841	30.641185
45	29.635197	29.708322	29.781524	29.854802	29.928155	30.001585	30.075090	30.148670
46	29.163161	29.236512	29.309940	29.383448	29.457033	29.530696	29.604436	29.678254
47	28.711806	28.785383	28.859040	28.932778	29.006595	29.080492	29.154469	29.228525
48	28.279840	28.353643	28.427530	28.501498	28.575548	28.649680	28.723894	28.798189
50	27.469414	27.543674	27.618020	27.692452	27.766970	27.841574	27.916263	27.991038
52	26.723466	26.798183	26.872991	26.947889	27.022877	27.097954	27.173121	27.248377
54	26.034824	26.110001	26.185272	26.260637	26.336096	26.411649	26.487294	26.563033
56	25.397340	25.472978	25.548714	25.624548	25.700479	25.776507	25.852632	25.928854
58	24.805717	24.881816	24.958017	25.034320	25.110724	25.187229	25.263834	25.340540
60	24.255359	24.331921	24.408587	24.485359	24.562237	24.639218	24.716304	24.793494
62	23.742268	23.819291	23.896424	23.973665	24.051016	24.128474	24.206040	24.283715
64	23.262941	23.340427	23.418025	23.495736	23.573559	23.651494	23.729540	23.807698
66	22.814303	22.892250	22.970314	23.048494	23.126789	23.205200	23.283726	23.362366
68	22.393638	22.472047	22.550575	22.629223	22.707990	22.786876	22.865880	22.945003
70	21.998543	22.077411	22.156404	22.235519	22.314757	22.394117	22.473599	22.553202
72	21.626878	21.706206	21.785662	21.865243	21.944951	22.024784	22.104742	22.184825
74	21.276738	21.356525	21.436441	21.516488	21.596664	21.676969	21.757402	21.837962
76	20.946416	21.026660	21.107037	21.187547	21.268190	21.348965	21.429871	21.510909
78	20.634380	20.715080	20.795916	20.876889	20.957997	21.039240	21.120618	21.202130
80	20.339254	20.420408	20.501701	20.583134	20.664706	20.746416	20.828264	20.910249
82	20.059791	20.141398	20.223147	20.305039	20.387073	20.469247	20.551563	20.634019
84	19.794868	19.876925	19.959128	20.041477	20.123970	20.206608	20.289389	20.372314
86	19.543462	19.625968	19.708623	19.791427	19.874378	19.957477	20.040721	20.124112
88	19.304645	19.387599	19.470704	19.553960	19.637367	19.720924	19.804630	19.888485
90	19.077572	19.160971	19.244524	19.328231	19.412091	19.496104	19.580269	19.664585
92	18.861470	18.945311	19.029310	19.113465	19.197777	19.282243	19.366864	19.451640
96	18.459410	18.544130	18.629013	18.714058	18.799264	18.884630	18.970157	19.055842
100	18.093481	18.179071	18.264828	18.350752	18.436843	18.523098	18.609519	18.696102
104	17.759464	17.845913	17.932535	18.019328	18.106292	18.193425	18.280728	18.368199
108	17.453765	17.541063	17.628537	17.716188	17.804014	17.892014	17.980187	18.068533
112	17.173300	17.261436	17.349752	17.438249	17.526926	17.615780	17.704811	17.794019
116	16.915413	17.004374	17.093521	17.182853	17.272367	17.362063	17.451939	17.541996
120	16.677797	16.767573	16.857539	16.947692	17.038031	17.128556	17.219265	17.310157
140	15.731533	15.825197	15.919063	16.013131	16.107398	16.201864	16.296526	16.391382
160	15.074027	15.171249	15.268682	15.366322	15.464169	15.562219	15.660471	15.758923

QUARTERLY WITHDRAWALS PER $1000

NUMBER OF QUARTRLY WTHDRWLS	EFFECTIVE ANNUAL YIELD							
	5.80%	5.85%	5.90%	5.95%	6.00%	6.05%	6.10%	6.15%
1	1014.194887	1014.314691	1014.434452	1014.554170	1014.673846	1014.793480	1014.913071	1015.032621
2	510.671175	510.761450	510.851696	510.941914	511.032104	511.122265	511.212398	511.302502
3	342.841052	342.921672	343.002269	343.082844	343.163397	343.243928	343.324436	343.404923
4	258.934326	259.010259	259.086173	259.162070	259.237949	259.313810	259.389652	259.465477
5	208.596957	208.670190	208.743409	208.816613	208.889803	208.962977	209.036138	209.109283
6	175.044266	175.115794	175.187310	175.258814	175.330306	175.401787	175.473257	175.544714
7	151.082819	151.153208	151.223589	151.293960	151.364323	151.434677	151.505022	151.575358
8	133.115897	133.185503	133.255103	133.324697	133.394284	133.463866	133.533441	133.603009
9	119.145325	119.214385	119.283440	119.352492	119.421541	119.490585	119.559626	119.628663
10	107.972197	108.040875	108.109552	108.178228	108.246902	108.315575	108.384247	108.452918
11	98.833573	98.901990	98.970408	99.038827	99.107248	99.175670	99.244093	99.312517
12	91.220824	91.289070	91.357320	91.425574	91.493831	91.562091	91.630356	91.698623
13	84.781825	84.849970	84.918121	84.986278	85.054441	85.122609	85.190784	85.258964
14	79.265058	79.333155	79.401262	79.469376	79.537499	79.605630	79.673769	79.741917
15	74.486053	74.554168	74.622273	74.690388	74.758515	74.826651	74.894799	74.962957
16	70.306537	70.374663	70.442802	70.510954	70.579119	70.647297	70.715488	70.783692
17	66.620662	66.688849	66.757052	66.825269	66.893502	66.961750	67.030013	67.098291
18	63.346171	63.414443	63.482733	63.551040	63.619365	63.687707	63.756067	63.824443
19	60.418107	60.486485	60.554882	60.623299	60.691736	60.760193	60.828669	60.897164
20	57.784505	57.853005	57.921527	57.990072	58.058638	58.127226	58.195836	58.264468
21	55.403297	55.471935	55.540597	55.609283	55.677993	55.746727	55.815486	55.884268
22	53.240066	53.308853	53.377667	53.446508	53.515374	53.584268	53.653187	53.722133
23	51.266377	51.335326	51.404303	51.473309	51.542343	51.611406	51.680498	51.749618
24	49.458538	49.527657	49.596806	49.665987	49.735199	49.804441	49.873714	49.943018
25	47.796644	47.865942	47.935273	48.004637	48.074034	48.143464	48.212927	48.282422
26	46.263855	46.333339	46.402858	46.472413	46.542003	46.611628	46.681288	46.750983
27	44.845824	44.915501	44.985216	45.054967	45.124757	45.194583	45.264447	45.334348
28	43.530256	43.600131	43.670046	43.740001	43.809995	43.880029	43.950102	44.020214
29	42.306548	42.376627	42.446748	42.516910	42.587115	42.657361	42.727648	42.797977
30	41.165514	41.235801	41.306132	41.376508	41.446927	41.517389	41.587896	41.658446
31	40.099151	40.169651	40.240197	40.310789	40.381426	40.452110	40.522839	40.593614
32	39.100459	39.171175	39.241939	39.312751	39.383611	39.454519	39.525475	39.596479
33	38.163284	38.234219	38.305204	38.376240	38.447325	38.518461	38.589647	38.660883
34	37.282196	37.353353	37.424563	37.495825	37.567139	37.638506	37.709924	37.781395
35	36.452388	36.523770	36.595207	36.666698	36.738243	36.809843	36.881497	36.953205
36	35.669584	35.741193	35.812859	35.884582	35.956361	36.028196	36.100088	36.172036
37	34.929972	35.001811	35.073709	35.145665	35.217680	35.289753	35.361884	35.434073
38	34.230141	34.302211	34.374343	34.446534	34.518787	34.591100	34.663473	34.735906
39	33.567030	33.639333	33.711700	33.784129	33.856621	33.929175	34.001791	34.074470
40	32.937883	33.010422	33.083025	33.155693	33.228425	33.301222	33.374084	33.447009
41	32.340215	32.412989	32.485831	32.558739	32.631714	32.704755	32.777863	32.851037
42	31.771774	31.844786	31.917867	31.991017	32.064235	32.137522	32.210878	32.284301
43	31.230522	31.303773	31.377094	31.450487	31.523950	31.009001	31.597483	31.744761
44	30.714603	30.788093	30.861656	30.935292	31.009001	31.082782	31.156636	31.230562
45	30.222326	30.296057	30.369863	30.443744	30.517699	30.591729	30.665833	30.740011
46	29.752150	29.826122	29.900171	29.974297	30.048500	30.122779	30.197134	30.271566
47	29.302661	29.376875	29.451169	29.525541	29.599992	29.674521	29.749128	29.823813
48	28.872566	28.947023	29.021561	29.096180	29.170880	29.245659	29.320519	29.395458
50	28.065898	28.140842	28.215872	28.290985	28.366184	28.441466	28.516832	28.592282
52	27.323722	27.399156	27.474678	27.550288	27.625987	27.701773	27.777647	27.853608
54	26.638864	26.714788	26.790804	26.866912	26.943112	27.019403	27.095786	27.172260
56	26.005173	26.081588	26.158098	26.234705	26.311407	26.388204	26.465096	26.542082
58	25.417346	25.494252	25.571258	25.648363	25.725567	25.802870	25.880271	25.957771
60	24.870788	24.948186	25.025686	25.103290	25.180996	25.258804	25.336715	25.414727
62	24.361496	24.439385	24.517380	24.595481	24.673689	24.752002	24.830421	24.908945
64	23.885966	23.964345	24.042835	24.121434	24.200142	24.278960	24.357887	24.436922
66	23.441121	23.519990	23.598972	23.678068	23.757276	23.836597	23.916030	23.995575
68	23.024243	23.103600	23.183075	23.262666	23.342373	23.422196	23.502134	23.582188
70	22.632926	22.712771	22.792736	22.872821	22.953026	23.033349	23.113791	23.194351
72	22.265032	22.345363	22.425817	22.506394	22.587094	22.667917	22.748861	22.829926
74	21.918651	21.999466	22.080408	22.161477	22.242670	22.323989	22.405433	22.487001
76	21.592077	21.673375	21.754803	21.836360	21.918045	21.999859	22.081801	22.163870
78	21.283776	21.365555	21.447467	21.529511	21.611686	21.693993	21.776430	21.858998
80	20.992370	21.074628	21.157021	21.239550	21.322213	21.405010	21.487941	21.571004
82	20.716614	20.799348	20.882221	20.965232	21.048380	21.131665	21.215086	21.298644
84	20.455381	20.538589	20.621939	20.705430	20.789061	20.872831	20.956740	21.040788
86	20.207648	20.291329	20.375153	20.459121	20.543232	20.627485	20.711880	20.796416
88	19.972487	20.056637	20.140934	20.225377	20.309965	20.394698	20.479575	20.564596
90	19.749052	19.833669	19.918435	20.003349	20.088412	20.173622	20.258979	20.344481
92	19.536568	19.621649	19.706882	19.792265	19.877800	19.963484	20.049317	20.135298
96	19.141685	19.227686	19.313843	19.400156	19.486624	19.573247	19.660023	19.746952
100	18.782849	18.869758	18.956827	19.044058	19.131447	19.218995	19.306701	19.394564
104	18.455837	18.543641	18.631611	18.719745	18.808043	18.896503	18.985125	19.073908
108	18.157050	18.245737	18.334593	18.423618	18.512810	18.602168	18.691692	18.781380
112	17.883401	17.972958	18.062687	18.152588	18.242660	18.332902	18.423313	18.513891
116	17.632231	17.722643	17.813231	17.903995	17.994932	18.086042	18.177325	18.268777
120	17.401230	17.492484	17.583917	17.675528	17.767316	17.859279	17.951417	18.043729
140	16.486432	16.581673	16.677104	16.772724	16.868530	16.964521	17.060696	17.157052
160	15.857572	15.956418	16.055456	16.154686	16.254106	16.353713	16.453505	16.553481

QUARTERLY WITHDRAWALS PER $1000

EFFECTIVE ANNUAL YIELD

NUMBER OF QUARTLY WTHDRWLS	6.20%	6.25%	6.30%	6.35%	6.40%	6.45%	6.50%	6.55%
1	1015.152128	1015.271592	1015.391015	1015.510396	1015.629734	1015.749030	1015.868285	1015.987497
2	511.392578	511.482626	511.572646	511.662637	511.752600	511.842535	511.932441	512.022320
3	343.485387	343.565828	343.646248	343.726645	343.807020	343.887373	343.967704	344.048013
4	259.541283	259.617071	259.692842	259.768594	259.844328	259.920045	259.995743	260.071423
5	209.182414	209.255530	209.328631	209.401718	209.474790	209.547847	209.620890	209.693919
6	175.616160	175.687594	175.759017	175.830428	175.901827	175.973215	176.044591	176.115955
7	151.645686	151.716004	151.786313	151.856614	151.926906	151.997188	152.067462	152.137727
8	133.672572	133.742128	133.811678	133.881221	133.950758	134.020289	134.089814	134.159333
9	119.697697	119.766726	119.835752	119.904774	119.973793	120.042807	120.111818	120.180825
10	108.521587	108.590255	108.658922	108.727588	108.796252	108.864915	108.933577	109.002237
11	99.380943	99.449369	99.517797	99.586226	99.654656	99.723087	99.791519	99.859952
12	91.766895	91.835170	91.903448	91.971730	92.040015	92.108304	92.176596	92.244892
13	85.327151	85.395343	85.463541	85.531745	85.599955	85.668171	85.736392	85.804619
14	79.810073	79.878237	79.946409	80.014589	80.082777	80.150974	80.219179	80.287391
15	75.031125	75.099304	75.167494	75.235694	75.303904	75.372125	75.440356	75.508597
16	70.851908	70.920137	70.988379	71.056634	71.124901	71.193181	71.261474	71.329779
17	67.166585	67.234893	67.303216	67.371555	67.439908	67.508276	67.576659	67.645057
18	63.892838	63.961249	64.029678	64.098124	64.166587	64.235067	64.303565	64.372079
19	60.965680	61.034215	61.102769	61.171343	61.239936	61.308549	61.377180	61.445832
20	58.333121	58.401797	58.470494	58.539212	58.607953	58.676715	58.745498	58.814303
21	55.953075	56.021905	56.090759	56.159638	56.228540	56.297466	56.366415	56.435388
22	53.791105	53.860103	53.929127	53.998178	54.067254	54.136356	54.205485	54.274639
23	51.818766	51.887943	51.957148	52.026381	52.095643	52.164932	52.234250	52.303596
24	50.012352	50.081717	50.151112	50.220538	50.289994	50.359480	50.428997	50.498544
25	48.351951	48.421512	48.491106	48.560732	48.630391	48.700083	48.769806	48.839562
26	46.820713	46.890478	46.960277	47.030112	47.099981	47.169884	47.239822	47.309795
27	45.404285	45.474260	45.544272	45.614321	45.684406	45.754529	45.824687	45.894883
28	44.090365	44.160556	44.230786	44.301055	44.371362	44.441709	44.512094	44.582518
29	42.868347	42.938759	43.009211	43.079705	43.150240	43.220815	43.291432	43.362089
30	41.729039	41.799676	41.870356	41.941079	42.011845	42.082655	42.153507	42.224402
31	40.664435	40.735301	40.806212	40.877169	40.948171	41.019218	41.090310	41.161447
32	39.667530	39.738629	39.809775	39.880969	39.952210	40.023498	40.094834	40.166216
33	38.732168	38.803503	38.874888	38.946322	39.017805	39.089338	39.160920	39.232550
34	37.852917	37.924491	37.996117	38.067794	38.139523	38.211302	38.283133	38.355016
35	37.024966	37.096782	37.168651	37.240574	37.312550	37.384580	37.456663	37.528799
36	36.244039	36.316098	36.388214	36.460384	36.532611	36.604892	36.677229	36.749621
37	35.506321	35.578626	35.650989	35.723410	35.795888	35.868424	35.941017	36.013667
38	34.808399	34.880952	34.953565	35.026238	35.098970	35.171761	35.244612	35.317522
39	34.147211	34.220013	34.292878	34.365804	34.438791	34.511840	34.584950	34.658122
40	33.519999	33.593053	33.666170	33.739351	33.812595	33.885903	33.959274	34.032709
41	32.924277	32.997582	33.070954	33.144391	33.217894	33.291462	33.365095	33.438794
42	32.357793	32.431352	32.504979	32.578674	32.652436	32.726265	32.800162	32.874125
43	31.818505	31.892319	31.966203	32.040156	32.114179	32.188270	32.262431	32.336661
44	31.304559	31.378629	31.452770	31.526982	31.601266	31.675621	31.750047	31.824544
45	30.814263	30.888589	30.962988	31.037461	31.112007	31.186625	31.261317	31.336082
46	30.346073	30.420655	30.495314	30.570047	30.644856	30.719740	30.794698	30.869731
47	29.898576	29.973416	30.048334	30.123329	30.198401	30.273550	30.348776	30.424078
48	29.470478	29.545576	29.620754	29.696011	29.771347	29.846762	29.922255	29.997826
50	28.667815	28.743431	28.819131	28.894913	28.970778	29.046725	29.122754	29.198866
52	27.929657	28.005792	28.082014	28.158323	28.234718	28.311198	28.387765	28.464417
54	27.248824	27.325480	27.402225	27.479061	27.555986	27.633001	27.710105	27.787299
56	26.619163	26.696339	26.773608	26.850970	26.928426	27.005976	27.083618	27.161352
58	26.035368	26.113063	26.190856	26.268746	26.346732	26.424815	26.502994	26.581269
60	25.492840	25.571055	25.649371	25.727787	25.806303	25.884919	25.963635	26.042450
62	24.987574	25.066308	25.145145	25.224087	25.303132	25.382280	25.461531	25.540885
64	24.516065	24.595316	24.674675	24.754140	24.833713	24.913392	24.993177	25.073068
66	24.075231	24.154999	24.234877	24.314866	24.394964	24.475172	24.555490	24.635916
68	23.662356	23.742638	23.823034	23.903544	23.984167	24.064902	24.145750	24.226710
70	23.275029	23.355825	23.436737	23.517766	23.598911	23.680172	23.761548	23.843039
72	22.911112	22.992418	23.073845	23.155391	23.237056	23.318840	23.400742	23.482763
74	22.568694	22.650509	22.732447	22.814508	22.896691	22.978996	23.061422	23.143968
76	22.246066	22.328388	22.410836	22.493409	22.576108	22.658930	22.741877	22.824947
78	21.941695	22.024521	22.107476	22.190559	22.273770	22.357108	22.440573	22.524164
80	21.654200	21.737528	21.820987	21.904578	21.988298	22.072149	22.156128	22.240236
82	21.382336	21.466162	21.550123	21.634218	21.718445	21.802805	21.887296	21.971919
84	21.124974	21.209297	21.293756	21.378351	21.463082	21.547948	21.632948	21.718082
86	20.881092	20.965907	21.050862	21.135956	21.221187	21.306556	21.392061	21.477702
88	20.649759	20.735065	20.820512	20.906100	20.991828	21.077696	21.163703	21.249849
90	20.430129	20.515921	20.601857	20.687937	20.774159	20.860523	20.947028	21.033673
92	20.221427	20.307702	20.394124	20.480692	20.567404	20.654260	20.741259	20.828401
96	19.834033	19.921265	20.008648	20.096180	20.183862	20.271691	20.359668	20.447791
100	19.482584	19.570758	19.659087	19.747570	19.836205	19.924992	20.013931	20.103019
104	19.162851	19.251953	19.341213	19.430630	19.520204	19.609933	19.699816	19.789853
108	18.871231	18.961245	19.051421	19.141757	19.232252	19.322906	19.413718	19.504686
112	18.604636	18.695546	18.786621	18.877859	18.969260	19.060822	19.152544	19.244426
116	18.360399	18.452190	18.544147	18.636271	18.728560	18.821012	18.913628	19.006405
120	18.136212	18.228866	18.321690	18.414682	18.507841	18.601166	18.694656	18.788310
140	17.253589	17.350304	17.447196	17.544264	17.641506	17.738919	17.836504	17.934258
160	16.653638	16.753975	16.854489	16.955179	17.056041	17.157076	17.258280	17.359651

QUARTERLY WITHDRAWALS PER $1000

EFFECTIVE ANNUAL YIELD

NUMBER OF QUARTLY WTHDRWLS	6.60%	6.65%	6.70%	6.75%	6.80%	6.85%	6.90%	6.95%
1	1016.106668	1016.225796	1016.344883	1016.463928	1016.582931	1016.701892	1016.820811	1016.939689
2	512.112170	512.201992	512.291786	512.381552	512.471289	512.560999	512.650681	512.740335
3	344.128300	344.208565	344.288807	344.369028	344.449226	344.529403	344.609557	344.689690
4	260.147086	260.222737	260.298357	260.373965	260.449556	260.525129	260.600683	260.676220
5	209.766932	209.839931	209.912916	209.985886	210.058841	210.131782	210.204708	210.277619
6	176.187307	176.258649	176.329978	176.401296	176.472602	176.543896	176.615179	176.686451
7	152.207983	152.278230	152.348469	152.418698	152.488919	152.559130	152.629333	152.699527
8	134.228845	134.298351	134.367850	134.437344	134.506831	134.576311	134.645786	134.715254
9	120.249829	120.318828	120.387824	120.456816	120.525804	120.594788	120.663769	120.732746
10	109.070896	109.139554	109.208210	109.276865	109.345519	109.414171	109.482822	109.551471
11	99.928386	99.996821	100.065258	100.133695	100.202133	100.270573	100.339013	100.407454
12	92.313191	92.381494	92.449800	92.518109	92.586422	92.654737	92.723057	92.791379
13	85.872852	85.941091	86.009335	86.077585	86.145841	86.214102	86.282369	86.350641
14	80.355612	80.423841	80.492077	80.560322	80.628575	80.696835	80.765104	80.833380
15	75.576849	75.645111	75.713383	75.781666	75.849959	75.918262	75.986575	76.054898
16	71.398097	71.466427	71.534770	71.603126	71.671493	71.739874	71.808266	71.876671
17	67.713470	67.781897	67.850339	67.918796	67.987268	68.055754	68.124255	68.192770
18	64.440611	64.509159	64.577725	64.646307	64.714906	64.783522	64.852155	64.920805
19	61.514502	61.583192	61.651901	61.720628	61.789375	61.858142	61.926927	61.995731
20	58.883129	58.951917	59.020846	59.089737	59.158648	59.227581	59.296536	59.365511
21	56.504385	56.573406	56.642450	56.711517	56.780608	56.849723	56.918860	56.988021
22	54.343914	54.413024	54.482256	54.551513	54.620795	54.690103	54.759437	54.828796
23	52.372969	52.442371	52.511800	52.581258	52.650743	52.720255	52.789796	52.859363
24	50.568121	50.637728	50.707365	50.777031	50.846728	50.916455	50.986211	51.055997
25	48.909351	48.979171	49.049024	49.118908	49.188825	49.258774	49.328754	49.398767
26	47.379802	47.449843	47.519919	47.590028	47.660172	47.730350	47.800562	47.870807
27	45.965115	46.035383	46.105688	46.176029	46.246406	46.316819	46.387268	46.457754
28	44.652980	44.723481	44.794021	44.864598	44.935215	45.005869	45.076561	45.147292
29	43.432787	43.503526	43.574305	43.645125	43.715985	43.786885	43.857826	43.928806
30	42.295340	42.366321	42.437344	42.508410	42.579518	42.650669	42.721862	42.793097
31	41.232629	41.303856	41.375127	41.446443	41.517804	41.589208	41.660657	41.732151
32	40.237646	40.309122	40.380645	40.452214	40.523830	40.595492	40.667201	40.738956
33	39.304230	39.375959	39.447736	39.519563	39.591437	39.663360	39.735332	39.807351
34	38.426949	38.498933	38.570968	38.643053	38.715189	38.787376	38.859613	38.931900
35	37.600988	37.673230	37.745524	37.817872	37.890272	37.962724	38.035229	38.107786
36	36.822068	36.894570	36.967127	37.039738	37.112404	37.185125	37.257899	37.330728
37	36.086374	36.159138	36.231959	36.304836	36.377770	36.450760	36.523807	36.596910
38	35.390491	35.463519	35.536605	35.609750	35.682954	35.756216	35.829536	35.902914
39	34.731354	34.804647	34.878001	34.951415	35.024890	35.098425	35.172021	35.245676
40	34.106206	34.179766	34.253388	34.327073	34.400821	34.474630	34.548502	34.622436
41	33.512557	33.586385	33.660277	33.734234	33.808255	33.882341	33.956490	34.030703
42	32.948156	33.022252	33.096416	33.170646	33.244942	33.319304	33.393732	33.468225
43	32.410959	32.485328	32.559762	32.634265	32.708837	32.783477	32.858184	32.932959
44	31.899111	31.973749	32.048457	32.123235	32.198083	32.273002	32.347989	32.423046
45	31.410919	31.485828	31.560810	31.635864	31.710989	31.786186	31.861455	31.936794
46	30.944838	31.020021	31.095276	31.170605	31.246008	31.321485	31.397035	31.472658
47	30.499456	30.574910	30.650440	30.726046	30.801728	30.877484	30.953316	31.029223
48	30.073476	30.149203	30.225008	30.300891	30.376851	30.452888	30.529002	30.605193
50	29.275059	29.351333	29.427689	29.504126	29.580644	29.657243	29.733922	29.810682
52	28.541155	28.617977	28.694885	28.771877	28.848954	28.926115	29.003359	29.080688
54	27.864581	27.941952	28.019411	28.096958	28.174594	28.252316	28.330127	28.408024
56	27.239179	27.317098	27.395109	27.473211	27.551404	27.629689	27.708064	27.786530
58	26.659640	26.738107	26.816668	26.895325	26.974076	27.052921	27.131860	27.210893
60	26.121364	26.200377	26.279488	26.358697	26.438004	26.517409	26.596911	26.676510
62	25.620341	25.699899	25.779558	25.859319	25.939181	26.019144	26.099207	26.179369
64	25.153064	25.233166	25.313372	25.393683	25.474097	25.554616	25.635238	25.715963
66	24.716451	24.797094	24.877845	24.958704	25.039669	25.120742	25.201920	25.283205
68	24.307782	24.388964	24.470258	24.551662	24.633176	24.714799	24.796532	24.878374
70	23.924645	24.006365	24.088199	24.170146	24.252206	24.334378	24.416663	24.499059
72	23.564900	23.647155	23.729526	23.812013	23.894616	23.977334	24.060167	24.143115
74	23.226635	23.309422	23.392327	23.475352	23.558495	23.641756	23.725135	23.808630
76	22.908140	22.991455	23.074893	23.158452	23.242132	23.325933	23.409853	23.493894
78	22.607880	22.691721	22.775687	22.859777	22.943991	23.028328	23.112787	23.197369
80	22.324473	22.408837	22.493328	22.577946	22.662690	22.747560	22.832554	22.917673
82	22.056672	22.141556	22.226569	22.311711	22.396981	22.482379	22.567905	22.653557
84	21.803349	21.888748	21.974279	22.059942	22.145735	22.231658	22.317711	22.403893
86	21.563479	21.649390	21.735436	21.821615	21.907927	21.994372	22.080948	22.167656
88	21.336132	21.422552	21.509108	21.595800	21.682627	21.769589	21.856684	21.943913
90	21.120459	21.207383	21.294446	21.381647	21.468985	21.556460	21.644070	21.731815
92	20.915686	21.003111	21.090677	21.178382	21.266227	21.354210	21.442330	21.530588
96	20.536061	20.624475	20.713034	20.801736	20.890581	20.979568	21.068696	21.157965
100	20.192257	20.281644	20.371178	20.460860	20.550687	20.640660	20.730777	20.821037
104	19.880043	19.970384	20.060877	20.151519	20.242311	20.333250	20.424337	20.515570
108	19.595810	19.687088	19.778521	19.870105	19.961842	20.053729	20.145766	20.237952
112	19.336646	19.428663	19.521016	19.613524	19.706186	19.799001	19.891968	19.985086
116	19.099342	19.192439	19.285694	19.379106	19.472674	19.566397	19.660273	19.754303
120	18.882126	18.976104	19.070241	19.164537	19.258991	19.353602	19.448368	19.543287
140	18.032179	18.130266	18.228517	18.326932	18.425507	18.524243	18.623136	18.722187
160	17.461188	17.562889	17.664752	17.766774	17.868954	17.971291	18.073782	18.176425

NUMBER OF QUARTRLY WTHDRWLS	EFFECTIVE ANNUAL YIELD							
	7.00%	7.05%	7.10%	7.15%	7.20%	7.25%	7.30%	7.35%
1	1017.058525	1017.177319	1017.296072	1017.414784	1017.533453	1017.652081	1017.770668	1017.889213
2	512.829960	512.919558	513.009128	513.098670	513.188184	513.277670	513.367128	513.456558
3	344.769800	344.849889	344.929955	345.010000	345.090023	345.170024	345.250003	345.329960
4	260.751739	260.827241	260.902724	260.978189	261.053637	261.129067	261.204479	261.279873
5	210.350516	210.423399	210.496267	210.569120	210.641959	210.714784	210.787593	210.860389
6	176.757710	176.828958	176.900195	176.971420	177.042633	177.113835	177.185025	177.256203
7	152.769712	152.839888	152.910055	152.980213	153.050363	153.120503	153.190635	153.260757
8	134.784715	134.854171	134.923620	134.993063	135.062499	135.131930	135.201354	135.270771
9	120.801719	120.870688	120.939653	121.008614	121.077572	121.146526	121.215476	121.284422
10	109.620119	109.688766	109.757411	109.826055	109.894697	109.963338	110.031977	110.100615
11	100.475897	100.544340	100.612784	100.681229	100.749675	100.818122	100.886570	100.955019
12	92.859705	92.928034	92.996367	93.064702	93.133041	93.201383	93.269729	93.338077
13	86.418919	86.487203	86.555492	86.623787	86.692087	86.760393	86.828704	86.897021
14	80.901664	80.969956	81.038256	81.106564	81.174879	81.243203	81.311533	81.379872
15	76.123231	76.191575	76.259928	76.328292	76.396665	76.465049	76.533442	76.601846
16	71.945089	72.013518	72.081960	72.150414	72.218881	72.287360	72.355850	72.424353
17	68.261300	68.329845	68.398404	68.466978	68.535565	68.604168	68.672784	68.741415
18	64.989472	65.058155	65.126855	65.195571	65.264305	65.333054	65.401821	65.470603
19	62.064554	62.133396	62.202256	62.271136	62.340034	62.408951	62.477887	62.546841
20	59.434507	59.503525	59.572563	59.641623	59.710703	59.779804	59.848926	59.918069
21	57.057205	57.126413	57.195643	57.264897	57.334174	57.403474	57.472797	57.542142
22	54.898180	54.967590	55.037025	55.106486	55.175971	55.245482	55.315018	55.384579
23	52.928959	52.998582	53.068232	53.137910	53.207615	53.277347	53.347107	53.416893
24	51.125813	51.195658	51.265533	51.335437	51.405371	51.475334	51.545326	51.615348
25	49.468811	49.538886	49.608994	49.679133	49.749303	49.819505	49.889738	49.960003
26	47.941087	48.011400	48.081747	48.152128	48.222542	48.292990	48.363471	48.433986
27	46.528275	46.598832	46.669425	46.740054	46.810718	46.881418	46.952153	47.022924
28	45.218061	45.288867	45.359711	45.430593	45.501513	45.572471	45.643466	45.714498
29	43.999827	44.070888	44.141988	44.213129	44.284309	44.355529	44.426788	44.498087
30	42.864374	42.935693	43.007054	43.078457	43.149902	43.221388	43.292916	43.364486
31	41.803688	41.875270	41.946895	42.018564	42.090278	42.162034	42.233835	42.305678
32	40.810757	40.882605	40.954498	41.026437	41.098421	41.170452	41.242528	41.314649
33	39.879419	39.951535	40.023699	40.095911	40.168170	40.240477	40.312832	40.385234
34	39.004237	39.076624	39.149062	39.221549	39.294086	39.366672	39.439308	39.511993
35	38.180395	38.253056	38.325769	38.398534	38.471350	38.544218	38.617138	38.690108
36	37.403611	37.476548	37.549539	37.622584	37.695682	37.768834	37.842039	37.915297
37	36.670069	36.743283	36.816554	36.889880	36.963262	37.036699	37.110192	37.183739
38	35.976351	36.049845	36.123397	36.197006	36.270673	36.344397	36.418179	36.492018
39	35.319391	35.393166	35.467001	35.540895	35.614849	35.688862	35.762933	35.837064
40	34.696431	34.770488	34.844607	34.918787	34.993029	35.067331	35.141695	35.216119
41	34.104980	34.179321	34.253724	34.328192	34.402722	34.477315	34.551971	34.626690
42	33.542785	33.617409	33.692099	33.766855	33.841675	33.916560	33.991509	34.066523
43	33.007802	33.082711	33.157688	33.232732	33.307843	33.383020	33.458264	33.533574
44	32.498173	32.573368	32.648633	32.723966	32.799368	32.874839	32.950377	33.025984
45	32.012205	32.087687	32.163240	32.238864	32.314557	32.390321	32.466155	32.542060
46	31.548354	31.624123	31.699964	31.775878	31.851864	31.927922	32.004052	32.080254
47	31.105204	31.181261	31.257391	31.333596	31.409874	31.486227	31.562653	31.639152
48	30.681460	30.757804	30.834224	30.910720	30.987291	31.063938	31.140660	31.217458
50	29.887521	29.964441	30.041440	30.118518	30.195675	30.272912	30.350227	30.427621
52	29.158100	29.235595	29.313173	29.390835	29.468578	29.546404	29.624313	29.702303
54	28.486008	28.564079	28.642237	28.720480	28.798810	28.877225	28.955725	29.034311
56	27.865086	27.943731	28.022467	28.101292	28.180206	28.259209	28.338300	28.417480
58	27.290019	27.369239	27.448551	27.527956	27.607454	27.687043	27.766724	27.846497
60	26.756205	26.835997	26.915884	26.995868	27.075947	27.156121	27.236389	27.316752
62	26.259632	26.339994	26.420455	26.501015	26.581673	26.662429	26.743283	26.824235
64	25.796790	25.877720	25.958753	26.039886	26.121121	26.202457	26.283894	26.365431
66	25.364595	25.446091	25.527692	25.609397	25.691206	25.773119	25.855135	25.937255
68	24.960325	25.042383	25.124549	25.206823	25.289203	25.371690	25.454283	25.536982
70	24.581566	24.664185	24.746913	24.829752	24.912700	24.995758	25.078925	25.162199
72	24.226176	24.309351	24.392640	24.476040	24.559553	24.643178	24.726914	24.810761
74	23.892243	23.975971	24.059815	24.143774	24.227848	24.312036	24.396338	24.480753
76	23.578053	23.662331	23.746727	23.831241	23.915872	24.000620	24.085483	24.170463
78	23.282072	23.366896	23.451840	23.536905	23.622089	23.707392	23.792813	23.878353
80	23.002915	23.088282	23.173770	23.259382	23.345115	23.430969	23.516944	23.603039
82	22.739336	22.825240	22.911269	22.997423	23.083700	23.170101	23.256625	23.343271
84	22.490203	22.576641	22.663207	22.749898	22.836716	22.923659	23.010727	23.097919
86	22.254493	22.341461	22.428558	22.515783	22.603136	22.690617	22.778225	22.865958
88	22.031273	22.118766	22.206390	22.294145	22.382029	22.470042	22.558184	22.646454
90	21.819695	21.907708	21.995855	22.084133	22.172544	22.261085	22.349757	22.438558
92	21.618982	21.707511	21.796175	21.884974	21.973905	22.062970	22.152166	22.241493
96	21.247373	21.336920	21.426605	21.516427	21.606386	21.696481	21.786711	21.877075
100	20.911441	21.001986	21.092672	21.183499	21.274464	21.365569	21.456811	21.548190
104	20.606949	20.698472	20.790139	20.881948	20.973899	21.065992	21.158224	21.250595
108	20.330285	20.422766	20.515392	20.608163	20.701078	20.794136	20.887336	20.980677
112	20.078354	20.171770	20.265335	20.359046	20.452903	20.546904	20.641049	20.735337
116	19.848484	19.942815	20.037296	20.131925	20.226701	20.321623	20.416690	20.511901
120	19.638360	19.733584	19.828959	19.924484	20.020156	20.115976	20.211941	20.308052
140	18.821392	18.920751	19.020262	19.119923	19.219734	19.319692	19.419796	19.520045
160	18.279218	18.382160	18.485249	18.588483	18.691860	18.795378	18.899036	19.002832

QUARTERLY WITHDRAWALS PER $1000

EFFECTIVE ANNUAL YIELD

NUMBER OF QUARTRLY WTHDRWLS	7.40%	7.45%	7.50%	7.55%	7.60%	7.65%	7.70%	7.75%
1	1018.007717	1018.126180	1018.244601	1018.362981	1018.481320	1018.599617	1018.717873	1018.836088
2	513.545961	513.635336	513.724683	513.814002	513.903294	513.992558	514.081794	514.171002
3	345.409895	345.489809	345.569700	345.649570	345.729418	345.809244	345.889049	345.968832
4	261.355250	261.430608	261.505949	261.581272	261.656578	261.731865	261.807135	261.882387
5	210.933170	211.005936	211.078688	211.151426	211.224149	211.296857	211.369551	211.442231
6	177.327370	177.398526	177.469670	177.540802	177.611923	177.683032	177.754129	177.825215
7	153.330871	153.400976	153.471072	153.541160	153.611238	153.681307	153.751368	153.821420
8	135.340182	135.409587	135.478986	135.548378	135.617764	135.687143	135.756516	135.825883
9	121.353364	121.422302	121.491236	121.560167	121.629093	121.698016	121.766935	121.835850
10	110.169251	110.237886	110.306520	110.375152	110.443782	110.512411	110.581039	110.649665
11	101.023468	101.091919	101.160370	101.228822	101.297275	101.365729	101.434183	101.502639
12	93.406429	93.474784	93.543142	93.611503	93.679867	93.748234	93.816605	93.884978
13	86.965343	87.033671	87.102004	87.170342	87.238686	87.307035	87.375390	87.443749
14	81.448218	81.516572	81.584934	81.653303	81.721680	81.790065	81.858457	81.926856
15	76.670259	76.738682	76.807115	76.875558	76.944011	77.012473	77.080946	77.149428
16	72.492868	72.561395	72.629935	72.698486	72.767049	72.835624	72.904211	72.972810
17	68.810061	68.878720	68.947394	69.016082	69.084784	69.153501	69.222231	69.290975
18	65.539403	65.608218	65.677050	65.745899	65.814763	65.883645	65.952542	66.021455
19	62.615815	62.684806	62.753816	62.822845	62.891892	62.960958	63.030042	63.099144
20	59.987233	60.056417	60.125622	60.194848	60.264094	60.333361	60.402649	60.471956
21	57.611511	57.680902	57.750317	57.819754	57.889213	57.958696	58.028201	58.097728
22	55.454165	55.523775	55.593411	55.663072	55.732757	55.802467	55.872202	55.941961
23	53.486707	53.556548	53.626415	53.696310	53.766232	53.836180	53.906155	53.976157
24	51.685399	51.755478	51.825587	51.895725	51.965892	52.036088	52.106313	52.176566
25	50.030299	50.100626	50.170984	50.241373	50.311793	50.382244	50.452726	50.523239
26	48.504534	48.575115	48.645729	48.716377	48.787057	48.857771	48.928517	48.999296
27	47.093730	47.164572	47.235448	47.306360	47.377307	47.448289	47.519306	47.590357
28	45.785568	45.856675	45.927819	45.999001	46.070219	46.141475	46.212767	46.284097
29	44.569425	44.640802	44.712219	44.783675	44.855170	44.926704	44.998277	45.069889
30	43.436097	43.507749	43.579442	43.651177	43.722952	43.794769	43.866627	43.938525
31	42.377566	42.449496	42.521470	42.593487	42.665547	42.737650	42.809795	42.881984
32	41.386816	41.459028	41.531286	41.603588	41.675936	41.748328	41.820765	41.893247
33	40.457684	40.530180	40.602724	40.675315	40.747953	40.820638	40.893369	40.966147
34	39.584728	39.657512	39.730344	39.803226	39.876157	39.949137	40.022165	40.095241
35	38.763130	38.836204	38.909328	38.982503	39.055729	39.129005	39.202332	39.275710
36	37.988609	38.061973	38.135391	38.208861	38.282384	38.355959	38.429587	38.503267
37	37.257342	37.331000	37.404712	37.478479	37.552301	37.626177	37.700108	37.774092
38	36.565913	36.639865	36.713874	36.787940	36.862062	36.936240	37.010475	37.084765
39	35.911254	35.985502	36.059809	36.134174	36.208598	36.283080	36.357619	36.432217
40	35.290640	35.365149	35.439755	35.514421	35.589147	35.663934	35.738780	35.813685
41	34.701471	34.776315	34.851221	34.926188	35.001218	35.076310	35.151463	35.226678
42	34.141602	34.216744	34.291951	34.367221	34.442556	34.517953	34.593415	34.668939
43	33.608951	33.684343	33.759901	33.835475	33.911114	33.986819	34.062589	34.138424
44	33.101659	33.177402	33.253212	33.329089	33.405034	33.481046	33.557125	33.151787
45	32.618033	32.694077	32.770189	32.846371	32.922622	32.998942	33.075330	32.692425
46	32.156527	32.232871	32.309287	32.385773	32.462331	32.538958	32.615657	32.253768
47	31.715725	31.792311	31.869089	31.945881	32.022744	32.099680	32.176688	31.834520
48	31.294330	31.371278	31.448300	31.525396	31.602566	31.679810	31.757128	31.834520
50	30.505094	30.582644	30.660272	30.737978	30.815762	30.893623	30.971561	31.049575
52	29.780375	29.858528	29.936762	30.015078	30.093474	30.171951	30.250508	30.329145
54	29.112981	29.191736	29.270576	29.349500	29.428508	29.507599	29.586773	29.666032
56	28.496748	28.576104	28.655548	28.735078	28.814696	28.894400	28.974191	29.054068
58	27.926360	28.006315	28.086360	28.166496	28.246721	28.327037	28.407441	28.487935
60	27.397210	27.477761	27.558406	27.639144	27.719975	27.800899	27.881915	27.963023
62	26.905283	26.986428	27.067670	27.149008	27.230442	27.311971	27.393595	27.475314
64	26.447068	26.528805	26.610640	26.692575	26.774608	26.856740	26.938969	27.021296
66	26.019477	26.101802	26.184229	26.266757	26.349386	26.432116	26.514947	26.597878
68	25.619786	25.702696	25.785710	25.868828	25.952050	26.035375	26.118804	26.202335
70	25.245582	25.329073	25.412670	25.496374	25.580185	25.664101	25.748123	25.832250
72	24.894719	24.978786	25.062963	25.147249	25.231644	25.316148	25.400759	25.485477
74	24.565281	24.649922	24.734675	24.819539	24.904514	24.989599	25.074795	25.160101
76	24.255558	24.340767	24.426091	24.511528	24.597079	24.682742	24.768518	24.854406
78	23.964010	24.049783	24.135674	24.221680	24.307801	24.394038	24.480388	24.566853
80	23.689253	23.775587	23.862039	23.948609	24.035296	24.122101	24.209021	24.296058
82	23.430039	23.516927	23.603936	23.691065	23.778314	23.865681	23.953166	24.040770
84	23.185235	23.272674	23.360235	23.447918	23.535722	23.623647	23.711692	23.799856
86	22.953817	23.041801	23.129909	23.218141	23.306495	23.394972	23.483571	23.572291
88	22.734852	22.823375	22.912025	23.000800	23.089700	23.178724	23.267871	23.357141
90	22.527489	22.616547	22.705733	22.795046	22.884485	22.974050	23.063740	23.153554
92	22.330952	22.420539	22.510256	22.600102	22.690075	22.780175	22.870402	22.960754
96	21.967573	22.058203	22.148965	22.239858	22.330882	22.422035	22.513317	22.604728
100	21.639704	21.731354	21.823139	21.915057	22.007107	22.099290	22.191604	22.284047
104	21.343105	21.435803	21.528535	21.621454	21.714507	21.807695	21.901015	21.994467
108	21.074159	21.167779	21.261537	21.355433	21.449465	21.543632	21.637933	21.732368
112	20.829766	20.924336	21.019045	21.113893	21.208878	21.304000	21.399257	21.494649
116	20.607254	20.702749	20.798385	20.894160	20.990074	21.086125	21.182312	21.278634
120	20.404305	20.500702	20.597239	20.693916	20.790733	20.887687	20.984778	21.082004
140	19.620437	19.720970	19.821644	19.922456	20.023405	20.124490	20.225709	20.327061
160	19.106763	19.210829	19.315027	19.419356	19.523814	19.628399	19.733110	19.837945

198

QUARTERLY WITHDRAWALS PER $1000

NUMBER OF QUARTRLY WTHDRWLS	EFFECTIVE ANNUAL YIELD							
	7.80%	7.85%	7.90%	7.95%	8.00%	8.05%	8.10%	8.15%
1	1018.954262	1019.072395	1019.190487	1019.308537	1019.426547	1019.544516	1019.662443	1019.780330
2	514.260183	514.349336	514.438462	514.527560	514.616630	514.705673	514.794689	514.883676
3	346.048593	346.128332	346.208050	346.287746	346.367420	346.447073	346.526704	346.606313
4	261.957622	262.032839	262.108038	262.183219	262.258383	262.333529	262.408658	262.483769
5	211.514896	211.587547	211.660183	211.732805	211.805413	211.878006	211.950585	212.023149
6	177.896290	177.967353	178.038404	178.109444	178.180472	178.251489	178.322494	178.393488
7	153.891462	153.961496	154.031521	154.101538	154.171545	154.241543	154.311533	154.381513
8	135.895244	135.964598	136.033946	136.103287	136.172622	136.241951	136.311273	136.380589
9	121.904761	121.973668	122.042571	122.111470	122.180365	122.249257	122.318144	122.387027
10	110.718289	110.786912	110.855533	110.924153	110.992771	111.061387	111.130002	111.198615
11	101.571095	101.639551	101.708009	101.776467	101.844926	101.913386	101.981846	102.050308
12	93.953355	94.021734	94.090117	94.158502	94.226891	94.295282	94.363677	94.432074
13	87.512114	87.580485	87.648860	87.717241	87.785627	87.854018	87.922415	87.990816
14	81.995263	82.063678	82.132100	82.200529	82.268966	82.337410	82.405862	82.474321
15	77.217919	77.286421	77.354932	77.423452	77.491983	77.560523	77.629072	77.697631
16	73.041421	73.110044	73.178679	73.247325	73.315983	73.384653	73.453335	73.522028
17	69.359734	69.428507	69.497293	69.566094	69.634908	69.703736	69.772578	69.841434
18	66.090385	66.159331	66.228293	66.297271	66.366265	66.435275	66.504301	66.573343
19	63.168265	63.237404	63.306561	63.375736	63.444929	63.514141	63.583371	63.652618
20	60.541285	60.610633	60.680002	60.749392	60.818801	60.888230	60.957680	61.027150
21	58.167278	58.236851	58.306446	58.376063	58.445703	58.515364	58.585049	58.654755
22	56.011745	56.081554	56.151387	56.221244	56.291126	56.361033	56.430963	56.500918
23	54.046185	54.116241	54.186322	54.256430	54.326565	54.396726	54.466913	54.537127
24	52.246848	52.317159	52.387498	52.457866	52.528262	52.598687	52.669140	52.739622
25	50.593783	50.664357	50.734962	50.805598	50.876264	50.946960	51.017687	51.088444
26	49.070108	49.140953	49.211830	49.282740	49.353683	49.424658	49.495665	49.566704
27	47.661444	47.732565	47.803721	47.874911	47.946136	48.017395	48.088689	48.160017
28	46.355463	46.426866	46.498305	46.569781	46.641294	46.712843	46.784428	46.856050
29	45.141540	45.213229	45.284957	45.356723	45.428528	45.500371	45.572253	45.644172
30	44.010464	44.082444	44.154464	44.226525	44.298626	44.370767	44.442949	44.515171
31	42.954215	43.026489	43.098805	43.171164	43.243565	43.316008	43.388493	43.461021
32	41.965774	42.038345	42.110960	42.183620	42.256324	42.329072	42.401864	42.474700
33	41.038972	41.111843	41.184760	41.257724	41.330733	41.403789	41.476891	41.550039
34	40.168367	40.241540	40.314762	40.388032	40.461350	40.534715	40.608129	40.681590
35	39.349138	39.422616	39.496144	39.569722	39.643350	39.717028	39.790756	39.864533
36	38.577000	38.650785	38.724621	38.798507	38.872450	38.946442	39.020485	39.094580
37	37.848131	37.922224	37.996370	38.070571	38.144824	38.219132	38.293492	38.367906
38	37.159112	37.233514	37.307972	37.382485	37.457054	37.531678	37.606357	37.681091
39	36.506872	36.581585	36.656356	36.731183	36.806068	36.881010	36.956009	37.031065
40	35.888651	35.963675	36.038759	36.113902	36.189104	36.264365	36.339685	36.415063
41	35.301954	35.377291	35.452690	35.528149	35.603669	35.679249	35.754890	35.830592
42	34.744527	34.820177	34.895891	34.971667	35.047505	35.123406	35.199369	35.275394
43	34.214323	34.290288	34.366316	34.442410	34.518568	34.594789	34.671075	34.747424
44	33.709483	33.785762	33.862107	33.938518	34.014995	34.091538	34.168147	34.244820
45	33.228312	33.304906	33.381567	33.458296	33.535093	33.611957	33.688889	33.765888
46	32.769263	32.846172	32.923149	33.000197	33.077314	33.154499	33.231754	33.309077
47	32.330920	32.408143	32.485438	32.562803	32.640240	32.717747	32.795325	32.872974
48	31.911985	31.989523	32.067134	32.144818	32.222575	32.300403	32.378304	32.456277
50	31.127667	31.205834	31.284078	31.362398	31.440794	31.519265	31.597812	31.676434
52	30.407861	30.486658	30.565531	30.644488	30.723522	30.802635	30.881826	30.961095
54	29.745373	29.824796	29.904302	29.983890	30.063561	30.143312	30.223146	30.303060
56	29.134031	29.214080	29.294217	29.374433	29.454738	29.535126	29.615599	29.696157
58	28.568518	28.649189	28.729949	28.810797	28.891732	28.972755	29.053865	29.135062
60	28.044222	28.125514	28.206896	28.288369	28.369933	28.451587	28.533331	28.615164
62	27.557128	27.639036	27.721038	27.803133	27.885321	27.967603	28.049976	28.132442
64	27.103720	27.186241	27.268858	27.351572	27.434381	27.517286	27.600286	27.683380
66	26.680909	26.764039	26.847268	26.930596	27.014022	27.097546	27.181168	27.264886
68	26.285968	26.369703	26.453540	26.537478	26.621516	26.705655	26.789894	26.874232
70	25.916482	26.000810	26.085258	26.169801	26.254447	26.339196	26.424047	26.508999
72	25.570303	25.655235	25.740273	25.825417	25.910666	25.996020	26.081478	26.167040
74	25.245515	25.331039	25.416670	25.502410	25.588256	25.674210	25.760270	25.846436
76	24.940404	25.026514	25.112734	25.199064	25.285503	25.372051	25.458707	25.545472
78	24.653431	24.740122	24.826925	24.913840	25.000866	25.088003	25.175250	25.262607
80	24.383210	24.470476	24.557857	24.645351	24.732959	24.820679	24.908511	24.996455
82	24.128490	24.216327	24.304279	24.392348	24.480531	24.568828	24.657239	24.745763
84	23.888139	23.976541	24.065060	24.153696	24.242449	24.331317	24.420301	24.509399
86	23.661132	23.750092	23.839171	23.928369	24.017686	24.107119	24.196669	24.286336
88	23.446532	23.536046	23.625680	23.715434	23.805307	23.895300	23.985410	24.075638
90	23.243491	23.333551	23.423734	23.514037	23.604462	23.695007	23.785671	23.876454
92	23.051230	23.141831	23.232556	23.323403	23.414372	23.505463	23.596674	23.688005
96	22.696265	22.787929	22.879719	22.971634	23.063673	23.155835	23.248121	23.340528
100	22.376620	22.469322	22.562151	22.655108	22.748190	22.841398	22.934730	23.028185
104	22.088050	22.181763	22.275609	22.369577	22.463675	22.557901	22.652252	22.746727
108	21.826935	21.921634	22.016463	22.111422	22.206509	22.301724	22.397066	22.492534
112	21.590174	21.685831	21.781620	21.877539	21.973587	22.069764	22.166068	22.262499
116	21.375090	21.471679	21.568400	21.665252	21.762233	21.859344	21.956582	22.053946
120	21.179365	21.276859	21.374485	21.472242	21.570129	21.668144	21.766287	21.864557
140	20.428545	20.530158	20.631900	20.733769	20.835764	20.937883	21.040126	21.142489
160	19.942901	20.047979	20.153175	20.258488	20.363917	20.469460	20.575115	20.680881

QUARTERLY WITHDRAWALS PER $1000

EFFECTIVE ANNUAL YIELD

NUMBER OF QUARTERLY WTHDRWLS	8.20%	8.25%	8.30%	8.35%	8.40%	8.45%	8.50%	8.55%
1	1019.898176	1020.015981	1020.133746	1020.251469	1020.369152	1020.486794	1020.604396	1020.721957
2	514.972637	515.061570	515.150475	515.239353	515.328204	515.417027	515.505823	515.594592
3	346.685901	346.765467	346.845011	346.924535	347.004036	347.083516	347.162974	347.242411
4	262.558862	262.633938	262.708996	262.784037	262.859059	262.934065	263.009053	263.084023
5	212.095699	212.168235	212.240756	212.313263	212.385756	212.458234	212.530698	212.603147
6	178.464470	178.535441	178.606400	178.677348	178.748284	178.819209	178.890122	178.961024
7	154.451485	154.521448	154.591402	154.661347	154.731284	154.801211	154.871130	154.941039
8	136.449899	136.519202	136.588499	136.657789	136.727073	136.796351	136.865622	136.934887
9	122.455907	122.524782	122.593654	122.662521	122.731385	122.800244	122.869100	122.937951
10	111.267227	111.335837	111.404445	111.473052	111.541657	111.610260	111.678862	111.747462
11	102.118769	102.187232	102.255695	102.324159	102.392623	102.461088	102.529554	102.598020
12	94.500474	94.568878	94.637284	94.705693	94.774105	94.842520	94.910937	94.979358
13	88.059223	88.127635	88.196052	88.264474	88.332901	88.401334	88.469771	88.538213
14	82.542787	82.611261	82.679742	82.748230	82.816726	82.885229	82.953739	83.022256
15	77.766199	77.834777	77.903365	77.971962	78.040568	78.109184	78.177809	78.246443
16	73.590733	73.659450	73.728178	73.796918	73.865670	73.934432	74.003207	74.071993
17	69.910304	69.979188	70.048085	70.116996	70.185921	70.254859	70.323811	70.392776
18	66.642401	66.711475	66.780565	66.849670	66.918791	66.987928	67.057081	67.126249
19	63.721884	63.791168	63.860469	63.929789	63.999126	64.068481	64.137854	64.207245
20	61.096640	61.166150	61.235681	61.305231	61.374801	61.444390	61.514000	61.583629
21	58.724483	58.794234	58.864007	58.933801	59.003618	59.073456	59.143317	59.213199
22	56.570897	56.640900	56.710927	56.780978	56.851054	56.921153	56.991276	57.061423
23	54.607367	54.677633	54.747925	54.818243	54.888587	54.958958	55.029354	55.099776
24	52.810132	52.880669	52.951236	53.021830	53.092452	53.163102	53.233780	53.304486
25	51.159231	51.230049	51.300896	51.371774	51.442682	51.513620	51.584587	51.655585
26	49.637776	49.708880	49.780016	49.851184	49.922384	49.993616	50.064880	50.136176
27	48.231379	48.302775	48.374206	48.445670	48.517168	48.588700	48.660266	48.731866
28	46.927707	46.999401	47.071131	47.142897	47.214698	47.286536	47.358409	47.430318
29	45.716130	45.788126	45.860160	45.932231	46.004341	46.076488	46.148673	46.220895
30	44.587433	44.659735	44.732076	44.804458	44.876879	44.949340	45.021840	45.094380
31	43.533590	43.606202	43.678855	43.751549	43.824286	43.897064	43.969883	44.042743
32	42.547580	42.620504	42.693472	42.766483	42.839537	42.912635	42.985776	43.058961
33	41.623232	41.696471	41.769755	41.843085	41.916460	41.989881	42.063347	42.136857
34	40.755099	40.828566	40.902260	40.975911	41.049609	41.123354	41.197147	41.270986
35	39.938360	40.012236	40.086161	40.160135	40.234158	40.308230	40.382351	40.456521
36	39.168726	39.242293	39.317171	39.391470	39.465820	39.540220	39.614672	39.689173
37	38.442373	38.516893	38.591466	38.666091	38.740769	38.815499	38.890282	38.965117
38	37.755880	37.830724	37.905623	37.980576	38.055583	38.130645	38.205760	38.280930
39	37.106177	37.181346	37.256571	37.331853	37.407191	37.482584	37.558034	37.633539
40	36.490500	36.565994	36.641547	36.717158	36.792827	36.868553	36.944337	37.020179
41	35.906353	35.982175	36.058056	36.133997	36.209997	36.286057	36.362177	36.438355
42	35.351481	35.427630	35.503840	35.580112	35.656445	35.732839	35.809294	35.885809
43	34.823837	34.900313	34.976853	35.053455	35.130121	35.206849	35.283640	35.360493
44	34.321560	34.398364	34.475233	34.552167	34.629165	34.706228	34.783355	34.860546
45	33.842953	33.920085	33.997284	34.074549	34.151881	34.229278	34.306741	34.384270
46	33.386469	33.463930	33.541458	33.619053	33.696719	33.774451	33.852251	33.930117
47	32.950692	33.028480	33.106339	33.184266	33.262264	33.340330	33.418465	33.496670
48	32.534322	32.612439	32.690626	32.768885	32.847215	32.925616	33.004087	33.082628
50	31.755130	31.833902	31.912748	31.991668	32.070662	32.149730	32.228871	32.308086
52	31.040442	31.119867	31.199369	31.278948	31.358605	31.438338	31.518148	31.598035
54	30.383055	30.463131	30.543288	30.623524	30.703841	30.784237	30.864713	30.945268
56	29.776798	29.857522	29.938330	30.019221	30.100194	30.181250	30.262388	30.343609
58	29.216346	29.297716	29.379172	29.460713	29.542340	29.624053	29.705850	29.787731
60	28.697087	28.779098	28.861199	28.943387	29.025664	29.108029	29.190481	29.273020
62	28.215000	28.297650	28.380391	28.463222	28.546144	28.629157	28.712259	28.795451
64	27.766569	27.849852	27.933229	28.016699	28.100262	28.183918	28.267666	28.351506
66	27.348702	27.432614	27.516622	27.600726	27.684925	27.769219	27.853607	27.938090
68	26.958669	27.043205	27.127839	27.212572	27.297402	27.382329	27.467352	27.552473
70	26.594053	26.679208	26.764464	26.849819	26.935275	27.020829	27.106482	27.192234
72	26.252705	26.338474	26.424345	26.510318	26.596393	26.682569	26.768846	26.855224
74	25.932707	26.019084	26.105565	26.192150	26.278839	26.365631	26.452525	26.539522
76	25.632344	25.719322	25.806407	25.893598	25.980895	26.068296	26.155802	26.243412
78	25.350073	25.437648	25.525331	25.613122	25.701020	25.789024	25.877135	25.965352
80	25.084509	25.172674	25.260949	25.349333	25.437826	25.526427	25.615136	25.703952
82	24.834400	24.923149	25.012009	25.100980	25.190061	25.279252	25.368553	25.457962
84	24.598612	24.687938	24.777377	24.866929	24.956592	25.046366	25.136251	25.226246
86	24.376118	24.466015	24.556026	24.646151	24.736389	24.826739	24.917202	25.007775
88	24.165983	24.256444	24.347020	24.437712	24.528518	24.619437	24.710470	24.801615
90	23.967355	24.058373	24.149508	24.240759	24.332126	24.423607	24.515203	24.606912
92	23.779456	23.871025	23.962711	24.054515	24.146435	24.238471	24.330622	24.422888
96	23.433056	23.525705	23.618474	23.711361	23.804367	23.897490	23.990729	24.084085
100	23.121764	23.215464	23.309285	23.403227	23.497289	23.591469	23.685767	23.780182
104	22.841207	22.936050	23.030896	23.125862	23.220949	23.316156	23.411482	23.506925
108	22.588126	22.683842	22.779682	22.875643	22.971726	23.067928	23.164251	23.260691
112	22.359055	22.455735	22.552538	22.649465	22.746512	22.843680	22.940967	23.038373
116	22.151436	22.249051	22.346789	22.444649	22.542631	22.640733	22.738954	22.837294
120	21.962922	22.061471	22.160114	22.258878	22.357763	22.456769	22.555892	22.655135
140	21.244973	21.347576	21.450296	21.553132	21.656082	21.759147	21.862323	21.965610
160	20.786756	20.892738	20.998827	21.105020	21.211316	21.317713	21.424210	21.530805

200

QUARTERLY WITHDRAWALS PER $1000

NUMBER OF QUARTERLY WTHDRWLS	EFFECTIVE ANNUAL YIELD							
	8.60%	8.65%	8.70%	8.75%	8.80%	8.85%	8.90%	8.95%
1	1020.839477	1020.956957	1021.074396	1021.191794	1021.309152	1021.426470	1021.543747	1021.660984
2	515.683333	515.772047	515.860734	515.949394	516.038026	516.126631	516.215209	516.303760
3	347.321827	347.401221	347.480593	347.559944	347.639274	347.718582	347.797869	347.877135
4	263.158976	263.233911	263.308829	263.383729	263.458612	263.533477	263.608325	263.683155
5	212.675583	212.748004	212.820410	212.892803	212.965181	213.037544	213.109894	213.182229
6	179.031914	179.102793	179.173660	179.244516	179.315360	179.386193	179.457014	179.527824
7	155.010940	155.080832	155.150715	155.220589	155.290455	155.360311	155.430159	155.499997
8	137.004146	137.073088	137.142643	137.211883	137.281116	137.350342	137.419562	137.488776
9	123.006799	123.075642	123.144482	123.213318	123.282149	123.350976	123.419800	123.488619
10	111.816061	111.884657	111.953252	112.021846	112.090437	112.159027	112.227615	112.296201
11	102.666487	102.734954	102.803422	102.871890	102.940359	103.008829	103.077299	103.145770
12	95.047781	95.116207	95.184636	95.253067	95.321502	95.389939	95.458378	95.526821
13	88.606660	88.675113	88.743570	88.812032	88.880499	88.948971	89.017448	89.085930
14	83.090780	83.159312	83.227851	83.296396	83.364949	83.433509	83.502076	83.570650
15	78.315087	78.383740	78.452402	78.521074	78.589755	78.658445	78.727144	78.795852
16	74.140790	74.209599	74.278419	74.347250	74.416093	74.484947	74.553813	74.622689
17	70.461755	70.530748	70.599754	70.668773	70.737806	70.806852	70.875912	70.944985
18	67.195433	67.264633	67.333848	67.403078	67.472324	67.541586	67.610863	67.680155
19	64.276653	64.346079	64.415523	64.484984	64.554463	64.623959	64.693473	64.763004
20	61.653279	61.722948	61.792636	61.862344	61.932072	62.001819	62.071586	62.141372
21	59.283103	59.353029	59.422976	59.492945	59.562936	59.632948	59.702982	59.773037
22	57.131594	57.201788	57.272006	57.342248	57.412514	57.482803	57.553115	57.623451
23	55.170223	55.240697	55.311196	55.381721	55.452271	55.522847	55.593449	55.664076
24	53.375219	53.445981	53.516770	53.587586	53.658431	53.729302	53.800201	53.871128
25	51.726612	51.797669	51.868755	51.939871	52.011017	52.082192	52.153396	52.224630
26	50.207503	50.278862	50.350253	50.421675	50.493128	50.564613	50.636130	50.707677
27	48.803499	48.875166	48.946867	49.018601	49.090368	49.162168	49.234002	49.305869
28	47.502262	47.574242	47.646257	47.718308	47.790394	47.862515	47.934671	48.006863
29	46.293155	46.365452	46.437787	46.510159	46.582569	46.655014	46.727497	46.800017
30	45.166959	45.239578	45.312235	45.384932	45.457668	45.530442	45.603256	45.676108
31	44.115645	44.188588	44.261572	44.334597	44.407663	44.480770	44.553917	44.627105
32	43.132188	43.205458	43.278772	43.352128	43.425527	43.498968	43.572452	43.645979
33	42.210413	42.284013	42.357658	42.431348	42.505082	42.578861	42.652684	42.726551
34	41.344872	41.418804	41.492783	41.566809	41.640881	41.714999	41.789163	41.863373
35	40.530739	40.605005	40.679320	40.753683	40.828095	40.902554	40.977061	41.051616
36	39.763725	39.838327	39.912980	39.987682	40.062434	40.137236	40.212087	40.286988
37	39.040004	39.114943	39.189934	39.264977	39.340071	39.415217	39.490414	39.565663
38	38.356153	38.431430	38.506760	38.582145	38.657583	38.733074	38.808617	38.884214
39	37.709099	37.784716	37.860387	37.936114	38.011895	38.087732	38.163623	38.239569
40	37.096078	37.172033	37.248046	37.324117	37.400247	37.476425	37.552665	37.628960
41	36.514592	36.590888	36.667243	36.743657	36.820128	36.896658	36.973246	37.049892
42	35.962385	36.039022	36.115719	36.192477	36.269294	36.346171	36.423108	36.500104
43	35.437409	35.514387	35.591426	35.668528	35.745691	35.822915	35.900201	35.977548
44	34.937801	35.015120	35.092502	35.169948	35.247456	35.325028	35.402663	35.480361
45	34.461865	34.539524	34.617249	34.695039	34.772894	34.850813	34.928797	35.006845
46	34.008051	34.086052	34.164119	34.242253	34.320453	34.398720	34.477052	34.555450
47	33.574943	33.653284	33.731694	33.810171	33.888717	33.967330	34.046011	34.124759
48	33.161240	33.239922	33.318673	33.397495	33.476385	33.555345	33.634373	33.713471
50	32.387375	32.466736	32.546170	32.625676	32.705255	32.784906	32.864629	32.944423
52	31.677997	31.758035	31.838149	31.918338	31.998603	32.078942	32.159356	32.239845
54	31.025901	31.106614	31.187405	31.268274	31.349221	31.430245	31.511347	31.592526
56	30.424910	30.506293	30.587758	30.669303	30.750929	30.832635	30.914421	30.996287
58	29.869697	29.951747	30.033881	30.116098	30.198399	30.280782	30.363247	30.445795
60	29.355646	29.438358	29.521157	29.604041	29.687011	29.770067	29.853207	29.936433
62	28.878732	28.962103	29.045561	29.129109	29.212744	29.296466	29.380276	29.464173
64	28.435438	28.519461	28.603574	28.687779	28.772073	28.856458	28.940932	29.025495
66	28.022667	28.107337	28.192100	28.276956	28.361904	28.446945	28.532077	28.617300
68	27.637689	27.723000	27.808407	27.893909	27.979505	28.065196	28.150979	28.236856
70	27.278084	27.364031	27.450076	27.536217	27.622455	27.708789	27.795218	27.881742
72	26.941701	27.028278	27.114954	27.201729	27.288601	27.375572	27.462640	27.549805
74	26.626621	26.713821	26.801122	26.888523	26.976024	27.063625	27.151324	27.239123
76	26.331126	26.418942	26.506861	26.594882	26.683005	26.771228	26.859553	26.947977
78	26.053673	26.142099	26.230630	26.319263	26.408000	26.496840	26.585781	26.674825
80	25.792875	25.881904	25.971039	26.060278	26.149622	26.239070	26.328622	26.418276
82	25.547479	25.637103	25.726835	25.816673	25.906616	25.996665	26.086819	26.177077
84	25.316350	25.406563	25.496884	25.587313	25.677848	25.768491	25.859239	25.950092
86	25.098459	25.189253	25.280156	25.371169	25.462289	25.553517	25.644851	25.736292
88	24.892871	24.984239	25.075717	25.167304	25.259001	25.350807	25.442720	25.534741
90	24.698733	24.790667	24.882712	24.974867	25.067133	25.159508	25.251992	25.344584
92	24.515266	24.607758	24.700362	24.793078	24.885904	24.978841	25.071887	25.165042
96	24.177556	24.271141	24.364840	24.458651	24.552575	24.646610	24.740756	24.835012
100	23.874713	23.969360	24.064122	24.158997	24.253986	24.349087	24.444299	24.539622
104	23.602486	23.698163	23.793955	23.889861	23.985881	24.082014	24.178259	24.274615
108	23.357249	23.453923	23.550713	23.647618	23.744637	23.841768	23.939012	24.036366
112	23.135896	23.233536	23.331292	23.429162	23.527145	23.625242	23.723450	23.821769
116	22.935751	23.034324	23.133012	23.231814	23.330730	23.429757	23.528896	23.628145
120	22.754493	22.853967	22.953555	23.053257	23.153071	23.252996	23.353032	23.453177
140	22.069006	22.172511	22.276122	22.379839	22.483660	22.587583	22.691609	22.795735
160	21.637497	21.744285	21.851166	21.958140	22.065205	22.172360	22.279602	22.386932

QUARTERLY WITHDRAWALS PER $1000

EFFECTIVE ANNUAL YIELD

NUMBER OF QUARTRLY WTHDRWLS	9.00%	9.05%	9.10%	9.15%	9.20%	9.25%	9.30%	9.35%
1	1021.778181	1021.895337	1022.012453	1022.129529	1022.246564	1022.363560	1022.480515	1022.597430
2	516.392283	516.480780	516.569249	516.657691	516.746106	516.834494	516.922856	517.011190
3	347.956379	348.035602	348.114803	348.193983	348.273142	348.352279	348.431396	348.510490
4	263.757968	263.832764	263.907542	263.982302	264.057046	264.131772	264.206480	264.281171
5	213.254550	213.326857	213.399149	213.471427	213.543691	213.615941	213.688177	213.760398
6	179.598623	179.669410	179.740185	179.810950	179.881702	179.952443	180.023173	180.093892
7	155.569827	155.639648	155.709460	155.779264	155.849058	155.918844	155.988620	156.058388
8	137.557983	137.627184	137.696379	137.765567	137.834749	137.903924	137.973093	138.042255
9	123.557435	123.626246	123.695053	123.763856	123.832655	123.901450	123.970241	124.039028
10	112.364786	112.433369	112.501950	112.570529	112.639107	112.707682	112.776256	112.844828
11	103.214241	103.282712	103.351184	103.419657	103.488129	103.556603	103.625076	103.693551
12	95.595266	95.663714	95.732165	95.800618	95.869074	95.937532	96.005993	96.074457
13	89.154417	89.222909	89.291405	89.359906	89.428412	89.496923	89.565438	89.633959
14	83.639231	83.707819	83.776414	83.845016	83.913625	83.982241	84.050863	84.119493
15	78.864569	78.933296	79.002032	79.070776	79.139530	79.208293	79.277064	79.345845
16	74.691577	74.760476	74.829386	74.898308	74.967240	75.036184	75.105138	75.174104
17	71.014071	71.083170	71.152283	71.221409	71.290548	71.359700	71.428866	71.498044
18	67.749463	67.818786	67.888124	67.957478	68.026847	68.096231	68.165630	68.235044
19	64.832552	64.902118	64.971702	65.041302	65.110920	65.180555	65.250207	65.319876
20	62.211178	62.281003	62.350847	62.420711	62.490594	62.560496	62.630417	62.700358
21	59.843114	59.913212	59.983331	60.053472	60.123633	60.193816	60.264021	60.334246
22	57.693811	57.764193	57.834599	57.905029	57.975481	58.045957	58.116456	58.186977
23	55.734728	55.805406	55.876108	55.946837	56.017590	56.088368	56.159171	56.230000
24	53.942082	54.013063	54.084071	54.155107	54.226169	54.297259	54.368376	54.439519
25	52.295893	52.367185	52.438506	52.509857	52.581236	52.652645	52.724082	52.795548
26	50.779256	50.850866	50.922506	50.994178	51.065881	51.137615	51.209379	51.281174
27	49.377769	49.449702	49.521668	49.593667	49.665699	49.737763	49.809860	49.881990
28	48.079089	48.151350	48.223646	48.295977	48.368342	48.440742	48.513177	48.585646
29	46.872573	46.945167	47.017797	47.090464	47.163168	47.235907	47.308684	47.381496
30	45.749000	45.821929	45.894897	45.967904	46.040949	46.114032	46.187154	46.260313
31	44.700334	44.773603	44.846912	44.920262	44.993652	45.067081	45.140551	45.214061
32	43.719548	43.793159	43.866812	43.940507	44.014244	44.088023	44.161844	44.235706
33	42.800463	42.874418	42.948418	43.022461	43.096548	43.170678	43.244853	43.319070
34	41.937629	42.011931	42.086279	42.160672	42.235111	42.309595	42.384124	42.458698
35	41.126218	41.200868	41.275566	41.350311	41.425103	41.499942	41.574828	41.649761
36	40.361939	40.436938	40.511987	40.587085	40.662232	40.737428	40.812672	40.887965
37	39.640962	39.716313	39.791714	39.867166	39.942669	40.018222	40.093826	40.169479
38	38.959864	39.035568	39.111321	39.187128	39.262987	39.338899	39.414863	39.490878
39	38.315569	38.391624	38.467733	38.543896	38.620113	38.696384	38.772708	38.849086
40	37.705312	37.781720	37.858184	37.934703	38.011278	38.087908	38.164594	38.241335
41	37.126595	37.203357	37.280175	37.357051	37.433985	37.510975	37.588022	37.665126
42	36.577160	36.654275	36.731449	36.808682	36.885973	36.963324	37.040732	37.118199
43	36.054956	36.132425	36.209954	36.287544	36.365194	36.442904	36.520675	36.598505
44	35.558121	35.635943	35.713828	35.791774	35.869783	35.947853	36.025985	36.104178
45	35.084957	35.163133	35.241372	35.319676	35.398042	35.476472	35.554965	35.633521
46	34.633914	34.712443	34.791038	34.869697	34.948421	35.027210	35.106064	35.184982
47	34.203574	34.282456	34.361405	34.440420	34.519502	34.598649	34.677863	34.757142
48	33.792637	33.871871	33.951174	34.030544	34.109982	34.189488	34.269061	34.348702
50	33.024289	33.104226	33.184234	33.264313	33.344463	33.424683	33.504973	33.585333
52	32.320408	32.401045	32.481755	32.562539	32.643397	32.724327	32.805331	32.886407
54	31.673783	31.755115	31.836525	31.918010	31.999571	32.081209	32.162921	32.244709
56	31.078232	31.160257	31.242360	31.324542	31.406803	31.489142	31.571559	31.654053
58	30.528425	30.611137	30.693930	30.776804	30.859759	30.942795	31.025911	31.109107
60	30.019742	30.103136	30.186615	30.270174	30.353818	30.437544	30.521354	30.605245
62	29.548157	29.632227	29.716383	29.800624	29.884951	29.969363	30.053860	30.138441
64	29.110147	29.194887	29.279716	29.364632	29.449636	29.534726	29.619904	29.705168
66	28.702614	28.788019	28.873514	28.959098	29.044772	29.130535	29.216387	29.302327
68	28.322826	28.408889	28.495043	28.581289	28.667627	28.754055	28.840574	28.927183
70	27.968361	28.055075	28.141882	28.228782	28.315776	28.402863	28.490041	28.577311
72	27.637066	27.724423	27.811876	27.899424	27.987067	28.074803	28.162634	28.250558
74	27.327019	27.415013	27.503104	27.591292	27.679576	27.767956	27.856431	27.945001
76	27.036501	27.125124	27.213846	27.302666	27.391584	27.480599	27.569710	27.658918
78	26.763969	26.853145	26.942558	27.032003	27.121546	27.211188	27.300928	27.390765
80	26.508033	26.597891	26.687851	26.777912	26.868073	26.958333	27.048693	27.139152
82	26.267438	26.357903	26.448470	26.539138	26.629909	26.720780	26.811751	26.902822
84	26.041050	26.132113	26.223278	26.314547	26.405918	26.497391	26.588965	26.680640
86	25.827839	25.919491	26.011247	26.103107	26.195071	26.287137	26.379305	26.471575
88	25.626868	25.719101	25.811439	25.903882	25.996430	26.089080	26.181834	26.274689
90	25.437283	25.530089	25.623001	25.716018	25.809141	25.902367	25.995697	26.089129
92	25.258305	25.351676	25.445153	25.538736	25.632424	25.726218	25.820115	25.914115
96	24.929377	25.023851	25.118432	25.213120	25.307915	25.402815	25.497819	25.592928
100	24.635055	24.730597	24.826247	24.922005	25.017870	25.113840	25.209916	25.306096
104	24.371081	24.467664	24.564341	24.661133	24.758032	24.855036	24.952146	25.049360
108	24.133831	24.231405	24.329088	24.426878	24.524774	24.622777	24.720884	24.819095
112	23.920197	24.018735	24.117380	24.216133	24.314992	24.413955	24.513023	24.612194
116	23.727503	23.826969	23.926542	24.026222	24.126006	24.225895	24.325887	24.425981
120	23.553430	23.653790	23.754256	23.854827	23.955502	24.056279	24.157159	24.258140
140	22.899960	23.004283	23.108702	23.213217	23.317826	23.422528	23.527322	23.632207
160	22.494346	22.601845	22.709426	22.817089	22.924831	23.032652	23.140550	23.248524

QUARTERLY WITHDRAWALS PER $1000

NUMBER OF QUARTRLY WTHDRWLS	EFFECTIVE ANNUAL YIELD							
	9.40%	9.45%	9.50%	9.55%	9.60%	9.65%	9.70%	9.75%
1	1022.714305	1022.831140	1022.947935	1023.064689	1023.181404	1023.298079	1023.414714	1023.531310
2	517.099497	517.187777	517.276030	517.364256	517.452456	517.540628	517.628774	517.716893
3	348.589564	348.668617	348.747648	348.826658	348.905647	348.984614	349.063561	349.142486
4	264.355845	264.430501	264.505140	264.579762	264.654367	264.728954	264.803524	264.878076
5	213.832605	213.904798	213.976977	214.049141	214.121292	214.193428	214.265550	214.337658
6	180.164599	180.235294	180.305978	180.376651	180.447312	180.517962	180.588601	180.659228
7	156.128147	156.197897	156.267639	156.337371	156.407095	156.476809	156.546515	156.616212
8	138.111411	138.180560	138.249703	138.318840	138.387970	138.457094	138.526211	138.595322
9	124.107811	124.176589	124.245364	124.314134	124.382901	124.451663	124.520421	124.589175
10	112.913399	112.981967	113.050534	113.119098	113.187661	113.256222	113.324782	113.393339
11	103.762025	103.830500	103.898975	103.967451	104.035927	104.104403	104.172880	104.241357
12	96.142923	96.211392	96.279863	96.348337	96.416813	96.485292	96.553774	96.622258
13	89.702484	89.771013	89.839548	89.908087	89.976631	90.045179	90.113732	90.182289
14	84.188129	84.256772	84.325422	84.394079	84.462742	84.531412	84.600089	84.668773
15	79.414634	79.483433	79.552240	79.621056	79.689881	79.758715	79.827558	79.896409
16	75.243081	75.312068	75.381067	75.450076	75.519097	75.588128	75.657170	75.726223
17	71.567236	71.636440	71.705658	71.774888	71.844132	71.913388	71.982657	72.051939
18	68.304473	68.373918	68.443377	68.512851	68.582341	68.651845	68.721364	68.790898
19	65.389562	65.459266	65.528986	65.598724	65.668478	65.738249	65.808037	65.877842
20	62.770317	62.840296	62.910293	62.980310	63.050345	63.120399	63.190473	63.260564
21	60.404492	60.474760	60.545048	60.615357	60.685687	60.756038	60.826410	60.896802
22	58.257522	58.328090	58.398681	58.469294	58.539931	58.610590	58.681272	58.751976
23	56.300853	56.371731	56.442634	56.513562	56.584515	56.655492	56.726494	56.797521
24	54.510690	54.581887	54.653111	54.724361	54.795639	54.866943	54.938274	55.009630
25	52.867043	52.938567	53.010119	53.081700	53.153309	53.224947	53.296613	53.368308
26	51.353000	51.424856	51.496743	51.568661	51.640608	51.712586	51.784595	51.856633
27	49.954152	50.026347	50.098574	50.170833	50.243125	50.315448	50.387804	50.460192
28	48.658149	48.730687	48.803259	48.875865	48.948505	49.021179	49.093887	49.166629
29	47.454345	47.527229	47.600150	47.673107	47.746100	47.819128	47.892193	47.965292
30	46.333511	46.406746	46.480020	46.553331	46.626679	46.700066	46.773490	46.846951
31	45.287610	45.361199	45.434828	45.508497	45.582204	45.655950	45.729738	45.803564
32	44.309610	44.383556	44.457543	44.531571	44.605641	44.679751	44.753903	44.828095
33	43.393331	43.467635	43.541982	43.616372	43.690806	43.765282	43.839800	43.914362
34	42.533318	42.607982	42.682692	42.757446	42.832245	42.907088	42.981975	43.056907
35	41.724741	41.799767	41.874840	41.949960	42.025126	42.100338	42.175596	42.250900
36	40.963066	41.038696	41.114134	41.189620	41.265154	41.340736	41.416365	41.492043
37	40.245183	40.320937	40.396741	40.472595	40.548498	40.624451	40.700453	40.776504
38	39.566946	39.643065	39.719235	39.795457	39.871730	39.948055	40.024430	40.100856
39	38.925518	39.002002	39.078540	39.155131	39.231774	39.308471	39.385220	39.462021
40	38.318131	38.394981	38.471887	38.548847	38.625861	38.702930	38.780052	38.857229
41	37.742286	37.819503	37.896776	37.974106	38.051491	38.128932	38.206429	38.283981
42	37.195725	37.273308	37.350949	37.428647	37.506403	37.584217	37.662088	37.740015
43	36.676394	36.754344	36.832352	36.910420	36.988547	37.066733	37.144977	37.223280
44	36.182432	36.260747	36.339123	36.417560	36.496057	36.574615	36.653233	36.731911
45	35.712139	35.790820	35.869563	35.948368	36.027235	36.106164	36.185155	36.264207
46	35.263964	35.343010	35.422119	35.501293	35.580529	35.659829	35.739192	35.818618
47	34.836487	34.915898	34.995373	35.074914	35.154519	35.234189	35.313924	35.393722
48	34.428409	34.508183	34.588024	34.667931	34.747905	34.827944	34.908049	34.988220
50	33.665762	33.746262	33.826830	33.907468	33.988174	34.068950	34.149793	34.230705
52	32.967555	33.048775	33.130068	33.211432	33.292867	33.374374	33.455952	33.537600
54	32.326571	32.408508	32.490520	32.572606	32.654765	32.736999	32.819306	32.901685
56	31.736625	31.819274	31.901999	31.984802	32.067680	32.150635	32.233665	32.316771
58	31.192382	31.275737	31.359171	31.442684	31.526275	31.609945	31.693693	31.777518
60	30.689219	30.773274	30.857410	30.941627	31.025925	31.110304	31.194762	31.279301
62	30.223106	30.307855	30.392687	30.477602	30.562600	30.647680	30.732843	30.818087
64	29.790518	29.875954	29.961475	30.047081	30.132771	30.218546	30.304405	30.390348
66	29.388355	29.474470	29.560673	29.646963	29.733339	29.819801	29.906349	29.992982
68	29.013881	29.100669	29.187546	29.274512	29.361565	29.448707	29.535936	29.623251
70	28.664673	28.752126	28.839669	28.927303	29.015026	29.102839	29.190740	29.278730
72	28.338576	28.426685	28.514887	28.603180	28.691565	28.780041	28.868606	28.957262
74	28.033665	28.122424	28.211276	28.300221	28.389258	28.478388	28.567609	28.656922
76	27.748222	27.837621	27.927114	28.016702	28.106384	28.196159	28.286027	28.375988
78	27.480699	27.570730	27.660857	27.751080	27.841397	27.931809	28.022314	28.112914
80	27.229708	27.320362	27.411113	27.501961	27.592905	27.683944	27.775078	27.866307
82	26.993992	27.085260	27.176627	27.268091	27.359652	27.451310	27.543063	27.634912
84	26.772414	26.864289	26.956262	27.048333	27.140502	27.232769	27.325132	27.417591
86	26.563945	26.656416	26.748986	26.841656	26.934423	27.027289	27.120252	27.213312
88	26.367646	26.460704	26.553863	26.647121	26.740478	26.833934	26.927487	27.021137
90	26.182664	26.276300	26.370037	26.463875	26.557812	26.651847	26.745981	26.840213
92	26.008218	26.102423	26.196730	26.291137	26.385644	26.480250	26.574955	26.669757
96	25.688140	25.783455	25.878871	25.974389	26.070007	26.165725	26.261542	26.357457
100	25.402380	25.498766	25.595255	25.691845	25.788535	25.885325	25.982215	26.079202
104	25.146678	25.244099	25.341621	25.439245	25.536969	25.634792	25.732714	25.830733
108	24.917410	25.015826	25.114344	25.212963	25.311681	25.410498	25.509413	25.608425
112	24.711468	24.810843	24.910318	25.009893	25.109567	25.209339	25.309207	25.409172
116	24.526177	24.626473	24.726868	24.827361	24.927952	25.028640	25.129423	25.230301
120	24.359221	24.460400	24.561678	24.663052	24.764523	24.866088	24.967747	25.069499
140	23.737180	23.842242	23.947391	24.052626	24.157946	24.263349	24.368834	24.474401
160	23.356573	23.464695	23.572889	23.681153	23.789487	23.897890	24.006359	24.114895

QUARTERLY WITHDRAWALS PER $1000

NUMBER OF QUARTLY WTHDRWLS	EFFECTIVE ANNUAL YIELD							
	9.80%	9.85%	9.90%	9.95%	10.00%	10.05%	10.10%	10.15%
1	1023.647865	1023.764381	1023.880857	1023.997293	1024.113689	1024.230046	1024.346363	1024.462640
2	517.804985	517.893050	517.981088	518.069100	518.157085	518.245043	518.332974	518.420879
3	349.221390	349.300274	349.379135	349.457976	349.536796	349.615595	349.694373	349.773129
4	264.952611	265.027129	265.101630	265.176114	265.250580	265.325029	265.399461	265.473875
5	214.409751	214.481831	214.553896	214.625948	214.697985	214.770008	214.842017	214.914012
6	180.729844	180.800448	180.871041	180.941622	181.012192	181.082751	181.153299	181.223835
7	156.685900	156.755580	156.825250	156.894912	156.964564	157.034208	157.103843	157.173469
8	138.664427	138.733525	138.802616	138.871701	138.940780	139.009852	139.078918	139.147977
9	124.657925	124.726670	124.795412	124.864149	124.932883	125.001612	125.070337	125.139057
10	113.461894	113.530448	113.598999	113.667549	113.736097	113.804643	113.873187	113.941729
11	104.309834	104.378312	104.446790	104.515268	104.583747	104.652225	104.720704	104.789183
12	96.690744	96.759233	96.827724	96.896217	96.964714	97.033212	97.101713	97.170216
13	90.250852	90.319418	90.387990	90.456565	90.525146	90.593730	90.662320	90.730914
14	84.737463	84.806160	84.874864	84.943574	85.012291	85.081014	85.149744	85.218481
15	79.965269	80.034138	80.103016	80.171902	80.240797	80.309700	80.378612	80.447533
16	75.795287	75.864361	75.933446	76.002542	76.071649	76.140766	76.209894	76.279032
17	72.121234	72.190541	72.259862	72.329195	72.398541	72.467899	72.537270	72.606653
18	68.860447	68.930010	68.999588	69.069181	69.138789	69.208411	69.278048	69.347700
19	65.947664	66.017502	66.087357	66.157229	66.227118	66.297023	66.366944	66.436882
20	63.330675	63.400804	63.470952	63.541119	63.611304	63.681508	63.751730	63.821971
21	60.967215	61.037649	61.108104	61.178579	61.249074	61.319590	61.390126	61.460683
22	58.822703	58.893453	58.964225	59.035020	59.105837	59.176677	59.247539	59.318423
23	56.868572	56.939647	57.010747	57.081871	57.153020	57.224193	57.295390	57.366611
24	55.081013	55.152423	55.223859	55.295321	55.366810	55.438324	55.509865	55.581432
25	53.440031	53.511782	53.583561	53.655369	53.727204	53.799067	53.870959	53.942878
26	51.928702	52.000801	52.072929	52.145088	52.217277	52.289495	52.361743	52.434021
27	50.532612	50.605064	50.677547	50.750063	50.822610	50.895188	50.967799	51.040440
28	49.239405	49.312214	49.385057	49.457934	49.530844	49.603787	49.676764	49.749774
29	48.038428	48.111599	48.184805	48.258047	48.331324	48.404636	48.477983	48.551365
30	46.920449	46.993985	47.067558	47.141169	47.214816	47.288500	47.362221	47.435978
31	45.877428	45.951332	46.025275	46.099256	46.173276	46.247335	46.321433	46.395568
32	44.902328	44.976602	45.050917	45.125272	45.199668	45.274104	45.348580	45.423096
33	43.988966	44.063612	44.138300	44.213031	44.287804	44.362619	44.437476	44.512375
34	43.131884	43.206904	43.281968	43.357077	43.432229	43.507424	43.582664	43.657946
35	42.326250	42.401646	42.477087	42.552574	42.628106	42.703684	42.779307	42.854975
36	41.567768	41.643540	41.719359	41.795226	41.871140	41.947100	42.023108	42.099162
37	40.852605	40.928754	41.004953	41.081200	41.157496	41.233841	41.310233	41.386674
38	40.177333	40.253861	40.330439	40.407067	40.483746	40.560474	40.637253	40.714081
39	39.538875	39.615781	39.692738	39.769748	39.846810	39.923923	40.001088	40.078304
40	38.934460	39.011744	39.089082	39.166474	39.243919	39.321416	39.398967	39.476571
41	38.361589	38.439252	38.516970	38.594743	38.672571	38.750453	38.828390	38.906382
42	37.818000	37.896042	37.974140	38.052294	38.130505	38.208771	38.287094	38.365473
43	37.301642	37.380061	37.458539	37.537074	37.615667	37.694318	37.773026	37.851792
44	36.810648	36.889445	36.968302	37.047218	37.126193	37.205228	37.284320	37.363472
45	36.343320	36.422495	36.501730	36.581026	36.660382	36.739799	36.819276	36.898813
46	35.898106	35.977657	36.057270	36.136945	36.216682	36.296481	36.376341	36.456263
47	35.473585	35.553511	35.633501	35.713555	35.793672	35.873852	35.954094	36.034400
48	35.068456	35.148757	35.229123	35.309554	35.390049	35.470609	35.551234	35.631922
50	34.311685	34.392732	34.473848	34.555030	34.636280	34.717596	34.798979	34.880429
52	33.619319	33.701108	33.782968	33.864897	33.946896	34.028964	34.111101	34.193307
54	32.984138	33.066664	33.149262	33.231932	33.314674	33.397488	33.480373	33.563329
56	32.399952	32.483208	32.566538	32.649943	32.733422	32.816975	32.900602	32.984302
58	31.861421	31.945401	32.029457	32.113591	32.197800	32.282085	32.366447	32.450883
60	31.363918	31.448615	31.533391	31.618245	31.703178	31.788188	31.873276	31.958442
62	30.903412	30.988819	31.074306	31.159874	31.245522	31.331250	31.417057	31.502944
64	30.476373	30.562482	30.648674	30.734947	30.821303	30.907739	30.994255	31.080857
66	30.079700	30.166503	30.253390	30.340361	30.427416	30.514553	30.601774	30.689077
68	29.710654	29.798142	29.885717	29.973377	30.061122	30.148951	30.236865	30.324863
70	29.366809	29.454974	29.543228	29.631568	29.719994	29.808507	29.897105	29.985789
72	29.046007	29.134842	29.223765	29.312776	29.401875	29.491061	29.580334	29.669694
74	28.746325	28.835819	28.925403	29.015076	29.104838	29.194688	29.284627	29.374653
76	28.466040	28.556184	28.646419	28.736745	28.827160	28.917665	29.008259	29.098942
78	28.203606	28.294391	28.385267	28.476236	28.567295	28.658444	28.749684	28.841013
80	27.957630	28.049046	28.140555	28.232156	28.323849	28.415633	28.507508	28.599474
82	27.726855	27.818893	27.911024	28.003248	28.095565	28.187974	28.280474	28.373066
84	27.510145	27.602794	27.695538	27.788375	27.881306	27.974329	28.067443	28.160651
86	27.306467	27.399719	27.493065	27.586505	27.680039	27.773666	27.867386	27.961198
88	27.114865	27.208728	27.302666	27.396699	27.490826	27.585047	27.679361	27.773767
90	26.934541	27.028966	27.123487	27.218103	27.312813	27.407616	27.502513	27.597503
92	26.764657	26.859654	26.954747	27.049934	27.145217	27.240593	27.336063	27.431625
96	26.453470	26.549579	26.645785	26.742086	26.838482	26.934972	27.031555	27.128231
100	26.176287	26.273469	26.370746	26.468119	26.565586	26.663147	26.760801	26.858548
104	25.928830	26.027053	26.125371	26.223774	26.322271	26.420861	26.519543	26.618317
108	25.707533	25.806737	25.906035	26.005427	26.104911	26.204488	26.304156	26.403914
112	25.509231	25.609383	25.709632	25.809972	25.910403	26.010925	26.111537	26.212237
116	25.331272	25.432336	25.533492	25.634739	25.736076	25.837502	25.939016	26.040618
120	25.171343	25.273278	25.375303	25.477418	25.579620	25.681910	25.784286	25.886747
140	24.580047	24.685773	24.791577	24.897457	25.003413	25.109444	25.215548	25.321725
160	24.223495	24.332158	24.440884	24.549671	24.658517	24.767423	24.876386	24.985405

QUARTERLY WITHDRAWALS PER $1000

NUMBER OF QUARTRLY WTHDRWLS	EFFECTIVE ANNUAL YIELD							
	10.20%	10.25%	10.30%	10.35%	10.40%	10.45%	10.50%	10.55%
1	1024.578878	1024.695077	1024.811235	1024.927355	1025.043435	1025.159475	1025.275476	1025.391438
2	518.508757	518.596609	518.684433	518.772232	518.860003	518.947748	519.035467	519.123159
3	349.851865	349.930580	350.009273	350.087946	350.166598	350.245229	350.323838	350.402427
4	265.548273	265.622653	265.697016	265.771362	265.845691	265.920003	265.994297	266.068574
5	214.985993	215.057959	215.129912	215.201850	215.273775	215.345685	215.417581	215.489464
6	181.294359	181.364873	181.435375	181.505865	181.576344	181.646812	181.717269	181.787714
7	157.243087	157.312695	157.382295	157.451886	157.521467	157.591041	157.660605	157.730160
8	139.217030	139.286076	139.355116	139.424149	139.493176	139.562197	139.631211	139.700218
9	125.207774	125.276486	125.345194	125.413898	125.482598	125.551294	125.619985	125.688672
10	114.010269	114.078807	114.147343	114.215877	114.284409	114.352939	114.421467	114.489993
11	104.857663	104.926142	104.994622	105.063102	105.131582	105.200063	105.268543	105.337024
12	97.238721	97.307229	97.375739	97.444252	97.512767	97.581284	97.649803	97.718325
13	90.799512	90.868114	90.936721	91.005333	91.073949	91.142569	91.211193	91.279822
14	85.287224	85.355973	85.424729	85.493491	85.562260	85.631035	85.699817	85.768605
15	80.516462	80.585400	80.654346	80.723301	80.792264	80.861236	80.930216	80.999205
16	76.348181	76.417341	76.486511	76.555691	76.624882	76.694084	76.763296	76.832518
17	72.676050	72.745458	72.814880	72.884313	72.953759	73.023218	73.092689	73.162172
18	69.417366	69.487046	69.556741	69.626450	69.696174	69.765912	69.835665	69.905432
19	66.506837	66.576808	66.646796	66.716800	66.786820	66.856857	66.926909	66.996978
20	63.892230	63.962508	64.032804	64.103118	64.173451	64.243801	64.314170	64.384557
21	61.531260	61.601858	61.672475	61.743113	61.813771	61.884449	61.955148	62.025866
22	59.389329	59.460258	59.531209	59.602181	59.673176	59.744193	59.815232	59.886293
23	57.437857	57.509126	57.580420	57.651737	57.723078	57.794443	57.865832	57.937245
24	55.653024	55.724643	55.796287	55.867957	55.939653	56.011375	56.083122	56.154895
25	54.014825	54.086800	54.158802	54.230832	54.302890	54.374975	54.447087	54.519227
26	52.506329	52.578665	52.651032	52.723428	52.795853	52.868308	52.940791	53.013304
27	51.113113	51.185818	51.258553	51.331320	51.404118	51.476947	51.549807	51.622698
28	49.822817	49.895893	49.969003	50.042145	50.115320	50.188528	50.261769	50.335042
29	48.624782	48.698234	48.771721	48.845243	48.918799	48.992389	49.066014	49.139674
30	47.509773	47.583603	47.657471	47.731375	47.805315	47.879291	47.953304	48.027352
31	46.469743	46.543955	46.618206	46.692495	46.766821	46.841186	46.915589	46.990029
32	45.497653	45.572249	45.646885	45.721561	45.796277	45.871032	45.945827	46.020661
33	44.587316	44.662298	44.737321	44.812387	44.887493	44.962641	45.037829	45.113059
34	43.733273	43.808642	43.884055	43.959510	44.035009	44.110550	44.186134	44.261761
35	42.930688	43.006446	43.082248	43.158096	43.233988	43.309924	43.385905	43.461930
36	42.175263	42.251410	42.327604	42.403844	42.480130	42.556462	42.632840	42.709263
37	41.463164	41.539701	41.616286	41.692919	41.769600	41.846328	41.923104	41.999927
38	40.790960	40.867887	40.944865	41.021891	41.098967	41.176092	41.253266	41.330488
39	40.155571	40.232890	40.310259	40.387679	40.465150	40.542672	40.620244	40.697866
40	39.554228	39.631937	39.709698	39.787512	39.865378	39.943296	40.021266	40.099288
41	38.984427	39.062527	39.140680	39.218888	39.297148	39.375463	39.453830	39.532251
42	38.443907	38.522397	38.600942	38.679542	38.758197	38.836908	38.915672	38.994492
43	37.930614	38.009494	38.088430	38.167422	38.246472	38.325577	38.404738	38.483956
44	37.442682	37.521951	37.601277	37.680662	37.760104	37.839604	37.919161	37.998776
45	36.978410	37.058067	37.137783	37.217559	37.297393	37.377287	37.457239	37.537250
46	36.536246	36.616290	36.696395	36.776560	36.856786	36.937072	37.017418	37.097824
47	36.114768	36.195198	36.275690	36.356245	36.436861	36.517538	36.598277	36.679077
48	35.712673	35.793489	35.874368	35.955310	36.036315	36.117383	36.198513	36.279706
50	34.961945	35.043527	35.125175	35.206889	35.288668	35.370512	35.452421	35.534395
52	34.275581	34.357925	34.440336	34.522815	34.605362	34.687977	34.770658	34.853407
54	33.646356	33.729454	33.812623	33.895861	33.979169	34.062547	34.145995	34.229512
56	33.068075	33.151921	33.235839	33.319830	33.403892	33.488027	33.572232	33.656509
58	32.535395	32.619981	32.704642	32.789377	32.874186	32.959069	33.044025	33.129055
60	32.043684	32.129003	32.214399	32.299871	32.385418	32.471041	32.556739	32.642513
62	31.588909	31.674952	31.761074	31.847274	31.933551	32.019906	32.106337	32.192845
64	31.167536	31.254296	31.341135	31.428054	31.515052	31.602129	31.689285	31.776518
66	30.776462	30.863928	30.951476	31.039105	31.126815	31.214605	31.302475	31.390424
68	30.412945	30.501109	30.589356	30.677686	30.766098	30.854591	30.943165	31.031820
70	30.074557	30.163410	30.252347	30.341367	30.430471	30.519657	30.608926	30.698277
72	29.759140	29.848671	29.938288	30.027989	30.117775	30.207644	30.297597	30.387634
74	29.464766	29.554966	29.645252	29.735624	29.826082	29.916624	30.007251	30.097962
76	29.189713	29.280571	29.371517	29.462549	29.553668	29.644872	29.736162	29.827537
78	28.932431	29.023938	29.115533	29.207215	29.298984	29.390840	29.482782	29.574809
80	28.691529	28.783673	28.875906	28.968227	29.060637	29.153133	29.245716	29.338385
82	28.465747	28.558519	28.651380	28.744329	28.837367	28.930493	29.023706	29.117005
84	28.253949	28.347337	28.440815	28.534382	28.628037	28.721781	28.815613	28.909531
86	28.055101	28.149094	28.243178	28.337352	28.431614	28.525965	28.620404	28.714930
88	27.868264	27.962853	28.057532	28.152301	28.247159	28.342106	28.437141	28.532263
90	27.692584	27.787757	27.883020	27.978373	28.073816	28.169348	28.264967	28.360674
92	27.527280	27.623025	27.718862	27.814788	27.910804	28.006909	28.103101	28.199382
96	27.224999	27.321858	27.418807	27.515846	27.612975	27.710192	27.807497	27.904889
100	26.956385	27.054314	27.152332	27.250440	27.348636	27.446920	27.545291	27.643748
104	26.717181	26.816135	26.915178	27.014310	27.113529	27.212835	27.312227	27.411704
108	26.503762	26.603698	26.703723	26.803834	26.904032	27.004315	27.104683	27.205135
112	26.313026	26.413902	26.514865	26.615912	26.717045	26.818261	26.919561	27.020942
116	26.142305	26.244079	26.345936	26.447878	26.549902	26.652009	26.754196	26.856463
120	25.989292	26.091921	26.194633	26.297426	26.400300	26.503253	26.606286	26.709396
140	25.427973	25.534291	25.640678	25.747134	25.853657	25.960247	26.066901	26.173620
160	25.094480	25.203609	25.312792	25.422026	25.531311	25.640647	25.750031	25.859464

QUARTERLY WITHDRAWALS PER $1000

EFFECTIVE ANNUAL YIELD

NUMBER OF QUARTERLY WTHDRWLS	10.60%	10.65%	10.70%	10.75%	10.80%	10.85%	10.90%	10.95%
1	1025.507360	1025.623243	1025.739087	1025.854892	1025.970657	1026.086383	1026.202070	1026.317718
2	519.210824	519.298463	519.386076	519.473662	519.561221	519.648755	519.736262	519.823742
3	350.480995	350.559542	350.638069	350.716574	350.795059	350.873522	350.951965	351.030387
4	266.142835	266.217078	266.291304	266.365513	266.439705	266.513880	266.588038	266.662178
5	215.561332	215.633186	215.705026	215.776853	215.848665	215.920463	215.992247	216.064017
6	181.858148	181.928521	181.998982	182.069382	182.139770	182.210147	182.280513	182.350868
7	157.799707	157.869245	157.938773	158.008293	158.077805	158.147307	158.216801	158.286285
8	139.769219	139.838213	139.907201	139.976183	140.045158	140.114127	140.183089	140.252044
9	125.757355	125.826034	125.894709	125.963379	126.032045	126.100707	126.169365	126.238018
10	114.558517	114.627040	114.695560	114.764078	114.832594	114.901107	114.969619	115.038129
11	105.405504	105.473985	105.542466	105.610947	105.679429	105.747910	105.816391	105.884873
12	97.786849	97.855375	97.923903	97.992433	98.060966	98.129501	98.198038	98.266577
13	91.348455	91.417093	91.485735	91.554381	91.623031	91.691685	91.760344	91.829007
14	85.837399	85.906200	85.975007	86.043820	86.112640	86.181466	86.250298	86.319136
15	81.068201	81.137207	81.206220	81.275242	81.344272	81.413310	81.482357	81.551411
16	76.901751	76.970994	77.040247	77.109510	77.178784	77.248068	77.317362	77.386667
17	73.231668	73.301176	73.370696	73.440228	73.509773	73.579330	73.648899	73.718480
18	69.975213	70.045008	70.114818	70.184641	70.254479	70.324331	70.394197	70.464077
19	67.067064	67.137165	67.207283	67.277416	67.347566	67.417732	67.487913	67.558111
20	64.454962	64.525386	64.595827	64.666286	64.736763	64.807257	64.877771	64.948302
21	62.096604	62.167362	62.238140	62.308938	62.379756	62.450593	62.521451	62.592328
22	59.957375	60.028479	60.099606	60.170753	60.241923	60.313114	60.384326	60.455561
23	58.008681	58.080141	58.151625	58.223132	58.294663	58.366217	58.437794	58.509395
24	56.226693	56.298517	56.370366	56.442241	56.514140	56.586066	56.658016	56.729991
25	54.591394	54.663589	54.735810	54.808059	54.880335	54.952638	55.024968	55.097324
26	53.085846	53.158417	53.231017	53.303646	53.376304	53.448990	53.521706	53.594449
27	51.695620	51.768573	51.841556	51.914570	51.987615	52.060690	52.133795	52.206931
28	50.408348	50.481687	50.555058	50.628461	50.701897	50.775364	50.848864	50.922397
29	49.213368	49.287006	49.360858	49.434654	49.508484	49.582348	49.656246	49.730178
30	48.101437	48.175558	48.249714	48.323906	48.398134	48.472397	48.546696	48.621030
31	47.064507	47.139023	47.213576	47.288166	47.362794	47.437459	47.512162	47.586901
32	46.095535	46.170448	46.245400	46.320391	46.395420	46.470489	46.545597	46.620743
33	45.188330	45.263642	45.338994	45.414387	45.489821	45.565295	45.640809	45.716363
34	44.337431	44.413142	44.488897	44.564693	44.640531	44.716412	44.792334	44.868298
35	43.537998	43.614111	43.690268	43.766469	43.842713	43.919001	43.995333	44.071707
36	42.785733	42.862248	42.938808	43.015414	43.092064	43.168760	43.245501	43.322287
37	42.076797	42.153714	42.230679	42.307690	42.384747	42.461852	42.539002	42.616199
38	41.407059	41.485079	41.562447	41.639864	41.717329	41.794841	41.872402	41.950010
39	40.775538	40.853261	40.931033	41.008855	41.086727	41.164648	41.242618	41.320638
40	40.177361	40.255486	40.333662	40.411889	40.490167	40.568497	40.646877	40.725307
41	39.610725	39.689252	39.767831	39.846463	39.925148	40.003885	40.082673	40.161514
42	39.073366	39.152294	39.231276	39.310312	39.389402	39.468546	39.547744	39.626994
43	38.563229	38.642558	38.721942	38.801382	38.880877	38.960426	39.040031	39.119690
44	38.078447	38.158176	38.237962	38.317804	38.397702	38.477657	38.557668	38.637735
45	37.617319	37.697447	37.777632	37.857876	37.938177	38.018536	38.098952	38.179425
46	37.178290	37.258815	37.339400	37.420044	37.500746	37.581508	37.662328	37.743207
47	36.759938	36.840860	36.921842	37.002885	37.083988	37.165151	37.246374	37.327656
48	36.360961	36.442278	36.523656	36.605097	36.686598	36.768161	36.849785	36.931470
50	35.616433	35.698536	35.780703	35.862934	35.945229	36.027587	36.110008	36.192492
52	34.936223	35.019105	35.102053	35.185068	35.268148	35.351294	35.434506	35.517783
54	34.313097	34.396751	34.480474	34.564265	34.648124	34.732050	34.816044	34.900106
56	33.740857	33.825276	33.909765	33.994324	34.078953	34.163652	34.248420	34.333257
58	33.214157	33.299331	33.384578	33.469897	33.555288	33.640750	33.726283	33.811887
60	32.728360	32.814282	32.900278	32.986348	33.072491	33.158707	33.244996	33.331357
62	32.279429	32.366089	32.452825	32.539636	32.626522	32.713483	32.800517	32.887626
64	31.863829	31.951218	32.038684	32.126226	32.213845	32.301540	32.389311	32.477156
66	31.478453	31.566560	31.654746	31.743009	31.831351	31.919770	32.008266	32.096838
68	31.120556	31.209372	31.298267	31.387242	31.476296	31.565428	31.654638	31.743926
70	30.787710	30.877223	30.966818	31.056493	31.146248	31.236082	31.325996	31.415989
72	30.477752	30.567953	30.658236	30.748601	30.839046	30.929572	31.020178	31.110863
74	30.188756	30.279634	30.370594	30.461636	30.552761	30.643966	30.735253	30.826620
76	29.918996	30.010538	30.102165	30.193874	30.285666	30.377540	30.469495	30.561532
78	29.666921	29.759118	29.851400	29.943764	30.036212	30.128743	30.221355	30.314050
80	29.431139	29.523979	29.616904	29.709912	29.803004	29.896180	29.989437	30.082778
82	29.210391	29.303862	29.397418	29.491059	29.584783	29.678591	29.772483	29.866456
84	29.003536	29.097627	29.191803	29.286065	29.380410	29.474839	29.569351	29.663946
86	28.809543	28.904242	28.999027	29.093897	29.188851	29.283888	29.379010	29.474214
88	28.627472	28.722768	28.818149	28.913615	29.009166	29.104801	29.200519	29.296319
90	28.456468	28.552348	28.648314	28.744365	28.840500	28.936720	29.033022	29.129407
92	28.295749	28.392202	28.488741	28.585364	28.682072	28.778864	28.875739	28.972696
96	28.002367	28.099931	28.197580	28.295313	28.393131	28.491031	28.589014	28.687078
100	27.742291	27.840919	27.939632	28.038427	28.137306	28.236266	28.335308	28.434431
104	27.511266	27.610911	27.710640	27.810451	27.910343	28.010316	28.110369	28.210501
108	27.305670	27.406287	27.506985	27.607765	27.708624	27.809562	27.910579	28.011673
112	27.122405	27.223949	27.325572	27.427274	27.529054	27.630911	27.732845	27.834854
116	26.958810	27.061235	27.163738	27.266318	27.368974	27.471704	27.574509	27.677387
120	26.812584	26.915847	27.019186	27.122600	27.226087	27.329647	27.433278	27.536981
140	26.280401	26.387245	26.494150	26.601116	26.708140	26.815223	26.922363	27.029560
160	25.968943	26.078468	26.188037	26.297651	26.407307	26.517006	26.626745	26.736524

QUARTERLY WITHDRAWALS PER $1000

EFFECTIVE ANNUAL YIELD

NUMBER OF QUARTRLY WTHDRWLS	11.00%	11.05%	11.10%	11.15%	11.20%	11.25%	11.30%	11.35%
1	1026.433327	1026.548897	1026.664428	1026.779920	1026.895373	1027.010786	1027.126161	1027.241498
2	519.911196	519.998624	520.086026	520.173401	520.260750	520.348072	520.435369	520.522639
3	351.108789	351.187169	351.265529	351.343868	351.422186	351.500484	351.578761	351.657017
4	266.736302	266.810409	266.884499	266.958571	267.032627	267.106666	267.180688	267.254693
5	216.135773	216.207515	216.279244	216.350958	216.422658	216.494345	216.566017	216.637675
6	182.421211	182.491543	182.561864	182.632174	182.702472	182.772759	182.843034	182.913298
7	158.355761	158.425228	158.494686	158.564136	158.633576	158.703008	158.772431	158.841845
8	140.320993	140.389936	140.458872	140.527801	140.596724	140.665641	140.734551	140.803454
9	126.306667	126.375312	126.443952	126.512589	126.581221	126.649848	126.718472	126.787091
10	115.106637	115.175142	115.243646	115.312147	115.380647	115.449144	115.517639	115.586132
11	105.953354	106.021835	106.090317	106.158798	106.227280	106.295761	106.364243	106.432724
12	98.335118	98.403661	98.472207	98.540754	98.609304	98.677856	98.746409	98.814965
13	91.897674	91.966345	92.035020	92.103700	92.172383	92.241071	92.309763	92.378459
14	86.387981	86.456831	86.525688	86.594551	86.663420	86.732295	86.801176	86.870064
15	81.620474	81.689546	81.758625	81.827712	81.896807	81.965911	82.035023	82.104142
16	77.455981	77.525306	77.594641	77.663985	77.733340	77.802705	77.872080	77.941465
17	73.788073	73.857678	73.927295	73.996925	74.066566	74.136219	74.205884	74.275561
18	70.533971	70.603879	70.673801	70.743737	70.813687	70.883651	70.953628	71.023619
19	67.628325	67.698554	67.768799	67.839060	67.909337	67.979630	68.049938	68.120262
20	65.018850	65.089417	65.160000	65.230602	65.301221	65.371858	65.442512	65.513184
21	62.663224	62.734140	62.805076	62.876031	62.947006	63.018000	63.089013	63.160046
22	60.526816	60.598093	60.669392	60.740711	60.812052	60.883414	60.954798	61.026202
23	58.581019	58.652666	58.724336	58.796030	58.867747	58.939486	59.011249	59.083034
24	56.801991	56.874017	56.946067	57.018142	57.090243	57.162367	57.234517	57.306691
25	55.169708	55.242118	55.314555	55.387019	55.459509	55.532026	55.604569	55.677139
26	53.667222	53.740023	53.812852	53.885710	53.958596	54.031510	54.104453	54.177424
27	52.280097	52.353294	52.426520	52.499777	52.573064	52.646380	52.719727	52.793103
28	50.995961	51.069557	51.143184	51.216844	51.290535	51.364258	51.438013	51.511799
29	49.804143	49.878142	49.952175	50.026241	50.100340	50.174473	50.248639	50.322838
30	48.695400	48.769805	48.844245	48.918720	48.993230	49.067775	49.142355	49.216969
31	47.661677	47.736490	47.811340	47.886226	47.961150	48.036109	48.111105	48.186138
32	46.695927	46.771151	46.846412	46.921712	46.997050	47.072426	47.147840	47.223292
33	45.791958	45.867593	45.943268	46.018982	46.094737	46.170530	46.246364	46.322237
34	44.944304	45.020352	45.096441	45.172571	45.248743	45.324956	45.401209	45.477504
35	44.148125	44.224586	44.301090	44.377637	44.454227	44.530859	44.607534	44.684251
36	43.399117	43.475992	43.552912	43.629876	43.706884	43.783936	43.861033	43.938173
37	42.693443	42.770732	42.848067	42.925448	43.002875	43.080348	43.157866	43.235429
38	42.027667	42.105370	42.183121	42.260919	42.338765	42.416657	42.494597	42.572583
39	41.398707	41.476824	41.554991	41.633206	41.711470	41.789782	41.868142	41.946551
40	40.803788	40.882319	40.960901	41.039533	41.118215	41.196945	41.275726	41.354557
41	40.240407	40.319351	40.398347	40.477395	40.556493	40.635643	40.714843	40.794095
42	39.706297	39.785654	39.865063	39.944526	40.024040	40.103608	40.183227	40.262899
43	39.199404	39.279172	39.358994	39.438870	39.518800	39.598784	39.678821	39.758911
44	38.717857	38.798036	38.878269	38.958558	39.038902	39.119301	39.199755	39.280263
45	38.259956	38.340543	38.421187	38.501888	38.582644	38.663457	38.744326	38.825250
46	37.824144	37.905138	37.986191	38.067302	38.148470	38.229695	38.310977	38.392317
47	37.408998	37.490399	37.571859	37.653378	37.734956	37.816592	37.898287	37.980039
48	37.013215	37.095021	37.176887	37.258813	37.340798	37.422844	37.504949	37.587113
50	36.275039	36.357649	36.440321	36.523056	36.605852	36.688710	36.771630	36.854611
52	35.601124	35.684531	35.768001	35.851537	35.935136	36.018799	36.102525	36.186315
54	34.984234	35.068428	35.152690	35.237017	35.321410	35.405870	35.490394	35.574984
56	34.418163	34.503137	34.588180	34.673291	34.758469	34.843715	34.929029	35.014409
58	33.897562	33.983306	34.069121	34.155006	34.240960	34.326983	34.413075	34.499235
60	33.417791	33.504296	33.590873	33.677521	33.764241	33.851031	33.937891	34.024821
62	32.974809	33.062065	33.149393	33.236795	33.324269	33.411815	33.499433	33.587122
64	32.565077	32.653073	32.741143	32.829286	32.917505	33.005796	33.094160	33.182597
66	32.185487	32.274212	32.363012	32.451887	32.540838	32.629863	32.718962	32.808134
68	31.833292	31.922734	32.012254	32.101849	32.191520	32.281267	32.371089	32.460986
70	31.506060	31.596209	31.686435	31.776739	31.867120	31.957577	32.048110	32.138718
72	31.201628	31.292472	31.383394	31.474394	31.565472	31.656627	31.747859	31.839167
74	30.918067	31.009593	31.101199	31.192884	31.284646	31.376487	31.468405	31.560400
76	30.653649	30.745847	30.838124	30.930481	31.022916	31.115430	31.208022	31.300691
78	30.406825	30.499681	30.592618	30.685634	30.778730	30.871904	30.965157	31.058487
80	30.176199	30.269702	30.363285	30.456949	30.550692	30.644514	30.738415	30.832394
82	29.960512	30.054648	30.148866	30.243164	30.337542	30.431999	30.526535	30.621149
84	29.758623	29.853381	29.948221	30.043141	30.138141	30.233220	30.328378	30.423615
86	29.569500	29.664867	29.760316	29.855845	29.951454	30.047143	30.142910	30.238756
88	29.392202	29.488166	29.584212	29.680337	29.776543	29.872828	29.969191	30.065633
90	29.225874	29.322423	29.419052	29.515761	29.612551	29.709419	29.806365	29.903390
92	29.069735	29.166855	29.264056	29.361336	29.458696	29.556135	29.653651	29.751245
96	28.785223	28.883449	28.981755	29.080139	29.178602	29.277143	29.375761	29.474455
100	28.533633	28.632915	28.732276	28.831714	28.931229	29.030821	29.130489	29.230232
104	28.310712	28.411001	28.511367	28.611809	28.712326	28.812919	28.913586	29.014326
108	28.112844	28.214091	28.315414	28.416811	28.518281	28.619825	28.721441	28.823129
112	27.936938	28.039096	28.141327	28.243631	28.346006	28.448453	28.550969	28.653555
116	27.780338	27.883361	27.986454	28.089618	28.192851	28.296152	28.399522	28.502958
120	27.640753	27.744595	27.848505	27.952483	28.056528	28.160638	28.264814	28.369054
140	27.136812	27.244118	27.351478	27.458891	27.566356	27.673871	27.781437	27.889052
160	26.846342	26.956199	27.066092	27.176022	27.285987	27.395986	27.506019	27.616085

NUMBER OF QUARTERLY WTHDRWLS	11.40%	11.45%	11.50%	11.55%	11.60%	11.65%	11.70%	11.75%
1	1027.356795	1027.472053	1027.587273	1027.702454	1027.817597	1027.932700	1028.047765	1028.162791
2	520.609883	520.697101	520.784293	520.871458	520.958598	521.045711	521.132798	521.219860
3	351.735252	351.813467	351.891661	351.969835	352.047988	352.126120	352.204232	352.282323
4	267.328681	267.402652	267.476606	267.550543	267.624463	267.698366	267.772253	267.846122
5	216.709320	216.780951	216.852567	216.924170	216.995759	217.067334	217.138895	217.210442
6	182.983551	183.053793	183.124024	183.194243	183.264451	183.334647	183.404833	183.475007
7	158.911250	158.980646	159.050034	159.119413	159.188783	159.258144	159.327496	159.396839
8	140.872351	140.941242	141.010125	141.079003	141.147874	141.216738	141.285596	141.354447
9	126.855706	126.924316	126.992922	127.061524	127.130122	127.198715	127.267304	127.335889
10	115.654622	115.723111	115.791597	115.860082	115.928564	115.997044	116.065522	116.133997
11	106.501205	106.569687	106.638168	106.706649	106.775130	106.843611	106.912092	106.980573
12	98.883523	98.952083	99.020644	99.089208	99.157774	99.226341	99.294911	99.363482
13	92.447158	92.515862	92.584570	92.653282	92.721998	92.790718	92.859441	92.928169
14	86.938957	87.007856	87.076761	87.145673	87.214590	87.283513	87.352442	87.421377
15	82.173270	82.242405	82.311549	82.380700	82.449859	82.519027	82.588202	82.657385
16	78.010860	78.080264	78.149679	78.219103	78.288537	78.357982	78.427435	78.496899
17	74.345250	74.414950	74.484663	74.554387	74.624123	74.693871	74.763630	74.833401
18	71.093624	71.163643	71.233675	71.303721	71.373781	71.443854	71.513941	71.584041
19	68.190601	68.260956	68.331327	68.401713	68.472114	68.542531	68.612964	68.683411
20	65.583814	65.654580	65.725304	65.796046	65.866805	65.937581	66.008374	66.079184
21	63.231098	63.302169	63.373260	63.444369	63.515498	63.586646	63.657812	63.728998
22	61.097628	61.169075	61.240542	61.312031	61.383540	61.455071	61.526622	61.598194
23	59.154843	59.226674	59.298528	59.370404	59.442304	59.514226	59.586170	59.658137
24	57.378890	57.451114	57.523362	57.595634	57.667931	57.740252	57.812598	57.884967
25	55.749735	55.822357	55.895006	55.967681	56.040381	56.113108	56.185861	56.258640
26	54.250422	54.323449	54.396504	54.469586	54.542697	54.615835	54.689001	54.762194
27	52.866510	52.939945	53.013411	53.086906	53.160430	53.233984	53.307567	53.381180
28	51.585616	51.659465	51.733345	51.807256	51.881199	51.955172	52.029177	52.103212
29	50.397070	50.471335	50.545632	50.619963	50.694327	50.768723	50.843151	50.917613
30	49.291619	49.366303	49.441021	49.515774	49.590561	49.665382	49.740238	49.815127
31	48.261206	48.336311	48.411452	48.486629	48.561842	48.637091	48.712373	48.787695
32	47.298782	47.374310	47.449875	47.525478	47.601118	47.676795	47.752510	47.828262
33	46.398149	46.474101	46.550091	46.626121	46.702190	46.778298	46.854444	46.930629
34	45.553840	45.630216	45.706634	45.783091	45.859589	45.936128	46.012707	46.089326
35	44.761011	44.837813	44.914657	44.991543	45.068471	45.145441	45.222453	45.299506
36	44.015357	44.092585	44.169856	44.247171	44.324529	44.401931	44.479375	44.556863
37	43.313037	43.390691	43.468390	43.546133	43.623921	43.701754	43.779631	43.857553
38	42.650616	42.728695	42.806820	42.884992	42.963210	43.041474	43.119784	43.198140
39	42.025007	42.103512	42.182064	42.260664	42.339311	42.418005	42.496747	42.575536
40	41.433436	41.512365	41.591343	41.670370	41.749446	41.828570	41.907743	41.986964
41	40.873397	40.952750	41.032153	41.111606	41.191109	41.270662	41.350265	41.429918
42	40.342622	40.422397	40.502224	40.582103	40.662033	40.742013	40.822045	40.902128
43	39.839055	39.919252	39.999502	40.079804	40.160159	40.240566	40.321026	40.401538
44	39.360826	39.441443	39.522114	39.602839	39.683618	39.764450	39.845336	39.926275
45	38.906230	38.987266	39.068357	39.149503	39.230704	39.311960	39.393270	39.474635
46	38.473713	38.555166	38.636675	38.718241	38.799862	38.881540	38.963273	39.045061
47	38.061850	38.143717	38.225644	38.307627	38.389667	38.471765	38.553919	38.636129
48	37.669336	37.751617	37.833958	37.916357	37.998814	38.081329	38.163902	38.246532
50	36.937653	37.020756	37.103920	37.187144	37.270429	37.353774	37.437178	37.520642
52	36.270168	36.354084	36.438062	36.522103	36.606207	36.690372	36.774599	36.858887
54	35.659639	35.744358	35.829142	35.913990	35.998902	36.083878	36.168918	36.254020
56	35.099856	35.185369	35.270948	35.356594	35.442305	35.528081	35.613923	35.699829
58	34.585464	34.671761	34.758125	34.844557	34.931057	35.017623	35.104255	35.190955
60	34.111821	34.198891	34.286030	34.373237	34.460514	34.547858	34.635271	34.722751
62	33.674882	33.762714	33.850615	33.938587	34.026629	34.114740	34.202920	34.291170
64	33.271106	33.359688	33.448340	33.537064	33.625860	33.714725	33.803662	33.892668
66	32.897381	32.986700	33.076092	33.165556	33.255092	33.344700	33.434380	33.524130
68	32.550957	32.641003	32.731121	32.821313	32.911578	33.001916	33.092326	33.182807
70	32.229402	32.320161	32.410994	32.501901	32.592882	32.683936	32.775063	32.866263
72	31.930551	32.022010	32.113545	32.205155	32.296838	32.388596	32.480427	32.572331
74	31.652472	31.744619	31.836843	31.929141	32.021515	32.113963	32.206484	32.299080
76	31.393437	31.486260	31.579159	31.672133	31.765183	31.858308	31.951507	32.044779
78	31.151895	31.245380	31.338941	31.432579	31.526291	31.620078	31.713941	31.807878
80	30.926450	31.020584	31.114794	31.209080	31.303443	31.397880	31.492392	31.586978
82	30.715841	30.810611	30.905457	31.000379	31.095377	31.190450	31.285598	31.380820
84	30.518929	30.614321	30.709789	30.805333	30.900953	30.996649	31.092419	31.188263
86	30.334679	30.430680	30.526757	30.622910	30.719138	30.815442	30.911820	31.008272
88	30.162152	30.258748	30.355420	30.452169	30.548992	30.645890	30.742863	30.839909
90	30.000491	30.097670	30.194924	30.292254	30.389659	30.487138	30.584690	30.682316
92	29.848916	29.946664	30.044486	30.142384	30.240357	30.338403	30.436522	30.534715
96	29.573225	29.672071	29.770991	29.869985	29.969052	30.068192	30.167403	30.266687
100	29.330049	29.429940	29.529904	29.629941	29.730049	29.830229	29.930479	30.030799
104	29.115139	29.216024	29.316981	29.418008	29.519105	29.620271	29.721506	29.822809
108	28.924887	29.026715	29.128613	29.230579	29.332614	29.434715	29.536883	29.639116
112	28.756209	28.858931	28.961720	29.064576	29.167497	29.270483	29.373532	29.476646
116	28.606460	28.710027	28.813659	28.917355	29.021114	29.124935	29.228818	29.332761
120	28.473357	28.577723	28.682151	28.786640	28.891189	28.995798	29.100465	29.205191
140	27.996715	28.104425	28.212182	28.319984	28.427831	28.535722	28.643657	28.751634
160	27.726183	27.836311	27.946470	28.056658	28.166874	28.277118	28.387389	28.497686

QUARTERLY WITHDRAWALS PER $1000

EFFECTIVE ANNUAL YIELD

NUMBER OF QUARTRLY WTHDRWLS	11.80%	11.85%	11.90%	11.95%	12.00%	12.05%	12.10%	12.15%
1	1028.277779	1028.392728	1028.507639	1028.622511	1028.737345	1028.852140	1028.966897	1029.081615
2	521.306895	521.393904	521.480887	521.567844	521.654776	521.741681	521.828560	521.915414
3	352.360394	352.438444	352.516473	352.594482	352.672470	352.750438	352.828386	352.906313
4	267.919975	267.993811	268.067630	268.141432	268.215217	268.288986	268.362738	268.436473
5	217.281975	217.353495	217.425001	217.496492	217.567970	217.639434	217.710884	217.782321
6	183.545170	183.615322	183.685462	183.755591	183.825709	183.895816	183.965912	184.035996
7	159.466174	159.535500	159.604817	159.674125	159.743424	159.812714	159.881996	159.951269
8	141.423292	141.492130	141.560962	141.629787	141.698605	141.767417	141.836223	141.905022
9	127.404469	127.473045	127.541617	127.610184	127.678747	127.747305	127.815859	127.884409
10	116.202470	116.270942	116.339410	116.407877	116.476342	116.544804	116.613264	116.681721
11	107.049054	107.117534	107.186015	107.254495	107.322975	107.391455	107.459934	107.528414
12	99.432056	99.500631	99.569208	99.637787	99.706368	99.774951	99.843535	99.912122
13	92.996890	93.065636	93.134375	93.203118	93.271865	93.340616	93.409371	93.478129
14	87.490318	87.559265	87.628217	87.697175	87.766140	87.835110	87.904085	87.973067
15	82.726575	82.795774	82.864980	82.934194	83.003416	83.072646	83.141883	83.211128
16	78.566372	78.635855	78.705348	78.774850	78.844362	78.913884	78.983415	79.052956
17	74.903183	74.972978	75.042783	75.112601	75.182429	75.252270	75.322121	75.391984
18	71.654155	71.724282	71.794423	71.864577	71.934744	72.004925	72.075119	72.145326
19	68.753874	68.824353	68.894846	68.965355	69.035879	69.106418	69.176973	69.247542
20	66.150012	66.220856	66.291718	66.362597	66.433492	66.504405	66.575335	66.646281
21	63.800203	63.871427	63.942669	64.013930	64.085210	64.156509	64.227826	64.299163
22	61.669786	61.741399	61.813033	61.884688	61.956363	62.028058	62.099774	62.171510
23	59.730127	59.802138	59.874173	59.946229	60.018308	60.090409	60.162532	60.234677
24	57.957361	58.029779	58.102221	58.174688	58.247178	58.319692	58.392229	58.464791
25	56.331445	56.404275	56.477132	56.550014	56.622921	56.695855	56.768814	56.841798
26	54.835415	54.908663	54.981939	55.055242	55.128573	55.201931	55.275316	55.348728
27	53.454821	53.528492	53.602192	53.675921	53.749679	53.823465	53.897281	53.971125
28	52.177278	52.251375	52.325502	52.399661	52.473849	52.548068	52.622318	52.696598
29	50.992106	51.066632	51.141190	51.215781	51.290403	51.365058	51.439745	51.514463
30	49.890051	49.965008	50.040000	50.115025	50.190084	50.265176	50.340302	50.415462
31	48.863051	48.938442	49.013868	49.089330	49.164827	49.240359	49.315926	49.391528
32	47.904051	47.979877	48.055740	48.131640	48.207576	48.283549	48.359559	48.435605
33	47.006853	47.083115	47.159415	47.235754	47.312131	47.388546	47.464999	47.541490
34	46.165984	46.242683	46.319422	46.396200	46.473018	46.549876	46.626773	46.703709
35	45.376600	45.453736	45.530914	45.608132	45.685391	45.762692	45.840033	45.917415
36	44.634393	44.711966	44.789582	44.867240	44.944941	45.022684	45.100469	45.178297
37	43.935519	44.013529	44.091584	44.169682	44.247823	44.326009	44.404238	44.482511
38	43.276541	43.354988	43.433480	43.512017	43.590599	43.669227	43.747899	43.826616
39	42.654372	42.733254	42.812183	42.891159	42.970181	43.049250	43.128364	43.207525
40	42.066234	42.145551	42.224917	42.304330	42.383791	42.463300	42.542856	42.622459
41	41.509620	41.589372	41.669172	41.749022	41.828921	41.908868	41.988864	42.068908
42	40.982262	41.062446	41.142680	41.222965	41.303300	41.383685	41.464120	41.544604
43	40.482101	40.562716	40.643383	40.724102	40.804871	40.885692	40.966564	41.047487
44	40.007267	40.088312	40.169410	40.250560	40.331763	40.413018	40.494325	40.575684
45	39.556054	39.637527	39.719054	39.800634	39.882268	39.963956	40.045696	40.127490
46	39.126905	39.208804	39.290758	39.372767	39.454831	39.536949	39.619121	39.701347
47	38.718396	38.800719	38.883099	38.965534	39.048025	39.130571	39.213172	39.295829
48	38.329221	38.411966	38.494768	38.577627	38.660543	38.743516	38.826544	38.909629
50	37.604166	37.687748	37.771390	37.855091	37.938850	38.022668	38.106543	38.190477
52	36.943237	37.027647	37.112119	37.196651	37.281244	37.365896	37.450609	37.535381
54	36.339186	36.424415	36.509706	36.595059	36.680474	36.765951	36.851490	36.937090
56	35.785800	35.871836	35.957935	36.044098	36.130325	36.216615	36.302968	36.389384
58	35.277720	35.364551	35.451447	35.538409	35.625435	35.712527	35.799682	35.886902
60	34.810298	34.897913	34.985594	35.073342	35.161157	35.249037	35.336982	35.424993
62	34.379487	34.467874	34.556328	34.644850	34.733439	34.822095	34.910818	34.999607
64	33.981743	34.070889	34.160103	34.249385	34.338736	34.428156	34.517642	34.607196
66	33.613951	33.703842	33.793803	33.883834	33.973933	34.064102	34.154339	34.244644
68	33.273360	33.363984	33.454679	33.545443	33.636278	33.727183	33.818156	33.909199
70	32.957535	33.048878	33.140292	33.231778	33.323334	33.414960	33.506657	33.598422
72	32.664308	32.756357	32.848478	32.940670	33.032934	33.125268	33.217672	33.310146
74	32.391748	32.484489	32.577303	32.670188	32.763144	32.856172	32.949270	33.042438
76	32.138126	32.231545	32.325036	32.418600	32.512236	32.605942	32.699720	32.793567
78	31.901888	31.995971	32.090127	32.184355	32.278655	32.373026	32.467468	32.561981
80	31.681638	31.776371	31.871177	31.966055	32.061005	32.156027	32.251119	32.346282
82	31.476116	31.571485	31.666926	31.762440	31.858026	31.953683	32.049410	32.145208
84	31.284180	31.380171	31.476234	31.572369	31.668576	31.764854	31.861202	31.957620
86	31.104797	31.201395	31.298066	31.394808	31.491621	31.588505	31.685459	31.782483
88	30.937028	31.034249	31.131482	31.228817	31.326222	31.423698	31.521244	31.618858
90	30.780015	30.877786	30.975628	31.073541	31.171524	31.269577	31.367699	31.465890
92	30.632979	30.731315	30.829721	30.928198	31.026745	31.125361	31.224045	31.322797
96	30.366041	30.465465	30.564958	30.664521	30.764152	30.863850	30.963616	31.063448
100	30.131188	30.231645	30.332170	30.432763	30.533422	30.634146	30.734936	30.835791
104	29.924179	30.025616	30.127118	30.228686	30.330318	30.432013	30.533772	30.635594
108	29.741415	29.843777	29.946204	30.048693	30.151245	30.253857	30.356531	30.459265
112	29.579621	29.683059	29.786558	29.889717	29.993135	30.096613	30.200149	30.303743
116	29.436764	29.540826	29.644947	29.749126	29.853361	29.957653	30.062000	30.166402
120	29.309973	29.414812	29.519706	29.624656	29.729659	29.834716	29.939825	30.044986
140	28.859652	28.967111	29.075810	29.183948	29.292124	29.400338	29.508588	29.616875
160	28.608008	28.718355	28.828725	28.939119	29.049534	29.159971	29.270429	29.380906

QUARTERLY WITHDRAWALS PER $1000

NUMBER OF QUARTRLY WTHDRWLS	EFFECTIVE ANNUAL YIELD							
	12.20%	12.25%	12.30%	12.35%	12.40%	12.45%	12.50%	12.55%
1	1029.196295	1029.310937	1029.425540	1029.540106	1029.654633	1029.769121	1029.883572	1029.997984
2	522.002241	522.089043	522.175819	522.262569	522.349293	522.435991	522.522664	522.609311
3	352.984219	353.062105	353.139971	353.217816	353.295641	353.373446	353.451230	353.528993
4	268.510191	268.583892	268.657577	268.731245	268.804896	268.878530	268.952148	269.025748
5	217.853743	217.925152	217.996547	218.067928	218.139295	218.210649	218.281989	218.353315
6	184.106069	184.176131	184.246182	184.316221	184.386250	184.456267	184.526273	184.596267
7	160.020533	160.089788	160.159035	160.228272	160.297501	160.366721	160.435932	160.505134
8	141.973814	142.042600	142.111379	142.180152	142.248918	142.317678	142.386431	142.455178
9	127.952955	128.021496	128.090032	128.158565	128.227093	128.295616	128.364135	128.432650
10	116.750177	116.818630	116.887081	116.955529	117.023976	117.092420	117.160861	117.229301
11	107.596893	107.665372	107.733851	107.802330	107.870808	107.939286	108.007764	108.076241
12	99.980710	100.049300	100.117892	100.186485	100.255081	100.323678	100.392276	100.460877
13	93.546892	93.615658	93.684427	93.753201	93.821978	93.890759	93.959544	94.028332
14	88.042054	88.111047	88.180045	88.249050	88.318059	88.387075	88.456096	88.525123
15	83.280380	83.349640	83.418908	83.488183	83.557466	83.626756	83.696054	83.765359
16	79.122506	79.192066	79.261635	79.331214	79.400802	79.470399	79.540006	79.609623
17	75.461859	75.531745	75.601642	75.671550	75.741470	75.811401	75.881343	75.951297
18	72.215546	72.285780	72.356027	72.426287	72.496560	72.566846	72.637145	72.707457
19	69.318126	69.388726	69.459340	69.529969	69.600613	69.671272	69.741946	69.812635
20	66.717244	66.788224	66.859221	66.930235	67.001265	67.072312	67.143375	67.214455
21	64.370517	64.441890	64.513282	64.584692	64.656121	64.727568	64.799033	64.870517
22	62.242657	62.315043	62.386840	62.458658	62.530495	62.602353	62.674230	62.746128
23	60.306844	60.379034	60.451245	60.523478	60.595733	60.668010	60.740308	60.812628
24	58.537376	58.609985	58.682618	58.755274	58.827954	58.900657	58.973384	59.046134
25	56.914807	56.987842	57.060903	57.133988	57.207099	57.280235	57.353395	57.426581
26	55.422167	55.495633	55.569126	55.642646	55.716193	55.789766	55.863366	55.936993
27	54.044998	54.118909	54.192829	54.266788	54.340775	54.414790	54.488833	54.562905
28	52.770908	52.845248	52.919619	52.994019	53.068450	53.142910	53.217400	53.291920
29	51.589213	51.663995	51.738809	51.813654	51.888531	51.963439	52.038378	52.113350
30	50.490654	50.565880	50.641139	50.716432	50.791757	50.867115	50.942506	51.017930
31	49.467165	49.542836	49.618543	49.694284	49.770059	49.845869	49.921713	49.997592
32	48.511687	48.587806	48.663960	48.740151	48.816378	48.892640	48.968939	49.045273
33	47.618018	47.694585	47.771188	47.847830	47.924509	48.001225	48.077978	48.154769
34	46.780684	46.857699	46.934753	47.011845	47.088976	47.166146	47.243355	47.320602
35	45.994837	46.072300	46.149803	46.227347	46.304931	46.382555	46.460218	46.537922
36	45.256166	45.334077	45.412030	45.490025	45.568061	45.646139	45.724257	45.802417
37	44.560826	44.639185	44.717587	44.796032	44.874520	44.953050	45.031623	45.110239
38	43.905377	43.984183	44.063034	44.141928	44.220867	44.299850	44.378876	44.457947
39	43.286731	43.365984	43.445281	43.524625	43.604013	43.683447	43.762926	43.842450
40	42.702109	42.781806	42.861550	42.941341	43.021178	43.101062	43.180992	43.260968
41	42.149001	42.229142	42.309331	42.389568	42.469853	42.550185	42.630564	42.710991
42	41.625138	41.705721	41.786353	41.867035	41.947765	42.028544	42.109372	42.190248
43	41.128460	41.209473	41.290558	41.371682	41.452856	41.534080	41.615354	41.696677
44	40.657095	40.738557	40.820071	40.901636	40.983252	41.064919	41.146637	41.228406
45	40.209337	40.291236	40.373187	40.455191	40.537247	40.619355	40.701515	40.783727
46	39.783627	39.865961	39.948348	40.030789	40.113282	40.195829	40.278429	40.361081
47	39.378360	39.461036	39.544127	39.627002	39.709931	39.792915	39.875951	39.959042
48	38.992769	39.075966	39.159217	39.242524	39.325887	39.409304	39.492775	39.576302
50	38.274468	38.358517	38.442623	38.526787	38.611007	38.695284	38.779617	38.864007
52	37.620213	37.705104	37.790054	37.875063	37.960130	38.045256	38.130439	38.215681
54	37.022751	37.108472	37.194255	37.280097	37.366000	37.451963	37.537985	37.624067
56	36.475863	36.562503	36.649006	36.735671	36.822397	36.909184	36.996032	37.082941
58	35.974186	36.061533	36.148943	36.236417	36.323953	36.411552	36.499213	36.586936
60	35.513070	35.601210	35.689416	35.777685	35.866018	35.954415	36.042875	36.131398
62	35.088462	35.177383	35.266370	35.355422	35.444538	35.533720	35.622965	35.712274
64	34.696818	34.786505	34.876260	34.966080	35.055966	35.145917	35.235932	35.326014
66	34.335017	34.425458	34.515966	34.606540	34.697181	34.787888	34.878660	34.969498
68	34.000310	34.091489	34.182736	34.274050	34.365431	34.456879	34.548393	34.639973
70	33.690256	33.782160	33.874131	33.966170	34.058277	34.150451	34.242691	34.334998
72	33.402690	33.495302	33.587984	33.680733	33.773550	33.866435	33.959387	34.052405
74	33.135676	33.228984	33.322360	33.415804	33.509317	33.602897	33.696545	33.790259
76	32.887485	32.981472	33.075528	33.169653	33.263846	33.358106	33.452434	33.546829
78	32.656564	32.751354	32.845937	32.940726	33.035584	33.130509	33.225502	33.320562
80	32.441514	32.536616	32.632187	32.727626	32.823133	32.918708	33.014350	33.110059
82	32.241075	32.337012	32.433018	32.529092	32.625233	32.721442	32.817718	32.914060
84	32.054107	32.150664	32.247289	32.343982	32.440743	32.537570	32.634464	32.731424
86	31.879576	31.976737	32.073967	32.171264	32.268628	32.366058	32.463555	32.561117
88	31.716541	31.814293	31.912112	32.009998	32.107950	32.205968	32.304052	32.402201
90	31.564149	31.662475	31.760868	31.859328	31.957854	32.056444	32.155100	32.253820
92	31.421617	31.520504	31.619457	31.718475	31.817559	31.916707	32.015919	32.115195
96	31.163346	31.263309	31.363337	31.463429	31.563584	31.663802	31.764083	31.864425
100	30.936710	31.037692	31.138737	31.239843	31.341012	31.442241	31.543530	31.644880
104	30.737477	30.839422	30.941427	31.043492	31.145616	31.247799	31.350040	31.452338
108	30.562059	30.664911	30.767821	30.870789	30.973813	31.076894	31.180030	31.283221
112	30.407393	30.511100	30.614862	30.718678	30.822549	30.926474	31.030451	31.134480
116	30.270858	30.375368	30.479930	30.584544	30.689209	30.793925	30.898691	31.003506
120	30.150199	30.255462	30.360774	30.466136	30.571545	30.677003	30.782507	30.888057
140	29.725197	29.833553	29.941943	30.050366	30.158822	30.267309	30.375827	30.484375
160	29.491403	29.601919	29.712452	29.823003	29.933570	30.044152	30.154750	30.265363

QUARTERLY WITHDRAWALS PER $1000

EFFECTIVE ANNUAL YIELD

NUMBER OF QUARTRLY WTHDRWLS	12.60%	12.65%	12.70%	12.75%	12.80%	12.85%	12.90%	12.95%
1	1030.112359	1030.226695	1030.340993	1030.455253	1030.569475	1030.683660	1030.797806	1030.911914
2	522.695932	522.782528	522.869097	522.955641	523.042160	523.128652	523.215120	523.301561
3	353.606737	353.684460	353.762162	353.839845	353.917507	353.995149	354.072770	354.150372
4	269.099333	269.172900	269.246451	269.319985	269.393503	269.467003	269.540488	269.613955
5	218.424627	218.495925	218.567210	218.638481	218.709738	218.780982	218.852211	218.923427
6	184.666251	184.736223	184.806184	184.876134	184.946073	185.016001	185.085917	185.155822
7	160.574328	160.643513	160.712689	160.781856	160.851014	160.920164	160.989304	161.058436
8	142.523918	142.592651	142.661378	142.730098	142.798812	142.867519	142.936219	143.004913
9	128.501160	128.569666	128.638167	128.706664	128.775157	128.843645	128.912129	128.980608
10	117.297738	117.366172	117.434605	117.503035	117.571462	117.639888	117.708311	117.776731
11	108.144718	108.213195	108.281672	108.350148	108.418624	108.487100	108.555575	108.624050
12	100.529479	100.598083	100.666688	100.735295	100.803904	100.872514	100.941126	101.009740
13	94.097124	94.165919	94.234718	94.303521	94.372327	94.441137	94.509951	94.578768
14	88.594155	88.663193	88.732236	88.801285	88.870339	88.939399	89.008464	89.077535
15	83.834672	83.903992	83.973320	84.042655	84.111997	84.181347	84.250704	84.320068
16	79.679248	79.748883	79.818527	79.888180	79.957843	80.027515	80.097196	80.166886
17	76.021261	76.091237	76.161224	76.231222	76.301230	76.371250	76.441281	76.511323
18	72.777782	72.848120	72.918471	72.988834	73.059211	73.129601	73.200003	73.270418
19	69.883338	69.954056	70.024789	70.095537	70.166299	70.237075	70.307866	70.378672
20	67.285551	67.356664	67.427794	67.498940	67.570102	67.641280	67.712475	67.783686
21	64.942019	65.013539	65.085077	65.156633	65.228208	65.299800	65.371411	65.443039
22	62.818045	62.889983	62.961940	63.033917	63.105914	63.177931	63.249967	63.322023
23	60.884970	60.957333	61.029718	61.102125	61.174553	61.247002	61.319473	61.391964
24	59.118907	59.191704	59.264523	59.337366	59.410232	59.483121	59.556033	59.628968
25	57.499792	57.573028	57.646288	57.719573	57.792883	57.866218	57.939577	58.012961
26	56.010646	56.084326	56.158032	56.231764	56.305523	56.379308	56.453119	56.526956
27	54.637005	54.711132	54.785288	54.859472	54.933683	55.007923	55.082190	55.156485
28	53.366470	53.441049	53.515658	53.590296	53.664963	53.739660	53.814386	53.889141
29	52.188352	52.263385	52.338449	52.413544	52.488670	52.563827	52.639015	52.714233
30	51.093387	51.168876	51.244397	51.319952	51.395538	51.471157	51.546808	51.622491
31	50.073504	50.149451	50.225431	50.301446	50.377494	50.453576	50.529692	50.605841
32	49.121643	49.198048	49.274488	49.350964	49.427476	49.504022	49.580603	49.657220
33	48.231596	48.308460	48.385361	48.462299	48.539274	48.616285	48.693332	48.770416
34	47.397887	47.475211	47.552573	47.629973	47.707411	47.784887	47.862400	47.939952
35	46.615665	46.693448	46.771271	46.849133	46.927034	47.004974	47.082954	47.160972
36	45.880618	45.958859	46.037142	46.115465	46.193829	46.272234	46.350679	46.429164
37	45.188897	45.267597	45.346339	45.425123	45.503949	45.582817	45.661726	45.740677
38	44.537060	44.616218	44.695418	44.774662	44.853949	44.933279	45.012652	45.092067
39	43.922019	44.001632	44.081290	44.160992	44.240739	44.320530	44.400364	44.480243
40	43.340990	43.421058	43.501172	43.581332	43.661536	43.741787	43.822082	43.902422
41	42.791465	42.871987	42.952556	43.033169	43.113831	43.194538	43.275292	43.356093
42	42.271172	42.352144	42.433165	42.514233	42.595349	42.676513	42.757723	42.838982
43	41.778050	41.859471	41.940942	42.022462	42.104031	42.185648	42.267313	42.349027
44	41.310225	41.392094	41.474013	41.555982	41.638001	41.720070	41.802188	41.884355
45	40.865990	40.948304	41.030669	41.113085	41.195553	41.278070	41.360638	41.443257
46	40.443786	40.526543	40.609352	40.692213	40.775125	40.858089	40.941105	41.024172
47	40.042186	40.125383	40.208633	40.291936	40.375292	40.458700	40.542160	40.625673
48	39.659882	39.743517	39.827206	39.910948	39.994744	40.078593	40.162496	40.246451
50	38.948453	39.032954	39.117512	39.202124	39.286792	39.371515	39.456293	39.541125
52	38.300981	38.386337	38.471751	38.557222	38.642750	38.728335	38.813975	38.899672
54	37.710208	37.796407	37.882665	37.968982	38.055357	38.141790	38.228280	38.314828
56	37.169910	37.256940	37.344029	37.431178	37.518387	37.605654	37.692981	37.780366
58	36.674720	36.762566	36.850473	36.938441	37.026469	37.114558	37.202706	37.290915
60	36.219984	36.308632	36.397343	36.486115	36.574949	36.663844	36.752800	36.841816
62	35.801647	35.891083	35.980583	36.070145	36.159769	36.249455	36.339203	36.429013
64	35.416160	35.506369	35.596642	35.686979	35.777379	35.867842	35.958367	36.048954
66	35.060401	35.151369	35.242401	35.333498	35.424657	35.515881	35.607167	35.698516
68	34.731618	34.823329	34.915105	35.006945	35.098850	35.190818	35.282849	35.374944
70	34.427371	34.519809	34.612313	34.704881	34.797514	34.890211	34.982972	35.075796
72	34.145490	34.238640	34.331856	34.425137	34.518482	34.611892	34.705366	34.798903
74	33.884040	33.977886	34.071799	34.165776	34.259818	34.353925	34.448095	34.542329
76	33.641290	33.735817	33.830410	33.925068	34.019790	34.114577	34.209428	34.304342
78	33.415687	33.510879	33.606136	33.701458	33.796845	33.892296	33.987811	34.083388
80	33.205833	33.301674	33.397580	33.493550	33.589585	33.685683	33.781845	33.878070
82	33.010467	33.106941	33.203479	33.300081	33.396748	33.493478	33.590271	33.687126
84	32.828449	32.925539	33.022694	33.119912	33.217194	33.314539	33.411947	33.509417
86	32.658744	32.756435	32.854190	32.952009	33.049891	33.147835	33.245841	33.343908
88	32.500414	32.598690	32.697030	32.795433	32.893898	32.992425	33.091013	33.189662
90	32.352603	32.451450	32.550359	32.649330	32.748363	32.847457	32.946611	33.045825
92	32.214534	32.313935	32.413397	32.512921	32.612506	32.712151	32.811855	32.911619
96	31.964828	32.065292	32.165815	32.266399	32.367040	32.467741	32.568498	32.669313
100	31.746288	31.847754	31.949279	32.050860	32.152499	32.254193	32.355942	32.457747
104	31.554693	31.657103	31.759570	31.862091	31.964666	32.067295	32.169977	32.272711
108	31.386466	31.489764	31.593115	31.696519	31.799974	31.903480	32.007036	32.110642
112	31.238560	31.342691	31.446873	31.551103	31.655383	31.759710	31.864086	31.968507
116	31.108369	31.213280	31.318239	31.423244	31.528294	31.633390	31.738531	31.843715
120	30.993653	31.099294	31.204979	31.310707	31.416478	31.522291	31.628145	31.734040
140	30.592952	30.701558	30.810192	30.918854	31.027542	31.136257	31.244996	31.353761
160	30.375989	30.486628	30.597280	30.707944	30.818619	30.929305	31.040000	31.150706

QUARTERLY WITHDRAWALS PER $1000

EFFECTIVE ANNUAL YIELD

NUMBER OF QUARTERLY WTHDRWLS	13.00%	13.05%	13.10%	13.15%	13.20%	13.25%	13.30%	13.35%
1	1031.025985	1031.140017	1031.254012	1031.367969	1031.481888	1031.595770	1031.709614	1031.823420
2	523.387977	523.474367	523.560732	523.647071	523.733385	523.819673	523.905936	523.992174
3	354.227953	354.305514	354.383054	354.460575	354.538075	354.615555	354.693015	354.770455
4	269.687406	269.760840	269.834258	269.907659	269.981044	270.054412	270.127763	270.201098
5	218.994630	219.065818	219.136993	219.208154	219.279302	219.350436	219.421556	219.492662
6	185.225717	185.295600	185.365471	185.435332	185.505182	185.575020	185.644847	185.714664
7	161.127559	161.196674	161.265779	161.334876	161.403964	161.473043	161.542113	161.611174
8	143.073600	143.142281	143.210955	143.279623	143.348284	143.416938	143.485586	143.554227
9	129.049083	129.117553	129.186019	129.254481	129.322937	129.391390	129.459838	129.528282
10	117.845149	117.913565	117.981978	118.050389	118.118798	118.187204	118.255608	118.324009
11	108.692524	108.760998	108.829472	108.897945	108.966418	109.034891	109.103363	109.171834
12	101.078355	101.146972	101.215591	101.284210	101.352832	101.421455	101.490079	101.558705
13	94.647588	94.716412	94.785240	94.854071	94.922905	94.991743	95.060584	95.129429
14	89.146611	89.215693	89.284780	89.353872	89.422969	89.492072	89.561181	89.630294
15	84.389440	84.458819	84.528205	84.597598	84.666999	84.736407	84.805822	84.875244
16	80.236585	80.306293	80.376011	80.445737	80.515473	80.585217	80.654970	80.724733
17	76.581376	76.651440	76.721514	76.791600	76.861696	76.931803	77.001921	77.072049
18	73.340846	73.411286	73.481739	73.552205	73.622683	73.693174	73.763677	73.834193
19	70.449492	70.520327	70.591176	70.662039	70.732917	70.803809	70.874715	70.945636
20	67.854913	67.926156	67.997416	68.068691	68.139983	68.211291	68.282614	68.353954
21	65.514685	65.586349	65.658031	65.729731	65.801449	65.873184	65.944937	66.016707
22	63.394098	63.466194	63.538308	63.610442	63.682596	63.754742	63.826960	63.899172
23	61.464478	61.537012	61.609567	61.682144	61.754742	61.827360	61.900000	61.972660
24	59.701926	59.774906	59.847910	59.920936	59.993985	60.067056	60.140150	60.213266
25	58.086369	58.159801	58.233258	58.306740	58.380245	58.453775	58.527328	58.600906
26	56.600820	56.674709	56.748624	56.822565	56.896532	56.970524	57.044543	57.118586
27	55.230807	55.305157	55.379534	55.453938	55.528370	55.602830	55.677316	55.751830
28	53.963926	54.038739	54.113582	54.188453	54.263353	54.338282	54.413239	54.488225
29	52.789482	52.864761	52.940071	53.015411	53.090782	53.166184	53.241613	53.317074
30	51.698206	51.773953	51.849732	51.925543	52.001386	52.077260	52.153166	52.229103
31	50.682024	50.758240	50.834490	50.910772	50.987088	51.063437	51.139819	51.216234
32	49.733871	49.810557	49.887277	49.964033	50.040822	50.117646	50.194505	50.271398
33	48.847536	48.924692	49.001884	49.079112	49.156376	49.233676	49.311011	49.388382
34	48.017540	48.095167	48.172830	48.250531	48.328269	48.406044	48.483857	48.561706
35	47.239030	47.317126	47.395261	47.473434	47.551646	47.629896	47.708184	47.786511
36	46.507689	46.586254	46.664860	46.743505	46.822189	46.900913	46.979677	47.058480
37	45.819669	45.898703	45.977777	46.056893	46.136049	46.215247	46.294485	46.373763
38	45.171525	45.251026	45.330568	45.410153	45.489781	45.569450	45.649161	45.728913
39	44.560165	44.640132	44.720141	44.800194	44.880290	44.960429	45.040612	45.120837
40	43.982807	44.063237	44.143712	44.224231	44.304794	44.385402	44.466054	44.546749
41	43.436939	43.517831	43.598769	43.679752	43.760781	43.841855	43.922974	44.004138
42	42.920287	43.001639	43.083038	43.164483	43.245975	43.327513	43.409098	43.490728
43	42.430789	42.512599	42.594457	42.676362	42.758315	42.840315	42.922362	43.004457
44	41.966571	42.048837	42.131151	42.213514	42.295925	42.378385	42.460892	42.543448
45	41.525925	41.608643	41.691411	41.774229	41.857096	41.940012	42.022978	42.105992
46	41.107289	41.190458	41.273677	41.356947	41.440267	41.523637	41.607058	41.690527
47	40.709237	40.792853	40.876521	40.960240	41.044010	41.127832	41.211704	41.295626
48	40.330459	40.414520	40.498633	40.582798	40.667016	40.751285	40.835606	40.919978
50	39.626012	39.710953	39.795948	39.880996	39.966099	40.051254	40.136463	40.221725
52	38.985425	39.071233	39.157097	39.243015	39.328989	39.415018	39.501101	39.587239
54	38.401434	38.488096	38.574815	38.661590	38.748422	38.835309	38.922253	39.009252
56	37.867810	37.955312	38.042872	38.130489	38.218164	38.305896	38.393685	38.481530
58	37.379182	37.467509	37.555895	37.644340	37.732843	37.821404	37.910023	37.998700
60	36.930893	37.020030	37.109227	37.198483	37.287799	37.377174	37.466607	37.556099
62	36.518884	36.608816	36.698808	36.788860	36.878973	36.969145	37.059376	37.149667
64	36.139603	36.230313	36.321085	36.411917	36.502810	36.593764	36.684778	36.775850
66	35.789927	35.881400	35.972935	36.064531	36.156189	36.247907	36.339685	36.431523
68	35.467101	35.559321	35.651603	35.743946	35.836351	35.928816	36.021343	36.113929
70	35.168683	35.261633	35.354645	35.447719	35.540854	35.634051	35.727308	35.820626
72	34.892504	34.986167	35.079892	35.173680	35.267529	35.361439	35.455410	35.549441
74	34.636626	34.730986	34.825408	34.919892	35.014438	35.109045	35.203712	35.298440
76	34.399319	34.494359	34.589461	34.684625	34.779850	34.875136	34.970483	35.065889
78	34.179029	34.274732	34.370497	34.466323	34.562211	34.658159	34.754168	34.850236
80	33.974357	34.070707	34.167118	34.263590	34.360123	34.456716	34.553369	34.650081
82	33.784044	33.881023	33.978063	34.075164	34.172325	34.269546	34.366826	34.464165
84	33.606948	33.704540	33.802193	33.899905	33.997678	34.095510	34.193400	34.291348
86	33.442036	33.540225	33.638473	33.736782	33.835148	33.933574	34.032057	34.130598
88	33.288371	33.387140	33.485968	33.584854	33.683799	33.782801	33.881861	33.980977
90	33.145099	33.244331	33.343622	33.443271	33.542777	33.642339	33.741958	33.841633
92	33.011441	33.111321	33.211258	33.311253	33.411303	33.511410	33.611572	33.711788
96	32.770185	32.871112	32.972095	33.073132	33.174224	33.275370	33.376569	33.477820
100	32.559606	32.661518	32.763484	32.865502	32.967572	33.069693	33.171866	33.274088
104	32.375497	32.478334	32.581222	32.684160	32.787147	32.890183	32.993267	33.096399
108	32.214297	32.318001	32.421752	32.525551	32.629396	32.733287	32.837224	32.941205
112	32.072975	32.177489	32.282048	32.386651	32.491297	32.595987	32.700719	32.805493
116	31.948942	32.054212	32.159524	32.264877	32.370271	32.475705	32.581178	32.686690
120	31.839975	31.945950	32.051964	32.158015	32.264105	32.370231	32.476393	32.582591
140	31.462549	31.571361	31.680196	31.789053	31.897931	32.006830	32.115750	32.224689
160	31.261420	31.372142	31.482872	31.593610	31.704354	31.815103	31.925859	32.036619

QUARTERLY WITHDRAWALS PER $1000

NUMBER OF QUARTRLY WTHDRWLS	EFFECTIVE ANNUAL YIELD							
	13.40%	13.45%	13.50%	13.55%	13.60%	13.65%	13.70%	13.75%
1	1031.937188	1032.050919	1032.164613	1032.278268	1032.391887	1032.505467	1032.619011	1032.732516
2	524.078385	524.164572	524.250733	524.336869	524.422979	524.509064	524.595124	524.681158
3	354.847874	354.925274	355.002653	355.080013	355.157352	355.234671	355.311970	355.389250
4	270.274416	270.347718	270.421003	270.494271	270.567524	270.640759	270.713978	270.787181
5	219.563755	219.634834	219.705900	219.776952	219.847990	219.919014	219.990025	220.061023
6	185.784469	185.854263	185.924045	185.993817	186.063578	186.133327	186.203065	186.272793
7	161.680227	161.749271	161.818306	161.887332	161.956350	162.025359	162.094359	162.163350
8	143.622862	143.691490	143.760112	143.828726	143.897335	143.965936	144.034531	144.103120
9	129.596721	129.665155	129.733585	129.802011	129.870432	129.938848	130.007260	130.075668
10	118.392408	118.460804	118.529198	118.597589	118.665978	118.734365	118.802749	118.871130
11	109.240306	109.308776	109.377246	109.445716	109.514185	109.582654	109.651122	109.719590
12	101.627333	101.695962	101.764592	101.833224	101.901857	101.970492	102.039128	102.107766
13	95.198277	95.267129	95.335983	95.404842	95.473703	95.542568	95.611436	95.680308
14	89.699413	89.768537	89.837666	89.906801	89.975940	90.045085	90.114235	90.183390
15	84.944673	85.014109	85.083552	85.153002	85.222460	85.291924	85.361395	85.430874
16	80.794504	80.864284	80.934073	81.003871	81.073678	81.143493	81.213318	81.283151
17	77.142188	77.212338	77.282499	77.352670	77.422852	77.493044	77.563247	77.633460
18	73.904721	73.975262	74.045815	74.116380	74.186958	74.257548	74.328151	74.398765
19	71.016570	71.087519	71.158482	71.229459	71.300450	71.371455	71.442474	71.513507
20	68.425309	68.496680	68.568068	68.639471	68.710889	68.782323	68.853773	68.925239
21	66.088495	66.160301	66.232124	66.303965	66.375823	66.447698	66.519590	66.591500
22	63.971402	64.043652	64.115921	64.188209	64.260516	64.332842	64.405187	64.477551
23	62.045342	62.118044	62.190767	62.263510	62.336274	62.409059	62.481864	62.554690
24	60.286405	60.359566	60.432749	60.505955	60.579183	60.652433	60.725706	60.799000
25	58.674508	58.748134	58.821783	58.895457	58.969154	59.042875	59.116620	59.190388
26	57.192656	57.266751	57.340871	57.415017	57.489187	57.563384	57.637605	57.711851
27	55.826370	55.900938	55.975532	56.050153	56.124801	56.199476	56.274178	56.348906
28	54.563240	54.638283	54.713354	54.788454	54.863582	54.938738	55.013922	55.089135
29	53.392565	53.468086	53.543636	53.619216	53.694826	53.770466	53.846135	53.921834
30	52.305071	52.381071	52.457102	52.533165	52.609258	52.685383	52.761538	52.837724
31	51.292681	51.369161	51.445674	51.522219	51.598797	51.675407	51.752049	51.828724
32	50.348324	50.425285	50.502280	50.579309	50.656371	50.733468	50.810597	50.887761
33	49.465789	49.543231	49.620708	49.698220	49.775767	49.853349	49.930967	50.008619
34	48.639591	48.717514	48.795473	48.873468	48.951500	49.029568	49.107672	49.185812
35	47.864875	47.943277	48.021718	48.100196	48.178711	48.257264	48.335854	48.414482
36	47.137323	47.216204	47.295124	47.374084	47.453082	47.532119	47.611194	47.690308
37	46.453082	46.532442	46.611841	46.691281	46.770760	46.850279	46.929839	47.009437
38	45.808707	45.888543	45.968420	46.048338	46.128298	46.208298	46.288339	46.368421
39	45.201105	45.281415	45.361768	45.442163	45.522600	45.603080	45.683601	45.764164
40	44.627489	44.708272	44.789099	44.869969	44.950882	45.031839	45.112838	45.193880
41	44.085347	44.166601	44.247899	44.329242	44.410629	44.492060	44.573535	44.655054
42	43.572405	43.654127	43.735894	43.817707	43.899566	43.981469	44.063418	44.145411
43	43.086598	43.168786	43.251020	43.333301	43.415628	43.498001	43.580421	43.662885
44	42.626051	42.708702	42.791401	42.874147	42.956940	43.039780	43.122667	43.205600
45	42.189055	42.272166	42.355326	42.438534	42.521790	42.605094	42.688446	42.771845
46	41.774047	41.857616	41.941234	42.024901	42.108617	42.192382	42.276196	42.360057
47	41.379599	41.463623	41.547696	41.631819	41.715992	41.800215	41.884487	41.968808
48	41.004402	41.088876	41.173402	41.257978	41.342604	41.427281	41.512008	41.596785
50	40.307039	40.392406	40.477826	40.563297	40.648820	40.734396	40.820022	40.905700
52	39.673430	39.759676	39.845975	39.932328	40.018734	40.105192	40.191704	40.278268
54	39.096306	39.183415	39.270580	39.357798	39.445072	39.532399	39.619780	39.707215
56	38.569432	38.657390	38.745404	38.833474	38.921599	39.009779	39.098014	39.186303
58	38.087433	38.176224	38.265072	38.353976	38.442937	38.531953	38.621025	38.710153
60	37.645649	37.735256	37.824921	37.914644	38.004423	38.094259	38.184152	38.274100
62	37.240016	37.330424	37.420890	37.511414	37.601995	37.692634	37.783329	37.874081
64	36.866982	36.958173	37.049422	37.140730	37.232096	37.323520	37.415001	37.506539
66	36.523421	36.615378	36.707394	36.799469	36.891602	36.983793	37.076042	37.168348
68	36.206575	36.299281	36.392047	36.484871	36.577753	36.670694	36.763693	36.856749
70	35.914003	36.007441	36.100937	36.194493	36.288107	36.381779	36.475510	36.569297
72	35.643533	35.737684	35.831894	35.926164	36.020491	36.114877	36.209321	36.303822
74	35.393228	35.488075	35.582981	35.677946	35.772970	35.868051	35.963190	36.058387
76	35.161356	35.256882	35.352466	35.448109	35.543810	35.639569	35.735385	35.831258
78	34.946363	35.042550	35.138795	35.235098	35.331459	35.427877	35.524351	35.620883
80	34.746852	34.843682	34.940570	35.037515	35.134518	35.231577	35.328692	35.425864
82	34.561563	34.659018	34.756531	34.854100	34.951727	35.049409	35.147147	35.244941
84	34.389355	34.487418	34.585538	34.683715	34.781947	34.880235	34.978578	35.076975
86	34.229196	34.327850	34.426561	34.525327	34.624148	34.723023	34.821953	34.920936
88	34.080150	34.179230	34.278661	34.377999	34.477391	34.576837	34.676336	34.775888
90	33.941363	34.041148	34.140987	34.240880	34.340826	34.440825	34.540876	34.640978
92	33.812059	33.912384	34.012762	34.113193	34.213676	34.314210	34.414796	34.515433
96	33.579124	33.680479	33.781885	33.883342	33.984849	34.086405	34.188010	34.289663
100	33.376360	33.478681	33.581051	33.683469	33.785934	33.888447	33.991005	34.093610
104	33.199577	33.302602	33.406074	33.509390	33.612751	33.716156	33.819605	33.923097
108	33.045231	33.149300	33.253412	33.357567	33.461764	33.566002	33.670280	33.774599
112	32.910309	33.015165	33.120061	33.224996	33.329970	33.434983	33.540034	33.645121
116	32.792240	32.897828	33.003453	33.109114	33.214811	33.320544	33.426311	33.532112
120	32.688825	32.795092	32.901394	33.007728	33.114096	33.220495	33.326926	33.433388
140	32.333647	32.442624	32.551618	32.660630	32.769659	32.878704	32.987764	33.096840
160	32.147384	32.258153	32.368925	32.479699	32.590477	32.701256	32.812036	32.922817

QUARTERLY WITHDRAWALS PER $1000

NUMBER OF QUARTRLY WTHDRWLS	EFFECTIVE ANNUAL YIELD							
	13.80%	13.85%	13.90%	13.95%	14.00%	14.05%	14.10%	14.15%
1	1032.845985	1032.959416	1033.072809	1033.186166	1033.299485	1033.412767	1033.526011	1033.639218
2	524.767167	524.853151	524.939109	525.025042	525.110951	525.196833	525.282691	525.368524
3	355.466509	355.543748	355.620967	355.698166	355.775345	355.852504	355.929643	356.006763
4	270.860367	270.933537	271.006690	271.079827	271.152947	271.226051	271.299139	271.372210
5	220.132007	220.202977	220.273933	220.344876	220.415805	220.486721	220.557623	220.628512
6	186.342509	186.412214	186.481908	186.551591	186.621262	186.690923	186.760573	186.830211
7	162.232332	162.301306	162.370271	162.439227	162.508174	162.577112	162.646042	162.714963
8	144.171701	144.240277	144.308845	144.377407	144.445963	144.514511	144.583053	144.651589
9	130.144071	130.212469	130.280863	130.349253	130.417638	130.486018	130.554394	130.622765
10	118.939509	119.007886	119.076260	119.144631	119.213000	119.281366	119.349730	119.418091
11	109.788057	109.856523	109.924989	109.993455	110.061920	110.130384	110.198848	110.267311
12	102.176405	102.245045	102.313687	102.382330	102.450974	102.519620	102.588267	102.656915
13	95.749182	95.818060	95.886941	95.955826	96.024713	96.093604	96.162498	96.231395
14	90.252550	90.321716	90.390886	90.460062	90.529242	90.598428	90.667618	90.736814
15	85.500359	85.569851	85.639350	85.708856	85.778369	85.847888	85.917415	85.986948
16	81.352992	81.422843	81.492702	81.562570	81.632446	81.702331	81.772225	81.842127
17	77.703684	77.773919	77.844163	77.914418	77.984684	78.054960	78.125246	78.195542
18	74.469392	74.540031	74.610682	74.681346	74.752021	74.822708	74.893408	74.964119
19	71.584554	71.655615	71.726690	71.797778	71.868881	71.939997	72.011126	72.082270
20	68.996720	69.068217	69.139729	69.211257	69.282800	69.354359	69.425933	69.497522
21	66.663428	66.735372	66.807333	66.879312	66.951308	67.023320	67.095350	67.167397
22	64.549934	64.622335	64.694755	64.767194	64.839652	64.912128	64.984623	65.057137
23	62.627536	62.700403	62.773290	62.846197	62.919125	62.992073	63.065041	63.138029
24	60.872316	60.945655	61.019015	61.092397	61.165801	61.239226	61.312674	61.386143
25	59.264180	59.337995	59.411834	59.485696	59.559581	59.633490	59.707421	59.781376
26	57.786123	57.860419	57.934741	58.009087	58.083458	58.157854	58.232274	58.306719
27	56.423660	56.498441	56.573249	56.648082	56.722942	56.797829	56.872741	56.947679
28	55.164375	55.239643	55.314939	55.390263	55.465614	55.540993	55.616400	55.691834
29	53.997562	54.073319	54.149105	54.224921	54.300765	54.376639	54.452542	54.528473
30	52.913941	52.990188	53.066467	53.142775	53.219114	53.295484	53.371883	53.448313
31	51.905430	51.982169	52.058940	52.135742	52.212576	52.289442	52.366340	52.443269
32	50.964957	51.042187	51.119451	51.196747	51.274077	51.351439	51.428834	51.506262
33	50.086305	50.164026	50.241782	50.319572	50.397397	50.475256	50.553149	50.631075
34	49.263988	49.342200	49.420448	49.498731	49.577050	49.655404	49.733794	49.812219
35	48.493146	48.571848	48.650587	48.729363	48.808175	48.887024	48.965909	49.044831
36	47.769460	47.848651	47.927879	48.007146	48.086450	48.165792	48.245172	48.324590
37	47.089075	47.168753	47.248470	47.328226	47.408021	47.487855	47.567727	47.647638
38	46.448544	46.528706	46.608910	46.689153	46.769437	46.849761	46.930124	47.010527
39	45.844769	45.925415	46.006103	46.086832	46.167602	46.248414	46.329266	46.410159
40	45.274965	45.356093	45.437263	45.518475	45.599730	45.681026	45.762364	45.843745
41	44.736617	44.818224	44.899873	44.981566	45.063303	45.145082	45.226904	45.308769
42	44.227449	44.309532	44.391658	44.473830	44.556045	44.638304	44.720607	44.802954
43	43.745396	43.827952	43.910553	43.993199	44.075891	44.158627	44.241408	44.324233
44	43.288580	43.371607	43.454679	43.537798	43.620962	43.704173	43.787428	43.870729
45	42.855292	42.938785	43.022326	43.105914	43.189548	43.273229	43.356957	43.440730
46	42.443967	42.527925	42.611931	42.695985	42.780086	42.864234	42.948429	43.032672
47	42.053178	42.137596	42.222061	42.306580	42.391144	42.475756	42.560416	42.645123
48	41.681611	41.766488	41.851413	41.936388	42.021411	42.106483	42.191604	42.276774
50	40.991429	41.077209	41.163040	41.248921	41.334852	41.420834	41.506865	41.592946
52	40.364885	40.451553	40.538274	40.625046	40.711870	40.798745	40.885671	40.972648
54	39.794704	39.882245	39.969840	40.057487	40.145187	40.232939	40.320743	40.408599
56	39.274647	39.363045	39.451497	39.540003	39.628562	39.717174	39.805839	39.894557
58	38.799336	38.888574	38.977866	39.067213	39.156614	39.246068	39.335577	39.425139
60	38.364105	38.454165	38.544287	38.634450	38.724676	38.814955	38.905289	38.995677
62	37.964890	38.055755	38.146675	38.237651	38.328682	38.419768	38.510909	38.602104
64	37.598134	37.689786	37.781493	37.873257	37.965076	38.056950	38.148879	38.240862
66	37.260711	37.353131	37.445608	37.538140	37.630728	37.723371	37.816070	37.908823
68	36.949862	37.043032	37.136259	37.229541	37.322880	37.416274	37.509723	37.603226
70	36.663142	36.757044	36.851002	36.945017	37.039087	37.133212	37.227392	37.321628
72	36.398381	36.492995	36.587667	36.682394	36.777176	36.872014	36.966907	37.061854
74	36.153640	36.248949	36.344314	36.439735	36.535212	36.630743	36.726329	36.821969
76	35.927187	36.023173	36.119214	36.215310	36.311461	36.407667	36.503926	36.600240
78	35.717470	35.814113	35.910811	36.007563	36.104371	36.201232	36.298146	36.395114
80	35.523090	35.620372	35.717709	35.815099	35.912543	36.010041	36.107591	36.205194
82	35.342789	35.440691	35.538647	35.636657	35.734720	35.832835	35.931003	36.029222
84	35.175427	35.273931	35.372489	35.471100	35.569763	35.668478	35.767244	35.866061
86	35.019973	35.119062	35.218204	35.317397	35.416642	35.515937	35.615283	35.714679
88	34.875492	34.975148	35.074855	35.174613	35.274421	35.374280	35.474187	35.574144
90	34.741133	34.841337	34.941593	35.041897	35.142252	35.242655	35.343106	35.443606
92	34.616120	34.716856	34.817642	34.918476	35.019359	35.120289	35.221266	35.322291
96	34.391364	34.493113	34.594908	34.696750	34.798637	34.900570	35.002548	35.104569
100	34.196259	34.298954	34.401692	34.504475	34.607300	34.710168	34.813079	34.916030
104	34.026632	34.130209	34.233827	34.337485	34.441185	34.544924	34.648702	34.752519
108	33.878958	33.983355	34.087791	34.192265	34.296777	34.401325	34.505909	34.610530
112	33.750245	33.855506	33.960601	34.065832	34.171097	34.276395	34.381727	34.487092
116	33.637946	33.743813	33.849713	33.955644	34.061607	34.167600	34.273623	34.379676
120	33.539880	33.646401	33.752952	33.859532	33.966139	34.072774	34.179436	34.286124
140	33.205930	33.315034	33.424151	33.533282	33.642424	33.751579	33.860744	33.969921
160	33.033599	33.144380	33.255161	33.365941	33.476719	33.587496	33.698270	33.809041

214

QUARTERLY WITHDRAWALS PER $1000

EFFECTIVE ANNUAL YIELD

NUMBER OF QUARTRLY WTHDRWLS	14.20%	14.25%	14.30%	14.35%	14.40%	14.45%	14.50%	14.55%
1	1033.752388	1033.865521	1033.978617	1034.091676	1034.204698	1034.317682	1034.430630	1034.543540
2	525.454331	525.540113	525.625870	525.711602	525.797309	525.882991	525.968648	526.054280
3	356.083862	356.160942	356.238001	356.315041	356.392061	356.469061	356.546041	356.623001
4	271.445265	271.518303	271.591325	271.664331	271.737320	271.810293	271.883249	271.956190
5	220.699387	220.770249	220.841097	220.911931	220.982752	221.053559	221.124353	221.195134
6	186.899839	186.969455	187.039061	187.108655	187.178238	187.247810	187.317371	187.386922
7	162.783875	162.852778	162.921673	162.990558	163.059435	163.128303	163.197163	163.266014
8	144.720118	144.788640	144.857156	144.925665	144.994167	145.062663	145.131152	145.199634
9	130.691131	130.759494	130.827851	130.896204	130.964552	131.032896	131.101235	131.169570
10	119.486450	119.554806	119.623160	119.691511	119.759859	119.828205	119.896548	119.964889
11	110.335773	110.404235	110.472696	110.541157	110.609617	110.678076	110.746534	110.814992
12	102.725564	102.794215	102.862867	102.931521	103.000175	103.068831	103.137488	103.206146
13	96.300295	96.369199	96.438105	96.507015	96.575928	96.644843	96.713762	96.782684
14	90.806014	90.875220	90.944430	91.013646	91.082866	91.152091	91.221321	91.290556
15	86.056488	86.126034	86.195588	86.265148	86.334714	86.404288	86.473868	86.543455
16	81.912037	81.981957	82.051884	82.121820	82.191765	82.261718	82.331679	82.401649
17	78.265849	78.336166	78.406493	78.476831	78.547178	78.617536	78.687903	78.758281
18	75.034843	75.105578	75.176325	75.247085	75.317855	75.388638	75.459433	75.530239
19	72.153427	72.224598	72.295782	72.366980	72.438191	72.509415	72.580654	72.651905
20	69.569127	69.640746	69.712381	69.784032	69.855697	69.927377	69.999073	70.070783
21	67.239460	67.311541	67.383638	67.455752	67.527883	67.600030	67.672194	67.744375
22	65.129669	65.202219	65.274788	65.347375	65.419981	65.492604	65.565246	65.637906
23	63.211037	63.284065	63.357113	63.430181	63.503269	63.576376	63.649504	63.722651
24	61.459833	61.533145	61.606679	61.680234	61.753810	61.827408	61.901027	61.974667
25	59.855354	59.929355	60.003380	60.077426	60.151496	60.225589	60.299704	60.373842
26	58.381189	58.455683	58.530201	58.604744	58.679312	58.753903	58.828519	58.903159
27	57.022644	57.097534	57.172650	57.247692	57.322760	57.397853	57.472972	57.548116
28	55.767295	55.842784	55.918300	55.993843	56.069414	56.145011	56.220636	56.296287
29	54.604433	54.680422	54.756440	54.832486	54.908560	54.984663	55.060795	55.136954
30	53.524773	53.601264	53.677784	53.754333	53.830913	53.907523	53.984162	54.060830
31	52.520229	52.597221	52.674244	52.751298	52.828383	52.905499	52.982647	53.059825
32	51.583723	51.661217	51.738743	51.816301	51.893892	51.971515	52.049170	52.126857
33	50.709036	50.787031	50.865059	50.943121	51.021217	51.099346	51.177509	51.255704
34	49.890679	49.969174	50.047704	50.126269	50.204869	50.283503	50.362172	50.440875
35	49.123789	49.202784	49.281814	49.360881	49.439983	49.519121	49.598295	49.677505
36	48.404045	48.483537	48.563066	48.642633	48.722236	48.801877	48.881554	48.961268
37	47.727588	47.807577	47.887603	47.967668	48.047771	48.127912	48.208090	48.288307
38	47.090707	47.171152	47.251974	47.332535	47.413135	47.493774	47.574452	47.655169
39	46.491092	46.572066	46.653081	46.734135	46.815230	46.896365	46.977540	47.058754
40	45.925166	46.006630	46.088134	46.169680	46.251267	46.332895	46.414546	46.496273
41	45.390676	45.472626	45.554618	45.636652	45.718729	45.800847	45.883007	45.965208
42	44.885344	44.967777	45.050254	45.132774	45.215336	45.297942	45.380590	45.463280
43	44.407103	44.490017	44.572975	44.655977	44.739023	44.822113	44.905245	44.988422
44	43.954076	44.037467	44.120903	44.204384	44.287910	44.371480	44.455094	44.538753
45	43.524549	43.608415	43.692326	43.776282	43.860284	43.944331	44.028424	44.112561
46	43.116961	43.201296	43.285679	43.370107	43.454582	43.539102	43.623669	43.708280
47	42.729879	42.814681	42.899531	42.984428	43.069371	43.154361	43.239398	43.324481
48	42.361991	42.447257	42.532570	42.617931	42.703340	42.788796	42.874299	42.959848
50	41.679077	41.765257	41.851486	41.937764	42.024090	42.110465	42.196888	42.283360
52	41.059675	41.146753	41.233881	41.321059	41.408287	41.495564	41.582891	41.670266
54	40.496506	40.584465	40.672475	40.760536	40.848648	40.936810	41.025022	41.113284
56	39.983327	40.072149	40.161024	40.249949	40.338927	40.427955	40.517035	40.606165
58	39.514754	39.604421	39.694141	39.783914	39.873739	39.963615	40.053543	40.143522
60	39.086118	39.176612	39.267160	39.357761	39.448414	39.539119	39.629876	39.720685
62	38.693353	38.784656	38.876012	38.967422	39.058884	39.150399	39.241966	39.333585
64	38.332900	38.424992	38.517138	38.609337	38.701589	38.793894	38.886251	38.978661
66	38.001631	38.094493	38.187408	38.280378	38.373400	38.466475	38.559603	38.652782
68	37.696785	37.790397	37.884063	37.977783	38.071555	38.165381	38.259259	38.353189
70	37.415917	37.510260	37.604657	37.699108	37.793611	37.888167	37.982775	38.077435
72	37.156855	37.251910	37.347018	37.442179	37.537393	37.632660	37.727978	37.823347
74	36.917662	37.013049	37.109209	37.205061	37.300966	37.396923	37.492931	37.588990
76	36.696606	36.793026	36.889498	36.986022	37.082598	37.179225	37.275903	37.372631
78	36.492134	36.589207	36.686331	36.783507	36.880734	36.978012	37.075340	37.172719
80	36.302849	36.400556	36.498313	36.596122	36.693981	36.791890	36.889848	36.987856
82	36.127493	36.225814	36.324186	36.422608	36.521079	36.619600	36.718169	36.816787
84	35.964928	36.063845	36.162812	36.261828	36.360893	36.460005	36.559166	36.658374
86	35.814125	35.913619	36.013162	36.112753	36.212392	36.312079	36.411812	36.511591
88	35.674149	35.774202	35.874303	35.974451	36.074646	36.174886	36.275173	36.375505
90	35.544153	35.644746	35.745386	35.846073	35.946804	36.047581	36.148402	36.249268
92	35.423361	35.524478	35.625639	35.726845	35.828096	35.929391	36.030729	36.132110
96	35.206635	35.308744	35.410895	35.513089	35.615325	35.717602	35.819920	35.922278
100	35.019023	35.122057	35.225130	35.328243	35.431396	35.534586	35.637815	35.741081
104	34.856374	34.960267	35.064197	35.168164	35.272167	35.376206	35.480280	35.584388
108	34.715185	34.819876	34.924600	35.029358	35.134149	35.238973	35.343829	35.448716
112	34.592488	34.697917	34.803376	34.908866	35.014386	35.119935	35.225514	35.331121
116	34.485758	34.591868	34.698006	34.804172	34.910364	35.016583	35.122828	35.229098
120	34.392838	34.499577	34.606341	34.713130	34.819941	34.926777	35.033634	35.140514
140	34.079108	34.188304	34.297510	34.406724	34.515947	34.625178	34.734416	34.843661
160	33.919809	34.030573	34.141334	34.252089	34.362840	34.473585	34.584325	34.695058

QUARTERLY WITHDRAWALS PER $1000

NUMBER OF QUARTRLY WTHDRWLS	EFFECTIVE ANNUAL YIELD							
	14.60%	14.65%	14.70%	14.75%	14.80%	14.85%	14.90%	14.95%
1	1034.656414	1034.769251	1034.882051	1034.994814	1035.107540	1035.220229	1035.332882	1035.445497
2	526.139887	526.225469	526.311025	526.396557	526.482064	526.567547	526.653004	526.738436
3	356.699942	356.776862	356.853763	356.930644	357.007506	357.084347	357.161169	357.237971
4	272.029114	272.102021	272.174913	272.247788	272.320646	272.393489	272.466315	272.539125
5	221.265900	221.336654	221.407394	221.478120	221.548833	221.619532	221.690218	221.760891
6	187.456461	187.525989	187.595506	187.665012	187.734507	187.803990	187.873463	187.942925
7	163.334855	163.403689	163.472513	163.541328	163.610135	163.678933	163.747722	163.816503
8	145.268110	145.336579	145.405042	145.473498	145.541947	145.610389	145.678825	145.747255
9	131.237900	131.306226	131.374546	131.442863	131.511174	131.579481	131.647784	131.716081
10	120.033227	120.101562	120.169895	120.238225	120.306552	120.374877	120.443199	120.511518
11	110.883450	110.951906	111.020362	111.088817	111.157271	111.225725	111.294178	111.362630
12	103.274806	103.343466	103.412128	103.480791	103.549455	103.618120	103.686786	103.755453
13	96.851609	96.920537	96.989468	97.058402	97.127338	97.196278	97.265221	97.334166
14	91.359795	91.429040	91.498289	91.567543	91.636802	91.706065	91.775333	91.844606
15	86.613048	86.682648	86.752254	86.821867	86.891486	86.961112	87.030745	87.100383
16	82.471627	82.541613	82.611607	82.681610	82.751621	82.821641	82.891668	82.961704
17	78.828669	78.899067	78.969474	79.039892	79.110320	79.180757	79.251205	79.321662
18	75.601087	75.671887	75.742728	75.813581	75.884446	75.955322	76.026210	76.097109
19	72.723170	72.794448	72.865740	72.937045	73.008363	73.079694	73.151039	73.222396
20	70.142509	70.214249	70.286005	70.357775	70.429560	70.501360	70.573175	70.645004
21	67.816572	67.888786	67.961016	68.033263	68.105526	68.177806	68.250102	68.322414
22	65.710585	65.783281	65.855996	65.928728	66.001478	66.074247	66.147033	66.219837
23	63.795818	63.869004	63.942210	64.015435	64.088680	64.161945	64.235228	64.308531
24	62.048328	62.122010	62.195714	62.269438	62.343184	62.416950	62.490737	62.564545
25	60.448003	60.522186	60.596392	60.670620	60.744871	60.819144	60.893439	60.967757
26	58.977822	59.052510	59.127222	59.201958	59.276717	59.351501	59.426308	59.501138
27	57.623286	57.698482	57.773702	57.848948	57.924219	57.999516	58.074837	58.150184
28	56.371965	56.447670	56.523401	56.599160	56.674944	56.750756	56.826593	56.902457
29	55.213142	55.289358	55.365601	55.441873	55.518173	55.594500	55.670856	55.747238
30	54.137528	54.214256	54.291013	54.367799	54.444614	54.521458	54.598331	54.675234
31	53.137033	53.214273	53.291543	53.368843	53.446174	53.523535	53.600927	53.678348
32	52.204576	52.282327	52.360110	52.437924	52.515771	52.593648	52.671558	52.749498
33	51.333933	51.412195	51.490490	51.568818	51.647179	51.725572	51.803998	51.882457
34	50.519613	50.598385	50.677191	50.756031	50.834905	50.913813	50.992754	51.071729
35	49.756750	49.836030	49.915346	49.994696	50.074082	50.153503	50.232958	50.312449
36	49.041019	49.120805	49.200629	49.280488	49.360384	49.440316	49.520284	49.600286
37	48.368561	48.448852	48.529181	48.609548	48.689951	48.770391	48.850869	48.931383
38	47.735924	47.816718	47.897550	47.978420	48.059329	48.140274	48.221260	48.302282
39	47.140008	47.221301	47.302634	47.384006	47.465418	47.546868	47.628357	47.709885
40	46.578023	46.659814	46.741644	46.823515	46.905426	46.987377	47.069367	47.151397
41	46.047451	46.129736	46.212061	46.294427	46.376835	46.459283	46.541772	46.624301
42	45.546013	45.628788	45.711605	45.794464	45.877365	45.960307	46.043290	46.126315
43	45.071641	45.154903	45.238208	45.321556	45.404947	45.488379	45.571854	45.655372
44	44.622455	44.706201	44.789991	44.873824	44.957701	45.041620	45.125583	45.209588
45	44.196742	44.280968	44.365239	44.449554	44.533913	44.618315	44.702762	44.787252
46	43.792938	43.877640	43.962388	44.047180	44.132017	44.216899	44.301825	44.386795
47	43.409769	43.494784	43.580005	43.665271	43.750582	43.835939	43.921341	44.006787
48	43.045445	43.131088	43.216777	43.302513	43.388295	43.474122	43.559995	43.645913
50	42.369879	42.456446	42.543060	42.629722	42.716431	42.803186	42.889989	42.976837
52	41.757691	41.845164	41.932686	42.020256	42.107874	42.195540	42.283253	42.371014
54	41.201596	41.289957	41.378368	41.466828	41.555336	41.643893	41.732499	41.821153
56	40.695345	40.784576	40.873857	40.963188	41.052568	41.141997	41.231475	41.321002
58	40.233553	40.323634	40.413765	40.503947	40.594179	40.684460	40.774791	40.865172
60	39.811546	39.902438	39.993420	40.084433	40.175497	40.266611	40.357774	40.448987
62	39.425256	39.516979	39.608752	39.700577	39.792452	39.884377	39.976352	40.068377
64	39.071122	39.163635	39.256200	39.348815	39.441481	39.534197	39.626964	39.719780
66	38.746014	38.839298	38.932632	39.026018	39.119454	39.212940	39.306477	39.400063
68	38.447171	38.541204	38.635288	38.729423	38.823609	38.917845	39.012131	39.106466
70	38.172146	38.266909	38.361723	38.456587	38.551501	38.646465	38.741479	38.836542
72	37.918768	38.014240	38.109762	38.205335	38.300957	38.396628	38.492349	38.588119
74	37.685100	37.781260	37.877471	37.973731	38.070040	38.166398	38.262805	38.359260
76	37.469410	37.566239	37.663117	37.760044	37.857020	37.954044	38.051116	38.148235
78	37.270146	37.367623	37.465148	37.562722	37.660344	37.758013	37.855729	37.953493
80	37.085913	37.184017	37.282170	37.380370	37.478618	37.576912	37.675252	37.773638
82	36.915452	37.014165	37.112925	37.211732	37.310585	37.409483	37.508428	37.607417
84	36.757629	36.856931	36.956279	37.055672	37.155110	37.254594	37.354122	37.453694
86	36.611416	36.711287	36.811203	36.911164	37.011168	37.111217	37.211309	37.311443
88	36.475881	36.576302	36.676767	36.777276	36.877827	36.978421	37.079058	37.179736
90	36.350177	36.451130	36.552125	36.653162	36.754242	36.855362	36.956524	37.057727
92	36.233533	36.334999	36.436506	36.538054	36.639642	36.741271	36.842940	36.944647
96	36.024676	36.127114	36.229590	36.332105	36.434657	36.537247	36.639875	36.742538
100	35.844385	35.947725	36.051101	36.154512	36.257959	36.361440	36.464956	36.568505
104	35.688530	35.792706	35.896916	36.001158	36.105432	36.209737	36.314074	36.418442
108	35.553635	35.658584	35.763563	35.868572	35.973610	36.078676	36.183771	36.288893
112	35.436756	35.542418	35.648107	35.753823	35.859565	35.965332	36.071124	36.176940
116	35.335393	35.441712	35.548055	35.654421	35.760810	35.867221	35.973654	36.080108
120	35.247416	35.354339	35.461282	35.568245	35.675228	35.782230	35.889251	35.996290
140	34.952912	35.062169	35.171432	35.280700	35.389972	35.499248	35.608528	35.717812
160	34.805785	34.916505	35.027218	35.137923	35.248620	35.359309	35.469989	35.580659

QUARTERLY WITHDRAWALS PER $1000

NUMBER OF QUARTERLY WTHDRWLS	EFFECTIVE ANNUAL YIELD							
	15.00%	15.05%	15.10%	15.15%	15.20%	15.25%	15.30%	15.35%
1	1035.558076	1035.670619	1035.783124	1035.895593	1036.008026	1036.120421	1036.232781	1036.345103
2	526.823844	526.909226	526.994584	527.079917	527.165225	527.250509	527.335767	527.421001
3	357.314754	357.391517	357.468260	357.544983	357.621687	357.698371	357.775036	357.851680
4	272.611919	272.684696	272.757457	272.830202	272.902931	272.975644	273.048340	273.121021
5	221.831550	221.902195	221.972827	222.043446	222.114051	222.184643	222.255222	222.325787
6	188.012376	188.081816	188.151245	188.220663	188.290070	188.359465	188.428850	188.498224
7	163.885275	163.954038	164.022792	164.091537	164.160274	164.229002	164.297721	164.366431
8	145.815677	145.884093	145.952503	146.020905	146.089301	146.157691	146.226074	146.294450
9	131.784375	131.852663	131.920947	131.989226	132.057501	132.125771	132.194036	132.262297
10	120.579835	120.648149	120.716461	120.784769	120.853076	120.921379	120.989679	121.057977
11	111.431081	111.499531	111.567981	111.636430	111.704878	111.773325	111.841772	111.910217
12	103.824122	103.892791	103.961462	104.030133	104.098806	104.167479	104.236154	104.304830
13	97.403115	97.472066	97.541020	97.609978	97.678938	97.747900	97.816866	97.885834
14	91.913884	91.983166	92.052453	92.121744	92.191040	92.260341	92.329646	92.398956
15	87.170029	87.239680	87.309338	87.379003	87.448673	87.518351	87.588034	87.657724
16	83.031747	83.101799	83.171859	83.241927	83.312003	83.382087	83.452180	83.522280
17	79.392129	79.462606	79.533093	79.603589	79.674096	79.744611	79.815137	79.885672
18	76.168020	76.238942	76.309875	76.380820	76.451776	76.522744	76.593723	76.664713
19	73.293767	73.365150	73.436547	73.507957	73.579380	73.650815	73.722264	73.793725
20	70.716848	70.788707	70.860580	70.932468	71.004370	71.076287	71.148219	71.220164
21	68.394742	68.467087	68.539448	68.611825	68.684218	68.756627	68.829052	68.901493
22	66.292659	66.365498	66.438355	66.511230	66.584123	66.657033	66.729960	66.802905
23	64.381854	64.455195	64.528556	64.601936	64.675335	64.748753	64.822190	64.895646
24	62.638374	62.712223	62.786093	62.859984	62.933895	63.007827	63.081779	63.155752
25	61.042096	61.116458	61.190842	61.265248	61.339676	61.414126	61.488597	61.563091
26	59.575992	59.650870	59.725771	59.800696	59.875644	59.950615	60.025610	60.100627
27	58.225555	58.300951	58.376372	58.451818	58.527289	58.602784	58.678303	58.753848
28	56.978348	57.054264	57.130207	57.206176	57.282170	57.358191	57.434238	57.510310
29	55.823649	55.900087	55.976552	56.053045	56.129565	56.206112	56.282687	56.359288
30	54.752165	54.829125	54.906113	54.983130	55.060176	55.137250	55.214353	55.291484
31	53.755800	53.833282	53.910793	53.988335	54.065906	54.143507	54.221137	54.298797
32	52.827470	52.905473	52.983507	53.061572	53.139668	53.217795	53.295953	53.374141
33	51.960948	52.039471	52.118027	52.196614	52.275234	52.353886	52.432570	52.511285
34	51.150738	51.229781	51.308856	51.387965	51.467107	51.546282	51.625490	51.704731
35	50.391974	50.471533	50.551127	50.630755	50.710418	50.790114	50.869845	50.949609
36	49.680325	49.760400	49.840510	49.920656	50.000836	50.081052	50.161303	50.241589
37	49.011933	49.092521	49.173145	49.253805	49.334501	49.415234	49.496002	49.576807
38	48.383342	48.464440	48.545575	48.626747	48.707957	48.789203	48.870486	48.951807
39	47.791451	47.873056	47.954699	48.036380	48.118100	48.199857	48.281652	48.363485
40	47.233467	47.315576	47.397724	47.479911	47.562138	47.644403	47.726707	47.809049
41	46.706871	46.789481	46.872131	46.954820	47.037550	47.120319	47.203128	47.285976
42	46.209382	46.292489	46.375637	46.458826	46.542055	46.625325	46.708635	46.791985
43	45.738931	45.822532	45.906174	45.989858	46.073583	46.157350	46.241157	46.325006
44	45.293637	45.377727	45.461860	45.546036	45.630253	45.714512	45.798813	45.883155
45	44.871785	44.956361	45.040981	45.125643	45.210348	45.295096	45.379886	45.464719
46	44.471810	44.556868	44.641970	44.727115	44.812304	44.897536	44.982811	45.068129
47	44.092278	44.177814	44.263394	44.349018	44.434686	44.520398	44.606153	44.691952
48	43.731877	43.817885	43.903939	43.990037	44.076180	44.162367	44.248598	44.334873
50	43.063732	43.150674	43.237661	43.324694	43.411772	43.498895	43.586064	43.673278
52	42.458822	42.546677	42.634579	42.722527	42.810522	42.898562	42.986649	43.074782
54	41.909854	41.998604	42.087401	42.176245	42.265136	42.354074	42.443058	42.532089
56	41.410578	41.500202	41.589873	41.679593	41.769361	41.859175	41.949037	42.038946
58	40.955601	41.046079	41.136605	41.227180	41.317802	41.408473	41.499191	41.589956
60	40.540249	40.631561	40.722921	40.814329	40.905786	40.997291	41.088844	41.180444
62	40.160452	40.252576	40.344748	40.436970	40.529239	40.621557	40.713922	40.806335
64	39.812646	39.905560	39.998524	40.091537	40.184597	40.277706	40.370863	40.464067
66	39.493699	39.587384	39.681117	39.774899	39.868730	39.962608	40.056533	40.150506
68	39.200850	39.295283	39.389765	39.484295	39.578873	39.673498	39.768171	39.862891
70	38.931653	39.026814	39.122022	39.217278	39.312582	39.407933	39.503331	39.598775
72	38.683936	38.779802	38.875716	38.971677	39.067685	39.163739	39.259840	39.355987
74	38.455763	38.552313	38.648910	38.745554	38.842245	38.938982	39.035764	39.132591
76	38.245402	38.342615	38.439875	38.537181	38.634533	38.731930	38.829371	38.926858
78	38.051302	38.149158	38.247059	38.345006	38.442997	38.541033	38.639113	38.737237
80	37.872070	37.970547	38.069069	38.167636	38.266246	38.364900	38.463597	38.562336
82	37.706451	37.805529	37.904650	38.003815	38.103024	38.202274	38.301567	38.400902
84	37.553309	37.652968	37.752669	37.852413	37.952199	38.052026	38.151894	38.251803
86	37.411621	37.511840	37.612101	37.712403	37.812746	37.913129	38.013553	38.114016
88	37.280455	37.381216	37.482017	37.582857	37.683738	37.784658	37.885616	37.986613
90	37.158969	37.260251	37.361573	37.462933	37.564331	37.665768	37.767242	37.868753
92	37.046394	37.148179	37.250002	37.351862	37.453760	37.555694	37.657664	37.759670
96	36.845238	36.947974	37.050745	37.153550	37.256390	37.359263	37.462170	37.565110
100	36.672088	36.775703	36.879350	36.983030	37.086741	37.190482	37.294254	37.398056
104	36.522839	36.627267	36.731724	36.836209	36.940723	37.045265	37.149835	37.254431
108	36.394042	36.499218	36.604420	36.709648	36.814901	36.920179	37.025482	37.130808
112	36.282781	36.388645	36.494532	36.600442	36.706374	36.812327	36.918302	37.024298
116	36.186583	36.293079	36.399595	36.506130	36.612683	36.719256	36.825846	36.932454
120	36.103347	36.210421	36.317512	36.424619	36.531742	36.638880	36.746033	36.853201
140	35.827098	35.936387	36.045677	36.154969	36.264263	36.373557	36.482851	36.592146
160	35.691321	35.801972	35.912614	36.023245	36.133865	36.244474	36.355071	36.465657

QUARTERLY WITHDRAWALS PER $1000

NUMBER OF QUARTERLY WTHDRWLS	EFFECTIVE ANNUAL YIELD							
	15.40%	15.45%	15.50%	15.55%	15.60%	15.65%	15.70%	15.75%
1	1036.457389	1036.569639	1036.681852	1036.794029	1036.906170	1037.018274	1037.130341	1037.242373
2	527.506210	527.591395	527.676555	527.761690	527.846800	527.931886	528.016948	528.101984
3	357.928306	358.004911	358.081497	358.158064	358.234611	358.311138	358.387646	358.464134
4	273.193685	273.266333	273.338964	273.411580	273.484180	273.556763	273.629330	273.701881
5	222.396338	222.466876	222.537401	222.607913	222.678411	222.748895	222.819367	222.889825
6	188.567587	188.636939	188.706280	188.775610	188.844929	188.914237	188.983534	189.052820
7	164.435133	164.503826	164.572510	164.641185	164.709852	164.778510	164.847159	164.915799
8	146.362819	146.431182	146.499538	146.567887	146.636230	146.704566	146.772895	146.841218
9	132.330553	132.398804	132.467050	132.535292	132.603530	132.671762	132.739990	132.808213
10	121.126272	121.194565	121.262855	121.331142	121.399426	121.467707	121.535986	121.604262
11	111.978662	112.047106	112.115549	112.183991	112.252433	112.320873	112.389313	112.457751
12	104.373506	104.442184	104.510862	104.579542	104.648222	104.716904	104.785586	104.854269
13	97.954805	98.023779	98.092756	98.161735	98.230717	98.299702	98.368690	98.437680
14	92.468270	92.537589	92.606913	92.676241	92.745573	92.814910	92.884251	92.953596
15	87.727419	87.797122	87.866830	87.936544	88.006265	88.075991	88.145725	88.215464
16	83.592388	83.662504	83.732627	83.802759	83.872899	83.943046	84.013201	84.083364
17	79.956217	80.026771	80.097335	80.167908	80.238491	80.309084	80.379686	80.450297
18	76.735714	76.806727	76.877751	76.948786	77.019832	77.090889	77.161957	77.233036
19	73.865199	73.936686	74.008186	74.079699	74.151224	74.222762	74.294312	74.365875
20	71.292125	71.364099	71.436088	71.508091	71.580109	71.652140	71.724186	71.796246
21	68.973950	69.046423	69.118912	69.191416	69.263936	69.336472	69.409024	69.481591
22	66.875867	66.948847	67.021844	67.094859	67.167890	67.240939	67.314005	67.387088
23	64.969121	65.042614	65.116127	65.189658	65.263208	65.336777	65.410364	65.483969
24	63.229744	63.303757	63.377791	63.451844	63.525918	63.600011	63.674125	63.748259
25	61.637606	61.712142	61.786701	61.861281	61.935882	62.010505	62.085150	62.159815
26	60.175668	60.250732	60.325818	60.400928	60.476060	60.551216	60.626394	60.701594
27	58.829416	58.905009	58.980626	59.056268	59.131934	59.207624	59.283337	59.359075
28	57.586408	57.662532	57.738681	57.814856	57.891057	57.967282	58.043534	58.119810
29	56.435917	56.512572	56.589254	56.665963	56.742699	56.819461	56.896250	56.973066
30	55.368643	55.445830	55.523045	55.600289	55.677560	55.754859	55.832186	55.909540
31	54.376487	54.454205	54.531953	54.609730	54.687537	54.765372	54.843236	54.921129
32	53.452360	53.530609	53.608889	53.687199	53.765539	53.843910	53.922310	54.000740
33	52.590032	52.668811	52.747621	52.826463	52.905335	52.984240	53.063175	53.142141
34	51.784005	51.863311	51.942650	52.022022	52.101425	52.180861	52.260330	52.339830
35	51.029407	51.109239	51.189105	51.269004	51.348937	51.428902	51.508901	51.588933
36	50.321909	50.402264	50.482654	50.563079	50.643537	50.724030	50.804557	50.885119
37	49.657647	49.738523	49.819434	49.900381	49.981363	50.062381	50.143433	50.224521
38	49.033164	49.114557	49.195987	49.277453	49.358956	49.440495	49.522069	49.603680
39	48.445356	48.527264	48.609209	48.691192	48.773211	48.855268	48.937361	49.019491
40	47.891430	47.973849	48.056306	48.138801	48.221334	48.303905	48.386514	48.469160
41	47.368864	47.451790	47.534755	47.617760	47.700803	47.783884	47.867004	47.950162
42	46.875375	46.958805	47.042275	47.125785	47.209334	47.292922	47.376549	47.460215
43	46.408895	46.492825	46.576795	46.660805	46.744856	46.828946	46.913077	46.997247
44	45.967539	46.051964	46.136431	46.220938	46.305486	46.390075	46.474704	46.559372
45	45.549593	45.634509	45.719467	45.804467	45.889508	45.974590	46.059714	46.144878
46	45.153489	45.238892	45.324338	45.409825	45.495355	45.580926	45.666539	45.752194
47	44.777794	44.863679	44.949607	45.035578	45.121591	45.207647	45.293745	45.379885
48	44.421192	44.507555	44.593961	44.680410	44.766902	44.853438	44.940015	45.026636
50	43.760536	43.847839	43.935186	44.022578	44.110013	44.197492	44.285015	44.372580
52	43.162959	43.251183	43.339431	43.427764	43.516122	43.604525	43.692971	43.781462
54	42.621166	42.710289	42.799458	42.888672	42.977932	43.067236	43.156586	43.245979
56	42.128901	42.218902	42.308950	42.399044	42.489183	42.579368	42.669598	42.759874
58	41.680768	41.771627	41.862532	41.953483	42.044481	42.135524	42.226613	42.317746
60	41.272091	41.363785	41.455525	41.547312	41.639145	41.731025	41.822949	41.914919
62	40.898796	40.991303	41.083857	41.176457	41.269103	41.361795	41.454533	41.547316
64	40.557318	40.650616	40.743961	40.837352	40.930788	41.024271	41.117799	41.211372
66	40.244526	40.338593	40.432706	40.526864	40.621069	40.715319	40.809615	40.903955
68	39.957657	40.052470	40.147329	40.242233	40.337183	40.432178	40.527217	40.622301
70	39.694266	39.789802	39.885384	39.981011	40.076684	40.172400	40.268161	40.363966
72	39.452180	39.548418	39.644701	39.741028	39.837400	39.933816	40.030275	40.126778
74	39.229464	39.326381	39.423343	39.520348	39.617397	39.714490	39.811625	39.908803
76	39.024389	39.121963	39.219581	39.317243	39.414947	39.512693	39.610482	39.708312
78	38.835404	38.933615	39.031867	39.130163	39.228500	39.326878	39.425298	39.523758
80	38.661119	38.759943	38.858809	38.957716	39.056665	39.155654	39.254683	39.353751
82	38.500279	38.599696	38.699154	38.798652	38.898190	38.997768	39.097384	39.197040
84	38.351753	38.451742	38.551771	38.651839	38.751946	38.852091	38.952274	39.052494
86	38.214518	38.315059	38.415638	38.516255	38.616910	38.717602	38.818330	38.919095
88	38.087648	38.188720	38.289829	38.390975	38.492158	38.593376	38.694630	38.795918
90	37.970300	38.071884	38.173504	38.275159	38.376849	38.478574	38.580333	38.682125
92	37.861711	37.963787	38.065898	38.168043	38.270221	38.372433	38.474677	38.576954
96	37.668083	37.771087	37.874123	37.977191	38.080269	38.183417	38.286576	38.389764
100	37.501888	37.605749	37.709639	37.813556	37.917502	38.021475	38.125475	38.229501
104	37.359054	37.463703	37.568377	37.673077	37.777801	37.882550	37.987323	38.092119
108	37.236157	37.341530	37.446925	37.552342	37.657781	37.763241	37.868721	37.974222
112	37.130313	37.236349	37.342404	37.448478	37.554570	37.660681	37.766809	37.872955
116	37.039080	37.145722	37.252380	37.359054	37.465743	37.572447	37.679166	37.785899
120	36.960383	37.067578	37.174787	37.282008	37.389241	37.496487	37.603744	37.711011
140	36.701440	36.810733	36.920025	37.029316	37.138604	37.247891	37.357174	37.466455
160	36.576231	36.686792	36.797340	36.907876	37.018398	37.128907	37.239402	37.349883

QUARTERLY WITHDRAWALS PER $1000

NUMBER OF QUARTRLY WTHDRWLS	EFFECTIVE ANNUAL YIELD							
	15.80%	15.85%	15.90%	15.95%	16.00%	16.05%	16.10%	16.15%
1	1037.354368	1037.466327	1037.578249	1037.690135	1037.801986	1037.913800	1038.025578	1038.137319
2	528.186996	528.271984	528.356947	528.441885	528.526799	528.611689	528.696554	528.781395
3	358.540603	358.617053	358.693483	358.769893	358.846284	358.922656	358.999008	359.075340
4	273.774416	273.846935	273.919438	273.991925	274.064396	274.136851	274.209289	274.281712
5	222.960269	223.030700	223.101118	223.171523	223.241914	223.312292	223.382657	223.453008
6	189.122096	189.191360	189.260613	189.329856	189.399087	189.468307	189.537517	189.606716
7	164.984431	165.053053	165.121668	165.190273	165.258870	165.327457	165.396036	165.464607
8	146.909534	146.977843	147.046146	147.114442	147.182731	147.251014	147.319290	147.387559
9	132.876432	132.944646	133.012855	133.081059	133.149259	133.217454	133.285644	133.353830
10	121.672535	121.740805	121.809073	121.877337	121.945599	122.013858	122.082115	122.150368
11	112.526189	112.594626	112.663061	112.731496	112.799930	112.868363	112.936795	113.005226
12	104.922953	104.991638	105.060324	105.129011	105.197698	105.266387	105.335076	105.403766
13	98.506673	98.575668	98.644667	98.713667	98.782671	98.851677	98.920685	98.989696
14	93.022946	93.092301	93.161660	93.231023	93.300390	93.369762	93.439138	93.508518
15	88.285209	88.354961	88.424718	88.494481	88.564251	88.634026	88.703808	88.773595
16	84.153535	84.223714	84.293900	84.364094	84.434295	84.504505	84.574721	84.644946
17	80.520917	80.591547	80.662187	80.732835	80.803493	80.874161	80.944837	81.015523
18	77.304126	77.375227	77.446339	77.517462	77.588596	77.659741	77.730896	77.802063
19	74.437451	74.509039	74.580640	74.652253	74.723878	74.795516	74.867167	74.938829
20	71.868637	71.940408	72.012510	72.084627	72.156757	72.228901	72.301059	72.373230
21	69.554174	69.626773	69.699387	69.772016	69.844661	69.917321	69.989997	70.062688
22	67.460189	67.533306	67.606440	67.679591	67.752759	67.825944	67.899146	67.972365
23	65.557594	65.631236	65.704898	65.778577	65.852275	65.925991	65.999725	66.073478
24	63.822412	63.896586	63.970779	64.044992	64.119225	64.193477	64.267749	64.342041
25	62.234502	62.309210	62.383940	62.458690	62.533462	62.608254	62.683068	62.757902
26	60.776818	60.852064	60.927332	61.002623	61.077936	61.153272	61.228629	61.304009
27	59.434837	59.510623	59.586432	59.662265	59.738122	59.814003	59.889907	59.965834
28	58.196111	58.272438	58.348790	58.425166	58.501568	58.577994	58.654446	58.730921
29	57.049908	57.126776	57.203670	57.280589	57.357537	57.434510	57.511509	57.588534
30	55.986922	56.064332	56.141769	56.219233	56.296725	56.374244	56.451790	56.529363
31	54.999051	55.077001	55.154980	55.232988	55.311023	55.389088	55.467180	55.545301
32	54.079201	54.157691	54.236210	54.314760	54.393339	54.471947	54.550585	54.629251
33	53.221138	53.300166	53.379225	53.458315	53.537435	53.616586	53.695767	53.774978
34	52.419362	52.498926	52.578522	52.658150	52.737809	52.817500	52.897222	52.976976
35	51.668998	51.749096	51.829227	51.909390	51.989586	52.069815	52.150076	52.230369
36	50.965714	51.046343	51.127005	51.207702	51.288432	51.369195	51.449991	51.530821
37	50.305643	50.386800	50.467992	50.549218	50.630478	50.711773	50.793102	50.874465
38	49.685326	49.767008	49.848725	49.930478	50.012266	50.094089	50.175947	50.257840
39	49.101658	49.183861	49.266101	49.348376	49.430688	49.513036	49.595420	49.677839
40	48.551843	48.634564	48.717322	48.800117	48.882949	48.965817	49.048722	49.131664
41	48.033359	48.116593	48.199865	48.283175	48.366523	48.449908	48.533330	48.616790
42	47.543920	47.627664	47.711447	47.795267	47.879127	47.963024	48.046959	48.130932
43	47.081456	47.165705	47.249994	47.334321	47.418687	47.503092	47.587536	47.672018
44	46.644083	46.728833	46.813622	46.898452	46.983320	47.068229	47.153176	47.238163
45	46.230083	46.315329	46.400615	46.485942	46.571309	46.656715	46.742162	46.827648
46	45.837890	45.923627	46.009405	46.095223	46.181083	46.266983	46.352923	46.438904
47	45.466066	45.552290	45.638555	45.724861	45.811208	45.897597	45.984026	46.070496
48	45.113298	45.200003	45.286750	45.373538	45.460369	45.547240	45.634153	45.721107
50	44.460190	44.547842	44.635537	44.723274	44.811054	44.898876	44.986740	45.074646
52	43.869996	43.958575	44.047196	44.135861	44.224569	44.313320	44.402113	44.490949
54	43.335418	43.424900	43.514427	43.603997	43.693610	43.783267	43.872967	43.962710
56	42.850193	42.940558	43.030967	43.121419	43.211916	43.302456	43.393040	43.483667
58	42.408925	42.500149	42.591417	42.682730	42.774086	42.865486	42.956930	43.048417
60	42.006934	42.098994	42.191099	42.283248	42.375440	42.467677	42.559957	42.652281
62	41.640145	41.733018	41.825935	41.918897	42.011902	42.104952	42.198045	42.291181
64	41.304991	41.398653	41.492360	41.586111	41.679907	41.773744	41.867626	41.961550
66	40.998340	41.092769	41.187242	41.281759	41.376319	41.470922	41.565568	41.660257
68	40.717429	40.812602	40.907817	41.003076	41.098378	41.193722	41.289109	41.384538
70	40.459815	40.555706	40.651641	40.747618	40.843638	40.939700	41.035804	41.131948
72	40.223324	40.319912	40.416543	40.513215	40.609930	40.706685	40.803482	40.900319
74	40.006023	40.103285	40.200588	40.297933	40.395318	40.492744	40.590211	40.687717
76	39.806184	39.904097	40.002050	40.100044	40.198078	40.296151	40.394264	40.492415
78	39.622259	39.720801	39.819381	39.918002	40.016661	40.115359	40.214095	40.312869
80	39.452860	39.552007	39.651193	39.750417	39.849680	39.948980	40.048317	40.147691
82	39.296733	39.396465	39.496234	39.596041	39.695884	39.795764	39.895680	39.995632
84	39.152752	39.253047	39.353378	39.453745	39.554148	39.654586	39.755059	39.855566
86	39.019896	39.120733	39.221604	39.322511	39.423452	39.524427	39.625435	39.726477
88	38.897242	38.998600	39.099991	39.201416	39.302875	39.404365	39.505889	39.607444
90	38.783951	38.885810	38.987701	39.089625	39.191580	39.293566	39.395584	39.497632
92	38.679262	38.781602	38.883975	38.986376	39.088808	39.191271	39.293762	39.396283
96	38.492981	38.596226	38.699500	38.802802	38.906131	39.009487	39.112870	39.216279
100	38.333553	38.437632	38.541735	38.645863	38.750016	38.854192	38.958393	39.062616
104	38.196938	38.301779	38.406643	38.511529	38.616436	38.721364	38.826312	38.931280
108	38.079743	38.185284	38.290843	38.396421	38.502017	38.607632	38.713263	38.818912
112	37.979116	38.085295	38.191489	38.297699	38.403924	38.510164	38.616418	38.722685
116	37.892646	37.999406	38.106178	38.212964	38.319761	38.426569	38.533389	38.640220
120	37.818290	37.925579	38.032877	38.140185	38.247502	38.354827	38.462161	38.569502
140	37.575732	37.685006	37.794275	37.903540	38.012800	38.122055	38.231305	38.340548
160	37.460349	37.570801	37.681237	37.791659	37.902065	38.012455	38.122829	38.233187

219

QUARTERLY WITHDRAWALS PER $1000

EFFECTIVE ANNUAL YIELD

NUMBER OF QUARTERLY WTHDRWLS	16.20%	16.25%	16.30%	16.35%	16.40%	16.45%	16.50%	16.55%
1	1038.249025	1038.360695	1038.472329	1038.583926	1038.695488	1038.807014	1038.918504	1039.029958
2	528.866211	528.951002	529.035770	529.120513	529.205231	529.289925	529.374595	529.459241
3	359.151654	359.227947	359.304222	359.380477	359.456713	359.532929	359.609126	359.685304
4	274.354119	274.426509	274.498884	274.571243	274.643585	274.715912	274.788223	274.860518
5	223.523346	223.593670	223.663982	223.734280	223.804565	223.874836	223.945095	224.015340
6	189.675903	189.745080	189.814246	189.883401	189.952545	190.021678	190.090800	190.159912
7	165.533168	165.601721	165.670266	165.738801	165.807328	165.875846	165.944355	166.012855
8	147.455821	147.524077	147.592326	147.660569	147.728805	147.797034	147.865256	147.933472
9	133.422011	133.490187	133.558358	133.626525	133.694687	133.762844	133.830996	133.899144
10	122.218619	122.286866	122.355111	122.423353	122.491593	122.559829	122.628062	122.696293
11	113.073656	113.142085	113.210513	113.278939	113.347365	113.415790	113.484214	113.552637
12	105.472457	105.541148	105.609840	105.678534	105.747227	105.815922	105.884617	105.953313
13	99.058211	99.127726	99.196745	99.265766	99.334789	99.403815	99.472844	99.541875
14	93.577903	93.647291	93.716684	93.786081	93.855483	93.924888	93.994298	94.063712
15	88.843388	88.913187	88.982992	89.052803	89.122620	89.192443	89.262271	89.332105
16	84.715178	84.785417	84.855664	84.925919	84.996181	85.066450	85.136727	85.207012
17	81.086217	81.156921	81.227634	81.298357	81.369088	81.439828	81.510578	81.581336
18	77.873240	77.944427	78.015626	78.086835	78.158055	78.229285	78.300526	78.371778
19	75.010504	75.082191	75.153891	75.225603	75.297326	75.369062	75.440810	75.512571
20	72.445416	72.517615	72.589828	72.662055	72.734295	72.806549	72.878817	72.951098
21	70.135394	70.208116	70.280853	70.353605	70.426372	70.499154	70.571951	70.644763
22	68.045600	68.118852	68.192120	68.265406	68.338707	68.412026	68.485360	68.558711
23	66.147249	66.221037	66.294844	66.368669	66.442512	66.516372	66.590251	66.664147
24	64.416352	64.490682	64.565032	64.639402	64.713790	64.788198	64.862625	64.937071
25	62.832758	62.907634	62.982530	63.057448	63.132386	63.207345	63.282324	63.357323
26	61.379412	61.454836	61.530282	61.605750	61.681241	61.756753	61.832286	61.907842
27	60.041785	60.117759	60.193757	60.269777	60.345821	60.421888	60.497978	60.574091
28	58.807422	58.883947	58.960497	59.037071	59.113669	59.190292	59.266939	59.343610
29	57.665584	57.742660	57.819762	57.896890	57.974043	58.051222	58.128426	58.205655
30	56.606963	56.684590	56.762244	56.839924	56.917632	56.995366	57.073126	57.150913
31	55.623450	55.701626	55.779831	55.858064	55.936324	56.014612	56.092928	56.171271
32	54.707948	54.786673	54.865427	54.944210	55.023022	55.101863	55.180732	55.259630
33	53.854219	53.933491	54.012793	54.092124	54.171486	54.250877	54.330298	54.409748
34	53.056760	53.136576	53.216423	53.296301	53.376209	53.456149	53.536119	53.616119
35	52.310694	52.391051	52.471440	52.551861	52.632314	52.712799	52.793315	52.873863
36	51.611684	51.692580	51.773508	51.854470	51.935464	52.016490	52.097549	52.178641
37	50.955863	51.037294	51.118758	51.200257	51.281788	51.363354	51.444952	51.526584
38	50.339768	50.421731	50.503728	50.585760	50.667826	50.749926	50.832060	50.914228
39	49.760294	49.842784	49.925310	50.007871	50.090467	50.173098	50.255764	50.338464
40	49.214641	49.297656	49.380706	49.463792	49.546914	49.630071	49.713265	49.796493
41	48.700286	48.783820	48.867390	48.950997	49.034641	49.118321	49.202037	49.285789
42	48.214943	48.298992	48.383078	48.467201	48.551361	48.635559	48.719793	48.804064
43	47.756539	47.841098	47.925695	48.010330	48.095002	48.179712	48.264460	48.349245
44	47.323188	47.408253	47.493356	47.578497	47.663677	47.748895	47.834151	47.919445
45	46.913173	46.998738	47.084342	47.169986	47.255668	47.341388	47.427147	47.512945
46	46.524925	46.610985	46.697085	46.783225	46.869404	46.955622	47.041879	47.128175
47	46.157006	46.243557	46.330148	46.416779	46.503449	46.590159	46.676909	46.763698
48	45.808102	45.895138	45.982214	46.069330	46.156487	46.243684	46.330920	46.418197
50	45.162594	45.250583	45.338613	45.426684	45.514797	45.602950	45.691143	45.779377
52	44.579827	44.668747	44.757709	44.846712	44.935757	45.024843	45.113970	45.203138
54	44.052496	44.142324	44.232194	44.322106	44.412060	44.502056	44.592093	44.682171
56	43.574336	43.665049	43.755804	43.846601	43.937440	44.028321	44.119243	44.210207
58	43.139947	43.231520	43.323136	43.414794	43.506494	43.598235	43.690019	43.781844
60	42.744647	42.837057	42.929509	43.022003	43.114539	43.207117	43.299737	43.392398
62	42.384360	42.477581	42.570845	42.664151	42.757499	42.850888	42.944319	43.037791
64	42.055517	42.149527	42.243578	42.337671	42.431806	42.525982	42.620199	42.714457
66	41.754987	41.849760	41.944575	42.039430	42.134327	42.229265	42.324243	42.419262
68	41.480008	41.575520	41.671073	41.766667	41.862301	41.957976	42.053690	42.149444
70	41.228135	41.324361	41.420629	41.516936	41.613283	41.709670	41.806096	41.902561
72	40.997197	41.094115	41.191072	41.288069	41.385105	41.482180	41.579293	41.676444
74	40.785263	40.882847	40.980471	41.078133	41.175834	41.273572	41.371348	41.469162
76	40.590606	40.688834	40.787101	40.885405	40.983746	41.082124	41.180539	41.278990
78	40.411681	40.510530	40.609416	40.708339	40.807297	40.906292	41.005322	41.104388
80	40.247101	40.346548	40.446031	40.545549	40.645102	40.744690	40.844312	40.943968
82	40.095619	40.195641	40.295697	40.395788	40.495913	40.596072	40.696263	40.796488
84	39.956108	40.056683	40.157292	40.257934	40.358608	40.459315	40.560054	40.660824
86	39.827552	39.928659	40.029798	40.130969	40.232171	40.333405	40.434669	40.535963
88	39.709031	39.810648	39.912297	40.013976	40.115685	40.217424	40.319192	40.420989
90	39.599710	39.701818	39.803956	39.906122	40.008317	40.110540	40.212792	40.315070
92	39.498833	39.601411	39.704017	39.806651	39.909312	40.012000	40.114714	40.217454
96	39.319714	39.423174	39.526660	39.630169	39.733704	39.837261	39.940843	40.044447
100	39.166862	39.271131	39.375421	39.479733	39.584067	39.688421	39.792795	39.897190
104	39.036268	39.141276	39.246302	39.351347	39.456410	39.561490	39.666588	39.771703
108	38.924577	39.030258	39.135955	39.241667	39.347395	39.453137	39.558893	39.664663
112	38.828967	38.935261	39.041568	39.147888	39.254219	39.360562	39.466916	39.573281
116	38.747062	38.853913	38.960774	39.067644	39.174523	39.281411	39.388306	39.495210
120	38.676851	38.784207	38.891570	38.998939	39.106314	39.213694	39.321079	39.428470
140	38.449786	38.559018	38.668242	38.777460	38.886670	38.995872	39.105067	39.214253
160	38.343528	38.453853	38.564161	38.674451	38.784724	38.894980	39.005217	39.115436

220

QUARTERLY WITHDRAWALS PER $1000

NUMBER OF QUARTRLY WTHDRWLS	EFFECTIVE ANNUAL YIELD							
	16.60%	16.65%	16.70%	16.75%	16.80%	16.85%	16.90%	16.95%
1	1039.141376	1039.252758	1039.364105	1039.475415	1039.586690	1039.697930	1039.809133	1039.920301
2	529.543862	529.628459	529.713031	529.797580	529.882104	529.966604	530.051080	530.135531
3	359.761463	359.837602	359.913722	359.989823	360.065904	360.141966	360.218009	360.294033
4	274.932796	275.005059	275.077306	275.149537	275.221752	275.293952	275.366135	275.438302
5	224.085572	224.155790	224.225995	224.296187	224.366366	224.436532	224.506684	224.576823
6	190.229012	190.298102	190.367180	190.436248	190.505305	190.574351	190.643386	190.712411
7	166.081347	166.149830	166.218304	166.286770	166.355226	166.423675	166.492114	166.560544
8	148.001681	148.069883	148.138079	148.206267	148.274450	148.342625	148.410794	148.478956
9	133.967287	134.035425	134.103558	134.171687	134.239810	134.307929	134.376044	134.444153
10	122.764521	122.832746	122.900968	122.969187	123.037403	123.105616	123.173826	123.242033
11	113.621058	113.689479	113.757898	113.826317	113.894734	113.963150	114.031565	114.099979
12	106.022010	106.090707	106.159405	106.228104	106.296803	106.365503	106.434204	106.502905
13	99.610908	99.679944	99.748983	99.818023	99.887066	99.956112	100.025159	100.094209
14	94.133130	94.202552	94.271978	94.341408	94.410842	94.480281	94.549723	94.619169
15	89.401945	89.471791	89.541642	89.611499	89.681362	89.751231	89.821105	89.890985
16	85.277304	85.347603	85.417909	85.488223	85.558544	85.628872	85.699208	85.769551
17	81.652103	81.722880	81.793665	81.864459	81.935262	82.006074	82.076894	82.147724
18	78.443040	78.514312	78.585595	78.656889	78.728193	78.799507	78.870831	78.942166
19	75.584343	75.656127	75.727923	75.799731	75.871551	75.943383	76.015227	76.087082
20	73.023393	73.095701	73.168022	73.240358	73.312706	73.385068	73.457443	73.529831
21	70.717590	70.790432	70.863289	70.936159	71.009048	71.081949	71.154865	71.227796
22	68.632079	68.705463	68.778863	68.852279	68.925712	68.999161	69.072626	69.146107
23	66.738061	66.811993	66.885942	66.959909	67.033894	67.107896	67.181916	67.255953
24	65.011537	65.086021	65.160524	65.235047	65.309588	65.384148	65.458727	65.533324
25	63.432344	63.507384	63.582445	63.657526	63.732627	63.807748	63.882889	63.958051
26	61.983419	62.059018	62.134638	62.210280	62.285944	62.361628	62.437334	62.513062
27	60.650227	60.726386	60.802567	60.878772	60.954998	61.031248	61.107520	61.183815
28	59.420305	59.497025	59.573768	59.650535	59.727326	59.804141	59.880979	59.957841
29	58.282910	58.360189	58.437494	58.514824	58.592179	58.669559	58.746963	58.824393
30	57.228726	57.306566	57.384431	57.462323	57.540241	57.618185	57.696155	57.774151
31	56.249642	56.328040	56.406465	56.484918	56.563398	56.641904	56.720438	56.798999
32	55.338556	55.417511	55.496494	55.575506	55.654545	55.733613	55.812708	55.891832
33	54.489228	54.568736	54.648276	54.727844	54.807441	54.887067	54.966722	55.046406
34	53.696150	53.776211	53.856303	53.936424	54.016576	54.096758	54.176969	54.257211
35	52.954441	53.035052	53.115693	53.196365	53.277069	53.357803	53.438568	53.519363
36	52.259765	52.340920	52.422108	52.503328	52.584579	52.665862	52.747177	52.828524
37	51.608249	51.689946	51.771677	51.853440	51.935236	52.017065	52.098925	52.180819
38	50.996430	51.078666	51.160935	51.243238	51.325574	51.407944	51.490347	51.572783
39	50.421199	50.503969	50.586773	50.669611	50.752484	50.835390	50.918330	51.001304
40	49.879757	49.963056	50.046391	50.129760	50.213164	50.296602	50.380076	50.463583
41	49.369577	49.453401	49.537261	49.621156	49.705087	49.789053	49.873054	49.957091
42	48.888372	48.972716	49.057097	49.141513	49.225966	49.310455	49.394979	49.479539
43	48.434067	48.518927	48.603823	48.688756	48.773725	48.858731	48.943774	49.028852
44	48.004777	48.090146	48.175553	48.260997	48.346478	48.431996	48.517551	48.603142
45	47.598781	47.684655	47.770567	47.856517	47.942504	48.028528	48.114590	48.200690
46	47.214510	47.300883	47.387295	47.473744	47.560232	47.646758	47.733321	47.819922
47	46.850526	46.937393	47.024299	47.111243	47.198226	47.285247	47.372306	47.459403
48	46.505512	46.592867	46.680262	46.767695	46.855167	46.942677	47.030226	47.117813
50	45.867651	45.955965	46.044318	46.132711	46.221144	46.309616	46.398126	46.486676
52	45.292347	45.381596	45.470885	45.560214	45.649583	45.738991	45.828439	45.917926
54	44.772290	44.862449	44.952649	45.042890	45.133171	45.223491	45.313851	45.404251
56	44.301212	44.392258	44.483344	44.574471	44.665638	44.756845	44.848092	44.939379
58	43.873710	43.965617	44.057564	44.149552	44.241580	44.333648	44.425756	44.517904
60	43.485100	43.577842	43.670626	43.763449	43.856313	43.949216	44.042159	44.135142
62	43.131304	43.224857	43.318450	43.412084	43.505757	43.599470	43.693222	43.787013
64	42.808755	42.903093	42.997471	43.091889	43.186346	43.280842	43.375378	43.469951
66	42.514320	42.609418	42.704555	42.799732	42.894947	42.990201	43.085493	43.180824
68	42.245238	42.341070	42.436942	42.532851	42.628799	42.724785	42.820809	42.916870
70	41.999065	42.095607	42.192187	42.288805	42.385460	42.482152	42.578882	42.675647
72	41.773633	41.870860	41.968124	42.065424	42.162762	42.260135	42.357545	42.454990
74	41.567012	41.664899	41.762822	41.860781	41.958775	42.056805	42.154870	42.252970
76	41.377478	41.476000	41.574558	41.673151	41.771779	41.870440	41.969136	42.067866
78	41.203488	41.302623	41.401792	41.500994	41.600231	41.699500	41.798802	41.898137
80	41.043659	41.143382	41.243138	41.342928	41.442749	41.542603	41.642488	41.742404
82	40.896745	40.997050	41.097355	41.197708	41.298091	41.398505	41.498950	41.599425
84	40.761625	40.862458	40.963321	41.064214	41.165137	41.266089	41.367071	41.468081
86	40.637287	40.738641	40.840024	40.941436	41.042876	41.144344	41.245840	41.347364
88	40.522814	40.624668	40.726549	40.828458	40.930394	41.032356	41.134345	41.236360
90	40.417376	40.519708	40.622067	40.724452	40.826863	40.929299	41.031759	41.134245
92	40.320220	40.423011	40.525827	40.628667	40.731532	40.834420	40.937332	41.040268
96	40.148075	40.251724	40.355395	40.459088	40.562803	40.666538	40.770293	40.874069
100	40.001604	40.106037	40.210490	40.314960	40.419449	40.523956	40.628480	40.733021
104	39.876835	39.981982	40.087146	40.192324	40.297518	40.402727	40.507949	40.613186
108	39.770447	39.876243	39.982053	40.087874	40.193708	40.299553	40.405410	40.511277
112	39.679656	39.786041	39.892436	39.998840	40.105254	40.211675	40.318105	40.424543
116	39.602121	39.709039	39.815963	39.922894	40.029831	40.136773	40.243721	40.350673
120	39.535865	39.643264	39.750666	39.858072	39.965482	40.072893	40.180308	40.287724
140	39.323431	39.432509	39.541759	39.650909	39.760050	39.869180	39.978301	40.087410
160	39.225637	39.335819	39.445983	39.556127	39.666253	39.776359	39.886445	39.996511

QUARTERLY WITHDRAWALS PER $1000

EFFECTIVE ANNUAL YIELD

NUMBER OF QUARTRLY WTHDRWLS	17.00%	17.05%	17.10%	17.15%	17.20%	17.25%	17.30%	17.35%
1	1040.031433	1040.142530	1040.253591	1040.364617	1040.475607	1040.586561	1040.697480	1040.808364
2	530.219959	530.304362	530.388741	530.473096	530.557427	530.641734	530.726017	530.810276
3	360.370037	360.446023	360.521989	360.597936	360.673864	360.749772	360.825662	360.901533
4	275.510454	275.582590	275.654710	275.726814	275.798902	275.870974	275.943031	276.015071
5	224.646949	224.717062	224.787162	224.857248	224.927321	224.997381	225.067428	225.137462
6	190.781424	190.850426	190.919418	190.988399	191.057369	191.126328	191.195276	191.264214
7	166.628966	166.697379	166.765784	166.834180	166.902567	166.970945	167.039314	167.107675
8	148.547111	148.615260	148.683402	148.751537	148.819665	148.887787	148.955902	149.024010
9	134.512258	134.580357	134.648453	134.716543	134.784628	134.852709	134.920785	134.988856
10	123.310238	123.378439	123.446638	123.514833	123.583026	123.651215	123.719402	123.787585
11	114.168392	114.236803	114.305214	114.373623	114.442031	114.510438	114.578844	114.647248
12	106.571607	106.640310	106.709013	106.777716	106.846420	106.915125	106.983830	107.052536
13	100.163262	100.232316	100.301373	100.370432	100.439494	100.508557	100.577623	100.646691
14	94.688620	94.758074	94.827532	94.896994	94.966460	95.035930	95.105404	95.174881
15	89.960870	90.030761	90.100658	90.170560	90.240467	90.310380	90.380299	90.450223
16	85.839901	85.910258	85.980622	86.050994	86.121372	86.191758	86.262151	86.332550
17	82.218562	82.289409	82.360264	82.431128	82.502001	82.572883	82.643773	82.714672
18	79.013511	79.084867	79.156232	79.227608	79.298994	79.370390	79.441797	79.513213
19	76.158949	76.230828	76.302719	76.374622	76.446536	76.518461	76.590399	76.662348
20	73.602233	73.674647	73.747075	73.819516	73.891970	73.964438	74.036918	74.109411
21	71.300742	71.373702	71.446676	71.519666	71.592669	71.665688	71.738720	71.811767
22	69.219460	69.293117	69.366646	69.440190	69.513751	69.587328	69.660920	69.734528
23	67.330007	67.404079	67.478168	67.552274	67.626398	67.700538	67.774696	67.848871
24	65.607941	65.682576	65.757229	65.831901	65.906592	65.981301	66.056028	66.130774
25	64.033232	64.108433	64.183655	64.258895	64.334156	64.409437	64.484737	64.560056
26	62.588810	62.664580	62.740371	62.816183	62.892015	62.967869	63.043744	63.119639
27	61.260131	61.336471	61.412832	61.489216	61.565622	61.642050	61.718500	61.794972
28	60.034727	60.111636	60.188569	60.265525	60.342504	60.419507	60.496532	60.573581
29	58.901847	58.979326	59.056829	59.134357	59.211909	59.289485	59.367086	59.444711
30	57.852172	57.930220	58.008292	58.086391	58.164515	58.242664	58.320838	58.399038
31	56.877586	56.956200	57.034841	57.113508	57.192202	57.270922	57.349669	57.428442
32	55.970983	56.050162	56.129368	56.208603	56.287864	56.367153	56.446469	56.525813
33	55.126119	55.205860	55.285630	55.365428	55.445255	55.525110	55.604993	55.684904
34	54.337482	54.417782	54.498112	54.578472	54.658861	54.739279	54.819726	54.900202
35	53.600190	53.681046	53.761933	53.842850	53.923798	54.004775	54.085783	54.166820
36	52.909901	52.991103	53.072750	53.154222	53.235724	53.317257	53.398821	53.480415
37	52.262744	52.344701	52.426691	52.508712	52.590765	52.672849	52.754965	52.837113
38	51.655251	51.737753	51.820287	51.902854	51.985453	52.068085	52.150748	52.233444
39	51.084312	51.167353	51.250428	51.333536	51.416676	51.499850	51.583057	51.666297
40	50.547125	50.630701	50.714311	50.797955	50.881633	50.965345	51.049090	51.132868
41	50.041162	50.125268	50.209409	50.293584	50.377794	50.462038	50.546316	50.630628
42	49.564135	49.648766	49.733432	49.818133	49.902869	49.987640	50.072446	50.157286
43	49.113967	49.199117	49.284303	49.369525	49.454782	49.540075	49.625403	49.710766
44	48.688771	48.774435	48.860136	48.945873	49.031645	49.117454	49.203298	49.289178
45	48.286826	48.372999	48.459208	48.545454	48.631737	48.718056	48.804410	48.890801
46	47.906561	47.993236	48.079949	48.166699	48.253485	48.340308	48.427168	48.514063
47	47.546538	47.633710	47.720920	47.808168	47.895452	47.982773	48.070131	48.157526
48	47.205439	47.293102	47.380803	47.468542	47.556318	47.644131	47.731982	47.819869
50	46.575264	46.663891	46.752556	46.841259	46.930000	47.018778	47.107595	47.196448
52	46.007453	46.097018	46.186621	46.276264	46.365944	46.455662	46.545419	46.635212
54	45.494690	45.585168	45.675684	45.766240	45.856834	45.947466	46.038136	46.128844
56	45.030704	45.122609	45.213475	45.304916	45.396397	45.487916	45.579473	45.671068
58	44.610090	44.702316	44.794581	44.886884	44.979225	45.071605	45.164022	45.256478
60	44.228163	44.321223	44.414322	44.507459	44.600634	44.693847	44.787098	44.880386
62	43.880843	43.974711	44.068618	44.162562	44.256544	44.350564	44.444621	44.538715
64	43.564563	43.659213	43.753901	43.848626	43.943388	44.038188	44.133024	44.227897
66	43.276192	43.371597	43.467039	43.562519	43.658035	43.753587	43.849176	43.944800
68	43.012967	43.109102	43.205273	43.301480	43.397723	43.494002	43.590316	43.686665
70	42.772449	42.869287	42.966161	43.063070	43.160014	43.256993	43.354006	43.451053
72	42.552471	42.649986	42.747537	42.845122	42.942741	43.040394	43.138080	43.235800
74	42.351104	42.449272	42.547474	42.645709	42.743978	42.842279	42.940613	43.038979
76	42.166628	42.265424	42.364253	42.463113	42.562006	42.660931	42.759887	42.858874
78	41.997504	42.096903	42.196334	42.295796	42.395288	42.494811	42.594365	42.693948
80	41.842352	41.942330	42.042338	42.142377	42.242445	42.342543	42.442669	42.542824
82	41.699929	41.800463	41.901026	42.001618	42.102238	42.202886	42.303562	42.404265
84	41.569120	41.670186	41.771281	41.872403	41.973552	42.074727	42.175929	42.277157
86	41.448914	41.550491	41.652095	41.753724	41.855380	41.957060	42.058766	42.160496
88	41.338401	41.440467	41.542557	41.644673	41.746813	41.848976	41.951163	42.053374
90	41.236754	41.339287	41.441844	41.544424	41.647027	41.749652	41.852300	41.954969
92	41.143225	41.246206	41.349208	41.452232	41.555277	41.658343	41.761430	41.864537
96	40.977864	41.081678	41.185512	41.289364	41.393235	41.497123	41.601029	41.704953
100	40.837579	40.942153	41.046743	41.151349	41.255969	41.360605	41.465255	41.569920
104	40.718437	40.823700	40.928977	41.034265	41.139567	41.244879	41.350204	41.455539
108	40.617155	40.723043	40.828941	40.934848	41.040765	41.146690	41.252624	41.358565
112	40.530988	40.637441	40.743900	40.850366	40.956837	41.063315	41.169798	41.276286
116	40.457631	40.564592	40.671557	40.778526	40.885498	40.992473	41.099450	41.206430
120	40.395142	40.502561	40.609982	40.717403	40.824824	40.932246	41.039667	41.147088
140	40.196509	40.305597	40.414674	40.523738	40.632791	40.741832	40.850861	40.959877
160	40.106558	40.216584	40.326590	40.436575	40.546540	40.656484	40.766406	40.876307

QUARTERLY WITHDRAWALS PER $1000

EFFECTIVE ANNUAL YIELD

NUMBER OF QUARTRLY WTHDRWLS	17.40%	17.45%	17.50%	17.55%	17.60%	17.65%	17.70%	17.75%
1	1040.919212	1041.030025	1041.140802	1041.251544	1041.362251	1041.472922	1041.583558	1041.694159
2	530.894510	530.978721	531.062908	531.147071	531.231209	531.315324	531.399415	531.483482
3	360.977384	361.053216	361.129029	361.204823	361.280598	361.356354	361.432091	361.507809
4	276.087096	276.159105	276.231099	276.303076	276.375038	276.446984	276.518914	276.590829
5	225.207483	225.277490	225.347484	225.417466	225.487434	225.557388	225.627330	225.697259
6	191.333140	191.402056	191.470961	191.539855	191.608739	191.677611	191.746473	191.815324
7	167.176027	167.244371	167.312706	167.381031	167.449349	167.517657	167.585957	167.654248
8	149.092112	149.160207	149.228295	149.296376	149.364451	149.432519	149.500580	149.568634
9	135.056922	135.124983	135.193040	135.261091	135.329138	135.397180	135.465217	135.533250
10	123.855766	123.923944	123.992118	124.060290	124.128459	124.196624	124.264787	124.332946
11	114.715652	114.784054	114.852454	114.920854	114.989252	115.057649	115.126045	115.194440
12	107.121242	107.189949	107.258657	107.327364	107.396073	107.464781	107.533490	107.602200
13	100.715762	100.784834	100.853909	100.922986	100.992065	101.061146	101.130229	101.199314
14	95.244363	95.313848	95.383337	95.452830	95.522327	95.591827	95.661331	95.730839
15	90.520153	90.590088	90.660028	90.729972	90.799925	90.869882	90.939843	91.009811
16	86.402957	86.473371	86.543792	86.614220	86.684654	86.755096	86.825544	86.896000
17	82.785579	82.856495	82.927419	82.998352	83.069294	83.140243	83.211201	83.282168
18	79.584639	79.656076	79.727522	79.798979	79.870445	79.941921	80.013408	80.084904
19	76.734308	76.806280	76.878263	76.950258	77.022264	77.094281	77.166310	77.238350
20	74.181917	74.254436	74.326968	74.399513	74.472071	74.544641	74.617224	74.689820
21	71.884828	71.957904	72.030994	72.104098	72.177216	72.250349	72.323495	72.396656
22	69.808152	69.881791	69.955446	70.029117	70.102803	70.176505	70.250222	70.323955
23	67.923063	67.997272	68.071498	68.145740	68.220000	68.294276	68.368569	68.442879
24	66.205538	66.280321	66.355121	66.429940	66.504777	66.579631	66.654504	66.729395
25	64.635396	64.710754	64.786132	64.861530	64.936947	65.012383	65.087838	65.163313
26	63.195555	63.271492	63.347450	63.423428	63.499426	63.575445	63.651485	63.727544
27	61.871466	61.947982	62.024519	62.101079	62.177660	62.254262	62.330886	62.407532
28	60.650653	60.727748	60.804865	60.882006	60.959169	61.036355	61.113564	61.190795
29	59.522360	59.600033	59.677730	59.755451	59.833196	59.910964	59.988756	60.066572
30	58.477263	58.555513	58.633788	58.712088	58.790413	58.868763	58.947137	59.025536
31	57.507241	57.586066	57.664917	57.743794	57.822697	57.901625	57.980579	58.059559
32	56.605184	56.684581	56.764006	56.843457	56.922936	57.002441	57.081972	57.161531
33	55.764844	55.844811	55.924807	56.004830	56.084880	56.164959	56.245065	56.325198
34	54.980707	55.061241	55.141803	55.222395	55.303014	55.383663	55.464339	55.545044
35	54.247887	54.328984	54.410110	54.491265	54.572451	54.653665	54.734908	54.816181
36	53.562040	53.643696	53.725381	53.807097	53.888844	53.970620	54.052426	54.134262
37	52.919291	53.001501	53.083742	53.166014	53.248317	53.330651	53.413015	53.495410
38	52.316172	52.398932	52.481724	52.564547	52.647402	52.730288	52.813206	52.896155
39	51.749569	51.832874	51.916212	51.999581	52.082983	52.166417	52.249883	52.333381
40	51.216680	51.300525	51.384403	51.468314	51.552257	51.636234	51.720242	51.804284
41	50.714974	50.799353	50.883766	50.968213	51.052693	51.137206	51.221753	51.306332
42	50.242160	50.327069	50.412012	50.496989	50.582000	50.667045	50.752123	50.837234
43	49.796163	49.881596	49.967063	50.052564	50.138100	50.223670	50.309274	50.394912
44	49.375093	49.461043	49.547028	49.633048	49.719103	49.805193	49.891317	49.977475
45	48.977228	49.063690	49.150187	49.236720	49.323288	49.409891	49.496528	49.583201
46	48.600995	48.687963	48.774966	48.862006	48.949080	49.036190	49.123335	49.210516
47	48.244957	48.332424	48.419927	48.507467	48.595042	48.682653	48.770299	48.857980
48	47.907793	47.995753	48.083750	48.171783	48.259853	48.347958	48.436098	48.524275
50	47.285339	47.374267	47.463231	47.552232	47.641270	47.730344	47.819453	47.908599
52	46.725044	46.814912	46.904818	46.994761	47.084740	47.174756	47.264808	47.354896
54	46.219589	46.310372	46.401192	46.492049	46.582943	46.673873	46.764840	46.855843
56	45.762701	45.854371	45.946078	46.037822	46.129602	46.221420	46.313273	46.405163
58	45.348970	45.441500	45.534067	45.626670	45.719310	45.811987	45.904699	45.997447
60	44.973712	45.067014	45.160473	45.253908	45.347379	45.440887	45.534430	45.628009
62	44.632846	44.727013	44.821216	44.915456	45.009731	45.104041	45.198387	45.292768
64	44.322805	44.417750	44.512731	44.607748	44.702797	44.797883	44.893004	44.988159
66	44.040460	44.136155	44.231885	44.327650	44.423449	44.519282	44.615150	44.711051
68	43.783049	43.879468	43.975920	44.072407	44.168927	44.265481	44.362068	44.458687
70	43.548135	43.645250	43.742398	43.839580	43.936794	44.034041	44.131320	44.228631
72	43.333553	43.431338	43.529156	43.627005	43.724887	43.822800	43.920745	44.018720
74	43.137377	43.235807	43.334268	43.432760	43.531283	43.629836	43.728419	43.827033
76	42.957892	43.056941	43.156019	43.255128	43.354266	43.453434	43.552630	43.651855
78	42.793561	42.893204	42.992876	43.092575	43.192303	43.292060	43.391844	43.491656
80	42.643008	42.743220	42.843459	42.943726	43.044020	43.144340	43.244688	43.345061
82	42.504996	42.605753	42.706536	42.807346	42.908181	43.009042	43.109928	43.210839
84	42.378411	42.479690	42.580995	42.682324	42.783677	42.885054	42.986455	43.087880
86	42.262251	42.364029	42.465831	42.567657	42.669505	42.771376	42.873270	42.975185
88	42.155607	42.257863	42.360141	42.462440	42.564762	42.667104	42.769468	42.871852
90	42.057659	42.160371	42.263103	42.365856	42.468628	42.571421	42.674233	42.777064
92	41.967664	42.070810	42.173976	42.277161	42.380364	42.483586	42.586825	42.690082
96	41.808893	41.912850	42.016823	42.120812	42.224816	42.328836	42.432870	42.536919
100	41.674598	41.779290	41.883995	41.988712	42.093443	42.198185	42.302939	42.407705
104	41.560886	41.666242	41.771609	41.876986	41.982372	42.087767	42.193171	42.298583
108	41.464515	41.570472	41.676436	41.782407	41.888384	41.994367	42.100357	42.206351
112	41.382779	41.489277	41.595778	41.702284	41.808793	41.915305	42.021820	42.128338
116	41.313412	41.420395	41.527379	41.634365	41.741351	41.848337	41.955324	42.062310
120	41.254508	41.361927	41.469344	41.576760	41.684173	41.791584	41.898993	42.006399
140	41.068880	41.177870	41.286847	41.395810	41.504759	41.613695	41.722616	41.831522
160	40.986187	41.096045	41.205881	41.315696	41.425488	41.535258	41.645006	41.754731

QUARTERLY WITHDRAWALS PER $1000

EFFECTIVE ANNUAL YIELD

NUMBER OF QUARTRLY WTHDRWLS	17.80%	17.85%	17.90%	18.00%	18.10%	18.20%	18.30%	18.40%
1	1041.804725	1041.915255	1042.025750	1042.246635	1042.467380	1042.687985	1042.908450	1043.128775
2	531.567525	531.651544	531.735540	531.903459	532.071283	532.239012	532.406645	532.574184
3	361.583508	361.659188	361.734849	361.886114	362.037304	362.188417	362.339455	362.490418
4	276.662728	276.734611	276.806478	276.950166	277.093791	277.237353	277.380853	277.524290
5	225.767174	225.837077	225.906966	226.046706	226.186393	226.326028	226.465611	226.605141
6	191.884164	191.952993	192.021811	192.159416	192.296977	192.434495	192.571970	192.709402
7	167.722531	167.790804	167.859069	167.995573	168.132042	168.268477	168.404876	168.541241
8	149.636682	149.704723	149.772757	149.908805	150.044827	150.180821	150.316788	150.452728
9	135.601277	135.669300	135.737317	135.873338	136.009340	136.145321	136.281284	136.417226
10	124.401103	124.469256	124.537406	124.673698	124.809977	124.946244	125.082499	125.218741
11	115.262833	115.331225	115.399616	115.536393	115.673165	115.809932	115.946693	116.083448
12	107.670910	107.739620	107.808331	107.945754	108.083178	108.220604	108.358030	108.495458
13	101.268402	101.337491	101.406583	101.544772	101.682969	101.821174	101.959387	102.097608
14	95.800351	95.869866	95.939385	96.078434	96.217497	96.356575	96.495667	96.634773
15	91.079783	91.149761	91.219744	91.359725	91.499728	91.639751	91.779794	91.919858
16	86.966462	87.036931	87.107407	87.248378	87.389377	87.530403	87.671455	87.812533
17	83.353143	83.424126	83.495118	83.637125	83.779166	83.921239	84.063345	84.205483
18	80.156409	80.227925	80.299450	80.442530	80.585649	80.728807	80.872002	81.015236
19	77.310402	77.382464	77.454538	77.598719	77.742945	77.887215	78.031528	78.175886
20	74.762428	74.835050	74.907683	75.052988	75.198343	75.343748	75.489202	75.634706
21	72.469831	72.543019	72.616222	72.762669	72.909171	73.055729	73.202341	73.349007
22	70.397702	70.471466	70.545244	70.692847	70.840510	70.988233	71.136017	71.283860
23	68.517205	68.591548	68.665908	68.814676	68.963510	69.112410	69.261375	69.410404
24	66.804304	66.879230	66.954175	67.104117	67.254129	67.404212	67.554365	67.704587
25	65.238806	65.314319	65.389851	65.540971	65.692166	65.843437	65.994782	66.146201
26	63.803624	63.879725	63.955845	64.108146	64.260527	64.412988	64.565528	64.718147
27	62.484199	62.560887	62.637597	62.791080	62.944647	63.098299	63.252034	63.405852
28	61.268049	61.345325	61.422623	61.577287	61.732040	61.886881	62.041810	62.196826
29	60.144412	60.222275	60.300161	60.456004	60.611940	60.767967	60.924087	61.080298
30	59.103960	59.182408	59.260880	59.417898	59.575013	59.732224	59.889530	60.046932
31	58.138565	58.217596	58.296652	58.454841	58.613130	58.771518	58.930007	59.088594
32	57.241115	57.320726	57.400364	57.559717	57.719174	57.878735	58.038399	58.198165
33	56.405359	56.485547	56.565762	56.726273	56.886892	57.047618	57.208450	57.369387
34	55.625777	55.706538	55.787328	55.948990	56.110762	56.272645	56.434637	56.596738
35	54.897482	54.978813	55.060172	55.222976	55.385895	55.548926	55.712070	55.875325
36	54.216128	54.298023	54.379948	54.543886	54.707940	54.872111	55.036397	55.200797
37	53.577835	53.660291	53.742777	53.907838	54.073020	54.238320	54.403738	54.569272
38	52.979134	53.062145	53.145187	53.311363	53.477661	53.644079	53.810619	53.977277
39	52.416910	52.500471	52.584064	52.751343	52.918746	53.086273	53.253922	53.421694
40	51.888357	51.972463	52.056601	52.224972	52.393470	52.562097	52.730842	52.899714
41	51.390944	51.475589	51.560266	51.729718	51.899299	52.069007	52.238842	52.408803
42	50.922379	51.007557	51.092768	51.263289	51.433941	51.604722	51.775631	51.946668
43	50.480584	50.566289	50.652028	50.823605	50.995315	51.167156	51.339127	51.511227
44	50.063668	50.149894	50.236154	50.408776	50.581532	50.754420	50.927439	51.100589
45	49.669908	49.756649	49.843424	50.017078	50.190866	50.364788	50.538843	50.713029
46	49.297731	49.384980	49.472265	49.646936	49.821744	49.996687	50.171763	50.346973
47	48.945697	49.033449	49.121235	49.296912	49.472725	49.648675	49.824760	50.000978
48	48.612486	48.700733	48.789015	48.965683	49.142490	49.319433	49.496511	49.673724
50	47.997781	48.086998	48.176250	48.354861	48.533610	48.712498	48.891522	49.070681
52	47.445020	47.535180	47.625375	47.805872	47.986508	48.167283	48.348195	48.529243
54	46.946881	47.037956	47.129066	47.311393	47.493859	47.676463	47.859205	48.042081
56	46.497089	46.589050	46.681046	46.865145	47.049383	47.233759	47.418271	47.602916
58	46.090231	46.183051	46.275905	46.461719	46.647671	46.833759	47.019982	47.206337
60	45.721623	45.815272	45.908955	46.096426	46.284034	46.471776	46.659651	46.847656
62	45.387184	45.481634	45.576118	45.765189	45.954394	46.143731	46.333199	46.522795
64	45.083348	45.178571	45.273827	45.464441	45.655185	45.846060	46.037062	46.228189
66	44.806985	44.902953	44.998954	45.191053	45.383280	45.575634	45.768112	45.960712
68	44.555340	44.652024	44.748741	44.942269	45.135922	45.329699	45.523595	45.717611
70	44.325973	44.423347	44.520752	44.715655	44.910678	45.105820	45.301080	45.496453
72	44.116726	44.214762	44.312828	44.509050	44.705389	44.901842	45.098408	45.295084
74	43.925675	44.024347	44.123048	44.320536	44.518136	44.715846	44.913664	45.111587
76	43.751109	43.850390	43.949700	44.148400	44.347209	44.546122	44.745139	44.944256
78	43.591494	43.691360	43.791252	43.991115	44.191080	44.391145	44.591309	44.791567
80	43.445460	43.545885	43.646335	43.847309	44.048381	44.249547	44.450806	44.652155
82	43.311774	43.412734	43.513717	43.715754	43.917883	44.120101	44.322406	44.524796
84	43.189328	43.290798	43.392291	43.595344	43.798482	44.001704	44.205007	44.408390
86	43.077122	43.179081	43.281061	43.485082	43.689183	43.893363	44.097617	44.301945
88	42.974256	43.076680	43.179124	43.384069	43.589089	43.794181	43.999342	44.204570
90	42.879914	42.982782	43.085668	43.291494	43.497388	43.703348	43.909372	44.115457
92	42.793357	42.896648	42.999956	43.206620	43.413346	43.620133	43.826978	44.033877
96	42.640982	42.745060	42.849150	43.057371	43.265643	43.473962	43.682327	43.890734
100	42.512482	42.617269	42.722068	42.931694	43.141359	43.351060	43.560794	43.770560
104	42.404004	42.509432	42.614868	42.825761	43.036681	43.247624	43.458588	43.669572
108	42.312351	42.418356	42.524365	42.736396	42.948441	43.160499	43.372566	43.584641
112	42.234858	42.341380	42.447903	42.660954	42.874008	43.087063	43.300116	43.513166
116	42.169296	42.276281	42.383265	42.597228	42.811184	43.025129	43.239062	43.452980
120	42.113801	42.221200	42.328595	42.543372	42.758132	42.972870	43.187586	43.402277
140	41.940414	42.049292	42.158153	42.375831	42.593446	42.810996	43.028480	43.245896
160	41.864433	41.974112	42.083768	42.303011	42.522160	42.741214	42.960172	43.179033

224

QUARTERLY WITHDRAWALS PER $1000

EFFECTIVE ANNUAL YIELD

NUMBER OF QUARTRLY WTHDRWLS	18.50%	18.60%	18.70%	18.80%	18.90%	19.00%	19.10%	19.20%
1	1043.348960	1043.569006	1043.788914	1044.008682	1044.228311	1044.447802	1044.667155	1044.886369
2	532.741629	532.908978	533.076233	533.243394	533.410461	533.577434	533.744312	533.911097
3	362.641305	362.792117	362.942853	363.093515	363.244101	363.394613	363.545050	363.695412
4	277.667664	277.810977	277.954226	278.097414	278.240540	278.383603	278.526604	278.669544
5	226.744620	226.884046	227.023421	227.162743	227.302014	227.441233	227.580400	227.719515
6	192.846791	192.984137	193.121440	193.258700	193.395917	193.533091	193.670222	193.807310
7	168.677571	168.813866	168.950126	169.086352	169.222543	169.358699	169.494820	169.630907
8	150.588642	150.724528	150.860387	150.996219	151.132025	151.267803	151.403554	151.539277
9	136.553149	136.689053	136.824937	136.960801	137.096645	137.232470	137.368275	137.504060
10	125.354971	125.491188	125.627392	125.763584	125.899763	126.035930	126.172083	126.308224
11	116.220199	116.356943	116.493682	116.630415	116.767142	116.903863	117.040578	117.177287
12	108.632888	108.770318	108.907749	109.045181	109.182613	109.320047	109.457481	109.594915
13	102.235836	102.374072	102.512315	102.650566	102.788824	102.927088	103.065360	103.203639
14	96.773893	96.913027	97.052175	97.191336	97.330511	97.469699	97.608900	97.748114
15	92.059942	92.200046	92.340170	92.480314	92.620477	92.760659	92.900861	93.041082
16	87.953638	88.094769	88.235925	88.377108	88.518315	88.659549	88.800807	88.942090
17	84.347654	84.489856	84.632090	84.774355	84.916652	85.058980	85.201339	85.343728
18	81.158507	81.301816	81.445163	81.588547	81.731967	81.875424	82.018918	82.162448
19	78.320287	78.464731	78.609218	78.753747	78.898319	79.042933	79.187590	79.332288
20	75.780258	75.925859	76.071508	76.217205	76.362950	76.508743	76.654582	76.800469
21	73.495728	73.642503	73.789331	73.936212	74.083147	74.230134	74.377173	74.524265
22	71.431762	71.579724	71.727743	71.875822	72.023958	72.172152	72.320403	72.468711
23	69.559497	69.708655	69.857876	70.007160	70.156507	70.305916	70.455388	70.604921
24	67.854878	68.005238	68.155666	68.306162	68.456724	68.607356	68.758054	68.908818
25	66.297694	66.449261	66.600900	66.752612	66.904395	67.056251	67.208177	67.360174
26	64.870843	65.023618	65.176469	65.329398	65.482403	65.635484	65.788641	65.941872
27	63.559752	63.713735	63.867799	64.021944	64.176169	64.330475	64.484861	64.639325
28	62.351928	62.507117	62.662391	62.817751	62.973195	63.128723	63.284334	63.440029
29	61.236599	61.392991	61.549472	61.706042	61.862701	62.019447	62.176281	62.333202
30	60.204428	60.362018	60.519701	60.677477	60.835345	60.993304	61.151355	61.309496
31	59.247279	59.406061	59.564941	59.723916	59.882987	60.042153	60.201414	60.360768
32	58.358032	58.518000	58.678069	58.838237	58.998504	59.158869	59.319332	59.479892
33	57.530429	57.691576	57.852826	58.014178	58.175633	58.337189	58.498845	58.660602
34	56.758947	56.921263	57.083686	57.246214	57.408847	57.571584	57.734425	57.897369
35	56.038691	56.202168	56.365753	56.529447	56.693249	56.857158	57.021173	57.185294
36	55.365311	55.529937	55.694676	55.859526	56.024486	56.189555	56.354734	56.520020
37	54.734923	54.900690	55.066570	55.232565	55.398672	55.564891	55.731221	55.897661
38	54.144055	54.310950	54.477961	54.645089	54.812331	54.979688	55.147158	55.314740
39	53.589586	53.757598	53.925728	54.093977	54.262343	54.430824	54.599421	54.768133
40	53.068708	53.237825	53.407063	53.576420	53.745896	53.915490	54.085202	54.255029
41	52.578888	52.749097	52.919429	53.089882	53.260455	53.431149	53.601961	53.772890
42	52.117831	52.289119	52.460532	52.632067	52.803725	52.975504	53.147403	53.319421
43	51.683455	51.855809	52.028289	52.200894	52.373622	52.546473	52.719445	52.892537
44	51.273868	51.447275	51.620809	51.794469	51.968253	52.142161	52.316192	52.490343
45	50.887346	51.061792	51.236366	51.411066	51.585893	51.760844	51.935918	52.111114
46	50.522313	50.697784	50.873383	51.049111	51.224964	51.400943	51.577046	51.753272
47	50.177328	50.353809	50.530420	50.707159	50.884025	51.061018	51.238134	51.415374
48	49.851070	50.028547	50.206154	50.383890	50.561754	50.739745	50.917860	51.096099
50	49.249974	49.429399	49.608955	49.788641	49.968454	50.148395	50.328461	50.508651
52	48.710424	48.891737	49.073182	49.254756	49.436458	49.618287	49.800241	49.982319
54	48.225091	48.408233	48.591505	48.774906	48.958435	49.142089	49.325868	49.509769
56	47.787695	47.972604	48.157643	48.342810	48.528102	48.713519	48.899059	49.084720
58	47.392824	47.579440	47.766184	47.953054	48.140048	48.327165	48.514403	48.701760
60	47.035791	47.224053	47.412441	47.600952	47.789586	47.978339	48.167212	48.356201
62	46.712518	46.902365	47.092336	47.282427	47.472638	47.662966	47.853410	48.043968
64	46.419440	46.610813	46.802306	46.993917	47.185644	47.377485	47.569438	47.761502
66	46.153433	46.346272	46.539228	46.732298	46.925480	47.118773	47.312174	47.505682
68	45.911743	46.105990	46.300349	46.494819	46.689397	46.884081	47.078870	47.273762
70	45.691940	45.887536	46.083241	46.279052	46.474967	46.670985	46.867102	47.063318
72	45.491868	45.688758	45.885752	46.082847	46.280042	46.477334	46.674722	46.872203
74	45.309614	45.507742	45.705969	45.904292	46.102711	46.301221	46.499822	46.698512
76	45.143472	45.342784	45.542189	45.741687	45.941273	46.140948	46.340707	46.540549
78	44.991919	45.192362	45.392893	45.593511	45.794213	45.994996	46.195860	46.396801
80	44.853592	45.055114	45.256720	45.458406	45.660171	45.862012	46.063928	46.265915
82	44.727268	44.929820	45.132449	45.335154	45.537931	45.740779	45.943696	46.146679
84	44.611848	44.815381	45.018986	45.222660	45.426401	45.630207	45.834076	46.038005
86	44.506344	44.710811	44.915344	45.119940	45.324598	45.529314	45.734088	45.938916
88	44.409863	44.615219	44.820634	45.026107	45.231636	45.437217	45.642850	45.848531
90	44.321601	44.527801	44.734056	44.940361	45.146717	45.353119	45.559566	45.766056
92	44.240830	44.447832	44.654883	44.861979	45.069118	45.276299	45.483518	45.690774
96	44.099183	44.307669	44.516192	44.724748	44.933336	45.141952	45.350595	45.559263
100	43.980354	44.190174	44.400018	44.609883	44.819768	45.029671	45.239588	45.449518
104	43.880573	44.091588	44.302615	44.513652	44.724697	44.935747	45.146801	45.357857
108	43.796721	44.008804	44.220888	44.432970	44.645049	44.857123	45.069188	45.281244
112	43.726209	43.939245	44.152270	44.365283	44.578282	44.791264	45.004228	45.217172
116	43.666882	43.880765	44.094627	44.308467	44.522282	44.736070	44.949830	45.163559
120	43.616942	43.831577	44.046182	44.260754	44.475292	44.689793	44.904257	45.118680
140	43.463243	43.680519	43.897723	44.114854	44.331909	44.548889	44.765791	44.982614
160	43.397796	43.616459	43.835023	44.053486	44.271848	44.490107	44.708262	44.926313

QUARTERLY WITHDRAWALS PER $1000

EFFECTIVE ANNUAL YIELD

NUMBER OF QUARTERLY WTHDRWLS	19.30%	19.40%	19.50%	19.60%	19.70%	19.80%	19.90%	20.00%
1	1045.105446	1045.324385	1045.543187	1045.761851	1045.980378	1046.198769	1046.417022	1046.635139
2	534.077788	534.244386	534.410890	534.577301	534.743619	534.909844	535.075975	535.242015
3	363.845699	363.995912	364.146050	364.296114	364.446104	364.596020	364.745861	364.895629
4	278.812421	278.955237	279.097991	279.240683	279.383314	279.525883	279.668390	279.810836
5	227.858578	227.997590	228.136550	228.275459	228.414316	228.553121	228.691875	228.830578
6	193.944356	194.081359	194.218318	194.355236	194.492110	194.628942	194.765731	194.902478
7	169.766959	169.902976	170.038959	170.174907	170.310820	170.446699	170.582543	170.718352
8	151.674974	151.810644	151.946287	152.081902	152.217490	152.353052	152.488586	152.624093
9	137.639825	137.775570	137.911295	138.047001	138.182686	138.318352	138.453997	138.589623
10	126.444352	126.580467	126.716569	126.852658	126.988734	127.124797	127.260847	127.396883
11	117.313990	117.450686	117.587377	117.724061	117.860738	117.997409	118.134074	118.270732
12	109.732350	109.869785	110.007220	110.144655	110.282091	110.419526	110.556962	110.694397
13	103.341924	103.480216	103.618515	103.756820	103.895131	104.033448	104.171772	104.310102
14	97.887342	98.026581	98.165834	98.305099	98.444377	98.583667	98.722969	98.862283
15	93.181322	93.321581	93.461858	93.602154	93.742468	93.882800	94.023151	94.163519
16	89.083398	89.224731	89.366088	89.507470	89.648875	89.790305	89.931758	90.073235
17	85.486148	85.628598	85.771079	85.913589	86.056129	86.198699	86.341298	86.483926
18	82.306015	82.449617	82.593254	82.736928	82.880636	83.024379	83.168157	83.311970
19	79.477027	79.621807	79.766629	79.911491	80.056394	80.201337	80.346320	80.491343
20	76.946402	77.092382	77.238408	77.384480	77.530597	77.676760	77.822968	77.969220
21	74.671408	74.818603	74.965848	75.113145	75.260492	75.407890	75.555338	75.702835
22	72.617076	72.765497	72.913974	73.062507	73.211095	73.359739	73.508437	73.657189
23	70.754515	70.904171	71.053888	71.203664	71.353501	71.503398	71.653353	71.803368
24	69.059648	69.210543	69.361504	69.512529	69.663619	69.814773	69.965991	70.117272
25	67.512242	67.664380	67.816587	67.968863	68.121209	68.273622	68.426104	68.578653
26	66.095178	66.248559	66.402013	66.555540	66.709140	66.862813	67.016558	67.170374
27	64.793868	64.948490	65.103189	65.257966	65.412819	65.567749	65.722754	65.877835
28	63.595806	63.751666	63.907607	64.063629	64.219731	64.375914	64.532176	64.688517
29	62.490209	62.647301	62.804479	62.961741	63.119088	63.276518	63.434032	63.591627
30	61.467726	61.626046	61.784455	61.942951	62.101535	62.260206	62.418964	62.577807
31	60.520215	60.679765	60.839387	60.999110	61.158924	61.318828	61.478821	61.638904
32	59.640548	59.801300	59.962147	60.123088	60.284123	60.445251	60.606471	60.767784
33	58.822458	58.984412	59.146465	59.308614	59.470861	59.633203	59.795640	59.958173
34	58.060415	58.223562	58.386810	58.550158	58.713605	58.877150	59.040794	59.204535
35	57.349519	57.513848	57.678280	57.842815	58.007452	58.172190	58.337027	58.501965
36	56.685413	56.850913	57.016518	57.182229	57.348043	57.513960	57.679980	57.846101
37	56.064211	56.230869	56.397636	56.564509	56.731488	56.898572	57.065761	57.233053
38	55.482434	55.650238	55.818152	55.986175	56.154306	56.322544	56.490888	56.659338
39	54.936957	55.105894	55.274943	55.444102	55.613372	55.782750	55.952235	56.121828
40	54.424971	54.595027	54.765197	54.935479	55.105872	55.276376	55.446989	55.617710
41	53.943936	54.115098	54.286375	54.457765	54.629268	54.800882	54.972607	55.144442
42	53.491557	53.663809	53.836178	54.008662	54.181259	54.353970	54.526792	54.699725
43	53.065748	53.239077	53.412523	53.586085	53.759763	53.933554	54.107457	54.281473
44	52.664615	52.839006	53.013514	53.188140	53.362881	53.537737	53.712706	53.887788
45	52.286431	52.461868	52.637424	52.813097	52.988887	53.164792	53.340811	53.516943
46	51.929619	52.106087	52.282674	52.459380	52.636202	52.813140	52.990193	53.167359
47	51.592737	51.770220	51.947823	52.125544	52.303383	52.481338	52.659407	52.837591
48	51.274460	51.452943	51.631546	51.810267	51.989106	52.168061	52.347131	52.526315
50	50.688963	50.869397	51.049951	51.230624	51.411414	51.592320	51.773341	51.954475
52	50.164518	50.346839	50.529279	50.711838	50.894512	51.077302	51.260206	51.443223
54	49.693792	49.877935	50.062195	50.246573	50.431066	50.615673	50.800392	50.985222
56	49.270501	49.456401	49.642416	49.828547	50.014791	50.201147	50.387614	50.574189
58	48.889234	49.076825	49.264530	49.452348	49.640277	49.828315	50.016461	50.204714
60	48.545305	48.734522	48.923851	49.113290	49.302837	49.492491	49.682250	49.872112
62	48.234638	48.425418	48.616306	48.807301	48.998402	49.189605	49.380910	49.572315
64	47.953674	48.145954	48.338337	48.530825	48.723413	48.916101	49.108886	49.301768
66	47.699295	47.893010	48.086827	48.280743	48.474756	48.668864	48.863066	49.057360
68	47.468754	47.663845	47.859032	48.054314	48.249689	48.445155	48.640710	48.836352
70	47.259629	47.456034	47.652532	47.849120	48.045795	48.242557	48.439404	48.636333
72	47.069775	47.267436	47.465185	47.663018	47.860935	48.058933	48.257011	48.455166
74	46.897287	47.096147	47.295089	47.494111	47.693210	47.892386	48.091636	48.290958
76	46.740472	46.940474	47.140553	47.340706	47.540932	47.741229	47.941594	48.142026
78	46.597818	46.798908	47.000069	47.201299	47.402596	47.603959	47.805384	48.006871
80	46.467972	46.670097	46.872288	47.074542	47.276858	47.479232	47.681665	47.884152
82	46.349726	46.552835	46.756004	46.959230	47.162513	47.365848	47.569236	47.772672
84	46.241993	46.446036	46.650134	46.854283	47.058483	47.262729	47.467022	47.671358
86	46.143796	46.348727	46.553705	46.758730	46.963798	47.168908	47.374058	47.579245
88	46.054258	46.260029	46.465843	46.671697	46.877588	47.083515	47.289476	47.495469
90	45.972586	46.179154	46.385758	46.592397	46.799067	47.005767	47.212495	47.419249
92	45.898065	46.105387	46.312740	46.520121	46.727527	46.934958	47.142411	47.349883
96	45.767954	45.976665	46.185394	46.394139	46.602898	46.811670	47.020452	47.229241
100	45.659459	45.869408	46.079365	46.289325	46.499289	46.709253	46.919216	47.129175
104	45.568911	45.779963	45.991011	46.202052	46.413084	46.624106	46.835115	47.046111
108	45.493289	45.705319	45.917335	46.129332	46.341311	46.553268	46.765203	46.977113
112	45.430093	45.642990	45.855862	46.068706	46.281520	46.494304	46.707054	46.919770
116	45.377256	45.590919	45.804547	46.018137	46.231688	46.445198	46.658666	46.872090
120	45.333062	45.547400	45.761694	45.975941	46.190139	46.404288	46.618386	46.832431
140	45.199357	45.416019	45.632599	45.849096	46.065508	46.281834	46.498074	46.714226
160	45.144260	45.362101	45.579835	45.797463	46.014983	46.232394	46.449697	46.666891

226

TABLE 7. ANNUAL WITHDRAWALS PER $1,000

ANNUAL WITHDRAWALS PER $1000

NUMBER OF ANNUAL WTHDRWLS	EFFECTIVE ANNUAL YIELD							
	5.00%	5.05%	5.10%	5.15%	5.20%	5.25%	5.30%	5.35%
1	1050.000000	1050.500000	1051.000000	1051.500000	1052.000000	1052.500000	1053.000000	1053.500000
2	537.804878	538.185930	538.567040	538.948209	539.329435	539.710719	540.092060	540.473460
3	367.208565	367.552653	367.896845	368.241139	368.585536	368.930036	369.274639	369.619344
4	282.011833	282.339449	282.667209	282.995114	283.323164	283.651358	283.979695	284.308177
5	230.974798	231.294133	231.613652	231.933356	232.253244	232.573317	232.893573	233.214014
6	197.017468	197.332611	197.647978	197.963569	198.279383	198.595420	198.911681	199.228164
7	172.819818	173.133101	173.446646	173.760453	174.074522	174.388852	174.703444	175.018297
8	154.721814	155.034687	155.347860	155.661333	155.975105	156.289177	156.603547	156.918216
9	140.690080	141.003504	141.317266	141.631365	141.945800	142.260571	142.575678	142.891121
10	129.504575	129.819217	130.134233	130.449622	130.765384	131.081519	131.398027	131.714906
11	120.388691	120.705229	121.021976	121.339133	121.656699	121.974674	122.293056	122.611845
12	112.825410	113.143795	113.462626	113.781901	114.101621	114.421784	114.742390	115.063439
13	106.455765	106.776463	107.097640	107.419297	107.741433	108.064047	108.387138	108.710705
14	101.023969	101.347181	101.670906	101.995144	102.319895	102.645158	102.970931	103.297215
15	96.342288	96.668167	96.994594	97.321567	97.649086	97.977149	98.305756	98.634905
16	92.269908	92.598575	92.927822	93.257647	93.588051	93.919030	94.250586	94.582715
17	88.699142	89.030688	89.362846	89.695614	90.028991	90.362976	90.697568	91.032764
18	85.546222	85.880718	86.215857	86.551636	86.888055	87.225112	87.562805	87.901134
19	82.745010	83.082509	83.420680	83.759522	84.099033	84.439211	84.780055	85.121563
20	80.242587	80.583127	80.924369	81.266310	81.608949	81.952283	82.296312	82.641033
21	77.996107	78.339716	78.684054	79.029120	79.374911	79.721425	80.068661	80.416616
22	75.970509	76.317204	76.664655	77.012861	77.361819	77.711526	78.061981	78.413182
23	74.136822	74.486612	74.837186	75.188539	75.540670	75.893576	76.247255	76.601704
24	72.470901	72.823789	73.177445	73.531986	73.887289	74.243392	74.600292	74.957986
25	70.952457	71.308440	71.665254	72.022897	72.381365	72.740657	73.100769	73.461697
26	69.564321	69.923388	70.283310	70.644084	71.005706	71.368174	71.731483	72.095630
27	68.291860	68.653999	69.017015	69.380904	69.745663	70.111288	70.477776	70.845123
28	67.122530	67.487724	67.853815	68.220800	68.588675	68.957436	69.327080	69.697602
29	66.045515	66.413742	66.782886	67.152944	67.523911	67.895783	68.268555	68.642225
30	65.051435	65.422671	65.794844	66.167948	66.541979	66.916934	67.292806	67.669593
31	64.132120	64.506339	64.881512	65.257633	65.634699	66.012705	66.391645	66.771515
32	63.280419	63.657591	64.035734	64.414841	64.794909	65.175932	65.557905	65.940822
33	62.490044	62.870138	63.251218	63.633278	64.016313	64.400318	64.785286	65.171213
34	61.755445	62.138428	62.522411	62.907389	63.293354	63.680303	64.068228	64.457124
35	61.071707	61.457544	61.844394	62.232251	62.621109	63.010962	63.401803	63.793626
36	60.434457	60.823111	61.212790	61.603488	61.995198	62.387915	62.781630	63.176337
37	59.839794	60.231227	60.623697	61.017196	61.411717	61.807254	62.203800	62.601348
38	59.284228	59.678401	60.073620	60.469879	60.867169	61.265484	61.664816	62.065157
39	58.764624	59.161497	59.559425	59.958400	60.358416	60.759464	61.161536	61.564625
40	58.278161	58.677692	59.078286	59.479936	59.882633	60.286368	60.691135	61.096923
41	57.822292	58.224440	58.627658	59.031937	59.437269	59.843647	60.251060	60.659500
42	57.394713	57.799434	58.205232	58.612096	59.020019	59.428990	59.839002	60.250046
43	56.993333	57.400584	57.808917	58.218321	58.628788	59.040307	59.452869	59.866466
44	56.616251	57.025989	57.436812	57.848710	58.261673	58.675692	59.090756	59.506856
45	56.261735	56.673915	57.087184	57.501529	57.916942	58.333412	58.750929	59.169483
46	55.928204	56.342782	56.758450	57.175197	57.593012	58.011885	58.431806	58.852763
47	55.614211	56.031142	56.449164	56.868265	57.288435	57.709663	58.131937	58.555248
48	55.318431	55.737669	56.157999	56.579408	57.001885	57.425419	57.849998	58.275611
49	55.039645	55.461147	55.883738	56.307408	56.732144	57.157935	57.584769	58.012634
50	54.776735	55.200454	55.625261	56.051145	56.478092	56.906092	57.335131	57.765199

ANNUAL WITHDRAWALS PER $1000

NUMBER OF ANNUAL WTHDRWLS	EFFECTIVE ANNUAL YIELD							
	5.40%	5.45%	5.50%	5.55%	5.60%	5.65%	5.70%	5.75%
1	1054.000000	1054.500000	1055.000000	1055.500000	1056.000000	1056.500000	1057.000000	1057.500000
2	540.854917	541.236432	541.618005	541.999635	542.381323	542.763068	543.144871	543.526731
3	369.964152	370.309062	370.654075	370.999190	371.344407	371.689726	372.035147	372.380670
4	284.636803	284.965572	285.294485	285.623542	285.952742	286.282085	286.611572	286.941202
5	233.534638	233.855445	234.176436	234.497610	234.818968	235.140508	235.462231	235.784137
6	199.544869	199.861797	200.178948	200.496320	200.813914	201.131730	201.449767	201.768025
7	175.333410	175.648784	175.964418	176.280312	176.596466	176.912879	177.229552	177.546483
8	157.233184	157.548449	157.864012	158.179872	158.496029	158.812483	159.129233	159.446280
9	143.206899	143.523012	143.839458	144.156239	144.473354	144.790802	145.108582	145.426695
10	132.032156	132.349777	132.667769	132.986130	133.304861	133.623961	133.943430	134.263267
11	122.931042	123.250645	123.570653	123.891067	124.211885	124.533108	124.854734	125.176764
12	115.384929	115.706860	116.029231	116.352042	116.675293	116.998982	117.323109	117.647673
13	109.034748	109.359266	109.684259	110.009725	110.335663	110.662074	110.988956	111.316309
14	103.624007	103.951308	104.279115	104.607430	104.936250	105.265575	105.595403	105.925735
15	98.964595	99.294827	99.625598	99.956907	100.288754	100.621138	100.954057	101.287511
16	94.915418	95.248692	95.582538	95.916953	96.251937	96.587489	96.923607	97.260290
17	91.368565	91.704968	92.041972	92.379577	92.717780	93.056581	93.395977	93.735969
18	88.240096	88.579691	88.919916	89.260771	89.602254	89.944363	90.287097	90.630454
19	85.463733	85.806565	86.150056	86.494204	86.839009	87.184468	87.530579	87.877342
20	82.986444	83.332544	83.679330	84.026801	84.374956	84.723791	85.073306	85.423499
21	80.765288	81.114675	81.464775	81.815587	82.167107	82.519335	82.872267	83.225902
22	78.765125	79.117809	79.471232	79.825391	80.180283	80.535908	80.892261	81.249342
23	76.956921	77.312902	77.669647	78.027152	78.385415	78.744432	79.104202	79.464723
24	75.316471	75.675744	76.035804	76.396646	76.758269	77.120669	77.483844	77.847791
25	73.823439	74.185992	74.549353	74.913519	75.278486	75.644252	76.010813	76.378167
26	72.460613	72.826428	73.193071	73.560540	73.928831	74.297940	74.667865	75.038601
27	71.213325	71.582379	71.952282	72.323029	72.694617	73.067043	73.440302	73.814392
28	70.068998	70.441266	70.814400	71.188396	71.563252	71.938963	72.315525	72.692935
29	69.016787	69.392237	69.768572	70.145786	70.523877	70.902838	71.282667	71.663359
30	68.047288	68.425889	68.805390	69.185786	69.567074	69.949248	70.332305	70.716239
31	67.152309	67.534024	67.916654	68.300195	68.684641	69.069987	69.456229	69.843362
32	66.324679	66.709470	67.095189	67.481833	67.869395	68.257871	68.647255	69.037542
33	65.558092	65.945918	66.334687	66.724391	67.115025	67.506585	67.899064	68.292457
34	64.846984	65.237804	65.629577	66.022297	66.415958	66.810555	67.206081	67.602530
35	64.186425	64.580194	64.974927	65.370616	65.767256	66.164841	66.563365	66.962820
36	63.572031	63.968704	64.366349	64.764960	65.164530	65.565053	65.966523	66.368931
37	62.999890	63.399419	63.799929	64.201413	64.603864	65.007274	65.411636	65.816944
38	62.466501	62.868840	63.272166	63.676472	64.081751	64.487996	64.895198	65.303352
39	61.968723	62.373822	62.779914	63.186992	63.595047	64.004073	64.414061	64.825004
40	61.503726	61.911536	62.320343	62.730141	63.140920	63.552673	63.965392	64.379069
41	61.068959	61.479429	61.890900	62.303365	62.716814	63.131240	63.546634	63.962988
42	60.662111	61.075190	61.489273	61.904352	62.320418	62.737462	63.155474	63.574448
43	60.281087	60.696724	61.113367	61.531007	61.949634	62.369240	62.789816	63.211352
44	59.923983	60.342126	60.761276	61.181423	61.602558	62.024671	62.447753	62.871793
45	59.589064	60.009661	60.431265	60.853866	61.277453	61.702017	62.127549	62.554037
46	59.274747	59.697746	60.121751	60.546750	60.972737	61.399696	61.827620	62.256499
47	58.979583	59.404933	59.831286	60.258632	60.686960	61.116259	61.546520	61.977731
48	58.702247	59.129894	59.558423	59.988180	60.418796	60.850380	61.282921	61.716408
49	58.441519	58.871413	59.302303	59.734179	60.167030	60.600843	61.035607	61.471312
50	58.196282	58.628370	59.061450	59.495511	59.930541	60.366528	60.803461	61.241328

ANNUAL WITHDRAWALS PER $1000

NUMBER OF ANNUAL WTHDRWLS	EFFECTIVE ANNUAL YIELD							
	5.80%	5.85%	5.90%	5.95%	6.00%	6.05%	6.10%	6.15%
1	1058.000000	1058.500000	1059.000000	1059.500000	1060.000000	1060.500000	1061.000000	1061.500000
2	543.908649	544.290624	544.672657	545.054746	545.436893	545.819097	546.201359	546.583677
3	372.726295	373.072022	373.417851	373.763781	374.109813	374.455946	374.802181	375.148517
4	287.270974	287.600890	287.930948	288.261149	288.591492	288.921978	289.252606	289.583377
5	236.106225	236.428496	236.750949	237.073584	237.396400	237.719399	238.042579	238.365940
6	202.086505	202.405205	202.724126	203.043267	203.362628	203.682210	204.002011	204.322032
7	177.863674	178.181123	178.498830	178.816795	179.135018	179.453499	179.772236	180.091231
8	159.763622	160.081260	160.399193	160.717420	161.035943	161.354759	161.673870	161.993274
9	145.745141	146.063918	146.383026	146.702465	147.022235	147.342335	147.662765	147.983524
10	134.583472	134.904044	135.224982	135.546287	135.867958	136.189995	136.512396	136.835162
11	125.499196	125.822030	126.145265	126.468901	126.792938	127.117375	127.442211	127.767445
12	117.972673	118.298110	118.623982	118.950289	119.277029	119.604203	119.931810	120.259849
13	111.644132	111.972423	112.301183	112.630411	112.960105	113.290266	113.620892	113.951982
14	106.256569	106.587904	106.919740	107.252075	107.584909	107.918241	108.252069	108.586394
15	101.621498	101.956018	102.291070	102.626652	102.962764	103.299404	103.636572	103.974267
16	97.597537	97.935347	98.273719	98.612652	98.952144	99.292194	99.632801	99.973964
17	94.076554	94.417732	94.759500	95.101858	95.444804	95.788337	96.132456	96.477159
18	90.974433	91.319033	91.664252	92.010088	92.356541	92.703607	93.051287	93.399578
19	88.224753	88.572813	88.921518	89.270868	89.620860	89.971494	90.322766	90.674676
20	85.774367	86.125908	86.478122	86.831005	87.184557	87.538775	87.893657	88.249201
21	83.580238	83.935273	84.291004	84.647429	85.004547	85.362355	85.720851	86.080033
22	81.607147	81.965675	82.324922	82.684888	83.045569	83.406962	83.769067	84.131880
23	79.825990	80.188003	80.550758	80.914253	81.278485	81.643451	82.009150	82.375578
24	78.212507	78.577989	78.944209	79.311241	79.679005	80.047524	80.416795	80.786815
25	76.746311	77.115241	77.484954	77.855448	78.226718	78.598763	78.971578	79.345162
26	75.410146	75.782497	76.155649	76.529600	76.904347	77.279885	77.656211	78.033323
27	74.189308	74.565048	74.941606	75.318980	75.697166	76.076161	76.455960	76.836560
28	73.071187	73.450279	73.830207	74.210965	74.592552	74.974961	75.358191	75.742235
29	72.044969	72.427314	72.810569	73.194671	73.579614	73.965394	74.352007	74.739450
30	71.101046	71.486721	71.873260	72.260658	72.648911	73.038015	73.427963	73.818753
31	70.231382	70.620282	71.010058	71.400706	71.792220	72.184595	72.577827	72.971911
32	69.428726	69.820803	70.213768	70.607614	71.002337	71.397932	71.794394	72.191716
33	68.686758	69.081962	69.478063	69.875056	70.272935	70.671694	71.071329	71.471832
34	67.999898	68.398177	68.797362	69.197447	69.598425	70.000293	70.403042	70.806668
35	67.363201	67.764502	68.166716	68.569837	68.973859	69.378776	69.784581	70.191268
36	66.772273	67.176540	67.581728	67.987828	68.394835	68.802742	69.211542	69.621229
37	66.223191	66.630370	67.038474	67.447495	67.857427	68.268264	68.679997	69.092621
38	65.712449	66.122481	66.533443	66.945326	67.358124	67.771829	68.186433	68.601930
39	65.236894	65.649724	66.063485	66.478171	66.893772	67.310283	67.727695	68.146002
40	64.793695	65.209263	65.625764	66.043191	66.461536	66.880790	67.300947	67.721997
41	64.380292	64.798540	65.217721	65.637829	66.058855	66.480790	66.903627	67.327357
42	63.994373	64.415241	64.837043	65.259770	65.683415	66.107968	66.533421	66.959765
43	63.633839	64.057268	64.481630	64.906916	65.333118	65.760225	66.188231	66.617076
44	63.296784	63.722715	64.149577	64.577361	65.006057	65.435656	65.866149	66.297527
45	62.981473	63.409846	63.839148	64.269367	64.700496	65.132523	65.565441	65.999238
46	62.686321	63.117078	63.548759	63.981354	64.414853	64.849246	65.284524	65.720677
47	62.409882	62.842963	63.276963	63.711872	64.147680	64.584377	65.021953	65.460397
48	62.150829	62.586176	63.022436	63.459599	63.897655	64.336593	64.776404	65.217076
49	61.907947	62.345500	62.783961	63.223319	63.663562	64.104680	64.546664	64.989501
50	61.680119	62.119821	62.560424	63.001916	63.444286	63.887524	64.331619	64.776559

ANNUAL WITHDRAWALS PER $1000

EFFECTIVE ANNUAL YIELD

NUMBER OF ANNUAL WTHDRWLS	6.20%	6.25%	6.30%	6.35%	6.40%	6.45%	6.50%	6.55%
1	1062.000000	1062.500000	1063.000000	1063.500000	1064.000000	1064.500000	1065.000000	1065.500000
2	546.966052	547.348485	547.730974	548.113521	548.496124	548.878784	549.261501	549.644275
3	375.494955	375.841493	376.188133	376.534874	376.881716	377.228658	377.575702	377.922846
4	289.914289	290.245343	290.576540	290.907877	291.239357	291.570978	291.902740	292.234644
5	238.689483	239.013207	239.337112	239.661197	239.985464	240.309910	240.634538	240.959345
6	204.642273	204.962732	205.283411	205.604309	205.925425	206.246759	206.568312	206.890083
7	180.410483	180.729991	181.049755	181.369775	181.690051	182.010583	182.331369	182.652411
8	162.312971	162.632961	162.953244	163.273820	163.594687	163.915846	164.237297	164.559039
9	148.304613	148.626030	148.947776	149.269849	149.592250	149.914978	150.238033	150.561414
10	137.158292	137.481785	137.805642	138.129861	138.454442	138.779386	139.104690	139.430355
11	128.093078	128.419108	128.745536	129.072360	129.399580	129.727195	130.055206	130.383610
12	120.588320	120.917221	121.246552	121.576313	121.906503	122.237121	122.568166	122.899638
13	114.283536	114.615553	114.948032	115.280973	115.614375	115.948236	116.282557	116.617336
14	108.921214	109.256528	109.592335	109.928635	110.265427	110.602709	110.940481	111.278741
15	104.312486	104.651231	104.990498	105.330289	105.670600	106.011432	106.352783	106.694652
16	100.315682	100.657954	101.000778	101.344153	101.688078	102.032552	102.377574	102.723142
17	96.822445	97.168312	97.514760	97.861787	98.209391	98.557571	98.906327	99.255655
18	93.748480	94.097989	94.448106	94.798828	95.150153	95.502081	95.854610	96.207738
19	91.027222	91.380401	91.734214	92.088656	92.443728	92.799427	93.155752	93.512700
20	88.605406	88.962269	89.319789	89.677963	90.036790	90.396268	90.756395	91.117169
21	86.439898	86.800446	87.161673	87.523578	87.886157	88.249410	88.613334	88.977927
22	84.495398	84.859621	85.224545	85.590167	85.956486	86.323499	86.691204	87.059599
23	82.742733	83.110612	83.479213	83.848533	84.218569	84.589319	84.960780	85.332950
24	81.157582	81.529093	81.901344	82.274333	82.648056	83.022512	83.397698	83.773609
25	79.719510	80.094619	80.470487	80.847111	81.224486	81.602611	81.981481	82.361094
26	78.411216	78.789887	79.169333	79.549551	79.930536	80.312287	80.694798	81.078068
27	77.217957	77.600148	77.983129	78.366896	78.751446	79.136774	79.522878	79.909753
28	76.127092	76.512756	76.899224	77.286491	77.674555	78.063409	78.453052	78.843479
29	75.127717	75.516804	75.906708	76.297423	76.688946	77.081272	77.474398	77.868317
30	74.210379	74.602837	74.996122	75.390230	75.785155	76.180894	76.577442	76.974795
31	73.366841	73.762614	74.159223	74.556665	74.954934	75.354025	75.753934	76.154655
32	72.589894	72.988924	73.388798	73.789513	74.191063	74.593443	74.996648	75.400672
33	71.873200	72.275426	72.678504	73.082430	73.487198	73.892802	74.299237	74.706496
34	71.211164	71.616525	72.022745	72.429818	72.837737	73.246499	73.656095	74.066522
35	70.598831	71.007264	71.416561	71.826715	72.237721	72.649571	73.062261	73.475783
36	70.031796	70.443237	70.855545	71.268714	71.682737	72.097608	72.513320	72.929868
37	69.506128	69.920512	70.335765	70.751882	71.168854	71.586676	72.005340	72.424840
38	69.018312	69.435573	69.853705	70.272700	70.692553	71.113255	71.534800	71.957180
39	68.565194	68.985265	69.406207	69.828014	70.250676	70.674188	71.098542	71.523729
40	68.143934	68.566749	68.990434	69.414982	69.840385	70.266636	70.693726	71.121648
41	67.751972	68.177464	68.603824	69.031045	69.459118	69.888037	70.317791	70.748375
42	67.386992	67.815094	68.244061	68.673886	69.104560	69.536075	69.968423	70.401595
43	67.046897	67.477541	67.909048	68.341408	68.774613	69.208654	69.643523	70.079211
44	66.729780	67.162000	67.596878	68.031705	68.467371	68.903868	69.341187	69.779320
45	66.433907	66.869436	67.305818	67.743043	68.181102	68.619985	69.059684	69.500189
46	66.157695	66.595568	67.034287	67.473843	67.914226	68.355426	68.797434	69.240242
47	65.899700	66.339851	66.780841	67.222661	67.665300	68.108748	68.552997	68.998037
48	65.658599	66.100964	66.544159	66.988176	67.433004	67.878634	68.325055	68.772258
49	65.433181	65.877695	66.323031	66.769180	67.216131	67.663874	68.112400	68.561698
50	65.222334	65.668933	66.116346	66.564562	67.013571	67.463362	67.913926	68.365251

ANNUAL WITHDRAWALS PER $1000

NUMBER OF ANNUAL WTHDRWLS	EFFECTIVE ANNUAL YIELD							
	6.60%	6.65%	6.70%	6.75%	6.80%	6.85%	6.90%	6.95%
1	1066.000000	1066.500000	1067.000000	1067.500000	1068.000000	1068.500000	1069.000000	1069.500000
2	550.027106	550.409993	550.792937	551.175937	551.558994	551.942108	552.325278	552.708504
3	378.270091	378.617437	378.964883	379.312429	379.660076	380.007823	380.355671	380.703618
4	292.566689	292.898875	293.231202	293.563670	293.896278	294.229027	294.561917	294.894946
5	241.284332	241.609500	241.934847	242.260373	242.586079	242.911964	243.238029	243.564272
6	207.212072	207.534278	207.856702	208.179343	208.502201	208.825276	209.148568	209.472076
7	182.973708	183.295259	183.617064	183.939123	184.261436	184.584002	184.906822	185.229894
8	164.881071	165.203394	165.526008	165.848911	166.172103	166.495585	166.819356	167.143415
9	150.885122	151.209154	151.533513	151.858196	152.183203	152.508535	152.834190	153.160169
10	139.756381	140.082767	140.409512	140.736615	141.064078	141.391898	141.720076	142.048611
11	130.712409	131.041601	131.371185	131.701161	132.031529	132.362288	132.693437	133.024976
12	123.231537	123.563861	123.896610	124.229783	124.563380	124.897399	125.231841	125.566704
13	116.952573	117.288267	117.624416	117.961021	118.298081	118.635594	118.973560	119.311978
14	111.617490	111.956726	112.296448	112.636655	112.977347	113.318522	113.660180	114.002319
15	107.037039	107.379942	107.723359	108.067291	108.411736	108.756693	109.102161	109.448138
16	103.069256	103.415913	103.763113	104.110855	104.459138	104.807959	105.157319	105.507216
17	99.605556	99.956027	100.307068	100.658677	101.010853	101.363593	101.716898	102.070765
18	96.561464	96.915786	97.270703	97.626212	97.982314	98.339005	98.696284	99.054150
19	93.870270	94.228461	94.587270	94.946695	95.306736	95.667390	96.028656	96.390531
20	91.478588	91.840650	92.203353	92.566696	92.930675	93.295290	93.660538	94.026417
21	89.343186	89.709110	90.075697	90.442943	90.810848	91.179408	91.548622	91.918487
22	87.428680	87.798446	88.168894	88.540022	88.911827	89.284307	89.657460	90.031283
23	85.705826	86.079405	86.453684	86.828662	87.204334	87.580700	87.957756	88.335499
24	84.150244	84.527599	84.905673	85.284461	85.663960	86.044169	86.425084	86.806702
25	82.741447	83.122536	83.504359	83.886912	84.270191	84.654195	85.038919	85.424361
26	81.462091	81.846866	82.232388	82.618654	83.005661	83.393406	83.781884	84.171092
27	80.297396	80.685802	81.074970	81.464894	81.855571	82.246997	82.639169	83.032082
28	79.234685	79.626667	80.019421	80.412942	80.807228	81.202273	81.598074	81.994627
29	78.263028	78.658524	79.054842	79.451858	79.849687	80.248286	80.647649	81.047772
30	77.372946	77.771894	78.171631	78.572155	78.973460	79.375542	79.778396	80.182018
31	76.556183	76.958515	77.361645	77.765567	78.170278	78.575772	78.982044	79.389091
32	75.805511	76.211159	76.617610	77.024861	77.432905	77.841738	78.251354	78.661748
33	75.114576	75.523470	75.933172	76.343678	76.754981	77.167077	77.579960	77.993625
34	74.477772	74.889840	75.302720	75.716407	76.130895	76.546177	76.962249	77.379105
35	73.890132	74.305302	74.721286	75.138079	75.555675	75.974066	76.393248	76.813215
36	73.347243	73.765441	74.184455	74.604277	75.024903	75.446326	75.868538	76.291535
37	72.845169	73.266321	73.688288	74.111064	74.534642	74.959017	75.384180	75.810126
38	72.380389	72.804419	73.229264	73.654916	74.081370	74.508617	74.936650	75.365464
39	71.949744	72.376578	72.804225	73.232677	73.661926	74.091967	74.522791	74.954392
40	71.550394	71.979958	72.410330	72.841504	73.273472	73.706227	74.139762	74.574068
41	71.179779	71.611996	72.045018	72.478838	72.913447	73.348838	73.785003	74.221934
42	70.835583	71.270380	71.705976	72.142365	72.579537	73.017485	73.456202	73.895678
43	70.515710	70.953012	71.391108	71.829989	72.269648	72.710076	73.151266	73.593208
44	70.218257	70.657990	71.098510	71.539810	71.981879	72.424710	72.868295	73.312625
45	69.941492	70.383584	70.826455	71.270098	71.714502	72.159660	72.605564	73.052203
46	69.683839	70.128217	70.573806	71.019278	71.465944	71.913354	72.361500	72.810373
47	69.443858	69.890451	70.337806	70.785915	71.234768	71.684356	72.134671	72.585702
48	69.220232	69.668970	70.118460	70.568695	71.019663	71.471356	71.923766	72.376882
49	69.011758	69.462571	69.914126	70.366415	70.819428	71.273155	71.727587	72.182715
50	68.817329	69.270149	69.723701	70.177976	70.632963	71.088654	71.545038	72.002106

232

ANNUAL WITHDRAWALS PER $1000

NUMBER OF ANNUAL WTHDRWLS	EFFECTIVE ANNUAL YIELD							
	7.00%	7.05%	7.10%	7.15%	7.20%	7.25%	7.30%	7.35%
1	1070.000000	1070.500000	1071.000000	1071.500000	1072.000000	1072.500000	1073.000000	1073.500000
2	553.091787	553.475127	553.858522	554.241974	554.625483	555.009047	555.392668	555.776344
3	381.051666	381.399813	381.748061	382.096408	382.444855	382.793402	383.142048	383.490794
4	295.228117	295.561427	295.894877	296.228468	296.562198	296.896068	297.230077	297.564226
5	243.890694	244.217295	244.544075	244.871032	245.198168	245.525482	245.852974	246.180644
6	209.795800	210.119740	210.443896	210.768268	211.092855	211.417658	211.742675	212.067907
7	185.553220	185.876797	186.200627	186.524709	186.849043	187.173628	187.498464	187.823551
8	167.467762	167.792398	168.117321	168.442532	168.768029	169.093813	169.419884	169.746240
9	153.486470	153.813094	154.140040	154.467308	154.794897	155.122808	155.451038	155.779589
10	142.377503	142.706750	143.036354	143.366312	143.696626	144.027293	144.358314	144.689689
11	133.356905	133.689222	134.021927	134.355020	134.688500	135.022366	135.356618	135.691256
12	125.901989	126.237693	126.573817	126.910360	127.247321	127.584700	127.922495	128.260706
13	119.650848	119.990168	120.329938	120.670158	121.010825	121.351940	121.693501	122.035508
14	114.344939	114.688038	115.031617	115.375673	115.720207	116.065216	116.410701	116.756660
15	109.794625	110.141619	110.489119	110.837126	111.185637	111.534651	111.884168	112.234185
16	105.857648	106.208614	106.560114	106.912145	107.264708	107.617799	107.971419	108.325566
17	102.425193	102.780181	103.135727	103.491830	103.848489	104.205702	104.563467	104.921784
18	99.412602	99.771637	100.131254	100.491452	100.852228	101.213583	101.575512	101.938016
19	96.753015	97.116104	97.479799	97.844095	98.208993	98.574490	98.940584	99.307274
20	94.392926	94.760062	95.127823	95.496208	95.865214	96.234840	96.605083	96.975942
21	92.289002	92.660163	93.031970	93.404419	93.777509	94.151237	94.525601	94.900599
22	90.405773	90.780929	91.156748	91.533227	91.910364	92.288157	92.666603	93.045700
23	88.713926	89.093036	89.472825	89.853291	90.234431	90.616243	90.998723	91.381869
24	87.189021	87.572036	87.955747	88.340148	88.725239	89.111015	89.497474	89.884613
25	85.810517	86.197385	86.584960	86.973240	87.362222	87.751902	88.142278	88.533346
26	84.561028	84.951687	85.343066	85.735162	86.127971	86.521490	86.915715	87.310644
27	83.425734	83.820120	84.215237	84.611081	85.007649	85.404936	85.802939	86.201654
28	82.391928	82.789973	83.188758	83.588279	83.988532	84.389513	84.791218	85.193643
29	81.448652	81.850284	82.252663	82.655786	83.059648	83.464245	83.869573	84.275628
30	80.586404	80.991547	81.397445	81.804093	82.211486	82.619619	83.028488	83.438089
31	79.796906	80.205485	80.614823	81.024916	81.435758	81.847345	82.259672	82.672734
32	79.072915	79.484851	79.897549	80.311005	80.725214	81.140170	81.555869	81.972305
33	78.408065	78.823276	79.239253	79.655989	80.073480	80.491720	80.910704	81.330427
34	77.796738	78.215144	78.634315	79.054248	79.474936	79.896374	80.318555	80.741475
35	77.233960	77.655477	78.077761	78.500805	78.924604	79.349151	79.774442	80.200469
36	76.715310	77.139856	77.565167	77.991237	78.418061	78.845631	79.273941	79.702987
37	76.236848	76.664339	77.092594	77.521605	77.951366	78.381871	78.813113	79.245086
38	75.795052	76.225405	76.656518	77.088385	77.520997	77.954349	78.388434	78.823245
39	75.386762	75.819894	76.253782	76.688418	77.123795	77.559907	77.996747	78.434307
40	75.009139	75.444967	75.881545	76.318867	76.756923	77.195708	77.635215	78.075436
41	74.659624	75.098046	75.537252	75.977174	76.417825	76.859197	77.301284	77.744078
42	74.335907	74.776681	75.218591	75.661030	76.104191	76.548066	76.992647	77.437927
43	74.035895	74.479320	74.923473	75.368347	75.813935	76.260228	76.707219	77.154899
44	73.757691	74.203486	74.650002	75.097230	75.545162	75.993791	76.443107	76.893105
45	73.499571	73.947658	74.396457	74.845958	75.296154	75.747036	76.198597	76.650828
46	73.259965	73.710266	74.161269	74.612965	75.065345	75.518401	75.972125	76.426508
47	73.037442	73.489882	73.943012	74.396824	74.851310	75.306462	75.762269	76.218726
48	72.830695	73.285198	73.740380	74.196233	74.652749	75.109918	75.567732	76.026183
49	72.638529	73.095021	73.552181	74.010001	74.468471	74.927582	75.387327	75.847697
50	72.459850	72.918258	73.377324	73.837036	74.297388	74.758368	75.219970	75.682183

ANNUAL WITHDRAWALS PER $1000

NUMBER OF ANNUAL WTHDRWLS	EFFECTIVE ANNUAL YIELD							
	7.40%	7.45%	7.50%	7.55%	7.60%	7.65%	7.70%	7.75%
1	1074.000000	1074.500000	1075.000000	1075.500000	1076.000000	1076.500000	1077.000000	1077.500000
2	556.160077	556.543866	556.927711	557.311612	557.695568	558.079581	558.463649	558.847774
3	383.839639	384.188584	384.537628	384.886771	385.236014	385.585355	385.934796	386.284335
4	297.898514	298.232942	298.567509	298.902214	299.237059	299.572043	299.907165	300.242426
5	246.508491	246.836516	247.164718	247.493097	247.821653	248.150386	248.479295	248.808382
6	212.393354	212.719016	213.044891	213.370981	213.697284	214.023801	214.350532	214.677476
7	188.148889	188.474477	188.800315	189.126404	189.452742	189.779329	190.106165	190.433251
8	170.072883	170.399810	170.727023	171.054521	171.382303	171.710369	172.038719	172.367352
9	156.108460	156.437650	156.767159	157.096987	157.427133	157.757597	158.088378	158.419476
10	145.021416	145.353496	145.685927	146.018710	146.351844	146.685328	147.019162	147.353346
11	136.026278	136.361684	136.697474	137.033647	137.370202	137.707139	138.044457	138.382156
12	128.599334	128.938375	129.277831	129.617701	129.957983	130.298677	130.639783	130.981299
13	122.377960	122.720856	123.064196	123.407979	123.752203	124.096868	124.441974	124.787518
14	117.103092	117.449996	117.797372	118.145218	118.493534	118.842319	119.191571	119.541290
15	112.584704	112.935721	113.287236	113.639249	113.991757	114.344760	114.698257	115.052246
16	108.680239	109.035436	109.391157	109.747400	110.104163	110.461446	110.819248	111.177567
17	105.280651	105.640066	106.000028	106.360536	106.721589	107.083184	107.445320	107.807997
18	102.301093	102.664741	103.028958	103.393743	103.759094	104.125010	104.491489	104.858529
19	99.674558	100.042433	100.410899	100.779954	101.149595	101.519821	101.890630	102.262020
20	97.347415	97.719498	98.092192	98.465492	98.839399	99.213909	99.589020	99.964731
21	95.276229	95.652488	96.029374	96.406886	96.785020	97.163775	97.543148	97.923138
22	93.425445	93.805837	94.186871	94.568546	94.950861	95.333811	95.717395	96.101610
23	91.765679	92.150149	92.535278	92.921062	93.307499	93.694585	94.082319	94.470698
24	90.272429	90.660918	91.050079	91.439909	91.830403	92.221560	92.613377	93.005850
25	88.925103	89.317546	89.710672	90.104477	90.498958	90.894113	91.289937	91.686429
26	87.706272	88.102596	88.499612	88.897318	89.295710	89.694785	90.094538	90.494967
27	86.601078	87.001207	87.402037	87.803564	88.205786	88.608698	89.012296	89.416577
28	85.596784	86.000638	86.405199	86.810465	87.216432	87.623095	88.030450	88.438494
29	84.682405	85.089899	85.498108	85.907026	86.316650	86.726975	87.137997	87.549713
30	83.848417	84.259467	84.671236	85.083718	85.496909	85.910805	86.325401	86.740693
31	83.086526	83.501044	83.916283	84.332238	84.748905	85.166278	85.584353	86.003126
32	82.389474	82.807370	83.225989	83.645325	84.065373	84.486129	84.907587	85.329743
33	81.750883	82.172066	82.593973	83.016597	83.439932	83.863975	84.288720	84.714161
34	81.165127	81.589507	82.014608	82.440426	82.866954	83.294188	83.722121	84.150748
35	80.627227	81.054711	81.482915	81.911832	82.341457	82.771784	83.202808	83.634523
36	80.132760	80.563256	80.994468	81.426390	81.859017	82.292342	82.726359	83.161063
37	79.677784	80.111199	80.545327	80.980161	81.415694	81.851920	82.288833	82.726428
38	79.258776	79.695020	80.131971	80.569622	81.007967	81.446999	81.886712	82.327099
39	78.872581	79.311563	79.751244	80.191620	80.632682	81.074425	81.516842	81.959926
40	78.516364	78.957992	79.400314	79.843322	80.287009	80.731370	81.176396	81.622081
41	78.187571	78.631757	79.076628	79.522178	79.968398	80.415283	80.862825	81.311018
42	77.883898	78.330554	78.777886	79.225887	79.674551	80.123869	80.573835	81.024442
43	77.603262	78.052300	78.502005	78.952370	79.403387	79.855049	80.307349	80.760279
44	77.343775	77.795109	78.247101	78.699743	79.153026	79.606944	80.061489	80.516654
45	77.103721	77.557269	78.011463	78.466296	78.921760	79.377848	79.834551	80.291862
46	76.881543	77.337222	77.793535	78.250476	78.708037	79.166210	79.624986	80.084359
47	76.675822	77.133550	77.591902	78.050870	78.510445	78.970620	79.431387	79.892738
48	76.485262	76.944962	77.405272	77.866187	78.327696	78.789794	79.252470	79.715718
49	76.308682	76.770275	77.232468	77.695251	78.158617	78.622558	79.087065	79.552131
50	76.145000	76.608412	77.072410	77.536987	78.002133	78.467841	78.934103	79.400910

ANNUAL WITHDRAWALS PER $1000

NUMBER OF ANNUAL WTHDRWLS	EFFECTIVE ANNUAL YIELD							
	7.80%	7.85%	7.90%	7.95%	8.00%	8.05%	8.10%	8.15%
1	1078.000000	1078.500000	1079.000000	1079.500000	1080.000000	1080.500000	1081.000000	1081.500000
2	559.231954	559.616190	560.000481	560.384828	560.769231	561.153689	561.538203	561.922772
3	386.633974	386.983711	387.333547	387.683481	388.033514	388.383646	388.733875	389.084204
4	300.577825	300.913362	301.249038	301.584852	301.920804	302.256894	302.593122	302.929488
5	249.137644	249.467083	249.796697	250.126488	250.456455	250.786597	251.116914	251.447407
6	215.004633	215.332002	215.659585	215.987379	216.315386	216.643605	216.972036	217.300678
7	190.760585	191.088167	191.415997	191.744076	192.072401	192.400975	192.729795	193.058862
8	172.696269	173.025468	173.354950	173.684715	174.014761	174.345088	174.675697	175.006587
9	158.750891	159.082622	159.414669	159.747032	160.079709	160.412701	160.746008	161.079628
10	147.687878	148.022760	148.357989	148.693565	149.029489	149.365759	149.702375	150.039337
11	138.720236	139.058694	139.397532	139.736748	140.076342	140.416313	140.756661	141.097385
12	131.323225	131.665561	132.008305	132.351457	132.695017	133.038983	133.383355	133.728132
13	125.133502	125.479923	125.826781	126.174076	126.521805	126.869969	127.218567	127.567598
14	119.891475	120.242124	120.593238	120.944814	121.296853	121.649352	122.002312	122.355731
15	115.406727	115.761699	116.117160	116.473109	116.829545	117.186467	117.543875	117.901766
16	111.536401	111.895750	112.255612	112.615987	112.976872	113.338267	113.700170	114.062580
17	108.171212	108.534965	108.899253	109.264076	109.629431	109.995319	110.361736	110.728681
18	105.226129	105.594287	105.963002	106.332272	106.702096	107.072471	107.443397	107.814871
19	102.633990	103.006537	103.379660	103.753358	104.127627	104.502468	104.877876	105.253852
20	100.341040	100.717944	101.095441	101.473530	101.852209	102.231475	102.611326	102.991761
21	98.303741	98.684956	99.066781	99.449213	99.832250	100.215890	100.600131	100.984970
22	96.486454	96.871924	97.258018	97.644734	98.032068	98.420020	98.808585	99.197762
23	94.859719	95.249379	95.639676	96.030607	96.422169	96.814360	97.207177	97.600617
24	93.398977	93.792754	94.187179	94.582249	94.977962	95.374313	95.771300	96.168921
25	92.083584	92.481400	92.879873	93.279001	93.678779	94.079205	94.480277	94.881990
26	90.896068	91.297838	91.700273	92.103371	92.507127	92.911538	93.316601	93.722312
27	89.821537	90.227172	90.633480	91.040456	91.448096	91.856398	92.265356	92.674968
28	88.847223	89.256632	89.666718	90.077477	90.488906	90.900999	91.313754	91.727166
29	87.962116	88.375205	88.788973	89.203418	89.618535	90.034320	90.450769	90.867877
30	87.156676	87.573346	87.990698	88.408729	88.827433	89.246807	89.666846	90.087545
31	86.422591	86.842744	87.263580	87.685095	88.107284	88.530143	88.953666	89.377849
32	85.752592	86.176128	86.600347	87.025243	87.450813	87.877051	88.303952	88.731512
33	85.140293	85.567111	85.994611	86.422786	86.851632	87.281144	87.711317	88.142145
34	84.580064	85.010064	85.440742	85.872092	86.304110	86.736790	87.170127	87.604115
35	84.066924	84.500003	84.933757	85.368179	85.803265	86.239007	86.675401	87.112442
36	83.596447	84.032507	84.469235	84.906626	85.344674	85.783374	86.222720	86.662706
37	83.164697	83.603635	84.043236	84.483494	84.924403	85.365956	85.808148	86.250974
38	82.768155	83.209873	83.652246	84.095270	84.538936	84.983240	85.428175	85.873735
39	82.403671	82.848070	83.293117	83.738806	84.185130	84.632082	85.079657	85.527848
40	82.068419	82.515402	82.963025	83.411280	83.860162	84.309662	84.759777	85.210498
41	81.759853	82.209326	82.659428	83.110153	83.561494	84.013445	84.465999	84.919150
42	81.475682	81.927549	82.380036	82.833135	83.286841	83.741145	84.196042	84.651525
43	81.213833	81.668002	82.122781	82.578162	83.034137	83.490701	83.947845	84.405565
44	80.972430	81.428812	81.885792	82.343362	82.801516	83.260246	83.719545	84.179408
45	80.749774	81.208280	81.667372	82.127042	82.587285	83.048091	83.509455	83.971369
46	80.544321	81.004864	81.465982	81.927665	82.389908	82.852704	83.316044	83.779921
47	80.354666	80.817163	81.280221	81.743833	82.207992	82.672690	83.137920	83.603676
48	80.179531	80.643899	81.108816	81.574274	82.040266	82.506784	82.973821	83.441370
49	80.017749	80.483909	80.950605	81.417829	81.885573	82.353830	82.822594	83.291855
50	79.868255	80.336130	80.804527	81.273439	81.742858	82.212777	82.683188	83.154083

ANNUAL WITHDRAWALS PER $1000

NUMBER OF ANNUAL WTHDRWLS	EFFECTIVE ANNUAL YIELD							
	8.20%	8.25%	8.30%	8.35%	8.40%	8.45%	8.50%	8.55%
1	1082.000000	1082.500000	1083.000000	1083.500000	1084.000000	1084.500000	1085.000000	1085.500000
2	562.307397	562.692077	563.076812	563.461603	563.846449	564.231350	564.616307	565.001319
3	389.434630	389.785155	390.135778	390.486499	390.837317	391.188234	391.539249	391.890361
4	303.265991	303.602631	303.939409	304.276325	304.613377	304.950566	305.287893	305.625356
5	251.778075	252.108918	252.439935	252.771128	253.102495	253.434036	253.765752	254.097642
6	217.629532	217.958597	218.287873	218.617360	218.947058	219.276966	219.607084	219.937412
7	193.388176	193.717736	194.047542	194.377594	194.707891	195.038434	195.369221	195.700254
8	175.337757	175.669208	176.000938	176.332948	176.665238	176.997806	177.330653	177.663779
9	161.413561	161.747808	162.082367	162.417239	162.752422	163.087917	163.423723	163.759840
10	150.376644	150.714295	151.052291	151.390630	151.729313	152.068338	152.407705	152.747414
11	141.438484	141.779958	142.121807	142.464029	142.806624	143.149592	143.492932	143.836643
12	134.073314	134.418899	134.764887	135.111278	135.458071	135.805264	136.152858	136.500852
13	127.917061	128.266955	128.617280	128.968034	129.319217	129.670828	130.022866	130.375331
14	122.709608	123.063942	123.418732	123.773978	124.129678	124.485832	124.842438	125.199496
15	118.260140	118.618996	118.978332	119.338148	119.698442	120.059214	120.420461	120.782184
16	114.425496	114.788917	115.152841	115.517267	115.882193	116.247620	116.613544	116.979965
17	111.096154	111.464153	111.832676	112.201722	112.571290	112.941377	113.311983	113.683106
18	108.186891	108.559458	108.932568	109.306220	109.680413	110.055144	110.430413	110.806217
19	105.620393	106.007497	106.385162	106.763387	107.142170	107.521509	107.901401	108.281847
20	103.372778	103.754374	104.136547	104.519296	104.902618	105.286511	105.670974	106.056005
21	101.370405	101.756434	102.143055	102.530266	102.918064	103.306446	103.695412	104.084958
22	99.587548	99.977941	100.368939	100.760538	101.152737	101.545533	101.938923	102.332906
23	97.994678	98.389356	98.784650	99.180557	99.577073	99.974197	100.371926	100.770256
24	96.567172	96.966051	97.365554	97.765679	98.166423	98.567782	98.969755	99.372337
25	95.284341	95.687328	96.090947	96.495195	96.900069	97.305566	97.711682	98.118416
26	94.128669	94.535667	94.943303	95.351575	95.760478	96.170009	96.580165	96.990943
27	93.085231	93.496140	93.907691	94.319882	94.732709	95.146167	95.560254	95.974966
28	92.141232	92.555947	92.971309	93.387312	93.803953	94.221229	94.639136	95.057669
29	91.285641	91.704057	92.123120	92.542827	92.963172	93.384153	93.805766	94.228005
30	90.508901	90.930909	91.353564	91.776862	92.200800	92.625372	93.050575	93.476404
31	89.802688	90.228178	90.654315	91.081093	91.508509	91.936558	92.365236	92.794537
32	89.159726	89.588588	90.018094	90.448240	90.879021	91.310431	91.742466	92.175122
33	88.573623	89.005747	89.438512	89.871912	90.305943	90.740599	91.175876	91.611769
34	88.038749	88.474025	88.909936	89.346478	89.783645	90.221433	90.659836	91.098849
35	87.550123	87.988440	88.427387	88.866959	89.307150	89.747955	90.189368	90.631386
36	87.103326	87.544576	87.986449	88.428939	88.872042	89.315751	89.760062	90.204968
37	86.694426	87.138500	87.583190	88.028490	88.474393	88.920895	89.367990	89.815673
38	86.319914	86.766706	87.214105	87.662106	88.110701	88.559887	89.009656	89.460002
39	85.976560	86.426055	86.876058	87.326653	87.777834	88.229594	88.681928	89.134830
40	85.661819	86.113734	86.566238	87.019323	87.472983	87.927213	88.382006	88.837356
41	85.372891	85.827215	86.282117	86.737590	87.193627	87.650222	88.107370	88.565064
42	85.107587	85.564222	86.021422	86.479183	86.937496	87.396356	87.855757	88.315692
43	84.863852	85.322700	85.782102	86.242052	86.702544	87.163570	87.625125	88.087201
44	84.639826	85.100793	85.562302	86.024347	86.486921	86.950018	87.413630	87.877752
45	84.433827	84.896822	85.360346	85.824393	86.288956	86.754030	87.219606	87.685679
46	84.244330	84.709262	85.174712	85.640671	86.107134	86.574094	87.041543	87.509477
47	84.069948	84.536732	85.004020	85.471804	85.940079	86.408838	86.878073	87.347779
48	83.909423	84.377974	84.847016	85.316541	85.786544	86.257016	86.727952	87.199345
49	83.761608	84.231845	84.702559	85.173743	85.645391	86.117496	86.590050	87.063048
50	83.625457	84.097301	84.569609	85.042374	85.515588	85.989246	86.463340	86.937863

ANNUAL WITHDRAWALS PER $1000

NUMBER OF ANNUAL WTHDRWLS	\multicolumn{8}{c}{EFFECTIVE ANNUAL YIELD}
	8.60%	8.65%	8.70%	8.75%	8.80%	8.85%	8.90%	8.95%
1	1086.000000	1086.500000	1087.000000	1087.500000	1088.000000	1088.500000	1089.000000	1089.500000
2	565.386385	565.771507	566.156684	566.541916	566.927203	567.312545	567.697942	568.083393
3	392.241571	392.592878	392.944283	393.295786	393.647386	393.999083	394.350877	394.702769
4	305.962956	306.300692	306.638565	306.976574	307.314720	307.653001	307.991419	308.329973
5	254.429705	254.761943	255.094354	255.426938	255.759696	256.092627	256.425731	256.759007
6	220.267950	220.598698	220.929655	221.260821	221.592196	221.923780	222.255573	222.587574
7	196.031530	196.363052	196.694817	197.026826	197.359078	197.691574	198.024312	198.357293
8	177.997182	178.330863	178.664822	178.999057	179.333569	179.668357	180.003422	180.338762
9	164.096267	164.433003	164.770050	165.107405	165.445068	165.783041	166.121320	166.459908
10	153.087464	153.427855	153.768586	154.109657	154.451067	154.792816	155.134903	155.477328
11	144.180725	144.525177	144.869998	145.215189	145.560748	145.906675	146.252969	146.599630
12	136.849244	137.198034	137.547222	137.896807	138.246788	138.597164	138.947935	139.299100
13	130.728221	131.081535	131.435274	131.789435	132.144019	132.499024	132.854450	133.210295
14	125.557004	125.914962	126.273368	126.632222	126.991523	127.351269	127.711460	128.072095
15	121.144381	121.507050	121.870191	122.233803	122.597885	122.962434	123.327451	123.692934
16	117.346882	117.714294	118.082198	118.450594	118.819481	119.188858	119.558722	119.929073
17	114.054745	114.426898	114.799564	115.172742	115.546429	115.920625	116.295328	116.670536
18	111.182555	111.559426	111.936827	112.314758	112.693216	113.072200	113.451708	113.831739
19	108.662843	109.044387	109.426479	109.809115	110.192295	110.576016	110.960277	111.345076
20	106.441600	106.827759	107.214479	107.601759	107.989596	108.377988	108.766933	109.156429
21	104.475083	104.865784	105.257058	105.648905	106.041321	106.434304	106.827852	107.221963
22	102.727478	103.122638	103.518382	103.914709	104.311615	104.709100	105.107159	105.505791
23	101.169186	101.568712	101.968833	102.369544	102.770845	103.172731	103.575201	103.978251
24	99.775527	100.179321	100.583717	100.988711	101.394301	101.800484	102.207257	102.614617
25	98.525763	98.933720	99.342284	99.751453	100.161222	100.571590	100.982553	101.394107
26	97.402338	97.814349	98.226971	98.640201	99.054037	99.468473	99.883508	100.299138
27	96.390299	96.806250	97.222815	97.639991	98.057774	98.476160	98.895146	99.314729
28	95.476825	95.896600	96.316991	96.737993	97.159603	97.581817	98.004632	98.428043
29	94.650868	95.074349	95.498446	95.923154	96.348469	96.774388	97.200905	97.628018
30	93.902856	94.329924	94.757607	95.185899	95.614795	96.044293	96.474388	96.905075
31	93.224458	93.654994	94.086141	94.517894	94.950249	95.383201	95.816747	96.250881
32	92.608394	93.042277	93.476767	93.911859	94.347548	94.783829	95.220699	95.658153
33	92.048273	92.485384	92.923095	93.361403	93.800303	94.239790	94.679859	95.120506
34	91.538467	91.978685	92.419499	92.860902	93.302890	93.745459	94.188603	94.632317
35	91.074001	91.517209	91.961005	92.405384	92.850340	93.295868	93.741964	94.188622
36	90.650464	91.096546	91.543207	91.990443	92.438247	92.886615	93.335542	93.785022
37	90.263937	90.712777	91.162187	91.612163	92.062698	92.513788	92.965427	93.417609
38	89.910921	90.362407	90.814453	91.267055	91.720206	92.173901	92.628135	93.082903
39	89.588295	90.042315	90.496886	90.952001	91.407655	91.863843	92.320558	92.777796
40	89.293257	89.749704	90.206690	90.664210	91.122257	91.580826	92.039912	92.499508
41	89.023297	89.482065	89.941360	90.401177	90.861510	91.322353	91.783700	92.245546
42	88.776155	89.237140	89.698640	90.160651	90.623165	91.086177	91.549681	92.013671
43	88.549794	89.012896	89.476502	89.940604	90.405198	90.870278	91.335836	91.801868
44	88.342377	88.807499	89.273111	89.739209	90.205784	90.672832	91.140346	91.608320
45	88.152243	88.619290	89.086815	89.554811	90.023273	90.492194	90.961568	91.431389
46	87.977887	88.446769	88.916114	89.385918	89.856174	90.326876	90.798017	91.269593
47	87.817948	88.288575	88.759653	89.231176	89.703137	90.175530	90.648350	91.121591
48	87.671188	88.143475	88.616200	89.089356	89.562937	90.036936	90.511349	90.986169
49	87.536483	88.010348	88.484637	88.959344	89.434462	89.909986	90.385909	90.862225
50	87.412810	87.888174	88.363948	88.840127	89.316703	89.793672	90.271026	90.748760

237

ANNUAL WITHDRAWALS PER $1000

EFFECTIVE ANNUAL YIELD

NUMBER OF ANNUAL WTHDRWLS	9.00%	9.05%	9.10%	9.15%	9.20%	9.25%	9.30%	9.35%
1	1090.000000	1090.500000	1091.000000	1091.500000	1092.000000	1092.500000	1093.000000	1093.500000
2	568.468900	568.854461	569.240077	569.625747	570.011472	570.397252	570.783086	571.168975
3	395.054757	395.406843	395.759026	396.111305	396.463681	396.816154	397.168724	397.521390
4	308.668662	309.007487	309.346448	309.685544	310.024776	310.364143	310.703645	311.043282
5	257.092457	257.426079	257.759873	258.093840	258.427979	258.762290	259.096772	259.431426
6	222.919783	223.252201	223.584826	223.917658	224.250698	224.583946	224.917400	225.251061
7	198.690517	199.023983	199.357690	199.691640	200.025830	200.360262	200.694935	201.029848
8	180.674378	181.010269	181.346434	181.682874	182.019588	182.356575	182.693836	183.031371
9	166.798802	167.138003	167.477510	167.817323	168.157442	168.497865	168.838593	169.179625
10	155.820090	156.163189	156.506624	156.850395	157.194501	157.538942	157.883717	158.228826
11	146.946657	147.294049	147.641806	147.989927	148.338412	148.687260	149.036471	149.386043
12	139.650658	140.002609	140.354952	140.707686	141.060810	141.414324	141.768227	142.122518
13	133.566560	133.923242	134.280342	134.637858	134.995789	135.354135	135.712895	136.072068
14	128.433173	128.794693	129.156653	129.519054	129.881893	130.245170	130.608885	130.973035
15	124.058883	124.425295	124.792170	125.159506	125.527303	125.895560	126.264275	126.633447
16	120.299910	120.671230	121.043034	121.415320	121.788085	122.161330	122.535053	122.909252
17	117.046248	117.422446	117.799180	118.176396	118.554111	118.932322	119.311029	119.690230
18	114.212291	114.593362	114.974951	115.357056	115.739675	116.122807	116.506451	116.890604
19	111.730411	112.116280	112.502681	112.889613	113.277073	113.665061	114.053573	114.442609
20	109.546475	109.937068	110.328206	110.719887	111.112110	111.504871	111.898170	112.292003
21	107.616635	108.011865	108.407651	108.803991	109.200883	109.598325	109.996313	110.394847
22	105.904993	106.304763	106.705098	107.105997	107.507455	107.909472	108.312045	108.715171
23	104.381880	104.786084	105.190861	105.596208	106.002123	106.408602	106.815644	107.223246
24	103.022561	103.431086	103.840190	104.249870	104.660123	105.070946	105.482335	105.894290
25	101.806251	102.218979	102.632291	103.046182	103.460650	103.875691	104.291303	104.707481
26	100.715360	101.132170	101.549565	101.967542	102.386097	102.805228	103.224931	103.645203
27	99.734900	100.155671	100.577023	100.998957	101.421470	101.844559	102.268220	102.692450
28	98.852047	99.276641	99.701819	100.127580	100.553919	100.980832	101.408316	101.836368
29	98.055723	98.484014	98.912890	99.342345	99.772376	100.202979	100.634150	101.065885
30	97.336351	97.768212	98.200653	98.633670	99.067259	99.501416	99.936138	100.371419
31	96.685600	97.120898	97.556773	97.993220	98.430233	98.867810	99.305946	99.744636
32	96.096186	96.534794	96.973972	97.413715	97.854021	98.294883	98.736297	99.178260
33	95.561726	96.003513	96.445865	96.888775	97.332240	97.776254	98.220814	98.665914
34	95.076597	95.521438	95.966834	96.412782	96.859275	97.306311	97.753883	98.201988
35	94.635837	95.083605	95.531920	95.980777	96.430172	96.880100	97.330555	97.781533
36	94.235050	94.685621	95.136730	95.588372	96.040542	96.493235	96.946445	97.400168
37	93.870329	94.323583	94.777364	95.231668	95.686490	96.141823	96.597664	97.054007
38	93.538198	93.994015	94.450349	94.907195	95.364548	95.822402	96.280751	96.739592
39	93.235550	93.693815	94.152586	94.611858	95.071624	95.531880	95.992620	96.453839
40	92.959609	93.420210	93.881304	94.342887	94.804952	95.267495	95.730511	96.193993
41	92.707885	93.170711	93.634019	94.097803	94.562057	95.026776	95.491955	95.957588
42	92.478142	92.943087	93.408501	93.874379	94.340714	94.807501	95.274736	95.742411
43	92.268368	92.735329	93.202746	93.670614	94.138926	94.607678	95.076863	95.546477
44	92.076749	92.545627	93.014947	93.484705	93.954894	94.425510	94.896546	95.367996
45	91.901651	92.372349	92.843477	93.315028	93.786997	94.259379	94.732169	95.205360
46	91.741596	92.214021	92.686862	93.160114	93.633771	94.107827	94.582276	95.057114
47	91.595245	92.069309	92.543775	93.018638	93.493892	93.969532	94.445553	94.921948
48	91.461389	91.937005	92.413010	92.889398	93.366164	93.843303	94.320808	94.798675
49	91.338929	91.816014	92.293476	92.771307	93.249503	93.728058	94.206966	94.686223
50	91.226868	91.705344	92.184183	92.663379	93.142926	93.622818	94.103051	94.583619

ANNUAL WITHDRAWALS PER $1000

EFFECTIVE ANNUAL YIELD

NUMBER OF ANNUAL WTHDRWLS	9.40%	9.45%	9.50%	9.55%	9.60%	9.65%	9.70%	9.75%
1	1094.000000	1094.500000	1095.000000	1095.500000	1096.000000	1096.500000	1097.000000	1097.500000
2	571.554919	571.940917	572.326969	572.713076	573.099237	573.485452	573.871722	574.258045
3	397.874152	398.227011	398.579967	398.933018	399.286166	399.639410	399.992750	400.346186
4	311.383054	311.722961	312.063002	312.403179	312.743489	313.083934	313.424514	313.765227
5	259.766252	260.101249	260.436417	260.771757	261.107267	261.442947	261.778799	262.114821
6	225.584928	225.919002	226.253283	226.587769	226.922461	227.257358	227.592461	227.927769
7	201.365002	201.700396	202.036030	202.371903	202.708015	203.044367	203.380957	203.717786
8	183.369178	183.707257	184.045608	184.384232	184.723126	185.062292	185.401729	185.741436
9	169.520961	169.862600	170.204543	170.546787	170.889334	171.232183	171.575333	171.918784
10	158.574269	158.920044	159.266152	159.612591	159.959362	160.306463	160.653895	161.001657
11	149.735977	150.086271	150.436926	150.787940	151.139312	151.491044	151.843132	152.195578
12	142.477197	142.832262	143.187714	143.543552	143.899774	144.256380	144.613369	144.970741
13	136.431654	136.791650	137.152057	137.512874	137.874100	138.235734	138.597775	138.960222
14	131.337620	131.702640	132.068002	132.433977	132.800293	133.167039	133.534214	133.901817
15	127.003075	127.373158	127.743695	128.114685	128.486126	128.858017	129.230358	129.603148
16	123.283926	123.659075	124.034696	124.410788	124.787351	125.164382	125.541881	125.919846
17	120.056929	120.450108	120.830782	121.211945	121.593594	121.975728	122.358346	122.741447
18	117.275265	117.660432	118.046104	118.432279	118.818955	119.206131	119.593806	119.981977
19	114.832167	115.222244	115.612838	116.003949	116.395574	116.787712	117.180360	117.573516
20	112.686370	113.081268	113.476695	113.872649	114.269129	114.666131	115.063654	115.461697
21	110.793924	111.193541	111.593697	111.994390	112.395616	112.797374	113.199662	113.602477
22	109.118847	109.523073	109.927844	110.333159	110.739015	111.145410	111.552342	111.959807
23	107.631404	108.040117	108.449382	108.859197	109.269557	109.680462	110.091909	110.503894
24	106.306806	106.719880	107.133511	107.547694	107.962428	108.377710	108.793536	109.209904
25	105.124225	105.541529	105.959392	106.377811	106.796781	107.216301	107.636368	108.056977
26	104.066040	104.487440	104.909399	105.331913	105.754981	106.178598	106.602761	107.027468
27	103.117245	103.542602	103.968517	104.394987	104.822009	105.249580	105.677695	106.106352
28	102.264982	102.694157	103.123888	103.554172	103.985005	104.416384	104.848304	105.280764
29	101.498181	101.931033	102.364439	102.798393	103.232893	103.667934	104.103513	104.539626
30	100.807257	101.243647	101.680584	102.118066	102.556089	102.994647	103.433738	103.873358
31	100.183877	100.623664	101.063994	101.504862	101.946263	102.388195	102.830652	103.273631
32	99.620767	100.063813	100.507395	100.951507	101.396146	101.841308	102.286988	102.733182
33	99.111550	99.557719	100.004414	100.451632	100.899369	101.347620	101.796380	102.245646
34	98.650620	99.099775	99.549449	99.999637	100.450333	100.901535	101.353237	101.805434
35	98.233029	98.685039	99.137558	99.590580	100.044102	100.498119	100.952625	101.407618
36	97.854400	98.309134	98.764367	99.220094	99.676309	100.133008	100.590187	101.047840
37	97.510848	97.968181	98.426001	98.884303	99.343083	99.802335	100.262056	100.722239
38	97.198919	97.658726	98.119009	98.579763	99.040982	99.502663	99.964799	100.427386
39	96.915532	97.377694	97.840320	98.303404	98.766942	99.230928	99.695358	100.160227
40	96.657937	97.122337	97.587188	98.052486	98.518224	98.984399	99.451004	99.918036
41	96.423670	96.890196	97.357160	97.824557	98.292383	98.760632	99.229298	99.698378
42	96.210523	96.679065	97.148033	97.617421	98.087225	98.557438	99.028056	99.499074
43	96.016513	96.486967	96.957834	97.429107	97.900782	98.372854	98.845318	99.318168
44	95.839857	96.312121	96.784785	97.257842	97.731288	98.205117	98.679324	99.153905
45	95.678947	96.152925	96.627288	97.102032	97.577151	98.052640	98.528494	99.004707
46	95.532334	96.007932	96.483903	96.960240	97.436938	97.913994	98.391401	98.869155
47	95.398712	95.875841	96.353328	96.831169	97.309358	97.787891	98.266762	98.745967
48	95.276898	95.755471	96.234391	96.713650	97.193245	97.673169	98.153420	98.633990
49	95.165822	95.645759	96.126028	96.606624	97.087543	97.568778	98.050326	98.532182
50	95.064516	95.545738	96.027280	96.509135	96.991300	97.473769	97.956538	98.439601

NUMBER OF ANNUAL WTHDRWLS	EFFECTIVE ANNUAL YIELD							
	9.80%	9.85%	9.90%	9.95%	10.00%	10.05%	10.10%	10.15%
1	1098.000000	1098.500000	1099.000000	1099.500000	1100.000000	1100.500000	1101.000000	1101.500000
2	574.644423	575.030855	575.417342	575.803882	576.190476	576.577124	576.963827	577.350583
3	400.699718	401.053346	401.407070	401.760889	402.114804	402.468814	402.822920	403.177121
4	314.106075	314.447056	314.788172	315.129421	315.470804	315.812320	316.153970	316.495753
5	262.451013	262.787375	263.123907	263.460609	263.797481	264.134522	264.471732	264.809112
6	228.263282	228.599000	228.934923	229.271049	229.607380	229.943915	230.280654	230.617596
7	204.054853	204.392159	204.729702	205.067482	205.405500	205.743754	206.082246	206.420973
8	186.081414	186.421661	186.762177	187.102963	187.444018	187.785341	188.126932	188.468791
9	172.262536	172.606588	172.950939	173.295590	173.640539	173.985787	174.331333	174.677177
10	161.349748	161.698167	162.046916	162.395992	162.745395	163.095125	163.445181	163.795564
11	152.548380	152.901538	153.255052	153.608920	153.963142	154.317718	154.672646	155.027927
12	145.328495	145.686630	146.045146	146.404041	146.763315	147.122968	147.482998	147.843405
13	139.323075	139.686332	140.049993	140.414057	140.778524	141.143391	141.508659	141.874327
14	134.269848	134.638305	135.007187	135.376493	135.746223	136.116375	136.486949	136.857943
15	129.976384	130.350066	130.724193	131.098764	131.473777	131.849232	132.225127	132.601461
16	126.298276	126.677170	127.056526	127.436344	127.816621	128.197356	128.578549	128.960198
17	123.125028	123.509099	123.893628	124.278644	124.664134	125.050099	125.436535	125.823442
18	120.370642	120.759802	121.149452	121.539593	121.930222	122.321338	122.712939	123.105024
19	117.967180	118.361349	118.756021	119.151195	119.546868	119.943040	120.339707	120.736869
20	115.860256	116.259331	116.658918	117.059017	117.459625	117.860740	118.262360	118.664483
21	114.005818	114.409682	114.814066	115.218970	115.624390	116.030324	116.436771	116.843727
22	112.367805	112.776331	113.185385	113.594963	114.005063	114.415683	114.826820	115.238473
23	110.916415	111.329471	111.743057	112.157172	112.571813	112.986977	113.402662	113.818866
24	109.626811	110.044255	110.462232	110.880740	111.299776	111.719338	112.139422	112.560026
25	108.478127	108.899815	109.322037	109.744790	110.168072	110.591880	111.016210	111.441060
26	107.452715	107.878498	108.304815	108.731663	109.159039	109.586938	110.015359	110.444298
27	106.535547	106.965277	107.395538	107.826328	108.257642	108.689478	109.121833	109.554702
28	105.713758	106.147283	106.581337	107.015914	107.451013	107.886629	108.322760	108.759401
29	104.976270	105.413440	105.851134	106.289346	106.728075	107.167315	107.607064	108.047318
30	104.313502	104.754167	105.195349	105.637044	106.079248	106.521958	106.965170	107.408880
31	103.717128	104.161139	104.605660	105.050686	105.496214	105.942240	106.388760	106.835770
32	103.179885	103.627095	104.074806	104.523015	104.971717	105.420908	105.870585	106.320743
33	102.695413	103.145677	103.596433	104.047678	104.499406	104.951615	105.404299	105.857455
34	102.258124	102.711300	103.164958	103.619095	104.073706	104.528787	104.984333	105.440340
35	101.863091	102.319041	102.775463	103.232352	103.689705	104.147517	104.605783	105.064499
36	101.505963	101.964551	102.423601	102.883106	103.343064	103.803469	104.264316	104.725602
37	101.182881	101.643077	102.105222	102.567511	103.029940	103.492805	103.956100	104.419822
38	100.890420	101.353896	101.817808	102.282153	102.746925	103.212120	103.677734	104.143761
39	100.622530	101.091261	101.557418	102.023993	102.490984	102.958385	103.426192	103.894399
40	100.385489	100.853358	101.321638	101.790325	102.259414	102.728901	103.198780	103.669047
41	100.167866	100.637758	101.108047	101.578731	102.049803	102.521259	102.993095	103.465306
42	99.970487	100.442290	100.914478	101.387047	101.859991	102.333306	102.806988	103.281031
43	99.791400	100.265008	100.738989	101.213337	101.688047	102.163114	102.638535	103.114304
44	99.628854	100.104167	100.579838	101.055863	101.532237	102.008955	102.486013	102.963406
45	99.481276	99.958195	100.435459	100.913064	101.391005	101.869276	102.347875	102.826795
46	99.347250	99.825682	100.304447	100.783538	101.262953	101.742685	102.222731	102.703085
47	99.225500	99.705357	100.185533	100.666022	101.146822	101.627927	102.109332	102.591033
48	99.114876	99.596072	100.077575	100.559379	101.041480	101.523873	102.006553	102.489517
49	99.014340	99.496796	99.979545	100.462582	100.945904	101.429506	101.913382	102.397530
50	98.922954	99.406593	99.890512	100.374707	100.859174	101.343908	101.828906	102.314162

ANNUAL WITHDRAWALS PER $1000

NUMBER OF ANNUAL WTHDRWLS	EFFECTIVE ANNUAL YIELD							
	10.20%	10.25%	10.30%	10.35%	10.40%	10.45%	10.50%	10.55%
1	1102.000000	1102.500000	1103.000000	1103.500000	1104.000000	1104.500000	1105.000000	1105.500000
2	577.737393	578.124257	578.511175	578.898146	579.285171	579.672250	580.059382	580.446569
3	403.531418	403.885810	404.240297	404.594879	404.949556	405.304328	405.659195	406.014157
4	316.837669	317.179718	317.521900	317.864215	318.206663	318.549243	318.891956	319.234802
5	265.146661	265.484379	265.822265	266.160320	266.498544	266.836935	267.175495	267.514223
6	230.954742	231.292091	231.629642	231.967397	232.305354	232.643513	232.981875	233.320438
7	206.759937	207.099137	207.438573	207.778244	208.118150	208.458291	208.798667	209.139277
8	188.810918	189.153311	189.495972	189.838899	190.182092	190.525552	190.869276	191.213266
9	175.023318	175.369756	175.716490	176.063520	176.410846	176.758467	177.106383	177.454593
10	164.146271	164.497304	164.848660	165.200341	165.552345	165.904672	166.257321	166.610291
11	155.383559	155.739543	156.095876	156.452560	156.809593	157.166975	157.524704	157.882781
12	148.204188	148.565347	148.926880	149.288787	149.651068	150.013721	150.376746	150.740142
13	142.240393	142.606857	142.973719	143.340976	143.708629	144.076676	144.445117	144.813951
14	137.229356	137.601187	137.973436	138.346102	138.719183	139.092678	139.466587	139.840908
15	132.978233	133.355442	133.733087	134.111166	134.489679	134.868625	135.248002	135.627808
16	129.342302	129.724859	130.107868	130.491328	130.875237	131.259595	131.644400	132.029650
17	126.210819	126.598663	126.986974	127.375750	127.764989	128.154690	128.544852	128.935473
18	123.497590	123.890637	124.284163	124.678165	125.072643	125.467594	125.863018	126.258913
19	121.134523	121.532668	121.931302	122.330422	122.730029	123.130118	123.530690	123.931741
20	119.067107	119.470230	119.873851	120.277967	120.682576	121.087676	121.493265	121.899342
21	117.251192	117.659162	118.067635	118.476610	118.886085	119.296056	119.706522	120.117481
22	115.650636	116.063314	116.476497	116.890187	117.304379	117.719073	118.134265	118.549953
23	114.235585	114.652817	115.070561	115.488812	115.907569	116.326829	116.746590	117.166849
24	112.981147	113.402783	113.824930	114.247586	114.670749	115.094415	115.518581	115.943247
25	111.866427	112.292308	112.718700	113.145600	113.573005	114.000913	114.429320	114.858224
26	110.873752	111.303718	111.734193	112.165173	112.596657	113.028640	113.461120	113.894093
27	109.988083	110.421973	110.856368	111.291265	111.726661	112.162552	112.598936	113.035809
28	109.196549	109.634200	110.072353	110.511002	110.950144	111.389777	111.829897	112.270500
29	108.488073	108.929326	109.371073	109.813311	110.256036	110.699245	111.142933	111.587098
30	107.853084	108.297778	108.742960	109.188625	109.634769	110.081389	110.528482	110.976043
31	107.283267	107.731246	108.179704	108.628636	109.078039	109.527910	109.978244	110.429038
32	106.771378	107.222487	107.674065	108.126108	108.578613	109.031576	109.484992	109.938859
33	106.311078	106.765165	107.219711	107.674713	108.130165	108.586066	109.042409	109.499192
34	105.896805	106.353722	106.811087	107.268898	107.727148	108.185835	108.644954	109.104502
35	105.523660	105.983264	106.443304	106.903778	107.364681	107.826008	108.287756	108.749921
36	105.187322	105.649472	106.112048	106.575044	107.038458	107.502284	107.966519	108.431158
37	104.883966	105.348527	105.813501	106.278885	106.744672	107.210860	107.677444	108.144420
38	104.610198	105.077040	105.544282	106.011920	106.479951	106.948369	107.417170	107.886350
39	104.363004	104.832000	105.301384	105.771151	106.241297	106.711818	107.182709	107.653966
40	104.139698	104.610728	105.082133	105.553907	106.026048	106.498549	106.971408	107.444620
41	103.937807	104.410834	104.884143	105.357808	105.831826	106.306193	106.780903	107.255953
42	103.755431	104.230184	104.705285	105.180730	105.656514	106.132633	106.609083	107.085860
43	103.590417	104.066869	104.543656	105.020774	105.498218	105.975983	106.454067	106.932463
44	103.441130	103.919180	104.397551	104.876240	105.355242	105.834553	106.314168	106.794084
45	103.306032	103.785583	104.265442	104.745606	105.226069	105.706829	106.187880	106.669218
46	103.183744	103.664704	104.145958	104.627505	105.109338	105.591455	106.073850	106.556520
47	103.073026	103.555306	104.037869	104.520710	105.003827	105.487213	105.970866	106.454782
48	102.972760	103.456278	103.940066	104.424121	104.908437	105.393012	105.877841	106.362920
49	102.881944	103.366621	103.851555	104.336744	104.822183	105.307868	105.793795	106.279961
50	102.799672	103.285433	103.771440	104.257689	104.744177	105.230899	105.717851	106.205030

ANNUAL WITHDRAWALS PER $1000

NUMBER OF ANNUAL WTHDRWLS	EFFECTIVE ANNUAL YIELD							
	10.60%	10.65%	10.70%	10.75%	10.80%	10.85%	10.90%	10.95%
1	1106.000000	1106.500000	1107.000000	1107.500000	1108.000000	1108.500000	1109.000000	1109.500000
2	580.833808	581.221101	581.608448	581.995848	582.383302	582.770809	583.158369	583.545982
3	406.369214	406.724365	407.079611	407.434952	407.790387	408.145916	408.501540	408.857258
4	319.577779	319.920889	320.264131	320.607505	320.951011	321.294649	321.638418	321.982319
5	267.853119	268.192183	268.531414	268.870812	269.210378	269.550110	269.890010	270.230076
6	233.659203	233.998170	234.337338	234.676707	235.016278	235.356048	235.696020	236.036192
7	209.480121	209.821199	210.162510	210.504055	210.845833	211.187843	211.530087	211.872562
8	191.557521	191.902040	192.246824	192.591871	192.937182	193.282756	193.628593	193.974692
9	177.803098	178.151895	178.500986	178.850370	179.200046	179.550014	179.900273	180.250823
10	166.963584	167.317196	167.671130	168.025383	168.379955	168.734846	169.090056	169.445583
11	158.241205	158.599975	158.959090	159.318551	159.678356	160.038505	160.398996	160.759831
12	151.103908	151.468044	151.832549	152.197422	152.562663	152.928271	153.294244	153.660583
13	145.183177	145.552794	145.922801	146.293198	146.663983	147.035156	147.406716	147.778661
14	140.215641	140.590785	140.966338	141.342299	141.718669	142.095444	142.472626	142.850212
15	136.008044	136.388708	136.769798	137.151314	137.533255	137.915619	138.298405	138.681612
16	132.415345	132.801483	133.188062	133.575083	133.962542	134.350440	134.738774	135.127543
17	129.326551	129.718086	130.110076	130.502519	130.895414	131.288760	131.682554	132.076796
18	126.655276	127.052106	127.449403	127.847163	128.245386	128.644070	129.043213	129.442813
19	124.333270	124.735276	125.137757	125.540710	125.944134	126.348027	126.752388	127.157214
20	122.305904	122.712949	123.120476	123.528483	123.936966	124.345926	124.755358	125.165263
21	120.528930	120.940868	121.353292	121.766200	122.179591	122.593461	123.007809	123.422633
22	118.966136	119.382810	119.799973	120.217624	120.635759	121.054377	121.473474	121.893050
23	117.587603	118.008851	118.430589	118.852815	119.275527	119.698722	120.122398	120.546552
24	116.368407	116.794061	117.220204	117.646835	118.073951	118.501550	118.929627	119.358182
25	115.287621	115.717510	116.147887	116.578749	117.010094	117.441918	117.874220	118.306995
26	114.327557	114.761509	115.195945	115.630863	116.066260	116.502133	116.938478	117.375293
27	113.473168	113.911010	114.349332	114.788131	115.227402	115.667145	116.107355	116.548029
28	112.711583	113.153144	113.595178	114.037682	114.480654	114.924089	115.367985	115.812338
29	112.031737	112.476845	112.922420	113.368457	113.814954	114.261907	114.709313	115.157168
30	111.424069	111.872557	112.321503	112.770903	113.220754	113.671053	114.121795	114.572978
31	110.880288	111.331990	111.784141	112.236737	112.689774	113.143250	113.597159	114.051499
32	110.393171	110.847926	111.303120	111.758749	112.214808	112.671296	113.128207	113.585538
33	109.956411	110.414061	110.872139	111.330641	111.789563	112.248902	112.708653	113.168814
34	109.564474	110.024866	110.485675	110.946896	111.408526	111.870560	112.332996	112.795829
35	109.212498	109.675484	110.138874	110.602665	111.066852	111.531432	111.996401	112.461755
36	108.896197	109.361633	109.827461	110.293677	110.760277	111.227257	111.694614	112.162343
37	108.611784	109.079531	109.547658	110.016160	110.485034	110.954275	111.423880	111.893844
38	108.355905	108.825831	109.296123	109.766778	110.237791	110.709159	111.180878	111.652943
39	108.125585	108.597562	109.069902	109.542572	110.015597	110.488963	110.962667	111.436704
40	107.918181	108.392086	108.866331	109.340913	109.815827	110.291070	110.766636	111.242523
41	107.731338	108.207055	108.683099	109.159466	109.636152	110.113153	110.590466	111.068085
42	107.562958	108.040375	108.518106	108.996147	109.474494	109.953143	110.432090	110.911332
43	107.411169	107.890180	108.369491	108.849100	109.329002	109.809193	110.289669	110.770427
44	107.274295	107.754799	108.235591	108.716667	109.198023	109.679656	110.161561	110.643735
45	107.150840	107.632741	108.114917	108.597365	109.080081	109.563060	110.046299	110.529794
46	107.039461	107.522668	108.006139	108.489868	108.973853	109.458089	109.942573	110.427300
47	106.938955	107.423384	107.908062	108.392988	108.878157	109.363565	109.849208	110.335084
48	106.848245	107.333813	107.819619	108.305660	108.791933	109.278433	109.765157	110.252101
49	106.766361	107.252991	107.739849	108.226930	108.714230	109.201747	109.689476	110.177415
50	106.692432	107.180053	107.667890	108.155939	108.644197	109.132659	109.621323	110.110186

ANNUAL WITHDRAWALS PER $1000

EFFECTIVE ANNUAL YIELD

NUMBER OF ANNUAL WTHDRWLS	11.00%	11.05%	11.10%	11.15%	11.20%	11.25%	11.30%	11.35%
1	1110.000000	1110.500000	1111.000000	1111.500000	1112.000000	1112.500000	1113.000000	1113.500000
2	583.933649	584.321369	584.709143	585.096969	585.484848	585.872781	586.260767	586.648805
3	409.213070	409.568976	409.924976	410.281070	410.637258	410.993540	411.349916	411.706386
4	322.326352	322.670515	323.014810	323.359236	323.703793	324.048481	324.393300	324.738249
5	270.570310	270.910709	271.251275	271.592007	271.932905	272.273969	272.615199	272.956594
6	236.376564	236.717135	237.057907	237.398878	237.740048	238.081418	238.422986	238.764754
7	212.215269	212.558209	212.901379	213.244781	213.588414	213.932278	214.276372	214.620696
8	194.321054	194.667678	195.014563	195.361709	195.709117	196.056784	196.404712	196.752900
9	180.601664	180.952796	181.304217	181.655927	182.007927	182.360215	182.712792	183.065656
10	169.801427	170.157588	170.514066	170.870859	171.227967	171.585391	171.943128	172.301179
11	161.121007	161.482525	161.844383	162.206582	162.569120	162.931997	163.295212	163.658765
12	154.027286	154.394354	154.761784	155.129577	155.497732	155.866247	156.235123	156.604359
13	148.150993	148.523708	148.896807	149.270288	149.644152	150.018396	150.393020	150.768024
14	143.228202	143.606594	143.985388	144.364583	144.744177	145.124170	145.504561	145.885349
15	139.065240	139.449286	139.833749	140.218630	140.603925	140.989636	141.375759	141.762294
16	135.516747	135.906384	136.296452	136.686950	137.077877	137.469233	137.861014	138.253221
17	132.471485	132.866617	133.262194	133.658212	134.054670	134.451567	134.848902	135.246673
18	129.842870	130.243381	130.644345	131.045760	131.447625	131.849938	132.252697	132.655901
19	127.562504	127.968256	128.374469	128.781140	129.188268	129.595851	130.003887	130.412375
20	125.575637	125.986479	126.397786	126.809558	127.221791	127.634485	128.047636	128.461244
21	123.837930	124.253699	124.669937	125.086642	125.503812	125.921445	126.339540	126.758093
22	122.313101	122.733625	123.154621	123.576085	123.998015	124.420410	124.843267	125.266583
23	120.971182	121.396285	121.821859	122.247901	122.674410	123.101382	123.528815	123.956707
24	119.787211	120.216712	120.646682	121.077119	121.508019	121.939381	122.371202	122.803478
25	118.740242	119.173957	119.608139	120.042783	120.477888	120.913450	121.349467	121.785937
26	117.812575	118.250321	118.688528	119.127194	119.566314	120.005887	120.445910	120.886379
27	116.989164	117.430757	117.872805	118.315305	118.758255	119.201650	119.645488	120.089766
28	116.257145	116.702404	117.148110	117.594261	118.040853	118.487884	118.935350	119.383249
29	115.605470	116.054214	116.503397	116.953016	117.403070	117.853553	118.304462	118.755795
30	115.024598	115.476652	115.929136	116.382047	116.835382	117.289136	117.743308	118.197893
31	114.506267	114.961458	115.417069	115.873097	116.329538	116.786389	117.243647	117.701307
32	114.043285	114.501446	114.960016	115.418992	115.878370	116.338146	116.798318	117.258882
33	113.629379	114.090346	114.551711	115.013470	115.475620	115.938157	116.401078	116.864378
34	113.259055	113.722671	114.186672	114.651053	115.115819	115.580957	116.046466	116.512343
35	112.927490	113.393602	113.860088	114.326944	114.794166	115.261751	115.729695	116.197993
36	112.630441	113.098903	113.567727	114.036907	114.506442	114.976325	115.446555	115.917128
37	112.364164	112.834836	113.305856	113.777220	114.248925	114.720967	115.193342	115.666046
38	112.125351	112.598097	113.071179	113.544592	114.018333	114.492397	114.966782	115.441483
39	111.911071	112.385764	112.860779	113.336112	113.811759	114.287717	114.763982	115.240551
40	111.718727	112.195243	112.672068	113.149198	113.626629	114.104359	114.582382	115.060695
41	111.546009	112.024231	112.502750	112.981561	113.460660	113.940043	114.419708	114.899651
42	111.390863	111.870682	112.350783	112.831164	113.311820	113.792748	114.273944	114.755405
43	111.251462	111.732771	112.214350	112.696196	113.178304	113.660672	114.143295	114.626171
44	111.126173	111.608873	112.091831	112.575042	113.058504	113.542213	114.026165	114.510357
45	111.013542	111.497539	111.981781	112.466265	112.950987	113.435944	113.921132	114.406548
46	110.912268	111.397473	111.882911	112.368579	112.854473	113.340591	113.826928	114.313481
47	110.821188	111.307518	111.794069	112.280838	112.767821	113.255017	113.742420	114.230029
48	110.739262	111.226637	111.714223	112.202015	112.690010	113.178206	113.666599	114.155187
49	110.665559	111.153906	111.642452	112.131194	112.620128	113.109252	113.598563	114.088057
50	110.599243	111.088492	111.577930	112.067553	112.557358	113.047343	113.537503	114.027837

ANNUAL WITHDRAWALS PER $1000

NUMBER OF ANNUAL WTHDRWLS	EFFECTIVE ANNUAL YIELD							
	11.40%	11.45%	11.50%	11.55%	11.60%	11.65%	11.70%	11.75%
1	1114.000000	1114.500000	1115.000000	1115.500000	1116.000000	1116.500000	1117.000000	1117.500000
2	587.036897	587.425041	587.813239	588.201489	588.589792	588.978148	589.366556	589.755018
3	412.062949	412.419605	412.776355	413.133198	413.490135	413.847165	414.204288	414.561505
4	325.083329	325.428540	325.773881	326.119352	326.464953	326.810685	327.156546	327.502537
5	273.298155	273.639881	273.981772	274.323828	274.666049	275.008435	275.350985	275.693699
6	239.106719	239.448883	239.791245	240.133805	240.476563	240.819518	241.162671	241.506021
7	214.965250	215.310033	215.655046	216.000289	216.345760	216.691459	217.037387	217.383544
8	197.101348	197.450054	197.799020	198.148244	198.497726	198.847467	199.197464	199.547720
9	183.418807	183.772246	184.125971	184.479982	184.834279	185.188861	185.543728	185.898879
10	172.659544	173.018221	173.377210	173.736511	174.096124	174.456047	174.816280	175.176822
11	164.022655	164.386881	164.751444	165.116341	165.481573	165.847140	166.213039	166.579272
12	156.973953	157.343905	157.714215	158.084881	158.455904	158.827281	159.199013	159.571099
13	151.143406	151.519165	151.895302	152.271814	152.648701	153.025962	153.403596	153.781603
14	146.266532	146.648110	147.030083	147.412447	147.795204	148.178352	148.561889	148.945815
15	142.149240	142.536597	142.924361	143.312534	143.701113	144.090097	144.479485	144.869276
16	138.645851	139.038905	139.432379	139.826274	140.220587	140.615318	141.010465	141.406027
17	135.644879	136.043518	136.442588	136.842089	137.242019	137.642376	138.043160	138.444368
18	133.059549	133.463638	133.868167	134.273134	134.678539	135.084378	135.490652	135.897357
19	130.821312	131.230698	131.640529	132.050806	132.461524	132.872684	133.284283	133.696320
20	128.875305	129.289819	129.704784	130.120197	130.536056	130.952360	131.369107	131.786295
21	127.177102	127.596567	128.016484	128.436851	128.857667	129.278929	129.700636	130.122785
22	125.690357	126.114585	126.539267	126.964400	127.389981	127.816008	128.242479	128.669392
23	124.385055	124.813858	125.243111	125.672814	126.102964	126.533559	126.964595	127.396071
24	123.236209	123.669391	124.103021	124.537097	124.971617	125.406578	125.841977	126.277812
25	122.222855	122.660221	123.098031	123.536282	123.974972	124.414098	124.853657	125.293647
26	121.327293	121.768647	122.210440	122.652668	123.095329	123.538419	123.981937	124.425879
27	120.534482	120.979631	121.425212	121.871221	122.317655	122.764511	123.211787	123.659480
28	119.831576	120.280329	120.729505	121.179102	121.629115	122.079542	122.530379	122.981625
29	119.207547	119.659717	120.112300	120.565294	121.018695	121.472501	121.926708	122.381313
30	118.652888	119.108290	119.564096	120.020302	120.476906	120.933904	121.391292	121.849069
31	118.159367	118.617823	119.076672	119.535911	119.995536	120.455544	120.915932	121.376697
32	117.719834	118.181171	118.642889	119.104986	119.567457	120.030300	120.493511	120.957087
33	117.328056	117.792106	118.256526	118.721312	119.186460	119.651968	120.117832	120.584049
34	116.978584	117.445186	117.912145	118.379458	118.847122	119.315132	119.783486	120.252180
35	116.666644	117.135643	117.604986	118.074670	118.544692	119.015049	119.485736	119.956751
36	116.388039	116.859286	117.330865	117.802771	118.275003	118.747556	119.220427	119.693612
37	116.139076	116.612429	117.086101	117.560087	118.034386	118.508993	118.983905	119.459118
38	115.916496	116.391819	116.867448	117.343380	117.819609	118.296135	118.772952	119.250058
39	115.717419	116.194584	116.672041	117.149788	117.627820	118.106135	118.584729	119.063599
40	115.539296	116.018180	116.497343	116.976783	117.456496	117.936478	118.416727	118.897238
41	115.379867	115.860354	116.341108	116.822125	117.303403	117.784937	118.266725	118.748764
42	115.237127	115.719108	116.201342	116.683828	117.166561	117.649539	118.132758	118.616215
43	115.109295	115.592665	116.076277	116.560128	117.044214	117.528533	118.013080	118.497853
44	114.994786	115.479448	115.964340	116.449459	116.934801	117.420364	117.906143	118.392137
45	114.892189	115.378051	115.864132	116.350427	116.836934	117.323650	117.810572	118.297696
46	114.800247	115.287223	115.774406	116.261792	116.749379	117.237164	117.725142	118.213313
47	114.717839	115.205848	115.694052	116.182450	116.671036	117.159809	117.648766	118.137904
48	114.643965	115.132931	115.622081	116.111414	116.600926	117.090613	117.580474	118.070506
49	114.577731	115.067583	115.557609	116.047807	116.538174	117.028707	117.519403	118.010259
50	114.518341	115.009012	115.499848	115.990846	116.482002	116.973315	117.464782	117.956399

ANNUAL WITHDRAWALS PER $1000

NUMBER OF ANNUAL WTHDRWLS	EFFECTIVE ANNUAL YIELD							
	11.80%	11.85%	11.90%	11.95%	12.00%	12.05%	12.10%	12.15%
1	1118.000000	1118.500000	1119.000000	1119.500000	1120.000000	1120.500000	1121.000000	1121.500000
2	590.143532	590.532098	590.920717	591.309389	591.698113	592.086890	592.475719	592.864601
3	414.918814	415.276216	415.633712	415.991300	416.348981	416.706754	417.064620	417.422579
4	327.848658	328.194908	328.541288	328.887798	329.234436	329.581204	329.928101	330.275127
5	276.036578	276.379621	276.722827	277.066198	277.409732	277.753430	278.097290	278.441314
6	241.849567	242.193310	242.537250	242.881386	243.225718	243.570246	243.914970	244.259889
7	217.729927	218.076539	218.423378	218.770443	219.117736	219.465255	219.813000	220.160971
8	199.898231	200.249000	200.600025	200.951305	201.302841	201.654633	202.006679	202.358980
9	186.254315	186.610034	186.966036	187.322321	187.678889	188.035738	188.392869	188.750282
10	175.537675	175.898835	176.260304	176.622081	176.984164	177.346554	177.709251	178.072253
11	166.945836	167.312732	167.679960	168.047517	168.415404	168.783621	169.152166	169.521038
12	159.943537	160.316328	160.689471	161.062964	161.436808	161.811000	162.185542	162.560431
13	154.159982	154.538731	154.917850	155.297339	155.677195	156.057419	156.438009	156.818965
14	149.330130	149.714831	150.099918	150.485390	150.871246	151.257485	151.644106	152.031108
15	145.259470	145.650064	146.041057	146.432450	146.824240	147.216426	147.609007	148.001983
16	141.802003	142.198391	142.595191	142.992400	143.390018	143.788043	144.186475	144.585311
17	138.845999	139.248052	139.650525	140.053418	140.456728	140.860454	141.264594	141.669148
18	136.304493	136.712058	137.120051	137.528469	137.937311	138.346577	138.756263	139.166369
19	134.108792	134.521699	134.935038	135.348807	135.763005	136.177630	136.592681	137.008155
20	132.203922	132.621985	133.040484	133.459416	133.878780	134.298573	134.718794	135.139441
21	130.545374	130.968401	131.391865	131.815762	132.240092	132.664851	133.090039	133.515652
22	129.096745	129.524535	129.952761	130.381419	130.810509	131.240027	131.669972	132.100341
23	127.827984	128.260333	128.693114	129.126325	129.559965	129.994030	130.428519	130.863429
24	126.714081	127.150781	127.587909	128.025464	128.463442	128.901841	129.340659	129.779893
25	125.734066	126.174910	126.616177	127.057865	127.499970	127.942490	128.385423	128.828767
26	124.870242	125.315025	125.760223	126.205835	126.651858	127.098289	127.545125	127.992364
27	124.107587	124.556104	125.005030	125.454360	125.904094	126.354227	126.804756	127.255680
28	123.433276	123.885329	124.337780	124.790628	125.243869	125.697500	126.151519	126.605923
29	122.836314	123.291706	123.747488	124.203656	124.660207	125.117138	125.574446	126.032128
30	122.307230	122.765772	123.224693	123.683989	124.143658	124.603695	125.064099	125.524866
31	121.837835	122.299343	122.761218	123.223457	123.686057	124.149015	124.612327	125.075990
32	121.421024	121.885320	122.349971	122.814974	123.280326	123.746024	124.212064	124.678443
33	121.050616	121.517528	121.984783	122.452378	122.920310	123.388574	123.857169	124.326091
34	120.721211	121.190576	121.660271	122.130293	122.600638	123.071305	123.542288	124.013586
35	120.428089	120.899749	121.371726	121.844017	122.316619	122.789529	123.262744	123.736260
36	120.167109	120.640913	121.115022	121.589432	122.064141	122.539144	123.014439	123.490022
37	119.934630	120.410436	120.886534	121.362921	121.839592	122.316546	122.793778	123.271286
38	119.727449	120.205122	120.683073	121.161301	121.639800	122.118568	122.597602	123.076899
39	119.542740	120.022151	120.501828	120.981768	121.461967	121.942422	122.423130	122.904089
40	119.378009	119.859037	120.340318	120.821848	121.303626	121.785647	122.267909	122.750408
41	119.231049	119.713759	120.196349	120.679356	121.162598	121.646072	122.129774	122.613701
42	119.099906	119.583829	120.067981	120.552358	121.036958	121.521777	122.006812	122.492061
43	118.982849	119.468065	119.953497	120.439142	120.924999	121.411063	121.897331	122.383802
44	118.878341	119.364754	119.851372	120.338191	120.825210	121.312425	121.799834	122.287433
45	118.785020	119.272540	119.760254	120.248159	120.736252	121.224531	121.712992	122.201632
46	118.701672	119.190216	119.678944	120.167851	120.656936	121.146196	121.635627	122.125228
47	118.627220	119.116710	119.606374	120.096206	120.586206	121.076371	121.566697	122.057182
48	118.560705	119.051069	119.541595	120.032281	120.523125	121.014123	121.505273	121.996572
49	118.501273	118.992443	119.483765	119.975238	120.466858	120.958623	121.450531	121.942579
50	118.448165	118.940077	119.432132	119.924329	120.416663	120.909134	121.401739	121.894476

245

ANNUAL WITHDRAWALS PER $1000

NUMBER OF ANNUAL WTHDRWLS	EFFECTIVE ANNUAL YIELD							
	12.20%	12.25%	12.30%	12.35%	12.40%	12.45%	12.50%	12.55%
1	1122.000000	1122.500000	1123.000000	1123.500000	1124.000000	1124.500000	1125.000000	1125.500000
2	593.253534	593.642521	594.031559	594.420650	594.809793	595.198988	595.588235	595.977535
3	417.780630	418.138774	418.497010	418.855338	419.213758	419.572271	419.930876	420.289572
4	330.622282	330.969565	331.316978	331.664518	332.012187	332.359985	332.707911	333.055965
5	278.785502	279.129851	279.474364	279.819039	280.163877	280.508877	280.854039	281.199363
6	244.605004	244.950314	245.295818	245.641517	245.987411	246.333499	246.679781	247.026257
7	220.509168	220.857591	221.206239	221.555111	221.904208	222.253530	222.603076	222.952845
8	202.711535	203.064344	203.417407	203.770722	204.124291	204.478112	204.832186	205.186511
9	189.107974	189.465948	189.824201	190.182734	190.541545	190.900636	191.260004	191.619651
10	178.435560	178.799172	179.163088	179.527307	179.891830	180.256655	180.621782	180.987211
11	169.890239	170.259765	170.629618	170.999797	171.370300	171.741127	172.112278	172.483752
12	162.935668	163.311251	163.687180	164.063454	164.440072	164.817034	165.194339	165.571986
13	157.200286	157.581971	157.964019	158.346429	158.729200	159.112332	159.495824	159.879675
14	152.418491	152.806252	153.194391	153.582908	153.971800	154.361068	154.750710	155.140725
15	148.395351	148.789111	149.183262	149.577803	149.972732	150.368049	150.763751	151.159839
16	144.984551	145.384193	145.784236	146.184679	146.585520	146.986759	147.388393	147.790423
17	142.074114	142.479490	142.885276	143.291472	143.698068	144.105072	144.512480	144.920290
18	139.576893	139.987833	140.399188	140.810957	141.223137	141.635727	142.048726	142.462133
19	137.424052	137.840368	138.257103	138.674255	139.091822	139.509803	139.928195	140.346998
20	135.560511	135.982004	136.403917	136.826248	137.248995	137.672158	138.095733	138.519719
21	133.941690	134.368149	134.795028	135.222326	135.650039	136.078167	136.506706	136.935655
22	132.531132	132.962343	133.393973	133.826018	134.258476	134.691347	135.124627	135.558314
23	131.298757	131.734502	132.170662	132.607233	133.044214	133.481603	133.919396	134.357593
24	130.219542	130.659601	131.100070	131.540945	131.982225	132.423907	132.865988	133.308466
25	129.272518	129.716674	130.161232	130.606190	131.051546	131.497297	131.943441	132.389975
26	128.440002	128.888038	129.336469	129.785292	130.234505	130.684104	131.134088	131.584454
27	127.706996	128.158700	128.610790	129.063263	129.516116	129.969348	130.422954	130.876933
28	127.060708	127.515872	127.971412	128.427326	128.883610	129.340262	129.797279	130.254658
29	126.490182	126.948604	127.407392	127.866543	128.326053	128.785920	129.246141	129.706714
30	125.985993	126.447478	126.909316	127.371506	127.834045	128.296929	128.760156	129.223722
31	125.540002	126.004360	126.469060	126.934100	127.399476	127.865186	128.331226	128.797595
32	125.145159	125.612208	126.079588	126.547294	127.015325	127.483677	127.952348	128.421334
33	124.795336	125.264903	125.734787	126.204986	126.675496	127.146315	127.617440	128.088868
34	124.485196	124.957113	125.429335	125.901859	126.374682	126.847801	127.321213	127.794915
35	124.210074	124.684184	125.158585	125.633276	126.108252	126.583512	127.059052	127.534869
36	123.965891	124.442042	124.918472	125.395178	125.872158	126.349408	126.826925	127.304706
37	123.749066	124.227116	124.705432	125.184011	125.662851	126.141948	126.621300	127.100904
38	123.556456	124.036269	124.516337	124.996654	125.477220	125.958030	126.439082	126.920373
39	123.385294	123.866744	124.348434	124.830363	125.312527	125.794924	126.277550	126.760402
40	123.233142	123.716108	124.199303	124.682723	125.166367	125.650231	126.134312	126.618607
41	123.097851	123.582220	124.066806	124.551606	125.036617	125.521837	126.007261	126.492889
42	122.977520	123.463187	123.949060	124.435134	124.921408	125.407878	125.894542	126.381398
43	122.870472	123.357338	123.844397	124.331648	124.819086	125.306710	125.794517	126.282504
44	122.775220	123.263192	123.751347	124.239682	124.728194	125.216880	125.705739	126.194767
45	122.690450	123.179442	123.668606	124.157940	124.647440	125.137104	125.626930	126.116916
46	122.614996	123.104928	123.595021	124.085273	124.575682	125.066246	125.556961	126.047826
47	122.547824	123.038621	123.529569	124.020666	124.511911	125.003300	125.494831	125.986503
48	122.488019	122.979610	123.471344	123.963218	124.455229	124.947376	125.439657	125.932068
49	122.434765	122.927087	123.419542	123.912129	124.404844	124.897687	125.390653	125.883743
50	122.387341	122.880334	123.373451	123.866691	124.360052	124.853531	125.347127	125.840837

ANNUAL WITHDRAWALS PER $1000

NUMBER OF ANNUAL WTHDRWLS	EFFECTIVE ANNUAL YIELD							
	12.60%	12.65%	12.70%	12.75%	12.80%	12.85%	12.90%	12.95%
1	1126.000000	1126.500000	1127.000000	1127.500000	1128.000000	1128.500000	1129.000000	1129.500000
2	596.366886	596.756290	597.145745	597.535253	597.924812	598.314423	598.704086	599.093801
3	420.648361	421.007241	421.366213	421.725277	422.084433	422.443680	422.803019	423.162449
4	333.404147	333.752456	334.100894	334.449459	334.798152	335.146972	335.495920	335.844995
5	281.544849	281.890496	282.236305	282.582276	282.928408	283.274700	283.621154	283.967768
6	247.372927	247.719790	248.066846	248.414096	248.761538	249.109173	249.457000	249.805020
7	223.302839	223.653055	224.003495	224.354158	224.705043	225.056150	225.407480	225.759031
8	205.541088	205.895916	206.250995	206.606325	206.961905	207.317734	207.673814	208.030142
9	191.979574	192.339775	192.700253	193.061006	193.422036	193.783340	194.144920	194.506774
10	181.352940	181.718971	182.085301	182.451931	182.818860	183.186087	183.553613	183.921436
11	172.855549	173.227667	173.600107	173.972867	174.345947	174.719346	175.093064	175.467101
12	165.949974	166.328303	166.706972	167.085980	167.465327	167.845012	168.225033	168.605391
13	160.263884	160.648450	161.033372	161.418650	161.804282	162.190268	162.576607	162.963299
14	155.531113	155.921871	156.313000	156.704499	157.096365	157.488599	157.881200	158.274166
15	151.556311	151.953166	152.350403	152.748020	153.146017	153.544393	153.943146	154.342275
16	148.192845	148.595661	148.998867	149.402463	149.806447	150.210819	150.615576	151.020719
17	145.328500	145.737110	146.146117	146.555521	146.965320	147.375512	147.786097	148.197073
18	142.875944	143.290160	143.704778	144.119798	144.535216	144.951033	145.367246	145.783854
19	140.766208	141.185826	141.605848	142.026274	142.447101	142.868329	143.289955	143.711977
20	138.944114	139.368917	139.794125	140.219737	140.645751	141.072165	141.498977	141.926185
21	137.365013	137.794776	138.224944	138.655514	139.086484	139.517852	139.949617	140.381776
22	135.992406	136.426901	136.861798	137.297093	137.732785	138.168872	138.605352	139.042222
23	134.796191	135.235187	135.674579	136.114366	136.554544	136.995112	137.436068	137.877409
24	133.751340	134.194605	134.638261	135.082305	135.526734	135.971547	136.416740	136.862312
25	132.836896	133.284202	133.731891	134.179961	134.628408	135.077231	135.526426	135.975993
26	132.035199	132.486320	132.937816	133.389683	133.841919	134.294522	134.747490	135.200818
27	131.331282	131.785998	132.241078	132.696521	133.152323	133.608481	134.064994	134.521859
28	130.712397	131.170492	131.628942	132.087743	132.546893	133.006390	133.466229	133.926410
29	130.167635	130.628902	131.090512	131.552463	132.014751	132.477373	132.940329	133.403613
30	129.687626	130.151863	130.616432	131.081330	131.546553	132.012100	132.477967	132.944151
31	129.264288	129.731303	130.198638	130.666289	131.134253	131.602528	132.071112	132.540001
32	128.890632	129.360240	129.830155	130.300374	130.770894	131.241712	131.712826	132.184232
33	128.560596	129.032620	129.504939	129.977549	130.450447	130.923631	131.397097	131.870844
34	128.268904	128.743177	129.217732	129.692567	130.167673	130.643054	131.118706	131.594624
35	128.010960	128.487323	128.963954	129.440851	129.918010	130.395430	130.873106	131.351038
36	127.782749	128.261050	128.739607	129.218417	129.697477	130.176785	130.656336	131.136130
37	127.580756	128.060853	128.541194	129.021776	129.502594	129.983648	130.464934	130.946449
38	127.401900	127.883661	128.365652	128.847871	129.330315	129.812982	130.295868	130.778972
39	127.243479	127.726776	128.210292	128.694024	129.177968	129.662123	130.146486	130.631054
40	127.103114	127.587831	128.072754	128.557881	129.043209	129.528735	130.014458	130.500374
41	126.978717	127.464742	127.950962	128.437374	128.923976	129.410765	129.897739	130.384895
42	126.868443	127.355673	127.843088	128.330683	128.818457	129.306407	129.794531	130.282826
43	126.770669	127.259009	127.747522	128.236205	128.725056	129.214073	129.703253	130.192593
44	126.683963	127.173323	127.662845	128.152528	128.642368	129.132363	129.622511	130.112810
45	126.607058	127.097355	127.587805	128.078404	128.569151	129.060043	129.551079	130.042255
46	126.538838	127.029994	127.521294	128.012734	128.504312	128.996026	129.487874	129.979854
47	126.478312	126.970258	127.462336	127.954546	128.446885	128.939351	129.431943	129.924657
48	126.424609	126.917276	127.410068	127.902983	128.396018	128.889172	129.382442	129.875828
49	126.376953	126.870281	127.363726	127.857285	128.350956	128.844739	129.338630	129.832628
50	126.334659	126.828592	127.322634	127.816782	128.311035	128.805391	129.299848	129.794404

ANNUAL WITHDRAWALS PER $1000

NUMBER OF ANNUAL WTHDRWLS	EFFECTIVE ANNUAL YIELD							
	13.00%	13.05%	13.10%	13.15%	13.20%	13.25%	13.30%	13.35%
1	1130.000000	1130.500000	1131.000000	1131.500000	1132.000000	1132.500000	1133.000000	1133.500000
2	599.483568	599.873387	600.263257	600.653179	601.043152	601.433177	601.823254	602.213382
3	423.521970	423.881583	424.241287	424.601082	424.960968	425.320945	425.681014	426.041173
4	336.194197	336.543527	336.892983	337.242566	337.592276	337.942112	338.292075	338.642164
5	284.314543	284.661479	285.008575	285.355831	285.703247	286.050823	286.398558	286.746454
6	250.153232	250.501636	250.850231	251.199018	251.547996	251.897165	252.246525	252.596076
7	226.110804	226.462798	226.815013	227.167449	227.520105	227.872982	228.226078	228.579394
8	208.386720	208.743546	209.100620	209.457942	209.815512	210.173329	210.531392	210.889703
9	194.868902	195.231304	195.593979	195.956927	196.320147	196.683639	197.047403	197.411439
10	184.289556	184.657972	185.026685	185.395693	185.764995	186.134593	186.504484	186.874668
11	175.841455	176.216125	176.591112	176.966415	177.342033	177.717965	178.094211	178.470771
12	168.986085	169.367113	169.748476	170.130172	170.512201	170.894562	171.277254	171.660277
13	163.350341	163.737734	164.125477	164.513568	164.902007	165.290793	165.679926	166.069404
14	158.667496	159.061190	159.455246	159.849664	160.244442	160.639580	161.035077	161.430931
15	154.741780	155.141658	155.541910	155.942533	156.343527	156.744891	157.146623	157.548723
16	151.426244	151.832153	152.238442	152.645111	153.052158	153.459583	153.867384	154.275560
17	148.608439	149.020192	149.432332	149.844858	150.257768	150.671060	151.084734	151.498787
18	146.200855	146.618248	147.036031	147.454203	147.872762	148.291707	148.711036	149.130748
19	144.134394	144.557205	144.980407	145.404000	145.827980	146.252348	146.677100	147.102236
20	142.353788	142.781784	143.210172	143.638948	144.068112	144.497662	144.927595	145.357911
21	140.814328	141.247270	141.680601	142.114318	142.548421	142.982906	143.417772	143.853018
22	139.479481	139.917127	140.355157	140.793569	141.232362	141.671534	142.111081	142.551004
23	138.319133	138.761238	139.203722	139.646583	140.089818	140.533426	140.977404	141.421750
24	137.308261	137.754583	138.201277	138.648341	139.095773	139.543569	139.991728	140.440248
25	136.425928	136.876228	137.326893	137.777918	138.229303	138.681044	139.133139	139.585587
26	135.654506	136.108551	136.562950	137.017701	137.472801	137.928249	138.384041	138.840175
27	134.979073	135.436633	135.894538	136.352784	136.811369	137.270291	137.729547	138.189135
28	134.386929	134.847784	135.308972	135.770490	136.232337	136.694509	137.157005	137.619821
29	133.867225	134.331160	134.795418	135.259994	135.724887	136.190094	136.655612	137.121439
30	133.410650	133.877462	134.344583	134.812012	135.279744	135.747779	136.216112	136.684742
31	133.009192	133.478683	133.948472	134.418555	134.888930	135.359595	135.830546	136.301782
32	132.655929	133.127913	133.600182	134.072732	134.545562	135.018669	135.492050	135.965702
33	132.344868	132.819167	133.293738	133.768578	134.243684	134.719055	135.194687	135.670578
34	132.070808	132.547523	133.023957	133.500918	133.978133	134.455599	134.933313	135.411274
35	131.829221	132.307653	132.786332	133.265255	133.744419	134.223821	134.703460	135.183332
36	131.616163	132.096433	132.576936	133.057671	133.538635	134.019825	134.501238	134.982872
37	131.428190	131.910156	132.392344	132.874750	133.357373	133.840210	134.323258	134.806515
38	131.262290	131.745820	132.229560	132.713506	133.197657	133.682009	134.166562	134.651311
39	131.115824	131.600795	132.085963	132.571326	133.056882	133.542629	134.028563	134.514683
40	130.986481	131.472777	131.959259	132.445924	132.932771	133.419797	133.906999	134.394376
41	130.872231	131.359744	131.847432	132.335293	132.823324	133.311523	133.799888	134.288417
42	130.771290	131.259921	131.748716	132.237673	132.726790	133.216064	133.705494	134.195076
43	130.682092	131.171747	131.661557	132.151518	132.641628	133.131866	133.622290	134.112837
44	130.603257	131.093851	131.584589	132.075469	132.566488	133.057646	133.548939	134.040367
45	130.533571	131.025024	131.516611	132.008331	132.500181	132.992160	133.484266	133.976497
46	130.471964	130.964201	131.456565	131.949052	132.441661	132.934390	133.427237	133.920200
47	130.417493	130.910448	131.403520	131.896707	132.390008	132.883420	133.376942	133.870573
48	130.369326	130.862936	131.356654	131.850480	132.344411	132.638446	133.332583	133.826821
49	130.326731	130.820937	131.315244	131.809652	132.304158	132.798759	133.293456	133.788246
50	130.289059	130.783809	131.278653	131.773590	132.268618	132.763736	133.258941	133.754233

ANNUAL WITHDRAWALS PER $1000

NUMBER OF ANNUAL WTHDRWLS	EFFECTIVE ANNUAL YIELD							
	13.40%	13.45%	13.50%	13.55%	13.60%	13.65%	13.70%	13.75%
1	1134.000000	1134.500000	1135.000000	1135.500000	1136.000000	1136.500000	1137.000000	1137.500000
2	602.603561	602.993792	603.384075	603.774409	604.164794	604.555231	604.945718	605.336257
3	426.401423	426.761763	427.122195	427.482717	427.843329	428.204032	428.564826	428.925709
4	338.992380	339.342722	339.693190	340.043784	340.394504	340.745350	341.096321	341.447418
5	287.094508	287.442722	287.791095	288.139628	288.488319	288.837168	289.186176	289.535343
6	252.945817	253.295749	253.645870	253.996182	254.346683	254.697374	255.048253	255.399322
7	228.932930	229.286685	229.640658	229.994851	230.349261	230.703890	231.058737	231.413801
8	211.248259	211.607062	211.966110	212.325403	212.684942	213.044724	213.404751	213.765022
9	197.775744	198.140321	198.505167	198.870283	199.235667	199.601321	199.967243	200.333432
10	187.245146	187.615916	187.986978	188.358331	188.729976	189.101910	189.474135	189.846649
11	178.847643	179.224827	179.602322	179.980129	180.358245	180.736671	181.115406	181.494450
12	172.043629	172.427311	172.811321	173.195659	173.580324	173.965315	174.350631	174.736273
13	166.459226	166.849392	167.239901	167.630752	168.021944	168.413477	168.805349	169.197559
14	161.827142	162.223708	162.620630	163.017905	163.415533	163.813513	164.211844	164.610525
15	157.951189	158.354021	158.757216	159.160775	159.564696	159.968977	160.373619	160.778619
16	154.684110	155.093031	155.502324	155.911987	156.322019	156.732418	157.143184	157.554314
17	151.913219	152.328028	152.743213	153.158773	153.574706	153.991010	154.407685	154.824728
18	149.550841	149.971314	150.392165	150.813393	151.234996	151.656972	152.079322	152.502041
19	147.527754	147.953652	148.379928	148.806582	149.233611	149.661013	150.088788	150.516933
20	145.788607	146.219682	146.651134	147.082961	147.515161	147.947734	148.380676	148.813986
21	144.288641	144.724639	145.161010	145.597753	146.034866	146.472347	146.910194	147.348406
22	142.991298	143.431963	143.872997	144.314397	144.756162	145.198289	145.640776	146.083623
23	141.866463	142.311539	142.756977	143.202776	143.648932	144.095443	144.542309	144.989526
24	140.889127	141.338361	141.787950	142.237891	142.688181	143.138820	143.589803	144.041130
25	140.038384	140.491529	140.945018	141.398851	141.853024	142.307536	142.762384	143.217566
26	139.296650	139.753462	140.210609	140.668089	141.125900	141.584039	142.042504	142.501293
27	138.649052	139.109297	139.569865	140.030756	140.491967	140.953495	141.415338	141.877494
28	138.082955	138.546404	139.010167	139.474240	139.938622	140.403310	140.868301	141.333593
29	137.587572	138.054009	138.520747	138.987784	139.455118	139.922745	140.390664	140.858872
30	137.153667	137.622882	138.092387	138.562179	139.032254	139.502611	139.973248	140.444161
31	136.773299	137.245095	137.717167	138.189514	138.662132	139.135019	139.608173	140.081591
32	136.439623	136.913811	137.388263	137.862975	138.337947	138.813176	139.288658	139.764392
33	136.146725	136.623126	137.099778	137.576678	138.053825	138.531216	139.008848	139.486719
34	135.889479	136.367924	136.846608	137.325528	137.804682	138.284067	138.763681	139.243521
35	135.663435	136.143767	136.624325	137.105106	137.586109	138.067330	138.548768	139.030420
36	135.464726	135.946795	136.429078	136.911572	137.394276	137.877186	138.360300	138.843616
37	135.289979	135.773647	136.257516	136.741585	137.225851	137.710312	138.194965	138.679808
38	135.136255	135.621391	136.106718	136.592232	137.077931	137.563813	138.049877	138.536119
39	135.000986	135.487469	135.974132	136.460970	136.947983	137.435168	137.922523	138.410045
40	134.881925	135.369644	135.857530	136.345582	136.833797	137.322173	137.810708	138.299400
41	134.777107	135.265956	135.754963	136.244124	136.733438	137.222902	137.712516	138.202276
42	134.684810	135.174693	135.664723	136.154898	136.645215	137.135673	137.626270	138.117004
43	134.603525	135.094352	135.585316	136.076416	136.567649	137.059013	137.550506	138.042127
44	134.531926	135.023615	135.515431	136.007374	136.499441	136.991630	137.483940	137.976368
45	134.468850	134.961325	135.453918	135.946629	136.439456	136.932396	137.425448	137.918610
46	134.413277	134.906467	135.399748	135.893178	136.386695	136.880318	137.374045	137.867873
47	134.364309	134.858151	135.352095	135.846140	136.340285	136.834528	137.328867	137.823301
48	134.321157	134.815591	135.310119	135.804742	136.299457	136.794262	137.289157	137.784140
49	134.283127	134.778099	135.273158	135.768305	136.263537	136.758853	137.254251	137.749731
50	134.249609	134.745069	135.240610	135.736232	136.231933	136.727711	137.223566	137.719495

EFFECTIVE ANNUAL YIELD

NUMBER OF ANNUAL WTHDRWLS	13.80%	13.85%	13.90%	13.95%	14.00%	14.05%	14.10%	14.15%
1	1138.000000	1138.500000	1139.000000	1139.500000	1140.000000	1140.500000	1141.000000	1141.500000
2	605.726848	606.117489	606.508181	606.898925	607.289720	607.680565	608.071462	608.462410
3	429.286683	429.647747	430.008902	430.370146	430.731480	431.092905	431.454419	431.816023
4	341.798641	342.149989	342.501462	342.853060	343.204783	343.556632	343.908605	344.260703
5	289.884668	290.234151	290.583792	290.933590	291.283546	291.633660	291.983931	292.334360
6	255.750580	256.102026	256.453661	256.805484	257.157496	257.509695	257.862082	258.214656
7	231.769083	232.124581	232.480297	232.836229	233.192377	233.548742	233.905322	234.262117
8	214.125537	214.486295	214.847295	215.208538	215.570024	215.931751	216.293720	216.655930
9	200.699889	201.066613	201.433604	201.800861	202.168384	202.536172	202.904225	203.272542
10	190.219451	190.592542	190.965921	191.339588	191.713541	192.087780	192.462306	192.837116
11	181.873801	182.253459	182.633424	183.013695	183.394271	183.775152	184.156337	184.537826
12	175.122238	175.508527	175.895139	176.282072	176.669327	177.056902	177.444797	177.833011
13	169.590108	169.982993	170.376215	170.769772	171.163663	171.557889	171.952447	172.347336
14	165.009555	165.408933	165.808657	166.208729	166.609145	167.009905	167.411009	167.812455
15	161.183977	161.589691	161.995761	162.402185	162.808963	163.216093	163.623574	164.031405
16	157.965809	158.377665	158.789884	159.202462	159.615400	160.028695	160.442347	160.856355
17	155.242140	155.659918	156.078061	156.496567	156.915436	157.334666	157.754255	158.174203
18	152.925131	153.348588	153.772411	154.196600	154.621152	155.046065	155.471340	155.896973
19	150.945447	151.374328	151.803575	152.233186	152.663159	153.093494	153.524188	153.955239
20	149.247663	149.681705	150.116110	150.550876	150.986002	151.421485	151.857326	152.293520
21	147.786979	148.225913	148.665206	149.104856	149.544861	149.985219	150.425929	150.866989
22	146.526826	146.970383	147.414294	147.858555	148.303165	148.748123	149.193425	149.639071
23	145.437092	145.885006	146.333266	146.781869	147.230813	147.680097	148.129718	148.579675
24	144.492798	144.944806	145.397150	145.849829	146.302841	146.756183	147.209854	147.663852
25	143.673079	144.128922	144.585093	145.041589	145.498408	145.955548	146.413006	146.870782
26	142.960403	143.419832	143.879579	144.339640	144.800014	145.260698	145.721690	146.182988
27	142.339960	142.802735	143.265815	143.729199	144.192884	144.656868	145.121149	145.585724
28	141.799185	142.265072	142.731254	143.197727	143.664490	144.131541	144.598876	145.066494
29	141.327367	141.796146	142.265207	142.734548	143.204166	143.674059	144.144225	144.614661
30	140.915348	141.386808	141.858537	142.330533	142.802794	143.275318	143.748102	144.221144
31	140.555271	141.029211	141.503407	141.977858	142.452561	142.927515	143.402716	143.878162
32	140.240375	140.716605	141.193079	141.669795	142.146751	142.623945	143.101373	143.579035
33	139.964827	140.443169	140.921742	141.400545	141.879576	142.358831	142.838309	143.318007
34	139.723585	140.203871	140.684377	141.165099	141.646037	142.127186	142.608547	143.090115
35	139.512284	139.994357	140.476637	140.959122	141.441810	141.924698	142.407784	142.891067
36	139.327132	139.810846	140.294754	140.778856	141.263148	141.747629	142.232296	142.717147
37	139.164839	139.650056	140.135456	140.621037	141.106798	141.592736	142.078849	142.565134
38	139.022538	139.509130	139.995896	140.482831	140.969934	141.457203	141.944636	142.432231
39	138.897732	139.385583	139.873596	140.361767	140.850096	141.338580	141.827217	142.316005
40	138.788247	139.277246	139.766397	140.255696	140.745143	141.234734	141.724468	142.214343
41	138.692180	139.182228	139.672416	140.162743	140.653207	141.143806	141.634538	142.125402
42	138.607873	139.098875	139.590008	140.081270	140.572660	141.064176	141.555815	142.047577
43	138.533874	139.025744	139.517737	140.009850	140.502081	140.994430	141.486893	141.979470
44	138.468914	138.961574	139.454448	139.947233	140.440228	140.933332	141.426543	141.919858
45	138.411881	138.905258	139.398741	139.892328	140.386016	140.879805	141.373693	141.867678
46	138.361803	138.855832	139.349958	139.844180	140.338496	140.832905	141.327406	141.821997
47	138.317828	138.812447	139.307156	139.801953	140.296838	140.791809	141.286864	141.782003
48	138.279208	138.774362	139.269599	139.764917	140.260317	140.755795	141.251352	141.746985
49	138.245290	138.740927	139.236642	139.732432	140.228296	140.724233	141.220242	141.716322
50	138.215498	138.711573	139.207719	139.703935	140.200219	140.696571	141.192988	141.689471

EFFECTIVE ANNUAL YIELD

NUMBER OF ANNUAL WTHDRWLS	14.20%	14.25%	14.30%	14.35%	14.40%	14.45%	14.50%	14.55%
1	1142.000000	1142.500000	1143.000000	1143.500000	1144.000000	1144.500000	1145.000000	1145.500000
2	608.853408	609.244457	609.635558	610.026709	610.417910	610.809163	611.200466	611.591820
3	432.177716	432.539500	432.901373	433.263335	433.625387	433.987528	434.349759	434.712079
4	344.612925	344.965272	345.317744	345.670340	346.023060	346.375904	346.728872	347.081964
5	292.684945	293.035688	293.386587	293.737643	294.088855	294.440223	294.791748	295.143429
6	258.567417	258.920366	259.273501	259.626823	259.980332	260.334027	260.687908	261.041974
7	234.619128	234.976354	235.333795	235.691450	236.049319	236.407402	236.765699	237.124210
8	217.018381	217.381073	217.744005	218.107176	218.470588	218.834238	219.198128	219.562256
9	203.641124	204.009970	204.379078	204.748450	205.118084	205.487980	205.858138	206.228557
10	193.212212	193.587592	193.963255	194.339202	194.715432	195.091944	195.468738	195.845813
11	184.919618	185.301711	185.684107	186.066803	186.449801	186.833098	187.216694	187.600589
12	178.221544	178.610394	178.999561	179.389044	179.778843	180.168956	180.559384	180.950124
13	172.742558	173.138109	173.533990	173.930199	174.326737	174.723601	175.120792	175.518308
14	168.214242	168.616370	169.018837	169.421643	169.824786	170.228266	170.632081	171.036232
15	164.439585	164.848112	165.256987	165.666208	166.075773	166.485682	166.895933	167.306526
16	161.270716	161.685430	162.100497	162.515913	162.931679	163.347794	163.764255	164.181062
17	158.594508	159.015168	159.436183	159.857551	160.279271	160.701341	161.123760	161.546526
18	156.322964	156.749312	157.176014	157.603069	158.030476	158.458234	158.886340	159.314794
19	154.386647	154.818409	155.250525	155.682992	156.115809	156.548974	156.982487	157.416344
20	152.730068	153.166967	153.604215	154.041811	154.479754	154.918041	155.356671	155.795642
21	151.308396	151.750149	152.192247	152.634687	153.077469	153.520589	153.964046	154.407839
22	150.085059	150.531385	150.978050	151.425050	151.872384	152.320050	152.768047	153.216371
23	149.029966	149.480588	149.931539	150.382819	150.834424	151.286353	151.738603	152.191174
24	148.118174	148.572819	149.027784	149.483068	149.938668	150.394583	150.850810	151.307347
25	147.328872	147.787274	148.245987	148.705008	149.164335	149.623966	150.083899	150.544133
26	146.644590	147.106493	147.568696	148.031196	148.493991	148.957080	149.420459	149.884128
27	146.050592	146.515750	146.981196	147.446928	147.912943	148.379240	148.845816	149.312669
28	145.534392	146.002569	146.471021	146.939747	147.408745	147.878013	148.347547	148.817347
29	145.085365	145.556336	146.027570	146.499066	146.970820	147.442833	147.915100	148.387619
30	144.694441	145.167993	145.641795	146.115846	146.590145	147.064688	147.539473	148.014499
31	144.353852	144.829783	145.305952	145.782358	146.258998	146.735870	147.212972	147.690302
32	144.056927	144.535047	145.013394	145.491965	145.970757	146.449769	146.928999	147.408444
33	143.797923	144.278056	144.758402	145.238960	145.719727	146.200702	146.681882	147.163265
34	143.571889	144.053867	144.536046	145.018425	145.501002	145.983773	146.466738	146.949893
35	143.374543	143.858211	144.342069	144.826114	145.310345	145.794759	146.279355	146.764130
36	143.202181	143.687395	144.172787	144.658354	145.144096	145.630010	146.116093	146.602345
37	143.051591	143.538216	144.025008	144.511965	144.999085	145.486365	145.973805	146.461401
38	142.919986	143.407898	143.895967	144.384189	144.872564	145.361089	145.849762	146.338582
39	142.804943	143.294028	143.783259	144.272633	144.762149	145.251805	145.741600	146.231530
40	142.704357	143.194509	143.684797	144.175218	144.665771	145.156454	145.647266	146.138205
41	142.616395	143.107516	143.598763	144.090135	144.581629	145.073244	145.564979	146.056831
42	142.539459	143.031460	143.523578	144.015812	144.508159	145.000618	145.493188	145.985866
43	142.472158	142.964957	143.457864	143.950878	144.443997	144.937221	145.430546	145.923972
44	142.413278	142.906799	143.400420	143.894141	144.387959	144.881873	145.375881	145.869983
45	142.361758	142.855934	143.350201	143.844561	144.339010	144.833548	145.328173	145.822884
46	142.316676	142.811442	143.306294	143.801230	144.296250	144.791351	145.286532	145.781792
47	142.277223	142.772523	143.267902	143.763359	144.258892	144.754501	145.250184	145.745939
48	142.242693	142.738475	143.234330	143.730257	144.226253	144.722319	145.218453	145.714654
49	142.212470	142.708687	143.204971	143.701321	144.197735	144.694212	145.190752	145.687354
50	142.186017	142.682625	143.179295	143.676026	144.172815	144.669663	145.166568	145.663530

NUMBER OF ANNUAL WTHDRWLS	EFFECTIVE ANNUAL YIELD							
	14.60%	14.65%	14.70%	14.75%	14.80%	14.85%	14.90%	14.95%
1	1146.000000	1146.500000	1147.000000	1147.500000	1148.000000	1148.500000	1149.000000	1149.500000
2	611.983225	612.374680	612.766185	613.157742	613.549348	613.941005	614.332713	614.724471
3	435.074488	435.436986	435.799573	436.162249	436.525014	436.887868	437.250810	437.613842
4	347.435180	347.788519	348.141983	348.495569	348.849279	349.203113	349.557069	349.911149
5	295.495265	295.847258	296.199406	296.551709	296.904168	297.256782	297.609550	297.962474
6	261.396227	261.750665	262.105288	262.460096	262.815089	263.170267	263.525629	263.881176
7	237.482933	237.841870	238.201019	238.560380	238.919954	239.279739	239.639736	239.999944
8	219.926622	220.291226	220.656068	221.021147	221.386463	221.752016	222.117805	222.483829
9	206.599237	206.970177	207.341377	207.712837	208.084556	208.456534	208.828770	209.201264
10	196.223168	196.600805	196.978720	197.356916	197.735389	198.114142	198.493171	198.872479
11	187.984782	188.369272	188.754059	189.139143	189.524522	189.910196	190.296165	190.682427
12	181.341178	181.732543	182.124220	182.516207	182.908504	183.301110	183.694025	184.087247
13	175.916148	176.314313	176.712800	177.111609	177.510739	177.910190	178.309960	178.710049
14	171.440716	171.845532	172.250681	172.656161	173.061970	173.468109	173.874576	174.281370
15	167.717459	168.128732	168.540342	168.952291	169.364575	169.777194	170.190148	170.603434
16	164.598214	165.015709	165.433546	165.851725	166.270243	166.689100	167.108294	167.527825
17	161.969640	162.393098	162.816900	163.241045	163.665531	164.090357	164.515522	164.941024
18	159.743595	160.172740	160.602228	161.032058	161.462228	161.892738	162.323585	162.754769
19	157.850546	158.285089	158.719974	159.155197	159.590759	160.026656	160.462888	160.899454
20	156.234953	156.674602	157.114587	157.554907	157.995560	158.436544	158.877859	159.319501
21	154.851966	155.296425	155.741215	156.186332	156.631777	157.077547	157.523641	157.970056
22	153.665023	154.113999	154.563297	155.012917	155.462857	155.913114	156.363686	156.814573
23	152.644063	153.097267	153.550786	154.004618	154.458760	154.913210	155.367967	155.823029
24	151.764193	152.221345	152.678802	153.136564	153.594621	154.052980	154.511636	154.970586
25	151.004664	151.465491	151.926613	152.388026	152.849729	153.311720	153.773997	154.236559
26	150.348083	150.812323	151.276846	151.741649	152.206731	152.672090	153.137723	153.603629
27	149.779798	150.247199	150.714872	151.182813	151.651021	152.119494	152.588230	153.057226
28	149.287410	149.757734	150.228316	150.699156	151.170250	151.641596	152.113193	152.585039
29	148.860390	149.333409	149.806674	150.280184	150.753936	151.227929	151.702159	152.176626
30	148.489763	148.965263	149.440997	149.916963	150.393158	150.869582	151.346231	151.823104
31	148.167858	148.645637	149.123638	149.601858	150.080296	150.558949	151.037815	151.516893
32	147.888102	148.367972	148.848050	149.328336	149.808827	150.289521	150.770416	151.251510
33	147.644849	148.126632	148.608612	149.090787	149.573154	150.055713	150.538461	151.021396
34	147.433238	147.916770	148.400487	148.884387	149.368468	149.852729	150.337166	150.821779
35	147.249082	147.734210	148.219511	148.704984	149.190626	149.676436	150.162412	150.648552
36	147.088763	147.575345	148.062089	148.548993	149.036056	149.523276	150.010651	150.498178
37	146.949153	147.437058	147.925114	148.413320	148.901674	149.390174	149.878819	150.367605
38	146.827546	147.316653	147.805901	148.295289	148.784814	149.274475	149.764271	150.254198
39	146.721596	147.211794	147.702123	148.192582	148.683169	149.173882	149.664719	150.155680
40	146.629268	147.120456	147.611764	148.103194	148.594741	149.086406	149.578185	150.070079
41	146.548799	147.040881	147.533076	148.025383	148.517799	149.010323	149.502954	149.995691
42	146.478653	146.971545	147.464541	147.957640	148.450841	148.944142	149.437541	149.931037
43	146.417498	146.911121	147.404841	147.898656	148.392564	148.886565	149.380656	149.874837
44	146.364176	146.858660	147.352832	147.847292	148.341838	148.836469	149.331184	149.825981
45	146.317679	146.812558	147.307518	147.802559	148.297680	148.792878	149.288154	149.783505
46	146.277130	146.772545	147.268035	147.763599	148.259236	148.754944	149.250724	149.746572
47	146.241766	146.737663	147.233629	147.729663	148.225764	148.721931	149.218163	149.714458
48	146.210920	146.707251	147.203645	147.700102	148.196620	148.693198	149.189836	149.686531
49	146.184015	146.680736	147.177515	147.674350	148.171242	148.668190	149.165191	149.662245
50	146.160546	146.657616	147.154740	147.651916	148.149144	148.646421	149.143749	149.641124

EFFECTIVE ANNUAL YIELD

NUMBER OF ANNUAL WTHDRWLS	15.00%	15.05%	15.10%	15.15%	15.20%	15.25%	15.30%	15.35%
1	1150.000000	1150.500000	1151.000000	1151.500000	1152.000000	1152.500000	1153.000000	1153.500000
2	615.116279	615.508138	615.900046	616.292006	616.684015	617.076074	617.468184	617.860344
3	437.976962	438.340170	438.703467	439.066853	439.430327	439.793889	440.157540	440.521278
4	350.265352	350.619677	350.974125	351.328696	351.683390	352.038206	352.393144	352.748204
5	298.315552	298.668785	299.022173	299.375714	299.729410	300.083260	300.437263	300.791420
6	264.236907	264.592821	264.948919	265.305201	265.661666	266.018314	266.375145	266.732159
7	240.360364	240.720994	241.081835	241.442886	241.804147	242.165618	242.527298	242.889188
8	222.850090	223.216585	223.583316	223.950281	224.317480	224.684913	225.052580	225.420481
9	209.574015	209.947024	210.320289	210.693810	211.067588	211.441621	211.815908	212.190451
10	199.252063	199.631923	200.012059	200.392470	200.773155	201.154116	201.535349	201.916856
11	191.068983	191.455831	191.842972	192.230403	192.618126	193.006139	193.394441	193.783033
12	184.480776	184.874611	185.268752	185.663198	186.057948	186.453001	186.848357	187.244015
13	179.110457	179.511181	179.912221	180.313577	180.715248	181.117232	181.519530	181.922140
14	174.688490	175.095935	175.503705	175.911799	176.320214	176.728952	177.138010	177.547388
15	171.017053	171.431002	171.845281	172.259889	172.674825	173.090087	173.505675	173.921588
16	167.947691	168.367891	168.788424	169.209289	169.630484	170.052009	170.473861	170.896041
17	165.366862	165.793035	166.219542	166.646381	167.073550	167.501050	167.928878	168.357033
18	163.186287	163.618139	164.050323	164.482838	164.915682	165.348853	165.782352	166.216175
19	161.336350	161.773577	162.211133	162.649016	163.087224	163.525757	163.964613	164.403789
20	159.761470	160.203765	160.646382	161.089322	161.532582	161.976161	162.420057	162.864268
21	158.416791	158.863845	159.311216	159.758901	160.206900	160.655211	161.103832	161.552761
22	157.265771	157.717280	158.169098	158.621223	159.073652	159.526386	159.979420	160.432755
23	156.278395	156.734061	157.190027	157.646291	158.102850	158.559703	159.016848	159.474284
24	155.429830	155.889364	156.349188	156.809299	157.269696	157.730376	158.191338	158.652580
25	154.699402	155.162526	155.625928	156.089606	156.553559	157.017784	157.482280	157.947045
26	154.069806	154.536251	155.002963	155.469940	155.937180	156.404680	156.872440	157.340456
27	153.526481	153.995993	154.465760	154.935779	155.406050	155.876569	156.347335	156.818346
28	153.057131	153.529468	154.002047	154.474866	154.947924	155.421219	155.894749	156.368511
29	152.651326	153.126259	153.601422	154.076813	154.552431	155.028272	155.504336	155.980620
30	152.300198	152.777512	153.255044	153.732792	154.210753	154.688927	155.167310	155.645901
31	151.996180	152.475674	152.955373	153.435276	153.915381	154.395685	154.876187	155.356885
32	151.732801	152.214287	152.695966	153.177837	153.659897	154.142145	154.624578	155.107196
33	151.504516	151.987819	152.471304	152.954968	153.438010	153.922827	154.407019	154.891382
34	151.306566	151.791524	152.276651	152.761947	153.247409	153.733035	154.218824	154.704773
35	151.134855	151.621317	152.107938	152.594716	153.081649	153.568735	154.055973	154.543361
36	150.985857	151.473686	151.961662	152.449784	152.938051	153.426460	153.915010	154.403700
37	150.856533	151.345600	151.834804	152.324144	152.813618	153.303224	153.792961	154.282828
38	150.744257	151.234445	151.724760	152.215201	152.705767	153.196455	153.687265	154.178194
39	150.646761	151.137963	151.629282	152.120718	152.612270	153.103935	153.595712	154.087599
40	150.562085	151.054202	151.546428	152.038762	152.531202	153.023747	153.516396	154.009146
41	150.488531	150.981473	151.474516	151.967659	152.460900	152.954238	153.447671	153.941198
42	150.424629	150.918315	151.412095	151.905966	152.399927	152.893977	153.388115	153.882340
43	150.369106	150.863462	151.357904	151.852429	152.347038	152.841729	153.336500	153.831351
44	150.320859	150.815817	151.310854	151.805968	152.301158	152.796423	153.291762	153.787174
45	150.278930	150.774429	151.270000	151.765642	152.261353	152.757134	153.252982	153.748897
46	150.242489	150.738473	151.234523	151.730639	152.226818	152.723060	153.219364	153.715729
47	150.210816	150.707235	151.203715	151.700254	152.196852	152.693507	153.190219	153.686986
48	150.183284	150.680093	151.176958	151.673877	152.170849	152.667874	153.164950	153.662077
49	150.159352	150.656510	151.153719	151.650977	152.148284	152.645639	153.143041	153.640489
50	150.138548	150.636018	151.133535	151.631097	152.128703	152.626352	153.124045	153.621779

EFFECTIVE ANNUAL YIELD

NUMBER OF ANNUAL WTHDRWLS	15.40%	15.45%	15.50%	15.55%	15.60%	15.65%	15.70%	15.75%
1	1154.000000	1154.500000	1155.000000	1155.500000	1156.000000	1156.500000	1157.000000	1157.500000
2	618.252553	618.644813	619.037123	619.429483	619.821892	620.214352	620.606861	620.999421
3	440.885105	441.249020	441.613022	441.977113	442.341291	442.705558	443.069911	443.434353
4	353.103387	353.458692	353.814119	354.169667	354.525337	354.881129	355.237043	355.593077
5	301.145731	301.500195	301.854812	302.209583	302.564506	302.919582	303.274811	303.630193
6	267.089355	267.446733	267.804294	268.162036	268.519960	268.878066	269.236353	269.594821
7	243.251286	243.613594	243.976109	244.338834	244.701766	245.064905	245.428252	245.791807
8	225.788614	226.156979	226.525577	226.894407	227.263469	227.632762	228.002286	228.372040
9	212.565248	212.940298	213.315602	213.691159	214.066968	214.443030	214.819343	215.195908
10	202.298636	202.680688	203.063012	203.445607	203.828472	204.211608	204.595014	204.978688
11	194.171913	194.561081	194.950536	195.340277	195.730305	196.120618	196.511216	196.902098
12	187.639975	188.036235	188.432794	188.829653	189.226811	189.624266	190.022019	190.420068
13	182.325061	182.728293	183.131834	183.535685	183.939844	184.344310	184.749082	185.154161
14	177.957084	178.367099	178.777430	179.188077	179.599040	180.010317	180.421906	180.833809
15	174.337824	174.754383	175.171263	175.588464	176.005984	176.423823	176.841979	177.260451
16	171.318546	171.741377	172.164531	172.588007	173.011805	173.435923	173.860359	174.285114
17	168.785514	169.214319	169.643448	170.072899	170.502671	170.932763	171.363173	171.793900
18	166.650323	167.084792	167.519583	167.954694	168.390122	168.825868	169.261930	169.698306
19	164.843286	165.283100	165.723222	166.163679	166.604440	167.045513	167.486897	167.928591
20	163.308793	163.753631	164.198780	164.644238	165.090004	165.536077	165.982454	166.429134
21	162.001997	162.451538	162.901383	163.351529	163.801976	164.252722	164.703764	165.155102
22	160.886388	161.340318	161.794542	162.249060	162.703869	163.158968	163.614355	164.070029
23	159.932009	160.390020	160.848317	161.306897	161.765758	162.224899	162.684319	163.144015
24	159.114100	159.575897	160.037968	160.500312	160.962926	161.425810	161.888962	162.352378
25	158.412077	158.877374	159.342934	159.808755	160.274836	160.741175	161.207770	161.674619
26	157.808728	158.277254	158.746030	159.215057	159.684331	160.153851	160.623615	161.093622
27	157.289601	157.761096	158.232831	158.704804	159.177012	159.649454	160.122128	160.595032
28	156.842504	157.316726	157.791176	158.265850	158.740748	159.215867	159.691206	160.166763
29	156.457123	156.933842	157.410776	157.887923	158.365281	158.842848	159.320623	159.798603
30	156.124699	156.603700	157.082905	157.562310	158.041913	158.521714	159.001709	159.481898
31	155.837776	156.318860	156.800134	157.281597	157.763246	158.245081	158.727098	159.209297
32	155.589995	156.072975	156.556133	157.039467	157.522977	158.006659	158.490513	158.974537
33	155.375916	155.860619	156.345488	156.830523	157.315720	157.801080	158.286599	158.772277
34	155.190882	155.677148	156.163569	156.650145	157.136872	157.623751	158.110778	158.597953
35	155.030896	155.518578	156.006405	156.494376	156.982487	157.470739	157.959129	158.447656
36	154.892527	155.381490	155.870588	156.359819	156.849181	157.338673	157.828293	158.318040
37	154.772823	155.262943	155.753188	156.243556	156.734046	157.224656	157.715385	158.206231
38	154.669242	155.160406	155.651686	156.143079	156.634585	157.126202	157.617928	158.109762
39	154.579596	155.071701	155.563912	156.056228	156.548648	157.041170	157.533793	158.026515
40	154.501998	154.994949	155.487997	155.981143	156.474384	156.967719	157.461147	157.954666
41	154.434818	154.928529	155.422330	155.916220	156.410198	156.904263	157.398412	157.892646
42	154.376650	154.871044	155.365520	155.860078	156.354717	156.849435	157.344231	157.839104
43	154.326280	154.821286	155.316368	155.811524	156.306754	156.802057	157.297432	157.792876
44	154.282658	154.778212	155.273836	155.769529	156.265288	156.761114	157.257005	157.752961
45	154.244878	154.740923	155.237031	155.733203	156.229435	156.725729	157.222082	157.718493
46	154.212154	154.708638	155.205180	155.701779	156.198434	156.695144	157.191909	157.688727
47	154.183809	154.680685	155.177613	155.674594	156.171626	156.668709	157.165840	157.663021
48	154.159254	154.656480	155.153754	155.651076	156.148444	156.645857	157.143316	157.640819
49	154.137983	154.635521	155.133103	155.630728	156.128395	156.626104	157.123853	157.621643
50	154.119555	154.617371	155.115227	155.613122	156.111056	156.609027	157.107035	157.605080

ANNUAL WITHDRAWALS PER $1000

EFFECTIVE ANNUAL YIELD

NUMBER OF ANNUAL WTHDRWLS	15.80%	15.85%	15.90%	15.95%	16.00%	16.05%	16.10%	16.15%
1	1158.000000	1158.500000	1159.000000	1159.500000	1160.000000	1160.500000	1161.000000	1161.500000
2	621.392030	621.784688	622.177397	622.570155	622.962963	623.355820	623.748727	624.141684
3	443.798882	444.163499	444.528203	444.892994	445.257873	445.622839	445.987892	446.353033
4	355.949234	356.305511	356.661909	357.018429	357.375069	357.731831	358.088713	358.445715
5	303.985726	304.341412	304.697250	305.053240	305.409382	305.765675	306.122120	306.478716
6	269.953469	270.312299	270.671309	271.030500	271.389870	271.749421	272.109151	272.469061
7	246.155568	246.519536	246.883710	247.248091	247.612677	247.977469	248.342467	248.707669
8	228.742025	229.112239	229.482684	229.853357	230.224260	230.595391	230.966751	231.338339
9	215.572723	215.949790	216.327106	216.704672	217.082487	217.460551	217.838863	218.217424
10	205.362632	205.746844	206.131323	206.516070	206.901083	207.286363	207.671908	208.057719
11	197.293264	197.684713	198.076444	198.468457	198.860751	199.253327	199.646182	200.039316
12	190.818412	191.217052	191.615986	192.015213	192.414733	192.814546	193.214650	193.615045
13	185.559544	185.965231	186.371222	186.777515	187.184110	187.591006	187.998202	188.405697
14	181.246022	181.658547	182.071380	182.484523	182.897973	183.311730	183.725793	184.140162
15	177.679239	178.098341	178.517756	178.937483	179.357522	179.777871	180.198529	180.619495
16	174.710186	175.135573	175.561274	175.987289	176.413616	176.840254	177.267203	177.694460
17	172.224943	172.656301	173.087972	173.519955	173.952249	174.384853	174.817766	175.250986
18	170.134994	170.571995	171.009306	171.446925	171.884853	172.323086	172.761625	173.200467
19	168.370594	168.812903	169.255517	169.698435	170.141656	170.585177	171.028999	171.473118
20	166.876117	167.323399	167.770980	168.218858	168.667032	169.115501	169.564262	170.013314
21	165.606734	166.058659	166.510873	166.963378	167.416169	167.869247	168.322609	168.776254
22	164.525987	164.982228	165.438715	165.895554	166.352635	166.809993	167.267626	167.725532
23	163.603986	164.064229	164.524744	164.985529	165.446582	165.907901	166.369485	166.831332
24	162.816059	163.280002	163.744205	164.208667	164.673386	165.138360	165.603588	166.069068
25	162.141721	162.609073	163.076674	163.544522	164.012615	164.480952	164.949532	165.418351
26	161.563869	162.034355	162.505077	162.976035	163.447227	163.918650	164.390303	164.862184
27	161.068164	161.541523	162.015107	162.488914	162.962942	163.437190	163.911655	164.386336
28	160.642536	161.118523	161.594723	162.071133	162.547753	163.024579	163.501612	163.978848
29	160.276787	160.755173	161.233759	161.712544	162.191525	162.670702	163.150071	163.629633
30	159.962279	160.442850	160.923608	161.404554	161.885683	162.366996	162.848490	163.330164
31	159.691675	160.174231	160.656964	161.139871	161.622951	162.106202	162.589623	163.073211
32	159.458728	159.943086	160.427609	160.912294	161.397141	161.882147	162.367312	162.852633
33	159.258111	159.744101	160.230244	160.716538	161.202983	161.689576	162.176316	162.663202
34	159.085273	159.572737	160.060344	160.548092	161.035980	161.524005	162.012167	162.500464
35	158.936318	159.425114	159.914042	160.403101	160.892289	161.381605	161.871047	162.360614
36	158.807912	159.297908	159.788026	160.278265	160.768624	161.259100	161.749693	162.240402
37	158.697192	159.188268	159.679457	160.170757	160.662168	161.153687	161.645314	162.137047
38	158.601704	159.093750	159.585901	160.078154	160.570509	161.062963	161.555517	162.048168
39	158.519336	159.012254	159.505267	159.998375	160.491576	160.984869	161.478253	161.971726
40	158.448276	158.941974	159.435761	159.929634	160.423593	160.917636	161.411762	161.905970
41	158.386642	158.881560	159.375389	159.870397	160.365033	160.859746	161.354536	161.849400
42	158.334053	158.829076	159.324173	159.819343	160.314585	160.809897	161.305278	161.800728
43	158.288391	158.783973	159.279623	159.775339	160.271120	160.766966	161.262875	161.758846
44	158.248980	158.745061	159.241204	159.737407	160.233670	160.729991	161.226370	161.722805
45	158.214962	158.711488	159.208070	159.704708	160.201399	160.698143	161.194940	161.691789
46	158.185598	158.682520	159.179494	159.676517	160.173589	160.670710	161.167879	161.665094
47	158.160249	158.657524	159.154845	159.652212	160.149624	160.647079	161.144578	161.642119
48	158.138365	158.635954	159.133585	159.631257	160.128969	160.626722	161.124513	161.622343
49	158.119472	158.617340	159.115245	159.613188	160.111168	160.609184	161.107235	161.605321
50	158.103160	158.601276	159.099425	159.597609	160.095825	160.594075	161.092356	161.590668

ANNUAL WITHDRAWALS PER $1000

NUMBER OF ANNUAL WTHDRWLS	EFFECTIVE ANNUAL YIELD							
	16.20%	16.25%	16.30%	16.35%	16.40%	16.45%	16.50%	16.55%
1	1162.000000	1162.500000	1163.000000	1163.500000	1164.000000	1164.500000	1165.000000	1165.500000
2	624.534690	624.927746	625.320851	625.714005	626.107209	626.500462	626.893764	627.287116
3	446.718260	447.083574	447.448975	447.814463	448.180038	448.545700	448.911448	449.277283
4	358.802838	359.160082	359.517446	359.874930	360.232534	360.590258	360.948102	361.306066
5	306.835463	307.192361	307.549411	307.906611	308.263961	308.621463	308.979114	309.336916
6	272.829150	273.189418	273.549865	273.910491	274.271295	274.632278	274.993439	275.354778
7	249.073076	249.438688	249.804504	250.170525	250.536749	250.903177	251.269808	251.636642
8	231.710154	232.082196	232.454466	232.826962	233.199685	233.572633	233.945808	234.319207
9	218.596232	218.975288	219.354590	219.734139	220.113933	220.493974	220.874259	221.254789
10	208.443794	208.830133	209.216737	209.603603	209.990732	210.378124	210.765777	211.153692
11	200.432730	200.826422	201.220391	201.614638	202.009161	202.403960	202.799034	203.194383
12	194.015730	194.416704	194.817967	195.219518	195.621357	196.023482	196.425893	196.828590
13	188.813491	189.221582	189.629971	190.038655	190.447635	190.856909	191.266477	191.676338
14	184.554834	184.969809	185.385087	185.800666	186.216546	186.632726	187.049204	187.465980
15	181.040768	181.462348	181.884232	182.306421	182.728913	183.151707	183.574802	183.998197
16	178.122024	178.549896	178.978073	179.406554	179.835339	180.264425	180.693813	181.123501
17	175.684511	176.118342	176.552477	176.986913	177.421651	177.856689	178.292026	178.727661
18	173.639612	174.079058	174.518803	174.958847	175.399188	175.839826	176.280757	176.721982
19	171.917535	172.362247	172.807253	173.252552	173.698142	174.144022	174.590191	175.036647
20	170.462656	170.912286	171.362204	171.812406	172.262893	172.713662	173.164712	173.616042
21	169.230180	169.684387	170.138871	170.593632	171.048669	171.503979	171.959562	172.415415
22	168.183710	168.642158	169.100875	169.559859	170.019108	170.478622	170.938398	171.398434
23	167.293440	167.755807	168.218433	168.681316	169.144453	169.607844	170.071486	170.535378
24	166.534798	167.000776	167.467001	167.933472	168.400186	168.867142	169.334339	169.801774
25	165.887409	166.356704	166.826234	167.295997	167.765992	168.236218	168.706672	169.177353
26	165.334292	165.806624	166.279180	166.751958	167.224955	167.698170	168.171601	168.645248
27	164.861232	165.336340	165.811660	166.287188	166.762925	167.238867	167.715013	168.191362
28	164.456286	164.933924	165.411762	165.889796	166.368024	166.846449	167.325065	167.803871
29	164.109384	164.589324	165.069450	165.549761	166.030256	166.510932	166.991789	167.472824
30	163.812016	164.294044	164.776246	165.258622	165.741169	166.223886	166.706772	167.189824
31	163.556966	164.040885	164.524968	165.009212	165.493616	165.978178	166.462897	166.947771
32	163.338109	163.823738	164.309519	164.795450	165.281531	165.767758	166.254131	166.740648
33	163.150232	163.637404	164.124717	164.612170	165.099760	165.587487	166.075350	166.563345
34	162.988894	163.477456	163.966149	164.454970	164.943920	165.432995	165.922196	166.411519
35	162.850304	163.340116	163.830049	164.320101	164.810270	165.300557	165.790958	166.281473
36	162.731224	163.222158	163.713204	164.204360	164.695624	165.186996	165.678473	166.170055
37	162.628885	163.120826	163.612870	164.105014	164.597258	165.089601	165.582042	166.074578
38	162.540916	163.033759	163.526695	164.019725	164.512846	165.006057	165.499357	165.992745
39	162.465288	162.958937	163.452671	163.946491	164.440395	164.934381	165.428449	165.922597
40	162.400259	162.894628	163.389076	163.883601	164.378203	164.872880	165.367632	165.862457
41	162.344339	162.839550	163.334433	163.829587	164.324811	164.820104	165.315465	165.810892
42	162.296245	162.791829	163.287478	163.783192	164.278970	164.774810	165.270712	165.766675
43	162.254879	162.750973	163.247126	163.743337	164.239607	164.735934	165.232317	165.728755
44	162.219297	162.715844	163.212445	163.709099	164.205806	164.702564	165.199374	165.696233
45	162.188688	162.685638	163.182636	163.679683	164.176778	164.673919	165.171107	165.668340
46	162.162356	162.659663	163.157014	163.654409	164.151848	164.649329	165.146851	165.644415
47	162.139702	162.637325	163.134990	163.632694	164.130436	164.628218	165.126037	165.623893
48	162.120211	162.618115	163.116057	163.614034	164.112046	164.610093	165.108174	165.606289
49	162.103441	162.601594	163.099781	163.598000	164.096250	164.594532	165.092845	165.591188
50	162.089012	162.587385	163.085789	163.584221	164.082683	164.581172	165.079689	165.578233

256

ANNUAL WITHDRAWALS PER $1000

NUMBER OF ANNUAL WTHDRWLS	EFFECTIVE ANNUAL YIELD							
	16.60%	16.65%	16.70%	16.75%	16.80%	16.85%	16.90%	16.95%
1	1166.000000	1166.500000	1167.000000	1167.500000	1168.000000	1168.500000	1169.000000	1169.500000
2	627.680517	628.073967	628.467467	628.861015	629.254613	629.648259	630.041955	630.435699
3	449.643204	450.009212	450.375306	450.741486	451.107753	451.474106	451.840545	452.207070
4	361.664149	362.022352	362.380675	362.739117	363.097678	363.456358	363.815158	364.174076
5	309.694867	310.052969	310.411220	310.769621	311.128171	311.486871	311.845720	312.204718
6	275.716294	276.077988	276.439860	276.801908	277.164134	277.526536	277.889115	278.251871
7	252.003679	252.370918	252.738360	253.106003	253.473849	253.841896	254.210144	254.578593
8	234.692832	235.066682	235.440755	235.815053	236.189575	236.564320	236.939288	237.314478
9	221.635564	222.016583	222.397845	222.779350	223.161098	223.543089	223.925321	224.307795
10	211.541867	211.930302	212.318998	212.707952	213.097165	213.486637	213.876366	214.266353
11	203.590007	203.985903	204.382073	204.778515	205.175229	205.572215	205.969470	206.366996
12	197.231571	197.634836	198.038384	198.442215	198.846327	199.250721	199.655395	200.060349
13	192.086491	192.496936	192.907671	193.318696	193.730009	194.141611	194.553501	194.965677
14	187.883052	188.300421	188.718085	189.136044	189.554295	189.972840	190.391675	190.810802
15	184.421891	184.845884	185.270173	185.694759	186.119640	186.544815	186.970283	187.396043
16	181.553488	181.983772	182.414353	182.845230	183.276402	183.707866	184.139623	184.571672
17	179.163592	179.599818	180.036338	180.473151	180.910256	181.347652	181.785336	182.223309
18	177.163499	177.605307	178.047404	178.489789	178.932462	179.375420	179.818662	180.262188
19	175.483389	175.930415	176.377725	176.825316	177.273187	177.721338	178.169767	178.618472
20	174.067650	174.519535	174.971695	175.424129	175.876836	176.329813	176.783061	177.236577
21	172.871538	173.327928	173.784585	174.241506	174.698691	175.156138	175.613845	176.071811
22	171.858730	172.319284	172.780094	173.241158	173.702476	174.164046	174.625865	175.087934
23	170.999519	171.463907	171.928540	172.393417	172.858536	173.323896	173.789495	174.255332
24	170.269446	170.737354	171.205495	171.673869	172.142474	172.611308	173.080370	173.549658
25	169.648259	170.119389	170.590741	171.062313	171.534105	172.006113	172.478338	172.950777
26	169.119108	169.593179	170.067460	170.541950	171.016647	171.491549	171.966654	172.441962
27	168.667913	169.144662	169.621610	170.098754	170.576092	171.053624	171.531347	172.009260
28	168.282866	168.762049	169.241417	169.720970	170.200705	170.680621	171.160716	171.640990
29	167.954036	168.435423	168.916984	169.398717	169.880622	170.362695	170.844936	171.327343
30	167.673042	168.156423	168.639966	169.123670	169.607533	170.091554	170.575730	171.060062
31	167.432800	167.917980	168.403312	168.888792	169.374421	169.860196	170.346116	170.832179
32	167.227308	167.714109	168.201051	168.688130	169.175347	169.662699	170.150186	170.637805
33	167.051473	167.539732	168.028120	168.516636	169.005279	169.494047	169.982939	170.471953
34	166.900965	167.390532	167.880218	168.370023	168.859944	169.349980	169.840131	170.330394
35	166.772101	167.262840	167.753689	168.244646	168.735711	169.226883	169.718159	170.209539
36	166.661741	167.153529	167.645418	168.137406	168.629493	169.121678	169.613959	170.106335
37	166.567209	167.059934	167.552751	168.045660	168.538660	169.031748	169.524924	170.018188
38	166.486221	166.979782	167.473427	167.967157	168.460969	168.954862	169.448835	169.942888
39	166.416825	166.911131	167.405514	167.899974	168.394509	168.889118	169.383801	169.878556
40	166.357355	166.852324	167.347364	167.842473	168.337651	168.832896	169.328208	169.823585
41	166.306386	166.801944	167.297567	167.793253	168.289001	168.784810	169.280681	169.776610
42	166.262697	166.758779	167.254919	167.751117	168.247371	168.743681	169.240046	169.736464
43	166.225247	166.721793	167.218392	167.715043	168.211745	168.708498	169.205300	169.702152
44	166.193142	166.690100	167.187105	167.684157	168.181256	168.678400	169.175590	169.672823
45	166.165618	166.662939	167.160304	167.657712	168.155161	168.652651	169.150183	169.647754
46	166.142019	166.639663	167.137345	167.635067	168.132826	168.630622	169.128454	169.626323
47	166.121785	166.619714	167.117677	167.615675	168.113708	168.611773	169.109872	169.608003
48	166.104436	166.602616	167.100827	167.599070	168.097343	168.595646	169.093979	169.592341
49	166.089560	166.587961	167.086391	167.584849	168.083335	168.581847	169.080386	169.578952
50	166.076804	166.575400	167.074023	167.572671	168.071343	168.570040	169.068760	169.567504

257

NUMBER OF ANNUAL WTHDRWLS	EFFECTIVE ANNUAL YIELD							
	17.00%	17.05%	17.10%	17.15%	17.20%	17.25%	17.30%	17.35%
1	1170.000000	1170.500000	1171.000000	1171.500000	1172.000000	1172.500000	1173.000000	1173.500000
2	630.829493	631.223336	631.617227	632.011167	632.405157	632.799194	633.193281	633.587417
3	452.573681	452.940378	453.307161	453.674030	454.040984	454.408024	454.775150	455.142361
4	364.533114	364.892270	365.251545	365.610938	365.970450	366.330080	366.689829	367.049695
5	312.563864	312.923160	313.282604	313.642196	314.001937	314.361826	314.721863	315.082048
6	278.614802	278.977910	279.341193	279.704652	280.068286	280.432095	280.796080	281.160239
7	254.947243	255.316093	255.685144	256.054394	256.423845	256.793494	257.163343	257.533391
8	237.689892	238.065527	238.441384	238.817462	239.193762	239.570282	239.947023	240.323984
9	224.690510	225.073466	225.456662	225.840098	226.223773	226.607688	226.991841	227.376233
10	214.656597	215.047097	215.437852	215.828863	216.220129	216.611649	217.003423	217.395451
11	206.764792	207.162856	207.561188	207.959788	208.358656	208.757790	209.157189	209.556855
12	200.465582	200.871093	201.276883	201.682949	202.089291	202.495910	202.902803	203.309971
13	195.378139	195.790886	196.203917	196.617232	197.030829	197.444708	197.858869	198.273310
14	191.230218	191.649923	192.069917	192.490197	192.910764	193.331616	193.752753	194.174173
15	187.822095	188.248437	188.675068	189.101987	189.529194	189.956687	190.384465	190.812527
16	185.004010	185.436638	185.869554	186.302756	186.736245	187.170018	187.604076	188.038416
17	182.661569	183.100115	183.538946	183.978060	184.417456	184.857134	185.297091	185.737328
18	180.705995	181.150084	181.594451	182.039097	182.484020	182.929218	183.374691	183.820437
19	179.067452	179.516706	179.966233	180.416031	180.866098	181.316435	181.767038	182.217908
20	177.690359	178.144408	178.598720	179.053295	179.508132	179.963229	180.418584	180.874197
21	176.530035	176.988515	177.447249	177.906237	178.365477	178.824967	179.284706	179.744693
22	175.550249	176.012811	176.475616	176.938665	177.401955	177.865485	178.329253	178.793258
23	174.721405	175.187713	175.654254	176.121027	176.588029	177.055261	177.522720	177.990404
24	174.019170	174.488906	174.958863	175.429040	175.899436	176.370048	176.840877	177.311919
25	173.423428	173.896291	174.369363	174.842643	175.316130	175.789822	176.263718	176.737816
26	172.917470	173.393178	173.869083	174.345184	174.821479	175.297968	175.774648	176.251518
27	172.487362	172.965651	173.444125	173.922783	174.401624	174.880646	175.359847	175.839226
28	172.121440	172.602066	173.082864	173.563835	174.044977	174.526287	175.007765	175.489410
29	171.809915	172.292651	172.775548	173.258605	173.741821	174.225195	174.708725	175.192410
30	171.544547	172.029183	172.513971	172.998907	173.483990	173.969220	174.454595	174.940113
31	171.318385	171.804732	172.291217	172.777841	173.264602	173.751498	174.238528	174.725691
32	171.125556	171.613438	172.101448	172.589585	173.077848	173.566238	174.054750	174.543385
33	170.961090	171.450346	171.939720	172.429213	172.918821	173.408545	173.898382	174.388332
34	170.820770	171.311256	171.801851	172.292553	172.783363	173.274278	173.765298	174.256421
35	170.701021	171.192605	171.684288	172.176071	172.667952	173.159930	173.652003	174.144170
36	170.598804	171.091367	171.584021	172.076766	172.569600	173.062523	173.555533	174.048630
37	170.511537	171.004971	171.498489	171.992089	172.485771	172.979534	173.473376	173.967297
38	170.437020	170.931229	171.425514	171.919874	172.414309	172.908817	173.403397	173.898050
39	170.373382	170.868278	171.363244	171.858279	172.353381	172.848550	173.343784	173.839084
40	170.319028	170.814534	171.310104	171.805736	172.301429	172.797182	173.292995	173.788867
41	170.272599	170.768646	171.264750	171.760910	172.257125	172.753396	173.249720	173.746098
42	170.232936	170.729461	171.226037	171.722665	172.219342	172.716069	173.212845	173.709669
43	170.199051	170.695998	171.192992	171.690032	172.187117	172.684247	173.181421	173.678638
44	170.170100	170.667420	171.164782	171.662186	172.159631	172.657115	173.154640	173.652203
45	170.145364	170.643013	171.140700	171.638424	172.136185	172.633982	173.131815	173.629684
46	170.124227	170.622166	171.120139	171.618146	172.116185	172.614258	173.112362	173.610498
47	170.106166	170.604360	171.102585	171.600840	172.099124	172.597438	173.095781	173.594152
48	170.090732	170.589150	171.087597	171.586070	172.084570	172.583096	173.081648	173.580225
49	170.077542	170.576159	171.074799	171.573465	172.072154	172.570866	173.069601	173.568360
50	170.066271	170.565061	171.063872	171.562706	172.061561	172.560436	173.059333	173.558249

ANNUAL WITHDRAWALS PER $1000

NUMBER OF ANNUAL WTHDRWLS	EFFECTIVE ANNUAL YIELD							
	17.40%	17.45%	17.50%	17.55%	17.60%	17.65%	17.70%	17.75%
1	1174.000000	1174.500000	1175.000000	1175.500000	1176.000000	1176.500000	1177.000000	1177.500000
2	633.981601	634.375834	634.770115	635.164445	635.558824	635.953251	636.347726	636.742250
3	455.509657	455.877040	456.244507	456.612060	456.979698	457.347421	457.715229	458.083122
4	367.409680	367.769783	368.130004	368.490342	368.850798	369.211372	369.572063	369.932871
5	315.442380	315.802861	316.163488	316.524263	316.885185	317.246254	317.607470	317.968833
6	281.524573	281.889081	282.253764	282.618621	282.983651	283.348855	283.714233	284.079783
7	257.903637	258.274082	258.644725	259.015566	259.386605	259.757841	260.129274	260.500904
8	240.701164	241.078565	241.456184	241.834022	242.212079	242.590354	242.968846	243.347556
9	227.760862	228.145729	228.530833	228.916174	229.301751	229.687564	230.073612	230.459895
10	217.787731	218.180264	218.573048	218.966084	219.359371	219.752909	220.146696	220.540733
11	209.956784	210.356979	210.757436	211.158157	211.559140	211.960386	212.361892	212.763659
12	203.717412	204.125127	204.533113	204.941371	205.349901	205.758700	206.167769	206.577108
13	198.688030	199.103030	199.518307	199.933862	200.349694	200.765801	201.182183	201.598839
14	194.595876	195.017862	195.440128	195.862674	196.285500	196.708604	197.131986	197.555644
15	191.240873	191.669502	192.098412	192.527602	192.957072	193.386821	193.816847	194.247150
16	188.473037	188.907939	189.343121	189.778581	190.214319	190.650333	191.086623	191.523186
17	186.177842	186.618633	187.059700	187.501041	187.942655	188.384541	188.826699	189.269126
18	184.266456	184.712745	185.159304	185.606131	186.053225	186.500586	186.948211	187.396100
19	182.669042	183.120440	183.572100	184.024020	184.476201	184.928639	185.381335	185.834287
20	181.330066	181.786190	182.242566	182.699195	183.156075	183.613204	184.070581	184.528205
21	180.204926	180.665404	181.126126	181.587089	182.048293	182.509737	182.971419	183.433337
22	179.257499	179.721974	180.186682	180.651621	181.116790	181.582188	182.047813	182.513664
23	178.458313	178.926445	179.394798	179.863371	180.332163	180.801172	181.270397	181.739836
24	177.783174	178.254640	178.726316	179.198200	179.670291	180.142588	180.615088	181.087791
25	177.212114	177.686612	178.161307	178.636199	179.111286	179.586566	180.062038	180.537701
26	176.728577	177.205823	177.683255	178.160871	178.638670	179.116651	179.594811	180.073150
27	176.318782	176.798513	177.278418	177.758496	178.238744	178.719162	179.199748	179.680501
28	175.971219	176.453192	176.935327	177.417622	177.900077	178.382689	178.865458	179.348382
29	175.676248	176.160238	176.644378	177.128669	177.613105	178.097689	178.582418	179.067291
30	175.425773	175.911574	176.397515	176.883594	177.369809	177.856160	178.342645	178.829264
31	175.212985	175.700409	176.187961	176.675642	177.163448	177.651380	178.139435	178.627613
32	175.032140	175.521016	176.010010	176.499121	176.988349	177.477692	177.967148	178.456717
33	174.878393	175.368564	175.858845	176.349233	176.839727	177.330327	177.821032	178.311839
34	174.747646	175.238972	175.730398	176.221922	176.713544	177.205263	177.697077	178.188985
35	174.636431	175.128784	175.621229	176.113764	176.606387	177.099099	177.591898	178.084783
36	174.541811	175.035077	175.528426	176.021857	176.515370	177.008962	177.502634	177.996385
37	174.461296	174.955371	175.449522	175.943748	176.438048	176.932420	177.426865	177.921380
38	174.392772	174.887565	175.382426	175.877355	176.372351	176.867413	177.362540	177.857732
39	174.334447	174.829874	175.325363	175.820913	176.316525	176.812196	177.307926	177.803714
40	174.284797	174.780784	175.276828	175.772927	176.269081	176.765289	177.261551	177.757865
41	174.242528	174.739010	175.235543	175.732126	176.228758	176.725439	177.222169	177.718946
42	174.206540	174.703458	175.200422	175.697431	176.194484	176.691582	177.188723	177.685906
43	174.175898	174.673199	175.170543	175.667926	176.165351	176.662814	177.160317	177.657857
44	174.149805	174.647445	175.145122	175.642835	176.140584	176.638369	177.136189	177.634044
45	174.127586	174.625523	175.123492	175.621495	176.119530	176.617597	177.115695	177.613824
46	174.108665	174.606862	175.105089	175.603346	176.101631	176.599945	177.098287	177.596657
47	174.092551	174.590977	175.089429	175.587908	176.086414	176.584944	177.083500	177.582080
48	174.078827	174.577454	175.076104	175.574778	176.073475	176.572195	177.070938	177.569702
49	174.067140	174.565942	175.064765	175.563610	176.062475	176.561361	177.060266	177.559191
50	174.057186	174.556142	175.055116	175.554110	176.053122	176.552153	177.051201	177.550266

NUMBER OF ANNUAL WTHDRWLS	EFFECTIVE ANNUAL YIELD							
	17.80%	17.85%	17.90%	18.00%	18.10%	18.20%	18.30%	18.40%
1	1178.000000	1178.500000	1179.000000	1180.000000	1181.000000	1182.000000	1183.000000	1184.000000
2	637.136823	637.531444	637.926113	638.715596	639.505273	640.295142	641.085204	641.875458
3	458.451100	458.819163	459.187311	459.923861	460.660749	461.397976	462.135540	462.873441
4	370.293797	370.654840	371.016000	371.738671	372.461809	373.185413	373.909483	374.634017
5	318.330342	318.691998	319.053800	319.777842	320.502467	321.227675	321.953465	322.679834
6	284.445507	284.811404	285.177473	285.910129	286.643474	287.377505	288.112221	288.847621
7	260.872731	261.244754	261.616974	262.361999	263.107807	263.854393	264.601757	265.349897
8	243.726484	244.105628	244.484989	245.244359	246.004591	246.765683	247.527632	248.290436
9	230.846413	231.233166	231.620152	232.394824	233.170427	233.946957	234.724411	235.502787
10	220.935018	221.329553	221.724335	222.514641	223.305934	224.098209	224.891462	225.685691
11	213.165687	213.567974	213.970520	214.776386	215.583282	216.391202	217.200142	218.010098
12	206.986714	207.396588	207.806729	208.627809	209.449949	210.273143	211.097386	211.922673
13	202.015769	202.432971	202.850446	203.686207	204.523048	205.360960	206.199940	207.039979
14	197.979579	198.403788	198.828272	199.678058	200.528931	201.380883	202.233909	203.088000
15	194.677729	195.108583	195.539710	196.402783	197.266939	198.132172	198.998475	199.865839
16	191.960023	192.397133	192.834513	193.710084	194.586727	195.464435	196.343199	197.223011
17	189.711822	190.154785	190.598016	191.485271	192.373579	193.262932	194.153320	195.044735
18	187.844251	188.292664	188.741336	189.639457	190.538604	191.438768	192.339940	193.242110
19	186.287493	186.740953	187.194664	188.102839	189.012007	189.922160	190.833286	191.745377
20	184.986075	185.444188	185.902545	186.819981	187.738374	188.657712	189.577987	190.499188
21	183.895491	184.357879	184.820499	185.746433	186.673281	187.601034	188.529681	189.459212
22	182.979739	183.446038	183.912558	184.846258	185.780828	186.716259	187.652539	188.589659
23	182.209488	182.679352	183.149426	184.090200	185.031798	185.974210	186.917425	187.861433
24	181.560696	182.033800	182.507102	183.454297	184.402270	185.351008	186.300503	187.250743
25	181.013553	181.489593	181.965819	182.918826	183.872563	184.827018	185.782181	186.738043
26	180.551667	181.030359	181.509226	182.467478	183.426412	184.386017	185.346284	186.307201
27	180.161419	180.642501	181.123746	182.086719	183.050328	184.014561	184.979408	185.944859
28	179.831460	180.314691	180.798073	181.765285	182.733086	183.701466	184.670415	185.639924
29	179.552307	180.037464	180.522761	181.493769	182.465323	183.437411	184.410025	185.383155
30	179.316014	179.802894	180.289904	181.264306	182.239210	183.214607	184.190488	185.166842
31	179.115913	179.604332	180.092870	181.070299	182.048189	183.026531	184.005318	184.984538
32	178.946398	179.436188	179.926088	180.906211	181.886756	182.867716	183.849082	184.830845
33	178.802749	179.293759	179.784870	180.767386	181.750289	182.733570	183.717221	184.701235
34	178.680986	179.173080	179.665265	180.649904	181.634896	182.620233	183.605906	184.591909
35	178.577753	179.070807	179.563944	180.550463	181.537303	182.524456	183.511915	184.499673
36	178.490212	178.984116	179.478095	180.466277	181.454749	182.443506	183.432539	184.421843
37	178.415966	178.910621	179.405345	180.394994	181.384906	182.375076	183.365496	184.356160
38	178.352988	178.848306	179.343686	180.334628	181.325809	182.317222	183.308861	184.300720
39	178.299560	178.795463	179.291421	180.283503	181.275800	182.268305	183.261015	184.253922
40	178.254231	178.750648	179.247115	180.240199	181.233476	182.226941	183.220589	184.214415
41	178.215769	178.712639	179.209554	180.203517	181.197655	182.191961	183.186431	184.181061
42	178.183132	178.680399	179.177707	180.172442	181.167334	182.162377	183.157567	184.152900
43	178.155436	178.653052	179.150704	180.146116	181.141668	182.137356	183.133175	184.129122
44	178.131932	178.629853	179.127807	180.123812	181.119942	182.116193	183.112561	184.109044
45	178.111984	178.610173	179.108391	180.104914	181.101549	182.098292	183.095140	184.092089
46	178.095054	178.593477	179.091927	180.088903	181.085978	182.083151	183.080416	184.077772
47	178.080684	178.579312	179.077964	180.075336	181.072796	182.070343	183.067972	184.065681
48	178.068488	178.567295	179.066123	180.063640	181.061636	182.059508	183.057454	184.055471
49	178.058136	178.557099	179.056081	180.054098	181.052187	182.050343	183.048564	184.046848
50	178.049349	178.548448	179.047564	180.045844	181.044187	182.042589	183.041050	184.039566

ANNUAL WITHDRAWALS PER $1000

NUMBER OF ANNUAL WTHDRWLS	EFFECTIVE ANNUAL YIELD							
	18.50%	18.60%	18.70%	18.80%	18.90%	19.00%	19.10%	19.20%
1	1185.000000	1186.000000	1187.000000	1188.000000	1189.000000	1190.000000	1191.000000	1192.000000
2	642.665904	643.456542	644.247371	645.038391	645.829603	646.621005	647.412597	648.204380
3	463.611678	464.350251	465.089160	465.828404	466.567983	467.307895	468.048141	468.788719
4	375.359015	376.084477	376.810401	377.536786	378.263632	378.990938	379.718703	380.446926
5	323.406782	324.134308	324.862410	325.591088	326.320341	327.050167	327.780564	328.511533
6	289.583703	290.320466	291.057908	291.796027	292.534822	293.274292	294.014435	294.755249
7	266.098810	266.848494	267.598947	268.350167	269.102153	269.854902	270.608412	271.362682
8	249.054092	249.818597	250.583949	251.350145	252.117183	252.885060	253.653774	254.423322
9	236.282080	237.062288	237.843407	238.625435	239.408368	240.192202	240.976936	241.762565
10	226.480889	227.277055	228.074184	228.872271	229.671315	230.471309	231.272252	232.074138
11	218.821064	219.633037	220.446012	221.259983	222.074948	222.890900	223.707837	224.525752
12	212.748999	213.576358	214.404745	215.234155	216.064582	216.896022	217.728469	218.561918
13	207.881074	208.723216	209.566401	210.410623	211.255876	212.102153	212.949449	213.797758
14	203.943151	204.799354	205.656604	206.514893	207.374215	208.234563	209.095931	209.958311
15	200.734257	201.603722	202.474227	203.345764	204.218326	205.091906	205.966497	206.842091
16	198.103863	198.985747	199.868656	200.752581	201.637514	202.523448	203.410375	204.298287
17	195.937168	196.830610	197.725054	198.620490	199.516911	200.414307	201.312671	202.211994
18	194.145269	195.049409	195.954521	196.860594	197.767622	198.675594	199.584502	200.494338
19	192.658423	193.572414	194.487342	195.403197	196.319969	197.237650	198.156230	199.075700
20	191.421304	192.344328	193.268247	194.193054	195.118738	196.045291	196.972702	197.900962
21	190.389617	191.320885	192.253008	193.185974	194.119774	195.054399	195.989839	196.926085
22	189.527608	190.466375	191.405951	192.346325	193.287488	194.229430	195.172142	196.115613
23	188.806223	189.751786	190.698110	191.645187	192.593005	193.541556	194.490829	195.440816
24	188.201719	189.153419	190.105834	191.058953	192.012767	192.967267	193.922441	194.878282
25	187.694592	188.651818	189.609712	190.568263	191.527462	192.487299	193.447765	194.408849
26	187.268758	188.230946	189.193755	190.157174	191.121195	192.085808	193.051003	194.016771
27	186.910905	187.877536	188.844741	189.812512	190.780839	191.749713	192.719124	193.689064
28	186.609982	187.580580	188.551709	189.523360	190.495522	191.468188	192.441349	193.414995
29	186.356791	187.330925	188.305546	189.280647	190.256218	191.232251	192.208738	193.185669
30	186.143662	187.120938	188.098662	189.076825	190.055418	191.034434	192.013864	192.993700
31	185.964185	186.944249	187.924723	188.905597	189.886865	190.868517	191.850547	192.832947
32	185.812947	186.795530	187.778436	188.761707	189.745335	190.729314	191.713636	192.698293
33	185.685603	186.670317	187.655371	188.640756	189.626466	190.612494	191.598832	192.585473
34	185.578233	186.564873	187.551819	188.539067	189.526608	190.514436	191.502545	192.490928
35	185.487723	186.476057	187.464670	188.453554	189.442704	190.432112	191.421774	192.411683
36	185.411411	186.401236	187.391312	188.381634	189.372194	190.362988	191.354009	192.345252
37	185.347062	186.338196	187.329556	188.321137	189.312933	190.304939	191.297148	192.289557
38	185.292793	186.285075	187.277561	188.270245	189.263121	190.256185	191.249433	192.242858
39	185.247022	186.240309	187.233779	188.227427	189.221247	190.215235	191.209387	192.203698
40	185.208414	186.202581	187.196911	188.191400	189.186044	190.180837	191.175777	192.170859
41	185.175846	186.170781	187.165862	188.161085	189.156446	190.151941	191.147566	192.143317
42	185.148371	186.143977	187.139713	188.135575	189.131561	190.127665	191.123886	192.120218
43	185.125192	186.121382	187.117688	188.114108	189.110636	190.107270	191.104007	192.100844
44	185.105636	186.102335	187.099138	188.096041	189.093041	190.090135	191.087320	192.084594
45	185.089136	186.086279	187.083513	188.080836	189.078245	190.075738	191.073311	192.070963
46	185.075215	186.072742	187.070351	188.068039	189.065803	190.063641	191.061551	192.059529
47	185.063468	186.061330	187.059265	188.057269	189.055340	190.053477	191.051677	192.049938
48	185.053557	186.051709	187.049926	188.048204	189.046541	190.044937	191.043388	192.041892
49	185.045194	186.043598	187.042059	188.040574	189.039142	190.037761	191.036428	192.035143
50	185.038137	186.036759	187.035431	188.034152	189.032919	190.031731	191.030585	192.029482

NUMBER OF ANNUAL WTHDRWLS	\multicolumn{8}{c}{EFFECTIVE ANNUAL YIELD}
	19.30%	19.40%	19.50%	19.60%	19.70%	19.80%	19.90%	20.00%
1	1193.000000	1194.000000	1195.000000	1196.000000	1197.000000	1198.000000	1199.000000	1200.000000
2	648.996352	649.788514	650.580866	651.373406	652.166136	652.959054	653.752160	654.545455
3	469.529631	470.270874	471.012448	471.754354	472.496589	473.239155	473.982051	474.725275
4	381.175607	381.904745	382.634339	383.364388	384.094891	384.825849	385.557259	386.289121
5	329.243072	329.975179	330.707854	331.441095	332.174902	332.909273	333.644207	334.379703
6	295.496733	296.238885	296.981704	297.725188	298.469335	299.214145	299.959616	300.705746
7	272.117708	272.873490	273.630025	274.387311	275.145346	275.904128	276.663656	277.423926
8	255.193701	255.964909	256.736943	257.509802	258.283481	259.057980	259.833294	260.609422
9	242.549086	243.336497	244.124794	244.913974	245.704034	246.494971	247.286781	248.079462
10	232.876965	233.680728	234.485423	235.291047	236.097597	236.905067	237.713455	238.522757
11	225.344643	226.164503	226.985330	227.807117	228.629862	229.453560	230.278205	231.103794
12	219.396364	220.231801	221.068225	221.905630	222.744012	223.583365	224.423685	225.264965
13	214.647074	215.497392	216.348705	217.201008	218.054294	218.908559	219.763797	220.620001
14	210.821699	211.686086	212.551467	213.417836	214.285185	215.153509	216.022801	216.893055
15	207.718681	208.596261	209.474823	210.354360	211.234865	212.116331	212.998752	213.882120
16	205.187177	206.077036	206.967858	207.859634	208.752357	209.646020	210.540615	211.436135
17	203.112269	204.013487	204.915639	205.818719	206.722717	207.627626	208.533439	209.440147
18	201.405092	202.316756	203.229322	204.142782	205.057126	205.972347	206.888436	207.805386
19	199.996051	200.917275	201.839363	202.762306	203.686095	204.610721	205.536177	206.462453
20	198.830062	199.759993	200.690747	201.622313	202.554683	203.487849	204.421801	205.356531
21	197.863126	198.800955	199.739561	200.678935	201.619069	202.559953	203.501580	204.443939
22	197.059835	198.004797	198.950491	199.896908	200.844038	201.791872	202.740402	203.689619
23	196.391505	197.342889	198.294958	199.247702	200.201113	201.155182	202.109900	203.065258
24	195.834779	196.791923	197.749705	198.708116	199.667147	200.626790	201.587034	202.547873
25	195.370544	196.332839	197.295726	198.259196	199.223239	200.187849	201.153015	202.118729
26	194.983104	195.949992	196.917426	197.885398	198.853900	199.822922	200.792457	201.762496
27	194.659525	195.630496	196.601970	197.573939	198.546393	199.519326	200.492728	201.466592
28	194.389119	195.363712	196.338766	197.314273	198.290224	199.266612	200.243429	201.220668
29	194.163037	195.140835	196.119053	197.097684	198.076721	199.056156	200.035981	201.016190
30	193.973935	194.954561	195.935570	196.916954	197.898708	198.880822	199.863292	200.846108
31	193.815709	194.798826	195.782291	196.766097	197.750237	198.734704	199.719492	200.704594
32	193.683279	194.668586	195.654209	196.640139	197.626372	198.612900	199.599717	200.586817
33	193.572412	194.559642	195.547155	196.534947	197.523011	198.511341	199.499931	200.488775
34	193.479579	194.468492	195.457661	196.447080	197.436744	198.426646	199.416783	200.407147
35	193.401832	194.392218	195.382833	196.373673	197.364732	198.356006	199.347488	200.339174
36	193.336712	194.328383	195.320260	196.312338	197.304613	198.297078	199.289731	200.282565
37	193.282160	194.274952	195.267928	196.261084	197.254415	198.247917	199.241585	200.235415
38	193.236457	194.230225	195.224157	196.218250	197.212499	198.206900	199.201448	200.196141
39	193.198164	194.192781	195.187544	196.182450	197.177495	198.172674	199.167985	200.163424
40	193.166078	194.161432	195.156916	196.152527	197.148261	198.144115	199.140085	200.136168
41	193.139191	194.135184	195.131293	196.127515	197.123845	198.120282	199.116821	200.113461
42	193.116660	194.113207	195.109857	196.106606	197.103452	198.100392	199.097423	200.094542
43	193.097777	194.094804	195.091922	196.089128	197.086419	198.083793	199.081247	200.078778
44	193.081952	194.079394	195.076916	196.074516	197.072191	198.069939	199.067757	200.065644
45	193.068690	194.066490	195.064361	196.062300	197.060306	198.058376	199.056508	200.054701
46	193.057574	194.055684	195.053856	196.052088	197.050379	198.048726	199.047127	200.045582
47	193.048258	194.046634	195.045065	196.043550	197.042086	198.040671	199.039304	200.037983
48	193.040449	194.039055	195.037710	196.036412	197.035158	198.033948	199.032780	200.031652
49	193.033904	194.032709	195.031556	196.030444	197.029371	198.028336	199.027338	200.026376
50	193.028418	194.027393	195.026406	196.025454	197.024537	198.023652	199.022800	200.021979

EFFECTIVE ANNUAL YIELD TABLE INSTRUCTIONS

Most fixed-rate investments call for the payment of interest at a nominal annual rate. The nominal annual rate is the named interest rate. In order to use the deposit tables or the withdrawal tables in this book, you must first convert the nominal annual rate paid by the investment into an effective annual yield.

Let's compare three fixed-rate investments so that you can see the differences between nominal annual rate and effective annual yield. A certificate of deposit (CD) issued by a bank pays interest at the nominal rate of 6% per annum, paid quarterly. A corporate bond having the same nominal rate, pays interest semiannually. A mortgage-backed security also carries the same nominal rate, but the payments are made monthly.

In general, the period for which interest is paid establishes the compounding period. Once the interest is received, it can be reinvested to begin earning interest on interest received. The receipt of interest on interest is called compounding. The more frequent the compounding period, the higher the amount of interest earned.

Let's look at our three examples. The bank CD interest is compounded quarterly, the corporate bond interest is compounded semiannually, and the mortgage-backed security interest is compounded monthly. All three investments have the same nominal annual rate. What are their respective effective annual yields?

First locate the 6% nominal annual rate in the left-hand column of page 266 of the table. Then read across this row to the column containing the compounding method in use. The effective annual yield (EAY) on the corporate bond is 6.090%, the EAY on the bank CD is 6.136%, and the EAY on the mortgage-backed security is 6.168%.

Methods of Compounding Interest. There are a variety of interest-compounding methods. This table contains the most commonly used compounding methods.

Annual compounding assumes that interest is figured at the end of each year. For this case, the nominal annual rate is the effective annual yield. There is no need to use the tables to find the EAY. The nominal annual rate when compounded annually is also called the simple interest annual rate.

263

Semiannual, quarterly, and monthly compounding assume that interest is figured at the end of each half-year, quarter, and month respectively. The nominal periodic rate for each of these compounding methods is the nominal annual rate divided by the number of periods in each year. For example, the corporate bond in the above example has a nominal annual rate of 6%, or a nominal semiannual rate of 3%. You might think of the bond as paying 3% simple interest semiannually.

There are three daily compounding methods; 360/360, 365/365, and 365/360. In the 360/360 daily method, the nominal daily rate is figured by dividing the nominal annual rate by 360, the daily basis. Interest at the nominal daily rate is then compounded for 360 days each year. Financial institutions refer to this day count and basis as the "ordinary interest" method for daily compounding of interest.

In the 365/365 daily method, the nominal daily rate is figured by dividing the nominal annual rate by 365, the daily basis. Interest at the nominal daily rate is then compounded for 365 days each year. This is the "exact day interest" method for daily compounding of interest.

In the 365/360 daily method, the nominal daily rate is figured by dividing the nominal annual rate by 360. Interest at the nominal daily rate is then compounded for 365 days each year. This is the "bank interest" method for daily compounding of interest.

Continuous compounding assumes that interest is figured for an infinitely small time period over an infinitely large number of such periods. Continuous compounding represents the natural maximum limit of interest that can be earned from a given nominal annual rate. In the 365/360 continuous compounding method, continuous compounding is applied to the adjusted nominal annual rate found from the "bank interest" method. To find this adjusted nominal rate, simply multiply the nominal rate by the fraction 365/360.

Comparison of Different Compounding Methods. A savings account has a nominal annual rate of 6.10%, compounded daily 365/360. What nominal rate must be earned on a zero-coupon bond to provide the investor with the same EAY? First find the 6.10% NAR in the left-hand column of page 266 of the table. Read across this row to the compounded daily 365/360 column and find the EAY of 6.379%. Since the zero-coupon bond EAY is based on semiannual compounding, scan down the semiannual compounding column until you find a 6.379% EAY. Read across to the left-hand column. The required zero-coupon bond nominal annual rate is 6.28%.

EFFECTIVE ANNUAL YIELDS

NOMINAL ANNUAL INTEREST RATE	COMPOUNDING METHOD							
	SEMI-ANNUALLY	QUARTERLY	MONTHLY	360/360 DAILY	365/365 DAILY	365/360 DAILY	CONTINUOUS	365/360 CONTINUOUS
5.00	5.062	5.095	5.116	5.127	5.127	5.200	5.127	5.200
5.01	5.073	5.105	5.127	5.137	5.137	5.210	5.138	5.211
5.02	5.083	5.115	5.137	5.148	5.148	5.221	5.148	5.221
5.03	5.093	5.126	5.148	5.158	5.158	5.232	5.159	5.232
5.04	5.104	5.136	5.158	5.169	5.169	5.242	5.169	5.243
5.05	5.114	5.146	5.169	5.179	5.179	5.253	5.180	5.253
5.06	5.124	5.137	5.179	5.190	5.190	5.264	5.190	5.264
5.07	5.134	5.167	5.189	5.200	5.200	5.274	5.201	5.275
5.08	5.145	5.178	5.200	5.211	5.211	5.285	5.211	5.286
5.09	5.155	5.188	5.210	5.221	5.221	5.296	5.222	5.296
5.10	5.165	5.198	5.221	5.232	5.232	5.306	5.232	5.307
5.11	5.175	5.209	5.231	5.242	5.242	5.317	5.243	5.318
5.12	5.186	5.219	5.242	5.253	5.253	5.328	5.253	5.328
5.13	5.196	5.230	5.252	5.263	5.263	5.339	5.264	5.339
5.14	5.206	5.240	5.263	5.274	5.274	5.349	5.274	5.350
5.15	5.216	5.250	5.273	5.285	5.285	5.360	5.285	5.360
5.16	5.227	5.261	5.284	5.295	5.295	5.371	5.295	5.371
5.17	5.237	5.271	5.294	5.306	5.306	5.381	5.306	5.382
5.18	5.247	5.281	5.305	5.316	5.316	5.392	5.317	5.392
5.19	5.257	5.292	5.315	5.327	5.327	5.403	5.327	5.403
5.20	5.268	5.302	5.326	5.337	5.337	5.413	5.338	5.414
5.21	5.278	5.313	5.336	5.348	5.348	5.424	5.348	5.424
5.22	5.288	5.323	5.347	5.358	5.358	5.435	5.359	5.435
5.23	5.298	5.333	5.357	5.369	5.369	5.445	5.369	5.446
5.24	5.309	5.344	5.368	5.379	5.379	5.456	5.380	5.456
5.25	5.319	5.354	5.378	5.390	5.390	5.467	5.390	5.467
5.26	5.329	5.365	5.389	5.400	5.400	5.477	5.401	5.478
5.27	5.339	5.375	5.399	5.411	5.411	5.488	5.411	5.489
5.28	5.350	5.385	5.410	5.421	5.421	5.499	5.422	5.499
5.29	5.360	5.396	5.420	5.432	5.432	5.509	5.432	5.510
5.30	5.370	5.406	5.431	5.443	5.443	5.520	5.443	5.521
5.31	5.380	5.417	5.441	5.453	5.453	5.531	5.454	5.531
5.32	5.391	5.427	5.452	5.464	5.464	5.542	5.464	5.542
5.33	5.401	5.437	5.462	5.474	5.474	5.552	5.475	5.553
5.34	5.411	5.448	5.473	5.485	5.485	5.563	5.485	5.563
5.35	5.422	5.458	5.483	5.495	5.495	5.574	5.496	5.574
5.36	5.432	5.469	5.494	5.506	5.506	5.584	5.506	5.585
5.37	5.442	5.479	5.504	5.516	5.516	5.595	5.517	5.596
5.38	5.452	5.490	5.515	5.527	5.527	5.606	5.527	5.606
5.39	5.463	5.500	5.525	5.537	5.537	5.617	5.538	5.617
5.40	5.473	5.510	5.536	5.548	5.548	5.627	5.548	5.628
5.41	5.483	5.521	5.546	5.559	5.559	5.638	5.559	5.638
5.42	5.493	5.531	5.557	5.569	5.569	5.649	5.570	5.649
5.43	5.504	5.542	5.567	5.580	5.580	5.659	5.580	5.660
5.44	5.514	5.552	5.578	5.590	5.590	5.670	5.591	5.670
5.45	5.524	5.562	5.588	5.601	5.601	5.681	5.601	5.681
5.46	5.535	5.573	5.599	5.611	5.611	5.691	5.612	5.692
5.47	5.545	5.583	5.609	5.622	5.622	5.702	5.622	5.703
5.48	5.555	5.594	5.620	5.632	5.632	5.713	5.633	5.713
5.49	5.565	5.604	5.630	5.643	5.643	5.724	5.643	5.724
5.50	5.576	5.614	5.641	5.654	5.654	5.734	5.654	5.735
5.51	5.586	5.625	5.651	5.664	5.664	5.745	5.665	5.746
5.52	5.596	5.635	5.662	5.675	5.675	5.756	5.675	5.756
5.53	5.606	5.646	5.672	5.685	5.685	5.767	5.686	5.767
5.54	5.617	5.656	5.683	5.696	5.696	5.777	5.696	5.778
5.55	5.627	5.667	5.693	5.706	5.706	5.788	5.707	5.788
5.56	5.637	5.677	5.704	5.717	5.717	5.799	5.717	5.799
5.57	5.648	5.687	5.714	5.728	5.728	5.809	5.728	5.810
5.58	5.658	5.698	5.725	5.738	5.738	5.820	5.739	5.821
5.59	5.668	5.708	5.735	5.749	5.749	5.831	5.749	5.831
5.60	5.678	5.719	5.746	5.759	5.759	5.842	5.760	5.842
5.61	5.689	5.729	5.757	5.770	5.770	5.852	5.770	5.853
5.62	5.699	5.740	5.767	5.780	5.780	5.863	5.781	5.864
5.63	5.709	5.750	5.778	5.791	5.791	5.874	5.792	5.874
5.64	5.720	5.760	5.788	5.802	5.802	5.885	5.802	5.885
5.65	5.730	5.771	5.799	5.812	5.812	5.895	5.813	5.896
5.66	5.740	5.781	5.809	5.823	5.823	5.906	5.823	5.906
5.67	5.750	5.792	5.820	5.833	5.833	5.917	5.834	5.917
5.68	5.761	5.802	5.830	5.844	5.844	5.927	5.844	5.928
5.69	5.771	5.813	5.841	5.855	5.855	5.938	5.855	5.939
5.70	5.781	5.823	5.851	5.865	5.865	5.949	5.866	5.949
5.71	5.792	5.833	5.862	5.876	5.876	5.960	5.876	5.960
5.72	5.802	5.844	5.872	5.886	5.886	5.970	5.887	5.971
5.73	5.812	5.854	5.883	5.897	5.897	5.981	5.897	5.982
5.74	5.822	5.865	5.893	5.907	5.907	5.992	5.908	5.992
5.75	5.833	5.875	5.904	5.918	5.918	6.003	5.919	6.003
5.76	5.843	5.886	5.915	5.929	5.929	6.013	5.929	6.014
5.77	5.853	5.896	5.925	5.939	5.939	6.024	5.940	6.025
5.78	5.864	5.906	5.936	5.950	5.950	6.035	5.950	6.035
5.79	5.874	5.917	5.946	5.960	5.960	6.046	5.961	6.046
5.80	5.884	5.927	5.957	5.971	5.971	6.056	5.971	6.057

EFFECTIVE ANNUAL YIELDS

NOMINAL ANNUAL INTEREST RATE	COMPOUNDING METHOD							
	SEMI-ANNUALLY	QUARTERLY	MONTHLY	360/360 DAILY	365/365 DAILY	365/360 DAILY	CONTINUOUS	365/360 CONTINUOUS
5.80	5.884	5.927	5.957	5.971	5.971	6.056	5.971	6.057
5.81	5.894	5.938	5.967	5.982	5.982	6.067	5.982	6.068
5.82	5.905	5.948	5.978	5.992	5.992	6.078	5.993	6.078
5.83	5.915	5.959	5.988	6.003	6.003	6.089	6.003	6.089
5.84	5.925	5.969	5.999	6.013	6.013	6.099	6.014	6.100
5.85	5.936	5.980	6.009	6.024	6.024	6.110	6.024	6.111
5.86	5.946	5.990	6.020	6.035	6.035	6.121	6.035	6.121
5.87	5.956	6.000	6.031	6.045	6.045	6.132	6.046	6.132
5.88	5.966	6.011	6.041	6.056	6.056	6.142	6.056	6.143
5.89	5.977	6.021	6.052	6.066	6.066	6.153	6.067	6.154
5.90	5.987	6.032	6.062	6.077	6.077	6.164	6.078	6.164
5.91	5.997	6.042	6.073	6.088	6.088	6.175	6.088	6.175
5.92	6.008	6.053	6.083	6.098	6.098	6.185	6.099	6.186
5.93	6.018	6.063	6.094	6.109	6.109	6.196	6.109	6.197
5.94	6.028	6.074	6.104	6.119	6.119	6.207	6.120	6.208
5.95	6.039	6.084	6.115	6.130	6.130	6.218	6.131	6.218
5.96	6.049	6.095	6.126	6.141	6.141	6.229	6.141	6.229
5.97	6.059	6.105	6.136	6.151	6.151	6.239	6.152	6.240
5.98	6.069	6.115	6.147	6.162	6.162	6.250	6.162	6.251
5.99	6.080	6.126	6.157	6.173	6.173	6.261	6.173	6.261
6.00	6.090	6.136	6.168	6.183	6.183	6.272	6.184	6.272
6.01	6.100	6.147	6.178	6.194	6.194	6.282	6.194	6.283
6.02	6.111	6.157	6.189	6.204	6.204	6.293	6.205	6.294
6.03	6.121	6.168	6.199	6.215	6.215	6.304	6.216	6.305
6.04	6.131	6.178	6.210	6.226	6.226	6.315	6.226	6.315
6.05	6.142	6.189	6.221	6.236	6.236	6.326	6.237	6.326
6.06	6.152	6.199	6.231	6.247	6.247	6.336	6.247	6.337
6.07	6.162	6.210	6.242	6.257	6.257	6.347	6.258	6.348
6.08	6.172	6.220	6.252	6.268	6.268	6.358	6.269	6.358
6.09	6.183	6.230	6.263	6.279	6.279	6.369	6.279	6.369
6.10	6.193	6.241	6.273	6.289	6.289	6.379	6.290	6.380
6.11	6.203	6.251	6.284	6.300	6.300	6.390	6.301	6.391
6.12	6.214	6.262	6.295	6.311	6.311	6.401	6.311	6.402
6.13	6.224	6.272	6.305	6.321	6.321	6.412	6.322	6.412
6.14	6.234	6.283	6.316	6.332	6.332	6.423	6.332	6.423
6.15	6.245	6.293	6.326	6.342	6.342	6.433	6.343	6.434
6.16	6.255	6.304	6.337	6.353	6.353	6.444	6.354	6.445
6.17	6.265	6.314	6.348	6.364	6.364	6.455	6.364	6.456
6.18	6.275	6.325	6.358	6.374	6.374	6.466	6.375	6.466
6.19	6.286	6.335	6.369	6.385	6.385	6.477	6.386	6.477
6.20	6.296	6.346	6.379	6.396	6.396	6.487	6.396	6.488
6.21	6.306	6.356	6.390	6.406	6.406	6.498	6.407	6.499
6.22	6.317	6.367	6.400	6.417	6.417	6.509	6.418	6.509
6.23	6.327	6.377	6.411	6.428	6.428	6.520	6.428	6.520
6.24	6.337	6.388	6.422	6.438	6.438	6.531	6.439	6.531
6.25	6.348	6.398	6.432	6.449	6.449	6.541	6.449	6.542
6.26	6.358	6.408	6.443	6.460	6.460	6.552	6.460	6.553
6.27	6.368	6.419	6.453	6.470	6.470	6.563	6.471	6.563
6.28	6.379	6.429	6.464	6.481	6.481	6.574	6.481	6.574
6.29	6.389	6.440	6.475	6.491	6.491	6.585	6.492	6.585
6.30	6.399	6.450	6.485	6.502	6.502	6.595	6.503	6.596
6.31	6.410	6.461	6.496	6.513	6.513	6.606	6.513	6.607
6.32	6.420	6.471	6.506	6.523	6.523	6.617	6.524	6.618
6.33	6.430	6.482	6.517	6.534	6.534	6.628	6.535	6.628
6.34	6.440	6.492	6.528	6.545	6.545	6.639	6.545	6.639
6.35	6.451	6.503	6.538	6.555	6.555	6.649	6.556	6.650
6.36	6.461	6.513	6.549	6.566	6.566	6.660	6.567	6.661
6.37	6.471	6.524	6.559	6.577	6.577	6.671	6.577	6.672
6.38	6.482	6.534	6.570	6.587	6.587	6.682	6.588	6.682
6.39	6.492	6.545	6.581	6.598	6.598	6.693	6.599	6.693
6.40	6.502	6.555	6.591	6.609	6.609	6.703	6.609	6.704
6.41	6.513	6.566	6.602	6.619	6.619	6.714	6.620	6.715
6.42	6.523	6.576	6.612	6.630	6.630	6.725	6.631	6.726
6.43	6.533	6.587	6.623	6.641	6.641	6.736	6.641	6.737
6.44	6.544	6.597	6.634	6.651	6.651	6.747	6.652	6.747
6.45	6.554	6.608	6.644	6.662	6.662	6.758	6.663	6.758
6.46	6.564	6.618	6.655	6.673	6.673	6.768	6.673	6.769
6.47	6.575	6.629	6.665	6.683	6.683	6.779	6.684	6.780
6.48	6.585	6.639	6.676	6.694	6.694	6.790	6.695	6.791
6.49	6.595	6.650	6.687	6.705	6.705	6.801	6.705	6.801
6.50	6.606	6.660	6.697	6.715	6.715	6.812	6.716	6.812
6.51	6.616	6.671	6.708	6.726	6.726	6.822	6.727	6.823
6.52	6.626	6.681	6.718	6.737	6.737	6.833	6.737	6.834
6.53	6.637	6.692	6.729	6.747	6.747	6.844	6.748	6.845
6.54	6.647	6.702	6.740	6.758	6.758	6.855	6.759	6.856
6.55	6.657	6.713	6.750	6.769	6.769	6.866	6.769	6.866
6.56	6.668	6.723	6.761	6.779	6.779	6.877	6.780	6.877
6.57	6.678	6.734	6.771	6.790	6.790	6.887	6.791	6.888
6.58	6.688	6.744	6.782	6.801	6.801	6.898	6.801	6.899
6.59	6.699	6.755	6.793	6.811	6.811	6.909	6.812	6.910
6.60	6.709	6.765	6.803	6.822	6.822	6.920	6.823	6.921

EFFECTIVE ANNUAL YIELDS

COMPOUNDING METHOD

NOMINAL ANNUAL INTEREST RATE	SEMI-ANNUALLY	QUARTERLY	MONTHLY	360/360 DAILY	365/365 DAILY	365/360 DAILY	CONTINUOUS	365/360 CONTINUOUS
6.60	6.709	6.765	6.803	6.822	6.822	6.920	6.823	6.921
6.61	6.719	6.776	6.814	6.833	6.833	6.931	6.833	6.931
6.62	6.730	6.786	6.825	6.843	6.843	6.942	6.844	6.942
6.63	6.740	6.797	6.835	6.854	6.854	6.953	6.855	6.953
6.64	6.750	6.807	6.846	6.865	6.865	6.963	6.865	6.964
6.65	6.761	6.818	6.856	6.875	6.875	6.974	6.876	6.975
6.66	6.771	6.828	6.867	6.886	6.886	6.985	6.887	6.986
6.67	6.781	6.839	6.878	6.897	6.897	6.996	6.897	6.997
6.68	6.792	6.849	6.888	6.908	6.908	7.007	6.908	7.007
6.69	6.802	6.860	6.899	6.918	6.918	7.018	6.919	7.018
6.70	6.812	6.870	6.910	6.929	6.929	7.028	6.930	7.029
6.71	6.823	6.881	6.920	6.940	6.940	7.039	6.940	7.040
6.72	6.833	6.891	6.931	6.950	6.950	7.050	6.951	7.051
6.73	6.843	6.902	6.942	6.961	6.961	7.061	6.962	7.062
6.74	6.854	6.912	6.952	6.972	6.972	7.072	6.972	7.073
6.75	6.864	6.923	6.963	6.982	6.982	7.083	6.983	7.083
6.76	6.874	6.933	6.973	6.993	6.993	7.094	6.994	7.094
6.77	6.885	6.944	6.984	7.004	7.004	7.104	7.004	7.105
6.78	6.895	6.954	6.995	7.014	7.014	7.115	7.015	7.116
6.79	6.905	6.965	7.005	7.025	7.025	7.126	7.026	7.127
6.80	6.916	6.975	7.016	7.036	7.036	7.137	7.037	7.138
6.81	6.926	6.986	7.027	7.047	7.047	7.148	7.047	7.149
6.82	6.936	6.996	7.037	7.057	7.057	7.159	7.058	7.159
6.83	6.947	7.007	7.048	7.068	7.068	7.170	7.069	7.170
6.84	6.957	7.017	7.059	7.079	7.079	7.180	7.079	7.181
6.85	6.967	7.028	7.069	7.089	7.089	7.191	7.090	7.192
6.86	6.978	7.038	7.080	7.100	7.100	7.202	7.101	7.203
6.87	6.988	7.049	7.091	7.111	7.111	7.213	7.111	7.214
6.88	6.998	7.060	7.101	7.121	7.121	7.224	7.122	7.225
6.89	7.009	7.070	7.112	7.132	7.132	7.235	7.133	7.235
6.90	7.019	7.081	7.122	7.143	7.143	7.246	7.144	7.246
6.91	7.029	7.091	7.133	7.154	7.154	7.257	7.154	7.257
6.92	7.040	7.102	7.144	7.164	7.164	7.267	7.165	7.268
6.93	7.050	7.112	7.154	7.175	7.175	7.278	7.176	7.279
6.94	7.060	7.123	7.165	7.186	7.186	7.289	7.186	7.290
6.95	7.071	7.133	7.176	7.196	7.196	7.300	7.197	7.301
6.96	7.081	7.144	7.186	7.207	7.207	7.311	7.208	7.312
6.97	7.091	7.154	7.197	7.218	7.218	7.322	7.219	7.322
6.98	7.102	7.165	7.208	7.229	7.229	7.333	7.229	7.333
6.99	7.112	7.175	7.218	7.239	7.239	7.344	7.240	7.344
7.00	7.122	7.186	7.229	7.250	7.250	7.354	7.251	7.355
7.01	7.133	7.196	7.240	7.261	7.261	7.365	7.262	7.366
7.02	7.143	7.207	7.250	7.272	7.272	7.376	7.272	7.377
7.03	7.154	7.218	7.261	7.282	7.282	7.387	7.283	7.388
7.04	7.164	7.228	7.272	7.293	7.293	7.398	7.294	7.399
7.05	7.174	7.239	7.282	7.304	7.304	7.409	7.304	7.410
7.06	7.185	7.249	7.293	7.314	7.314	7.420	7.315	7.420
7.07	7.195	7.260	7.304	7.325	7.325	7.431	7.326	7.431
7.08	7.205	7.270	7.314	7.336	7.336	7.441	7.337	7.442
7.09	7.216	7.281	7.325	7.347	7.347	7.452	7.347	7.453
7.10	7.226	7.291	7.336	7.357	7.357	7.463	7.358	7.464
7.11	7.236	7.302	7.346	7.368	7.368	7.474	7.369	7.475
7.12	7.247	7.312	7.357	7.379	7.379	7.485	7.380	7.486
7.13	7.257	7.323	7.368	7.390	7.390	7.496	7.390	7.497
7.14	7.267	7.333	7.378	7.400	7.400	7.507	7.401	7.508
7.15	7.278	7.344	7.389	7.411	7.411	7.518	7.412	7.519
7.16	7.288	7.355	7.400	7.422	7.422	7.529	7.423	7.529
7.17	7.299	7.365	7.410	7.433	7.433	7.540	7.433	7.540
7.18	7.309	7.376	7.421	7.443	7.443	7.550	7.444	7.551
7.19	7.319	7.386	7.432	7.454	7.454	7.561	7.455	7.562
7.20	7.330	7.397	7.442	7.465	7.465	7.572	7.466	7.573
7.21	7.340	7.407	7.453	7.476	7.476	7.583	7.476	7.584
7.22	7.350	7.418	7.464	7.486	7.486	7.594	7.487	7.595
7.23	7.361	7.428	7.474	7.497	7.497	7.605	7.498	7.606
7.24	7.371	7.439	7.485	7.508	7.508	7.616	7.509	7.617
7.25	7.381	7.450	7.496	7.518	7.519	7.627	7.519	7.628
7.26	7.392	7.460	7.507	7.529	7.529	7.638	7.530	7.639
7.27	7.402	7.471	7.517	7.540	7.540	7.649	7.541	7.649
7.28	7.412	7.481	7.528	7.551	7.551	7.660	7.552	7.660
7.29	7.423	7.492	7.539	7.562	7.562	7.670	7.562	7.671
7.30	7.433	7.502	7.549	7.572	7.572	7.681	7.573	7.682
7.31	7.444	7.513	7.560	7.583	7.583	7.692	7.584	7.693
7.32	7.454	7.523	7.571	7.594	7.594	7.703	7.595	7.704
7.33	7.464	7.534	7.581	7.605	7.605	7.714	7.605	7.715
7.34	7.475	7.545	7.592	7.615	7.615	7.725	7.616	7.726
7.35	7.485	7.555	7.603	7.626	7.626	7.736	7.627	7.737
7.36	7.495	7.566	7.613	7.637	7.637	7.747	7.638	7.748
7.37	7.506	7.576	7.624	7.648	7.648	7.758	7.648	7.759
7.38	7.516	7.587	7.635	7.658	7.658	7.769	7.659	7.770
7.39	7.527	7.597	7.646	7.669	7.669	7.780	7.670	7.780
7.40	7.537	7.608	7.656	7.680	7.680	7.791	7.681	7.791

EFFECTIVE ANNUAL YIELDS

NOMINAL ANNUAL INTEREST RATE	COMPOUNDING METHOD							
	SEMI-ANNUALLY	QUARTERLY	MONTHLY	360/360 DAILY	365/365 DAILY	365/360 DAILY	CONTINUOUS	365/360 CONTINUOUS
7.40	7.537	7.608	7.656	7.680	7.680	7.791	7.681	7.791
7.41	7.547	7.618	7.667	7.691	7.691	7.802	7.691	7.802
7.42	7.558	7.629	7.678	7.701	7.701	7.812	7.702	7.813
7.43	7.568	7.640	7.688	7.712	7.712	7.823	7.713	7.824
7.44	7.578	7.650	7.699	7.723	7.723	7.834	7.724	7.835
7.45	7.589	7.661	7.710	7.734	7.734	7.845	7.735	7.846
7.46	7.599	7.671	7.720	7.744	7.744	7.856	7.745	7.857
7.47	7.610	7.682	7.731	7.755	7.755	7.867	7.756	7.868
7.48	7.620	7.692	7.742	7.766	7.766	7.878	7.767	7.879
7.49	7.630	7.703	7.753	7.777	7.777	7.889	7.778	7.890
7.50	7.641	7.714	7.763	7.788	7.788	7.900	7.788	7.901
7.51	7.651	7.724	7.774	7.798	7.798	7.911	7.799	7.912
7.52	7.661	7.735	7.785	7.809	7.809	7.922	7.810	7.923
7.53	7.672	7.745	7.795	7.820	7.820	7.933	7.821	7.934
7.54	7.682	7.756	7.806	7.831	7.831	7.944	7.832	7.945
7.55	7.693	7.766	7.817	7.841	7.841	7.955	7.842	7.955
7.56	7.703	7.777	7.828	7.852	7.852	7.966	7.853	7.966
7.57	7.713	7.788	7.838	7.863	7.863	7.976	7.864	7.977
7.58	7.724	7.798	7.849	7.874	7.874	7.987	7.875	7.988
7.59	7.734	7.809	7.860	7.885	7.885	7.998	7.885	7.999
7.60	7.744	7.819	7.870	7.895	7.895	8.009	7.896	8.010
7.61	7.755	7.830	7.881	7.906	7.906	8.020	7.907	8.021
7.62	7.765	7.841	7.892	7.917	7.917	8.031	7.918	8.032
7.63	7.776	7.851	7.903	7.928	7.928	8.042	7.929	8.043
7.64	7.786	7.862	7.913	7.939	7.939	8.053	7.939	8.054
7.65	7.796	7.872	7.924	7.949	7.949	8.064	7.950	8.065
7.66	7.807	7.883	7.935	7.960	7.960	8.075	7.961	8.076
7.67	7.817	7.893	7.945	7.971	7.971	8.086	7.972	8.087
7.68	7.827	7.904	7.956	7.982	7.982	8.097	7.983	8.098
7.69	7.838	7.915	7.967	7.993	7.993	8.108	7.993	8.109
7.70	7.848	7.925	7.978	8.003	8.003	8.119	8.004	8.120
7.71	7.859	7.936	7.988	8.014	8.014	8.130	8.015	8.131
7.72	7.869	7.946	7.999	8.025	8.025	8.141	8.026	8.142
7.73	7.879	7.957	8.010	8.036	8.036	8.152	8.037	8.153
7.74	7.890	7.968	8.021	8.047	8.047	8.163	8.047	8.164
7.75	7.900	7.978	8.031	8.057	8.057	8.174	8.058	8.175
7.76	7.911	7.989	8.042	8.068	8.068	8.185	8.069	8.186
7.77	7.921	7.999	8.053	8.079	8.079	8.196	8.080	8.197
7.78	7.931	8.010	8.064	8.090	8.090	8.207	8.091	8.208
7.79	7.942	8.021	8.074	8.101	8.101	8.218	8.101	8.218
7.80	7.952	8.031	8.085	8.111	8.111	8.229	8.112	8.229
7.81	7.962	8.042	8.096	8.122	8.122	8.239	8.123	8.240
7.82	7.973	8.052	8.106	8.133	8.133	8.250	8.134	8.251
7.83	7.983	8.063	8.117	8.144	8.144	8.261	8.145	8.262
7.84	7.994	8.074	8.128	8.155	8.155	8.272	8.156	8.273
7.85	8.004	8.084	8.139	8.165	8.165	8.283	8.166	8.284
7.86	8.014	8.095	8.149	8.176	8.176	8.294	8.177	8.295
7.87	8.025	8.105	8.160	8.187	8.187	8.305	8.188	8.306
7.88	8.035	8.116	8.171	8.198	8.198	8.316	8.199	8.317
7.89	8.046	8.127	8.182	8.209	8.209	8.327	8.210	8.328
7.90	8.056	8.137	8.192	8.219	8.220	8.338	8.220	8.339
7.91	8.066	8.148	8.203	8.230	8.230	8.349	8.231	8.350
7.92	8.077	8.158	8.214	8.241	8.241	8.360	8.242	8.361
7.93	8.087	8.169	8.225	8.252	8.252	8.371	8.253	8.372
7.94	8.098	8.180	8.235	8.263	8.263	8.382	8.264	8.383
7.95	8.108	8.190	8.246	8.274	8.274	8.393	8.275	8.394
7.96	8.118	8.201	8.257	8.284	8.284	8.404	8.285	8.405
7.97	8.129	8.211	8.268	8.295	8.295	8.415	8.296	8.416
7.98	8.139	8.222	8.278	8.306	8.306	8.426	8.307	8.427
7.99	8.150	8.233	8.289	8.317	8.317	8.437	8.318	8.438
8.00	8.160	8.243	8.300	8.328	8.328	8.448	8.329	8.449
8.01	8.170	8.254	8.311	8.339	8.339	8.459	8.340	8.460
8.02	8.181	8.264	8.321	8.349	8.349	8.470	8.350	8.471
8.03	8.191	8.275	8.332	8.360	8.360	8.481	8.361	8.482
8.04	8.202	8.286	8.343	8.371	8.371	8.492	8.372	8.493
8.05	8.212	8.296	8.354	8.382	8.382	8.503	8.383	8.504
8.06	8.222	8.307	8.365	8.393	8.393	8.514	8.394	8.515
8.07	8.233	8.318	8.375	8.404	8.404	8.525	8.405	8.526
8.08	8.243	8.328	8.386	8.414	8.414	8.536	8.415	8.537
8.09	8.254	8.339	8.397	8.425	8.425	8.547	8.426	8.548
8.10	8.264	8.349	8.408	8.436	8.436	8.558	8.437	8.559
8.11	8.274	8.360	8.418	8.447	8.447	8.569	8.448	8.570
8.12	8.285	8.371	8.429	8.458	8.458	8.580	8.459	8.581
8.13	8.295	8.381	8.440	8.469	8.469	8.591	8.470	8.592
8.14	8.306	8.392	8.451	8.479	8.479	8.602	8.480	8.603
8.15	8.316	8.402	8.461	8.490	8.490	8.613	8.491	8.614
8.16	8.326	8.413	8.472	8.501	8.501	8.624	8.502	8.625
8.17	8.337	8.424	8.483	8.512	8.512	8.635	8.513	8.636
8.18	8.347	8.434	8.494	8.523	8.523	8.646	8.524	8.647
8.19	8.358	8.445	8.505	8.534	8.534	8.657	8.535	8.658
8.20	8.368	8.456	8.515	8.545	8.545	8.668	8.546	8.669

EFFECTIVE ANNUAL YIELDS

NOMINAL ANNUAL INTEREST RATE	COMPOUNDING METHOD							
	SEMI-ANNUALLY	QUARTERLY	MONTHLY	360/360 DAILY	365/365 DAILY	365/360 DAILY	CONTINUOUS	365/360 CONTINUOUS
8.20	8.368	8.456	8.515	8.545	8.545	8.668	8.546	8.669
8.21	8.379	8.466	8.526	8.555	8.555	8.679	8.556	8.680
8.22	8.389	8.477	8.537	8.566	8.566	8.690	8.567	8.691
8.23	8.399	8.488	8.548	8.577	8.577	8.701	8.578	8.702
8.24	8.410	8.498	8.558	8.588	8.588	8.712	8.589	8.713
8.25	8.420	8.509	8.569	8.599	8.599	8.723	8.600	8.724
8.26	8.431	8.519	8.580	8.610	8.610	8.734	8.611	8.735
8.27	8.441	8.530	8.591	8.621	8.621	8.745	8.622	8.746
8.28	8.451	8.541	8.602	8.631	8.631	8.756	8.632	8.757
8.29	8.462	8.551	8.612	8.642	8.642	8.767	8.643	8.768
8.30	8.472	8.562	8.623	8.653	8.653	8.778	8.654	8.780
8.31	8.483	8.573	8.634	8.664	8.664	8.789	8.665	8.791
8.32	8.493	8.583	8.645	8.675	8.675	8.801	8.676	8.802
8.33	8.503	8.594	8.656	8.686	8.686	8.812	8.687	8.813
8.34	8.514	8.604	8.666	8.697	8.697	8.823	8.698	8.824
8.35	8.524	8.615	8.677	8.707	8.707	8.834	8.709	8.835
8.36	8.535	8.626	8.688	8.718	8.718	8.845	8.719	8.846
8.37	8.545	8.636	8.699	8.729	8.729	8.856	8.730	8.857
8.38	8.556	8.647	8.709	8.740	8.740	8.867	8.741	8.868
8.39	8.566	8.658	8.720	8.751	8.751	8.878	8.752	8.879
8.40	8.576	8.668	8.731	8.762	8.762	8.889	8.763	8.890
8.41	8.587	8.679	8.742	8.773	8.773	8.900	8.774	8.901
8.42	8.597	8.690	8.753	8.784	8.784	8.911	8.785	8.912
8.43	8.608	8.700	8.763	8.794	8.794	8.922	8.796	8.923
8.44	8.618	8.711	8.774	8.805	8.805	8.933	8.806	8.934
8.45	8.629	8.722	8.785	8.816	8.816	8.944	8.817	8.945
8.46	8.639	8.732	8.796	8.827	8.827	8.955	8.828	8.956
8.47	8.649	8.743	8.807	8.838	8.838	8.966	8.839	8.967
8.48	8.660	8.753	8.817	8.849	8.849	8.977	8.850	8.978
8.49	8.670	8.764	8.828	8.860	8.860	8.988	8.861	8.989
8.50	8.681	8.775	8.839	8.871	8.871	8.999	8.872	9.000
8.51	8.691	8.785	8.850	8.881	8.882	9.010	8.883	9.011
8.52	8.701	8.796	8.861	8.892	8.892	9.021	8.893	9.022
8.53	8.712	8.807	8.872	8.903	8.903	9.032	8.904	9.033
8.54	8.722	8.817	8.882	8.914	8.914	9.043	8.915	9.045
8.55	8.733	8.828	8.893	8.925	8.925	9.054	8.926	9.056
8.56	8.743	8.839	8.904	8.936	8.936	9.066	8.937	9.067
8.57	8.754	8.849	8.915	8.947	8.947	9.077	8.948	9.078
8.58	8.764	8.860	8.926	8.958	8.958	9.088	8.959	9.089
8.59	8.774	8.871	8.936	8.969	8.969	9.099	8.970	9.100
8.60	8.785	8.881	8.947	8.980	8.980	9.110	8.981	9.111
8.61	8.795	8.892	8.958	8.990	8.990	9.121	8.992	9.122
8.62	8.806	8.903	8.969	9.001	9.001	9.132	9.002	9.133
8.63	8.816	8.913	8.980	9.012	9.012	9.143	9.013	9.144
8.64	8.827	8.924	8.990	9.023	9.023	9.154	9.024	9.155
8.65	8.837	8.935	9.001	9.034	9.034	9.165	9.035	9.166
8.66	8.847	8.945	9.012	9.045	9.045	9.176	9.046	9.177
8.67	8.858	8.956	9.023	9.056	9.056	9.187	9.057	9.188
8.68	8.868	8.967	9.034	9.067	9.067	9.198	9.068	9.199
8.69	8.879	8.977	9.045	9.078	9.078	9.209	9.079	9.210
8.70	8.889	8.988	9.055	9.089	9.089	9.220	9.090	9.222
8.71	8.900	8.999	9.066	9.099	9.099	9.231	9.101	9.233
8.72	8.910	9.009	9.077	9.110	9.110	9.243	9.111	9.244
8.73	8.921	9.020	9.088	9.121	9.121	9.254	9.122	9.255
8.74	8.931	9.031	9.099	9.132	9.132	9.265	9.133	9.266
8.75	8.941	9.041	9.110	9.143	9.143	9.276	9.144	9.277
8.76	8.952	9.052	9.120	9.154	9.154	9.287	9.155	9.288
8.77	8.962	9.063	9.131	9.165	9.165	9.298	9.166	9.299
8.78	8.973	9.073	9.142	9.176	9.176	9.309	9.177	9.310
8.79	8.983	9.084	9.153	9.187	9.187	9.320	9.188	9.321
8.80	8.994	9.095	9.164	9.198	9.198	9.331	9.199	9.332
8.81	9.004	9.105	9.175	9.209	9.209	9.342	9.210	9.343
8.82	9.014	9.116	9.185	9.219	9.219	9.353	9.221	9.355
8.83	9.025	9.127	9.196	9.230	9.230	9.364	9.232	9.366
8.84	9.035	9.137	9.207	9.241	9.241	9.376	9.243	9.377
8.85	9.046	9.148	9.218	9.252	9.252	9.387	9.253	9.388
8.86	9.056	9.159	9.229	9.263	9.263	9.398	9.264	9.399
8.87	9.067	9.169	9.240	9.274	9.274	9.409	9.275	9.410
8.88	9.077	9.180	9.250	9.285	9.285	9.420	9.286	9.421
8.89	9.088	9.191	9.261	9.296	9.296	9.431	9.297	9.432
8.90	9.098	9.201	9.272	9.307	9.307	9.442	9.308	9.443
8.91	9.108	9.212	9.283	9.318	9.318	9.453	9.319	9.454
8.92	9.119	9.223	9.294	9.329	9.329	9.464	9.330	9.465
8.93	9.129	9.234	9.305	9.340	9.340	9.475	9.341	9.477
8.94	9.140	9.244	9.316	9.351	9.351	9.486	9.352	9.488
8.95	9.150	9.255	9.326	9.362	9.362	9.498	9.363	9.499
8.96	9.161	9.266	9.337	9.372	9.372	9.509	9.374	9.510
8.97	9.171	9.276	9.348	9.383	9.383	9.520	9.385	9.521
8.98	9.182	9.287	9.359	9.394	9.394	9.531	9.396	9.532
8.99	9.192	9.298	9.370	9.405	9.405	9.542	9.406	9.543
9.00	9.202	9.308	9.381	9.416	9.416	9.553	9.417	9.554

EFFECTIVE ANNUAL YIELDS

NOMINAL ANNUAL INTEREST RATE	COMPOUNDING METHOD							
	SEMI-ANNUALLY	QUARTERLY	MONTHLY	360/360 DAILY	365/365 DAILY	365/360 DAILY	CONTINUOUS	365/360 CONTINUOUS
9.00	9.202	9.308	9.381	9.416	9.416	9.553	9.417	9.554
9.01	9.213	9.319	9.392	9.427	9.427	9.564	9.428	9.565
9.02	9.223	9.330	9.402	9.438	9.438	9.575	9.439	9.577
9.03	9.234	9.340	9.413	9.449	9.449	9.586	9.450	9.588
9.04	9.244	9.351	9.424	9.460	9.460	9.597	9.461	9.599
9.05	9.255	9.362	9.435	9.471	9.471	9.609	9.472	9.610
9.06	9.265	9.372	9.446	9.482	9.482	9.620	9.483	9.621
9.07	9.276	9.383	9.457	9.493	9.493	9.631	9.494	9.632
9.08	9.286	9.394	9.468	9.504	9.504	9.642	9.505	9.643
9.09	9.297	9.405	9.478	9.515	9.515	9.653	9.516	9.654
9.10	9.307	9.415	9.489	9.526	9.526	9.664	9.527	9.665
9.11	9.317	9.426	9.500	9.537	9.537	9.675	9.538	9.677
9.12	9.328	9.437	9.511	9.548	9.548	9.686	9.549	9.688
9.13	9.338	9.447	9.522	9.558	9.559	9.697	9.560	9.699
9.14	9.349	9.458	9.533	9.569	9.569	9.709	9.571	9.710
9.15	9.359	9.469	9.544	9.580	9.580	9.720	9.582	9.721
9.16	9.370	9.479	9.555	9.591	9.591	9.731	9.593	9.732
9.17	9.380	9.490	9.565	9.602	9.602	9.742	9.604	9.743
9.18	9.391	9.501	9.576	9.613	9.613	9.753	9.615	9.754
9.19	9.401	9.512	9.587	9.624	9.624	9.764	9.626	9.766
9.20	9.412	9.522	9.598	9.635	9.635	9.775	9.636	9.777
9.21	9.422	9.533	9.609	9.646	9.646	9.786	9.647	9.788
9.22	9.433	9.544	9.620	9.657	9.657	9.798	9.658	9.799
9.23	9.443	9.554	9.631	9.668	9.668	9.809	9.669	9.810
9.24	9.453	9.565	9.642	9.679	9.679	9.820	9.680	9.821
9.25	9.464	9.576	9.652	9.690	9.690	9.831	9.691	9.832
9.26	9.474	9.587	9.663	9.701	9.701	9.842	9.702	9.843
9.27	9.485	9.597	9.674	9.712	9.712	9.853	9.713	9.855
9.28	9.495	9.608	9.685	9.723	9.723	9.864	9.724	9.866
9.29	9.506	9.619	9.696	9.734	9.734	9.876	9.735	9.877
9.30	9.516	9.629	9.707	9.745	9.745	9.887	9.746	9.888
9.31	9.527	9.640	9.718	9.756	9.756	9.898	9.757	9.899
9.32	9.537	9.651	9.729	9.767	9.767	9.909	9.768	9.910
9.33	9.548	9.662	9.739	9.778	9.778	9.920	9.779	9.921
9.34	9.558	9.672	9.750	9.789	9.789	9.931	9.790	9.933
9.35	9.569	9.683	9.761	9.800	9.800	9.942	9.801	9.944
9.36	9.579	9.694	9.772	9.811	9.811	9.954	9.812	9.955
9.37	9.589	9.704	9.783	9.822	9.822	9.965	9.823	9.966
9.38	9.600	9.715	9.794	9.833	9.833	9.976	9.834	9.977
9.39	9.610	9.726	9.805	9.844	9.844	9.987	9.845	9.988
9.40	9.621	9.737	9.816	9.855	9.855	9.998	9.856	9.999
9.41	9.631	9.747	9.827	9.866	9.866	10.009	9.867	10.011
9.42	9.642	9.758	9.838	9.877	9.877	10.020	9.878	10.022
9.43	9.652	9.769	9.848	9.888	9.888	10.032	9.889	10.033
9.44	9.663	9.779	9.859	9.899	9.899	10.043	9.900	10.044
9.45	9.673	9.790	9.870	9.910	9.910	10.054	9.911	10.055
9.46	9.684	9.801	9.881	9.921	9.921	10.065	9.922	10.066
9.47	9.694	9.812	9.892	9.932	9.932	10.076	9.933	10.078
9.48	9.705	9.822	9.903	9.943	9.943	10.087	9.944	10.089
9.49	9.715	9.833	9.914	9.954	9.954	10.099	9.955	10.100
9.50	9.726	9.844	9.925	9.965	9.965	10.110	9.966	10.111
9.51	9.736	9.855	9.936	9.976	9.976	10.121	9.977	10.122
9.52	9.747	9.865	9.947	9.986	9.987	10.132	9.988	10.133
9.53	9.757	9.876	9.957	9.997	9.998	10.143	9.999	10.145
9.54	9.768	9.887	9.968	10.008	10.009	10.154	10.010	10.156
9.55	9.778	9.897	9.979	10.019	10.020	10.165	10.021	10.167
9.56	9.788	9.908	9.990	10.030	10.031	10.177	10.032	10.178
9.57	9.799	9.919	10.001	10.041	10.042	10.188	10.043	10.189
9.58	9.809	9.930	10.012	10.052	10.053	10.199	10.054	10.200
9.59	9.820	9.940	10.023	10.063	10.064	10.210	10.065	10.212
9.60	9.830	9.951	10.034	10.074	10.075	10.221	10.076	10.223
9.61	9.841	9.962	10.045	10.086	10.086	10.233	10.087	10.234
9.62	9.851	9.973	10.056	10.097	10.097	10.244	10.098	10.245
9.63	9.862	9.983	10.067	10.108	10.108	10.255	10.109	10.256
9.64	9.872	9.994	10.078	10.119	10.119	10.266	10.120	10.267
9.65	9.883	10.005	10.088	10.130	10.130	10.277	10.131	10.279
9.66	9.893	10.016	10.099	10.141	10.141	10.288	10.142	10.290
9.67	9.904	10.026	10.110	10.152	10.152	10.300	10.153	10.301
9.68	9.914	10.037	10.121	10.163	10.163	10.311	10.164	10.312
9.69	9.925	10.048	10.132	10.174	10.174	10.322	10.175	10.323
9.70	9.935	10.059	10.143	10.185	10.185	10.333	10.186	10.335
9.71	9.946	10.069	10.154	10.196	10.196	10.344	10.197	10.346
9.72	9.956	10.080	10.165	10.207	10.207	10.355	10.208	10.357
9.73	9.967	10.091	10.176	10.218	10.218	10.367	10.219	10.368
9.74	9.977	10.102	10.187	10.229	10.229	10.378	10.230	10.379
9.75	9.988	10.112	10.198	10.240	10.240	10.389	10.241	10.391
9.76	9.998	10.123	10.209	10.251	10.251	10.400	10.252	10.402
9.77	10.009	10.134	10.220	10.262	10.262	10.411	10.263	10.413
9.78	10.019	10.145	10.231	10.273	10.273	10.423	10.274	10.424
9.79	10.030	10.155	10.241	10.284	10.284	10.434	10.285	10.435
9.80	10.040	10.166	10.252	10.295	10.295	10.445	10.296	10.447

EFFECTIVE ANNUAL YIELDS

NOMINAL ANNUAL INTEREST RATE	SEMI-ANNUALLY	QUARTERLY	MONTHLY	360/360 DAILY	365/365 DAILY	365/360 DAILY	CONTINUOUS	365/360 CONTINUOUS
9.80	10.040	10.166	10.252	10.295	10.295	10.445	10.296	10.447
9.81	10.051	10.177	10.263	10.306	10.306	10.456	10.307	10.458
9.82	10.061	10.188	10.274	10.317	10.317	10.467	10.318	10.469
9.83	10.072	10.198	10.285	10.328	10.328	10.479	10.329	10.480
9.84	10.082	10.209	10.296	10.339	10.339	10.490	10.340	10.491
9.85	10.093	10.220	10.307	10.350	10.350	10.501	10.351	10.503
9.86	10.103	10.231	10.318	10.361	10.361	10.512	10.362	10.514
9.87	10.114	10.241	10.329	10.372	10.372	10.523	10.374	10.525
9.88	10.124	10.252	10.340	10.383	10.383	10.535	10.385	10.536
9.89	10.135	10.263	10.351	10.394	10.394	10.546	10.396	10.547
9.90	10.145	10.274	10.362	10.405	10.405	10.557	10.407	10.559
9.91	10.156	10.284	10.373	10.416	10.416	10.568	10.418	10.570
9.92	10.166	10.295	10.384	10.427	10.427	10.579	10.429	10.581
9.93	10.177	10.306	10.395	10.438	10.438	10.591	10.440	10.592
9.94	10.187	10.317	10.406	10.449	10.449	10.602	10.451	10.603
9.95	10.198	10.327	10.417	10.460	10.460	10.613	10.462	10.615
9.96	10.208	10.338	10.427	10.471	10.471	10.624	10.473	10.626
9.97	10.219	10.349	10.438	10.482	10.482	10.635	10.484	10.637
9.98	10.229	10.360	10.449	10.493	10.493	10.647	10.495	10.648
9.99	10.240	10.371	10.460	10.505	10.505	10.658	10.506	10.659
10.00	10.250	10.381	10.471	10.516	10.516	10.669	10.517	10.671
10.01	10.261	10.392	10.482	10.527	10.527	10.680	10.528	10.682
10.02	10.271	10.403	10.493	10.538	10.538	10.692	10.539	10.693
10.03	10.282	10.414	10.504	10.549	10.549	10.703	10.550	10.704
10.04	10.292	10.424	10.515	10.560	10.560	10.714	10.561	10.716
10.05	10.303	10.435	10.526	10.571	10.571	10.725	10.572	10.727
10.06	10.313	10.446	10.537	10.582	10.582	10.736	10.583	10.738
10.07	10.324	10.457	10.548	10.593	10.593	10.748	10.594	10.749
10.08	10.334	10.467	10.559	10.604	10.604	10.759	10.606	10.760
10.09	10.345	10.478	10.570	10.615	10.615	10.770	10.617	10.772
10.10	10.355	10.489	10.581	10.626	10.626	10.781	10.628	10.783
10.11	10.366	10.500	10.592	10.637	10.637	10.793	10.639	10.794
10.12	10.376	10.511	10.603	10.648	10.648	10.804	10.650	10.805
10.13	10.387	10.521	10.614	10.659	10.659	10.815	10.661	10.817
10.14	10.397	10.532	10.625	10.670	10.670	10.826	10.672	10.828
10.15	10.408	10.543	10.636	10.681	10.681	10.838	10.683	10.839
10.16	10.418	10.554	10.647	10.692	10.692	10.849	10.694	10.850
10.17	10.429	10.564	10.658	10.704	10.704	10.860	10.705	10.862
10.18	10.439	10.575	10.669	10.715	10.715	10.871	10.716	10.873
10.19	10.450	10.586	10.680	10.726	10.726	10.882	10.727	10.884
10.20	10.460	10.597	10.691	10.737	10.737	10.894	10.738	10.895
10.21	10.471	10.608	10.702	10.748	10.748	10.905	10.749	10.907
10.22	10.481	10.618	10.713	10.759	10.759	10.916	10.760	10.918
10.23	10.492	10.629	10.724	10.770	10.770	10.927	10.772	10.929
10.24	10.502	10.640	10.735	10.781	10.781	10.939	10.783	10.940
10.25	10.513	10.651	10.746	10.792	10.792	10.950	10.794	10.952
10.26	10.523	10.662	10.756	10.803	10.803	10.961	10.805	10.963
10.27	10.534	10.672	10.767	10.814	10.814	10.972	10.816	10.974
10.28	10.544	10.683	10.778	10.825	10.825	10.984	10.827	10.985
10.29	10.555	10.694	10.789	10.836	10.836	10.995	10.838	10.997
10.30	10.565	10.705	10.800	10.848	10.848	11.006	10.849	11.008
10.31	10.576	10.716	10.811	10.859	10.859	11.017	10.860	11.019
10.32	10.586	10.726	10.822	10.870	10.870	11.029	10.871	11.030
10.33	10.597	10.737	10.833	10.881	10.881	11.040	10.882	11.042
10.34	10.607	10.748	10.844	10.892	10.892	11.051	10.893	11.053
10.35	10.618	10.759	10.855	10.903	10.903	11.062	10.905	11.064
10.36	10.628	10.769	10.866	10.914	10.914	11.074	10.916	11.075
10.37	10.639	10.780	10.877	10.925	10.925	11.085	10.927	11.087
10.38	10.649	10.791	10.888	10.936	10.936	11.096	10.938	11.098
10.39	10.660	10.802	10.899	10.947	10.947	11.107	10.949	11.109
10.40	10.670	10.813	10.910	10.958	10.958	11.119	10.960	11.120
10.41	10.681	10.823	10.921	10.969	10.969	11.130	10.971	11.132
10.42	10.691	10.834	10.932	10.981	10.981	11.141	10.982	11.143
10.43	10.702	10.845	10.943	10.992	10.992	11.153	10.993	11.154
10.44	10.712	10.856	10.954	11.003	11.003	11.164	11.004	11.166
10.45	10.723	10.867	10.965	11.014	11.014	11.175	11.016	11.177
10.46	10.734	10.877	10.976	11.025	11.025	11.186	11.027	11.188
10.47	10.744	10.888	10.987	11.036	11.036	11.198	11.038	11.199
10.48	10.755	10.899	10.998	11.047	11.047	11.209	11.049	11.211
10.49	10.765	10.910	11.009	11.058	11.058	11.220	11.060	11.222
10.50	10.776	10.921	11.020	11.069	11.069	11.231	11.071	11.233
10.51	10.786	10.932	11.031	11.080	11.080	11.243	11.082	11.244
10.52	10.797	10.942	11.042	11.092	11.092	11.254	11.093	11.256
10.53	10.807	10.953	11.053	11.103	11.103	11.265	11.104	11.267
10.54	10.818	10.964	11.064	11.114	11.114	11.277	11.115	11.278
10.55	10.828	10.975	11.075	11.125	11.125	11.288	11.127	11.290
10.56	10.839	10.986	11.086	11.136	11.136	11.299	11.138	11.301
10.57	10.849	10.996	11.097	11.147	11.147	11.310	11.149	11.312
10.58	10.860	11.007	11.108	11.158	11.158	11.322	11.160	11.323
10.59	10.870	11.018	11.119	11.169	11.169	11.333	11.171	11.335
10.60	10.881	11.029	11.130	11.180	11.180	11.344	11.182	11.346

271

EFFECTIVE ANNUAL YIELDS

NOMINAL ANNUAL INTEREST RATE	COMPOUNDING METHOD							
	SEMI-ANNUALLY	QUARTERLY	MONTHLY	360/360 DAILY	365/365 DAILY	365/360 DAILY	CONTINUOUS	365/360 CONTINUOUS
10.60	10.881	11.029	11.130	11.180	11.180	11.344	11.182	11.346
10.61	10.891	11.040	11.141	11.192	11.192	11.356	11.193	11.357
10.62	10.902	11.050	11.152	11.203	11.203	11.367	11.204	11.369
10.63	10.912	11.061	11.164	11.214	11.214	11.378	11.216	11.380
10.64	10.923	11.072	11.175	11.225	11.225	11.389	11.227	11.391
10.65	10.934	11.083	11.186	11.236	11.236	11.401	11.238	11.402
10.66	10.944	11.094	11.197	11.247	11.247	11.412	11.249	11.414
10.67	10.955	11.105	11.208	11.258	11.258	11.423	11.260	11.425
10.68	10.965	11.115	11.219	11.269	11.269	11.435	11.271	11.436
10.69	10.976	11.126	11.230	11.281	11.281	11.446	11.282	11.448
10.70	10.986	11.137	11.241	11.292	11.292	11.457	11.293	11.459
10.71	10.997	11.148	11.252	11.303	11.303	11.468	11.305	11.470
10.72	11.007	11.159	11.263	11.314	11.314	11.480	11.316	11.482
10.73	11.018	11.170	11.274	11.325	11.325	11.491	11.327	11.493
10.74	11.028	11.180	11.285	11.336	11.336	11.502	11.338	11.504
10.75	11.039	11.191	11.296	11.347	11.347	11.514	11.349	11.515
10.76	11.049	11.202	11.307	11.358	11.358	11.525	11.360	11.527
10.77	11.060	11.213	11.318	11.370	11.370	11.536	11.371	11.538
10.78	11.071	11.224	11.329	11.381	11.381	11.548	11.382	11.549
10.79	11.081	11.234	11.340	11.392	11.392	11.559	11.394	11.561
10.80	11.092	11.245	11.351	11.403	11.403	11.570	11.405	11.572
10.81	11.102	11.256	11.362	11.414	11.414	11.581	11.416	11.583
10.82	11.113	11.267	11.373	11.425	11.425	11.593	11.427	11.595
10.83	11.123	11.278	11.384	11.436	11.436	11.604	11.438	11.606
10.84	11.134	11.289	11.395	11.448	11.448	11.615	11.449	11.617
10.85	11.144	11.299	11.406	11.459	11.459	11.627	11.460	11.629
10.86	11.155	11.310	11.417	11.470	11.470	11.638	11.472	11.640
10.87	11.165	11.321	11.428	11.481	11.481	11.649	11.483	11.651
10.88	11.176	11.332	11.439	11.492	11.492	11.661	11.494	11.663
10.89	11.186	11.343	11.450	11.503	11.503	11.672	11.505	11.674
10.90	11.197	11.354	11.461	11.514	11.514	11.683	11.516	11.685
10.91	11.208	11.365	11.472	11.526	11.526	11.695	11.527	11.697
10.92	11.218	11.375	11.483	11.537	11.537	11.706	11.539	11.708
10.93	11.229	11.386	11.495	11.548	11.548	11.717	11.550	11.719
10.94	11.239	11.397	11.506	11.559	11.559	11.729	11.561	11.730
10.95	11.250	11.408	11.517	11.570	11.570	11.740	11.572	11.742
10.96	11.260	11.419	11.528	11.581	11.581	11.751	11.583	11.753
10.97	11.271	11.430	11.539	11.592	11.592	11.763	11.594	11.764
10.98	11.281	11.440	11.550	11.604	11.604	11.774	11.605	11.776
10.99	11.292	11.451	11.561	11.615	11.615	11.785	11.617	11.787
11.00	11.302	11.462	11.572	11.626	11.626	11.797	11.628	11.798
11.01	11.313	11.473	11.583	11.637	11.637	11.808	11.639	11.810
11.02	11.324	11.484	11.594	11.648	11.648	11.819	11.650	11.821
11.03	11.334	11.495	11.605	11.659	11.659	11.831	11.661	11.832
11.04	11.345	11.506	11.616	11.671	11.671	11.842	11.672	11.844
11.05	11.355	11.516	11.627	11.682	11.682	11.853	11.684	11.855
11.06	11.366	11.527	11.638	11.693	11.693	11.865	11.695	11.867
11.07	11.376	11.538	11.649	11.704	11.704	11.876	11.706	11.878
11.08	11.387	11.549	11.660	11.715	11.715	11.887	11.717	11.889
11.09	11.397	11.560	11.671	11.726	11.726	11.899	11.728	11.901
11.10	11.408	11.571	11.682	11.738	11.738	11.910	11.739	11.912
11.11	11.419	11.582	11.694	11.749	11.749	11.921	11.751	11.923
11.12	11.429	11.592	11.705	11.760	11.760	11.933	11.762	11.935
11.13	11.440	11.603	11.716	11.771	11.771	11.944	11.773	11.946
11.14	11.450	11.614	11.727	11.782	11.782	11.955	11.784	11.957
11.15	11.461	11.625	11.738	11.793	11.793	11.967	11.795	11.969
11.16	11.471	11.636	11.749	11.805	11.805	11.978	11.807	11.980
11.17	11.482	11.647	11.760	11.816	11.816	11.989	11.818	11.991
11.18	11.492	11.658	11.771	11.827	11.827	12.001	11.829	12.003
11.19	11.503	11.668	11.782	11.838	11.838	12.012	11.840	12.014
11.20	11.514	11.679	11.793	11.849	11.849	12.023	11.851	12.025
11.21	11.524	11.690	11.804	11.861	11.861	12.035	11.862	12.037
11.22	11.535	11.701	11.815	11.872	11.872	12.046	11.874	12.048
11.23	11.545	11.712	11.826	11.883	11.883	12.058	11.885	12.059
11.24	11.556	11.723	11.838	11.894	11.894	12.069	11.896	12.071
11.25	11.566	11.734	11.849	11.905	11.905	12.080	11.907	12.082
11.26	11.577	11.744	11.860	11.916	11.916	12.092	11.918	12.094
11.27	11.588	11.755	11.871	11.928	11.928	12.103	11.930	12.105
11.28	11.598	11.766	11.882	11.939	11.939	12.114	11.941	12.116
11.29	11.609	11.777	11.893	11.950	11.950	12.126	11.952	12.128
11.30	11.619	11.788	11.904	11.961	11.961	12.137	11.963	12.139
11.31	11.630	11.799	11.915	11.972	11.972	12.148	11.974	12.150
11.32	11.640	11.810	11.926	11.984	11.984	12.160	11.986	12.162
11.33	11.651	11.821	11.937	11.995	11.995	12.171	11.997	12.173
11.34	11.661	11.831	11.948	12.006	12.006	12.183	12.008	12.185
11.35	11.672	11.842	11.959	12.017	12.017	12.194	12.019	12.196
11.36	11.683	11.853	11.971	12.028	12.028	12.205	12.030	12.207
11.37	11.693	11.864	11.982	12.040	12.040	12.217	12.042	12.219
11.38	11.704	11.875	11.993	12.051	12.051	12.228	12.053	12.230
11.39	11.714	11.886	12.004	12.062	12.062	12.239	12.064	12.241
11.40	11.725	11.897	12.015	12.073	12.073	12.251	12.075	12.253

EFFECTIVE ANNUAL YIELDS

COMPOUNDING METHOD

NOMINAL ANNUAL INTEREST RATE	SEMI-ANNUALLY	QUARTERLY	MONTHLY	360/360 DAILY	365/365 DAILY	365/360 DAILY	CONTINUOUS	365/360 CONTINUOUS
11.40	11.725	11.897	12.015	12.073	12.073	12.251	12.075	12.253
11.41	11.735	11.908	12.026	12.084	12.084	12.262	12.086	12.264
11.42	11.746	11.918	12.037	12.096	12.096	12.274	12.098	12.276
11.43	11.757	11.929	12.048	12.107	12.107	12.285	12.109	12.287
11.44	11.767	11.940	12.059	12.118	12.118	12.296	12.120	12.298
11.45	11.778	11.951	12.070	12.129	12.129	12.308	12.131	12.310
11.46	11.788	11.962	12.082	12.140	12.140	12.319	12.142	12.321
11.47	11.799	11.973	12.093	12.152	12.152	12.330	12.154	12.333
11.48	11.809	11.984	12.104	12.163	12.163	12.342	12.165	12.344
11.49	11.820	11.995	12.115	12.174	12.174	12.353	12.176	12.355
11.50	11.831	12.006	12.126	12.185	12.185	12.365	12.187	12.367
11.51	11.841	12.016	12.137	12.196	12.197	12.376	12.199	12.378
11.52	11.852	12.027	12.148	12.208	12.208	12.387	12.210	12.389
11.53	11.862	12.038	12.159	12.219	12.219	12.399	12.221	12.401
11.54	11.873	12.049	12.170	12.230	12.230	12.410	12.232	12.412
11.55	11.884	12.060	12.181	12.241	12.241	12.422	12.243	12.424
11.56	11.894	12.071	12.193	12.253	12.253	12.433	12.255	12.435
11.57	11.905	12.082	12.204	12.264	12.264	12.444	12.266	12.446
11.58	11.915	12.093	12.215	12.275	12.275	12.456	12.277	12.458
11.59	11.926	12.104	12.226	12.286	12.286	12.467	12.288	12.469
11.60	11.936	12.114	12.237	12.297	12.298	12.479	12.300	12.481
11.61	11.947	12.125	12.248	12.309	12.309	12.490	12.311	12.492
11.62	11.958	12.136	12.259	12.320	12.320	12.501	12.322	12.503
11.63	11.968	12.147	12.270	12.331	12.331	12.513	12.333	12.515
11.64	11.979	12.158	12.282	12.342	12.342	12.524	12.345	12.526
11.65	11.989	12.169	12.293	12.354	12.354	12.536	12.356	12.538
11.66	12.000	12.180	12.304	12.365	12.365	12.547	12.367	12.549
11.67	12.010	12.191	12.315	12.376	12.376	12.558	12.378	12.561
11.68	12.021	12.202	12.326	12.387	12.387	12.570	12.389	12.572
11.69	12.032	12.213	12.337	12.399	12.399	12.581	12.401	12.583
11.70	12.042	12.223	12.348	12.410	12.410	12.593	12.412	12.595
11.71	12.053	12.234	12.359	12.421	12.421	12.604	12.423	12.606
11.72	12.063	12.245	12.371	12.432	12.432	12.615	12.434	12.618
11.73	12.074	12.256	12.382	12.444	12.444	12.627	12.446	12.629
11.74	12.085	12.267	12.393	12.455	12.455	12.638	12.457	12.640
11.75	12.095	12.278	12.404	12.466	12.466	12.650	12.468	12.652
11.76	12.106	12.289	12.415	12.477	12.477	12.661	12.479	12.663
11.77	12.116	12.300	12.426	12.488	12.489	12.673	12.491	12.675
11.78	12.127	12.311	12.437	12.500	12.500	12.684	12.502	12.686
11.79	12.138	12.322	12.448	12.511	12.511	12.695	12.513	12.698
11.80	12.148	12.332	12.460	12.522	12.522	12.707	12.524	12.709
11.81	12.159	12.343	12.471	12.533	12.534	12.718	12.536	12.720
11.82	12.169	12.354	12.482	12.545	12.545	12.730	12.547	12.732
11.83	12.180	12.365	12.493	12.556	12.556	12.741	12.558	12.743
11.84	12.190	12.376	12.504	12.567	12.567	12.752	12.569	12.755
11.85	12.201	12.387	12.515	12.578	12.579	12.764	12.581	12.766
11.86	12.212	12.398	12.526	12.590	12.590	12.775	12.592	12.778
11.87	12.222	12.409	12.538	12.601	12.601	12.787	12.603	12.789
11.88	12.233	12.420	12.549	12.612	12.612	12.798	12.614	12.800
11.89	12.243	12.431	12.560	12.624	12.624	12.810	12.626	12.812
11.90	12.254	12.442	12.571	12.635	12.635	12.821	12.637	12.823
11.91	12.265	12.453	12.582	12.646	12.646	12.832	12.648	12.835
11.92	12.275	12.463	12.593	12.657	12.657	12.844	12.660	12.846
11.93	12.286	12.474	12.604	12.669	12.669	12.855	12.671	12.858
11.94	12.296	12.485	12.616	12.680	12.680	12.867	12.682	12.869
11.95	12.307	12.496	12.627	12.691	12.691	12.878	12.693	12.881
11.96	12.318	12.507	12.638	12.702	12.702	12.890	12.705	12.892
11.97	12.328	12.518	12.649	12.714	12.714	12.901	12.716	12.903
11.98	12.339	12.529	12.660	12.725	12.725	12.913	12.727	12.915
11.99	12.349	12.540	12.671	12.736	12.736	12.924	12.738	12.926
12.00	12.360	12.551	12.683	12.747	12.747	12.935	12.750	12.938
12.01	12.371	12.562	12.694	12.759	12.759	12.947	12.761	12.949
12.02	12.381	12.573	12.705	12.770	12.770	12.958	12.772	12.961
12.03	12.392	12.584	12.716	12.781	12.781	12.970	12.784	12.972
12.04	12.402	12.595	12.727	12.793	12.793	12.981	12.795	12.984
12.05	12.413	12.606	12.738	12.804	12.804	12.993	12.806	12.995
12.06	12.424	12.616	12.749	12.815	12.815	13.004	12.817	13.006
12.07	12.434	12.627	12.761	12.826	12.826	13.016	12.829	13.018
12.08	12.445	12.638	12.772	12.838	12.838	13.027	12.840	13.029
12.09	12.455	12.649	12.783	12.849	12.849	13.039	12.851	13.041
12.10	12.466	12.660	12.794	12.860	12.860	13.050	12.862	13.052
12.11	12.477	12.671	12.805	12.871	12.872	13.061	12.874	13.064
12.12	12.487	12.682	12.816	12.883	12.883	13.073	12.885	13.075
12.13	12.498	12.693	12.828	12.894	12.894	13.084	12.896	13.087
12.14	12.508	12.704	12.839	12.905	12.905	13.096	12.908	13.098
12.15	12.519	12.715	12.850	12.917	12.917	13.107	12.919	13.110
12.16	12.530	12.726	12.861	12.928	12.928	13.119	12.930	13.121
12.17	12.540	12.737	12.872	12.939	12.939	13.130	12.942	13.133
12.18	12.551	12.748	12.883	12.950	12.951	13.142	12.953	13.144
12.19	12.561	12.759	12.895	12.962	12.962	13.153	12.964	13.156
12.20	12.572	12.770	12.906	12.973	12.973	13.165	12.975	13.167

273

EFFECTIVE ANNUAL YIELDS

COMPOUNDING METHOD

NOMINAL ANNUAL INTEREST RATE	SEMI-ANNUALLY	QUARTERLY	MONTHLY	360/360 DAILY	365/365 DAILY	365/360 DAILY	CONTINUOUS	365/360 CONTINUOUS
12.20	12.572	12.770	12.906	12.973	12.973	13.165	12.975	13.167
12.21	12.583	12.781	12.917	12.984	12.984	13.176	12.987	13.178
12.22	12.593	12.791	12.928	12.996	12.996	13.188	12.998	13.190
12.23	12.604	12.802	12.939	13.007	13.007	13.199	13.009	13.201
12.24	12.615	12.813	12.951	13.018	13.018	13.211	13.021	13.213
12.25	12.625	12.824	12.962	13.030	13.030	13.222	13.032	13.224
12.26	12.636	12.835	12.973	13.041	13.041	13.233	13.043	13.236
12.27	12.646	12.846	12.984	13.052	13.052	13.245	13.055	13.247
12.28	12.657	12.857	12.995	13.063	13.063	13.256	13.066	13.259
12.29	12.668	12.868	13.006	13.075	13.075	13.268	13.077	13.270
12.30	12.678	12.879	13.018	13.086	13.086	13.279	13.088	13.282
12.31	12.689	12.890	13.029	13.097	13.097	13.291	13.100	13.293
12.32	12.699	12.901	13.040	13.109	13.109	13.302	13.111	13.305
12.33	12.710	12.912	13.051	13.120	13.120	13.314	13.122	13.316
12.34	12.721	12.923	13.062	13.131	13.131	13.325	13.134	13.328
12.35	12.731	12.934	13.074	13.143	13.143	13.337	13.145	13.339
12.36	12.742	12.945	13.085	13.154	13.154	13.348	13.156	13.351
12.37	12.753	12.956	13.096	13.165	13.165	13.360	13.168	13.362
12.38	12.763	12.967	13.107	13.177	13.177	13.371	13.179	13.374
12.39	12.774	12.978	13.118	13.188	13.188	13.383	13.190	13.385
12.40	12.784	12.989	13.130	13.199	13.199	13.394	13.202	13.397
12.41	12.795	13.000	13.141	13.210	13.211	13.406	13.213	13.408
12.42	12.806	13.011	13.152	13.222	13.222	13.417	13.224	13.420
12.43	12.816	13.021	13.163	13.233	13.233	13.429	13.236	13.431
12.44	12.827	13.032	13.174	13.244	13.244	13.440	13.247	13.443
12.45	12.838	13.043	13.186	13.256	13.256	13.452	13.258	13.454
12.46	12.848	13.054	13.197	13.267	13.267	13.463	13.270	13.466
12.47	12.859	13.065	13.208	13.278	13.278	13.475	13.281	13.477
12.48	12.869	13.076	13.219	13.290	13.290	13.486	13.292	13.489
12.49	12.880	13.087	13.230	13.301	13.301	13.498	13.304	13.500
12.50	12.891	13.098	13.242	13.312	13.312	13.509	13.315	13.512
12.51	12.901	13.109	13.253	13.324	13.324	13.521	13.326	13.523
12.52	12.912	13.120	13.264	13.335	13.335	13.532	13.338	13.535
12.53	12.923	13.131	13.275	13.346	13.346	13.544	13.349	13.546
12.54	12.933	13.142	13.286	13.358	13.358	13.555	13.360	13.558
12.55	12.944	13.153	13.298	13.369	13.369	13.567	13.372	13.569
12.56	12.954	13.164	13.309	13.380	13.380	13.578	13.383	13.581
12.57	12.965	13.175	13.320	13.392	13.392	13.590	13.394	13.592
12.58	12.976	13.186	13.331	13.403	13.403	13.601	13.406	13.604
12.59	12.986	13.197	13.343	13.414	13.414	13.613	13.417	13.615
12.60	12.997	13.208	13.354	13.426	13.426	13.624	13.428	13.627
12.61	13.008	13.219	13.365	13.437	13.437	13.636	13.440	13.638
12.62	13.018	13.230	13.376	13.448	13.448	13.647	13.451	13.650
12.63	13.029	13.241	13.387	13.460	13.460	13.659	13.462	13.661
12.64	13.039	13.252	13.399	13.471	13.471	13.670	13.474	13.673
12.65	13.050	13.263	13.410	13.482	13.482	13.682	13.485	13.685
12.66	13.061	13.274	13.421	13.494	13.494	13.693	13.496	13.696
12.67	13.071	13.285	13.432	13.505	13.505	13.705	13.508	13.708
12.68	13.082	13.296	13.444	13.516	13.516	13.717	13.519	13.719
12.69	13.093	13.307	13.455	13.528	13.528	13.728	13.530	13.731
12.70	13.103	13.318	13.466	13.539	13.539	13.740	13.542	13.742
12.71	13.114	13.329	13.477	13.551	13.551	13.751	13.553	13.754
12.72	13.124	13.340	13.488	13.562	13.562	13.763	13.564	13.765
12.73	13.135	13.351	13.500	13.573	13.573	13.774	13.576	13.777
12.74	13.146	13.362	13.511	13.585	13.585	13.786	13.587	13.788
12.75	13.156	13.373	13.522	13.596	13.596	13.797	13.598	13.800
12.76	13.167	13.384	13.533	13.607	13.607	13.809	13.610	13.811
12.77	13.178	13.395	13.545	13.619	13.619	13.820	13.621	13.823
12.78	13.188	13.406	13.556	13.630	13.630	13.832	13.633	13.834
12.79	13.199	13.417	13.567	13.641	13.641	13.843	13.644	13.846
12.80	13.210	13.428	13.578	13.653	13.653	13.855	13.655	13.858
12.81	13.220	13.439	13.590	13.664	13.664	13.866	13.667	13.869
12.82	13.231	13.450	13.601	13.675	13.675	13.878	13.678	13.881
12.83	13.242	13.461	13.612	13.687	13.687	13.890	13.689	13.892
12.84	13.252	13.472	13.623	13.698	13.698	13.901	13.701	13.904
12.85	13.263	13.483	13.634	13.710	13.710	13.913	13.712	13.915
12.86	13.273	13.494	13.646	13.721	13.721	13.924	13.724	13.927
12.87	13.284	13.505	13.657	13.732	13.732	13.936	13.735	13.938
12.88	13.295	13.516	13.668	13.744	13.744	13.947	13.746	13.950
12.89	13.305	13.527	13.679	13.755	13.755	13.959	13.758	13.961
12.90	13.316	13.538	13.691	13.766	13.766	13.970	13.769	13.973
12.91	13.327	13.549	13.702	13.778	13.778	13.982	13.780	13.985
12.92	13.337	13.560	13.713	13.789	13.789	13.993	13.792	13.996
12.93	13.348	13.571	13.724	13.801	13.801	14.005	13.803	14.008
12.94	13.359	13.582	13.736	13.812	13.812	14.017	13.815	14.019
12.95	13.369	13.593	13.747	13.823	13.823	14.028	13.826	14.031
12.96	13.380	13.604	13.758	13.835	13.835	14.040	13.837	14.042
12.97	13.391	13.615	13.769	13.846	13.846	14.051	13.849	14.054
12.98	13.401	13.626	13.781	13.857	13.857	14.063	13.860	14.066
12.99	13.412	13.637	13.792	13.869	13.869	14.074	13.871	14.077
13.00	13.422	13.648	13.803	13.880	13.880	14.086	13.883	14.089

EFFECTIVE ANNUAL YIELDS

COMPOUNDING METHOD

NOMINAL ANNUAL INTEREST RATE	SEMI-ANNUALLY	QUARTERLY	MONTHLY	360/360 DAILY	365/365 DAILY	365/360 DAILY	CONTINUOUS	365/360 CONTINUOUS
13.00	13.422	13.648	13.803	13.880	13.880	14.086	13.883	14.089
13.01	13.433	13.659	13.815	13.892	13.892	14.097	13.894	14.100
13.02	13.444	13.670	13.826	13.903	13.903	14.109	13.906	14.112
13.03	13.454	13.681	13.837	13.914	13.914	14.121	13.917	14.123
13.04	13.465	13.692	13.848	13.926	13.926	14.132	13.928	14.135
13.05	13.476	13.703	13.860	13.937	13.937	14.144	13.940	14.146
13.06	13.486	13.714	13.871	13.948	13.949	14.155	13.951	14.158
13.07	13.497	13.725	13.882	13.960	13.960	14.167	13.963	14.170
13.08	13.508	13.736	13.893	13.971	13.971	14.178	13.974	14.181
13.09	13.518	13.747	13.905	13.983	13.983	14.190	13.985	14.193
13.10	13.529	13.758	13.916	13.994	13.994	14.202	13.997	14.204
13.11	13.540	13.769	13.927	14.005	14.005	14.213	14.008	14.216
13.12	13.550	13.780	13.938	14.017	14.017	14.225	14.020	14.228
13.13	13.561	13.791	13.950	14.028	14.028	14.236	14.031	14.239
13.14	13.572	13.802	13.961	14.040	14.040	14.248	14.042	14.251
13.15	13.582	13.813	13.972	14.051	14.051	14.260	14.054	14.262
13.16	13.593	13.824	13.984	14.062	14.062	14.271	14.065	14.274
13.17	13.604	13.835	13.995	14.074	14.074	14.283	14.077	14.285
13.18	13.614	13.846	14.006	14.085	14.085	14.294	14.088	14.297
13.19	13.625	13.857	14.017	14.097	14.097	14.306	14.099	14.309
13.20	13.636	13.868	14.029	14.108	14.108	14.317	14.111	14.320
13.21	13.646	13.879	14.040	14.119	14.120	14.329	14.122	14.332
13.22	13.657	13.890	14.051	14.131	14.131	14.341	14.134	14.343
13.23	13.668	13.901	14.062	14.142	14.142	14.352	14.145	14.355
13.24	13.678	13.912	14.074	14.154	14.154	14.364	14.156	14.367
13.25	13.689	13.923	14.085	14.165	14.165	14.375	14.168	14.378
13.26	13.700	13.934	14.096	14.177	14.177	14.387	14.179	14.390
13.27	13.710	13.945	14.108	14.188	14.188	14.399	14.191	14.401
13.28	13.721	13.956	14.119	14.199	14.199	14.410	14.202	14.413
13.29	13.732	13.967	14.130	14.211	14.211	14.422	14.214	14.425
13.30	13.742	13.978	14.141	14.222	14.222	14.433	14.225	14.436
13.31	13.753	13.989	14.153	14.234	14.234	14.445	14.236	14.448
13.32	13.764	14.000	14.164	14.245	14.245	14.457	14.248	14.459
13.33	13.774	14.011	14.175	14.256	14.256	14.468	14.259	14.471
13.34	13.785	14.022	14.187	14.268	14.268	14.480	14.271	14.483
13.35	13.796	14.033	14.198	14.279	14.279	14.491	14.282	14.494
13.36	13.806	14.044	14.209	14.291	14.291	14.503	14.294	14.506
13.37	13.817	14.055	14.221	14.302	14.302	14.515	14.305	14.517
13.38	13.828	14.066	14.232	14.314	14.314	14.526	14.316	14.529
13.39	13.838	14.077	14.243	14.325	14.325	14.538	14.328	14.541
13.40	13.849	14.089	14.254	14.336	14.336	14.549	14.339	14.552
13.41	13.860	14.100	14.266	14.348	14.348	14.561	14.351	14.564
13.42	13.870	14.111	14.277	14.359	14.359	14.573	14.362	14.576
13.43	13.881	14.122	14.288	14.371	14.371	14.584	14.374	14.587
13.44	13.892	14.133	14.300	14.382	14.382	14.596	14.385	14.599
13.45	13.902	14.144	14.311	14.394	14.394	14.607	14.396	14.610
13.46	13.913	14.155	14.322	14.405	14.405	14.619	14.408	14.622
13.47	13.924	14.166	14.334	14.416	14.417	14.631	14.419	14.634
13.48	13.934	14.177	14.345	14.428	14.428	14.642	14.431	14.645
13.49	13.945	14.188	14.356	14.439	14.439	14.654	14.442	14.657
13.50	13.956	14.199	14.367	14.451	14.451	14.666	14.454	14.668
13.51	13.966	14.210	14.379	14.462	14.462	14.677	14.465	14.680
13.52	13.977	14.221	14.390	14.474	14.474	14.689	14.477	14.692
13.53	13.988	14.232	14.401	14.485	14.485	14.700	14.488	14.703
13.54	13.998	14.243	14.413	14.497	14.497	14.712	14.499	14.715
13.55	14.009	14.254	14.424	14.508	14.508	14.724	14.511	14.727
13.56	14.020	14.265	14.435	14.519	14.519	14.735	14.522	14.738
13.57	14.030	14.276	14.447	14.531	14.531	14.747	14.534	14.750
13.58	14.041	14.287	14.458	14.542	14.542	14.759	14.545	14.762
13.59	14.052	14.298	14.469	14.554	14.554	14.770	14.557	14.773
13.60	14.062	14.309	14.481	14.565	14.565	14.782	14.568	14.785
13.61	14.073	14.321	14.492	14.577	14.577	14.793	14.580	14.796
13.62	14.084	14.332	14.503	14.588	14.588	14.805	14.591	14.808
13.63	14.094	14.343	14.515	14.600	14.600	14.817	14.603	14.820
13.64	14.105	14.354	14.526	14.611	14.611	14.828	14.614	14.831
13.65	14.116	14.365	14.537	14.623	14.623	14.840	14.625	14.843
13.66	14.126	14.376	14.549	14.634	14.634	14.852	14.637	14.855
13.67	14.137	14.387	14.560	14.645	14.645	14.863	14.648	14.866
13.68	14.148	14.398	14.571	14.657	14.657	14.875	14.660	14.878
13.69	14.159	14.409	14.583	14.668	14.668	14.887	14.671	14.890
13.70	14.169	14.420	14.594	14.680	14.680	14.898	14.683	14.901
13.71	14.180	14.431	14.605	14.691	14.691	14.910	14.694	14.913
13.72	14.191	14.442	14.617	14.703	14.703	14.921	14.706	14.925
13.73	14.201	14.453	14.628	14.714	14.714	14.933	14.717	14.936
13.74	14.212	14.464	14.639	14.726	14.726	14.945	14.729	14.948
13.75	14.223	14.475	14.651	14.737	14.737	14.956	14.740	14.960
13.76	14.233	14.486	14.662	14.749	14.749	14.968	14.752	14.971
13.77	14.244	14.498	14.673	14.760	14.760	14.980	14.763	14.983
13.78	14.255	14.509	14.685	14.772	14.772	14.991	14.775	14.994
13.79	14.265	14.520	14.696	14.783	14.783	15.003	14.786	15.006
13.80	14.276	14.531	14.707	14.795	14.795	15.015	14.798	15.018

EFFECTIVE ANNUAL YIELDS

COMPOUNDING METHOD

NOMINAL ANNUAL INTEREST RATE	SEMI-ANNUALLY	QUARTERLY	MONTHLY	360/360 DAILY	365/365 DAILY	365/360 DAILY	CONTINUOUS	365/360 CONTINUOUS
13.80	14.276	14.531	14.707	14.795	14.795	15.015	14.798	15.018
13.81	14.287	14.542	14.719	14.806	14.806	15.026	14.809	15.029
13.82	14.297	14.553	14.730	14.817	14.818	15.038	14.821	15.041
13.83	14.308	14.564	14.741	14.829	14.829	15.050	14.832	15.053
13.84	14.319	14.575	14.753	14.840	14.840	15.061	14.843	15.064
13.85	14.330	14.586	14.764	14.852	14.852	15.073	14.855	15.076
13.86	14.340	14.597	14.775	14.863	14.863	15.085	14.866	15.088
13.87	14.351	14.608	14.787	14.875	14.875	15.096	14.878	15.099
13.88	14.362	14.619	14.798	14.886	14.886	15.108	14.889	15.111
13.89	14.372	14.630	14.809	14.898	14.898	15.120	14.901	15.123
13.90	14.383	14.641	14.821	14.909	14.909	15.131	14.912	15.134
13.91	14.394	14.653	14.832	14.921	14.921	15.143	14.924	15.146
13.92	14.404	14.664	14.843	14.932	14.932	15.155	14.935	15.158
13.93	14.415	14.675	14.855	14.944	14.944	15.166	14.947	15.169
13.94	14.426	14.686	14.866	14.955	14.955	15.178	14.958	15.181
13.95	14.437	14.697	14.877	14.967	14.967	15.190	14.970	15.193
13.96	14.447	14.708	14.889	14.978	14.978	15.201	14.981	15.205
13.97	14.458	14.719	14.900	14.990	14.990	15.213	14.993	15.216
13.98	14.469	14.730	14.911	15.001	15.001	15.225	15.004	15.228
13.99	14.479	14.741	14.923	15.013	15.013	15.236	15.016	15.240
14.00	14.490	14.752	14.934	15.024	15.024	15.248	15.027	15.251
14.01	14.501	14.763	14.946	15.036	15.036	15.260	15.039	15.263
14.02	14.511	14.774	14.957	15.047	15.047	15.271	15.050	15.275
14.03	14.522	14.786	14.968	15.059	15.059	15.283	15.062	15.286
14.04	14.533	14.797	14.980	15.070	15.070	15.295	15.073	15.298
14.05	14.544	14.808	14.991	15.082	15.082	15.306	15.085	15.310
14.06	14.554	14.819	15.002	15.093	15.093	15.318	15.096	15.321
14.07	14.565	14.830	15.014	15.105	15.105	15.330	15.108	15.333
14.08	14.576	14.841	15.025	15.116	15.116	15.342	15.119	15.345
14.09	14.586	14.852	15.036	15.128	15.128	15.353	15.131	15.356
14.10	14.597	14.863	15.048	15.139	15.139	15.365	15.142	15.368
14.11	14.608	14.874	15.059	15.151	15.151	15.377	15.154	15.380
14.12	14.618	14.885	15.071	15.162	15.162	15.388	15.165	15.392
14.13	14.629	14.897	15.082	15.174	15.174	15.400	15.177	15.403
14.14	14.640	14.908	15.093	15.185	15.185	15.412	15.189	15.415
14.15	14.651	14.919	15.105	15.197	15.197	15.423	15.200	15.427
14.16	14.661	14.930	15.116	15.208	15.208	15.435	15.212	15.438
14.17	14.672	14.941	15.127	15.220	15.220	15.447	15.223	15.450
14.18	14.683	14.952	15.139	15.231	15.231	15.459	15.235	15.462
14.19	14.693	14.963	15.150	15.243	15.243	15.470	15.246	15.473
14.20	14.704	14.974	15.162	15.254	15.254	15.482	15.258	15.485
14.21	14.715	14.985	15.173	15.266	15.266	15.494	15.269	15.497
14.22	14.726	14.996	15.184	15.277	15.278	15.505	15.281	15.509
14.23	14.736	15.008	15.196	15.289	15.289	15.517	15.292	15.520
14.24	14.747	15.019	15.207	15.301	15.301	15.529	15.304	15.532
14.25	14.758	15.030	15.219	15.312	15.312	15.540	15.315	15.544
14.26	14.768	15.041	15.230	15.324	15.324	15.552	15.327	15.555
14.27	14.779	15.052	15.241	15.335	15.335	15.564	15.338	15.567
14.28	14.790	15.063	15.253	15.347	15.347	15.576	15.350	15.579
14.29	14.801	15.074	15.264	15.358	15.358	15.587	15.361	15.591
14.30	14.811	15.085	15.275	15.370	15.370	15.599	15.373	15.602
14.31	14.822	15.096	15.287	15.381	15.381	15.611	15.385	15.614
14.32	14.833	15.108	15.298	15.393	15.393	15.622	15.396	15.626
14.33	14.843	15.119	15.310	15.404	15.404	15.634	15.408	15.638
14.34	14.854	15.130	15.321	15.416	15.416	15.646	15.419	15.649
14.35	14.865	15.141	15.332	15.427	15.427	15.658	15.431	15.661
14.36	14.876	15.152	15.344	15.439	15.439	15.669	15.442	15.673
14.37	14.886	15.163	15.355	15.450	15.451	15.681	15.454	15.684
14.38	14.897	15.174	15.367	15.462	15.462	15.693	15.465	15.696
14.39	14.908	15.185	15.378	15.474	15.474	15.705	15.477	15.708
14.40	14.918	15.196	15.389	15.485	15.485	15.716	15.488	15.720
14.41	14.929	15.208	15.401	15.497	15.497	15.728	15.500	15.731
14.42	14.940	15.219	15.412	15.508	15.508	15.740	15.512	15.743
14.43	14.951	15.230	15.424	15.520	15.520	15.751	15.523	15.755
14.44	14.961	15.241	15.435	15.531	15.531	15.763	15.535	15.767
14.45	14.972	15.252	15.446	15.543	15.543	15.775	15.546	15.778
14.46	14.983	15.263	15.458	15.554	15.554	15.787	15.558	15.790
14.47	14.993	15.274	15.469	15.566	15.566	15.798	15.569	15.802
14.48	15.004	15.285	15.481	15.577	15.578	15.810	15.581	15.814
14.49	15.015	15.297	15.492	15.589	15.589	15.822	15.592	15.825
14.50	15.026	15.308	15.504	15.601	15.601	15.834	15.604	15.837
14.51	15.036	15.319	15.515	15.612	15.612	15.845	15.616	15.849
14.52	15.047	15.330	15.526	15.624	15.624	15.857	15.627	15.860
14.53	15.058	15.341	15.538	15.635	15.635	15.869	15.639	15.872
14.54	15.069	15.352	15.549	15.647	15.647	15.881	15.650	15.884
14.55	15.079	15.363	15.561	15.658	15.658	15.892	15.662	15.896
14.56	15.090	15.374	15.572	15.670	15.670	15.904	15.673	15.907
14.57	15.101	15.386	15.583	15.681	15.682	15.916	15.685	15.919
14.58	15.111	15.397	15.595	15.693	15.693	15.928	15.696	15.931
14.59	15.122	15.408	15.606	15.705	15.705	15.939	15.708	15.943
14.60	15.133	15.419	15.618	15.716	15.716	15.951	15.720	15.955

EFFECTIVE ANNUAL YIELDS

NOMINAL ANNUAL INTEREST RATE	COMPOUNDING METHOD							
	SEMI-ANNUALLY	QUARTERLY	MONTHLY	360/360 DAILY	365/365 DAILY	365/360 DAILY	CONTINUOUS	365/360 CONTINUOUS
14.60	15.133	15.419	15.618	15.716	15.716	15.951	15.720	15.955
14.61	15.144	15.430	15.629	15.728	15.728	15.963	15.731	15.966
14.62	15.154	15.441	15.641	15.739	15.739	15.975	15.743	15.978
14.63	15.165	15.452	15.652	15.751	15.751	15.986	15.754	15.990
14.64	15.176	15.464	15.663	15.762	15.763	15.998	15.766	16.002
14.65	15.187	15.475	15.675	15.774	15.774	16.010	15.777	16.013
14.66	15.197	15.486	15.686	15.786	15.786	16.022	15.789	16.025
14.67	15.208	15.497	15.698	15.797	15.797	16.033	15.801	16.037
14.68	15.219	15.508	15.709	15.809	15.809	16.045	15.812	16.049
14.69	15.229	15.519	15.721	15.820	15.820	16.057	15.824	16.060
14.70	15.240	15.530	15.732	15.832	15.832	16.069	15.835	16.072
14.71	15.251	15.542	15.743	15.843	15.844	16.080	15.847	16.084
14.72	15.262	15.553	15.755	15.855	15.855	16.092	15.859	16.096
14.73	15.272	15.564	15.766	15.867	15.867	16.104	15.870	16.107
14.74	15.283	15.575	15.778	15.878	15.878	16.116	15.882	16.119
14.75	15.294	15.586	15.789	15.890	15.890	16.127	15.893	16.131
14.76	15.305	15.597	15.801	15.901	15.901	16.139	15.905	16.143
14.77	15.315	15.608	15.812	15.913	15.913	16.151	15.917	16.155
14.78	15.326	15.620	15.823	15.925	15.925	16.163	15.928	16.166
14.79	15.337	15.631	15.835	15.936	15.936	16.175	15.940	16.178
14.80	15.348	15.642	15.846	15.948	15.948	16.186	15.951	16.190
14.81	15.358	15.653	15.858	15.959	15.959	16.198	15.963	16.202
14.82	15.369	15.664	15.869	15.971	15.971	16.210	15.974	16.213
14.83	15.380	15.675	15.881	15.983	15.983	16.222	15.986	16.225
14.84	15.391	15.686	15.892	15.994	15.994	16.233	15.998	16.237
14.85	15.401	15.698	15.904	16.006	16.006	16.245	16.009	16.249
14.86	15.412	15.709	15.915	16.017	16.017	16.257	16.021	16.261
14.87	15.423	15.720	15.927	16.029	16.029	16.269	16.032	16.272
14.88	15.434	15.731	15.938	16.041	16.041	16.281	16.044	16.284
14.89	15.444	15.742	15.949	16.052	16.052	16.292	16.056	16.296
14.90	15.455	15.753	15.961	16.064	16.064	16.304	16.067	16.308
14.91	15.466	15.765	15.972	16.075	16.075	16.316	16.079	16.320
14.92	15.477	15.776	15.984	16.087	16.087	16.328	16.091	16.331
14.93	15.487	15.787	15.995	16.099	16.099	16.339	16.102	16.343
14.94	15.498	15.798	16.007	16.110	16.110	16.351	16.114	16.355
14.95	15.509	15.809	16.018	16.122	16.122	16.363	16.125	16.367
14.96	15.520	15.820	16.030	16.133	16.133	16.375	16.137	16.379
14.97	15.530	15.832	16.041	16.145	16.145	16.387	16.149	16.390
14.98	15.541	15.843	16.053	16.157	16.157	16.398	16.160	16.402
14.99	15.552	15.854	16.064	16.168	16.168	16.410	16.172	16.414
15.00	15.562	15.865	16.075	16.180	16.180	16.422	16.183	16.426
15.01	15.573	15.876	16.087	16.191	16.191	16.434	16.195	16.438
15.02	15.584	15.887	16.098	16.203	16.203	16.446	16.207	16.449
15.03	15.595	15.899	16.110	16.215	16.215	16.457	16.218	16.461
15.04	15.606	15.910	16.121	16.226	16.226	16.469	16.230	16.473
15.05	15.616	15.921	16.133	16.238	16.238	16.481	16.242	16.485
15.06	15.627	15.932	16.144	16.249	16.250	16.493	16.253	16.497
15.07	15.638	15.943	16.156	16.261	16.261	16.505	16.265	16.508
15.08	15.649	15.954	16.167	16.273	16.273	16.516	16.276	16.520
15.09	15.659	15.966	16.179	16.284	16.284	16.528	16.288	16.532
15.10	15.670	15.977	16.190	16.296	16.296	16.540	16.300	16.544
15.11	15.681	15.988	16.202	16.308	16.308	16.552	16.311	16.556
15.12	15.692	15.999	16.213	16.319	16.319	16.564	16.323	16.567
15.13	15.702	16.010	16.225	16.331	16.331	16.576	16.335	16.579
15.14	15.713	16.021	16.236	16.342	16.343	16.587	16.346	16.591
15.15	15.724	16.033	16.248	16.354	16.354	16.599	16.358	16.603
15.16	15.735	16.044	16.259	16.366	16.366	16.611	16.369	16.615
15.17	15.745	16.055	16.270	16.377	16.377	16.623	16.381	16.627
15.18	15.756	16.066	16.282	16.389	16.389	16.635	16.393	16.638
15.19	15.767	16.077	16.293	16.401	16.401	16.646	16.404	16.650
15.20	15.778	16.089	16.305	16.412	16.412	16.658	16.416	16.662
15.21	15.788	16.100	16.316	16.424	16.424	16.670	16.428	16.674
15.22	15.799	16.111	16.328	16.436	16.436	16.682	16.439	16.686
15.23	15.810	16.122	16.339	16.447	16.447	16.694	16.451	16.698
15.24	15.821	16.133	16.351	16.459	16.459	16.706	16.463	16.709
15.25	15.831	16.144	16.362	16.470	16.471	16.717	16.474	16.721
15.26	15.842	16.156	16.374	16.482	16.482	16.729	16.486	16.733
15.27	15.853	16.167	16.385	16.494	16.494	16.741	16.498	16.745
15.28	15.864	16.178	16.397	16.505	16.505	16.753	16.509	16.757
15.29	15.874	16.189	16.408	16.517	16.517	16.765	16.521	16.769
15.30	15.885	16.200	16.420	16.529	16.529	16.777	16.532	16.780
15.31	15.896	16.212	16.431	16.540	16.540	16.788	16.544	16.792
15.32	15.907	16.223	16.443	16.552	16.552	16.800	16.556	16.804
15.33	15.918	16.234	16.454	16.564	16.564	16.812	16.567	16.816
15.34	15.928	16.245	16.466	16.575	16.575	16.824	16.579	16.828
15.35	15.939	16.256	16.477	16.587	16.587	16.836	16.591	16.840
15.36	15.950	16.268	16.489	16.599	16.599	16.848	16.602	16.851
15.37	15.961	16.279	16.500	16.610	16.610	16.859	16.614	16.863
15.38	15.971	16.290	16.512	16.622	16.622	16.871	16.626	16.875
15.39	15.982	16.301	16.523	16.634	16.634	16.883	16.637	16.887
15.40	15.993	16.312	16.535	16.645	16.645	16.895	16.649	16.899

EFFECTIVE ANNUAL YIELDS

NOMINAL ANNUAL INTEREST RATE	COMPOUNDING METHOD							
	SEMI-ANNUALLY	QUARTERLY	MONTHLY	360/360 DAILY	365/365 DAILY	365/360 DAILY	CONTINUOUS	365/360 CONTINUOUS
15.40	15.993	16.312	16.535	16.645	16.645	16.895	16.649	16.899
15.41	16.004	16.324	16.546	16.657	16.657	16.907	16.661	16.911
15.42	16.014	16.335	16.558	16.669	16.669	16.919	16.672	16.923
15.43	16.025	16.346	16.569	16.680	16.680	16.930	16.684	16.934
15.44	16.036	16.357	16.581	16.692	16.692	16.942	16.696	16.946
15.45	16.047	16.368	16.592	16.704	16.704	16.954	16.707	16.958
15.46	16.058	16.380	16.604	16.715	16.715	16.966	16.719	16.970
15.47	16.068	16.391	16.615	16.727	16.727	16.978	16.731	16.982
15.48	16.079	16.402	16.627	16.739	16.739	16.990	16.742	16.994
15.49	16.090	16.413	16.638	16.750	16.750	17.002	16.754	17.006
15.50	16.101	16.424	16.650	16.762	16.762	17.013	16.766	17.017
15.51	16.111	16.436	16.661	16.774	16.774	17.025	16.777	17.029
15.52	16.122	16.447	16.673	16.785	16.785	17.037	16.789	17.041
15.53	16.133	16.458	16.685	16.797	16.797	17.049	16.801	17.053
15.54	16.144	16.469	16.696	16.809	16.809	17.061	16.813	17.065
15.55	16.155	16.480	16.708	16.820	16.820	17.073	16.824	17.077
15.56	16.165	16.492	16.719	16.832	16.832	17.085	16.836	17.089
15.57	16.176	16.503	16.731	16.844	16.844	17.097	16.848	17.101
15.58	16.187	16.514	16.742	16.855	16.855	17.108	16.859	17.112
15.59	16.198	16.525	16.754	16.867	16.867	17.120	16.871	17.124
15.60	16.208	16.537	16.765	16.879	16.879	17.132	16.883	17.136
15.61	16.219	16.548	16.777	16.890	16.890	17.144	16.894	17.148
15.62	16.230	16.559	16.788	16.902	16.902	17.156	16.906	17.160
15.63	16.241	16.570	16.800	16.914	16.914	17.168	16.918	17.172
15.64	16.252	16.581	16.811	16.925	16.925	17.180	16.929	17.184
15.65	16.262	16.593	16.823	16.937	16.937	17.191	16.941	17.196
15.66	16.273	16.604	16.834	16.949	16.949	17.203	16.953	17.207
15.67	16.284	16.615	16.846	16.960	16.961	17.215	16.964	17.219
15.68	16.295	16.626	16.857	16.972	16.972	17.227	16.976	17.231
15.69	16.305	16.638	16.869	16.984	16.984	17.239	16.988	17.243
15.70	16.316	16.649	16.880	16.996	16.996	17.251	17.000	17.255
15.71	16.327	16.660	16.892	17.007	17.007	17.263	17.011	17.267
15.72	16.338	16.671	16.904	17.019	17.019	17.275	17.023	17.279
15.73	16.349	16.682	16.915	17.031	17.031	17.287	17.035	17.291
15.74	16.359	16.694	16.927	17.042	17.042	17.298	17.046	17.303
15.75	16.370	16.705	16.938	17.054	17.054	17.310	17.058	17.314
15.76	16.381	16.716	16.950	17.066	17.066	17.322	17.070	17.326
15.77	16.392	16.727	16.961	17.077	17.078	17.334	17.081	17.338
15.78	16.403	16.739	16.973	17.089	17.089	17.346	17.093	17.350
15.79	16.413	16.750	16.984	17.101	17.101	17.358	17.105	17.362
15.80	16.424	16.761	16.996	17.113	17.113	17.370	17.117	17.374
15.81	16.435	16.772	17.007	17.124	17.124	17.382	17.128	17.386
15.82	16.446	16.784	17.019	17.136	17.136	17.394	17.140	17.398
15.83	16.456	16.795	17.031	17.148	17.148	17.405	17.152	17.410
15.84	16.467	16.806	17.042	17.159	17.159	17.417	17.163	17.422
15.85	16.478	16.817	17.054	17.171	17.171	17.429	17.175	17.433
15.86	16.489	16.828	17.065	17.183	17.183	17.441	17.187	17.445
15.87	16.500	16.840	17.077	17.195	17.195	17.453	17.199	17.457
15.88	16.510	16.851	17.088	17.206	17.206	17.465	17.210	17.469
15.89	16.521	16.862	17.100	17.218	17.218	17.477	17.222	17.481
15.90	16.532	16.873	17.111	17.230	17.230	17.489	17.234	17.493
15.91	16.543	16.885	17.123	17.241	17.241	17.501	17.246	17.505
15.92	16.554	16.896	17.135	17.253	17.253	17.513	17.257	17.517
15.93	16.564	16.907	17.146	17.265	17.265	17.525	17.269	17.529
15.94	16.575	16.918	17.158	17.277	17.277	17.536	17.281	17.541
15.95	16.586	16.930	17.169	17.288	17.288	17.548	17.292	17.553
15.96	16.597	16.941	17.181	17.300	17.300	17.560	17.304	17.564
15.97	16.608	16.952	17.192	17.312	17.312	17.572	17.316	17.576
15.98	16.618	16.963	17.204	17.323	17.324	17.584	17.328	17.588
15.99	16.629	16.975	17.216	17.335	17.335	17.596	17.339	17.600
16.00	16.640	16.986	17.227	17.347	17.347	17.608	17.351	17.612
16.01	16.651	16.997	17.239	17.359	17.359	17.620	17.363	17.624
16.02	16.662	17.008	17.250	17.370	17.370	17.632	17.375	17.636
16.03	16.672	17.020	17.262	17.382	17.382	17.644	17.386	17.648
16.04	16.683	17.031	17.273	17.394	17.394	17.656	17.398	17.660
16.05	16.694	17.042	17.285	17.406	17.406	17.668	17.410	17.672
16.06	16.705	17.053	17.297	17.417	17.417	17.679	17.422	17.684
16.07	16.716	17.065	17.308	17.429	17.429	17.691	17.433	17.696
16.08	16.726	17.076	17.320	17.441	17.441	17.703	17.445	17.708
16.09	16.737	17.087	17.331	17.453	17.453	17.715	17.457	17.720
16.10	16.748	17.098	17.343	17.464	17.464	17.727	17.468	17.731
16.11	16.759	17.110	17.354	17.476	17.476	17.739	17.480	17.743
16.12	16.770	17.121	17.366	17.488	17.488	17.751	17.492	17.755
16.13	16.780	17.132	17.378	17.499	17.500	17.763	17.504	17.767
16.14	16.791	17.143	17.389	17.511	17.511	17.775	17.515	17.779
16.15	16.802	17.155	17.401	17.523	17.523	17.787	17.527	17.791
16.16	16.813	17.166	17.412	17.535	17.535	17.799	17.539	17.803
16.17	16.824	17.177	17.424	17.546	17.547	17.811	17.551	17.815
16.18	16.834	17.188	17.435	17.558	17.558	17.823	17.563	17.827
16.19	16.845	17.200	17.447	17.570	17.570	17.835	17.574	17.839
16.20	16.856	17.211	17.459	17.582	17.582	17.847	17.586	17.851

278

EFFECTIVE ANNUAL YIELDS

COMPOUNDING METHOD

NOMINAL ANNUAL INTEREST RATE	SEMI-ANNUALLY	QUARTERLY	MONTHLY	360/360 DAILY	365/365 DAILY	365/360 DAILY	CONTINUOUS	365/360 CONTINUOUS
16.20	16.856	17.211	17.459	17.582	17.582	17.847	17.586	17.851
16.21	16.867	17.222	17.470	17.593	17.594	17.858	17.598	17.863
16.22	16.878	17.234	17.482	17.605	17.605	17.870	17.610	17.875
16.23	16.889	17.245	17.493	17.617	17.617	17.882	17.621	17.887
16.24	16.899	17.256	17.505	17.629	17.629	17.894	17.633	17.899
16.25	16.910	17.267	17.517	17.641	17.641	17.906	17.645	17.911
16.26	16.921	17.279	17.528	17.652	17.652	17.918	17.657	17.923
16.27	16.932	17.290	17.540	17.664	17.664	17.930	17.668	17.935
16.28	16.943	17.301	17.551	17.676	17.676	17.942	17.680	17.947
16.29	16.953	17.312	17.563	17.688	17.688	17.954	17.692	17.958
16.30	16.964	17.324	17.575	17.699	17.699	17.966	17.704	17.970
16.31	16.975	17.335	17.586	17.711	17.711	17.978	17.715	17.982
16.32	16.986	17.346	17.598	17.723	17.723	17.990	17.727	17.994
16.33	16.997	17.358	17.609	17.735	17.735	18.002	17.739	18.006
16.34	17.007	17.369	17.621	17.746	17.746	18.014	17.751	18.018
16.35	17.018	17.380	17.633	17.758	17.758	18.026	17.763	18.030
16.36	17.029	17.391	17.644	17.770	17.770	18.038	17.774	18.042
16.37	17.040	17.403	17.656	17.782	17.782	18.050	17.786	18.054
16.38	17.051	17.414	17.667	17.793	17.794	18.062	17.798	18.066
16.39	17.062	17.425	17.679	17.805	17.805	18.074	17.810	18.078
16.40	17.072	17.436	17.691	17.817	17.817	18.086	17.821	18.090
16.41	17.083	17.448	17.702	17.829	17.829	18.098	17.833	18.102
16.42	17.094	17.459	17.714	17.841	17.841	18.110	17.845	18.114
16.43	17.105	17.470	17.725	17.852	17.852	18.122	17.857	18.126
16.44	17.116	17.482	17.737	17.864	17.864	18.134	17.869	18.138
16.45	17.127	17.493	17.749	17.876	17.876	18.145	17.880	18.150
16.46	17.137	17.504	17.760	17.888	17.888	18.157	17.892	18.162
16.47	17.148	17.515	17.772	17.899	17.900	18.169	17.904	18.174
16.48	17.159	17.527	17.784	17.911	17.911	18.181	17.916	18.186
16.49	17.170	17.538	17.795	17.923	17.923	18.193	17.928	18.198
16.50	17.181	17.549	17.807	17.935	17.935	18.205	17.939	18.210
16.51	17.191	17.561	17.818	17.947	17.947	18.217	17.951	18.222
16.52	17.202	17.572	17.830	17.958	17.958	18.229	17.963	18.234
16.53	17.213	17.583	17.842	17.970	17.970	18.241	17.975	18.246
16.54	17.224	17.594	17.853	17.982	17.982	18.253	17.986	18.258
16.55	17.235	17.606	17.865	17.994	17.994	18.265	17.998	18.270
16.56	17.246	17.617	17.877	18.006	18.006	18.277	18.010	18.282
16.57	17.256	17.628	17.888	18.017	18.017	18.289	18.022	18.294
16.58	17.267	17.640	17.900	18.029	18.029	18.301	18.034	18.306
16.59	17.278	17.651	17.911	18.041	18.041	18.313	18.046	18.318
16.60	17.289	17.662	17.923	18.053	18.053	18.325	18.057	18.330
16.61	17.300	17.674	17.935	18.065	18.065	18.337	18.069	18.342
16.62	17.311	17.685	17.946	18.076	18.076	18.349	18.081	18.354
16.63	17.321	17.696	17.958	18.088	18.088	18.361	18.093	18.366
16.64	17.332	17.707	17.970	18.100	18.100	18.373	18.105	18.378
16.65	17.343	17.719	17.981	18.112	18.112	18.385	18.116	18.390
16.66	17.354	17.730	17.993	18.124	18.124	18.397	18.128	18.402
16.67	17.365	17.741	18.005	18.135	18.135	18.409	18.140	18.414
16.68	17.376	17.753	18.016	18.147	18.147	18.421	18.152	18.426
16.69	17.386	17.764	18.028	18.159	18.159	18.433	18.164	18.438
16.70	17.397	17.775	18.039	18.171	18.171	18.445	18.175	18.450
16.71	17.408	17.787	18.051	18.183	18.183	18.457	18.187	18.462
16.72	17.419	17.798	18.063	18.194	18.195	18.469	18.199	18.474
16.73	17.430	17.809	18.074	18.206	18.206	18.481	18.211	18.486
16.74	17.441	17.820	18.086	18.218	18.218	18.493	18.223	18.498
16.75	17.451	17.832	18.098	18.230	18.230	18.505	18.235	18.510
16.76	17.462	17.843	18.109	18.242	18.242	18.517	18.246	18.522
16.77	17.473	17.854	18.121	18.254	18.254	18.529	18.258	18.534
16.78	17.484	17.866	18.133	18.265	18.265	18.541	18.270	18.546
16.79	17.495	17.877	18.144	18.277	18.277	18.553	18.282	18.558
16.80	17.506	17.888	18.156	18.289	18.289	18.565	18.294	18.570
16.81	17.516	17.900	18.168	18.301	18.301	18.577	18.305	18.582
16.82	17.527	17.911	18.179	18.313	18.313	18.589	18.317	18.594
16.83	17.538	17.922	18.191	18.325	18.325	18.601	18.329	18.606
16.84	17.549	17.934	18.203	18.336	18.336	18.613	18.341	18.618
16.85	17.560	17.945	18.214	18.348	18.348	18.625	18.353	18.630
16.86	17.571	17.956	18.226	18.360	18.360	18.637	18.365	18.642
16.87	17.581	17.968	18.238	18.372	18.372	18.649	18.376	18.654
16.88	17.592	17.979	18.249	18.384	18.384	18.661	18.388	18.666
16.89	17.603	17.990	18.261	18.395	18.396	18.673	18.400	18.678
16.90	17.614	18.002	18.272	18.407	18.407	18.686	18.412	18.690
16.91	17.625	18.013	18.284	18.419	18.419	18.698	18.424	18.702
16.92	17.636	18.024	18.296	18.431	18.431	18.710	18.436	18.714
16.93	17.647	18.035	18.307	18.443	18.443	18.722	18.448	18.726
16.94	17.657	18.047	18.319	18.455	18.455	18.734	18.459	18.738
16.95	17.668	18.058	18.331	18.467	18.467	18.746	18.471	18.750
16.96	17.679	18.069	18.342	18.478	18.478	18.758	18.483	18.763
16.97	17.690	18.081	18.354	18.490	18.490	18.770	18.495	18.775
16.98	17.701	18.092	18.366	18.502	18.502	18.782	18.507	18.787
16.99	17.712	18.103	18.377	18.514	18.514	18.794	18.519	18.799
17.00	17.722	18.115	18.389	18.526	18.526	18.806	18.530	18.811

EFFECTIVE ANNUAL YIELDS

COMPOUNDING METHOD

NOMINAL ANNUAL INTEREST RATE	SEMI-ANNUALLY	QUARTERLY	MONTHLY	360/360 DAILY	365/365 DAILY	365/360 DAILY	CONTINUOUS	365/360 CONTINUOUS
17.00	17.722	18.115	18.389	18.526	18.526	18.806	18.530	18.811
17.01	17.733	18.126	18.401	18.538	18.538	18.818	18.542	18.823
17.02	17.744	18.137	18.413	18.549	18.549	18.830	18.554	18.835
17.03	17.755	18.149	18.424	18.561	18.561	18.842	18.566	18.847
17.04	17.766	18.160	18.436	18.573	18.573	18.854	18.578	18.859
17.05	17.777	18.171	18.448	18.585	18.585	18.866	18.590	18.871
17.06	17.788	18.183	18.459	18.597	18.597	18.878	18.602	18.883
17.07	17.798	18.194	18.471	18.609	18.609	18.890	18.613	18.895
17.08	17.809	18.205	18.483	18.621	18.621	18.902	18.625	18.907
17.09	17.820	18.217	18.494	18.632	18.632	18.914	18.637	18.919
17.10	17.831	18.228	18.506	18.644	18.644	18.926	18.649	18.931
17.11	17.842	18.239	18.518	18.656	18.656	18.938	18.661	18.943
17.12	17.853	18.251	18.529	18.668	18.668	18.950	18.673	18.955
17.13	17.864	18.262	18.541	18.680	18.680	18.962	18.685	18.967
17.14	17.874	18.273	18.553	18.692	18.692	18.975	18.697	18.979
17.15	17.885	18.285	18.564	18.704	18.704	18.987	18.708	18.992
17.16	17.896	18.296	18.576	18.715	18.715	18.999	18.720	19.004
17.17	17.907	18.308	18.588	18.727	18.727	19.011	18.732	19.016
17.18	17.918	18.319	18.599	18.739	18.739	19.023	18.744	19.028
17.19	17.929	18.330	18.611	18.751	18.751	19.035	18.756	19.040
17.20	17.940	18.342	18.623	18.763	18.763	19.047	18.768	19.052
17.21	17.950	18.353	18.635	18.775	18.775	19.059	18.780	19.064
17.22	17.961	18.364	18.646	18.787	18.787	19.071	18.792	19.076
17.23	17.972	18.376	18.658	18.799	18.799	19.083	18.803	19.088
17.24	17.983	18.387	18.670	18.810	18.810	19.095	18.815	19.100
17.25	17.994	18.398	18.681	18.822	18.822	19.107	18.827	19.112
17.26	18.005	18.410	18.693	18.834	18.834	19.119	18.839	19.124
17.27	18.016	18.421	18.705	18.846	18.846	19.131	18.851	19.136
17.28	18.026	18.432	18.716	18.858	18.858	19.143	18.863	19.148
17.29	18.037	18.444	18.728	18.870	18.870	19.156	18.875	19.161
17.30	18.048	18.455	18.740	18.882	18.882	19.168	18.887	19.173
17.31	18.059	18.466	18.752	18.894	18.894	19.180	18.898	19.185
17.32	18.070	18.478	18.763	18.905	18.906	19.192	18.910	19.197
17.33	18.081	18.489	18.775	18.917	18.917	19.204	18.922	19.209
17.34	18.092	18.500	18.787	18.929	18.929	19.216	18.934	19.221
17.35	18.103	18.512	18.798	18.941	18.941	19.228	18.946	19.233
17.36	18.113	18.523	18.810	18.953	18.953	19.240	18.958	19.245
17.37	18.124	18.535	18.822	18.965	18.965	19.252	18.970	19.257
17.38	18.135	18.546	18.834	18.977	18.977	19.264	18.982	19.269
17.39	18.146	18.557	18.845	18.989	18.989	19.276	18.994	19.281
17.40	18.157	18.569	18.857	19.001	19.001	19.288	19.006	19.294
17.41	18.168	18.580	18.869	19.012	19.013	19.301	19.017	19.306
17.42	18.179	18.591	18.880	19.024	19.024	19.313	19.029	19.318
17.43	18.190	18.603	18.892	19.036	19.036	19.325	19.041	19.330
17.44	18.200	18.614	18.904	19.048	19.048	19.337	19.053	19.342
17.45	18.211	18.625	18.916	19.060	19.060	19.349	19.065	19.354
17.46	18.222	18.637	18.927	19.072	19.072	19.361	19.077	19.366
17.47	18.233	18.648	18.939	19.084	19.084	19.373	19.089	19.378
17.48	18.244	18.660	18.951	19.096	19.096	19.385	19.101	19.390
17.49	18.255	18.671	18.962	19.108	19.108	19.397	19.113	19.402
17.50	18.266	18.682	18.974	19.120	19.120	19.409	19.125	19.415
17.51	18.277	18.694	18.986	19.131	19.132	19.421	19.137	19.427
17.52	18.287	18.705	18.998	19.143	19.143	19.434	19.148	19.439
17.53	18.298	18.716	19.009	19.155	19.155	19.446	19.160	19.451
17.54	18.309	18.728	19.021	19.167	19.167	19.458	19.172	19.463
17.55	18.320	18.739	19.033	19.179	19.179	19.470	19.184	19.475
17.56	18.331	18.751	19.045	19.191	19.191	19.482	19.196	19.487
17.57	18.342	18.762	19.056	19.203	19.203	19.494	19.208	19.499
17.58	18.353	18.773	19.068	19.215	19.215	19.506	19.220	19.511
17.59	18.364	18.785	19.080	19.227	19.227	19.518	19.232	19.524
17.60	18.374	18.796	19.091	19.239	19.239	19.530	19.244	19.536
17.61	18.385	18.807	19.103	19.251	19.251	19.543	19.256	19.548
17.62	18.396	18.819	19.115	19.263	19.263	19.555	19.268	19.560
17.63	18.407	18.830	19.127	19.274	19.275	19.567	19.280	19.572
17.64	18.418	18.842	19.138	19.286	19.286	19.579	19.292	19.584
17.65	18.429	18.853	19.150	19.298	19.298	19.591	19.303	19.596
17.66	18.440	18.864	19.162	19.310	19.310	19.603	19.315	19.608
17.67	18.451	18.876	19.174	19.322	19.322	19.615	19.327	19.621
17.68	18.461	18.887	19.185	19.334	19.334	19.627	19.339	19.633
17.69	18.472	18.898	19.197	19.346	19.346	19.640	19.351	19.645
17.70	18.483	18.910	19.209	19.358	19.358	19.652	19.363	19.657
17.71	18.494	18.921	19.221	19.370	19.370	19.664	19.375	19.669
17.72	18.505	18.933	19.232	19.382	19.382	19.676	19.387	19.681
17.73	18.516	18.944	19.244	19.394	19.394	19.688	19.399	19.693
17.74	18.527	18.955	19.256	19.406	19.406	19.700	19.411	19.705
17.75	18.538	18.967	19.268	19.418	19.418	19.712	19.423	19.718
17.76	18.549	18.978	19.279	19.430	19.430	19.724	19.435	19.730
17.77	18.559	18.990	19.291	19.441	19.442	19.737	19.447	19.742
17.78	18.570	19.001	19.303	19.453	19.453	19.749	19.459	19.754
17.79	18.581	19.012	19.315	19.465	19.465	19.761	19.471	19.766
17.80	18.592	19.024	19.326	19.477	19.477	19.773	19.483	19.778

EFFECTIVE ANNUAL YIELDS

COMPOUNDING METHOD

NOMINAL ANNUAL INTEREST RATE	SEMI-ANNUALLY	QUARTERLY	MONTHLY	360/360 DAILY	365/365 DAILY	365/360 DAILY	CONTINUOUS	365/360 CONTINUOUS
17.80	18.592	19.024	19.326	19.477	19.477	19.773	19.483	19.778
17.81	18.603	19.035	19.338	19.489	19.489	19.785	19.494	19.790
17.82	18.614	19.047	19.350	19.501	19.501	19.797	19.506	19.803
17.83	18.625	19.058	19.362	19.513	19.513	19.809	19.518	19.815
17.84	18.636	19.069	19.373	19.525	19.525	19.822	19.530	19.827
17.85	18.647	19.081	19.385	19.537	19.537	19.834	19.542	19.839
17.86	18.657	19.092	19.397	19.549	19.549	19.846	19.554	19.851
17.87	18.668	19.104	19.409	19.561	19.561	19.858	19.566	19.863
17.88	18.679	19.115	19.421	19.573	19.573	19.870	19.578	19.875
17.89	18.690	19.126	19.432	19.585	19.585	19.882	19.590	19.888
17.90	18.701	19.138	19.444	19.597	19.597	19.894	19.602	19.900
17.91	18.712	19.149	19.456	19.609	19.609	19.907	19.614	19.912
17.92	18.723	19.161	19.468	19.621	19.621	19.919	19.626	19.924
17.93	18.734	19.172	19.479	19.633	19.633	19.931	19.638	19.936
17.94	18.745	19.183	19.491	19.645	19.645	19.943	19.650	19.948
17.95	18.756	19.195	19.503	19.657	19.657	19.955	19.662	19.961
17.96	18.766	19.206	19.515	19.668	19.669	19.967	19.674	19.973
17.97	18.777	19.218	19.526	19.680	19.681	19.979	19.686	19.985
17.98	18.788	19.229	19.538	19.692	19.692	19.992	19.698	19.997
17.99	18.799	19.240	19.550	19.704	19.704	20.004	19.710	20.009
18.00	18.810	19.252	19.562	19.716	19.716	20.016	19.722	20.021
18.01	18.821	19.263	19.574	19.728	19.728	20.028	19.734	20.034
18.02	18.832	19.275	19.585	19.740	19.740	20.040	19.746	20.046
18.03	18.843	19.286	19.597	19.752	19.752	20.052	19.758	20.058
18.04	18.854	19.298	19.609	19.764	19.764	20.065	19.770	20.070
18.05	18.865	19.309	19.621	19.776	19.776	20.077	19.782	20.082
18.06	18.875	19.320	19.633	19.788	19.788	20.089	19.794	20.094
18.07	18.886	19.332	19.644	19.800	19.800	20.101	19.806	20.107
18.08	18.897	19.343	19.656	19.812	19.812	20.113	19.818	20.119
18.09	18.908	19.355	19.668	19.824	19.824	20.125	19.830	20.131
18.10	18.919	19.366	19.680	19.836	19.836	20.138	19.842	20.143
18.11	18.930	19.377	19.691	19.848	19.848	20.150	19.854	20.155
18.12	18.941	19.389	19.703	19.860	19.860	20.162	19.865	20.168
18.13	18.952	19.400	19.715	19.872	19.872	20.174	19.877	20.180
18.14	18.963	19.412	19.727	19.884	19.884	20.186	19.889	20.192
18.15	18.974	19.423	19.739	19.896	19.896	20.199	19.901	20.204
18.16	18.984	19.435	19.750	19.908	19.908	20.211	19.913	20.216
18.17	18.995	19.446	19.762	19.920	19.920	20.223	19.925	20.228
18.18	19.006	19.457	19.774	19.932	19.932	20.235	19.937	20.241
18.19	19.017	19.469	19.786	19.944	19.944	20.247	19.949	20.253
18.20	19.028	19.480	19.798	19.956	19.956	20.259	19.961	20.265
18.21	19.039	19.492	19.809	19.968	19.968	20.272	19.973	20.277
18.22	19.050	19.503	19.821	19.980	19.980	20.284	19.985	20.289
18.23	19.061	19.515	19.833	19.992	19.992	20.296	19.997	20.302
18.24	19.072	19.526	19.845	20.004	20.004	20.308	20.009	20.314
18.25	19.083	19.537	19.857	20.016	20.016	20.320	20.021	20.326
18.26	19.094	19.549	19.868	20.028	20.028	20.333	20.033	20.338
18.27	19.104	19.560	19.880	20.040	20.040	20.345	20.045	20.350
18.28	19.115	19.572	19.892	20.052	20.052	20.357	20.057	20.363
18.29	19.126	19.583	19.904	20.064	20.064	20.369	20.069	20.375
18.30	19.137	19.595	19.916	20.076	20.076	20.381	20.081	20.387
18.31	19.148	19.606	19.927	20.088	20.088	20.394	20.093	20.399
18.32	19.159	19.617	19.939	20.100	20.100	20.406	20.105	20.411
18.33	19.170	19.629	19.951	20.112	20.112	20.418	20.117	20.424
18.34	19.181	19.640	19.963	20.124	20.124	20.430	20.129	20.436
18.35	19.192	19.652	19.975	20.136	20.136	20.442	20.141	20.448
18.36	19.203	19.663	19.987	20.148	20.148	20.455	20.154	20.460
18.37	19.214	19.675	19.998	20.160	20.160	20.467	20.166	20.473
18.38	19.225	19.686	20.010	20.172	20.172	20.479	20.178	20.485
18.39	19.235	19.698	20.022	20.184	20.184	20.491	20.190	20.497
18.40	19.246	19.709	20.034	20.196	20.196	20.503	20.202	20.509
18.41	19.257	19.720	20.046	20.208	20.208	20.516	20.214	20.521
18.42	19.268	19.732	20.057	20.220	20.220	20.528	20.226	20.534
18.43	19.279	19.743	20.069	20.232	20.232	20.540	20.238	20.546
18.44	19.290	19.755	20.081	20.244	20.244	20.552	20.250	20.558
18.45	19.301	19.766	20.093	20.256	20.256	20.564	20.262	20.570
18.46	19.312	19.778	20.105	20.268	20.268	20.577	20.274	20.582
18.47	19.323	19.789	20.117	20.280	20.280	20.589	20.286	20.595
18.48	19.334	19.801	20.128	20.292	20.292	20.601	20.298	20.607
18.49	19.345	19.812	20.140	20.304	20.304	20.613	20.310	20.619
18.50	19.356	19.823	20.152	20.316	20.316	20.626	20.322	20.631
18.51	19.367	19.835	20.164	20.328	20.328	20.638	20.334	20.644
18.52	19.377	19.846	20.176	20.340	20.340	20.650	20.346	20.656
18.53	19.388	19.858	20.188	20.352	20.352	20.662	20.358	20.668
18.54	19.399	19.869	20.199	20.364	20.364	20.674	20.370	20.680
18.55	19.410	19.881	20.211	20.376	20.376	20.687	20.382	20.693
18.56	19.421	19.892	20.223	20.388	20.388	20.699	20.394	20.705
18.57	19.432	19.904	20.235	20.400	20.400	20.711	20.406	20.717
18.58	19.443	19.915	20.247	20.412	20.412	20.723	20.418	20.729
18.59	19.454	19.927	20.259	20.424	20.424	20.736	20.430	20.742
18.60	19.465	19.938	20.271	20.436	20.437	20.748	20.442	20.754

EFFECTIVE ANNUAL YIELDS

NOMINAL ANNUAL INTEREST RATE	COMPOUNDING METHOD							
	SEMI-ANNUALLY	QUARTERLY	MONTHLY	360/360 DAILY	365/365 DAILY	365/360 DAILY	CONTINUOUS	365/360 CONTINUOUS
18.60	19.465	19.938	20.271	20.436	20.437	20.748	20.442	20.754
18.61	19.476	19.949	20.282	20.448	20.449	20.760	20.454	20.766
18.62	19.487	19.961	20.294	20.461	20.461	20.772	20.466	20.778
18.63	19.498	19.972	20.306	20.473	20.473	20.785	20.478	20.791
18.64	19.509	19.984	20.318	20.485	20.485	20.797	20.490	20.803
18.65	19.520	19.995	20.330	20.497	20.497	20.809	20.502	20.815
18.66	19.530	20.007	20.342	20.509	20.509	20.821	20.515	20.827
18.67	19.541	20.018	20.353	20.521	20.521	20.834	20.527	20.840
18.68	19.552	20.030	20.365	20.533	20.533	20.846	20.539	20.852
18.69	19.563	20.041	20.377	20.545	20.545	20.858	20.551	20.864
18.70	19.574	20.053	20.389	20.557	20.557	20.870	20.563	20.876
18.71	19.585	20.064	20.401	20.569	20.569	20.883	20.575	20.889
18.72	19.596	20.076	20.413	20.581	20.581	20.895	20.587	20.901
18.73	19.607	20.087	20.425	20.593	20.593	20.907	20.599	20.913
18.74	19.618	20.099	20.436	20.605	20.605	20.919	20.611	20.925
18.75	19.629	20.110	20.448	20.617	20.617	20.932	20.623	20.938
18.76	19.640	20.122	20.460	20.629	20.629	20.944	20.635	20.950
18.77	19.651	20.133	20.472	20.641	20.641	20.956	20.647	20.962
18.78	19.662	20.144	20.484	20.653	20.653	20.968	20.659	20.974
18.79	19.673	20.156	20.496	20.665	20.665	20.981	20.671	20.987
18.80	19.684	20.167	20.508	20.677	20.678	20.993	20.683	20.999
18.81	19.695	20.179	20.519	20.689	20.690	21.005	20.695	21.011
18.82	19.705	20.190	20.531	20.702	20.702	21.017	20.707	21.023
18.83	19.716	20.202	20.543	20.714	20.714	21.030	20.720	21.036
18.84	19.727	20.213	20.555	20.726	20.726	21.042	20.732	21.048
18.85	19.738	20.225	20.567	20.738	20.738	21.054	20.744	21.060
18.86	19.749	20.236	20.579	20.750	20.750	21.066	20.756	21.073
18.87	19.760	20.248	20.591	20.762	20.762	21.079	20.768	21.085
18.88	19.771	20.259	20.603	20.774	20.774	21.091	20.780	21.097
18.89	19.782	20.271	20.614	20.786	20.786	21.103	20.792	21.109
18.90	19.793	20.282	20.626	20.798	20.798	21.116	20.804	21.122
18.91	19.804	20.294	20.638	20.810	20.810	21.128	20.816	21.134
18.92	19.815	20.305	20.650	20.822	20.822	21.140	20.828	21.146
18.93	19.826	20.317	20.662	20.834	20.834	21.152	20.840	21.158
18.94	19.837	20.328	20.674	20.846	20.846	21.165	20.852	21.171
18.95	19.848	20.340	20.686	20.858	20.859	21.177	20.865	21.183
18.96	19.859	20.351	20.698	20.871	20.871	21.189	20.877	21.195
18.97	19.870	20.363	20.709	20.883	20.883	21.201	20.889	21.208
18.98	19.881	20.374	20.721	20.895	20.895	21.214	20.901	21.220
18.99	19.892	20.386	20.733	20.907	20.907	21.226	20.913	21.232
19.00	19.902	20.397	20.745	20.919	20.919	21.238	20.925	21.244
19.01	19.913	20.409	20.757	20.931	20.931	21.251	20.937	21.257
19.02	19.924	20.420	20.769	20.943	20.943	21.263	20.949	21.269
19.03	19.935	20.432	20.781	20.955	20.955	21.275	20.961	21.281
19.04	19.946	20.443	20.793	20.967	20.967	21.287	20.973	21.294
19.05	19.957	20.455	20.805	20.979	20.979	21.300	20.985	21.306
19.06	19.968	20.466	20.816	20.991	20.992	21.312	20.998	21.318
19.07	19.979	20.478	20.828	21.004	21.004	21.324	21.010	21.331
19.08	19.990	20.489	20.840	21.016	21.016	21.337	21.022	21.343
19.09	20.001	20.501	20.852	21.028	21.028	21.349	21.034	21.355
19.10	20.012	20.512	20.864	21.040	21.040	21.361	21.046	21.367
19.11	20.023	20.524	20.876	21.052	21.052	21.374	21.058	21.380
19.12	20.034	20.535	20.888	21.064	21.064	21.386	21.070	21.392
19.13	20.045	20.547	20.900	21.076	21.076	21.398	21.082	21.404
19.14	20.056	20.558	20.912	21.088	21.088	21.410	21.094	21.417
19.15	20.067	20.570	20.924	21.100	21.100	21.423	21.106	21.429
19.16	20.078	20.581	20.935	21.112	21.113	21.435	21.119	21.441
19.17	20.089	20.593	20.947	21.125	21.125	21.447	21.131	21.454
19.18	20.100	20.604	20.959	21.137	21.137	21.460	21.143	21.466
19.19	20.111	20.616	20.971	21.149	21.149	21.472	21.155	21.478
19.20	20.122	20.627	20.983	21.161	21.161	21.484	21.167	21.491
19.21	20.133	20.639	20.995	21.173	21.173	21.497	21.179	21.503
19.22	20.144	20.650	21.007	21.185	21.185	21.509	21.191	21.515
19.23	20.154	20.662	21.019	21.197	21.197	21.521	21.203	21.528
19.24	20.165	20.673	21.031	21.209	21.209	21.534	21.216	21.540
19.25	20.176	20.685	21.043	21.221	21.221	21.546	21.228	21.552
19.26	20.187	20.696	21.055	21.234	21.234	21.558	21.240	21.565
19.27	20.198	20.708	21.066	21.246	21.246	21.570	21.252	21.577
19.28	20.209	20.719	21.078	21.258	21.258	21.583	21.264	21.589
19.29	20.220	20.731	21.090	21.270	21.270	21.595	21.276	21.602
19.30	20.231	20.742	21.102	21.282	21.282	21.607	21.288	21.614
19.31	20.242	20.754	21.114	21.294	21.294	21.620	21.300	21.626
19.32	20.253	20.765	21.126	21.306	21.306	21.632	21.313	21.638
19.33	20.264	20.777	21.138	21.318	21.318	21.644	21.325	21.651
19.34	20.275	20.788	21.150	21.331	21.331	21.657	21.337	21.663
19.35	20.286	20.800	21.162	21.343	21.343	21.669	21.349	21.676
19.36	20.297	20.811	21.174	21.355	21.355	21.681	21.361	21.688
19.37	20.308	20.823	21.186	21.367	21.367	21.694	21.373	21.700
19.38	20.319	20.834	21.198	21.379	21.379	21.706	21.385	21.713
19.39	20.330	20.846	21.209	21.391	21.391	21.718	21.397	21.725
19.40	20.341	20.858	21.221	21.403	21.403	21.731	21.410	21.737

EFFECTIVE ANNUAL YIELDS

COMPOUNDING METHOD

NOMINAL ANNUAL INTEREST RATE	SEMI-ANNUALLY	QUARTERLY	MONTHLY	360/360 DAILY	365/365 DAILY	365/360 DAILY	CONTINUOUS	365/360 CONTINUOUS
19.40	20.341	20.858	21.221	21.403	21.403	21.731	21.410	21.737
19.41	20.352	20.869	21.233	21.415	21.416	21.743	21.422	21.750
19.42	20.363	20.881	21.245	21.428	21.428	21.755	21.434	21.762
19.43	20.374	20.892	21.257	21.440	21.440	21.768	21.446	21.774
19.44	20.385	20.904	21.269	21.452	21.452	21.780	21.458	21.787
19.45	20.396	20.915	21.281	21.464	21.464	21.792	21.470	21.799
19.46	20.407	20.927	21.293	21.476	21.476	21.805	21.482	21.811
19.47	20.418	20.938	21.305	21.488	21.488	21.817	21.495	21.824
19.48	20.429	20.950	21.317	21.500	21.500	21.829	21.507	21.836
19.49	20.440	20.961	21.329	21.513	21.513	21.842	21.519	21.848
19.50	20.451	20.973	21.341	21.525	21.525	21.854	21.531	21.861
19.51	20.462	20.984	21.353	21.537	21.537	21.867	21.543	21.873
19.52	20.473	20.996	21.365	21.549	21.549	21.879	21.555	21.885
19.53	20.484	21.007	21.377	21.561	21.561	21.891	21.568	21.898
19.54	20.495	21.019	21.389	21.573	21.573	21.904	21.580	21.910
19.55	20.506	21.031	21.400	21.585	21.586	21.916	21.592	21.922
19.56	20.516	21.042	21.412	21.598	21.598	21.928	21.604	21.935
19.57	20.527	21.054	21.424	21.610	21.610	21.941	21.616	21.947
19.58	20.538	21.065	21.436	21.622	21.622	21.953	21.628	21.960
19.59	20.549	21.077	21.448	21.634	21.634	21.965	21.641	21.972
19.60	20.560	21.088	21.460	21.646	21.646	21.978	21.653	21.984
19.61	20.571	21.100	21.472	21.658	21.658	21.990	21.665	21.997
19.62	20.582	21.111	21.484	21.671	21.671	22.002	21.677	22.009
19.63	20.593	21.123	21.496	21.683	21.683	22.015	21.689	22.021
19.64	20.604	21.134	21.508	21.695	21.695	22.027	21.701	22.034
19.65	20.615	21.146	21.520	21.707	21.707	22.040	21.714	22.046
19.66	20.626	21.158	21.532	21.719	21.719	22.052	21.726	22.059
19.67	20.637	21.169	21.544	21.731	21.731	22.064	21.738	22.071
19.68	20.648	21.181	21.556	21.744	21.744	22.077	21.750	22.083
19.69	20.659	21.192	21.568	21.756	21.756	22.089	21.762	22.096
19.70	20.670	21.204	21.580	21.768	21.768	22.101	21.774	22.108
19.71	20.681	21.215	21.592	21.780	21.780	22.114	21.787	22.120
19.72	20.692	21.227	21.604	21.792	21.792	22.126	21.799	22.133
19.73	20.703	21.238	21.616	21.804	21.804	22.139	21.811	22.145
19.74	20.714	21.250	21.628	21.817	21.817	22.151	21.823	22.158
19.75	20.725	21.261	21.640	21.829	21.829	22.163	21.835	22.170
19.76	20.736	21.273	21.652	21.841	21.841	22.176	21.847	22.182
19.77	20.747	21.285	21.664	21.853	21.853	22.188	21.860	22.195
19.78	20.758	21.296	21.676	21.865	21.865	22.200	21.872	22.207
19.79	20.769	21.308	21.687	21.877	21.878	22.213	21.884	22.220
19.80	20.780	21.319	21.699	21.890	21.890	22.225	21.896	22.232
19.81	20.791	21.331	21.711	21.902	21.902	22.238	21.908	22.244
19.82	20.802	21.342	21.723	21.914	21.914	22.250	21.921	22.257
19.83	20.813	21.354	21.735	21.926	21.926	22.262	21.933	22.269
19.84	20.824	21.366	21.747	21.938	21.938	22.275	21.945	22.281
19.85	20.835	21.377	21.759	21.951	21.951	22.287	21.957	22.294
19.86	20.846	21.389	21.771	21.963	21.963	22.300	21.969	22.306
19.87	20.857	21.400	21.783	21.975	21.975	22.312	21.982	22.319
19.88	20.868	21.412	21.795	21.987	21.987	22.324	21.994	22.331
19.89	20.879	21.423	21.807	21.999	21.999	22.337	22.006	22.344
19.90	20.890	21.435	21.819	22.011	22.012	22.349	22.018	22.356
19.91	20.901	21.446	21.831	22.024	22.024	22.361	22.030	22.368
19.92	20.912	21.458	21.843	22.036	22.036	22.374	22.043	22.381
19.93	20.923	21.470	21.855	22.048	22.048	22.386	22.055	22.393
19.94	20.934	21.481	21.867	22.060	22.060	22.399	22.067	22.406
19.95	20.945	21.493	21.879	22.072	22.073	22.411	22.079	22.418
19.96	20.956	21.504	21.891	22.085	22.085	22.423	22.091	22.430
19.97	20.967	21.516	21.903	22.097	22.097	22.436	22.104	22.443
19.98	20.978	21.527	21.915	22.109	22.109	22.448	22.116	22.455
19.99	20.989	21.539	21.927	22.121	22.121	22.461	22.128	22.468
20.00	21.000	21.551	21.939	22.133	22.134	22.473	22.140	22.480
20.01	21.011	21.562	21.951	22.146	22.146	22.486	22.152	22.492
20.02	21.022	21.574	21.963	22.158	22.158	22.498	22.165	22.505
20.03	21.033	21.585	21.975	22.170	22.170	22.510	22.177	22.517
20.04	21.044	21.597	21.987	22.182	22.182	22.523	22.189	22.530
20.05	21.055	21.609	21.999	22.195	22.195	22.535	22.201	22.542
20.06	21.066	21.620	22.011	22.207	22.207	22.548	22.214	22.555
20.07	21.077	21.632	22.023	22.219	22.219	22.560	22.226	22.567
20.08	21.088	21.643	22.035	22.231	22.231	22.572	22.238	22.579
20.09	21.099	21.655	22.047	22.243	22.243	22.585	22.250	22.592
20.10	21.110	21.666	22.059	22.256	22.256	22.597	22.262	22.604
20.11	21.121	21.678	22.071	22.268	22.268	22.610	22.275	22.617
20.12	21.132	21.690	22.083	22.280	22.280	22.622	22.287	22.629
20.13	21.143	21.701	22.095	22.292	22.292	22.635	22.299	22.642
20.14	21.154	21.713	22.107	22.305	22.305	22.647	22.311	22.654
20.15	21.165	21.724	22.119	22.317	22.317	22.659	22.324	22.666
20.16	21.176	21.736	22.131	22.329	22.329	22.672	22.336	22.679
20.17	21.187	21.748	22.143	22.341	22.341	22.684	22.348	22.691
20.18	21.198	21.759	22.155	22.353	22.354	22.697	22.360	22.704
20.19	21.209	21.771	22.167	22.366	22.366	22.709	22.373	22.716
20.20	21.220	21.782	22.179	22.378	22.378	22.722	22.385	22.729

EFFECTIVE ANNUAL YIELDS

NOMINAL ANNUAL INTEREST RATE	COMPOUNDING METHOD							
	SEMI-ANNUALLY	QUARTERLY	MONTHLY	360/360 DAILY	365/365 DAILY	365/360 DAILY	CONTINUOUS	365/360 CONTINUOUS
20.20	21.220	21.782	22.179	22.378	22.378	22.722	22.385	22.729
20.21	21.231	21.794	22.191	22.390	22.390	22.734	22.397	22.741
20.22	21.242	21.806	22.203	22.402	22.402	22.746	22.409	22.754
20.23	21.253	21.817	22.215	22.415	22.415	22.759	22.422	22.766
20.24	21.264	21.829	22.227	22.427	22.427	22.771	22.434	22.778
20.25	21.275	21.840	22.239	22.439	22.439	22.784	22.446	22.791
20.26	21.286	21.852	22.251	22.451	22.451	22.796	22.458	22.803
20.27	21.297	21.863	22.263	22.464	22.464	22.809	22.471	22.816
20.28	21.308	21.875	22.275	22.476	22.476	22.821	22.483	22.828
20.29	21.319	21.887	22.287	22.488	22.488	22.834	22.495	22.841
20.30	21.330	21.898	22.299	22.500	22.500	22.846	22.507	22.853
20.31	21.341	21.910	22.311	22.512	22.513	22.858	22.519	22.866
20.32	21.352	21.921	22.323	22.525	22.525	22.871	22.532	22.878
20.33	21.363	21.933	22.336	22.537	22.537	22.883	22.544	22.891
20.34	21.374	21.945	22.348	22.549	22.549	22.896	22.556	22.903
20.35	21.385	21.956	22.360	22.561	22.562	22.908	22.569	22.915
20.36	21.396	21.968	22.372	22.574	22.574	22.921	22.581	22.928
20.37	21.407	21.980	22.384	22.586	22.586	22.933	22.593	22.940
20.38	21.418	21.991	22.396	22.598	22.598	22.946	22.605	22.953
20.39	21.429	22.003	22.408	22.610	22.611	22.958	22.618	22.965
20.40	21.440	22.014	22.420	22.623	22.623	22.971	22.630	22.978
20.41	21.451	22.026	22.432	22.635	22.635	22.983	22.642	22.990
20.42	21.462	22.038	22.444	22.647	22.647	22.995	22.654	23.003
20.43	21.473	22.049	22.456	22.660	22.660	23.008	22.667	23.015
20.44	21.484	22.061	22.468	22.672	22.672	23.020	22.679	23.028
20.45	21.496	22.072	22.480	22.684	22.684	23.033	22.691	23.040
20.46	21.507	22.084	22.492	22.696	22.696	23.045	22.703	23.053
20.47	21.518	22.096	22.504	22.709	22.709	23.058	22.716	23.065
20.48	21.529	22.107	22.516	22.721	22.721	23.070	22.728	23.078
20.49	21.540	22.119	22.528	22.733	22.733	23.083	22.740	23.090
20.50	21.551	22.130	22.540	22.745	22.745	23.095	22.753	23.103
20.51	21.562	22.142	22.552	22.758	22.758	23.108	22.765	23.115
20.52	21.573	22.154	22.564	22.770	22.770	23.120	22.777	23.127
20.53	21.584	22.165	22.576	22.782	22.782	23.133	22.789	23.140
20.54	21.595	22.177	22.588	22.794	22.795	23.145	22.802	23.152
20.55	21.606	22.189	22.600	22.807	22.807	23.158	22.814	23.165
20.56	21.617	22.200	22.612	22.819	22.819	23.170	22.826	23.177
20.57	21.628	22.212	22.625	22.831	22.831	23.183	22.838	23.190
20.58	21.639	22.223	22.637	22.844	22.844	23.195	22.851	23.202
20.59	21.650	22.235	22.649	22.856	22.856	23.208	22.863	23.215
20.60	21.661	22.247	22.661	22.868	22.868	23.220	22.875	23.227
20.61	21.672	22.258	22.673	22.880	22.880	23.233	22.888	23.240
20.62	21.683	22.270	22.685	22.893	22.893	23.245	22.900	23.252
20.63	21.694	22.282	22.697	22.905	22.905	23.257	22.912	23.265
20.64	21.705	22.293	22.709	22.917	22.917	23.270	22.924	23.277
20.65	21.716	22.305	22.721	22.929	22.930	23.282	22.937	23.290
20.66	21.727	22.316	22.733	22.942	22.942	23.295	22.949	23.302
20.67	21.738	22.328	22.745	22.954	22.954	23.307	22.961	23.315
20.68	21.749	22.340	22.757	22.966	22.966	23.320	22.974	23.327
20.69	21.760	22.351	22.769	22.979	22.979	23.332	22.986	23.340
20.70	21.771	22.363	22.781	22.991	22.991	23.345	22.998	23.352
20.71	21.782	22.375	22.793	23.003	23.003	23.357	23.011	23.365
20.72	21.793	22.386	22.805	23.016	23.016	23.370	23.023	23.377
20.73	21.804	22.398	22.818	23.028	23.028	23.382	23.035	23.390
20.74	21.815	22.410	22.830	23.040	23.040	23.395	23.047	23.402
20.75	21.826	22.421	22.842	23.052	23.053	23.407	23.060	23.415
20.76	21.837	22.433	22.854	23.065	23.065	23.420	23.072	23.427
20.77	21.848	22.444	22.866	23.077	23.077	23.432	23.084	23.440
20.78	21.860	22.456	22.878	23.089	23.089	23.445	23.097	23.452
20.79	21.871	22.468	22.890	23.102	23.102	23.457	23.109	23.465
20.80	21.882	22.479	22.902	23.114	23.114	23.470	23.121	23.478
20.81	21.893	22.491	22.914	23.126	23.126	23.483	23.134	23.490
20.82	21.904	22.503	22.926	23.139	23.139	23.495	23.146	23.503
20.83	21.915	22.514	22.938	23.151	23.151	23.508	23.158	23.515
20.84	21.926	22.526	22.950	23.163	23.163	23.520	23.171	23.528
20.85	21.937	22.538	22.963	23.175	23.176	23.533	23.183	23.540
20.86	21.948	22.549	22.975	23.188	23.188	23.545	23.195	23.553
20.87	21.959	22.561	22.987	23.200	23.200	23.558	23.208	23.565
20.88	21.970	22.573	22.999	23.212	23.212	23.570	23.220	23.578
20.89	21.981	22.584	23.011	23.225	23.225	23.583	23.232	23.590
20.90	21.992	22.596	23.023	23.237	23.237	23.595	23.244	23.603
20.91	22.003	22.607	23.035	23.249	23.249	23.608	23.257	23.615
20.92	22.014	22.619	23.047	23.262	23.262	23.620	23.269	23.628
20.93	22.025	22.631	23.059	23.274	23.274	23.633	23.281	23.640
20.94	22.036	22.642	23.071	23.286	23.286	23.645	23.294	23.653
20.95	22.047	22.654	23.083	23.299	23.299	23.658	23.306	23.665
20.96	22.058	22.666	23.096	23.311	23.311	23.670	23.318	23.678
20.97	22.069	22.677	23.108	23.323	23.323	23.683	23.331	23.691
20.98	22.080	22.689	23.120	23.336	23.336	23.695	23.343	23.703
20.99	22.091	22.701	23.132	23.348	23.348	23.708	23.355	23.716
21.00	22.102	22.712	23.144	23.360	23.360	23.720	23.368	23.728